Handbook of Research on Gaming Trends in P-12 Education

Donna Russell
Walden University, USA

James M. Laffey
University of Missouri at Columbia, USA

A volume in the Advances in Game-Based Learning (AGBL) Book Series

Information Science REFERENCE
An Imprint of IGI Global

Published in the United States of America by
Information Science Reference (an imprint of IGI Global)
701 E. Chocolate Avenue
Hershey PA, USA 17033
Tel: 717-533-8845
Fax: 717-533-8661
E-mail: cust@igi-global.com
Web site: http://www.igi-global.com

Library of Congress Cataloging-in-Publication Data

CIP Data Pending
ISBN: 978-1-4666-9629-7
eISBN: 978-1-4666-9630-3

This book is published in the IGI Global book series Advances in Game-Based Learning (AGBL) (ISSN: 2327-1825; eISSN: 2327-1833)

British Cataloguing in Publication Data
A Cataloguing in Publication record for this book is available from the British Library.

For electronic access to this publication, please contact: eresources@igi-global.com.

Advances in Game-Based Learning (AGBL) Book Series

Robert D. Tennyson
University of Minnesota, USA

ISSN: 2327-1825
EISSN: 2327-1833

Mission

The **Advances in Game-Based Learning (AGBL) Book Series** aims to cover all aspects of serious games applied to any area of education. The definition and concept of education has begun to morph significantly in the past decades and game-based learning has become a popular way to encourage more active learning in a creative and alternative manner for students in K-12 classrooms, higher education, and adult education. **AGBL** presents titles that address many applications, theories, and principles surrounding this growing area of educational theory and practice.

Coverage

- Curriculum Development Using Educational Games
- Digital Game-Based Learning
- Edutainment
- Electronic Educational Games
- Game Design and Development of Educational Games
- MMOs in Education
- Pedagogical Theory of Game-Based Learning
- Psychological Study of Students Involved in Game-Based Learning
- Role of instructors
- Virtual worlds and Game-Based Learning

IGI Global is currently accepting manuscripts for publication within this series. To submit a proposal for a volume in this series, please contact our Acquisition Editors at Acquisitions@igi-global.com or visit: http://www.igi-global.com/publish/.

The Advances in Game-Based Learning (AGBL) Book Series (ISSN 2327-1825) is published by IGI Global, 701 E. Chocolate Avenue, Hershey, PA 17033-1240, USA, www.igi-global.com. This series is composed of titles available for purchase individually; each title is edited to be contextually exclusive from any other title within the series. For pricing and ordering information please visit http://www.igi-global.com/book-series/advances-game-based-learning/73680. Postmaster: Send all address changes to above address.

Titles in this Series

For a list of additional titles in this series, please visit: www.igi-global.com

Cases on the Assessment of Scenario and Game-Based Virtual Worlds in Higher Education
Shannon Kennedy-Clark (Australian Catholic University, Australia) Kristina Everett (Australian Catholic University, Australia) and Penny Wheeler (Australian Catholic University, Australia)
Information Science Reference • copyright 2014 • 333pp • H/C (ISBN: 9781466644700) • US $205.00 (our price)

Psychology, Pedagogy, and Assessment in Serious Games
Thomas M. Connolly (University of the West of Scotland, UK) Thomas Hainey (University of the West of Scotland, UK) Elizabeth Boyle (University of the West of Scotland, UK) Gavin Baxter (University of the West of Scotland, UK) and Pablo Moreno-Ger (Universidad Complutense de Madrid, Spain)
Information Science Reference • copyright 2014 • 522pp • H/C (ISBN: 9781466647732) • US $175.00 (our price)

Student Usability in Educational Software and Games Improving Experiences
Carina Gonzalez (University of La Laguna, Spain)
Information Science Reference • copyright 2013 • 439pp • H/C (ISBN: 9781466619876) • US $175.00 (our price)

Interactivity in E-Learning Case Studies and Frameworks
Haomin Wang (Dakota State University, USA)
Information Science Reference • copyright 2012 • 408pp • H/C (ISBN: 9781613504413) • US $175.00 (our price)

Handbook of Research on Improving Learning and Motivation through Educational Games Multidisciplinary Approaches
Patrick Felicia (Waterford Institute of Technology, Ireland)
Information Science Reference • copyright 2011 • 1462pp • H/C (ISBN: 9781609604950) • US $475.00 (our price)

Simulation and Gaming for Mathematical Education Epistemology and Teaching Strategies
Angela Piu (University of L'Aquila, Italy) and Cesare Fregola (Roma Tre University, Italy)
Information Science Reference • copyright 2011 • 256pp • H/C (ISBN: 9781605669304) • US $180.00 (our price)

Gaming for Classroom-Based Learning Digital Role Playing as a Motivator of Study
Young Kyun Baek (Korea National University of Education, Korea)
Information Science Reference • copyright 2010 • 358pp • H/C (ISBN: 9781615207138) • US $180.00 (our price)

Ethics and Game Design Teaching Values through Play
Karen Schrier (Columbia University, USA) and David Gibson (University of Vermont, USA)
Information Science Reference • copyright 2010 • 396pp • H/C (ISBN: 9781615208456) • US $180.00 (our price)

Editorial Advisory Board

List of Reviewers

List of Contributors

Table of Contents

Section 4
Gaming Innovations

Detailed Table of Contents

A central goal of education involves helping students develop deep understandings of complex models at the heart of core learning goals. Interestingly, an analogous goal of commercial recreational digital games involves helping players develop deep understandings of the models at the heart of those games. Given that games can motivate players to engage voluntarily over extended periods of time in developing understandings of complex game models, one may ask whether and how one might foster similar engagement with educational concepts and models. Much fanfare has accompanied claims about games' potential for engagement and motivation, but many of those claims have focused on a shallow idea of "fun". This chapter takes a deeper view of motivation and learning by employing Pintrich's synthesis of research on motivation to learn as a lens for examining (a) how popular game design conventions currently scaffold motivation to learn and (b) how game design conventions might be augmented to more effectively scaffold motivation to learn in the future.

The purpose of this chapter is to describe the design of template for the design of an immersive virtual learning environment that includes collaborative learning virtual worlds as problem-solving scenarios that engage students in virtual explorations of worlds. The problem-based learning 3d model incorporates a curriculum design model that includes a real-world issue that correlates to the virtual scenarios or games. This virtual PBL design model also includes a learning assessment process that utilizes sociocultural learning theories to develop an ongoing feedback model for assessment of learning in a 3d problem-based learning environment. This problem-based learning model combines the benefits of games, such as high-levels of learner engagement, real-life simulations, with research on cognition and instructional design to create a design model that can be modified to develop advanced knowledge, skills and concepts in multiple educational settings.

Kinesthetic gaming, which is also called full-body gaming, is the rising star of digital gaming trends of recent years. With the integration of commercially available motion tracking systems into game consoles, players are able to control the games with kinesthetic movements without any handheld controllers. This new form of advanced human-computer interaction (HCI) allows players to interact with games in more realistic and natural ways. Because of its novelty, research in kinesthetic gameplay is limited, and experimental research on the effects of kinesthetic gaming on learning is almost non-existent. The purpose of the chapter is to investigate the philosophical foundations of kinesthetic game-playing by emphasizing the role of physical action on learning under the framework of cognitive theories and to discuss possible implications in P-12 education. The author aims to introduce kinesthetic game-playing as a powerful tool for learning and to develop new insights on gaming in P-12 education.

This chapter explores the issues associated with training teachers to become effective Augmented Reality game designers in their own educational settings. Within the context of defining and defending the use of games as instructional tools, the authors of this chapter describe a project in Queensland, Australia which involved training 26 teachers from the greater Brisbane area on the theory and process of designing narrative-based Augmented Reality games. This process resulted in usable games that the participants could then implement in their own educational setting. This chapter includes a discussion of the issues and challenges that were faced throughout this training process, and the authors propose potential solutions to address those challenges. Additionally, the authors propose future directions for further research into this area.

The purpose of this chapter is to define a prototype for a comprehensive educational program that integrates virtual immersive learning environments into traditional educational settings to develop innovative educational programs. The Future of Learning (FoL) protocol combines an integrative curriculum guide providing educators with thematic modular units of study that are designed based on problem-based learning principles and a FoL learning management system where online learning environments are structured to be integrated into p-12 educational settings and provide a login protected interface for educators and learners to access all the aspects of the FoL protocol including 1) a home page for the educational program linking all aspects of the protocol, 2) a learner home page, 3) a learning analytic system and 4) access to a 3d simulation world. The comprehensive and modular design of the Future of Learning protocol means that it can be integrated in a multitude of p-12 educational programs and define the future of learning.

This chapter examined pre-service teachers' attitudes toward game-based learning. Research participants included 30 pre-service teachers at a Midwest public university. The research participants took an online course in which game elements such as online mini games as either warm-up or wrap-up activities were integrated. After the course, the researchers analyzed participants' login data and collected their responses to an open online survey. The research results showed that students enjoyed playing games integrated into the course. They spent time playing the games and found them enjoyable and useful. The participants valued the usefulness of integrating games into the classroom. Playing games helped them focus on the topic and review what they had learned from the lecture. They also indicated that they would integrate games into their teaching.

This chapter describes and defines role-play simulations. Reviews of two undergraduate role-play studies highlight the advantages and benefits of using simulations. Few secondary students participate in science or STEM role-plays during their high school careers. This chapter portrays the CyberSurgeons live simulation where teams of students use critical thinking skills and scientific knowledge to solve emergency

ended interview, training session, and post-project open-ended interview. The researchers analyzed participants' responses to the interviews and the quality of the games they created, using the Educational Electronic Games Rubric. Results showed that students not only enjoyed learning about digital games, but also were able to create quality games without coding knowledge or advanced technology skills. Five participants indicated that they plan on creating and integrating digital games into their future teaching.

The paper presents results of a study that was focused on testing the hypothesis that the levels of kindergarten and primary school students' positive emotions, engagement and positive experience will be significantly different while they play free-form and structured digital games. In the context of this study, students' emotion, engagement and experience were assessed through three corresponding questionnaires drawn from the literature. These questionnaires were completed for approx. 500 students of public kindergartens and primary schools located in Athens, Greece. From the analysis of the data collected, free-form digital games are found to lead students towards more positive emotions, higher engagement and more positive player experience. On top of that, a significant correlation is found between positive emotions, engagement and positive experience; the more positive the students' emotion while playing digital games, the higher appears to be their engagement and positive player experience.

Distance Learning through game-based 3D virtual learning environments has promise for helping rural and other communities that have become increasingly dependent upon online learning to meet the Next Generation Science Standards. The team developing Mission HydroSci (MHS) envisions a learning product that integrates a game-based 3D VLE with a learning progressions approach to curriculum and innovative methods for teacher support and learning analytics. MHS uses an eight level game which at each level immerses students in a simulation environment for learning about water systems and then requires the student to put that knowledge into practice in a context of developing their competencies for scientific argumentation. This chapter describes the vision for MHS at the beginning of the development process funded by a grant award from the Investing in Innovation (i3) Fund of the U.S. Department of Education.

The purpose of this chapter is to develop a template for the evaluation of learning in an educational game. In this case, gaming is referred to as 3D immersive virtual learning environments. Problem-based learning is the design template for the IVLE as it engages learners in defined learning behaviors that have been shown to encourage advanced problem-based learning. As a result of this holistic design procedure the learning analytic system proposed in this chapter is an integrated system that can be linked to P-12 educational programs augmenting their traditional programs and providing alternative instructional procedures, alternative learning processes for students and a standards-based but a more individualistic and thus viable assessment of learning to replace an outdated learning assessment model.

With the rise and success of digital games over the past few decades, path planning algorithms have become an important aspect in modern game development for all types of genres. Indirectly-controlled playable characters as well as non-player characters have to find their way through the game's environment to reach their goal destinations. Modern gaming hardware and new algorithms enable the simulation of large crowds with thousands of individual characters. Still, the task of generating feasible and believable paths in a time- and storage-efficient way is a big challenge in this emerging and exciting research field. In this chapter, the authors describe classical algorithms and data structures, as well as recent approaches that enable the simulation of new and immersive features related to path planning and crowd simulation in modern games. The authors discuss the pros and cons of such algorithms, give an overview of current research questions and show why graph-based methods will soon be replaced by novel approaches that work on a surface-based representation of the environment.

Learning through games is a promising field for the future of education. In this research study the authors describe the development process of an educational application, a game targeting P-12 students. This application is meant to be used with the Leap Motion Controller, a small 3D infrared camera, which while in use, tracks the user's hands and finger movements in the 3D space. The chapter describes the application itself and presents the outcomes of a field study, which was carried out with a small group of students at an elementary school. It can be pointed out that there is a huge potential of using innovative input devices in school education.

Foreword

GAMES: LITTLE 'g' AND BIG 'G'

We don't want games going to school in the way textbooks went to school. Textbooks are a very poor educational tool. They standardize education rather than customize it. They are a one-size-fits-all-all-purpose-tool that is too blunt for any of the jobs they need to do. They stress summary rather than inquiry and exploration. They stay always at the surface rather than go on deep dives. And they are too often private reading experiences rather than fuel for collaborative interactions and collective intelligence. Let's not let games become yet another stand-alone-all-purpose tool.

Games are good for lots of things. For example, they are good for motivation, preparation for future learning, developing persistence past failure, and for coming to see failure as a form of (and necessity for) learning. They are good for giving people experiences they cannot necessarily have in the real world and for tying these experience to words, discussion, texts, and dialogue often outside the game. And they can be good for getting students to think about and think like designers and for getting them to see problem solving as social and collaborative interaction among people and smart tools. But they are not good at everything. We need to combine them with texts, social media, and many other sorts of tools and activities.

In the world of entertainment games—games like *Civilization*, *League of Legends*, *the Sims*, *Zelda*, *World of Warcraft*, or *Minecraft*—games as software are only part of the action. They are (often social and collaborative) problem solving spaces that fuel all sorts of interactions outside and around the game. Players gather on all sorts of sites to review, discuss, debate, and mod the game. They discuss strategies, answer questions, write fan fiction, and make videos. They relate the game to other games, texts, media, activities, and experiences in the world. They create all sorts of teaching and learning practices customized to the needs of different sorts of players, things like tutorials, strategy guides, in-game coaching, annotated video, and models of how to build, spec, design, and play at different levels in different ways. They theory craft in an attempt to understand the deep properties of the game's design and to use this understanding for deeper forms of play and collaboration. They help turn interests into passions—passions that might be orthogonal to the game or devoted to related skill areas beyond the game—passions that can fuel thousands of hours of practice as the necessary route to real mastery.

The combination of a game as software and all this hive of interest, passion, teaching and learning around the game I call the "Big G Game" (for me the "little g game" is the game as software). We need to bring Big G Games to school. When we do this, the game is one tool networked with many others and with all sorts of teaching and learning practices, all in the service of discovery, problem solving, and collective intelligence (collective intelligence = networking people, tools, and practices so that the system is smarter than anything in it and can solve "hard problems").

We have major problems in our world today. We face great danger from a variety of interacting complex systems that human greed and stupidity have set on a course to disaster. We face global warming; massive and growing inequality; large-scale environmental degradation; massive immigration flows; speculative capitalism conducted by computers; global wars and violence; and a deterioration of work and wages thanks to the Internet, automation, global competition, and rampant forms of social Darwinism in the United States and spreading across the world. It is time to end business as usual and start working on the really hard problems that face us all. Let's use Games (note the capital) to finally change the paradigm. This book is a great place to start, but it is up to readers to jump into the new paradigm pool and swim for their lives.

James Paul Gee
Arizona State University, USA

James Paul Gee is Mary Lou Fulton Presidential Professor of Literacy Studies and Regents' Professor at Arizona State University.

Preface

INTRODUCTION

The term gaming has radically changed in the last few years as technologies that are mobile, multi-media, interactive, and collaborative have become more advanced and sophisticated. The process of gaming holds promise for advancing learning in P-12 education if designed and developed with educational goals and standards. The premise for this book is that gaming in P-12 Education has the potential to develop advanced knowledge and skills required by the learners while providing a transformative educational experience for both learners and teachers. In order to understand the potential of games in P-12 education this book brings together experts in multiple fields to develop a new understanding of the trends of gaming in education. As a result it provides a definitive guide for educators, researchers and game designers as we take early, but substantial steps towards a future where gaming is a core process in education. The Handbook is designed in strands that will bring together experts' and practitioners' voices on gaming in education. The result is that the Handbook of Research on Gaming Trends in P-12 Education is a holistic guide for trends in virtual immersive learning environments, gaming, as a transformative aspect of P-12 education.

To too great an extent current educational practice relies on past concepts of learning and knowledge that Carl Bereiter called "folk theories" (2002, pg.IX) of the mind. Folk theories of the mind are that the mind is a container that is filled by education. Advances in the cognitive sciences over the last 50 years have revised concepts of learning, mind and education but have not resulted in any major advances in the practical, day-to-day aspects of P-12 education. Most educational programs are struggling to meet standards that require high-stakes testing and a dictated curriculum that is taught in didactic methods based more on economic models of education than pedagogic models. As a result, most technologies are employed in ways that sustain the old system rather than challenge it with innovative new educational forums.

In a parallel path to the advances in cognitive science have been advances in computational capacity and networking bringing about waves of progressing interactive and visual computing connected by the Internet. Around 40% of the world population has an internet connection today. In 1995, it was less than 1%. The third billion was reached by the end of 2014. This has led to a rapid increase in the total information base known as the Knowledge Doubling Curve. Buckminster Fuller identified the Knowledge Doubling Curve noting that until 1900 human knowledge doubled approximately every century. By the end of World War II knowledge was doubling every 25 years. Today, on average, human knowledge is doubling every 13 months. Additionally, the current theory is that as a result of the "internet of things", the Internet added to multiple devices, will lead to the doubling of knowledge every 12 hours (internetworldstatscom).

The folk theory of education as putting information into learners becomes increasingly impossible when the sum total of all knowledge, the information base, is doubling twice a day! Education must instead focus on helping learners become knowledge workers who can respond to this constant deluge of information by using information to solve problems. Learner who, when faced with failure or challenges, can explore, research, and create knowledge.

There are many definitions of these knowledge workers but there are main ideas that run through them all. Knowledge workers are able to do complex problem-solving, drill down into information to understand patterns, evaluate information for relevance and accuracy, and create functional projects. The shift is from passive to active learning, from a focus on teaching about content to enabling learning through the application and search for knowledge, from standardization to customization, from breaking information down to building knowledge. These knowledge workers must be able to navigate the exponentially increasing information base and become the builders, creators and leaders who will be the core of the knowledge economies of the future. Education must change in core ways to develop knowledge workers. This requires a major rethinking- a paradigm shift- in the educational system.

Educational games, or immersive virtual learning environments, can provide engaging, relevant, and personalized learning experiences for all learners that mirror students' daily lives and the reality of their futures as knowledge workers. These games may be the solution making the necessary paradigm shift in education possible.

SOLUTIONS

Into this complex changing dynamic of emerging transformative technologies, changing nature of teaching and learning, increased pedagogical challenges, increased diversity in classrooms, and the necessity for alternative assessments is the concept of gaming in education. Can gaming provide productive forums that are responsive to these issues? It is the premise of this book and the many authors that have contributed to it, that they can. Gaming when considered as an immersive learning environment designed for engagement, motivation, problem-solving and meaningful interactions can develop the types and qualities of learning processes, skills and knowledge required for knowledge workers. Gaming when it is designed and implemented as a forum for immersive virtual learning environment can flip the paradigm of education.

We believe that the nature of games as experiential, interactive, leveled, engaging, and challenging is the basis for systemic reform in education. The type of reform needed to create knowledge workers requires a comprehensive redesign of the nature of education that is based on the attributes of these learning environments, the characteristics of immersive learning, the constructivist pedagogy of the teaching and learning, and the necessity for education to develop immersive virtual learning environments that are tagged to standards and outcomes.

This book is a beginning of a systemic discussion of trends in gaming with chapters by experts in evaluative research of games, academics describing conceptual principals for gaming, gaming companies designing games for education and educators who are implementing games in their classrooms. This discussion on the viability of these transformative technologies and their potential gives us a broad perspective on the future of gaming in P-12 education and a starting point for creating a future for education that matches the challenges of our times.

ORGANIZATION OF THE BOOK

The Handbook of Research on Gaming Trends in P-12 Education is divided into four sections, theoretical research on gaming, pedagogical considerations of games, content specific cases, and gaming innovations research.

Section 1 contains chapters on theoretical research on gaming and includes essays on related philosophies of immersive learning including constructivism, cultural historical activity theory, telepresence, and the evaluation of learning in immersive learning environments,

In Chapter 1, *Beyond Fun: Pintrich, Motivation to Learn, and Games for Learning*, the authors, Mario Martinez-Garza, Douglas Clark, Deanne Adams and Stephen Killingsworth, present a discussion of a deeper view of motivation and learning by employing Pintrich's synthesis of research on motivation to learn as a lens for examining (a) how popular game design conventions currently scaffold motivation to learn and (b) how game design conventions might be augmented to more effectively scaffold motivation to learn in the future.

In Chapter 2, *Design and Implementation of an MMO: Approaches to Support Inquiry Learning with Games,* Louisa Rosenheck, Susannah Gordon-Messer, Eric Klopfer and Jody Clarke-Midura examine how key elements of an implementation of The Radix Endeavor, a multiplayer online game for inquiry-based STEM learning, impact student and teacher experiences and support problem-solving and inquiry learning.

In Chapter 3, *Games and their Embodied Learning Principles in the Classroom: Connecting Learning Theory to Practice,* the author, Sam von Gillern, explores how educators can use games and their embodied learning principles as a source for student learning, motivation, and engagement. Each learning principle and activity is addressed with a summary of the concept, an example of how video games exemplify the concept, and practical methods for integrating the idea into classroom instruction through games and activities.

Chapter 4, In *Game Design Frameworks and Reality Guides*, Jouni Smed, Tomi Suovuo and Ilmari Lahti use the concept of reality guides to analyse the characteristics as applications that aim at assisting the user in the real world and to investigate the applicability of game design frameworks in a wider context of gaming in education.

In Chapter 5, *The Design of Immersive Virtual Learning Environments Utilizing Problem-Based Learning Templates*, Donna Russell describes the design of templates for the design of an immersive virtual learning environment that includes collaborative learning virtual worlds as problem-solving scenarios that engage students in virtual explorations of worlds.

Erdem Demiroz in Chapter 6, *Kinesthetic Gaming, Cognition and Learning: Implications for P-12 Education*, provides an overview of kinesthetic gaming, which is also called full-body gaming, as a new form of advanced human-computer interaction (HCI) allowing players to interact with games in more realistic and natural ways and investigates the philosophical foundations of kinesthetic game-playing by emphasizing the role of physical action on learning under the framework of cognitive theories and goes on to discuss possible implications in P-12 education.

Patrick O'Shea and Chris Campbell in Chapter 7, *The Theory and Process Involved with Educational Augmented Reality Game Design*, explore the issues associated with training teachers to become effective Augmented Reality game designers in their own educational settings.

In Section 2, *Pedagogical Concepts and Related Practice*, the chapters identify and explore the pedagogical aspects of learning in games such as problem-based learning, and collaborative learning environments.

In chapter 8, *Information Literacy in Virtual Environments: Changing Needs of P-12 Learners*, Valerie Hill provides an overview of information literacy needs of P-12 learners in virtual environments. Using standards for 21st century learning from the American Library Association, examples highlight information literacy elements embedded in immersive learning environments, such as the Anne Frank simulation (a 3D replica of Amsterdam and the annex where Anne's family hid) and a digital citizenship game built by students in the game of Minecraft where learners in virtual environments take on digital citizenship responsibilities.

In Chapter 9, *Disciplinarily-Integrated Games: Generalizing Across Domains and Model Types,* the authors Douglas Clark, Pratim Sengupta and Satyugjit Virk advance the idea that disciplinarily-integrated games are a generalizable template for supporting students in interpreting, manipulating, and translating across phenomenological and formal representations in support of a Science as Practice perspective.

Chapter 10, *Playful Transition: Serious Games for the Middle School Years*, Anne Snyder and Victori Van Voorhis provide game designers, instructors, and other stakeholders with an overview of the typical middle school student, as well as the role of serious games in middle school education. Drawing from a case study of an actual game under development, the authors present specific design principles in order to guide stakeholders in the design and use of serious games in the middle school classroom.

Chapter 11, *Designing Alien Mysteries in Chatterdale: An Instructor's Perspective*, the authors, Stella K. Hadjistassou and Judith Molka-Danielsen, describe the design of a virtual science fiction scenario that was student-instigated. Students' quests to unravel a mystery afford opportunities for active involvement and collaborative actions, engagement in verbal exchanges, and interaction with content and context.

In Chapter 12, *Designing Digital Objects to Scaffold Learning*, Grant Van Eaton and Douglas B Clark discuss the importance of digital objects in learning games to provide opportunities to scaffold teacher and student learning toward deeper epistemological understanding of the concepts they represent. Their fiindings highlight the importance of designs that (a) explicitly model the meaning of the representations in the learning environment, (b) provide opportunities for teachers and students to interact with the full range of the properties of the representational object, and (c) incentivize players to utilize representations in the environment to their full extent, such that the learning environment repeatedly reinforces the core concepts of the representation.

In chapter 13, *Flipping the Paradigm of Education, Developing a Comprehensive Educational Program Integrating Virtual Immersive Learning Environments*, Donna Russell defines a prototype for a comprehensive educational program that integrates virtual immersive learning environments into traditional educational settings to develop innovative educational programs.

In Chapter 14, *An Examination of Pre-Service teachers' Attitudes Toward Game-Based Learning,* Scott Fredrickson, Patricia Hoehner, and Jane Ziebarth examine pre-service teachers' attitudes toward game-based learning. Research participants included 30 pre-service teachers at a Midwest public university. The participants valued the usefulness of integrating games into the classroom. Playing games helped them focus on the topic and review what they had learned from the lecture.

In section 3 the chapters include conceptual chapters as well as research that describe current implementation or future trends in gaming in P-12 education. These chapters focus on practical issues including lessons learned and best practices.

In Chapter 15, *Using a Live Simulation to Teach Human Anatomy and the Diagnostic Process to High School Students,* Debra C. Burkey Piecka and Manetta Calinger describe and define role-play simulations as virtual missions for students. In this simulation, students become part of an emergency medical team aboard a National Institutes of Health (NIH) mercy ship traveling up the Amazon River.

Chapter 16, *Using Video Gameplay to Measure Achievement for Students with Disabilities: A New Perspective to Grading and Achievement Reporting Video*, the authors, Benjamin Gallegos, Michelle Kepple and Caitlyn Bukaty focus on the benefits and use of educational video game-based learning for students with disabilities. The authors discuss (1) current barriers hindering widespread adoption of video games for learning and assessment, (2) characteristics of video games being used for learning and assessment, (3) how gameplay data represents academic achievement for grading, and (4) the types of assessments available and considerations for implementation.

Philip Chappell and Douglas Agar in chapter 17, *The Creation of a Rubric for the Evaluation of Language Teaching and Learning Videogames*, report on the creation and evaluation of the Language Education Videogame Evaluation Rubric (LEVER) which will be of benefit to those involved in the teaching and learning of foreign languages.

In Chapter 18, *Can Pre-service Teachers Create Digital Game-Based Activities without Coding Knowledge?,* the authors, Phu Vu and Martonia Gaskill, examine five cases of pre-service teachers' abilities and attitudes towards creating and using digital games in their future teaching.

Chapter 19, *Exploring the Impact of Free-form and Structured Digital Games on the Player Experience of Kindergarten and Primary School Students*, the authors, Sotiris Kirginas and Dimitris Gouscos, present results of a study that tested the hypothesis that the levels of kindergarten and primary school students' positive emotions, engagement and positive experience are significantly different when playing free-form or structured digital games.

In Chapter 20, *Mission HydroSci: Distance Learning through Game-Based 3D Virtual Learning Environments*, that authors, James Laffey, Troy Sadler, Sean Goggins, Joseph Griffin and Ryan Babiuch, envision a learning product that integrates a game-based 3D VLE with a learning progressions approach to curriculum and innovative methods for teacher support and learning analytics. MHS uses an eight level game which at each level immerses students in a simulation environment for learning about water systems and then requires the student to put that knowledge into practice in a context of developing their competencies for scientific argumentation.

Elizabeth Rowe, Erin Bardar, Jodi Asbell-Clark, Christina Shane-Simpso and Su-Jen Roberts in Chapter 21, *Building Bridges, Teachers Leveraging Game-Based Implicit Science Learning in Physics Classrooms*, examine the student and teacher demographics, science content, instructional materials and methods, and game-based pedagogies as potential explanations for differences in learning outcomes.

Section 4, *Gaming Innovations*, contains chapters which are descriptive cases of new games or gaming related technologies. These chapters focus on highly innovative new aspects that are being developed or being planned.

In chapter 22, *The Use of Smart Toys in Learning Games*, Peter A. Smith and Shelly Welch describe use of toys and videogames in learning with the advent of new games like Activision's Skylanders and Disney Infinity. These new approaches are introducing kids to a new level of interaction between the real and virtual. The chapter explores what smart toys are, how they are being used, and future applications of the technology.

The authors of Chapter 23, *Minecraft Schooling: Digital learning for Junior Years,* Leonard Busuttil, Christina Gruppetta, Vanessa Camilleri outline how Minecraft is being used in junior year settings by referring to academic literature as well as communities of practice available on the internet. The authors outline a set of activities incorporating Minecraft aimed at seven year olds which were designed to introduce a series of curricular topics in a class in a Maltese school.

Chapter 24, *Designing a Learning Analytic System for Assessing Immersive Virtual Learning Environments*, the authors, Donna Russell and Steve Wallis describe a template for the evaluation of learning in an educational game through an integrated system that can be linked to P-12 educational programs thereby augmenting their traditional programs and providing alternative instructional procedures, alternative learning processes for students and a standards-based assessment model.

Norman Jaklin and Roland Geraerts describe in Chapter 25, *Navigating through Virtual Worlds: From Single Characters to Large Crowds*, the implications of approaches for the design of crowd simulations and the features that impact learner navigation for games in education.

Chapter 26, *Game-Based Learning with the Leap Motion Controller*, Martin Ebner and Norbert Spot describe the development process of an educational application, a game targeting P-12 students. The authors describe the application itself and present the outcomes of a field study.

In Chapter 27, *A Future Focus of Gaming: Soft Skills*, the authors, DeAnna Proctor and Lenora Justice, discuss the instruction of soft skills training, such as communication, collaboration, decision-making, problem-solving, negotiation, and leadership in games and simulations as a future direction for the use of educational gaming in P-12 education.

This comprehensive Handbook of Research provides a thorough review of research on the multifaceted topic of gaming in education. As the technologies evolve and the educational system responds, this type of systematic review of trends can provide educators, parents, and academics a core conceptual basis for new understandings of the potential of gaming in education.

Donna Russell
Walden University, USA

James Laffey
University of Missouri, USA

REFERENCES

Bereiter, C. (2002). *Education and Mind in the Knowledge Age*. New York, NY: Lawrence Erlbaum Assoc.

Acknowledgment

The editors would like to acknowledge the help of all the people involved in this project and, more specifically, to the authors and reviewers that took part in the review process. Without their support, this book would not have become a reality.

First, the editors would like to thank each one of the authors for their contributions. Our sincere gratitude goes to the chapters' authors who contributed their time and expertise to this book.

Second, the editors wish to acknowledge the valuable contributions of the reviewers regarding the improvement of quality, coherence, and content presentation of chapters. Most of the authors also served as referees; we highly appreciate their double task.

Finally, we would like to thank Dr. James Gee for writing the Foreword and adding his insight to the Handbook of Research on Gaming Trends in P-12 Education.

Donna Russell
Walden University, USA

James Laffey
University of Missouri, USA

Section 1
Theoretical Research

Chapter 1
Beyond Fun:
Pintrich, Motivation to Learn, and Games for Learning

Mario M Martinez-Garza
Vanderbilt University, USA

Stephen S Killingsworth
Vanderbilt University, USA

Douglas B Clark
Vanderbilt University, USA

Deanne M. Adams
University of Notre Dame, USA

ABSTRACT

A central goal of education involves helping students develop deep understandings of complex models at the heart of core learning goals. Interestingly, an analogous goal of commercial recreational digital games involves helping players develop deep understandings of the models at the heart of those games. Given that games can motivate players to engage voluntarily over extended periods of time in developing understandings of complex game models, one may ask whether and how one might foster similar engagement with educational concepts and models. Much fanfare has accompanied claims about games' potential for engagement and motivation, but many of those claims have focused on a shallow idea of "fun". This chapter takes a deeper view of motivation and learning by employing Pintrich's synthesis of research on motivation to learn as a lens for examining (a) how popular game design conventions currently scaffold motivation to learn and (b) how game design conventions might be augmented to more effectively scaffold motivation to learn in the future.

INTRODUCTION

"Kids like games, and they are motivated to play them." This statement, while simple and perhaps self-evident, forms the cornerstone of many arguments advocating digital games as learning tools. Motivation to engage and play, the argument further reads, can be parlayed into positive educational outcomes through skillful design of the game's various elements. Essentially, if students are provided an opportunity to play a game, they will eagerly play it. As a result, if the game is about mathematics (or whatever other subject), the students will learn mathematics because they are motivated to play the game. This line of reasoning acknowledges that digital games are

DOI: 10.4018/978-1-4666-9629-7.ch001

an important part of the lives of young learners. Many school age children invest substantial time in recreational digital games, and in return, these games provide:

1. A collective culture and vocabulary,
2. A set of signifiers of skill, achievement, and hierarchy, and
3. A sense of community, shared enterprise, and self-image (Kafai, Heeter, Denner, & Sun, 2008; Squire, 2003; Thai, Lowenstein, Ching & Rejesky, 2009).

That said, digital games present an interesting puzzle from an educational perspective. Successful recreational games can be challenging and involve complex models and systems at their core. Games must therefore effectively motivate and scaffold the player in learning to master these models in order to be playable. Remarkably, successful recreational games must motivate players to engage voluntarily in this learning process and to pay for the opportunity.

What makes people, especially young people, want to learn, master, and persist at difficult games that require substantial understanding of complex models and systems? It must be that well-designed games successfully motivate players not only to *play,* but also to *learn.* Thus, we may find the answer by investigating certain traits of well-designed games. After all, if all recreational games are not equally motivating to all players, then it stands to reason that games that are more motivating to large numbers of players must share certain traits, and that these traits may be stable and reproducible. And while these traits have evolved independently of research efforts in psychology and education, these traits may provide significant affordances for supporting learning and motivation to learn in the context of games for learning.

GOAL AND STRUCTURE OF THIS CHAPTER

The principal goal of this chapter is to expand and refine the theory of games for learning by situating the unique affordances and features of digital games within Pintrich's widely cited framework on motivation to learn (Pintrich, 2003). Pintrich reviewed and synthesized the literature on motivation to learn in terms of five motivational generalizations that are robustly supported by research and then proposed sample design principles for supporting motivation to learn in classrooms based on these five foundational factors. Our intention is to demonstrate that many design features common across games (what we call *design conventions)* are not simply genre rules that structure play. Rather, these design conventions reify well-founded and agreed upon practices that motivate learning reflected in Pintrich's synthesized framework. From this point of view, when researchers and instructional designers build these design conventions into educational games, they not only make learning environments more game-like: they also introduce elements that strongly affect students' motivation to learn the underlying content.

A more distal goal of this chapter is to address two underlying assumptions that researchers, teachers, and policy makers may have regarding motivation and games for learning:

Assumption 1: Digital games are inherently motivating, and so learners are more likely to engage with a learning environment that is game-like, due solely to its ludic appeal. This assumption drives, at least partly, the well-meaning yet unsubtle infusion of game elements into a digital learning environment in an effort to make it more motivating. Bruckman (1999) famously described these combinations as "chocolate-covered broccoli." We will argue that game design conventions are not motivating because they signal "gameness"; rather, they are motivating because they encode interactions demonstrated by research in psychology and education to be motivating in themselves.

Assumption 2: "Motivation to play" and "motivation to learn" are distinct and uncorrelated. This assumption suggests that a learner that engages with a learning game is responding only to a motivation to play in the sense of having "fun." We will show that there is a high level of overlap between the practices that drive "motivation to learn" and the design conventions that we know are "motivating to play," and that this overlap suggests that these concepts might be related.

Pintrich's Synthetic Framework on Motivation to Learn

The report by the National Research Council (2003) on schools and engagement affirms the key role of motivation in learning. The potential to motivate students is a persuasive argument for including digital games in classrooms. This motivational potential can be understood more deeply when analyzed through the broader research literature on motivation and learning. This literature is extensive and several excellent reviews have catalogued the domain of motivational science and learning (Eccles, Wigfield, & Schiefele, 1998; Pintrich & Schunk, 2002). While many reviews and syntheses of research on motivation have been conducted recently (e.g., Hasni & Potvin, 2014; Graham & Weiner, 2012), Pintrich's synthesis of research on motivation to learn (Pintrich, 2003) is especially useful because of its use-inspired focus on motivation to learn, and the design of environments to support learning, rather than more general aspects of motivation or more specific disciplinary foci. Specifically, while Pintrich's synthetic framework is geared towards the design of classroom activities, this framework also easily supports a deeper structural understanding of the motivational design aspects of recreational games to inform the design of educational games. Pintrich's review distills the literature into five *motivational generalizations*:

1. Adaptive self-efficacy and competence beliefs motivate students.
2. Adaptive attributions and control beliefs motivate students.
3. Higher levels of interest and intrinsic motivation motivate students.
4. Higher levels of value motivate students.
5. Goals motivate and direct students.

We will refer to these propositions hereafter as *core constructs*, to indicate that each one has its own evidence base and can be understood and analyzed separately. Pintrich argues that teachers and instructional designers can use these constructs to develop learning activities that scaffold students' motivation to learn. Pintrich also outlines *design principles* for applying these five motivational generalizations in instructional practice. In the following sections, we explore

1. How popular game design conventions scaffold motivation to learn in light of Pintrich's framework, and
2. How game design conventions might be augmented based on Pintrich's framework.

A Brief Note Regarding Comparisons between Recreational and Educational Games

Throughout our analysis, we often refer to design elements from recreational games, not educational games. This is not to say that no educational games have these same design elements, and the lack of mention of a given educational game is not intended as commentary on its merits. Rather, our comparatively spare use of educational game exemplars is a pragmatic acknowledgement that

Table 1. Pintrich's first core construct and design principles with examples of game design conventions that embody those design principles

First Core Construct: • Adaptive self-efficacy and competence beliefs motivate students. **Design Principles:** • Provide clear and accurate feedback on the development of competence and self-efficacy, focusing on development of competence, expertise and skill. • Design tasks that offer opportunities to be successful but also challenge students. **Example Game Design Conventions That Embody Pintrich's Design Principles:** • **Narrative of Practice:** A well-designed game creates and consistently enforces a narrative of practice leading to improved performance. In other words, recreational games uniformly communicate to players that they can learn to play the game, can develop their expertise with time, and should expect to succeed. • **Difficulty Curves:** Difficulty curves in recreational games increase challenge over time in line with a player's skill – reinforcing a player's belief that he or she can succeed through effort and practice. • **Boss Encounters:** "Boss encounters" provide assessments of a player's ability and also opportunities for players to develop and experiment with new strategies and tactics not necessarily involved in the normal flow of the game, thus helping to scaffold development of players' skill.

1. Recreational games are the source of the design language that educational games extensively borrow from, a trend that is not likely change;
2. Recreational games are more effective as examples because they are probably more familiar and available to the reader; and
3. Recreational games might be considered cleaner examples of motivation to learn, given that players choose to play them freely, rather than playing because they are induced to play by teachers or parents, which can be the case for educational games.

Another important caveat to mention is that, even though we cite many recreational games in our examples of motivation to learn, our analysis applies mainly to a subset of games which contain a complex underlying system, model, or set of rules with which the player must engage and master. Not all popular recreational digital games fall under this description; some popular recreational games, for example, have very simple systems that focus on fast-paced action and reflexes (e.g., *Asteroids*, 1979, or *Call of Duty: Modern Warfare 3*, 2011), simple systems focusing on slow-paced collection and socializing (e.g., Farmville, 2009), or other simple systems that don't involve the mastery of complex models or sets of rules. Given their general simplicity, their reliance on alternate forms of player motivation, and their limited potential to drive player learning, our discussion does not focus on these types of games.

CORE CONSTRUCT 1: ADAPTIVE SELF-EFFICACY AND COMPETENCE PERCEPTIONS MOTIVATE STUDENTS

The first core construct reviewed by Pintrich focuses on the repeated finding that people tend to work hard, persist, and demonstrate enhanced performance when they expect to do well (Bandura, 1997; Pintrich, 1999; Pintrich & Schunk, 2002). This core construct is closely related to the expectancy value model of motivation, which suggests that a person's motivation for a given goal can be roughly computed by multiplying *expectancy* (the subjectively estimated probability of success in achieving that goal) by *value* (the subjective importance of achieving the goal) (Atkinson, 1957; Schunk, 1991; Weiner, 2010). Therefore, as the perceived expectancy of a task increases, so does the person's motivation to engage in the task. Pintrich proposes two design principles to leverage self-efficacy and competence perceptions (Table 1). We discuss these design principles in terms of

1. Providing feedback to players, and
2. Modulating challenges for players.

Scaffolding Self-Efficacy

Self-efficacy refers to an individual's beliefs about their own personal capabilities to learn and employ skills and knowledge (Schunk, 1991; Weiner, 2010). The development of self-efficacy beliefs is influenced by how a student attributes success to internal as well as external factors (Schunk, 1991). The importance of supporting self-efficacy in learning environments is clearly voiced in the following design principle:

- **Design Principle:** Provide clear and accurate feedback on the development of competence and self-efficacy, focusing on development of competence, expertise and skill (Pintrich, 2003, p. 671)

Recreational games must necessarily address the self-efficacy goals of this principle. Games must consistently deliver a certain level of challenge, or the player will quickly lose interest (Koster, 2004). Concurrently, games must contain mechanisms that guide the player in developing the skills necessary to overcome the game's challenges, reinforce the player's feelings of self-efficacy, and reward players for achieving success. A well-designed game thus creates and consistently enforces a narrative of practice leading to improved performance. In other words, recreational games uniformly communicate to players that they can learn to play the game, can increase their skill over time, and should expect to eventually succeed.

The implementation of "difficulty curves" in recreational games exemplifies a design convention that aligns with this theme. In most contemporary games, difficulty curves ensure that players will rarely face a game challenge that requires substantially more skill or understanding than what they currently possess. In this sense, we say that recreational games implement a design property of *guided trajectory*. The player's trajectory typically begins with an "introductory" phase that introduces the game's rules, controls, and conventions. These introductory phases take various forms. Examples include pre-scripted introductory sections of a game in which players develop familiarity with the game mechanics while stakes are low and failure is not possible (as found in *Elder Scrolls V: Skyrim*, 2011, and *Deus Ex: Human Revolution*, 2011); relatively simple levels that are explicitly framed as training (*Star Wars: Knights of the Old Republic*, 2003, and *Call of Duty: Modern Warfare 3*, 2011); or levels in which the player easily outmatches any enemies that may appear (*Torchlight*, 2009). Once the introductory phase has ended, the game gradually increases the level of challenge across the entirety of the player's experience. By keeping the difficulty curve trending upward and ensuring that the player's skill keeps pace, the game may reinforce the player's perception of self-efficacy and encourages a mastery goal orientation (p. 37, this chapter) by suggesting that the player can overcome anything through effort and repeated practice.

Recreational game companies carefully tune games during development to support players' self-efficacy. Supports (such as "difficulty curves") have long been tuned through the process of play testing, in which numerous individuals play the game prior to its release to ensure that the game is neither too easy nor too difficult. Certain companies have also recently begun to incorporate physiological data into this process. For example, Valve Software, the maker of *Left 4 Dead* (2008) and *Portal* (2007), has analyzed heart rate, galvanic skin response, pupil dilation, and even EEG as way to infer the player's emotional state during play; this data is then applied in the service of refining the game's design (Ambinder, 2009; 2011). Further discussion of the connection between emotional state and motivation to learn is somewhat beyond the scope of this chapter (see

Meyer & Turner, 2006), but this novel approach highlights the importance that recreational game designers attribute to supporting players' sense of self-efficacy.

Beyond supporting self-efficacy directly through careful design of tasks (or games), Pintrich's first design principle emphasizes the role of feedback. Recreational games provide several forms of explicit feedback regarding performance. Examples include multi-tiered scoring systems that grade different aspects of player performance (*Vanquish*, 2010), scoring systems that explicitly give bonuses when the player meets certain criteria for outstanding play (e.g., a streak of consecutive notes in *Guitar Hero*, 2010), leaderboards that update frequently (*Counter-Strike*, 2000), and "ghost" versions of the player-avatar that appear on-screen and allow a player to gauge their performance relative to previous instances of play (*Gran Turismo 5*, 2010). These systems help players directly assess their performance and measure their progress.

Future work on games for learning should consider how these forms of feedback may best be deployed in an educational game and how to scaffold the self-efficacy such that it translates beyond the game context. Most of the feedback presented in games highlights how well players complete in-game tasks; this type of feedback has been shown to have an important role in learning (Cameron & Dwyer, 2005; Mayer and Johnson, 2010). Feedback need not be uniformly positive, particularly in the case of occasional failure during game play. Bandura (1986) suggests that failures can have less impact on motivation after a strong sense of efficacy is developed. Bandura has also noted that self-efficacy can be specific to learning domains, environments, and tasks; this raises important questions regarding the transfer of self-efficacy developed within a game to the broader targeted learning domain. Specifically, Bandura's work implies that students may need explicit supports to promote such transfer. This is an important consideration for designing educational games because the design conventions of recreational games do not account for such transfer. More research is necessary to understand this transfer relationship between self-efficacy in a game and self-efficacy beyond the game.

Optimizing Challenge

In addition to the emphasis of Pintrich's first construct on promoting competence and self-efficacy, the first construct also focuses on the motivating effect of challenge. The design principle below suggests that supporting self-efficacy may be motivating in the face of adequate challenge, but may not be motivating if a task is too trivial or difficult:

- **Design Principle:** Design tasks that offer opportunities to be successful but also challenge students (Pintrich, 2003, p. 671)

Pintrich explains that this design principle is a particularly good example of how his framework is guided by both cognitive and motivational considerations. To this he adds, "This congruence is not just serendipitous, but reflects the interpenetration of motivational and cognitive systems when considering the whole learner in context" (Pintrich, 2003, p. 674). Motivational frameworks introduced since Pintrich's review have further articulated the integrated nature of their motivational and cognitive components (e.g., Keller, 2008). In this section, we explore how cognitive and motivational factors influence the relationship between challenge and motivation to learn by analyzing how popular game design conventions modulate difficulty.

As suggested by the idea of "difficulty curves" noted earlier, recreational games are designed to provide an appropriate level of challenge to a player based on the player's expertise. For a game to reach a broad audience, it is crucial that it should not appeal only to the fastest, smartest, and most skilled players. Game design conventions scaffold players through guided trajectories to master increasingly complex sets of skills and capabilities relevant for understanding the underlying models in the game. Thus, recreational games iteratively introduce complexity as players demonstrate increased proficiency. Players may encounter

1. New challenges requiring more sophisticated application of existing skills, or
2. Challenges requiring a demonstration of acquired mastery.

New game challenges can appear in various forms or combinations. Players commonly face more powerful and capable adversaries (*Halo*, 2009) or more complex environments (*Portal*, 2007). In some cases, the environment and opponents remain largely unchanged while the rules within the game increase in complexity as the player advances (*SimCity 4,* 2003, and *Railroad Tycoon,* 1990). Games have recently been developed that either

1. Adjust the difficulty-level of any portion of a game to the player's current skill regardless of the order in which the player encounters that portion of the game (*Elder Scrolls V: Skyrim,* 2011), or
2. Adjust the adversary strategies to provide an appropriate level of challenge based on an assessment of the player's actions (*A.I. War: Fleet Command,* 2010).

A less common (though still popular) method involves gradually increasing the speed (*Tetris*, 1989, *Geometry Wars,* 2003) and dexterity (*Guitar Hero,* 2010) required for the player to advance. While this manner of escalating difficulty is arguably the most primitive and least effective for learning, it has the advantage of making the requirements for advancement clear to the player.

Another common design convention for modulating challenge involves periodically requiring players to demonstrate increasing mastery in very challenging scenarios in order to advance to the next phase or tier of a game. These scenarios are often referred to as "boss" encounters; the name comes from the traditional plot device of the protagonist facing the lead antagonist's senior henchmen (i.e., the "mid-bosses") at the end of each progressive stage of the game before the climactic clash with the lead antagonist at the end of the final stage of the game. Boss encounters have long been a part of video games, from early "platformers" such as *Mega Man,* (1990), and *Contra,* (1988) to more modern multiplayer games like *World of Warcraft* (2004). While boss encounters serve a narrative function in games, they also perform an important pacing and gatekeeping role. If players' skills are not yet advanced enough so that they can progress in the remaining portion of the game, the boss encounter will halt their advancement and provide an opportunity for practice and refinement.

Boss encounters not only provide assessments of a player's ability, but they also provide opportunities for players to develop and experiment with new strategies and tactics that the normal flow of the game would not necessarily demand, thus helping to extend players' skills. Boss encounters often require players to test and develop situation-specific schemata and may require near expert level automaticity in implementing these schemata. However, because boss encounters are a standard design convention, players recognize and accept that boss encounters should be difficult, that repeated failure is likely, and that they will need to integrate and refine all of the skills they have been mastering in order to succeed. Players' understanding of this convention generally helps them to persist in the face of these challenges, and boss encounters are likely to invoke high degrees of player observation, reflection, and experimentation. Players tend to adopt strongly analytical frames of mind for boss encounters, priming players for effortful and purposeful learning. These analytical frames of mind are evidenced in online forums where players discuss games and strategies. Steinkuehler and Chmiel (2006) and Steinkuehler and Duncan (2008), for example, have studied online game forums and found that games have the effect of fostering scientific habits of mind in approaching particularly difficult or complex challenges.

These design features demonstrate how recreational games modulate their perceived difficulty. However, the importance of these features becomes more salient in light of a crucial difference between players of recreational and educational games. Players in informal contexts tend to choose a game in accordance with their current mindsets, experience, and skill levels, but learners in formal contexts tend to be recruited into specific games (and thus have lesser agency in selecting games that match their current experiences, expertise, and skill levels). Thus, players of games in informal contexts essentially provide a degree of "adaptive difficulty" functionality themselves as expressed through their choices. Games for learners in classrooms and other formal contexts typically are not allowed such choice, and thus educational games themselves need to provide adaptive difficulty.

Several research perspectives can be leveraged to theoretically conceptualize the optimization of challenge in game design. One such theoretical frame comes from cognitive load theory. This theory suggests that what an individual can learn within a window of time is limited by how much information can be maintained in working memory (Sweller, Merrienboer, & Paas, 1998). A further conceptualization afforded by cognitive load theory is that of "free resources" that are not occupied by the intrinsic and extraneous loads imposed by the task. This notion of free resources is important because most learning is an effortful process of constructing schemas and developing automaticity that requires deploying these free resources (Kalyuga, 2011). Higher motivation leads students to persist in a task (Vollmeyer & Rheinberg, 2000) and, within reason, this persistence can help learners overcome high cognitive demands, whereas a lack of motivation and persistence may lead students to feel overwhelmed by much lower cognitive demands.

Vygotsky's idea of the zone of proximal development (Vygotsky, 1978) provides another lens for conceptualizing challenge from the other end of the theoretical spectrum. Vygotsky proposed that optimal learning occurs for tasks that are just above an individual's capabilities, but that the individual can accomplish with scaffolding (Vygotsky, 1986). The concept of the zone of proximal development highlights that challenge is individually specified and shifts over time for each individual. The tasks that one individual can perform with and without assistance are typically different from those that another can perform at any given point in the learning process. Thus, degree of challenge is dependent upon prior experience and knowledge. With repeated, effortful individual practice, a previously challenging activity will no longer require scaffolding and, eventually, these effortful tasks can even be transformed and internalized into relatively automatic behaviors (Chi, 1978; Chi, Feltovich, & Glaser, 1981; De Groot, 1965; Kalyuga Ayres, Chandler, & Sweller, 2003).

This shift in challenge across time within and across individuals is also recognized in cognitive load or free resource perspectives (Kalyuga, et al., 2003; Schnotz, Fries, & Horz, 2009). As a person gains experience with a task, he or she may develop a schema to efficiently maintain an optimal balance between attentional and working memory resources in order to achieve high levels of performance fairly automatically (for an example of how this happens in the case of visual processing for a simple action, see Droll & Hayhoe, 2007, or Hayhoe, Shrivastava, Mruczek, & Pelz, 2003). Brophy (1999) integrates cognitive and zone of proximal development perspectives in his work with motivation in the domain of task difficulty. Specifically, Brophy suggests that tasks should not be

1. So unfamiliar that they cannot to be recognized as learning opportunities,
2. So over-familiar that a learner is temporarily satiated with them, or
3. Associated with past unrewarding experiences.

Thus, optimizing challenge in game design from either theoretical perspective recognizes intra-individual and inter-individual variation based on prior experience.

As noted, players of educational games have fewer choices and resources available to them to control the overall difficulty of their play experience, and this increases the importance of adaptive functionality for adjusting challenge in educational games designed for classrooms or other formal contexts. Each of the research perspectives discussed above provides a workable framework for designing such additional supports.

CORE CONSTRUCT 2: ADAPTIVE ATTRIBUTIONS AND CONTROL BELIEFS MOTIVATE STUDENTS

The second construct discussed by Pintrich (2003) focuses on attributions and control beliefs (Table 2). The central idea common to models of attributions and control beliefs focuses on learners' perceptions of their control over outcomes and the causes of success and failure (Pintrich, 2003). As Pintrich explains:

Although there are some mixed results (cf. Findley & Cooper, 1983; Stipek & Weisz, 1981), the general trend is that students who believe they have more personal control of their own learning and behavior are more likely to do well and achieve at higher levels than students who do not feel in control, such as those who are often labeled as learned helpless (Pintrich & Schunk, 2002; Skinner, Zimmer-Gembeck, & Connell, 1998). (p. 673, emphasis added)

Pintrich synthesizes diverse perspectives in this area. Perry and colleagues (e.g., Perry, Hladkyj, Pekrun, & Pelletier, 2001), for example, show that "higher levels of perceived control are positively related to a host of cognitive, motivational, affective, and academic achievement outcomes" (Pintrich, 2003, p. 673). Similarly, Skinner et al. (1998) conducted a longitudinal study demonstrating that productive patterns of perceived control were connected to increased engagement in school and higher levels of academic achievement. Finally, research from self-determination theory, which is especially relevant to game design, demonstrates "the importance of an internal locus of causality and perceptions of autonomy and competence in adaptive behavior (Deci & Ryan, 1985; Ryan & Deci, 2000)" (Pintrich, 2003, p. 673).

The first design principle that Pintrich outlines in this second construct on attributions and control beliefs (Table 2) resonates with the first construct's focus on feedback

- **Design Principle:** "Provide feedback that stresses process nature of learning, including importance of effort, strategies, and potential self-control of learning" (Pintrich, 2003, p. 671)

Providing immediate and detailed responsive feedback is a central hallmark of good game design. Detailed and responsive feedback stresses the process of learning and rewards experimentation. Game design conventions focus on developing a strong narrative of practice in terms of providing feedback to the player that highlights growth, self-improvement, and mastery. We discussed the design conventions that align with feedback in the previous section. Also, this design principle applies to achievement goal orientations; these will be discussed in depth later in this chapter.

The second design principle of this construct focuses on choice and control. This section discusses the application of the following design

Table 2. Pintrich's second core construct and design principles with examples of game design conventions that embody those design principles

Second Core Construct: • Adaptive attributions and control beliefs motivate students. **Design Principles:** • Provide feedback that stresses process nature of learning, including importance of effort, strategies, and potential self-control of learning. • Provide opportunities to exercise some choice and control. • Build supportive and caring personal relationships in the community of learners in the classroom. [This design principle is discussed later in terms of the role of the teacher rather than in the current section in terms of game design conventions]. **Example Game Design Conventions That Embody Pintrich's Design Principles:** • **Narrative of Practice:** Recreational games have a long tradition of encapsulating gameplay as narratives of growth, self-improvement, and mastery. The general principle of these recreational games is that the game experience should not remain static but should expand along with the players' growing skills to offer new challenges and possibilities for play, promoting self-improvement, effort, and mastery among players. • **Dynamic Control:** Unlike more established media (such as books, movies or radio), which are largely non-interactive and passive, the player in a digital game is an active, central, and necessary participant in the construction of the activity. The centrality of the player can be observed in various forms, and different game genres provide various types of player control. • **Customization:** Customization is an increasingly popular component of successful recreational games that allows for choices and control of game features such as character appearance, equipment, and skill sets.

principle to digital games in light of self-determination theory and research on choice in learning environments.

- **Design Principle:** "Provide opportunities to exercise some choice and control" (Pintrich, 2003, p. 671)

Games generally situate players as largely in control of their experiences. This player-centered control aligns with the implications of self-determination theory and motivation. Self-determination theory proposes that three general psychological needs support intrinsic motivation: competence, relatedness, and autonomy. Competence generally relates to the ideas discussed previously regarding self-efficacy and optimal challenge. The idea of relatedness will not be discussed in detail here, but generally suggests that the level of security and concern provided by an adult moderates competence and autonomy factors (Ryan & Deci, 2000). Research on the final type of need, autonomy, suggests that intrinsic motivation is supported by choice and control (Deci, Connell, & Ryan, 1989; Ryan & Deci, 2000). This aspect of self-determination theory suggests that intrinsic motivation is high when individuals feel that they control the outcomes they experience and when feedback is provided about their competence at autonomously navigating the environment (Deci, Connell, & Ryan, 1989; Ryan & Deci, 2000).

Opportunities to exercise choice and control over the progress and direction of the narrative are central features of many digital games. Unlike more established media (such as books, movies or radio), which are largely non-interactive, the player of a digital game is not a passive receptor but an active, central, and necessary participant in the construction of the activity.

The centrality of the player can be observed in various forms, and different game genres provide one or more of the following types of player control. Players can have low-level *moment-to-moment control* in which they perform a simple task that is still important (e.g. travel by mounted creature in *World of Warcraft,* 2004). Players can have *tactical control*, where quick decisions lead to decisive actions on the basis of whatever information is immediately at hand (as in *Tetris,* 1989, *Street Fighter*, 1998, or *Starcraft,* 1998). Players can make informed *strategic control* choices about which goals to pursue, in what order to pursue them, and which resources to deploy (as in *Civilization V,* 2010). Players can have *narrative control*, where the long-term development of the plot depends on choices that only the player can make (as in *Dragon Age: Origins,* 2009). Lastly, players can have *moral control* when they choose a set of permissible actions from a broader range of behaviors allowable by the game (e.g. *Fable II,* 2008, or *Grand Theft Auto IV,* 2008).

One important point is that opportunities for control in recreational games need to be legitimate in order for players to value them. Players quickly detect false control and tend to hold strong negative opinions of game mechanics that offer only illusory choice. Games with otherwise strong narratives (such as *Final Fantasy XIII,* 2010) have been harshly criticized by gamers for restricting players' opportunity for choice (by limiting gameplay to traveling down long corridors with little possibility of choice) and for excessive use of non-interactive animated sequences, or "cut scenes." Therefore, there exists a tension between restricting the space of player choice (in order to present a strong narrative or simplify the game experience) and expanding it (to provide an enhanced feeling of control); how this tension plays out in terms of motivation to learn is still not well understood.

The motivating effects and other positive outcomes due to introducing choice have been demonstrated by numerous studies in addition to the work of Deci and colleagues (e.g. Becker, 1997; Cordova & Lepper, 1996; Iyengar & Lepper, 1999). Some research, however, has reported negative outcomes from introducing choice (e.g. Baumeister, Bratslavsky, Muraven, & Tice, 1998; Flowerday, Schraw, & Stevens, 2004). To address these contradictions in research on choice, Patall, Cooper, and Robinson (2008) conducted a meta-analysis of numerous studies. These authors found that choice can produce positive outcomes, but only with certain important restrictions on the characteristics of the relevant choices. Overall, the authors found that choice has positive impacts on intrinsic motivation (measured by self-report and task-persistence following the manipulation) and related outcomes of effort, perceived competence, and task performance. Thus, in line with Pintrich's design principle and with the principles of self-determination theory, choice generally seems to be motivating.

Patall et al. (2008) identified several variables, however, moderating the effects of choice. Their most interesting finding was that *instructionally-irrelevant* choices (e.g. the music played during an aerobics class) had the largest positive effects on intrinsic motivation. The authors suggest that students may perceive these irrelevant choices as opportunities to express their personal identities. In the case of *instructionally-relevant* choices (e.g., choosing which color names to learn in a foreign language), or choices that could change the effectiveness of the task for learning purposes, Patall and colleagues suggest that these choices can produce a reduction in self-regulatory resources that interferes with the possible positive effects of choice. Instructionally-irrelevant choices also showed stronger effects on motivation than manipulations involving choices between activities or choices between versions of a task, reinforcing the idea that more removed choices may be more intrinsically motivating. Patall et al. also found that the number of choices moderated the effect; making two to four choices in a single experimental manipulation (rather than one choice or five or more choices) seemed to have the greatest positive effect on measures of intrinsic motivation. The authors explain their results in terms of a trade-off between the positive effects of choice predicted by self-determination theory (greater motivation from more than one choice) and the negative effects of choice from resource expenditure (lowered motivation for five or more choices).

In terms of "instructionally-irrelevant choices," recreational games contain several mechanics that allow choices about details of the game that do not affect game mechanics. These choices can, however, strongly enhance a players' identification with the character or game. Games offer a wide and increasing array of options, for example, for customization of a player's avatar. Avatar customization and design is a compelling mechanic for male and female players (see Kafai, Fields, & Cook, 2010). These options have always been present to some extent, but they have grown more sophisticated and varied in recent years. Many different kinds of games provide for extensive customization of the player character's appearance (e.g. *Dragon Age: Origins,* 2009) that can inscribe not only the player's aesthetic preferences but also make visible his or her decisions and achievements in the game by modifying appearance based on choices during game play (e.g. *Fable II,* 2008) or accomplishments during game play (e.g., *World of Warcraft*, 2004). These customizations can be displayed publically and serve as identifying features in multiplayer games (e.g., *Team Fortress 2,* 2007, and *World of Warcraft,* 2004).

It remains less clear how the research on instructionally-relevant choices maps onto the moment-to-moment, tactical, strategic, narrative, and moral control provided in games. Though each of these types of control may be central to understanding the models at the heart of a digital game, this does not necessarily align with nature of instructionally-relevant choices studied in the literature surveyed by Patall et al. (e.g. choosing color names to learn in a foreign language). One important distinction between the types of instructionally-relevant choices studied in that research and the types of instructionally-relevant choices players make in games involve *consequentiality*.

Consequentiality refers to the observable, logical impact of the player's choices on the simulated world (e.g. if a player makes a choice that initiates a narrative that differentially influences learning the core models of the game). When a player is certain that his or her choices matter, and that the game will extrapolate outcomes based largely on the player's actions, these actions become laden with meaning. Such *consequential engagement* is theorized to be critical for conceptual understanding (Gresalfi, Barab, Siyahhan & Christensen, 2009). Consequential engagement arises when learners must consider the consequences of their choices, not only in the proximal sense of analyzing their impact on the simulated world, but also in the more reflective sense of examining the context in which those choices were made and their appropriateness under the circumstances. This form of engagement goes beyond the kinds of choices considered by Patall et al. (2008) and is rare in typical educational practice or even in discussions of educational reform (Gresalfi et al., 2009).

Patall and colleagues note that the manipulations of instructionally-irrelevant choices (e.g. choosing what color pen to use or choosing what music to listen to) included in their meta-analysis may have facilitated a greater expression of individuality in a way that the manipulations of instructionally-relevant choices did not. If supporting individual expression is a critical factor in what makes a choice motivating, then the consequential engagement supported by the "instructionally-irrelevant choices" in games is likely to be even more motivating than the forms of instructionally-irrelevant choices reviewed by Patall and colleagues. The intersection between broader educational research on choice and the ubiquitous presence of choice in recreational games is an important area for future research, for instance, by examining the benefits and possible tradeoffs involved in consequential choice.

CORE CONSTRUCT 3: HIGHER LEVELS OF INTEREST AND INTRINSIC MOTIVATION MOTIVATE STUDENTS

Pintrich's third core construct (Table 3) focuses on the role of interest and intrinsic motivation (e.g., Renninger, Hidi, & Krapp, 1992). This includes both personal interest (i.e., a learner's relatively enduring dispositions and preferences) and situational interest (i.e., the psychological state of being that provides interest in an activity based on characteristics of the activity itself). As Pintrich explains:

Table 3. Pintrich's third core construct and design principles with examples of game design conventions that embody those design principles

Third Core Construct: • Higher levels of interest and intrinsic motivation motivate students. **Design Principles:** • Provide stimulating and interesting tasks, activities, and materials, including some novelty and variety in tasks and activities. • Provide content material and tasks that are personally meaningful and interesting to students. • Display and model interest and involvement in the content and activities. [This design principle is discussed later in terms of the role of the teacher rather than in the current section in terms of game design conventions]. **Example Game Design Conventions That Embody Pintrich's Design Principles:** • **Novelty and Emergent Experiences:** The nature of digital games demands that the central challenge of a game evolve and emerge. Koster (2004) observed that games that do not provide emergent experiences cannot remain challenging. • **"Mini-Games":** Mini-games provide a secondary (and sometimes optional) game experience used as a diversion to slow the pace of the narrative and make it more light-hearted. • **Meaningful Play:** Meaningful play is a defined by Salen and Zimmerman (2004) as a form of action through which the player can create new meanings within the system. Through having a direct impact on new meanings within a game, this can promote intrinsic interest.

Research on both personal and situational interest has shown that higher levels of both are associated with more cognitive engagement, more learning, and higher levels of achievement (Eccles et al., 1998; Hidi, 1990; Pintrich & Schunk, 2002; Schiefele, Krapp, & Winteler, 1992) (Pintrich, 2003, p. 674).

Novelty and Emergent Experiences

As with his other core constructs, Pintrich's design principles and synthesis of the research on interest and intrinsic motivation align closely with game design conventions. The first design principle for this construct focuses on novelty and variety, which are defining features of contemporary digital games in terms of the staggering diversity of their designs.

- **Design Principle:** Provide stimulating and interesting tasks, activities, and materials, including some novelty and variety in tasks and activities (Pintrich, 2003, p. 671)

Recreational games have evolved since the days of fast-paced arcade games like *Space Invaders* (1978) and *Galaga* (1981). These older games followed paradigms that were very narrowly defined. Games had not yet explored the full range of forms that exist today. Novelty in digital games has greatly increased since; new gaming genres have since emerged and recombined with classic forms to produce a very broad range of gaming experiences. This high level of novelty stands in stark contrast to the narrower range of activities that often define traditional classrooms.

In addition to variety across games, a player may be called upon to engage in a variety of tasks within a single game. These tasks are termed "mini-games" and are usually a secondary (and sometimes optional) part of the game experience. Many successful game designs use mini-games in an integrated fashion to provide variety to the game experience and to keep novelty high. An example of this is the "hacking" mini-game (in the form of a timed puzzle) built into the first-person shooter *Deus Ex: Human Revolution,* (2011) or the role-playing game *Mass Effect 2* (2010). More commonly, mini-games are used as diversions intended to slow the pace of the narrative and make it more light-hearted. For instance, players can take a break from questing in *The Legend of Zelda: Ocarina of Time* (1998) to go fishing, rest from saving the galaxy in *Mass Effect* (2008) by gambling at a space casino, or recover from fighting evil in *Final Fantasy VII* (1997) by racing ostrich-like Chocobos.

Furthermore, the very nature of digital games demands that the central challenge of a game evolve and emerge. Koster (2004) observed that games that do not provide emergent experiences cannot remain challenging in the face of the inevitable (and desirable) progressive mastery of the player. Such games become boring and are cast aside. A boring game is a failure not only on the commercial level but also at the level of evolutionary design: boring games typically leave no successors or sequels. Consequently, their game mechanics typically do not propagate into the general design space of digital games. Recreational game designers therefore have tremendous incentive to create games that are interesting, novel, and varied in a manner that evolves with the progressive mastery of the player.

Interestingly, well-designed games occasionally break the aforementioned boredom rule in ways that players find acceptable. Some games include a dynamic through which a player can obtain desirable in-game rewards or advantages if the player dedicates an extended period of time to a certain repetitive form of play. Players will often tolerate bouts of this repetitive play (known as "grinding") for the rewards (e.g., "gold farming" in *Diablo III,* 2012), but game designers are constantly searching for more varied and interesting designs to maintain popularity with their player base. For example, *World of Warcraft* (2004) created "daily quests" as a more varied alternative to gold farming, and *Warhammer Online* (2008), *Rift* (2011), and *Guild Wars 2* (2012) all include further evolutions on this theme. This commercially-necessitated ongoing design evolution toward more interesting alternatives attests to the motivational value of variety and novelty.

Personally Meaningful and Interesting Tasks

Throughout our discussion of Pintrich's framework and how it applies to digital games for learning, our goal has been to clearly identify where Pintrich's design principles for instruction can be instantiated in digital games. Calling them "design principles", as Pintrich does, suggests that motivation is a factor that can be purposefully built into a game or activity. However, motivation is not a response that can be triggered in an individual at-will; rather, it is an outcome of the game or task as designed and the learner's personal attitudes and values. While psychological research has identified in general terms what elements people find broadly motivating (and we cite some of these findings here), it remains true nonetheless that it is the learner who ultimately filters, shapes, and accepts or rejects these elements. The central, active role of the learner in motivation to learn is acknowledged in Pintrich's next design principle:

- **Design Principle:** Provide content material and tasks that are personally meaningful and interesting to students (Pintrich, 2003, p. 671)

Understanding what constitutes "personal meaning" is a difficult task, perhaps better suited to philosophy. Nonetheless, some scholars have noted that game playing is not an activity inherently devoid of personal significance. One way in which games build personal meaning and sustain interest is through *meaningful play,* defined by Salen and Zimmerman (2004) as a form of action through which the player can create new meanings within a system. These meanings arise when the player interacts with both the formal relationships defined by the game rules and the interpretable context of the play experience. Since these meanings are not built into the game, they arise only through the player's actions and can strongly vary from one player to the next. These mechanisms can scaffold players' intrinsic motivation in line with Pintrich's (2003) research synthesis.

One example of meaningful play comes from the *SimCity* franchise (e.g., *SimCity 4,* 2003) in which players create cities by making design choices within the affordances and constraints of the game. Some players of *SimCity 4* (2003), for example, may choose to build park-like cities with ample public spaces and efficient mass transit; others might prefer to create industrial powerhouses or bustling high-tech towns. We argue that these alternatives are not merely stylistic choices, nor do they represent any "best" way to play the game. Rather, players produce artifacts that encapsulate core personal notions of what a "good city" is and how it functions; the "SimCities" they create are not just solutions to a simulation, but *authored works* laden with meaning. Some contemporary games even provide support for public sharing of game play as individually authored works. For example, the logic puzzle game *SpaceChem* (2011) allows players to submit their solutions as videos to YouTube from within the game interface so that their individual approaches may be shared and acknowledged by other players.

Aside from opportunities for personal meaning-making, in some cases the structure and challenges of the game may be intrinsically interesting for students. This intrinsic source of interest stands in contrast to extrinsic sources; this distinction has been the focus of a significant amount of research. Before discussing the second design principle of this construct, it is important to understand prior distinctions that have been made between intrinsic and extrinsic motivation. Intrinsic motivation is repeatedly mentioned in this and other discussions of motivation to learn. Ryan and Deci (2000) define intrinsic motivation as, "doing an activity for its inherent satisfactions rather than for some separable consequence" (p. 56). These authors further state, "when intrinsically motivated, a person is moved to act for the fun or challenge entailed rather than because of external prods, pressures, or rewards" (p. 56). In contrast to this, Ryan and Deci (2000) define extrinsic motivation as "...whenever an activity is done in order to attain some separable outcome" (p. 60). Beyond the coarse division above, self-determination theory also suggests that extrinsic motivation can be internalized (and identified with the self) to varying degrees. The least internalized form of extrinsic motivation proposed is externally regulated behavior (Ryan & Deci, 2000). These behaviors involve an external demand or reward such that the behavior is performed (or performed to a particular specification) in order to receive the reward.

The intrinsic-extrinsic duality is less clear in games because it is not always clear what is intrinsic and what is extrinsic. Several studies suggest that games support intrinsic motivation as measured by self-report (Huang, Huang, & Tschopp, 2010; Papastergiou, 2009; Tüzün, Yilmaz-Soylu, Karakus, Inal, & Kizilkaya, 2009). However, as mentioned by Huang et al. (2010), games employ numerous external rewards. Games often introduce coins, stars, medals, or points to measure students' progress and performance. Each of these features could be viewed as external to game play. Much of the research on self-determination theory has been concerned with evaluating the influences of tangible external rewards on motivation and performance. This work generally finds that engagement-contingent, completion-contingent, and performance-contingent tangible rewards reduce intrinsic motivation (Deci, Koestner, & Ryan, 1999). Though rewards can increase desired behaviors (see Slavin, 2009), students' free choice of an activity (a behavioral measure of intrinsic motivation) and self-reported measures of intrinsic motivation seem to be negatively impacted by tangible external rewards.

Designing educational games adds an extra challenge in terms of integrating the intrinsically motivating aspects of a game success and the broader learning goals targeted by the game. This is highlighted in the literature in terms of the discussion of intrinsic and extrinsic design of games for learning (e.g., Habgood & Ainsworth, 2011). Intrinsic design incorporates the learning goals directly into the most inherently motivating and interesting aspects of the game, while extrinsic design separates the learning goals from the inherently motivating and interesting aspects of the game (e.g., *Math Blaster!*, 1983). Intrinsic design can be further divided into *conceptually-embedded design* where the learning goals are embedded in central game activities set in various locations in a virtual world or space versus *conceptually integrated design* where the learning goals are integrated into the core game mechanics for manipulating or navigating the game space itself (Clark and Martinez-Garza, 2012). Rather than including the learning goals as mandatory but less interesting aspects of the game, these intrinsic design approaches thus connect the learning goals into the inherently motivating and interesting aspects of the game, which may potentially promote transfer of that motivation to learn beyond the game.

CORE CONSTRUCT 4: HIGHER LEVELS OF VALUE MOTIVATE STUDENTS

The fourth general construct supported across the research literature focuses on the motivational implications of an activity's perceived value (Table 4). Expectancy-value theory identifies four components of task-value beliefs: intrinsic interest, utility, importance, and cost (Eccles & Wigfield, 1995; Wigfield, 1994; Wigfield & Eccles, 1992). Furthermore, Wigfield and Eccles (1989) found that these value components can differentially impact intentions to persist in learning at different grade levels. Pintrich provides a useful summary of the model's components:

In this model, intrinsic interest is similar to personal interest, whereas utility is defined in terms of individuals' perceptions of the usefulness of the content or task to them, a more extrinsic orientation to the task. Importance or attainment value refers to how important it is to do well on the task for the individual as well as how central the task is perceived to be to the individual's personal identity. Cost beliefs refer to the perceptions of the costs or negative consequences of engaging in the task, although it has not been empirically investigated as much as the other three components of task value (Pintrich & Schunk, 2002) (Pintrich, 2003, p. 675).

- **Design Principle:** Provide tasks, material, and activities that are relevant and useful to students, allowing for some personal identification with school (Pintrich, 2003, p. 671)

Game-based learning environments clearly leverage the "intrinsic interest" component of the expectancy-value theory at the heart of this construct. Furthermore, the "cost" component of expectancy-value theory is low for students

Table 4. Pintrich's fourth core construct and design principles with examples of game design conventions that embody those design principles

Fourth Core Construct: • Higher levels of value motivate students. **Design Principles:** • Provide tasks, material, and activities that are relevant and useful to students, allowing for some personal identification with school. • Classroom discourse should focus on importance and utility of content and activities. [This design principle is discussed at the end of this chapter in terms of the role of the teacher rather than in the current section in terms of game design conventions]. **Example Game Design Conventions That Embody Pintrich's Design Principles:** • **Training and Simulation:** Some games engender value by ostensibly cultivating a set of cognitive and or physical abilities or attributes that have real-world relevance that the player considers valuable or desirable. • **Epistemic Games:** These games offer an emerging area of increased value in gaming by engaging players in situated roles that are designed to align the players' actions, goals, and attitudes with those typical of a professional operating within the field of expertise being modeled by the game.

because of the focus on game-design conventions in supporting success and minimizing the costs of failure. This leaves "utility" and "importance" as the two remaining features suggested by expectancy-value theory that can frame our discussion.

Whether or not digital games have or are perceived to have utility, beyond the gratification of immediate needs for distraction, is quite debatable. We interpret the persistence of digital gaming in the cultural landscape and the growing evidence that gaming is a life-long pursuit (Electronic Software Association, 2014) as indications that people are finding some form of value in digital games. Digital gaming has moved beyond a "boys only" enterprise and has spread across age groups, cultures, and nations (see Kafai, Heeter, Denner, & Sun, 2008). According to surveys published by the Entertainment Software Association, the average age of a gamer in 2004 was 29; in 2011 it was 37 (with an average of 12 years of digital game playing). That said, some game designs have attempted to make their claims to utility more explicit. For example, some games have billed themselves as ways to learn to play musical instruments (*Rocksmith*, 2011), or forms of physical exercise (e.g. *Wii Fit*, 2008, *Dance Dance Revolution*, 2010, *Your Shape: Fitness Evolved,* 2010), largely through the use of game controllers that respond to body motions. Similarly, games have been designed for the purpose of training cognitive abilities (e.g., *Brain Age,* 2009, *Big Brain Academy,* 2006). While these cognitive games may not deliver their promised effect (e.g. Owen et al., 2010), players clearly find some value at least in the training metaphor based on the popularity of the genre. Similarly, some games are perceived as relevant because they train a specific skill that the player finds valuable. Recent simulation games such as *iRacing* (2008) and *Flight Simulator X* (2006) are realistic enough that gamers may be getting more than just "a sense of what it means" to drive a race car or pilot an aircraft and are actually learning the true skill. A telling example is the case of Greger Huttu, the *iRacing* (2008) champion who, when placed in a real race car for the first time, posted outstanding lap times despite not even having a driver's license (Read, 2010).

In terms of "importance", digital games generally make very limited claims. However, a developing niche for importance in games comes from online crowd-sourced puzzle games. Games such as *FoldIt* (2008) allow players to interact with a game-based version of a real-world scientific puzzle. In *FoldIt,* players obey accurate rules of amino-acid folding to create various possible configurations of enzymatic proteins. Researchers can then synthesize real versions of promising player-generated proteins to improve the efficiency of bio-chemical processes (see Cooper et al., 2010; Khatib et al., 2011). Games such as *FoldIt* are perceived by some players as genuinely important because the players' efforts contribute directly to genuine published scientific progress. Along these lines, *EteRNA* (2011) focuses on the design of RNA, the molecules that control protein synthesis. *EteRNA* also allows players to contribute directly to scientific progress because the player community is substantially more effective than the current scientific algorithms at predicting and planning RNA folding (Koerner, 2012).

Finally, educational games can leverage the capabilities of current recreational games to better address issues of "utility" and "importance" by allowing players to take on robust identities in rich authentic contexts in service of socially valued skills and practices (rather than the more destructive goals typical in many current recreational games). The term *instrumentality* (essentially a synonym for "utility") refers to the subjective perception of how useful a task is in terms of some particular external goal. One example of instrumentality that has an important effect on an individual's motivation to pursue a task is the individual's beliefs about how closely a task relates to that individual's desired future profession. If an individual has a positive outlook toward his or her future, then a closer connection between a task and a desired profession can increase motivation

Table 5. Pintrich's fifth core construct and design principles with examples of game design conventions that embody those design principles

Fifth Core Construct: • Goals motivate and direct students. **Design Principles:** • Use cooperative and collaborative groups to allow for opportunities to attain both social and academic goals. • Use task, reward, and evaluation structures that promote mastery, learning, effort, progress, and self-improvement standards and less reliance on social comparison or norm referenced standards. • Classroom discourse should focus on mastery, learning, and understanding course and lesson content. • Use organizational and management structures that encourage personal and social responsibility and provide a safe, comfortable, and predictable environment. [See "Across Constructs", below, for main discussion]. **Example Game Design Conventions That Embody Pintrich's Design Principles:** • **MMORPGs (Massively Multiplayer Online Roleplaying Games):** MMORPGs involve enduring collaborations between players as an inherent structure and foundation of the game. • **Affinity Spaces:** Places where people interact around a common passion. The online communities formed around recreational games constitute affinity spaces with multiple avenues for exploring one's interests such as discussing tactics, developing and obtaining modifications and add-ons to games, and even mathematically analyzing game mechanics.

(see Creten, Lens, & Simons, 2001; Raynor, 1969; van Calster, Lens, & Nuttin, 1987; Vroom, 1964).

Along these lines, some educational games allow players to take on other socially valuable roles that may match or overlap with future professional aspirations. For example, *Operation: Resilient Planet* (2008) allows players to take on the role of a marine ecologist and perform many tasks relevant to this profession. Substantial theoretical research focuses on developing "epistemic games" and augmented reality games in which players take on the roles of professionals such as urban planners or nanotechnology engineers (e.g., Shaffer & Gee, 2007; Shaffer, 2009). In summary, research on the motivational benefits of developing discernible instrumentality within game-based curricula and research on opportunities to take on authentic roles as practitioners of science or other disciplines offer rich possibilities for building strong cognitive and motivational connections among the kinds of knowledge and reasoning that will be required throughout an individual's academic and career paths.

Furthermore, it is important to note that external goals and intrinsic interest are not mutually incompatible. Lens (2001) distinguishes several different relationships between the locus of goals and motivation. External goals can produce "endogenous instrumentality," for example, in which the alignment between the demands of the current learning context (e.g. learning math) and the future goal (e.g. being an engineer) will enhance intrinsic motivation. Alternatively, external goals can produce "exogenous instrumentality" in which interest in a task (e.g. taking a history class) that is required for achieving an external goal (e.g. becoming an engineer) creates extrinsic interest. However, Lens (2001) suggests that this extrinsic interest can still be motivating because the task is viewed as an important step to achieving the external goal and the individual will thus internalize the responsibility of regulating task performance. Thus, educational games as a medium can also be leveraged to address both intrinsic interest and external goals without placing a player directly in the role of a long-term targeted profession.

CORE CONSTRUCT 5: GOALS MOTIVATE AND DIRECT STUDENTS

Pintrich's fifth construct synthesizes research on goals and goal orientation (Table 5). Pintrich focuses specifically on

1. Goal content and the multiple goals that students can pursue in school settings, and

2. The nature of achievement goals or goal orientations.

Pintrich makes clear that this fifth construct is more fragmented than the other constructs in terms of its implications for design. He accordingly outlines a larger number of design principles. We discuss these design principles in the following sections in terms of leveraging social goals and building productive goal orientations.

The Socially-Situated Nature of Modern Gaming and Motivation to Learn

Although social goals are often assumed to distract from academic pursuits, social goals can be harnessed in the service of academic goals. Wentzel (1991, 1999, 2000) examined, for example, how different goals interrelate in terms of learning, adjustment, and achievement with an emphasis on the role of social goals. Pintrich's first design principle for this construct focuses on the affordances of cooperative and collaborative groups for scaffolding social and academic goals:

- **Design Principle:** Use cooperative and collaborative groups to allow for opportunities to attain both social and academic goals (Pintrich, 2003, p. 671)

This social design principle is not universally leveraged across all genres of recreational games, but features prominently in several genres. Some games are designed so that players can form collaborations to reach certain in-game goals. These collaborations can be brief and *ad hoc*, lasting only as long as the current game session (e.g., teams formed for a match of *Team Fortress 2,* 2007). But in certain genres, particularly Massively Multiplayer Online Roleplaying Games ("MMORPGs"), these collaborations tend to be more enduring and comprehensive in scope. As discussed earlier, persistent player associations are a fixture of MMORPGs in the form of "guilds" (*World of Warcraft,* 2004), "clans" (*Call of Duty: Modern Warfare 3,* 2011), "corporations" (*EVE Online,* 2007), "fleets" (*Star Trek Online, 2010*), and "supergroups" (*City of Heroes,* 2004). These MMORPGs focus explicitly on cooperative and collaborative groups as a core structure.

Collaborative social interactivity, however, can also be designed into single-player games. Even when the nature of the game reduces or eliminates opportunities for direct collaboration, modern games often provide in-game features that link players' individual play with the wider community of players. As discussed earlier, for example, some contemporary games like *SpaceChem* (2011) even provide support for public sharing of game play as individually authored works on YouTube and other venues.

Collaboration around games does not, however, require specific in-game functionality. Communities arise spontaneously around games based on shared interests. Examples of these extra-game collaborations include the *Skyrim Nexus* (a "modding" community dedicated to creating modifications for *Elder Scrolls V: Skyrim,* 2011); the *Apolyton University* (a forum group intended to teach novice players the nuances of *Civilization V,* 2010); and *Elitist Jerks* (a research community devoted to mathematically analyzing the game mechanics of *World of Warcraft*, 2004).

Modern game designers of both single and multiplayer games have therefore become highly attuned to issues of community building and apprenticeship. Designers understand that games are more successful when players are motivated to work with one another, to help novices learn, and to induct newcomers into the community. The result of this focus on community is that games increasingly become nuclei for what James Gee calls "affinity spaces" (Gee, 2003/2007). In the broadest sense, affinity spaces are defined as places where people interact around a common passion. As Gee explains, affinity spaces have powerful features that provide resources and mentoring for learners. Affinity spaces encourage people to gain both intensive and extensive knowledge, enable multiple routes to participation, support the creation of new material and knowledge resources for everyone to use, and encourage tacit, individual, and dispersed knowledge (Hayes & Gee, 2009; see also Gee, 2004).

Gee proposes that affinity spaces are functionally similar to Wenger's communities of practice (Wenger, 1998), but Gee argues that the concept of communities of practice are difficult to extend into forms of co-participation with no defined group membership (Gee, 2005). That said, contemporary recreational game designers embrace concepts of mutual engagement and shared enterprise that parallel Wenger's perspectives on communities of practice, and continue to explore new ways in which these concepts can be incorporated into the game experience. Recent approaches to community building in MMORPGs, for example, provide extensive frameworks for groups of players of all sizes and levels of expertise to band together in service of community goals. As discussed above, collaboration is thus possible not only at the level of small temporary teams or more permanent "guilds" but also at the level of larger factions (e.g., the Horde and Alliance factions that include all characters in *World of Warcraft,* 2004, and coalitions that span thousands of players on *EVE Online,* 2007) or even server-wide communities (e.g., competitions between entire servers that result in server-wide benefits in *Guild Wars 2,* 2012). Future research needs to further explore collaborative synergies for learning at these large scales.

Building Productive Achievement Goal Orientations

Pintrich's next two design principles focus on achievement goals and goal orientations. Distilling the most uncontroversial recommendations from the relevant research, Pintrich focuses on promoting a mastery orientation and promoting specific aspects of approach behavior relevant to goal-setting within a mastery orientation.

- **Design Principle:** Use task, reward, and evaluation structures that promote mastery, learning, effort, progress, and self-improvement standards and less reliance on social comparison or norm referenced standards
- **Design Principle:** Classroom discourse should focus on mastery, learning, and understanding course and lesson content (Pintrich, 2003, p. 671)

These design principles relate specifically to the idea of achievement goals and goal orientation (Ames & Archer, 1988; Elliot & Dweck, 1988; Nicholls, 1984) and to the idea of a theory of intelligence, or mindset (Dweck, 2006). Pintrich describes achievement goals as "purposes or reasons an individual is pursuing an achievement task" (Pintrich, 2000, p. 93). Generally speaking, achievement goal perspectives describe *mastery orientation*, which focuses on the desire to develop competence and increase knowledge and understanding through effortful learning; *performance orientation*, which focuses on gaining favorable judgments and avoiding negative judgments of one's competence; and *work-avoidance orientation,* which focuses on getting work done with minimum effort (Pintrich, 2000; Thrash & Elliot, 2001; see also Murphy & Alexander, 2000). These goal orientations may be activated in a context-dependent manner based on factors like competition, although certain individuals may have greater degrees of stability or higher probabilities for a given goal orientation (Pintrich, 2000).

Furthermore, work-avoidance goals have often been characterized as maladaptive (Fellonar, Román, & Cuestas, 2007; Seifert & O'Keefe, 2001) while mastery goals have been regarded as promoting better learning outcomes than performance goals (see Harackiewicz, Barron, Pintrich, Elliot, & Thrash, 2002). Also, individuals may hold multiple goal orientations simultaneously with mastery and performance goals having an additive influence (Harackiewicz et al., 2002).

These findings and theoretical perspectives help us understand the affordances of digital games for manipulating players' goal orientations. Recreational games have a long tradition of encouraging mastery orientations among players by encapsulating gameplay as narratives of growth, self-improvement, and mastery. The greatest concentration of this narrative can be found in the role-playing game (or "RPG") genre. In these games, a player's character gains "levels" as he or she makes progress in the game, and each new level gained brings an increase in the character's power and ability. The skills that the character gains are also graded in "levels" and, in some cases, these skill levels increase with practice (e.g., *Elder Scrolls V: Skyrim,* 2011). With play, characters accrue "experience points" commensurate with the challenges the player has solved, and players are often provided with visual indicators that signal their progress towards the next level. Characters can also obtain diverse equipment to improve their capabilities, such as weapons, armor, magical items, etc., that have some quantitative measure attached to them. In summary, players of RPGs frequently experience a variety of elements that reinforce the idea that every success they achieve counts towards progress.

These mechanics of growth (generically termed "role-playing elements") have been adopted by a variety of genres beyond what is commonly acknowledged as the role-playing genre. In the cartoonish "shoot'em-up" *Jamestown* (2011), for example, players gain access to more capable aircraft as more "boss" enemies are dispatched. Similarly, players in the "tower-defense" game *Revenge of the Titans* (2011) earn currency by defeating invading Martian Titans, which can then be used to research and purchase more advanced defensive weaponry. The general principle of these recreational games is that the game experience should not remain static but should expand along with the players' growing skills to offer new challenges and possibilities for play, promoting self-improvement, effort, and mastery among players.

Features and gaming practices that emphasize performance orientations are also common in both single- and multiplayer games. In single-player games, an increasingly common practice for players is to record outstanding examples of their own play so they can be published on the Internet. An example of this type of play is the "speed run" (i.e., a complete run through a game, from start to finish, in an extremely short amount of time). Speed runs require extreme skill, but also a remarkable willingness to repeat an identical run many times until the shortest possible time has been achieved. There are over 110,000 "speed run" videos posted on YouTube, most of them for platform games (e.g. *Super Mario Bros.*, 1985), but extending to other genres as well. Moreover, as discussed earlier, some games like *SpaceChem* (2011) streamline the process of sharing examples of play by automatically recording and uploading the player's solutions to YouTube.

In the realm of multiplayer games, performance orientations are further emphasized when players engage in high-risk group endeavors such as "raiding" in *World of Warcraft* or "fleet ops" in *Eve Online*. These games have features that make it easy to observe and critique performance in the context of group play. *Eve Online*, for example, makes a detailed record of every player-vs.-player combat available via a direct link to their server's database. These records become public at the victor's discretion. These public records create an incentive for players to perform their best, but negative consequences are common in group play for players who show a lack of skill or discipline during "fleet ops" or "raids". Performance orientation is encouraged by a somewhat unique mechanic in *World of Tanks* (2010), where a third-party service called XVM collects individual players' game logs and calculates a unofficial "player rating", similar to a chess player's FIDE rating.

While these emphases on performance orientations in recreational games can drive refinement at the highest levels of play, this emphasis on social comparison is at odds with Pintrich's first design principle for this construct (i.e., "Use task, reward, and evaluation structures that promote mastery, learning, effort, progress, and self-improvement standards and less reliance on social comparison or norm referenced standards"). In light of this design principle, future research should examine how this balance between mastery and performance orientation impacts motivation to learn in more formal learning contexts in which players have less opportunity to opt in and out of playing.

In summary, recreational game design conventions encode numerous mechanics that promote a variety of goal and performance orientations in players. Further research on scaffolding productive goal and performance orientations could thus prove valuable to both recreational and educational game designers by

1. Improving the quality of players' experiences,
2. Maximizing their learning opportunities, and
3. Potentially promoting transfer of productive goal orientations beyond the game.

ACROSS CONSTRUCTS: THE OFTEN OVERLOOKED ROLE OF TEACHERS AND COACHES IN FORMAL CONTEXTS

Thus far, this chapter has outlined the congruence between recreational game design conventions and Pintrich's (2003) design principles for encouraging motivation to learn in classrooms. We have discussed ten of the fourteen design principles proposed by Pintrich because of their close parallels with recreational game design conventions. The remaining four design principles focus on the role of the teacher, and recreational game design conventions generally do not focus on a role for teachers or other formal coaches (Martinez-Garza and Clark, 2013). Unfortunately, in leveraging recreational game design conventions, designers of educational games often focus on tight parallels with recreational design conventions, thus focusing on players' interactions with the game environment, rather than also considering the role of the teacher or coach. This lack of articulation of a role for the teacher often extends even to the literature on games intended for classroom use (Martinez-Garza and Clark, 2013).

Pintrich's remaining four design principles highlight the lost opportunities resulting from this oversight. These design principles focus on the teacher's orchestration of the classroom, rather than the nature of the activities themselves, and thus apply to games along with all other activities in formal learning environments:

- Build supportive and caring personal relationships in the community of learners in the classroom. (Second Construct)
- Display and model interest and involvement in the content and activities. (Third Construct)
- Classroom discourse should focus on the importance and utility of content and activities. (Fourth Construct)
- Use organizational and management structures that encourage personal and social responsibility and provide a safe, comfortable, and predictable environment. (Fifth Construct)

Aligning educational game design to these principles is a challenge because, as discussed above, games for learning are often designed and discussed solely in relation to the learner. Kebritchi, Hirumi, Kappers, and Henry (2009) found, for example, that only four out of ten educational games surveyed provided a teacher's manual, and only one provided teacher aids, lesson plans, or unit plans. In the absence of guidance or resources, teachers must design and plan their own curricular integrations and scaffolding around the edges (Millstone & Levy, 2012; see also Ng, Zeng, and Plass, 2009). This is a missed opportunity; teachers possess extensive expertise on how to personalize and adapt instructional tools to the individual needs of students. Educational reform perspectives emphasize the central role of teachers in students' learning even when the tools that support that learning have their own embedded forms of guidance (e.g. Duschl, Schweingruber & Shouse, 2007). Less time is available for teachers to engage in such student-specific adaptation if teachers must also develop all of the overarching curricular integration and scaffolding.

The role of the teacher is not only important from the perspectives of adoption and implementation but also for students' cognition and metacognition (Squire, Barnett, Grant, & Higginbotham, 2004). Moreover, teachers are the principal proponents of classroom initiatives (such as educational games) and teachers are an important source of guidance and support for other teachers (Kirriemuir & McFarlane, 2004). Pintrich's final four design principles thus highlight a critical gap in the design of many educational games for formal learning contexts at the most fundamental level.

In addition to highlighting the role of the teacher, these design principles also highlight the role of digital games as *organizational tools* to structure interaction between peers in a learning context. Digital games can be designed, for example, to provoke and scaffold certain forms of discourse that are conducive to learning. This view is in keeping with existing perspectives on computer-supported collaborative learning, where computer environments are seen as tools for scaffolding interactions between peers (e.g., Ertl, 2010; Weinberger, Kollar, Dimitriadis, Mäkitalo-Siegl, & Fischer, 2009) and cultivating tacit forms of knowledge that are crucial to participation in disciplinary communities (e.g., Tabak & Reiser, 2008).

MMORPGs represent the closest parallel in terms of scaffolding and structuring interactions between peers in current recreational games. As discussed in previous sections, MMORPGs share many features that motivate players to collaborate, participate meaningfully in the shared enterprise, and hold each other accountable for their performance. While Pintrich's framework places responsibility for these aspects of motivation to learn on the teacher, MMORPGs generate analogous processes without requiring a central agent (i.e. a teacher). These processes are partly self-organizing but also reflect the design choices that the game's creators selected. Future research on educational games should explore how existing design choices for social interactions in these contexts can be reframed or elaborated in a manner that supports the role of the teacher within or around educational games while also leveraging the role of the teacher through game mechanics that effectively implement these final four design principles.

CONCLUSION

Moving forward in the field of educational research on games will depend on focusing beyond shallow superficial elements in games and instead focusing on deeper structures that encourage motivation to play and learn. To advance understanding of the learning affordances of games, research should thus attend to deeper structures which connect to foundational issues of motivation. That said, nuanced discussion of motivation to play has often been preempted by basic assumptions that "educational games are motivating because they are games."

In our discussion, we have addressed these assumptions by transposing a well-known and accepted framework for motivation to learn unto the design elements that underpin many popular recreational games in hopes of encouraging more nuanced and thoughtful design efforts of educational games. We used Pintrich's framework as an analytic lens given its comprehensive nature, its specific focus on design, and its generativity for educational games. However, while Pintrich's framework is compatible with educational games research, it is clearly not a complete answer. While educational games, like any other school intervention, are certainly unlikely to yield positive outcomes if students are not motivated to engage with them, the converse is not necessarily true; motivation to learn means little if a given game's underlying systems are not well aligned with learning goals and processes (Clark, Sengupta, Brady, Martinez-Garza, and Killingsworth, 2015). Thus, principled and thoughtful design efforts to design educational games must also focus on learning goals and player's learning processes in support of those goals. Furthermore, Pintrich's framework highlights areas where the affordances for the design of educational games remain unclear (e.g. the role of the teacher as a social mediator of learning). More research and innovation is clearly warranted in these areas to fully leverage motivation to learn in educational games.

In closing, we return to two final ideas that introduced in the beginning of the chapter. First, that motivation to learn is much deeper than "fun". Learning is motivated by a complex interplay of both individual perceptions and dispositions and external factors in the environment. Second, as Pintrich's framework makes clear, motivation to learn is not an inherent property of the medium in which learning happens (i.e., digital games). Rather, motivation to learn is an outcome of purposeful, principled design. Thus, our discussion is meant to encourage educational game design that focuses more on specific principles and elements that reify these principles, and less on a general assumption that "kids like games and are motivated to play them." We feel that this view is more empowering to educational game designers, and ultimately, to students.

ACKNOWLEDGMENT

This material is based upon work supported by the National Science Foundation under Grant No. 1119290. Any opinions, findings, and conclusions or recommendations expressed in this material are those of the author(s) and do not necessarily reflect the views of the National Science Foundation.

REFERENCES

A.I. War: Fleet Command [Digital Game]. (2009). NC: Arcen Games, Arcen Games.

Ambinder, M. (2009, March). Valve's Approach to Playtesting: The Application of Empiricism. Presentation and the Game Developers Conference. Retrieved from http://www.valvesoftware.com/publications/2009/GDC2009_ValvesApproachToPlaytesting.pdf

Ambinder, M. (2011, March). Biofeedback in Gameplay: How Valve Measures Physiology to Enhance Gaming Experience. Presentation at the Game Developers Conference. Retrieved from http://www.valvesoftware.com/publications/2011/ValveBiofeedback-Ambinder.pdf

Ames, C., & Archer, J. (1988). Achievement goals in the classroom: Students' learning strategies and motivation processes. *Journal of Educational Psychology*, *80*(3), 260–267. doi:10.1037/0022-0663.80.3.260

Atkinson, J. W. (1957). Motivational determinants of risk-taking behavior. *Psychological Review; Psychological Review, 64*(6p1), 359.

Bandura, A. (1986). *Social foundations of thought and action: A social cognitive theory*. Englewood Cliffs, NJ: Prentice Hall.

Bandura, A. (1997). *Self-efficacy: The exercise of control*. New York: Freeman.

Baumeister, R. F., Bratslavsky, E., Muraven, M., & Tice, D. M. (1998). Ego depletion: Is the active self a limited resource? *Journal of Personality and Social Psychology*, *74*(5), 1252–1265. doi:10.1037/0022-3514.74.5.1252 PMID:9599441

Becker, D. A. (1997). The effects of choice on auditors' intrinsic motivation and performance. Retrieved from http://papers.ssrn.com/sol3/papers.cfm?abstract_id=2918

Big Brain Academy [Digital Game]. (2006). Kyoto, Japan: Nintendo.

Brain Age [Digital Game]. (2009). Kyoto, Japan: Nintendo.

Brophy, J. (1999). Toward a model of the value aspects of motivation in education: Developing appreciation for. *Educational Psychologist*, *34*(2), 75–85. doi:10.1207/s15326985ep3402_1

Bruckman, A. (1999). Can educational be fun? Paper presented at the Game Developers Conference '99, San Jose, CA.

Call of Duty: Modern Warfare 3 [Digital Game]. (2011). Santa Monica, CA: Activision, Infinity Ward Sledgehammer Games.

Cameron, B., & Dwyer, F. (2005). The effect of online gaming, cognition and feedback type in facilitating delayed achievement of different learning objectives. *Journal of Interactive Learning Research*, *16*(3), 243–258.

Chi, M. T., Feltovich, P. J., & Glaser, R. (1981). Categorization and representation of physics problems by experts and novices. *Cognitive Science*, *5*(2), 121–152. doi:10.1207/s15516709cog0502_2

Chi, M. T. H. (1978). Knowledge structure and memory development. In R. Siegler (Ed.), *Children's thinking: What develops?* (pp. 73–96). Hillsdale, NJ: Erlbaum.

City of Heroes [Digital Game]. (2004). Seoul, Korea: NCsoft, Cryptic Studios.

Civilization V [Digital Game]. (2010). Novato, CA: 2K Games, Firaxis.

Clark, D. B., & Martinez-Garza, M. (2012). Prediction and explanation as design mechanics in conceptually integrated digital games to help players articulate the tacit understandings they build through game play. In C. Steinkuhler, K. Squire, & S. Barab (Eds.), *Games, learning, and society: Learning and meaning in the digital age*. Cambridge: Cambridge University Press. doi:10.1017/CBO9781139031127.023

Clark, D. B., Sengupta, P., Brady, C., Martinez-Garza, M., & Killingsworth, S. (2015). Disciplinary Integration in Digital Games for Science Learning. *International STEM Education Journal*, *2*(2), 1–21. doi: 10.1186/s40594-014-0014-4

Contra [Digital Game]. (1988). Tokyo, Japan: Konami, Konami.

Cooper, S., Khatib, F., Treuille, A., Barbero, J., Lee, J., & Beenen, M. et al. (2010). Predicting protein structures with a multiplayer online game. *Nature*, *466*(7307), 756–760. doi:10.1038/nature09304 PMID:20686574

Cordova, D. I., & Lepper, M. R. (1996). Intrinsic motivation and the process of learning: Beneficial effects of contextualization, personalization, and choice. *Journal of Educational Psychology*, *88*(4), 715–730. doi:10.1037/0022-0663.88.4.715

Counter-Strike [Digital Game]. (2000). Redwood City, CA: Electronic Arts, Valve.

Creten, H., Lens, W., & Simons, J. (2001). The role of perceived instrumentality in student motivation. In A. Efklides, J. Kuhl, & R. M. Sorrentino (Eds.), *Trends and prospects in motivation research* (pp. 33–45). Dordrecht, The Netherlands: Kluwer Academic Publishers.

Dance Dance Revolution [Digital Game]. (2010). Tokyo, Japan: Konami.

De Groot, A. (1965). *Thought and choice in chess*. The Hague: Mouton.

Deci, E. L., Connell, J. P., & Ryan, R. M. (1989). Self-determination in a work organization. *The Journal of Applied Psychology*, *74*(4), 580–590. doi:10.1037/0021-9010.74.4.580

Deci, E. L., Koestner, R., & Ryan, R. M. (1999). A meta-analytic review of experiments examining the effects of extrinsic rewards on intrinsic motivation. *Psychological Bulletin*, *125*(6), 627–668. doi:10.1037/0033-2909.125.6.627 PMID:10589297

Deci, E. L., & Ryan, R. M. (1985). *Intrinsic motivation and self-determination in human behavior*. New York: Plenum. doi:10.1007/978-1-4899-2271-7

Deus Ex: Human Revolution [Digital Game]. (2011). Montreal: Square Enix, Eidos Studios.

Diablo III [Digital Game]. (2012). Irvine, CA: Blizzard Entertainment, Blizzard Entertainment.

Dragon Age: Origins [Digital Game]. (2009). Redwood City, CA: Electronic Arts, BioWare.

Droll, J. A., & Hayhoe, M. M. (2007). Trade-offs Between Gaze and Working Memory Use. *Journal of Experimental Psychology. Human Perception and Performance*, *33*(6), 1352–1365. doi:10.1037/0096-1523.33.6.1352 PMID:18085948

Duschl, R. A., Schweingruber, H. A., & Shouse, A. W. (Eds.). (2007). *Taking Science to School: Learning and Teaching Science in Grades K-8*. Washington, D.C.: The National Academies Press.

Dweck, C. S. (2006). *Mindset: The new psychology of success*. New York: Random House.

Eccles, J., & Wigfield, A. (1995). In the mind of the actor: The structure of adolescents' achievement task values and expectancy-related beliefs. *Personality and Social Psychology Bulletin*, *21*(3), 215–225. doi:10.1177/0146167295213003

Eccles, J., Wigfield, A., & Schiefele, U. (1998). Motivation to succeed. In W. Damon (Series Ed.) & N. Eisenberg (Vol. Ed.), Handbook of child psychology: Vol. 3. Social, emotional, and personality development (5th ed., pp. 1017–1095). New York: Wiley.

Elder Scrolls: Skyrim [Digital Game]. (2011). Rockville, MD: Bethesda Softworks, Bethesda Game Studios.

Electronic Software Association. (2014, April) Essential facts about the computer and video game industry: 2014 sales, demographic, and usage data. Retrieved from http://www.theesa.com/wp-content/uploads/2014/10/ESA_EF_2014.pdf

Elliott, E. S., & Dweck, C. S. (1988). Goals: An approach to motivation and achievement. *Journal of Personality and Social Psychology*, *54*(1), 5–12. doi:10.1037/0022-3514.54.1.5 PMID:3346808

Ertl, B. (Ed.). (2010). *E-Collaborative Knowledge Construction: Learning from Computer-Supported and Virtual Environments*. New York: IGI Global. doi:10.4018/978-1-61520-729-9

EteRNA [Digital Game] (2011). Pittsburgh, PA: Carnegie Mellon University and Stanford University, Carnegie Mellon University. Retrieved from http://eterna.cmu.edu/

EVE Online [Digital Game]. (2007). New York: Simon & Schuster Interactive, CCP TransGaming.

Fable II [Digital Game]. (2008). Redmond, WA: Microsoft, Lionhead Studios.

Final Fantasy VII [Digital Game]. (1997). Foster City, CA: Sony Computer Entertainment, Square.

Final Fantasy XIII [Digital Game]. (2010). Tokyo, Japan: Square Enix.

Findley, M. J., & Cooper, H. M. (1983). Locus of control and academic achievement: A literature review. *Journal of Personality and Social Psychology*. *Journal of Personality and Social Psychology*, *44*(2), 419–427. doi:10.1037/0022-3514.44.2.419

Flight Simulator X [Digital Game]. (2006). Redmond, WA: Microsoft, ACES Game Studio.

Flowerday, T., Schraw, G., & Stevens, J. (2004). The role of choice and interest in reader engagement. *Journal of Experimental Education*, *72*(2), 93–114. doi:10.3200/JEXE.72.2.93-114

FoldIt [Digital Game]. (2008). Seattle, WA: University of Washington, University of Washington.

Galaga [Digital Game]. (1981). Chicago, IL: Namco, Midway.

Gee, J. P. (2003/2007). *What video games have to teach us about learning and literacy*. New York: Palgrave Macmillan.

Gee, J. P. (2004). *Situated language and learning: A critique of traditional schooling*. Routledge.

Gee, J. P. (2005). *Why Video Games Are Good for Your Soul: Pleasure and Learning*. Common Ground.

Geometry Wars [Digital Game]. (2003). Liverpool, U.K.: Bizarre Creations.

Graham, S., & Weiner, B. (2012). Motivation: Past, present, and future. In K. Harris, S. Graham, T. Urdan, C. McCormick, G. Sinatra, J. Sweller (Eds.) APA Educational Psychology Handbook, Vol 1: Theories, Constructs, And Critical Issues (pp. 367-397). Washington, DC, US: American Psychological Association.

Gran Turismo 5 [Digital Game]. (2010). Foster City, CA: Sony Computer Entertainment, Polyphony Digital.

Grand Theft Auto IV [Digital Game]. (2008). New York: Rockstar Games, Rockstar North.

Gresalfi, M., Barab, S., Siyahhan, S., & Christensen, T. (2009). Virtual worlds, conceptual understanding, and me: Designing for consequential engagement. *On the Horizon*, *17*(1), 21–34. doi:10.1108/10748120910936126

Guild Wars 2 [Digital Game]. (2012). Seoul, Korea: NCsoft, ArenaNet.

Guitar Hero [Digital Game]. (2010). Santa Monica, CA: Activision, Vicarious Visions.

Habgood, M. P. J., & Ainsworth, S. E. (2011). Motivating Children to Learn Effectively: Exploring the Value of Intrinsic Integration in Educational Games. *Journal of the Learning Sciences*, *20*(2), 169–206. doi:10.1080/10508406.2010.508029

Halo [Digital Game]. (2009). Redmond, WA: Microsoft, Bungie Software.

Harackiewicz, B., & Pintrich, E. (2002). Revision of Achievement Goal Theory: Necessary and Illuminating. *Journal of Educational Psychology*, *94*(3), 638–645. doi:10.1037/0022-0663.94.3.638

Hayes, E. R., & Gee, J. P. (2009). Public Pedagogy through Video Games. Handbook of public pedagogy: education and learning beyond schooling, 185.

Hayhoe, M. M., Shrivastava, A., Mruczek, R., & Pelz, J. B. (2003). Visual memory and motor planning in a natural task. *Journal of Vision (Charlottesville, Va.)*, *3*(1), 49–63. doi:10.1167/3.1.6 PMID:12678625

Hidi, S. (1990). Interest and its contribution as a mental resource for learning. *Review of Educational Research*, *60*(4), 549–571. doi:10.3102/00346543060004549

Huang, W. H., Huang, W. Y., & Tschopp, J. (2010). Sustaining iterative game playing processes in DGBL: The relationship between motivational processing and outcome processing. *Computers & Education*, *55*(2), 789–797. doi:10.1016/j.compedu.2010.03.011

iRacing [Digital Game]. (2008). Redmond, WA: iRacing.com Motorsport Simulations.

Iyengar, S. S., & Lepper, M. R. (1999). Rethinking the value of choice: A cultural perspective on intrinsic motivation. *Journal of Personality and Social Psychology*, *76*(3), 349–366. doi:10.1037/0022-3514.76.3.349 PMID:10101874

Jamestown: Legend of the Lost Colony [Digital Game]. (2011). Philadelphia: Final Form Games.

Kafai, Y. B., Fields, D. A., & Cook, M. S. (2010). Your Second Selves: Player Designed Avatar Designs. *Games and Culture*, *5*(1), 23–42. doi:10.1177/1555412009351260

Kafai, Y. B., Heeter, C., Denner, J., & Sun, J. (2008). (Eds.), Beyond Barbie and Mortal Kombat: New Perspectives on Gender and Gaming. Cambridge, MA: MIT Press.

Kalyuga, S. (2011). Cognitive Load Theory: How Many Types of Load Does It Really Need? *Educational Psychology Review*, *23*(1), 1–19. doi:10.1007/s10648-010-9150-7

Kalyuga, S., Ayres, P., Chandler, P., & Sweller, J. (2003). The expertise reversal effect. *Educational Psychologist*, *38*(1), 23–31. doi:10.1207/S15326985EP3801_4

Kebritchi, M., Hirumi, A., Kappers, W., & Henry, R. (2009). Analysis of the supporting websites for the use of instructional games in K-12 settings. *British Journal of Educational Technology*, *40*(4), 733–754. doi:10.1111/j.1467-8535.2008.00854.x

Keller, J. M. (2008). First principles of motivation to learn and e3-learning. *Distance Education*, *29*(2), 175–185. doi:10.1080/01587910802154970

Khatib, F., Cooper, S., Tyka, M. D., Xu, K., Makedon, I., & Popovic, Z. et al. (2011). Algorithm discovery by protein folding game players. *Proceedings of the National Academy of Sciences of the United States of America*, *108*(47), 18949–18953. doi:10.1073/pnas.1115898108 PMID:22065763

Kirriemuir, J., & Mcfarlane, A. (2004). Literature Review in Games and Learning. Retrieved from http://halshs.archives-ouvertes.fr/hal-00190453/

Koerner, B. I. (2012). Popular science. *Wired Magazine*, July 2012, 138-145.

Koster, R. (2004). *A Theory of Fun for Game Design* (1st ed.). Phoenix, AZ: Paraglyph Press.

Left 4 Dead [Digital Game]. (2008). Redwood City, CA, Kirkland, WA: Electronic Arts, Valve, Certain Affinity.

Lens, W. (2001). How to Combine Intrinsic Task-Motivation with the Motivational Effects of the Instrumentality of Present Tasks for Future Goals. In A. Efklides, J. Kuhl, & R. M. Sorrentino (Eds.), *Trends and Prospects in Motivation Research* (pp. 23–36). New York, NY: Kluwer Academic Publishers.

Martinez-Garza, M., & Clark, D. B. (2013). Teachers and Teaching in Game-Based Learning Theory and Practice. In M. Khine & I. Saleh (Eds.), *Approaches and Strategies in Next Generation Science Learning* (pp. 147–163). Hershey, PA: IGI Global; doi:10.4018/978-1-4666-2809-0.ch008

Mass Effect [Digital Game]. (2008). Redwood City, CA: Electronic Arts, BioWare.

Mass Effect 2 [Digital Game]. (2010). Redwood City, CA: Electronic Arts, BioWare.

Math Blaster! [Digital Game]. (1983). Torrance, CA: Davidson & Associates.

Mega Man [Digital Game]. (1990). Osaka, Japan: Hi Tech Expressions, Capcom.

Meyer, D. K., & Turner, J. C. (2006). Re-conceptualizing Emotion and Motivation to Learn in Classroom Contexts. *Educational Psychology Review, 18*(4), 377–390. doi:10.1007/s10648-006-9032-1

Millstone, J., & Levy, A. (2012) *What do teachers really think about using video games in the classroom?* Paper presented at the 9th Annual Games for Change Summit, New York.

Murphy, P. K., & Alexander, P. A. (2000). A motivated exploration of motivation terminology. *Contemporary Educational Psychology, 25*(1), 3–53. doi:10.1006/ceps.1999.1019 PMID:10620380

National Research Council. (2003). *Engaging Schools: Fostering High School Students' Motivation to Learn.* Washington, DC: The National Academies Press.

Ng, F., Zeng, H., & Plass, J. (2009) Research on Educational Impact of Games: A Literature Review. (Report No. 02/2009) New York, NY: Institute for Games for Learning, NYU/CUNY.

Nicholls, J. G. (1984). Achievement motivation: Conceptions of ability, subjective experience, task choice, and performance. *Psychological Review, 91*(3), 328–346. doi:10.1037/0033-295X.91.3.328

Operation: Resilient Planet [Digital Game]. (2008). Madison, WI: Filament Games.

Owen, A. M., Hampshire, A., Grahn, J. A., Stenton, R., Dajani, S., & Burns, A. S. et al. (2010). Putting brain training to the test. *Nature, 465*(7299), 775–778. doi:10.1038/nature09042 PMID:20407435

Papastergiou, M. (2009). Digital Game-Based Learning in high school Computer Science education: Impact on educational effectiveness and student motivation. *Computers & Education, 52*(1), 1–12. doi:10.1016/j.compedu.2008.06.004

Patall, E. A., Cooper, H., & Robinson, J. C. (2008). The effects of choice on intrinsic motivation and related outcomes: A meta-analysis of research findings. *Psychological Bulletin, 134*(2), 270–300. doi:10.1037/0033-2909.134.2.270 PMID:18298272

Perry, R., Hladkyj, S., Pekrun, R., & Pelletier, S. (2001). Academic control and action control in the achievement of college students: A longitudinal field study. *Journal of Educational Psychology, 93*(4), 776–789. doi:10.1037/0022-0663.93.4.776

Philip, S. (2010, September 23). Geek, Rebooted. *Top Gear*, (Front End), 53–58. Retrieved from http://www.iracing.com/wp-content/uploads/2010/10/Huttu-PDF.pdf

Pintrich, P. R. (2003). A motivational science perspective on the role of student motivation in learning and teaching contexts. *Journal of Educational Psychology, 95*(4), 667–686. doi:10.1037/0022-0663.95.4.667

Pintrich, P. R., & Schunk, D. H. (2002). *Motivation in education: Theory, research, and applications* (2nd ed.). Upper Saddle River, NJ: Prentice Hall.

Portal [Digital Game]. (2007). Redwood City, CA: Electronic Arts - Valve, Valve Nuclear Monkey Software.

Potvin, P., & Hasni, H. (2014). Interest, motivation and attitude towards science and technology at K-12 levels: A systematic review of 12 years of educational research. *Studies in Science Education, 50*(1), 85–129. doi:10.1080/03057267.2014.881626

Railroad Tycoon [Digital Game]. (1990). Wilmington, DE: Micropose, Micropose.

Raynor, J. O. (1969). Future orientation and motivation of immediate activity: An elaboration of the theory of achievement motivation. *Psychological Review, 76*(6), 606–610. doi:10.1037/h0028291

Renninger, K. A., Hidi, S., & Krapp, A. (1992). *The role of interest in learning and development*. Hillsdale, NJ: Erlbaum.

Revenge of the Titans [Digital Game]. (2011). New York: Puppygames.

Rift [Digital Game]. (2011). Redwood Shores, CA: Trion Worlds.

Rocksmith [Digital Game]. (2011). Montreuil, France: Ubisoft San Francisco, Ubisoft.

Ryan, R. M., & Deci, E. L. (2000). Intrinsic and Extrinsic Motivations: Classic Definitions and New Directions. *Contemporary Educational Psychology*, *25*(1), 54–67. doi:10.1006/ceps.1999.1020 PMID:10620381

Salen, K., & Zimmerman, E. (2004). *Rules of play: game design fundamentals*. Cambridge, MA: The MIT Press.

Schiefele, U., Krapp, A., & Winteler, A. (1992). Interest as a predictor of academic achievement: A meta-analysis of research. In K. A. Renninger, S. Hidi, & A. Krapp (Eds.), *The role of interest in learning and development* (pp. 183–212). Hillsdale, NJ: Erlbaum.

Schnotz, W., Fries, S., & Horz, H. (2009). Motivational aspects of cognitive load theory. (M. Wosnita, S. Karabenick, A. Efklides, & P. Nenniger, Eds.) Hogrefe & Huber, Contemporary motivation research: from multiple perspectives, 69–96.

Schunk, D. H. (1991). Self-efficacy and academic motivation. *Educational Psychologist*, *26*(3-4), 207–231. doi:10.1080/00461520.1991.9653133

Seifert, T. L., & O'Keefe, B. A. (2001). The relationship of work avoidance and learning goals to perceived competence, externality and meaning. *The British Journal of Educational Psychology*, *71*(Pt 1), 81–92. Retrieved from http://www.ncbi.nlm.nih.gov/pubmed/11307710 doi:10.1348/000709901158406 PMID:11307710

Shaffer, D. W. (2009). Computers and the End of Progressive Education. In D. Gibson (Ed.), *Digital Simulations for Improving Education: Learning Through Artificial Teaching Environments* (pp. 68–85). Hershey, PA: IGI Global. doi:10.4018/978-1-60566-322-7.ch004

Shaffer, D. W., & Gee, J. P. (2007). Epistemic Games as Education for Innovation. In J. D. M. Underwood & J. Dockrell (Eds.), *Learning through digital technologies* (pp. 71–82). Leicester, UK: British Journal of Educational Psychology.

SimCity [Digital Game]. (1989). Redwood City, CA: Electronic Arts, Maxis.

SimCity 4 [Digital Game]. (2003). Redwood City, CA: Electronic Arts, Maxis.

Skinner, E., Zimmer-Gembeck, M., & Connell, J. (1998). Individual differences and the development of perceived control. *Monographs of the Society for Research in Child Development, 63(2–3,* Serial No. 254).

Slavin, R. E., Madden, N. A., Chambers, B., & Haxby, B. (2009). *Two million children: Success for All*. CA: Corwin Thousand Oaks.

Space Invaders [Digital Game]. (1978). Tokyo, Japan: Taito, Midway.

SpaceChem [Digital Game]. (2011). Redwood City, CA: Zachtronics Industries.

Squire, K. (2003). Video games in education. *International Journal of Intelligent Simulations and Gaming*, *2*(1), 49–62.

Squire, K. (2011). *Video games and learning: teaching and participatory culture in the digital age*. New York: Teachers College Press.

Squire, K., Barnett, M., Grant, J. M., & Higginbotham, T. (2004). Electromagnetism supercharged!: Learning physics with digital simulation games. *Proceedings of the 6th International Conference of the Learning Sciences* (pp. 513–520).

Star Trek Online [Digital Game]. (2010). San Jose, CA: Atari, Cryptic Studios.

Star Wars: Knights of the Old Republic [Digital Game]. (2003). San Francisco: LucasArts, BioWare.

Starcraft [Digital Game]. (1998). Irvine, CA: Blizzard Entertainment.

Steinkuehler, C., & Chmiel, M. (2006). *Fostering scientific habits of mind in the context of online play* (pp. 723–729). International Society of the Learning Sciences.

Steinkuehler, D., & Duncan, S. (2008). Scientific habits of mind in virtual worlds. *Journal of Science Education and Technology*, *17*(6), 530–543. doi:10.1007/s10956-008-9120-8

Stipek, D. J., & Weisz, J. R. (1981). Perceived personal control and academic achievement. *Review of Educational Research*, *51*(1), 101–137. doi:10.3102/00346543051001101

Street Fighter [Digital Game]. (1988). Osaka, Japan: Capcom.

Super Mario Bros. [Digital Game]. (1985). Kyoto, Japan: Nintendo R&D4.

Sweller, J., Merrienboer, J. J. G. V., & Paas, F. G. W. C. (1998). Cognitive Architecture and Instructional Design. *Educational Psychology Review*, *10*(3), 251–296. doi:10.1023/A:1022193728205

Tabak, I., & Reiser, B. J. (2008). Software-realized inquiry for cultivating a disciplinary stance. *Pragmatics & Cognition*, *16*(2), 307–355.

Team Fortress 2 [Digital Game]. (2007). Redwood City, CA: Electronic Arts, Valve.

Tetris [Digital Game]. (1989). Alameda, CA: Spectrum HoloByte.

The Legend of Zelda: Ocarina of Time [Digital Game]. (1998). Kyoto, Japan: Nintendo EAD.

Thrash, T. M., & Elliot, A. J. (2001). Delimiting and integrating achieve-ment motive and goal constructs. In A. Efklides, J. Kuhl, & R. M. Sorrentino (Eds.), *Trends and prospects in motivation research* (pp. 3–21). Boston: Kluwer.

Torchlight [Digital Game]. (2009). Gardena, CA: EncorePerfect World Entertainment, Runic Games.

Tüzün, H., Yılmaz-Soylu, M., Karakuş, T., İnal, Y., & Kızılkaya, G. (2009). The effects of computer games on primary school students' achievement and motivation in geography learning. *Computers & Education*, *52*(1), 68–77. doi:10.1016/j.compedu.2008.06.008

Van Calster, K., Lens, W., & Nuttin, J. R. (1987). Affective attitude toward the personal future: Impact on motivation in high school boys. *The American Journal of Psychology*, 1–13.

Vanquish, 2010 [Digital Game]. (2010). Tokyo, Japan: Sega, PlatinumGames.

Vollmeyer, R., & Rheinberg, F. (2000). Does motivation affect performance via persistence? *Learning and Instruction*, *10*(4), 293–309. doi:10.1016/S0959-4752(99)00031-6

Vroom, V. (1964). *Work and motivation*. Oxford, England: Wiley.

Vygotsky, L. (1986). *Thought and Language* (Revised Edition). Cambridge, MA: The MIT Press.

Vygotsky, L. S. (1978). *Mind in society. The development of higher psychological processes*. Cambridge: Harvard University Press.

Warhammer Online [Digital Game]. (2008). Redwood City, CA: Electronic Arts, Mythic Entertainment.

Weinberger, A., Kollar, I., Dimitriadis, Y., Mäkitalo-Siegl, K., & Fischer, F. (2009). Computer-supported collaboration scripts. Perspectives from educational psychology and computer science. In N. Balacheff, S. R. Ludvigsen, T. de Jong, S. Barnes, & A. W. Lazonder (Eds.), *Technology-enhanced learning. Principles and products* (pp. 155–173). Berlin: Springer. doi:10.1007/978-1-4020-9827-7_10

Weiner, B. (2010). The development of an attribution-based theory of motivation: A history of ideas. *Educational Psychologist*, *45*(1), 28–36. doi:10.1080/00461520903433596

Wenger, E. (1998). *Communities of practice: Learning, meaning, and identity*. Cambridge University Press. doi:10.1017/CBO9780511803932

Wentzel, K. (1991). Social competence at school: Relation between social responsibility and academic achievement. *Review of Educational Research*, *61*(1), 1–24. doi:10.3102/00346543061001001

Wentzel, K. (1999). Social-motivational processes and interpersonal relationships: Implications for understanding students' academic success. *Journal of Educational Psychology*, *91*, 76–97. doi:10.1037/0022-0663.91.1.76

Wentzel, K. (2000). What is it that I'm trying to achieve? Classroom goals from a content perspective. *Contemporary Educational Psychology*, *25*(1), 105–115. doi:10.1006/ceps.1999.1021 PMID:10620385

Wigfield, A. (1994). Expectancy-value theory of achievement motivation: A developmental perspective. *Educational Psychology Review*, *6*(1), 49–78. doi:10.1007/BF02209024

Wigfield, A., & Eccles, J. S. (1989). Test anxiety in elementary and secondary school students. *Educational Psychologist*, *24*(2), 159–183. doi:10.1207/s15326985ep2402_3

Wigfield, A., & Eccles, J. S. (1992). The development of achievement task values: A theoretical analysis. *Developmental Review*, *12*(3), 265–310. doi:10.1016/0273-2297(92)90011-P

Wii Fit [Digital Game]. (2008). Kyoto, Japan: Nintendo, Nintendo.

World of Warcraft [Digital Game]. (2004). Irvine, CA: Blizzard Entertainment, Blizzard Entertainment.

Your Shape: Fitness Evolved [Digital Game]. (2010). Montreal, Canada: Ubisoft, Ubisoft Montreal.

KEY TERMS AND DEFINITIONS

Boss Encounter: A set-piece challenge presented by a game, usually at a dramatic point in the narrative, in which a player must demonstrate a higher level of skill in order to advance.

Design Convention: An element or interaction that is frequently found in digital games (qv.) as a whole, and is identifiable across game genres, time periods, and technological platforms.

Difficulty Curve: The increase in a game's level of challenge that a player experiences over time.

Digital Game: A set of challenging and/or novel experiences, scenarios, or decisions, structured by rules and/or goals, and mediated by a digital electronic device.

Educational Game: A digital game (qv.) whose main purpose is to teach, demonstrate, or scaffold a specific content or skill.

Motivation: The willingness to act in a certain way or perform a certain task, including the reasons for that willingness.

Recreational Game: A digital game (qv.) whose main purpose is to entertain, regardless of its educational affordances.

Chapter 2
Design and Implementation of an MMO:
Approaches to Support Inquiry Learning with Games

Louisa Rosenheck
MIT, USA

Jody Clarke-Midura
Utah State University, USA

Susannah Gordon-Messer
MIT, USA

Eric Klopfer
MIT, USA

ABSTRACT

Games can be a powerful tool for learning not only content knowledge but also skills and ways of thinking. In a classroom, the instructional design that goes into the implementation of a learning game is as important as the game itself. The Radix Endeavor is a multiplayer online game for inquiry-based STEM learning in which players explore mathematical and biological systems and use their understanding of those systems to solve problems in a virtual world. This chapter will present case studies of teachers implementing Radix in their classroom with a wide variety of formats, approaches, and learning goals. The authors will examine how key elements of an implementation impact student and teacher experiences and support problem-solving and inquiry learning. The chapter will explain the importance of implementation decisions, which will aid teachers and instructional designers integrating game-based learning into their own curriculum.

INTRODUCTION

Multiple research studies support the idea that games are powerful tools for learning (e.g. Clark, Tanner-Smith, Killingsworth, in press; Wouters et al, 2013; Squire, 2011; Steinkuehler & Duncan, 2008). Well-designed games provide scaffolding and motivation for a player to learn skills and apply knowledge in service of meeting specified goals. In addition, they create a safe space to fail, enabling players to take risks they might not take in other learning environments (Gee, 2003). However, how games are implemented in classrooms affects the learning and engagement outcomes

DOI: 10.4018/978-1-4666-9629-7.ch002

and therefore their efficacy. The problem is that teachers do not always know how to integrate games into their teaching. For example, Fishman et al (2014), found that 33% of the teachers they surveyed as part of the A-Games Project claimed that not being sure how to integrate games into instruction was a barrier to using them. This is a difficult problem to solve because a game that works well in one context may not work well in another. As such, rather than simply identifying successful games for learning, the learning games community must also identify types of successful implementations for games.

Critiquing an implementation is no easy task given the wide array of factors within classrooms and schools. The ideal implementation model for a given game will depend on the goals of the game and how those goals can be met. Whether that model will be successful with a given group of students will depend on what the students are accustomed to and how they respond to changes in their teacher's approach. There are many options for an implementation of even one game, and how that is carried out can have a great effect on the experiences of both students and teachers. The experience of a game or any educational intervention, rather than simply exposure to it, is what ultimately leads to learning and growth. Therefore, implementation style is a key piece in planning any successful game-based learning unit.

It is pointless to try to designate a "best" implementation for learning games, or even one specific game, in the classroom. We can however catalog different types of implementation models and call attention to important considerations and how they may impact the overall experience. We can begin to identify approaches that do or don't support problem-solving and inquiry learning. In this chapter, the authors take the game *The Radix Endeavor* as an example. Radix is a multiplayer online game for inquiry-based STEM learning developed at the MIT Education Arcade. It has been implemented in a number of different ways as part of a pilot research study. After taking a close look at the goals of the game and the player experience, five case studies of Radix teachers will be presented. We will describe the ways in which these teachers implemented Radix in their classroom, along with how they made those decisions. Most importantly, each case study will show the types of interactions that occurred in the classroom – between teachers, students, and the game itself – as a way to characterize the experience for those involved. The case studies will highlight many of the ways that one game can be used, and present choices that led to either successful or frustrating classroom experiences. After considering each teacher's case study we will draw out common themes and identify important factors and the effects they have on teachers' and students' experiences as well as on learning outcomes. The goal of this chapter is to highlight the importance of each implementation-related decision that a teacher makes, as well as to gain a clearer picture of the types of approaches that support deep learning and inquiry activities. Doing this will aid teachers and instructional designers who are integrating game-based learning into their own curriculum.

BACKGROUND

Massively Multiplayer Online Games (MMOGs) are open worlds that encourage exploration and experimentation. Learning in these environments is often situated in problem spaces that involve hypothesizing, probing, observing, reflecting, and recycling these steps (Gee, 2003). Typically in a game of this genre, players find themselves in an unfamiliar virtual world but equipped with an array of tools and in-game abilities. They are presented with a series of tasks, often called quests, which set specific goals but don't tell the players exactly how to accomplish those goals. In order to progress, players must experiment with the tools at hand to see how they can interact with the world and its inhabitants. Through this process of experimentation and discovery, they construct an understanding of the world's underlying systems and how to work within them to accomplish their goals and complete quests. While in the world, players in an MMO can see the avatars of other players nearby, and are commonly motivated to chat with each other to give each other advice or even collaborate on quests.

The unique affordances of massively multiplayer environments have been shown to foster scientific thinking, scientific identity and inquiry skills both inside and outside of the educational gaming space in places like Quest Atlantis, Whyville and River City (Kafai, Quintero & Feldon, 2010; Barab, 2007; Ketelhut 2007; Ketelhut et al. 2007; Nelson et al. 2007). Since the game world is massive and persistent, the open ended game play encourages a sustained investment in "systems based reasoning, model-based reasoning, [and] evaluative epistemology in which knowledge is treated as an open-ended process of evaluation and argument" (Steinkuehler & Duncan, 2008). To capitalize on the affordances of MMOs and build on the commonalities between this type of game and authentic science inquiry, the designers of *The Radix Endeavor* set out to design an environment that deeply integrates STEM practices as core game mechanics and allows players to learn by doing in authentic contexts.

To support these goals, the Radix game world is designed around systems that players can interact with and manipulate. Figure 1 shows players in the forest region, one of the five distinct biomes with unique fauna, flora, structures, and characters. In each of these biomes, players can engage in activities such as collecting data to compare the heights of plants in different regions. They can also experiment with running simulations to see how a species in a biome has evolved over time and manipulate variables to test out changes in the environment, as seen in Figure 2. Players also have a variety of tools that allow them to engage in the authentic practices of biologists and mathematicians. Some of the tools are open-ended and creative, allowing players to draw geometric objects on scale maps, build fences, or create and

Figure 1. Radix players exploring the forest biome

share food web diagrams. The gameplay is centered on quests that target specific content areas in biology and math. These quests are designed to encourage players to explore the different systems and biomes as well as to engage in inquiry, problem-solving, and collaborative learning in order to complete the task and provide evidence needed to support their solution.

When a new player enters the Radix game, she finds herself in a grassland biome on the island of Ysola, an earth-like world full of fictional plants and animals. She is likely to see the avatars of other players moving around the world working on tasks in the same area. There is a character nearby with an exclamation point over her head, so she talks to her to take on her first challenge, which starts the series of introductory quests. Once she has completed those quests she will be familiar with navigating the world, talking with in-game characters, and using the basic tools for collecting objects, examining them, and analyzing data about them. From there, a wide array of other questlines is unlocked. The player can explore any topic area she is interested in, or the specific ones that her teacher has asked her to work on. Each questline starts with one of the island's residents explaining some problem or question that is causing the people trouble. This way, the game's challenges are situated in a contextual narrative that gives the player a reason to care, and a motivation to solve problems that will save the island or its people. The player will then use her tools to explore the environment, ostensibly "messing around" but in reality experimenting and making discoveries. Through collecting and analyzing data, the player gains an understanding of the mathematical and biological systems embedded within the game world, such as Mendelian genetics or evolution. Once she understands each system, she can adjust the inputs to that system in order to get the outputs necessary to solve the problem. She then returns to the character in need of help to turn in an artifact or explain a solution, which requires not only an answer but also data that explains how they know their solution will work. Quests take place across the Radix world in rich biomes, with different

Figure 2. The evo globe lets players simulate changes in a trait over time

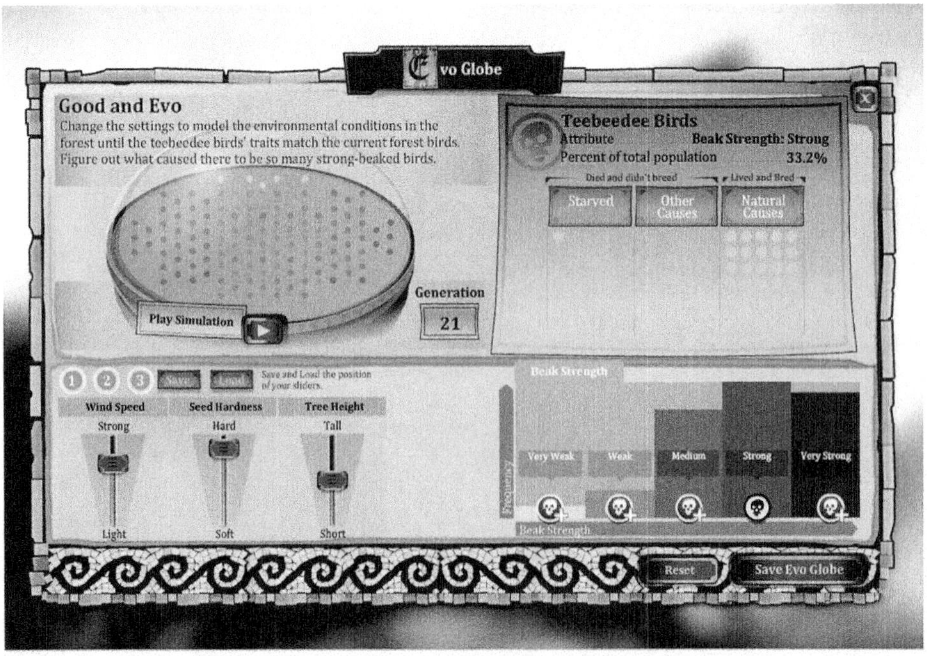

Figure 3. Players must choose which tests to perform to diagnose their patients

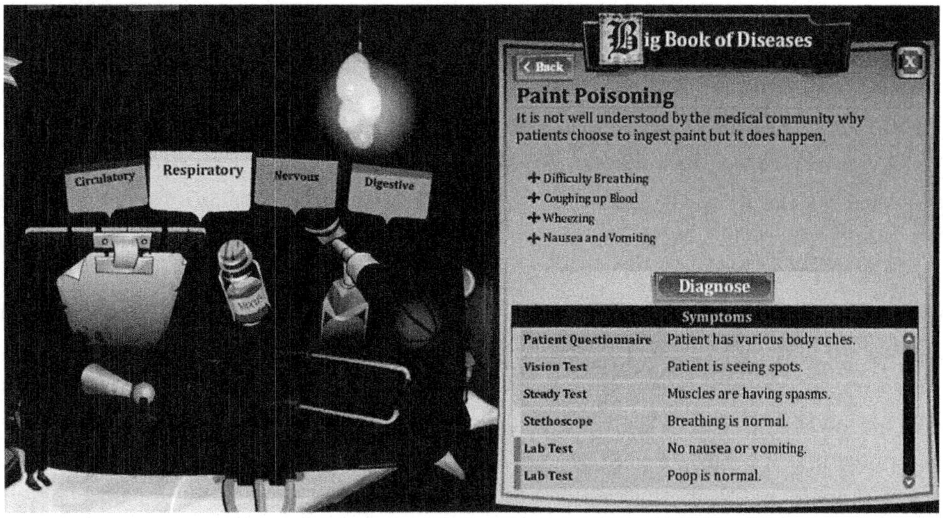

tools becoming useful in different domains. This brief overview provides a sense of the format of the game and the player's experience, setting the stage to next understand how STEM content and practices are embedded into the inquiry-based play style of Radix.

The virtual Radix world provides an environment where students can gain both content knowledge and the skills and practices critical to science understanding. The game covers four topics in biology: genetics, ecology, evolution and human body systems. These content areas were carefully selected to complement what students might be able to do in a hands-on lab, with simulations and longer time-scale activities that are only possible in a virtual world. The particular content for each of the topic areas is aligned with standards from the Next Generation Science Standards (NGSS) for high school and middle school, including an emphasis on science practices. The NGSS encourage the teaching of cross cutting concepts such as model building and practices such as investigation, interpreting data and evaluating information, which are incorporated into game tasks. In the evolution questlines, players collect data about the traits of animals in different regions of the world in order to learn about adaptation. As the players investigate, they study patterns, interpret data, and construct explanations, all key practices laid out in the NGSS. Throughout all of the questlines in the game, players must use 21st century skills such as collaboration and critical thinking in order to solve problems. This emphasis on skill and practices is critical to students as they learn concepts from science, and Radix provides an innovative place for students to engage with these skills.

One of the key components in designing the game content and quests was to create a space where students could practice inquiry. This means that when players encounter a problem in the game, they must think through how to solve the problem and determine their own course of action. For example, in the human body systems quests shown in Figure 3, players diagnose and treat islanders by making decisions about which body systems to test and which tests they would like to do. They are not directed step by step, but rather are free to decide how best to make their discoveries and what path they would like to take.

Although Radix was designed to create a space that fosters inquiry learning and exploration, a completely open-ended game would leave players confused about where to start and what to work on. Therefore, in regards to the player experience, game designers aimed to strike a balance between directed quests and open-ended experimentation. In many quests, this means that a problem is presented to the player, and a question is posed. Often the game goes so far as to suggest a tool that may be useful in solving the problem, and players are aware of what type of artifact they are expected to turn in. As for what to do and how to solve the problem though, players are on their own to experiment and see what works before ultimately settling on a solution. This creates a space for inquiry activities that may take some students outside of their comfort zone, but provides the opportunity for authentic discovery and problem-solving.

IMPLEMENTATION

Radix launched as a free tool available across the US and internationally in late January 2014. Teachers were encouraged to sign up for an account and begin to use the game as they saw fit in their classroom. At the time of writing this chapter, Radix had over 12,000 user accounts, and was being played in all 50 states and 7 different countries. While the game was designed with high school math and biology teachers in mind, Radix has been used by upper elementary, middle, and high school teachers as well as by a few instructors at community colleges and universities. Outside of the formal school environment, the game has also been picked up by various after school groups, enrichment programs, and the homeschool community who are using it with a wide variety of ages.

Radix was not designed to be a stand-alone game. It was designed as a supplemental tool for teachers to use in conjunction with other curricula. Therefore, the game provides many important resources for teachers. There is a teacher dashboard with links to resources, tutorials, and tools for monitoring student play. Every questline in the game has curriculum materials that accompany it. One element of these materials lists both the standards and the practices that are covered for

Figure 4. The bridge curriculum shows standards alignment

Home Play Game Teachers About News FAQ Forums Log in Teachers Join Mailing List!

Menji Family Reunion

Menji Family Reunion: Investigate Menji traits across three regions and collect data to find out which varieties are most prevalent in each biome. Talk with locals in each area to gather clues about how the menjis that live there came to be that way. Using that evidence and the concepts of selection pressures and inheritance, figure out how evolution has shaped the current menji populations.

Standards Covered in Quest line:

Disciplinary Core Ideas:

- LS4.A: Evidence of Common Ancestry and Diversity
- LS4.B: Natural Selection
- LS4.C: Adaptation

Practices:

- Analyzing and Interpreting Data
- Constructing Explanations and Designing Solutions
- Engaging in Argument from Evidence
- Obtaining, Evaluating, and Communicating Information

Cross Cutting Concepts:

- Patterns
- Cause and Effect

HS-LS4-2. Construct an explanation based on evidence that the process of evolution primarily results from four factors: (1) the potential for a species to increase in number, (2) the heritable genetic variation of individuals in a species due to mutation and sexual reproduction, (3) competition for limited resources, and (4) the proliferation of those organisms that are better able to survive and reproduce in the environment. [Clarification Statement: Emphasis is on using evidence to explain the influence each of the four factors has on number of organisms, behaviors, morphology, or physiology in terms of ability to compete for limited resources and subsequent survival of individuals and adaptation of species. Examples of evidence could include mathematical models such as simple distribution graphs and proportional

Figure 5. Teachers can track student progress in the game

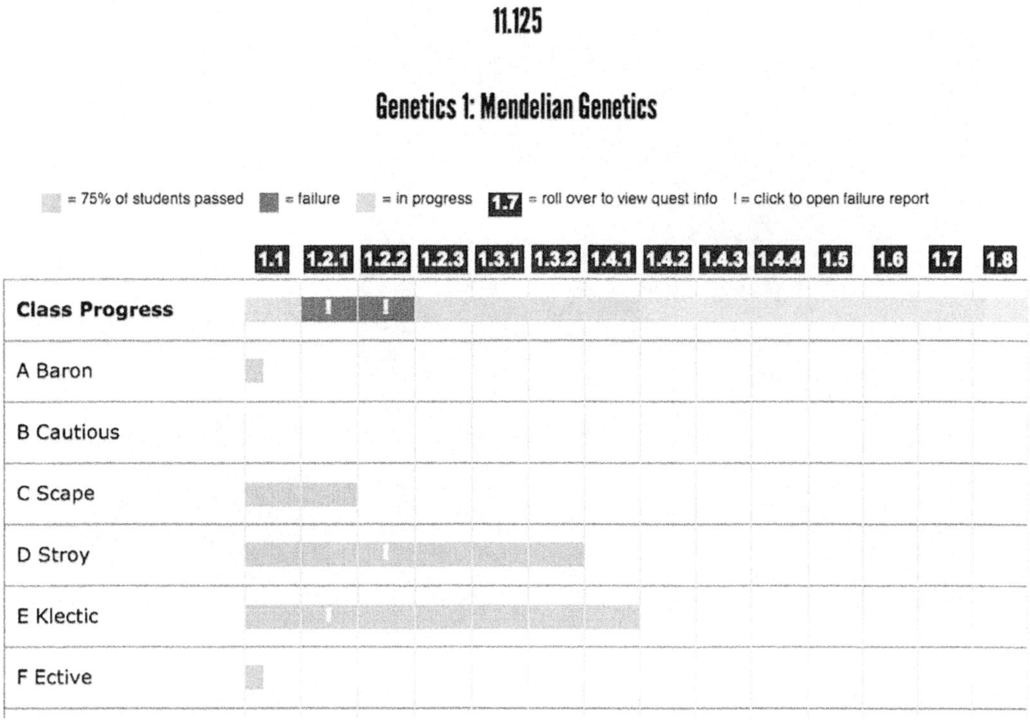

the particular questline, as seen in Figure 4. This gives teachers an easy way to see how the game aligns with standards already being covered and is particularly helpful for those teachers who are required to turn in lesson plans detailing what standards will be addressed daily in class. Additionally, these curriculum materials contain a set of "connecting questions" for every quest. The connecting questions are meant to help students reflect on their gameplay experience. Teachers can watch videos showing how to use the tools or explaining the main purpose of a quest. They can also track their students' progress in the game in real time, with focused information provided around students' "quest failures." As shown in Figure 5, teachers can see when students are struggling with quests and may need help or review on specific content. Those content areas are highlighted and linked back to the teacher resource section.

When Radix launched, teachers were offered both online and face-to-face professional development, much of which focused on the inquiry-based nature of the game. They also had access to webinars and virtual office hours throughout the pilot period, which provided a chance to vent frustrations, share successes, and get help from staff and peers. When they signed up for the pilot, teachers were given several suggested implementation models, and the ones they actually used spanned an even wider range of possibilities. There are teachers who used it as an introduction to material, some who used it during a unit and some who used it as an assessment at the end of a unit. Some used only one quest line while others had students play the material freely over the course of several months.

Figure 6. Players breed multiple generations for a specific trait

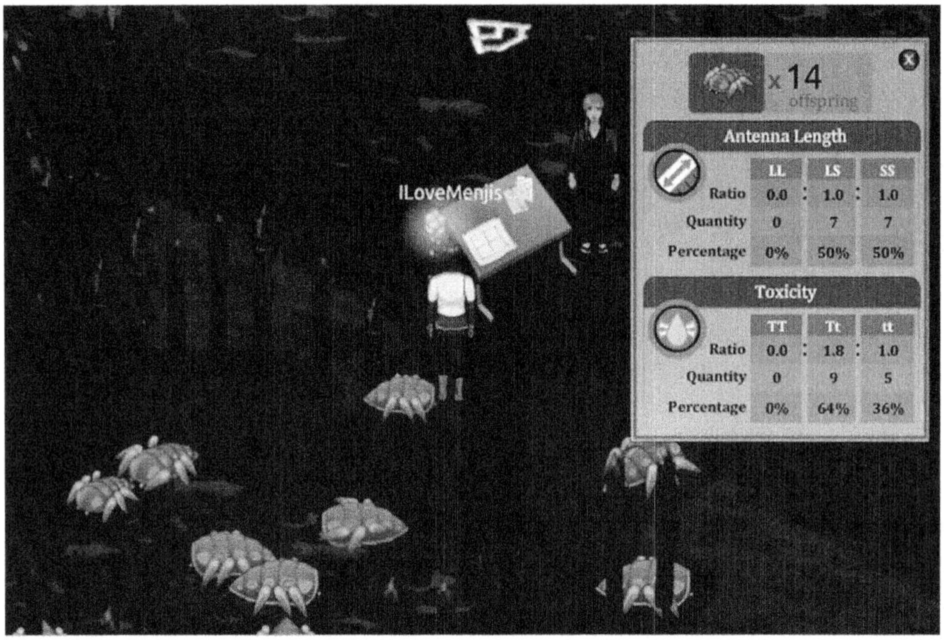

Radix is designed for students to first play and explore and then reflect. The reflection piece is critical for their learning. For example, in the genetics quests students explore the traits and varieties of different species in the virtual world, experimenting with different genetic crosses and the resulting offspring, shown in Figure 6. However, the game does not explicitly mention genotypes and phenotypes, or directly explain the relevant inheritance patterns. It is up to the teacher to do this through classroom discussion, small group work, or individual student reflection. The game provides students with hands-on experiences of the systems that they can later connect to vocabulary and concepts through discussions. For example, a teacher may say, "Remember in Radix when you were breeding glumbugs and you had babies with medium antennae, not only long and short? That is an example of incomplete dominance." The role of teachers in implementing Radix is to help students form these links and provide the time and space for reflection during game play.

RESEARCH DESIGN

The research presented in this chapter was part of a larger pilot that has collected a wide range of data including what students did in the game (log data), pre and post assessments of content, student interviews, teacher interviews, teacher surveys, and classroom observation data. In order to learn more about how teachers were integrating Radix into their curriculum and what that looks like in the classroom, the research team invited teachers participating in the pilot to opt into this research. Participation involved allowing researchers to conduct classroom observations, student interviews, and teacher interviews, and completing a teacher survey. Due to logistics, 10 teachers and 27 classrooms were selected for the observations and student interviews. However, an additional 10 teachers completed surveys and video conference interviews. These teachers received ongoing support from Radix staff and were encouraged to experiment with the type of implementation they thought would work best for their students. The data presented in this chapter focuses specifically on the teacher survey, classroom observations, and interviews with those teachers and their students.

The classroom observation protocol focuses on the types of interactions teachers have with their students during the Radix session in order to understand how often teachers address the whole class, give direct instructions to individual students, provide guiding questions to a group of students, etc. The student interviews were conducted during class in 5-minute segments during which students were asked to explain what quest they were playing and what they thought they were learning. The teacher interviews were conducted after completing the implementation, and the protocol attempted to understand how teachers made their implementation decisions, what they and the students struggled with, and how students did or didn't make connections across topics. The teacher survey asked about their comfort level using Radix, how they used it, and what kind of supports they used.

This study did not aim to draw conclusions about the most effective implementation methods. Rather, the goal was to catalog some of the different implementation models, analyze their pros and cons, and examine the effects that various factors in the classroom had on each other. By understanding the effects of certain implementation choices, researchers hoped to identify the types of pedagogical approaches that can best support an inquiry-based game like Radix.

IMPLEMENTATION FINDINGS

From the observation, interview, and survey data, there emerged two main dimensions on which teachers' methods greatly differed: format and approach. Choices in these two areas impacted the ways in which teachers were able to facilitate transfer and create a student-led learning experience, and it is therefore important to make these explicit.

The format of a Radix implementation describes when and where students play. The following formats cover most of the implementations seen in the pilot study.

- **In Class:** By far the most common format, teachers took their class to the computer lab, used a laptop cart, or students' own computers in 1-to-1 schools. They used class time to have all the students log in and play Radix. Usually students were asked to play through specific assigned questlines but they worked at their own pace. This format let teachers help students that needed it and keep them on task, but it took up valuable class time.
- **Out of Class:** Possibly the least common format, teachers assigned their students to play Radix outside of class time, as homework or extra credit. They decided whether to require certain quests and how to translate that work into grades. While teachers were encouraged to use this format in order to save class time for discussion and facilitating transfer, the main roadblock was that too many students didn't have internet access outside of school.
- **Blended:** Sometimes teachers used a blended format, where they started students off playing Radix in class in order to make sure they could log in and knew how to use the basic tools of the game. Then they asked students to finish the quests at some point after class. This seemed to work well for some students but not as well for others, potentially causing a larger disparity between the progress of each student.
- **After School Program:** There were a small number of groups who used Radix in after school programs rather than a formal class environment. In these cases, students played during the after school program time, in a computer lab or on a set of laptops, and were often given free reign

to play any and all of the quests that interested them. Despite not having specific content goals, students responded well to this level of autonomy.

The approach of a Radix implementation is harder to define. This factor describes a teaching philosophy that influences how a teacher interacts with and guides the students. The two extreme ends of the spectrum can be described, but in reality it is just that – a spectrum – and teachers may fall at different points along it and even vary at different times in a day.

- **Traditional Approach:** This describes the times when the teacher had the information and the students got that information from the teacher. It fits with the "sage on the stage" model where information flows in one direction and there is typically a correct answer. In a Radix implementation characterized by a traditional approach, students often asked the teacher what they should do or what the right answer was, and teachers often provided as much information as they could to help students make their way through the game.
- **Inquiry-Based Approach:** This describes the times when the students were working to construct their own knowledge, with the teacher asking guiding questions and promoting collaboration. It fits with the "guide on the side" model where the teacher helps students think through their ideas and provides resources, but wants them to figure out a solution on their own, especially when there are multiple possible solutions to a problem. In a Radix implementation characterized by an inquiry-based approach, students often explained their strategies to each other, and teachers often stood back or did more listening than talking.

There are appropriate times for each of these approaches, but when to use which method should be a conscious choice rather than simply a default. The important idea is that the approach a teacher takes has a very strong influence on how students experience the game, as the following case studies will illustrate.

CASE STUDIES

The following five case studies of Radix teachers illustrate different combinations of format and approach in their implementations, and describe the implications on the student and teacher experiences.

Case Study 1: The Traditional Teacher

Name: Jessica.
Subject/Grade Level: 10th grade biology.
Location: Northeast US.
Type of School: Urban/rural mix, 40% free or reduced lunch.
Technology Environment: 1 to 1 laptops.
Technology Comfort Level: Willing to try new things but often anxious about the time required.
Format: In-class.
Approach: Traditional.

Among the Radix teachers, Jessica is a clear example of a teacher who wants to promote inquiry learning but hasn't yet made the shift away from a teacher-centered classroom. In preparation for her biology students to use Radix, she dutifully created a number of guides available to them via Google Docs. These guides included a list of the quests she asked them to complete, a list of tools they would need to use in those quests, and even detailed walkthrough instructions describing how to complete the quests. In class, she began by projecting the game and giving a demo of how to start the evolution questline. She then had students play on their individual laptops, asking them to complete the quests during the class period. Students began to play and they had many questions. Where is the critter catcher tool? How do I get to Lednem Wilds? How many menjis do I need to investigate? What should I do next? Is this right? Hands were continuously raised and Jessica hustled busily from student to student explaining what she understood of how to progress through the tasks. In interviews about their Radix experience, students were asked how they figured out what to do in the game and for more than half of the students, their first response was either "My teacher told me." or "I read it in my teacher's instruction sheet." While there is nothing inherently negative about these interactions, they do demonstrate a traditional, teacher-centered classroom culture. The teacher was the sole source of information in the classroom, all knowledge transmission went through her, and students were in search of a "right answer."

How did this approach play out in a Radix implementation? Students were frustrated because of the disconnect between their expectations and their assignment. They were used to a linear path of learning where the teacher outlined what they needed to do and defined the steps to completion. Radix, however, is more open-ended and requires exploration and inquiry, skills that students didn't expect, and perhaps weren't able to apply. Jessica was flustered and had difficulty responding to all of her students' questions – an ultimately unsustainable practice to keep up during gameplay. Those questions were focused on the technical aspects or mechanics of the game, with very little discussion of the actual biology concepts being explored. Overall, the class had an emphasis on checking off the steps on the list rather than solving interesting problems. This seemed largely due to the classroom culture both teacher and students were used to – lectures, book work, and proscribed lab assignments were the norm for these biology students. Additionally, the documents Jessica provided to help students along the way set expectations that this was another activity that could be completed by simply following instructions and getting to the "correct" answer. While this may be an effective approach in certain settings, Radix and other inquiry-based activities don't fit that mold and it seemed to frustrate both teacher and students, resulting in an implementation deemed unsuccessful.

After some discussion with Jessica about how much work it was for her to keep the students going and how reluctantly they were playing the game, she agreed to let one of the Radix staff model a different approach for her next class, which was another section of the same course with students from the same school population. With this class, the facilitator skipped over the whole-class introduction and encouraged students to jump right in and play. Students began with much the same type of interactions as the first class. They asked questions about the game mechanics and what to do. However, instead of running around trying to answer every question, the facilitator took a step back. She asked students guiding questions and encouraged them to get up and go see if their classmates had figured that part out. She asked students that were further ahead to explain to each other why the data analyzer tool worked the way it did, rather than simply which settings to choose. In this way, she managed the class in a way more consistent with an inquiry-based approach, trying to guide students to keep trying and figure out what to do on their own or with each other's help. Compared with the first class, this one had many more students talking to each other about Radix. Students were similarly frustrated at first, but once they began to really dig in, there were more "aha"s and "I get it!"s to be heard. They were beginning to take ownership of their game experience, and interacting with the game on a deeper level, to the point where the facilitator could lead a discussion about evolution with students providing evidence they remembered from the game. The second class, while by no means perfect, began to take on a very different character than the first class – one that included problem-solving and collaboration.

We present these contrasting classrooms not to show that the key to a successful Radix implementation is having a Radix staff member run the show, but rather to illustrate two key points. The first is that existing classroom culture has a huge impact on the expectations students have around any new activity. However, culture shifts can occur with a few basic changes in teaching style and a commitment to keeping it up. The second is that a given learning game implemented with a clashing approach may appear not to work, and should not be discounted but rather have its classroom ecosystem more carefully examined. Jessica was open-minded enough that she was willing to engage in some self-reflection. In a debrief interview she said, "That was really a fun and interesting time watching the students enjoy learning and really helped me to know how to guide them from here in the game." By sitting back and being an observer, she could see that what felt like giving up control could actually lead to deeper learning and a more relaxed atmosphere. This also gave her the confidence to continue using Radix and to practice developing an inquiry-based approach to teaching.

Case Study 2: Transfer Techniques

Name: Nancy.
Subject/Grade Level: 9th grade honors biology.
Location: Northeast US.
Type of School: Urban, 30% free or reduced lunch.
Technology Environment: Difficult-to-book computer lab, a few laptops in her own classroom.
Technology Comfort Level: An early adopter, passionate about the power of games for learning.
Format: Blended.
Approach: Somewhat inquiry-based.

One of the big questions around Radix and many other educational games is where does the transfer happen? Students play through the game and get very good at playing that game, but can they apply concepts they explored in the game world to other situations? We know that transfer often doesn't happen spontaneously, and that's where Nancy's implementation of Radix comes into play. Class time and computer lab time is always limited, but Nancy put a lot of effort into trying different ways to get students to connect Radix to other activities and ideas.

Nancy is an experienced teacher who works hard to make her lessons as hands-on and student-led as possible. She says students don't always love that because for many of them it's easier and more comforting to do straightforward book work, but she knows that inquiry-based activities lead to deeper learning and provide an opportunity to practice important skills and competencies. Nancy's typical strategy for teaching a given topic is to provide a variety of different modalities and types of experiences that involve the content, then ask her students to connect and reflect on what they've learned.

Nancy booked the computer lab when she could, so that all of her students could play Radix while she kept them on task. Early in the school year, she only used an in-class format and in order to support her students' learning of the game, she answered many of their questions about technical aspects of the game, much as Jessica did in the first case study. However, in post-class interviews with Nancy, she recognized that she was giving a lot more direct instruction about the game than she really wanted to, and she felt that was mainly because it was early in the year. Sure enough, as the semester progressed Nancy adjusted both her approach and format. Once students were more comfortable with the basics of the Radix world, she spent class time talking in more depth with individual students that were stuck on the content or needed guidance. The other students responded well to her suggestions of using her as a sounding board for whatever they were stuck on, and they often looked to their classmates for help progressing through the game. It's not that her students were all model pupils, but she worked hard to create an environment where they could work both independently and collaboratively when they needed to. Nancy felt that one of the benefits of Radix was that students could work through the quests at their own pace. Naturally, that led to everyone being at different places by the end of the class. For this reason, Nancy decided to move to a more blended format where students could finish what they didn't complete in the game on her classroom computers after school, or at home if they had Internet access there. This seemed to provide the most flexibility for students to go at their own pace and work in the environment that best suited them.

The most interesting part of Nancy's method however, was that her integration of Radix into her classroom didn't stop there. Once all students had a chance to experience the challenges of the game and solve some of the problems, she looked for opportunities to synthesize what was presented in the game, connect it to other class activities, and model how to use that knowledge to solve new problems. Nancy's methods for doing this were simple, but quite powerful. Three examples of methods she experimented with are described here.

- Where possible, Nancy took class time to facilitate discussion around problem-solving strategies in the game or to have students summarize their Radix discoveries in order to describe biology concepts in their own words. As all teachers know, the drawbacks of class discussion are that it can be hard to find class time and more importantly not all students' voices will be heard.
- As an alternate approach, which gave every individual student a chance to reflect on their Radix experience and get feedback from their teacher, Nancy sometimes assigned students to respond to journal prompts related to recent quests. For example, after an ecology questline she asked them: *Why would animals found in different locations have different food sources?* This method took a format students were familiar with, their reflection journals, and used it to encourage students to reflect on what they did in Radix and why their discoveries there mattered.
- Another strategy Nancy had been developing in conjunction with Radix and other areas of her teaching was to design inquiry-based short answer questions. These questions started with what students learned in Radix and took it a step further so that students had to predict what they thought would happen in a new situation. One example of this type of scenario is: *What do you think might happen if a group of menjis migrated from the grassland to an area that was full of deep caves that contained an easy source of food for the menjis?* This question didn't have a correct answer and students couldn't find the answers in Radix or in a book. Rather, they had to take what they knew to make an educated guess about what adaptations might develop. By handing in their response to questions like this, Nancy could then assess whether they actually understood what they were doing in the game and challenge them to some higher-order critical thinking.

These three strategies were just some of the ways in which Nancy experimented with her Radix implementation. This type of experimentation is extremely important in game-based learning, and good teachers do this in every new lesson they introduce into their curriculum. Instructional designers can provide the software, the professional development, and even supporting curricular materials, but ultimately each teacher must try a variety of things to see what works best for her students. This is exactly what Nancy has done with Radix, and as a result, her students learned to engage with the game in a deeper way and apply their in-game discoveries to other contexts. This type of implementation and the promising results Nancy got underscore the importance of incorporating transfer activities into a game-based curriculum like Radix.

Case Study 3: Team Teachers

Names: Steve and Sam.
Subject/Grade Level: 7th grade life science.
Location: Northeast US.
Type of School: Rural, 52% free or reduced lunch.
Technology Environment: 1 to 1 laptops.
Technology Comfort Level: Moderate tech experience, excited about new ways to engage students.
Format: Blended.
Approach: Student-directed.

Often the teachers participating in the Radix pilot were sole implementers in their school. This can make it difficult for teachers who feel they are "going it alone." While there is a larger Radix community, it is helpful to have close colleagues to turn to when issues arise ranging from technical problems to how best to support students through a particular quest. This case presents a situation where two middle school science teachers teamed up to support their students as they played through Radix.

Steve and Sam are enthusiastic teachers who are always up for something new and place a heavy emphasis on having their students be responsible for their own learning. They didn't want to spend the majority of their Radix class time answering questions about how to use tools and navigate around the world. To help the students manage their play experience as well as to help them along, the two teachers set up a wiki page to be used by all of their students. This page gave the students information about the game, listed the quests they were supposed to complete as well as linked to all of the tutorial videos for the different tools in the game. During classroom observations, the teachers were frequently heard referring students to the page the minute they had questions about how to use in-game tools. Students were also encouraged to ask each other questions and to move around the room to see what others were doing as they played through. All classrooms used the "ask three before me" rule where the students were required to have asked three classmates before they could come to the teacher for help. In this way, Steve and Sam worked to build a community of practice among students figuring out how to make their way through Radix.

Both teachers worked hard to foster an environment of independent learning in the class rather than a culture where the teacher held all of the answers. Their frequent response to student questions was "Well, what have you tried?" This resulted in a classroom environment where the students felt like they were the ones figuring things out for the first time. Students reported that while the game was challenging at times, they felt very satisfied when they finally figured things out on their own. There was a particular level of satisfaction that came from being the first person in the class to figure out how to solve a certain quest. Steve and Sam's classrooms were noisy, a healthy mix of chatter, frustration and excitement.

When they began discussing their implementation, they decided together to primarily let students have a free play experience. They assigned the same quests to both classes, but agreed that the students were free to play in any order they would like. This would make it harder to keep track of where the students were at all times, but they felt that with a large group playing, there would always be some other students working on the same material. Students played during class, during study hall periods, and at home if they wanted to. Chat permissions were set so that the students could talk with anyone from the same school, allowing the students from different classes to interact in the world even though they would otherwise not interact in the classroom. During visits to both classrooms, students reported that it was nice to be able to work on school work with friends who were in another class and wouldn't usually have the same classwork or homework. This indicates that students enjoyed being a part of the Radix community in their school.

One of the key successes to Steve and Sam's implementation was how they supported each other. Beyond just sharing the wiki resources, they regularly checked in with each other about how their students were responding to the game. They compared student progress and even had a bit of friendly competition about whose students were completing more quests. They also went to each other if there were certain parts of the game that were mystifying their students. On occasion, one would walk into the other's classroom to check in on whether anyone had figured out how to use the population survey tool or how to handle a student who had thrown away a critical data summary needed for a quest. They also commented that it was easier to get administrative support given that there were multiple teachers using the game. They introduced their tech support officer to Radix and moved on to persuade their math teachers to try using the game as well. For Steve and Sam, creating their own community of practice of Radix teachers, however small it may have been, was a key component of their implementation. Their concerted effort shows just how valuable Radix can be when used by multiple teachers in a school.

Case Study 4: Designs for Learning

Name: Jeff.
Subject/Grade Level: 9-12th grade, 21st century skills and video game design.
Location: Northeast US.
Type of School: Suburban, 36% free or reduced lunch.
Technology Environment: Computer lab.
Technology Comfort Level: Low, but with access to tech coordinator support.
Format: After school program.
Approach: Exploratory.

Though Radix was designed primarily to be a formal education tool, it was used in after school programs as well. In the spring of 2014, Radix was used as the basis for an after school class in video game design. The focus of the program was on 21st century skills and giving students experiences after school that they otherwise would not have. Jeff emphasized that this was a program designed for "a group of students who haven't been targeted by other after school activities such as sports or drama." In the course, Radix was used as a model to help kids learn about the different stages in designing a game, and as a final project students were asked to make a paper prototype of their own educational game. This acted as the hook to encourage students to analyze what learning was going on in Radix, and then apply those observations to their own designs.

The after school program took place two afternoons a week, with hour-long sessions for 12 weeks. On any given day, there were between 8 and 15 students in attendance, the majority of which were avid gamers and excited to learn about the process of game design. The course took place in one of the computer labs in the school, but the room was set up such that the students could either be working on the computers or at a large table in the middle of the room. Students in computer labs often have trouble focusing on non-computer tasks when they are still seated in front of the machines so having the extra space provided an excellent place in which to conduct discussions and work on projects.

During the initial weeks of the program the students played Radix and gave feedback about each aspect of the game that they could identify – mechanics, tools, art style, etc. Jeff facilitated discussions about the feedback and the students also completed written questions. This feedback was passed along to the Radix team, but the real value of this exercise was to motivate students to think critically about the design decisions that went into Radix. They began to understand why those decisions were made and how they impacted gameplay and learning, ultimately resulting in students coming to think like designers.

To take this a step further, and to prepare for designing their own games, the students spent four sessions coming up with ideas for new elements for Radix. They were asked to create the following:

- One new tool to be used for either math or biology.
- One new plant or animal for the world.
- One food web for an area of the island.
- Danger/toxicity levels for a set of plants in a certain region.

These were short tasks. Students were not asked to design an entirely new tool, but rather to think about what might make the game more engaging and add to both the biology content in the game as well as the overall play experience. The students worked in pairs to brainstorm their additional game content. Students then shared out their ideas and with some prompting, challenged each other to think about what their designs would add to the game beyond the common response of "We thought it would be really cool if…". Jeff reported that he was surprised at how much the students had taken to playing Radix—coming early, staying late, and even playing at home on their own in order to really dive in to the game.

As the culminating activity, the students worked in pairs to design and create a paper prototype for an educational game. This gave them hands on experience with the early stages of game design. Jeff was very hands-off as the students began designing their games, letting them take ownership of their work. Once the students had finished a minimally playable game, they had a chance to play test each other's projects and give feedback. Jeff got more involved at this stage, playing along with the students, but gave limited feedback, purposely letting the majority of it come from peers. By the end of the session students were struck by how difficult it was to make a really great game. With Jeff's facilitation, they had taken the experience of playing Radix to a deeper level by reflecting on the designs and intentions of the game. They also practiced 21st century skills like critical thinking, creativity, and collaboration by designing their own games inspired by Radix. Jeff's after school program is a great example of an alterative Radix implementation where the game was used not as the content delivery method but as an "object to think with," (Papert, 1980) in a way that matched his students' interests and learning goals.

Case Study 5: The Need for Community Supports

Name: A group of OHS instructors.
Subject/Grade Level: 9-12th grade STEM.
Location: Western US.
Type of School: Blended learning (online and in-person).
Technology Environment: Home computers, individual on-site computers.
Technology Comfort Level: High.
Format: Primarily virtual classroom.
Approach: Free play.

Virtual and distance learning high schools are slowly becoming more common as parents, students and teachers look for alternative ways to earn a high school education. One virtual high school decided to implement Radix as part of their curriculum in the spring of 2014. Radix was set up as its own course that students could enroll in for credit, but was not integrated with existing math or biology classes. In order to support the students as they played, OHS instructors set up a web site with detailed instructions for the students. Before students began to play, they were instructed to watch a series of YouTube videos including a trailer of the game as well as several tutorial videos explaining navigation and tool use in Radix. To direct them in their gameplay, the website had a document that listed all of the assigned quests, summaries of those quests and links to additional videos for how to use quest specific tools.

The requirements of the course were based on quest completion. In order to get credit in science, they had to complete all of the biology quests and to receive math credit, they needed to complete all of the math quests. In order to receive credit in both areas, students needed to complete all 110 quests in the game. The Radix course began with 50 students enrolled, but ended with only five who had successfully completed all of those assigned quests. There was no requirement around the sequence in which to complete the quests and there were no checkpoints throughout the semester, so students were free to play when and how they liked. OHS instructors were available throughout the semester to provide support both through online chat as well as in person to students who came to work at the various site locations. However, the OHS instructors said that having students playing all different quests at different times made it difficult to provide adequate support. They felt that they weren't comfortable enough with the game to be able to provide support for every quest and that tracking progress to know where students were at all times got complicated. Whereas teachers in other schools often encouraged their students to use each other as a resource for solving problems in the game, the distributed nature of the virtual classroom meant that there wasn't a readily available community for these students to tap into.

When researchers met with a group of OHS instructors upon completion, they discussed the challenges they had encountered throughout the semester and concerns regarding the low completion rate. Unfortunately data was not collected on the causes for the high attrition rate in the course, but it is reasonable to hypothesize that lack of teacher and peer support could be a main factor. Radix was not designed as standalone curriculum, and the need for connections to biology content and support for student communication becomes even more evident in an online course format. A school like OHS might consider incorporating the game into existing math and biology courses as supplemental material rather than having students' ability to pass a course be entirely dependent on one game. They might also be able to come up with innovative ways to connect students within the game and encourage collaboration across distances. Creating an implementation in which Radix could be effective in this format would take some additional instructional design but could be well worth it for the benefit of students in a self-paced course of study.

DISCUSSION

These case studies of teachers who have designed implementations of The Radix Endeavor illustrate a number of interesting differences and also highlight some commonalities. It is apparent that there is not one right way to use a game like this, and there is no clear path to finding the best implementation. In this pilot, teachers were given materials on gameplay and curriculum, offered professional development opportunities, and had access to Radix staff, but there was no required format or method. As a result, teachers used this opportunity to explore how Radix could work best in their environment and for their students, and they helped researchers learn a number of lessons about practices that do and don't support an inquiry-based game for learning. The most important lessons are described here.

Lesson 1: Radix Can Work in Many Different Ways

Each of the formats used by Radix teachers, such as in class, out of class, and during after school programs, gave students an opportunity to explore the game world and make discoveries in science and math. Nancy used her in class time for gameplay and out of class time for transfer activities in specific content areas. Steve and Sam used in class time as well but gave their students free reign to explore the content. The OHS students essentially only had unguided out of class time, though they were required to explore not only anything in the game, but in fact everything. Jeff used informal learning time on Radix to explore an entirely different domain. These implementations had a variety of formats, student requirements, and available resources, but the teachers were all mostly happy with how Radix worked in their classrooms. This suggests that in the appropriate ecosystem, any of these combinations can support a successful Radix implementation.

Lesson 2: The Implementation's Design Should Match Its Goals

The implementation of an educational intervention involves many factors in its design. As discussed, the Radix Endeavor can work in a variety of formats and with any number of other elements such as different types of pacing, required milestones, and accompanying curriculum. However, this doesn't mean that they can all work in any combination. Every teacher should be able to clearly state the goals of the implementation, and these may vary widely. Jessica wanted her students to learn about natural selection and be able to identify evolutionary patterns. Nancy wanted her students to be able to think critically about science-related problems they may encounter. Jeff wanted his students to understand all that goes into game design. OHS instructors wanted their students to gain content knowledge in both biology and math. Given these disparate goals, they made corresponding choices in how to support their students during their Radix experience. Nancy included specific activities designed to connect Radix to other experiences and facilitate transfer. Jeff's students compared their experience in Radix to other types of games they played. These choices made sense as ways for the teachers to help their students reach the learning goals. OHS on the other hand, required their students to complete every quest in the game in order to get credit, despite integrating the game into a course with few constraints and few supports. This suggests that students who are more interested in certain topic areas, or who struggled with others, might not be able to pass the class. Missing some area of the game does not negate learning in other areas, but setting up the requirements in this way may have led to students disengaging from all areas and dropping out of the class. This is an example of an implementation design choice that did not necessarily match or support the learning goals. In cases such as this, where final completion numbers of the course were low, it may look like Radix as a tool did not engage students and made it too hard for them to pass the class, when in reality the teachers simply needed a more critical eye on the implementation, or perhaps another chance at iteration. By identifying what went wrong and whether or not it was due to something inherent in Radix, then making adjustments to support specific goals, teachers can build a stronger and more effective implementation.

Lesson 3: An Inquiry-Based Approach Supports an Inquiry-Based Game

While these case studies display a number of different formats that can be successful, this may not be the case when it comes to approach. We see a common theme where the approach categorized as more traditional tends to cause frustration and confusion. In Jessica's class, students and the teacher herself were bogged down by game logistics because it wasn't feasible for Jessica to be the sole source of guidance for both gameplay and content. This dynamic was also seen in a number of other classrooms not profiled here, and in those classrooms as well it often felt to the teacher like Radix wasn't "working." However, this dynamic is not necessarily a result of the game itself, but rather the interaction between the game and the approach. In contrast to Jessica, Steve and Sam chose to avoid directly answering students' questions about how to do specific things, thereby encouraging them to persist on their own or seek other sources such as classmates or the wiki. Removing the option to obtain the "right" answer from the teacher, and instead responding with guiding questions and encouragement, creates a more inquiry-based environment. In these classrooms that led to students feeling more ownership over their learning and showing more excitement at each accomplishment. For this reason, the case studies suggest that the teacher's pedagogical approach has a significant impact on the implementation.

Thoughtful choices on how to interact with students can strongly support a specific implementation, but another factor that plays a big role is the existing classroom culture. In Jessica's class, it wasn't only the expectations she set for the students during Radix play time that led them to expect every answer from her. It was a classroom culture that she, and everyone else involved in the students' educational careers, had built over time. Students in most of these schools are used to the traditional model of learning in a classroom and they naturally expect that to apply in new activities as well. To change that assumption takes consistency and a strong belief in inquiry learning. A teacher with a traditional approach who would like to implement Radix in the classroom is absolutely capable of doing so but needs to be committed to setting shared expectations and building a classroom culture around more independent, inquiry-based learning.

Lesson 4: Radix Cannot Exist in a Vacuum

Despite being a large-scale game with hours of gameplay, by design Radix doesn't work as a standalone tool or teacher replacement. In cases where teachers expected students to understand inheritance patterns or natural selection simply from playing the game during a few class periods, they were often disappointed with the tool. Radix can provide a meaningful foundation as students' initial experience with a topic area, and it is a place to explore and engage in a variety of math and science practices. Despite this, one tool on its own can't easily facilitate transfer or ensure reflection and synthesis of ideas. This was well understood by teachers like Nancy and Jeff. Nancy created her own bridge materials and treated Radix as one valuable experience in a collection of biology activities. Jeff selected Radix as one example of an educational game to be analyzed and to inspire students in their own game design. These are examples of integrating Radix into an ecosystem where each piece connects to and supports the other pieces, combining content learning and skill building to create a more meaningful and comprehensive learning experience.

Lesson 5: Communities of Practice Can Be Fostered

Games are often designed as a social experience, and Radix provides key opportunities to hypothesize about systems in the game and rework those theories together with peers. Because of this, a community of practice around a game can be just as important as the game itself. In a face-to-face classroom these communities may emerge organically, though as we've seen in Steve and Sam's classes, even in brick and mortar schools some facilitation is often necessary to create a strong community. Steve and Sam did this by starting a wiki for students to use together, and by explicitly and consistently reminding students to ask each other for help. In an online course, with a group of students who may not know each other and don't interact regularly, it becomes even more important for a teacher or facilitator to model that community of practice and help it grow. This was a key piece that was missing in the OHS implementation, where teachers did their best to support students but did not connect students who could support each other. Building a community of practice is not an easy task and community management may be a new skill for many teachers. However, looking at the difference between students engaging in inquiry in Radix on their own versus with the support of a community shows that communities of practice can have a great impact on the student experience. Therefore, there is value to be added by teachers who can consciously incorporate this into their implementations of learning games.

Lesson 6: Teacher Supports Are Essential

As with any new learning tool, teachers need to feel that they are well informed and supported as they try to implement something new in the classroom. The bridge materials developed to accompany the game were critical to helping teachers with their implementation. The standards alignment information helped the teachers to better understand the learning objectives of the game and ensured administrators that this was a worthwhile use of class time. The connecting questions helped teachers facilitate transfer between the game and content learning in the classroom. The video walkthroughs allowed teachers to easily see how to play through a quest, helped students figure out how to use certain tools.

In addition to these resources, face-to-face professional development and online support is crucial for an intervention that asks teachers to change their approach. Being able to model implementations as in the case of Jessica's class helped teachers see how to realize the full potential of the game. Webinars and virtual office hours that were offered throughout the pilot period let teachers ask questions about anything ranging from technical issues to content. Through these, teachers like Nancy were able to share their experiences with others and the after school students were able to ask questions of the Radix staff directly. These events worked to build a supportive community for teachers using Radix in individual schools, which turned out to be a key resource for teachers' implementation choices and their own professional development. It is this combination of readily available materials and social supports that can make the difference between an unsuccessful and at times difficult implementation, and one in which the teacher experiences the value of a tool such as Radix.

CONCLUSION

The Radix Endeavor is a game that was designed to foster an inquiry-based experience with STEM content and practices. As described, there are features in the game that are meant to support the inquiry process, but there are many more external elements that are necessary for a successful implementation of the game. Teachers need to consider how the game fits into their classroom culture and pay attention to how that impacts the interactions among students and teachers. They also need to carefully plan activities or experiences outside of the game to take students to the next level of conceptual understanding. Additionally they need to consciously foster the growth of communities of practice around the game. The case studies presented serve as examples of how the same game can appear frustrating when not well supported, but very valuable when thoughtfully implemented.

It may seem like common sense that an educational intervention should be well supported and thoughtfully implemented, but unfortunately it is not always the case due to time constraints and standards requirements. Many teachers tend to choose games that are more standalone and require less customization. This style of game can ensure that students are learning on their own simply by spending time in front of the computer. When it comes to game-based learning and educational technologies, certainly there are tools out there that fit this description. Starfall and Coolmath are sites with small, focused games that are commonly found in classrooms (Takeuchi & Vaala, 2014), and some teachers will gravitate toward those, deeming them more feasible to implement and more effective as a learning tool.

Radix doesn't fit the bill as a standalone type of tool. Instead, the stories of teachers like Nancy, and Steve and Sam, suggest that the most successful implementations are the ones where teachers match their approach to the game, and find the right connections between the in-game and out-of-game experiences. They lead discussions and construct assignments that facilitate transfer. They provide resources with the right balance of guidance and open-endedness. They monitor their responses to create a culture of exploration and peer support. All of this takes time and energy in the preparation and the execution to match the class's needs and goals. In the end though, these are the teachers that feel they have provided their students with a unique and rich learning experience. Their students are not only mastering specific topics in biology, but they are learning to ask questions, evaluate information sources, locate resources for problem-solving, and apply these skills to new contexts. They are taking ownership of their learning, experiencing the satisfaction of solving problems independently, and building 21st century skills. This is the learning that lies at the heart of an immersive, experiential game like Radix and to get all this out of the experience, implementation matters.

New literacies such as the ones described above are essential in this digital age where information is readily available but needs to be synthesized and applied. New emphasis is being placed on teaching these skills in schools to enable students to adapt and thrive in an ever-changing society. In order to effectively teach these different types of skills, new pedagogical approaches must also be developed – approaches that match the learning goals and support deep thinking in ways that traditional classroom instruction hasn't done. Games, including inquiry-based experiences such as Radix, are tools that are gaining in popularity for building 21st century skills. However, the pedagogical approaches and implementation methods to support them and ensure that the learning goals are met are still in the early stages of development. The next steps in educational research in this area should include exploring the rich variety of practices being used, and gaining an understanding of the approaches that can best support deep learning experiences. Doing so will enable more teachers to learn to effectively implement inquiry-based games, thereby supporting the movement toward student-centered classrooms fostering deep learning.

REFERENCES

Barab, S. A., Sadler, T., Heiselt, C., Hickey, D., & Zuiker, S. (2007). Relating narrative, inquiry, and inscriptions: A framework for socio- scientific inquiry. *Journal of Science Education and Technology*, *16*(1), 59–82. doi:10.1007/s10956-006-9033-3

Clark, D. B., Tanner-Smith, E., & Killingsworth, S. (revised and resubmitted). *Digital games, design, and learning: A systematic review and meta-analysis.* Review of Educational Research.

Fishman, B., Riconscente, M., Snider, R., Tsai, T., & Plass, J. (2014). Empowering Educators: Supporting Student Progress in the Classroom with Digital Games. Ann Arbor: University of Michigan. Retrieved from gamesandlearning.umich.edu/agames

Gee, J. P. (2003). *What video games have to teach us about learning and literacy*. New York: Palgrave/Macmillan.

Kafai, Y. B., Quintero, M., & Feldon, D. (2010). Investigating the ''why'' in whypox: Casual and systematic explorations of a virtual epidemic. *Games and Culture*, *5*(1), 116–135. doi:10.1177/1555412009351265

Ketelhut, D. J. (2007). The impact of student self-efficacy on scientific inquiry skills: An exploratory investigation in River City, a multi- user virtual environment. *Journal of Science Education and Technology*, *16*(1), 99–111. doi:10.1007/s10956-006-9038-y

Ketelhut, D. J., Dede, C., Clarke, J., Nelson, B., & Bowman, C. (2007). Studying situated learning in a multi-user virtual environment. In E. Baker, J. Dickieson, W. Wulfeck, & H. O'Neil (Eds.), *Assessment of problem solving using simulations*. Mahwah, NJ: Lawrence Erlbaum Associates.

Nelson, B., Ketelhut, D. J., Clarke, J., Dieterle, E., Dede, C., & Erlandson, B. (in press). Robust design strategies for scaling educational innovations: The River City MUVE case study. In B. E. Shelton & D. A. Wiley (Eds.), *The educational design and use of computer simulation games*. Rotterdam, The Netherlands: Sense Press.

Papert, S. (1980). *Mindstorms: Children, computers, and powerful ideas*. Basic Books, Inc.

Squire, K. (2011). *Video games and learning: Teaching and participatory culture in the digital age*. New York: Teachers College Press.

Steinkuehler, C., & Duncan, S. (2008). Scientific habits of mind in virtual worlds. *Journal of Science Education and Technology*, *17*(6), 530–543. doi:10.1007/s10956-008-9120-8

Takeuchi, L. M., & Vaala, S. (2014). *Level up learning: A national survey on teaching with digital games*. New York: The Joan Ganz Cooney Center at Sesame Workshop.

Wouters, P., van Nimwegen, C., van Oostendorp, H., & van der Spek, E. D. (2013). A meta- Analysis of the Cognitive and Motivational Effects of Serious Games. *Journal of Educational Psychology*, *105*(2), 249–265. doi:10.1037/a0031311

Chapter 3
Games and Their Embodied Learning Principles in the Classroom:
Connecting Learning Theory to Practice

Sam von Gillern
Iowa State University

ABSTRACT

This chapter explores how educators can use games and their embodied learning principles as a source for student learning, motivation, and engagement. It begins by highlighting important educational issues, such as lack of motivation and how technology has affected students and communication (Prensky, 2005). It then illustrates how digital games can address these issues and support learning and foster meaningful engagement by exploring Gee's (2007) learning principles and Prensky's (2005) activities and learning techniques. Each learning principle and activity is addressed with a summary of the concept, an example of how video games exemplify the concept, and practical methods for integrating the idea into classroom instruction through games and activities. The chapter concludes with an overview of main concepts and highlights future directions for research connecting learning theories to digital games.

INTRODUCTION

Games are the most elevated form of investigation. – Albert Einstein

Both schools and educators can learn something from video games (Gee, 2007). Why do young people eagerly pay sixty dollars for a video game that may lead to expenditure of great effort and significant frustration, but we struggle to get them to sit still, learn, and persevere in schools, even for five minutes? The answer is that they find choice, pleasure, and empowerment in video games in ways unmatched by schoolwork. Numerous scholars have explored how such games can produce engaging and effective learning (Gee, 2007; Prensky, 2005; Squire, 2011). Pedagogical principles exist in gaming that may when utilized effectively result in deepened learning, mastery, engagement, and motivation.

DOI: 10.4018/978-1-4666-9629-7.ch003

Prensky (2005) draws attention to two significant reasons that educators should consider the value of video games in education: "Learners have changed radically [and] computer games can provide a new way to motivate today's students to learn" (p. 97). Technology permeates the lives of children. Computers and digital games are normal parts of their lives, and the use of such technologies has influenced how they learn and experience the world (Prensky, 2005). This influence should be considered by educators striving to provide both effective and engaging learning opportunities for their students. Additionally, when students lack motivation to learn in school settings—as many often do—it can be even more difficult to promote learning in the classroom. "Motivation is important because learning requires putting out effort" (Prensky, 2005, p. 97). Many students are clearly motivated to play video games, and educators can harness this motivation to promote positive learning gains for students and teachers alike. The primary objective of this chapter is to inform the audience how video games and their embodied learning principles and techniques (Gee, 2007; Prensky, 2005) can be used by schools and educators to promote student learning, motivation, and engagement.

BACKGROUND

Prensky (2005) and other researchers (Becker, 2008; McGonigal, 2011; Squire, 2011) illustrate that video games can promote valuable educational outcomes, but we must ask why video games motivate and engage students in ways that schools typically do not? Most likely it is because

Good video games give people pleasures. These pleasures are connected to control, agency, and meaningfulness. But good games are problem-solving spaces that create deep learning, learning that is better than what we often see today in our schools...Pleasure is the basis of learning for humans and learning is, like sex and eating, deeply pleasurable for human beings. Learning is a basic drive for human beings [but] school has taught people to fear and avoid learning, (Gee, 2007).

As Gee (2007) notes, video game engagement is related to pleasure, learning, agency, and meaningfulness. Given the way humans are drawn to pleasure, it makes sense that educators should strive to make educational environments warm and enjoyable. While some might say that learning X is not necessarily fun, given Gee's position on the deep pleasure of learning, one might benefit from thinking that a shift in methods or activities might make learning X more enjoyable and thereby increase student motivation and learning. Agency is another important element of Gee's perspective. Although many educators believe in the importance of active learning in which the student has a significant role to play in the learning process, tasks assigned to children are often unclear or too difficult to allow them to develop a deep sense of self-efficacy, negatively impacting their achievement. Video games and their embodied pedagogical principles can promote pleasure, learning, and agency, all things that students (and humans in general) care about. Students find these experiences meaningful and their engagement may therefore be enhanced. Additionally, with a little creativity and planning, educators can use games and the pedagogical principles explored within this chapter to help them and their students achieve a variety of educational goals, ranging from personal goals to the Common Core. Ideas such as well-ordered problems and system thinking (Gee, 2007) to situated learning and role playing (Prensky, 2005) have tremendous potential for helping educators and students reach their goals.

Educators, researchers, and policy makers can benefit from a deeper understanding of both the theoretical foundations of learning principles embodied in video games and their practical applications in educational settings. It is important to note that while good video games embody such principles, these principles are not limited to video games. In fact, they largely exist independently of video games and have been developed through research in areas of learning and cognition. However, good video games often capitalize on these principles, which leads to the deep engagement and learning video games often promote. Thus, this chapter explores how video games embody these principles, and how educators can use video games in the classroom to harness these principles and promote learning. Additionally, these principles can be utilized with non-digital games as well as non-gaming educational activities, so this chapter will also illustrate how various ideas can be harnessed independent from their use in video games.

While the main focus of this chapter is to highlight important elements of the works of Gee (2007) and Prensky (2005) and illustrate how these ideas can be used in the classroom, a variety of relevant concepts related to learning theories and cognition are also integrated to demonstrate how the work of Gee and Prensky aligns with existing conceptions of learning and cognition more broadly. This includes ideas such as situated cognition (Brown, Collins, & Duguid, 1989), systems thinking (Checkland, 1999), inquiry-based learning (Edelson, Gordin, & Pea, 1999; Kuhn, Black, Keselman, & Kaplan, 2000), constructivism (Fosnot, 2005; Piaget, 1954), and a variety of others, which will be addressed in more detail in the sections below. Through exploring important concepts on learning and cognition along with the work of Gee and Prensky as well as incorporating practical ideas for the classroom implementation, this chapter aims to tie theory to practice in ways helpful for researchers and educators alike.

The following sections will use Gee's (2007) learning principles and Prensky's (2005) activities and learning techniques to illustrate how games and gaming principles can be utilized in schools to achieve educational gains. First, Gee's (2007) learning principles will each be explored in three steps:

1. An overview of the concept;
2. The manner in which a contemporary video game harnesses that concept; and
3. How educators can use the concept through games in their classrooms.

Next, Prensky's activities and learning techniques will be examined by describing

1. An overview of the concept;
2. How video games in general utilize that concept; and
3. How educators can harness the concept more generally without the use of games.

This differentiated presentation between Gee's and Prensky's concepts is intended to illustrate how specific games can be useful in education as well as how games in general and their underlying principles can be used by educators. The chapter concludes with an overview of major ideas and directions for future research.

JAMES GEE'S LEARNING PRICIPLES

Co-Design

- **Concept:** Students experience deeper learning when they feel that their decisions and actions matter. Students actively involved in educational processes are more likely to experience deeper learning than unengaged students (Gee, 2007). Learners may therefore benefit from participating through actions and decisions in co-designing curricula with educators.
- **Video Game Example:** Telltale's The Walking Dead video game clearly illustrates how player choice influences engagement, appreciation, and outcome. In this game, the player assumes the role of Lee Everett, a man dedicated to protect-

ing a young girl, Clementine, in an apocalyptic, zombie-ridden world. As events unfold, the player (Lee) makes clear decisions through both dialogue with other characters and his actions, and these decisions affect how subsequent events unfold and how non-playable characters perceive him. For example, while under zombie attack, Lee has a choice: he can save one of two people, but not both. His decision directly influences subsequent events and therefore represents a process of co-design. The knowledge that one's decisions are important influences the player's experience and engagement.

- **Classroom Example:** Creating opportunities for students to influence curricula can influence learning and engagement. These opportunities include both:
  - Allowing students to make important decisions about classroom activities (e.g., providing several options for students to choose from or even allowing them to vote on a topic or method of inquiry).
  - Using student behavior as a guide for future planning, something that good teachers do all the time. A teacher's thought processes with respect to influence of student behavior on planning can be either covert (unexpressed) or explicit (e.g., informing students that "Because of X, we will do Y").

Co-design demands engagement and interactivity, two strengths of video games that can be harnessed in classrooms to promote co-design. Squire (2011) illustrates how games such as *Civilization* and *SimCity* promote engagement and interactivity while simultaneously illustrating important concepts relating to how civilizations and cities function and grow. These games illustrate how humans may utilize limited goods to try to achieve goals such as development. These concepts are clearly important in social studies, history, economics, and numerous other areas. When thoughtfully integrated into classrooms, video games can provide opportunities for co-design by which students learn important concepts and are increasingly engaged and motivated through recognition of the importance of their actions.

Customize

- **Concept:** Different people prefer different styles and approaches to learning. Allowing students to harness their own preferred learning styles and to actively explore new styles promotes opportunities for learning and engagement (Gee, 2007).
- **Video Game Example:** SSX, a snowboarding-related video game, allows players to customize characters and equipment to achieve their goals. Players can, for example, spend experience points (gained from accomplishing various tasks) on equipment to help them achieve new goals. For example, one can upgrade to new snowboards that are better for a particular use, either stunts or racing, or they can select a balance between the two types. Some players may value speed over stunts and can customize accordingly. Providing opportunities for players to customize their characters and gear promotes engagement and allows them to achieve both personal goals and goals set by the game while using their own chosen style.
- **Classroom Example:** Students, like all of us, have preferences, strengths, and areas for growth. Educators can provide opportunities for students to harness their individual strengths and strengthen their individual weaknesses. Educators can encourage students to accomplish particular tasks in different ways, allowing various styles to emerge in accomplishing the same (or similar) tasks; they may also promote growth through such encouragement.

Teachers can incorporate a variety of role playing games into their classrooms. *The Adventurer's Atlas* (The Escapist, n.d.), a component of The Escapist's Young Person's Adventure League, provides an extensive list of various role playing games, including their central concepts and required materials. Incorporating such games into classrooms provides opportunities for teachers to promote collaboration, creativity, and critical thinking through engaging activities in which children can harness their personal strengths and explore new skills and styles for development.

Identity

- **Concept:** Engagement is often enhanced when an individual is able to assume a new identity (Gee, 2007). Individuals often enjoy harnessing distinctive perspectives that allow them to see the world in new and unique ways; it can be both natural and useful for people to take on roles that influence the way they interpret the world. For example, soccer players watch and play soccer with their soccer knowledge and identity in mind, which influences the way they think about and interpret the game. The same observation can be made for teachers, engineers, accountants, and a nearly endless variety of other positions and roles. Fostering children's abilities to adopt alternate identities can prepare them for the future while enhancing engagement, motivation, and learning in the present.
- **Video Game Example:** In Rocksteady Studios' Batman: Arkham City (2011), players take on the role of Batman, using his tools and skills to investigate crimes throughout the city. They can use Batman's Detective Vision to investigate crime scenes and pursue enemies. Players, in trying to think like Batman, often find it beneficial to keep hidden and quiet in the shadows, to avoid enemy attention and incapacitate them while remaining unnoticed. If an enemy becomes aware of your presence, you may find it difficult to defend yourself. Players are deeply engaged in wanting to help Batman succeed and, in order to win, they must think and act like Batman.
- **Classroom Example:** Because most students tend to enjoy taking on new identities and this can be beneficial in terms of enhancing engagement and learning, teachers should facilitate opportunities for students to assume new perspectives and roles. There are a great number of detective-oriented video games available for use with computers and tablets. Sampling highly-rated games and seeing if/how they can help accomplish learning goals is a great way for teachers to incorporate such games into classroom activities. For example, in a detective game, learning objectives might include getting students to determine relevant and valuable information as well as to make evidence-based decisions.

Teachers can promote learning and engagement by creating and integrating non-digital games into their classroom activities. Mock trials, for example, can be great aids for teaching students about the legal system. Students can assume roles of lawyers, judges, jury members, and witnesses, and a trial becomes a game in which they can learn about how courts and trials function while simultaneously engaging in a variety of valuable social processes.

Manipulation and Distributed Knowledge

- **Concept:** People tend to experience enjoyment and empowerment when they can achieve personal goals through manipulating objects (including digital objects); this helps them feel they are in control of their environment (Gee, 2007). Manipulating digital objects such as digital characters and avatars can allow humans to achieve their goals in virtual worlds. Digitally-based characters typically have knowledge that humans do not, (e.g., how to walk and open doors in the digital world), and humans also have knowledge that digital characters do not, such as where to walk and which doors to open (Gee, 2007). This results in knowledge being distributed between humans and digital characters in an environment where digital characters are "smart tools" that humans can use to achieve their goals in the virtual world, often resulting in a satisfying feeling of empowerment.

- **Video Game Example:** Minecraft is a hugely successfully game that has achieved popularity among over 100 million registered users (Makuch, 2014). In Minecraft, humans control a virtual character, Steve, who they guide through exploration, collecting resources, and building objects and structures from cubes. The human players have their own goals, such as exploring a vast land or building a house (or castle), and they use Steve to help them achieve these goals. Through using the virtual character as a smart tool, players can create incredible structures that are personally fulfilling, creative, and worth boasting about to friends. Without the help of Steve (a virtual character who knows about gathering resources and building structures), players would be unable to create such truly magnificent structures and worlds.
- **Classroom Example:** Children often enjoy interacting with virtual characters and teachers can harness this interest in their classrooms. Given Minecraft's popularity and the range of activities within the game, Minecraft could serve as a platform for getting students actively engaged in activities with valuable educational outcomes. For example, students could explore the world and classify types of blocks and elements within the game. They could write a story about their Minecraft world. Students could design a house (or palace) on paper and then attempt to transfer the design into the game. Minecraft could also help students understand principles of logic, because Minecraft players have the ability to create complex virtual devices through the use of logic gates (Farwell, 2014). Teachers have a multitude of ways for harnessing student interest in virtual characters and worlds to promote valuable real-world learning experiences.

Well-Ordered Problems

- **Concept:** Problems should be organized in such a way that beginners can learn important elements and concepts that allow them to accurately hypothesize ideas that assist them in completing more difficult puzzles in the future (Gee, 2007). When relatively easy problems have key concepts, processes, and elements that don't align with difficult problems encountered in the future, students can become frustrated and disengaged. Problems should thus be well-ordered to promote success and engagement.
- **Video Game Example:** A characteristic of good video games is the inclusion of well-ordered problems. Overcoming early challenges should clearly and directly influence a player's thinking about approaching later challenges, and early challenges should thus prepare a player for future success. An example is the Rayman series of games, most recently Rayman Legends by Ubisoft. In this platforming game (a genre featuring jumping from one platform to another and attacking enemies who get in your way), Rayman, a cartoon character,

works his way through colorful worlds and accumulates new abilities over time. He begins with simple abilities such as running and punching, and then over time develops more sophisticated abilities such as wall-jumping and gliding. As the game progresses, the player must use skills he or she mastered earlier in the game (i.e., running and punching) along with new skills (e.g., wall-jumping and gliding). The game is structured in such a way in that players must initially master certain skills that will directly increase their abilities for advancing to and completing more challenging levels.

- **Classroom Example:** Creating well-ordered problems can result in significant benefits for learning and engagement. Teachers should present problems in a manner that allows students to develop an understanding of important basic processes and concepts that help prepare them for more complicated tasks in the future. Mathematics education often succeeds in this process. . First, students learn to count, then to add, subtract, multiply, and divide; they then move to solving equations that include a variety of these processes. Teachers can also consider using well-ordered problems in logic games and puzzles. For example, teachers can incorporate "whodunit" logic games in their classrooms; these may begin by highlighting important concepts related to logic, and then gradually move from simple games of deduction to highly complex ones. Logic games can be gripping if they tell a story, have rules, set a clear goal (e.g., finding out whodunit), and allow students to individually or collaboratively use their intellectual capabilities to solve a problem.

Pleasantly Frustrating

- **Concept:** People often enjoy learning new concepts and materials when they are engaged with pleasantly frustrating tasks. When students feel they can accomplish a task that is difficult—but manageable—they may experience deep and enjoyable learning (Gee, 2007). This idea compliments Vygotsky's (1978) idea of Zone of Proximal Development that highlights the benefits of engaging students in activities that they complete with support, as opposed to an activity that is either very easy to complete independently or too difficult even with support. Teachers should try to incorporate pleasantly frustrating tasks to promote learning and engagement.
- **Video Game Example:** In Metal Gear Solid V: Ground Zeroes, players assume the role of Snake, a spy who needs to infiltrate a military base to rescue hostages. This can be a difficult game, and players must be careful, observant, and capable of learning from their mistakes as they try to covertly accomplish their mission. Most people playing this game will become discovered by enemies at some point, at which point they will likely die or at least compromise their mission. However, this typically represents a pleasantly frustrating experience in which people learn from their environment and from their mistakes. Through experimentation, via feedback from gameplay, players learn that certain strategies are better than others. For example, players may learn that some routes are more difficult than others, that there are various ways to distract guards, and that they can use the environment (e.g., lighting, structures, and objects) to their advantage. Additionally,

one can tackle bonus objectives to increase the challenge of the mission. Playing this game can be difficult—but highly enjoyable—and while learners feel capable of accomplishing the mission, to do so they must experiment and learn along the way.

- **Classroom Example:** Educators should carefully consider their students' level of development, because this is key for finding their instructional level and Zone of Proximal Development. This observation is applicable to a wide variety of subjects and activities. One such subject is language learning, including first- and second-language development. Language arts educators can use pleasantly frustrating tasks and games to promote learning and engagement. For example, language arts educators can use a variety of word study games, such as memory or vocabulary and phonics board games, to help students learn (Bear, Invernizzi, Templeton, & Johnson, 2012). Additionally, second-language teachers can use role playing games in which some students assume the role of a store clerk or bus station attendant while other students assume the role of a shopper or traveler with the goal of purchasing various goods and services. With thoughtful planning and support from teachers, such games can be pleasantly frustrating experiences that result in meaningful learning.

Cycles of Expertise

- **Concept:** Mastery and growth occur when learners repeatedly practice skills until they become experts and then face new, but similar, challenges that require them to think in new ways (Gee, 2007). Combining new challenges with mastered skills allows learners to draw deeply from their schemata (Mandler, 1984) and helps them integrate prior knowledge with new concepts. Cycles of expertise mirror levels and boss battles in video games in which players face new challenges in each level and gradually develop relevant skills, and ultimately face bosses as a test of mastery. After defeating a boss, the player advances to the subsequent level, often requiring incorporation of new challenges, enemies, and tasks that build upon previously mastered skills (Gee, 2007). This structure assists players in developing and mastering basic skills before advancing to more complex skills that ultimately must be combined to beat the game.
- **Video Game Example:** The Legend of Zelda series by Nintendo exemplifies cycles of expertise in video games. Link, the protagonist, starts with minimal skills and equipment, and gradually gains new abilities and gear by completing tasks and conquering dungeons. For example, in classic The Legend of Zelda: Ocarina of Time, one of the most highly-acclaimed games of all time, having received a 99/100 through Metacritic based on 22 critical reviews (Legend of Zelda, n.d.), players begin with a small sword and wooden shield whose use they master through various tasks. As players progress, they upgrade these weapons as well as acquire new ones, such as a bow and a grappling hook, that can be used in combination with their existing arsenal to overcome enemies and obstacles. Gaining new tools and abilities and combining them with existing skills allows players to progress through this world while intermittently facing dungeon bosses to prove their mastery.
- **Classroom Example:** Incorporating cycles of expertise into classroom activities provides students with opportunities to master basic skills before integrating the more advanced skills necessary to ultimately promote expertise and success in a

given area. One way of incorporating cycles of expertise into classrooms is through gamification, the process of incorporating game-like structures and activities in non-gaming environments (Werbach & Hunter, 2012). Using game elements in educational settings has significant potential (Lee & Hammer, 2011). Codecademy is one platform that offers opportunities for incorporating a gamified platform into educational settings. Codecademy allows beginners to develop computer programming skills by completing a series of activities related to various computer programming languages, and it uses a badge system (Werbach & Hunter, 2012) that functions similarly to Boy or Girl Scout badges; this system keeps track of individual progress in terms of completed training modules that represent their acquired skills. In addition to highlighting work completed and skills acquired, badge systems also raise awareness of unearned badges that represent future goals and opportunities for learning and growth. Furthermore, badges illustrate achievement and can serve as a source of pride for badge holders, who often interpret them as trophies. Codecademy could be directly incorporated into a variety of disciplines such as computer science, math, and even language arts. Teachers could additionally gamify their courses through creating and incorporating a badge system that recognizes students'personal, social, and academic accomplishments.

Information "On Demand" and "Just in Time"

- **Concept:** People often have difficulty processing and harnessing information when they are unable to immediately apply it to a real-world situation. Learning is enhanced when "information…is given 'just in time' (when [people] can put it to use) and 'on demand' (when they feel they need it)" (Gee, 2007, p. 37). These features help learners understand information and processes by presenting information in context and with immediate opportunity for practical application.
- **Video Game Example:** Guacamelee is a platforming game inspired by Mexican folklore in which a farmer, Juan, becomes a powerful luchador (wrestler) who fights evil. Throughout the game, Juan develops new skills that enable him to combat new enemies and traverse new environments. Each new ability is introduced by a sage who informs Juan of his new ability (and how to use it) along with an immediate opportunity for application; the information is thus presented "just in time." Additionally, as Juan gains various new abilities throughout the game, it may be difficult for the player to remember exactly how to execute each one, but at any given time the player can pause the game to refamiliarize him- or herself with button commands for each ability, and thus information is available "on demand." These features, common in video games, allow players to immediately put information to use, a process that facilitates learning (Gee, 2007).
- **Classroom Example:** Educators in a variety of disciplines can present information just in time and on demand through careful planning. Many teachers already present certain information just in time (i.e., right before or just when the students need it); although, being conscious of the importance of presenting information just in time is also helpful because it can influence planning. The use of computers and course management systems may additionally make it easier for teachers to present information on demand, as well as just in time. For example, information and ideas

can be explained just in time by introducing an activity through a course management system. Students can also access explanations, examples, and definitions on demand by going to a relevant page of the management system.

An example of how information can presented just in time and on demand may be found in chess clubs in many schools around the country. Ferguson (2006) highlights potential benefits of chess for student development and raises the idea of including chess more broadly in school curricula, as is the case in a variety of places around the world. Educators and their tools (such as computers) can help players learn the game of chess by providing information (e.g., which moves are legal and strategies that may be helpful) just in time and on demand. In addition to its potential educational benefits (Ferguson, 2006), chess is a particularly exciting prospect for inclusion at school, because chess—unlike most games—often engages players throughout their entire lives and can become an object of life-long appreciation and study (McGonigal, 2011).

Fish Tanks

- **Concept:** A fish tank is a metaphor for a "simplified eco-system that clearly displays some critical variables and their interactions that are otherwise obscured in the highly complex eco-system in the real world" (Gee, 2007, pp. 38-39). Students would most likely be overwhelmed if their teachers tried to explain how a multitude of elements interact in any system, whether it be the ocean, outer space, or even the human mind. It is thus important for educators to present simplified systems that illustrate fundamental elements and relationships of a more complex system to help students better understand the overall system. Once basic principles are learned, students have a better chance for understanding the overall system as well as its intricacies than if they were presented all the information at once.
- **Video Game Example:** LittleBigPlanet 3 utilizes the fish-tank principle through introducing important elements of gameplay, such as how to run, jump, grab, and customize a character, in the first few levels. Early-provided explicit instruction highlights important elements that will be used throughout the game and, by initially understanding basic features, players can begin to form a better idea of how the larger system (or game) works as challenges become more complicated. Video games commonly use tutorials and initial levels to introduce a simplified version of the game to prepare players for more complicated tasks in the future.
- **Classroom Example:** Teachers can create and utilize simplified representations of complex systems in a wide variety of subject areas, and study of the sciences is an obvious area to harness the fish-tank concept. Teachers can create representations of environmental ecosystems to include fundamental elements and processes, such as rain, sunlight, vegetation, animals, and evaporation. Teachers can also find valuable "fish tanks" online by carefully searching. The fish-tank concept is not just for teachers of ecology and biology; it can be used in virtually any discipline, ranging from economics to language arts and psychology to dance.

Economics, finance, and social studies teachers could incorporate games using fish tanks to highlight important variables and relationships in economics. Teachers can find a variety of online economics games, e.g., various prisoners' dilemmas or stock market simulations, from websites such as federalreserveeducation.org ("Classroom activities," n.d.) or economics-games.com (Gruyer & Toublanc, n.d.). Teachers can harness the power of games and fish tanks to promote deep learning of complex systems by highlighting key elements and relationships before introducing more detailed information and intricacies of the larger system.

Sandboxes

- **Concept:** Children often experience learning when they feel they are in a safe environment that allows them to explore without the fear of failing. Sandboxes are "safe havens for children that still look and feel like the real world" (Gee, 2007, p. 39). When teachers offer opportunities for children to safely explore concepts and activities, students do not need to worry about failing and can instead focus their energy on discovery and learning, leading to significant educational gains.
- **Video Game Example:** In addition to being a fun game that introduces important gameplay elements through its first few levels, LittleBigPlanet 3 is a game that inspires creativity by allowing players to construct their own levels that can be shared with the online community. Players of the LittleBigPlanet series have to date created over 9 million levels (Siegal, 2014). To help would-be level creators familiarize themselves with level-creation software, LittleBigPlanet 3 offers modules for players to learn about basic elements and relationships that can be used in level creation. Countless objects, tools, and stickers can be combined in a nearly infinite number of ways (hence 9 million levels and counting). Exhaustively explaining every element would be impossible, but through guided practice, LittleBigPlanet 3 helps players develop level creation skills by representing important elements and relationships through its modules.
- **Classroom Example:** Creating a safe environment is an important consideration for all educators. Teachers want their students to feel safe in their classrooms, but sometimes a student's biggest fear is the fear of failure. Since grades and evaluation (and their implications for the future) comprise part of nearly every classroom, student fears are understandable, making it difficult to establish a truly safe environment in a school setting without the fear of failure. However, while mandatory tests might never be totally free from fear of failure, teachers can create activities that help students focus on the present and significantly limit their worries regarding failure. Teachers can structure activities that focus on processes such as group exploration and collaboration rather than a specific end product. Teachers can also create activities that emphasize creativity and expression over correctness, and, particularly for younger children, teachers should never forget the value of play (Vygotsky, 1967).

Physical education teachers can create cooperative games to promote student development. In such games, students simply need to participate and are not expected to achieve a specific score, decreasing the fear of failure. One such game is Mine Field ("PE central," n.d.), in which students work in pairs. One student verbally guides his or her blindfolded partner through a mine field (obstacles placed throughout the gym). After one student successfully crosses the mine field, they switch positions. If the blindfolded student hits a mine, the teacher can decide if the student should start over or should switch places with their partner. This is a low-risk game that can foster trust and collaboration. There are a variety of physical education games that can create a safe place for students to learn valuable skills through collaboration, and such games are worthy of inclusion.

Skills as Strategies

- **Concept:** People do not enjoy repeatedly practicing skills out of context, but it is hard for students to succeed in tasks without having necessary skills (Gee, 2007). An effective way of addressing this dilemma is to have students practice skills as a strategy for attaining a larger personal goal. Through creating situations in which skill practice is part of a larger desirable goal, teachers can help students master the skills necessary for accomplishing various tasks.
- **Video Game Example:** Middle Earth: Shadow of Mordor is an expansion of J. R. R. Tolkien's Lord of the Rings universe in which players are essentially half human and half wraith, with goals of defeating enemies, becoming more powerful, and learning more about the history of Middle Earth. To accomplish these goals, the player must gain and use skills, e.g., a variety of attacks and abilities. Players learn that various skills can be used as strategies for accomplishing objectives. For example, using stealth skills may be a beneficial strategy for one's goal of rescuing hostages, because stealth skills can decrease the chance of enemies calling for reinforcements. Skills are not practiced out of context; they are used as specific strategies to help a player achieve his or her goals.
- **Classroom Example:** Students are often expected to complete various tasks out of context; consider the variety of rote drills in schools today. These drills are designed to get students to practice skills to be (hopefully) used when they are really needed. However, when students do not see immediate application (drills are often out-of-context experiences) they are less likely to engage with and learn from these drills. To deal with such a situation, a teacher can structure activities to help students use skills as strategies to accomplish goals; games can be great activities for this purpose. Math games, both digital and non-digital, have potential to harness student interest to help them develop skills as they work toward larger goals, and teachers can use existing games or create their own on topics ranging from addition to geometry to calculus. One aspect of such games should be establishing a larger goal; a goal of simply finishing a worksheet fails to motivate many students, so teachers must be creative here. Point systems, rewards, and badges (Werbach & Hunter, 2012) might serve as larger goals to be attained through using skills as strategies and resulting in engagement and learning.

System Thinking

- **Concept:** Students experience deep learning when they understand how elements and concepts relate to a larger system rather than viewing such elements only as discrete pieces of information (Gee, 2007). A video games is a system created by humans ("a designed system") that is more than the sum of its parts (Checkland, 1999). Graphics, rules, problems, goals, and possibilities for user input create a system, an opportunity for users to play and learn from the game. "Players…must learn to see each game (actually each genre of game) as a distinctive semiotic system affording and discouraging certain sorts of actions and interactions" (Gee, 2007, p. 42). When people understand interconnectedness of information in a larger system, they are better able to make informed decisions about how to interpret information in a contextual manner and to act accordingly.

- **Video Game Example:** Portal 2 is a unique puzzle game in which players strive to escape rooms (solve puzzles) using a portal gun to place one orange and one blue portal around the room (e.g., on the ceiling, floor, and walls); when a player steps into one portal, he or she emerges from the other. (Objects can also pass through portals). Players conceptualize the game as a system in which certain actions such as maintaining momentum through portals are allowed, (which helps players use gravity and speed to solve puzzles), and certain other actions are prohibited. For example, some surfaces (walls, floors, and ceilings) can hold a portal while others cannot. (Players can differentiate them through visual clues.) It is only through learning the system and how elements and features work together that players can successfully escape rooms, solve puzzles, and advance in the game.
- **Classroom Example:** Teachers can help students think about interconnected elements in systems; such elements can occur in a variety of areas ranging from biology to computer science, and from literature to physics. Highlighting important elements and relationships in any system can help teachers stimulate this type of thinking. As illustrated in the previous section, Portal 2 facilitates such system thinking while also being a great deal of fun. Shute, Ventura, and Ke (2015) conducted a study in which college students were divided into two groups: one played Portal 2 and the other played Luminosity, a brain-training game. They found that

Portal 2 [players] showed a statistically significant advantage over Lumosity [players] on each of the three composite measures—problem solving, spatial skill, and persistence. Portal 2 players also showed significant increases from pretest to posttest on specific small- and large scale spatial tests while those in the Lumosity condition did not show any pretest to posttest differences on any measure. (p. 58)

Such findings might be appealing to some educators. However, it is important to note that some scientists cast doubt on the efficacy of brain-training games (Stanford Center on Longevity, 2014). Nonetheless, many students would certainly enjoy playing Portal 2 (not a brain-training game) as part of their curriculum, and as Shute et al., (2015) noted, playing Portal 2 may in fact lead to some worthy educational gains.

Meaning as Action Image

- **Concept:** People generally use personal experiences, not textbook definitions, to give meaning to concepts (Gee, 2007). For example, people do not think about the concept of "schools" based on some definition; rather, they use their own experiences in schools as well as experiences they've heard about other schools through friends, family, and media to create "imaginative reconstructions" of schools. Thus, experiences determine how we make meaning of things rather than using textbook definitions. "Furthermore, for humans, words and concepts have their deepest meanings when they are clearly tied to perception and action in the world" (Gee, 2007, p. 43).
- **Video Game Example:** Far Cry 4 allows players to explore the fictional country of Kyrat, a country influenced by the cultures and geography of Nepal and Tibet. Beautiful Himalayan landscapes, marked with villages, temples, and hidden valuables, are ripe for exploration in this open-world adventure game. The player assumes the role of Ajay Ghale, whose

father created a rebel group, The Golden Path, to overthrow a brutal dictator, Pagan Min. Players experience deep immersion traversing the mountains and admiring Buddhist-inspired artifacts such as prayer flags, prayer wheels, statues, and temples. In addition to defeating enemies, players act through their role as Ajay Ghale to destroy propaganda such as radio broadcasts and posters in an effort to diminish Pagan Min's power. In reality, many people will not actually explore the Himalayas, nor will they rebel against a brutal dictator. However, this game allows players to simulate an experience of rebellion in a safe manner, allowing players to expand their understanding of rebellions as well as purposes and strategies of rebellions. This experience results in a greater depth of understanding that a textbook definition would not.

- **Classroom Example:** Experience trumps textbook definitions when we make meaning in the world, and teachers should consider this fact in their pedagogy. In recent years, educators have harnessed the power of experience by using video games to achieve educational gains in social studies within both in-school and after-school programs (Squire, DeVane, and Durga, 2008; Watson, Mong, & Harris, 2011). Squire et al., (2008) highlight several video games that have potential to promote significant learning gains in history and social studies; they include "*Europa Universalis, the Patrician, Sid Meier's Pirates, Railroad Tycoon, Colonization,* and the *Rome: Total War*" (p. 250). Social studies educators can thoughtfully integrate video games in their classrooms to help students develop experiences that enhance their understanding of complex social phenomena.

PRENSKY'S ACTIVITIES AND LEARNING TECHNIQUES

Prensky's (2005) activities and learning techniques focus on how digital games incorporate various principles and activities to facilitate learning. However, this section will extract these principles from a highly digital game context and illustrate how they can be harnessed by educators to promote learning in general, even without the use of games. This also contrasts with the discussion of the previous section, in which Gee's learning principles were also explored through the use of games in the classroom. The purpose of this alternate structure is to illustrate that, while games can be utilized to promote educational engagement and learning, the principles that games employ can also be harnessed by educators in non-game contexts to promote student learning. Educators can thus use both games and their underlying principles in a wide variety of contexts. Let's turn to Prensky's activities and learning techniques to find out how.

Practice and Feedback

- **Concept:** Learning new things requires practice and feedback, and these features work together to allow learners to gain skills through experience. Practice provides repetition, and feedback helps learners make adjustments to their technique. Interactivity is an important element of practice and feedback that can promote engagement and learning that "drill and kill" practice is unlikely to achieve (Prensky, 2005).
- **Video Game Example:** Gamers enjoy practicing and mastering new games, skills, and abilities. Practicing can be a reward in itself because improving one's skills is often intrinsically satisfying, but players may also regularly use such skills

to also help them achieve larger goals in the game; for example, "beating a level" may demonstrate that practice has paid off. The primary form of feedback in video games is nearly omnipresent, and this feedback is obtained through player experience. For example, players may attempt various actions (e.g., trying to climb an object or use a certain attack on a particular enemy) and the game either allows them to succeed using that action (e.g., climb or attack successfully) or indicates that the action will not work in this particular environment. Such feedback is constant and helps learners discover how the game works.

- **Classroom Example:** This concept is supported through Hattie's (2009, 2012) work. Hattie (2009) states that it is important for teachers to provide "multiple opportunities for deliberative practice" and "openly discuss…three feedback questions: 'Where are they going?' 'How are they going?' and 'Where to next?' ('they' refers to both the teacher and to the student)" (pp. 36-37). Teachers should help students understand these issues and provide opportunities to incorporate meaningful feedback into practice.

Learning by Doing

- **Concept:** People experience significant learning when they *do* things as opposed to when others *tell* them things. This concept represents an underlying strength of games. Prensky (2005) illustrates this point by asking "When was the last time you played a game that spent a lot of the time 'telling' you anything?" (p. 114). People are likely to benefit from "exploring, discovering, and problem solving" in ways that require "active participation and decision making [from] the learner" (Prensky, 2005, p. 114).
- **Video Game Example:** Gamers play games. Another way to look at it is "Gamers *do* games" like students do math or do homework. Playing, however, is typically more fun and more engaging. Video games require players to be actively engaged. Games reward exploration and problem solving, and they honor players' decisions, goals, and preferences. Players create unique experiences when playing games. They can proceed in a variety of ways and integrate their personal goals and decisions into their game experience, and games encourage this. This is part of the beauty of games. No two players have the same experience. Gamers *do*. Gamers explore and make the game their own.
- **Classroom Example:** Educators should consider the value of learning by doing. Students can achieve incredible learning gains when they are actively engaged. Exploration and discovery are likely to promote learning that simply telling will not (Prensky, 2005). This is not to say that teachers should never lecture on a topic or inform students about important aspects of some phenomenon. As with many things, finding a balance is important and, while many people recognize the importance of learning by doing, educators should try to creatively craft ways of incorporating activities into their classrooms through which students can experience active participation, exploration, and problem solving. Classrooms that incorporate these features are often enjoyable places that promote deep learning.

Learning from Mistakes

- **Concept:** Feedback should help students recognize and understand their mistakes so they can improve upon them. Mistakes provide great learning opportunities, and teachers should seize them. Prensky (2005) highlights a typical difference between educational and game feedback: educational feedback *tells* you your mistakes (e.g., written comments), while game feedback uses *actions* to illustrate your mistakes (e.g., your character dies or you have to restart a level). Prensky illustrates how game-like feedback is often more engaging and fun, which may provide benefits in educational settings.

- **Video Game Example:** Games require players to learn from their mistakes. Good video games are challenging and gamers may fail often and spectacularly. "Gamers aren't afraid to fail. Failing in a good game is at the very least fun and interesting; it can also be instructive and even empowering" (McGonigal, 2011, pp. 248-249). Mistakes inform gamers on how to adjust their decisions and actions to conquer a task at hand. Learning from mistakes to overcome obstacles and achieve goals can indeed be empowering.
- **Classroom Example:** Teachers should try to create experiences in which students can use feedback, whether educational or game-like, to help them understand the goal, their progress, and necessary next steps; this aligns with Hattie's (2009) ideas on feedback. Teachers can create educational feedback through explicitly addressing goals, progress, and next steps with students via written and oral feedback. They can also creatively incorporate game-like feedback in non-game settings or by incorporating digital games that support learning goals, often naturally providing interesting types of feedback described by Prensky (2005).

Goal-Oriented Learning

- **Concept:** Goals impact learning (Hattie, 2009). "A goal is a key element of a game… [they are] usually considered worth reaching, [and] give players the incentive to push on through repeated failure" (Prensky, 2005, p. 114). Educators can harness goals to set clear objectives and guide student action.
- **Video Game Example:** Gamers set and accomplish various goals throughout the playing of a video game. Notably, not all gamers have the same goals for a particular game. While beating the game is often a goal for many players, other goals they may set for themselves in games often vary greatly. Some players may want to maximize a certain ability or weapon, while other players may want to locate every hidden item or beat the game within a certain amount of time. A strength of video games is that they provide a range of possible goals for players, who can choose their goals and a manner of accomplishing them (multiple paths exist for achieving each goal); games can also do an incredibly satisfying job of informing gamers when they accomplish a goal, often through the use of visual and auditory feedback as well as a list of achievements and trophies.
- **Classroom Example:** Locke and Latham (1990) make a persuasive case that goals affect performance; teachers should thus consider harnessing the power of goals in their classrooms. Teachers can help students set goals through conferences or documents and monitor their progress to help them enhance their performance. Goals can furthermore provide a structure for feedback. Teachers can provide explicit

feedback related to student goal progression and attainment, and once goals are reached, teachers can help students set new goals for further growth. Goals can be incorporated into classrooms at the individual, small group, or entire-class levels.

Discovery Learning and Guided Discovery

- **Concept:** "Discovery learning is based on the idea that you learn something better if you find it out for yourself, rather than having it told to you" (Prensky, 2005, p. 114). The discovery process is sometimes very open-ended (i.e., learners explore without a specific goal or problem to solve), while at other times it can be more structured (i.e., learners explore a concept or environment, but an underlying problem or goal influences student action).
- **Video Game Example:** Most learning in video games is accomplished through discovery. Games rarely explicitly inform players what their goal is and exactly how they should accomplish it. Games typically in an initial step briefly inform players about basic skills and abilities, but they leave players to discover how using such skills at various times and in various combinations can help them achieve their goals. Thus, learning in games is highly based on discovery.
- **Classroom Example:** Teachers can incorporate discovery learning into their classrooms by offering opportunities for students to explore ideas, materials, and activities either individually or in groups. For example, science teachers might allow students to experiment with various objects to make generalizations about how the objects function together and relate to a larger system. Teachers can provide varying degrees of guidance through mentoring and/or other support, including establishing goals. Teachers can also ask students about their interests, and provide opportunities for democratic engagement in the classroom as well as letting students choose for themselves what they want to discover.

Task-Based Learning

- **Concept:** Educational activities often begin with significant explanations and demonstrations before allowing students to begin work on some task or activity; however, task-based learning often reduces or skips lengthy explanations and hands-off time to provide students with greater time to work towards a specific task or goal (Prensky, 2005). During hands-on time teachers can provide support and modeling to help students better understand the material. A key concept in task-based learning is that students learn by doing.
- **Video Game Example:** Modern video games are full of task-based activities in which players must collect items, explore new areas, and unlock new abilities. The "how-to" explanations of these tasks are often minimal or non-existent. Some items might be marked on a map while others are not. Some explicit direction or monitoring system may be available to help players accomplish their goals, while at other times careful searching, creativity, hard work, and a little bit of luck may make all the difference. While all games have tasks, some more transparent than others, video games are exceptionally good at rewarding players when tasks are accomplished, often through power-ups, new items, and trophies.
- **Classroom Example:** Teachers naturally incorporate a variety of tasks into their classrooms, but not all such tasks are equally valuable. A variety of schol-

ars from a range of disciplines, including literacy education (Beach, Campano, Edmiston, & Borgmann, 2010) and science education (Chinn & Malhorta, 2002), have argued that creating authentic tasks and activities promotes meaningful learning experiences. Beach et al., (2010) argue that "Literacy learning best occurs when students are engaged in meaningful activities that have authentic purposes...[which] may seem obvious...But literacy policy has been geared toward the teaching of reading and writing as a discrete set of skills" (p. 15). Teachers can create *authentic* tasks for students that carry real meaning. The task of finding such authentic tasks obviously varies by discipline. It may take the form of drafting a letter to a real person or creating a public service announcement in language arts, creating a useful computer program in computer science, or engaging in authentic experiments that utilize the scientific method in a science class. Promoting hands-on time for students to engage in authentic tasks can result in valuable learning experiences.

Question-Led Learning

- **Concept:** Harnessing questions as a central pedagogical tool has various benefits. For example, "Attempting to respond as best as you can to a question whose answer you don't know forces you to think about the information and reason among the answers, rather than just being told the response" (Prensky, 2005, p. 114). This idea is related to the concept of inquiry-based learning, which revolves heavily around the use of open-ended and learner-generated questions to facilitate learning (Edelson, Gordon, & Pea, 1999).
- **Video Game Example:** Video games rely much more on implicit questions than on explicit questions. For example, games rarely ask questions like "How are you going to beat this level?" However, the objectives in most games could be translated into questions like "What are the weaknesses of this boss?" or "What information is important to help me solve this puzzle?" These types of implicit questions are constantly in the minds of gamers trying to answer questions and solve problems through experimentation with a variety of actions and strategies, receiving feedback from the game, and adjusting actions to accomplish goals.
- **Classroom Example:** While questions can be a great asset for teachers, many, if not most, questions are "low-level cognitive questions" related to recalling facts and procedures, and to which students often only have about one second to respond (Hattie, 2009, 2012). Teachers should consider what types of questions they are asking (e.g., factual, procedural, open-ended, etc.), their frequency of occurrence, and the response time given to students. Inclusion of more meaningful questions and providing ample response time is important because "higher-order questions can enhance deeper understanding" (Hattie, 2009). Kuhn, Black, Keselman, and Kaplan (2000) also note the value of inquiry in education, particularly science education, in which students can develop questions and utilize the scientific method to learn more about the world, a helpful and authentic task for promoting learning. Not all questions are equally valuable, and pedagogies that incorporate higher-order questions that drive deep investigations can facilitate learning in any discipline.

Situated Learning

- **Concept:** This approach focuses on creating environments for learning experiences that are comparable to the future environments in which the ideas and activities will be utilized (Prensky, 2005). "According to this approach, when students learn in such an environment they benefit not only from the learning material that is taught but also from the culture that is in that environment, the vocabulary used, and the behavior associated with that environment" (Prensky, 2005, p. 114), which complements the work of Brown, Collins, and Duguid (1989) and their conceptions of situated cognition and cognitive apprenticeship. Learning is enhanced, perceived value is increased, and the ability to transfer concepts and abilities to new environments develops when learning occurs in a contextualized environment and students understand the activities have an authentic purpose, and practical applications for the future.
- **Video Game Example:** It is in the nature of games to promote situated learning. Almost all initial learning presented in the context of a game (or game genre), allows players to learn skills and gain information in simplified environments (early levels) that is directly related to and prepares them for future experiences in the game (more challenging tasks and levels). Additionally, game skills and knowledge often transfer across games, particularly within a specific genre (e.g., understanding jumping mechanics in one game may help one achieve success in jumping tasks in other games).
- **Classroom Example:** Teachers can help students understand that different roles and occupations have unique ways of thinking, communicating, and acting in the world; these are all situated in the context of that role and its purposes. For example, students may take on the role of a scientist (Gee, 2007) and utilize the scientific method for learning new things about the world, or they may become citizen scientists through various programs and applications (Malykhina, 2013). Students can harness identities and learn situated ways of thinking and acting to promote authentic learning experiences that improve their ability to function in such roles in the future, a process that aligns with the concept of Brown, Collins, and Duguid's (1989) idea of cognitive apprenticeship. Teachers can harness these opportunities to promote deep learning, motivation, and engagement.

Role Playing

- **Concept:** Role playing is often used in games and trainings to help individuals learn about key concepts and actions related to a variety of roles and positions. This concept is related to Gee's (2007) principle of Identity: "Learners need to know what the 'rules of the game' are and who plays it. They need to know how to take on the identity…[and] operate by a certain set of values, attitudes, and actions" (p. 32). Role playing helps with this process.
- **Video Game Example:** Players assume new roles and identities when playing video games; gamers may become treasure hunters, soldiers, and detectives. Through role playing, players learn what information, actions, and objects are important to those roles. For example, when assuming the role of a detective, players learn that searching for, interpreting, and connecting evidence helps detectives, both in real life and in the game, achieve goals such as locating a suspect or solving a crime. Video games provide safe places for gamers to assume new identities that help them under-

stand the thought processes, actions, and value systems of that role (Gee, 2007).

- **Classroom Example:** Teachers can promote opportunities for students to role play. These opportunities can take many forms. As previously mentioned, one might take the form of English language learners assuming the roles of customers and clerks to learn language related to shopping or traveling. One would expect such an activity to promote learning based on Interactionist Second Language Acquisition (SLA) Theory, which posits that meaningful interaction and engagement with the target language leads to language learning (Chapelle, 2005). Other opportunities may consist of students taking on the role of scientists (Gee, 2007) or engaging in role playing through dramatic inquiry (Beach et al., 2010). Students can assume different roles that can lead them to understand other people's perspectives and develop empathy for them. Dramatic inquiry can be a form of role playing that permits students to safely engage with a multitude of identities. Beach et al., (2010) illustrate one such example in which one student becomes a gorilla poacher and other students essentially become anti-poaching activists. This leads to a rich discussion about the rights of humans and gorillas, a discussion that might be less fruitful if it emerged from a top-down approach. There are a vast number of possibilities for role playing in education, and teachers can benefit from thinking of creative ways of incorporating role playing into their classrooms.

Constructivist Learning

- **Concept:** Piaget (1954) believed that people created (constructed) knowledge through assimilation and accommodation of new experiences with existing knowledge, a process influenced by various thought processes and social interactions. "Constructivism is a theory about knowledge and learning…[and] describes knowledge not as truths to be transmitted or discovered, but as emergent, developmental, nonobjective, viable constructed explanations by humans engaged in meaning-making in cultural and social communities" (Fosnot, 2005, p. ix). Prensky (2005) argues that humans experience deep learning when they are actively engaged in educational experiences, rather than in a top-down lecture format, as well as when we produce "personally meaningful physical artifacts" (p. 115).
- **Video Game Example:** Gamers constantly construct meaning when they play games. There are few instances of top-down transmission of knowledge in video games. Players regularly connect their past experiences with their present situation to understand how the game works and how to establish and achieve goals. Gamers additionally draw on a variety of experiences and past media interaction (e.g., books read, movies watched, etc.) to help them make meaning of the story. Video games are a useful medium for helping gamers construct and extract meaning from their experiences, both inside and outside the game world.
- **Classroom Example:** These ideas can be helpful for classroom teachers who can incorporate hands-on activities and facilitate the production of meaningful artifacts that can help their students learn. Teachers in a variety of disciplines can provide opportunities for creativity and self-expression, can affirm that students have valuable ways of thinking about the world, and can help them understand there is often not a single correct answer to many of the world's problems and issues. Savery and Duffy

(2001) illustrate a variety of ways that educators can combine a constructivist framework with problem-based learning. Tying smaller tasks to a larger problem, helping students cultivate a sense of ownership of the activity, and encouraging students to think about issues from multiple perspectives incorporates both constructivism and problem-based learning (Savery & Duffy, 1995). Incorporating such ideas, using hand-on projects, and integrating higher-order questions can help teachers promote student learning, engagement, and creativity while simultaneously helping students understand that they have valuable and legitimate perspectives and skills.

Multisensory Learning

- **Concept:** This idea highlights the value of incorporating multiple senses into instruction to engage students in a variety of ways. Shams and Seitz (2008) highlight the benefits of multisensory learning and found "that learning mechanisms operate optimally under multisensory conditions" (p. 5). Prensky (2005) also connects this concept to Gardner's (2011) multiple intelligences, representing the idea that there is not a singular intelligence for humans; rather, there are multiple intelligences that people draw from to think about and engage in a variety of activities. Multisensory and multiple intelligence perspectives recognize the value of incorporating a diverse set of stimulating activities that allow students to develop their abilities in a balanced fashion rather than using only a single sense or intelligence.
- **Video Game Example:** Multiple senses are regularly activated when playing video games. Two obvious examples are sight and hearing, each of which can obviously be used to promote learning in and of itself; games also incorporate tactile feedback from controllers via both interaction with buttons and the rumbling (or vibrating) effects that occur in tandem with related events in the game like experiencing damage. There are a variety of games that also regularly require kinesthetic movement; examples include Nintendo's Wii system and games for the X-Box Kinect. Such games may require players to move around the room, to swing their arms, and even to dance. Video games incorporate multisensory learning in various ways to promote stimulation and engagement.
- **Classroom Example:** Students can benefit from instruction and activities that harness multiple senses and intelligences, and teachers can create a variety of activities to help students in this regard. Modern technology allows students to creatively engage multiple senses and technologies. For example, Glogster allows users to create graphical blogs (glogs) incorporating written text, oral language, videos, and more. As students create, view, and interact with glogs they engage in multisensory activities that harness their multiple intelligences. Teachers can create activities that allow students to utilize multiple senses and intelligences to promote learning and development.

Learning Objects

- **Concept:** "The idea of learning objects grows out of object-oriented programming, where pieces of a program are built as stand-alone units with input and output 'hooks' to link them together in whatever order is needed for the particular task at hand" (Prensky, 2005, p. 115). Such a modular structure works well for computers and can also work well in classrooms. Through exploring tasks and concepts that are worthy of independent study, and then connecting them with other ideas and activities, students can transfer concepts and skills to new environments while simultaneously developing their system thinking skills (Gee, 2007).

- **Video Game Example:** Video games help players learn discrete skills related to movement and action, such as running, climbing, attacking, and opening doors, that must be combined in various ways at different points in the game to help a player achieve his or her goals. These concepts and skills may be used discretely or hooked together (combined). Typically in video games, skills are initially used in a more discrete fashion and then connected together in more complex arrangements as the game progresses.
- **Classroom Example:** Teachers can harness learning objects in units of study in which different key concepts or skills are individually developed and then combined for a final unit project, a process regularly utilized by many educators. For example, in chemistry students might sequentially learn about characteristics of a group of elements and substances, how to measure mass and volume, and then how to use lab equipment and interpret results; they are subsequently required to use all of these discrete skills in tandem, each process influencing the others, to create a system that "hooks" multiple learning objects (concepts and skills) together. Generally speaking, teachers can illustrate the interconnectedness of significant ideas and skills to promote learning.

Coaching

- **Concept:** Coaches, like teachers, are people who help learners develop and realize their potential; this may happen in a classroom, on a sports team, or somewhere else entirely. Hawes (2004) notes that "teaching is not telling" and that interactive learning should be a priority for modern educators (p. 47). Coaching and teaching involves *showing* students how to do things and illustrate their importance. Prensky (2005) notes that digital games are creating unique ways to coach learners and guide them to success. Conati and VanLehn (2000) also illustrate how computer programs can serve as coaches to promote metacognition and learning among student users. In addition to being a coach, teachers can also incorporate technology and other resources to facilitate coaching and learning.
- **Video Game Example:** Games coach players to succeed in a variety of ways. One example lies in how many games, particularly during their initial levels, provide an explanation of a task and then help players accomplish that task through providing a visual demonstration (e.g., a computer-produced simulation of the task) in which the computer illustrates the action. However, there is a more common and prominent method for coaching implemented through feedback systems built into the game. For example, the player may receive feedback when he or she accomplishes a task, experiences damage, or unsuccessfully attempts an action. In all of these examples, the game's feedback will promote player learning that influences future actions. Video games *show* players how various techniques and actions can help them accomplish their goals.
- **Classroom Example:** Teachers regularly coach students in a variety of ways, and there are at least a couple of ways to extend coaching beyond the teacher, which can result in desirable learning outcomes. Prensky (2005) illustrates that games and technology can create beneficial coach-

ing experiences. For example, in a digital environment, non-playable characters can guide students towards their goal, perhaps solving a math problem or understanding a concept in physics or economics. These digital coaches can harness multimodal resources (e.g., text, audio, video, graphics, etc.) to help convey their points in an interactive fashion. Technology and games can also serve as coaches themselves, even without introducing a digital character, because technology can present information, facilitate activities, and provide feedback. Teachers can also harness the intrinsic power of students themselves who invariably have varying degrees of knowledge and skills in a variety of disciplines. Students can coach other students, a process teachers can facilitate. In such circumstances both students may learn: the novice learns from the expert and, as the classic Latin maxim *docendo discimus* reminds us, "we learn by teaching" (Merriam-Webster, n.d.). There is no replacement for skilled teachers in classrooms; teachers can, however, draw upon other resources to increase coaching opportunities in the classroom to promote learning and engagement.

Intelligent Tutors

- **Concept:** An intelligent tutor system (ITS) is a computer program that harnesses artificial intelligence that understands the domain of study, provides various tasks to students, assesses student input, and provides feedback tailored to student performance to help students learn concepts and skills (Burns & Capps, 1988; Corbett, Koedinger, & Anderson, 1997). Intelligent tutors compare student performance to expert performance to create feedback and "understands most common misconceptions and tries to correct them early on, as well as giving problems and hints to mediate the misconceptions" (Prensky, 2005, p. 115).
- **Video Game Example:** While intelligent tutoring systems are generally thought of in terms of educational outcomes, video games incorporate a form of intelligent tutoring through monitoring players' actions, goals, and progress and providing feedback to help them accomplish their goals given their actions and progress. For example, many games provide tips and hints if a player is struggling with a task such as defeating a boss. The game understands the goal (e.g., beating the boss), analyzes players' actions (e.g., attacking but not exploiting the boss' weakness), monitors progress (e.g., the player is currently stuck on the boss), and then provides feedback such as directing the player to look for the boss's weakness or explicitly telling the player what that weakness is. This process illustrates intelligent tutoring in game systems to help players accomplish their goals.
- **Classroom Example:** Given the prominence and power of computers, teachers should consider integrating intelligent tutoring systems into their classrooms. *The International Journal of Artificial Intelligence in Education* offers a variety of research that can introduce educators to various intelligent tutoring systems based on their particular disciplines. Intelligent tutors exist in fields ranging from second language acquisition (Kukulska-Hulme & Shield, 2008) to mathematics (Khachatryan et al., 2014) and from logic (Lanzilotti & Roselli, 2007) to physics (Dzikovska, Steinhauser, Farrow, Moore, & Campbell, 2014). Incorporating intelligent tutors provides tailored feedback for each student; this can serve as a helpful supplement to

teacher feedback and can create opportunities for teachers to work in person with individuals or small groups while other students interact with the intelligent tutoring system.

SOLUTIONS AND RECOMMENDATIONS

This chapter has identified video games as an important platform for promoting learning and engagement. Prensky (2005) states that "learners have changed…[and] need to be motivated in new ways" (p. 97) Video games have incredible potential for application in educational settings. Prensky (2005) illustrates that video games promote motivation and engagement, two features that positively influence school success (Hattie, 2009). Students love video games; they are drawn to them because gaming is a source of pleasure, learning, agency, and meaningfulness (Gee, 2007). Teachers should think about these issues. They are the very reason why gamers choose to pay significant money and to experience considerable frustration in playing them. Educators should consider using both digital and non-digital games in their classrooms as well as recognize the principles embodied in video games that influence learning (Gee, 2007; Prensky, 2005). These ideas complement the work of Becker (2008) and her chapter "Video Game Pedagogy: Good Games = Good Pedagogy", which highlights the benefits and potential of a pedagogy that harnesses video games to promote significant learning gains. This chapter, though, aims to take a slightly broader perspective that can be described as a gaming pedagogy more generally. This perspective highlights the benefits and potential of video games, non-digital games, and the embodied learning principles and techniques of games as well as gamification to facilitate learning in educational contexts. Adopting this type of gaming pedagogy has tremendous potential to help educators promote learning, engagement, and motivation in their classrooms, and educators may consider harnessing these ideas to help them attain their educational goals. It is important to note, though, that the promise of games lies not just in their current state—but in their potential.

Games have already been shown to produce great learning, but not always the type of learning we value in classrooms; this has at least two significant implications. First, teachers should recognize the value of video games and how they can facilitate important meaning-making processes through multimodal interaction. Gamers develop abilities to assume new identities, develop system thinking, creatively solve problems, and much more. These are valuable educational skills, and teachers can incorporate video games into their classrooms to develop such skills and explain their importance to students who are often of the mind that games are fun and learning is not (Gee, 2007). Educators can help students recognize that "fun non-school stuff" is valuable and contributes to learning that can transfer to a variety of both school and non-school settings, and we do children a favor by helping them understand that learning can be fun while simultaneously encouraging them to utilize and share their diverse out-of-school experiences and skills in educational contexts.

Second, collaborative efforts between researchers, policy makers, teachers, parents, game developers, and students should focus on creating games that promote deep learning of knowledge and skills related to academic disciplines and are designed specifically for educational purposes. This is no easy task, but given the potential of video games as educational tools, it is a worthy endeavor.

Integrating games into classrooms is important and has tremendous potential, but there are a few points to mention with respect to potential pitfalls. First, there is no substitute for skilled teachers; simply placing video games in front of students is not likely to help educators achieve all their goals, and teachers should carefully consider their educational goals and resources before implementing any technology (Hutchison & Woodward, 2014). Second, some educational games and brain games may claim to promote somewhat unbelievable outcomes, and there is good reason to be cautious of such claims (Stanford Center on Longevity, 2014). Educators can be understandably skeptical about any miracle product or program, whether it be a video game, a basal program, or a teaching technique. However, this concern does not negate the fact that video games often carry significant benefits and potential (Gee, 2007; Prensky, 2005, McGonigal, 2011). This leads to a third consideration; as with most things, it is not what you use but how you use it. Educators should harness video games to promote educational gains, and this often takes careful planning. Teachers should first consider their goals then plan accordingly. Sometimes games can be tremendously helpful in attaining one's current educational goals, other times they may not be helpful at all. Teacher creativity and collaboration can promote effective integration of video games resulting in valuable learning gains.

Gaming in education, like any area, has opportunities and challenges. In the future, it is likely there will be a continued give-and-take between incorporating games in classrooms and pushback by various stakeholders, such as parents, teachers, administrators, and even students. However, as the population ages and a greater proportion of students, teachers, and parents are familiar with technology and gaming, an increased general acceptance of gaming to promote educational gains is likely to occur. As video games have enormous potential in education, an increased acceptance of gaming is likely to be helpful for students and teachers in a variety of ways. However, not all games are equally good; some games when incorporated in certain ways will be much more likely to promote valuable educational outcomes than other games that are incorporated poorly. This will be a struggle for many educators, deciding what games to include and how to utilize them. There is no magic answer, and what works well in one classroom may not succeed in another classroom. This highlights the importance of professional discretion and collaboration among educators. Teachers who deeply understand games, their benefits, and adopt a gaming pedagogy will likely be more successful with harnessing the power of games in their classrooms than their peers who incorporate them simply as a reward or time-filler. The educators who deeply understand games will be a driving force for the expansion of gaming in education in the future. They will be able to share their insights with colleagues and demonstrate the efficacy and potential of gaming in the classroom. These educators already exist, but their numbers can be expanded and repertoire increased through additional research that illustrates specific ways that games can support education.

Gaming in education will also be affected by the growing technologies of augmented and virtual reality. "Augmented reality refers to technologies that project digital materials onto real world objects" (Cuendet, Bonnard, Do-Lenh, & Dillenbourg, 2013, p. 557). The potential for augmented reality in education is enormous. Cuedet et al., (2013) illustrate how it can be used to promote learning in a variety of disciplines, ranging from logistics to carpentry to geometric symmetry. Augmented reality gaming opportunities also exist that allow users to merge the digital and real world while playing a game and learning. The extensive presence of mobile technologies in schools will help educators incorporate augmented reality. Additionally, virtual reality (VR) technologies are being developed and becoming more accessible to a range of users including educators. "There are basically two types of VR: immersive VR and non-immersive VR" (Lee & Wong, 2014, p. 50). Non-immersive VR facilitates user interaction in digital worlds through the use of everyday devices ranging from game consoles to tablets and laptops to mobile phones. Immersive VR, on the other hand, uses technologies that are currently uncommon in educational environments such as VR headsets and "immersive project technology systems (IPT), where images are projected on surface(s) around the users" (Limniou, Roberts, & Papadopoulos, 2008, p. 585), such systems facilitate a deep sense of immersion can encapsulate the user and his or her full field of vision. Users may explore recreations of ancient parts of the world or be transported to microscopic environments. As immersive VR technologies become more affordable, they will likely be integrated into educational environments. As augmented reality and virtual reality technologies become more prevalent in schools, they will also integrate games and gaming principles to promote student learning and engagement. The future of games in education is bright, but it is important to build upon existing research and knowledge to try to maximize the effectiveness of games in education.

FUTURE RESEARCH DIRECTIONS

While much has been learned and studied regarding video games and education, significant work still remains. A primary direction for future research relates to studying how educators are integrating games into their classrooms and which of their practices are highly effective and which are not. Further research is also warranted with respect to connecting video games and the concept of Flow (Csikszentmihalyi, 1991). Squire (2003) has noted the experience of Flow in video games and summarized Flow as "state of optimal experience, whereby a person is so engaged in activity that self-consciousness disappears, time becomes distorted, and people engage in complex, goal-directed activity not for external rewards, but for simply the exhilaration of doing" (p. 50). Harnessing Flow as a "state of optimal experience" in schools through video games holds promise and deserves further research attention. Furthermore, it is important to continue to develop the concept of video game literacies (Squire, 2008), and its relationship to New Literacies (Leu, Kinzer, Coiro, and Kammack, 2004), multiliteracies (The New London Group, 2000), and education in general. Developing an understanding of this range of perspectives on literacies and how they are connected can help researchers and educators understand video games in new and valuable ways.

One final direction for future research is also warranted. While video games may have tremendous potential in education (Gee, 2007; McGonigal; 2011, Prensky; 2005; Squire, 2011), that potential is ultimately influenced by various stakeholders and gatekeepers, including parents, administrators, teachers, and students. If one or more of such stakeholder groups dismisses video games as unworthy, a waste of time, or simply not fit for educational purposes, it will be difficult to capitalize on the potential of video games. Therefore, further research should build upon the limited existing research (Bourgonjon, Valcke, Soetaert, De Wever, & Schellens, 2011; Bourgonjon, Valcke, Soetaert, & Schellens, 2010; Schrader, Zheng, & Young, 2006) to develop an understanding of the perceptions and practices of these stakeholders as they relate to video games as educational tools.

CONCLUSION

Video games are a valuable asset for educators and can promote motivation, engagement, and learning. Creative and passionate teachers can harness the power of games in classrooms. Various scholars (Gee, 2007; McGonigal, 2011; Prensky, 2005; Squire, 2011) recognize games and their potential to facilitate meaningful educational outcomes. This chapter illustrates how educators can harness games and their embodied learning principles and activities to create valuable educational outcomes for their students and utilize a gaming pedagogy in their classrooms. While much work remains to be done, the expansion of the use of video games as learning tools is an exciting prospect for many students and educators alike.

REFERENCES

Beach, R., Campano, G., Edmiston, B., & Borgmann, M. (2010). Literacy tools in the classroom: Teaching through critical inquiry, grades 5-12. New York, NY: Teachers College Press.

Bear, D., Invernizzi, M., Templeton, S., & Johnston, F. (2012). *Words their way: Word study for phonics, vocabulary, and spelling instruction* (5th ed.). Upper Saddle River, NJ: Pearson Inc.

Becker, K. (2008). Video game pedagogy: Good games = good pedagogy. In C. T. Miller (Ed.), *Games: Purpose and potential in education* (pp. 73–125). New York, NY: Springer.

Bourgonjon, J., Valcke, M., Soetaert, R., De Wever, B., & Schellens, T. (2011). Parental acceptance of digital game-based learning. *Computers & Education, 57*(1), 1434–1444. doi:10.1016/j.compedu.2010.12.012

Bourgonjon, J., Valcke, M., Soetaert, R., & Schellens, T. (2010). Students' perceptions about the use of video games in the classroom. *Computers & Education, 54*(4), 1145–1156. doi:10.1016/j.compedu.2009.10.022

Brown, J. S., Collins, A., & Duguid, P. (1989). Situated cognition and the culture of learning. *Educational Researcher, 18*(1), 32–42. doi:10.3102/0013189X018001032

Burns, H. L., & Capps, C. G. (1988). Foundations of intelligent tutoring systems: An introduction. In M. C. Polson & J. J. Richardson (Eds.), *Foundations of Intelligent Tutoring Systems* (pp. 1–19). Hillsdale, NJ: Lawrence Earlbaum Associates.

Chapelle, C. A. (2005). Interactionist SLA theory in CALL research. In J. Egbert & G. M. Petrie (Eds.), *CALL research perspectives* (pp. 53–64). Mahwah, NJ: Lawrence Erlbaum.

Checkland, P. (1999). Systems Thinking. In W. L. Currie & R. Galliers (Eds.), *Rethinking Management Information Systems* (pp. 45–56). Oxford: Oxford University Press.

Chinn, C. A., & Malhotra, B. A. (2002). Epistemologically authentic inquiry in schools: A theoretical framework for evaluating inquiry tasks. *Science Education, 86*(2), 175–218. doi:10.1002/sce.10001

Conati, C., & VanLehn, K. (2000). Toward computer-based support of meta-cognitive skills: A computational framework to coach self-explanation. *International Journal of Artificial Intelligence in Education, 11*(1), 389–415.

Corbett, A. T., Koedinger, K. R., & Anderson, J. R. (1997). Intelligent tutoring systems. In M. G. Helander, T. K. Landauer, & P. Prabhu (Eds.), *Handbook of human-computer interaction* (2nd ed., pp. 849–874). Amsterdam: Elsevier Science.

Csikszentmihalyi, M. (1991). *Flow: The psychology of optimal experience.* New York, NY: Harper Perennial.

Cuendet, S., Bonnard, Q., Do-Lenh, S., & Dillenbourg, P. (2013). Designing augmented reality for the classroom. *Computers & Education, 68*, 557–569. doi:10.1016/j.compedu.2013.02.015

Dzikovska, M., Steinhauser, N., Farrow, E., Moore, J., & Campbell, G. (2014). BEETLE II: Deep Natural Language Understanding and Automatic Feedback Generation for Intelligent Tutoring in Basic Electricity and Electronics. *International Journal of Artificial Intelligence in Education, 24*(3), 284–332. doi:10.1007/s40593-014-0017-9

Edelson, D. C., Gordin, D. N., & Pea, R. D. (1999). Addressing the challenges of inquiry-based learning through technology and curriculum design. *Journal of the Learning Sciences, 8*(3-4), 391–450. doi:10.1080/10508406.1999.9672075

Farwell, N. (2014). *Minecraft: Redstone handbook*. New York, NY: Scholastic Inc.

Ferguson, R. C. (2006). *Teacher's guide: Research and benefits of chess.*

Fosnot, C. (Ed.). (2005). *Constructivism: Theory, perspectives, and practice*. New York, NY: Teachers College Press.

Gee, J. P. (2007). *Good video games + good learning: Collected essays on video games, learning, and literacy*. New York, NY: Peter Lang.

Gruyer, N., & Toublanc, N. (n.d.). *Online classroom games for teaching economics*. Retrieved from http://economics-games.com/

Hattie, J. (2009). *Visible learning: A synthesis of over 800 meta-analyses relating to achievement*. New York, NY: Routledge.

Hattie, J. (2012). *Visible learning for teachers: Maximizing impact on learning*. New York, NY: Routledge.

Khachatryan, G. A., Romashov, A. V., Khachatryan, A. R., Gaudino, S. J., Khachatryan, J. M., Guarian, K. R., & Yufa, N. V. (2014). Reasoning Mind Genie 2: An Intelligent Tutoring System as a Vehicle for International Transfer of Instructional Methods in Mathematics. *International Journal of Artificial Intelligence in Education, 24*(3), 333–382. doi:10.1007/s40593-014-0019-7

Kuhn, D., Black, J., Keselman, A., & Kaplan, D. (2000). The development of cognitive skills to support inquiry learning. *Cognition and Instruction, 18*(4), 495–523. doi:10.1207/S1532690XCI1804_3

Kukulska-Hulme, A., & Shield, L. (2008). An overview of mobile assisted language learning: From content delivery to supported collaboration and interaction. *ReCALL, 20*(03), 271–289. doi:10.1017/S0958344008000335

Lanzilotti, R., & Roselli, T. (2007). An experimental evaluation of Logiocando, an intelligent tutoring hypermedia system. *International Journal of Artificial Intelligence in Education, 17*(1), 41–56.

Lee, E. A.-L., & Wong, K. W. (2014). Learning with desktop virtual reality: Low spatial ability learners are more positively affected. *Computers & Education, 79*, 49–58. doi:10.1016/j.compedu.2014.07.010

Lee, J. J., & Hammer, J. (2011). Gamification in education: What, how, why bother? *Academic Exchange Quarterly, 15*(2), 146–151.

Leu, D. J., Kinzer, C. K., Coiro, J. L., & Cammack, D. W. (2004). Toward a theory of new literacies emerging from the Internet and other information and communication technologies. *Theoretical models and processes of reading, 5*(1), 1570-1613.

Limniou, M., Roberts, D., & Papadopoulos, N. (2008). Full immersive virtual environment CAVE™ in chemistry education. *Computers & Education, 51*(2), 584–593. doi:10.1016/j.compedu.2007.06.014

Locke, E. A., & Latham, G. P. (1990). *A theory of goal setting & task performance*. Englewood Cliffs, NJ: Prentice-Hall, Inc.

Makuch, E. (2014, February 26). *Minecraft passes 100 million registered users, 14.3 million sales on PC*. Retrieved from http://www.gamespot.com/articles/minecraft-passes-100-million-registered-users-14-3-million-sales-on-pc/1100-6417972/

Malykhina, E. (2013, November 5). 8 apps that turn citizens into scientists. *Scientific American*, Retrieved from http://www.scientificamerican.com/article/8-apps-that-turn-citizens-into-scientists/

Mandler, J. M. (1984). *Stories, Scripts, and Scenes: Aspects of Schema Theory*. Hillsdale, NJ: Lawrence Erlbaum Associates.

McGonigal, J. (2011). *Reality is broken: Why games make us better and how they can change the world*. New York, NY: Random House.

Merriam-Webster. (n.d.). *Docendo discimus*. Retrieved from http://www.merriam-webster.com/dictionary/docendodiscimus

Piaget, J. (1954). *The construction of reality in the child*. New York, NY: Basic Books. doi:10.1037/11168-000

Prensky, M. (2005). Computer games and learning: Digital game-based learning. In J. Raessens & J. Goldstein (Eds.), *Handbook of Computer Game Studies* (pp. 97–122). Cambridge, MA: MIT Press.

Savery, J. R., & Duffy, T. M. (1995). Problem-based learning: An instructional model and its constructivist framework. *Educational Technology*, *35*(5), 31–38.

Schrader, P. G., Zheng, D., & Young, M. (2006). Teachers' perceptions of video games: MMOGs and the future of preservice teacher education. *Innovate: Journal of Online Education*, *2*(3), 1–10.

Shams, L., & Seitz, A. R. (2008). Benefits of multisensory learning. *Trends in Cognitive Sciences*, *12*(11), 411–417. doi:10.1016/j.tics.2008.07.006 PMID:18805039

Shute, V. J., Ventura, M., & Ke, F. (2015). The power of play: The effects of Portal 2 and Lumosity on cognitive and noncognitive skills. *Computers & Education*, *80*, 58–67. doi:10.1016/j.compedu.2014.08.013

Siegal, J. (2014, November 19). *Littlebigplanet 3 review: Small worlds after all*. Retrieved from http://bgr.com/2014/11/19/littlebigplanet-3-review/

Squire, K. (2003). Video games in education. *International Journal of Intelligent Games & Simulation*, *2*(1), 49–62.

Squire, K. (2008). Video-game literacy: A literacy of expertise. In J. Coiro, M. Knobel, C. Lankshear, & D. Leu (Eds.), *Handbook of Research on New Literacies* (pp. 635–670). New York, NY: Rutledge - Taylor & Francis Group.

Squire, K. (2011). *Video Games and Learning: Teaching and Participatory Culture in the Digital Age*. New York, NY: Teachers College Press.

Stanford Center on Longevity. (2014, October 20). A consensus on the brain training industry from the scientific community. Retrieved from http://longevity3.stanford.edu/blog/2014/10/15/the-consensus-on-the-brain-training-industry-from-the-scientific-community/

The Escapist. (n. d.). *The adventurer's atlas*. Retrieved from http://www.theescapist.com/ypal/atlas.htm

The New London Group. (2000). A pedagogy of multiliteracies: Designing social futures. In W. Cope & M. Kalantzis (Eds.), *Multiliteracies: Literacy learning and the design of social futures* (pp. 9–37). New York, NY: Rutledge.

United States Chess Federation. (n. d.). Retrieved from http://www.quadcitychess.com/benefits_of_chess.html

Vygotsky, L. S. (1967). Play and its role in the mental development of the child. *Journal of Russian & East European Psychology*, *5*(3), 6–18. doi:10.2753/RPO1061-040505036

Vygotsky, L. S. (1978). *Mind in society: The development of higher psychological processes*. Cambridge, MA: Harvard University Press.

Werbach, K., & Hunter, D. (2012). *For the win: How game thinking can revolutionize your business*. Philadelphia, PA: Wharton Digital Press.

KEY TERMS AND DEFINITIONS

Badge System: A structure of symbols (badges) that people can earn through accomplishing various tasks that illustrate their knowledge and skills.

Engagement: A process of high-level student interest and participation.

Gamification: The process and phenomenon of incorporating game-like structures and activities into non-gaming environments.

Gaming Pedagogy: An educational philosophy, style, and approach to promoting learning in educational contexts through the use of video games, non-digital games, the embodied learning principles and techniques of games, and gamification.

Learning Theory: A model that explicates how people develop and acquire knowledge and skills through their experiences in world.

Learning Tool: A means or instrument such as a program, process, or device that facilitates educational gains.

Chapter 4
Game Design Frameworks and Reality Guides

Tomi "bgt" Suovuo
University of Turku, Finland

Ilmari Lahti
University of Turku, Finland

Jouni Smed
University of Turku, Finland

ABSTRACT

The gamification trend has cultivated a wide variety of game design frameworks. In this chapter, we use the concept of reality guides to analyse the characteristics of a few of these. Reality guides are applications that aim at assisting the user in the real world. As such they are not games, which is why we can use them to investigate the applicability of game design frameworks in a wider context than they are originally introduced for. Although these frameworks are for games, we find them at least partially applicable in the design of any kind of software and services. We also further refine the concept of reality guides as a type of application and consider the apparent usefulness of these frameworks on them.

INTRODUCTION

The term 'reality guide' (RG) groups applications that aim at assisting, teaching or supporting the user in the real world. Among other things they are used to illustrate history, to educate students or to provide services to visitors. They include applications such as city guides, virtual museums or location-aware games that are nowadays commonplace. Many cities and institutes employ them, for instance, to provide service for visitors, to illustrate history or architecture or simply to promote their possibilities. RGs are, therefore, enhanced replacements of the traditional paper printed guides.

RGs can be one-directional guides to, for example, a museum where the visitors are given information about the exhibition as they arrive at different locations, but where they cannot give their own input. Alternatively, RGs can be bi-directional social media applications where people share reviews of locations where they visit and

DOI: 10.4018/978-1-4666-9629-7.ch004

can find the reviews of others. There are different approaches to RGs: some of them are games, while others are more like social media applications. Also, they are often applying augmented reality (or augmented virtuality) – in one way or another – to transmit information. Some well-known examples of RGs are *FourSquare*, *Paris3DSaga*, *Ingress*, *Geocaching*, *Google Maps*, and – to some extent – Wikipedia. Our project *Lost Turku* (Mäntylä, Lahti, Ketamo, Luimula, & Smed, 2014), which is currently a virtually reality of a reconstructed real location 200 years from history, is a one-directional guide that uses a student's story as a narrative (see Figure 1). *Vares* (Mäntylä et al., 2014) is another of our RG applications. It guides people to visit various locations in Turku where the fictitious events of the Vares detective books and filmatisations are placed. The application reminds the user of scenes in the original stories and movies and fuses them into the story of the user traversing from a hotspot to another.

Our motivation in this article is to look into different frameworks for understanding games, RGs and narratives: What they are, what they are not, and what distinguishes them from each other. The field of game research has seen new terms, such as gamification and serious games, which are basically already established. However, there is still work to be done to make clear distinctions in terminology, as the word "game" itself already has several meanings, ranging from hunted animals to even acting in a live-action roleplaying game. The success of Foursquare has been an elementary part of sparking out several different innovative categories of applications, including RGs and gamification, for example. (Detering, Dixon, Khaled & Nacke, 2011) This new field is very young and we are joining the effort with Detering et al. to help keeping sense and order in the terminology.

For game designers, children and youngsters form a challenging audience. Rogers (2014, pp. 35–36) makes the practical observation that children usually want what is made for an audience older than their own age group. This is often due to the game developers' tendency to oversimplify and talk down to younger audience. This observation is accompanied by Burgun (2013, p. 57) who emphasizes that although children's games might not do a lot, what they do they should do with elegance as it is of utmost importance with children. Game designers have found ways use stealth learning, which inspires players to learn without being aware that they are being taught

Figure 1. Augmentation of the current real Turku Cathedral area with an image from the history in the Lost Turku reality guide

(Adams, 2014, p. 27). The benefits of gaming in learning include increased memory, class performance, social benefits and improving the transfer of learning (Sharp, 2012). According to Crawford (1984) games are "most ancient and time-honored vehicle for education", which make them natural tool for teaching pupils, especially when they are unaware or uninterested in learning.

In this paper, we tackle RGs from various directions based on relevant literature. We begin by looking at RGs from the human user's point-of-view: We consider Bartle's player taxonomy, Octalysis, Myers-Briggs and Keirsey, DGD and Brainhex, and Radoff's FUNdamentals. After that, we approach RGs from the direction of game design by evaluating Schell's game design lenses, after which we apply contextual game experience model to RGs. Then we consider RGs with respect to the environment using Benford's classification of shared spaces and Ermi's and Mäyrä's contextual game experience model. Our last approach is narrativity, where we review models by Aarseth, Murray and Aylett. After that, we will discuss other possible approaches and the implications of our work.

Figure 2. Bartle's four player types

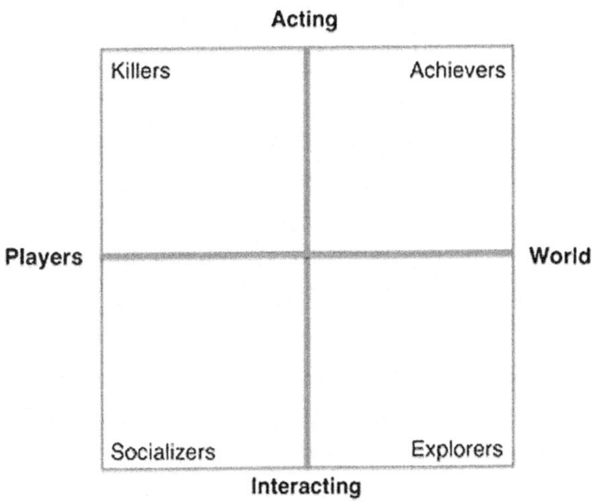

BARTLES'S TAXONOMY

Based on his observations on multi-user dungeons (MUDs) Richard Bartle (1996) presented a taxonomy of different player types, which divides the players into four groups according to their activities (see Figure 2):

1. **Achievers:** People who set themselves game-related goals that they then try achieve.
2. **Explorers:** People who try find out what is in the game world and map it for others.
3. **Socialisers:** People who want to converse and interact with the other players.
4. **Killers:** People who use the game to dominate to other people.

The player's motivations should be understood as a mix of these, and the type of play for a single player can change during gameplay. For example, in the early game the player can act more like an explorer, whereas towards the end he can turn out to play more like a killer.

Andrzej Marczewski (2013) gives another perspective into these four player types. He adds one dimension to the chart, based on the user's motivations being intrinsic (self-rewarding) or extrinsic (expecting an external reward); see Table 1. Marczewski's killers are either philanthropists, who "seek a sense of purpose from a system", for example, by "answering questions on Quora", or self seekers, who "seek rewards from acting on others", for example, by "answering peoples questions just for points". Marczewski sees that "self seekers have no real interest in the people within

Table 1. Marczewski's player types

	Intrinsic	Extrinsic
Killer	Philanthropist	Self Seeker
Achiever	Achiever	Consumer
Explorer	Free Spirit	Exploiter
Socializer	Socializer	Networker

Figure 3. Bartle's eight player types

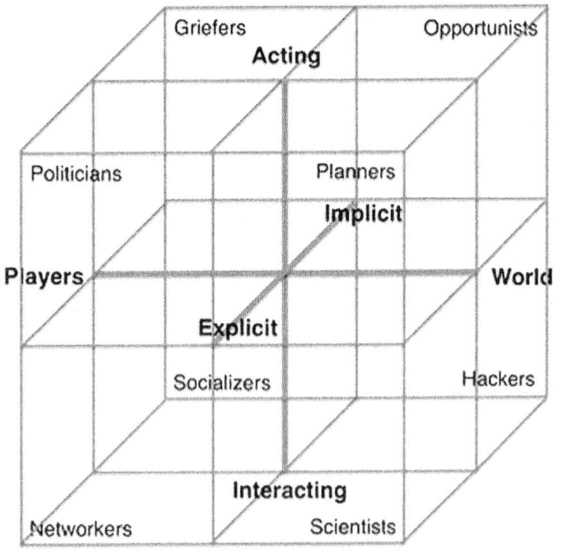

a system, they are just a means to an end", and "philanthropists are the parent figure. They are the ones who are likely to want to help anybody they can, no matter of the other person's motives".

Bartle (2005) also expands his taxonomy from four to eight player types by adding a new axis: implicit (spontaneous behaviour) and explicit (premeditated behaviour); see Figure 3.

The proper application of Bartle's model is somewhat unclear. Edvard Castronova (2005) uses Bartle's four-type model to examine "synthetic worlds". He looks at the games through users. He considers who would be an *achiever*, *explorer*, *socialiser*, or *controller* in a game and what kind of game they would best enjoy. Bartle (2005) proposes that users advance through certain typical *development paths* within the game, starting most typically as *griefers*, developing to *scientist* to *planner* to *friend* as they come more and more familiar with the game. This would suggest that a player has individual player types for each game. Bartle looks at the users through the game.

Bartle's player type model seems to excel as a lens-like design tool, such as Radoff's FUNdamentals and Schell's lenses that we will discuss further later in this chapter. These tools help the designer by giving different angles to look at the design. We have not found yet, however, why precisely eight different categories would suffice to cover all the necessary aspects of human behaviour. We believe that we would benefit, on the field of game studies, from the input that the researchers of psychology could give to the models.

It would be interesting to make a similar study on RG users as Bartle has done on MUD players, and discover the relevant axes there. Bartle's methodology is based on his wide experience on the MUD players, both personal and from his fellow players. This methodology is difficult to apply on single-player games and one-directional RGs as they have no other users to observe and report on the user's behaviour. Also, we do not currently enjoy the deep insight of a strong experience on user behaviour in RGs as Bartle does in MUDs. What we can do is to apply Castronova's method to the player types and consider how different personalities would find RGs.

Opportunists in games take every opportunity they see without bothering with tackling obstacles or spending lots of time with any single feature. This behaviour is easily perceivable for an RG user as well. Also the explicit *achiever* type, *planner* would act the same in RGs as in games – set themselves goals and persistently pursue their way towards them.

Scientists in games experiment with the game mechanics to find out and explain how they work. This behaviour is world-oriented and therefore directly transferable to any RGs as well. The same applies with the explicit *explorer* type, the *hacker*, who seeks to discover new phenomena and experiment to reveal meaning.

Networkers in games search for interesting and worthwhile people to interact and want to get to know their fellow players. If the RG is bi-directional, they can demonstrate such behaviour there as well, but it is not clear how they would consider one-directional RGs, especially if there are not even proper computer controlled characters to interact with. The implicit *socializer* type, the *friends*, who enjoy a familiar company of other players they know well, suffer the same problem. A networker might not play single player games at all, but unlike for games, for RGs the purpose of use is usually not the application in itself, but the reality it gives guidance to. Hence, one might assume that lack of social interactions in an RG would cause discomfort in the networker type of users and that these users would probably try to apply social interaction in the use of the RG anyways, for example by posting screenshots or text captions in social media.

Griefers in games attack other players to get a big, bad reputation. Such behaviour is demonstrable in bi-directional RGs as well. Bartle does not clearly point that griefers would attack the game system (e.g., the application and servers) as well as other players. Attacking the system would be some kind of mix of a griefer and hacker or scientist. One might assume that in one-directional RGs a griefer would be interested in causing problems in the application big enough to be recognized by people. They might, for example, spread story spoilers that would ruin the suspense of the story of the application from other users. The explicit *killer* type, the *politicians* aim for a big, good reputation in games. This behaviour might be demonstrated with one-directional RGs through writing insightful reviews and helpful hints on personal blogs, again outside the actual application.

To consider Bartle's *development paths* in one-directional RGs, we should take the *world*-oriented one, as in one-directional RGs the user cannot act player oriented. This development path in Bartle's theory progresses from *opportunist* to *scientist* to *planner* to *hacker*. The initial player type would be *opportunist*, who goes through every easily available feature in the application to discover the first glance and the easy pickings of the system. Then the user would start to experiment with the system more methodologically, being *scientists* who try to understand its workings. They would then have formed some kind of idea of the system's possibilities and set themselves goals that they pursue as *planners*. Finally, they would have found the application as a casual part of their lives, or mostly abandon it, only finding interest in the system when they come up with some exotic idea they want to try in the system, which they now master perfectly as *hackers*.

Figure 4. The core drives of Octalysis

OCTALYSIS

Not all type profiling on games is done on the players. A recent taxonomy by Yu-kai Chou (2013), called Octalysis, is used to profile a game rather than the player. Octalysis consists of eight "Core Drives of Gamification" – Meaning, Accomplishment, Ownership, Scarcity, Avoidance, Unpredictability, Social Pressure and Empowerment – which Chou identifies as things that motivate people and tries to map how well a gamified system meets these eight core drives (see Figure 4).

More specifically, the eight core drives are:

1. **Epic Meaning and Calling:** Players believe that they are something greater or they were "chosen" to do something. This core drive makes the users, for example, to devote much time to create things for the community (e.g., writing to Wikipedia or participating in Open Source Projects).
2. **Development and Accomplishment:** This is the internal drive pushing the players to make progress, develop skills and overcome challenges. It is the easiest core drive to tap into in game design (e.g., with points, badges, or leaderboards).
3. **Empowerment of Creativity and Feedback:** Players are engaged in a creative process where they continuosly have to figure out things and try different combinations. This core drive reflects the need to see the results of creativity, to receive feedback, and to respond in turn.
4. **Ownership and Possession:** When players feel ownership, they want to make what they own better and own even more (e.g., virtual goods, virtual currencies or customizations for avatars).
5. **Social Influence and Relatedness:** This core drive reflects the social elements driving people (e.g., companionship, competition or mentorship).
6. **Scarcity and Impatience:** When players cannot have it now, they will keep thinking about it, which is the focus of this core drive.
7. **Unpredictability and Curiosity:** This core drive represents the want to find out what happens next, which is, for example, the drive behind reading stories.
8. **Loss and Avoidance:** This core drive steers players to avoid something negative from happening.

According Chou (2013) the core drives on right-hand side of Figure 4 – related to creativity, self-expression and social aspects – represent intrinsic motivations, whereas the core drives on left-hand side – related to logic, calculation and ownership – represent extrinsic motivations. Moreover, the core drives on the top (which Chou calls "white hat") are positive motivations, and the core drives on bottom ("black hat") reflect to negative motivations. Black hat drives appeal to the players, but do not make them feel good – and one could argue that they are alike to an addiction. White hat drives make people feel good and attract them to return to the game to create something more rather than seek for thrills.

Chou himself has made an Octalysis analysis for web services that are not actually games such as Facebook and Twitter. This suggests that the tool is really not specifically a game design tool, but a tool to analyse the attractiveness factors of RGs or any application. Epic meaning and calling, as well as scarcity and impatience might first appear as something that dedicate the framework for games, as one hardly considers a word processor, for example, as having an epic meaning, or would appreciate scarcity or impatience there. However, a word processor would be likely to gain popularity, if it managed to give the feeling of epic outcomes for important documents for the user, and, indeed, Microsoft Word is more succesfull in easily including great looking styles to a document in real-time during editing, unlike for example LaTeX. Although, LaTeX appeals to many users in its professionality, which makes use of the same epic meaning and calling – to be cool and epic by using something that is "a professional tool, rather than a shiny play thing" as some LaTeX fans might describe Word. Scarcity and impatience motivations can be also appealed by providing style libraries and functionalities that are attractive and not available in other products.

The Level 2 of Octalysis tries to better approach gamification, by describing a matrix of Level 1 Octalyses. One dimension here is the Bartle's Taxonomy, already discussed earlier. The other dimension contains discovery, onboarding, scaffolding and endgame phases. This Level 2 does not add anything fundamentally more to the framework. Only difference to Level 1 is that the signifigance of the drives vary depending on the player's point of view in aims and time with the application.

MYERS-BRIGGS, KEIRSEY, AND THE BIG FIVE

Bartle's and Chou's taxonomies both are tools for psychological profiling, However, neither have a background in psychology. They are both experts in games and have created their taxonomies based on their personal experiences. Next, we take a look at two strands on theories of personality. One strand includes the popular Myers-Briggs Type Indicator (MBTI) (Myers & Myers 1980) and the Keirsey Temperament Sorter (KTS) based on David Keirsey's critique on the MBTI (Keirsey 1998). These two are popular among consultants of various sorts, but heavily criticized by personality researchers. The other strand includes personality trait theories that, opposite to the former strand, enjoy a wide support of the contemporary psychologists. The most popular of the trait theories is the Five Factor Model – also known as the Big Five (McCrae & John 1992). In the upcoming sections we compare these to the game player taxonomies.

After World War II, Isabel Myers and Kathrun Briggs devised the MBTI questionnaire for identifying different types of personalities based on Carl Jung's Psychological Types. Later David Keirsey criticized the work and published a questionnaire of his own, the KTS. Based on Jung's theory of psychological types, they both consider four fundamental personality types that are each further divided into four subtypes, totaling in sixteen types.

These sixteen types are denoted with four-letter combinations such as ESTP. According to Myers-Briggs, the first letter is E for extraverted or I for introverted; the second letter is S for sensory or N for intuitive; the third letter is T for thinking or F for feeling; and the fourth letter is J for judging and P for perceiving.

The main difference in MBTI and KTS is the hierarchy of the 16 types. Myers focused on perception and judgement, partitioning the 16 types into four groups: the *sensing plus thinking* ST, the *sensing plus feeling* SF, the *intuitive plus feeling* NF, and the *intuitive plus thinking* NT. The extravertion-introvertion and the perveiving-judging preferences were considered only to further modify these four main personality types. Keirsey disagreed on this finding that the subtypes in ST had very little in common, as well as the subtypes in SF. However, he found it more feasible to first partition the types on the intuitive-sensing preferences and then, further partition the intuitive types on the judging-feeling preferences, but the sensing types on the perceiving-judging preferences. His four main groups were: the *sensing plus perceiving* SP, the *sensing plus judging* SJ, the *intuitive plus feeling* NF, and the *intuitive plus thinking* NT. (Keirsey 1998)

These personality assessment tools predate the game player type taxonomies. They are invented by "consulting psychologists" and therefore the focus of their creators has been in the practical usability.

The scientific study of personality accuses the MBTI and KTS of lack of empirical evidence. The trait theories originate from 1930's and are being built with rigorous scientific rigor. However, even the most popular of them, the Five Factor Model (also known as the Big Five) is not as commonly applied in practice as MBTI and KTS, although, for example, Jason VandenBerghe (2012) has promoted its use for game designers to understand players' behaviour.

DGD AND BrainHex

Chris Bateman and Richard Boon (2005) devised the Demographic Game Design model (DGD1), which is an adaptation of the Myers-Briggs typology to games. This work has continued as an empiric survey study that resulted in a further version, DGD1.5, which took distance from the Myers-Briggs typology. Later on, the DGD2 by Berens was again transformable to the Myers-Briggs. Nacke and Bateman have later on focused more on neuropsychology in their work and the currently worked on typology survey, BrainHex, has discarded the Myers-Briggs model altogether and is based on more recent theories in psychology. (Bateman, Lowenhaupt & Nacke, 2011)

The game research field contains models that are based on psychological theories as well as models that are based on personal experiences. Scientifically the most solid models would be the fusions of the two, where theoretical understanding of psychology is combined with empirical studies on games. One example of such is the fresh BrainHex player satisfaction model (Nacke, Bateman & Mandryk, 2011), which applies neuropsychological studies among others in effort to understand the reasons behind the models.

At the least, player typing helps the game designer to look their design from multiple perspectives. We dare say that even if a player type system is not a perfect model of the human psyche, a good model will, nevertheless, help the game designer even to better understand different kinds of players and significantly improve the game experience for them. Optimally future player type models should follow closely the research done by psychologists as they improve their understanding of the general human psyche. The fact that theories are abandoned does not mean that the research results are unreliable, but that they are gaining better and better understanding that clears the way from missunderstandings. It is worth noting that even though the MBTI is generally considered as an outdated and faulty model in psychology, it still is used to help open new perspectives to problems in social dynamics. Both game design typology and personality psychology are in progress of refining their understanding on how and why people behave, and both should benefit from working together.

42 FUNdamentals

In his game design book *Game On*, Jon Radoff (2011) seems to apply a short definition for games: "games are fun". Schell's (2008) definition goes: "A game is a problem-solving activity, approached with a playful attitude", but while analysing the definition, Schell also focuses on fun: "fun is pleasure with surprises". Radoff continues to define what is fun, by listing 42 of the most important fun things, backed by the psychologist Steven Reiss' (2002) 16 basic desires. These things are generally known as Radoff's 42 FUNdamentals.

We agree that a game can be designed to provide the user with any and all of Radoff's 42 FUNdamentals. We now proceed to take the FUNdamentals from their context of games and inspect them in the context of RGs. Many of them (18 out of the 42) can be provided by any kind of RG as well, and even more (26) by any kind of bi-directional RG. There are 14 further FUNdamentals that could be implemented on RGs, but that would be through gamification. Such are, for example, "being a rebel", "competition" and "nurturing".

"Achieving a sense of completion" is a FUNdamental that RGs rarely provide. Most of them are perpentual with nothing ever really being completed. Others contain finite stories, but it can easily remain unclear for the user, whether they have already really seen the whole of the story. A sense of completion tends to play a low role in RGs.

Finally, there are two FUNdamentals that the users cannot typically do within RGs: "recognizing patterns" and "creating order out of chaos".

The reason for this is that RGs are usually tools that do this for the users. *Google Maps* will find the best route for the user from place A to place B. *FourSquare* recognizes patterns around and in the user and recommends places the user might wish to visit.

Radoff's FUNdamentals is a good tool in making any application more appealing by making it more fun. They offer 42 good perspectives even for serious applications.

RGs typically do not contain intentional resisting forces, which is a significant difference to games. RGs are mainly cooperative. The aim of the RGs is to provide information, not to limit access to it. Certainly, opposing challenges may be motivating for some users, and intentional hindrances can actually help the system to deliver more information to the users by motivating them, but this is more about gamification placed on top of the RG than about RGs as such.

SCHELL'S LENSES

Jesse Schell's (2008) *The Art of Game Design: A Book of Lenses* sets out to teach the readers "how to be a better video game designer", stating that the principles explored in the book "are more broadly applicable than that". The book introduces 100 "lenses" that designers can use to switch their perspectives to their design. This is the same concept that lies in the heart of Bartle's taxonomy of players, Radoff's FUNdamentals and even Benford's model.

Although in the second edition of the book Schell (2015) has increased the number of lenses to 112, we focus here on the original set of 100 lenses. When looking at RGs through Schell's 100 lenses, we perceive that most of them suit at least in certain cases, but there are 13 lenses that are really effective only with games, 4 lenses that need some adjustment and 10 lenses that do not suit RGs at all.

The lenses that do not fit RGs at all have to do with challenges and uncertainty. For games it is good to sustain tension by making the achieving of the goals difficult and uncertain. The point of RGs is to help in the transfer of information, which makes challenges and uncertainty typically counterproductive. One could consider inversing the lenses, to see that the feature described by the lense is minimized. However, the lens *#33: Triangularity*, where big risks are supposed to give great value and low risks less value, is symmetrical in a way that inversion is impossible. These lenses could be applied in gamified RGs, at least in the gamified part of the application. Assuming that *Ingress* can be considered as a RG, it is clearly a game, where the RG part is in finding the portals and the game part is in the challenges involved handling the portals.

One peculiar lens that does not seem to fit RGs is *#21: Functional Space*. Most typically for RGs, the functional space is the reality (be it physical or virtual). With some cases, like *Lost Turku*, this space may be focused on certain areas. Looking around anywhere else but on that one bridge, you do not see any game pieces. However, in the concept of the reality, the functional space, technically speaking, spans everywhere. This problem can also be found on some games. A live action role playing game can be focused, for example within one city, but there need not be restrictions for the players to travel outside – only that the other players and game events are unlikely to be found there.

Some lenses suit games better than RGs. They can be used in RGs, but they do not really give much extra value, especially comparing to how they help games. These are lenses about pleasure and punishment, rules, competition and cooperation. *FourSquare* clearly applies competition and cooperation, but if the users do not perceive *FourSquare* as a game, but rather as an application for finding one's friends, or good restaurants nearby, the competitive part of the application does not really play much of a part.

Some of the lenses suit certain types of RGs. There are lenses concerning character development and narrative in general that work well for RGs with strong narrative, but not so well, for example, for *FourSquare*. On the other hand, *FourSquare* can be seen through lenses that have to do with social visibility, such as *#80: Status*. This does not, however, fit *Vares*. Some RGs are made for a company as a *#90: Client*, but some have the company being built around the RG. Puzzles can be seen as an obstruction for transffering information, or a tool or a motivator for it.

There are four lenses that should be changed to suit RGs:

#19 - Needs: For games, the need that the game fulfills is deeper in the psychological imagination. The question is how the game creates a need and satisfies it to give pleasure. For RGs, one should consider what actual need the RG satisfies. Games generally do not feed a hungry player, but *FourSquare* can find you a restaurant nearby.

#32 - Meaningful Choises: This should be *Meaningful information*. The information transferred should be meaningful. In games this is not similarly within the ontology, as basically the only meaningful information is the information needed to win the game. For RGs, it is important that the information the user receives is meaningful.

#34 - Skill vs. Chance: This should be *Intention vs. Serendipity*. For serendipity, especially, users may wish to ask for suggestions (the application of "chance") from the RG. An alternative is to have the information to be transferred only per given parameters (the equivalent of a skill).

#74 - The World: RGs typically do not try to make an imaginative world better than the real world, but rather they try to improve the real world, either by helping people to make things better, or by bringing fantasy into the real world through augmentation. *FourSquare* and *Lost Turku* attempt to make the reality they are guiding the user to, somehow better and more interesting.

We have been studying the lenses against RGs through surveys and found 42 of the lenses such that they are generally applicable to all kinds of software development. One example is the lens *#12: The Problem Statement*, which recommends the designer to ask oneself questions such as: "What problem am I really trying to solve?" and "Is a game [Why not RG, or any other type of application?] the best solution? Why?" Another lens that fits RGs perfectly is the lens *#16: The Player*, which recommends the designer to consider what the intended players will like and how and what they expect to see in an application such as this. This lens encourages the use of player type analysis tools, such as Bartle's player types, which Schell even describes in his book.

BENFORD'S SHARED SPACES

Steve Benford et al. (1998) provide a general framework to understand the differences of shared-space technologies. This is a framework that was not originally developed for game design, but it has been often used for game design analysis, especially for virtual, mixed, altered and augmented reality games. The framework is originally three dimensional, but the third dimension, *spatiality* was not as powerfully portrayed together with the other two dimensions, *transportation and artificiality*, which were portrayed together. Therefore, the *spatiality* dimension is often omitted as the framework is cited.

The *transportation* axis indicates the level to which the users leave behind their local space, and the *artificiality* axis the level to which a space is computer generated. By using these two dimensions, four types of technology can be classified: Physical reality resides in the local, physical world (i.e., the things are tangible and the participants are corporeal). Conversely, virtual reality allows the participants to be transported to a remote, synthetic world. In telepresence, the participants have and experience presence at a real world location remote from their physical location (e.g., remote controlled drones with sensory feedback). In augmented reality, synthetic objects are overlaid on the local environment.

RGs can typically be used on-site and off-site. Depending on the case, the application is used either as augmented reality or virtual reality. Either the inherent artificial model of the location is used to add synthetic artefacts to the actual reality where the user is, or the model is used for a virtual world into which the user immerses. At the moment, all effects of the user's actions in reality guides are virtual without physical substance. The user may move a digital marker from one location to another, but cannot move an actual stone anywhere. This border may blur as 3D-printing technology evolves and the Internet of Things arises, where network connected devices in our environment may start reacting to the virtual models. If a user generates a chair in a room within a RG, an automated 3D-printer may start and print the chair. Strictly speaking, it would still appear here that the border of virtual and physical will not get breached, but it is only physical artefacts reacting to virtual events and artefacts.

Starting from the original physical location of the user, on the bottom left corner of Benford's diagram, RGs initially move the user higher towards the augmented reality. With Oculus Rift, it is possible to attain *a complete augmentation of reality* at the top of the diagram. For any horizontal movement, the service must be engaging enough to create immersion on the user.

Benford's transition seems to focus on where the user's actions have effect. With teleconferencing, certainly your voice (and image) are transferred to the other location, but all manipulation you do is local. In telepresence you generally have some kind of agent to relay your actions to the external location. Augmented reality gives you local virtual artefacts that you can manipulate. Even though their essence is stored in a database in some distant location, the conceptual location of them is "here". In virtual reality the user manipulates objects that are located in a virtual environment, to which the user is transferred.

RGs are typically located on the border of augmented reality and virtual reality, as shown on Figure 5. For example, in our RG project *Lost Turku*, we have a virtually reality of a reconstructed real location of Turku 200 years from history. It can be observed in its current location, and it can be visited off-site as well. It is our intention that the visitors can leave their marks there and later visitors can find them. Off-site visitors will find the virtual reality touched. On-site visitors will observe exactly the same, except that the virtual reality serves as an augmentation of their physical reality.

CONTEXTUAL GAME EXPERIENCE MODEL

Frans Mäyrä (2007) and Laura Ermi (2005) have been working on a framework for analysing game experiences. The earlier SCI-model of gameplay experience concerns what is happening *prima facie* during the performance of play and the later Contextual Game Experience Model considers the involved contexts.

At the SCI-model core are three kinds of immersion: *Sensory*, *Challenge-based* and *Imaginative*. (Later Mäyrä (2007) uses the terms *action-based immersion* instead of *challenge-based immersion* and *mental immersion* instead of *imaginative immersion.*)

Sensory immersion is typically related to the audiovisual and kinetic execution of games. The sensory immersion is beneficial to certain types of RGs, but actually harmful for certain other types. Virtual museums attempt to take the user back in time and immerse the user in the guide. Car navigators aim at being as invisible as possible,

Figure 5. Reality guides in Benford's taxonomy

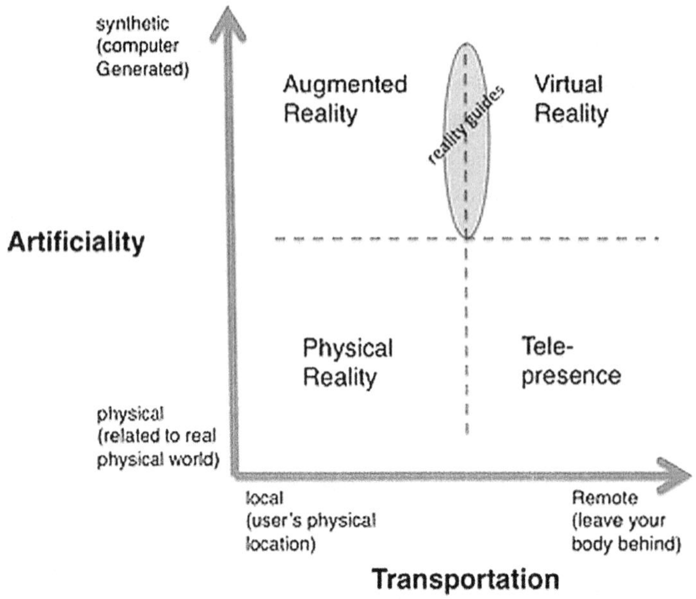

keeping the driver aware of the driving situation while trying to augment the driver's understanding of the situation with information on where their overall destination is. For all kinds of games, where the SCI-model has been designed to be used, it is desirable for the players to immerse their senses in the game as deeply as possible. With RGs this immersion can go either way: Either the user's senses are immersed in the guide, or the guide is embedded in the user's senses.

The *challenge-based (or action-based) immersion* of the SCI-model is the one that is least applicable in a RG. It can be applied in a RG that is a game, but there the application has a dualistic essence and the challenge-based immersion is involved in the game part. RGs are more like assistants that attempt to make transfer of information as easy as possible. For example, in *Ingress* the RG part tells the user without any challenge where the portals are and to which faction they belong. The challenge arises in that the player has to physically go to the enemy portal location and stay there for a period of time, in effort to claim the portal.

The *imaginative (or mental) immersion* has the user immerse in the application due to a captivating narrative. This works equally with RGs and games. Games like *Ingress* and virtual museums like *Paris 3D Saga* and *Lost Turku* all aim at immersing the players in the story of the application. A car navigator could be incorporating the car drive as a story of how they are taking the evil ring to a volcano at a distance. On longer stretches of driving straight on a freeway, the navigator could generate dialogue for the fictional characters and upon an approaching turn it could alert the characters as well as the driver about something looming ahead – as long as the driver is not being excited by the narrative too much to cause reckless or careless driving. The story may augment the reality, but not obfuscate it. The application could easily be better in this than the traditional listening of audio books, music or radio, none of which are in any way aware of the driving situation. An RG could know to alert the user to the foct of the upcoming intersection rather than to the exiting fiction.

In the Contextual Game Experience Model, Mäyrä embedded the SCI-model inside five contexts. According to the new model, playing game is linked with the *immediate personal contexts* – how they play and what motivates their play. This would involve Radoff's 42 FUNdamentals and Reiss's 16 basic desires. Clearly this is equally significant for RGs, as it is for any applications or services that are selected by consumers directly and not imposed by authorities.

Another context in the model is the *immediate social context* – how the player's closest people regard game playing. Mäyrä takes this apart from the FUNdamentals ("Strengthening a Family Relationship") and basic desires ("Acceptance", "Family", "Social contact", "Social status") possibly because it is to be regarded differently as a context that is external to the game, instead of a motivator that is internal to the game and fulfilled within the game. This context relates with the technology acceptance model and is equally significant for RGs as it is for games. If a person's closest people all generally look down upon RGs, the person is a rebel in their immediate social context, if they choose to use them. People are more likely to use RGs, if other people in their immediate social context have a positive attitude towards them, and even already use them.

Third context is the *context provided by the earlier forms for Game and Play*. In addition to how the immediate social context considers using RG applications, also the person's familiarity to them affects their attitude towards single applications. Also, this context exists for all kinds of applications, including RGs. Users will always compare applications to their known frameworks of reference. Familiar concepts are comfortable, but clearly different concepts can stand out greatly, either for the better or the worse.

The fourth context is the *context for digital games' production*. In addition that new applications seek their place in the user's own frame of reference applications and experiences, they become related also to all other contemporary applications, even if the user has not even heard of all of them. This context affects the culture around the user and has an indirect impact. One of the clearest effects is the visibility an application gets and how popular it becomes with other people. The direct equivalent for this context, of course, exists for all kinds of applications.

The fifth context, which includes all the four other contexts, is the *wider context of social norms and values*. This, of course, applies also to RGs just as well as to any other applications.

It is clear to see that the contextual game experience model is drawn out of game design analysis, but still the outcome is something that can be applied much more widely. Only the challenge-based immersion in the SCI-model core has very little use anywhere else than in games. Even this can be helped by considering the negative challenge, which would be how easily the application provides the user with what they are searching for.

NARRATIVITY FRAMEWORKS

To understand the difference between storytelling and games, Espen Aarseth (2012) separates the narrative content into two groups: kernel and satellite. The term *kernel* refers to the essential content of the story or game that is repeated when it is experienced anew. Basically, the kernels form the identity of the story: If we change a kernel, we will end up having a different story. In comparison, *satellite* refers to content that could be omitted or altered without changing the identity of the story. For example, the identity of the story of Cinderella remains the same, whether she has one or two stepsisters or whether her chores include cleaning the house or peeling potatoes; however, the identity of the story would change, if Cinderella's father had died and her mother would have remarried.

Within the kernel–satellite framework the reader or player could have three kinds of influence: no, limited or full (see Table 2):

Table 2. Using kernels and satellites to differentiate stories and games

Kernel Influence	Satellite Influence Not Possible	Satellite Influence Possible
No influence	Linear story	Linear game
Choose from alternatives	Non-linear story	Quest game
Full influence	N/A	Pure game

1. If the user has no influence on the kernels and the satellites, we have a linear story (e.g., a novel or a film).
2. If the user has no influence on the kernels but can influence the satellites, we have a linear game (e.g., *Half-Life*).
3. If the user can choose the kernels from a set of alternatives but has no influence on the satellites, we have a non-linear story (e.g., hyperfiction).
4. If the user can choose the kernels from a set of alternative and can influence the satellites, we have a quest game (e.g., *Star Wars: Knights of the Old Republic*).
5. If the user can influence both the kernels and the satellite, we have a (pure) game (e.g., chess).

With respect to RGs, the key question is whether we want to impose a narrative structure that the users have to follow. To compare with the previous list, we can have following types of RGs:

1. The users are limited to follow one ideal path (e.g., a car navigator leading the driver to the desired destination).
2. The users follow a path through different locations, and at each location they can wander around and create their own content (e.g., guided tourist group visiting different sights).
3. The users can choose from given alternatives where they go next, but at each location they have beforehand-prepared content waiting for them (e.g., orienteering, *Geocaching*, or *Vares*).
4. The users can choose from given alternatives where they go next, and and at each location they can wander around and create their own content. (e.g., *FourSquare*)
5. The users are free go wherever they want and to act however they want. (e.g. *Wikipedia*)

We can compare different narrative forms based on their four typical features (Aylett & Louchart, 2003):

- **Contingency:** How much does the story time and space depend on the real time and space?
- **Narrative Representation:** How is the story presented?
- **Presence:** How far does the viewer/participant share the story time and space?
- **Interactivity:** How much does the viewer/participant participate in the story generation process?

Based on these four features we can divide different narrative forms as shown in Table 3. Virtual reality (e.g., computer games) differs from the other forms of storytelling in that the story time and real time are highly contingent, whereas in traditional forms of storytelling (e.g., cinema or literature) this dependency can be quite loose. For example, we can jump forward or backward or even construct the narrative in an unusual way such as in the film *Memento* which inverts the chronology of the narrative. Another differentiating factor is interactivity, which is non-existent or rather restricted in other forms of storytelling, whereas in computer games it is an essential part of how the narrative is presented in the medium.

In RGs the contingency is strong as it is linked in real-time to the user's position, and the current status of the augmentation data on the service. The narrative representation is most commonly

Table 3. Comparison of different narrative forms

Feature/Form	Cinema	Theatre	Literature	Virtual Reality	Reality Guides
Contingency on time and space	low	medium	low	strong	strong
Narrative representation	visual	visual	mental	visual	visual
Presence	not physical	physical	not physical	not physical but immersive	physical with non-physical augmentation
Interactivity	no	no/yes	no	yes	no/yes

visual, but can also be mental depending on how much textual information is included. The presence is typically physical with non-physical, as the user is following the RG in real-world locations; otherwise, it is not physical. RGs allow the user to interact with the story.

A digital medium offers the user *affordances*, which are opportunities for action made available by an interface. According to Murray (1997, pp. 71–90; 2012, pp. 51–80) a digital medium has four affordances:

- **Encyclopaedic Affordance:** Digital medium can store a vast amount of (possibly semantically segmented) information in various formats.
- **Spatial Affordance:** Digital medium can represent a navigable space.
- **Procedural Affordance:** Digital medium allows us to specify conditional, executable instructions.
- **Participatory Affordance:** Digital medium allows the user to manipulate the content and processing.

These affordances make the digital medium a vehicle for literary creation: the procedural and participatory affordances make it interactive, and the encyclopaedic and spatial affordances make it immersive. We can recognize all of these features also in RGs.

Aarseth's framework is a convenient tool for analyzing digital narratives. However, its terminology need not be as game oriented as it is. Not all narratives where you can influence the satellites are games. People can tell each other stories and stories may emerge from RGs, social media and other types of innovative applications without restrictions to kernels or satellites, and yet these are not necessarily games.

DISCUSSION

Observing the frameworks presented in this paper, we have discovered a lack of scientific foundation and foundations of subjectively restrained empiric experience. This begs the question whether they have missed certain points. Are Bartle's eight player types sufficient or should there be something that combines features, for example, from the *griefer* and the *hacker*? Why are there precisely 42 FUNdamentals in Radoff's set or eight core drives in Octalysis? Even more suspicious is the nicely round amount of 100 lenses that Schell offers.

Furthermore, the frameworks are not exclusive to games. What differentiates RGs from games would appear to be that games benefit from challenges and uncertainty of success. As we observed when analysing Schell's lenses, the point of RGs is to help in the transfer of information, which is why challenges and uncertainty are counterproductive. RGs can act as a platform for games that offers challenges, but the RG part provides its own function and the challenges lay on the game part of the application. RGs differ from games by helping us to satisfy our intrinsic needs, such as hunger or trying to find things, rather than extrinsic needs that are created and exist within the application, such as achieving a goal or scoring points. RGs typically try to improve the real world, rather than present us with an imaginative world better than the real one. Regarding the distinction of RGs and game, we can ask if a RG has game-like features, are those mainly just laid on top of the RG using it as a platform, or should they be considered as a fundamental part of the RG.

The concepts of gamification and game are still defying definitions. We can easily imagine using the Octalysis as a framework to help creating interesting RGs. Putting in "epic meaning and calling" is a part of having an interesting story within the application to help the user better understand what to expect from the application. However, is this already about building a serious game, or at least just gamifying the design concept? If putting storylike features in an application makes it gamified, does this mean that all ebooks are gamified applications or even games? If not, then what is the definition of 'game', where Octalysis, or any other of these frameworks is clearly more efficient tool for specifically game design, rather than general interaction design? One reason for this disintegration might lay in the inorganization of game research field. We are having different people coming from different fields with their own perspectives and concepts. This is richness, but it also causes people coming from the game industry talk only about the design of games, neglecting the idea that the ideas could be even more general. Eventually, there will always be pigeons that do not fit any hole, because reality defies all classifications. Yet, the field of game research is still on its early phases of building definitions and in these times a lot of results can be gained with relatively small amounts of work.

RGs are an outcome of mobile and ubiquitous services, social media and global positioning system. The rise of new technology, such as the Google Glass and Microsoft HoloLens are paving way for greatly enhanced new augmentations of reality and thereafter for RGs. Also between hardware and software, programming tools such as the Unity game engine have increasing support for connecting computer-generated assets to mobile device camera input.

The features of RGs are formed now in an era of agile methodologies and gamification. We still hesitate to include Wikipedia in the category of RGs, but to clearly cross the threshold all they need a mobile application that taps into user location data and quickly gives the users information about places and things near to them.

We find the transfer of information as an essential part of RGs. Before the written word, history was stored in stories told verbally by one generation to the next. Narrativity is, therefore, understandably present basically in any RGs, although its presence can vary greatly. It can be explicit, when the RG is in the form of a story, or implicit, when the user sees a story in the information given by the RG, although it is not actually in a story form. This is related to the anthropomorphizing phenomenon, where people state how "the phone refuses to work", even though the phone device obviously has no sentience required to actively "refuse".

In the oral tradition of storytelling, a bard would adapt the story depending on the audience – even the structure of the story could vary within a certain confines. The development of digital storytelling devices is also putting an effort on this aspect. In RG applications, we can consider, for example, a tour guide visiting the same location and telling different stories depending on whether the tour group consists of schoolchildren or pensioners and on the group's questions and reactions. Similarly, a good RG can adapt to the feedback from the user.

In narrative theories, the concept of a magic circle (Huizinga, 1955), where the user is immersed in a sealed reality of the story, plays an important role. All experiences come from this world in the fashion of a virtual reality. The magic circle can be broken, if the user's phone starts to ring or someone in the real world begins to talk with them. Input from the real world does not always necessarily break the circle, if the other person is also within the circle such as in a role-playing game. What is still developing, however, is the application of social media as a source of material for a digital story. Most RGs allow sharing the in-RG actions and events in the social media. This could also be bi-directional, where people not directly involved in the particular RG could some way to affect the story within the RG. The RGs could maintain polls or questionnaires in social media to have people answer, or they could look into material people publish, for example, with certain hashtags. A fantasy story could find descriptions for dragons by looking for the hashtag #dragon. In addition to the questions arising on the immaterial rights, there are others concerning how well the magic circle can be sustained with this kind of mining of material.

Aki Järvinen (2009) discusses how games built for social media as a platform should be designed using the paradigms of the social media server in question. A person playing a game in Facebook should not find the game interface and mechanics alien to Facebook. How should one design a game that is not built to run on a social media service, but to apply social media, for example, for social connectivity and content harvesting? What are the juridical issues?

Our intention for this chapter was also to consider the exploitation of social media in RGs, but there seems to be little research on this topic so far and we are yet only about to conduct our own empirical research. Social media seems to be currently as high in popularity as games and gamification. However, where the users of gamification consists of system and product developers, social media has been found most interesting by the marketing people, media and politicians. In games, social media is typically used to announce the players' friends that they are playing the game, which is hoped to attract the friends to also start playing. We perceive that social media could be used as a mechanism in games and RGs, at least for user communication and to provide raw material for a story engine through text mining.

Applying social media as a part of a game mechanism is not simple. In the beginning of the popularization of personal home computers, the applications were delivered as finished and polished products. In the next phase, the applications were provided with bug-fixing patches, and after a year or two the application would finally be fully functional in the user's computer. With the further spread of the Internet, it is now more typical that any application gets almost regular updates that often even add new features in the application and the application is never really finished or even error-free. The next interesting phase in this line is the interconnectivity with third-party service interfaces, especially social media. Nowadays applications are often used online and they include buttons to share content in *Facebook* or *Twitter*, for example. If one of these services change their application interfaces remarkably – let alone that they completely cease to exist – the question arises, how usable are the applications with interconnectivity to them.

It is also easy to stumble and fall in the social media (Mäntylä, 2014). One cause for abusive attacks from the social media would appear to be brands being forced into the social media. The social media is perceived as "People's Web" and the users retaliate the violation of this (Fournier & Avery, 2011). The important task is then to offer people something they want, instead of coercing them into something you want, which leads to the idea of gamifying your service – to appeal to the intrinsic motivators of the users.

CONCLUSION

In this paper, we reviewed different frameworks that aim at helping the design and analysis of games. Often these frameworks are rather holistic for the game design process, considering also general application and service design issues, rather than focusing on issues explicit for games. This becomes easy to see, when trying to apply the frameworks on other kinds of applications, such as RGs as we have done in this paper. There are, however, several issues addressed in these frameworks that are explicit for games, and issues in-between. Some parts of the tools are therefore inapplicable on RG design. Other parts are applicable on both games and RGs, but likely inapplicable for some other types of applications.

ACKNOWLEDGMENT

The authors wish to thank the folks at Turku Game Lab for their support. Also, the students of the course "Gamification" (organized jointly by University of Turku and Turku University of Applied Sciences in November–December 2014) have provided us with invaluable help in analysing Schell's lenses in a broader context. The authors express their gratitude to the teachers Mika Luimula and Balsam Abdulghani for their co-operation on the course.

REFERENCES

Aarseth, E. (2012). A narrative theory of games. *Proceedings of the International Conference on the Foundations of Digital Games* (pp. 129–133). DOI= doi:10.1145/2282338.2282365

Adams, E. (2014). *Fundamentals of Game Design* (3rd ed.). San Francisco, CA, USA: New Riders.

Aylett, R., & Louchart, S. (2003). Towards a narrative theory of virtual reality. *Virtual Reality (Waltham Cross)*, *7*(1), 2–9. doi:10.1007/s10055-003-0114-9

Bartle, R. A. (1996). Hearts, clubs, diamonds, spades: Players who suit MUDs. *Journal of MUD Research*, *1*(1). Retrieved from http://www.mud.co.uk/richard/hcds.htm

Bartle, R. A. (2005). Virtual worlds: Why people play. *Massively multiplayer game development*, *2*, 3–18.

Bateman, C., & Boon, R. (2005). *21st Century Game Design (Game Development Series). Newton Center.* MA: Charles River Media, Inc.

Bateman, C., Lowenhaupt, R., & Nacke, L. E. (2011, September). Player typology in theory and practice. *Proceedings of DiGRA*.

Benford, S., Greenhalgh, C., Reynard, G., Brown, C., & Koleva, B. (1998). Understanding and constructing shared spaces with mixed-reality boundaries. *ACM Transactions on Computer-Human Interaction*, *5*(3), 185–223. doi:10.1145/292834.292836

Burgun, K. (2013). *Game Design Theory: A New Philosophy for Understanding Game*. Boca Raton, FL, USA: CRC Press.

Castronova, E. (2005). *Synthetic Worlds: The Business and Culture of Online Games*. Chicago, IL, USA: University of Chicago Press.

Chou, Y.-K. (2013). Octalysis: Complete Gamification Framework. Yu-Kai Chou & Gamification. Retrieved from http://www.yukaichou.com/gamification-examples/octalysis-complete-gamification-framework/

Crawford, C. (1984). *The Art of Computer Game Design*. Berkeley, CA, USA: Osborne/McGraw-Hill.

Deterding, S., Dixon, D., Khaled, R., & Nacke, L. (2011, September). From game design elements to gamefulness: defining gamification. *Proceedings of the 15th International Academic MindTrek Conference: Envisioning Future Media Environments* (pp. 9-15). ACM. doi:10.1145/2181037.2181040

Ermi, L., & Mäyrä, F. (2005). Fundamental components of the gameplay experience: Analysing immersion. In Worlds in Play: International Perspectives on Digital Games Research (37).

Fournier, S., & Avery, J. (2011). The uninvited brand. *Business Horizons, 54*(3), 193–207. DOI=10.1016/j.bushor.2011.01.001

Huizinga, J. (1955). *Homo Ludens: A Study of the Play-Element in Culture*. Boston, MA: The Beacon Press.

Järvinen, A. (2009). Game design for social networks: Interaction design for playful dispositions. *Proceedings of the 2009 ACM SIGGRAPH Symposium on Video Games* (pp. 95–102). doi:10.1145/1581073.1581088

Keirsey, D. (1998). *Please Understand Me II: Temperament, Character, Intelligence*. San Diego, CA: Prometheus Nemesis Book Company.

Mäntylä, T. (2014). Nimenehdotuskilpailut netissä. Retrieved from http://tomibgt.wordpress.com/2014/02/04/nimenehdotuskilpailut-netissa/

Mäntylä, T., Lahti, I., Ketamo, H., Luimula, M., & Smed, J. (2014). Designing reality guides. Proceedings of the *Sixth International Conference on Virtual Worlds and Games for Serious Applications, VS-Games* (pp. 69–76).

Marczewski, A. (2013). *Gamification: A Simple Introduction*. Andrzej Marczewski.

Mäyrä, F. (2007). The contextual game experience: On the socio-cultural contexts for meaning in digital play. In *Proceedings of DiGRA* (pp. 810–814).

McCrae, R. R., & John, O. P. (1992). An introduction to the five-factor model and its applications. *Journal of Personality, 60*(2), 175–215. doi:10.1111/j.1467-6494.1992.tb00970.x PMID:1635039

Murray, J. (1997). *Hamlet on the Holodeck: The Future of Narrative in Cyberspace*. Cambridge, MA: The MIT Press.

Murray, J. (2012). *Inventing the Medium: Principles of Interaction Design as a Cultural Practice*. Cambridge, MA: The MIT Press.

Myers, I. B., & Myers, P. B. (1980). *Gifts Differing: Understanding Personality Type*. Palo Alto, CA: Davies-Black Publishing.

Nacke, L. E., Bateman, C., & Mandryk, R. L. (2011). BrainHex: preliminary results from a neurobiological gamer typology survey. In Entertainment Computing–ICEC 2011 (pp. 288-293). Springer Berlin Heidelberg. doi:10.1007/978-3-642-24500-8_31

Radoff, J. (2011). *Game On: Energize Your Business with Social Media Games*. Chichester, UK: John Wiley & Sons.

Reiss, S. (2002). Basic Desires that Motivate Our Actions Define Our Persona. *Who Am I*, 16.

Rogers, S. (2014). *Level Up: The Guide to Great Video Game Design* (2nd ed.). Chichester, UK: John Wiley & Sons.

Schell, J. (2008). *The Art of Game Design: A Book of Lenses*. Boca Raton, FL: CRC Press.

Schell, J. (2015). *The Art of Game Design: A Book of Lenses* (2nd ed.). Boca Raton, FL: CRC Press.

Sharp, L. A. (2012). Stealth learning: Unexpected learning opportunities through games. *Journal of Instructional Research, 1*(1), 42–48. doi:10.9743/JIR.2013.6

VandenBerghe, J. (2012). The 5 domains of play. Presentation at the Game Developers Conference 2012, San Francisco, CA, USA. Retrieved from http://www.darklorde.com/2012/03/the-5-domains-of-play-slides/

KEY TERMS AND DEFINITIONS

Affordance: An opportunity for action made available by an interface.

Augmented Reality: A real-world environment that is supplemented with computer-generated elements.

Game Design Lense: A tool for reviewing and reassessing game design, which comprises thematic questions that the game designers should ask themselves.

Game Design: The art of creating rules, goals and challenges for a game.

Interactive Storytelling: An interactive system where the player's decisions affect on run-time how a dramatically compelling story is being generated.

Kernels and Satellites: Kernels are the essential parts of a story, which cannot be changed without the identity of story being changed as well. Satellites are part of story that can be changed while the story remains identifiable.

Octalysis: A tool for analysing game design based on players' eight core drives.

Player Type: An abstraction of common attributes that many players share.

Reality Guide: An application that aims at assisting, teaching or supporting the user in the real world.

Shared Space Technology: Distributed electronic environments that allow participants to make use of spatial properties to manage their communication.

Chapter 5
The Design of Immersive Virtual Learning Environments Utilizing Problem-Based Learning Templates

Donna Russell
Walden University, USA

ABSTRACT

The purpose of this chapter is to describe the design of template for the design of an immersive virtual learning environment that includes collaborative learning virtual worlds as problem-solving scenarios that engage students in virtual explorations of worlds. The problem-based learning 3d model incorporates a curriculum design model that includes a real-world issue that correlates to the virtual scenarios or games. This virtual PBL design model also includes a learning assessment process that utilizes sociocultural learning theories to develop an ongoing feedback model for assessment of learning in a 3d problem-based learning environment. This problem-based learning model combines the benefits of games, such as high-levels of learner engagement, real-life simulations, with research on cognition and instructional design to create a design model that can be modified to develop advanced knowledge, skills and concepts in multiple educational settings.

INTRODUCTION

The potential of educational games that are designed based on constructivist learning theories, a problem-based learning educational model and assessed using holistic assessment rubics is to redefine what education and learning is today from a passive learner model to an active immersive learning model where engagement and meaning-making result in effective and efficient learning. This chapter will define the core learning theories that underlie problem-based learning, the design protocol for a virtual problem-based learning educational forum and discuss future trends for games in education.

Problem-Based Learning (PBL) is an instructional method that addresses the complex knowledge and skill applications that students will face

DOI: 10.4018/978-1-4666-9629-7.ch005

in the future by participating as problems solvers to tackle complex, ill-structured problems that mirror real world problems. One of the tenets of PBL is that it is difficult to give meaning to knowledge once it is removed out of context. PBL immerses the students in a context similar to the one the problem would normally occur outside the classroom. The students additionally can consider themselves active members of their community of students within the context of the problem but respond with less risk and intensity than those in actual practice, a phenomena Lave and Wenger (1991) called legitimate peripheral participation (LPP). Although the there are varied designs of PBL environments the design of the problem space should involve an ill-structured problem of "wicked" complexity (Rittel, 1984).

Problem-based learning (PBL) has gained attention as a potential for educational settings as a result of several recent developments including

1. An increasing need to correlate theoretical models and practical realities into varied educational settings,
2. Increasing information accessibility and the resulting knowledge age,
3. The increased use of multidisciplinary approaches to problem simulations,
4. Emphasis on multi-dimensional modeling and virtual reality, and
5. New developments in cognitive science

Problem-Based Learning proposes that learning experiences build on the interdependent attributes of meaningful learning including authentic, intentional, active, constructive, and cooperative learning and involve meaningful application of knowledge and skills (Jonassen, Peck & Wilson, 1999). In PBL environments a problem triggers cognitive engagement including the psychological processes of context for engagement, curiosity, inquiry and a quest to address a real-world issue. Examples of cognitive processes embedded in PBL design include confronting ill-structuredness and novelty, active search for information, proactive immersion in task, conscious and subconscious investment of time on task, motivation to solve the problem, need for meaning and explanation, a learning goal orientation, and a requirement of generative thinking, analytical thinking, divergent thinking and synthesis (Tan, 2003). In productive problem-based learning environments, learners consider themselves active members of their community of learners within the context of solving the problem, a phenomena Lave and Wenger (1991) call legitimate peripheral participation (LPP). As a result problem-based learning has an incredible potential to develop advanced learning and knowledge responses. When integrated into immersive virtual learning environments, educational game, PBL becomes the core design feature for developing advanced learning processes and skills necessary for the knowledge workers of the future.

BACKGROUND

Constructivist Learning Principles

Research in constructivist learning environments suggests that instructional design grounded in constructivist principles engaged students in purposeful activity as the students attempt to respond to a complex problem in a guided learning context, overcome an obstacle, or negotiate a contradiction in their thinking (von Glasersfeld, 1998). In addition, instructional design based on constructivist learning principles allows students to apply their knowledge more effectively under appropriate conditions (Brown, Collins, & Druguid, 1989). In studies of constructive learning environments research have shown that learners can develop higher levels of awareness and knowledge as a result of their dialog and interactions in online environment (Russell, 2005a). When students have the opportunity to articulate what they have learned and reflect on the process they went through and the knowledge they acquired in that process, they understand more and are better able to use that knowledge in new situations. Interacting in this manner of intentional learning allows students to focus on their learning and on satisfying their personal goals (Jonassen, Peck & Wison, 1999). Additional instances of constructivist-based learning theories incorporated in the PBL Design Model include situated theories of learning Cole (Cole & Engestrom, 1993) and Lave (Lave & Wneger, 1991) and distributed cognition theories including Pea, (1993) Resnick, (1987) and Salomon (1993). These cognitive theories emphasize how the design of the learning environment impacts the cognitive development of learners through dialogic processes.

The design of the PBL Design Template (Figure 1) is based on theories of sociocultural learning which define the importance of culture, the social aspects of the inter/intrapersonal aspects of learning and the concepts of problem-based learning with the potential to develop advanced knowledge (Vygotsky, 1987; Jonassen, Peck, &Wilson, 1999; Bereiter, 2001). The theoretical grounding for the design of the learning environments is sociocultural theory of human interaction, and development (Vygotsky, 1978; Bruner, 1990) with an emphasis on understanding the processes of mediated activity (Wertsch, 1998). These theories focus on learners who create meaning by comparing what they already know to new experiences. They either resolve the inconsistency by adapting or assimilating the new knowledge into their existing knowledge. Bruner (1990) called this process meaning making. In sociocultural learning theory learning is an active and engaged process whereby "students are actively engaged in working at tasks and activities that are authentic to the environment in which they would be used" (Savery & Duffy, 1996, p. 37). Knowledge and meaning are not fixed but instead constructed by the individual within the context of meaningful learning.

The Virtual PBL Design Model (Figure 2) uses a PBL Design Model as a template to design the virtual scenarios and the supporting curriculum. The Virtual PBL Design Model is based on research in the cognitive sciences on the premise that instructional design grounded in constructivist principles engages students in purposeful activity as the students attempt to tackle a complex problem, overcome an obstacle, or negotiate a contradiction in their thinking (Jonassen, 2000). In addition, constructivist learning principles propose that learners apply their knowledge more effectively if engaged in purposeful learning (Vygotsky, 1978)

Through the process of responding to that problem, students acquire knowledge and skill that enable them to revise their theories, develop new theories, and compare their theories with other students through discussions (Russell, 2008). When students have the opportunity to articulate what they have learned and reflect on the process they went through and the knowledge they acquired in that process, they understand more and are better able to use that knowledge in new situations. Jonassen (2000) refers to this as intentional learning since students are focusing their learning on satisfying their personal goals. Instances of constructivist-based learning theories include situated theories of learning (Greeno, 1997; Lave & Wenger, 1991) and distributed cognition theory (Pea, 1993; Resnick, Levine, & Teasley, 1991; Salomon, 1993), which emphasize how the responses of the learner and the design of the learning environment affect the cognitive development of knowledge in students.

Problem-based learning (PBL) is a constructivist learning model providing contextual meaning-making for students. (Barrows, 1983; Norman and Schmidt, 1992). A growing body of research demonstrates the increased learning potential of PBL (Hinrichs, T.R., 1992: Knuth, R.A., & Cunningham D. J. 1993: Jonassen, 2000) in science, technology, engineering and math (STEM) area. In some cases this curriculum design model demonstrated significant increases in conceptual understanding as well as content knowledge. (Patterson and Harbor, 2005). This pedagogic approach addresses the complex knowledge and skill applications that students will face in the future by having them participate as problem solvers in tackling complex, ill-structured situations based on authentic issues. These are also the associated design principles resulting in a model for designing games that will be productive for multiple educational settings.

Assessment of Learning in PBL Environments

The process of learning in a PBL environment is difficult to define and assess as the learning is immersed in the learners' responses to the problem space. Additional consideration has to focused on a model for defining, qualifying and assessing the level of response in problem-based learning environments. The PBL Design template uses Carl Bereiter's Scheme of Knowledge to design assessment of learning in immersive PBL environments (2002). In his taxonomy he contends that knowledge implies the purposeful use, recombination, evaluation, and redistribution of information as the core abilities of a knowledge-based society (2001). According to Bereiter (2001) a productive learning response includes two aspects,

1. The learner sees information as something functional or useful, and
2. The learner sees him or herself in control of the process and uses information in pursuit of a particular goal.

He identifies knowledge development in these settings as a complex relationship between culture, humans, objects, and tools where mental content is a status of a metaphor thereby useful for some purposes and not for others, not to be taken literally. Abstract knowledge are objects, such as theories, numbers and designs with which people may develop perceptions of characteristics. Understanding and the development of advanced learning is then the understanding of these relationships. Advancement of knowledge is then the process of creating and improving of these abstract knowledge objects (Bereiter, 2001).

Bereiter separates his concept of knowledge development from previous concepts of learning by defining learning as the development of conceptual artifacts. Conceptual is meant to define any discussible idea including theories, plans, or concepts. Artifacts are purposeful human creations. One of the difficulties in the changes from the Industrial Age to the Knowledge Age is that more human work deals with conceptual objects instead of the physical objects to which they are related. Identifying these conceptual artifacts is an important aspect of defining and assessing the learning in complex PBL environments (2001).

The Problem-Based Learning (PBL) Design Model was developed as a template for the creation and implementation of a PBL curriculum. It has been used to design successful k-12 and university level courses (Russell, 2008). The PBL Design Model is implemented in three phases. Each phase has the potential to develop higher levels of thinking. Phase 1 of the PBL Design Model engages the learner in challenging the students to recognize the legitimacy of the dilemma (Barab, & Duffy, 2000). In Phase 2 the students work to develop an area of expertise within their inquiry process. This method of collaborative learning is supported by research on the nature of developing conceptual understanding of complex issues (Jonassen, Howland, Moore, & Marra, 2003). In Phase 3 the students work in groups to create and present a strategy for solution of the problem. In this final phase learners are asked to bring together the areas of expertise and respond to the problem by identifying a justifiable course of action that resolves all the sub issues identified by the group in Phase 2. This final phase is based on research on developing community of learners. This group interaction is called a Jigsaw (Aronson, Blaney, Stepan, Sikes & Snapp, 1978). This process is also supported by research on the nature of apprenticeship and expertise (Brown, Collins, & Duguid, 1989). Figure 1 is a problem-based learning design template based on constructivist learning theories.

MAIN FOCUS OF THE CHAPTER

The use of games within educational settings has been debated often. McClarty et al (2012) performed a review of literature and found "mixed empirical support" for using digital games in education while at the same time finding "the research supports that digital games can facilitate learning" (p. 23). Similar studies with mixed results based on the games' potential for learning and the lack of effective integration methods have identified major issues with gaming in education. Several issues with what is a game have also defined the debate on gaming in education. Caillois described a game as activity that is voluntary, uncertain, unproductive, and make believe. Juul discussed games as a rule-based system with a variable and quanitifiable outcomes that are assigned different values and engage the player in defining the level of effort to produce the chosen outcome. The first definition is of a process that has no place in education. The second definition could be used to develop a viable educational setting .

Using this second definition as a guide for designing and educational game, Gee's (2007) conception of role-playing within computer games and his description of the various roles that game players can fill during the experience provides guides for learner engagement and interaction in an educational game. The issue with engagement is the relationship between the real-world identity of the player and the virtual identify, the avatar. This relationship is defined by Gee as the third identity occuring in games, called the projective identity or "the interface between one's real-world identities and the virtual identity" (p. 50). In this third identity the player/learner creates a gaming interaction that defines their capabilities to succeed in the educational game. This third identity is also relevant to the term telepresence, the persence everyone feels in their virtual encounter. The potential then for this type of well-designed educational game is that learners can be empowered in these roles to engage in high level learning responses, in the case for this chapter, through problem-based learning processes and projects.

The problem-based learning design model places gamers/learners in the role of interacting with a real-world issue using real-world cognitive processes and projects. This process of epistemic gaming (Shaffer et.al, 2009) is a system that is based on learning theory and an accompanying method of assessment. Epistemic gaming integrates a problem-space with real-world problem-solving skills with the design of a virtual game or simulation that engages the learner. The benefit of games in education are based on the design of a game that engage the learners in responding to authentic issues in a simulation of a real-world response. It is the purpose of this chapter to coalesce these issues with a modular problem-based learning model that provides learners with access to complex problem-spaces and interactions that are simply not possible in traditional classrooms.

Immersive Learning

Immersion is defined as the subjective impression that one is participating in a comprehensive, realistic experience. Interactive media now enable various degrees of digital immersion. The more a virtual immersive experience is based on design strategies that combine actional, symbolic, and sensory factors increasing the participant's suspension of disbelief that she or he is "inside" a digitally enhanced setting. Studies have shown that immersion in a digital environment can enhance education in at least three ways: by allowing mul-

Figure 1. Standard PBL design

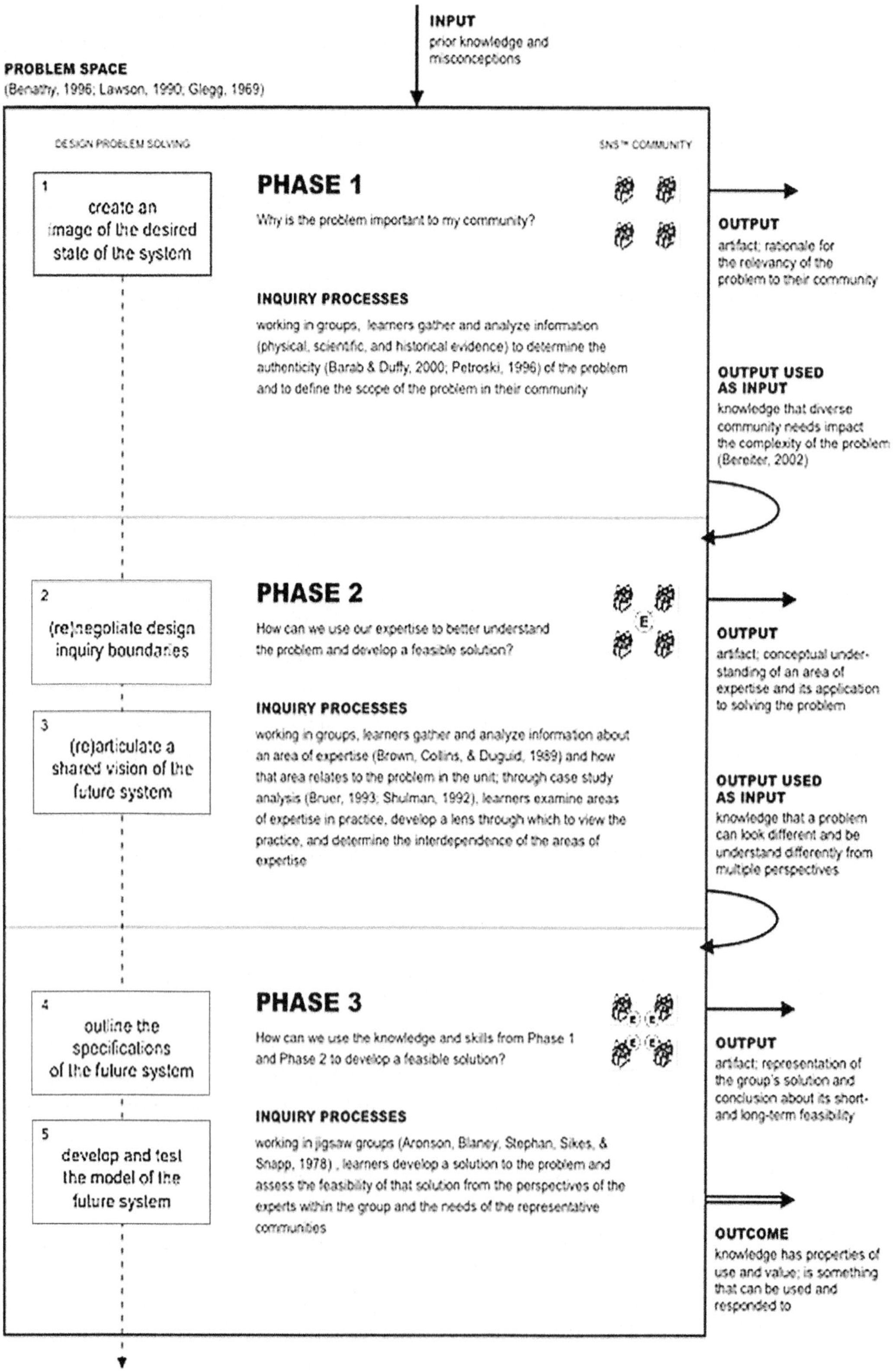

tiple perspectives, situated learning, and transfer. (Dede, 2009) Immersion in a digital experience involves the willing suspension of disbelief, and the design of immersive learning experiences that induce this disbelief draws on sensory, actional, and symbolic factors. Immersive virtual learning environments can be designed to develop advanced learning environments where students can explore and experience phenomena, where learning is active, social and participatatory, and can be customized for differentiation. The result is a learning environment that can be exceptionally productive and effective at developing advanced knowledge.

IMMERSIVE VIRTUAL LEARNING ENVIRONMENTS

Immersive virtual learning environments have many benefits for educational programs wanting to develop advanced learning processes and knowledge. The salient factors include

1. **Presence:** Learners have presence in 3D virtual through their avatar. They engage in interactions in the environment and modify the environment through their character. This higher, more immediate level of engagement, telepresence, means that the learner can integrate more advanced knowledge and processes.
2. **Interactivity:** The 3D virtual environments provide multiple interactive, media-rich forums for the learner. This also means a higher level of engagement as the virtual worlds are designed to be visually rich and provide opportunities for the learner to interact with others in the environment through audio, text and visual media.
3. **Collaborative:** The 3D VLE also provides a social context for the learner that increases engagement as they interact in the virtual worlds providing opportunities for training in simulated events that are live and collaborative such as a live simulation of an emergency room event for training medical and nursing students or the live simulation of a classroom activity for training teachers.
4. **Immersive:** Virtual 3D environments are immersive learning experiences that engage students in proactive activities providing the students with the opportunity to problem-solve and collaborate. This type of ubiquitous learning empowers the students and motivates them to higher levels of cognitive response. reality rooms, stereoscopic sound, and through haptic technologies that apply forces, vibrations, and motions to the user—the ability to touch virtual objects.

The process of immersion is a critical aspect of the potential for learning in immersive virtual learning environments. Actional immersion involves empowering the participant in an experience to initiate actions impossible in the real world. Symbolic immersion involves the evoking of semantic and psychological associations through immersion in the content of an experience. These immersive experiences tap into the participant's beliefs, emotions, and values about the real world. Themoreavirtual immersive experiences are based on design strategies that combine actional, symbolic, and sensory factors to create the potential for increasingly powerful immersive experiences (Dede, 2014). As a result of these immersive experiences the learner in a virtual immersive learning environment can be increasingly engaged in the learning process and through this engagement potentially learn more advanced cognitive processes and development more complex responses.

Immersive virtual learning environments have become viable constructivist learning forums with new advances in virtual reality devices. Learners can immerse themselves in distributed, synthetic environments, becoming avatars who actively experience the learning (Walker, 1990). Moving forward from technology-mediated interactions between students and phenomena to immersive virtual learning shifts the focus of constructivism from peripherally enhancing how a student interprets a typical interaction with the external world to shaping the fundamental nature of how learners experience their physical and social context by creating simulations of real-world environments and experiences.

Immersive virtual learning environments combines 3D and virtual reality (VR) technologies with digital media to develop highly interactive and engaging virtual worlds. In these virtual worlds simulations with rules and consequences are designed that provide a developmentally designed scenario to develop learners' advanced knowledge. Virtual immersive learning enviornments combine virtual worlds, simulators, learning games and sophisticated digital media (voice chat, game-based learning modules, audio/video, and so forth) with collaborative online learning environments, study rooms, and classrooms. Immersive virtual learning gives learners a sense of presence when real participation is not possible or practical. This, in turn provides educators and remote learners with the ability to connect, communicate, and collaborate in a way that greatly enhances the learning experience.

The virtual immersive learning environments are distinguished from other learning methods by their ability to simulate realistic scenarios and environments that give learners the opportunity to practice skills and interact with other learners. The critical distinction is that these environments are immersive with high levels of learner engagement and autonomy, and engaging, with emerging technologies that provide the learner with high levels of presence. As a result of these two powerful learning modalities, the design issues them become how to merge these new technologies and capabilities with solid research in teaching and learning. It is the premise of this chapter that a design model based on problem-based learning, an immersive learning pedagogy, with advanced simulations is a way to benefit from these transformative learning tools and the resultant experiential learning that is possible in immersive virtual learning environments.

These concepts were used to develop a model for the design of a Virtual PBL Design model. Figure 2 identifies the modified PBL design template for the Virtual PBL Design model. Currently technologies have advanced that make the design of these PBL-based gaming environments possible. The potential of highly complex virtual worlds with physics engines running their simulations makes the design of a complex problem-space that are highly interactive. This increase the potential for a problem-based game that can be integrated into multiple educational settings based on core design features. Figure 2 identifies the aspects of problem-based learning as well as the virtual learning environment characteristics incorporated into the design. This design template creates a viable potential for designing PBL scenarios capable of developing advanced learning abilities and being implemented in varied educational settings.

Virtual PBL Model

In the phased design model of the Virtual PBL, the teacher moderates all the activities in the virtual environment by correlating the virtual experiences to the real world issue and problem resolution. the Virtual PBL model, like the standard PBL model is based on a three phase design process.

Phase 1

For each Virtual PBL world there is an overarching concept that underlies the development of the virtual PBL scenario. This big idea is the problem space. This problem space is an integrated curriculum theme that can be based on major issues such as environmental issues, social issues and technological issues. The students enter the world in a Base Camp location. In each world there will be an AI Guide and inquiry tools in the base camp.

Figure 2. 3D PBL design

3D Problem-Based Learning
Collaborative Virtual Learning Environments
Design Template

Virtual Design	**Problem Space (Banathy, 1996; Lawson, 1990)** Simulation designed as an interactive virtual environment that relates to a real world problem space.
Pedagogical Agent used as Guide to aid learners as they explore the problem space. **Output** Virtual artifact including a rationale for relevancy of the problem.	**PHASE 1** Why is the problem Important? **Inquiry Processes** Working in pairs, learners gather and analyze information in the virtual simulation to determine nature of the problem and to define the scope of the problem. (Barab & Duffy, 2000; Petroski, 1996). **Output used as input.** Knowledge that a diverse community needs impact the complexity of the problem. (Bereiter, 2001).
Pedagogical Agent used as a Resource Mentor to answer questions and find resources. **Output** Virtual artifact including a conceptual understanding of an area of expertise and its application to solve the problem	**PHASE 2** How can we use our expertise to better understand the problem and develop a feasible solution? **Inquiry Processes** Working groups, learners gather and analyze information about an area of expertise (Brown, Collins & Duguid, 1989) and how that area relates to the problem, (Bruer, 1993, Shulman, 1992) learners examine areas of expertise in simulated environments, determine the interdependence of the areas of expertise. **Output used as input** Knowledge that a problem can look different and be understood differently from multiple perspectives.
Pedagogical Agent used as Survey Buddy to assess new knowledge and final projects. **Output** Virtual artifact including a representation of the group's solution and conclusion about its short-term and long-term feasibility.	**PHASE 3** How can we use the knowledge and skills from Phase 1 and Phase 2 to develop a feasible solution? **Inquiry Processes** Working in jigsaw groups (Aronson, Blaney, Stephan, Sikes & Snapp, 1978), learners develop a solution to the problem and assess the feasibility of that solution from the perspectives of the experts within the group and the needs of the community. **Outcome** Knowledge has properties of use and value; is something that can be used and responded to.

There will be a series of interactive presentations in this location to build background knowledge of the problem space. Students go to these locations to open a kiosk and respond to a variety of media on their theme. It is recommended that students work in pairs. The students will be asked to summarize the information to progress to go to the next activity, the field experiences, by writing in their field books, moveable kiosks, and posting them to their main 2-D website for the classroom teacher. Phase 1 includes the benchmark activities that give students the background information that they need to go into the field experiences. The assessment of student products in this phase will be a rubric coding the student summary notes and student dialogs based on Bereiter's Scheme of Knowledge.

Phase 2

During Phase 2 activities the students go into the 'field' to develop expertise on the problem. It is again recommended that students go into the virtual worlds in pairs. Their typed dialogs with each other will become part of their field notes and data collection process. They are given some background material and information on finding their information and collecting the information. The students respond to this mission by collecting 'data' in the field experiences. The students will write down new data in their Field Books. This should be a portable device that the students can carry with open access to a kiosk for storage of their responses. The information in the Field Books will be used to assess the level of student responses, develop the final real-world project and give students' access to the next level of the scenario. Each environment includes AI bots that have information about the different expert knowledge and can help student's answer questions. The goal of the learner is to collect the data in their Field Books and go to the next level of the virtual game.

Once all the field activities are complete, the students will create a summary multi-media project in the Base Camp that will summarize their ideas from their field experiences. This project will be posted in a kiosk for subsequent learners and discussed live in group in the Base Camp's Sand Box. This summary media project is the final student artifact for Phase 2. This live dialogic activity can be supported by a teacher, a mentor avatar or occur independently with the student's posting their presentations in their classroom website. These dialogs will be assessed for their level of knowledge response using a coded rubric of student dialogs in field teams and of the final summary reflective presentations.

Phase 3

In the final phase students will work in small groups to create a response to their field experiences. They will create this future world in a virtual sandbox at the main base camp. They will use media tools in the sandbox. They will work in jigsaw groups to create and then present their future world. They will be assessed based on the credibility of their design based on the information learned in Phases 1 and 2. In their real-world classrooms the students will create a statement of the unifying issue. The student generated statement of how government, business and people can respond to this issue locally. The students will design a succinct overview of the responses to the knowledge learned in the virtual scenarios including all the social and cultural ramifications of the problem issue that they identified as critical in Phase 1. This overview statement will be shared with an audience outside of the classroom. The students have become experts in this problem and are now capable of identifying and evaluating the strategies for responding to the problem. This final response, a statement of a plan of action for addressing the problem space, is assessed using a rubric scaled on Bereiter's Scheme of Knowledge.

The design of the Virtual PBL model is based on research on core cognitive theories and a sound pedagogical model of learning. Additionally the Virtual PBL model is based on concepts endemic to the immersive virtual learning environments.

Virtual Interactions

Facilitating inquiry for deeper learning and developing the learner's abilities to ask key questions is an important aspect of the design of the Virtual PBL scenarios. In Virtual PBL the interactions of the learners with the virtual environment, with the other learner's avatars and with the avatar guides will be designed to develop these questioning and thinking processes. The development of these learning processes in Virtual PBL includes interactions with virtual mentors designed to scaffold the learner through the PBL environments. These mentors will be designed to use the learner's telepresence to advance their thinking processes. Using a curriculum template based on educational best practice, the Virtual PBL model engages learners in simulations in virtual worlds to interact with experts in related fields and gather information for their problem-solving activities (Pea, 1993). As a result of these collaborative constructivist activities students develop advanced problem-solving abilities that are needed aspects of functioning in a knowledge-based society of the future (Savery, and Duffy, 1996).

Virtual Learning Places

A definition of place according to Norber-Schulz is that it is closely linked to meaning. "The places are goals where we experience the meaningful events of our existence, but thery are also points of departure from which we orient ourselves and take possession of the environment" (as cited in Noormohammadi, 2012, p. 27). When discussing the essence of place Relph believes that belonging to a place is identification with it. Identity is a function of intersubjecitve intent and experiences not the buildings and scenary. (Relph, E., 2008). This concept of place is critical when designing an educational game. The purposefulness of these learning environments is understood as the design of a learning place where all aspects of design are considered in relation to the development of learning outcomes. No aspect of the vitual worlds are unrecognized as a potential developmental interaction.

3D virtual worlds provide a basis for creating a new kind of place that provides context for human action and intention not available for education previously. The theory underlying these new concepts of virtual place was explored by Kalay (2003). He defined place as a setting that transforms spaces and activities in unique sociocultural events. The relationships of people in the the virtual space, the activities in the context and the virtual space all are considered the virtual place. Time and space become malleable constructs that can be designed to encourage an awareness of others, the qualities of the content and the activities for constructing learning (Kalay, 2003). Recently educational research has identified that the use of immersive 3D virtual worlds for education can afford learners with opportunities for experiential and situated learning within a collaborative learning environment They have shown that 3D virtual environments can lend themselves to supporting a constructivist approach to learning. Studies into constructivist 3D learning environments by Di Blas, Paolini, and Poggi (2004) have studied the pedagogical, technical and organizational issues inherent in virtual world design. A study by Kiili (2007) identified authenticity, collaboration and active learning as the characteristics of an effective 3D learning environment. The learner's level of engagement as a result of the authenticity of the learning space, their collaboration with other and an active learning dynamic are all aspects of telepresence in virtual worlds.

Telepresence

Telepresence is the sense that a person using certain technologies has that he/she is present in a location other than their real world location. In the book Natural Born Cyborgs, Andy Clark (2003) describes the ability of the human brain to develop new concepts using technological tools as explosively opportunistic. He further states that " We should not underestimate the capacity of human brains in general—young human brains in particular—to simultaneously alter and grow so they can better exploit the problem-solving opportunities our technologies provide." (pg. 86). McLuhan (1964) writing about the then new media of television describes the electric consciousness as "putting our physical bodies inside our extended nervous systems, by means of electronic media, we set up a dynamic by which all previous technologies that are extensions of our bodies will be translated into information systems." (p. 57). These are aspects of the potential for high levels of engagement in virtual worlds called telepresence. This concept was studied by Hayes (1999) who described telepresence as "extending embodied awareness in highly specific, local and material ways that would be impossible without electronic prosthesis" (pg. 291). Learners engage and develop telepresence through their virtual person, their avatar, or through the use of augmented reality devices. In the Virtual PBL model telepresence is defined and understood through the interactions and the responses of the learners based on coding of the dialogic and interactivity of the learners in the learning analytic system (Hui, & Russell, 2008).

Telepresence can allow the learner to feel high levels of engagement in the virtual environments and create the potential for high levels of learning responses. Understanding how the learner's level of engagement in the inquiry process is related to their sense of telepresence then becomes an important aspect of the potential for learning in these collaborative virtual learning environments. Subsequently the evaluation of this aspect of virtual reality scenarios should be addressed in the design of these environments.

Pedagogical Agents

The Virtual PBL design protocol also incorporates the use of artificial intelligence in these virtual learning environments to develop student levels of telepresence and monitor student responses. When you correlate the natural language processing and reasoning control of artificial intelligence (AI) with an avatar it becomes a powerful personification of knowledge. The AI is the agent to the ontological knowledge base of information. This separation results in modularity and dynamic abilities to change and update knowledge representation. With the AI seeming to respond as a regular avatar does, social interaction and engagement are increased. The student level of telepresence is maintained by ongoing interactions with these pedagogical agents. These AI avatars can be guides, mentors and even become points of assessment for the educator and for self-monitoring by the learners for the development of meta-cognitive learning processes.

Used to develop advanced learning processes, these pedagogical agents provide for the development of the critical interactions important to productive integration of problem-based learning environments in real-world classrooms. Without the ability to discuss, share and observe students in the classroom, these pedagogical agents are a critical link in the development of these PBL environments in classrooms. The dialogs among the students and with the pedagogical agents creates the potential for evaluation of the level of student discourse using qualitative research methodologies and the assessment of student response using the principals of social cognitive science (Johnson, Rickel, & Lester, 2000).

Additionally extensive interactions including access to information and web applications become feasible. The Virtual PBL models integrate web interfaces to assist with guide conversation review. This allows approved individuals to go over conversation logs and even to enter desired responses to questions if the automatically generated replies are not desired. This allows the designer to develop surveys and measures of learning to assess the effectiveness of the interactions in the virtual environments when the teacher cannot be directly involved in these interactions. This means that the teacher can monitor and evaluate the learning of the students during and after their experiences in the virtual scenarios using the AI bots.

The PBL design template includes a learning assessment model to understand how the virtual interactions and the students' levels of telepresence are related to the development of both cognitive processes and content knowledge. This learner's sense of telepresence will be defined for research as an aspect of the collaborative virtual learning environment that is related to the development of cognitive apprenticeship as defined by Anderson (1999) who described this cognitive apprenticeship as a guided learning process where the guide mentors the learner by making the expert processes explicit. Additionally interactions with the virtual mentors will be correlated to the process of the development of learning in the Zone of Proximal Development as described by Vygtosky (1978) where a mentor scaffolds the learner through higher and higher levels of difficulty toward mastery. In the virtual worlds students will respond to surveys that define their relationship with the mentor guides and the teacher can then correlate this information to formative and summative assessments of their learning and knowledge responses. The designers can modify these interactions based on the assessment feedback from the students about the avatar guides.

There are two types of AI software agents in the Virtual PBL Protocol that are designed to scaffold the learning of the students and aid in the advancement of their knowledge of the content area (Slator, Juell, McClean, Saini-Eidukat, Schwert, White & Hill, 1999). The main avatar guide is located at the main portal into the gaming environment and is designed to interact with the learners during Phase 1. The Guide AI bots help students develop the background information and the context for the next level interactions in the field experiences. This guide will have access to a live data feed from an SQL database that includes primary sources for the interrelated content areas. This database includes background information on the problem space, information about the virtual space, and contains the opening narrative for the world. Student avatars interact with this guide by responding to the opening narrative for each world, gathering information about the problem space for this virtual world, and asking questions about the content topics embedded in the problem space. This guide is designed to provide background context for the problem scenario in both the virtual and in the correlated real world issues that are interrelated to the virtual scenarios.

In Phase 2 there is a second form of guide is a mentor guide who will respond to the student questions with varying levels of specificity. By repeatedly querying about the facts to obtain a clear mental picture, problem solvers also learn to develop systematic and more thorough information gathering (Barrows, 1983). These avatar guides aid learners in the development of productive inquiry to solve problems. These avatar guides will also be connected to SQL databases that will allow them to modify their responses to the students. They are the main source of mentoring for the student's avatars as they move through this complex open-ended virtual PBL scenario. Mentor guides in virtual PBL gaming environment provide scaffolding as the students travel in their field experiences mentoring them as they develop higher and higher levels of expertise in the learning processes and develop higher levels of content knowledge as assessed by Bereiter's Scheme of Knowledge (2001). Subsequently the design of the virtual scenarios in Virtual PBL will include developmentally phased interactions of the learners with the mentor guides as a way to move students through the Zone of Proximal development as they develop conceptual artifacts in response to meaningful real-world issues.

This overview of a potential integration into a classroom identifies the ways that the Virtual PBL model can be integrated into myriad classrooms. It is modular and developmentally scaled to develop high levels of responses. The overview is provided an example of the integrated nature of linking problem-based learning design with the transformative nature of virtual simulations.

FUTURE RESEARCH DIRECTIONS

In these interactive collaborative gaming environments the learner's mind is engaged and social awareness is developed through active play that leads to a complete paradigm shift in education's consideration of the process and product of learning. Engagement, motive, affect, and meaning become the core issues inherent in the design of these environments. The successful virtual immersive learning environment then becomes the one where play becomes structured learning. "In the standard school environment the old adage that child's play is imagination in action must be reversed; we can say that imagination in adolescents and school children is play without action." (Vygotsky, 1978, p.93).

Design Issues and Trends

There are important trends in the development of games for learning in the future. There is a trend toward design processes to build the game specifically for learning and education and instead of games that are arbitrarily injected into education. Games can be productive educational experiences that occur in immersive learning environments. However, the design of the game must be linked to current research in the learning sciences, the pedagogy of effective educational models, such as problem-based learning, and finally the game must fit the needs of the p-12 educational setting.

Currently and in the past teachers have been asked to integrate new technologies and games from the outside into their already full curriculum. In this case, the PBL Design model links with standards-based education, albeit non-traditional education, and provides the educator with a productive learning environment with the assessment of learning linked to standards and built into the learning management system. In the Introduction to the chapter, I referred to a definition of games as a rule-based system with a variable and quantifiable outcomes that are assigned different values and engage the player in defining the level of effort to produce the chosen outcome. This is the crux of how games can become valuable learning environments by creating a problem-space with rules for productive or less productive outcomes based on an assessment model linked to standards and engaging the learner in defining their own learning and response. This is the future of educational gaming- real-world learning in virtual reality.

Virtual reality is an image or an environment that can be interacted with in through special electronic equipment such as a helmet with a screen or gloves fitted with sensors. It is considered an immersive multimedia environment that recreates sensory experiences such as virtual taste, sight, smell, sound and touch. The trend in virtual reality is for the use of augmented reality and haptic devices to exponentially increase the sensory experiences in virtual reality thus potentially increasing the learner's level of engagement and response.

Augmented Reality

A technological change that will make a difference in the future of educational gaming is the emerging field of augmented reality and its influence on the development of telepresence and engagement in educational games. Augmented Reality (AR) is an enhanced version of reality created by the use of technology to overlay digital information on an image of something being viewed through a device (Merriam-Webster.com, 2015). This use of these emergent technologies in educational settings has been the subject of speculation since the 2010 Horizon Report for K-12 predicted that educational Augmented Reality would be adopted within "four to five years" (New Media Consortium, 2010, p. 26). There are several companies that have begun developing Augmented Reality applications for use in educational settings. These increasingly realistic simulations that are comprehensively designed to provide as similar as possible reality to the real-world context have the potential to develop advanced learning skills and processes in many educational settings as games that are linked with visual devices allow students to explore and engage.

Students in Ireland have recreated a historic landscape in OpenSim and then explored it with an Oculus Rift headset (Abrosimova, 2014). Using the visual headset provides a more productive link to the virtual world and creates a strong motivational bond to the learning process in the virtual world. Augmented reality can also be used by students to develop real-world abilities such as engineering, architecture, science by providing a safe, cost-effective place for students to engage in complex scenarios with high levels of detail and engagement. As gaming design moves toward more productive integration in p-12 educational settings, and AR creates more defined and realist worlds for developing specific levels of expertise and knowledge, games then become increasingly viable as very efficient and effective learning environments for the development of advanced knowledge and skills not possible in any other learning environments.

Haptic Devices

Additionally, as gaming design becomes more focused on defining learning environments, virtual reality technologies becomes more engaging and augmented reality increases the virtual world's association with real worlds, haptic devices are also becoming more prevalent. Haptic devices are artificial touch technology. These new devices are becoming increasingly pervasive in their ability to provide feedback to the user through sensory feedback loop that increases telepresence and the potential for increasing the effectiveness of the learning environment. A haptic interface is a device that provides the user with the ability to interact with the computer through tactile and kinesthetic feedback. This can be in the form of gloves and eyewear.

Haptic learning from a constructivist perspective of learning provides additional augmentation of AR environments by increasing the learner's sensory interaction in virtual games (Klopfer, 2008). For instance, paired with an AR virtual world that simulates a chemical procedure with a haptic device that allows the learner to manipulate the chemical reaction using haptic gloves and eyewear, the educator can provide the learner with access to a virtual immersive learning environment, a game, that allows them to manipulate chemicals to identify chemical bonding.

There are a myriad of uses for haptic devices in education. They provide a very high of sensory input, visual or tactile, and thus are extremely effective, if designed well, at providing learners with the ability to manipulate objects to understand relationships, cause and effect, design prototypes and test these prototypes. It is only a matter of productive design that considers the affordances of these new devices in relationship to the educational goals. The new devices are also becoming increasingly facile and provide educators with the development of increasingly more engaging and potentially more productive and efficient virtual learning environments.

The potential of gaming scenarios built in virtual reality with augmented reality worlds where the learner interacts through visual and tactile haptic devices will in the future completely flip the paradigm of education. If these 'games' are designed to build on the potential of these new technologies to create an immersive learning experience that is designed based on cognitive sciences and sound pedagogical principles of teaching and learning, then these virtual worlds of play may provide the most effective and efficient of learning environments to develop advanced content knowledge and learning processes thereby supporting the development of the knowledge workers of the future.

CONCLUSION

The PBL design templates described in this chapter have been designed to develop advanced learning processes through structured interactions in a collaborative virtual learning environment. The Virtual PBL protocol includes

1. A virtual world scenario guide which includes game-like problem-based scenarios during which they interact with pedagogical agents that guide them through the virtual worlds,
2. A curriculum design template that includes assessments linked to federal standards, and
3. An evaluative qualitative research program to understand the levels and qualities of the learning and content knowledge resulting from the virtual learning environments.

The Virtual PBL protocol has the potential to meet the needs of all schools. The virtual scenarios are highly engaging providing motivation for the students. The students respond to the initial issue by working together in the virtual space to solve the problem by finding the information needed. The AI bots, pedagogical agents, provide scaffolding support to the students. The environment is highly interactive providing for another form of productive feedback to the students in the virtual space.

The Virtual PBL project incorporates the development of complex gaming-like scenarios to develop interest, motive and higher levels of engagement in students. The youngest generations spend significant time engaged and interacting with computer games (Bereiter, 2001). This protocol capitalizes on the current level of student interest in computer games to encourage focus on inquiry using gaming technology as an educational tool. Specifically these virtual gaming environments have the potential to develop the engagement of under-represented minorities and females (Vogel, Connon-Bowers, Bowers, Muse, & Wright, 2006). Another aspect of the potential for these environments is the process of collaboration as students can interact with others in these virtual worlds. When learning experiences are contextualized as meaningful problem-based scenarios, learning, retention, and productive engagement of students can be realized in dramatic and successful ways (Jonassen, et al, 2003).

Virtual PBL is an opportunity to utilize the emerging field of virtual modeling and simulation to design virtual problem scenarios that are based on current research in the cognitive sciences on the development of advanced thinking processes and new instructional design models to develop productive educational experiences for diverse students. The design of these environments when correlated with the needs of the learners and the affordances of the technologies can become a model for productive virtual learning environments designed to meet the needs of the diverse students to be productive in an increasingly complex technological society.

REFERENCES

American Association for the Advancement of Science. (1990). Science for All Americans. Retrieved from http://www.project2061.org/publications/sfaa/online/sfaatoc.htm

Anderson, C. (2001). Situative versus cognitive perspectives: Form versus substance. *Educational Researcher*, *26*(1), 18–21.

Aronson, E., Blaney, N., Stephan, C., Sikes, J., & Snapp, M. (1978). *The jigsaw classroom*. Beverly Hills, CA: Sage Publications.

Barab, S., & Duffy, T. (2000). From practice fields to communities of practice. In D. Jonassen (Ed.), *Theoretical Foundations of Learning Environments*. NJ: Lawerence Erlbaum Associates, Inc.

Barrows. H., (1983). Problem-based, self-directed learning, *Journal of the American Medical Association,* 250(30), 77-308.

Bereiter, C. (2001). *Education and Mind in the Knowledge Age*. New York, NY: Lawrence Erlbaum Assoc.

Bransford, J., Brown, A., & Cocking, R. (1999). *How people learn: Brain, mind, experience, and school.* Washington, DC: National Academy Press.

Brown, A., Ash, D., Rutherford, M., Nakagawa, N., Gordon, A., & Campione, J. (1993). Distributed expertise in the classroom. In G. Salomon (Ed.), *Distributed cognitions: Psychological and educational considerations*. New York, NY: Cambridge University Press.

Brown, A., & Campione, J. (1996). Communities of learning and thinking or a context by any other name. In Woods, P. (Ed), Contemporary Issues in Teaching and Learning. New York, NY: Routledge. 21,108-126.

Brown, J., Collins, A., & Duguid, P. (1989). Situated cognition and the culture of learning. *Educational Researcher*, *18*(1), 32–42. doi:10.3102/0013189X018001032

Clark, A. (2003). *Natural Born Cyborgs; Minds, Technologies and the Future of Human Intelligence*. Oxford, UK: Oxford University Press.

Cole, M., & Engeström, Y. (1993). A cultural-historical approach to distributed cognition. In G. Salomon (Ed.), *Distributed cognition: Psychological and educational considerations*. Cambridge, MA: Cambridge University Press.

Dede, C. (2014). Immersive interfaces for engagement and learning. Retrieved from http://isites.harvard.edu/fs/docs/icb.topic443490.files/Immersive%20Interfaces%20for%20Learning.pdf

Di Blas, N., Paolini, P., & Poggi, C. (2004). Learning by playing. an eductainment 3D environment for schools. Presented at the World Conference on Educational Multimedia, Hypermedia and Telecommunications. Chesapeake, VA. ISBN 978-1-880094-53-2

Gee, J. (2007). *What video games have to teach us about learning and literacy.* New York, NY: Palgrave Macmillan. ISBN-13: 9781-4039-8453-1

Gordon, P., Rogers, A., Comfort, M., Gavula, N., & McGee, B. (2001). A taste of problem-based learning increases achievement of urban minority middle school students. *Educational Horizons*, *79*(4), 171–175.

Greeno, (1997).

Hayles, N. K. (1999). How We Became Post-Human. Chicago, IL: University of Chicago Press. Retrieved from http://gamestudies.org/0102/squire/ doi:10.7208/chicago/9780226321394.001.0001

Hinrichs, T. R. (1992). *Problem solving in open worlds: A case study in design*. Hillsdale, NJ: Lawrence Erlbaum Associates.

Johnson, L., Laurence, F., Levine, A., & Smith, R. (2009). *The 2010 horizon report*. Austin, TX: The New Media Consortium.

Johnson, W., Rickel, J., & Lester, J. (2000). Animated pedagogical agents: Face-to-face interaction in interactive learning environments. *International Journal of Artificial Intelligence in Education*, *1*, 47–78.

Jonassen, D. (2000). Toward a design theory of problem solving. *Educational Technology Research and Development*, *48*(4), 63–85. doi:10.1007/BF02300500

Jonassen, D., Howland, J., Moore, J., & Marra, J. (2003). *Learning to Solve Problems with Technology: A Constructivist Perspective*. Upper Saddle River, NJ: Merrill-Prentice Hall.

Jonassen, D., Peck, K., & Wilson, B. G. (1999). *Learning with technology: A constructivist perspective*. Upper Saddle River, New Jersey: Merrill-Prentice Hall.

Jonassen, D., Peck, K. L., & Wilson, B. G. (1999). *Learning with technology: A constructivist perspective*. Upper Saddle River, N.J.: Merrill-Prentice Hall.

Kalay, Y., Jeony, Y., & Kim, J. (2003). Virtual Learning Environments. *Journal of Information Technology in Mathematical Surfaces*. doi=10.1.1.120.8491

Kiili, K. (2007). *Foundation for problem-based gaming*. British Journal of Educational Technology. Doi: doi:10.111/j.1467-8535.2007.00704x

Klopfer, E. (2008). *Augmented learning: Research and design of mobile educational games*. USA: MIT Press. doi:10.7551/mitpress/9780262113151.001.0001

Knuth, R. A., & Cunningham, D. J. (1993). Tools for constructivism. In T. M. Dufffy, J. Lowyck, & D. H. Jonassen (Eds.), *Designing environments for constructive learning* (pp. 163–188). Berlin, Heidelberg: Springer-Verlag. doi:10.1007/978-3-642-78069-1_9

Lave, J., & Wenger, E. (1991). *Situated learning: Legitimate peripheral participation*. Cambridge, UK: Cambridge University Press. doi:10.1017/CBO9780511815355

McLuhan, M. (1964). *Understanding Media: The Extensions of Man*. New York, NY: McGraw Hill. 'Merriam Webster. Encyclopedia Britannica Company. Retrieved from http://www.merriam-webster.com/dictionary/augmented%20reality

Noormohammadi, S. (2012). Essential human qualities in strengthening place identity as expressed in Louis Kahn's architectural theory. In H. Casakin, & F. Bernardo (Eds), The Role of Place Identity in the Perception, Understanding and Design of Built Environments. Bentham eBooks. eISBN: 978-60805-413-8, 22-35.

Norman, G., & Schidt, H. (1992). The psychological basis of problem-based learning: A review of the evidence. *National Institutes of Health*, 67(9), 557-65. Retrieved from http://www.ncbi.nlm.nih.gov/pubmed/1520409

Pea, R. (1993). Practices of distributed intelligence and designs for education. In G. Salomon (Ed.), *Distributed cognitions: Psychological and educational considerations*. Cambridge, UK: Cambridge University Press.

Relph, E. (2008). sense of place and emerging social and evnironmental challenges. In J. Eyeles, & A. Williams (Eds), Sense of place, health and quality of life (pp. 66-78). Burlington, VT: Ashgate.

Resnick, L. (1987). Learning in school and out. *Educational Researcher*, *16*, 13–20.

Resnick, Levine, & Teasley (1991).

Russell, D. (2004a). *The Vashon Education Compact Youth Leadership and Technology Program: Community Renewal*. Presentation at the National Association of Multicultural Education, Kansas City, MO.

Russell, D. (2004b). Paradigm shift: A case study of innovation in an educational setting. *International Journal of Instructional Technology & Distance Learning*, *1*(12).

Russell, D. (2005a). Implementing an Innovation cluster in educational settings in order develop constructivist-based learning environments. *Journal of Educational Technology & Society*, *8*(2).

Russell, D. (2005b). Transformation in an urban school: Using systemic analysis to understand an innovative urban teacher's implementation of an online problem-based unit. *International Journal of Instructional Technology & Distance Learning*, *2*(2).

Russell, D. (2007). The impact of group Collaboration on an online problem-based university course. In *O. Tan (Ed.), Problem-Based Learning and Creativity*. Singapore: Thomson Publications.

Salomon, G. (1993). No distribution without individuals' cognition: A dynamic interactional view. In G. Salomon (Ed.), *Distributed cognitions: Psychological and educational considerations*. NY: Cambridge University Press.

Shaffer, D., Hatfield, D., Svaronvsky, G., Nash, P., Nulty, A., Bagley, E., . . . Mislevey, R. (2009). Epistemic Network Analysis: A Prototype for 21st-Century Assessment of Learning. *International Journal of Learning and Media,* 1(2). MIT Press. Retrieved from http://www.mitpressjournals.org/doi/abs/10.1162/ijlm.2009.0013#VMb7qWTF8QU

Shaw, D., Becker, H., Bransford, J., Davidson, J., Hawkins, J., Malcom, S., & Lehoczky, S. et al. (1998). Report to the president of the use of technology to strengthen k-12 education in the United States: Findings related to research and evaluation. *Journal of Science Education and Technology*, 7(2), 115–126. Retrieved from http://link.springer.com/article/10.1023/A:1022539822660#page-1 doi:10.1023/A:1022539822660

Slator, B., Juell, P., McClean, P., & Saini-Eidukat, B., Schwert, D., White, D. A., & Hill. C., (1999). Virtual Environments in Education. paper presented at ED-MEDIA 99; AACE Conference.

Squire, K. (2007). Cultural framing of computer/video games. *International Journal of Computer Games*, *2*(1). Retrieved from http://www.gamestudies.org/0102/squire/

Tan, O. (2003). *Problem-based learning innovation: Using problems to power learning in the 21st century*. Singapore: Thomson Learning.

Vogel, J., Cannon-Bowers, J., Bowers, C., Muse, K., & Wright, M. (2006). Computer gaming and interactive simulations for learning: A meta-analysis. *Journal of Educational Computing Research*, *6*(34), 229–243. doi:10.2190/FLHV-K4WA-WPVQ-H0YM

Vygotsky, L. (1978). *Mind in society: The development of higher psychological processes*. Cambridge, MA: Harvard University Press.

Chapter 6
Kinesthetic Gaming, Cognition, and Learning:
Implications for P-12 Education

Erdem Demiroz
University of Missouri – Kansas City, USA

ABSTRACT

Kinesthetic gaming, which is also called full-body gaming, is the rising star of digital gaming trends of recent years. With the integration of commercially available motion tracking systems into game consoles, players are able to control the games with kinesthetic movements without any handheld controllers. This new form of advanced human-computer interaction (HCI) allows players to interact with games in more realistic and natural ways. Because of its novelty, research in kinesthetic gameplay is limited, and experimental research on the effects of kinesthetic gaming on learning is almost non-existent. The purpose of the chapter is to investigate the philosophical foundations of kinesthetic game-playing by emphasizing the role of physical action on learning under the framework of cognitive theories and to discuss possible implications in P-12 education. The author aims to introduce kinesthetic game-playing as a powerful tool for learning and to develop new insights on gaming in P-12 education.

INTRODUCTION

Due to new developments in gaming technology, motion tracking systems that use players' physical actions as inputs are becoming widely available. As of today, almost all gaming consoles are coming with motion tracking systems such as Microsoft Kinect©, Nintendo Wii© or Sony Move©. These motion tracking systems provide unique opportunities to evaluate game-play not only from an educational perspective but also from a cognitive perspective since players' gaming experiences become more realistic and natural with the integration of physical action into gaming. Such controller-free gaming experiences provide opportunities to attribute new meanings to physical movements that are not game-related especially when they are evaluated under the principles of cognitive theories. This new meaning attributed to the non-registered inputs might be helpful to investigate the mutual relationship between physical action, environment and cognitive development.

DOI: 10.4018/978-1-4666-9629-7.ch006

Kinesthetic gaming has an extreme potential for educational implementation and practice through virtual experiential learning. Educational content can be delivered in an effective way, and learners can interact and engage with the content as they learn in real life settings through gaming. The kinesthetic gaming in P-12 can be integrated into any content area or field of teaching. For instance, learners could collect virtual apples from trees in virtual learning environments in which learners are physically active to learn counting in mathematics in early grades; an adult learner can learn how to play piano by physically practicing a virtual piano; a graduate student could complete a dangerous experiment in a virtual chemistry laboratory; a 5th grader could take a field-trip to a virtual museum by physically wandering around in real-life settings; or a medical student could complete a virtual surgery by physically acting in real life settings. These are basic ideas, and more mature and complex tasks can be proposed for educational purposes.

There is an increasing number of research studies that investigate the role of kinesthetic engagement and physical action on learning processes in gaming, cognitive science, and learning literature (e.g. Bautista, Roth, & Thom, 2011; Bianchi-Berthouze, 2013; Chang, Chien, Chiang, Lin, & Lai, 2013; Chao, Huang, Fang, & Chen, 2013; Chen, Hsu, Hsieh, & Chou, 2014; Ferrai, 2007; Nakamura et al., 2013; Rambusch, 2006; Rambusch & Ziemke, 2005; and Xu & Ke, 2014). Generally speaking, research on kinesthetic game-playing and its effects on educational outcomes are promising; however, there is a lack of experimental research. Although basic requirement of learning settings are satisfied in virtual learning settings that offers engaging educational experiences, educational theory and game design cannot meet on a common ground through a well-designed model (Kiili, 2005). Therefore, virtual learning environments in which players are totally immersed and physically active should be developed by considering design principles of gaming in order to investigate the effects of kinesthetic gaming on learning progress. Kinesthetic movements not only impact players' experiences of game-playing and cognitive development in virtual learning settings, but also affect the learning experiences and cognitive development in real life.

Prominent names of 20th century in the fields of pedagogy and cognition evaluate experiences and physical actions of cognitive agents in real life settings from different perspectives. For example, Piaget (1952) evaluates the role of physical actions from a cognitive perspective whereas Bruner (1966) and Kolb (1984) look from educational perspectives. Bruner's studies initiate the development of student-centered discovery learning approach that focuses on active participation and creative problem solving whereas Piaget's studies along with Lewin's model of action research and laboratory training, and Dewey's model of learning underlie experiential learning model developed by Kolb. According to Kolb, learning is "the process whereby knowledge is created through the transformation of experience. Knowledge results from the combination of grasping and transforming experience" (as cited in Kolb and Kolb, 2009, p. 297). Lainema (2003) explains that designers of virtual learning environments have been inspired by the experiential learning theory (as cited in Kiili, 2005), and "[t]he ideology of experiential learning provides a fruitful basis for integration of gameplay and pedagogy" (Kiili, p. 17).

Piaget defines four stages of cognitive development as sensorimotor, pre-operational, concrete operational and formal operational (Huitt & Hummel, 2003). Likewise, Bruner (1966) introduces three modes of representation which explains how information or knowledge is processed and stored in memory: enactive, iconic and symbolic (McLeod, 2012). Physical actions and experiments are essentials for cognitive development in early stages of development at Piaget's sensorimotor stage (from birth to 18-24 months) and Bruner's enactive mode of representation (from birth to 12 months). More attention should be paid to these two stages of development which emphasize the role of physical actions on learning and cognitive development. According to Kolb (1984), "learning is predominantly enactive through feeling, touching and handling" (p.23) in sensorimotor stage of Piaget's cognitive development model. McLeod (2010) summarizes that "[i]nitially equipped with a set of reflex movements and a set of perceptual systems, an infant quickly begins to build up direct knowledge of world around her, by relating physical actions to perceived results of those actions [at sensorimotor stage]" (para. 3). McLeod also discusses that enactive mode of representation emphasizes the action based information processing and storing such as remembering the action of shaking a rattle in the form of movement as muscle memory. However, physical actions, kinesthetic movements or reflective behaviors are not only observed at the sensorimotor stage of cognitive development and enactive mode of representation, but also throughout the lifecycle of the cognitive agents. Indeed, cognitive agents are physically active during their life cycle starting not from birth, but from the early stages of pregnancy. Therefore, the role of kinesthetic movements and physical actions in lifelong cognitive development cannot be ignored at any time of the life cycle, as they cannot be ignored at the sensorimotor stage of cognitive development and learning or the enactive mode of representation.

Recent technological innovations allow game designers and researchers to develop virtual learning environments in which players are physically active and cognitively engaged. By constructing on this notion, this chapter

1. Summarizes emergent cognitive theories,
2. Evaluates kinesthetic gameplay and physical actions in virtual learning settings by enhancing the discussions on immersion, presence and player-avatar identity,
3. Discusses impacts of kinesthetic gameplay on learning and cognitive development by emphasizing the similarities between virtual settings that allow cognitive agents being physically active and real life settings.

The chapter is constructed on theoretical discussions that evaluate potential impacts of kinesthetic gameplay on cognitive development and learning progress under the light of cognitive theories, so the chapter does not necessarily focus on a specific kinesthetic gaming technology, in-class implementation strategies, or practical implications in P-12 education. The underlying thesis statement of the chapter is that kinesthetic gaming, which offers new opportunities for virtual experimental learning, supports cognitive development of learners at all grade levels as a result of intertwined interaction between high level immersion and presence, physical actions and virtual environment. Thus, as a non-traditional gaming experience, kinesthetic gaming is a unique advancement from an educational perspective, and it has potential to leverage use of educational games to achieve desired learning outcomes in P-12 education.

Kinesthetic Gaming and Technological Advancements

Ferrai (2007) calls for novel ways of interaction that plays a significant role on the immersion of players with games such as an interaction which is not only limited to handheld controllers, but also includes body movements. Recent technological innovations have moved human-computer interaction (HCI) to a new dimension in which users are able to control the technological devices through gesture, voice, and kinesthetic movement. New generation human-computer interaction that is supported by motion tracking and capturing systems developed by game designers has an influence not only on the gaming and entertainment industry, but also on players' gaming experiences. The idea of motion capturing and tracking is not new, and it has been used specifically for gaming and entertainment to design 2D and 3D animations and avatars for a long time. However, recent innovations reveal their potential for changing and advancing human computer interaction in addition to game design.

During the past few years, commercially available depth sensors, voice, and motion controlling systems have become a turning point in gaming because such devices present a new way of controlling game consoles and allowing game players to be physically active in game playing. Beforehand, game players were passive, and their actions were limited by controllers that required only finger movements to interact with the virtual gaming environment. Since kinesthetic gaming was announced, game players have become active players who are able to control their virtual representations (avatars) through physical motions as they control their bodies in real life environment. One of the most effective new generation gaming controllers which operates through motion sensors tracking body movements to generate input data for the game is the Kinect©, which was first introduced with XBOX 360© the game console of Microsoft©.

The discussions on gaming and gameplay focus on Kinect rather than other motion sensing controlling devices for two reasons:

1. Kinect, which can be used for personal programming and software development, has been commercially available separately from the XBOX 360© gaming console, and
2. Kinect provides full-body gaming experience without using controllers.

Kinect gaming and programming have dramatically increased after Microsoft© released its free Software Development Kit (SDK) for the Kinect© in 2011. Since then, several Kinect© applications have been developed for different purposes in different fields such as education, health, business and military purposes in addition to several on-the-shelf commercially available digital games such as Kinect Sports©, Kinect Rush©, Kinect Star Wars©, Kinect Dance Party©, Majesco Zumba Fitness World Party©, and Body and Brain Connection©. Some of these professionally developed entertainment games have been used for educational purposes, but there are also third-party Kinect games developed by researchers and educators for education purposes. For example, Kinect Sports© is a commercially available digital game that has potential to be used in physical education. Using full-body kinesthetic gaming for physical activities and exercises introduces a new term, exergaming. According to Best (2013), exergaming does not only support physical engagement, but also facilitates cognitive engagement. Lwin and Malik (2012) examined the possible outcomes of using exergaming in physical education and concluded that "[i]ncorporating exergaming into PE [physical education] lessons can be more effective than regular PE in enhancing PA [physical activity] beliefs and behaviors, particularly among younger children" (p. 756). Likewise, Homer et al. (2014) examined a Kinect-based literacy game for beginning readers by comparing three randomly-assigned groups and concluded that all groups showed significant gains on reading components, but only Kinect-Activities group had significant gain for sight words, which are recognizable by sight, such as children, where, home, and, morning, the, etc. On the other hand, Xdigit© and Scoop© were developed to teach mathematics through kinesthetic movements, but no experimental research is available in the mathematics education literature about them.

Kinesthetic Gameplay from Educational Perspective

Kinesthetic engagement authenticates game-players' experiences in virtual settings, and relatively increases their immersion, presence, and cognitive engagement in gaming. The relationship between actual game players and their virtual representations in virtual settings has been one of the well-discussed topics in cognitive science (see Froese & Di Paolo, 2009; Nijhar, Bianchi-Berthouze, & Boguslawski, 2012; Nørgård, 2011; Rehak, 2003; Slater, Steed, McCarthy, & Maringelli, 1998; Steinkuehler, 2008). However, the impacts of being physically active in game playing are not fully investigated from an educational perspective by considering its role in advanced human computer interaction and in cognitive engagement in virtual settings. It is a fact that this new generation game-playing creates new opportunities for game developers and possibly for educators and promises to advance learning experiences of game players.

Kinesthetic gaming is relatively new and has not become popular in professional educational games and applications yet. Commercially available over-the-counter games are designed for entertainment, and educational use of such games are limited. Third party educational games developed mostly by researchers do not completely address the design principles of game development. There are individual efforts to develop educational applications in which players are able to manipulate the game content by kinesthetic movements, but such efforts are not sufficient for in-depth evaluation of the impact of kinesthetic gaming in P-12 education. Enhanced discussions on gesture-based learning and its educational and theoretical foundations of gameplay could deepen our understanding on kinesthetic gaming and its impact on P-12 education. In conjunction with the gesture based learning approach, whose principles and outcomes could possibly shed light on kinesthetic educational gaming, discussion on simulations, role playing, non-Cartesian cognitive theories could help us to understand the connections between cognition, physical movement and environment from an educational perspective.

Motion tracking systems allow users to interact with virtual worlds in more natural and realistic ways. Research on full-body game playing indicates that kinesthetic gaming potentially enriches players' gaming experiences by allowing them to be physically active during gameplay. Bianchi-Berthouze (2013), for example, investigated the role of body movement on player engagement by comparing two different types of input devices, the traditional control pad and a motion-sensing guitar shaped controller, and concluded that body movement or physical action during game play increased the engagement level of the players. Other comparative studies have been completed to analyze the effectiveness of kinesthetic gameplay from an educational perspective. Chao, Huang, Fang, and Chen (2013) examined the embodied game-play on learning and compared the memory performances of students who were assigned for the Kinect-controlled condition and the traditional mouse-controlled condition. They concluded that students in the Kinect-controlled condition not only outperformed their peers who were in the mouse-controlled condition, but also retained memory gains over a long-term period. Although limited research is available in the literature, the impact of kinesthetic gaming on cognitive development and learning is promising.

Based on real life experiences, the following argument might be useful to estimate the impact of kinesthetic game-play on learning. Assume that twin game players are playing an identical dancing game in two different game consoles. One of them is sitting in front of the game console and is playing by using a controller and his fingers to move the dancer avatar in the game. The other player is using physical movements to control the dancer avatar in the game and needs to physically dance in the real life setting. The question that needs to be asked is how such a dramatic change in being physically active in gaming affects the second player's cognitive process, learning, and understanding. In order to be more specific, which of the following learns to dance better: a player who controls the avatar by a controller, or a player who controls the avatar by physically dancing? The author constructs the answers of these questions throughout the chapter by investigating the topic from an enactivist perspective.

COGNITION, KINESTHETIC GAMEPLAY, AND LEARNING

Cognitive theories such as enacted mind, embodied cognition, and situated cognition emphasize that the interaction between body, physical actions/perceptions and environment has significant role in cognitive development and learning. According to recent cognitive theories, which challenge with Cartesian Dualism, cognitive development and learning are interactive processes which occur as a result of the interactivity between these three intertwined factors in real life settings. Chalmers (2008) summarizes the interconnection between mind, action, and environment as "[i]t is natural to hold that perception is the interface where the world affects the mind, and that action is the interface where the mind affects the world" (p. 2-3). Non-Cartesian cognitive theories assume that mind and body are inseparable. Mind and body strongly depend on and affect each other, so they cannot be separated (Clancey, 1997; Clark, 1997; Varela, Thompson, & Rosch, 1991 as cited in Rambusch, 2006). If this notion is embedded into Chalmers' statement, then it could be assumed that body and environment are essentially interrelated, and perceptions are the ways that the real world interacts with the body, and actions are the ways that the body interacts with the world. As a result, cognition and learning are constructed because of this perceptual and active interconnectivity. The role of the body and physical actions, which include gestures, is undeniable in this interaction. Klemmer, Hartmann, and Takayama (2006) emphasize that "[o]ur physical bodies play a central role in shaping human experience in the world, understanding of the world, and interactions in the world" (p. 140). As an indispensable part of the cognitive organism, being physically active in the real world should be considered an important factor in learning and constructing meaning. Theoretically, this is true for virtual worlds which include digital games in which players are cognitively engaged and immersed. However, lack of physical activity or bodily engagement is a disadvantage for learning and cognitive development in virtual worlds. Therefore, kinesthetic game play is a unique advancement which has potential to overcome this challenge in order to design better virtual educational settings for mastery learning.

Cognition from a General Perspective

Cartesian Dualism

The traditional cognitive science that is built on Cartesian Dualism assumes that all the cognitive processes occur in the brain, and mind and body are separated. "Whatever else is true of cognitive processes, they are processes occurring inside the brains of cognizing organisms. That is something on which both classical approaches to cognition and the connectionist alternative can agree" (Rowlands, 2010, p. 52). Traditional cognitive science hypothesizes that the brain of any living organism is the location of mental states, and claims that "[c]ognitive processes consist in the manipulation and transformation of structures that carry information about the world; these information-bearing structures are known as mental representations; mental representations are structures located in the brains of cognizing organisms" (Rowlands, p. 51). On the other hand, some cognitive scientists challenge and reject the assumptions of traditional cognitive science. This new generation cognitive science is known as a non-Cartesian form of cognitive science. To sum up, traditional cognitive science which is deeply rooted in Cartesian dualism assumes that mind and body are separate, and cognitive processes occur only inside the brain, but other cognitive theories, which reject this claim, have been widely accepted in cognitive science for more than two decades.

The Cartesian tradition is mistaken in supposing that the mind is an inner entity of any kind, whether mind-stuff, brain states, or whatever. Ontologi-

cally, mind is much more a matter of what we do within environmental and social possibilities and bounds. Twentieth-century anti-Cartesianism thus draws much of mind out, and in particular outside the skull. (van Gelder, 1995, p. 380)

Embedded Cognition

Embedded cognition advocates that cognition is intensely rooted in the natural and social environment of the organism, and cognitive activity is shared by the agent and environment since agents use various strategies to off-load cognitive processing onto the environment (Suchman, 1987; Hutchins, 1995; Wilson & Foglia, 2011). According to Rowlands (2010), embedded cognition hypothesizes that certain environmental structures are required for some mental processes to function, and some mental processes are designed to function only with these environmental structures, so the mental processes cannot function in a way that they are supposed to function if these environmental structures are not available. The main idea of the embedded cognition is that cognitive organisms manipulate the environmental structures in order to reduce the internal cognitive load by off-loading the complex cognitive load of the cognitive tasks accomplished (Rowlands, 2010). Relocating objects in the house not to step on them or using post-its or planners as reminders are the two simple examples of the ways that agents change and construct the environment by spreading information in it, and such activities help agents to release some of the complexity of internal cognitive processes in the environment (Fenici, 2012). According to Fenici, embedded cognition theory emphasizes the role of external structures in cognitive activity. The cognitive load on memory is discharged and perception and action planning are simplified because of such environmental alterations made by cognitive agents (Kirsh, 1995; Clark, 1997; Fenici, 2012).

Extended Cognition

Extended cognition has similarities with embedded mind, but focuses on actions to manipulate the environment rather than focusing on environmental structures in which the agent off-loads cognitive processing and considers these structures as information resources. In other words, according to the extended cognition theory, cognitive agents are capable of extending their cognitive systems beyond the individual organism, and physical, social and cultural features of the environment might form the agents' cognitive systems (Clark, 2008; Clark & Chalmers, 1998; Menary, 2010; Wilson, 2004; Wilson & Foglia, 2011). Rowlands (2010) summarizes that a cognitive organism performs actions to manipulate, exploit, and transform external structures that carry information which facilitates accomplishing given cognitive tasks, and agents are able to make the information stored by environmental structures available to themselves and to related cognitive operations by acting properly in these structures. Wilson and Foglia discuss that the thesis of extended cognition asserts that "an agent's mind and associated cognitive processing are neither skull-bound nor even body-bound, but extend into the agent's world" (Sec. 6.3, para. 1). Extended mind claims that information is externally stored in the environment and is processed by "perceiving, remembering, reasoning and experiencing" through internal cognitive processes which include supporting the agent to use the relevant structures appropriately to accomplish the given cognitive tasks and external cognitive processes which include the actions such as the "manipulation, exploitation, and transformation of environmental structures" (Rowlands, p. 59). Robbins and Aydede (2009) discuss that from the perspective of extended cognition, "the mind leaks out into the world, and cognitive activity is distributed across individuals and situations" (p. 8).

Situated Cognition

Rambusch and Ziemke (2005) state that "cognition is for action" (p. 1804) is the key theme of situated cognition. Fenici (2012) states that according to theory of situated cognition agents –body- and environment are intertwined, and cannot be separated. Situated cognition emphasizes the external environmental structures and the role of these structures on the control of behavior (Norman, 1993). Thus action or social activity is at the center of situated cognition, which is generally used interchangeably with the term situated learning. Rambusch and Ziemke discuss that situated learning theories, which also reject the idea that the mind could be studied and comprehended in isolation from the body and environment, consider social interactions and tool use as the main focus of learning activities. In addition, the ecological approach, which also claims that behavior cannot be studied in isolation from environment, is closely related to situated cognition (Gibson, 1974; Fenici, 2012). Rambusch and Ziemke summarize that "[c]ognition, and learning in particular, are seen as processes that are situated as they emerge through interaction between agent and environment" (p. 1806).

Embodied Cognition

The common ground of non-Cartesian strands of cognition is that they reject the assumption that all mental processes occur in the brain. Rambusch and Ziemke (2005) claim that "[i]n embodied cognition research, on the other hand, there is an increasing awareness that mind and body are inextricably intertwined and cannot be viewed in isolation" (p. 1803). There is an ever increasing number of research studies in embodied cognition literature. Wilson and Foglia (2011) define cognition as "embodied when it is deeply dependent upon features of the physical body of an agent, that is, when aspects of the agent's body beyond the brain play a significant causal or physically constitutive role in cognitive processing" (para. 1). Embodied cognition theory takes the body and physical actions into account while discussing cognitive processing. Rambusch and Ziemke explain that "[t]he underlying assumption in the theoretical framework of embodied cognition is that cognition arises from bodily interactions with the world and is, thus, grounded in and linked to sensorimotor activity" (p. 1807). Interactions of the body with the environment is essential in embodied cognition. The theory of embodied cognition defines humans as acting beings or embodied agents and cognitive processes of acting beings are strongly dependent on the interaction of the agent with the world (Anderson, 2003; Shapiro, 2011; Wilson, 2002; Xu & Ke, 2014). "[O]ur powers of advanced cognition vitally depend on a substrate of abilities for moving around in and coping with the world which we inherited from our evolutionary forbears" (Anderson, p.126). Fenici (2012) claims that embodied cognition stresses that agent's body has an important role in understanding cognitive processes because it is the body that actively interacts and engages the agent with the environment. Rocha (2012) believes that the relationship between body and cognition is mutually inclusive because body is directly related to cognitive processes which are naturally linked to the body.

According to the embodied perspective, cognition is situated in the interaction of body and world, dynamic bodily process such a motor activity can be part of reasoning process, and offline cognition is body-based too. Finally embodiment assumes that cognition evolved for action, and because of this, perception and action are not separate systems, but are inextricably linked to each other and to cognition. This last idea is a near relative to the core idea of enaction. (Hutchins, 2010, p. 428)

Enactivism

Froese (2009) summarizes that the enactive approach, which dates back to the early 1990s, emerges as part of embodied-embedded cognitive science, and "[i]t has recently distinguished itself by more explicitly placing the phenomenon of life at the heart of cognitive science" (p. 22). Varela, Thomson, and Rosch (1991) introduce enaction as a framework which emphasizes that the experienced environment is perceived through "mutual interactions between physiology of the cognitive organism, its sensorimotor circuit, and the environment" (Wilson & Foglia, 2011, Sec. 2.2., para. 2). The core idea of enactivism is that agents act through the situated living bodies in an environment and interact with the environment through physical actions. "Cognition is enactive - that is, dependent on aspects of the activity of the cognizing organism" (Hurley, 1998; Noë, 2004; Thompson 2007; Varela, Thompson, & Rosch, 1991 as cited in Ward & Stapleton, 2012, p.2).

Thus we confront the problem of understanding how our experience – the praxis of our living – is coupled to a surrounding world, which appears filled with regularities that are at every instant the result of our biological and social histories. [...] our world, as the world which we bring forth in our coexistence with others, will always have precisely that mixture of regularity and mutability, that combination of solidity and shifting sand, so typical of human experience when we look at it up close. (Maturana & Varela, 1992, p. 241)

Wilson and Foglia (2011) claim "that cognition is a dynamic sensorimotor activity, and the world that is given and experienced is not only conditioned by the neural activity of the subject, but is essentially enacted in that it emerges through the bodily activities of the organism" (Sec. 2.2, para. 3). Ward and Stapleton (2012) examine the relationship between embodied cognition, enactivist cognition, embedded cognition, affective cognition, and extended cognition, and introduce ecumenical enactivism, which advocates that "if cognition is enactive then it is also embodied, embedded, affective and potentially extended." (Ward & Stapleton, p. 2). There is a thin line between enactive cognition and embodied-embedded cognition since enactive cognition is grounded in embodied-embedded cognitive science. Rocha (2012) summarizes the relationship between embodied cognition and enactivist cognition simply by stating that:

Embodiment means that the cognitive process is embedded in our bodies and Enaction suggests a future potential action and both concepts are related. Also according to several researchers (Varela, Thompson and Rosch 1991; Thompson, 2005) we can identify five linked ideas that constitute the notion of Enaction. These are Autonomy, sense-making, emergence, embodiment and experience. (Rocha, 2012, p. 7)

Kinesthetic Gameplay

Psychological and physiological dynamics of game-play such as kinesthetic movements, immersion, perception, and gaming environment should be well-portrayed before discussing the kinesthetic gaming from an enactivist perspective and emphasizing the similarity between gaming experience and real life experience. Isbister, Karlesky, Frye, and Rao (2012) state that "as game designers, we are only beginning to understand the interrelation of movement, gaming, and experience" (p. 228). Unfortunately, the situation is the same for educators and educational technology designers. However, educators are more experienced than game designers in terms of physical activities because cognitive theories shed light on learning theories.

Kinesthetic gameplay is promising for better gaming experience, cognitive development, and learning experience from the perspectives of cognitive theories, especially when these topics are considered under the framework of enactivism. The discussion of gaming experience from an enactivist perspective is almost non-existent because one of the main factors of enactivism, physical action, was limited prior to the introduction of kinesthetic or full-body gaming experience which is more natural and authentic. Before kinesthetic gaming, players were physically restricted, and their non-game-task movements were widely accepted as disengagement or as evidences of presence.

Kinesthetic Gaming and Virtual Environments

Embodied mixed-reality environments as discussed in Cheok, Yang, Ying, Billinghurst, and Kato (2002) and well-designed simulations are ideal for kinesthetic game playing and enhanced gaming experience. On the other hand, one of the most advanced and commercially available motion tracking system, Microsoft Kinect©, has potential to convert digital games into mixed-reality environments and simulations if the gaming environment is well-designed and immersive enough. Virtual environments, which provide high-level presence and immersion and physical action, could possibly be considered as embodied mixed-reality learning environments. Johnson-Glenberg, Koziupa, Birchfield, and Li (2011) define these learning environments as platforms in which users are able to learn through visual, auditory, and kinesthetic engagement. Mixed-reality environments like simulations attempt to imitate real life settings, so the similarities between the way users interact in embodied mixed-reality settings and in the real life environments are notable. It is a fact that simulations and games have been used by educators for decades to support learning (Gredler 1996; Heinich, Molenda, Russell, & Smaldino, 1996; Reigeluth & Schwartz, 1989; Squire, 2003). However, games ignore the rules of real life in order to implement the rules of the game whereas simulations try to model reality (Heinich et al., 1996 as cited in Squire, 2003). Kinesthetically controllable educational games can be designed for mastery learning by considering the pedagogical principles and design characteristics of embodied mixed-reality environments and simulations.

Immersion and Presence in Virtual Settings

In movies I do not identify with the main character at all. I just watch what he does. But in a book, if I read about the actions of some main character, then I identify with him as I would be the character myself. Or at least I immerse myself more into it. But in a game you immerse into it most of all, because you actually do things with that guy, with that character, most of all. (Boy, 11 years (n.d.) as cited in Ermi & Mäyrä, 2005, p. 6)

The literature on Artificial Intelligence (AI), Virtual Reality (VR) and digital gaming includes several studies on immersion and presence. Slater, Linakis, Usoh, Kooper, and Street (1996) define immersion as a “quantifiable description of technology” (p. 3). Slater et al. identify five characteristics of immersion and immersive virtual environment: extensive, surrounding, inclusive, vivid, and matching. Extensiveness refers to the quality of the displays which are supported by sensory systems; virtual settings should be surrounding, which means the information transferred goes through all sense organs of the agent; being inclusive refers to the isolation from the real life environment; vividness considers the enhancement, content of the information delivered, resolution and quality of displays in addition to the quality of sensory information created; and matching addresses the appropriate feedback to the players’ actions which requires body tracking sensors (Slater et al., 1996; Steuer, 1992). McMahan (2003) suggests that immersive virtual reality or 3-D games should have three characteristics: the conventions of the digital environment should closely satisfy the expectations of the user; the user should be challenged in the virtual learning environment; and there should be a consistent virtual environment design.

Ermi and Mäyrä (2005) define sensory immersion as the impact of audio-visual components on the user; imaginative immersion as empathizing with the game character –avatar; and challenge-based immersion as the feeling of achievement. On the other hand, Brown and Cairns (2004) identify three steps of being immersed in virtual environments. Brown and Cairns consider engagement as the first step in immersion followed by engrossment and full immersion. Virtual settings should provide engaging experiences for the users. According to Brown and Cairns, two conditions need to be addressed for engagement: addressing users' preferences and expectations, and easy investigation of the game and how to play. Users move to the second level (engrossment) when they overcome the challenges from the engagement level. The biggest challenge at the engrossment level is game design and construction, which affect the players' emotions and could make them feel more isolated from their real life setting (Brown & Cairns). One of the users who participated in the study of Brown and Cairns describes his feelings as "A Zen-like state where your hands just seem to know what to do, and your mind just carries on with the story" (p. 1299).

The relation between immersion and presence is not clear although it is a fact that one takes strength from the other. For example, Brown and Cairns (2004) define the final stage of immersion, which is total immersion, as presence while Schuemie, Van Der Straaten, Krijn and Van Der Mast (2001) think both involvement and immersion are necessary conditions to experience presence. It is also notable what Brown and Cairns quote from the participants of their study in order to develop a better understanding of presence because all these quotations are evidences of how virtual settings become the actual environments while interacting with the digitally-generated virtual settings. The participants reported that "When you stop thinking about the fact that you're playing a computer game and you're just in a computer"; "I suppose it's best described as a sense of being cut off from the world you actually inhabit."; "You just forget about the things around you and you're focused on what you're doing in the game"; "You feel like you're there" (Brown & Cairns, p. 7). Newman (2002a) also reports that "[i]n recounting their play, videogame players talk of 'inhabiting worlds' and the experience of 'being there' rather than remotely controlling or manipulating icons or characters" (p. 405). Ferrai (2007) claims that research on immersion and presence in gaming emphasizes the subjective experiences of users. For example, the degree of subjective presence is examined through a questionnaire, and the study concludes that presence in virtual settings depends on the natural interactions with the virtual world that imitates the real world (Witmer & Singer, 1998 as cited in Jennett, Cox, Cairns, Dhoparee, Epps, Tijs, & Walton, 2008). However, as Jennett et al. claim, presence can be measured without subjective approaches from a Gibsonian perspective since "presence is defined as tantamount to successfully supported action in the environment" (p.7).

Zahorik and Jenison (1998) claim that when the environment responds to the user's actions in a way which is perceived as lawful, presence is more likely to occur. Therefore they argue that presence should be measured by investigating the coupling between perception and action and assessing the degree of lawfulness between the virtual environment and the real world (Jennett et al., 2008, p. 7)

Jennett et al. (2008) summarize that "whereas presence is often viewed as a state of mind, we argue that immersion is an experience in time" (p.643). Actions or physical movements and perceptions have an important role on presence in virtual settings as they are important in real life settings. Slater, Usoh, and Steed (1995) note that presence in virtual settings could be enriched when players' body movements and sensory feedback generated by digital displays strongly overlaps. Level and typology of immersion in virtual settings can be evaluated through the players' body movements (Ferrai, 2007). As the importance of actions and perceptions are discussed under the framework of cognitive theories, hereafter, the chapter focuses on player-avatar identity development in relation to kinesthetic gameplay.

Immersion, Presence, and Kinesthetic Gameplay

Gaming and virtual reality literature include numerous research studies on presence and immersion (see Bianchi-Berthouze, 2013; Ermi & Mäyrä, 2005). Rehak (2006) emphasizes that players actually feel being and existing in virtual learning environments because of their avatars. Thus, in virtual settings which include digital games, avatars that are the digital characters controlled by players represent the body of the players because immersion and presence studies show that there is a strong connection between players and avatars during game-play. In order to clarify the close relationship between players and avatars, Nørgård (2011) claims that "in player-avatar identity it is the avatars that are being embedded within the players' body schema rather than it is the players that are being prosthetically extended to the avatars" (p. 1). Avatars (digital body) act within virtual environments as physical bodies act in real life settings. When the strong connection between avatars and players is considered, it is natural to hold that players theoretically act in virtual settings when they feel high-level immersion and presence which is a feeling of being there.

The relation between avatars and players cannot be well supported by physical actions in virtual settings since the flexibility for physical activity is limited by handheld controllers and input devices. Indeed, the body tries to tolerate this deficiency through conscious or unconscious physical actions in the real world during gameplay. For example, Bianchi-Berthouze (2013) observes non-game related body movements that include "task-facilitating movements supporting the control of the game" (p. 11). Newman (1998) terms these body movements "non-registered inputs and responses" (as cited in Newman, 2002a, p. 410). Such non-registered inputs are generally considered evidence for presence and engagement or disengagement. Bianchi-Berthouze summarizes that body movements which are not required to play the game include fidgeting movements that represent affective expressions such as boredom, discomfort, disengagement; stillness which is the evidence of concentration and engagement in the game; and movements that support gameplay.

From the author's perspective such non-registered inputs are evidence of the need for physical action to complete the intertwined interaction between cognition, environment, and physical action-perception in virtual settings to satisfy the requirements for natural cognitive development and learning. This notion will be discussed in detail throughout the chapter by providing real life examples and observations during gameplay or interaction in virtual settings. In order to discuss game-play, cognitive development, and learning under the framework of ecumenical enactivism, the author theoretically matches the physical body with avatars by emphasizing the presence and immersion in virtual settings, real world environments with virtual environments by looking through an ecological perspective, and physical action with kinesthetic gameplay by emphasizing the role of recent advancements in digital gaming. Hereafter, enactivism refers to ecumenical enactivism, cognitive agent refers to human being, and virtual settings refer to virtual reality and digital games.

Player-Avatar Identity

The relationship between the player and the avatar is critical because avatars are the digital characters in which players enact during gameplay. Gee (2008) defines player-avatar identity as "projective beings" (p. 260) because avatars are labeled as projects managed by players whose goals and objectives are embedded into them. Nørgård (2011) emphasizes that "avatars become players' embodied minds which are used to carry out players' cognitive goals and intentions in the digital sphere" (p. 3). According to Nørgård, avatars are: the cognitive tools used by players which means players think with the avatars; containers of players' minds which explains how players think in avatars; players' new mind so that players think as avatars; or projects that players transfer their intentionality through avatars. The latter considers player-avatar-identity as "a relation of mentalism where players are immersed in the projection, transmission or transportation to avatars as embodied minds" (Nørgård, p. 1). Gregersen and Grodal (2009) emphasize thinking through avatars to discuss avatar-player identity by noting that computer games are digital mediums that provide opportunities for embodied brains to interact with the world and other players (as cited in Nørgård, p. 3). Nørgård claims that the literature of player-avatar identity yields five common themes: visuality, cognition, dramaturgy, prosthesis, and sociality. In addition to these five themes, Nørgård proposes a sixth stance for player-avatar identity which is corporeal connection that also makes sense under the framework of enactivism.

This [corporeal connection] is done by moving through the stereotypical stances within player-avatar identity once more, but now with a viewpoint explicitly grounded in corporeality and locomotion, thus, enabling an overall movement: from body images to body schemas and from visual perspectives to 'handsight,'; from instrumental/intentional transmission to corporeal locomotion and form projected minds to body memory; from role-play, pretense and performance to digital corporeality; from corporeal extension, prostheses and extending tools to corporeal incorporation, handcraft and implemented tools; and from self-representation and identity-play to self-being and self-doing (Nørgård, 2011, p. 5).

Role of Physical Actions

Recent advancements in gaming technology introduce players to experience new models of human computer interaction. Newman (2002b) emphasizes that "the pleasures of videogame play are not principally visual, but rather are kinaesthetic" (para. 5). Players are able to control avatars in virtual settings through natural physical movements which also possibly affect their immersion and presence because of motion tracking systems shipped with gaming consoles. Bianchi-Berthouze, Kim, and Patel (2007) emphasize that "new types of controllers and the involvement of the body not only affect the level of immersion but also the type of immersion" (as cited in Ferrai, 2007, p. 8). Heeter (1992) explains that "[i]n immersion VR, a sense of personal presence is based in part on simulating real world perceptions. You know you are "there" because sounds and images in the virtual world respond like the real world to your head movements. Seeing your virtual hand move when your real hand moves adds to the illusion" (para. 13). Slater, Steed, McCarthy and Maringelli (1998) clarify that the sense of presence in virtual settings is affected by body movements. In a recent study, Bianchi-Berthouze (2013) investigates how the perception of the players' own body-movements impacts the players' cognitive and emotional experience and concludes that the increased physical motion is positively correlated with the engagement level of the player. Likewise, Bianchi-Berthouze, Kim, and Patel report similar results which emphasize that the engagement level of the player increases and affective experience of the player strengthens when body movement increases. Full-body experience supports the sense of presence, triggers the affective domains of interaction, and employs the regulatory assets of affect (Bianchi-Berthouze, Kim, & Patel). Ferrai concludes that game players report more satisfactory and exciting gaming experience when they are physically active during game-play. Slater et al. report that there is a significant positive correlation between the amount of physical action and reported sense of presence, and suggest that body movement and sense of presence creates a loop in which increases in body movement cause high level presence, and high level presence generates increased physical action.

The sixth stance, corporeal connection, of player-avatar identity becomes more important in kinesthetic game-play when the role of the physical actions in cognition is considered. Nørgård (2011) claims that players and avatars are corporeally engaged, and players' body schemas absorb the avatars regardless of their appearance hence "[p]layers and avatars become dynamically interacting units where learning to play as player-avatar is to enrich one's body schema and acquire new digital-locomotive possibilities through corporeal locomotion" (p. 6). Nørgård defines that corporeal locomotion is "what establishes and upholds their [players'] avatarian connection; players can only 'become' avatars by letting corporeal locomotion flow from their hands" (p. 8). According to Nørgård, player avatar-identity raises in a virtual setting where "identity exists within and through the player's hands and only emerge through corporeal effort" (p. 6). Nørgård believes that avatars are the expressions of players' corporeal work and they are "players' body schemas in action" (p. 6), and discusses body schematic interaction as kinaesthetic action in virtual settings to criticize player-avatar identity from a cognitive perspective. Nørgård proposes strong arguments on memory by describing the player-avatar identity as "a relation stored and recalled as body memory" (p. 8) which puts more emphasis on enactivist cognition than embodied and situated cognition.

Player avatar identity emerges from the inseparable kin-aesthetic streams of players' locomotive corporeality fused with avatars' locomotive digitality. Entailing that player-avatar identity is based on the coming together of corporeal digitality and digital corporeality within players' unified body schemas as players develop and derive pleasure from their handcrafting skills, rather than based on the transmission of their thinking minds. (Nørgård, 2011, p. 8)

Nørgård (2011) claims that there is a two way connection between player and avatar in player-avatar identity, and "[i]n games [or virtual settings] players are concurrently existing as 'players-as-avatars' and as 'avatars-as-players'" (p. 10).

[T]he avatarian connection is not an in-technology or in-bodies experience but an in-body experience; where the avatarian connection is contained within the process of making. As a result, a body schematic fusion between players-as-avatars and avatars-as-players occurs, making the avatar part of the players' body rather than the other way around... [T]hey [players] become players-as avatars- as-players; they move their hands as they move on the screen. Whenever they want to make something happen as avatars in the digital sphere, they have to take action as players in the corporeal sphere. Players-as-avatars-as-players are fundamentally characterized, not by inhabiting, but by being corporeal digital bodies inhabiting the gameworld (Nørgård, 2011, p. 12-13)

Impacts on Learning and Cognitive Development

Kinesthetic Gameplay from an Enactive Perspective: Mutual Relationship

Enactivism is an emerging approach in relation to life-mind continuity thesis (see Froese, 2009). It is possible and appropriate to discuss game-play, physical actions, learning and cognitive development from an educational perspective under the framework of the enactivist approach since enactivism has a natural and realistic perspective on cognition and learning. Gaming experience provides great opportunities to study enactivism and vice versa enactivist principles provide supportive arguments for better –educational- game design. The author poses several analogies from real life to discuss the mutual relationship between enactivism and gameplay by emphasizing the similarities and differences of being a cognitive agent in virtual and real life settings.

Enactivism is built on embodied-embedded cognition, and the core element of enactivism is the cognitive agent's actions. The cognitive agent is enacting in real life settings, and it is not appropriate to evaluate body, cognition and environment in isolation. As discussed previously, body and cognition are inseparable, and body acts in the environment. The physical actions of a cognitive agent in real life settings are extremely natural, and it is difficult to study the impact of each factor separately. When traditional (handheld-controller) gaming is considered, the situation changes since all the factors of enactivism are artificially satisfied except physical action. When immersion and presence occur at optimum level and player-avatar identity increases, two hypothetical assumptions could possibly be made:

1. Players isolate themselves from the real world and feel that they are in the virtual setting, so the virtual environment becomes their real environment.
2. Players become avatars as avatars become players in virtual settings, and avatars' actions become players' actions.

The latter is the place where the intertwined interaction between body, actions, perceptions, cognition and environment is broken because the players' physical actions are limited to finger movements, and there is a mismatch between what the avatar performs and what the player is capable of performing. At that moment, the mutual relationship between enactivism and kinesthetic gameplay becomes more obvious because of non-registered inputs that are observed by researchers and game players. These non-registered inputs which are emphasized as evidence of disengagement in research studies (e.g. Bianchi-Berthouze, 2013) are the observed physical responses performed by the cognitive agents' body when the physical actions of the cognitive agent are limited. These non-registered inputs are the physical attempts of the body to complete intertwined interaction between body, actions, perceptions, cognition and environment to achieve perfect naturalism. In real life settings, it is difficult to observe the actions in relation to cognition and environment since the flow is so natural. However, when the cognitive agent is in virtual settings, players' are forced to be in a new environment in which they are not physically active. Because of the mismatch between the players' physical actions in real life and the actions of the avatars in virtual settings, the role of physical action in cognition and interaction with environment becomes more evident. The following real-life analogies might help to clarify the notion behind non-registered inputs in gameplay.

Starting from the early days of digital gaming, totally immersive players move the controllers up, down, right or left while playing the Super Mario game when they want the character to jump, slow down or accelerate. Such physical responses are not limited with controller movements, and it is possible to observe highly immersed players' attempts to jump during the gameplay. This is because their physical actions are limited, and their body physically responds to match the character's actions at most. Second, highly immersive players lean right or left while playing car race games. Such leaning movements are also the physical responses of the body to match the physical actions performed by the character. Third, when they are totally immersed, audiences react to a thrown arrow in a 3-D movie, scream, laugh or cry. Although there are several affective factors behind such behaviors, these are the physical responses of our bodies to reach perfect naturalism. Forth, some cognitive agents agitate their legs when they are bored or feel stressed in a meeting or in a doctor appointment, but they are not able to leave. Likewise, the body of the cognitive agent consciously or unconsciously respond to musical rhythm by tapping foot. Indeed, whatever the cognitive agent experiences and shows as reflective behaviors in the real life environment might also be given as examples. Non-immersive players who do not feel high level presence might not perform such physical responses since they are not fully isolated from the real life settings and they are aware of their real life surroundings, so their cognitive loop is strongly tied in the real life settings.

The question that needs to be asked is why does the body perform non-registered inputs under certain physical limitations in both real and virtual settings if the enactivism hypothesis is false? If the cognition is only embodied, embedded, extended or affective, why does the body consciously or unconsciously physically respond when the agent is fully engaged with the environment but physically limited? The human body physically acts because this is what it has cognitively constructed and learned. A baby starts its first movements in the womb. The baby knows how to get milk from the mother because he drinks amniotic fluid and sucks his finger starting at early stages of pregnancy. The body leans right or left during gameplay because it has constructed the cognition and has learned in real life that it needs to lean to resist centrifugal force while a car is turning a curve. The body is aware of the arrow in a 3-D movie because the cognitive agent has learned that s/he needs to escape from it. After few attempts, either the body learns that it is harmless, or it becomes aware of its real surrounding and realizes that it is in movie-theater, not in a battle field. The leg agitates because the cognitive agent has learned based on his previous experiences that either he needs to walk away, or manipulate the environment or direct attention to something else when he is bored or feels stressed.

If learners are not provided opportunities for being physically active, they imagine that they are physically active to achieve the learning goal, but this process causes delays to achieve desired learning outcomes. This notion is also true for all living cognitive agents and can be generalized to learning abstract concepts such as mathematics and language. For example, finger counting is one of the first steps in learning mathematics, and geometry has been practiced by drawing. Cognitive development starts with first movements in the womb, and since then whatever cognitive agents learn which includes language and abstract concepts such as love and happiness is built on physical actions far deep in the subconscious. For instance, if a toddler is asked to define love at early ages, first few words could possibly include action verbs such as hugging, kissing, touching or caressing. If cognitive agents are not capable of physically acting or doing, they imagine as they do it in order to construct cognition and learning as they do in many educational settings today. Salthouse (2009) reports that "age-related cognitive decline begin in healthy educated adults when they are in their 20s and 30s" (p. 507). Can it be a coincidence cognitive decline begins when physical actions decline?

Kinesthetic Gameplay, Cognitive Development, and Learning

One learns by doing a thing; for though you think you know it, you have not certainty until you try. (Sophocles, n. d.)

The physical action-perception, cognition, body (avatars) and (virtual) environment loop is complete in gaming settings with the introduction of kinesthetic game-playing or full-body control. If the assumptions of enactivism are considered, cognition and learning increase as a result of the intertwined interaction between body, physical action-perception, and environment. Bautista, Roth and Thom (2011) investigated the embodied-enactivist account on mathematical learning and concluded that "mathematical knowing and learning is only possible when the kinetic movement of the body – or rather, the flesh – is conceptualized as a necessary pre-requisite for mathematical sense, and when mind and living/lived body are conceived of as indistinguishable and irreducible structures" (p. 366). Jaimes and Sebe (2007) describe that "[e]nactive knowledge is not simply multisensory mediated knowledge, but knowledge stored in the form of motor responses and acquired by the act of 'doing'" (p. 118). Thus, people need to be in learning environments in which learners are physically active and cognitively engaged to learn in real life settings, and the situation is the same for virtual settings including games for education. An absolutely perfect learning environment in which learners are fully cognitively engaged can be designed in virtual settings, but it is possible that players will not be able to learn at mastery level without being physically active in the virtual learning setting. Theoretically, in this new virtual learning setting, learners are forced to be cognitively engaged, but not to be physically active. In one sense, this is against the nature of cognitive development and learning from an enactivist perspective. Educational games could possibly become more effective learning tools in P-12 education if virtual learning settings that support the triangle of body, actions-perceptions, and environment in coordination are designed.

Physical actions are as closely related to learning and cognitive development in virtual settings as they are essential in real life settings. "Kinetic movement constitutes the ground of all human knowing" (Bautista, Roth, and Thom, 2011, p. 363). The role of the human body and its motor processes in interpreting meaning and understanding sentences about abstract concepts is significant (Barsalou, 1999; Glenberg & Robertson, 2000; Glenberg & Kaschak, 2002; Zwaan & Taylor, 2006 as cited in Cook, Mitchell & Goldin-Meadow, 2008, p. 1054). As a result of an experimental study on the role of gestures on learning mathematics, Cook, Mitchell and Goldin-Meadow report that children retain the knowledge learned from instruction longer when they are encouraged to instantiate a new concept in their hands. Similarly, Chang et al. (2013) adopted Microsoft Kinect© for teaching through gesture-based multimedia to analyze the retention of the knowledge learned from the presentation, which is about multiple intelligences and reported that immediate and delayed test results indicated that knowledge retention was at the desired level. Although the authors report satisfactory knowledge retention, one of the limitations of their study is to use single group pretest-posttest design, so there is no control group to compare the results. Bautista, Roth, and Thom focus on insight learning in mathematics by emphasizing incarnation and theory of mathematics in the flesh, and claim that "[i]n our approach, mathematical knowing is not thought as arising from 'intellectual' forms of consciousness, such as sensorimotor image schemas (Johnson, 1987), but from 'incarnate' forms of consciousness such as the kinetic movements of our lived/living body" (p. 366). As increasing numbers of studies investigate the effectiveness of physical actions on learning and cognitive development in real life studies, it might not be surprising to experience similar outcomes in virtual settings after kinesthetic game play becomes available for learners.

Acting on the objects in virtual settings allows users to learn by doing, to receive feedback on their actions, to examine the world, and to think on their own comprehension (Chee, 2007). Nørgård (2011) emphasizes Edward Casey's ideas on body memory in player-avatar identity which becomes more important when the relationship between physical actions and learning is considered. According to Nørgård, "as the avatarian connection is not an out-of-body experience, but an in-body experience characterized by corporeal handcraft and locomotion it is also within players' bodies that the avatarian connection is stored and recalled" (p. 9).

The memories of heavily played games are just as much recalled as corporeal-locomotive patterns and memories in the body. Players' bodies resonate with the avatar-shaped corporeal movements, im-

printed in their body schemas as unique rhythmic compositions. My hands still remember Summer Games (Epyx/U.S. Gold, 1984) for the Commodore 64; how my left hand, in sprinting, franticly but rhythmically pushed the joystick from side to side as I sprinted on the screen. My memories of Summer Games are (also) corporeal-locomotive memories - The platform diving exercise remembered as the gyrating of the joystick in a carefully metered tempo in perfect unison with my digital corporeality as my hands crafted a flawlessly executed dive from the springboard. In this way, players acquire and recall their avatarian connections through handcraft, not through 'mindcraft' (or 'eyecraft'). (Nørgård, 2011, p. 9).

Casey (1987) states that "I speak of 'body memory,' not of 'memory of the body.' Body memory alludes to memory that is intrinsic to the body, to its own ways of remembering: how we remember in and by and through the body" (p. 147). Nørgård (2011) clarifies that players' hands remember their ways to controllers during gaming activity since players' bodies remember their own activity. Referring to the question the author asked in the introduction section of the chapter about learning how to dance, the answer, "player who controls the avatar by physically dancing learns better" seems to be true since the whole body of the player learns and remembers the movements and figures whereas only the fingers of the second player remember how to dance with the help of corporeal connection and body memory. Although immediate evaluation and comparison of players' dance performances might yield similar results, it is possible that the player who plays the game kinesthetically retains the knowledge longer.

CONCLUSION

Virtual settings have become more effective learning mediums after the introduction of kinesthetic gameplay, full-body gaming or in a general term being physically active in virtual settings. Players experience more natural and enriched human-computer interaction because of recent advancements in gaming technology. Kinesthetic game playing, enactivism and cognitive development in enactivism shed light on designing better virtual worlds and educational games for mastery learning. Digital games or virtual learning environments that use traditional controllers or mouse-keyboard combinations limit the players' physical action. As a result, desired learning outcomes cannot always be achieved in virtual settings at mastery level, or they cannot be retained longer. As it is emphasized, current educational games force learners to become highly engaged but physically inactive. Despite the fact that there is limited physical action such as using a keyboard or controller, learning occurs in virtual learning environments because of raised player-avatar identity, high level immersion, and imagination of being physically active. However, these learning outcomes should be approached with caution by considering the difference between memorization and actual learning because there is a lack of bodily involvement which also affect player-avatar identity development and cognitive construction. Current educational games, which do not offer kinesthetic game-play, provide learning opportunities for short-time memorization whereas as it is supported by research studies (e.g. Chang et al., 2013; Cook, Mitchell, & Goldin-Meadow, 2008), virtual learning opportunities which includes physical action supports long-term knowledge gains.

Implications for Educational Gaming

Direct physical interaction with the world is an essential factor of cognitive development, and being physically active and interactive provides unique opportunities for learning and cognitive development which reading and listening do not. According to Piaget (1952), cognitive development should be supported by not only mental activity but also physical activity (as cited in Klemmer, Hartmann, & Takayama, 2006, p. 141). Unfortunately, a majority of the educational settings fall short providing hands-on learning in which learners are physically active although there is a dramatic shift from teacher-centered pedagogy to student-centered pedagogy. Some of these student-centered pedagogies such as the Montessori Approach, the Reggio Emilia Approach, and the Waldorf Approach have shown great success. The common ground of all these three approaches is to provide activity-based self-learning opportunities in which learners are physically active to some degree.

Call for a New Educational Approach

The popular educational philosophy of 21st century is constructivism which emphasizes interactivity and hands-on learning, and there are several learning approaches such as discovery learning, experiential learning, problem-based learning and situated learning. However, with the rise of enactivism, a more comprehensive and natural pedagogical approach which involves the principles of all previous pedagogical approaches is needed. Such a natural learning approach, which is also ecumenical, considers learning and cognitive development as it occurs naturally in the real world and centers cognitive development in the middle of the body, action-perception, and environment loop, and integrates learning theories in a way to support cognitive development from an enactivist perspective. The natural learning approach is built on ecumenical enactivism which assumes that cognition is embodied, embedded, extended and affected if it is enacted (Ward & Stapleton, 2012). It hypothesizes that learning and cognitive development cannot be explained by a single learning theory such as constructivism since constructivism explains only one aspect of cognitive development which is cognition is constructive. If it is natural, it is affective, behaviorist, constructivist, and humanist. This notion is expandable, and should be investigated in further research studies.

Kinesthetic game playing is a cornerstone in educational games. Motion tracking systems which are commercially available provide full body gaming for everyone and have a great potential for enhancing learning settings either by supporting real-world learning environments or creating their own learning environments. Although several digital games controlled by physical action are available on the shelves, they emphasize entertainment more than pedagogy, and their implementation in current school curricula is challenging. By considering the design principles of digital gaming which provides total immersion and raises high level player-avatar identity, unique educational (serious) games which allow kinesthetic gameplay can be produced for all levels of P-12 education. Indeed, it does not necessarily need to be a digital game, and designers who are experts in developing any kind of virtual setting are able to design perfect learning environments in which learning occurs naturally through interaction between body, environment, physical actions and perceptions.

Directions for Future Research

Both enactivism and kinesthetic gaming are relatively new concepts and there is limited experimental research available in the literature. Although the effects of kinesthetic movement on learning has emerged in recent years, more comprehensive experimental research is needed. On the other hand, enactivism could possibly be investigated as a central cognitive approach in learning, and its effects on learning and knowledge retention could be examined through longitudinal studies. Kinesthetic gaming has attracted researchers' attention not only in education, but also in cognitive science. However, current games that provide kinesthetic movement are not pedagogically well-designed. Thus, it is essential to examine kinesthetic game-play in a well-designed virtual environment in which players are totally immersed and physically active.

In conclusion, kinesthetic game-play has its roots in cognitive science and education. A comparison of kinesthetic-game play and traditional gameplay which uses handheld controllers by considering the non-registered inputs as cognitive agents' efforts to complete the enactive loop could possibly yield strong arguments in terms of cognitive development and learning. It is difficult to discuss mastery learning in educational settings unless the cognitive agents interact with an environment in which they are physically active and highly engaged. Current virtual learning environments force students to be totally immersed but physically inactive. This educational practice is against the nature of cognitive development and learning. As it is discussed, learning occurs not only in educational virtual settings but also in real life educational settings in which the cognitive agent is not physically active. However, this is a form of short-term memorization, and it is challenging to retain knowledge gained from educational activities for a long time unless participants cognitively or physically relate what they learn with previous experiences through physical actions. Learning theories such as behaviorism, constructivism and cognitivism emphasize different aspects of learning. As the ecumenical enactivism approach brings several cognitive theories together, the natural (ecumenical) approach, which combines all the previous learning theories through enactivism is proposed. All living organisms physically act and move. Not only every single cell of a cognitive organism is constantly in physical action, but also the whole universe and whatever is living in between two are in action and constantly moving. Keep in mind that life begins with a moving single cell, and we are living in an environment which is spinning at the speed of 1670 kilometers per hour (NASA, 2014).

REFERENCES

Anderson, M. L. (2003). Embodied cognition: A field guide. *Artificial Intelligence*, *149*(1), 91–130. doi:10.1016/S0004-3702(03)00054-7

Barsalou, L. (1999). Perceptions of perceptual symbols. *Behavioral and Brain Sciences*, *22*(4), 637–660. doi:10.1017/S0140525X99532147 PMID:11301525

Bautista, A., Roth, W. M., & Thom, J. S. (2011). Knowing, insight learning, and the integrity of kinetic movement. *Interchange*, *42*(4), 363–388. doi:10.1007/s10780-012-9164-9

Best, J. R. (2013). Exergaming in youth: Effects on physical and cognitive health. *Zeitschrift fur Psychologie mit Zeitschrift fur Angewandte Psychologie*, *221*(2), 72–78. doi:10.1027/2151-2604/a000137 PMID:25097828

Bianchi-Berthouze, N. (2013). Understanding the role of body movement in player engagement. *Human-Computer Interaction*, *28*(1), 40–75.

Bianchi-Berthouze, N., Kim, W., & Patel, D. (2007). Does body movement engage you more in digital game play? And Why? In A. Paiva, R. Prada, R.W. Picard (Eds.), Lecture Notes in Computer Science: Affective Computing and Intelligent Interaction. (Vol. LNCS 4738, pp. 102-113). Berlin, Germany: Springer doi:10.1007/978-3-540-74889-2_10

Brown, E., & Cairns, P. (2004). A grounded investigation of game immersion. In E. Dykstra-Erickson & M. Tscheligi (Eds.), *CHI'04 Extended Abstracts on Human Factors in Computing Systems* (pp. 1297–1300). New York, NY: ACM; doi:10.1145/985921.986048

Bruner, J. S. (1966). *Toward a theory of instruction*. Cambridge, MA: Belkapp Press.

Casey, E. S. (1987). *Remembering: A Phenomenological Study*. Bloomington, IN: Indiana University Press.

Chalmers, D. (2008). Foreword to Andy Clark's supersizing the mind. In A. Clark (Ed.), *Supersizing the mind: Embodiment, action, and cognitive extension* (pp. ix–xvi). New York, NY: Oxford University Press.

Chang, C. Y., Chien, Y. T., Chiang, C. Y., Lin, M. C., & Lai, H. C. (2013). Embodying gesture-based multimedia to improve learning. *British Journal of Educational Technology*, *44*(1), E5–E9. doi:10.1111/j.1467-8535.2012.01311.x

Chao, K. J., Huang, H. W., Fang, W. C., & Chen, N. S. (2013). Embodied play to learn: Exploring Kinect-facilitated memory performance. *British Journal of Educational Technology*, *44*(5), 151–155. doi:10.1111/bjet.12018

Chee, Y. S. (2007). Embodiment, embeddedness, and experience: Game-based learning and the construction of identity. *Research and Practice in Technology Enhanced Learning*, *2*(1), 3–30. doi:10.1142/S1793206807000282

Chen, K. W., Hsu, F. C., Hsieh, Y. Z., & Chou, C. H. (2014). *To design an interactive learning system for child by integrating blocks with Kinect*. Paper presented at the Global Engineering Education Conference (EDUCON) (pp. 20-22). Istanbul, Turkey. IEEE

Cheok, A. D., Yang, X., Ying, Z. Z., Billinghurst, M., & Kato, H. (2002). Touch-space: Mixed reality game space based on ubiquitous, tangible, and social computing. *Personal and Ubiquitous Computing*, *6*(5), 430–442. doi:10.1007/s007790200047

Clancey, W. J. (1997). *Situated cognition: On human knowledge and computer representations*. Cambridge, U.K.: Cambridge University Press.

Clark, A. (1997). *Being there: Putting brain, body, and world together again*. Cambridge, MA: MIT Press.

Clark, A. (2008). *Supersizing the mind: Embodiment, action, and cognitive extension*. Oxford, U.K.: Oxford University Press. doi:10.1093/acprof:oso/9780195333213.001.0001

Clark, A., & Chalmers, D. (1998). The extended mind. *Analysis*, *58*(1), 7–19. doi:10.1093/analys/58.1.7

Cook, S. W., Mitchell, Z., & Goldin-Meadow, S. (2008). Gesturing makes learning last. *Cognition*, *106*(2), 1047–1058. doi:10.1016/j.cognition.2007.04.010 PMID:17560971

Ermi, L., & Mäyrä, F. (2005). *Fundamental Components of the Gameplay Experience: Analysing Immersion*. Paper presented at DiGRA 2005 Conference: Changing Views–Worlds in Play (pp. 88-115).Vancouver, Canada.

Fenici, M. (2012). Embodied social cognition and embedded theory of mind. *Biolinguistics*, *6*, 276–307.

Ferrai, D. A. (2007). *An investigation on the relationships between immersion, body movements and extraversion in computer games play* [Unpublished master's thesis]. UCL. Retrieved from https://www.ucl.ac.uk/uclic/studying/taught-courses/distinction-projects/2006_theses/ferrai.pdf

Froese, T. (2009). *Sociality and the life-mind continuity thesis: A study in evolutionary robotics*. [Unpublished doctoral dissertation]. University of Sussex. U.K. Retrieved from https://www.academia.edu/584795/Sociality_and_the_Life-Mind_Continuity_Thesis_A_Study_in_Evolutionary_Robotics

Froese, T., & Di Paolo, E. A. (2009). Sociality and the life–mind continuity thesis. *Phenomenology and the Cognitive Sciences, 8*(4), 439-463.

Gee, J. P. (2008). Video games and embodiment. *Games and Culture*, *3*(3-4), 253–263. doi:10.1177/1555412008317309

Gibson, J. J. (1979). *The ecological approach to visual perception*. Boston, MA: Houghton Mifflin.

Glenberg, A. M., & Kaschak, M. P. (2002). Grounding language in action. *Psychonomic Bulletin & Review*, *9*(3), 558–565. doi:10.3758/BF03196313 PMID:12412897

Glenberg, A. M., & Robertson, D. A. (2000). Symbol grounding and meaning: A comparison of high-dimensional and embodied theories of meaning. *Journal of Memory and Language*, *43*(3), 379–401. doi:10.1006/jmla.2000.2714

Gredler, M. E. (1996). 17 educational games and simulations: A technology in search of a (research) paradigm. *Technology (Elmsford, N.Y.)*, *39*, 521–540.

Gregersen, A., & Grodal, T. (2009). Embodiment and interface. In Wolf (Ed.), The video game theory reader (pp. 65-85), New York, NY: Routlege

Heeter, C. (1992). Being there: The subjective experience of presence. *Presence (Cambridge, Mass.)*, *1*(2), 262–271.

Heinich, R., Molenda, M., Russell, J. D., & Smaldino, S. E. (1996). *Instructional media and technologies for learning* (5th ed.). Englewood Cliffs, NJ: Prentice Hall.

Hew, K. F., & Cheung, W. S. (2010). Use of three-dimensional (3-D) immersive virtual worlds in K-12 and higher education settings: A review of the research. *British Journal of Educational Technology*, *41*(1), 33–55. doi:10.1111/j.1467-8535.2008.00900.x

Homer, B. D., Kinzer, C. K., Plass, J. L., Letourneau, S. M., Hoffman, D., Bromley, M., & Kornak, Y. et al. (2014). Moved to learn: The effects of interactivity in a Kinect-based literacy game for beginning readers. *Computers & Education*, *74*, 37–49. doi:10.1016/j.compedu.2014.01.007

Huitt, W., & Hummel, J. (2003). Piaget's theory of cognitive development. *Educational Psychology Interactive*, *3*(2), 1–24.

Hurley, S. (2008). The shared circuits model (SCM): How control, mirroring, and simulation can enable imitation, deliberation, and mindreading. *Behavioral and Brain Sciences*, *31*(1), 1–22. doi:10.1017/S0140525X07003123 PMID:18394222

Hutchins, E. (1995). *Cognition in the Wild*. Cambridge, MA: MIT Press.

Hutchins, E. (2010). Enaction, imagination, and insight. In J. R. Stewart, O. Gapenne, & E. A. Di Paolo (Eds.), *Enaction: Towards a new paradigm for cognitive science* (pp. 425–450). Cambridge, MA: MIT Press. doi:10.7551/mitpress/9780262014601.003.0016

Isbister, K., Karlesky, M., Frye, J., & Rao, R. (2012). Scoop: A movement-based math game designed to reduce math anxiety. In J. A. Konstan, E. H. Chi, & K. Höök (Eds.), *CHI'12 Extended Abstracts on Human Factors in Computing Systems,* Austin, TX (pp. 1075–1078). ACM. doi:10.1145/2212776.2212389

Jaimes, A., & Sebe, N. (2007). Multimodal human–computer interaction: A survey. *Computer Vision and Image Understanding*, *108*(1-2), 116–134. doi:10.1016/j.cviu.2006.10.019

Jennett, C., Cox, A. L., Cairns, P., Dhoparee, S., Epps, A., Tijs, T., & Walton, A. (2008). Measuring and defining the experience of immersion in games. *International Journal of Human-Computer Studies*, *66*(9), 641–661. doi:10.1016/j.ijhcs.2008.04.004

Johnson, M. (1987). *The body in the mind: The bodily basis of imagination, reason, and meaning*. Chicago, IL: Chicago University Press.

Johnson-Glenberg, M. C., Koziupa, T., Birchfield, D., & Li, K. (2011). Games for learning in embodied mixed-reality environments: Principles and results. In C. Steinkuehler, C. Martin, & A. Ochsner (Eds.), *Proceedings of the 7th International Conference on Games+ Learning+ Society Conference* (pp. 129-137). Madison, WI: ETC Press.

Kirsh, D. (1995). The intelligent use of space. *Artificial Intelligence*, *73*(1-2), 31–68. doi:10.1016/0004-3702(94)00017-U

Klemmer, S. R., Hartmann, B., & Takayama, L. (2006). How bodies matter: Five themes for interaction design. In J. M. Carroll, S. Bødker, & J. Coughlin (Eds.), *Proceedings of the 6th Conference on Designing Interactive Systems* (pp. 140-149). University Park, PA. ACM. doi:10.1145/1142405.1142429

Kolb, A. Y., & Kolb, D. A. (2009). The learning way meta-cognitive aspects of experiential learning. *Simulation & Gaming*, *40*(3), 297–327. doi:10.1177/1046878108325713

Kolb, D. A. (1984). *Experiential learning: Experience as the source of learning and development*. Englewood Cliffs, NJ: Prentice Hall.

Lainema, T. (2003). *Enhancing organizational business process perception: Experiences from constructing and applying a dynamic business simulation game*. [Unpublished doctoral dissertation]. Turku School of Economics and Business Administration, Turku, FIN

Lwin, M. O., & Malik, S. (2012). The efficacy of exergames-incorporated physical education lessons in influencing drivers of physical activity: A comparison of children and pre-adolescents. *Psychology of Sport and Exercise*, *13*(6), 756–760. doi:10.1016/j.psychsport.2012.04.013

Maturana, H. R., & Varela, F. J. (1992). *The tree of knowledge: The biological roots of human understanding*. Boston, MA: Shambhala.

McLeod, S. A. (2010). Sensorimotor Stage. Retrieved from http://www.simplypsychology.org/sensorimotor.html

McLeod, S. A. (2012). Bruner. Retrieved from http://www.simplypsychology.org/bruner.html

McMahan, A. (2003). Immersion, engagement and presence. In M. J. P. Wolf & B. Perron (Eds.), *The video game theory reader* (pp. 67–86). New York, NY: Routledge.

Menary, R. (2010). *The extended mind*. Cambridge, MA: MIT Press. doi:10.7551/mitpress/9780262014038.001.0001

Nakamura, M., Kitajima, Y., Ota, J., Ogata, T., Huang, Z., Nagata, A., . . . Kanai-Pak, M. (2013). The relationship between nursing students' attitudes towards learning and effects of self-learning system using Kinect. In V.G. Duffy (Ed.), *4th international conference on digital human modeling and applications in health, safety, ergonomics, and risk management, part II: Human body modeling and ergonomics*. (Vol. LNCS 8026, pp. 111-116). Berlin, Germany: Springer.

Newman, J. (2002a). In search of the videogame player: The lives of Mario. *New Media & Society*, *4*(3), 405–422. doi:10.1177/146144480200400305

Newman, J. (2002b). The myth of the ergodic videogame. *Game studies*, *2*(1), 1-17.

Newman, J. A. (1998) *Gameworlds: Videogames, space and experience. Critically examining a player's perspective* [Unpublished doctoral dissertation]. Lancaster University (Edge Hill College), Lancashire, UK.

Nijhar, J., Bianchi-Berthouze, N., & Boguslawski, G. (2012). Does movement recognition precision affect the player experience in exertion games? In A. Nijholt, H. Hondorp, & D. Reidsma (Eds.), *Intelligent technologies for interactive entertainment* (Vol. 9, pp. 73–82). Berlin, Germany: Springer. doi:10.1007/978-3-642-30214-5_9

Noë, A. (2004). *Action in Perception*. Cambridge, MA: The MIT Press.

Nørgård, R. T. (2011). The joy of doing: The corporeal connection in player-avatar identity. Paper presented at *Philosophy of Computer Games Conference*, Athens, Greece. Retrieved from https://gameconference2011.files.wordpress.com/2010/10/thejoy1.pdf

Norman, D. A. (1993). *Things that make us smart: Defending human attributes in the age of the machine*. Reading, MA: Addison-Wesley Pub. Co.

Odenwald, S. (n. d.) What is the speed of the Earth's rotation? Retrieved from http://image.gsfc.nasa.gov/poetry/ask/a10840.html

Piaget, J. (1952). *The origins of intelligence in children*. New York, NY: International Universities Press. doi:10.1037/11494-000

Rambusch, J. (2006). The embodied and situated nature of computer game play. In proceedings of the workshop on the cognitive science of games and game play, Vancouver, Canada (pp. 1-8). Retrieved from http://jana-rambusch.net/publications/rambusch-vancouver.pdf

Rambusch, J., & Ziemke, T. (2005). The role of embodiment in situated learning. In B.G. Bara, L. Barsalou, & M. Bucciarelli (Eds.), *Proceedings of the 27th Annual Conference of the Cognitive Science Society* (pp. 1803-1808). Mahwah, NJ: Lawrence Erlbaum.

Rehak, B. (2003). Playing at being. In M. Wolf & B. Perron (Eds.), *The Video Game Theory Reader* (pp. 103–127). New York, NY: Routledge.

Reigeluth, C., & Schwartz, E. (1989). An instructional theory for the design of computer-based simulations. *Journal of Computer-Based Instruction, 16*(1), 1–10.

Robbins, P., & Aydede, M. (2009). *The Cambridge handbook of situated cognition*. Cambridge, U.K.: Cambridge University Press.

Rocha, M. (2012). Cognitive, embodied or enacted? Contemporary perspectives for HCI and interaction. Retrieved from http://trans-techresearch.net/wp-content/uploads/2010/11/Rocha-01.pdf

Roth, W. M. (2010). Incarnation: Radicalizing the embodiment of mathematics. *For the Learning of Mathematics, 30*(2), 8–17.

Roth, W. M. (2011). *Geometry as objective science in elementary classrooms. Mathematics in the flesh*. New York, NY: Routledge.

Rowlands, M. (2010). *The new science of the mind: From extended mind to embodied phenomenology*. Cambridge, MA: MIT Press. doi:10.7551/mitpress/9780262014557.001.0001

Salthouse, T. A. (2009). When does age-related cognitive decline begin? *Neurobiology of Aging, 30*(4), 507–514. doi:10.1016/j.neurobiolaging.2008.09.023 PMID:19231028

Schuemie, M. J., Van Der Straaten, P., Krijn, M., & Van Der Mast, C. A. (2001). Research on presence in virtual reality: A survey. *Cyberpsychology & Behavior*, *4*(2), 183–201. doi:10.1089/109493101300117884 PMID:11710246

Shapiro, L. A. (2011). *Embodied cognition*. New York, NY: Routledge.

Sheets-Johnstone, M. (2009). *The corporeal turn: An interdisciplinary reader*. Exeter, UK: Imprint Academic.

Slater, M., Linakis, V., Usoh, M., & Kooper, R. (1996). Immersion, presence, and performance in virtual environments: An experiment with tri-dimensional chess. Paper presented at ACM Virtual Reality Software and Technology Conference, Hong Kong (pp. 163–172). VRST. Retrieved from http://citeseerx.ist.psu.edu/viewdoc/download?doi=10.1.1.34.6594&rep=rep1&type=pdf

Slater, M., Steed, A., McCarthy, J., & Maringelli, F. (1998). The influence of body movement on subjective presence in virtual environments. *Human Factors: The Journal of the Human Factors and Ergonomics Society*, *40*(3), 469–477. doi:10.1518/001872098779591368 PMID:9849105

Slater, M., Usoh, M., & Steed, A. (1995). Taking steps: The influence of a walking technique on presence in virtual reality. *ACM Transactions on Computer-Human Interaction*, *2*(3), 201–219. doi:10.1145/210079.210084

Sophocles. (n. d.). *Experiential learning*. Retrieved from http://www.psychology.pitt.edu/experiential-learning

Squire, K. (2002). Cultural framing of computer/video games. *The International Journal of Computer Game Research*, *2*(1). Retrieved from http://www.gamestudies.org/0102/squire/

Squire, K. (2003). Video games in education. *International Journal of Intelligent Games & Simulation*, *2*(1), 49–62.

Steinkuehler, C. (2008). Massively multiplayer online games as an educational technology: An outline for research. *Educational Technology*, *48*(1), 10–21.

Steuer, J. (1992). Defining virtual reality: Dimensions determining telepresence. *Journal of Communication*, *42*(4), 73–93. doi:10.1111/j.1460-2466.1992.tb00812.x

Suchman, L. A. (1987). *Plans and situated actions: The problem of human-machine communication*. Cambridge, U.K.: Cambridge University Press.

Thompson, E. (2007). *Mind in life: Biology, phenomenology, and the sciences of mind*. Cambridge, MA: The Belknap Press of Harvard University Press.

Van Gelder, T. (1995). What might cognition be, if not computation? *The Journal of Philosophy*, *91*(7), 345–381. doi:10.2307/2941061

Varela, A. H., Thompson, E., & Rosch, E. (1991). *The embodied mind*. Cambridge, MA: MIT Press.

Ward, D., & Stapleton, M. (2012). Es are good: Cognition as enacted, embodied, embedded, affective and extended. *Advances in Consciousness Research*, *86*, 89–106. doi:10.1075/aicr.86.06war

Wilson, M. (2002). Six views of embodied cognition. *Psychonomic Bulletin & Review*, *9*(4), 625–636. doi:10.3758/BF03196322 PMID:12613670

Wilson, R. A. (2004). *Boundaries of the mind: The individual in the fragile sciences: Cognition*. Cambridge, U.K.: Cambridge University Press.

Wilson, R. A., & Foglia, L. (2011). Embodied cognition. In E.N. Zalta (Ed.), *The Stanford Encyclopedia of Philosophy, Fall 2011 Edition*. Retrieved from http://plato.stanford.edu/archives/fall2011/entries/embodied-cognition

Witmer, B. G., & Singer, M. J. (1998). Measuring presence in virtual environments: A presence questionnaire. *Presence (Cambridge, Mass.)*, *7*(3), 225–240. doi:10.1162/105474698565686

Xu, X., & Ke, F. (2014). From psychomotor to 'motorpsycho': Learning through gestures with body sensory technologies. *Educational Technology Research and Development*, *62*(6), 711–741. doi:10.1007/s11423-014-9351-8

Zahorik, P., & Jenison, R. (1998). Presence as being-in-the-world. *Presence (Cambridge, Mass.)*, *7*(1), 78–89. doi:10.1162/105474698565541

Zwaan, R. A., & Taylor, L. J. (2006). Seeing, acting, understanding: Motor resonance in language comprehension. *Journal of Experimental Psychology. General*, *135*(1), 1–11. doi:10.1037/0096-3445.135.1.1 PMID:16478313

ADDITIONAL READING

Boot, W. R., Blakely, D. P., & Simons, D. J. (2011). Do action video games improve perception and cognition? *Frontiers in Psychology*, *2*, 1–6. doi:10.3389/fpsyg.2011.00226 PMID:21949513

Cameron, B., & Dwyer, F. (2005). The effect of online gaming, cognition and feedback type in facilitating delayed achievement of different learning objectives. *Journal of Interactive Learning Research*, *16*(3), 243–258.

DiPietro, M. (2009). Experience, cognition, and video game play. In R. E. Ferdig (Ed.), *Handbook of research on effective electronic gaming in education* (Vol. 2, pp. 776–790). Hershey, PA: Medical Information Science Reference. doi:10.4018/978-1-59904-808-6.ch044

Eck, R. V. (2010). *Gaming and cognition: Theories and practice from the learning sciences*. Hershey, PA: Information Science Reference.

Feng, J., Spence, I., & Pratt, J. (2007). Playing an action video game reduces gender differences in spatial cognition. *Psychological Science*, *18*(10), 850–855. doi:10.1111/j.1467-9280.2007.01990.x PMID:17894600

Gamberini, L., Raya, M. A., Barresi, G., Fabregat, M., Ibanez, F., & Prontu, L. (2006). Cognition, technology and games for the elderly: An introduction to ELDERGAMES Project. *PsychNology Journal*, *4*(3), 285–308.

Ke, F. (2008). A case study of computer gaming for math: Engaged learning from gameplay? *Computers & Education*, *51*(4), 1609–1620. doi:10.1016/j.compedu.2008.03.003

Kiili, K. (2005). Digital game-based learning: Towards an experiential gaming model. *The Internet and Higher Education*, *8*(1), 13–24. doi:10.1016/j.iheduc.2004.12.001

Latham, A. J., Patston, L. L., & Tippett, L. J. (2013). The virtual brain: 30 years of video-game play and cognitive abilities. *Frontiers in Psychology*, *4*, 1–10. doi:10.3389/fpsyg.2013.00629 PMID:24062712

Seok, S., Meyen, E. L., & DaCosta, B. (2010). *Handbook of Research on Human Cognition and Assistive Technology: Design, Accessibility and Transdisciplinary Perspectives*. Hershey, PA: Medical Information Science Reference. doi:10.4018/978-1-61520-817-3

Spence, I., & Feng, J. (2010). Video games and spatial cognition. *Review of General Psychology*, *14*(2), 92–104. doi:10.1037/a0019491

Steinkuehler, C. A. (2008). Cognition and literacy in massively multiplayer online games. In J. Coiro, M. Knobel, C. Lankshear, & D. J. Leu (Eds.), *Handbook of Research on New Literacies* (pp. 611–634). Mahwah, NJ: Erlbaum.

KEY TERMS AND DEFINITIONS

Avatar: Computer generated digital characters controlled by players in virtual settings.

Cognitive Agent: Living organism that is capable of acting and interacting to the environment for cognitive development and learning.

Enactivism: Cognitive approach that assumes cognition is embodied, extended, affected and situated if it is enacted, and places kinesthetic movements at the center of cognitive development.

Kinesthetic Gameplay: Full-body gaming. Controlling the game mechanisms through physical action and body movements.

Motion Tracking: Motion sensing electronic devices that converts players' physical actions to digital inputs to control virtual learning environments.

Natural (Ecumenical) Learning Approach: An educational approach that is built on enactivist cognitive development and learning.

Non-Registered Inputs: Physical actions that are consciously or unconsciously performed by cognitive agent under high level immersion and presence in virtual setting.

Player-Avatar Identity: Corporeal connection between avatar and active player who controls the avatar.

Virtual Settings: Computer-generated digital environments that include digital games, educational games, mixed-reality environments, and virtual realities.

Chapter 7
The Theory and Process Involved with Educational Augmented Reality Game Design

Patrick O'Shea
Appalachian State University, USA

Chris Campbell
The University of Queensland, Australia

ABSTRACT

This chapter explores the issues associated with training teachers to become effective Augmented Reality game designers in their own educational settings. Within the context of defining and defending the use of games as instructional tools, the authors of this chapter describe a project in Queensland, Australia which involved training 26 teachers from the greater Brisbane area on the theory and process of designing narrative-based Augmented Reality games. This process resulted in usable games that the participants could then implement in their own educational setting. This chapter includes a discussion of the issues and challenges that were faced throughout this training process, and the authors propose potential solutions to address those challenges. Additionally, the authors propose future directions for further research into this area.

INTRODUCTION

It is a relatively well-worn maxim in education that the best way to learn something is to teach it. In fact, it is so well worn that it reaches all the way back to Seneca the Younger in ancient Roman society, and the Latin phrase "Docendo Discimus" (by teaching, we learn) has been adopted as the motto of educational institutions around the globe (Classical Academic Press, 2014). Yet, the educational use of games has historically relied, to a great extent, on the use of pre-packaged, self-contained materials. These games are purchased by educators or districts and are implemented in the classroom (with varying degrees of success), but aside from learning the rules of the games, their

DOI: 10.4018/978-1-4666-9629-7.ch007

use rarely embodies the philosophy of "Docendo Discimus". Educational game design and development have usually been accomplished separately from where those games are implemented. It is the purpose of this chapter to explore ways that design, development and implementation can be accomplished by the same individuals.

This chapter will provide an exploration of an alternative approach to designing and utilizing games in educational settings. Through a discussion of a teacher training program undertaken through The University of Queensland in Brisbane, Australia in conjunction with faculty from Appalachian State University in Boone, North Carolina, this chapter will lay out an argument for an alternate approach to educational game use through training teachers how to build their own specifically designed games. This training was intended to instruct K-12 teachers in and around the greater Brisbane area on how to design and build educational Augmented Reality games.

BACKGROUND

The use of games within educational settings has been debated for quite some time. McClarty et al (2012) performed a review of literature and found "mixed empirical support" for the use of digital games in educational settings while simultaneously concluding "the research supports that digital games can facilitate learning" (p. 23). Of course, this kind of mixed finding can cause confusion about the short- and long-term viability of the use of digital games in education. However, this uncertainty is a separate issue from larger concerns associated with "games" in educational settings. Many schools and school districts are wary of using "games" because they are viewed as frivolous or non-educational. What this means in practice is that before we can effectively incorporate games of any sort into educational settings, we must defend the very idea of gaming as being educationally worthy and appropriate for a classroom setting.

Nature of Games in Education

Part of the difficulty in making an argument for the use of games in education is that there is no clear-cut definition for the term "game." The Merriam-Webster dictionary defines games, among other things, as activities "engaged in for diversion or amusement" (Merriam-Webster, Inc., 2014a), which causes difficulties for many educators who see "diversion or amusement" as a distraction from education. This area does not become any clearer, however, when other definitions are explored. Koster (2005) dismissively quotes definitions by Roger Caillois, ("activity which is…voluntary… uncertain, unproductive, governed by rules, make believe"), Johan Huizinga ("free activity…outside 'ordinary' life…") and Jesper Juul ("a rule-based formal system with a variable and quantifiable outcome, where different outcomes are assigned different values, the player exerts effort in order to influence the outcome, the player feels attached to the outcome, and the consequences of the activity are optional and negotiable") because he fails to see how their definitions make games "fun" (cited in Koster, 2005, p. 12).

Recently, efforts have been made to move beyond the view of games as "unproductive" or "diversions." McGonigal (2011) cites Bernard Suits definition of games as "the voluntary attempt to overcome unnecessary obstacles" (p. 22) which is a much more educationally sound view of games as it speaks directly to the type of engagement that educators wish to engender in their classrooms. For that reason, this definition acted as the starting point for the work we undertook to train the Australian teachers about how to build their own games.

Once an education-friendly definition can be agreed upon, the next step is to build further and describe the nature of games and what they can offer for students and teachers. The natural starting point for this conversation would be Gee's (2003) conception of role-playing within computer games and his description of the various roles that game players can fill during the experience. First is the real-world identity of the player (that is, the player him or herself). Second is the virtual identity (that is, the character that is assumed within the game). The third identity is what Gee calls the projective identity, or "the interface between one's real-world identities and the virtual identity" (p. 63). It is at this point where the player of an experience starts to see him or herself as capable of undertaking the roles of the virtual identity. It is also this third identity that is important for educational endeavors as it is a natural means through which students can begin to view themselves differently than they would otherwise.

The natural question that flows from this line of thought, though, is "what do we do with the projective identity that is educational sound?" The answer lies in Shaffer's conception of "Epistemic Gaming", that is, games that focus on placing students within the context of a profession in order to learn as they simulate professional practice (see, for example, Shaffer, 2007 or Nash & Shaffer, 2011). In this sense, students learn the skills and knowledge associated with real-world settings rather than though the artificial environment of teacher-lead classrooms. For example, a game could be developed that asked the students to play as if they were engineers (or doctors, or lawyers, or politicians, or any of a myriad other professions). As they play the game, they interact with the materials and characters that they meet within the gameplay environment as if they were that profession. Of course, it is naive to think that a student can learn to be a physician by playing a game (who wants to visit that doctor, right?), but such an epistemic game may introduce that student to a field that he or she may not have thought of before, and the projective identity can help them to begin to see themselves as actually being capable of reaching that professional level.

Of course, the training with the Australian teachers did not focus solely on educational gaming, it also included introducing them to the technologies and capabilities of Augmented Reality (in some cases) or furthering their familiarity with these tools (in other cases).

Augmented Reality

Augmented Reality (AR) is "an enhanced version of reality created by the use of technology to overlay digital information on an image of something being viewed through a device (as a smartphone camera)" (Merriam-Webster, Inc, 2014b). In practice, this is a suite of technologies that use markers or geo-location capabilities to trigger information to appear on the screen of a handheld device. The use of this technology in educational settings has been the subject of speculation since the 2010 Horizon Report for K-12 predicted that educational Augmented Reality would be adopted within "four to five years" (New Media Consortium, 2010, p. 26). As that time window is about to close in 2015, and widespread adoption of these kinds of technologies has yet to materialize, the prediction can now be seen as slightly incorrect. However, that does not mean that these tools are not being used around the globe educationally. There are several companies that have begun developing Augmented Reality applications for use in educational settings, however, a recent review of commercially available educational Augmented Reality apps for Android and iOS indicated that the majority of these apps were either non-functional or consisted of very low-level educational value (O'Shea & Elliott, in press). Keating, Gregor, Fitzgerald, Campbell & Steele's (2014) work focused on developing an information systems design for location-aware educational events in informal learning environments. The design theory that they developed built upon the earlier work of Gregor & Jones (2007, as cited by Keating et al, 2014), who identified the following eight elements that would be required for an information system design theory (p. 4):

- Purpose and scope,
- Constructs,
- Principles of form and function,
- Artifact mutability,
- Testable propositions,
- Justificatory knowledge,
- Principles of implementation,
- Expository instantiation.

Augmented Reality technologies themselves, however, are relatively easy to categorize and explain. Augmented Reality apps tend to fall into one of two categories: Marker-based Augmented Reality and Markerless Augmented Reality.

- **Marker-Based Augmented Reality:** These applications of Augmented Reality will use the device's camera in conjunction with some trigger image (e.g. a QR code or a picture). When the device is pointed at the appropriate trigger image the device performs some sort of action. These actions may entail a webpage opening, a video playing, a 3D object appearing, an audio file playing, or many other options.
- **Markerless Augmented Reality:** Applications that utilize this technology depend upon the internal technology of the device to identify the user's geographic location and directionality. By determining a series of pre-identified "Points of Interest" that are pinned to geographic locations, the device can present information about the surroundings. For example, the device can be used as a "viewfinder", through which the user can see the real world but may also see additional information about the items in the field of view (e.g. distance to a landmark, price of a specific piece of property, location of a pub, etc.)

Each of these types of Augmented Reality can be, and have been, used in educational settings. Marker-based Augmented Reality tends to function best for indoor activities, however, it has the limitation of being tied to a specific set of markers that are required to be placed within the setting and made available to trigger. Markerless Augmented Reality, on the other hand, can be used with activities requiring students to be outdoors for all or part of the time, however, it has the limitation of often requiring devices with mobile access to data plans (something that schools are unlikely to support through their own purchasing) and placing the game play at the whims of the elements.

Augmented Reality experiences (as distinct from the technology used to serve those experiences) tend to fall into two categories of their own: Place Dependent and Place Independent.

- **Place Dependent Augmented Reality:** These experiences are generally tied to a specific geographic location or space (e.g. the Eiffel Tower or the Smithsonian Air and Space Museum), and usually include specific items that can be found in those locations as key elements of the experience.
- **Place Independent Augmented Reality:** These experiences are not tied to specific locations, instead they are able to be "played" at any location where markers or trigger locations can be placed, even if they are incongruous to the locale.

As with Marker-based and Markerless Augmented Reality, these two categories have strengths and weaknesses. Place dependent Augmented Reality has the potential to more fully utilize the space where the event is occurring (for example, the device can trigger the user to look to their left and find a grove of trees and those trees will actually exist in the physical space). The difficulty with this type of experience is that it has relatively low scalability. In order to actually experience the Augmented Reality, the user must be in that location, and this is not always (or even often) possible for educators and students. Place independent Augmented Reality, on the other hand, isn't constrained by being tied to a specific location; however, the inverse problem arises as these experiences are not as fully integrated into the setting as they could be if the game were designed for the locale.

Of course, all of this discussion of the types of Augmented Reality technologies and types of Augmented Reality experiences is foundation to the true question, "how can we most effectively leverage these technologies and experiences to build epistemic games?"

Educational Uses

The educational use of these types of tools rests on building narrative structures through which the story of the game can be told. Well-designed educational Augmented Reality experiences will involve students solving a central mystery either individually or in a group. The students utilize a technological medium, such as an iPod Touch, as they gather virtual data from their environment. This data provides the content that makes up the story and incorporates academic challenges that "push" the narrative forward. In this way, academics are needed to successfully complete the experience, but they are not the main reason for undertaking the challenge. This type of experience has a powerful pedagogical benefit: it can alter the instructional dynamic. In traditional educational settings, teachers often focus on teaching discrete "chunks" of information, assess mastery of that "chunk" of content, and then move on to the next "chunk". Although the means through which the process is conducted may be very student-centered (for example, incorporating student-lead discussions or group work), the underlying concept remains the same. The goal is to master a specific piece of material or skill and then move on to the next piece of material or skill.

Designing Augmented Reality experiences as described earlier, however, requires a re-envisioning of that underlying goal. The objective is no longer to teach and master a discrete piece of information. Rather, the objective is to build a compelling mystery that integrates many different pieces of information or skills, and that information is used as the means to unravel the mystery.

Additionally, there are several affordances that these kinds of experiences offer for students.

- **Engagement and Motivation:** The research that has been done on these types of experiences so far has been generally positive about the impact of these types of Augmented Reality games on student engagement and motivation (Klopfer, Yoon, & Perry, 2005; O'Shea & Folkestad, 2010; O'Shea, Mitchell, Johnstong, & Dede, 2009; Papadimitriou, Komis, Tselios, & Avouris, 2006; and Squire & Jan, 2007). Students who participate are engaged by the content and motivated to participate. This may be due to the relative novelty of the technology and experiences, however.
- **Active Motion:** The very nature of using Augmented Reality technologies in these types of experiences requires students to move around, a feature that is not often found in educational settings (and, quite honestly, is actively frowned upon in some settings). Aside from the engaging aspects of this active motion, there is the potential for health benefits – a particularly important feature given current rates of childhood obesity.
- **Altered Relationship with Setting:** This is the area about which the least is known, and is perhaps the ripest for further study. Specifically, the potential is there to impact the ways that individuals view and interact with their surroundings by designing Augmented Reality games effectively. For example, if the students came in each day and interact with their school as if it were the African savannah or the Great Barrier Reef or a Super-hero battle scene or a pirate ship or a fairy-filled forest (the list could go

> on), then the potential is there to begin altering how they view that physical space. It is possible that they could begin to see physical spaces as the canvas upon which adventures can be painted. Again, there is little to no research into this area, however, the logic behind such a thought is intriguing and suitable for further exploration.

It is worth exploring how the actual Augmented Reality elements of any such game are used within the structure of that game. Elliott (2013) developed an evaluation tool to measure and define the use of immersive learning technologies. The purpose and function of the technology are defined across levels from basic utility, content delivery, and assessment, to experience (see Table 1).

This framework is useful in determining how well the specific app or game uses the augmented reality technology for educational purposes. This was the evaluation instrument that was at the core of O'Shea and Elliott's (in press) review of commercially available apps, during which they found the vast majority of these apps failed to go beyond the utility stage. What O'Shea and Elliott's review demonstrates is that there is much work to be done in preparing educationally appropriate augmented reality apps, but there is also work to be done in preparing educators to effectively leverage those apps when they become available.

Table 1. Technology purpose and function

Technology Purpose	Technology Function
Trigger	Technology launches another website, movie, or other (generally) static image or video
Utility	Technology serves a functional purpose that is not directly related to learning
Content Deliver/ Information Access	Technology is used to cover content, deliver content or access data, but does not require the user to interact with the content in a way that is meaningful for learning
Content Delivery+ Assessment	Technology is used in a way that delivers content, but also requires the user to respond interactively
Content Delivery+ Assessment+ Experience/ Context	Technology helps learner experiences content, learns from it, and does so in meaningful context and through and experiential process

TEACHER TRAINING PROCESS AND ISSUES

Keeping with the philosophy of Docendo Discimus, a project was undertaken to train teachers in the theory and skills necessary to design Augmented Reality games for their own classroom use. In all cases, the teachers who consented to participate had no pre-existing familiarity with developing AR games, and had little (if any) familiarity with the AR tools beforehand. They had varying levels of ICT skills, but all were capable of creating materials using production tools on the computer (e.g. Microsoft Word, GIMP, nVU, Google Sites, etc). The remainder of this chapter will be dedicated to describing this project, exploring the nature of the training, and discussing the issues and opportunities that arose as a result.

Teacher Training

The project was the result of a partnership between Faculty at The University of Queensland (Brisbane, Queensland, Australia) and Appalachian State University (Boone, North Carolina, USA). Each of these two institutions provided support for the project through travel and research grants, which were in turn used to provide Augmented Reality game design training to a cohort of Australian K-12 teachers. This training took place at The University of Queensland in Brisbane, Australia in August, 2014. The focus of this training was on developing the skills required to build a functional Augmented Reality game. A total of 26 individuals participated in the workshops, which consisted of four two-hour sessions held on Tuesday and Wednesday evenings over two consecutive weeks. A series of face-to-face, individual or small group meetings were held over the following weeks to finish the games that were started during the large group instruction. The participants were split into two small groups of 14 and 12 teachers and the workshops were held at two different times (4pm and 6pm). This was beneficial as it allowed the participants to change their preferred meeting time if they had other commitments on one of the days.

Teacher Recruitment

Teachers were recruited in various ways. This depended on the school system, namely government, independent or Catholic. Government teachers were recruited through advertisement in schools through their central email address. Independent schools were emailed depending on personal contacts with individual schools. With regards to the Catholic system an email was sent to a generic email account and they then distributed the email. The University of Queensland School of Education distribution list was also emailed and staff members were asked to distribute to their contacts within schools. All emails contained a flyer advertising the workshops and asked to distribute it. These methods were very productive as inquiry rates were high.

NATURE OF THE TRAINING

The training itself followed a similar pattern as had been conducted in other educational settings previously; however, it was condensed by necessity of the two-week time constraints. The structure of the training followed a modified scaffolding model that involved a large group effort to develop the framework for a game, then splitting up into pairs (or individually, if they preferred) and working on building their own game with guidance from the training instructor. Large portions of the meeting times were dedicated to individual or pair-based work to develop the concept and materials associated with their own Augmented Reality game, and the instructional staff was there to help guide these efforts. Additionally, the training included tailored instruction on technologies that best fit the needs and requirements of each individual. As there are a great many possible Augmented Reality development tools available, the individual circumstances of each participant were used to determine which tools would best suit their needs.

In terms of specifics of the sessions themselves, the training focused on introducing, exploring, designing and building the following game-design elements:

- **Concept Identification:** E.g. "This will be a police crime story".
- **Development of a Story Arc:** E.g. "The detective will solve the mystery of the stolen painting".
- **Player Role Identification:** E.g. "The student will play the game as Detective Henderson". Additional complexity can be added to the game by having multiple roles that students can play, either individually or in teams.
- **Identification of In-Game Interactions:** E.g. "Detective Henderson will find a ransom note from the art thief, a riddle to be solved to stop the thief from selling the art, and a final geographic clue to capture the thief". As with the previous stage, complexity can be added by providing multiple "paths" for the various players to reach the end state or by "jigsawing" content to provide only portions of the material to individuals, effectively forcing them to share information.
- **Identification of Academic Content:** E.g. "Students will learn latitude and longitude, division of fractions, and the chemical process for creating paint". Identifying academic material comes late in the process to ensure that it is not the driving force for the game. Academic content should be the means through which success can be

achieved, not the success state itself. Very few individuals are excited about playing a dividing fractions game, however, if that is a skill that is needed in order to succeed as a detective, they are more likely to be interested in mastering it.

- **Storyboarding and Scripting of Game Elements:** Detailed interactions are written out for each element of the game. These materials will be viewed by students through the use of Augmented Reality technologies so they must be designed in enough detail that the actual production of the web pages, videos, audio clips, and images (and any other materials) will go smoothly.
- **Material Production:** The production of the materials storyboarded and scripted in the previous step. This can usually be done relatively quickly if enough detail was provided as a result of the previous step. For example, an actor in front of a green screen playing the art thief can be recorded in a matter of minutes if the script has been completed beforehand.
- **Post-Production Finishing:** This stage is where all of the materials are put together into a finished product. It usually entails created the actual Auras and Aurasma Channels or QR codes (or whatever other technology has been selected) to successfully play the game.
- **De-Bugging and Revision:** The final step in the game design process is to play the game to identify any logical or technological errors. At that point, those issues can be fixed and the game can be finalized.

The sessions focused on specific applications of the elements listed above. The initial two-hour session was used to describe the theoretical and philosophical foundations that support educational Augmented Reality games. Once that was done, the session moved into a practical group exercise that allowed the whole group to participate in the initial design stages of a shared game. This game wasn't actually created, though, as this activity was used to simply demonstrate the game development process. Participants (either individually or in pairs) used the remaining time to begin the design of their own unique game.

The second two-hour session was used to provide time for the students to work individually or in pairs to further develop their game concept, story arc, player roles and in-game interactions. The session finished with the participants working on identifying academic content for their game and starting to storyboard the interactions (which were to be completed in the time between the second and third sessions). The third and fourth sessions along with any one-on-one or small group meetings were dedicated to actually producing materials, testing and de-bugging the games.

Participants were encouraged to work in pairs to develop the games as this allowed them to build on each other's ideas. Although not all teachers were from the same schools, pairings were formed through common interests, thus allowing the teachers to expand networks and create teams from various schools.

Results

As was intended, the training lead to the development of a series of games by the participant attendees, and, by extension, it can fairly be said that the participants learned the processes, skills and technologies associated with developing Augmented Reality games. For the most part, participants utilized Aurasma (2014) as their Augmented Reality technology of choice, however, some utilized QR codes as well, and at least one individual showed interest in expanding into ARIS (ARISgames, 2014) as their Augmented Reality delivery mechanism. Beyond the technology, several groups learned to use relatively advanced Javascript coding to set cookies on devices in order to better control the flow and direction of the user experience.

The games that were designed tended to be fairly rudimentary, however, that would be expected with an initial development. In many cases, the games were simple, linear progressions through the tasks and were available for students to play as only one role. Again, these types of simplistic designs should be expected when first learning a process.

In addition to the actual game elements that were created, another aspect of the project was interviewing the participants afterwards to determine how the training may have impacted their thinking about their educational practices. This was done as a follow up to the pre-survey, which asked them to describe an instructional event that they were particularly proud of from their past, and then during the interview to reflect back on how they might change that event based on what they learned during the trainings. These interviews were inconclusive in terms of showing a clear growth in the participants thinking about their role within the educational setting, however, that could perhaps be due to the relatively short duration of the training. One participant stated that he would set up his computer lab differently to provide greater opportunity to collaborate and communicate. Another participant focused on how she would incorporate Aurasma in future educational settings, while a third participant stated that the "augmented reality workshop showed me how to frame [student knowledge] in a different way to the classroom". As would be expected, these kinds of diverse thoughts demonstrate that participants in professional development will value different elements of the training and will learn different lessons from them. In terms of trying to pinpoint a common effect that the training might have had, however, the interviews proved inconclusive.

ISSUES, CONTROVERSIES, PROBLEMS

The issues associated with this project demonstrated some of the biggest problems with any technological integration within a classroom setting. Among those are finding tools that will work for the intended purpose while also being acceptable to use in educational settings. For example, Facebook may be a good tool for connecting and group work, however schools and districts may have policies or politics that stand in the way of implementing it as a tool. Along those lines, the biggest difficulty presented within the context of selecting technologies for use in this training was the fact that many of the participants were not allowed to utilize cloud-based resources (such as Google Sites and YouTube). In fact, the policies put in place by the governing body within Queensland state schools were more restrictive than most seen in the US in that teachers were prohibited from even creating Google Site websites that students would purely have access to. This made it much more difficult to troubleshoot potential sources for the content of the Augmented Reality games. In every case, however, appropriate web-based resources were identified, and games were successfully built. This is possibly due to the teachers from that school system regularly having to solve these types of problems and learning to be creative in how to work within that system.

Another issue that is usually confronted when integrating technology and the associated training is that of time. Teachers have a great many responsibilities that call upon their time, and it is sometimes difficult to find enough time to effectively train teachers on the pedagogical and technical aspects of different tools. The training within this project was no different, and, in fact, may have been even more problematic since the process itself can be rather daunting. Experience has shown that this type of training requires a substantial amount of time to master. Undertaking the process over the course of eight instructional hours provides an introduction to the concepts and skills, and can lead to a rudimentary game, but it is unlikely to lead to sustained practice or advanced skillset development. One participant commented that she "wondered where the balance was…between effort and output" while another stated that she liked having the time to work on the project because "if you had watched a 20 min clip online you never put in the next hour to figure it out." There is a balance to be sought in terms of the cost and benefits of this type of activity.

These issues lead to another, and perhaps the largest, difficulty with successfully training teachers to build their own games. Namely, the time and effort that is required is only possible for dedicated and passionate individuals. It is unlikely that a large number of people will be willing to put that effort in, and that is no indictment of those individuals who do not choose to do so. It is simply to say that, while it is possible to take a group of interested individuals to a stage where they can actually create games in a relatively short time, the full implementation and realization of the power of learning how to develop these games would only be realized with sustained effort and time. And that effort and time is only available to those individuals who are willing to find ways to make it happen.

SOLUTIONS AND RECOMMENDATIONS

The issues that were identified in the previous section are not simple or easy to fix. If they were so, then they would have been fixed already and many teachers would be creating Augmented Reality games. However, having said that, as described below there are means through which the issues of technology identification, time and dedication can be tackled.

Technology Identification

The issue of identifying appropriate technologies for the needs of this kind of project can be daunting since there are a great deal of practical and policy issues that must be addressed along the way. This is one of the benefits of being "technologically agnostic". A tool can usually be found to address a problem, however, if training or staff development is dependent upon a specific tool (for example, YouTube) it is not always possible to utilize that in educational settings. Adaptability is the key to this approach. As long as the participants have a clear sense of what they want the instructional activity to accomplish, then a tool can usually be found that will make that possible.

Time

The issue of time is much more difficult to address because it involves structural issues within a school setting which stand in the way of sustained practice or advanced skillset development. In order to ensure those things occur, the training would have to be quite a bit more intensive and perhaps expand across months, semesters or even years. This is not to say that all participation would be intense (for instance, daily meetings that can last for hours) over the course of creating the game, however, it should be sustained so that the learning becomes ingrained, opportunities are provided to learn, practice and master skills, and games are able to be implemented, observed and modified based on need.

Additionally, providing that sort of sustained staff development would allow for expanded skills in the development of games. More advanced and complex games would incorporate multiple student roles, jigsawed content (where only part of the material is shown to individual students, thus forcing them to work together to see the whole picture), and branching tree-structured architecture that allows the game to be played in different ways over time.

Dedication

Unfortunately, the issue of dedication is the most difficult to address. It must simply be accepted that not all teachers will be dedicated enough to this type of process to make it work, particularly as teachers have competing interests with their time. Again, this is not an indictment of those people who are not excited by the process or willing enough to dedicate their time to mastering game design. It is not controversial to say that people are motivated by different things, and thus some will be dedicated to this type of game design process while others (and, quite honestly, the majority of others) will not.

Having said that, though, it is possible to envision a two-pronged approach to developing and using Augmented Reality games within educational settings. The first would be to find and train those individuals who are sufficiently motivated by the concept of Augmented Reality game design to a point where they can build games. Those games can be made available to the larger audience of individuals who are interested in playing the games but are not interested in building them. In this way, the process is serving both levels of interest in Augmented Reality game design and utilization.

FUTURE RESEARCH DIRECTIONS

There are several fruitful directions that could be undertaken in relation to the design and implementation of Augmented Reality games by teachers (or anyone else who wishes to design them). The first area of inquiry would be associated with the game development and design training. First, teacher skill development could be studied. The actual quality of the games that teachers design could be studied to determine if their skills improve over time and they become better able to build complexity and depth to their games. Following in that same vein, a second avenue of exploration would be to study teacher-build games and their usage. It would be possible to research how successful those games are at their intended purpose (that is, do they help students learn) and how well those games are being utilized by other teachers who were not involved with the design process.

A second avenue for potential research would be to explore the effects of these games on students. As was mentioned earlier, there is potential in terms of the affordances of these technologies for impacting students' interaction with the games and their environment. In this area, the first, and most logical starting point, would be to further study these games impact on engagement and motivation. As was mentioned earlier, the current research supports the assertion that these games will engage and motivate students to participate. The natural next step in this research progression would be to find out if this is due to the relative novelty of the tools and games. This would require a series of longer games spread across a year or multiple years to determine if engagement and motivation levels change over time. Second, it would be worth exploring how these games use of active motion impacts student outcomes. As games become more complex and require greater activity of the students who are playing them, then it will be possible to study the effect of such activity on student health outcomes. Third, and perhaps most exciting, is the avenue of research into how these games impact participant's relationship with their settings. This may be a long way off, and may require a full immersion into the Augmented Reality gaming experience (that is, multiple games with different virtual locales played over sustained timeframes), but the potential for these types of experiences to alter the ways in which participants view and interact with their environments would be well worth exploring.

CONCLUSION

This chapter describes the process through which teachers can learn how to create augmented reality games for their classes. Although a certain amount of time was given during the training sessions so that they could work on creating their own games, time was limited and thus teachers needed to find their own time to actually finish the games. Many of the teachers did this and were able to finish their games to a standard to teach with their classes. This shows that the teachers were sufficiently motivated to learn the skills and thus complete the games.

As with Clarke (2013) the technologies associated with building QR codes and Aurasma Auras are reasonably easy for the teachers to learn, however the conceptualization of a 'good' game they could develop that would be able to meet the needs of their students was much more difficult and time consuming.

There are some issues and problems that can arise when creating Augmented Reality games. This includes that learning how to create augmented reality games does tend to be time consuming and labor intensive. This means that the process may not suit all teachers, however, the ones that do put in the time and effort can succeed with guidance and assistance (at least initially).

Overall the workshops were beneficial to the participants, who reported on them in a positive way. These teachers now have enough skill to create more Augmented Reality games on their own in the future and perhaps collaborate with others and thus share their newfound skills with them.

REFERENCES

ARISgames. (2014). ARIS. Retrieved from https://arisgames.org/

Aurasma (2014). Aurasma Augmented Reality Browser. Retrieved from http://www.aurasma.com/

Clarke, J. (2013). Augmented reality, multimodal literacy and mobile technology: An experiment in teacher engagement. *QScience Proceedings*: Vol. 2013, 12th World Conference on Mobile and Contextual Learning (mLearn 2013), 28. DOI: doi:10.5339/qproc.2013.mlearn.28

Classical Academic Press. (2014). Docendo Discimus. Classical Academic Press. Retrieved from http://classicalacademicpress.com/docendo-discimus/

Elliott, J. (2013) Analog Thinking: Digital Times. Invited workshop presentation at *American Education Research Association Annual Conference*, San Francisco, CA.

Gee, J. P. (2003). *What Video Games Have to Teach Us about Learning and Literacy*. New York, NY: Palgrave Macmillan.

Keating, B., Gregor, S., Fitzgerald, R., Campbell, J., & Steele, J. (2014, December 8-10). *Information Systems Design Theory for Location-Based Educational Services in Informal Learning Environments*. Paper presented at the 25th Australasian Conference on Information Systems, Auckland, New Zealand.

Klopfer, E., Yoon, S., & Perry, J. (2005). Using Palm technology in participatory simulations of complex systems: A new take on ubiquitous and accessible mobile computing. *Journal of Science Education and Technology*, *14*(3), 285–297. doi:10.1007/s10956-005-7194-0

Koster, R. (2005). *A Theory of Fun for Game Design*. Scottsdale, AZ: Paraglyph Press, Inc.

McClarty, K., Orr, A., Frey, P., Dolan, R., Vassileva, V., & McVay, A. (2012). A literature review of gaming in education. Pearson Education. Retrieved from http://researchnetwork.pearson.com/wp-content/uploads/Lit_Review_of_Gaming_in_Education.pdf

McGonigal, J. (2011). *Reality is broken: Why Games Make Us Better and How They Can Change the World*. London: The Penguin Press HC.

Merriam-Webster, Inc. (2014a). Game. Merriam-Webster Online Dictionary. Retrieved from http://www.merriam-webster.com/dictionary/game

Merriam-Webster, Inc. (2014b). Augmented Reality. Merriam-Webster, Incorporated. Retrieved from http://www.merriam-webster.com/dictionary/augmented%20reality

Nash, P., & Shaffer, D. W. (2011). Mentor modeling: The internalization of modeled professional thinking in an epistemic game. *Journal of Computer Assisted Learning*, *27*(2), 173–189. doi:10.1111/j.1365-2729.2010.00385.x

New Media Consortium. (2010). 2010 Horizons Report: The K-12 Edition. *New Media Consortium*. Retrieved from http://wp.nmc.org/horizon-k12-2010/

O'Shea, P. & Elliott, J. (in press). Augmented reality in education: An exploration and analysis of currently available educational apps. *Research Highlights in Technology and Teacher Education* a publication of the Society for Information Technology and Teacher Education.

O'Shea, P., & Folkestad, J. (2010). *Evaluation of the augmented reality project at the School in the Park* [Unpublished Manuscript].

O'Shea, P., Mitchell, R., Johnston, C., & Dede, C. (2009). Lessons learned about designing augmented realities. *The International Journal of Games and Computer Mediated Simulations*, *1*(1).

Papadimitriou, I., Komis, V., Tselios, N., & Avouris, N. (2006, December 8-10). Designing PDA mediated educational ctivities in the frame of a museum visit. IADIS Cognition and Exploratory Learning in Digital Age (CELDA) 2006 Conference, Barcelona, Spain.

Shaffer, D. W. (2007). The educational value of computer games. Principle, March/April, 66-67.

Shaffer, D. W. (2008). *How Computer Games Help Children Learn*. New York, NY: Palgrave MacMillan.

Squire, K. D., & Jan, M. (2007). Mad city mystery: Developing scientific argumentation skills with a place-based augmented reality game on handheld computers. *Journal of Science Education and Technology*, *16*(1), 1, 5–29. doi:10.1007/s10956-006-9037-z

KEY TERMS AND DEFINITIONS

Augmented Reality: The use of a technological medium to display virtual information "on top" of the real world.

Epistemic Gaming: Educational games that as the students to play the game using a professional role (e.g. an engineer) in order to learn skills and knowledge associated with that role.

Games: There are many different definitions for this term, however, the one used in this paper is "the voluntary attempt to overcome unnecessary obstacles."

Professional Development: The training of in-service or pre-service teachers on a specific skill or content area applicable to their professional practice.

Projective Identity: As identified by James Paul Gee, this is "the interface between one's real-world identities and the virtual identity."

Section 2

Pedagogical Concepts and Related Practice

Chapter 8

Information Literacy in Virtual Environments:

Changing Needs of P-12 Learners

Valerie J Hill
Lewisville ISD, USA

ABSTRACT

This chapter provides an overview of information literacy needs of P-12 learners in virtual environments. As more of life is spent in global digital participatory culture, information literacy skills have moved from primarily print-based to include digital content evaluation, content curation, and a personal responsibility for digital citizenship. Using standards for 21st century learning from the American Library Association, examples highlight information literacy elements embedded in immersive learning environments, such as the Anne Frank simulation (a 3D replica of Amsterdam and the annex where Anne's family hid) and a digital citizenship game built by students in the game of Minecraft. Creators of immersive learning environments in virtual worlds must accurately depict historical eras and cite sources for authority and accuracy of information. These 3D simulations provide opportunities to teach information literacy in virtual spaces with a shared "sense of presence". Learners in virtual environments have digital citizenship responsibilities from a very young age.

INTRODUCTION

As more of life is spent in *global digital participatory culture*, information literacy skills have moved from primarily print-based to include digital content evaluation, content curation, and a personal responsibility for digital citizenship. Global digital participatory culture refers to the immediate access across distance (global) through mobile devices (digital). The majority of students today (92 percent) have mobile devices which are used daily, sometimes instantly according to the Pew Internet Report (2015) and are expected to demonstrate learning using technology tools (participatory culture). The importance of information literacy in the information age, where today's youth live, cannot be over emphasized. In fact, the future of civilization and the successful education of the citizens of tomorrow may depend upon understanding information literacy in the

DOI: 10.4018/978-1-4666-9629-7.ch008

information age and encouraging young people to take personal responsibility for digital citizenship. Identifying the information literacy needs of learners, particularly in virtual environments, is fundamental to educators, librarians, students, parents, and society. Through discussion of the revolutionary changes taking place in digital culture, we can develop a better understanding of the need for information literacy embedded in virtual environments.

BACKGROUND

Learners growing up in global digital participatory culture have new information literacy needs that differ greatly from the needs of prior generations. Reading and writing were of utmost importance for P-12 learners just decades ago, but information literacy now includes numerous other formats: listening, viewing, creating, evaluating, and curating content. Futurist, Alvin Toffler, suggested back in 1980 that individuals are now *prosumers,* meaning both consumers and producers of content (Kotler, 1986). Prosumerism impacts all aspects of our lives, including the education of youth growing up in a culture where user-generated content is more prevalent than content from traditional publishing sources. The move from a primarily print-based world into digital and virtual world learning environments puts personal responsibility for digital citizenship on each learner.

The expectation of learners to produce content illustrating learning concepts, particularly in digital formats, such as uploading electronic Web 2.0 products, has become common in classrooms through free technology applications and websites. Glogster, Edublogs, Livebinder are a few examples of online resources that provide students with digital tools. Sometimes digital applications can be deceiving because the high quality graphics are exceptional but the critical thinking underlying them may be minimal. Librarians and teachers are encouraged to scaffold learning through guided inquiry (Kulthau and Maniotes, 2010), modeling good questioning techniques and a critical stance on issues.

Deep learning requires rigor. Learners of all ages, not just the younger learners, can run into trouble evaluating electronic resources and digital tools. Fontichiaro (2010) shares strategies for developing a questioning stance regarding digital content that can "nudge learners toward inquiry". Learning to ask better questions when seeking information helps students think deeply and critically and makes learning a rigorous activity. This rigor applies to immersive gaming environments where participants must concentrate on difficult tasks even though the game-like state is interpreted as play (Gee, 2003). The first academic article to use the term 'playbour' (often spelled *playbor*), a portmanteaux combining *play* and *labor*, was Julian Kucklich (2005). The playbor concept illustrates that learning in a gaming environment can be both enjoyable and challenging; however, education has been far behind commercial business in utilizing videogames (Rey, 2012).

The rise in digital content online coincided with the popularity of video games and the birth of immersive learning environments or virtual worlds, like Second Life and Minecraft over the past decade. Children ages 10-14 represents the largest user group within virtual worlds with millions of registered users in environments like Habbo Hotel, Club Penguin and Minecraft (Kzero, 2014). These environments can be synchronous and multi-player or asynchronous and entered alone. Either way, learning in virtual environments or videogames requires many elements of information literacy.

Merriam Webster defines *gamification* as "the process of adding games or game-like elements to something (as a task) so as to encourage participation". This definition aligns with global digital participatory culture and suggests that students may be able to learn rigorously in virtual immersive learning environments that have been designed with embedded information literacy alongside curriculum for various subjects. In a study in the field of art education, Parks states, "Computers, digital media, and video games have revolutionized the way young people today communicate and make meaning with the world" (Parks, 2008, p. 236). This 'revolution' within global digital participatory culture has influenced the expectations of students about how and when learning takes place and includes elements of gamification.

Libraries have listened to young people who desire interesting programs, such as video game clubs. Brown and Kasper (2013) assessed literacy learning outcomes through a case study of a library video game club using grounded theory framework. Findings included a positive impact on youth's academic life and a renewed interest in reading. The case study suggested potential for measuring information literacy skills through gamification and for motivating reluctant learners through a reward-based system of play.

THE NEED FOR INFORMATION LITERACY

The American Library Association (ALA, 2000) defines information literacy as a "set of abilities requiring individuals to recognize when information is needed and have the ability to locate, evaluate, and use effectively the needed information". Young learners from P-12 need information literacy embedded throughout all areas of the curriculum as they learn in settings that utilize digital spaces, particularly as gamification in education increases.

The Association of College and Research Libraries (ACRL) currently will investigate the term *metaliteracy* in a framework for revising the information literacy standards adopted in 2000. This framework "draws significantly upon the concept of metaliteracy, which offers a renewed vision of information literacy as an overarching set of abilities in which students are both consumers and creators of information who can participate successfully in collaborative spaces" (ACRL, 2015, p.2). While ACRL serves learners in higher education settings, students in P-12 are also living in global digital participatory culture and the information literacy needs of these learners are just as complex as those of adults. Nomenclature of information literacy terms is evolving as new media formats rapidly change information seeking behavior. Mackey and Jacobson (2011) propose reframing the overall umbrella of information literacy concepts with the overarching metaliteracy term; however, many experts still prefer using the term *information literacy* to encompass the many formats of information needs necessary for success in physical, digital, virtual or augmented learning environments (Grassian and Kaplowitz, 2009).

21st Century Learning Standards

ALA provides information literacy standards for 21st century learners with emphasis on ethical behavior in an inquiry based learning framework through the American Association of School Librarians (AASL). These learning standards are organized in four parts: skills, dispositions in action, responsibilities, and self-assessment strategies. ALA believes "multiple literacies, including digital, visual, textual, and technological, have now joined information literacy as crucial skills for this century" (ALA AASL, 2007, p.3).

The standards for 21st century learning describe how learners use skills, resources and tools four ways. First, learners use available skills, resources and tools to inquire, think critically, and gain knowledge. Secondly, learners draw conclusions, make informed decisions, apply knowledge to new situations, and create new knowledge. Next, they share knowledge and participate ethically and productively as members of our democratic society. Finally, learners pursue personal and aesthetic growth. These learning descriptions are specifically applicable to educational games and immersive learning environments because they exemplify the digital culture in which students now live with access to resource on mobile devices at any time.

Funding for game-based learning from the Bill and Melinda Gates Foundation for over 20 million US dollars in 2011 and increased numbers of educators in virtual worlds, such as Second Life, provide evidence of gamification becoming widely recognized as a powerful learning tool (Weaver, 2011). Gates Foundation also invested in game-based learning tools developed by Digital Youth Network, Institute of Play, and Quest Atlantis with literacy based trajectories (Gates Foundation, 2011). Research on the Gates Foundation funded project, conducted by the Institute of Play and GlassLab, was designed to evaluate assessment of learning in gaming environments where learners enter a "state of flow". The findings illustrate that "assessment design helps game designers see how theory and experience in some learning domains can be applied to build the situations, the challenges, and the actions that players interact with (Institute of Play, 2014, p. 7). Understanding how information literacy needs can be met through virtual environments is an important challenge for librarians and educators working with 21st century youth.

Immersive Learning Environments

Students today visit virtual worlds, such as Club Penguin or Minecraft, from an early age. Educators are beginning to understand the value of immersive learning for many different curriculum areas, such as mathematics, reading, art, history, social studies or any subject. Virtual worlds, according to Bulu (2012), provide students with a *sense of presence* unlike traditional learning experiences such as reading literature or viewing multi-media in physical classrooms. A virtual world is not considered a game, but often games are offered with them. Mastel and Huston (2009) believe video games are now considered (by educators who embrace them) to be a literary genre.

School age children P-12 as well as adults find opportunities within virtual worlds for immersive learning. A study by Hew and Cheung (2010) found that virtual worlds are utilized for communication spaces, simulation of space (spatial), and experiential spaces through action, such as role-play.

Information literacy specialists, Grassian and Trueman (2012), document benefits of professional development in virtual worlds through workshops, opportunities to share interests in particular subjects and issues, and the ability to seek a community, for networking, creative problem-solving and feedback on current issues and projects. Educators and librarians lead learners into historical simulations, role-play scenarios, and challenging 3D experiences, such as an emergency rescue documented by Taylor-Nelms and Hill (2014). Some of these simulations provide experiences that could not be done in the physical world, such as a tsunami hitting the shore or a trip to space.

Anne Frank's Life in Hiding

An example of an historic era brought to life through an immersive learning experience is Anne Frank's life in hiding at the Understanding the Holocaust Project (ISTE, 2011). As part of the project, educators took part in a ten-week MOOC (massive open online course) designed to experience how middle school students learn through a virtual simulation of Anne Frank's surroundings during World War II. During the ten weeks, these educators were given weekly assignments exemplifying the learning experience students might encounter.

For example, students (as avatars) entered a 3D simulation of Anne's tiny sleeping quarters in the annex and were asked to compare the space with the bedroom they have at home or to compare the wildlife Anne might have seen out her window with that outside their own. The educators met weekly to experience the immersive space together but could also visit alone at any time during the week to explore the annex, a virtual museum, and other buildings from the era. A Star of David icon was placed throughout the simulation to link additional resources, such as websites, photos, or videos to provide a rich learning experience.

Weekly assignments could be accomplished through new media content creation, such as video, podcasts, photos, blogging, or other formats. The four ways learners use skills, resources and tools for 21st century learning (information literacy standards) were evident within this immersive learning experience and required by the assignments presented. Learners were provided with authentic content and encouraged to evaluate and self-assess through giving credit to sources. Information literacy skills needed directly correlate with AASL Standard 2.1.6, which states, "Use the writing process, media and visual literacy, and technology skills to create products that express new understandings" (ALA AASL, 2007, p.5; see Figures 1 and 2).

In the past, students traditionally read about history (through both historical fiction and non-fiction) and viewed videos or listened to audio materials. While those experiences were effective and important for learning, traditional literacy modes were often passive and sometimes isolating rather than collaborative. Immersive learning experiences allow opportunities to collaborate with other learners across distance or work alone as needed, providing both synchronous and asynchronous learning.

Experiencing the Anne Frank simulation required learners to use many of the AASL Information Literacy Standards, particularly *demonstrating mastering of technology tools for accessing information and pursuing inquiry* (AASL Standard 1.1.8). In addition to demonstration of skills, the AASL Standards propose learners display "Dispositions in Action" putting emphasis on the intrinsic learning motivation required for deep learning. The Anne Frank immersive learning environment provided opportunity to *demonstrate creativity by using multiple resources and formats* (AASL Standard 1.2.3).

The final assignment for the Anne Frank MOOC was given at week ten. Participants were asked to "light a 3D virtual candle" with a note containing a personal reflection about the experience. The candles of various sizes and colors were all placed together in a virtual room. This shared experience was both collaborative and personal, addressing the AASL Standards for self-assessment and the pursuit of personal growth through personal responsibility. Participants described the experience as "more personal than simply reading a book about Anne" (Hill, 2012; see Figure 3).

Figure 1. Anne Frank MOOC shares virtual Amsterdam

Figure 2. Anne Frank at a writing desk (The Independent online)

Figure 3. Anne Frank reflection candles

Minecraft Digital Citizenship Game

Information literacy encompasses both the consumption (or *intake*- such as reading) and production (or *output*- such as writing) of resources. In video games and virtual immersive learning environments, both consumption and production are possible because the individual may simply "play" the game or "create and build" the game or both. Hence, embedding information literacy into video games and virtual worlds is a critical need for the creators as well as the players, learners, or "residents" (as individuals are sometimes called in virtual worlds).

Video games can be educational, such as the best reading games listed online through Common Sense Media (CSM, 2015), just for entertainment, or a combination commonly referred to as *edutainment*. Corporations, of course, create games for profit for all three purposes. Digital citizenship requires parents and children alike to become responsible for choosing best digital content in a culture that provides huge numbers of apps and games on any number of devices and platforms. Common Sense Media offers educators and schools a certification in digital citizenship with resources for teachers, students, and parents.

An example of user-generated production of an immersive learning environment is a Minecraft Digital Citizenship Game designed and created by 5th graders in an after school library club. The students were challenge by the librarian to create and build a Minecraft Game for younger students to promote information literacy, particularly digital citizenship (Hill, 2015). Using the AASL Standards for 21st Century Learning and resources from Common Sense Media, the 5th grade students wrote questions for younger students and hid clues inside a virtual library which resembled the students' own school library. Machinima shots archived the student project on YouTube (Hill, 2014; see Figure 4).

Questions the students hid inside the Minecraft Digital Citizenship game included topics such as cyber safety, respect for intellectual property, online privacy, and evaluation of online resources. One of the AASL Standards for Dispositions in Action addressed through the creation of this digital citizenship game was AASL Standard 1.2.4 "Maintain a critical stance by questioning the validity and accuracy of all information". Using a constructivist learning pedagogy, these students combined teaching others as they learned information literacy concepts themselves. Constructivist Learning Theory promotes application, synthesis, and creation of new knowledge through social collaboration rather than individual memorization and collection of knowledge, facts and skills (Duffy and Cunningham, 2001).

Figure 4. Minecraft digital citizenship game courtyard

Information Literacy in Second Life and Other Virtual Worlds

Librarians have been actively working in virtual worlds for nearly a decade, particularly in Second Life at the Community Virtual Library. The American Library Association hosted an island in Second Life from 2007 -2012 and currently volunteers continue to collaborate around the globe through member initiative groups such as ALA Virtual Communities in Libraries and the ACRL Virtual Worlds Interest Group. School librarians, public librarians, academic and special librarians connect virtually with educators in Second Life and other virtual worlds. Virtual worlds provide immersive learning experiences through collaboration on a global scale for both children and adults. While Second Life (SL) is only one of many virtual worlds, Hill and Lee (2009) document many universities and colleges have chosen SL as a virtual space for building virtual campuses and immersive learning spaces for particular experiences (such as medical simulations).

Professor Sheila Webber, at the University of Sheffield in the United Kingdom, teaches information literacy in Second Life at the InfoLit Ischool. Information literacy responsibilities, such as ethical behavior, understanding diverse perspectives, and respect for copyright and intellectual property are obviously abundant in Second Life. Webber actively participates in the European Conference on Information Literacy annually and believes "the increase in the options for acquiring, remixing, creating and sharing information, in all formats, has increased the complexity of IL, and made it more challenging to help people become truly information literate" (Webber, 2013, p 1).

The exploration of virtual worlds as a platform for the information science profession led librarians to "gridhop" from Second Life to other virtual worlds such as Unity 3D, Reaction Grid, Sococo, and others. As virtual reality continues to rise in popularity with virtual reality tools like Oculus Rift, educators struggle to keep up with best practices (Education Week, 2015). Librarians often lead the way in exploring new media formats and platforms to promote information literacy (See Figure 5). Sometimes learning new platforms can be difficult and these librarians model AASL Standards for Dispositions in Action, such as a willingness to "display persistence by continuing to pursue information to gain a broad perspective" (AASL Standard 1.2.7). Teaching information literacy is impossible without modeling best practices through relevant real world applications. Virtual world librarians understand that children are now growing up in virtual world spaces and seek opportunities to explore and build them.

Commercial Video Games and Information Literacy

Virtual environments include open-ended virtual worlds, which may or may not include video games but are often perceived as such, and online video games. Critics of video games for young people often list violence and crime as potentially harmful elements in popular games, such as Grand Theft Auto, a top selling game on several gaming platforms. A literature review, conducted by the Australia Government, presenting research studies of the effects of violent video games was inconclusive. After examination of numerous studies, the results were "very mixed and more research is needed to directly compare effects, leaving the question of whether VVGs (violent video games) have a greater impact than other violent media unresolved" (Commonwealth of Australia, 2010 p. 41).

Because profit is top priority for most video game creators, the educational value is often seen as neglected entirely. However, most video game creators embed choices for the player as *agent* with consequences for actions taken and studies in ethics and gaming are underway. Sicart states, "The constructivist argument proposes that for a game to create ethical game play, players have to be made responsible for their choices, as well as for their development as moral agents" (Sicart, 2013, p. 35).

Figure 5. Librarians explore and collaborate in virtual worlds

Commercially popular games, like Assassin's Creed Unity, utilize a research department for accuracy in historical dates and events for battles such as the Storming the Bastille during the French Revolution. The facts generated during play in Assassin's Creed Unity French Revolution are not imperative to the game but contain additional factual information for those interested in information about the era. Common Sense Media (2015) rates this video game as "Not For Kids"

Figure 6. Storming the Bastille in Assassin's Creed French Unity

and informs parents of the violence encountered through role-play as a hit man. Many young people share popular video games without the knowledge of parents who sometimes lack understanding of computer literacy. Evaluating video games for educational value and ethical value can be challenging but most experts would agree that violent video games are outside the arena of education even though information literacy concepts, such as accuracy and authority, may be embraced by creators. Often these games lack citation of sources and use storytelling techniques, while cinematic, that fail to depict accurate cultural perspectives (see Figure 6).

Commercial video games should be addressed when examining the virtual spaces encountered by youth because the lines between home and school and the lines between personal and professional learning have become blurred due to instant access to information in digital culture. Popular video games, like Assassin's Creed, remind us once again of the personal responsibility required by each individual to become a good digital citizen. Just as librarians once recommended excellent books for reading, we now recommend the best digital content for learning. Choices for spending time outside of the classroom are left not only to parents, but also certainly to students themselves. Information literacy is a personal responsibility.

FUTURE RESEARCH DIRECTIONS

Future studies are needed to understand best practices for embedding information literacy in 21st century learning resources, particularly in virtual environments, and best pedagogical strategies for guiding learners toward digital citizenship. Research is needed in evaluating information literacy standards of immersive learning environments and other digital platforms that merge and blend content, such as MOOCs (massive open online courses). Studies might compare learning outcomes of both physical classroom techniques and activities and video games or virtual world activities. As virtual reality tools emerge, such as Oculus Rift, research is needed to determine how concepts can be learned best in virtual reality with information literacy standards assuring educational use, including accuracy, authority, respect for intellectual property and foundation of digital citizenship.

CONCLUSION

Both creators of virtual environments, video games and immersive learning spaces and users of those environments need to understand the critical necessity for information literacy in global digital participatory culture. Without information literacy skills, intellectual property becomes lost in the chaos of the Internet. Without personal responsibility for learning, we are headed for trouble. Barlow and Leston compare the Internet to a 'book of sand', stating, "...[the book of sand] is the Internet, but without the possibility of organization, is information but with no system (or no discernible system), the centuries old-nightmare of the librarian and, today, of every serious researcher working through the web" (Barlow and Leston, 2012, p. 51). Information literacy is not only critical because it will help students achieve greater academic success (although it may help them get better grades) but because the future of civilization depends upon it.

REFERENCES

ACRL (Association for College and Research Libraries). (2015). ACRL information literacy framework for higher education. Retrieved from http://acrl.ala.org/ilstandards/wp-content/uploads/2015/01/Framework-MW15-Board-Docs.pdf

ALA AASL (American Association of School Librarians). (2007). Standards for the 21st century learner. Retrieved from http://www.ala.org/aasl/standards-guidelines/learning-standards

ALA (American Library Association). (2000). Information literacy standards. Retrieved from http://www.ala.org/acrl/standards/informationliteracycompetency#ildef

Barlow, A., & Leston, R. (2012). *Beyond the blogosphere: information and its children*. Santa Barbara, CA: ABC-CLIO, LLC.

Best Selling Video Games. (2015). Retrieved from http://en.wikipedia.org/wiki/List_of_best-selling_video_games

Brown, R., & Kasper, T. (2013). The fusion of literacy and games: A case study in assessing the goals of a library video game program. *Library Trends*, *61*(4), 755–558. doi:10.1353/lib.2013.0012

Bulu, S. T. (2012). Place presence, social presence, co-presence, and satisfaction in virtual worlds. *Computers & Education*, *58*(1), 154–161. doi:10.1016/j.compedu.2011.08.024

Common Sense Media. (2015). Best reading games. Retrieved from https://www.commonsensemedia.org/lists/reading-games

Commonwealth of Australia. (2010). Literature review on the impact of playing violent video games on aggression. Retrieved from http://www.classification.govau/Pages/Public/Media-And-Student-Resources/Other%20Resources/Literature%20review%20on%20the%20impact%20of%20playing%20violent%20video%20games%20on%20aggression.pdf

Duffy, T. M., & Cunningham, D. J. (2001). Constructivism: Implications for the design and delivery of instruction. In D. H. Jonassen (Ed.), *Handbook of Research for Educational Communications and Technology*. New York, NY: Simon and Schuster.

Education Week. (2015). Oculus Rift fueling new vision for virtual reality in K-12. Retrieved from http://www.edweek.org/ew/articles/2014/08/27/02oculus.h34.html

Fontichiaro, K. (2010). Research strategies grades 3-5. *School Library Monthly* [serial online]. 29 (3): 48-50. Retrieved from http://www.schoollibrarymonthly.com/articles/Fontichiaro2010-v27n3p12.html

Gates Foundation. (2011). Press release for innovative grants to develop new teaching and learning tools. Retrieved from http://www.gatesfoundation.org/Media-Center/Press-Releases/2011/04/Gates-Foundation-Announces-Portfolio-of-Innovative-Grants-to-Develop-New-Teaching-and-Learning-Tools-that-Support-Teachers-and-Help-Students

Gee, J. P. (2003). *What video games have to teach us about learning and literacy*. New York: Palgrave Macmillan.

Grassian, E., & Kaplowitz, J. R. (2009). *Information literacy instruction: theory and practice* (2nd ed.). ALA Neal Schuman.

Grassian, E., & Trueman, R. (2013). What's in it for me?: Professional development in virtual worlds. In A. Sigal (Ed.), *Advancing Library Education: Technological Innovation and Instructional Design* (pp. 91–109). Hershey, PA: Information Science Reference. doi:10.4018/978-1-4666-3688-0.ch006

Hew, K. F., & Cheung, W. S. (2010). Use of three-dimensional (3-D) immersive virtual worlds in K-12 and higher education settings: A review of the research. *British Journal of Educational Technology*, *41*(1), 33–55. doi:10.1111/j.1467-8535.2008.00900.x

Hill, V. (2012). Valibrarian's Anne Frank MOOC experience. Retrieved from http://www.livebinders.com/play/play?id=694451

Hill, V. (2014). Ethridge Minecraft digital citizens library. https://youtu.be/BQiBtD7fD1k

Hill, V. (2015). Digital citizenship through game design in minecraft. *New Library World*, *116*(7/8), 369–382. doi:10.1108/NLW-09-2014-0112

Hill, V., & Lee, H. (2009). Libraries and immersive learning environments unite in second life. *Library Hi Tech*, *27*(3), 338–356. doi:10.1108/07378830910988487

InfoLit Ischool in Second Life. (2015). http://secondlife.com/destination/infolit-ischool

Institute of Play. (2014). Psychometric considerations in game-based learning assessment executive summary. Retrieved from http://www.instituteofplay.org/wp-content/uploads/2014/02/GlassLab_GBA1_Summary.pdf

ISTE (International Society for Technology in Education). (2011). Understanding the holocaust project. Retrieved from http://sigve.iste.wikispaces.net/file/view/ISTE+2011+Newsletter+Final.pdf

Karlova, N., & Fisher, K. (2013). A Social diffusion model of misinformation and disinformation for understanding human information behavior. *Information Research* [serial online], 18(1), 1-12. Retrieved from http://www.informationr.net/ir/18-1/paper573.html#VVEXW2RViko

Kotler, P. (1986). The prosumer movement: a new challenge for marketers in NA - advances in consumer research eds. Richard J. Lutz, Provo, UT: *Association for Consumer Research,* (13): 510-513. Retrieved March 12, 2015, from http://acrwebsite.org/volumes/6542/volumes/v13/NA-13

Kucklich, J. (2005). Precarious playbour: modders and the digital games industry. *Fibreculture,* 5. Retrieved from http://five.fibreculturejournal.org/fcj-025-precarious-playbour-modders-and-the-digital-games-industry/

Kuhlthau, C., & Maniotes, L. (2010). Building guided inquiry teams for 21st century learners. *School Library Monthly* [serial online], 26(5), 18-21. Retrieved from http://www.schoollibrarymonthly.com/articles/Kuhlthau&Maniotes2010-v26n5p18.html

Kzero Worldswide. (2014). Virtual world reports. Retrieved from http://www.kzero.co.uk/

Mackey, T. P., & Jacobson, T. E. (2011). Reframing information literacy as a metaliteracy. *College & Research Libraries*, *72*(1), 62–78. doi:10.5860/crl-76r1

Maddux, C., & Johnson, D. (n. d.). The need for a research Focus on the possible causal link between violent behavior and videogames. *Computers in the Schools*, *30*(1/2), 1–3.

Mastel, K., & Huston, D. (2009). Using video games to teach game design: A gaming collection for libraries. *Computers in Libraries*, *29*(3), 41–44.

Merriam Webster. (2015). Online dictionary. Retrieved from http://www.merriam-webster.com/dictionary/gamification

Parks, N. (2008). Video games as reconstructionist sites of learning in art education. *Studies in Art Education: A Journal of Issues and Research in Art Education*, 49(3), 235-250.

Pew Research Center. (2015). Teens, social media, and technology overview 2015. Retrieved from http://www.pewinternet.org/topics/mobile/

Rey, P.J. (2012). Gamification, playbor, and expoitation. *Cyborgology*. Retrieved from http://thesocietypages.org/cyborgology/2012/10/15/gamification-playbor-exploitation-2/

Sicart, M. (2013). Moral dilemmas in computer games. *Design Issues*, *29*(3), 28–37. doi:10.1162/DESI_a_00219

The Independent. Photo of Anne Frank. Retrieved from http://www.independent.co.uk/incoming/article8673682.ece/alternates/w460/web-frank-rex.jpg

Webber, S. (2013). Information literacy: A subject for the 21st century. *Pakistan Journal of Library and Information Science*. Retrieved from http://www.academia.edu/6956094/Information_Literacy_A_Subject_for_the_21st_Century

KEY TERMS AND DEFINITIONS

Constructivist Learning Theory: A belief that learners construct knowledge themselves through personal interest, knowledge, experience and social interaction.

Digital Culture: Society (post Internet) is connected online through mobile devices and computer networks across time and space.

Immersive Learning Environment: A digital space built in 3D for individuals to interact and learn through simulation across a computer network or grid.

Information Literacy: The ability for an individual to locate, access and use information effectively in multiple formats.

Massive Open Online Course (MOOC): An open access course developed for online users at low cost or no cost on a large scale.

Metaliteracy: The ability to utilize information across many formats, including print, audio, digital, virtual, or augmented resources.

Virtual World: A persistent digital environment hosted online for participants to build, create, or interact across a computer network or grid.

Chapter 9
Disciplinarily-Integrated Games:
Generalizing Across Domains and Model Types

Douglas B Clark
Vanderbilt University, USA

Pratim Sengupta
University of Calgary, Canada

Satyugjit Virk
Vanderbilt University, USA

ABSTRACT

Clark, Sengupta, Brady, Martinez-Garza, and Killingsworth (2015) and Sengupta and Clark (submitted) propose disciplinarily-integrated games as a generalizable template for supporting students in interpreting, manipulating, and translating across phenomenological and formal representations in support of a Science as Practice perspective (Pickering, 1995; Lehrer & Schauble, 2006). To explore the generalizability of disciplinarily-integrated games, this chapter proposes other hypothetical examples of disciplinarily-integrated games in physics, biology, chemistry, and the social sciences. We explore disciplinarily-integrated games in three categories, beginning with the category involving the nearest and simplest transfer of the template and extending to the category involving the furthest and most complex transfer: (1) time-series analyses with Cartesian formal representations, (2) constraint-system analyses with Cartesian formal representations, and (3) other model types and non-Cartesian formal representations. We close with the discussion of the implications of this generalizability.

DOI: 10.4018/978-1-4666-9629-7.ch009

INTRODUCTION

Clark, Sengupta, Brady, Martinez-Garza, and Killingsworth (2015) outline an approach for leveraging digital games as a medium to support the development of scientific modeling in K-12 classrooms based on the Science as Practice perspective (Pickering, 1995; Lehrer & Schauble, 2006). Clark et al. name this approach disciplinary integration and outline its development though a program of iterative research on student learning. Sengupta and Clark (submitted) extend the theoretical framing of disciplinarily-integrated games in terms of materiality within the classroom and the iterative design of multiple complementary symbolic inscriptional systems.

Clark et al. (2015) and Sengupta and Clark (submitted) propose that disciplinarily-integrated games represent a highly generalizable genre. To explore this claim of generalizability, the current chapter proposes other hypothetical examples of disciplinarily-integrated games (which we will refer to as DIGs for brevity) in physics, biology, chemistry, and the social sciences. We explore DIGs in three categories, beginning with model types and modeling strategies involving the nearest and simplest transfer of the DIG template and extending to those involving the furthest and most complex transfer:

1. Time-series analyses with Cartesian formal representations,
2. Constraint-system analyses with Cartesian formal representations, and
3. Other model types and non-Cartesian formal representations. We close with the discussion of the implications of this generalizability.

BACKGROUND

The Science as Practice (or SaP) perspective (Pickering, 1995; Lehrer & Schauble, 2006a, 2006b; Duschl et al., 2007) argues that the development of scientific concepts is deeply intertwined with the development of epistemic and representational practices (e.g., modeling). Models are inscriptions and fictive representations of real things (e.g., planes, cars, or buildings) or systems (e.g., atomic structure, weather patterns, traffic flow, ecosystems, or social systems) that are simpler than the real objects and systems they represent, but preferentially highlight certain properties of the referent (Rapp & Sengupta, 2012). Modeling is generally recognized as the core disciplinary practice in science, and involves the iterative generation and refinement of inscriptions, which in turn serve as, or provide mechanistic explanations of a referent phenomenon (Giere, 1988; Nercessian, 2002; Lehrer & Schauble, 2002).

Science and math education researchers have shown that engaging in modeling and progressively refining one's representation of some aspect of the world (e.g., a model or an inscription) can contribute to a deeper understanding of mathematical and scientific knowledge and practices (Gravemeijer, Cobb, Bowers, & Whitenack, 2000; Hall & Stevens, 1995). Enyedy (2005) refers to this process as "progressive symbolization". Lehrer (2009) makes clear that, while students need to see and handle models of abstract concepts in order for meaningful conceptual change to happen, the nature of the model is key. Developing a good model involves designing representations that capture essential dynamic features of the relationships they describe, but these representations also edit the relationships, by foregrounding some elements and obscuring or omitting others (Lehrer & Schauble, 2010; Lynch, 1990). Pedagogically, this involves creating opportunities for model evaluation by way of model comparison, i.e., designing curricula that involve the iterative creation of and comparison between different types of inscriptions or models of the same phenomenon (Lehrer & Schauble, 2010; Lesh & Doerr, 2003). This is because models are fundamentally analogies that can only be evaluated in light of comparison with competing models (Lehrer & Schauble, 2010).

As proposed in Clark, Sengupta, Brady, Martinez-Garza, and Killingsworth (2015), disciplinary integration is an approach to designing games in terms of a Science as Practice perspective. More specifically, disciplinary integration can be thought of in terms of Allan Collins's and colleagues' analyses of "model types" and "modeling strategies" (Collins, White, & Fadel, in preparation), which Collins and colleagues have termed "epistemic forms" and "epistemic games" in earlier work (Collins, 2011; Collins & Ferguson, 1993; Morrison & Collins, 1995). Collins and colleagues argue that the professional work of scientists can be understood in terms of model types (epistemic forms) that are the target structures guiding scientific inquiry and modeling strategies (epistemic games) that are the sets of rules and strategies for creating, manipulating, and refining those model types. While Collins and colleagues did not write with the intention of informing the design of actual digital games (they used the term "game" as a metaphor), DIGs can leverage the ideas of Collins and colleagues by structuring digital game play around modeling strategies (epistemic games) of designing and manipulating formal disciplinary model types (epistemic forms). More specifically, the puzzles and game-play mechanics of DIGs distill model types and the modeling strategies for navigating and manipulating those models.

As discussed in Clark, Sengupta, Brady, Martinez-Garza, and Killingsworth (2015), this specific emphasis on modeling as game play around disciplinary model types stands in contrast to engaging in "inquiry" more broadly, as is common in 3D virtual worlds (e.g., *Quest Atlantis*, *River City*, or *Crystal Island*). A key distinction between these two forms of virtual environments involves the nature and breadth of focus of the inquiry undertaken by students. Virtual inquiry worlds generally engage students in the practices and discourses (Gee, 1990) of a discipline at the level of inquiry writ large. Much of the pedagogical power and engagement of 3D virtual inquiry worlds tends to focus heavily on their impressive affordances for roleplaying, narrative, and identity-building (cf. Gee, 2007; Squire, 2011). As Clark, Sengupta, Brady, Martinez-Garza, and Killingsworth explain, however, while 3D virtual inquiry worlds are compelling and powerful, their scope and structure involve tradeoffs in terms of the individual tasks or puzzles. More specifically, individual tasks and puzzles are often relatively mundane (e.g., click on a character to be told a piece of evidence, click on a location to get a reading on oxygen levels, or click on a location to bring up another mini-game to collect evidence). Essentially, whereas 3D virtual inquiry worlds tend to cast students as scientists investigating a "mystery" at the level of overarching inquiry, DIGs do not attempt the depth of immersion, identity-building, and role-playing of virtual inquiry worlds (nor do we dispute their importance or value in virtual inquiry worlds). Instead, however, DIGs are designed to engage students more deeply in specific modeling and representational practices of developing, interpreting, manipulating, and translating across specific model types. This focus allows DIGs to progressively deepen the puzzle at the heart of the game and, more broadly, allows all elements of the game to emphasize that puzzle.

HOW WOULD DISCIPLINARY INTEGRATION LOOK ACROSS MODEL TYPES?

To explore the generalizability of disciplinarily-integrated games, this chapter proposes other hypothetical examples of disciplinarily-integrated games in physics, biology, chemistry, and the social sciences. We explore disciplinarily-integrated games in three categories, beginning with the category involving the nearest and simplest transfer of the template and extending to the category involving the furthest and most complex transfer:

1. TIME-series analyses with Cartesian formal representations,
2. Constraint-system analyses with Cartesian formal representations, and
3. Other model types and non-Cartesian formal representations. We close with the discussion of the implications of this generalizability.

Core DIG Template: SURGE Symbolic

SURGE Symbolic is the prototypical DIG template that we will consider in terms of generalizability to hypothetical DIGs for other disciplinary topics (Figure 1). More information and playable demos of *SURGE Symbolic* and other *SURGE* games are available at www.surgeuniverse.com. *SURGE Symbolic* is a game that is the result of the evolution of design, research, and thinking chronicled in Clark et al. (2015). Whereas earlier versions of *SURGE (i.e., SURGE Classic, SURGE Next,* and *SURGE: Fuzzy Chronicles)* focused on layering formal representations over informal representations, *SURGE Symbolic* inverts this order, layering informal representations over formal representations while organizing gameplay explicitly around navigating, translating, and coordinating across representations.

Earlier versions of *SURGE* supported reflection on the results of game play through formal representations as a means to support strategy-refinement, but the formal representations were not the medium through which players planned, implemented, and manipulated their game strategies. Earlier versions of *SURGE* provided vector representations, for example, to help students understand what was happening and how they might adjust their control strategy, but these formal representations only communicated information that a player might or might not use. The challenges and opportunities in a given game level, however, were communicated through the layout of elements in the game world, not in the formal representations. Similarly, the player's controls for executing a strategy were also independent of the formal representations. Thus, while attending to the formal representations might help a player succeed in a level, earlier *SURGE* games did not use formal representations as the medium through which challenges and opportunities were communicated to the player, nor did earlier *SURGE* games use diagrammatic formal representations as the medium of control.

SURGE Symbolic builds on research on teaching physics using simulations and motion sensors (e.g., Brasell, 1987; diSessa et al., 1991; Mokros & Tinker, 1987), research on constructing graphs based on assembling relevant "pieces" of trajectories of motion, and research on SimCalc (e.g., Hegedus & Roschelle, 2013; Kaput, 1992; Roschelle, Knudsen, & Hegedus, 2010). In the work of Tinker and colleagues, students have often been provided graphs of position or velocity that they were asked to replicate using the controls of the system, which might involve a motion sensor. Sengupta and Farris (2012) developed an agent-based modeling toolkit in which learners as young as 3th graders could generate trajectories of motion by providing simple rules to a computational agent (e.g., a Logo Turtle). These trajectories themselves were programmable; students were able to select portions of the trajectories and rearrange them vertically to generate speed vs. time and distance vs. time graphs. Similarly, students have been provided with a dot trace representation overlaid on their phenomenological view that they worked to interpret in terms of a graph (diSessa et al., 1991), and SimCalc pioneered in scaffolding students' integration and differentiation between and across Cartesian graphs of position, velocity, and acceleration over time by dynamically linking across representations (Kaput, 1992; Hegedus & Roschelle, 2013).

DIGs build on these bodies of research by pushing more deeply on approaches for leveraging formal representations as the means of communicating challenges to players, as well as leveraging abstract formal representations as

Figure 1. SURGE Symbolic level where the player is halfway through launching a trial; Surge is moving in the phenomenological world on the left and this motion is being graphed in the Cartesian Control and Communication graphs on the right. Colored regions in the position and velocity graphs display when and where the player will encounter hazards and goals.

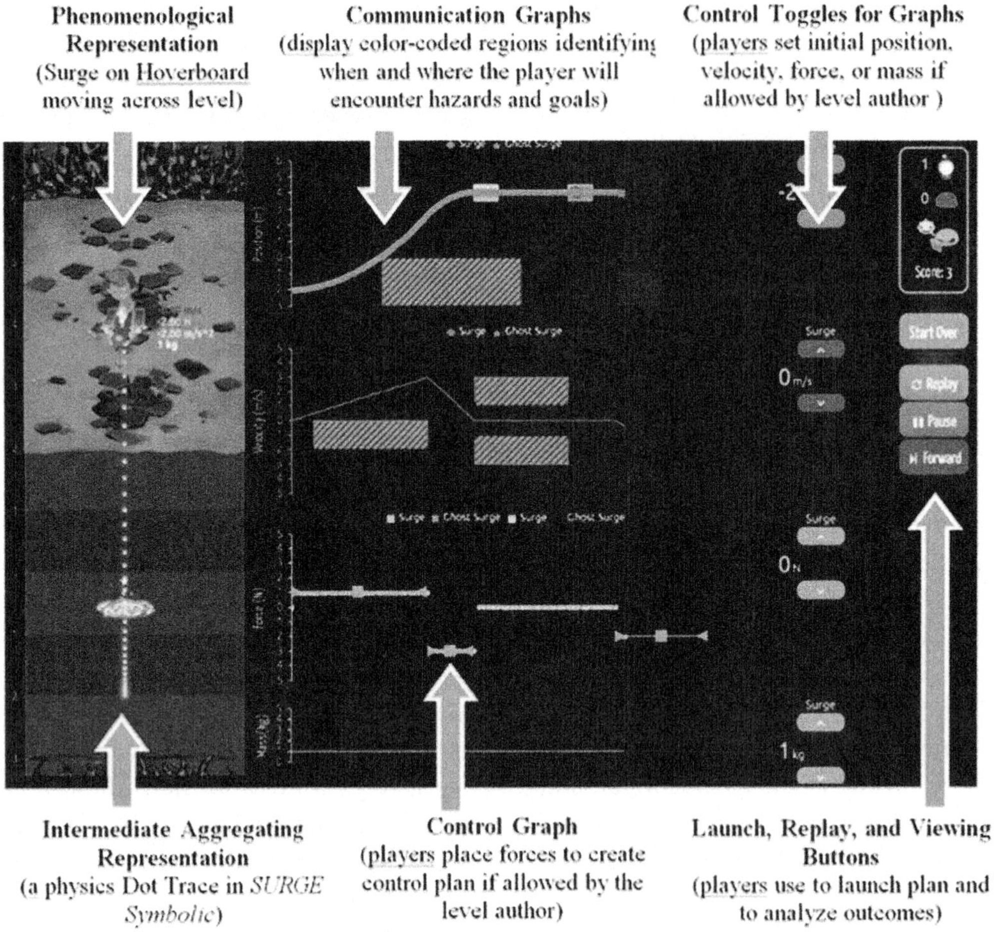

the players' means of control within the game. Furthermore, we propose that DIGs generalize beyond time-series analyses and multiple representation systems involving Cartesian graphs of change over time (the central claim we explore in this chapter).

DIGs, by definition, use formal representations as the medium through which challenges and opportunities are communicated to the player (Communication Representations), and DIGs use formal representations as the medium through which the player implements strategies and exerts control over the game (Control Representations). Some DIGs might use the same representation for both control and communication, while other DIGs might use one or more formal representations for communication and one or more other representations for control. All DIGs include a phenomenological representation (which in traditional digital games would be the primary focus). Furthermore, all DIGs include an intermediate representation to support players in translating from the phenomenological representation to the formal representations and to constrain their interpretation of the formal representation. The goal in all DIGs involves interpreting, creating, modifying, and translating across these formal and phenomenological representations.

The template for *SURGE Symbolic*, for example, presents the phenomenological representation (which we refer to as "the world") on the left side of Figure 1. The phenomenological representation portrays the heroine, Surge, on her hoverboard moving forward and backward along a game map. The formal Cartesian graphs on the right side are the communication and control representations. The position and velocity graphs in Figure 1, for example, can present information about the specific regions of the game-world that will be affected by dangerous electrical storms at given times, as well as information about locations and times where rewards or allies will rendezvous with Surge. As a result of this design approach, the Cartesian space emerges as a set of scientific instruments for the player by communicating data about the game world that are not available through other means. While Figure 1 shows an example where the challenges and opportunities are communicated through the position graph and velocity graphs, any subset (or all) of the Cartesian graphs could serve this role. Simultaneously, the Cartesian graphs also play the role of an instrument panel or mission planner, offering fine-grained control over the movement of the Surge spacecraft. In Figure 1, for example, the player can exert control by placing forces of various magnitudes and durations at different time points in the force graph. Alternatively, the player can exert control through the other graphs using the toggles to the right of the graphs. The author of a game level designates which graphs are visible to the player, which graphs are used for which purposes (communication or control), and what challenges and goals constitute the level.

Thus, all DIGs have the following characteristics:

1. Formal representations for controlling the game,
2. Formal representations for communicating challenges and opportunities,
3. A phenomenological representation presenting the phenomenon being modeled,
4. An intermediate aggregating representation, and
5. Game mechanics and goals focused on engaging the player in interpreting, creating, modifying, and translating across these formal and phenomenological representations.

To have value, the proposed specific template and broader DIG genre must be generalizable. To explore this claim of generalizability, the following sections propose other hypothetical examples of DIGs in physics, biology, chemistry, and the social sciences. We will explore DIGs in terms of three model types, beginning with the model type involving the nearest and simplest transfer of the DIG template to model types involving the furthest and most complex transfer:

1. Time-series analyses with Cartesian formal representations,
2. Constraint-system analyses with Cartesian formal representations, and
3. Other model types and non-Cartesian formal representations.

Time Series Analyses with Cartesian Representations

The nearest transfer of the template is to other topics focusing on time-series analyses where Cartesian graphs of change over time remain the focal formal representation. In such cases, the template outlined in this paper transfers relatively directly and requires minimal discussion because the template remains essentially identical with time series analyses as the modeling strategy and Cartesian representations of change over time as the model type.

One example would involve exploring predator-prey relationships in population ecology. The time-series analyses would focus on changes and relationships between populations over time depicting the classic Lotka-Volterra equation relationships (Figure 2). The phenomenological representation could be in the form of a multi-agent simulation in which predator and prey animals within a given area run around reproducing, eating, and being eaten. An advantage of such simulations is that they enable learners to investigate the system-level behaviors (e.g., graphs of population change over time) while taking on the perspective of the individual agents (Wilenksy & Reisman, 2006; Dickes & Sengupta, 2013). Research also shows, however, that students' interactions with multi-agent simulations need to be scaffolded so that students can identify the appropriate agent-level interactions and events (Dickes & Sengupta, 2013; Basu, Sengupta & Biswas, 2015). Herein, we posit that the bridging representations in DIGs could indeed act as such a scaffold. For example, the phenomenological and formal representations under consideration here could be bridged by an intermediate representation that dynamically aggregates or stacks the different agent-types of animals in the simulation to represent the population levels of each agent-type. In terms of narrative, the game might be called *Alien Populations*, and perhaps the player is an alien zoo keeper who needs to manage populations within the zoo. Perhaps the keeper can adjust temperature and irrigation in the zoo. As per the DIG template, the challenges and opportunities in each game level are depicted within the formal representations. The Cartesian graphs might, for example, depict target levels for various populations at various times to avoid or attain. Also in line with the DIG template, the player specifies her strategy for an attempt in another formal representation, perhaps a Cartesian graph of temperature and irrigation levels over time to influence plant growth and animal activity levels.

Figure 2. Classic Lotka-Volterra predator-prey population graph

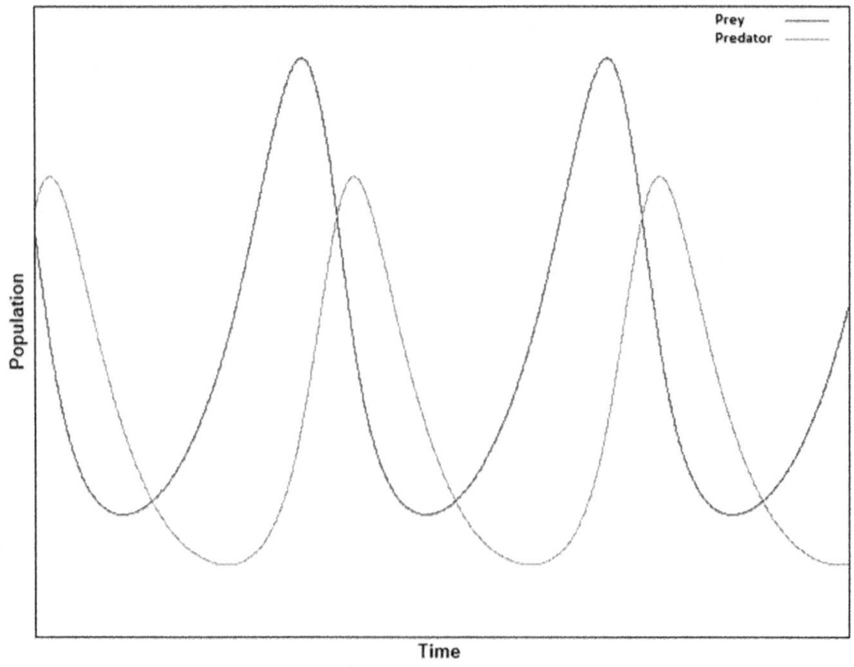

In terms of other possible topics, the phenomenological view in a DIG for teaching chemical reaction kinetics might be a cylinder with various reactant molecules mixing together to create products. In terms of narrative, the player might need to get a certain number of products by a certain time because the cylinder is being used to create a series of pills to help cure a disease. A DIG about action potential in neurons might include a phenomenological representation that is a dynamic visualizations showing how sodium and potassium ions flow into and out of the neuron at the axon hillock. In terms of narrative, a player might need to generate specific membrane-potential over time graphs to remotely control an alien organism she has engineered and set loose on a foreign planet. In designing a DIG to teach about glacial retreat, the phenomenological representation might depict a dynamic glacial tongue protruding from an arctic land mass towards the ocean. The narrative might involve connecting families of walruses while also shielding them from intermittent incursions of polar bears by adjusting the glacial tongue.

All of these proposed DIGs focus on Time Series Analyses with Cartesian formal representations. All of these DIGs could thus build on the *SURGE Symbolic* design template. Essentially, challenges and opportunities are presented to the player in the formal representations, and the player manipulates and creates her strategies and actions through the formal representations. Across all of these DIGs, the interfaces, representational forms, and intermediate aggregating representations would remain relatively consistent.

Constraint-Systems with Cartesian Representations

What about generalizing beyond Cartesian time-series analyses? Collins and colleagues outline a wealth of model types and modeling strategies in terms of structural, functional/causal, and process/behavioral analyses. We propose that the next most proximal category of DIGs focuses on constraint-systems that include Cartesian representations with axes other than time. Collins and colleagues define constraint-systems as process/behavioral analyses where: (a) the model type is the equation (or equations) describing the steady state of the system and (b) the most common modeling strategy involves controlling variables by manipulating one variable at a time while all others are held constant to determine the behavior of each on the system. Constraint-system analyses therefore lend themselves to displaying relationships using Cartesian graphs as the formal representations with one variable along each axis and the other variables as controls for manipulating the Cartesian graphs.

In the domain of chemistry, the ideal gas law presents one possible context for a constraint-system analysis DIG. The ideal gas law is governed by the equation PV = nRT, where "P" stands for pressure, "V" stands for volume, and "T" stands for temperature. The phenomenological representation might comprise a simulation where molecules move around in a container and the player can make the container larger or smaller (volume) and increase or decrease the temperature by altering the size of a flame on the system. Pressure in this system is visualized by a series of red marks on the container that occur every time a gas molecule collides with it. In this game, perhaps called *Kinetic Explorer*, the player has to manipulate pressure, volume, and temperature to manage specialized cells that power a hovercraft she uses to explore an alien world. Cartesian graphs of pressure vs. volume, volume vs. temperature, and temperature vs. pressure become the control and communication representations. Power cells burst if pressure remains too high for too long, but the cells provide minimal power to the craft when the pressure is low.

In the domain of physics, Coulomb's force of repulsion and attraction presents another context for a constraint-system analysis DIG. Coulomb's force of repulsion and attraction is particularly interesting for Cartesian graphs because it involves both multiplicative and exponential relationships ($F = k * q1 * q2/r^2$). The phenomenological representation might depict a series of charge spheres where the player can control the distance between the spheres (r) and the charges on each sphere (q1, q2). The narrative might cast the player as a space explorer who needs to achieve the right amount of repulsion or attraction between charge spheres in an alien device in order to navigate across the game world (parallel to game-play in *SuperCharged*, Squire et al., 2004, but played out in formal Cartesian representations rather than in a simulated world).

These proposed constraint-system analysis DIGs parallel the time-series analysis DIGs in their focus on Cartesian graphs as the formal control and communication representations. Thus, these constraint analysis DIGs might also build on very similar design templates and interfaces to present the challenges and opportunities in a game level as well as a very similar design templates and interfaces through which the player plans, authors, and executes her strategy for the game level.

FUTURE DIRECTIONS: EPISTEMIC FORMS BEYOND CARTESIAN REPRESENTATIONS

The previous sections suggest that the DIG template and genre proposed in this paper are generalizable to topics focusing on time-series analyses and constraint-system analyses where the formal representations of communication and control are Cartesian graphs. This opens up a wide range topics across which the genre might apply. But what about other model types and modeling strategies beyond these?

Collins and colleagues (Collins & Ferguson, 1993; Collins, 2011; Collins et al., in preparation) discuss three different major groups of model types:

1. *Structural models for analyzing the structure of phenomena,*
2. *Causal and functional models for analyzing causal or functional aspects of phenomena, and*
3. *Behavioral models for describing the dynamic behavior of phenomena (Collins, personal communication).*

The time-series and constraint-system model types we have focused on thus far in terms of possible DIGs are behavioral models (which Collins and Ferguson, 1993, originally termed "process analyses"). Process/behavioral models focus on the dynamic behavior of phenomena. The major behavioral/process model types discussed by Collins and colleagues include: system-dynamics models, aggregate-behavior models, constraint-system analyses, situation-action models, and trend and cyclical analysis (with time-series analyses being a subset of trend analyses). With that in mind, behavioral/process model types seem the next most proximal group in terms of generalization given that a focus on dynamic behavior lends itself well to the medium of digital games.

System-dynamics models, for example, seem promising for DIGs because they involve specifying relationships and action sequences that determine/predict outcomes given a scenario or set of parameters. In a system-dynamics model, variables are linked together by positive or negative links. Variables can be increased or decreased. These changes, in turn, influence other variables in the system though the links. These models can be qualitative or quantitative. Various lag, homeostatic, or feedback functions can be built into the models. Climate, economic, ecological models, and models in many other disciplines can be structured as system-dynamics models. Figure 3 presents simple system-dynamics models for economics and population ecology.

Figure 3. System dynamics model in economics (top) and ecology (bottom)

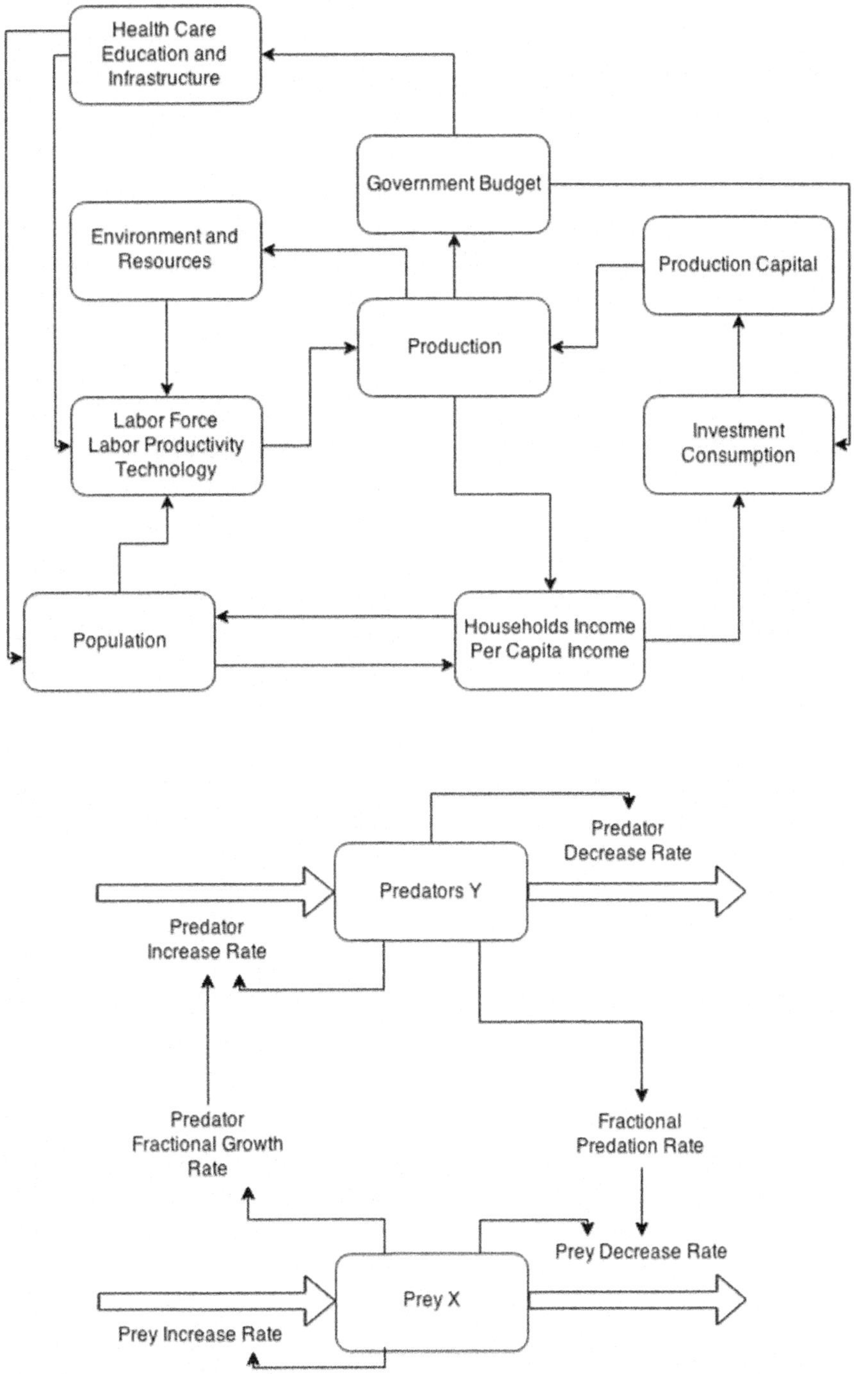

Could interesting game-play be built around interpreting and manipulating a system-dynamics model? Actually, a commercially and critically successful franchise of "indie" recreational games has already done so. *Democracy I, II,* and *III* are essentially system-dynamics models (http://www.positech.co.uk) where the changes you make to one variable influences all of the connected variables (either positively or negatively depending on the valence and magnitude of the link). *Democracy* is a great example because all of the game play is located and focused in the formal representations. The models in *Democracy* games are incredibly complex with huge numbers of nodes, but the models would not need to be so complex for other games. Nonetheless, the *Democracy* games focus entirely on reading and manipulating a single formal system-dynamics representation while monitoring other formal representations for information and changes across variables. Thus system-dynamics models, in conjunction with other formal representations, clearly are viable for DIGs. System dynamics models could thus be implemented in other DIGs. In the earlier *Alien Zoo Keeper* example about population dynamics, for example, rather than using Cartesian change-over-time graphs for the player to plan and author her strategy, she might manipulate the population system-dynamics model in Figure 3 to plan and author her strategy while a Cartesian graph of populations over time might still be employed as the representations that present the challenges and opportunities for the level (perhaps *Zoo Keeper System Dynamics*).

In terms of other process/behavioral model types, situation-action models are also promising for DIGs set in various science, social science, and robotics disciplines. Situation-action models specify a set of if/then rules that specify what actions an agent will take in what situations. As situations change, either because of previous actions or because of changes in the agent's environment, the rules specify the next actions (or inaction). Such situation-action model rule sets could be used either for player control or for game communication of challenges and opportunities in a level. In *Zoo Keeper Situation Action*, for example, a situation-action model might be used for the player to author her strategy by specifying the actions and properties of the animals being modeled, which might then play out in a system-dynamics model or an agent-based model (another type of behavioral/process model).

Behavioral/process models thus seem fertile ground for generalizing DIGs. Beyond behavioral/process models, however, Collins's and colleagues' structural-analysis model types and causal/functional model types seem potentially more challenging for designing DIGs with our current templates. Structural-analysis model types "include compare and contrast, cost-benefit analysis, primitive elements analysis, tables or cross-product analysis, tree structures or hierarchical analysis, and axiom systems. Structural-analysis [model types] answer the question 'What is the nature of x?' by breaking x down into subsets or constituents and describing the relationships among the constituents" (Collins & Ferguson, 1993, p. 29). Causal/functional analysis model types specify "the causal or functional structures that relate elements in a system. These include critical-event analysis, cause-and-effect analysis, problem-centered analysis, multicausal analysis, and form-and-function analysis" (Collins & Ferguson, 1993, p. 33). Structural-analysis (e.g., the structured tree model, Figure 4) as well as causal/functional analysis model types (e.g., the multi-factor analysis model) are therefore less dynamic than process/behavioral analysis model types. Because they are less dynamic, they will require more fundamental design shifts for DIGs.

In DIGs, structural-analysis model types and causal/functional model types might support more static or less dynamic puzzle-like or mystery types of games where the player is working to construct or discover the relationships in the model. Structural-analysis model types and causal/functional model types might be incorporated into DIGs, however, in tandem with other more dynamic models for more dynamic game-play. The model that articulates the challenge and goals for a DIG, for example, might be a dynamic agent-based model from which the player needs to deduce the relationships of the elements/agents within some structural-analysis or causal/functional model type. In this case, intermediate representations would likely be very helpful for

Figure 4. Structured tree model of fish relationships

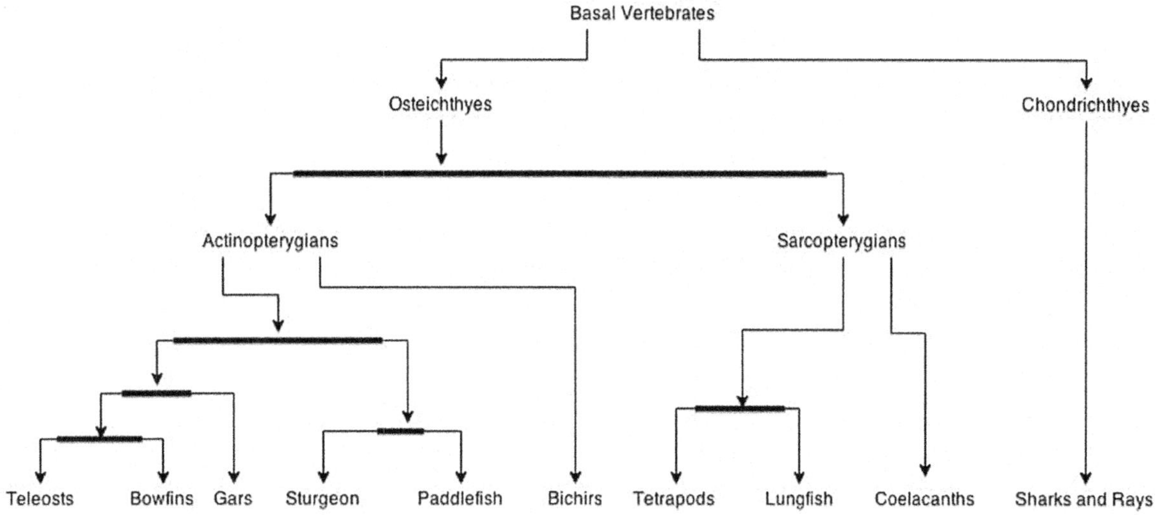

players in translating between the different formal representations. While these examples suggest that the overarching genre of DIGs might indeed be generalizable for structural-analysis model types and causal/functional model types, the DIG genre outlined in this paper seem most generalizable across behavioral/process analysis model types.

CONCLUSION

We propose that these examples are only a subset of possible DIGs, potentially making DIGs a highly generalizable template for integrating digital games into the curriculum. Furthermore, the puzzles and mechanics in these games are highly focused, providing clean, challenging, and engaging puzzles. Disciplinary integration also responds to calls for greater emphasis on problem-solving, 21st century skills, and engaging students in the practices of disciplines to develop deeper understanding. We now close the paper by considering the implications of this proposed generalizability in terms of the propagation of digital learning games across the curriculum and the conceptual development of students within this integrated curriculum.

Economically Feasible Propagation of Games in the Curriculum

Up to now, developing digital games for learning in multiple disciplines at an economically feasible budget has often devolved into simple forms of gamification (i.e., simply layering points and badges over mechanics that are not themselves game-like). Developing a game where core disciplinary ideas drive game-mechanics, on the other hand, has proven time-intensive and cost-intensive. This, in turn, has created a barrier to the systematic integration of digital games as a medium across the curriculum. A potential advantage of the generalizability of the DIG genre and the design implications proposed in this chapter is that once a DIG is honed and refined through iterative cycles of design and research, other games can be developed building on the conceptual, design, functional, and software foundations of that DIG to create DIGs in other disciplines focusing on the same epistemic forms and games. These important economies of scale in terms of development time and cost could therefore make possible broad and systematic integration of digital games across the curriculum.

Beyond Learning Within the Game: Development Across the Curriculum

Even more importantly, this generalizability has critical implications in terms of integration and students' development across the curriculum. Sengupta and Clark (submitted) explore the affordances of DIGs in terms of their integration into the larger curriculum both in terms of the materiality of the curriculum as well as leveraging teachers' existing pedagogical resources and epistemological framing around modeling. Sengupta and Clark (in preparation) explore and theoretically frame the developmental process across the span of multiple curricular units, semesters, and years. Essentially, much research on digital environments in the classroom focuses at the level of the activity rather than the level of the longer-term curriculum because of the limitations of the development of technology. The conceptualization of DIGs as multiple representational systems, however, lends itself well to thinking about the connections between and across curricula beyond DIGs in terms of underlying foundational epistemic and representational forms.

As explained in Clark et al. (2015) and Sengupta and Clark (submitted), the "Science as Practice" perspective is rooted in the long-term production of scientific knowledge through the long-term development of epistemic and representational practices. Sengupta and Clark (in preparation) point out, however, that students in a typical K-12 science classroom have to learn several different domains during the same academic year, thereby minimizing opportunities of meaningful long-term engagement within a single curricular unit. By considering the epistemic and representational forms within each unit, though, a few DIGs could be interspersed throughout the academic year with the goal of meaningfully connecting these forms across the sequence of curricular units. Within a DIG, the multiple representational systems can be designed in a manner that players begin with a familiar representational form, develop intermediate abstractions, and then generate new representational forms that are not only canonically more sophisticated, but can also become representational forms that extend through succeeding curricular units.

In their strongest form, therefore, DIGs can help us conceptualize the year-long science curriculum as a careful assembly of curricular units, arranged in terms of meaningful connections between epistemic and representational forms, designed to create meaningful coherence across the curriculum. From the perspective of student learning, such integration across curricular units shifts the focus from thinking about students' learning within a game – i.e., a short-term focus on learning – to students' long-term development. This emphasis on long-term development parallels calls across reform standards for students' development of epistemic and representational practices central to scientific expertise in an authentic manner representative of the professional practice of scientists.

ACKNOWLEDGMENT

This material is based upon work supported by the National Science Foundation under Grant No. 1119290. Any opinions, findings, and conclusions or recommendations expressed in this material are those of the author(s) and do not necessarily reflect the views of the National Science Foundation.

REFERENCES

Basu, S., Sengupta, P., & Biswas, G. (2015). A scaffolding framework to support learning of emergent phenomena using multi-agent based simulation environments. *Research in Science Education*, *45*(2), 293–324. doi:10.1007/s11165-014-9424-z

Brasell, H. (1987). The effect of real-time laboratory graphing on learning graphic representations of distance and velocity. *Journal of Research in Science Teaching*, *24*(4), 385–395. doi:10.1002/tea.3660240409

Clark, D.B., Sengupta, P., Brady, C., Martinez-Garza, M., & Killingsworth, S. (2015). Disciplinary Integration in Digital Games for Science Learning. *International STEM Education Journal*, *2*(2), 1-21. Retrieved from http://www.stemeducationjournal.com/content/pdf/s40594-014-0014-4.pdf DOI 10.1186/s40594-014-0014-4

Collins, A. (2011). A study of expert theory formation: The role of model types and domain frameworks. In M. S. Khine & I. Saleh (Eds.), *Models and Modeling: Cognitive Tools for Scientific Enquiry* (pp. 23–40). London: Springer. doi:10.1007/978-94-007-0449-7_2

Collins, A., & Ferguson, W. (1993). Epistemic forms and epistemic games. *Educational Psychologist*, *28*(1), 25–42. doi:10.1207/s15326985ep2801_3

Collins, A., White, B., & Fadel, C. (in preparation). What's worth learning: That school won't teach you.

Dickes, A., & Sengupta, P. (2013). Learning Natural Selection in 4th Grade with Agent-Based Models. *Research in Science Education*, *43*(3), 921–953. doi:10.1007/s11165-012-9293-2

diSessa, A., Hammer, D., Sherin, B., & Kolpakowski, T. (1991). Inventing Graphing: MetaRepresentational Expertise in Children. *The Journal of Mathematical Behavior*, *10*, 117–160.

Duschl, R. A., Schweingruber, H. A., & Shouse, A. W. (Eds.). (2007). *Taking Science to School: Learning and Teaching Science in Grades K-8. National Research Council Board on Science Education, Center for Education, Division of Behavioral and Social Sciences and Education*. Washington, DC: The National Academies Press.

Enyedy, N. (2005). Inventing mapping: Creating cultural forms to solve collective problems. *Cognition and Instruction*, *23*(4), 427–466. doi:10.1207/s1532690xci2304_1

Gee, J. P. (1990). *Social Linguistics and Literacies: Ideology in Discourses*. London: Falmer Press.

Gee, J. P. (2007a). *Good Video Games and Good Learning: Collected Essays on Video Games, Learning, and Literacy (New Literacies and Digital Epistemologies)*. New York: Peter Lang Pub Inc.

Gee, J. P. (2007b). What Video Games Have to Teach us About Learning and Literacy (2nd ed.). New York: Palgrave Macmillan.

Giere, R. N. (1988). *Explaining science: A cognitive approach*. Chicago: University of Chicago Press. doi:10.7208/chicago/9780226292038.001.0001

Gravemeijer, K., Cobb, P., Bowers, J., & Whitenack, J. (2000). Symbolizing, modeling, and instructional design. In P. Cobb, E. Yackel, & K. McClain (Eds.), *Symbolizing and communicating in mathematics classrooms: Perspectives on discourse, tools, and instructional design*. Mahwah, NJ: Lawrence Erlbaum Associates.

Hall, R., & Stevens, R. (1995). Making space: A comparison of mathematical work in school and professional design practices. In S. L. Star (Ed.), *The cultures of computing* (pp. 118–145). London, UK: Basil Blackwell.

Lehrer, R., & Schauble, L. (2002). Symbolic communication in mathematics and science: Co-constituting inscription and thought. In E. Amsel & J. Byrnes (Eds.), *The development of symbolic communication*. Mahwah, NJ: Lawrence Erlbaum Associates.

Lehrer, R., & Schauble, L. (2006a). Cultivating model-based reasoning in science education. In R. K. Sawyer (Ed.), *The Cambridge Handbook of the Learning Sciences* (pp. 371–388). Cambridge, England: Cambridge University Press.

Lehrer, R., & Schauble, L. (2006b). In W. Damon, R. M. Lerner, K. A. Renninger, & I. E. Sigel (Eds.), Handbook of Child Psychology: Vol. 4. *Scientific thinking and science literacy: supporting development in learning in contexts* (6th ed.). Hoboken, NJ: John Wiley and Sons.

Lehrer, R., & Schauble, L. (2010). What kind of explanation is a model? In M. K. Stein (Ed.), *Instructional explanations in the disciplines* (pp. 9–22). New York: Springer. doi:10.1007/978-1-4419-0594-9_2

Lesh, R. A., & Doer, H. (2003). Foundations of a models and modeling perspec-tive on mathematics teaching, learning, and problem solving. In H. Doer & R. A. Lesh (Eds.), *Beyond constructivism: Models and modeling perspectives on mathematics teaching, learning, and problem solving*. Mahwah, NJ: Erlbaum.

Lynch, M. (1990). The Externalized Retina: Selection and Mathematization in the Visual Documentation of Objects in the Life Sciences. In M. Lynch & S. Woolgar (Eds.), *Representation in Scientific Practice* (pp. 153–186). Cambridge, MA: MIT Press.

Mokros, J. R., & Tinker, R. F. (1987). The impact of microcomputer-based labs on children's ability to interpret graphs. *Journal of Research in Science Teaching*, *24*(4), 369–383. doi:10.1002/tea.3660240408

Morrison, D., & Collins, A. (1995). Epistemic fluency and constructivist learning environments. *Educational Technology*, *35*(5), 39–45.

Nersessian, N. J. (2002). The cognitive basis of model-based reasoning in science. In P. Carruthers, S. Stich, & M. Siegal (Eds.), *The cognitive basis of science* (pp. 133–155). Cambridge: Cambridge University Press. doi:10.1017/CBO9780511613517.008

Pickering, A. (1995). *The Mangle of Practice: Time, Agency, and Science*. Chicago: University of Chicago Press. doi:10.7208/chicago/9780226668253.001.0001

Rapp, D. N., & Sengupta, P. (2012). *Models and modeling in science learning. Encyclopedia of the Sciences of Learning* (pp. 2320–2322). New York: Springer.

Roschelle, J., Knudsen, J., & Hegedus, S. (2010). From new technological infrastructures to curricular activity systems: Advanced designs for teaching and learning. In M. J. Jacobson & P. Reimann (Eds.), *Designs for Learning Environments of the Future: International Perspectives from the Learning Sciences* (pp. 233–262). New York: Springer. doi:10.1007/978-0-387-88279-6_9

Sengupta, P. & Clark, D. B. (in preparation). Disciplinarily-integrated games: Shifting from perceptual and cognitive to developmental trajectories across the curriculum.

Sengupta, P. & Clark, D. B. (submitted). Playing Modeling Games in the Science Classroom: The Case for Disciplinary Integration. Educational Technology special issue on games and playful learning.

Sengupta, P., & Farris, A. V. (2012). Learning Kinematics in Elementary Grades Using Agent-based Computational Modeling: A Visual Programming Based Approach. *Proceedings of the 11th International Conference on Interaction Design & Children* (pp 78–87). ACM. doi:10.1145/2307096.2307106

Squire, K. (2011). *Video Games and Learning: Teaching and Participatory Culture in the Digital age*. New York: Teachers College Press.

Squire, K., Barnett, M., Grant, J. M., & Higginbotham, T. (2004). Electromagnetism supercharged!: Learning physics with digital simulation games. *Proceedings of the 6th International Conference of the Learning Sciences* (pp. 513–520).

Wilensky, U., & Reisman, K. (2006). Thinking like a wolf, a sheep or a firefly: Learning biology through constructing and testing computational theories – An embodied modeling approach. *Cognition and Instruction*, *24*(2), 171–209. doi:10.1207/s1532690xci2402_1

ADDITIONAL READING

Duschl, R. A., Schweingruber, H. A., & Shouse, A. W. (Eds.). (2007). *Taking Science to School: Learning and Teaching Science in Grades K-8. National Research Council Board on Science Education, Center for Education, Division of Behavioral and Social Sciences and Education*. Washington, DC: The National Academies Press.

Enyedy, N. (2005). Inventing mapping: Creating cultural forms to solve collective problems. *Cognition and Instruction*, *23*(4), 427–466. doi:10.1207/s1532690xci2304_1

Gee, J. P. (2008). Learning and Games. In K. Salen (Ed.), *The ecology of games: Connecting youth, games, and learning. The John D. and Catherine T. MacArthur Foundation Series on Digital Media and Learning* (pp. 21–40). Cambridge, MA: The MIT Press; doi:10.1162/dmal.9780262693646.021

Gravemeijer, K., Cobb, P., Bowers, J., & Whitenack, J. (2000). Symbolizing, modeling, and instructional design. In P. Cobb, E. Yackel, & K. McClain (Eds.), *Symbolizing and communicating in mathematics classrooms: Perspectives on discourse, tools, and instructional design*. Mahwah, NJ: Lawrence Erlbaum Associates.

Hegedus, S., & Roschelle, J. (Eds.). (2013). *The SimCalc vision and contributions: Democratizing access to important mathematics*. New York, NY: Springer. doi:10.1007/978-94-007-5696-0

Hegedus, S. J., & Moreno-Armella, L. (2009). Intersecting representation and communication infrastructures. *ZDM*, *41*(4), 399–412. doi:10.1007/s11858-009-0191-7

Hestenes, D. (1992). Modeling Games in the Newtonian World. *American Journal of Physics*, *60*(8), 732–748. doi:10.1119/1.17080

Hestenes, D. (1993). MODELING is the name of the game. Presentation at the NSF Modeling Conference, Washington, DC.

Hestenes, D., & Halloun, I. (1995). Interpreting the Force Concept Inventory: A response to March 1995 critique by Huffman and Heller. *The Physics Teacher*, *33*(8), 502–506. doi:10.1119/1.2344278

Hestenes, D., Wells, M., & Swackhamer, G. (1992). Force Concept Inventory. *The Physics Teacher*, *30*(3), 141–158. doi:10.1119/1.2343497

Kaput, J. (1994). Democratizing access to calculus: New routes to old roots. In A. Schoenfeld (Ed.), *Mathematical thinking and problem solving* (pp. 77–156). Hillsdale, NJ: Lawrence Erlbaum Associates.

Latour, B. (1990). Drawing things together. In M. Lynch & S. Woolgar (Eds.), *Representation in scientific practice* (pp. 19–68). Cambridge, MA: MIT Press.

Lehrer, R., & Pritchard, C. (2002). Symbolizing space into being. In K. Gravemeijer, R. Lehrer, B. van Oers, & L. Verschaffel (Eds.), *Symbolization, modeling and tool use in mathematics education* (pp. 59–86). Dordrecht, Netherlands: Kluwer Academic Press. doi:10.1007/978-94-017-3194-2_5

Lehrer, R., Schauble, L., Carpenter, S., & Penner, D. (2000). The inter-related development of inscriptions and conceptual understanding. In P. Cobb, E. Yackel, & K. McClain (Eds.), *Symbolizing and communicating in mathematics classrooms: Perspectives on discourse, tools, and instructional design* (pp. 325–360). Mahwah, NJ: Lawrence Erlbaum Associates.

Radford, L. (2009). Signifying relative motion: Time, space and the semiotics of Cartesian graphs. In W. M. Roth (Ed.), *Mathematical representation at the interface of body and culture* (pp. 45–69). Charlotte, NC: Information Age Publishing.

Rochelle, J., & Kaput, J. (1996). Educational software architecture and systemic impact: The promise of component software. *Journal of Educational Computing Research, 14*(3), 217–228. doi:10.2190/YLTR-MLTH-WKE8-L9G3

KEY TERMS AND DEFINITIONS

Cartesian Representation: Graphically representing relationships between multiple variables in a coordinate system where the variables specify signed distance perpendicular to an axis for each variable. Most commonly two dimensional relationships represented along an X and Y axis, but greater dimensionality is also feasible.

Disciplinary Integration: An approach for leveraging digital games as a medium to support the development of scientific modeling in K-12 classrooms based on the Science as Practice perspective.

Model Types (Epistemic Forms): Target structures guiding scientific inquiry for scientists.

Modeling Strategies (Epistemic Games): The sets of rules and strategies for creating, manipulating, and refining specific model types.

Situation Action Models: Situation-action models specify a set of if/then rules that specify what actions an agent will take in what situations. As situations change, either because of previous actions or because of changes in agent's environment, the rules then specify the next actions (or inaction).

Structural-Analysis Models: Model types that include compare and contrast, cost-benefit analysis, primitive elements analysis, tables or cross-product analysis, tree structures or hierarchical analysis, and axiom systems.

System Dynamics Model: In a system-dynamics model, variables are linked together by positive or negative links. Variables can be increased or decreased, which in turn changes other variables in the system though the links. These models can be qualitative or quantitative. Various lag, homeostatic, or feedback functions can be built into the models.

Chapter 10
Playful Transition:
Serious Games for the Middle School Years

Anne Elizabeth Snyder
Second Avenue Learning, USA

Victoria Van Voorhis
Second Avenue Learning, USA

ABSTRACT

What is the role of play in middle school education? Typically, play is not integrated into the middle school day to the same degree as in elementary school, yet researchers have found that children in this age group are perfectly primed to learn from the rich experiences offered through play. Serious games, which blend content and skill instruction with entertaining play, provide an ideal mechanism for addressing the unique needs of the middle school student. This chapter provides game designers, instructors, and other stakeholders with an overview of the typical middle school student, as well as the role of serious games in middle school education. Drawing from a case study of an actual game under development, the authors present specific design principles in order to guide stakeholders in the design and use of serious and learning games in the middle school classroom.

INTRODUCTION

Middle school. These two words conjure up numerous others, many of them negative. Nouns such as *anxiety, puberty,* and *drama.* Verbs such as *changing* or *bullying* or *struggling*. The adjectives associated with middle school are perhaps most telling of all; words such as *awkward, confused, sullen, doubtful,* and *hypocritical.* Yet middle school also heralds a positive, magical time, when children become more self-sufficient and aware of the world, themselves, and each other. In the middle school years, children have the capacity to learn at astonishing rates and tackle complex problems in and out of the classroom. This juxtaposition of positive and negative, awkwardness and magic, highlights the incredible contradictions that go hand in hand with pre-adolescence.

From a purely physiological standpoint, the middle school years constitute one of the most remarkable periods in all of human development. At the same time that puberty begins and children transition into their adult bodies, their brains transform as well. As a result, middle-schoolers

DOI: 10.4018/978-1-4666-9629-7.ch010

enter a critical period in cognitive development, second only to the critical period experienced during the first few years of life. During this time, children acquire skills, knowledge, and habits that influence the entire rest of their lives.

One of the most fascinating, and poignant, aspects of the middle school years is the disparity between the physical appearance of students and their state of cognitive and emotional maturity. While students at this age begin to look and behave like adults, they still retain many of the qualities of younger children. Notably, students in middle school continue to want (and need!) to play. The type of play that pre-adolescents and early adolescents enjoy is somewhat different than that of younger children, but the urge to participate in play remains strong.

Taken together, the overall picture of a middle school student is quite intriguing. A middle school student possesses the playfulness of a child, yet demonstrates a growing capacity for complex thought. Is it possible to harness these two qualities, and use them to support learning during one of the most dramatic and important transitions in the human life span?

Game-based learning is one way to do just this. Games, by their very nature, invite players to engage in thoughtful, exciting, and rich interaction with content – just the sort of experiential learning that has been shown to be most effective with middle school students. By providing a game that blends the fun and joy of play with instruction and practice in specific key concepts and skills, a middle school educator can offer students a bridge between the elementary school environment and the more rigorous, structured middle school setting.

This chapter provides game designers, instructors, and other stakeholders with an overview of the role of serious games in middle school education, as well as best practices for designing effective learning and serious games for the middle school audience. In order to create quality game designs for this audience, it is essential to first build a clear understanding of the needs of the average middle school student. Within this context, we review existing research and theory relating to the changing role of play in the middle school years, and survey current play practices of students in this age range. Because much of this play now takes place socially and/or digitally, we also discuss current technology use among middle school students. Finally, we present guiding principles for middle school serious game design, drawing upon a case study of an actual game in development for this audience.

BACKGROUND

Play

Play is a remarkable phenomenon. The act of playing does not serve to feed, clothe, shelter, or provide humans with any tangible benefits or protections. Yet all humans feel the instinct to play, and in fact engage in play behaviors beginning in infancy and continuing throughout the lifespan (Casby, 2003). Why is this? What *is* play? What role does it fill in our lives?

Although play is often viewed as a frivolous, childish, and purposeless activity, many researchers have found that play is critical to human development. Though it is notoriously difficult to define as a whole, most agree that play involves behaviors and activities that are voluntary, organized by the players, and are undertaken for their own sake rather than as a means to another end (Bergen & Fromberg, 2009; Cohen, 2007; Conklin, 2014; Gray, 2011). As noted by prominent play researcher Brian Sutton-Smith (2009), play can take infinite form, and can be adapted or built to accommodate any environment. Some types of play are momentary, such as the wordplay that is involved in telling a joke, while other types of play span long periods of time, such as the sports play that takes place in the Olympics or the play involved when engaging in a massively multiplayer online role-playing game (MMORPG). Play theorists are also careful to note that play, while commonly associated with childhood, in fact persists throughout adolescence and adulthood (Conklin, 2014; Singer, Golinkoff, & Hirsch-Pasek, 2006; Sutton-Smith, 2009).

Many theorists posit that play develops in distinct phases, increasing in complexity as humans grow from infants to children, adolescents to young adults, and on into middle and old age. Parten (1932) was one of the first researchers to categorize play, creating a classification system based on her observations of children. This classification, which is still used today, begins with a stage termed *unoccupied play*, in which the player is merely an observer, and progresses to *solitary independent play, parallel play, associative play,* and *cooperative play;* with this last stage representing the most complex and critical phase in terms of its translation to real-world skills. Piaget (1962) in turn suggested that play corresponds to his described stages of cognitive development, such that infants engaged in basic repetitive motor play, children take part in pretend play as they develop more symbolic thinking, and finally progress to playing games with rules as a result of an increased capacity for abstract thinking. Others have rejected the notion of distinct stages of play, yet agree that play changes in form and function throughout human development (Hughes, 2009).

Perhaps one of the greatest mysteries surrounding play is why we engage in it at all. We know that play is fun and motivating, but does it serve any other purpose? Researchers have long speculated on this question. Previously, it was thought that play is simply a result of superfluous energy - a “leftover” once children’s other primary needs are met by caregivers (Rubin, 1982; Saracho & Spodek, 1995). Others, such as Bruner (1972), suggested an alternative view, in which play is more specific to childhood and reflects the extended immature period of humans, during which it is necessary to practice motor skills and object manipulation in order to develop these skills for use as adults.

More recently, however, experts in education and human development have linked play with learning, creativity, problem-solving ability, and overall cognitive and social development. It is thought that beginning in infancy, it is through play that humans first learn how to positively engage with caregivers and later, other children (Bruce, 2011; Newland, Roggman, & Boyce, 2001). Play offers open-ended opportunities to explore foundational concepts, and is motivating enough to encourage the persistence needed to achieve skill mastery (Isenberg & Quisenberry, 2002; Jalongo, 2003). Brain imaging studies have lent further credence to the idea that play and cognition are related, providing concrete evidence that play influences neural growth, connection, and functioning (Rushton, Juola-Rushton, & Larkin, 2010). Play and cognition are so tightly linked, in fact, that it is nearly impossible to isolate each variable in experimental research. Rather, by necessity most research into play has focused on correlations, such that we cannot determine whether play causes changes in cognition, cognitive development causes changes in play, or whether the two factors share a much more complex relationship (Hughes, 2009).

Play has also been associated with positive social and emotional growth. When humans play with others, they build their understanding of the social world. Play behaviors and activities encourage the active exploration of emotions, behaviors, and consequences (Ginsburg, 2007). Sociodramatic play is particularly important for socio-emotional development. This form of play, in which the players engage with others in role-acting, creative play, and/or problem-solving, can foster an understanding of social roles and context-appropriate social behaviors; all skills that are critical to group interaction in real-world settings (Hirsh-Pasek, Golinkoff, Berk, & Singer, 2008).

Play in the Middle School Years?

The starkly obvious difference between games and traditional schooling is that good games always involve play, and schooling rarely does, (Klopfer, Osterweil, & Salen, 2009).

The benefits of play, its function in childhood, and its role in early childhood education have been formally recognized in the United States since the late 1800s. In 1897, George Stanley Hall began formally studying and reporting on play. In 1907, in part due to Hall's work, President Roosevelt called for the introduction of playgrounds into U.S. cities; today, playgrounds are found not only in parks and city centers, but also on the grounds of many primary and elementary schools. Similarly, efforts have been made to include play as part of many early childhood programs, including programs with a strong academic focus (Frost, 2010).

When students enter middle school, however, play is suddenly no longer part of the school day. Recess, if it is offered, is typically short, and often middle schools do not have a playground or play area. While middle school students may receive physical education or break periods, there are typically no periods of time set aside for unstructured play (Schumacher, 1998). In her overview of play in the middle school years, Conklin (2014) notes that "in the current age of accountability, play, creativity and joy are not only absent from prominent frameworks for effective teaching, they are increasingly absent from young people's classrooms and lives" (p. 1228).

Do middle school students suddenly, at the age of 11 or 12, stop feeling the urge to play? Does the beginning of adolescence herald an immediate, innate need to shift away from the playful action of childhood toward the behaviors and patterns of an adult work day? Though very little formal research has been conducted into the play of early adolescents, it has been suggested that middle school students maintain the need to play, even (or especially!) as they face a myriad of other significant changes (Conklin, 2014; Millar, Patel, & Hornsby, 2011; Packman, 2002). To gain a better picture of the needs of middle school students, it is helpful to first examine those significant changes, both in body and in environment, that accompany the transition to adolescence.

Puberty, the Brain, and School

Though it depends on the individual, the beginning of the middle school years frequently coincides with the onset of puberty. A period of dramatic physiological growth, puberty involves a wide range of significant physical changes, including the emergence of primary and secondary sex characteristics, changes in height and musculature, and transformations in the brain (Caskey & Anfara, 2007; Kail & Cavanaugh, 2012). Age of onset is typically between 10 and 13 years of age, though this varies by ethnicity and sex. Girls typically enter puberty an average of 18 months earlier than boys, and children worldwide are now beginning puberty much earlier than in the past (in the 1840s, for example, puberty began at 16 or 17) (Ge, Natsuaki, Neiderhiser, & Reiss, 2007).

The behaviors, language patterns, and emotional changes that emerge during the onset of puberty are often baffling to adults, and are commonly attributed to the surge of hormones that are released during this period. Recently, however, it has been revealed that many of these changes are in fact due to a dynamic and rapid synaptic reorganization that occurs in the brain (Roaten & Roaten, 2012). Magnetic resonance imaging (MRI) studies have revealed evidence that the brain begins to change in composition at puberty, such that the prefrontal cortex contains a greater proportion of white matter and a smaller proportion of gray matter than it did in childhood. Such changes are indicative of synaptic pruning, a neural process by which the brain selectively refines certain neural pathways while eliminating others, thus increasing the overall efficiency of the system (Barnea-Goraly et al., 2005; Giedd, et al.,

1999). It has been found that between the ages of 11 and 15, synaptic pruning is so extensive that over twenty percent of the neural networking built in earlier childhood is destroyed or reconfigured (Strauch, 2003).

Research of real-time brain functioning in preadolescents and adolescents has suggested that the brain undergoes changes in prefrontal cortex functioning as a result of this synaptic pruning. More specifically, functional MRI (fMRI) research has revealed that the prefrontal cortex is the last part of the brain to receive myelin, a fatty substance that increases the speed of information flow (Paus, 2005). Thus, the synaptic pruning of puberty allows students to build and refine lasting knowledge and skills - in effect serving a second critical stage of learning - yet the prefrontal cortex remains immature (Roaten & Roaten, 2012).

It is this last finding that is perhaps most critical to understanding the seeming inconsistencies of middle school students. The prefrontal cortex is the area of the brain that provides humans with the powers of reasoning, planning, and insight. In addition, the prefrontal cortex also serves as a gatekeeper for information that is transmitted by the amygdala, a separate area of the brain that processes incoming sensory inputs from the outside world and interprets those inputs in terms of emotion. As the gatekeeper for output from the amygdala, the prefrontal cortex assists in mood regulation (Roaten & Roaten, 2012). When the amygdala sends negative or "danger" signals to the mature prefrontal cortex of an adult, the adult can effectively reason about those signals and adjust or adapt the resulting emotions and actions that take place as a result. However, full myelination of the prefrontal cortex does not take place until the early twenties. This means that students in the middle and high school years do not yet possess either the more mature reasoning skills or the emotional control of adults, even as their brains enter one of the most plastic stages in the entire life span (Barnea-Goraly, et al., 2005; Steinberg, 2011). This combination can lead pre-adolescents and teens to engage in risky behaviors, simply because they are responding first to emotion, and second to logical reasoning.

It is worth noting that the prefrontal cortex plays a role in the production of language as well. Again, the slower development of this brain area, in comparison to other brain structures, influences the behaviors of students at this age. Sowell and colleagues (1999) found that pre-adolescents struggle to fully express themselves and generate new phrases, a trait that can cause confusion or problems in social engagement, both with peers and with adults.

An additional neurological change during puberty, one that has great implications for educators and game designers alike, involves heightened excitability and sensitivity to chemical neurotransmitters such as dopamine and noradrenalin. This increased activity leads to heightened sensitivity to sensory input and experiences, which in turn can cause a rush of dopamine, the neurotransmitter responsible for pleasure (Steinberg, 2011). Many have posited that this dopamine rush, combined with relatively immature prefrontal cortex functioning, is a primary factor behind the risky behaviors and lack of forethought that are the hallmarks of this developmental stage.

Interestingly, dopamine is also involved in curiosity, attention, learning, and memory (Gruber, Gelman, & Ranganath, 2014; Willis, 2007). Therefore, the same rush of sensation and pleasure that can accompany a strong experience (e.g. a rollercoaster) can also be experienced when learning a new skill or solving a problem, which in turn improves the processing of new information. This system of neurotransmitter response and reward is thought to be the basis of motivation and the natural human inclination to be curious (Gruber, Gelman, & Ranganath, 2014).

Pre-Adolescent Learning Needs and School

Because of the marked changes in the neurology of the pre-adolescent, the learning needs of students in this age group change as well. Given that the plasticity of the brain in middle school is remarkably high at this time, students of this age are primed and ready to assimilate new information into the foundational knowledge that has been learned in elementary school. The phrase "thirsty for knowledge," while a cliché, is thus quite apropos for the middle school audience. At the same time, these intense neural changes expend a student's cognitive resources, such that the attention span of the typical middle-schooler is quite short, averaging only 12 minutes (Vawter, 2010). Consequently, effective middle school instruction ideally involves shorter tasks or periods of lecture or discussion, with opportunities to work on other tasks, engage in movement, or take a brief rest.

The increased neurotransmitter activity in the middle school-age brain means that students of this age tend to be experiential learners, often preferring to immerse themselves in a topic and explore it in depth (Carrington, 2006). The more interactive the project or task, the better, as these interactions can lead to increased dopaminergic activity, motivating students to persist in their learning. Social engagement throughout the day is highly important for middle-schoolers as well, meaning that collaborative learning opportunities, such as brainstorming with peers, engaging in constructive debates, or participating in group design projects, are particularly appropriate for this age group (Jackson & Davis, 2000; Roeser, Eccles, & Sameroff, 2000).

At the same time, middle school students require extra support and practice in tasks that rely on the prefrontal cortex, such as sequential and logical reasoning, understanding cause and effect, and making predictions. Strategies such as providing graphic organizers or roadmaps for complex topics, offering scaffolded instructional hints, and outlining expected effort and outcomes are all methods that can assist in ensuring a middle-schooler's success in content learning (Jensen, 2005). Similarly, many middle school students struggle with organization and study skills, which are dependent on the higher-order reasoning that accompanies prefrontal cortex development (Jackson & Davis, 2000).

Since students at this age tend to respond to emotion before thinking about circumstance or consequences, middle school students also benefit from guidance in examining and re-examining a question or situation before making a choice or performing an action. Activities that involve objective observation, consideration of options as well as the opinions of others, and impartial peer review can be particularly helpful in encouraging students to develop their capacity to think critically before responding to emotion.

Does the traditional middle school address these age specific-needs of its students? Unfortunately, in many respects the transition from elementary to middle school represents a transition *away* from the type of environment that would most benefit its students. The structure of the average middle school day involves changing classes, learning from multiple teachers, and interacting with a much larger set of peers than the more enclosed elementary school classroom (Im, Hughes, Kwok, Puckett, & Cerdia, 2014). The shift from the structured single-classroom environment to the much larger and fluid middle school setting demands organizational skills, sequential thinking, and the ability to handle complex social interactions with both peers and numerous authority figures; in short, the exact skills that students in this age group have not yet developed.

The middle school day itself typically begins significantly earlier than the elementary day. This change takes place just as the circadian rhythm of middle school students shifts later, which leads, in essence, to a state of continual sleep deprivation. In fact, this disparity between start times and the natural sleep rhythms of middle school students is so significant that it has been found that waking a pre-adolescent at 7 a.m. is the equivalent to waking a fully-grown adult at 4 a.m. This is a major problem considering that sleep is essential both for memory and attention (Yan & Slagle, 2007). Once at school, student encounter class periods that are longer than the instructional periods in elementary school. These periods can range from 50 minutes to 150 minutes, depending on whether or not a school chooses to implement the block scheduling approach (longer periods and fewer subjects taught per day) (Jacob & Rockoff, 2011).

The changes in school environment from elementary to middle school often extend beyond class scheduling. Though this is not true of every middle school, in general it has been found that students are expected to sit for longer periods of time, listen to longer lectures or other forms of teacher-led direct instruction, and spend much of their time at work rather than at play. The more open-ended, creative, and playful atmosphere of the elementary setting gives way to a setting that looks and feels more like a college lecture course. Opportunities for social engagement, collaborative problem-solving, field trips, or design projects may not be provided as frequently (Gray, 2011).

The consequences of this shift have been noted in a variety of studies of middle school adjustment and psychological well-being. Researchers have noted a significant drop in both effort and academic performance during the transition period (Burchinal, Roberts, Zeisel, & Rowley, 2008; Chung, Elias, & Schneider, 1998). Students' sense of school belonging tends to decline (Anderman, 2003) as do feelings of self-esteem and academic competency (Cantin & Boivin, 2004; Duchesne, Ratelle, Poitras, & Drouin, 2009). Simultaneously, the incidence of depression, anxiety, and other psychological disorders during the middle school transition increases (Gray, 2011; Duchesne, Ratelle, Poitras, & Drouin, 2009). Increases in high school dropout rates have also been linked to issues in the middle school years (cf. Balfanz, 2009).

In sum, a middle school student is often ready to tackle the challenges of more complex, cognitively-demanding learning and social skills and tasks (Manning, 2002). However, the rapid shift to the new, less playful and more rigid middle school environment, in combination with the dramatic changes brought on by puberty, places many students at risk of academic and emotional decline.

Digital Game-Based Learning: Easing the Middle School Transition through Play

How do students cope with the changes introduced by the transition from elementary into middle school? Interestingly, it has been found that many middle school students turn toward play and games. Most of this play occurs outside of the classroom, and increasingly, it occurs in a digital world. In fact, children between the ages of 11 and 14 spend more time playing video games than any other school age bracket (Greenberg, Sherry, Lachlan, Lucas, & Holmstrom, 2010; Rideout, Foehr, & Roberts, 2010). As technology continues to improve and become more affordable, students are increasingly owning and using a myriad of devices in order to engage in such gameplay. Engel and Green (2011), for example, report that nearly 60% of middle-schoolers own a cell phone, and spend a considerable amount of time using the phone to play games.

In essence, students in the middle school years continue to play, but the play shifts from the rough and tumble or imaginative play behaviors of elementary school to digital play.

It is here, in this digital play space, that a remarkable opportunity exists.

As we have seen, the average middle school student lives between worlds, in more ways than one. The middle-schooler craves complex experiential learning and a sense of autonomy, yet requires support and guidance in both organization and in considering the possible outcomes of a decision (Hayenga and Corpus, 2010). This same student is ready for multifaceted problem-based learning and collaborative tasks, but also benefits from a safe space in which to not only explore, but to make mistakes. Above all, a middle school student continues to seek the creativity and joy that naturally result from play, even as play fades from the classroom (Conklin, 2014).

Serious and/or educational games offer a safe yet dynamic approach to re-introducing joy and play into the middle school setting. Indeed, high quality game-based learning can serve as an ideal bridge between elementary and middle school instruction by harnessing the power of play, while honoring the more mature cognitive and social skills that develop during pre-adolescence.

In addition, research in the field of game-based learning has uncovered other potential benefits of this approach:

- **Students Can Become Better Problem-Solvers:** Several recent studies have demonstrated that students develop more efficient strategies and approaches to problems when playing games, compared to more traditional classroom activities (Chuang & Chen, 2009; Kim, Park, & Baek, 2009; Kolovou & Heuvel-Panhuizen, 2010; Spires, Rowe, Mott, & Lester, 2011). Games allow players to take on new personas and try novel tactics or approaches, allowing for experimentation and "learning by doing" (Shaffer, Halverson, Squire, & Gee, 2005).
- **Students Can Learn New Content through Games:** When observing children playing a game, it is often striking to note just how easily and quickly children acquire information about that game. Children can frequently name large numbers of characters, recite statistics, provide and analyze in-game strategies, and connect related concepts, without realizing that they have learned anything at all (Squire, 2006). Children are able to do these things because games are very effective at teaching content, often without players recognizing that anything new has been taught. Effective educational games often teach using the same methods as entertainment games, but replace or supplement fictional game content with academic content (Chuang & Chen, 2009; Egert & Phelps, 2011; Papastergiou, 2009).
- **Students Have Opportunities to Create:** The act of creation is believed to be one of the highest forms of learning. When we create, we must not only remember and apply relevant concepts, but also use those concepts in new ways to build something that does not yet exist. By creating something in-game, students also build the ability to think deeply about design as well as engage in testing and revisions: all skills that are important not only for standardized tests, but activities outside of school, and eventually, the work world (Kangas, 2010; Yang, 2012).
- **Games Can Combine "Soft Skills" with Social Learning:** In discussing the learning inherent in gameplay, Klopfer, Osterweil, and Salen (2009) note that games naturally reinforce the 21st century skills referenced in education circles (Trilling & Fadel, 2009), including metacognition, technology fluencies, development of ethical understanding, and collaboration in cross-functional teams. Moreover, games can help students build these skills in a situated social context, fostering positive social interaction. Lenhart, et al. (2008) report that younger teenagers may especially benefit from this combination of soft skills and social learning.

Game-Based Learning as a Growing Movement

In the past, games were relegated to the world outside of the classroom, and game-based learning was a concept that stood on the fringes of standard educational practice. Although games were used on sporadic occasions to support instruction or to motivate students to engage in skill and drill activities, games were rarely front and center in the classroom (Spires, Rowe, Mott, & Lester, 2011).

Then, in 2003, a psycholinguistics professor named Dr. James Gee published the now-famous book titled, *What Video Games Have to Teach Us About Learning and Literacy.* After playing videogames with his young son, and then again on his own, Gee was struck by the difficulty, complexity, and richness of many of these games. Drawing from his own studies of how people learn and interact, Gee identified a number of learning principles that apply both to good videogames as well as effective instruction in schools.

Gee's book, along with others, opened the door for further conversation. Not long after its publication, the field of game-based learning began to truly emerge. Game developers turned their attention to the creation of more rigorous learning games based on research and standards. Federal policy-makers created funds and forums for exploring the use of games in schools, and began subsidizing the technology needed to play them. Researchers began studying how children learn from games.

Perhaps most importantly, teachers began to think about integrating games into instruction. Today, teachers are increasingly using tools, programs, and apps that are either gamified (not games per se, but that use elements of games) or that are designed to teach or reinforce learning through full games. Just as teachers have long used non-academic materials and media (e.g. entertainment films) and in-person experiences such as field trips to enhance instruction and learning, teachers are now turning to the game offerings of the Internet age to build student interest and learning (Klopfer, Osterweil, & Salen, 2009).

The field of game-based learning is now growing at a remarkable rate (Coiro, Knobel, Lankshear, & Leu, 2014). However, there is a marked dearth of games specifically designed for the middle school audience. Given that games are an ideal mechanism for supporting student success in these grades, it is time to address this gap. How do we do this? As Klopfer, Osterweil, and Salen (2009) note, "to succeed, we must look at where the strengths and challenges of both classrooms and games lie and situate 'learning games' at the most productive intersection of these separate environments" (p. 3).

PRINCIPLES OF MIDDLE SCHOOL GAME DESIGN

In creating games for the middle school audience, the authors have drawn from best practices in education *and* game design to establish a set of essential principles that can inform the design and use of serious games for students in this age range. Drawing from a case study of the design and development of *Martha Madison*, a middle school physical science game, these essential principles are explained and illustrated with real-world examples. These principles can guide teachers, families, administrators, game designers, and any other stakeholders who are interested in assessing existing middle school serious games or in designing their own.

It should be noted that, because middle school students are not quite children, yet not quite teenagers, serious and learning games that are designed for this age group must be not quite like those designed for either younger or older students. An ideal middle school game acknowledges the more advanced capabilities of the older child, while simultaneously providing a greater proportion of support (and a slightly more juvenile design) than games for teenagers. It can be quite challenging to find this balance, whether the goal is to design a game or evaluate it for potential use in the classroom. The key is to incorporate a backwards/forwards perspective when considering all aspects of serious games, including learning design, game mechanics, and aesthetics. That is, it is important to look backwards to the needs and preferences of elementary-aged children to inform design decisions, while also looking forward toward the more advanced and sophisticated leanings of the adolescent.

Case Study Introduction: *Martha Madison*

Product History and Purpose

STEM performance in the United States is markedly low, as demonstrated in the Programme for International Student Assessment (PISA, 2012). Among the 34 developed countries taking part in the 2012 PISA study, the U.S. ranked 27th in math and 20th in science. In addition, other research has demonstrated that middle school students, particularly girls, tend to disengage with the STEM fields during the transition years (Britner & Pajares, 2006). To address these issues, an entertainment-style videogame suite for the physical sciences, entitled *Martha Madison,* was designed and developed for use in middle school science instruction.

The initial prototype for *Martha Madison* was built as part of a grant for the National Science Foundation. Initial research and feedback conducted during Phase I of this grant led to the award of Phase II and Phase IIB funding. The prototype was fully developed into *Martha Madison: Simple Machines,* followed by the development of *Optics, Waves,* and *Forces* physical science games. The *Martha Madison* games are designed to be played in pairs on a Mac or PC via a web browser. Players may use keyboard controls or may play with an Xbox controller with USB adaptor.

Primary goals of the suite are to improve STEM content learning, confidence, self-efficacy, and collaboration in STEM. As such, each game in the suite is designed for paired collaborative play, such that students must work together in order to succeed. All gameplay is untimed; students may take as long as they need to solve each level, and replay options are provided at all times.

Due to the educational and motivational power of narrative, every game in the suite is situated inside a story, led by a protagonist meerkat character named Martha Madison. Martha is a scientist who uses her skill and knowledge to solve problems in the animal community. Players each choose an animal character who serves as a fellow scientist, traveling throughout Martha's world and helping her solve each problem. In the *Martha Madison: Forces* game, for example, students navigate through an arctic landscape and solve problems involving physical forces in order to transport blocks of ice to penguins, who need the blocks to build their ice homes.

The games are designed to help students begin to explore and play with concepts of physical science, even before formal instruction has taken place. In fact, gameplay ideally takes place at the beginning of an instructional unit on that topic, which can allow students to encounter key concepts, vocabulary, and representative problem types early on in an engaging and safe environment. The game may be played again at the end of a unit, either as a formative assessment or as a reinforcement of material that has been learned through classroom instruction.

To provide insight into student interactions and progress in the game, real-time gameplay data is collected during play, which is reported to a dashboard interface. A teacher interface allows an instructor to view game progress and achievement for an entire class or an individual student, while student and family interfaces display data for an individual student. Based on feedback from middle school educators, supporting instructional materials (lesson plans, rubrics, guided notes, activities) were also developed to support each game.

Guiding Principles for Middle School Game Design

The design, implementation, and testing of the *Martha Madison* games led to the identification of a number of guiding principles for middle school game design, described below:

Research, Research, Research!

Whether the stakeholder is an educator deciding whether to use a serious game, or a designer looking to create one, research is a key component of the process. By reviewing existing research, as well as collecting and examining data through new research, it becomes possible to ensure that serious middle school games provide the desired outcomes. Note that this principle is critical to serious game design for the middle school audience specifically, but is also applicable to designs for other target audiences as well.

Serious game research takes many forms. One form may be better suited for an early stage in the design or evaluation process, while another form for the same game is more appropriate for a later stage. Fortunately, because research approaches are varied and extensive, each study may be tailored in type and scope in order to answer specific questions for any stage in the process.

For example, consider this question: how does a designer decide the premise of a middle school game? Sometimes, the main purpose and thrust of a serious game emerges from a sudden flash of insight, but more often it stems from a desire to address a specific issue. Before attempting to solve that issue, however, it is beneficial to investigate existing literature and research surrounding that problem. This type of informal research, which often entails examining existing empirical studies, can be invaluable in uncovering the factors that contribute to the problem. These factors may directly impact the design of features, mechanics, narratives, and other aspects of the game. A literature review is often an important component of grant proposals and pre-marketing efforts, so this form of research can often serve more than one purpose for a designer and can provide important information for an instructor considering adoption of the product.

Benchmarking is another form of informal research that can take place prior to product conception and/or product adoption. By examining existing products and solutions within and outside the industry, it becomes easier to gain an understanding of practices, solutions, and methods that have proven successful in the past. For a designer, this research, particularly when combined with a literature review, can also identify gaps, areas for improvement, and opportunities for new solutions.

Once a game design is established and product development begins, a relatively low-cost form of research called playtesting can begin as well. Davis, Steury, and Pagulayan (2005) describe playtesting as a practice that goes beyond standard usability and beta testing, stating that "the goal of the playtest is to obtain feedback from consumers about their experiences with a specific game in a systematic manner using scientific methods" (p. 5). Playtesting works best by establishing a somewhat controlled environment, in which all participants answer the same surveys and play the same game for the same amount of time. When playtesting, observers should strive to refrain from intervening (however tempting it may be!) and instead take careful note of where in the game players struggle or become stuck, what they choose to comment on, how they progress through the flow of the game, and any areas in which their behavior deviates from what is expected. Feedback from pre- and post-surveys can provide additional feedback on the player experience as well as content learning

(Davis, Steury, & Pagulayan, 2005). Instructors may engage in playtesting as well, but in this case, instructor involvement typically occurs as part of a more formal pilot or trial for a fully-developed game. Playtesting can also assist teachers and districts in deciding whether to invest in a serious game.

In some cases, more rigorous research may also be warranted. For example, many games claim to improve content learning, but do they actually impact student outcomes? Efficacy research, in the form of quasi-experimental or experimental studies, can answer this type of question by allowing the researcher to compare use of the game with another intervention (see All, Castellar, and Van Looy, 2014 as well as Wouters, van der Spek, & Van Oostendorp, 2009 for more detailed discussions of recommended study approaches). Ideally, efficacy studies take place with a representative sample of the target population, within the setting(s) in which the game is most likely to be used. Key aspects to look for in a high quality efficacy study include use of a control group (a comparison group of participants using similar or more traditional products or materials), a representative and relatively large sample of participants, random assignment (participants or groups of participants are randomly chosen to engage in the control or treatment), and measures and assessments that are valid, reliable, and relevant to the product and the needs of students and teachers (Wouters, van der Spek, & Oostendorp, 2009).

Examples from *Martha Madison:* The designers of *Martha Madison* utilized both literature reviews and benchmarking to create the initial game ideas and lay the foundation for the general requirements, framework, and narrative of the game. *Little Big Planet,* a puzzle platform created by Media Molecule for the PlayStation, served as one of the primary games used in benchmarking. Cooperative play and a strong central protagonist are features that were identified as important to the target age group within this game. Other physics-based games across a variety of platforms were also examined, and the team identified themes and game mechanics that were especially compelling for middle school students. Similarly, findings from a review of the literature additionally highlighted the importance of collaborative work in middle school science education, as well as middle school girls' preference for collaborative play and puzzles in games. Given the results of this early-stage research, the entire product was framed as a collaborative puzzle-platformer game.

Development began at the conclusion of this initial research review, and playtesting took place even before a playable digital prototype was built. Paper and mechanical prototypes of the game, with sketches of levels, puzzle elements, and possible mechanics, were used by the playtesters in place of digital assets. A paper lever held in place by a pin, for example, was pushed up and down in order to examine how a similar lever could be used by players in the game to reach various floors on a windmill. Playtesting with the paper prototype assisted in establishing the initial game mechanics, puzzle layout, dimensions, and the flow of the game. At each subsequent stage of game development (Alpha, Beta, and Gold) one or more playtesting sessions were held in order to gather additional feedback. These sessions not only uncovered technical issues, bugs, problems with game mechanics, and layout and design concerns, they also led to the development of entirely new features. For example, students who playtested the *Simple Machines* and *Optics* games consistently indicated a desire to have greater control over the placement of game objects, as well as the layout of the level. As a result of this, and in tandem with a literature review of research on creation and gameplay, Second Avenue built "Freeplay," a special unlockable game mode in which players can use a modified level editor to create their own levels and puzzles (see Figure 1). This in turn

Figure 1. Freeplay mode in Martha Madison: Forces

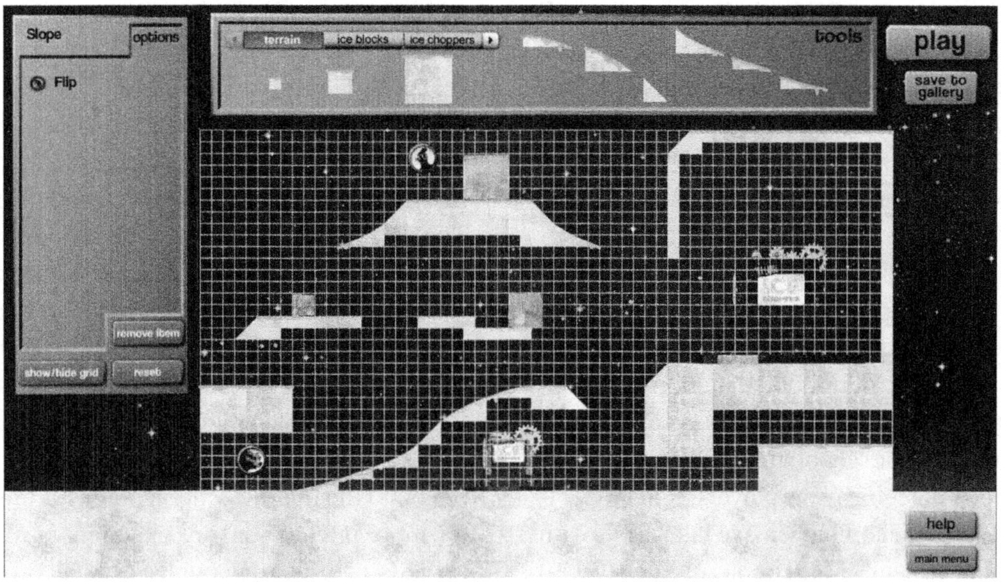

has opened the door to new designs and ideas for meeting the needs of students and teachers, such as the creation of a standalone *Martha Madison* science creator application or an assessment and homework tool for teachers.

In addition to engaging students in playtesting, Second Avenue conducted efficacy research with middle school students in lab and classroom settings. These studies allowed Second Avenue to examine how the *Martha Madison* games influenced student engagement, collaboration, communication, content learning, and feelings of self-efficacy and interest in the STEM fields. By examining the effects of the games on these student factors, Second Avenue was not only able to modify the game to better suit the needs of students, but also to provide teachers, district administrators, and other stakeholders with valuable information that they can use to inform their decision to adopt the games and integrate them into existing instruction.

Incorporate Intrinsic and Extrinsic Motivations

Because middle school is a period of great transition, the motivations of middle school students are often rapidly shifting as well. In order to maintain engagement, promote deeper immersion in the material, ensure persistence, and thus enhance content learning, it is necessary to provide continual sources of motivation throughout gameplay, as well as within any instructional or affinity space that exists outside the game (Gee, 2003; Liu, Horton, Olmanson, & Toprac, 2011; Olson, 2010). Motivation has been shown to be associated with academic achievement among middle school students, such that students with higher levels of motivation tend to receive higher grades (Hayenga & Corpus, 2010).

Intrinsic motivation, or the internal desire to perform a task for a task's sake, has been a topic of interest in the fields of psychology, education, and game design for some time. Beginning in the

1970s, Edward Deci and Richard Ryan began investigating the innate psychology needs of all humans, and found that the actions, perceptions, or objects that meet these innate needs are intrinsically motivating (Deci, 1975; Deci & Ryan, 1985). Deci and Ryan have posited that actions and objects that address the need for autonomy, as well as a sense of competence, are sources of particularly high intrinsic motivation. This finding has direct implications for game design and the use of serious games for instruction, as games naturally offer the player both autonomy and opportunities to continually develop competence.

What do middle school students, as a particular subgroup of potential game players, find motivating? In a series of comprehensive interviews with sixth-grade students, Liu, Toprac, & Yuen (2009) found that when students engaged with digital media, they were particularly motivated by eleven elements: choice, sensory engagement, fantasy, challenge, cognitive engagement, authenticity, competence, interactivity, novelty, identity, and social relations. In many respects, these same elements echo the qualities of written literature for the middle school audience, which often incorporate fantasy, a hero's journey, complex challenges, and exploration (e.g. the *Harry Potter* series, *Hatchet*, *Walk Two Moons*, or *The Book Thief*).

Gameplay allows middle school students to tap into these elements by encouraging them to try on different identities, bond with protagonists and/or fellow players, and embark on their own hero's journey. Middle-schoolers are at a stage when they are beginning to separate from the familial unit (Anfara & Mertens, 2007); games can offer an opportunity to test this separation in a safe space, exploring causes and consequences in an environment where such exploration is not only *not* punished, but actively encouraged. Indeed, several studies have found that game-based learning improves overall student motivation, self-confidence, and engagement, at least in part due to goal-focused exploration and adventure within the game (Papastergiou, 2009; Schaaf, 2012; Ya-Ting, 2012).

High quality serious games for the middle school tap into both intrinsic and extrinsic motivation by including game features and structures that are closely tied to the needs of this age group. The best games for this age may include extrinsic rewards such as badges, win state animations, sound effects or music, currency, and aesthetic options (e.g. costumes for a digital avatar). While these rewards are typically less effective over time than more intrinsic motivators, they can serve as a "hook" for initially engaging a learner by tapping into the middle-schooler's increasing desire for more intense sensory experiences. Extrinsic rewards can also encourage students to persist in a game when a task becomes challenging or they may otherwise turn away (Garris, Ahlers, & Driskell, 2002).

A well-designed serious game will, by design, intrinsically motivate students by providing open-ended problem-solving play spaces. Ideally, these spaces include tasks in which students can collaborate (in real-time or asynchronously) to create and test their ideas for solving problems. Just as in real-life, some of the in-game problems should include more than one possible solution. This design principle encourages deeper learning by requiring students to think critically about the problem itself, apply existing knowledge, and seek out new information that may assist in solving the problem.

Game mechanics are another important motivator in games, as they are the core means by which students interact with the game. Game mechanics are the systems, constructs, and/or rules through which a player engages and explores a game space (Sicart, 2008). Because middle school students have more developed cognitive abilities than their younger peers, the mechanics of play need to be sophisticated enough to interest students, as well as remain closely correlated with the core learning objectives. However, these mechanics should not be so complicated that they distract from the purpose of the game. Finding this balance can be challenging; as such, playtesting (see *Principle 1*) is highly recommended for both designers and adopters of serious games, to ensure that the mechanics encourage and maintain engagement.

Examples from *Martha Madison*: The overall aesthetic design of the *Martha Madison* games was determined to be an important source of both extrinsic and intrinsic motivation for students taking part in early testing, particularly among girls. To establish this design, SAL conducted an "art slam" study with middle school students from urban, suburban, and rural school districts. The aesthetics of the games needed to appeal to both middle school males and females, while also allowing for accurate depictions of scientific content across multiple hardware platforms.

Prior to the art slam, several artists created sample art treatments for the project. Each artist was tasked with reading a creative brief and designing the Martha Madison character, an additional playable animal, Martha Madison's lab, and one outdoor level. Middle school participants reviewed each of the five resulting art treatments, rating each component using a Likert scale (1-5). In addition, each art treatment was presented to game design faculty at New York University and the Rochester Institute of Technology. Based on the data and feedback gathered during the art slam, two components were selected to serve as design guides for the remainder of the games.

Similarly, focus groups with a representative sample of middle school students provided data on student preferences for extrinsic rewards. A badging system was created for one platform of the game, awarding new badges for both learning achievement (e.g. solving a specific number of puzzles using a given tool, such as a convex lens) as well as non-learning goals (e.g. solving an in-game problem not tied to a learning objective, such as using a bucket to catch water from a leaking roof). Short win-state animations were developed for each game, providing sensory rewards for solving puzzles (see Figure 2). In addition, students are provided with extrinsic motivation in the form of textual praise and encouragement from non-player characters.

Figure 2. Sample win-state animation from Martha Madison: Forces

Figure 3. Sample narrative in Martha Madison: Optics

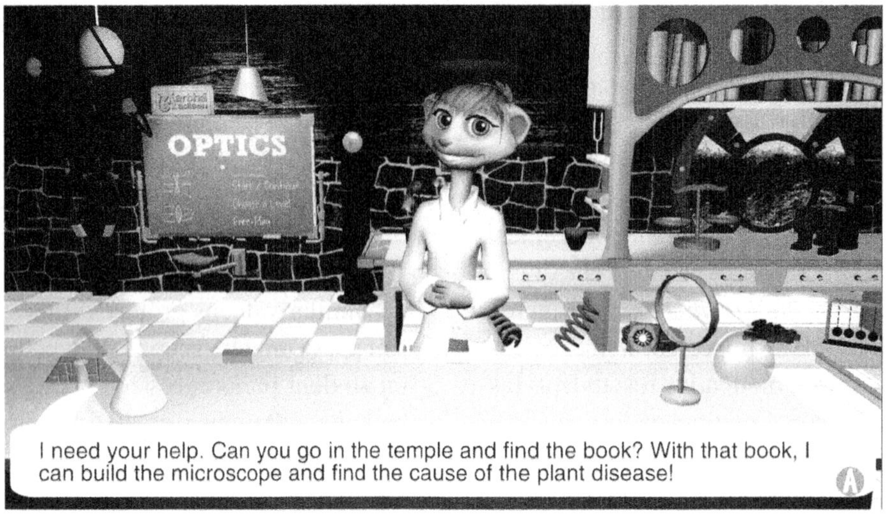

Because a primary goal of *Martha Madison* is to develop students' intrinsic desire to engage in STEM, intrinsic motivators were the primary focus of the design of each game. In keeping with Gee's (2003) assertion that games offer learning in context, each game was built to fit within an authentic yet whimsical narrative. For example, in *Martha Madison: Optics*, students play as animal characters who are traveling through an ancient temple in order to find a much-needed book. The book contains the schematics for building a microscope, a tool that Martha Madison requires in order to determine the cause of a plant blight. The narrative drives students to pursue play, while also tapping into their innate interest in fantasy, adventure, and novelty (see Figure 3).

Martha Madison was designed to be played by both male and female students. However, because a secondary goal of the games was to build games that support the specific needs of middle school girls, special consideration was taken in regards to the intrinsic motivations of this population. For example, studies have found that when playing games, girls tend to prefer collaborative and social play over competitive play or games that involve violence (Dickey, 2006; Miller, Chaika, & Groppe, 1996; Vorderer, Hartmann, & Klimmt, 2006); as such, each of the *Martha Madison* games requires students to play together to solve each in-game puzzle. Similarly, some have found that females tend to prefer games and tasks that do not involve time constraints, instead favoring opportunities to reason through a situation under minimal or no time pressure (Homer, Hayward, Frye, & Plass, 2012; Shurchkov, 2012). Given these findings, SAL created game levels that do not include timers or other forms of time constraints.

Guide Play through Learning, Guide Learning through Play

Typically, the primary purpose of a serious or educational game for middle school students is to help that student learn. The game may teach new content, reinforce skills taught in the classroom, provide scenarios for small group discussions, or offer any number of other learning opportunities. Regardless of the specific educational goal(s) of a game, it is important to consider both the learning needs and prior preparation of middle-schoolers. As noted previously, students at this age are capable of accomplishing a wide variety of complex academic tasks, particularly when those tasks are tied to authentic problems (Conklin,

2014). Young adolescents crave work that allows for increased independence from adult authority, that builds on social engagement, and that encourages the exploration of abstract concepts. In addition, opportunities to create new content, both within and outside of the game, are key to middle school learning and motivation (Liu, Toprac, & Yuen, 2009). Overarching all of these features is the student's inherent need to *play*, whether it is structured play, social play, or open-ended play.

Interestingly, as Gee (2003) often notes in his discussions of video games, many popular entertainment games offer players the exact sorts of learning opportunities that are perfectly suited to young adolescents. For example, *the Sims* games (the *Sims 1, 2, 3, 4,* and various spin-off games) encourage open play and complex social engagement, albeit with virtual characters. *World of Warcraft*, a massively multiplayer online role-playing game (MMORPG) that boasts the greatest number of subscribers in the world, attracts its players with a design that allows for autonomy and flexible group problem-solving. Similarly, *Minecraft* offers flexibility and open-play, and encourages players to engage in creation in-game, sometimes in order to solve a problem (such as creating shelter from dangerous monsters) but more often purely for the sake of creation itself.

Serious games for middle school students can and should utilize the same sorts of designs, while simultaneously teaching or offering practice with key skills and content that are tied to a curriculum. When introducing content, however, it is critical to avoid assumptions about students' prior knowledge and training. It should not be assumed that a student has adult knowledge or experience with any given subject matter. Moreover, due to the extensive synaptic pruning that occurs at this age, a student may have forgotten basic skills or concepts that were learned earlier and that are prerequisites for new subject understnading. Thus, when establishing or evaluating the learning objectives in a middle school game, it is essential to not only look at current and future standards and curricula, but also to identify the skills and content covered in earlier grades.

Current entertainment games also offer insight into how to introduce new skills and content sequentially, with each achievement building upon what has been learned previously. These games offer a slight challenge outside the player's current experience or ability. In essence, well-designed games offer learning opportunities within the *Zone of Proximal Development* (ZPD),a concept first introduced by psychologist Lev Vygotsky. According to this theory, learners enter the ZPD when attempting to learn a skill that is slightly outside of reach (Vygotsky, 1978). With assistance from a peer, teacher, or in the case of videogames, a character or in-game scaffolding system, the learner can master the skill. Gee (2003) argues that a game is an effective teaching approach because much of what occurs remains within the learner's ZPD, such that "the game operates within, but at the outer edge of, the learner's resources, so that at many points the game is felt as challenging but not 'undoable'" (p. 70).

Portal, a game developed by Valve in 2007, offers an excellent illustration of how players are sequentially taught key game skills by offering learning challenges within a player's ZPD. In the game, players must solve puzzles by placing "portals" in the environment and subsequently maneuvering themselves and other objects in ways that are not possible in the real world. To succeed, players must discard their previous understanding of physical space and momentum; a significant feat of learning. To support this learning, players are guided through a series of introductory puzzles, each of which builds upon skills learned earlier. A non-playable character in the form of a computer voice offers some support, but the main learning takes place through guided play. This same principle is effective for the learning design of middle school games as well.

Figure 4. Storyboard frame and final design for Martha Madison: Optics

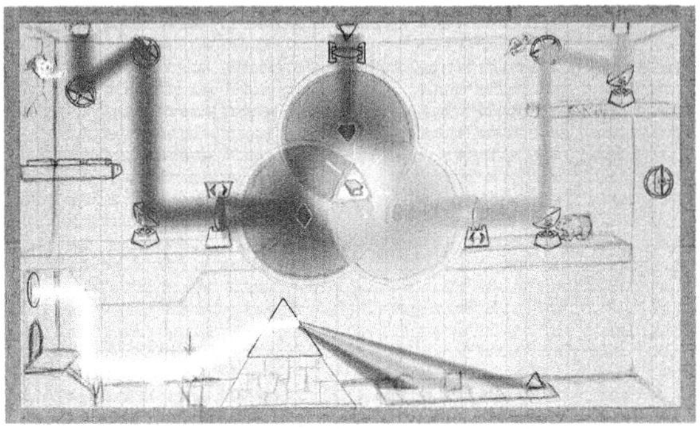

- **Examples from Martha Madison:** After establishing the overall flow and mechanics of the game, the design team at Second Avenue Learning identified a set of learning objectives that sequentially moved students through a progression of key concepts. Each specific learning objective utilized skills or concepts introduced in previous objectives. These learning objectives were then used to build storyboards, mock-ups, and flow diagrams, matching the learning sequence to a proposed game flow and adjusting each as necessary. Each level design included a scenario or set of mechanics meant to encourage open exploration. When possible, every level was also built such that students could solve a problem in more than one way. As a result, players learn core concepts through guided play. Players must use each science concept (as well as those learned earlier) to solve the problems or puzzles in a level; deep learning then occurs even without direct instruction. This open-ended yet logical design specifically addresses the middle school student's need for a complex, constructive set of learning tasks (see Figure 4 for a storyboard frame and final design for the culminating level of *Martha Madison: Optics*).

Once again, however, a game design that offers deep experiential learning can often overlook students' levels of preparation prior to gameplay. The importance of examining prior knowledge as part of design was underscored in the initial efficacy testing of the first *Martha* game prototype, *Martha Madison's Marvelous Machines.* An assessment of knowledge transfer and application indicated that students were able to more successfully solve problems involving simple machines after playing the game, as compared to their problem-solving prior to gameplay. However, these same students struggled to describe their solutions and answer vocabulary identification questions.

Essentially, though the game helped students learn how to apply concepts, they were not able to find the words to describe what they were doing. The original design of the game included terminology such as *lever, inclined plane,* and *force.* However, it was found that some cohorts of students demonstrated very little prior knowledge or experience with these terms in a scientific context. As a result, the *Martha Madison* games were modified to include in-game support for terminology acquisition, both through interactions with non-playable characters, and through labels, signs, and other cues in the game environment itself. These modifications led to significant improvement in students' ability to identify and discuss scientific tools, solutions, and theories.

Make Usability and Ease of Use a Priority

Thus far, our focus has been on the needs of the middle school student. However, the needs of middle school teachers also warrant attention, as these are the professionals who are tasked with guiding the social, emotional, and cognitive growth of large numbers of students. Typically, the job of a middle school teacher involves far more than providing instruction. These teachers must also juggle many other high-stakes, high-pressure responsibilities, a few of which are listed here (Cushman & Rogers, 2013; Kellough & Kellough, 1999):

- Preparing students for standardized exams.
- Preparing lesson plans that correlate to curricula and state standards.
- Creating supporting materials (e.g. worksheets) and assessments.
- Grading homework and assessments.
- Maintaining communication with many disparate groups (students, parents, teachers, staff, administration).
- Developing curriculum.
- Managing individual student and whole class behavior.
- Integrating technology into instruction.
- Providing additional support outside of class (e.g. help room).
- Counseling students on a wide range of issues (behavior, academic performance, health, etc.).
- Writing grant proposals.
- Participating in professional development activities.

All of these responsibilities must be met in order to support middle school student growth and learning; moreover, they often must be met under significant constraints. Preparation time is often minimal, teachers must cover vast amounts of material within defined periods of time, and they are under great pressure to *differentiate*, or adjust instruction to support learners of all abilities and motivation levels. In addition, teachers are given only a limited number of resources each year (or a defined budget for purchasing resources), such that any additional materials must be funded by other sources, including their own salaries. Because of these constraints, teachers search for solutions and technologies that maximize instruction time, are cost-effective, can be used in multiple environments, and that are relatively flexible (Cushman & Rogers, 2013). By necessity, however, teachers are cautious in their purchases and adoptions of new approaches or technologies in the classroom. As some experts have noted, "teachers will not use a technology in the classroom, unless they understand how it will help their current practice by offering either administrative or teaching advantages" (Bourgonjon, De Grove, De Smet, Van Looy, Soetart, and Valcke, 2013, p.22).

To encourage the adoption of a game in the classroom, it needs to be clear how that game can ease the burden of the teachers while also benefiting students. As we have found, a high quality game can provide instruction, which is naturally differentiated to learners of different abilities. The well-designed game also offers opportunities to explore concepts in depth, practice key concepts, take on new identities, and collaborate with others; all key characteristics that will motivate use in the classroom.

In addition, teachers today are eager for game solutions that are aligned with existing learning standards and curricula, with documented evidence of how gameplay helps students achieve the goals listed in the standards. A standards correlation document, for example, not only assists teachers in deciding when and how to use the game as part of instruction (or homework), it also helps them justify the use of the game in discussions with administrators, parents, and caregivers. Similarly, designers may wish to provide printable lesson plans, unit plans, student and instructor guides, supplementary worksheets, or other resources that can facilitate discussion or further learning surrounding the game. While not strictly part of the game, per se, these resources can support teachers in their planning, and encourage re-use of the game throughout a unit of instruction or even the entire academic year, again maximizing the value of the product from a teacher's perspective.

Ideally, middle school serious games are also easy to download and install across multiple platforms, as technology varies from school to school. Some districts may have adopted a BYOD (bring your own device) model, others may have a tablet cart that is wheeled into the classroom, while still others may follow the more traditional computer lab approach to technology; digital games must be playable in any of these cases if widespread adoption is to take place (Rice, 2007). Maintenance, like installation, must place as little burden on a teacher as possible. Student accounts and set up should be straightforward, and by middle school, many students are capable of establishing and maintaining their accounts completely independently.

These investments in terms of ease of use and teacher support pay great dividends, as they facilitate teachers and administrators in the decision to adopt a game, as well as in the implementation of the game itself in the classroom. This, in turn, sets the stage for a positive, seamless game experience that enriches rather than disrupts classroom instruction.

Examples from Martha Madison: Because the *Martha Madison* games were intended to support existing science instruction, it was necessary to build the game design to suit this use case. Second Avenue consulted with several practicing middle school science teachers, and found that most of them taught in 45- to 50-minute blocks, with approximately 25 minutes of that time to devoted to lab work or group activities. As a result of this feedback, each *Martha Madison* game was designed to be completed within a 25-minute time span, allowing for instructional time before gameplay, as well as review of relevant concepts at the end of class.

The data dashboard that is integrated with the *Martha Madison* games was also developed based on the needs of both students and teachers (see Figure 5). Dashboards are becoming a standard feature in many serious/educational games, not only because they provide records of student progress and assist in classroom management, but also because they can assist teachers and other

Figure 5. Sample screen from teacher interface of the Martha Madison dashboard

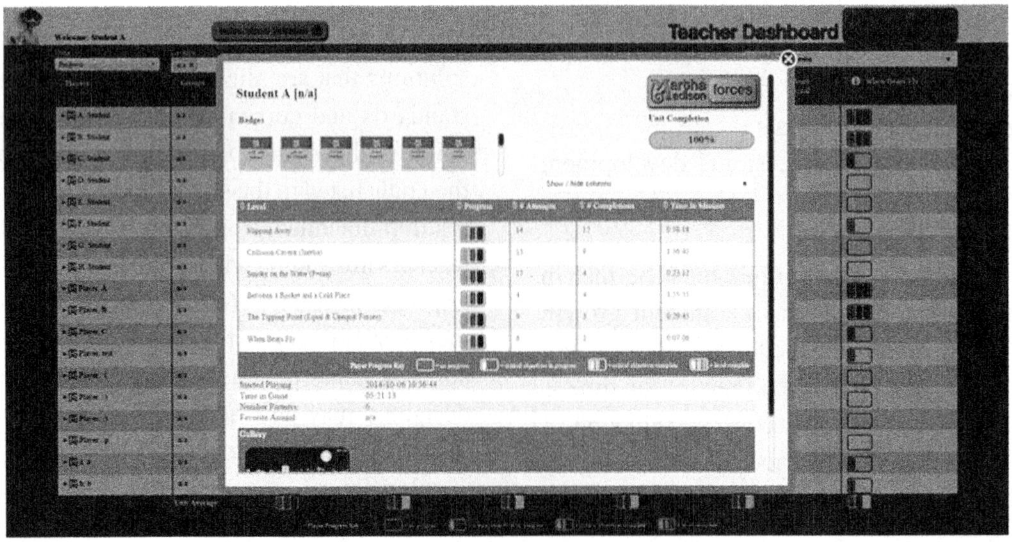

stakeholders in determining the efficacy of the game in supporting learning. As such, dashboards or other mechanisms of collecting student data are highly recommended features for games that are intended for use in the classroom.

To support the integration of *Martha Madison* into existing instruction, learning designers worked with teachers and game developers to create a set of supporting resources outside of the game. This package is continually evolving, as playtesting and classroom tests have highlighted potential new resources that can extend or reinforce the science concepts explored in-game. For example, the original resource package included a unit plan, sample lesson plans, and a set of guided notes to provide instructors with basic factual information. Teachers expressed a desire for paper/pencil assessments and student worksheets; these were then added to the package, along with extension activities and scoring rubrics.

As the technology trends have changed within the average middle school classroom, the design of *Martha Madison* is changing accordingly. The games are now being redesigned to accommodate new technologies, with a special focus on tablets and mobile devices.

THE FUTURE OF MIDDLE SCHOOL GAME-BASED LEARNING

Many have joked that middle school is the "Bermuda triangle of education." While a joke, there is truth in this comparison. Middle school can indeed become a time and place where students get lost, academic achievement falls, and teachers lose stamina. Students are caught in a sort of educational and physical limbo, faced with extraordinary challenges while still possessing many of the traits of young children.

We would rather our middle school students enjoy Bermuda, rather than disappear into the Bermuda triangle, and one way to do this is to capitalize on the strengths of middle school students and teachers. Middle school is a place where so much can be found. Students bring much to the table: energy, drive, excitement, and an astonishing capacity to learn. These students are ready to engage in deep learning, especially if that learning can occur via hands-on, collaborative experiences. The teachers who "brave" the middle school years are eager to support their students, and many are willing to try new approaches to instruction, provided those approaches address their needs and the needs of their students.

Game-based learning offers an approach that is tailor-made for the needs and motivations of today's middle-schoolers. As new technologies continue to emerge, the game possibilities will expand in kind. We foresee that augmented reality, wearable technologies, adaptive engines, user-generated content platforms, in-game social networks, digital "maker spaces," 3D printing, and several other digital and gaming trends will merge with game-based learning, creating learning environments that are both effective and transformative.

If this transformation is to take place in the middle school environment, however, it will be imperative that *all* stakeholders collaborate toward the development of a strong body of research and product creation in this domain. Until recently, few game developers and even fewer researchers have chosen to examine on producing or researching serious games for the middle school audience.

The time is ripe to develop a focus on the development, implementation, and assessment of serious games specifically for the middle school audience. Acceptance of game-based learning as a whole is growing, and this is occurring concurrently with a rise in the availability and decrease in cost of a multitude of new technologies. Together, students, teachers, and game designers have the potential give rise to a new generation of games that not only teach, but reintroduce play into the classroom, building a much-needed bridge from the elementary years into middle school and beyond.

REFERENCES

All, A., Castellar, E.P.N., & Van Looy, J. (2014). Measuring Effectiveness in Digital Game-Based Learning: A Methodological Review. *International Journal of Serious Games*, *1*(2), 3–21. doi:10.17083/ijsg.v1i2.18

Anderman, L. H. (2003). Academic and social perceptions as predictors of change in middle school students' sense of school belonging. *Journal of Experimental Education*, *72*(1), 5–22. doi:10.1080/00220970309600877

Anfara, V. A., & Mertens, S. B. (Eds.). (2007). *The young adolescent and the middle school*. IAP.

Balfanz, R. (2009). *Putting middle grades students on the graduation path: A policy and practice brief*. Baltimore, MD: Johns Hopkins University, Everyone Graduates Center and Talent Development Middle Grades Program.

Barnea-Goraly, N., Menon, V., Eckert, M., Tamm, L., Bammer, R., Karchemskiy, A., & Reiss, A. L. et al. (2005). White matter development during childhood and adolescence: A cross-sectional diffusion tensor imaging study. *Cerebral Cortex*, *15*(12), 1848–1854. doi:10.1093/cercor/bhi062 PMID:15758200

Bergen, D., & Fromberg, D. P. (2009). Play and social interaction in middle childhood. *Phi Delta Kappan*, *90*(6), 426–430. doi:10.1177/003172170909000610

Bourgonjon, J., De Grove, F., De Smet, C., Van Looy, J., Soetaert, R., & Valcke, M. (2013). Acceptance of game-based learning by secondary school teachers. *Computers & Education*, *67*, 21–35. doi:10.1016/j.compedu.2013.02.010

Britner, S. L., & Pajares, F. (2006). Sources of science self-efficacy beliefs of middle school students. *Journal of Research in Science Teaching*, *43*(5), 485–499. doi:10.1002/tea.20131

Bruce, T. (2011). *Learning Through Play*. Hachette, UK: For Babies, Toddlers and Young Children.

Bruner, J. S. (1972). Nature and uses of immaturity. *The American Psychologist*, *27*(8), 28–60. doi:10.1037/h0033144

Burchinal, M. R., Roberts, J. E., Zeisel, S. A., & Rowley, S. J. (2008). Social risk and protective factors for African American children's academic achievement and adjustment during the transition to middle school. *Developmental Psychology*, *44*(1), 286–292. doi:10.1037/0012-1649.44.1.286 PMID:18194027

Cantin, S., & Boivin, M. (2004). Change and stability in children's social network and self-perceptions during transition from elementary to junior high school. *International Journal of Behavioral Development*, *28*(6), 561–570. doi:10.1080/01650250444000289

Carrington, V. (2006). *Rethinking middle years: early adolescents, schooling and digital culture*. Allen & Unwin.

Casby, M. W. (2003). The development of play in infants, toddlers, and young children. *Communication Disorders Quarterly*, *24*(4), 163–174. doi:10.1177/15257401030240040201

Caskey, M.M., & Anfara Jr, V.A. (2007). Research summary: Young adolescents' developmental characteristics.

Chuang, T. Y., & Chen, W. F. (2009). Effect of computer-based video games on children: An experimental study. *Journal of Educational Technology & Society*, *12*(2), 1–10.

Chung, H., Elias, M., & Schneider, K. (1998). Patterns of individual adjustment changes during middle school transition. *Journal of School Psychology*, *36*(1), 83–101. doi:10.1016/S0022-4405(97)00051-4

Cohen, D. (Ed.). (2007). *The development of play*. Routledge.

Coiro, J., Knobel, M., Lankshear, C., & Leu, D.J. (Eds.), (2014). *Handbook of research on new literacies*. Routledge.

Conklin, H. G. (2014). Toward more joyful learning: Integrating play into frameworks of middle grades teaching. *American Educational Research Journal, 51*(6), 1227–1255. doi:10.3102/0002831214549451

Creech, S. (2001). *Walk Two Moons*. Pan Macmillan.

Cushman, K., & Rogers, L. (2009). *Fires in the middle school bathroom: Advice for teachers from middle schoolers*. The New Press.

Davis, J. P., Steury, K., & Pagulvan, R. (2005). A survey method for assessing perceptions of a game: The consumer playtest in game design. *The International Journal of Computer Game Research, 5*(1).

Deci, E. L. (1975). *Intrinsic motivation*. New York: Plenum Press. doi:10.1007/978-1-4613-4446-9

Deci, E. L., & Ryan, R. M. (1985). *Intrinsic motivation and self-determination in human behavior*. New York: Plenum Press. doi:10.1007/978-1-4899-2271-7

Dickey, M. D. (2006). Girl gamers: The controversy of girl games and the relevance of female-oriented game design for instructional design. *British Journal of Educational Technology, 37*(5), 785–793. doi:10.1111/j.1467-8535.2006.00561.x

Duchesne, S., Ratelle, C. F., Poitras, S. C., & Drouin, E. (2009). Early adolescent attachment to parents, emotional problems, and teacher–academic worries about the middle school transition. *The Journal of Early Adolescence, 29*(5), 743–766. doi:10.1177/0272431608325502

Egert, C. A., & Phelps, A. M. (2011). Motivating Science Education through Games. *Learning to Play: Exploring the Future of Education with Video Games, 53*, 129.

Engel, G., & Green, T. (2011). Cell Phones in the Classroom: Are We Dialing up Disaster? *TechTrends, 55*(2), 39–45. doi:10.1007/s11528-011-0482-z

Frost, J. L. (2009). *A history of children's play and play environments: Toward a contemporary child- saving movement*. Routledge.

Garris, R., Ahlers, R., & Driskell, J. E. (2002). Games, motivation, and learning: A research and practice model. *Simulation & Gaming, 33*(4), 441–467. doi:10.1177/1046878102238607

Ge, X., Natsuaki, M., Neiderhiser, J. M., & Reiss, D. (2007). Genetic and environmental influences on pubertal timing: Results from two national sibling studies. *Journal of Research on Adolescence, 17*(4), 767–788. doi:10.1111/j.1532-7795.2007.00546.x

Gee, J. P. (2003). What video games have to teach us about learning and literacy. *Computers in Entertainment, 1*(1), 20–20. doi:10.1145/950566.950595

Giedd, J. N., Blumenthal, J., Jeffries, N. O., Castellanos, F. X., Liu, H., Zijdenbos, A., & Rapoport, J. L. et al. (1999). Brain development during childhood and adolescence: A longitudinal MRI study. *Nature Neuroscience, 2*(10), 861–863. doi:10.1038/13158 PMID:10491603

Ginsburg, K. R. (2007). The importance of play in promoting healthy child development and maintaining strong parent-child bonds. *Pediatrics, 119*(1), 182–191. doi:10.1542/peds.2006-2697 PMID:17200287

Gray, P. (2011). The decline of play and the rise of psychopathology in children and adolescents. *American Journal of Play, 3*(4), 443–463.

Greenberg, B. S., Sherry, J., Lachlan, K., Lucas, K., & Holmstrom, A. (2010). Orientations to video games among gender and age groups. *Simulation & Gaming*, *41*(2), 238–259. doi:10.1177/1046878108319930

Gruber, M. J., Gelman, B. D., & Ranganath, C. (2014). States of Curiosity Modulate Hippocampus-Dependent Learning via the Dopaminergic Circuit. *Neuron*, *84*(2), 486–496. doi:10.1016/j.neuron.2014.08.060 PMID:25284006

Hayenga, A. O., & Corpus, J. H. (2010). Profiles of intrinsic and extrinsic motivations: A person-centered approach to motivation and achievement in middle school. *Motivation and Emotion*, *34*(4), 371–383. doi:10.1007/s11031-010-9181-x

Hirsh-Pasek, K., Golinkoff, R. M., Berk, L. E., & Singer, D. (2008). *A mandate for playful learning in preschool: Applying the scientific evidence*. Oxford University Press. doi:10.1093/acprof:oso/9780195382716.001.0001

Homer, B. D., Hayward, E. O., Frye, J., & Plass, J. L. (2012). Gender and player characteristics in video game play of preadolescents. *Computers in Human Behavior*, *28*(5), 1782–1789. doi:10.1016/j.chb.2012.04.018

Hughes, F. P. (2009). Children, play, and development. *Sage (Atlanta, Ga.)*.

Im, M. H., Hughes, J. H., Kwok, O., Puckett, S., & Cerdia, C. A. (2014). Effect of retention in elementary grades on transition to middle school. *Journal of School Psychology*, *51*(3), 349–365. doi:10.1016/j.jsp.2013.01.004 PMID:23816229

Isenberg, J. P., & Quisenberry, N. (2002). A position paper of the Association for Childhood Education International PLAY: Essential for all Children. *Childhood Education*, *79*(1), 33–39. doi:10.1080/00094056.2002.10522763

Jackson, A., & Davis, G. A. (2000). *Turning points 2000: Educating adolescents in the 21st century*. New York, NY: Teachers College Press.

Jacob, B. A., & Rockoff, J. E. (2011). *Organizing schools to improve student achievement: start times, grade configurations, and teacher assignments*. Brookings Institution, Hamilton Project.

Jalongo, M. R. (2003). A Position Paper of the Association for Childhood Education International: The Child's Right to Creative Thought and Expression. *Childhood Education*, *79*(4), 218–228. doi:10.1080/00094056.2003.10521196

Jensen, E. (2005). *Teaching with the brain in mind*. Alexandria, VA: Association for Supervision and Curriculum Development.

Kail, R., & Cavanaugh, J. (2012). *Human development: A life-span view*. Cengage Learning.

Kangas, M. (2010). Creative and playful learning: Learning through game co-creation and games in a playful learning environment. *Thinking Skills and Creativity*, *5*(1), 1–15. doi:10.1016/j.tsc.2009.11.001

Kellough, R. D., & Kellough, N. G. (1999). Middle school teaching: A guide to methods and resources. Saddle River, NJ: Merrill.

Kim, B., Park, H., & Baek, Y. (2009). Not just fun, but serious strategies: Using meta- cognitive strategies in game-based learning. *Computers & Education*, *52*(4), 800–810. doi:10.1016/j.compedu.2008.12.004

Klopfer, E., Osterweil, S., & Salen, K. (2009). *Moving learning games forward*. Cambridge, MA: Education Arcade.

Kolovou, A., & Heuvel-Panhuizen, M. V. D. (2010). Online game-generated feedback as a way to support early algebraic reasoning. *International Journal of Continuing Engineering Education and Lifelong Learning*, *20*(2), 224–238. doi:10.1504/IJCEELL.2010.036817

Lenhart, A., Kahne, J., Middaugh, E., Macgill, A. R., Evans, C., & Vitak, J. (2008). *Teens, Video Games, and Civics: Teens' Gaming Experiences Are Diverse and Include Significant Social Interaction and Civic Engagement.* Pew Internet & American Life Project.

Liu, M., Horton, L., Olmanson, J., & Toprac, P. (2011). A study of learning and motivation in a new media enriched environment for middle school science. *Educational Technology Research and Development, 59*(2), 249–265. doi:10.1007/s11423-011-9192-7

Liu, M., Toprac, P., & Yuen, T. (2009). What factors make a multimedia learning environment engaging: A case study. *Cognitive effects of multimedia learning*, 173-192.

Manning, M. L. (2002). Revisiting developmentally appropriate middle level schools. *Childhood Education, 78*(4), 225–227. doi:10.1080/00094056.2002.10522187

Millar, D., Patel, R., & Hornsby, A. J. (2011, November). Solving preadolescent anti socialism through play. *Proceedings of the 7th Australasian Conference on Interactive Entertainment* (p. 13). Interactive Entertainment.

Miller, L., Chaika, M., & Groppe, L. (1996). Girls' preferences in software design: Insights from a focus group. *Technology and Electronic Journal of the 21st Century, 4*(2), 1-6.

Newland, L. A., Roggman, L. A., & Boyce, L. K. (2001). The development of social toy play and language in infancy. *Infant Behavior and Development, 24*(1), 1–25. doi:10.1016/S0163-6383(01)00067-4

Olson, C. K. (2010). Children's motivations for video game play in the context of normal development. *Review of General Psychology, 14*(2), 180–187. doi:10.1037/a0018984

Packman, J. (2002). *Group activity therapy with learning disabled preadolescents exhibiting behavior problems* [Doctoral dissertation]. University of North Texas.

Papastergiou, M. (2009). Digital game-based learning in high school computer science education: Impact on educational effectiveness and student motivation. *Computers & Education, 52*(1), 1–12. doi:10.1016/j.compedu.2008.06.004

Parten, M. B. (1932). Social participation among pre-school children. *Journal of Abnormal and Social Psychology, 27*(3), 243–269. doi:10.1037/h0074524

Paulsen, G. (2006). *Hatchet.* Simon and Schuster.

Paus, T. (2005). Mapping brain maturation and cognitive development during adolescence. *Trends in Cognitive Sciences, 9*(2), 60–68. doi:10.1016/j.tics.2004.12.008 PMID:15668098

Piaget, J. (1962). *Play, dreams and imitation in childhood.* New York: Norton.

Rice, J. W. (2007). New media resistance: Barriers to implementation of computer video games in the classroom. *Journal of Educational Multimedia and Hypermedia, 16*(3), 249–261.

Rideout, V. J., Foehr, U. G., & Roberts, D. F. (2011). *Generation M2: Media in the Lives of 8 to 18 year Olds: A Kaiser Family Foundation Study.*

Roaten, G. K., & Roaten, D. J. (2012). Adolescent Brain Development: Current Research and the Impact on Secondary School Counseling Programs. *Journal of School Counseling, 10*(18), 18.

Roeser, R. W., Eccles, J. S., & Sameroff, A. J. (2000). School as a context of early adolescents' academic and social-emotional development: A summary of research findings. *The Elementary School Journal, 100*(5), 443–471. doi:10.1086/499650

Rowling, J. K. (1999). *The Chamber of Secrets*. New York: Scholastic.

Rubin, K. H. (1982). Early play theories revisited: Contributions to contemporary research and theory. In D. J. Pepler & K. H. Rubin (Eds.), *The play of children: Current theory and research*. New York: Karger. doi:10.1159/000407155

Rushton, S., Juola-Rushton, A., & Larkin, E. (2010). Neuroscience, play and early childhood education: Connections, implications and assessment. *Early Childhood Education Journal*, *37*(5), 351–361. doi:10.1007/s10643-009-0359-3

Saracho, O. N., & Spodek, B. (1995). Children's play and early childhood education: Insights from history and theory. *Journal of Education*, *177*(3), 129–149.

Schaaf, R. (2012). Does digital game-based learning improve student time-on-task behavior and engagement in comparison to alternative instructional strategies? *The Canadian Journal of Action Research*, *13*(1), 50–64.

Schumacher, D. (1998). *The transition to middle school. ERIC Clearinghouse on Elementary and Early Childhood Education*. University of Illinois.

Shaffer, D. W., Halverson, R., Squire, K. R., & Gee, J. P. (2005). Video Games and the Future of Learning (WCER Working Paper No. 2005-4). *Wisconsin Center for Education Research (NJ1)*.

Shurchkov, O. (2012). Under pressure: Gender differences in output quality and quantity under competition and time constraints. *Journal of the European Economic Association*, *10*(5), 1189–1213. doi:10.1111/j.1542-4774.2012.01084.x

Sicart, M. (2008). Defining game mechanics. *Game Studies*, *8*(2), 1–14.

Singer, D. G., Golinkoff, R. M., & Hirsh-Pasek, K. (Eds.). (2006). *Play= Learning: How play motivates and enhances children's cognitive and social-emotional growth*. Oxford University Press. doi:10.1093/acprof:oso/9780195304381.001.0001

Sowell, E. R., Thompson, P. M., Holmes, C. J., Jernigan, T. L., & Toga, A. W. (1999). In vivo evidence for post-adolescent brain maturation in frontal and striatal regions. *Nature Neuroscience*, *2*(10), 859–861. doi:10.1038/13154 PMID:10491602

Spires, H. A., Rowe, J. P., Mott, B. W., & Lester, J. C. (2011). Problem solving and game- based learning: Effects of middle grade students' hypothesis testing strategies on learning outcomes. *Journal of Educational Computing Research*, *44*(4), 453–472. doi:10.2190/EC.44.4.e

Squire, K. (2006). From content to context: Videogames as designed experience. *Educational Researcher*, *35*(8), 19–29. doi:10.3102/0013189X035008019

Steinberg, L. (2011). Demystifying the adolescent brain. *Educational Leadership*, *68*(7), 42–46.

Strauch, B. (2003). *The primal teen: What the new discoveries about the teenage brain tell us about our kids*. New York: Doubleday.

Sutton-Smith, B. (2009). *The ambiguity of play*. Harvard University Press.

Trilling, B., & Fadel, C. (2009). *21st century skills: Learning for life in our times*. John Wiley & Sons.

Valve Corporation. (2007). *Portal*. Bellevue, WA: Valve Corporation.

Vawter, D. (2010). Mining the Middle School Mind. *Education Digest: Essential Readings Condensed for Quick Review*, *75*(5), 47–49.

Vorderer, P., Hartmann, T., & Klimmt, C. (2006). Explaining the enjoyment of playing video games: The role of competition. In D. Marinelli (Ed.), *ICEC Conference Proceedings 2003: Essays on the Future of Interactive Entertainment* (pp. 107– 120). Pittsburgh, PA: Carnegie Mellon University Press.

Vygotsky, L. S. (1978). *Mind in society: The development of higher psychological processes*. Cambridge, MA: Harvard University Press.

Willis, J. (2007). Cooperative Learning Is a Brain Turn-On. *Middle School Journal (J1)*, 38(4), 4-13.

Wouters, P., van der Spek, E. D., & Van Oostendorp, H. (2009). Current practices in serious game research: a review from a learning outcomes perspective. *Games- based learning advancements for multisensory human computer interfaces: techniques and effective practices* (pp. 232-255).

Yan, B., & Slagle, M. (2006). School Start Time and Academic Achievement: A Literature Review. *Blue Valley School District Series*, 1-19.

Yang, Y.T.C. (2012). Building virtual cities, inspiring intelligent citizens: Digital games for developing students' problem solving and learning motivation. *Computers & Education*, *59*(2), 365–377. doi:10.1016/j.compedu.2012.01.012

Zusak, M. (2007). *The Book Thief*. Knopf Books for Young Readers.

Chapter 11
Designing Alien Mysteries in Chatterdale:
An Instructor's Perspective

Stella K. Hadjistassou
KIOS Research Center for Intelligent Systems and Networks, Cyprus

Judith Molka-Danielsen
Molde University College, Norway

ABSTRACT

As part of a larger, three-year long European project, Franziska reflected on her experiences in designing and implementing age-appropriate, immersive learning experiences in the virtual village of Chatterdale in OpenSim. Thirteen-year-old German and Norwegian students learning English as a target language engaged in collaborative goal-driven actions, task-oriented activities, and verbal interactions in a quest to solve a mystery involving extraterrestrials and the local residents' disappearance. Building on Barab, Gresalfi, and Arici's (2009) conceptualization of game-oriented environments as transformational activities, the focus was placed on investigating how the emerging affordances can empower learners and enact opportunities to actively participate in these game-driven learning experiences and mold the content and context. The study illustrated that the design of this virtual Chatterdale science fiction scenario was student-instigated, while students' quest to unravel the mystery afforded opportunities for active involvement and collaborative actions, engagement in verbal exchanges, and interaction with content and context.

INTRODUCTION

Multi-user virtual learning environments, such as OpenSim, Second Life, and Minecraft, can transform teachers' teaching practices and students' learning experiences if immersive, game-like but task-driven learning experiences are effectively designed and implemented in the language curriculum. Many foreign language educators tend to agree that the semiotic resources enacted by the virtual characters, sculpted three-dimensional interactive environments featuring a wide multiplicity of objects, communication modes, the collaborative and playful nature of the virtual

DOI: 10.4018/978-1-4666-9629-7.ch011

platform, the rich repertoire of engaging game-like activities and experiences can be deployed to build affordances for social interaction, creativity, intercultural exchanges, immersive language learning experiences, task-driven activities, and collaboration (see Gee, 2003, 2007; Young, Schrader, & Zheng, 2006; Allison, Cambell, Davies, Dow, Kennedy, McCafferty, Miller, Oliver, & Perera, 2012; Zheng, 2012; Godwin-Jones, 2014). Most studies in second or foreign language learning have been conducted in Second Life and more recently in Minecraft (see Molka-Danielsen & Deutchmann, 2009; Clark, 2009; Jauregi, Canto, de Graaff, Koenraad, & Moonen, 2012; Zheng, Newgarden, & Young, 2012; Zheng, 2012). The open-source virtual platform of Open Simulator (OpenSim) has received considerably less attention than other virtual platforms. Despite some initially promising findings on the prospect of enacting technological and cultural affordances in this virtual environment to immerse students in challenging, thought-provoking, motivating, fun, imaginary, and collaborative game-like activities (see Berns, Gonzalez-Pardo, & Camacho, 2011; Berns, Gonzalez-Pardo, & Camacho, 2013), few studies have been published on how second or foreign language educators can design transformational game-related activities in OpenSim (Barab, Gresalfi, & Arici, 2009). As Barab et al. (2009) demonstrate, "To play transformationally, a player must become a protagonist who uses the knowledge, skills, and concepts embedded in curricular content to make sense of a fictional situation and make choices that transform that situation" (p. 77). Such game-driven activities can also guide second or foreign language educators in investigating how "players deploy their agency in organizing their actions and interactions" (Zheng, Newgarden, & Young, 2012). That is, transformation is an agent-directed behavior where affordances emerge in the virtual learning environment, in this case OpenSim, that galvanize learners' interactions and collaboratively enacted actions. Utilizing these semiotic resources, i.e., artifacts, avatars, and actions, to immerse students in transformational learning activities, however, requires dexterity, extensive knowledge, and expertise. Language educators that are newly adopters of virtual learning environments, such as OpenSim, are often confronted with "technological barriers, institutional opposition, limited familiarity, and other concerns [that] may be preventing" them from fully exploring and utilizing such virtual environments in their language curricula (Neely, Bowers, & Ragas, 2010, p.3). Not all institutions have the technological infrastructure or the technical, pedagogical, and institutional support to train their teachers to design and deliver goal-determined activities in virtual environments (see Hubbard & Levy, 2006; Arnold, 2007; Arnold & Ducate, 2011). Some useful online pedagogical resources have been created for educators using OpenSim to enhance students' learning experiences, such as OPENSIM-EDU (http://opensim-edu.org/blog/). However, even though these resources are insightful and extremely useful, they do not suffice for the successful implementation of OpenSim in the language curriculum as a path to enact affordances for transforming second/foreign language learners' learning experiences. Second or foreign language educators need to go beyond these successful integrations in the different institutionally-supported contexts to explore new teaching possibilities and identify institutional, technological, and technical support and constraints for implementing OpenSim in their own curricula.

Moreover, Berns, Gonzalez-Pardo, & Camacho (2013) warn that the integration of game-based learning experiences in virtual platforms pose a particular challenge since they often fail to be designed around clearly exemplified learning goals and specifically defined tasks and activities. As a result, "many users get lost in the virtual environment and loose finally their interest in it" (p. 212). Other users, on the other hand, often get carried away by the interactive, game-driven nature of such virtual spaces and instead of focusing on task completion, they interact with the multiplicity of semiotic resources, navigate through the open spaces, and engage in long conversations with students from all over the globe (see Clark, 2008; Cookie-Plagwitz, 2008; Berns, et al. 2013). OpenSim might galvanize students' interest by immersing them in cultural and linguistic experiences but, at the same time, educators need to contemplate students' learning styles and needs, level of motivation, the instructional materials, and the required conditions under which this virtual environment can form a constructive tool or a hindering mechanism for language learning. Educators need to also explore the teaching contexts where OpenSim might not form the most compelling tool for language learning, i.e., in cases where students' limited technological knowledge or low proficiency level in the target language can impede their capacity to engage in constructive conversations with their peers. In cases where second or foreign language educators determine that OpenSim can be dynamically tailored to transform their learning experiences, the learning objectives and activities need to be carefully enacted on clear game-designed learning goals, which can be a taunting task for educators who have no or limited experience in teaching in virtual world environments. Creating a network of experienced practitioners who can share their expertise, practices, knowledge, and perceptions about the pedagogical and learning value of a particular tool and the emerging contradictions during their use in particular situated contexts can form an empowering tool for language educators. Expanding on Barab et al. (2009) framework on transformational play, in this paper, we provide an educator's perception and experience in using the semiotic resources of the multi-user virtual environment of OpenSim to enact transformational learning experiences through collaborative quests and other gaming activities. More precisely, the study addressed the following research questions:

1. How can students' reflective and insightful inquiries be used to design game-driven learning experiences in OpenSim?
2. How can student-inspired game-based scenarios be used to immerse students in roles that enact affordances for active and demanding participation trajectories but are laden with opportunities for verbal interaction, collaborative actions, and goal-driven experiences in the target language?
3. How can content be turned from a formal textbook-situated activity to a meaningful and practical game-determined activity?
4. How can a virtual setting be turned into an interactive contextualized learning experience?

TRANSFORMATIONAL PLAY AND LEARNING EXPERIENCES IN OPENSIM

Confronting the conventional argument that game-playing experiences are trivial, addictive, time-consuming experiences that inhibit learning and real world experiences, Gee (2003) perceives situated game-playing experiences as engaging and crucial activities where "They situate meaning in a multimodal space through embodied experiences to solve problems and reflect on the intricacies of the design of imagined worlds and the design of both real and imaged social relationships and identities in the modern world" (p.48). Even though Gee's (2003) underlying principles on gaming experiences refer to video games, many of these principles can also be extended to quests or well planned activities in OpenSim that involve interacting with avatars or objects, performing specific collaborative tasks, such as solving mysteries, using postcards and utilizing other modes of communication or setting strategies that can aid in solving a particular mystery and learning a second or foreign language. OpenSim is an open source 3D virtual platform written in C#, a widely used multi-paradigm programming language. Second or foreign language educators can build in OpenSim, customize the virtual environment, and add additional software modules to enhance its functionality and design game-driven applications and experiences (see Berns, Gonzalez-Pardo, & Camacho, 2011). Both real-life and imaginary activities can be enacted or simulated in such virtual environments, which can transform learning by turning such experiences into immersive, highly engaging learning experiences (Helmer, 2007; Clark, 2009; Molka-Danielsen, 2009). Language learners can use their imagination, creativity, and engage in "long-term, joint coordinated action. In these spaces, cultures and meanings emerge from a complex set of interactions among the participants, rather than as part of a predefined story or narrative arc" (Brown & Thomas, 2009, p.2). Taking it a step further, Zheng (2012) advocates that "Built-in material and cultural artifacts are able to become affordances for players to create teams, groups, in which joint actions can be coordinated and sustained" (p. 547). But even in cases where students engage in collaborative actions with assigned peers, the actions can still be collaboratively coordinated through the assigned tasks, unpredictable turn of events during such game-based quests, or joint quests for solutions to inworld problem-solving events. Zheng, Newgarden, and Young (2012) maintain that such gaming experiences enact affordances not simply for coaction but also for a wide range of communicative activities, such as asking for help, exchanging strategies, and offering directions. In a similar vein, Cornillie, Thorne, and Desmet (2012) contend, game-enacted activities situate human development in theoretical frameworks grounded in problem-solving activities, experiential, collaborative, and distributed paths of learning. Most scholars would consent that game-based activities tailored for language learning are more effective if implemented in project-driven curricula where second or foreign language learners engage in goal-driven activities. In language contexts where the wide variation of gaming activities in such virtual settings is not explicitly linked to the learning goals and objectives, language learning will not materialize.

Barab et al. (2009) accentuate the transformational value of game-driven learning experiences, which "transform learners in three ways:

1. They transform a person from a passive recipient to an empowered actor,
2. They transform content from information that the learner has to remember to a tool that the learner can use to accomplish the desired ends, and
3. They transform context from an assurance that 'this knowledge will be relevant in the future to a present reality that responds to the learner's actions" (p.78).

In essence, Barab et al. (2009) propose curriculum-enacted activities that are intended to immerse learners in roles that require asserting a sense of agency. The content is molded through meaningful goal-seeking actions that promote deeper learner engagement, and finally context is transformed by using such contextual information to perform actions in the current situation and not dwell on its future value. Initiatives to integrate in the curriculum such transforming learning experiences in OpenSim would require the design of goal-seeking activities where language learners would jointly partake in and coordinate their participation in goal-seeking actions, would jointly strive to complete tasks, engage in verbal interactions that would guide them in accomplishing a particular goal, and would use the artifacts and game-nature setting of this virtual environment to achieve their intended goal. Transformational learning during such game-like experiences would invite language learners to assume agency in deploying the artifacts, i.e., postcards, engaging in written or oral communications to organize and coordinate their actions. Interestingly, scholarly discussions highlight the experiential, socially-organized and goal-seeking nature of such cooperative game-afforded virtual experiences. However, very few resources exist on instructors' insightful perspectives on the actual and multiplicity of processes and contradictions involved in designing, launching, and delivering successful game-like experiences in virtual learning environments, such as OpenSim. Instructors usually come across institutionally-organized initiatives and successful implementations of OpenSims and other virtual environments for educational purposes. However, not all instructors that are new to virtual learning environments form part of such organized and funded institutional initiatives. Consequently, there is a need to obtain experienced instructors' perspectives on these complex design and delivering processes in virtual environments in order to build new more powerful, immersive, and transformative learning experiences for language learners (see Figure 1).

Figure 1. Barab, Gresalfi, and Arici's (2009) conceptualization of transformational play

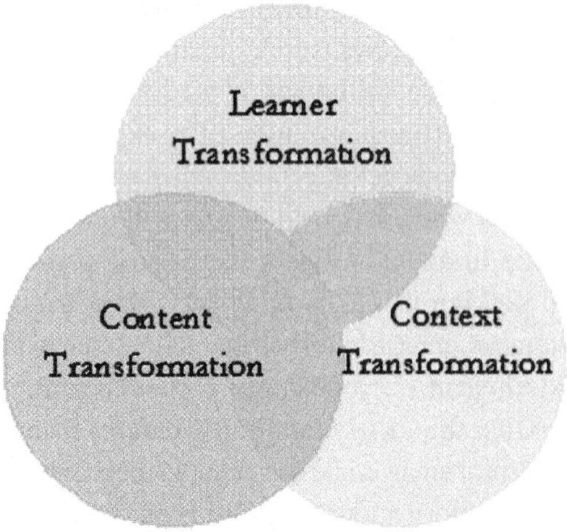

Method

The study formed part of the Euroversity project, a three-year long study funded by the Executive Agency, Education, Audiovisual and Culture in 2011. Euroversity was composed of a large network of 19 organizations of educators, researchers, and practitioners in a wide multiplicity of fields who shared their expertise and knowledge and compiled multiple resources and guidelines to guide educators in teaching in virtual environments and launched new teaching courses in such virtual settings. In the second year of the project, educators, who were involved in compiling these resources or offering new courses or learning events in virtual environments, were interviewed. The interviews were to evaluate the effectiveness of these resources and enhance the guidelines in planning, designing, and offering courses in virtual environments. Instructors' perceptions, opinions, experiences, and feedback were then used to revise these resources. Out of the nine interviews conducted via Skype, this study focuses on one educator, Franziska, a forty-three-year-old Austrian female learning consultant and educator who was actively involved in different aspects of the project. Franziska consented to participate in this study. A pseudonym was used to protect her identity. Franziska was selected mainly for her technological and pedagogical knowledge, extensive experience, and expertise in teaching and training in OpenSim and Second Life. Franziska was adept at combining students' imagination, the semiotic resources of OpenSim, and task-oriented activities to design collaborative and transforming learning experiences for both students and instructors. Reflecting on her own teaching practices and collaborative language learning projects launched with other academic institutions, Franziska used her expert knowledge not simply to train teachers and educators to teach in OpenSim but also to devise practical, immersive, and transforming experiences for the students. Franziska was not apprehensive at all in sharing the institutional, technological, technical, pedagogical, and learning contradictions emerging while designing and teaching in OpenSim or in other virtual learning environments.

THE CHATTERDALE MYSTERY IN OPENSIM

The Chatterdale mystery was designed in the virtual village of Chatterdale in OpenSim, which is a multi-user virtual platform often used by educators, schools, and academic institutions, such as the University of Cincinnati and Rutgers University for a wide multiplicity of teaching, research, learning, training, and even counselling purposes. Like many educators, for Franziska, OpenSim formed a gateway for designing highly immersive game-like scenarios that promoted student interactions through cooperative task-driven, goal-determined actions. The village of Chatterdale was carefully designed to feature a unique suburban community landscape design, combining elements of grass, scattered trees, and its craftily constructed buildings and structures, lighthouse, and various community resources and amenities. Chatterdale was a virtual microcosmic community, with its intricacies, mysteries, and above all extraterrestrial activities. The game was designed after students' initial visit to Chatterdale, where they were intrigued by the absence of local residents. Consequently, 4 classes of 13 year old Norwegian and Austrian students, a total of 100 students, were immersed in a quest to explore what truly transpired in this virtual setting that had led to the disappearance of the local residents and later on to Professor Jones, a hunter who had confessed his suspicions on alien involvement in the local residents' disappearance. Professor Jones' aunt reported his disappearance to the local authorities.

This game-like experience was set in motion by an e-mail distributed to each team of Norwegian and Austrian students. Three different teams on three different missions were devised:

1. A debt collection team which was sent to Chatterdale to unveil what had led these local residents to stop paying their bills;
2. A newspaper team which was invited to investigate local residents disappearance and compose a newspaper article on the topic;
3. A railway team which was invited to investigate, report on the railway damage, and propose suggestions for its improvement.

Each team was comprised of two Norwegian and two Austrian students, who eventually searched for clues, talked to the two remaining local residents, a priest and a drunk Chatterdale resident, and used inductive reasoning to discover Professor Jones' and local Chatterdale residents' mysterious disappearance. The award for the team completing the task first included some accessories for their avatars, while the team who discovered Professor Jones first won the competition. Each team had to compose a final writing assignment based on their role and assigned tasks in this game-like activity.

RESEARCH INSTRUMENTS AND DATA ANALYSIS

The data were collected during an hour-long interview via Skype and recorded using the screen recording software Camtasia. A questionnaire comprised of twenty-one questions was offered to Franziska prior to the interview. The questions were devised to solicit crucial information on educators' previous experiences, training, and teaching in virtual environments, their perceptions, beliefs, and feedback suggestions on the relevance, usefulness, practicality, and applicability of these proffered project resources in teaching in multi-user virtual learning environments and suggestions for revising these resources. The questionnaire was only intended as a guideline during the interview and additional questions or clarifications were requested during that process. For a detailed discussion on these guidelines on teaching in multi-user virtual learning environments, please refer to the wiki set for the Euroversity project (http://euroversity.pbworks.com/w/page/64358485/Final%20draft%209-March-2013#heading1). The data were transcribed using Och's (1979) conversational analysis procedures. Using Barab, Gresalfi, and Arici's (2009) call for immersing students in transformational play, particular attention was paid on investigating Franziska's use of the contextual affordances and constraints of the virtual village of Chatterdale to engage students in joint collaborative actions, interactions, and communications to solve a mystery. Students invitation to engage in game-like experiences where they were asserted a sense of agency in solving the mystery, coordinating, and engaging in dialogic exchanges with their peers and using the semiotic resources and constraints to reach their intended goal. Further, focus was also placed on Franziska's design of goal-oriented actions that promoted, through the different demands imposed by the slightly different tasks that students needed to jointly complete, a more comprehensive understanding of the content, i.e., brief e-mails inviting students to visit the virtual village to investigate the disappearance of the Chatterdale residents. Finally, following Barab et al.(2009) and van Lier's (2004) insightful discussion on the complexity and crucial significance of context, the study examined how Franziska used some of the contextual affordances and constraints a virtual environment shrouded in mysteries, rumors, and constant turn of events to help students solve the mystery. As van Lier (2004) notes, "in ecology, context is the heart of the matter" (p.5). Consequently, attention was placed on how Franziska perceived context and deployed those semiotic resources that turned it into a more interactive, immersive, and goal-driven virtual learning environment.

RESULTS AND DISCUSSION

Student-Inspiration on the Design of a Riddle in a Virtual Microcosmic Scenario

Designing and integrating in the curriculum, game-driven scenarios that enact affordances for engagement, agency deployment, action, and interaction is a dynamic but complex and multifaceted activity. Multiple contextual variables and constraints, as well as scenarios and genres, that promoted immersive game-driven experience and could contribute to learner engagement in actions, dialogical, and interactive communicative-oriented activities needed to be taken in consideration. In Excerpt 1 lines 1-5, Franziska contemplated with her Norwegian colleagues multiple imaginative scenarios, such as vampire fiction, that would galvanize students' interest and motivate them to engage and collaborate in imaginary game-play actions. However, instead of collaboratively developing a vampire fiction plot or any other game-driven scenario, Franziska became very perceptive of her students' needs. She was inspired by her students' repeated inquiries during a training session about a virtually enacted microcosmic society that featured some of the physical and material artifacts of a human society, such as shops and restaurants, but showed no signs of human life. Building on her students' relentless quests to discover what really happened to the residents of this virtual microcosmic community, Franziska devised an intriguing science fiction scenario initially involving a scavenger hunt, where a granny who owned a lighthouse in the village of Chatterdale passed on but, in her will, informed all heirs that they could inherit the lighthouse only if they could locate it and solve the mystery behind it. Similarly,

Excerpt 1.

I mean there were many interesting aspects in it. One was certainly the story itself. We really thought it took us some time to: to come up with this kind of story. We really thought what topics would those students be interested in. And we thought about vampires, something and then many different ideas and then finally the inspiration came from the students themselves because, when they had this introduction session, one question they asked me is 'where' 'Why are there no people?' There are so many nice buildings, and there is a hotel, shop, and restaurant, and everything but where are no people. And I thought, yes, this is a good question ((laughs)) Where did people? So maybe let's pick it up and build a quest around this question where: 'what happened to the people?' And to do it with Professor Jones and aliens.

the actual plot involved alien abductions of local residents, vanishing of material artifacts, such as bikes, unlawful imprisonment of professor Jones, a mystery hunter who initially offered students clues about alien involvement in the mysterious disappearance of the local residents, and students' role as investigators jointly collaborating to solve this mystery and free professor Jones who was suddenly imprisoned by aliens.

For Franziska, instructional goals should be aligned with students' interests, expectations, and what they perceived as salient in a virtual scenario embedded in goal-driven actions. Game-driven scenarios would enact affordances for verbal interactions, collaborative actions, and task-driven learning. As Franziska revealed in Excerpt 2, lines 1-2, some students might have initially felt overwhelmed by the demands imposed by this multiscale storyline and might have solicited Franziska's assistance, but none of the twenty-four students, who were so immersed and involved in their joint quest to solve the mystery, took a break during a one-and-a-half-hour session.

Franziska perceived and evaluated the meaning potential that a student-inspired quest could have had in creating new action-driven opportunities for engagement, interaction, and further action and new joint goals. In return, even though some students had initially struggled with the complexity of the enacted tasks in the game-driven virtual setting, they were so intensively engaged in their embodied experiences and the meaning-potential that these action-driven tasks generated that they persistently continued to pursue their joint goal of solving the mystery.

Excerpt 2.

…some students were a bit over challenged by doing this, so they needed a bit more help than I originally thought, but it was anyway it was very nice to see how they how they engaged, how they got immersed into the whole thing. I had one class with 22 boys and only two girls and I'd never seen this class so concentrated, so focused. We had a 90 minute session and they had a break in between but nobody left the room, nobody wanted to use the break, they just stayed there and wanted to go on talking to the priest and looking for the code.

Virtual Investigations with Real Learning Implications

Students' participation in transformative play where they were constantly engaged in collective interactions, actions, and negotiations also enacted further affordances for transformation. In Excerpts 3 and 4, Franziska provided a synoptic overview of how she utilized second-order resources, such as fabricated letters from Professor Jones to his aunt (lines 1-3) or written instructions in an e-mail from Amazon's vice-president to thrust students out of the classroom to a virtual environment with new virtual identities, roles, and task-driven goals. Second-order resources also formed the pillars upon which affordances were enacted for joint actions, goals, and interactions. Each group had slightly different tasks, but all tasks were designed to enact affordances for meaningful joint engagement through embodied action-instigated experiences. Whether asserting the role of a private investigator (Excerpt 3) or a debt collection agent (Excerpt 4), students embarked on a joint mission: to investigate the disappearance of the residents of Chatterdale.

Each group of students perceived the *action potential* of these second ordering resources and jointly collaborated to unravel the perplexing puzzle of Chatterdale.

As Franziska indicated in Excerpt 5, lines 1-4, the two Norwegian students and two Austrian students in each team needed to collectively strive to unravel the clues by first locating the hotel and then exploring the different clues. Students also needed to exercise collective agency and take initiatives by soliciting information from the two survivors: an intoxicated Chatterdale resident and a local priest (lines 4-5). Both survivors were played by real actors. Consequently, students engaged in dialogic interactions in the target language, English, with their peers and the actors. They also engaged in deductive reasoning to collectively explore the clues, determine their actions, and reach their collective goal to be the first group to solve the Chatterdale mystery. The rich participation trajectories were contingent upon students'

Excerpt 3.

1: …Involved is also Professor Jones who is a kind of mystery hunter, who was
2: suspicious that some aliens were involved, and he wrote letters to his aunt, and
3: suddenly he: there were no more letters, so the aunt went to this private
4: investigation company and asked them to send people there to look for him.

Excerpt 4.

1: Therefore: \ Mr.\ big \ vice-president of Amazon sent his debt collection
2: agents to Chatterdale on a debt finding mission. So these people who Well, the
3: group who formed this team, the debt collection agents of Amazon.com, I
4: distributed an email to them, yeah? So there they it just said that people
5: from Chatterdale don't pay their bill anymore. There is a list of people who
6: should have paid. Go there immediately and find them and report about the
7: status… And then they locked in there. They had their assignment find those
8: people. They had the role. They had the context, and each of the teams had a
9: slightly different assignment. So for all of them it was the same: find out what
10: is going on there, but they had slightly different roles.

Excerpt 5.

…Then they went to Chatterdale. They had this mixed teams, two Austrians, two Norwegians, and they had to: In this email, there: was the start-up point was indicated. For example, first go to the Health hotel and talk to my friend there, yeah? And they found a hint there, and then they found two survivors one drunken guy in the bar, and one priest in the church. And those two obviously survived and nobody really knows why. And then later on, they found out that indeed Professor Jones was right there were aliens who had used this location thousands years before and they had stored some secret source of power there. And when they [aliens] came back to fetch to fetch these power balls, they saw that there was a village there and they thought that people there spoiled this holy place, and therefore they teleported them away. But the alien who operated the teleporter, made a mistake with the set co-ordinates, so all the people who were below ground, like the priest in the catacombs and the drunk guy in the cellar were not taken by this teleporting radiation, so there is a reason why they survived… And then finally, the students found Professor Jones who had found out about this, who found the secret cave…

interactions, collaboratively set goals, conscious choices, and participation in this dynamically emerging scenario. Students needed to engage in interactions in English in order to unravel the multiscale plot, which included the verification of Professor Jones suspicions of the existence of aliens (line 7), the aliens return to Chatterdale to retrieve their salient power source (lines 8-9), and the Chatterdale residents' disrespect against this sacred place, which resulted to the residents' and Professor Jones' imprisonment in the secret cave (line 16), and the aliens' series of miscalculations and mistakes in imprisoning all Chatterdale residents (lines 11-14). Students were engaged in an emergent and ongoing scenario which required first-order languaging to instigate and participate in verbal interactions, goal-driven actions, enact a group identity, and set new goals in unraveling this extraterrestrial mystery.

Engagement in first-order languaging was also the primary goal of this game-driven scenario. Franziska situated this scenario in a virtual space where student-instigated verbal interactions in English would galvanize their actions, perceptions, and generate new cultural meaning by solving this mystery. Composing a reflective written report, in the form a newspaper article, a billing report, or a report for the railway damage, also prompted students to jointly collaborate to generate this final piece of writing.

Unraveling the Chatterdale Riddle: Situating Content in an Ecosocial System

The Norwegian and Austrian students were teamed-up in this ecosocial system of the virtual village of Chatterdale where their learning of the target language was not contingent upon traditional institutional curricula or scripted dialogues in assigned textbooks to promote verbal interactions in English. Instead, as Franziska noted in Excerpt 6, the learning landscape was transformed by the meaningful participation in a sociocultural environment where Austrian students teamed-up with Norwegian students to engage in verbal interactions in English to collectively explore this string of clues and solve this extraterrestrial riddle.

Excerpt 6.

What I liked about it was, of course, this teaming up with Norwegian students because I think this is really one of the big advantages of the virtual worlds that you can draw language courses out of this artificial classroom, where everybody speaks German, but now we do as if we could do only English, and this is so artificial. But as soon as you are in this world and your peers only speak English and Norwegian, you just have to speak English. And It was very nice to see how the students got into this. How they were a little bit shy at the beginning and then later on it came very natural to them.

This traditional ESL classroom in Austria was subject to the limitations arising from the physical set-up of the classroom, where the students were facing their teacher, and the geographic limitations which inhibited interactions with other second or foreign language learners. All students spoke German (lines 3-4) and were learning English in a rather artificial, non-authentic context. In this new virtual game-driven environment, Austrian students used first-order languaging by being immersed in these embodied experiences, jointly determining their actions, understanding the importance of using the target language to successfully solve this riddle, and finally to compose a newspaper article, a report for the Amazon vice-president justifying the billing and other related costs, a report on the damage of the Chatterdale railway, and offer suggestions to resolve the situation. As Franziska indicated in a follow-up e-mail, "the writing assignment was closely linked to the fictitious identity of each team." Here, it could be argued that Franziska's design of the game-play script also promoted identity construction in a virtual environment as a path to enact new affordances for joint collaboration, meaningful participation in actions, verbal interactions, and learning. Even though the students hesitated at the beginning because they were "shy," they were gradually immersed in this learning excavation (lines 7-8). The game-driven scenario did not inhibit students' learning. To the contrary, this historical game-driven learning experience transformed students' learning in distinctive ways by enacting affordances for dynamic and emergent engagement in collaborative actions and interactions to successfully achieve their goal. Instead of recalling grammatical structures, pragmatics, or etiquettes in dialogic interactions, students engaged with content in historically and culturally changing ways that are not afforded by traditional classrooms. Their engagement in joint actions was constructed on meaningful game-driven quests with real learning implications in culturally and historically emerging virtual communities (see Gee, 2003, 2007 for a discussion on content in game-driven contexts).

Chatterdale as an Interactive Contextual Experience

The virtual game-play experiences in Chatterdale redefined context, collaborative engagement, and transcended learning in interactive, embodied experiences where students and instructors needed to contemplate the material, cultural, and technological values, constraints, and contradictions of the virtual context. As Franziska discussed, engaging with such a virtual environment was a novel experience for the students: "…For many of them [the students], this whole idea of being thrown into such a quest was quite new." In this contextualized virtual learning experience, students needed to develop and apply in practice a set of skills required to control their avatar, navigate through

Chatterdale, use the oral and written modes of communication to interact with their peers (lines 2-3), tune out distractions, and focus on the task (line 5). It is a cognitively taxing process, where students needed to explore and interact with the environment, its wide multiplicity of artifacts, content, and their peers, but at the same to master the socially, historically, and culturally acceptable rules and constraints of their participation. As Franziska advocated in Excerpt 7, the participation trajectories often drew on real-life social, cultural, and learning values (lines 10-11). However, to collaboratively participate in actions, purposeful game-driven activities, and verbal interactions, students needed to overcome these contextual constraints, make conscious choices, and focus on their joint goals (see Zheng et al. 2012 and Zheng, 2012 for a discussion on students' participation in collaborative actions). Students needed to direct their attention, identify, and to pick up the second-order resources, such as fabricated letters from Professor Jones, as path to enact affordances that would galvanize students' collaborative actions, dialogic interactions, and would guide them in solving this virtual extraterrestrial riddle.

For Franziska, *access and engagement* with the virtual village Chatterdale did not suffice for active and productive language learning experiences, but students should also pay *attention* to and take up those contextual affordances that would engage them in productive game-driven learning activities (see Van Lier, 2004 for a discussion on *access, engagement, and attention*).

DISCUSSION

Game-driven learning experiences should be envisaged as part of an ecosocial environment where participation, exploration, and engagement with the semiotic resources enacts affordances for understanding, evaluating, and determining their potential and constraints for learning, collaboration, and design of meaningful and engaging scenarios. Van Lier (2004) strikes a core when he deftly notes that "A learning environment is not one in which a teacher throws linguistic signs around like an eccentric billionaire might throw dollar bills, nor one in which bills of various linguistic denominations are doled out piecemeal by a grammar miser" (p. 81). Game-driven learning activities in a virtual learning environment should be designed and integrated as part of learning by drawing on those critical connections between students' interests, instructional goals, objectives, and intended outcomes. In this study, Franziska's teaching experience in Chatterdale indicated the role students could play in the decision-making process of designing the game-driven learning scenarios. Consequently, to address the first research

Excerpt 7.

…They [students] have to handle the environment. To make sure that they see properly, that their avatar walks where they want him to walk. They have to manage communication with their peers, via text chat, via voice. Uhm Maybe in a noisy environment where others speak as well, maybe with voice not being very clear. And on top of all of these, they have to find hints. Uhm see what's lying around. There is a letter lying on the floor in front of the post office, for example. And it's a bit difficult to understand, but in a virtual world often people don't see this le: letter laying [lying] there, because there is so much else going on at the same time. So they really have to get a bit into this and learn to behave in the virtual world as they would in real world as well.

question of the study, students' expectations of encountering a virtual community with its local residents formed the grounds for designing more immersive game-driven learning experiences. However, Franziska used her imagination, innovation, and creativity to enrich the plot and devise a scenario that was aligned with students' interests, learning needs, and imaginations. She did not reach a conclusive decision beforehand instead she relied on her students' inquiries. Involving students in the decision-making process of the game-driven activities contributed to the design of more immersive and pedagogical potent learning activities. As an instructor, Franziska proved to be very perceptive and attentive to her students' interests and learning needs, which guided her in finally designing with her Norwegian partner the mystery plot in Chatterdale that captivated her students' interest. In terms of the second research question, students were immersed in different virtual roles and ventured out on a quest searching for clues and evidence that could shed some light to Chatterdale residents' disappearance. Their roles were no longer bound to the traditional classroom participation trajectories or roles, but were more engaging, collaborative, and active. The students not only participated in virtual learning community of Chatterdale, but also had to jointly set goals, engage in action, identify further clues, and put the pieces of the puzzle together. All these jointly enacted actions were afforded by students' verbal interactions. As Zheng et al. (2012) indicates, such game-driven experiences require *agency* to set goals, actions, and verbal interactions (see also Zheng, 2012; Barab et al., 2009). Barab et al. (2009) also show that "Rather than working on problems in which they must imagine the implications of their decisions (as in most project-based works), students experience consequentially" (p.77). Franziska discussed how the activity was designed to engage students in a constant flow of events where students needed to instigate, participate, and coordinate collaborative actions. These engagement trajectories were contingent upon students' verbal interactions and collaborations. In reference to the third research question, regarding content transformation, Franziska reflected on the importance of not simply transforming engagement in language learning where all students spoke German but attempted to learn English. In Chatterdale, students had to actually initiate and participate in verbal interactions in English because most of their Norwegian partners did not speak German. Initially, the game-driven environment appeared to be artificial but as the quest became meaningful and immersive, students became engaged in socially and historically collaborative and emerging practices and communities. Gee (2003) asserts that "it is in these social practices that 'content' is generated, debated, and transformed via certain distinctive ways of thinking, talking, valuing, acting, and, often, writing and reading" (p.21). In the process, Franziska illustrated the importance of identity construction in this emerging scientific scenario virtual learning experience. Finally, to address the fourth research question, Franziska demonstrated that contextualizing students' learning experiences in this ecosocial environment was cognitively demanding, often generating tensions with engagement with the multiplicity of semiotic resources which can often act as distractors (see Thorne, 2003 and Hadjistassou, 2012 for a discussion on contradictions in virtual settings). However, as students overcame these contextual constraints and contradictions, their engagement with context was deeper and more meaningful than a traditional classroom context. Students also focused on the affordances that opened the path to participate in game-oriented experiences. To borrow van Lier's (2004) powerful claim, in this ecosocially enacted environment, "context... [was] the heart of the matter" (p.5).

CONCLUSION

Moving content, context, and language learning to virtual realms can expand learning in an ecosocial environment where imagination, game, learning, joint participation, and interactions afford transformative learning experiences. As Franziska indicated in this study, the nature of game-driven activities and the dynamics involved in the design and actual implementation of these activities are rather complex and multifaceted and require student feedback, engagement, and active participation in captivating scientific scenario plots. The virtual Chatterdale village transcended the imaginary scientific scenarios of extraterrestrial activity and enacted affordances to experience, engage, and jointly undertake multiple actions to unveil the extraterrestrials involvement in mysterious disappearances. However, whether involving quests or collaborative explorations, language teachers should be well aware of the benefits, constraints, and contradictions of teaching, learning, and collaborating in virtual environments like OpenSim. At the same time, they should also be aware that involving students in such fantasy role-playing and problem-solving activities can enact affordances for active engagement, instigation of and participation in collaborative actions, actual verbal interactions in the target language, which are often required to reach a particular goal, and can immerse students in an exploratory quest with real language learning implications.

REFERENCES

Allison, C., Campbell, A., Davies, C. J., Dow, L., Kennedy, S., McCafferty, J., & Perera, I. et al. (2012). Growing the use of virtual worlds in education: An OpenSim perspective. *Proceedings of the 2nd European Immersive Education Summit.*

Arnold, N. (2007). Technology-mediated learning ten years later: Emphasizing pedagogical or utilitarian applications? *Foreign Language Annals, 40*(1), 161–181. doi:10.1111/j.1944-9720.2007.tb02859.x

Arnold, N., & Ducate, L. (2011). Technology, CALL, and the Net generation: Where are we headed from here? In N. Arnold & L. Ducate (Eds.), Present and future promises of CALL: From theory and research to new directions in language teaching (pp. 1-22). CALICO Monograph Series, 5 (2).

Barab, S. A., Gresalfi, M., & Arici, A. (2009). Why educators should care about games. *Educational Leadership*, 76–80.

Berns, A., Gonzalez-Pardo, A., & Camacho, D. (2011). Implementing the use of virtual worlds in the teaching of foreign languages (level a1). *Proceedings of Learning a Language in Virtual Worlds: A Review of Innovation and ICT in Language Teaching Methodology* (pp. 33–40). Warsaw: Warsaw Academy of Computer Science.

Berns, A., Gonzalez-Pardo, A., & Camacho, D. (2013). Game-like language learning in 3-D virtual environments. *Computers & Education, 60*(1), 210–220. doi:10.1016/j.compedu.2012.07.001

Gee, J. P. (2003). *What video games have to teach us about learning and literacy*. New York, NY: Palgrave MacMillan.

Gee, J. P. (2007). *What video games have to teach us about learning and literacy: Revised and updated edition*. New York, NY: Palgrave MacMillan.

Godwin-Jones, R. (2014). Emerging technologies. Games in language learning: Opportunities and challenges. *Language Learning & Technology, 18*(2), 9–19.

Hadjistassou, S. (2012). An Activity Theory exegesis on conflict and contradictions in Networked discussions and feedback exchanges. *CALICO Journal*, *29*(2), 367–388. doi:10.11139/cj.29.2.367-388

Hubbard, P., & Levy, M. (2006). *Teacher education in CALL*. Amsterdam: John Benjamin Publishing Co. doi:10.1075/lllt.14

Jauregi, K., Canto, S., de Graaff, R., Koenraad, T., & Moonen, M. (2011). Verbal interaction in Second Life: Towards a pedagogic framework for task design. *Computer Assisted Language Learning*, *24*(1), 77–101. doi:10.1080/09588221.2010.538699

Lord, G., & Lomicka, L. (2011). Calling on educators: Paving the way for the future of technology and CALL. In N. Arnold & L. Ducate (Eds.), Present and future promises of CALL: From theory and research to new directions in language teaching (pp. 441-470). CALICO Monograph Series, 5 (2).

Molka-Danielsen, J., & Deutchmann, M. (2009). *Learning and teaching in the virtual world of Second Life*. Trondheim: Tapir Academy Press.

Neely, J., Bowers, K. W., & Ragas, M. W. (2010). Virtual possibilities: A constructivist examination of the educational applications of Second Life. *Journal of Interactive Learning Research*, *21*(1), 93–110.

van Lier, L. (1996). *Interaction in the language curriculum: Awareness, autonomy, and authenticity*. New York: Longman.

van Lier, L. (2004). *The ecology and semiotics of language learning: A sociocultural perspective*. Boston: Kluwer. doi:10.1007/1-4020-7912-5

Young, M. F., Schrader, P. G., & Zheng, D. (2006). MMOGs as learning environments: An ecological journey into Quest Atlantis and Sims Online. *Innovate: Journal of Online Education*, *2*(4), 1–7.

Zheng, D. (2012). Caring in the dynamics of design and languaging: Exploring language learning in 3D virtual spaces. *Language Sciences*, *34*(5), 543–558. doi:10.1016/j.langsci.2012.03.010

Zheng, D., Newgarden, K., & Young, M. (2012). Multimodal analysis of language learning in World of Warcraft play: Languaging as values-realizing. *ReCALL*, *24*, 339–360.

Chapter 12
Designing Digital Objects to Scaffold Learning

Grant Van Eaton
Vanderbilt University, USA

Douglas B Clark
Vanderbilt University, USA

ABSTRACT

The design of digital objects and representations in digital games is highly consequential for learning. Digital objects in learning games provide opportunities to scaffold teacher and student learning toward deeper epistemological understanding of the concepts they represent, but objects and representations can also be interpreted in a manner that misrepresents the concepts in whose place they stand. For the current study, one teacher was observed using the SURGE learning environment. During the study, the teacher combined the learning environment with direct instruction to teach Newton's laws of force and motion. Findings highlight the importance of designs that (a) explicitly model the meaning of the representations in the learning environment, (b) provide opportunities for teachers and students to interact with the full range of the properties of the representational object, and (c) incentivize players to utilize representations in the environment to their full extent, such that the learning environment repeatedly reinforces the core concepts of the representation.

INTRODUCTION

In their review of the literature on digital games and simulations for science education, Clark, et al (2009) call on researchers to move beyond proofs of concept in terms of the possible efficacy of simulations and games to instead focus on ascertaining design principles that best support learning and conceptual change. Design principles in digital learning environments necessarily rely on the use of representations. These representations model core concepts and have the power to scaffold the learning trajectories of both teachers and students. Representations, however, are malleable and have the potential to be interpreted by both teachers and students in ways other than intended by the designer. The current study analyzes extended interviews and video footage of a teacher and his

DOI: 10.4018/978-1-4666-9629-7.ch012

students playing, learning, and teaching with a digital physics game designed for learning. The teacher was observed using the SURGE learning environment with four class periods totaling 136 students over the course of two weeks. During the study, the teacher combined the learning environment with direct instruction to teach Newton's laws of force and motion. Analyses focus on the teacher's and students' appropriation of the representational objects corresponding to the concepts of force, time, distance, and mass and the effects of these interactions on scaffolding the teacher and student's epistemology of force and motion. The primary data for this study include:

1. The video and audio of the teacher throughout the run in class,
2. Video and audio of interviews with the teacher outside of class before, during, and after the run,
3. Video and audio of the 68 student formative assessments that the teacher conducted during the classes.

The analyses of these data are supplemented by

1. Pre-post test data for the 122 students who completed the pre and post-tests, and
2. Post-gameplay interviews with the teacher and four students two months after gameplay.

This chapter analyzes these data in terms of two questions central to the interplay between design, representation, and epistemology:

- How do teachers and students interpret representations in the *Fuzzy Chronicles* learning environment?
- How do representations in *Fuzzy Chronicles* scaffold the development of teachers' and students' epistemology of force?

THEORETICAL FRAMEWORK

When thinking about how to use representations to scaffold concepts in a digital learning environment, Ball and Cohen's (1996) *educative curriculum* framework provides an orientation that positions the learning environment to scaffold learning not only for students, but also their teachers. As teachers play games in order to develop an understanding of their mechanics and how best to integrate them into curricula, the potential exists for games to scaffold teachers' learning of content as they interact with the game or simulation. Developing canonically aligned understandings of science content in teachers is especially important for students, as this development affects the quality of instruction students, in turn, receive. Teachers' understanding of Newtonian relationships influence not only the questions teachers ask when scaffolding their students' understanding, but also the tasks teachers plan for classroom instruction and the concepts these tasks reinforce (Feiman-Nemser, 2001). Using learning games to develop deeper content knowledge in teachers, however, will only be effective insofar as

1. The representations in the learning environment properly embody the focus concept(s), and
2. The correct scaffolds are in place to bridge teachers' intuitive understanding with the canonical understanding of concepts as represented in the game.

Representations in the Learning Environment

In order to discuss the potential for learning games to educate both teachers and students, and the role of representations, this chapter focuses on four representations in the *Fuzzy Chronicles* learning environment, which is a digital game designed to support students learning about Newtonian physics ideas and relationships. *Fuzzy Chronicles* and other early SURGE games are "conceptually-integrated games" for learning (Clark & Martinez-Garza, 2012), as opposed to merely "conceptually-embedded games." This means that the science to be learned is integrated directly into the mechanics as the central focus of navigating or manipulating the game world, rather than being embedded as an activity to be visited at some location in the game environment (i.e., isolated from the process of navigating or manipulating the overall game word and confined to challenges experienced at particular moments in time and/or special locations in the game-world). The latter structure is typical of many virtual worlds designed for science learning. Conceptual integration was the initial approach of our research group to the design of games for physics learning, and provided the foundation for our current approach, which we term "disciplinary integration" (please see Clark, Sengupta, Brady, Martinez-Garza, & Killingsworth, in press, for a full discussion of the rationale for conceptual integration, disciplinary integration, and the shift from one to the other in our research and designs).

Essentially, conceptual integration requires a two-pronged design approach:

1. Designing levels around popular game-play mechanics from appropriate game genres, while also
2. Designing challenges that directly explore, rather than merely contain, targeted physics relationships.

Along the first dimension, key ideas from recreational game design conventions include

1. Supporting engagement and approachable entry (Koster, 2004; Squire, 2011),
2. Situating the player with a principled stance and perspective (McGonigal, 2011),
3. Providing context and identification for the player with a role and narrative (Pelletier, 2008; Gee, 2007; Squire, 2005),
4. Monitoring and providing actionable feedback for the player (Annetta et al., 2009; Garris, Ahlers & Driskell, 2002; Munz, Schumm, Wiesebrock & Allgower, 2007), and
5. Using pacing and gatekeeping to guide the player through cycles of performance (Squire, 2006).

Along the second dimension, *Fuzzy Chronicles* is designed to require students to apply and coordinate many principles related to Newtonian dynamics to complete levels (e.g., force, time, acceleration, velocity, mass, and the relationships between them). Physics ideas and terminology were built into pre-level and post-level story and feedback screens and within the levels of the game itself. The levels are designed so that physics concepts built upon one another and gradually introduced the student to new ideas and ways of interacting with the game world. Each level highlights one or two topics, and levels allow students to connect the concepts together and to see the relationships among the topics.

Players must navigate a spaceship around obstacles to reach an exit portal. This is accomplished by placing commands on a timeline specifying the magnitude and direction of forces that the ship should apply to achieve the desired path. All forces are applied for a duration of 0.1 seconds. Within the game, these representations are represented by force tiles (force), a timeline delineated in one-second increments (time), a grid within the simulation space of the game along which the spaceship must travel (distance), and Fuzzies that the ship may pick up, release, and throw (mass). These representations are shown within the simulation space of the game in Figure 1. The design emphasizes prediction over mere reaction by

Figure 1. Representations in the Fuzzy Chronicles learning environment

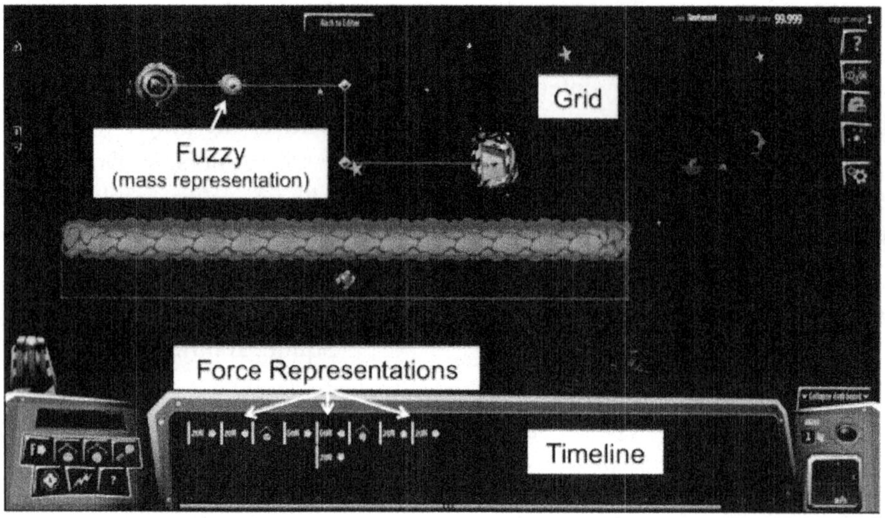

1. Creating challenges that require players to make fewer but higher impact decisions, and
2. Requiring players to spatially place all of these commands in advance.

Thus, in order to move along a particular path, the learner creates a predictive model of the trajectory by placing "force tiles" on the timeline to guide the ship along the player's intended path. The learner then deploys his or her model by "launching" the level to "run" the plan. Players watch their plans unfold and then revise them accordingly.

The current chapter focuses specifically on the representations in the game and how the teacher and students interpret the representations in terms of intuitive and formal Newtonian ideas and relationships (see Figure 1). Force tiles are representations in the game that embody a command to the ship to fire a force of a specific magnitude and direction at a certain time. This representation is not a digital embodiment of the actual force being applied, but rather a command to the ship to fire the desired force. Force tiles are placed within the timeline at the bottom of the simulation space, which is a representation of when the ship should issue the command to fire the force indicated on the force tile. The timeline is thus intended to represent and visualize the amount of time between commands to fire forces. The grid within the simulation space represents distance intervals of one meter. Within the design of the simulation space, the grid is an aid to the student or teacher for specifying the amount of force needed to accelerate the ship along a desired path, as well as the duration for which the ship should move at the velocity achieved by application of the force. Finally, Fuzzies, small creatures with a mass of one kilogram, are representations used to increase the mass of the spaceship (which also has a mass of one kilogram), providing opportunities for teachers and students to simulate the effects of mass on acceleration.

Impact of Representations on Scaffolding Learning

Lehrer and Schauble (2002) have shown that representations edit concepts in the sense that they reduce and enhance various aspects of the information representations contain to focus the attention of the viewer. In the best case scenario, these reductions and enhancements effectively scaffold student and teacher understanding toward the concept that the representation intends to stand in for (by focusing the viewer on salient aspects and relationships of the phenomena under study while minimizing other less salient aspects). Representations, however, also have the potential to be misinterpreted to such an extent that, despite the best design intentions, students and teachers emerge from interaction with the representation holding a fundamentally different concept than intended by designer. This study, therefore, seeks to better understand the impact of the representations of force, time, distance, and mass in *Fuzzy Chronicles* in terms of how they support or detract from students' and teachers' development of a canonically-aligned epistemology of force and motion.

It is also worth taking a moment to examine the ontology of the representations in the learning environment. Western philosophy has grappled for centuries with the ontological status of objects in the natural world. In the wake of Kant's transcendental idealism, the dominant view in western philosophy focused on a dichotomy of subjects and objects, with the existence of objects dependent on their perception by subjects (Kant, 1999). In the last two decades, however, a new strain of philosophy under the banner of object-oriented ontology (Harman, 2001) and (Bryant, 2011) posits that this dichotomy is false and that all objects are on equal ontological footing, existing independent of the perception of subjects. Such elevation of ontological status resonates with the actor-networks of Latour (1987) and Ingold's (2011) meshwork of objects.

This distinction is important for the current study because representations in the digital learning environment take on an ontological status as objects in their own right (2012). Representations are not simply passive entities subject to the perception of students and teachers, but rather independent objects that have the ability to interact with other human and non-human objects in the sense of taking on new meanings through interaction with viewers and guiding the resulting perceptions of the viewers. This will become increasingly important as the ways in which students and teachers relate to the representations is discussed in the analysis below.

Force

Throughout the teacher and student interviews, the teacher and students perceive force tiles as taking on independent agency in the game's simulation space, contrary to the intent of the designers. In other words, rather than the force tiles being perceived as a mere representation of a command given by the user to the ship to fire a particular magnitude of force in a particular direction, the student sees the force tile as the actor applying a particular magnitude of force in a particular direction directly on the ship. The student repeatedly talks of 'sending' a force from the timeline into the simulation space in order to do work, even gesturing from force tiles in the timeline to the point in the simulation space in which the force is applied:

Student: Like, where it sends... where you send a 60 Newton force over here to get to this point, and then you'd send another 60 Newton force to stop it [student gestures from 60 Newton force on timeline to the spot where the force is applied in the simulation space] ... and then a 20 Newton force... [repeats gesture] and then a 20 Newton force to stop it and go up... [repeats gesture]

In addition to the student misperceiving the force tile representation by conferring agency upon the object and "sending" it to do work, the force tile also takes on ontological independence to act within the simulation space as an object in its own right, with the student describing an interaction between the force tile and ship in the simulation space as "the force would go backward and stop [the ship]". The student also sends a 20 Newton force "to stop" the ship. In the student's mind, the force tile does not represent a mere command for

Table 1. Canonical formulations of Newton's three laws of motion, with teacher's memory aids

Law	Canonical Definition	Teacher's Definition *Net Force*	*Teacher's Definition Classroom Device*
1st	An object at rest (in motion) will stay at rest (in motion) unless acted upon by an unbalanced force – Law of Inertia	=	Balanced
2nd	Heavier objects require more force to accelerate at the same rate *Force = Mass x Acceleration*	+/-	Unbalanced
3rd	For every action there is an equal and opposite reaction		Opposite

the ship to apply force and decelerate, but rather the force tile object itself travels into the simulation space to oppose the movement of the ship.

This distinction is important with regard to the student's developing epistemology of force. Within the framework of the force tile merely representing a command of the ship to apply force, the action of the ship carrying out the force tile's command represents a change in velocity to decelerate the ship, exemplifying Newton's second law of motion. The student's conception of the force tile being 'sent' into the simulation space to 'oppose' the ship, however, gives agency to the force tile to travel into the simulation space and push backward on the ship in order to stop it, an enactment Newton's third law of motion. This unintended consequence is directly related to the design of the force representation, the means by which the object scaffolds student learning, and the way in which the student interacts with the object in the learning environment. It is also illustrative of an object-oriented ontology in which the force tile's ontological status grants it agency to participate in the simulation and not only oppose another digital object, but also interact (or interfere, even) with the student's epistemological development.

The teacher's epistemological development as a result of interacting with force representations in the game is further complicated by the framework he developed in order to explain and simplify Newton's three laws of motion for his students. Utilizing key words from canonical formulations of each law, the teacher developed the memory aid B-U-O: **B**alanced (Newton's first law), **U**nbalanced (Newton's second law) and **O**pposite (Newton's third law). Following gameplay, the teacher was given an example level from the game and asked to identify each of Newton's laws in the level. Canonical definitions of each of Newton's three laws, as well as their mapping to the teacher's memory aid, can be found in Table 1.

In the teacher's description of each of the laws in the simulation space, his classroom framework for remembering Newton's laws, as well as the misperception of the force tiles as independent actors in the simulation space, is evident:

Teacher: Newton's second... of course, when I change from at rest to in motion I've applied a force. So [the ship] starts moving from left to right. When I stopped [the ship] here I had to put an unbalanced force on it to go up to down.

[...]

Teacher: Newton's third law... opposites. When I stopped the ship I had to apply an opposite force of the same force amount to make my ship stop.

In these two statements, the teacher's epistemology of force becomes evident: unbalanced forces (Newton's second law) start the motion of the ship and opposing forces (Newton's third law) stop the ship (see Figure 2 and Figure 3). Parsing the teacher's response, the verb 'to apply' takes center stage. In his second law formulation,

Figure 2. Canonical epistemology of force

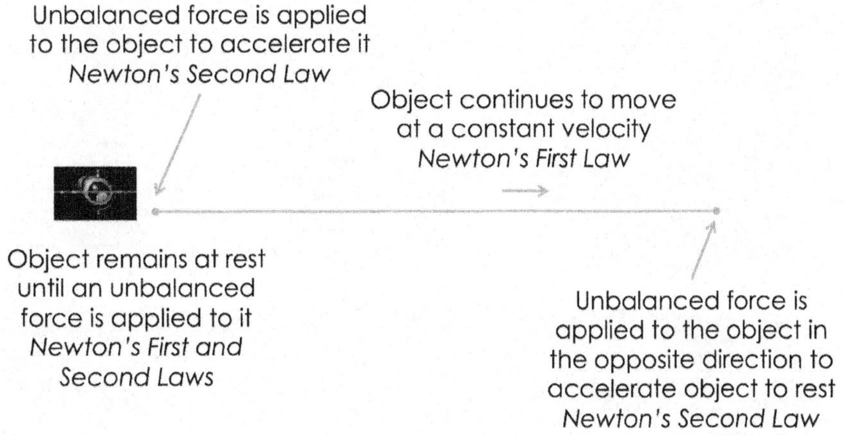

the teacher "applied a force" and in his third law formulation, the teacher also "had to apply an opposite force" in order to achieve the outcome he desired in the simulation space. Within the semantic frame of application, force is no longer applied by the ship, but by the teacher. What and where this force is, however, remains elusive. It is conceivable, based on the teacher's formulation of Newton's third law as the force to 'stop the ship', that the ability to apply force in the simulation environment is a property of the force tile, which pushes on the ship to cause it to stop. As the teacher seeks to answer the question 'What is force?', the representations of the learning game lead to the conclusion that force is a property of an acting object opposing another acting object, scaffolded by the representation of the force tile opposing the ship.

Time, Distance, and Mass

Representations of time, distance, and mass in the *Fuzzy Chronicles* learning environment also have implications for games' ability to scaffold the student and teacher's epistemology of force. When describing the path of the spaceship in an example level given to the teacher, the teacher describes the motion of the spaceship as moving "20 Newtons to the right" (region A in Figure 4) as it travels two boxes (representing two meters)

Figure 3. Teacher's epistemology of force

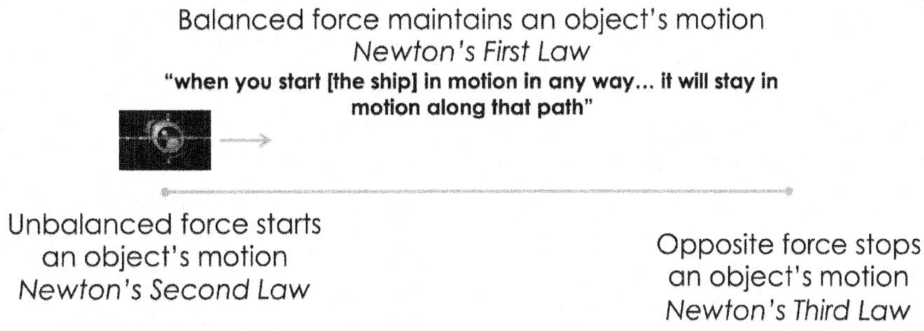

Figure 4. Example level shown to the teacher

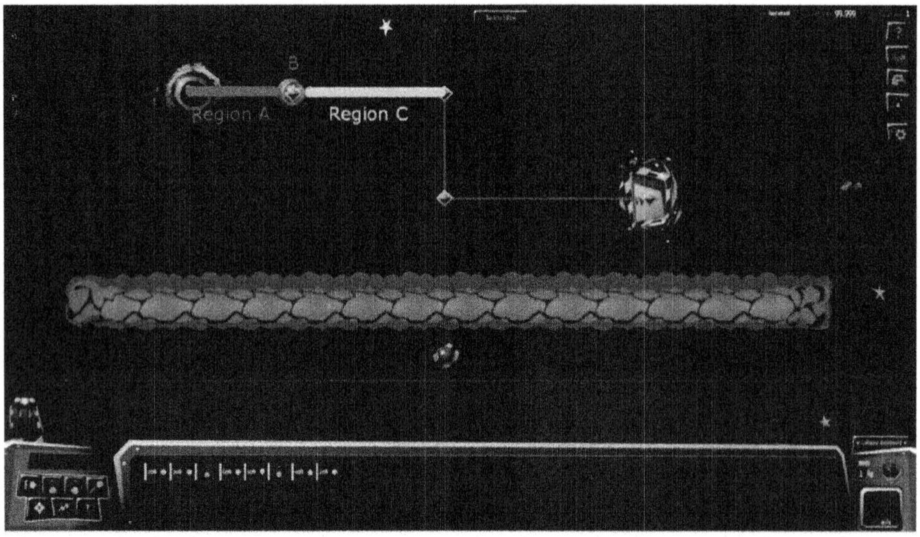

on the grid. As the example level continues, the spaceship picks up a Fuzzy (letter B in Figure 4), effectively doubling its digital mass, and then needs to travel another three meters in order to complete its trajectory (region C in Figure 4). Analyzing the pre-set force tiles in the timeline, the teacher remarks that the 60 Newton force in the timeline will be "twice as much as [the spaceship] would need since there are three squares".

This episode suggests two key points. First, force and distance are conflated in these statements in terms of the interplay between the timeline, force tile, and grid representations. Second, as a result of this conflation, the teacher's epistemology of force and motion (especially in relation to Newton's second law) incorrectly foregrounds the explanatory importance of distance instead of time.

In terms of the first point, each force fired by the spaceship in the Fuzzy Chronicles has a duration of 0.1 seconds. According to Newton's second law (change in velocity = [force(time)]/mass), the application of a 20 Newton force for 0.1 seconds on a 1 kilogram object (the mass of the ship) would change in the ship's velocity by 2 m/s in the selected direction. Since the timeline is delineated in one second intervals, it becomes convenient for students and teachers to develop a heuristic that equates applying a 20 Newton force with moving two spaces on the grid every second. Furthermore, level design decisions that constrain the number of force tiles available to place in the timeline have encouraged students and teachers to select force tile magnitudes that correspond with traveling the length of their path in a particular direction in one second. Thus, "traveling 20 Newtons to the right" becomes the equivalent in their minds with traveling two boxes to the right, the desired distance to complete the path of the spaceship.

In terms of the second point, students' and teachers' talk foregrounds the use of a force to travel a particular distance, rather than the use of a force to change the ship's velocity until changed again by the firing of another force at a subsequent time interval. This explanation reinforces the Aristotelian notion of force being 'used up' or 'spread out' over a distance, rather than velocity remaining constant until another force acts upon the object. The teacher highlights this with his concern that a 60 Newton force shouldn't be used to travel three squares. While 60 Newtons is, in fact, the appropriate amount of force needed since the mass of the ship is now 2 kilograms after picking up the Fuzzy, the teacher employs the heuristic of 3 squares = 30 Newtons. Focusing on the distance the ship must travel rather than the effects of the force on the ship's velocity and the amount of time it will need to travel at that velocity in order to travel three meters, the teacher communicates an inaccurate epistemology of force and motion that privileges force being applied over a set distance, rather than distance being a function of the time an object remains at a particular velocity, as achieved by the firing of a force. The representation thus scaffolds and reinforces the teacher's non-normative understanding of force and motion with regard to Newton's second law. Representations are, therefore, powerful agents to scaffold both understanding and misunderstanding. More specifically, the design features of representations can direct conceptual understanding in unintended ways away from canonically aligned conceptions of force and motion by reinforcing intuitive understandings of force and motion that are not consistent with Newtonian relationships.

Patterns Across the 68 Formative Assessment Interviews

As discussed, the video footage included 68 formative assessment interviews that the teacher conducted with individual students as he circulated within the room on the 4th day of the curriculum. His stated goal was to better understand students' evolving understanding of Newton's three laws of force and motion as a result of students having played *Fuzzy Chronicles*. These interviews highlight, however, that the students have picked up his interpretation of BUO and the underlying non-normative interpretations of the representations in the game, as well as the underlying physics. The following sections distil the findings from across those formative assessments for relationships relevant to each of Newton's laws.

FIRST LAW RELATIONSHIPS

The canonical formulation of Newton's first law of motion states that an object will remain in motion or at rest unless acted upon by an unbalanced force. The teacher's formulation of this Newtonian relationship, however, is incomplete. His self-definition, taken from interviews and observations of instruction, is Newton's first law states that "an object at rest will stay at rest". Within the *Fuzzy Chronicles* learning environment, the teacher's definition of Newton's first law is represented by the player's spaceship is not moving. The teacher's incomplete formulation of Newton's first law is evident in students' formulations of the law across the formative interviews.

Example Exchange A:

Teacher: *Ok, tell me where I see Newton's First Law right now happening?*

Student A: *Where the ship's not moving; because the forces are unbalanced.*

Example Exchange B:

Teacher: *Show me right now on your screen, where Newton's First Law's occurring.*

Student B: *Right there. [points to spaceship at rest]*

Teacher: *Why?*

Student B: *Because it's at rest, and an object at rest will stay at rest.*

Across the 68 formative assessments conducted by the teacher, he asked students for an example of Newton's first law in 28 interviews. In those 28 interviews, 24 of the students (86%) provided formulations of Newton's first law that were aligned

Figure 5. Percentage of students aligned with the teacher's non-normative interpretation of 1st law relationships

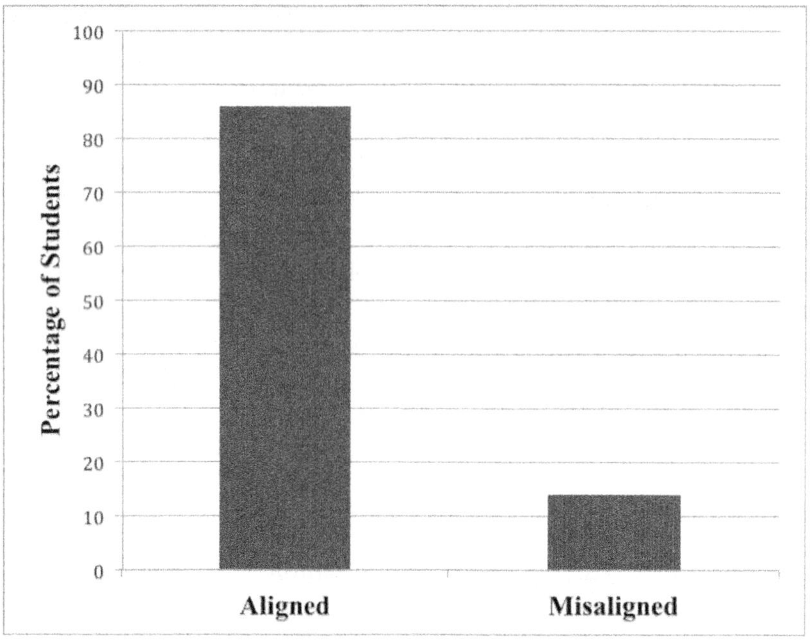

with the teacher's formulation, and 4 students (14%) provided formulations of Newton's first law that did not align with the teacher's formulation (see Figure 5). On the whole, both the teacher and students offer similar formulations of Newton's first law that are consistent with the canonical formulation, although incomplete.

SECOND LAW RELATIONSHIPS

With regard to Newton's second law of force and motion, the alignment between the teacher and students' formulation of the relationship remain strong. The consistency of their formulation with the canonical formulation, however, begins to diverge. The canonical formulation of second law relationships states that heavier objects require more force to accelerate at the same rate. This formulation is often expressed mathematically as "Force = Mass x Acceleration". In the teacher's formulation, however, this relationship is overly simplified to "when [a student's spaceship] changes from rest to motion… I apply a force, so it starts". The teacher finds evidence for this interpretation in the *Fuzzy Chronicles* learning environment when he applies a force in the timeline to start the movement of the spaceship. Students go on to interpret second law relationships as "unbalanced forces make [my spaceship] move" – sourcing the word 'unbalanced' from the U in the teacher's BUO mnemonic.

Example Exchange C:

Teacher: *Ok, show me, when you click go on this path what law happens, when you click go?*

Student C: *Newton's First Law, I mean, Newton's Second.*

Teacher: *Why?*

Student C: *Because, since you put (inaudible) it's gonna like, put effort into it.*

Teacher: *You apply a force, which will cause what?*

Student C: *Um, the spaceship to move?*

Teacher: *To accelerate, or move. All right.*

Across the 68 formative assessments conducted by the teacher, he asked students for an example of Newton's second law in 9 interviews. In those 9 interviews, 9 of the students provided formulations of Newton's second law that were aligned with the teacher's formulation, and 0 students provided formulations of Newton's second law that did not align with the teacher's formulation (see Figure 6). While students' and teacher's conceptualization aligned with each other, they were not consistent with the canonical formulation. In their reinterpretation, the teacher and students operationalize the second law relationship as the force needed to start movement, limiting its explanatory power for accelerating their spaceship from rest and changing velocity while in motion.

THIRD LAW RELATIONSHIPS

With regard to third law relationships, the canonical formulation of the law states that for every action there is an equal and opposite reaction. It is in regard to this relationship that teacher and student formulations different most significantly from the canonical formulation. In the teacher's formulation, third law relationships are "when I stopped the ship, I had to apply an opposite force of the same amount to make my ship stop". In other words, where second law relationships started the ship's movement (in the teacher's framework), third law relationships stop the ship's movement. This formulation was equally clear in student interviews.

Figure 6. Percentage of students aligned with the teacher's non-normative interpretation of 2nd law relationships

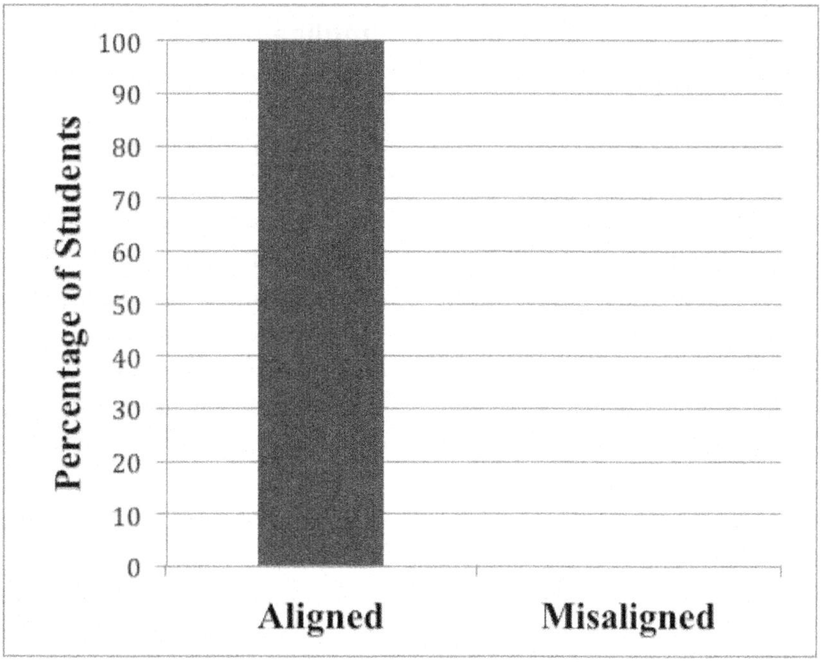

Figure 7. Percentage of students aligned with the teacher's non-normative interpretation of 3rd law relationships

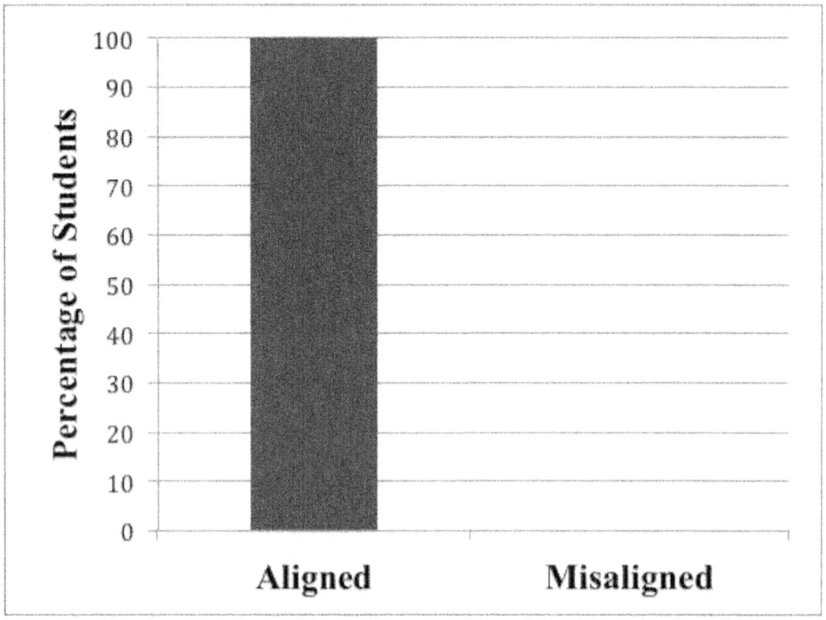

Example Exchange D:

Student D: *The opposing force would be where it'd, where the force would go backwards and stop it.*

Example Exchange E:

Teacher: *When would you use an opposing force?*

Student E: *So, like, to make it stop.*

Across the 68 formative assessments conducted by the teacher, he asked students for an example of Newton's third law in 35 interviews. In those 35 interviews, 35 of the students provided formulations of Newton's third law that were aligned with the teacher's formulation, and 0 students provided formulations of Newton's third law that did not align with the teacher's formulation (see Figure 7). Furthermore, the students' and teacher's conceptualization aligned with each other, but not with the canonical interpretation. In their reinterpretation, the teacher and students operationalize third law relationships as a force that opposes their spaceship to stop its motion, rather than the result of another object's force acting on their spaceship in an opposing direction, such as when the spaceship launches another mass into space.

Implications from the Formative Assessments

The teacher's interpretation of Newtonian relationships had significant impact on his interpretation and students' interpretation of representations during and after gameplay. Students' ideas and explanations of force and motion aligned with their teacher's interpretation and these formulations endured two months after instruction, as evidenced in post-interviews. These assessments highlight two important realities:

1. Even the most well-intentioned representation designs can be reinterpreted in light of teacher's and students' preconceived theories of force and motion, and that

2. Teachers hold powerful sway over the ways in which students perceive and interpret representations in a digital learning environment.

Pre-Post Assessment of Intervention Efficacy

In addition to the formative assessments, students took a modified version of the Force Concept Inventory (Hestenes et al, 1992) before and after gameplay as a measure of the change that occurred in students' understanding of Newtonian relationships after playing *Fuzzy Chronicles*. Analysis of these data using a repeated-measures ANOVA for the 122 students who completed the pre and post-tests revealed statistically significant differences between students' test scores before and after playing *Fuzzy Chronicles* ($F(1, 121) = 8.68, p < 0.01, R^2 = 0.81$). The practical significance, however, was an increase of only 0.75 test questions (Table 2). More specifically, student averages increase from 7.05 on the pre-test to 7.80 on the post-test out of 16 total possible questions. While these results show that students did learn while playing the game, the learning was marginal, potentially due to the effect of the teacher reinforcing incorrect interpretations of the representations in the game.

FINAL THOUGHTS: IMPLICATIONS AND DESIGN PRINCIPLES

As a result of the effects of representations on scaffolding epistemological formation evidenced in the teacher and student interviews, four considerations for future design of scaffolding in digital learning environments emerge:

1. Exploration of the nature of core concepts represented in the learning environment,
2. Explicit modeling of the meaning of the representations in the learning environment,
3. Opportunities to interact with the full range of the properties of the representational object, and
4. Learning environment design that privileges using representations in the environment to their full extent in order that they repeatedly reinforce canonical properties of the representation.

EXPLORATION OF CORE CONCEPTS

In the current study, confusion emerges on the part of the teacher and the student as to the nature of force. Integrating opportunities within the game to explore the question "what is force?" could potentially clarify for students and teachers what the force tiles represent, allow for the representation to better scaffold understanding of force and motion, and further reinforce canonical understanding of Newton's laws. In the absence of such an exploration, students and teachers are free to ascribe their own properties to the objects, 'sending' them to do work that the objects are actually incapable of doing.

Explicit Modeling of Representations

Beyond exploration, however, teachers and students must have the nature of representations in gaming environments explicitly modeled to ensure properties of the object are correctly ascribed. In

Table 2. Means and standard deviations for students' pre and post-test scores

	Pre-Test			Post-Test		
	M	SD	n	M	SD	n
Test Score	7.05	3.10	122	7.80	3.28	122

the *Fuzzy Chronicles* example, a simple statement that the force tiles are not, in fact, independent objects that travel to the simulation space and push on the ship, but rather are simply commands given to the ship to fire its rockets, could potentially alleviate the confusion as to the tile's agency in the simulation space. In conjunction, the features of the representations that scaffold non-normative interpretations could be altered or muted to highlight normative interpretations. Coupled with a deeper understanding of the nature of force, much of the epistemology confusion evidenced in the teacher and student interview could be rectified. Such explicit modeling also aligns with Ball and Cohen's principles of educative curriculum, scaffolding teachers and students alike toward canonical understandings of force and motion.

Opportunities for Interaction with Representations

Students and teachers also should be given the opportunity to interact with the full range of the representation's properties. In *Fuzzy Chronicles*, a designed tutorial that allows students and teachers to see the effects of the same force tile as the time between the first tile and a second force tile of the same magnitude but opposite direction is fired would foreground the effects of time on distance traveled, rather than conflating force and distance within the simulated space. In its educative capacity, the learning environment would not only scaffold teachers' and students' understanding of canonical applications of Newton's second law, but also shift their intuitive understanding of force's relationship with distance to a relationship with time. Exploration of these properties would also strengthen the agency of the digital objects to scaffold learning as teachers and students fully realize the potential for digital objects to act independently in the simulation space.

Full Utilization of Representations

Finally, students and teachers must have opportunities to utilize the full range of the representation's properties while playing the game to avoid limited interpretations of the features of the representations and the concepts that they portray. Instead of repeatedly playing levels in which students can solve the level by applying forces for only one second to travel along a successful path to the level's exit, levels should be purposefully designed to require the student or teacher to remain at a specific velocity for multiple seconds, reinforcing the primacy of time, rather than distance, in developing an epistemology of force and motion. As the culmination of the previous three considerations, repeated use of the full and appropriate properties of the representational objects in the learning environment would not only provide accurate representations of force and motion, but scaffold teachers' and students' epistemology of force and motion toward an epistemology aligned with the canon of Newton's three laws.

ACKNOWLEDGMENT

The research reported here was supported by the Institute of Education Sciences, U.S. Department of Education, through Grant R305A110782 to Vanderbilt University. The opinions expressed are those of the authors and do not represent views of the Institute or the U.S. Department of Education.

REFERENCES

Annetta, L. A., Minogue, J., Holmes, S. Y., & Cheng, M. (2009). Investigating the impact of vid eo games on high school students' engagement and learning about genetics. *Computers & Education*, *53*(1), 74–85. doi:10.1016/j.compedu.2008.12.020

Ball, D. L., & Cohen, D. K. (1996). Reform by the book: What is: Or might be: The role of curriculum materials in teacher learning and instructional reform? *Educational Researcher*, *25*(9), 6–14.

Bogost, I. (2012). *Alien Phenomenology, Or What It's Like to Be a Thing*. University of Minnesota Press.

Bryant, L. (2011). *The Democracy of Objects*. http://quod.lib.umich.edu/o/ohp/9750134.0001.001

Clark, D., Nelson, B., Sengupta, P., & D'Angelo, C. (2009). Rethinking science learning through digital games and simulations: Genres, examples, and evidence. In Learning science: Computer games, simulations, and education workshop sponsored by the National Academy of Sciences, Washington, DC.

Clark, D. B., Sengupta, P., Brady, C., Martinez-Garza, M., & Killingsworth, S. (2015). Disciplinary Integration in Digital Games for Science Learning. *International STEM Education Journal*, 2(2), 1-21. DOI . http://www.stemeducationjournal.com/content/pdf/s40594-014-0014-4.pdf10.1186/s40594-014-0014-4

Feiman-Nemser, S. (2001). From preparation to practice: Designing a continuum to strengthen and sustain teaching. *Teachers College Record*, *103*(6), 1013–1055. doi:10.1111/0161-4681.00141

Garris, R., Ahlers, R., & Driskell, J. E. (2002). Games, motivation, and learning: A research and practice model. *Simulation & Gaming*, *33*(4), 441–467. doi:10.1177/1046878102238607

Gee, J. P. (2007). Good Video Games and Good Learning: Collected Essays on Video Games, Learning, and Literacy (New Literacies and Digital Epistemologies). New York: Peter Lang Pub Inc.

Harman, G. (2001). Object-oriented philosophy. *Towards Speculative Realism: Essays and Lectures* (pp. 93-104). Ripley: Zero Books.

Hestenes, D., Wells, M., & Swackhamer, G. (1992). Force concept inventory. *The Physics Teacher*, *30*(3), 141–158. doi:10.1119/1.2343497

Ingold, T. (2011). *Being Alive: Essays on movement, knowledge and description*. London, New York: Taylor & Francis Group.

Kant, I. (1999). *Critique of pure reason*. Cambridge University Press.

Koster, R. (2004). *A Theory of Fun for Game Design*. Scottsdale, AZ: Paraglyph Press.

Latour, B. (1987). *Science in action: How to follow scientists and engineers through society*. Harvard University Press.

Lehrer, R., & Schauble, L. (2002). Symbolic communication in mathematics and science: Co-constituting inscription and thought. In E. Amsel & J. Byrnes (Eds.), *The development of symbolic communication* (pp. 167–192). Mahwah, NJ: Erlbaum.

McGonigal, J. (2011). *Reality is Broken: Why Games Make Us Better and How They Can Change the World*. New York: Penguin Press.

Munz, U., Schumm, P., Wiesebrock, A., & Allgower, F. (2007). Motivation and learning progress through educational games. Industrial Electronics. *IEEE Transactions on*, *54*(6), 3141–3144. doi: 10.1109/TIE.2007.907030

Pelletier, C. (2008). Gaming in context: How young people construct their gendered identities in playing and making games. In Y. B. Kafai, C. Heeter, J. Denner, & J. Y. Sun (Eds.), *Beyond Barbie and Mortal Kombat: New Perspectives on Gender and Gaming*. Cambridge, Mass: The MIT Press.

Squire, K. (2005). Changing the game: What happens when video games enter the classroom. *Innovate*, *1*(6), 25–49.

Squire, K. (2006). From content to context: Videogames as designed experience. *Educational Researcher*, *35*(8), 19–29. doi:10.3102/0013189X035008019

KEY TERMS AND DEFINITIONS

Conceptually-Embedded Game: Games in which content is presented as an activity within the game.

Conceptually-Integrated Game: Games in which content and concepts are woven into the mechanics of gameplay.

Educative Curriculum: Curriculum that educates teachers, as well as students, through its implementation.

Epistemology: The study of how knowledge is developed within a discipline.

Ontology: The study of the nature of being, of what exists and does not exist.

Representation: A depiction or model of a concept within a game.

Scaffolding: The act of supporting the learning process by providing resources to aid the learning process, which are slowly taken away as learners become more autonomous.

Chapter 13
Flipping the Paradigm of Education:
Developing a Comprehensive Educational Program Integrating Virtual Immersive Learning Environments

Donna Russell
Walden University, USA

ABSTRACT

The purpose of this chapter is to define a prototype for a comprehensive educational program that integrates virtual immersive learning environments into traditional educational settings to develop innovative educational programs. The Future of Learning (FoL) protocol combines an integrative curriculum guide providing educators with thematic modular units of study that are designed based on problem-based learning principles and a FoL learning management system where online learning environments are structured to be integrated into p-12 educational settings and provide a login protected interface for educators and learners to access all the aspects of the FoL protocol including 1) a home page for the educational program linking all aspects of the protocol, 2) a learner home page, 3) a learning analytic system and 4) access to a 3d simulation world. The comprehensive and modular design of the Future of Learning protocol means that it can be integrated in a multitude of p-12 educational programs and define the future of learning.

INTRODUCTION

The Future of Learning protocol's goal is to develop a comprehensive educational program that will focus on the development of advanced problem-solving abilities of learners through Units of Study that are designed around future trends. The purpose of this chapter is to define a prototype for a comprehensive educational program that integrates virtual immersive learning environments into traditional educational settings to develop innovative educational programs. The Future of Learning (FoL) protocol combines an integrative curriculum guide providing educators

DOI: 10.4018/978-1-4666-9629-7.ch013

with thematic modular units of study that are designed based on problem-based learning principles and a FoL learning management system where online learning environments are structured to be integrated into p-12 educational settings and provide a login protected interface for educators and learners to access all the aspects of the FoL protocol including

1. A home page for the educational program linking all aspects of the protocol,
2. A learner home page,
3. A learning analytic system, and
4. Access to a 3d simulation world.

The comprehensive and modular design of the Future of Learning protocol means that it can be integrated in a multitude of p-12 educational programs and define the future of learning.

BACKGROUND

The nature of learning has changed as the internet has radically increased the amount and type of knowledge needed to be successful in a knowledge economy. Around 40% of the world population has an internet connection today. In 1995, it was less than 1%. In 2014 there were 2,980,719,590 Internet users in the world. The first billion was reached in 2005. The second billion in 2010. The third billion will be reached by the end of 2014. This has led to a rapid increase in the knowledge doubling curve. Buckminster Fuller identified the Knowledge Doubling Curve when he noticed that until 1900 human knowledge doubled approximately every century. By the end of World War II knowledge was doubling every 25 years. Today, on average human knowledge is doubling every 13 months. The current theory is that as a result of the "internet of things", the internet added to varied devices, will lead to the doubling of knowledge every 12 hours (internetworldstatscom).

However, in current p-12 programs standardized testing is the definition of learning. All knowledge learned is produced in the form of a test. As a result, the processes of teaching and learning, knowledge development has become preparing a learner to reproduce small isolated bits of information. This type of learning, memorizing these factoids for a test, is the antithesis of developing knowledge workers that can respond to the data deluge of an exponentially complex information base. As online technologies provide more open access to an increasing and changing base of information the knowledge workers of the future must be able to use information to solve problems, addresses issues, and create responses to authentic issues. The ability to do this is by learning how to infer, hypothesize, synthesize, relate, generalize, value, and evaluate information in a purposeful manner, not memorization for testing recall on a standardized test. The knowledge economy of the future is based on how effectively knowledge workers can use information productively in this expanding knowledge-based global economy. In order to do this knowledge workers must be productive and efficient learners. Learning is the commodity of the future that will separate out successful or less successful organizations and nations in the global technology-based knowledge economy.

The Future of Learning protocol is designed to develop these abilities in a program that can be integrated into traditional educational programs as a result of a comprehensive design procedure. The FOL educational program is modular and functional for integration in multiple learning environments because of the nature of the design template. By shifting the educational experience from passive to active learning, from a focus on teaching to a focus on learning, from the standardization of instruction and assessment to the individualization of the development of learning processes, and from breaking knowledge down to building functional knowledge to solve problems, the Future of Learning educational program is designed to develop knowledge workers capable of functioning in the future knowledge economy.

This chapter describes the design of this protocol that uses 3-D collaborative learning virtual worlds as problem-solving scenarios that engage students in virtual explorations of worlds. Additionally the problem-based learning (PBL) scenarios incorporate a curriculum design model that includes a real-world issue that correlates to the virtual scenarios. This virtual PBL design protocol also includes a research program that utilizes sociocultural learning theories to develop an analytical systemic analysis of the learning processes of the students to assess the effectiveness of these immersive virtual learning environment, educational games, to develop advanced cognitive abilities and knowledge in students.

MAIN FOCUS OF THE CHAPTER

The Future of Learning protocol for the design of learning environments is a unique pedagogy of immersive learning environments with the integration of transformative new technologies, interactive virtual simulations and game-like scenarios. The result is an integrated curriculum that is both differentiated and compacted for individualization of the learner response incorporated with virtual worlds that engage learners in simulations that immersive them in the problem space. The FoL protocol is based on constructivist principles of learning and the design of problem-based learning environments. The PBL design process for the FOL protocol is based on three phases that are based on inquiry-based learning principles (Russell and Schneiderheinze, 2004). Phase 1 is designed to respond to the question 'why is the problem important?' In this phase learners enter the world to identify the problem and develop an artifact. Phase 2 is designed to answer the question 'how can we use our expertise to better understand the problem and develop a feasible solution?' In this phase the students identify the subissues in the problem and develop a response. In Phase 3 the students respond to 'how can we use the knowledge and skills from Phase 1 and Phase 2 to develop a feasible solution?' In this last phase they create an artifact that is a feasible solution to the problem and build an object in the virtual world as a response. A chart of the design of these live events, including interactions with the pedagogical agents designed to be guides and assessment points and references to learning theories, is shown in Figure 1, the 3D problem-based learning template for the design of a virtual immersive learning environment.

The 3D simulations are designed to develop advanced cognitive skills and knowledge through problem-based learning processes. The simulations are designed to promote and assess the development of advanced cognitive skills and content knowledge. The simulations are based on scenarios of real-world events giving the students opportunities to respond to real-world problem scenarios. As a result, the virtual worlds are designed to be engaging and fun but also be designed to define the learning activities and responses. The assessment process included in the FoL protocol is designed to be part of the interactions in the game or simulation. The learner will respond to questions and interactions in the virtual world that are part of the game itself with the learning analytic system tracking the learning throughout.

The Future of Learning protocol is based on current theories of learning and developed with the mission to flip the paradigm of education to shape the learning of the knowledge workers of the future. The Future of Learning protocol curriculum is based on theories of sociocultural learning (Vygotsky, 1995; Wertsch, 2008), problem-based learning (Jonanssen, 2006; Russell, 2005) and a design template based on these principles (Russell, 2006). The FOL protocol is based on the integration of transformative new technologies into collaborative multi-national classrooms designed around the principles of problem-based

Figure 1. 3D PBL design template

3D Problem-Based Learning
Collaborative Virtual Learning Environments
Design Template

Virtual Design	**Problem Space (Banathy, 1996; Lawson, 1990)** Simulation designed as an interactive virtual environment that relates to a real world problem space.
Pedagogical Agent used as Guide to aid learners as they explore the problem space. **Output** Virtual artifact including a rationale for relevancy of the problem.	**PHASE 1** Why is the problem Important? **Inquiry Processes** Working in pairs, learners gather and analyze information in the virtual simulation to determine nature of the problem and to define the scope of the problem. (Barab & Duffy, 2000; Petroski, 1996). **Output used as input.** Knowledge that a diverse community needs impact the complexity of the problem. (Bereiter, 2001).
Pedagogical Agent used as a Resource Mentor to answer questions and find resources. **Output** Virtual artifact including a conceptual understanding of an area of expertise and its application to solve the problem	**PHASE 2** How can we use our expertise to better understand the problem and develop a feasible solution? **Inquiry Processes** Working groups, learners gather and analyze information about an area of expertise (Brown, Collins & Duguid, 1989) and how that area relates to the problem, (Bruer, 1993, Shulman, 1992) learners examine areas of expertise in simulated environments, determine the interdependence of the areas of expertise. **Output used as input** Knowledge that a problem can look different and be understood differently from multiple perspectives.
Pedagogical Agent used as Survey Buddy to assess new knowledge and final projects. **Output** Virtual artifact including a representation of the group's solution and conclusion about its short-term and long-term feasibility.	**PHASE 3** How can we use the knowledge and skills from Phase 1 and Phase 2 to develop a feasible solution? **Inquiry Processes** Working in jigsaw groups (Aronson, Blaney, Stephan, Sikes & Snapp, 1978), learners develop a solution to the problem and assess the feasibility of that solution from the perspectives of the experts within the group and the needs of the community. **Outcome** Knowledge has properties of use and value; is something that can be used and responded to.

learning to develop advanced cognitive processes and functional content knowledge. The immersive virtual learning environment is a learning management system (LMS) composed of 5 major aspects:

1. **Problem-Based Learning Curriculum Design:** The design of each unit of study is built around a PBL curriculum design template and modified to develop the advanced cognitive processes needed for progress through each learning environment.
2. **Learning Management System:** The LMS is a login protected system that provides ongoing interactive courses and learning activities.

3. **Immersive Virtual Learning Environments:** The immersive virtual learning environments are incorporated into the LMS and includes 3D virtual events where learners can participate in complex scenarios to prepare them for the decision-making critical thinking skills needed for their development.
4. **Learning Analytics System:** The learning analytics system is a data management system designed into each LMS that is structured around evaluating the development of the advanced learning processes designed into the educational programs. The learning analytics system (LAS) is a unique system designed by an educational researcher who has advanced theoretical and practical knowledge of defining and assessing the development of advanced thinking skills and knowledge in online data management systems.
5. **Evaluative Research Program:** The evaluative research program is a module available for all LMS programs. It is a holistic, systemic evaluation program that is modified to meet the educational goals of each organization. It is aligned with the design and the evaluation of learning programs in the FOL protocol. It provides insight for administrators and educators on the effectiveness of the learning environments for each organization's goals.
6. **Future of Teaching:** The FOL protocol includes a teacher professional development program that supports educators as they implement this integrated educational protocol. The Future of Teaching program provides any level of ongoing teacher training with access to multiple forums.

As a result of the comprehensive protocol for education the Future of Learning protocol is able to provide modular educational programs that meet the needs of multiple educational settings. The current prototype of the Future of Learning LMS will support the development of standards for P-12 educational programs and can be modified by the district, state or school to fit their educational goals and technological resources. This prototype gives P-12 programs access to the LMS, a curriculum guide and template for implementation of the curriculum, assessment guides and models, and choices among several units of study with access to all the modules. For example the FoL includes simulations based on core science, technology, engineering, and math (STEM) standards such as a unit on Exploring for Life on Mars, Designing a Green City, and Feeding the World. The mission of the Future of Learning protocol is to develop global citizens both aware of and able to respond to the critical issues of the future. The Future of Learning protocol will succeed in this mission by the comprehensive design of immersion learning activities that engage the learner in the active response to the units of study, that integration of authentic global issues with a response to local problems in order to build the knowledge workers of the future.

Curriculum Design Principles

The design of the FoL protocol curriculum is built around a holistic integrated design protocol that develops and assesses advanced learning capabilities. There are four main design structures to provide opportunities for learners to engage in advanced knowledge creation:

1. An overarching *Core IDEA* that are concepts critical to future knowledge workers and embedded in all instructional activities,
2. The *Learning Strands* that are critical learning processes needed by future knowledge workers,
3. *Themes* which are curricular structures for integrated content learning and instruction that includes multiple and
4. *Units of Study* and are designed to develop the concepts, learning processes and integrated content in defined teaching and learning activities and outcomes.

CORE IDEA

The design of the FoL protocol is based on the development of integrated, thematic units that are linked to a Core IDEA. A Core IDEA is a holistic conceptual base that is a critical awareness for global citizens and knowledge workers. An example of a Core IDEA is Resource Management. The educational goal is to develop learners' awareness of human role in managing the Earth's resources with all the attendant social, political and ethical issues inherent in the future. The Core IDEAs are included in the mission statement for each unit of study. Each Core IDEA Unit includes global issues relevant to developing a comprehensive understanding and responses to the Core IDEA. These issues include a multi-disciplinary base in content knowledge. An example of an issue in Resource Management is Climate Change Theme. Climate Change then results in multiple Units of Study that can be taught based on local issues such as drought and climate change, extreme weather, and pollution.

Core IDEA: Learning Strands

The Learning Strands are cognitive processes that are developed in each unit of study and integrated in the development of the content knowledge and skills. The Learning Strands are integrated into each unit of study and linked to the Core IDEAs. The Learning Strands for the FoL protocol are:

1. **Understanding Media:** Media is a critical aspect for global citizens as it is endemic in the interactions of all citizens. The forums for media include more traditional forums such as books, TV, and radio. The new evolving media include social media, and the internet. Each Unit of Study develops relevant awareness of media throughout the interactions as students discuss, analyze and create media. New media awareness is assessed through their projects and their interactions formatively and summatively.
2. **Human Computer Interface:** HCI is an ongoing strand for students as they identify, analyze and create technology-based projects. Each Unit of Study will include a Strand on the critical aspects of technology inherent in the unit and the curriculum themes. Students will both use technology and create projects using technology but they will also develop insight into how technologies influence social, individual and cultural dynamics.
3. **Advanced Problem Solving Processes:** Students will develop advanced problem solving processes throughout each unit. Examples of the cognitive processes integrated and assessed in each unit include critical thinking, advanced decision-making, problem solving, analysis, evaluation, collaborative problem solving, and effective communication processes. All units will include holistic rubrics to assess the development of these advanced cognitive processes.
4. **Social Awareness:** Each unit will engage the students in discussions of social issues. The students will present their responses that include a social awareness component. The units will all include an assessment that identifies the social awareness component in the learners' activities and interactions.
5. **Awareness of Areas of Expertise:** Each unit will involve students in interactions with the community of private and public experts. Students will understand the areas of expertise involved each Core IDEA to reduce the isolationist aspect of education and support these learners become knowledge workers in the future.

Curricular Themes

Curricular themes are specific curriculum structures that provide an instructional space for content knowledge. Curricular Themes will be modular and designed on a problem-based learning educational setting (Russell, 2005). Themes all include a Core IDEA as a basis and the Learning Strands which are included in the ongoing formative and summative assessment model. Themes include assessment of the learner's responses to

1. Content knowledge,
2. Conceptual knowledge, and
3. Process skills.

A Curricular Theme is a complete modular educational program that can be integrated into a traditional educational setting with associated standards, a complete curriculum guide, assessments, the LMS with access to virtual worlds and a teacher training protocol. The Theme is a curriculum structure with defined responses that engage students in developing advanced concepts, skills and knowledge based on the global theme.

Units of Study

Each Theme has multiple Units of Study. These are individual modular units that can be isolated and taught individually. For example, the Climate Change Theme in the Core IDEA Resource Management includes

1. Water Management, and
2. Land Management units of study.

Water management will engage students in understanding water globally including drought and climate change effects on water access. Students will develop new understandings of pollution, loss of marker species such as the coral reef, changes in global ocean patterns, coastal degradation and other patterns of change associated with Climate Change. Land Management will engage students in understanding issues related to land resources such as mining, carbon emissions, air pollution, health effects of pollution, greenhouse effect and clear cutting of forests. Below is an overview of some of the Units of Study in the FoL protocol.

Resource Management: Curricular Theme, Climate Change, Units of Study – Water World

Water World is a unit of study that engages students in understanding and creating a response to the issues inherent in Climate Change as they relate to changes in oceans including weather related events such as drought or extreme storms.

Major Science Concepts

The science concepts for Water World include developing an understanding of geochemical cycles is a major benchmark in Earth and Space Science benchmarks and National science standards. Students will develop new understanding of the hydrological cycle involves flows and reservoirs of matter and energy, changing physical properties as it passes through solid earth, oceans, atmosphere, and organisms. As the water planet, student understanding of the role of the hydrologic cycle is critical to their understanding of geochemical cycling, weathering of the surface, global temperature regulation, and significance for all life. The Water World unit supports the benchmark in science in Personal and Social Perspectives. Particularly, water's uniqueness to biological life makes understanding human interactions with water essential. Students will learn about issues of global warming and water vulnerability such as that more than half the world's population relies on mountain glaciers for water and these water sources are disappearing as temperatures rise (Price, Jansky, and Iatsenia, 2004).

- **Learning Activities:** In the virtual world, Water World, students will explore the geochemical cycling of water and its constituents, it role in climate change, and human impacts. Specifically, the virtual world scenarios will involve students in the flow and interactions of a water as it passes through all the stages of the hydrologic cycle solving problems at each stage. Through their accumulated information they will explore water's role in atmospheric processes and climate regulation. They will explore the power of water to erode and deposit as it sculpts the landscape. At the watershed level, students will investigate the pathways of the mineral and nutrient constituents of water.

Students will work in blended environments where they move from their classroom activities (whether online or face-to-face), to online activities and immersive virtual learning environments that are virtual worlds designed to simulate aspects of the theme issue and provide the learners with the opportunity respond to real-world issues in a virtual simulation, a game, that engages them in an advanced problem-based scenario.

In their local contexts, students will identify a local issue related to the issue of global warming or an environmental issue such as soil loss due to drought/urbanization or pollution of groundwater. Students will bring their collaborative knowledge and virtual experiences to apply to understanding their local watershed. This will include interviewing local authorities and stakeholders about transboundary water issues and policies. They will learn protocols for measuring hydrological parameters (i.e. Globe Protocols) to characterize local hydrological conditions and predict future hydrologic scenarios.

In their virtual worlds, students will experience and respond to online simulations and interactive field trips that explore the cycling of water, energy transfer, and the chemical phases of water at increasingly smaller scales. They will examine global water distribution through space and time coming to understand the relationship of the regional bedrock and its origin as ocean bottom. Students will explore issues of global climate change and the implications for both drought and flood.

The Water World Unit of Study curriculum includes a formative and assessment process that is integrated into the online FoL learning assessment system. Throughout the learning experiences, students will respond to self-assessments using a variety of integrative online assessments assessing their interactions, reflections, and knowledge-based surveys. Teacher/Facilitators will assess students and their knowledge levels by monitoring interactions, reviewing student products, and interactions within the virtual world, IDEA World. As students engage in the 2D and 3D learning environments, they collaboratively build projects. Their projects are shared in a variety of forums that occur in the real world in the virtual Idea World Media Center including

1. Ed-TED Talks,
2. Museum Exhibits,
3. Live Conference Presentations,
4. Symposium Discussions,
5. International Virtual Events, and Inventions modeled and protyped in the Virtual Worlds.

As a result of the core cognitive principles underlying the design of the Future of Learning Protocol, the functional, the practical and classroom functional design aspects of the problem-based learning environments, and the comprehensive and integrative modular aspects of the protocol the Future of Learning Protocol can be readily modified to meet the needs of varied educational programs and implemented in P-12 classrooms.

SOLUTIONS AND RECOMMENDATIONS

Assessment of Learning

It is the premise of the design and the evaluation of this online problem-based learning protocol that learning online can be productive based on theories of sociocultural learning which define the importance of culture, the social aspects of the inter/intrapersonal aspects of learning and the concepts of problem-based learning with the potential to develop advanced knowledge (Vygotsky, 1987; Jonassen, Peck, &Wilson, 1999; Bereiter, 2001). Bereiter & Scardamalia (2001), defined a knowledge response as a complex relationship between culture, humans, objects, and tools that results in conceptual artifacts. Conceptual is any discussible idea including theories, plans, or concepts. Artifacts are purposeful human creations. One of the difficulties in the changes from the Industrial Age to the Knowledge Age is that more human work deals with conceptual objects instead of the physical objects to which they are related. This concept of knowledge as object is based on a historical analysis of the development of a knowledge-based society (Bereiter, 2002).

In all Units of Study student activities are assessed both formatively and summatively using a rubrics and evaluative scales based on the development of learning processes and projects based on Bereiter's Scheme of Knowledge (Bereiter, 2002). Bereiter's Scheme of Knowledge provides educators with a scaled delineation of learning responses that can be used to create scaled rubrics of higher-level thinking skills (Russell, 2005a). The learning analytic system (LAS) is built into the FOL protocol that defines these levels of response using holistic rubric for cognitive processes, coding of interactivity in the learning environment and definition of the qualities of the learner responses to the virtual worlds. These assessment tools will be included in the Curriculum Guides, designed into all the LMS activities, the IDEA World scenarios, as well as linked to the Learning Analytic System, online data management system.

Future of Learning Online Learning Management System

The FoL protocol includes access to an online learning management system (LMS) that includes an immersive virtual learning management system, IDEA World. This unique virtual learning space is designed to develop the advanced cognitive processes, concepts and knowledge that are developed in the Curriculum Guideline for the FoL. There are specific areas of the FOL LMS that blend the real-world and the virtual-world to create a highly interactive and authentic blended learning environments. Each aspect is described in more detail after the outline listed below.

Specific Internet Design Characteristics of the FOL LMS

LMS home with the six main components below:

1. MyMedia.
2. MyCourses – Modify Digital Learning Tree LMS. Access to Problem-Based Learning Units. Design of Unit of Study Guide:
    a. Curriculum CK12
    b. Integration of core standards
    c. Integration of common instructional resources
    d. Development modular units including
        i. Scope and sequence
        ii. Modular units include teachers' Curriculum Guide: Assessments, Content and resources, Reflective journaling for redesign, Access to Training Resources.
3. MyLearning:
    a. includes Pedagogical Agent, an Artificial Intelligence Bot (AI bot):
        i. Mentors for learners
        ii. Guides for learners
        iii. Source of formative assessments for educators

4. Learning Analytics System – Data management system:
    a. linked to holistic rubrics assessing knowledge
    b. Interface with learners to develop metacognitive awareness and processes
    c. Tagged to coding of learning responses. Includes Tests/quizzes/assessment of assignments (rubrics), Interactions in virtual world:
        i. Access/exit points in worlds/lms
        ii. Interactions with worlds (where; how long)
        iii. Semantic data algorithm designed with Dr. Russell on interactivity with components: AI bots- ped agents, Kiosks, Other learners.
5. Virtual Worlds, immersive virtual worlds for gaming simulations
    a. The Virtual IDEA World where students engage in simulations and games designed to advance their knowledge of Core Ideas through quests, collaborative problem-solving, investigations, mentoring by experts and interactions with other FoL students.
6. Community Mentoring
    a. All virtual worlds include a Community Mentoring aspect where experts in the fields interact with students including answering questions, providing feedback on projects, developing projects and supporting innovative, entrepreneurial projects resulting from the Units of Study.

Learning Analytics System

The Learning Analytics System is designed into the FOL protocol. It is a data mashup that is linked to activity and assessment of activity in the LMS. It is coded to identify learning activities and, in some cases, present an evaluation of the learning activity to both the educators and the learners based on predesignated response times, quality of response and interactivity levels. It provides a nearly real-time visual mapping of the learning responses to both learner and instructor of the interactions of the learner and is tagged to the rubrics for the holistic assessments. The coding structure for the assessment of learning is based on research on sociocognitive learning theories, (Vygotsky, 1998), intersubjectivity (Hui and Russell, 2008), and semantic analysis (Russell, 2008) that will define the learning in the virtual learning management system.

Virtual IDEA World

The virtual games and simulations occur in IDEA World in the FOL protocol. It is a virtual world that includes IDEA City, IDEA Farm, IDEA University, IDEA Schools and open quests that are linked to Units of Study such as a virtual replica of Mars, and a replica of a prehistoric world to understand past climate change. The Media Center is the Sim World main entrance and includes conference areas with large screens, interactive forums that allow for texting and talking in live sessions, small group work areas where international groups can schedule meetings, post and share information and develop their projects resulting from the experiments, exploration and completion of the Scenarios. The virtual IDEA World sections are listed and explained below.

1. **Experimenter Labs:** In the virtual IDEA World there are experimenter labs in the various locations that allow students to test theories or develop projects. They are virtual rooms setup with deliminated objects and interaction between objects that can be reset once they are used by students. These include chemistry labs, biology labs, experiments, and research labs. Experimenter labs are closed systems that can be reset over and

over with one path to solution; procedural learning with levels 1-3 knowledge response on a Bereiter Scale.

2. **Designer Toolbox:** Designer Toolboxes are also designed to be in specific locations throughout IDEA World. They are sandboxes which allow students to modify and create new objects in response to the units. Students can build a solar car or develop a new object in the 3d virtual world, or design an app using the coding structure in the virtual world. Each activity is linked to the curriculum learning goals and objectives and include associated learning assessment methods.
3. **Explorer Worlds:** Explorer worlds are scenario worlds. These are the large worlds designed for live interactive events that are open-ended dilemma problem spaces. The students will go into these world to respond to a live event, build, design, or present through their avatar. In IDEA City they can design a solar grid working with a group including civic contact, e.g. citizen groups, civic engineers etc. The virtual city can be reset for multiple scenarios and events. Over time the students' projects will build and redesign the city as part of the learning activities.
4. **Media Center:** The Media Center is the main conference hall in IDEA World. It includes presentation forums for student projects including interactive museums, symposiums, High School TED talks, and interactive kiosks. Learners build their presentations in the online LMS or in their classroom but present in the main conference halls on a global stage with varying levels of live interactive presentations. The media in the Media Center gives tools for learners to build their electronic portfolios which is the main source of ongoing assessment for the students' experiences. STEM Conferences for presentations and response to audiences where groups justify their research and development. Examples of the interactive forums are listed below.
    a. Innovation Symposiums are scheduled for dialog on specific topics and the development of collaborative models and protocols. Innovation Symposiums result in major publications and prototypes that incorporate the Core Themes from the student-generated research and projects.
    b. Science Museums for the dissemination of presentations, models, and prototype. Each artifact are included in the development of comprehensive e-portfolios for students.
    c. **TED Talks:** Ed-TED Talks are live presentations chosen to demonstrate advanced knowledge on a specific innovative project or program. Students and groups will apply to present live in TED talks and for the dissemination of their Talks in social media.
5. **Pedagogical Agents:** Pedagogical Agents are designed into all IDEA virtual worlds to automatize some of the interactions in virtual worlds. These programmed AI bots act as mentor bots, guide bots, and learner bots. The mentor bots provide feedback to learners in defined manners and locations in the virtual worlds. The guide bots provide support to learners as they work on successfully completing the scenarios. The learner bots are linked to specific learner's progress and are used to track the learner's progress as a source of metacognitive feedback on learning activities and assessment.

All pedagogical agents are linked to the Learning Analytics System and used as both formative and summative assessments. The pedagogical agents (AI bots) use an artificial Intelligence coding structure to populate IDEA Worlds with AI Guides. These avatars will be responsive to the students during their investigations in the 3-D scenarios. They will be coded to a SQL database that can adapt as the students interact with the guides in the environments. Thus the AI Guides can respond to questions, requests for information or directions. They can develop new information so the students can diverge from the pre assigned questions or topics given to them in their Unit of Study Field Books for the 3-D scenarios.

6. **Community Mentors:** Community Mentors will be linked to the Units of Study through a database of experts and companies who are partnering with the Future of Learning protocol. The Curriculum Guides for Themes and Units of Study include public and private community mentors and organizations in fields related to the Core IDEA such as medicine, engineering, genetics, mechanical engineering, aerospace, chemistry, biology and others. These mentors also provide a forum for students to be engaged in real-world authentic activities as a result of these interactions with these mentors. Mentors Organizations will have an interactive presence in the IDEAL World. They will provide support for the design of virtual worlds. Engineers, professors and other professionals will give students directives and instruct, in the form of interactive online discussions or in the form of pedagogical agents.

Simulation Design Guide

The FOL protocol includes a simulation design guide for developing advanced learning in IDEA World. The simulations will occur in three phases each one designed to develop higher levels of problem-solving capabilities in the students. As the students progress, they will 'win' badges by completing the activities in each phase and responding to the formative assessments, such as checking into a kiosk and uploading their answers to the survey, posting an artifact that they have created in that Phase, dialoging with others in the game, with their mentors, interacting with pedagogical agents and presenting in the Sim World Media Center in a series of international interactive forums. There are specific design procedures for the live interactive learning environments in IDEA World. Below are examples of several simulations designed using this design guide.

- **Orientation to IDEA World:** Students enter Idea World through the home page for the Unit of Study in the LMS. The main portal into and out of IDEA World is IDEAL City. Students will build an avatar to move about the virtual worlds. Next they will explore the futuristic city that will be the catalyst for all the scenarios they will respond to throughout the initial phase of development. They will get a brief orientation to the city from an avatar that will also direct them to several organizations and businesses that are resources to the city and later mentors for the students. Finally this character, the mayor for instance, will provide them with a series of problems and issues plaguing this city that they can respond to in order to save the city and provide a safer, cleaner, more energy efficient place for the people. After orientation the students will respond to the virtual scenarios. Below are examples of Problem Scenarios in the Future of Learning protocol.

Problem Scenario 1: Design a Green Building.

In the Resource Management/Climate Change/ Global Warming Unit of study students design a Green Building for IDEA City. They will be able to participate in a real-world competition using materials created in the scenario. They meet their guide, another character in the game, who will give them a set of guidelines including cost, environmental impact to build, and brief overview of city guidelines. They will then be able to go into an interactive workspace where they can work with other students, or individually, to design their building.

They will be able to go into a Sand Box and get all the materials needed to build an object for the building including solar panels, energy saving materials for building, landscaping that aids the building, clean water sources etc. However each of these will come with a price tag, an area of expertise and other issues that will be considered as they build their green building. They will be briefly surveyed for comments throughout and at the end of this process as a form of formative assessment and a feedback for redesign of the simulation itself.

Throughout this experience they will be given clues for information sources, feedback on costs and other parameters, and support from the guide character or instructors. At the end of this scenario,

1. They will have created their building,
2. Tested their prototype in the virtual world,
3. They will have communicated with mentors, others in the sim, and teachers,
4. They will have uploaded their design pics: comments: survey results into their portfolio and
5. They will have created a presentation of their building modification, their prototype testing data, and a justification for the efficiency of the green building based on LEED guidelines.

Problem Scenario 2: Solar Design: Energy from the Sun.

In IDEAL World main area, IDEA City students will be able to go into a local university, IDEAL U., and design a solar car. They will participate in a real-world competition in association with this scenario. They will go into the scenario and the guide character will describe the problem parameters including time lines, resources, and the how they will 'win' the solar race at the end. They will be able to go into a workspace and use resources and create artifacts each activity being guided by the problem parameters. They can collaborate in the game and use resources from the real-world and virtual world and their mentors. Ultimately they will race the cars and redesign based on the differing environmental conditions and the physics of their design.

The students will then set up in international collaborative groups to develop a solar-powered program for their city or the rural farms associated with IDEAL City. The will develop solar panels, do lab experiments, integrate solar panels in new areas and innovative ways. They will present their prototype for their solar project in the Media Center during the international Alternative Energies Conference. Projects will be designed in international groups that are responsive to both their country's needs and the global issues inherent in the development of alternative energies.

Problem Scenario 3: BioDesign – Designing a New World.

As a result of the Feeding the World Unit of Study students develop projects in response to international agriculture and economic issues. Students receive core instruction on the nature of world hunger and then develop projects to reduce world hunger. The core simulation includes weather patterns such as amount of rain for the region, soil conditions, anticipated plant growth for core species used in the region. The simulation will introduce problems, such as drought or crop failure, for the students to develop a potential solution (e.g. new species of yams that are drought resistant). Finally students will be able to go into the environment and 'plant' their new crop and monitor its growth.

In Virtual World there are virtual farms designed around the parameters of agriculture and its environmental and economic aspects in various places in the world. This is a simulation of a biotechnology company research lab including a multidisciplinary overview and evaluation of biotechnology influence on farming, food distribution, medicine, health care, and future issues. The core content areas include biology, chemistry, math-graphing geometry, and algebra. The advanced learning processes include communication, presentation, group work skills, social skills, writing, and speech. The advanced conceptual artifacts include scientific methods and business ethics. The advanced technologies reviewed as part of the human computer interface theme include cloning, DNA mapping and smart medicine. The sumative projects include the development of an innovative farming model that reduces waste, drought resistant, and can reduce global hunger. Students will present on their international collaborative models in the Media Center Conference on Hunger.

Problem Scenario 4: Water as Life – Planning for a Water.

In IDEA World water is limited and drought is endemic. The students enter an island in the World and discover ways to conserve, clean and protect water. As a result of the scenario students will survive in a drought-ridden environment by conserving water and purifying water. Students will do experiments on how to purify ocean water, develop solar panels for cleaning water, plants that are drought resistant and other projects that conserve water. They will also respond to the inhabitants of the world that do not understand how to share and conserve this critical resource and they will develop presentations that identify how everyone can support water conservation. After completion of the scenario, students will group in international groups for interactions and develop a project for an urban and rural water conservation model that involves reduction of ocean waste, purification models, and conservation effort globally. Students will present their models in a Water Conference in the Media Lab.

Problem Scenario 5: Humans and Computers – Innovative Technologies.

In this scenario on Innovative Technologies, students will study and use advanced technologies to integrate into their innovative projects. They will respond to their Learning Strands of Media and HCI by building virtual objects that are used in the innovative projects. They will study and use innovative technologies including biology, advanced technologies and analyze the issues of trends in HCI in multiple fields. The learning includes:

1. **Content Knowledge:** Technology, neuroscience, math, coding languages,
2. **Advanced Processes:** Communication skills, group work skills, social awareness,
3. **Problem-Based Learning:** Evaluation of the potential for HCI,
4. **Advanced Technologies:** Artificial Intelligence, Social Media, Gaming.

Their projects will include collaborative International project to develop and 'sell' an Innovation HCI Prototype in a Media Center Entrepreneur Symposium scheduled with international innovators that creates a more efficient and effective interface between technology and humans for a beneficial purpose such as learning, smart homes, reducing waste in all areas, and increasing productivity. They will present their projects in an international high school version of the TED talk in the Media Center Conference Hall.

Problem Scenario 6: Future World – The Mission to Mars.

During the unit Mission to Mars the students respond to STEM content information by building a model of a Mars habitat that will support human life on the Mars World in IDEA World. The students receive core content information in biology, chemistry, physics and astronomy. The students respond to this information by designing several projects including papers, models and presentations. With the addition of the virtual simulations however, the students will be able to design and test their models in a virtual Mars environment. This environment will include

1. The needed resources for the students to build their habitat based on their knowledge of the core requirements for humans to live and work on Mars, and
2. Basic environmental characteristics of Mars including atmospheric content and conditions such as wind storms, and geographic features such as Olympus Mons and red soil.

As a result of the physics engine that runs the virtual worlds, the students' habitats can be 'tested' for their capacity to sustain human life. For instance if the students design a hydroponics garden to provide oxygen for the astronauts, the garden's oxygen output can be configured and the simulation can 'fail' if it is not sufficient.

Future of Learning Academy Program

The Future of Learning protocol includes the Future of Learning Academy. The Future of Learning Academy, an online LMS that supports teachers implementing the FoL protocol by providing them with

1. Professional development specific for implementing the FoL educational units,
2. Professional development including courses on cognition and technology,
3. Curriculum guides,
4. Resources for instructional design,
5. Links to a myriad of instructional resources,
6. Dialogic spaces for reflection and development of community, and
7. A Future of Teaching virtual space for collaborations and presentations in an international forum.

Professional development for educators is an essential aspect of the FoL protocol. Teachers engaging in developing and implementing these innovative units incorporating the virtual worlds need initial and ongoing support to be successful. The Future of Learning Protocol focuses on developing the Facilitator Model of teaching.

1. From teaching to facilitating learning (theories of learning).
2. From direct instruction to mass audiences to mentoring learners (interactions with learners).
3. From delivery of prepackaged curriculum and content to instructional design specialists able to design, modify and develop content for educational settings (design components of PBL).
4. From the Sage on the Stage concept of knowledge to a community of learners where all engage in developing a shared understanding (role of the instructor).
5. Utilizing learning technologies in appropriate manners to engage learners and advance learning goals.

Professional Development then focuses on these major concepts:

1. Develop teachers' understanding of constructivist learning and problem-based learning.
2. Develop teachers' concepts of how to interact productively with learners in the immersive learning environments.

Table 1. Curriculum guide

<table>
<tr><th colspan="2">Instructional Design Template for Idea City: Climate Change</th></tr>
<tr><td colspan="2">The purpose of this instructional design template is to guide the teacher through the implementation of a problem-based unit based on constructivist learning principles.</td></tr>
<tr><td colspan="2">What is the nature of the Real World problem students will study as they do their Climate Change unit?
• Hydology Problem: The central region water reservoir is running out of water. How can the water reserve be protected from depletion?
• Geology Problem: The state has a major earthquake fault. How can IDEA City prepare for a potential earthquake?
• Water Problem: Local city has am experienced continued growth and construction. The region has also suffered a drought over the past 5 years. How can the city maintain and protect their waterways from erosion and pollution caused by construction?
• Air Problem: The EPA has established an air pollution goal for -local city-. What are actions that the city can take to improve the quality of the air?</td></tr>
<tr><th colspan="2">Meaningfulness for Students</th></tr>
<tr><td colspan="2">Why do you think students will find the problem in this unit meaningful?</td></tr>
<tr><th colspan="2">Relevant Standards</th></tr>
<tr><td colspan="2">Although several of the Standards could relate to the content in this unit, which knowledge standards will you integrate into the activities and projects of this unit?
suggestions include: Earth Science Literacy Standards and the National Science Education Standards (NSES).</td></tr>
<tr><th colspan="2">Communication Arts</th></tr>
<tr><td>4.</td><td>Writing formally (such as reports, narratives, essays) and informally (such as outlines, notes)</td></tr>
<tr><td>6.</td><td>Participating in formal and informal presentations and discussions of issues and ideas</td></tr>
<tr><th colspan="2">Mathematics</th></tr>
<tr><td>3.</td><td>Data analysis, probability and statistics</td></tr>
<tr><th colspan="2">Science</th></tr>
<tr><td>7.</td><td>Processes of scientific inquiry (such as formulating and testing hypotheses)</td></tr>
<tr><td>8.</td><td>Impact of science, technology and human activity on resources and the environment</td></tr>
<tr><th colspan="2">Social Studies</th></tr>
<tr><td>6.</td><td>Relationships of the individual and groups to institutions and cultural traditions</td></tr>
<tr><td>7.</td><td>Processes of scientific inquiry (such as formulating and testing hypotheses)</td></tr>
<tr><th colspan="2">Others</th></tr>
<tr><td>1.</td><td></td></tr>
<tr><th colspan="2">Goals and Objectives</th></tr>
<tr><td colspan="2">Based on the National Science Education Standards, what are the goals of the unit and what objectives will help students meet those goals throughout the three phases of the unit?</td></tr>
<tr><td rowspan="2">1.</td><td>Working as a researcher exploring water issues in the unit the student will gather, organize, analyze, and apply information ideas.</td></tr>
<tr><td>Objectives:
• Conduct research to answer questions and evaluate information and ideas.
• Use technological tools and other resources to locate, select, and organize information.
• Organize data, information and ideas into useful forms (including charts, graphs, outlines) for analysis or presentation.</td></tr>
<tr><td rowspan="2">2.</td><td>While analyzing potential problems and solutions, the student will communicate effectively within and beyond the classroom.</td></tr>
<tr><td>Objectives:
• Plan and make written, oral and visual presentations for a variety of purposes and audiences.
• Exchange information, questions and ideas while recognizing the perspectives of others.
• Use technological tools to exchange information and ideas.</td></tr>
</table>

continued on following page

Table 1. Continued

3.	*Using the tools of inquiry to develop a plan of action, the student will recognize and solve problems.*
	Objectives: • Identify problems and define their scope and elements. • Examine problems and propose solutions from multiple perspectives. • Assess costs, benefits and other consequences of proposed solutions
Pre-Assessment	
What knowledge and skills do you think are important for students to have in order to complete the projects in this unit successfully?	
How will you identify students' prior knowledge and misconceptions about the problem?	

Table 2. Phase 1

Facilitating Activities	
What activities do you think are important in Phase 1 to help your students meet the objectives of this phase of the unit and to successfully complete the project?	
1.	
2.	
3.	
Initial Inquiry Questions	
What kind of questions do you anticipate students posing at the beginning of Phase 1 that will guide them in answering the critical question in this phase of the unit?	
1.	
Important Implementation Dates	
What aspects of the activities in Phase 1 need to be scheduled or arranged ahead of time?	
1.	
2.	
Resources and Tools	
What resources and/or tools within your classroom, in your building, or in your community are necessary to help students during Phase 1?	
1.	
2.	

3. Develop teachers' skills to design, redesign and evaluate the effectiveness of the design of immersive educational settings.
4. Develop teachers' ability to engage in a social dynamic in student centered learning environments.
5. Develop teachers' understanding of the integration of advanced technologies into immersive learning environments.

The Future of Teaching professional development model is a community of teachers and administrators focused on developing the most efficient and effective learning environment for their diverse students by using advanced innovative technologies that flip the paradigm of education by focusing on developing advanced knowledge for the knowledge age.

Table 3. Phase 2

Critical Question	
What is the critical question that students will respond to throughout Phase 2 of the unit?	
How can we use our expertise in an area related to Climate Change to better understand the problem and develop a feasible solution?	
Objectives	
Considering the goals of this unit, what are the objectives for students during this phase of the unit? You might consider the performance and knowledge skills required for students to complete the project in Phase 2 with little or no teacher support.	
1. Conduct research to answer questions and evaluate information and ideas 2. Exchange information, questions and ideas while recognizing the perspectives of others 3. Examine problems and proposed solutions from multiple perspectives 4. Reason inductively from facts and deductively from general premises 5. Develop, monitor, and revise plans of action to meet deadlines and accomplish goals	
Problem-Solving Model	
What part of the model for design problem solving best illustrates the problem solving that will occur in the work groups during Phase 2?	
In Phase 2, students will acquire expertise in an area related to Climate Change, including problem solving strategies and conceptual knowledge. This will help them know where change could be effected in the system and help the revise their original vision for Climate Change.	
How does the problem solving process in this phase of the unit relate to the way experts in related fields solve problems?	
Experts draw upon their prior experiences and knowledge and relate these to the unique characteristics of a current design problem.	
Phase 2 Project Criteria	
What project will students work collaboratively to complete during Phase 2 that relates to the critical question of this phase of the unit?	
After gathering and analyzing relevant, accurate, and clear facts and statistics about an area related to Climate Change, the group will determine how the area of expertise applies to development of a feasible solution to the Climate Change problem that impacts multiple communities in Missouri.	
What criteria will you expect students to complete when they work on the project collaboratively? Consider the objectives you identified for students' learning during Phase 2.	
1. Locate relevant, accurate, and clear facts from different sources that help you understand your expert area related to Climate Change. 2. Talk in your expert area group about how your expert area affects the way we will solve the Climate Change problem and how it affects each of your communities. 3. Develop a plan for how to accurately communicate the following to students in your group: (1) the main ideas about the expert area and (2) how you think your expert area will help us solve the Climate Change problem better. 4. Develop your plan for communicating to students in your group. 5. Talk in your group about how the areas of expertise are related and how the expert areas will help you solve the Climate Change problem better	
Formative and Summative Assessment	
How will you assess students' learning in regards to the objectives at the end of Phase 2?	
See Phase 2 Group Scoring Guide for assessment of group products based on Bereiter's Scheme of Knowledge (levels 3-5).	
Facilitating Activities	
What activities do you think are important in Phase 2 to help your students meet the objectives of this phase of the unit and to successfully complete the project?	
1. Case study analyses of similar projects.	
Areas of Expertise	
What areas of expertise are important to the Climate Change problem that students will investigate in their groups?	
1. Ecology, 2. Socioeconomics, 3. Design, 4. Public affairs,	5. Natural environment (e.g., wetlands, habitat, species), 6. Human environment, 7. Financing, 8. Construction.

continued on following page

Table 3. Continued

Important Implementation Dates	
What aspects of the activities in Phase 2 need to be scheduled or arranged ahead of time?	
1.	
2.	
Resources and Tools	
What resources and/or tools within your classroom, in your building, or in your community are necessary to help students during Phase 2?	
1.	
2.	

Table 4. Phase 3

Critical Question
What is the critical question that students will respond to throughout Phase 3 of the unit?
How can we use the knowledge and skills from Phase 1 and Phase 2 to develop a feasible solution to the Climate Change problem?
Objectives
Considering the goals of this unit, what are the objectives for students during this phase of the unit? You might consider the performance and knowledge skills required for students to complete the project in Phase 3 with little or no teacher support.
6. Organize data, information and ideas into useful forms (including charts, graphs, outlines) for analysis or presentation. 7. Use technological tools to exchange information and ideas. 8. Assess costs, benefits and other consequences of proposed solutions. 9. Explain reasoning and identify information used to support decisions. 10. Work with others to complete tasks that require a coordinated effort.
Problem-Solving Model
In Phase 3, students will work in their local group to propose a solution to the Climate Change problem that incorporates a plan of action for their community and multiple communities. They will apply the expert areas and assess their solution to determine feasibility.
How does the problem solving process in this phase of the unit relate to the way experts in related fields solve problems?
Phase 3 Project Criteria
What project will students work collaboratively to complete during Phase 3 that relates to the critical question of this phase of the unit?
After gathering relevant, accurate, and clear facts and statistics about Climate Change in their community, the group will determine why the Climate Change problem is important to their community. Their knowledge and ideas for the future of Climate Change will be shared with other groups in the class with other groups of students from our partner schools.
What criteria will you expect students to complete when they work on the project collaboratively? Consider the objectives you identified for students' learning during Phase 3.
6. Write a description of the problem, including facts and statistics, of the current condition of Climate Change as well as a prediction for its future. 7. Develop a hypothesis, or a statement describing how your group thinks the local organizations should develop Climate Change to better meet the needs of people in Missouri. 8. Outline a procedure, or a logically-defined plan of action, about how your group's idea would be implemented. 9. Talk in your group about how to "test the feasibility" of your solution and plan; determine whether your solution could feasibly be implemented locally. 10. Using the results of your feasibility test, predict the success of your solution and plan and identify short-term and long-term problems that might occur because of your solution and plan of action.

continued on following page

Table 4. Continued

Formative and Summative Assessment	
How will you assess students' learning in regards to the objectives at the end of Phase 3?	
See Phase 3 Group Scoring Guide for assessment of group products based on Bereiter's Scheme of Knowledge (levels 4-6).	
Facilitating Activities	
What activities do you think are important in Phase 3 to help your students meet the objectives of this phase of the unit and to successfully complete the project?	
1.	
2.	
Solution Generation	
How will you motivate students to develop solutions to the Climate Change problem that incorporates state and local community needs from Phase 1 and the different areas of expertise from Phase 2?	
1.	
Important Implementation Dates	
What aspects of the activities in Phase 3 need to be scheduled or arranged ahead of time?	
1.	
2.	
Resources and Tools	
What resources and/or tools within your classroom, in your building, or in your community are necessary to help students during Phase 3?	
1.	
2.	

Curriculum Guide

The educational programs that decide to utilize the Future of Learning protocol will receive a modular Curriculum Guide that includes the curriculum needed to integrate the units they choose into their traditional educational programs. The Curriculum Guide includes the scope and sequence, assessments, and learning activities. An example of a curriculum guide for a unit on Climate Change in IDEA City is below. In this unit students engage in exploration of a virtual world undergoing climate change. Tables 1-5 are the Curriculum Guide.

The Curriculum Guide for teachers as shown above is a modular template that can be modified for multiple virtual problem-based learning units. Appendix 1 is an overview scope and sequence of a Resources Management unit designed from the Future of Learning protocol focusing on STEM content areas. This virtual learning environment will be developed based on standards including the common core standards that will be integrated into problem-based learning units that combine several sciences into a holistic unit of study that provides the learner access to understanding problem-solving in multiple disciplines utilizing international collaboration on global issues.

FUTURE RESEARCH DIRECTIONS

The need for radical changes in the nature of education in the US is becoming increasingly obvious. The needs of the increasingly diverse learners are not being met in a traditional testing model of teaching and lerning. Direct instruction with itemized decontextualized content does not lead to the development of advanced knowledge forma-

Table 5. Phase 1 group artifact scoring guide

	Learning	Accomplishing	Excelling	Exceptional
Gathering Information	Working with the teacher, the students found and used at least two resources.	With some teacher help, the students found and used at least two resources and identified if the information gathered was relevant.	The students found and used information from different types of resources, determined if the information was relevant, and explained if the information was reliable.	The students independently found and used information from different types of resources, judged the relevancy of information, and verified the reliability of information by cross-referencing.
Using Facts and Statistics	The students and teacher worked together to identify and use facts and statistics to support their ideas.	With some teacher assistance, the students determined facts and statistics to support their ideas and could explain how some facts and statistics were connected.	The students could combine information, make connections between information, and identify relevant prior knowledge to support their ideas.	The students independently combined information, made connections between facts and statistics, recognized contradictions, and integrated prior knowledge.
Presenting the Message	The students used minimal eye contact, needed few reminders about distracting body movements, yet needed some reminders to speak so all could hear.	The students attempted some eye contact, stood straight and relaxed, and used good volume and were easy to understand.	The students made eye contact with many audience members, used several appropriate gestures and facial expressions, and used good volume and varied voice for important points in the presentation.	The student made eye contact with all audience members used many appropriate gestures and facial expressions that added to the presentation, and consistently used good volume and varied voice.
Working on a Team	With teacher help, the students listened to one others' ideas and shared in the responsibility for completing work.	With encouragement, the students listened to one others' ideas, tried to compromise with each group members, and shared in the responsibility of completing work.	The students listened to one others' ideas, encouraged all group members to compromise, and actively shared in the responsibility for completing work.	The student listened to others' ideas, motivated all group members to compromise, and proposed a plan for sharing responsibility for completing work.
Setting up the Problem	With teacher support, the students identified and/or explained constraints in the Climate Change system and stated a vision for the future of interstate.	As they described a vision for the future of Climate Change, the students identified and explained constraints in the Climate Change system including some that are related to the students' community.	As they described a specific vision for the future of Climate Change in their community, the students identified and explained constraints in the Climate Change system that are directly related to the students' community.	As they described a specific vision for the future of Climate Change in their community, the students identified, explained, and prioritized constraints in the Climate Change system that are directly related to the students' community, including constraints that are not apparent or are external to the Climate Change system.

tion. It is the premise of the Future of Learning curriculum model can be the comprehensive foci for educational programs that are more student-centric, based on immersive learning principles, designed to advance problem-solving, critical thinking, advanced decision making and knowledge formation and assessed in a recursive cycle of formative and summative assessments built into the learning environment itself. The Future of Learning protocol provides an integrated curriculum is blended and modular for integration as a completely online mode or a blended mode of instruction and learning. The Future of Learning provides a curriculum guide for teachers to use, a training protocol for teachers and advanced simulation-based learning environments based on problem-based learning concepts of learning and development. As a result, the protocol can be implemented readily into multiple p-12 learning environments providing a basis for innovative teachers and programs to flip the paradigm of education in their educational programs.

CONCLUSION

In response to a rapidly changing information age with a need for knowledge workers as economic drivers of our country, p-12 education must adapt to become relevant. Knowledge workers understand how to use information to solve problems, how to think critically, how to create, how to communicate their vision effectively and share their ideas in a variety of forums. The integration of immersive virtual learning environments into a problem-based learning program is the future of learning necessary for the adaptation of -12 education to meet the needs of the knowledge workers of the future.

REFERENCES

Barab, S., Kling, R., & Gray, J. (2006). *Designing for Virtual Communities in the Service of Learning*. Cambridge, UK: Cambridge University Press.

Bereiter, C. (2001). *Education and mind in the knowledge age*. New York, NY: Lawrence Erlbaum Assoc.

Clark, and M.L. Maher, The effects of a sense of place on the learning experience in a 3 virtual world, *Proc. 10th Association for Learning Technologies Conf. on Communities of Practice*, Sheffield, UK, 2003, 82-101.

Di Blas, N., Paolini, P., & Poggi, C. 3D worlds for edutainment: educational, relational and organizational principles. *Proc. 3rd IEEE PerCom2005 Workshops. On Pervasive eLearning*, Hawaii, (pp. 291-295). doi:10.1109/PERCOMW.2005.1

Dickey, M. (2005). Three-dimensional virtual worlds and distance learning: Two case studies of Active Worlds as a medium for distance education. *British Journal of Educational Technology*, *36*(3), 439–451. doi:10.1111/j.1467-8535.2005.00477.x

Kalay, Y., Jeong, S., Kim, W., & Lee, J. (n. d.). Virtual Learning Environments. *Proc. 9th CAADRIA2004 conf. on Culture, Technology and Architecture*, Seoul, Korea (pp. 871-890).

Norbert-Schulz. (1971). *Existence, space and architecture*. New York, NY: Praeger Publishing.

Relph, E. (1976). *Place and placelessness*. London, UK: Pion Ltd.

Rosenman, M., Smith, G., Ding, L., Marchant D., & Maher, M.L. (2005). Multidisciplinary design in virtual worlds. *Proc. 11th CAAD Futures conf. on Learning from the Past – a Foundation for the Future*, Vienna, Austria (pp. 433-442).

Russell, D. (2005a). Implementing an Innovation cluster in educational settings in order develop constructivist-based learning environments. *Journal of Educational Technology & Society*, *8*(2).

Russell, D., (2005b, February). Transformation in an Urban School: Using Systemic Analysis to Understand an Innovative Urban Teacher's Implementation of an Online Problem-Based Unit. *International Journal of Instructional Technology & Distance Learning*, 2(2).

Vogel, J. J., Vogel, D. S., Cannon-Bowers, J., Bowers, C. A., Muse, K., & Wright, M. (2006). Computer Gaming and Interactive Simulations for Learning: A meta-analysis. *Journal of Educational Computing Research*, *34*(3), 229–243. doi:10.2190/FLHV-K4WA-WPVQ-H0YM

APPENDIX 1

Below is an overview scope and sequence based on the Future of Learning protocol. This is an aspect of a Resource Management core theme. All assessment models are linked to core National and International standards. All assessments of learning activities are designed into the online learning management system.

1. High School AP-based 3D virtual simulations:
   a. This program will develop immersive 3D virtual simulations that are evaluated based on High School AP criteria. This includes a common meeting area, content areas to support the development of advanced learning processes and knowledge such as
      i. Chemistry and biology labs for developing experiments,
      ii. Interactive units of study that engage all learners in addressing a global issues e.g. climate change, and
      iii. Common rooms for interaction, presentation and discussion among the students and teachers as appropriate.
2. Online Problem-Based Learning (PBL) curriculum and Curriculum Guide for teachers.
   a. The program will result in a comprehensive PBL curriculum for the vPBL High School that is based on social cultural learning theories and the philosophy of constructivist learning. This will include the development of 3D simulations based on integrated units of study. Dr. Russell has a background in the assessment of immersive learning environments.
      i. Based on Common Core Standards and national content standards.
      ii. Includes holistic formative and summative assessments.
      iii. STEM Worlds will include feedback systems designed into the environment.
3. Modified Learning Management System for the Virtual Schools:
   a. The program will result in modifications to the LMS to incorporate 3D immersive learning environments and additional tools including apps, a revised portal and a comprehensive learning analytic tool that is linked to the holistic assessment processes that will be incorporated into the assessment model for the immersive learning environments.
4. Research protocols for these environments.
   a. Dr. Russell will develop evaluative research protocols for assessing the implementation of these projects including international presentations and publications on the program.

Four Main Components Included in the LMS for the Virtual HS

1. Home Portal the home page for the LMS: MetaLearning Focus on metacognition and self-regulation of learning:
   a. The link to the learning analytics system provides live feedback to the learner.
   b. Includes a graphic linked to the assessment modes.
   c. Includes a Mentor Bot for the learners:
      i. A form of AI to provide feedback to the learners
      ii. Pedagogical Agent tagged to Learning Analytics. Includes feedback loop for learners for metacognitive and Student self-monitors throughout movement through the units (development of portfolio, assessments including rubrics for projects; tests in LMS)

   d. Unit Courseroom:
      i. Access to the instructional resources including a curriculum.
      ii. Access to links to resources.
      iii. Access to the assessment tools.
2. Sim Worlds; a gaming scenario that is designed based on problem-based learning dilemma scenarios.
   a. 3D Sim World (simulation/gaming scenario) for each unit of study.
   b. Worlds include a gaming scenario that provides the students with opportunities to develop advanced knowledge and skills through interactions in the environment:
      i. Games/Simulation engages students in a high-stakes simulation to develop content knowledge, skills, and awareness.
      ii. Students/instructors engage through an avatar
      iii. Students earn points/prizes for moving successfully through simulation. Assessments tagged to the simulation through Reporting In Kiosks.
   c. Access to the Media Center to develop projects; disseminate projects; present; schedule international conferences:
      i. Media Center is common location reached through each Sim World.
      ii. **Media Center:** 2d and 3d common area for group meetings; presentations; conferences; and access to resources to build, store and disseminate their portfolio artifacts. Media Center includes sand boxes to build projects and conference Center with rooms for small group presentations.
   d. Guide Bots to support the learner movement; monitor learning.
   e. **Reporting in Kiosks:** Learners engage in reporting or receiving feedback from the instructor.
3. Learning Analytics System:
   a. Data management system that combines information from the Home Portal and Sim Worlds to provide as close as possible real-time analytics.
      i. Student responses to formative and summative assessments built into Unit Courseroom and Sim Worlds (Student response graphics).
      ii. Instructor feedback on student progress in the LAS.
   b. Instructor training site The Instructor site will include TPCK-based courses that focus on
      i. Development and implement of virtual PBL units, including characteristics of PBL environments.
      ii. Assessment of learning in immersive virtual learning environments (cognitive theories, Bereiter Scheme of Knowledge).
      iii. **Technology Meditated Learning Principles:** Characteristics of technology, Characteristics of innovation in education (Rogers, Russell), Integration of learning technologies into immersive learning environments (Jonassen).
      iv. **Implementation of the vPBL for High School STEM Learning:** Specific training for units of study, training on the LMS, training on the assessment of the Learning Analytics Program, online international collaborative website for discussion and meetings with others implementing the vPBL HS STEM program (Blog site).

Courseroom Site vPBL for High School STEM Learning

1. IDEAL World: Are We the Problem or the Solution?
    a. A global systemic overview of issues such as climate change, hunger; alternative energies including the overarching concept of ecosystems and human interactions and consequences globally.
        i. **Content Knowledge:** Geology, geography, math; mapping, charts, civics, engineering.
        ii. **Advanced Processes:** Communication, presentation, group work skills, social skills, writing, speech.
        iii. **Problem-Based Learning:** Issue of the consequence of human interactions on environments.
        iv. **Advanced Technologies:** Global mapping, design of innovations.

Learning Goal

Develop a virtual 2D and 3D interactive immersive PBL-based virtual learning environment that:

1. Develops advanced knowledge responses as assessed by holistic rubrics based on Bereiter's Scheme of Knowledge.
2. Engages and motivates students in problems and issues based on STEM career areas.

Learning Activities

The learners will:

1. Respond to 3D immersive interactive virtual simulations designed to develop advanced problem-based learning processes and skills including
    a. Critical thinking,
    b. Collaborative skills,
    c. Inquiry skills, and
    d. Evaluative thinking.
2. Create an interactive virtual e-portfolio for dissemination to their IDEAL mentors.
3. Present on the results of their simulations in the 3D VLE.

Assessment Model

The learning will be assessed using

1. Formative assessment will be built into the 3D simulations and will be part of the immersive experience allowing students to continue the game, e.g. go to the next level of the game, without taking them out of the game experience. These formative assessments will include holistic rubrics designed by Dr. Russell and based on research on knowledge formation and the development of advanced cognitive functions. These rubrics will be immersed in the 3D VLE in kiosks or other

interactive forums for the students to respond to at the end of each phase of their interactive simulations. In later iterations the formative assessments can be done through the students' interaction with a pedagogical agent, an AI bot, programmed to 'talk' to the students about their interactions and responses.

2. Pre and Post Likert surveys that will assess the development of students'
   a. Feelings of self-attribution,
   b. Motivation to engage in STEM careers, and
   c. A pre/post holistic rubric identifying advanced problem-solving processes and skills using a case scenario with multiple outcomes and decisions.

All assessment data will be stored and accessed through a learning management system that will be correlated to the learning goals, learning activities and 3D design characteristics to be used for assessment of learning, evaluation of effectiveness of the simulations, and redesign of the virtual context.

Description

The Ideal World will be a 3d virtual world. The 3d world would include:

1. A main area for students to enter and leave the virtual world. The IDEAL City simulation will be a place for students and mentors to
   a. Enter/exit the 3d world simulations,
   b. Collaborate and present,
   c. Receive basic information about the simulations,
   d. Post e-portfolio project to their LMS.
2. Two virtual simulations will be designed for IDEAL city
   a. **Simulation 1:** Build a green building.
      i. Using materials on-site students build a green building making choices. concerning economics, effectiveness, environmental impact and codes.
   b. **Simulation 2:** Design an energy efficient vehicle.
      i. Students collaboratively design a solar/hydrogen/electric car.
      ii. Students race cars.
3. A learning management system to manage assessment data from students' interactions in the world.
4. A 2d website that will be a restricted login forum for:
   a. Student collaborations.
   b. Entry/exit from the virtual world.
   c. Curriculum dissemination.
5. An open site for disseminating information about the project.
6. An evaluative research protocol that will
   a. Evaluate the learning responses and their correlation to the virtual experiences.
   b. Develop new understandings about professional development.
   c. Understand design characteristics of immersive 3D environment.
   d. Understand motive/affect in 3D immersive learning environments.

The vPBL STEM High School Learning Management System student's login flowchart is outlined below.

Student Logins to Learning Management System

1. Digital Learning Tree
2. Access Home Page Portal:
    a. **MySocialMedia:** Communication window (lists all connections in the Portal), check in with AI bot, Eportfolio (links to all courses and virtual worlds media projects).
    b. **MyLearning:** MetaLearning graphs identifying, what current grades are, what projects/assignments are in progress, interactions in courserooms (last time in courseroom, what activity, how long), interactions in virtual world (last time in courseroom, what they did. how long).
    c. **MyCourses:** List of all courses (units) in window, access to courses (links to Unit of Study, problem Space e.g. Sustainable City Life. Modules include lessons, assignments, assessment, and learner activities), virtual world – IDEAL World (access related scenarios, e.g. Build a Solar Car, develop project, race Car), media center (Collaborative Project in Media Center, including solar Car finished design and presentation for Design Symposiums).

Virtual World Interactions

Below is a flowchart for student interactions in the 3D virtual world, IDEAL World

Students access the Virtual World in the Courseroom site.

As a result of their progress through the unit of study in the Courseroom, they will be directed to a scenario in the 3D world.

IDEAL World

1. Students enter into the IDEAL World in the main area, the Media Center.
2. The students will be guided to their main World
    a. Pedagogical agents or kiosks/signage.
    b. IDEAL City.
    c. IDEAL Country.
3. IDEAL City:
    a. Students in specific units will respond to Scenarios (simulations with defined responses and projects) in each IDEAL world.
    b. Sustainable City unit includes 3 Scenarios:
        i. Solar Scenario.
        ii. Students go to the IDEAL City and enter the IDEAL University to go to test lab for building a solar car.
        iii. Students have components for building a solar car.
        iv. Students work in groups to develop a solar car.

    v. Students respond to info kiosks that give them the information on topics. Students respond to comments in the kiosks (short quiz) to access components and design (solar panels, solar power, car design, car mechanics).
    vi. Project Completed: Students will be able to test their cars in the IDEAL U lab.
    vii. Students will complete a Solar Race in the IDEAL World City Race.

4. IDEAL Country
    a. Students in specific units will respond to Scenarios related to the rural IDEAL Country
    b. Feeding the World – world hunger, gmo foods, biotechnology
    c. Students will go to Main Farm to get information on the Build a Drought Resistant Food Scenario
        i. Students will find a Greenhouse set for Drought conditions
        ii. Students will grow plants with differing characteristics: Info kiosks on genetics, World food production, World hunger (Choose plant, Interaction with international groups) Genetic modification, Biotechnology, Short comments after each info (survey or quiz), Students get additional biotechnology tools, In groups students will biodesign a drought resistant plant, Students will test their plants in the greenhouse.
    d. In international groups students will present their biodesigned plant in a biotech Conference:
        i. Students will justify their use of biotech tools for human food production

Instructional Activities

Below is an outline of instructional activities for this high school unit.

The Problem-Based Unit of Study will be Climate Change.

The instructional activities are also structured around the Phases in the PBL Template.

- Phases are approximately 3-4 lessons each.
- Total Issue response is 9-12 lessons of approx. 90 minutes each.
- Courses: Content Instruction: 5-7 lessons each content area.

PBL Design Template: Phase 1

Develop knowledge of the global issue Climate Change
The Content Knowledge are STEM focused but include interdisciplinary activities such as

- Communication arts (focus on writing, presenting, and media integration),
- Math (focus on data analysis and representation), and
- Social Sciences (focus on geological time, community activities' and engagement).

Instructional Activities

Teacher develops initial instruction on the issues inherent in the problem space:

- Overview of Climate Change.
- Description of the issues inherent in this problem.
- Review of entire unit with students.
- Brainstorming session to setup groups for development of Phase 2 Expertise.
- Pair students to research aspects that they are interested in for presentation to the class.
- Establish phase 2 groups for expertise.
- Approx. 3-5 lessons.

Learning Activities:

- Students discuss topic.
- Research aspects of the topic they wish to understand more fully.
- Develop presentation to share with the class.
- **LMS:** Exploration of Idea World: Future World.

Assessment:

- **Response in Class:** Checklist of engagement and collaboration.
- **Research Process:** Develop a question and identify multiple sources of information.
- **Presentation of Sub Issues:** Presentation Rubric.

PBL Design Template: Phase 2

- Develop expert knowledge of sub issues in the global issue.
- **Teacher Activities:** Teacher instructs in content area needed to understand the subissues:
    - AP Geology
    - AP Zoology
    - AP Chemistry
    - **LMS:** Courses
    - **Labs:** Chemistry; Biology
    - Sub issues:
        - Oceanic changes,
        - Marker species-Coral Reef,
        - Atmospheric Changes,
        - Carbon in Atmosphere: Pollution,
        - Biosphere changes,
        - Trends in animal and plant marker species,
        - Weather: Drought.
- Learner Activities:
    - Respond to Direct Instruction.
    - In groups research sub issues and prepare a presentation.
    - LMS: Exploration of Water World and Terra World.

- Assessment:
    - Test.
    - Presentation Rubric.

Phase 3: Create a Strategy for Addressing the Problem Issues

Develop a strategy for addressing Climate Change through local plan of action.

- Jigsaw Groups:
    - Large groups with experts from each area of expertise.
    - Develop a strategy to address the issues.
    - Presentation of Plan of Action.
- LMS:
    - Groups meet in LMS and use Media Center to develop presentation.
    - Design Sandbox to test prototype for Project.
- Learning Assessment:
    - Rubric for assessing the Presentation: quality of data; referencing; efficacy.
    - The Community Mentors for this unit include experts in the following areas.

STEM Virtual Career Scenarios

- **Green Building Industry:** LEED building simulator, LEED residential house simulator.
- **Clean Tech Transportation:** Designing, building and testing an all-electric drag racer.
- **Operate Clean Tech Power Utility:** Design a "smart grid" to make the most of energy sources.
- **Medicine:** Performing functions in an emergency room, in surgery, dentistry, or pathology, creating technology devices, exploring genetic codes for cures.
- **Clean Tech Chemistry:** Converting algae to fuel while saving oceans and generating power.
- **Landscape Architecture:** Landscape construction and design, irrigation repair and installation, and organic maintenance.
- **Large Land Owner:** Community farming.
- **Solar Power and Architectural and Mechanical Engineering:** Construct solar panels, create solar-powered vehicles.
- **Wind Power Technology:** Creating small and large turbines.Private Space Colonization—Star Wars for real.
- **CSI-Style Forensic Science:** Solve mysteries using forensic science.
- **Interactive Museums:** QuantumWorks' Proteus edutainment system list of Interactive Museums and Pavilions range from the Seven Wonders of the Ancient World, Forgotten Inventors, Leonardo Machines Come Alive, to Mayan Empire, Rome Alive, and Mesozoic Time Traveler.

APPENDIX 2

Curriculum Design Template for vPBLE

The PBL Design Template is shown in Figure 2.

Figure 2.

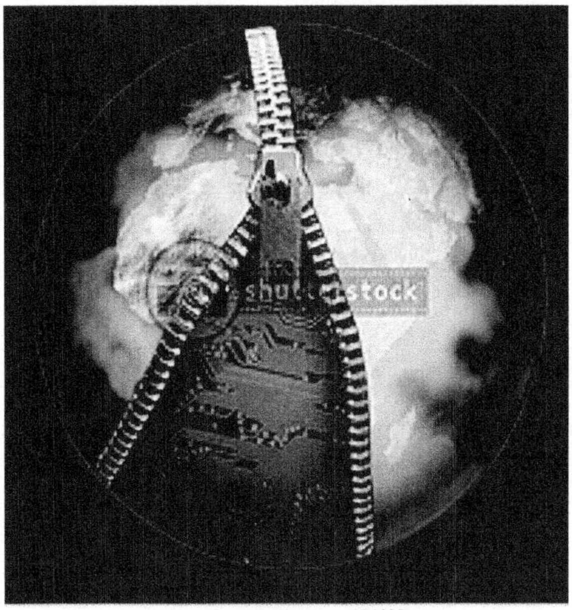

1. Instructional Design Template

The purpose of this instructional design template is to guide the teacher through the development of a unit based on constructivist learning principles.

Table 6.

<table>
<tr><td colspan="2">Teacher</td><td>Grade Level</td></tr>
<tr><td colspan="2"></td><td></td></tr>
<tr><td colspan="2">School</td><td>City and State</td></tr>
<tr><td colspan="2"></td><td></td></tr>
<tr><td>Number of Students</td><td colspan="2">Email Address</td></tr>
<tr><td></td><td colspan="2"></td></tr>
</table>

Table 7. Unit overview

<table>
<tr><th colspan="2">Description</th></tr>
<tr><td colspan="2">What is the nature of the problem students will tackle in this unit?</td></tr>
<tr><th colspan="2">Meaningfulness for Students</th></tr>
<tr><td colspan="2">Why do you think students will find the problem in this unit meaningful?</td></tr>
<tr><th colspan="2">Relevant Missouri Show-Me Knowledge Standards</th></tr>
<tr><td colspan="2">Although several of the Missouri Show-Me Knowledge Standards could relate to the content in this unit, which knowledge standards will you integrate into the activities and projects of this unit?</td></tr>
<tr><th colspan="2">Communication Arts</th></tr>
<tr><td>4.</td><td>Writing formally (such as reports, narratives, essays) and informally (such as outlines, notes)</td></tr>
<tr><td>6.</td><td>Participating in formal and informal presentations and discussions of issues and ideas</td></tr>
<tr><th colspan="2">Mathematics</th></tr>
<tr><td>3.</td><td>Data analysis, probability and statistics</td></tr>
<tr><th colspan="2">Science</th></tr>
<tr><td>7.</td><td>Processes of scientific inquiry (such as formulating and testing hypotheses)</td></tr>
<tr><td>8.</td><td>Impact of science, technology and human activity on resources and the environment</td></tr>
<tr><th colspan="2">Social Studies</th></tr>
<tr><td>6.</td><td>Relationships of the individual and groups to institutions and cultural traditions</td></tr>
<tr><td>7.</td><td>Processes of scientific inquiry (such as formulating and testing hypotheses)</td></tr>
<tr><th colspan="2">Others</th></tr>
<tr><td>1.</td><td></td></tr>
<tr><th colspan="2">Goals and Objectives</th></tr>
<tr><td colspan="2">Based on the Missouri Show-Me Performance Standards, what are the goals of the unit and what objectives will help students meet those goals throughout the three phases of the unit?</td></tr>
<tr><td rowspan="2">1.</td><td>Working as a researcher exploring water issues in the unit the student will gather, organize, analyze, and apply information ideas.</td></tr>
<tr><td>Objectives:
• Conduct research to answer questions and evaluate information and ideas.
• Use technological tools and other resources to locate, select, and organize information.
• Organize data, information and ideas into useful forms (including charts, graphs, outlines) for analysis or presentation.</td></tr>
<tr><td rowspan="2">2.</td><td>While analyzing potential problems and solutions, the student will communicate effectively within and beyond the classroom.</td></tr>
<tr><td>Objectives:
• Plan and make written, oral and visual presentations for a variety of purposes and audiences.
• Exchange information, questions and ideas while recognizing the perspectives of others.
• Use technological tools to exchange information and ideas.</td></tr>
<tr><td rowspan="2">3.</td><td>Using the tools of inquiry to develop a plan of action, the student will recognize and solve problems.</td></tr>
<tr><td>Objectives:
• Identify problems and define their scope and elements.
• Examine problems and propose solutions from multiple perspectives.
• Assess costs, benefits and other consequences of proposed solutions</td></tr>
<tr><td rowspan="2">4.</td><td>While considering the interdependence of community and state needs, the student will use critical thinking to defend decisions.</td></tr>
<tr><td>Objectives:
• Explain reasoning and identify information used to support decisions.
• Reason inductively from facts and deductively from general premises.</td></tr>
</table>

continued on following page

Table 7. Continued

5.	*As an engineer working with other engineers, the student will be a responsible group member and demonstrate positive leadership skills.*
	Objectives: • Develop, monitor, and revise plans of action to meet deadlines and accomplish goals. • Work with others to complete tasks that require a coordinated effort.
Expert Contacts	
What experts in fields related to this unit will contribute to the design, development, and implementation of this unit with students?	
1. 2. 3. 4. 5.	
Pre-Assessment	
What knowledge and skills do you think are important for students to have in order to complete the projects in this unit successfully?	
How will you identify students' prior knowledge and misconceptions about the problem?	

Table 8. Phase 1

Critical Question
What is the critical question that students will respond to throughout Phase 1 of the unit?
Objectives
Considering the goals of this unit, what are the objectives for students during this phase of the unit? You might consider the performance and knowledge skills required for students to complete the project in Phase 1 with little or no teacher support.
6. Use technological tools and other resources to locate, select, and organize information. 7. Make oral and visual presentations for a variety of purposes and audiences. 8. Identify problems and define their scope and elements. 9. Explain reasoning and identify information used to support decisions. 10. Work with others to complete tasks that require a coordinated effort.
Problem-Solving Model
What part of the model for design problem solving best illustrates the problem solving that will occur in the work groups during Phase 1?
How does the problem solving process in this phase of the unit relate to the way experts in related fields solve problems?
Phase 1 Project Criteria
What project will students work collaboratively to complete during Phase 1 that relates to the critical question of this phase of the unit?
What criteria will you expect students to complete when they work on the project collaboratively? Consider the objectives you identified for students' learning during Phase 1.
6. Locate relevant, accurate, and clear facts from different sources that help your group explain why the problem is important to your community. 7. Talk in your group about whether or not your group thinks the topic without changes, can meet the needs of people in your community. 8. Talk in your group about what your group thinks the topic of study should do to better meet the needs of people in your community. 9. Develop a plan for how to convince students from other communities why the problem needs improvement in order to better meet the needs of people in your community. 10. Present the plan to other workgroups in your classroom and improve your presentation before sharing it with students from other communities.
Formative and Summative Assessment
How will you assess students' learning in regards to the objectives at the end of Phase 1?
See Phase 1 Group Scoring Guide for assessment of group products based on Bereiter's Scheme of Knowledge (levels 1-3).

continued on following page

Table 8. Continued

Facilitating Activities
What activities do you think are important in Phase 1 to help your students meet the objectives of this phase of the unit and to successfully complete the project?
1. 2. 3. 4. 5.
Initial Inquiry Questions
What kind of questions do you anticipate students posing at the beginning of Phase 1 that will guide them in answering the critical question in this phase of the unit?
Important Implementation Dates
What aspects of the activities in Phase 1 need to be scheduled or arranged ahead of time?
1. 2. 3. 4. 5.
Resources and Tools
What resources and/or tools within your classroom, in your building, or in your community are necessary to help students during Phase 1?
1. 2. 3. 4. 5.

Table 9. Phase 2

Critical Question
What is the critical question that students will respond to throughout Phase 2 of the unit?
Objectives
Considering the goals of this unit, what are the objectives for students during this phase of the unit? You might consider the performance and knowledge skills required for students to complete the project in Phase 2 with little or no teacher support.
6. Conduct research to answer questions and evaluate information and ideas. 7. Exchange information, questions and ideas while recognizing the perspectives of others. 8. Examine problems and proposed solutions from multiple perspectives. 9. Reason inductively from facts and deductively from general premises. 10. Develop, monitor, and revise plans of action to meet deadlines and accomplish goals.
Problem-Solving Model
What part of the model for design problem solving best illustrates the problem solving that will occur in the work groups during Phase 2?
How does the problem solving process in this phase of the unit relate to the way experts in related fields solve problems?
Phase 2 Project Criteria
What project will students work collaboratively to complete during Phase 2 that relates to the critical question of this phase of the unit?
What criteria will you expect students to complete when they work on the project collaboratively? Consider the objectives you identified for students' learning during Phase 2.

continued on following page

Table 9. Continued

<table>
<tr><td colspan="2">1. Locate relevant, accurate, and clear facts from different sources that help you understand your expert area related to the problem space.
2. Talk in your expert area group about how your expert area affects the way we will solve the the problem and how it affects each of your communities.
3. Develop a plan for how to accurately communicate the following to students in your group:(1) the main ideas about the expert area and (2) how you think your expert area will help us solve the problem better.
4. Develop your plan for communicating to students in your group.
5. Talk in your group about how the areas of expertise are related and how the expert areas will help you solve the problem better.</td></tr>
<tr><td colspan="2">Formative and Summative Assessment</td></tr>
<tr><td colspan="2">How will you assess students' learning in regards to the objectives at the end of Phase 2?</td></tr>
<tr><td colspan="2">see Phase 2 Group Scoring Guide for assessment of group products based on Bereiter's Scheme of Knowledge (levels 3-5)</td></tr>
<tr><td colspan="2">Facilitating Activities</td></tr>
<tr><td colspan="2">What activities do you think are important in Phase 2 to help your students meet the objectives of this phase of the unit and to successfully complete the project?</td></tr>
<tr><td colspan="2">1. Case study analyses of similar projects.</td></tr>
<tr><td colspan="2">Areas of Expertise</td></tr>
<tr><td colspan="2">What areas of expertise are important to the problem that students will investigate in jigsaw groups?</td></tr>
<tr><td>1.
2.
3.
4.
5.</td><td>6.
7.
8.
9.
10.</td></tr>
<tr><td colspan="2">Important Implementation Dates</td></tr>
<tr><td colspan="2">What aspects of the activities in Phase 2 need to be scheduled or arranged ahead of time?</td></tr>
<tr><td colspan="2">1.
2.
3.
4.
5.</td></tr>
<tr><td colspan="2">Resources and Tools</td></tr>
<tr><td colspan="2">What resources and/or tools within your classroom, in your building, or in your community are necessary to help students during Phase 2?</td></tr>
<tr><td colspan="2">1.
2.
3.
4.
5.</td></tr>
</table>

APPENDIX 3: CURRICULUM DESIGIN ASSESSMENT RUBRICS

2. Phase 1 Scoring Guide

The teachers can use the following scoring guide for the group products created by students in response to the critical question, "Why is the problem important to your community?"

The scoring guide assumes one thing: *all groups of students complete the work.* The scoring guide does not include a level to assess non-performance. It does include four levels of performance, ranging from "learning" to "exceptional".

Theoretically, groups that meet the criteria for a project perform at the level, "accomplishing". For some groups, it may be their first time developing a skill; therefore, they might perform at the level, "learning", which means they required additional teacher help at this time of their development. Some students exceed the criteria not necessarily by quantity but by quality, or level of sophisticated response. The last two levels of performance accommodate for these groups of students.

The five components of the scoring guide (Table 11) relate to the five goals of the unit and the objectives of Phase 1 identified in the instructional design template.

Table 10. Phase 3

Critical Question
What is the critical question that students will respond to throughout Phase 3 of the unit?
How can we use the knowledge and skills from Phase 1 and Phase 2 to develop a feasible solution to the problem?
Objectives
Considering the goals of this unit, what are the objectives for students during this phase of the unit? You might consider the performance and knowledge skills required for students to complete the project in Phase 3 with little or no teacher support.
6. Organize data, information and ideas into useful forms (including charts, graphs, outlines) for analysis or presentation. 7. Use technological tools to exchange information and ideas. 8. Assess costs, benefits and other consequences of proposed solutions. 9. Explain reasoning and identify information used to support decisions. 10. Work with others to complete tasks that require a coordinated effort.
Problem-Solving Model
What part of the model for design problem solving best illustrates the problem solving that will occur in the work groups during Phase 3?
How does the problem solving process in this phase of the unit relate to the way experts in related fields solve problems?
Phase 3 Project Criteria
What project will students work collaboratively to complete during Phase 3 that relates to the critical question of this phase of the unit?
After gathering relevant, accurate, and clear facts and statistics about the problem in their community, the group will determine why the problem is important to their community. Their knowledge and ideas for the future of the problem will be shared with other groups.
What criteria will you expect students to complete when they work on the project collaboratively? Consider the objectives you identified for students' learning during Phase 3.

continued on following page

Table 10. Continued

6. Write a description of the problem, including facts and statistics, of the current condition of the problem as well as a prediction for its future. 7. Develop a hypothesis, or a statement describing how your group thinks their strategy would better meet the needs of people in their community. 8. Outline a procedure, or a logically-defined plan of action, about how your group's idea would be implemented. 9. Talk in your group about how to "test the feasibility" of your solution and plan; determine whether your solution could feasibly be implemented. 10. Using the results of your feasibility test, predict the success of your solution and plan and identify short-term and long-term problems that might occur because of your solution and plan of action.
Formative and Summative Assessment
How will you assess students' learning in regards to the objectives at the end of Phase 3?
See Phase 3 Group Scoring Guide for assessment of group products based on Bereiter's Scheme of Knowledge (levels 4-6).
Facilitating Activities
What activities do you think are important in Phase 3 to help your students meet the objectives of this phase of the unit and to successfully complete the project?
1. 2. 3. 4. 5.
Solution Generation
How will you motivate students to develop solutions to the problem that incorporates state and local community needs from Phase 1 and the different areas of expertise from Phase 2?
Important Implementation Dates
What aspects of the activities in Phase 3 need to be scheduled or arranged ahead of time?
1. 2. 3. 4. 5.
Resources and Tools
What resources and/or tools within your classroom, in your building, or in your community are necessary to help students during Phase 3?
1. 2. 3.

Table 11. Phase 1 scoring guide

Understanding the Problem: Phase I Group Assessment Names: ______		
Scoring Guide	**Expected Group Performance**	**Phase 1 Objectives**
Gathering information	Found relevant information about The problem and their community from different sources	Use technological tools and other resources to locate, select, and organize information
Using facts and information	Used the information they gathered to support their ideas and explained how facts and statistics were connected	Explain reasoning and identify information used to support decisions
Presenting the message	While presenting to the class, attempted some eye contact, stood straight and relaxed, and used good volume and were easy to understand	Make oral and visual presentations for a variety of purposes and audiences
Working on a team	Listened to one others' ideas, tried to compromise with each group member, and shared in the responsibility of completing work	Work with others to complete tasks that require a coordinated effort
Setting up the problem	Described a vision for the future of The problem, identified and explained constraints (current limitations) in the The problem system including some that are related to their community	Identify problems and define their scope and elements

2.1 Purpose

After gathering relevant, accurate, and clear facts and statistics about the problem in a particular community, your group will determine why tackling the problems related to the problem is important to your community. A ✓ notes the level at which your group met the standards (See Table 12).

Table 12.

	Learning	Accomplishing	Excelling	Exceptional
Gathering Information	Working with the teacher, you found and used at least two resources.	With some teacher help, you found and used at least two resources and identified if the information gathered was relevant.	You found and used information from different types of resources, determined if the information was relevant, and explained if the information was reliable.	You independently found and used information from different types of resources, judged the relevancy of information, and verified the reliability of information by cross-referencing.
Using Facts and Statistics	You and the teacher worked together to identify and use facts and statistics to support your ideas.	With some teacher assistance, you determined facts and statistics to support your ideas and could explain how some facts and statistics were connected.	You could combine information, make connections between information, and identify relevant prior knowledge to support your ideas.	You independently combined information, made connections between facts and statistics, recognized contradictions, and integrated prior knowledge.
Presenting the Message	You used minimal eye contact, needed few reminders about distracting body movements, yet needed some reminders to speak so all could hear.	You attempted some eye contact, stood straight and relaxed, and used good volume and were easy to understand.	You made eye contact with many audience members, used several appropriate gestures and facial expressions, and used good volume and varied voice for important points in the presentation.	The student made eye contact with all audience members used many appropriate gestures and facial expressions that added to the presentation, and consistently used good volume and varied voice.
Working on a Team	With teacher help, you listened to one others' ideas and shared in the responsibility for completing work.	With encouragement, you listened to one others' ideas, tried to compromise with each group member, and shared in the responsibility of completing work.	You listened to one others' ideas, encouraged all group members to compromise, and actively shared in the responsibility for completing work.	The student listened to others' ideas, motivated all group members to compromise, and proposed a plan for sharing responsibility for completing work.
Setting up the Problem	With teacher support, you identified and/or explained constraints in the problem and /or issue and stated a reasonable strategy for responding to the problem or issue.	As you described a vision for the future of The problem, you identified and explained constraints in the problem system including some that are related to your community.	As you described a specific vision for the future of The problem in your community, you identified and explained constraints in the problem systems that are directly related to your community.	As you described a specific vision for the future of The problem in your community, you identified, explained, and prioritized constraints in the problem system that are directly related to your community, including constraints that are not apparent or are external to the problem system.

2.2 Additional Teacher Feedback

____

____

____

____

3. Phase 2 Scoring Guide

The teachers can use the following scoring guide for the group products created by students in response to the critical question, "How can we use our expertise in an area related to Problem to better understand the problem and develop a feasible solution?"

The scoring guide assumes one thing: *all groups of students complete the work.* The scoring guide does not include a level to assess non-performance. It does include four levels of performance, ranging from "learning" to "exceptional".

Theoretically, groups that meet the criteria for a project perform at the level, "accomplishing". For some groups, it may be their first time developing a skill; therefore, they might perform at the level, "learning", which means they required additional teacher help at this time of their development. Some students exceed the criteria not necessarily by quantity but by quality, or level of sophisticated response. The last two levels of performance accommodate for these groups of students.

The five components of the scoring guide relate to the five goals of the unit and the objectives of Phase 1 identified in the instructional design template.

Table 13. Phase 2 scoring guide

Developing Expertise: Phase 2 Group Assessment Names: ____________		
Scoring Guide	**Expected Group Performance**	**Phase 1 Objectives**
Analyzing information	Described information about the subtopics related to an area of expertise and explained the importance of the area of expertise to the problem	Conduct research to answer questions and evaluate information and ideas
Reasoning	Made recommendations about the area of expertise that were based on logical conclusions concerning the information gathered	Reason inductively from facts and deductively from general premises
Planning the message	Created a plan and reviewed and revised the plan to present the expert workgroup's recommendations to students in the group.	Exchange information, questions and ideas while recognizing the perspectives of others
Managing a team	Compromise to decide what resources to use, what part of the project to complete, and how to use the time allowed	Develop, monitor, and revise plans of action to meet deadlines and accomplish goals
Developing problem solving strategies	Made recommendations about the area of expertise that included justification of the usefulness of the recommendations as strategies for solving the problem and communicated an awareness of community similarities and differences	Examine problems and proposed solutions from multiple perspectives

3.1 Purpose

After deciding to become experts in an area related to the Problem problem, your group will work collaboratively with students from three other classrooms in Missouri to make recommendations about how your expert area offers strategies that might be useful in Phase 3 to develop solutions to the Problem. A ✓ notes the level at which your group met the standards.

Table 14.

	Learning	Accomplishing	Excelling	Exceptional
Analyzing Information	You identified information about the area of expertise that may be relevant, and, working with the teacher, you explained the importance of the area of expertise to the Problem problem.	You described information about the subtopics related to your area of expertise and explained the importance of the area of expertise to the Problem problem.	You described information about the subtopics related to your area of expertise, determined how the subtopics were related, and explained the importance of the area of expertise to the Problem problem.	You described information about the subtopics related to your area of expertise, determined how the subtopics were related, and proposed creative insights into how the area of expertise relates to solving the Problem problem.
Reasoning	You worked with the teacher to make recommendations that were based on the conclusions you made about the information gathered.	You made recommendations about the area of expertise that were based on logical conclusions concerning the information you gathered.	You made recommendations about the area of expertise that were based on logical conclusions concerning the information you gathered, and you stated an awareness of potential intended system or community consequences.	You made recommendations about the area of expertise that were based on logical conclusions concerning the information you gathered, and you describe potential unintended system or community consequences.
Planning the Message	You and the teacher worked together to create a plan to present your expert workgroup's recommendations to students in your group.	You created a plan and reviewed and revised the plan to present your expert workgroup's recommendations to students in your group	You created a plan, reviewed and revised the plan, and developed a quality (accurate and complete) presentation of your expert workgroup's recommendations to students in your group.	You created a plan and continually reviewed and revised the plan to develop a high-quality (accurate, complete, creative, and well-organized) presentation of your expert workgroup's recommendations to students in your group
Managing a Team	With teacher facilitation, you decided what resources to use, what part of the project to complete, and how to use the time allowed.	With assistance, you tried to compromise to decide what resources to use, what part of the project to complete, and how to use the time allowed.	You encouraged the one other to compromise when proposing a plan for sharing resources and responsibilities and effectively using the time allowed.	You motivated one another to compromise by setting an example, and proposed a plan for sharing resources and responsibilities, and delegating work according to one another's strengths.
Developing Problem Solving Strategies	You made recommendations about the area of expertise, and, with teacher questioning, explained the usefulness of the recommendations as strategies for solving the problem.	You made recommendations about the area of expertise that included justification of the usefulness of the recommendations as strategies for solving the problem and communicated an awareness of community similarities and differences.	You made recommendations about the area of expertise that included justification, with validation, of the usefulness of the recommendations as strategies for solving the problem and communicated an awareness of community similarities and differences.	You made recommendations about the area of expertise that included justification, through demonstration of its validity, of the usefulness of the recommendations as strategies for solving the problem and communicated an awareness of community similarities and differences.

3.2 Additional Teacher Feedback

Chapter 14
An Examination of Pre-Service Teachers' Attitudes towards Game-Based Learning

Phu Vu
University of Nebraska at Kearney, USA

Patricia Hoehner
University of Nebraska at Kearney, USA

Scott Fredrickson
University of Nebraska at Kearney, USA

Jane K. Ziebarth-Bovill
University of Nebraska at Kearney, USA

ABSTRACT

This chapter examined pre-service teachers' attitudes toward game-based learning. Research participants included 30 pre-service teachers at a Midwest public university. The research participants took an online course in which game elements such as online mini games as either warm-up or wrap-up activities were integrated. After the course, the researchers analyzed participants' login data and collected their responses to an open online survey. The research results showed that students enjoyed playing games integrated into the course. They spent time playing the games and found them enjoyable and useful. The participants valued the usefulness of integrating games into the classroom. Playing games helped them focus on the topic and review what they had learned from the lecture. They also indicated that they would integrate games into their teaching.

INTRODUCTION

The use of digital or video games in educational settings has appropriately garnered the attention of individuals in education and also in the game industry (Garris, Ahlers, & Driskell, 2002; Squire, 2003; Shaffer, Squire, Halverson, & Gee, 2005; Van Eck, 2006; Moreno-Ger, Burgos, Martinez-Ortiz, Sierra, & Fernández-Manjón, 2008). In November of 2014, the researchers found 2538 articles using the term "game- based learning" or "games in the classroom" when searching the *Chronicle of Higher Education.* That is an increase of more than 2400 from the approximately 100 that Epper, Derryberry, & Jackson (2012) found a mere two years earlier. Epper, Derryberry, & Jackson noted that adoption and institutional implementation of game-based learning is still in the experimental stage in American higher education. In an effort to examine the literature

DOI: 10.4018/978-1-4666-9629-7.ch014

surrounding the use of game-based learning in online learning settings, the researchers found that empirical research related to this topic is fairly limited, especially in regards to pre-service teachers. To this end, via this research project, the researchers aims to examine pre-service teachers' attitudes toward game-based learning by finding the answers to the following research questions.

1. Do pre-service teachers enjoy playing games integrated in the course?
2. What do they think about the roles of games in education?
3. Will they integrate games into their future teaching?

TERMINOLOGY

It is important that the reader understands the definition of game-based learning as the researchers are using it. Salters notes that "when a game is designed with a primary purpose other than entertainment, it is generally labeled a serious game" (Salter, 2011, para. 3) while Dickey (2011) explained "the notion of 'game' as an ambiguous term used to describe structured recreational activities. Typically, components of games include goals, rules, challenges and some form of interaction" (p. 458). Dickey continues the delineation of the term with:while individual definitions may vary, games are primarily recreational, including challenges or some form of stimulation, and typically, in varying degrees, have some type of victory/loss conditions. In contrast, serious games are games designed with a purpose beyond that of recreation or entertainment. Serious games encompass games designed to educate, train, incite activism, and inform. (p. 458)

Differentiating worthwhile educational games from mere entertainment-style games, Hirumi, Appelman, Rieber, & Van Eck (2010) described them as "'serious' and 'educational' [video] games…" (p 27). Torrente, Moreno-Ger, Martinez-Ortiz, & Fernandez-Manjon, (2009) suggested that "game-based learning is a very broad field, with varied initiatives and heterogeneous approaches" (p. 362). For this study, the term game-based learning will include all of the following: serious games, instructional games, instructional video games, instructional computer games, structuring learning experiences in a gaming environment, and education games when used in an educational environment. The definition of game-based learning used in this study is "instructional content presented to learners in a game-based learning environment or activity with the intention of facilitating learning and increasing the knowledge base of the learners."

REVIEW OF LITERATURE

I agree with Rousseau, that the aim of education should be, to teach us rather how to think, than what to think; rather to improve our minds so as to enable us to think for ourselves, than to load the memory with the thoughts of other men (Beattie, 1809, pp. 330-331).

If we teach today as we taught yesterday, we rob our children of tomorrow (Dewey, as cited in Peake, 2010, p. 4).

Both Drs. Dewey and Beattie would likely be distressed if they were to visit schools in the early part of this 21st century. In many schools, they would find rote memorization occurring in a variety of disciplines in the quest to succeed on standardized testing. Due to the requirements of *No Child Left Behind* (NCLB), many teachers have shifted their focus from teaching learners how to learn to scoring well on standardized testing.

Dewey would not be alone in his concern. Holmes (2009) stated "… there is such great pressure for students to receive a certain score or show the amount of growth required that curriculum has become too narrow and focusing only on getting through the test and less on real learning" (p. 7).

The National Center for Fair and Open Testing's report on standardized testing also noted that "... the emphasis on testing yielded little learning progress but caused significant harm. NCLB demonstrated what happens when tests are misused" (para. 2). Those "...consequences include narrowing the curriculum, teaching to the test, pushing students out of school, driving teachers out of the profession, and undermining student engagement and school climate" (para. 2).

It is the researchers' contention that to enable students to not only do well on the required standardized tests, but to actually learn how to learn, game-based learning must be employed. Due to the collaborative efforts of game-based learning, the motivational aspects of game-based learning, and the natures of young adults entering the teaching profession with strong technology-centric backgrounds, the researchers have concluded that pre-service teachers must be prepared to teach game-based learning.

Most of the students from the Generation Z have grown up in a world with computers and multiple forms of technology readily available to them and are therefore very comfortable using technology. Unlike their grandparents and parents, many of these students likely had their nursery rhymes read to them, not from books while sitting on their mothers' laps, but from Kindles or similar devices. Some Gen Zs may have even learned how to interact with their computers playing basic games before learning to walk (Cross-Bystrom, 2010; Fudin, 2012).

Involvement with technology, both socially and academically, has vastly expanded over the past decades. In 2014, friendships and relationships are typically validated on Facebook, Snapchat, Twitter, and/or Instagram. Generation Z students have not known life without social networking or texting. They were reared in social-savvy environments (Cross-Bystrom; Fudin). "To say Generation Z is well-integrated with technology is to say marketing flirts with consumer needs" (Cross-Bystrom, para. 2). She indicates that from an early age, the Gen Zs have honed their digital skills and have taken multitasking to a new level. Concurrently, they can text, listen to music, and browse the Internet. From the very beginning, Generation Zs have grown up in a world that is connected through technology.

According to various studies (Cross-Bystrom, 2010; Fudin, 2012; Gershenfeld, 2011), these Generation Z digital natives have some shortcomings in the classroom. A side effect of their intense involvement in technology is that they depend on instant feedback and their skills with multitasking can lead to limited attention spans. In addition, they are more prone to be less gregarious and more apt to spend time indoors than previous generations.

In addition to the interpersonal relationship issues cited above, Gershenfeld (2011, para. 6) discussed a presidential speech in which President Obama noted Generation Z students encounter a number of educational challenges. They are in schools which are severely underfunded and a quarter of American students are dropping out of school prior to completion of high school, partly because schools are not engaging them. Hence, American students are falling further behind students in other industrial countries.

If indeed American students are lagging behind their international as revealed by poor test results, Fudin (2012) provides suggestions for bridging the gap between Generation Zs affinity for technology and the delivery of instruction. Teaching activities need to provide immediate feedback, provide engagement by planning and then teaching projects and activities which includes online collaboration, using visual media, and "... developing critical thinking and problem solving skills, especially in the use of technology" (para. 5). In addition, Fudin notes that game-based learning helps to "train students to focus their attention on a single task that has depth and complexity... and requires concentrated effort for success" (para. 5).

To address poor test scores, while utilizing Generation Z students' skills in visual learning, the use of video games has increased over the past twenty years (Ruggiero, 2013; Trybus, 2014). Gershenfeld (2012, para. 10) notes game-based-learning "…can be a powerful tool… because there is a unique … alignment between the core elements that make video games so deeply engaging and the best practices that many of the most effective teachers are employing in the classroom."

Trybus (2014) reinforces the power of game-based learning by noting that: "To progress in a game is to learn; where we are actively engaged again, our minds are experiencing the pleasure of grappling with (and coming to understand) a new system. This is true whether the game is considered 'entertainment' (e.g., World of Watercraft) or 'serious' (e.g., an FAA – approved flight simulator) (para. 2).

She states that in an effective game-based learning environment, students are goal oriented. To be successful in the game, they must make choices and perform actions and then benefit or suffer from the consequences.

We make mistakes in a risk-free setting, and through experimentation, we actively learn and practice the right way to do things. This keeps us highly engaged in practicing behaviors and thought processes that we can easily transfer from the simulated environment to real life. Research supports the effectiveness of game-based learning in virtual environments – for example, according to a meta-analysis of flight simulator training effectiveness, simulators combined with aircraft training consistently produced training improvements compared to aircraft–only training (para. 8).

Several publishers have moved into the game-based learning area. Random House has introductory videos for four of their game-based learning programs. In one of them, *Government in Action*, the student/player is a member of Congress attempting to be productive and to get reelected. A second game-based learning program is a management operations game, while a third focuses on using Spanish in a natural setting, and the fourth is on medical technology. They can be accessed at http://www.mhpractice.com and in the researchers' opinions are worth the reader's time to visit.

Motivation is a key component to effective learning. Multiple researchers agree that games are highly motivational (De Freitas, Rebolledo-Mendez, Liarokapis, Magoulas & Poulovassilis, 2010; Dickey, 2011, Eseryel, Law, Ifenthaler, Xun, & Miller, 2014, Fitó-Bertran, Beatriz Hernández-Lara., Serradell-López, 2014; Kapp, 2014; Malone, 1982, Robinson, 2013, Salter, 2013, Hsu & Chiou, 2011). If the reader has ever watched adults and/or children playing digital games such as *Warcraft* or *Clash of Clans*, you will have seen very motivated, intense, and focused concentration being exhibited by the gamers as well as effective collaboration among players. This intensity and the collaboration are major benefits of game-based learning.

In the mid-1970s, one of the researchers, working with high school freshman, used a text-based computer game called "Oregon Trail." The game essentially had students leaving from Missouri in a covered wagon and attempting to arrive in Oregon without "dying" *en route*. Prior to leaving Missouri and along the trail the students had to make a variety of choices. If they took too many farm implements with them, the wagon might be too heavy for the animals pulling the wagons, which would kill the animals and thereby strand the traveler, and hence cause the student to lose the game. If the student or students did not take enough weapons, they could not fight off villains or hunt for meat and they would possibly succumb along the trail, as many actual westbound travelers did. If they took items such as beds and chairs, often they would have to leave them along the trail or they could not get up the hills and across rivers. They would lose once again. If they failed to take enough seed, they would not have anything to plant when they reached Oregon and, again they would lose. The students had to balance what they took with them in order to survive on the trail and after arriving in Oregon. This required planning, analyzing errors, making more effective choices, and learning new behaviors on the part of the gamers/students.

The students were highly engaged in this game, even though it had none of the graphics that today's games have. They would work cooperatively in groups and many would come in before and after school to attempt their westward passage repeatedly. The students learned it was best to make joint decisions, and think of the future goal and not just the next "few minutes." Those problem solving and planning skills were then put to use in other classroom-related activities allowing the students to internalize those skills and hence benefit substantially. Current games have similar results. With today's beautiful graphics and sounds and the processing speeds of computers and online activity, if anything the students become more engrossed, are strongly motivated, and work longer and harder accomplishing the tasks.

Educators are constantly seeking new approaches for the delivery of instruction. A key question facing pre-service teachers and teacher educators is how best to provide instruction that matches the digital savvy backgrounds of their Generation Z students. Online game-based learning is a trend that is shifting the focus from *the digital generation* to a focus on *the interaction generation*. The online aspect is important because, in a gaming environment, it fosters collaboration. Boller (2012) states emphatically that "40 years of research says yes, games are effective learning tools. People learn from games… and they will learn more from a game than from other forms of learning" (para. 1). Games are not only simply "fun" because of the collaborating, the exploring, and naturally the winning along with other aspects, but because they are also motivational, relevant, provide timely feedback, and students are able to repeat aspects of the game as often as they necessary. Kapp (2012, slides 9–11) noted in a keynote speech that gaming provides a 20% increase in the confidence level of learners over traditional classroom instruction and that knowledge retention was 9% higher with game-based learning than with traditional classroom instruction.

Through an email conversation, Jan Hoegh noted the importance of an effective game-based learning environment and noted that games:… incorporate physical movement, inconsequential competition, as well as an opportunity to practice and deepen important academic content." In her experience she found that "…games typically result in higher levels of student engagement … (and) the likelihood for increased learning is greater!" (Hoegh, personal communication, August 26, 2014).

The rapid growth of the gaming industry has impacted students in both academic and nonacademic arenas, but of equal importance is how it has impacted teachers, and how it must impact pre-service teachers. How do teachers view the successes and shortcomings of game-based instruction? According to Marzano (2010) "students play games throughout the day on their computers, the Internet, and their cell phones. One of the few places they don't regularly play games is in their classrooms" (p.1).

It becomes the role of the teacher educators to include game-based learning activities and resources and to provide the necessary preparation to ensure that future teachers can align games with their instructional strategies. According to the research, many teacher preparation institutions have incorporated game-based learning methods; however, a single game inserted within a course is not a systematic approach nor will it be a very valuable/usable experience. To ensure that future teachers view games as valid tools for learning, it is important to understand how pre-service teachers view the role of games. A key question facing pre-service teachers is how best to provide instruction that matches the technological savvy backgrounds of their students.

Although there have been a number of studies about gaming in education, there have been limited studies published about game-based learning and pre-service teachers (Redekopp, 2013). There is a small yet growing body of recent research related to game-based learning and pre-service teachers (Can & Cagiltay, 2006; Pastore & Falvo, 2010; Ruggiero, 2013; Sardone & Devlin-Scherer, 2010; Schrader, Zheng, & Young, 2006). The most recent studies have identified the increasing role that game-based learning plays in the preparation of teachers (Ruggiero). Schrader, Zheng, & Young found that the majority (71.4%) of pre-service teachers surveyed believed game-based learning was a valuable and useful tool in the classroom. In addition, the pre-service teachers surveyed were receptive to using games in their own teaching.

In a similar study, Hsu & Chiou (2011) found that the majority (85.6%) of pre-service teachers planned to use game-based learning in the content area in which they will teach and 82.4% believed that games can be integrated into academic subjects. Hsu & Chiou also reported that 93.6% of the pre-service teachers thought game-based learning motivated students to learn. A majority of pre-service teachers in Hsu and Chiou's study believed game-based learning can help students get better grades (85.6%), promote imagination (88%), encourage higher-level thinking (85.6%), and facilitate problem-solving (75.2%). Although Hsu & Chiou indicated that the majority of pre-service teachers have a favorable outlook for using game-based learning in the classroom, they did find that some pre-service teachers had perceived barriers to educational gaming. Those barriers included a lack of preparation to obtain the skills and knowledge to effectively integrate game-based learning in the classroom.

King, Schneider, Kozdras, Minick, Welsh, Brindley, Feger & Kirby (2013) echo this finding with this statement, "Although pre-service teachers are exposed to a variety of innovative uses of technology…there seems to be a disconnect between the learning of innovative and generative uses of technology and the implementation of these new literacies into traditional classroom settings" (p. 15).

A number of researchers are calling for a more proactive teacher preparation plan to prepare pre-service teachers for 21st Century technology skills and the use of game-based learning in the classroom (Becker, 2007; Devlin-Scherer & Sardone, 2010; Hsu & Chiou, 2011; King, et al., 2013; Li, Lemieux, Vandermeiden & Nathoo, 2013; Redekopp, 2013; Tiong & Yong, 2008). According to Redekopp, "pre-service teachers should be made aware of the potential and the issues of using digital games. Education programs should teach about and model the use of educational games for gaining curricular understanding, building 21C skills, and assessing, and reporting the results" (p. 5).

METHODOLOGY

This descriptive research used two sources of data: students' login data in a learning management system and an online survey to find the answers to the following questions.

1. Do pre-service teachers enjoyed playing games integrated in the course?
2. What do they think about the roles of games in education?
3. Will they integrate games into their future teaching?

In the spring semester 2014, an instructor at a Midwest public university offered an online course in technology integration in classrooms for 30 pre-service teachers, the majority of whom were female students in the age range of 23-26. During the semester, the instructor integrated game elements into his class such as online mini games as either warm-up or wrap-up activities. According to the instructor, the content of those mini games were based on the content of the lectures. For instance, in week three, the course topic was about "Netiquettes and Cyber security". The instructor created mini games which included information related to the topic "Netiquettes and Cyber security." Students were also introduced to different game-based learning platforms and taught how to create web-based simple games for classroom uses. After the course was completed, the researchers got access to his course to collect all of students' login data in the learning management system during the whole semester such as students' time spending in courses, students' time playing games, and students' responses to our online survey upon having the instructor's approval. The online survey had ten questions in different formats, five of which were open-ended questions, two were closed questions, and three were five-point Likert items. Twenty-eight of 30 participants' completed the survey, for a response rate of 93%.

The use of two different data sources in this study allowed for triangulation, which increased the reliability and validity of the findings. According to Maxwell (2005), the triangulation process of collecting information from different sources using a variety of methods reduced the risk that conclusions would reflect systematic biases and allowed a broader understanding of the study's issues. The comparison of the data gathered supported the triangulation process and therefore enhanced internal validity. Efforts to control any threats to theoretical validity were also conducted by collecting and drawing attention to any discrepant data or alternative explanations.

RESULTS

Question 1: Do Pre-Service Teachers Enjoyed Playing Games Integrated in the Course?

To find the answer to this research question, the researchers combined three sub-questions in the online survey with data collected by the learning management system. The first sub-question in the survey was "Did you play warm-up or wrap-up games in the course?" Twenty-eight out of twenty eight participants (100%) said that they played the games in the course. On the scale from Zero (never) to Four (often play the games), twenty-three participants selected item three to indicate how often they played the games, while five participants selected level four. Analyzing participants' responses to the third sub-question "Why did or did not you play the games?" the researchers identified and categorized the following themes: playing games is fun, playing games to experience game integration in the classroom, and playing games to test pre-knowledge or review the lesson. The first theme is "playing games is fun." Thirteen participants indicated that they had fun while playing those games. One of the participants explained in the response, "I thought they were fun games. Games make learning fun. It also helped me when trying to come up with games to play." Another participant said, "I like playing the games because they helped me get started and put a fun twist in learning. I love challenges and trying to figure things out." The second theme that emerged in the participants' responses was "playing games to experience game integration in the classroom." One participant said, "I felt they were part of the required learning. I liked playing them. They were the perfect way to learn a new game, many of which I then made a game with myself." The last theme was "playing games to test pre-knowledge or review the lesson." Many participants indicated that they played the warm-up and wrap-up games because they "found them to be helpful for review of the previous lessons or material that I have just read."

To validate what the participants responded to the online survey, the researchers pulled out students' login data in the learning management system including students' time spending in the course and the total number of students' clicking/playing the games. The researchers found that on average each student hit/played the games at least

Table 1. Participants' responses to the impact of games on their lecture understanding

Number	Min	Max	Median	Mode	Mean	S.D
28	1	5	4	4	4.15	0.85

one time per week. It is noteworthy that this course was conducted on a weekly basis. There were sixteen weeks in a semester. Each week, students were expected to login to the course to learn and complete the assignments. In this study, the researchers used the term "hit" instead of "played" because technically the learning management system could track whether students hit a certain activity or game in the system, but could not tell whether the students actually played the games or not. The researchers made the assumption that if they "hit" the game, they played it. The amount of time maintained by the learning management system tends to support the researchers assumption. The data of students' time spent in the course also showed that students tended to spend more time in the course during the weeks the instructor included the games in the lecture than during the weeks the instructor did not include games into his lecture.

In summary, based on the responses to the three sub-questions and students' login data in the management system, the researchers concluded that students enjoyed playing games integrated into the course. They spent time playing the games and found them enjoyable and useful.

Question 2: What Do They Think about the Roles of Games in Education?

To find the answer to this research questions, the researchers included one open-ended question and one Likert item. The purpose of having one Likert item was to validate what the participants said in the open-ended question. When asked "Do you see any educational values in those games? Please also explain your response." Two participants did not reply to the question. Twenty- six out of 28 participants confirmed that they saw the educational values in the games they played in the course. One of the participants stated, "Yes, all those games were connected to learning in the classroom. It proves that 'gaming' works and is successful and helps students". Another participant said that the educational values that she saw in the games were giving her another way of learning the material through technology. In the same vein, one participant explained that it was a great to way to focus on the topic, and he or she practiced some application before learning about a particular topic. In a Likert item asked the participants to select from "5 - strongly agree" to "1 - strongly disagree" with the statement "Playing those games helped me understand the content of the lecture deeply" the result indicated that the participants agreed that playing those games integrated into the course helped them understand the content of the lectures deeply as shown in Table 1.

Participants' responses to both the open-ended questions and a Likert item showed that pre-service teachers in that course valued the usefulness of integrating games into the classroom. Playing games helped them focus on the topic and review what they had learned from the lecture.

Question 3: Will They Integrate Games into Their Future Teaching?

The researchers included two open-ended questions to find the answer to the above research question. In the first sub-question of "As a future educator, do you think that game-based learning should be included into learning environments?"

twenty-eight out of twenty eight participants (100%) agreed that game-based learning should be integrated into the classroom. Two themes emerged as to why the participants thought that game-based learning should be integrated into the classroom: gaming increases student engagement and gaming makes learning fun.

The first theme was "playing games make students more engaged in the learning process." One student explained that game-based learning increased student engagement and when students are engaged in their education, they increase the quality of their learning. Similarly, another participant stated, "Game based learning helps to keep students engaged in the task at hand. So including them only helps to keep everyone focused."

The second theme was "Games make the learning process fun." According to the participants, students are so in-tune with technology that it gives them the opportunity to feel as though they are playing while learning a lesson. In addition, there is less resistance to learning if the material is covered through games. In the second question, "will you plan to use games in your teaching?" twenty- eight out of 28 participants (100%) indicated that they would integrate games into their teaching. The reason that they would infuse games into their teaching was in line with what they said about why game-based learning should be included into learning environments.

DISCUSSIONS

Findings of the first research question yielded interesting insight into how pre-service teachers perceived game-based learning activities. The result indicated that the students in this research enjoyed playing games that were integrated into the course. They spent additional time playing the games and found them enjoyable and useful. Most of students said that they enjoyed playing the games in the course, which was similar to what was reported by Siwek (2014) and in the Entertainment Software Association Report (2014). Accordingly, women age 18 or older account for a significantly greater portion of the game-playing population (36%) than boys age 18 or younger (17%). It is noted that most of students in this research were female between 23-26 years old.

Findings of the second research question reinforced what had previously been reported about pre-service teachers' attitude toward using games in classroom. In this study, the researchers found that pre-service teachers valued the usefulness of integrating games into the classroom. Similarly, in their study, Schrader, Zheng, & Young (2006) found that the majority (71.4%) of pre-service teachers believed game-based learning was a valuable and useful tool in the classroom. The finding of this study also extended a study by Hsu & Chiou (2011) in which they reported that a majority of pre-service teachers in their study believed game-based learning can help students get better grades (85.6%). In this study, the students indicated that playing games helped them to focus on the topic and review what they had learned from the lecture.

To answer the third research question, all of the research participants agreed that game-based learning should be integrated into the classroom and that they would integrate games into their future teaching. This finding corroborates a study by Hsu & Chiou (2011) that the majority (85.6%) of pre-service teachers in their survey planned to use digital games in their future teaching.

CONCLUSION

Is game-based learning the panacea for which American education has been looking? Will it by itself eliminate all of the problems currently being faced by teachers, schools, and students? It is not deemed likely by the researchers. However, game-based learning is absolutely a positive and impactful methodology that needs to be used in schools. Pre-service teachers have played various forms of electronic games most of their lives and, as this study indicates, they enjoy and are comfortable with using game-based learning activities. The pre-service teachers in this study also view game-based learning's role in education very positively. They also plan to integrate game-based learning into their own classrooms. These pre-service teachers will be the teachers for the next several generations of students and must be very comfortable with and have the expertise creating and developing game-based learning modules. Given the available data from the literature and from the results of this study, pre-service teachers are prepared and willing to engage in both learning with and teaching using game-based learning. As noted, they have played digital games most of their lives and are very adept at gaming. If they are properly prepared, the literature and this study would indicate that pre-service teachers will enthusiastically use game-based learning activities in their future classes. Therefore, it is incumbent upon teacher preparation programs to have a strong focus on game-based learning. Game-based learning is motivational, collaborative, requires focus and tenacity, and will prepare students to know how to think instead of just what to think. Pre-service teachers are ready and willing to play and teacher education programs need to prepare them for the classrooms they will enter.

REFERENCES

Beattie, J. (1809). *Remarks on the utility of classical learning*. Philadelphia: Hopkins and Earle.

Becker, K. (2007). Digital game-based learning, once removed: Teaching teachers. *British Journal of Educational Technology*, *38*(3), 478–488. doi:10.1111/j.1467-8535.2007.00711.x

Boller, S. (2012, October 20). *Game-based learning – why does it work?* Bottom-line Performance. Retrieved from http://www.bottomlineperformance.com/

Can, G., & Cagiltay, K. (2006). Turkish prospective teachers' perceptions regarding the use of computer games with educational features. *Journal of Educational Technology & Society*, *9*(1), 308–321.

Cross–Bystrom, A. (2010, August 20). What you need to know about Generation Z. iMedia Connections. Retrieved from http://www.imediaconnection.com/content/27425.asp

De Freitas, S., Rebolledo-Mendez, G., Liarokapis, F., Magoulas, G., & Poulovassilis, A. (2010). Learning as immersive experiences: Using the four-dimensional framework for designing and evaluating immersive learning experiences in a virtual world. *British Journal of Educational Technology*, *41*(1), 69–85. doi:10.1111/j.1467-8535.2009.01024.x

Devlin-Scherer, R., & Sardone, N. (2010). Digital simulation games for social studies classrooms. *The Clearing House: A Journal of Educational Strategies, Issues and Ideas*, *83*(4), 138–144. doi:10.1080/00098651003774836

Dickey, M. D. (2011). Murder on Grimm Isle: The impact of game narrative design in an educational game-based learning environment. *British Journal of Educational Technology*, *42*(3), 456–469. doi:10.1111/j.1467-8535.2009.01032.x

Entertainment Software Association. (2014, September 25). *Millions of Americans embrace video games on mobile devices: New study reveals mobile games attract new players to video game community*. Retrieved from http://www.theesa.com/newsroom/release_detail.asp?releaseID=236

Epper, R. M., Derryberry, A., & Jackson, S. (2012, August 9). Game-based learning: Developing and institutional strategy. Educause. Retrieved from http://www.educause.edu/

Eseryel, D., Law, V., Ifenthaler, D., Xun, G., & Miller, R. (2014). An Investigation of the Interrelationships between Motivation, Engagement, and Complex Problem Solving in Game-based Learning. *Journal of Educational Technology & Society*, *17*(1), 42–53.

FairTest. (2012, July). How Standardized Testing Damages Education. Retrieved from http://fairtest.org/how-standardized-testing-damages-education-pdf

Fitó-Bertran, A., Beatriz Hernández-Lara, A., & Serradell-López, E. (2014). Comparing student competences in a face-to-face and online business. *Computers in Human Behavior*, *30*, 452–459. doi:10.1016/j.chb.2013.06.023

Fudin, S. (2012, March 29). Gen Z & What does it mean in your classroom? Inside USC Rossier Online Blog. Retrieved from http://rossieronline.usc.edu/gen-z-what-does-it-mean-in-your-classroom-2

Garris, R., Ahlers, R., & Driskell, J. E. (2002). Games, motivation, and learning: A research and practice model. *Simulation & Gaming*, *33*(4), 441–467. doi:10.1177/1046878102238607

Gershenfeld, A. (2011, April 3). Game-based learning: Hype vs. versus reality. Retrieved from http://www.huffingtonpost.com/education/

Hirumi, A., Appelman, R. L., Rieber, L. P., & Van Eck, R. (2010). Preparing Instructional Designers for Game-Based Learning: Part 2. *Techtrends. Linking Research & Practice to Improve Learning*, *54*(1), 19–27.

Holmes, S. E. (2009) *Standardized testing and the No Child Left Behind Act: A failing attempt at reform.* Retrieved from http://www.ecu.edu/cs-lib/awards/upload/Sarah_Holmes_First_Place.pdf

Hsu, T. Y., & Chiou, G. F. (2011). Pre-service teachers' awareness of digital game-supported learning. In M. Koehler & P. Mishra (Eds.), *Proceedings of Society for Information Technology & Teacher Education International Conference 2011* (pp. 2135-2141). Chesapeake, VA: AACE.

Kapp, K. M. (2012, 2 Oct). The gamification of learning: What research says about simulations & serious games. Retrieved from http://www.slideshare.net/kkapp/spbt-kapp-keynote2012

Kapp, K. M. (2014, 11 Sep). Abstracts of Three Meta-Analysis Studies of Serious Games. Kapp Notes Blog. Retrieved from http://karlkapp.com/abstracts-of-three-meta-analysis-studies-of-serious-games

King, J., Schneider, J., Kozdras, D., Minick, V., Welsh, J., Brindley, R., & Kirby, A. et al. (2013). The multiple ways technology supports pre-service teacher education: A foray into multimedia literacies. *Journal of Reading Education*, *38*(3), 14–20.

Li, Q., Lemieux, C., Vandermeiden, E., & Nathoo, S. (2013). Are you ready to teach secondary mathematics in the 21st Century? A study of Pre-service teachers' digital game design experience. *Journal of Research on Technology in Education*, *45*(4), 309–337. doi:10.1080/15391523.2013.10782608

Malone, T. W. (1982). Toward a theory of intrinsically motivating instruction. *Cognitive Science*, *4*, 333–369.

Marzano, R. J. (2010). The art and science of teaching/using games to enhance student achievement. *Educational Leadership*, *5*(67), 71–72.

Moreno-Ger, P., Burgos, D., Martinez-Ortiz, I., Sierra, J., & Fernández-Manjón, B. (2008). Educational game design for online education. *Computers in Human Behavior*, *24*(6), 2530–2540. doi:10.1016/j.chb.2008.03.012

Pastore, R., & Falvo, D. (2010). Video games in the classroom: Pre-service and in-service teachers' perceptions of games in K-12 classrooms. *International Journal of Instructional Technology and Distance Learning*, *7*(12), 49–57.

Peake, J. (2010). If we teach today as we taught yesterday, we rob our children of tomorrow. *The Agricultural Education Magazine*, *83*(3), 4.

Redekopp, R. (2013). Teaching digital games in pre-service teacher education. *International Journal of Technology and Inclusive Education*, *2*(1), 124–129.

Robison, W. (2013, August). Stimulation, Not simulation: An alternate approach to history teaching games. *The History Teacher*, *46*(4), 577–588. Retrieved from http://www.societyforhistoryeducation.org/A13Preview.html

Ruggiero, D. (2013). Video games in the classroom: The teacher point of view. Paper presented at the *Games for Learning workshop of the Foundations of Digital Games conference*, Chania, Greece.

Salter, A. (2011, September 22). *Games in the classroom (part 2)* [Web log article]. Retrieved from http://chronicle.com/blogs/profhacker/games-in-the-classroom-part-2/36075

Salter, A. (2013, January 28). *Make games in the classroom with Inform 7.* [Web log article]. Retrieved from http://chronicle.com/section/Home/5

Sardone, N., & Devlin-Scherer, R. (2010). Teacher candidate responses to Digital games: 21st Century skills development. *Journal of Research on Technology in Education*, *42*(4), 409–425. doi:10.1080/15391523.2010.10782558

Schrader, P. G., Zheng, D., & Young, M. (2006). Teachers' perceptions of video games: MMOGs and the future of Pre-service teacher education. *Innovate: Journal of Online Education*, *2*(3), 1-10. Retrieved from http://www.slideshare.net/rredekopp/ijtie-the-use-of-games-in-preservice-teacher-education

Shaffer, D. W., Squire, K. R., & Halverson, R. (2005). Video Games and the Future of Learning. *Phi Delta Kappan*, *87*(2), 104-111.\Siwek, S. (2014) Video games in the 21st century: The 2014 report. Retrieved from http://www.theesa.com/facts/pdfs/VideoGames21stCentury_2014.pdf

Tiong, K., & Yong, S. (2008). Learning through computer game design: Possible success (or failure) factors. *Proceedings of the 16th International Conference on Computers in Education*, Taipei, Taiwan.

Trybus, J. (2014). *Game-based learning: What it is, why it works, and where it's going* (New Media Institute White Paper). Retrieved from http://www.newmedia.org/game-based-learning--what-it-is-why-it-works-and-where-its-going.html

KEY TERMS AND DEFINITIONS

Gamed-Based Learning: Instructional content presented to learners in a game-based learning environment or activity with the intention of facilitating learning and increasing the knowledge base of the learners.

Pre-Service Teachers: Students admitted to a teacher education program.

Section 3
Discipline Cases

Chapter 15
Using a Live Simulation to Teach Human Anatomy and the Diagnostic Process to High School Students

Debra C. Burkey Piecka
Wheeling Jesuit University, USA

Manetta Calinger
Wheeling Jesuit University, USA

ABSTRACT

This chapter describes and defines role-play simulations. Reviews of two undergraduate role-play studies highlight the advantages and benefits of using simulations. Few secondary students participate in science or STEM role-plays during their high school careers. This chapter portrays the CyberSurgeons live simulation where teams of students use critical thinking skills and scientific knowledge to solve emergency medical problems. During their virtual mission students become part of an emergency medical team aboard a National Institutes of Health (NIH) mercy ship traveling up the Amazon River. Authors describe CyberSurgeons' learning goals, design features, mission day experiences, and the summative evaluation. Findings from the summative evaluation indicate that the CyberSurgeons program provides an authentic context for high school students to apply their knowledge of biology, physiology, and the diagnostic process to analyze data and make decisions as professionals in the biomedical field. Recommendations and future research considerations close this chapter.

INTRODUCTION

This chapter aligns with Strand 2, Pedagogical Concepts and Related Practice, and identifies pedagogical aspects of learning in the *CyberSurgeons* live, role-based, clinical simulation for high school students. The chapter describes the pedagogical concepts and related best practices for the online simulation learning goals and design/development, simulation mission preparation, mission day, literature review, summative evaluation results, and recommendations for research about role-playing simulations.

DOI: 10.4018/978-1-4666-9629-7.ch015

Innovative ways that teach students about real-world applications of anatomy and physiology, biology, and health professions in a cost-effective, authentic manner are needed to prepare high school students for biomedical careers. Immersing students in didactic content while providing limited hands-on experience can teach content but does not inform high school students about the complexities of clinical diagnosis and treatment involved in the biomedical workplace. To advance the research literature about the use of role-playing simulations in high school science classrooms, this chapter provides a literature review about the use of role-based simulations in secondary classrooms. The review highlights two role-play studies conducted at the undergraduate level (one medical student and one interdisciplinary health) to describe the benefits and advantages of using simulations. The next section of the chapter focuses on multiple aspects of the *CyberSurgeons* live-simulation experience including learning goals and design/development, simulation design features, facilitator's programming features, simulation mission preparation, simulation/mission day, the summative evaluation, and potential conditions that may negatively impact *CyberSurgeons*. This chapter closes with recommendations, future research directions, and the conclusion. After reviewing this chapter, readers will be able to

1. Define a role-play simulation.
2. Discuss the benefits and advantages of using role-play simulations in secondary science classrooms.
3. Understand the development and design features of the *CyberSurgeons* live simulation.
4. Review the summative evaluation results for *CyberSurgeons* and realize the challenges for evaluation of online, role-playing simulations in secondary science classrooms.
5. Identify opportunities for introducing science simulations into high school curriculum.

BACKGROUND

What Is a Role-Play Simulation?

A role-play simulation is a form of experiential learning that provides students with an active opportunity to practice and apply new content and skills in a real situation (Shaw, 2012). Good simulations must contain high levels of integration of the material in addition to interactivity between the facilitator/teacher and the student (Wheeler, 2006). High levels of interactivity result in more advanced levels of learning using Bloom's (Bloom & Krathwohl, 1956) taxonomy criteria (Wheeler, 2006). Studies show that role-playing simulations are an effective instructional method to give students the opportunity to engage in higher-level learning (Silvia, 2010). During a role-play simulation, students transition from a passive learning style that is more common in traditional lecture to a more active style. It is important to clarify the students' responsibility in role-playing simulations. In this chapter no consideration is given in situations where students play parts in scientific phenomena such as electrons in an electrical circuit, molecules from food in digestion (Aubusson, Fogwill, Barr, & Perkovic, 1997), or human chromosomes in mitosis and meiosis (Chinnici, Yue, & Torres, 2004). The simulation scenarios discussed in the literature review pertain to situations where students analyze and synthesize data in order to complete the tasks designed for their role play.

During role play, students develop their problem-solving skills by taking on different roles and confronting unstructured problems in scenarios involving the content and given roles. Clapper (2010) discussed the pedagogical advantages of using role-play simulations as "returning to teaching for understanding" (p. 39). Classroom simulations provide an opportunity for students to problem solve, think critically, and make decisions during the play of near-real situations and complex systems (Clapper, 2010; Silvia, 2010). As role-play simulation advances, students evaluate and synthesize data, decisions, and consequences based on their prior knowledge. Students complete tasks to learn how the real-world system functions and practice making decisions within the scenario.

High School Students' Role-Play Simulation Experiences

Students participate in few science or STEM role-play simulations during their high school careers. However, high school role-play simulations in social studies and business/economics classes occur more frequently. Examples of role-play exercises in social studies include the dramatization of pivotal moments (e.g., Constitutional Convention of 1787 [Maloy & LaRoche, 2010] and Byford's (2012) Iron Curtain and Berlin Wall); re-enactment of key events such as the 1955 Montgomery Bus Boycott (Maloy & LaRoche, 2010) and constitutional convention (Pavao, 2009); and organization of mock trials or senates (Carnegie Corporation of New York and The Center for Information and Research on Civic Learning and Engagement [CIRCLE], 2003; Maloy & LaRoche, 2010). Social studies teachers employ role-playing simulations as a strategy to address the topics of diversity, group identity, and citizenship education (Banks, 2008). The *Guardian of Democracy: The Civic Mission of Schools* (Gould & Annenberg Public Policy Center, 2011) report identified several proven practices that constitute a well-rounded, quality civic-learning experience for students. One of the proven practices specifically identified role-play simulations as a way to encourage students' participation in democratic processes and procedures that can "lead to heightened political knowledge and interest" (Gould & Annenberg Public Policy Center, 2011, p. 34).

Many high school students participate in business or economics-related simulations during their secondary education. Stock market games such as The Stock Market Game (The SIFMA Foundation, 2013) and National Stock Market Simulation (StockTrack Global Portfolio Simulations, 2014) introduce students to the stock market, allowing them to buy and sell stocks, bonds, and mutual funds within a mock portfolio. Economics classroom simulations inform students about issues surrounding wages, budgeting, banking, supply and demand, and poverty. In *The Organic Goodie Simulation* (Bigelow & Diamond, 2007), an economics exercise, teachers select students to work on the Organic Goodie Machine. Students earn wages while working on the machine and producing the perfect food (yields no waste or emissions and requires no soil or sunlight). Working students receive money to buy goodies; unemployed students make no wages to buy goodies. In 2008, an Executive Order created a President's Advisory Council on Financial Literacy whose charge was to improve financial literacy among all Americans (The Department of the Treasury, 2009). In order to meet financial education mandates, many states include role-play simulations as a method for addressing financial literacy standards in high school.

Why do high school role-playing simulations focus mostly on social studies and business/finance topics? Where are the science and STEM role-playing simulations? The *CyberSurgeons* curriculum provides a unique opportunity for students in anatomy and physiology, biology, and health courses to learn about patient diagnosis and treatment, clinical trials research, and patient assignment to clinical trials.

Role-play simulation in clinical education occurs frequently at the undergraduate and graduate levels. Multiple research studies of role-play simulations exist in the medical, nursing, health care, and clinical education studies. In order to illustrate and capture the use of role-playing simulations and their impact, two research studies from undergraduate healthcare students are highlighted in this chapter. One study focuses on interdisciplinary undergraduate health students and the other on third-year undergraduate medical students.

Health-care professionals face increasing pressure to work across discipline borders to better patient outcomes. To better understand the impact of interdisciplinary collaboration for patient care and diagnosis, McCormick, Burton, and Werts (2010) examined the effectiveness of a case-study and simulation curriculum to teach students enrolled in several health programs about asthma care and patient education. The purpose of the study was to examine what effect the interdisciplinary curriculum had on students' knowledge, confidence, and satisfaction level about their ability to care for a patient with asthma and obesity. The study used a pretest-posttest design to compare the difference in means between a control and an experimental group of students. The tests focused on the analysis, synthesis, and evaluation levels of the cognitive domain; the tests were used to measure the student's critical thinking knowledge about the care and management of a respiratory patient before and after the intervention of current clinical asthma guidelines and physical examination findings for patents with both asthma and obesity. Participants were undergraduates at a college of health professionals located in the Mideastern United States.

The interdisciplinary group consisted of 17 students in their first year as nursing, respiratory therapy, and health education. The control group included 17 students from the health assessments class. Students received content in the form of an online seminar. Part of the seminar included a clinical scenario that described a case study involving a male patient with an acute asthma exacerbation and comorbid condition of obesity. Students reviewed the online curriculum content before attending their first face-to-face class. Once the course started, students received a PowerPoint-delivered, clinical lecture material, including content on four topics:

1. Basic facts about asthma and its causes,
2. Asthma medications and treatments,
3. Nutritional guidelines, and
4. Physical assessment techniques and past medical history.

After the PowerPoint presentation, students participated in clinical-simulation experience, using a human patient simulator and role play. The role-play exercise included four roles of primary nurse, student, family member, and observer. Students questioned the patient and family members about asthma severity during the admission history. Students had telephone access to call in orders and report physical changes. They also charted rate and quality of respirations. Students debriefed and groups of students worked in small groups to develop asthma actions plans for the patient's discharge. Repeated-measures, paired, and independent sample *t* tests were performed to determine between and within-group differences. The mean simulation satisfaction rating for the interdisciplinary group was higher than for the nurses-only group. Additionally, the interdisciplinary group showed greater confidence in being able to coordinate care and educate patients about asthma.

Radomski and Russell (2010) investigated how 8, third-year undergraduate medical students could learn how to think like doctors in their early educational experiences. Using a model of collaborative integrated case learning (ICL) and simulated clinical reasoning, the study used a sociocultural perspective to investigate the reflective learning interactions and practices of clinical thinking that emerged in the ICL environment. The study also explored how the undergraduate medical students perceived their ICL experiences in relation to the clinical experiences in the faced in the hospital setting in Australia. Radomski and Russell used a qualitative case study methodology following the eight students through their school year. Data collection methods included individual and group interviews, along with observations and document/artifact analysis. Narrative and content methods were used to analyze data.

In the Radomski and Russell simulation, the simulation opened with a short narrative scenario of a doctor/patient interview. Simulation roles (Radomski & Russell, 2010) included

- The doctor is played by two students. As the doctor, students verbalized their thinking processes and formulated questions they could ask to the patient, each other and the rest of the group. Sometimes the doctor's role included summation of the case so far in order to practice synthesis and focused case presentations on the fly.
- The patient is played by the clinical educator. The educator played the role of both the simulated patient and clinician facilitator, switching between the roles to provide feedback to the students as the scenario progressed. The clinical educator also mediated and redirected students' issues by asking reflective questions such as, "What were you thinking about when you mentioned…? Could you follow that idea through from a cardiovascular point of view? Why did you order liver function tests when there wasn't any indication of that? How useful is this X-ray? Would you do any investigations to sort this situation out?" (Radomski & Russell, 2010, p. 255).
- The scribe is played by a student. The scribe captures a detailed patient history/ health story. The scribe also structures parts of the differential diagnosis as it progresses and participated in the clinical discussion.
- Participant–observers are played by the students. The participant observers pose clinical questions, differential diagnosis, and reflective comments when the doctor (clinical educator) invites their input during lag periods in the doctor/patient interview or generation of diagnosis options.

Case selections increased in complexity as the academic year progressed, moving from the beginning focus on diagnosis with progression to patient management. Radomski and Russell (2010) described the process,

The patient/doctor interactions offer the beginnings of an 'interesting clinical story' that the students 'reconstruct', analsze and subsequently 'unravel' together, by taking different clinical reasoning roles and reflective thinking positions within the ICL environment…As the ICL session proceeds, uncertainties related to the simulated patient's health issues are revealed and discussed. A working differential is generated, investigations proposed, copies of X-rays and test results interpreted and potential diagnosis pathways justified by 'the doctor' in consultation with the group. (p. 254)

The role-playing simulation for medical students displayed an emergent and collaborative process of rehearsal and deliberations for successful clinical decision-making and did not focus on a set time for debriefing. Instead, the simulation integrated feedback into the process (Radomski & Russell, 2010).

Results from the participant interviews revealed the authentic and realistic nature of the role-play simulation for the students. Students commented about the opportunity to close the gap between theoretical learning and application of patient diagnosis and management. Radomski and Russell (2010) termed this theme "becoming a doctor" (p. 259). In her interview, Jacqui (pseudonym) discussed having the chance to practice finding the correct clinical decisions,

I've found it's helpful …not just when it comes to talking to a patient but also when you're presenting a case to another doctor, or if you're listening to a presentation. You know what important bits to pull out… (Radomski & Russell, 2010, p. 259)

Another theme that emerged from the study of undergraduate medical students focused on putting clinical reasoning in context. Radomski and Russell (2010) recounted how Jacqui identified a connection between the scribe role's medical note taking requirements and high level synthesis of the content. Several students mentioned how the role-play simulation mimicked meeting a patient for the first time. Krysten contributed,

In the ICL sessions ... the patient comes in with something that could be a lot of different things. You get back negative test results that don't help you very much and it's sort of what it would be like in real life. The patient's not perfect, the situation's not perfect and it's not that easy. It's a narrative but its got twists and turns. It's good that way. (Radomski & Russell, 2010, p. 259)

The final themes identified by Radomski and Russell (2010) centered on connecting knowing with doing and the idea of integrated case learning "'hot seats' and 'rehearsals': learning to think, talk and 'be' like doctors" (p. 260). Two students mentioned having transformational moments in their clinical learning where their previous, inert theoretical knowledge became useful and mobilized in the application of their content. Adam (pseudonym) remarked about the role-playing simulations practical support and cognitive scaffolding design that included a second student in the shared doctor role,

It takes a little bit of pressure off you. If you have a mind-blank you just stop and ask the other doc, or pass. (Radomski & Russell, 2010, p. 261).

In other words, students felt that the role-play design scaffolded hot-seat moments when they presented patient histories or diagnoses.

These two clinical research studies demonstrate many of the benefits and advantages identified by role-play, simulation researchers. First, they realize learning objectives that are not easily communicated through lecture format (Doody & Condon, 2013; Druckman & Ebner, 2013, Smith & Boyer, 1996). Students received scaffolded support in the forms of supplemental data such as lab reports and guidelines along with facilitator-led guiding questions. These role-play exercises simulate complex processes of admitting patients for diagnosis and treatment (Jeffries, 2005; Shaw, 2012) and decision making (Shaw, 2012; Silvia, 2010). Students in both research studies were engaged and motivated to learn (Aldrich, 2009; Barab & Dede, 2007; Shaw, 2012). Feedback from the student participants in Radomski and Russell's (2010) study indicated that they perceived the role-playing process to be significantly more engaging than their problem-based learning experiences.

Both studies reached different levels of learners. McCormick et al.'s (2010) study extended to multiple levels of learners in the interdisciplinary fields of nursing, respiratory therapy, and health education. Whether the simulation reaches different grades of learners, students majoring in different disciplines, or different professions, role-playing activities provide a way to reach a mixed level of learners (Clapper, 2010; Shaw, 2012). Radomski and Russell (2010) and McCormick et al. (2010) reported that students participated in authentic communities of practice (Barab & Dodge, 2008) while improving their cognitive learning (Barab & Dede, 2007; Clapper, 2010; Shaw, 2012) during the role-playing simulations. In the Radomski and Russell study, Ann (pseudonym) reported that

In the course we get surprisingly little practise at actually learning what a doctor does and getting a patient for the first time and working through it. The ICL [role-playing simulation] process is pretty much the only practise we get at doing that. (2010, p. 258).

Ben, a student in Radomski and Russell's study, noted his shift from a passive observer position to active learner, clinical thinker, and real doctor who can recognize patterns of clinical reasoning in this statement:

You apply your ICL [role-play simulation] skills in clinical situations and it means that you pick up things you wouldn't have picked up before. You actually question why. Why would you do this test? It encourages you to think critically all the time... rather than being a passive observer. (p. 260)

Ben's experience demonstrated that role-playing simulations provide students with the ability to perform tasks that students would otherwise not experience (Hennessy, Deaney, & Ruthven, 2006). The same concept holds true for McCormick et al.'s (2010) study where interdisciplinary health-care students worked in simulation teams to care for patients. Likewise, both role-play studies provided students with career awareness information unavailable to them without the simulation (Piecka et al., 2012).

As in another study about improvement in student self-efficacy for students participating in simulations (Goldenberg, Andrusyszyn, & Iwasiw, 2005), the McCormick et al. (2010) and Radomski and Russell (2010) research showed improved students' perceptions about their capacities (self-efficacy) to deal with clinical situations involving patient diagnosis and management after participating in the simulations. McCormick et al. (2010) noted that the interdisciplinary group of health students expressed more confidence in their abilities to organize care and educate their patients about asthma. They also recommended that interdisciplinary simulations be used to improve confidence in nursing and allied health students and to succeed in clinical-based settings. Medical students in the Radomski and Russell's (2010) study felt better about their abilities to practice *doctor talk*, publicly justify their diagnostic thinking and reasoning, and deal with patients. While Radomski and Russell did not talk directly about students' improved self-efficacy, the students' reflections indicate their improved perceptions. In line with improved self-efficacy, the McCormick et al. (2010) and Radomski and Russell (2010) studies showed that students improved and practiced affective learning (Shaw, 2012) during their interactions with facilitators and patients. The interdisciplinary health and nursing students displayed concern for their patient's asthma and general health concerns (McCormick et al., 2010). The interdisciplinary students also practiced their team building and collaboration skills with other health-related students. The Radomski and Russell (2010) study did not emphasize affective learning; however, in reading the students reflections, the confidence expressed by the students after participating in the role-play situation in addition to the appreciation for the experience and passion about becoming doctors emerged from the students' reflections.

While researchers stress the importance of providing a debriefing and feedback period of the learning process for role-based simulations (Doody & Condon, 2013), the two selected literature reviews did not discuss feedback in great detail McCormick et al. (2010) mentioned that students debriefed after their simulation experience but added little additional detail. The Radomski and Russell (2010) research emphasized the feedback given by the clinical facilitator during the role play through the use of guided prompts.

Students in the McCormick et al. (2010) and Radomski and Russell (2012) created an engaging, constructivist classroom (Shaw, 2012). Nursing, respiratory therapy, and nutrition students learned from each other during their experiential role play. Their collaboration during the simulation's task-oriented activities served as a tool for joint construction of knowledge (McCormick et al., 2010). Medical students also identified transformational moments when their inert theoretical knowledge became mobilized in meaningful ways. They also commented about the co-construction of clinical meaning and problem-solving dialogue as a central feature of the role play. Students reflected on moments when individual learning transitioned to group-level learning through "social interaction while using domain specific language/clinical tools [doctor talk] and mediation" (Radomski

& Russell, 2012, p. 263). Students' recognition of transformational experiences in knowledge and skills points to the creation of an engaging, constructivist classroom.

CYBERSURGEONS[1]

Online Role-Playing Simulation Experience

Via Internet connection and video camera, students connect live with a chief medical officer (CMO) played by an educator at a simulation center at a university. Together, teams of students use critical-thinking skills and scientific knowledge to solve emergency medical problems. During their virtual mission, students become part of an emergency medical team aboard a National Institutes of Health (NIH) Mercy ship traveling up the Amazon River. The ship is equipped with high-tech hospital equipment and medical research capabilities. Students prepare for the mission through lesson plans that address biology, anatomy, and physiology, or human health standards and clinical trials. Each mission supports from 5 to 32 students.

Learning Goals and Design/Development

The goals of the *CyberSurgeons* simulation are threefold: to increase science literacy among high school students taking biology, anatomy and physiology, or related classes; to promote career awareness for biomedical fields within the target population; and to increase students' knowledge about clinical trials. The design and development of *CyberSurgeons* employed the analysis, design, development, implementation, and evaluation (ADDIE) model to guide the instructional designers in their instructional decision making (Branch, 2008). The project meets high school contexts of varying lengths of time for class schedules and can be customized for different time constraints. By varying the patient cases, the simulation can also be modified to meet the needs of different student groups according to the type of science class and differing grade and ability levels. *CyberSurgeons* provides a realistic context to study human body systems where students are immersed in the clinical environment of translational science and bridging textbook concepts to authentic health issues. Science content covered in the simulation includes the diagnostic process, clinical-trial protocol, human anatomy and physiology, and clinical science. Development of the simulation's task analysis aligns with national and state standards and supports identification of learning objects, activities, and assessment.

CyberSurgeons' design uses a combination of innovative tools such as online database simulation; communications resources for diagnosis, treatment, and follow-up; images of medical and surgical conditions; selective push/pull strategies from the facilitator; inquiry prompts; and clinical trials' database to create a collaborative and authentic environment where students use critical thinking skills and scientific knowledge to diagnose and treat the researchers aboard the Mercy ship as well as the indigenous Amazon population.

CyberSurgeons Simulation Design Features

The simulation was designed to address the learning objectives as stated in the funded proposal and also specifically designed to meet research-based objectives to deliver more effectively science content and science-career motivation to high school students. Although there are many articles concerning projects with research-based science learning objectives, there are few that address educational projects that utilize features to optimize learning science through a live simulation.

Multiple features were considered and incorporated into the *CyberSurgeons* live-simulation design to accomplish the goals and objectives. Key to design and development decisions was keep-

Figure 1. Image of fictional patient Cassandra Lighting chosen by Team Alpha
Screenshot from CyberSurgeons program. Copyright 2015 by the Center for Educational Technologies, Wheeling Jesuit University.

ing in mind the needs and characteristics of the target audience in order to produce a simulation that *delivered real science content* and *emphasized critical thinking skills* in the most effective way. The content focused on human anatomy and physiology, the diagnostic process, disease and health conditions, and clinical trials. The critical thinking skills were embedded in each student specialty on each team.

The core of *CyberSurgeons*' science-content delivery is the patient case. Each patient case immerses the students in a different scenario that puts the outcome of a patient's care in the hands of the student team. It is stressed through pre-mission preparation, the scene-setting introduction by the Chief Medical Officer, and student instructions that the team is responsible for the medical care of the patient chosen from the waiting room by the team case manager. Student interest and engagement in the patient is strengthened through an image of the patient in the chart (see Figure 1).

Images of patients on the medical chart can be enlarged to cover the chart for increased student engagement with each patient in their care. This young girl (see Figure 1) has a painful infection on her left leg. Students view the image of the ruptured cyst (see Figure 2) included in the physical exam results on the chart, order lab cultures,

Figure 2. A ruptured MRSA cyst. "Mrsa_cyst_exploded.jpg," by Jbtank
http://commons.wikimedia.org/wiki/File:Mrsa_cyst_exploded.jpg. Copyright 2009 by Wikipedia Commons, Creative Commons.

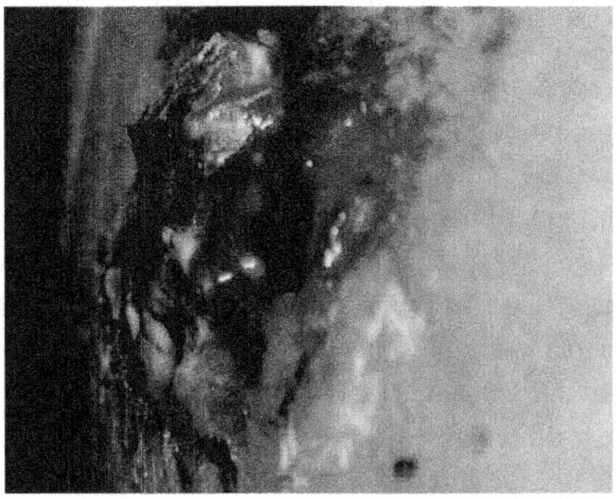

and find out that she has an antibiotic-resistant infection. Treatment is described in their Medi-Net resource, and students finish the case by possibly recommending inclusion in a clinical trial.

The Chief Complaint, a mini-scenario for each patient, also includes details that allow the student to connect to the patient's life. For instance, one team chooses a patient from the waiting room and finds out that bats, living in the family's hut, often bite family members at night, a common occurrence in some villages. Their patient, a 5 year-old boy, has rabies.

Another team chooses a young man from the waiting room who is brought in complaining of pain from multiple injuries. Students learn from the medical chart that the patient is vacationing in the Amazon and has fallen from a makeshift bungee cord hitting several tree limbs on the way down, injuring his right ankle, left shoulder, and left wrist. He is somewhat intoxicated, but is sobering up quickly, and still feels intense pain. Student specialists order tests and review images of x-rays of each fracture. Images show human bone anatomy for the injuries described and reports from the radiologist use anatomical terms (see Figure 3). In addition to learning more anatomy and seeing x-rays of fractures, students are given the subtle message that alcohol played a significant role in this painful accident that was entirely avoidable and most high school students can, in some way, relate to this young man's predicament.

In another case, a team chooses a man who comes in complaining of abdominal pain, nausea, and vomiting; the team goes through the diagnostic process to find out he has dead gut syndrome. Students learn what dead gut syndrome is and must become more aware of intestinal structure and function to work the case.

Each case has images that are delivered through the student interface, which includes a medical chart and a PDA (personal digital assistant) device that delivers additional information students use to work the case or to receive information about the disease or condition.

Figure 3. A triplane fracture of the ankle as seen on plain X ray. "TriplanefractureXa" by James Heilman, MD
http://commons.wikimedia.org/wiki/File:TriplanefractureXa.png#mediaviewer/File:TriplanefractureXa.png. Copyright 2011 by Wikimedia Commons, Creative Commons.

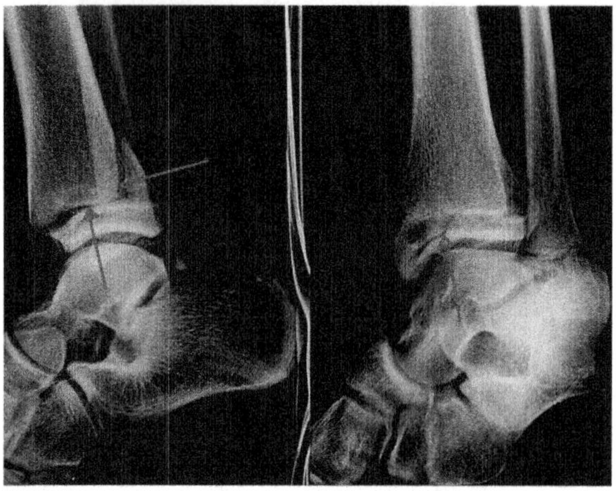

Patient cases also present an effective way to immerse students in *problem-solving, decision-making situations*. Student specialists are given the information they need to solve the case, but they must use critical thinking skills to manage the case from patient acceptance from the waiting room to patient discharge. Some scenarios create heightened emergency situations in which students are informed that the patient had to be put on life support; the Chief Medical Officer requests an initial diagnosis or treatment protocol as soon as possible. Individual patient scenarios use *affective learning strategies* to more thoroughly engage the student and *increase content learning and retention*.

The *delivery of science content* is also accomplished through the PDA-like device on the student interface desktop. Students receive alerts throughout the case concerning patient status and content related to the patient's disease or condition. For instance, they learn about disease vectors, risk factors, anatomy and physiology, and geographical information about outbreaks of infectious diseases (see Figure 4). Each case has information delivered in this manner. Questions from the Chief Medical Officer require them to access the information received through the PDA. Also, if they are having difficulties solving any tasks within the diagnostic process, and they haven't utilized the PDA information, the Chief Medical Officer knows, by prompts on the simulation facilitator's interface, to refer the students to the PDA. Students then know they have to read all the information available in order to solve the case. The Chief Medical Officer is not supposed to give the answers; students are supposed to apply critical thinking skills to solve each task within the case.

Facilitator's Programming Features

The Chief Medical Officer's interface provides multiple opportunities to deliver a high quality educational experience. Having prompts on the sim facilitator's interface not only ensures that students employ more critical thinking skills as mentioned above, but allows for the delivery of a more consistent and high quality education experience; the student experience is not as affected by inexperienced or ill-informed facilitators. The facilitator programming on the sim backend has been populated with timed, informative, and engaging content. As the students progress through each case, the Chief Medical Officer passes along facts about the occurrence of the disease or condition, the prevalence in a certain population or age group, or especially any significance in the target population of high school students.

For example, when the students treat fictional patient Eddie Little for a tongue piercing infection, the Chief Medical Officer prompts the students with information that tongue piercing infections sometimes travel to other parts of the body, especially the heart. Piercing infections also carry the risk that other infections result from the piercing equipment. Do they want to test for these secondary conditions? Students order more tests and discover that in addition to the serious (and unattractive) tongue piercing infection, Eddie Little also suf-

Figure 4. The PDA showing an x-ray of surgical correction of scoliosis
Screenshot from CyberSurgeons program. Copyright 2015 by the Center for Educational Technologies, Wheeling Jesuit University.

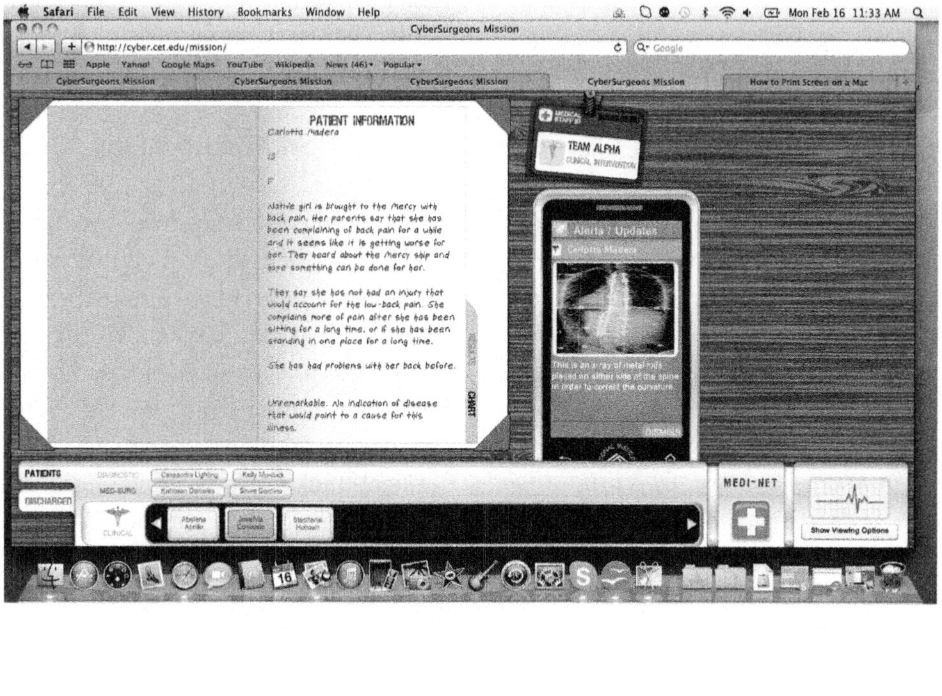

fers from secondary endocarditis (inflammation of the lining of the heart) and hepatitis B from a contaminated piercing needle.

Similarly, students working a nasty tattoo infection are led, by facilitator prompts, to discover that fictional patient Nick Gaudiski's infection is Methicillin Resistant *Staphylococcus aureus* (MRSA), and he is unfortunately also HIV positive from contaminated tattooing needles.

CyberSurgeons is programmed to allow facilitators to choose patient cases to push to the waiting room for student selection. This design feature allows for customization for *mixed levels of learners*. Patient cases are designed for varying grade levels, ability levels, and specific science-subject classes. Facilitators push easier cases, such as chicken pox or appendicitis, to ninth or tenth graders in integrated science classes, and more difficult cases to upper-level science classes with more biology and anatomy and physiology mastery. For one case, a fictional patient presents with no apparent injuries and no swelling or rashes on the upper body, abdominal wall, or extremities. He is, however, very agitated and hostile, his movements are spastic, speech is slurred, and stethoscope sounds are rapid and irregular. The symptoms do not immediately lead to an obvious diagnosis and students have to consider several options and test for several conditions before they arrive at a correct diagnosis. This reflects an authentic situation for this condition. Students finally suggest possible inhalant abuse; they find out later that the patient has died.

Specialists are paired, which not only *promotes collaborative learning*, but allows for students with *varying learning styles* and strengths to better learn the science content and have a successful experience. Specialist tasks are designed to target *varying student abilities. Major CyberSurgeons strengths include a design which allows all specialists teams to do science, all students to become a critical part of the diagnostic process, and all students to know that they have each contributed to "patient" care.*

CyberSurgeons live simulation embodies every concept of *constructivist teaching*. Students are continually actively engaged in the process of knowledge construction as they choose patients by reviewing the medical chart and working through the diagnostic process from formulating an initial diagnosis, ordering tests, recommending treatment, and possible inclusion in a clinical trial.

Simulation Mission Preparation

Prior to participating in the live simulation, teachers receive a virtual professional development session that allows them to experience the simulation in a similar way to the students (Johnson, Zerwic, & Theis, 1999). The online session walks the teachers through the sequence of events, reinforces the need for student pre-mission preparation, and allows them to understand the experience from their students' point of view. This also improves the teachers' abilities to enhance student learning through post-mission classroom discussion and activities. Before the live simulation, students spend a week of class in preparation for the event. All materials and resources for the preparation are provided and available for download by teachers. Pre-mission classroom materials ensure that students obtain the background knowledge and skills necessary for successful completion of the mission tasks.

Simulation/Mission Day

On the simulation day, the *CyberSurgeons* teams connect to the CMO, an educator at the simulation center, via video over Internet connection. The CMO guides students through the mission, accepts or rejects diagnoses and treatments, and uses questioning strategies built into the CMO mission program as a means to increase student critical-thinking skills. Providing critical-thinking questioning strategies on the CMO program backend provides for a more consistent delivery and effectiveness of the simulation.

As the scenario develops, the CMO at the fictional NIH headquarters shows students a video of the ship traveling up the Amazon River in Brazil and alerts the students to patients awaiting diagnosis and treatment. Students take on the roles of various experts and begin working together on different aspects of each patient's care. Students are members of one of four teams: case managers, diagnostic specialists, med-surg specialists, and clinical intervention specialists. To respond to each patient case, teams use the live Medi-Net database and communication resource for diagnosis, testing, and treatment. The case managers assign patients to teams and manage all aspects of patient status as the case moves through the diagnostic process.. As the students receive case histories and medical charts for each patient, the diagnostic specialists access the Medi-Net database that links symptoms with possible diagnoses. Team members evaluate and identify possible diagnoses and work with the med-surg specialists to order diagnostic tests.

The results of laboratory tests eliminate unlikely diagnoses, and team members continue ordering tests and analyzing results until they achieve a final diagnosis. The clinical intervention specialists review the diagnosis and test results and recommend treatment. They also use a clinical trials database in Medi-Net to match patient cases for possible clinical trials inclusion. Throughout the simulation the CMO selects relevant digital video clips to show students the results of their decision-making. This instructional strategy allows students to see the outcomes of their problem-solving and decision-making skills. Students also update a classroom mission wall chart that keeps track of each team's patient work. After the mission is over, the wall chart provides an artifact of patient cases, diseases students worked on, and how they progressed through the case. Other communication tools include a Patient Status Board interface that allows case managers to follow the patient's progress through the diagnostic and treatment process. Students and teachers monitor their progress through these features as well as through CMO comments throughout the mission. At the end of the simulation, the CMO debriefs teams to learn about their most difficult or perplexing case. The debriefs provide teachers and students with examples of critical thinking, favorite cases, learning moments, vocabulary applications, and other comments indicative of content learned.

Design team members observed all simulations during the main development phase of the project and all new patient cases added to the *CyberSurgeons* suite of cases. Extensive observation of student work through cases allowed for edits and enhancements, particularly addressing critical thinking skills and problem solving.

CyberSurgeons Summative Evaluation Results

CyberSurgeons used a mixed methods approach for evaluation during project year. An evaluation team composed of an internal evaluator, the design team, and an external evaluator contributed to the analysis and summative evaluation. Each *CyberSurgeons* team used four computers; up to four teams in a classroom participate in each mission. Teacher participants received free *CyberSurgeons* programs and stipends for completing all permission/consent forms and mission surveys.

After recruiting existing teacher customers, additional teachers were recruited through word of mouth, emails, and professional development sessions and conferences. Participating teachers signed consent forms and coordinated and returned parental/guardian permission and student consent forms. Teachers were assigned unique mission codes to access the system database, where they created a confidential login and password and entered ID numbers for their students. Before conducting pre-mission activities in the classroom, teachers and students completed online surveys comprised of quantitative and qualitative questions for several key variables: mission preparation, content knowledge and process skills associated with diagnosing and treating various maladies, personal attitudes toward challenges (self-efficacy), communication and collaboration skills, critical-thinking and problem-solving skills, career awareness of biomedical fields, and mission effectiveness. After the simulation teachers and students completed online surveys for the same variables as the pre-mission surveys with the addition of mission effectiveness.

Data were available from 82 teachers and 1,785 students. The chapter includes detailed information about the evaluation results including participant demographics, detailed multilevel repeated-measures multivariate analysis of variance results, and multiple structural equation modeling results. Of the 1,785 students providing data, 1,304 completed all pretest and posttest items and were included in the summative evaluation analysis. Statistically significant effects were found for the difference between student pre-mission and post-mission scores, $p < .001$, combined over the four types of skills (content knowledge, critical thinking/problem solving, collaboration/communication, and personal attributes). Students' pre-mission and post-mission self-reported means showed gains for all four skill types with the greatest gains reported in content knowledge.

Teachers reported widespread agreement with statements indicating better student skills in content knowledge, critical thinking/problem skills, and communication/ collaboration as a result of the mission. They also reported that students learned more about clinical research and clinical trials. Teachers agreed strongly that the mission was a valuable experience, that they were satisfied with the curriculum, and that they would recommend the program to other teachers. The most commonly noted valuable aspects of the program mentioned by teachers were the teamwork/interactive nature of the program, exposure to symptoms and diseases, real-life/practical experiences and problems, and application of critical thinking skills to solve problems. Students reported increased consideration of careers in medical fields, most especially in medical research and technology. Students' rating of program effectiveness was very positive, with most of them agreeing or strongly agreeing with statements indicating engagement in the mission. When asked in an open-ended question what they liked best about the program, most common student responses cited the realistic nature of the mission, teamwork, diagnosing, and fun/excitement/enjoyment. Asked what was most valuable in the experience, students cited motivation to enter health care, understanding diagnosis, and realism. Students reported the most enjoyable aspects of the program to be the hands-on experience, the realistic nature of the experience, teamwork, and having to think.

POTENTIAL CONDITIONS THAT MAY NEGATIVELY IMPACT *CYBERSURGEONS*

In spite of all the educational benefits that a well-designed, role-playing simulation affords, there are a few circumstances that negatively impact its effectiveness. Recognizing these circumstances can go a long way to preventing or lessening potential negative impacts. Four situations may pose challenges for running *CyberSurgeons*:

1. Programming failures,
2. Lack of pre-mission preparation,
3. Simulation facilitator preferences, and
4. Simulation cost.

Programming failures may interrupt simulations. Examples of programming failures range from student work not "saving" or pushing to the next specialist team in the diagnostic process to patient cases not going into the waiting room for student selection. Some of these program failure scenarios represent complete stops to simulation work although designers became adept at work-arounds during the pilot testing phase.

For students to experience the most benefit from the simulation, they should know the learning objectives as well as their roles in the activity. Reaching optimal goals can sometimes be sabotaged by *lack of pre-mission preparation* by teachers only looking for a free period while their students take part in a school field trip. The *CyberSurgeons* team recognized learner unpreparedness as a possible problem and took proactive measures to build support into the interfaces and instructions. Interfaces were designed to be intuitive while instructions for each role contained screen captures for ease of use and student support.

The *CyberSurgeons* design team observed that *simulation facilitators displayed preferences* for some fictional cases over others. Simulation facilitators preferred easier cases that presented fewer possibilities for student questions to the Chief Medical Officer. They also showed a preference for cases they had facilitated many times over cases with complications, difficult diagnoses, or any sexually transmitted disease (STD). Although a needs assessment given to high school teachers early in the project showed a demand for STD education in 9-12 grade levels, the facilitators avoided these cases. These preferences adversely affected potential students' gains in content knowledge, science process skills, and critical thinking practice through loss of ideal customization for grade level, ability level, and science class subject matter.

The *simulation costs* about $600 depending on discounts through multiple bookings and grant funding incentives. This expense is often prohibitive for schools.

SOLUTIONS AND RECOMMENDATIONS

These findings indicate that the *CyberSurgeons* program provides an authentic context for high school students to apply their knowledge of biology, physiology, and the diagnostic process to analyze data and make decisions as professionals in the biomedical field. Students need more opportunities for role-playing simulations in their science classes to delve into biomedical careers. NIH is the sole funding agency for STEM programs in the biomedical field. As role-playing simulations become more prevalent in the science classroom, it is imperative to learn what works in designing and evaluation an effective learning experience.

As modeled by *CyberSurgeons* (Piecka et al., 2012), Radomski and Russell (2010), and McCormick et al. (2010), and put into words by Griffiths and Guile (2003), establishing opportunities for students to "us[e] context-specific language to clarify understanding and resolve problems associated with different 'communities of practice' are central to learning through work experience" (p. 58). Educators need to "anticipate the needs of future health care workers by developing program changes in the curriculum that are innovative, use technology, and are on the cutting edge of evidence-based practice" (McCormick, et al., 2010, p. 21). Role-play simulations evolve as technology options emerge. For instance, health-care training simulations often include programmable digital mannequins that accompany learners in role play. The focus for role-playing simulations should emphasize the clinical-thinking process and deliberate rehearsal of clinical reasoning aimed not just on resolving unstructured, clinical problems, but investigating pathways for proceeding. (Radomski & Russell, 2010). Likewise, attention should be paid to the immediacy and timing of reflective prompts by the clinical educator/facilitator in the role-play simulation in order to provide students with a safe-learning environment where they can take risk and explore decision-making paths.

More role-play simulations should be delivered via distance. *CyberSurgeons* provides distance education role-playing simulations via videoconferencing. More educators should explore online and live role-playing simulations such as Hou (2012), Mclaughlan and Kirkpatrick (2005), and Nelson and Blenkin (2007).

FUTURE RESEARCH DIRECTIONS

This chapter adds valuable information about a unique genre of role-playing simulation for P-12 education. More research needs to be done on the transformative learning effects of *CyberSurgeons*. Although originally funded by NIH for a 5-year grant, future research related to *CyberSurgeo*ns should investigate learning gains and explore longitudinal/retention effects (Shaw, 2012) of role-based simulations. More research (using rigorous designs) is needed about using science role-playing simulations in high school. Targeting secondary students necessitates specific considerations to state and federal education standards, time limitations, and prior knowledge of the learners.

CyberSurgeons fills a gap in STEM instruction for high school students. The live, role-playing simulation provides a feasible, authentic, and sustainable, learning activity that teachers use year after year. Many teachers (some who were in the original fifth-year summative evaluation), continue to fly the mission. While many curriculum efforts work to build STEM "pipeline persistence" (Maltese & Tai, 2011), content knowledge alone is not adequate to inspire students to continue in STEM professions. Recent research shows promise for technology-based, role-play simulations to engage and increase students' interest in science careers while improving their content knowledge (Berk et al., 2014; Miller, 2015; Piecka et al., 2012) simulations. The authors plan to design more science-based, live simulations for secondary students as their proposals become accepted. They anticipate wider examination of role-playing simulations and their effectiveness through both case study and quasi-experimental research.

The authors foresee the following emerging trends related to designing and researching role-play simulations in science education:

- Role-playing simulations will include more types of technology such as tablets, smartphones, QR codes, social media, specialized digital mannequins, and online course management systems.
- More science and STEM-related role-play simulations for high school students will be developed.
- The number of role-playing simulations delivered online will increase.
- Additional qualitative research design studies need to be conducted during the design and development of role-playing simulations.
- More role-play simulations need to be evaluated and researched involving a greater number of P-12 participants.
- Additional science role-play simulations will be funded by the National Institutes of Health Science Education Partnership Award (SEPA) program to encourage more students, and especially minority and underrepresented students, to pursue biomedical careers.

CONCLUSION

A role-playing simulation is an educational strategy that provides students with a unique platform upon which to apply previously learned knowledge to new content in real-world situations—and so much more. An effective role-playing simulation engages students in complex processes not easily learned in regular classroom settings, reaches a mixed level of learners, improves cognitive learning, improves affective learning and self-efficacy, inspires careers in the sim topic, and enhances long-term knowledge retention.

More research and evaluation is needed on the effectiveness of role-playing simulations and their key design features in order to achieve a highly effective simulation. Unfortunately, little research has been done that evaluates the many aspects of design that must coalesce to produce the most effective learning strategy for specific target groups.

REFERENCES

Aldrich, C. (2009). *The complete guide to simulations and serious games: How the most valuable content will be created in the age beyond Gutenberg to Google*. San Francisco, CA: Pfeiffer.

Aubusson, P., Fogwill, S., Barr, R., & Perkovic, L. (1997). What happens when students do simulation-role-play in science? *Research in Science Education*, *27*(4), 565–579. doi:10.1007/BF02461481

Banks, J. A. (2008). Diversity, group identity, and citizenship education in a global age. *Educational Researcher*, *37*(3), 129–139. doi:10.3102/0013189X08317501

Barab, S., & Dede, C. (2007). Games and immersive participatory simulations for science education: An emerging type of curricula. *Journal of Science Education and Technology*, *16*(1), 1–3. doi:10.1007/s10956-007-9043-9

Barab, S. A., & Dodge, T. (2008). Strategies for designing embodied curriculum. In J. M. Spector, M. D. Merrill, J. van Merrienboër, & M. P. Driscoll (Eds.), *Handbook of research on educational communications and technology* (pp. 97–110). New York: Routledge.

Berk, L. J., Muret-Wagstaff, S. L., Goyal, R., Joyal, J. A., Gordon, J. A., Faux, R., & Oriol, N. E. (2014). Inspiring careers in STEM and healthcare fields through medical simulation embedded in high school science education. *Advances in Physiology Education*, *38*(3), 210–215. doi:10.1152/advan.00143.2013 PMID:25179609

Bigelow, B., & Diamond, N. (2007). The organic goodie simulation. In *Rethinking our classrooms: Teaching for equity and justice* (Vol. 1, pp. 100–102). Milwaukee, WI: Rethinking Schools.

Bloom, B. S., & Krathwohl, D. R. (1956). *Taxonomy of educational objectives: The classification of educational goals. Handbook I: Cognitive domain*. White Plains, NY: Longman.

Branch, R. M. (2008). *Instructional design: The ADDIE approach*. New York: Springer.

Byford, J. M. (2012). *Behind the Iron Curtain: A teacher's guide to West Germany and Cold War activities*. Lanham, MD: University Press of America.

Carnegie Corporation of New York and The Center for Information and Research on Civic Learning and Engagement (CIRCLE). (2003). *The Civic Mission of Schools*. New York, NY: Author.

Chinnici, J. P., Yue, J. W., & Torres, K. M. (2004). Students as "humans chromosomes" in role-playing mitosis and meiosis. *The American Biology Teacher*, *66*(1), 35–39. doi:10.1662/0002-7685(2004)066[0035:SAHCIR]2.0.CO;2

Clapper, T. (2010). Role play and simulation. *Education Digest*, *75*(8), 39–43. doi: 10.1016/b978-0-7506-0617-2.50014-2

Doody, O., & Condon, M. (2013). Using a simulated environment to support students learning clinical skills. *Nurse Education in Practice*, *13*(6), 561–566. doi:10.1016/j.nepr.2013.03.011 PMID:23602694

Druckman, D., & Ebner, N. (2013). Games, claims, and new frames: Rethinking the use of simulation in negotiation education. *Negotiation Journal*, *29*(1), 61–92. doi:10.1111/nejo.12005

Goldenberg, D., Andrusyszyn, M. A., & Iwasiw, C. (2005). The effect of classroom simulation on nursing students' self-efficacy related to health teaching. *The Journal of Nursing Education*, *44*, 310–314. Retrieved from http://europepmc.org/abstract/med/16094789 PMID:16094789

Gould, J., & Annenberg Public Policy Center. (2011). *Guardian of democracy: The civic mission of schools*. Retrieved from http://civicmission.s3.amazonaws.com/118/f0/5/171/1/Guardian-of-Democracy-report.pdf

Griffiths, T., & Guile, D. (2003). A connective model of learning: Implications for work process knowledge. *European Educational Research Journal*, *2*(1), 56–73. doi:10.2304/eerj.2003.2.1.10

Hennessy, S., Deaney, R., & Ruthven, K. (2006). Situated expertise in integrating use of multimedia simulation into secondary science teaching. *International Journal of Science Education*, *28*(7), 701–732. doi:10.1080/09500690500404656

Hou, H.-T. (2012). Analyzing the learning process of an online role-playing discussion activity. *Journal of Educational Technology & Society*, *15*(1), 211–222. Retrieved from http://www.ifets.info/journals/15_1/19.pdf

Jeffries, P. R. (2005). A framework for designing, implementing, and evaluating simulations used as teaching strategies in nursing. *Nursing Education Perspectives*, *26*(2), 96–103. doi: 10.1043/1536-5026(2005)026%3C0096%3AAFWFDI%3E2.0.CO%3B2 PMID:15921126

Johnson, J. H., Zerwic, J. J., & Theis, S. L. (1999). Clinical simulation laboratory: An adjunct to clinical teaching. *Nurse Educator*, *24*(5), 37–41. doi:10.1097/00006223-199909000-00016 PMID:10795255

Maloy, R. W., & LaRoche, I. (2010). Student-centered teaching methods in the history classroom: Ideas, issues, and insights for new teachers. *Social Studies Research and Practice*, *5*(2), 46-61. Retrieved from http://www.academia.edu/420967/Student-Centered_Teaching_Methods_In_the_History_Classroom_Ideas_Issues_and_Insights_for_New_Teachers

Maltese, A. V., & Tai, R. H. (2011, September 01). Pipeline persistence: Examining the association of educational experiences with earned degrees in STEM among U.S. students. *Science Education*, *95*(5), 877–907. doi:10.1002/sce.20441

McCormick, M. J., Burton, T., & Werts, N. (2010). Case scenarios and simulations as techniques to facilitate asthma education and team building among health care students. *Journal of Asthma & Allergy Educators*, *1*(1), 18–22. doi:10.1177/2150129709355459

Mclaughlan, R., & Kirkpatrick, D. (2005, April). *Online text-based roleplay-simulation: The challenges ahead.* Paper presented at the Simulation Industry Association of Australia (SIAA), Sydney, Australia. Retrieved from http://hdl.handle.net/10453/7195

Miller, L. (2015). Role-play games as a tool for STEM career inspiration and the development of scientific possible selves. In T. Bastiaens & G. Marks (Eds.), *Proceedings of Global Learn 2015* (pp. 385-389). Waynesville, NC: Association for the Advancement of Computing in Education (AACE). Retrieved From http://www.editlib.org/p/150883/proceeding_150883.pdf

Nelson, D. L., & Blenkin, C. (2007). The power of online role-play simulations: Technology in nursing education. *International Journal of Nursing Education Scholarship*, *4*(1), 1–14. doi:10.2202/1548-923X.1263 PMID:17402925

Pavao, W. (2009). *Constitutional convention: A decision-making activity.* Retrieved from http://ssecamoreperfectunion.com/PDFs/Constitutional_Convention_Lesson_Plan_Web_Version_by_Pavao.pdf

Piecka, D. C. B., Calinger, M., Wood, C., Shia, J., Kudlak, L., & Tabachnick, B. G. (2012, April). *Evaluation of a live high school clinical science education simulation*. Paper presented at the annual meeting of the American Educational Research Association, Vancouver, BC, Canada.

Radomski, N., & Russell, J. (2010). Integrated case learning: Teaching clinical reasoning. *Advances in Health Sciences Education: Theory and Practice*, *15*(2), 251–264. doi:10.1007/s10459-009-9195-x PMID:19760511

Shaw, C. M. (2012). Designing and using simulations and role-play exercises. In R. A. Denemark (Ed.), The International Studies Encyclopedia. New York, NY: Blackwell. Retrieved from http://webs.wichita.edu/depttools/depttoolsmemberfiles/carolynshaw/Shaw%20in%20Compendium.pdf

Silvia, C. (2010). The impact of simulations on higher-level learning. *Journal of Public Affairs Education*, *18*, 397–422. Retrieved from http://www.naspaa.org/jpaemessenger/article/vol18-2/10_silva.pdf

Smith, E. T., & Boyer, M. A. (1996). Designing in-class simulations. *Political Science & Politics*, *29*(4), 690–694. doi:10.1017/S1049096500045686

StockTrack Global Portfolio Simulations. (2014). *National stock market simulation high school stock market game*. Retrieved from http://www.stocktrak.com/Public/products/National-SMS-High-School-Stock-Market-Game.aspx

The Department of the Treasury. (2009). *President's advisory council on financial literacy: 2008 annual report to the President*. Retrieved from https://www.wdfi.org/_resources/indexed/ site/ymm/PACFL_ANNUAL_REPORT_1-16-09.pdf

The SIFMA Foundation. (2013). The stock market game. Retrieved from http://www. stockmarketgame.org/impact.html

Wheeler, S. M. (2006). Role-playing games and simulations for international issues courses. *Journal of Political Science Education*, *2*(3), 331–347. doi:10.1080/15512160600840814

ENDNOTE

1 Additional notes: The NIH project was supported by the National Center for Research Resources and the Division of Program Coordination, Planning, and Strategic Initiatives of the National Institutes of Health through Grant Number 5R25RR023299-05. *CyberSurgeons* is a Science Education Partnership Award, SEPA.

Chapter 16
Using Video Gameplay to Measure Achievement for Students with Disabilities:
A New Perspective to Grading and Achievement Reporting

Benjamin Gallegos
University of Central Florida, USA

Michelle T. Kepple
University of Central Florida, USA

Caitlyn A. Bukaty
University of Central Florida, USA

ABSTRACT

Video gaming in the classroom offers students and educators the opportunity to conceptualize learning in new ways and address 21st century skills. This construct appears in research-based literature by leading trans-disciplinary experts in the field of special education and video gaming. Empirical research has established the application of video games as leaning tools in schools, and the benefits of video games for students with disabilities (Ke & Abras, 2013). This chapter focuses on the benefits and use of educational video game based learning for students with disabilities. The authors discuss (1) current barriers hindering widespread adoption of video games for learning and assessment, (2) characteristics of video games being used for learning and assessment, (3) how gameplay data represents academic achievement for grading, and (4) the types of assessments available and considerations for implementation. Finally, the authors explore avenues to prepare educators to use video gaming for learning and assessment in classrooms for students with disabilities.

DOI: 10.4018/978-1-4666-9629-7.ch016

INTRODUCTION

Video games are often used as interventions or methods of integrating supportive content for students with disabilities (SWD), but should also be considered as a means of alternative assessment for learners (Marino, Basham, & Beecher, 2011). Traditionally, large-scale school assessments are administered with accommodations for SWD to ensure that: (a) all students can access and take the test and (b) SWDs are graded on a fair scale that measures their performance outcomes (Lovett, 2010). There are 6.4 million SWDs ages 3 to 21 years old served under the Individual with Disabilities Education Act (IDEA) receiving special education services (Kena et al., 2014). Delacruz, Chung, and Baker (2010) indicated evidence to support of using video games as an assessment alternative for measuring students learning outcomes, underscoring the importance of reform initiatives for K-12 educational assessment. According to the National Research Council report on games and simulation, "science games and simulations can be adapted for students with special needs, allowing them to be mainstreamed in science classrooms" (Honey & Hilton, 2011, p. 61). It is important to give consideration to the video games as an instructional and assessment tool given that 2.4 million SWDs have been classified as having specific learning disabilities (SLD) which affect students' cognitive learning process, and subsequently, academic outcomes (Cortiella, & Horowitz, 2014). In the field of special education research on video games as a support for students with disabilities is limited (Durkin, Boyle, Hunter, & Conti-Ramsden, 2013). This chapter will provide insight on the use of video games to facilitate academic success for students with disabilities in inclusive classroom settings.

Use of video games for game based learning (GBL), as an alternative assessment could be valuable considering the rich amount of feedback, data collection capabilities and accessibility features available within many games (Marino et al., 2011). Video game feedback components can have a significant impact on academic success rates for SWD especially those with SLD. Teachers can use students' video gameplay performance data to provide specific, detailed feedback. Such feedback is crucial when using educational simulation activities to increase students' academic performance (Savoldelli et al., 2006). In an empirical study on game-based feedback in virtual learning environments Serge and colleagues (2013) reported that participants who received detailed feedback during GBL tasks outperformed those who received general feedback. Students with disabilities sought activities in simulation-based scenarios and used this virtual medium to reflect and view their own successes (Anstadt, Bradley, & Burnette, 2013). With the increasing use of GBL curriculum as a support and intervention in educational settings many SWDs already have achievements from playing educational video games that can represent their academic performance (Manusos, Busby, & Clark, 2013).

This chapter will include the intellectual merits and broader impacts of video games and possible grading systems that can be used in the classroom. The authors have included references to how GBL has been utilized in inclusive classrooms and support the consideration that video games should be used as tools for learning, presenting content, grading, and assessing students' abilities. The purpose of this chapter is to initiate dialogue on benefits of further developments and research for SWD and their use of video games. Video games (regardless of game types or genres) can have the accessibility features, flexibility of creating environments, and feedback components beneficial for SWDs and not found in traditional educational content.

BACKGROUND AND CONTEXT

Video games have been used in the classroom to present content that was once considered too complex for SWDs as engaging tasks, beneficial for critical thinking, and have turned assignments into interactive learning missions (Marino et al., 2011). Learning and entertainment activities are more engaging for SWDs when they have the opportunity to select the content from digital media (Kagohara, 2011). Many gaming consoles, smart phones, tablet computers, and personal electronic devices house sophisticated software that can provide educational content. Mobile devices allow for more flexibility with classroom content than traditional methods due to the limited information that is typically printed and produced under a 'one size fits all' model.

Traditional curriculum materials have evolved slightly with the introduction of updated, packaged programs including grade appropriate and leveled material designed to accommodate students' reading, or English language learning levels. This material may include software or downloadable content that serves as supplemental support. Video games have the ability to provide an expanse of traditional information plus innovative, engaging activities in one medium. A teacher's instruction using traditional classroom materials coupled with GBL can offer accessibility features that are unique to each individual learner in the class. For effective use of video games as assessment tools videogames must also be part of the students' regular learning curriculum (Brown, 2014).

Universal Design for Learning

Today's K-12 teachers have a classroom full of diverse learners who excel in different ways. Traditional classroom content delivery methods (e.g., textbooks, worksheets, workbooks, and presentations) include vocabulary, terms, and information that SWDs may have difficulty comprehending and connecting to on a personal level (Marino, Black, Hayes, & Beecher, 2010). The Universal Design for Learning (UDL) framework was developed to help educators create learning objectives and content that includes accessible features to promote successful learning outcomes for all learners and learning styles (Messinger-Willman & Marino, 2010). The three UDL principals for successful student academic outcomes provide learners with multiple means of

1. Representation,
2. Action and expression, and
3. Engagement (CAST, 2013).

The application of UDL principles is integral to lesson planning, because "without the knowledge and ability to increase students' access to curricula, many general education teachers do not create a responsive environment designed to best meet the individual needs of their students" (Courey, Tappe, Siker, & LePage, 2013, p. 11).

The idea of a UDL-based educational environment does not refer only to the physical setting but also the content being learned and the material that is delivered to students daily. The degree to which students receive or maintain what they have been presented from their teacher should also be considered in how students' achievements are measured. Often teachers supplement traditional materials (e.g., textbooks, worksheets, and digital content provided through packaged curriculum materials) with hands-on lab settings and project based curriculum. The means to measure the students' competencies from such activities may include an assessment that does not reflect the characteristics of a responsive environment. Assessment characteristics and delivery modes through the UDL framework may provide a strong base for turning to video game-based assessments over traditional paper pencil assessments.

Textbooks and worksheets are created for students to engage with content, yet many students, including some SWDs do not excel when working with printed medium and instead benefit when content is presented with a UDL lens (Rose, 2000). Using UDL aligned video games for learning and achievement reporting in the classroom may provide elements of promoting all learners' academic achievements. The UDL framework has attributes to provide successful inclusive classroom models that foster success for all learners (Katz, 2013). Courey and colleagues (2013) investigated the use of UDL for lesson planning and delivery by graduate students who were seeking credentials as teachers of SWDs. Findings indicated that when the graduate students received UDL training and applied the UDL framework, they had a better understanding of how to develop lesson plans that were accessible and beneficial to all learners. The incorporation of UDL and digital content formats for interactive science notebooks was shown to be more effective than traditional paper-pencil science notebook tasks for students of underrepresented populations such as SWDs and minority students (Rappolt-Schlichtmann et al., 2013). Universal Design for Learning further provides a learning environment where students who have behavior disorders can have positive attitudes and behaviors based on content that was provided to them according to their individual needs and interests (Johnson-Harris & Mundschenk, 2014). One result of UDL implementation is the decreased need to address behavior issues during the delivery of academic content.

Video Gaming for All Learners

The use of video games in the classroom is not limited to students with learning disabilities but can also be valuable for any students. "Video games have become an essential part of the way people play and learn" (Kenny & McDaniel, 2011, p. 197). Video games offer an engaging and unconventional method of adding physical activity for students with physical disabilities (Rowland & Rimmer, 2012). Game-based learning also has potential applications for students with physical disabilities receiving rehabilitation therapy in school (i.e., physical and occupational therapy). As Acosta, Dewald, and Dewald (2011) highlighted in their study individuals recovering from a stroke were actively engaged when using video games for physical rehabilitation exercises. Students with disabilities learning vocational skills in class benefited from use of a virtual video game training environment because of the software's ability to individualize the students' learning activities (Brooks, Rose, Attree, & Elliot-Square, 2002). Individuals with cerebral palsy using virtual simulation increased the frequency of physical tasks completed when instant visual feedback was given (de Mello Monteiro et al., 2014). The researchers then were able to evaluate the game-like assessments taken from the participants' performance outcomes and found that among different simulation modes abstract tasks were more difficult for participants to perform than concrete tasks. The study conducted by de Mello Monteiro and colleagues (2014) is a good example of the potential alternative assessment methods can provide to teachers evaluating students' needs and strengths.

The use of video games for learning has the potential of being used beyond the classroom (Honey & Hilton, 2011). Researchers conducting one study used video games to increase physical arm and shoulder movement in stroke patients (Acosta et al., 2011). Anecdotal accounts from the research included discussion of the subjects' continuous play of the video game for personal leisure after the study was completed. Student use of video games to enhance physical therapy can take place at home and serve as an extension of daily school interventions. Furthermore, teachers can establish remote access to the SWDs gameplay data, allowing students to continue the gameplay intervention at home and while teachers are able to monitor progress.

When working with students with any type of disability, teachers can use the gameplay data to determine whether learning milestones are being met. Inclusive schools are made up of students with different learning styles, processing skills, and personalized learning accommodations in place to help students be successful (Marino & Hayes, 2012). Video games can also serve as a virtual reality platform that can take SWDs to realistic simulated environments. This can include situations and responsibilities individuals may encounter in real life (Chan, Leung, Tang, & Komura, 2011). Game based assessments are similar to classroom assessments in that they are most commonly portrayed in two types: summative and formative assessments. Summative assessments are designed to measure a learner's proficiency of content against predetermined benchmarks, whereas the goal of formative assessment is to gather data on learners and provide rich feedback to the instructor and student so modifications to the learning processes can take place (Carnegie Mellon University, n.d.). Similarly, games can be designed to utilize and report either formative or summative assessments, or an integration of the two.

Extended research on GBL has shown positive perceptions on the use of video games for science instruction (Marino, Israel, Beecher, & Basham, 2013). Many of the middle school teachers participating in a study by Marino, Israel, Beecher, and Basham (2013) reported that their students with disabilities were engaged, comprehended material, and excelled academically as a result of learning science through the science video games. One teacher reported that an individual student with a reading disability increased his gains on a science assessment by approximately 30% following the use of video game play when compared to the typical lesson plan without incorporating GBL. Additional benefits associated with interactive virtual learning environments (i.e., video games) is decreased classroom behavior issues such as "off-task behavior, noise level, and inappropriate behaviors" (Retter, Anderson, & Kieran, 2013, p. 459). Peer-reviewed empirical research has supported what many educational video game researchers already believe: well-designed educational video games can be engaging, provide immediate performance feedback and interventions, and can be utilized as a sufficient learning alternative when compared to traditional curriculum. The remarkable approach students use when playing a video game in order to master a level or to be identified as a master level expert is fueled by their relentless perseverance through trial and error (Hamlen, 2012). Today's students often learn and take on difficult concepts and challenges through a self-satisfying approach by playing video games (O'Rourke, Main, & Ellis, 2013). Teaching today's students essential academic skills and applicable approaches to successfully achieving academic outcomes is not the same as teaching the generations before them (Zydney & Hasselbring, 2014). If the original purpose of assessment was to measure students' true performance outcomes and address areas in need of intervention based on scores, then subject matter needs to be presented in a way that SWDs can easily access so all student needs can be addressed (Qi & Mitchell, 2012). It is time to not only continue the efforts of incorporating video games in the classroom as an engagement or exploring tool but to extend the use of video games as a grading system reflecting the rich GBL data that reflects the effort and time invested by students with disabilities in educational video gaming as a means for assessing academic achievements.

Need for Educator Support

Any time there is a new technological advancement or program (e.g., educational video games played through iPads, tablets, or smart phones) that may benefit learners, educators are often quick to adopt the latest trends (Hall, Soderstrom, Ahlqvist, & Nilsson, 2011). For educators who provide assistive technology and instructional supports for SWD, using technology that will not be surpassed by newer technologies regularly with optimal implementation is often an issue (Edyburn, 2013). Much like assistive technology devices for supporting the SWDs in their classroom, teachers reported the need for proper training and support in implementing technology supports (Flanagan, Bouck, & Richardson, 2012). When using technology in the classroom it is important teachers and schools receive the technical support, infrastructure, and training to ensure implementation for the enhancement of SWD (Kenny & McDaniel, 2011).

The demands on today's teachers require support for implementing new technologies into daily lesson plans and activities (Wilson et al., 2011). Teachers receiving support to implement GBL can make the pedagogical paradigm change to influence the adoption of grading through video games. Switching to video games from the traditional learning methods (e.g., paper, pencil, and notebooks) in schools was shown to promote a genuine measurement of students' comprehension and performance outcomes as opposed to the typical 'standardized tests' previously used for assessment (Morris, Croker, Zimmerman, Gill, & Romig, 2013). This parallels the trends of many corporations and other fields that have recently turned to video games for training and learning (Vlasak & Ranaldo, 2012).

MAIN FOCUS OF THE CHAPTER

This chapter focuses on the benefits and use of educational video games for students with disabilities. The authors discuss

1. Current barriers hindering widespread adoption of video games for learning and assessment,
2. Characteristics of video games being used for learning and assessment,
3. How gameplay data represents academic achievement for grading, and
4. Considerations for the types of assessments available and considerations for implementation.

Currently there are several barriers within educational communities that cause issues, controversies, and problems with video game play within inclusive classrooms.

Before discussing the considerations needed for educational video games, it is important to recognize the main issues, controversies and problems surrounding GBL in inclusive classrooms including

1. Perceptions of video games,
2. Incongruence in student achievement and assessment reporting in gaming, and
3. Lack of or underdeveloped professional learning opportunities for teachers.

Issues, Controversies, Problems

Perceptions: Perceived Characteristics of Video Games

Teachers are always looking for opportunities to increase their students' problem solving skills and academic performance, yet teachers do not always recognize the potential application of video gaming as a learning intervention for struggling students (Marino & Beecher, 2010). It is often the student who was struggling with paper pencil content or who had poor academic outcomes who was not allowed to play the educational video games and instead was 'caught up' with one-on-one instruction with the teacher (Marino & Beecher, 2010). Video games are a multibillion dollar industry responsible for captivating many youth for over well over two decades and until recently the field of education has begun to explore the potential of using video games for learning in schools (Annetta et al., 2013)

Another issue towards the advancement of educational video game use in the classroom is the attitudes of school personnel towards the uses of video games; even more so than not that the technology available, or lack of district funding. While there may be a variety of reasons why video games are associated with negative connotations instead, this chapter focuses on exploring reasons brought up on why video games have not garnered more noteworthy positive attention in schools. These factors may have contributed to the reasons why video games have not been thoroughly considered.

The development of a GBL environment must first overcome longstanding negative perceptions on the general use of video games. The use of video games has had a long reputation associated with negative behaviors and may be seen as a vehicle for unproductive activities (Oswald, Prorock, & Murphy, 2014). There have been reports of individuals' obsessive behaviors of playing video games, and the notion that time spent on video games can contribute to students' time away from schoolwork (Bavelier et al., 2011). Bavelier and colleagues (2011) wrote a perspective piece on the role video games have played in studies and how video games are a not just a tool for learning but a complex software with both positive potential for learning outcomes and negative pitfalls. An important factor the researchers suggested was the emerging development of video game behavior supports and interventions for individuals who may become obsessed with video games at an unhealthy level.

In a study of elementary personnel and staff perceptions of children's health and activities conducted by Odum, McKyer, Tisone, and Outley (2013) the researchers reported that many respondents noted video games as a negative factor to children's health. Video games have also been strongly perceived in the public as a factor to invoking violent behaviors and actions in young people (Ybarra, Huesmann, Korchmaros, & Reisner, 2014). Even though the use of video games has been associated with user violence, Przybylski, Ryan, and Rigby (2009) noted that game players engagement in specific games was not tied into violent video gameplay activities. The study focused on whether the participants' engagement in a game was dependent on the game's inclusion of graphic violence. There is clear evidence of this perception in many pieces of qualitative research examining the uses of video games and negative connotations. The expectations of the views of state and district stakeholders on the use of video games as an assessment tool may be one of the biggest factors on serious consideration of overall implementation. Kenny and McDaniel's (2009) study reconfirmed that minimal exposure to GBL tools can change teachers' preconceived notions about using a game as tool for instructional outcomes.

Positive teacher perceptions on video games for learning have also been noted in current literature, for example science teachers who received training on science video game development and how to use those video games as a content support for their students' learning indicated they perceived video games as a valuable learning tool (Annetta et al., 2012). For many SWD video games are an activity they invest their time in. In a study completed by Mazurek, Shattuck, Wagner, and Cooper (2012) the researchers examined the use of video games from SWDs, specifically those with autism spectrum disorders (ASD). The researchers' found almost half of the students with ASD spent their recreational time playing video games (Mazurek, Shattuck, Wagner & Cooper, 2012). With the growing use of video games in classrooms as a content support a drawback of being well received in the educational community is the potential for teachers to accept video games indiscriminately without thorough evaluation (Annetta, Lamb, & Stone, 2011).

Lack of Understanding of Student Achievement and Assessment in Gaming

There is a shared understanding among policy makers, educators, and school administrators on student learning outcomes derived from exposure to high quality education from teachers' delivery of instruction and academic measurements (Jones, Buzick, & Turkan, 2013). In today's evaluation models traditional paper and pencil assessments are the primary vehicle for measuring student learning outcomes. Current assessment protocols for measuring and representing students' academic performance has hindered the progression of the field of education (Shaffer & Gee, 2012). Assessments taken in schools have a disheartening disconnect to students' comprehension, learning potential, and information for the implementation of interventions that will address student deficits (Shute & Ventura, 2013). The national perspective of students' engagement and persistence in academics under the traditional delivery of content has been at an all-time low (Simpson, 2009).

Nationwide, schools are measured on the assessment performance of all students, including SWDs, receiving a rating indicating students' academic growth (Buzick & Laitusis, 2010). Implications for teachers and schools not meeting rating benchmarks include consequences that reflect in funding and teacher evaluations. With the current emphasis on assessment and performance of SWDs the adoption of video game assessment initiatives should strongly be considered. The use of interactive assessment delivered through computers will be the next step for developers to consider when creating measures that accurately represent students' comprehension (Almond et al., 2010). Incorporation of accessible features and measures should be reflected in schools' and districts' assessment procedures.

The field of K-12 education across the United States has introduced initiatives to measure and report academic outcomes and performance increases for SWDs based on testing accommodations (Thurlow, Lazarus, Thompson, & Morse, 2005). Some states have extended these initiatives and assessment accommodations to all students, not just those with disabilities. These assessment accommodations and initiatives were developed from the need to ensure students' assessment performance measured actual student achievement and was not reflective of how the students struggled with interpreting the exam (Tindal, Heath, Hollenbeck, Almond, & Harniss, 1998).

In terms of accessibility and alternative testing measures for SWDs, Computer Adaptive Testing (CAT) has been developed to create measures that meet the needs of all students (Stone & Davey, 2011). Including video games as a CAT platform would be strategic in aligning assessments to SWDs' performance. Such developments are needed as a recent investigation on state standardized assessments for individuals who were deaf or hard of hearing found that the accommodations allowing the students to have some or all of a test read aloud were not acceptable for reading assessments in many states. Still, it was considered an acceptable practice for students with other disabilities that required the accommodation (Steinberg, Cline, Ling, Cook, & Tognatta, 2014). Assessments through video games, following UDL guidelines have the ability to meet the accommodation needs of all SWDs (Izzo, 2012). Video games have multiple benefits for SWDs beyond leisurely use and can enhance students' learning experiences in the classroom setting with the promising potential of decreasing their likelihood of dropping out of school (Wilson et al., 2011).

In Hamlen's (2014) study that compared students' problem solving strategies between video gameplay and regular school-based homework, she found that participants reported using video game guided 'walkthroughs' that served as learning supports to master video gameplay. On the contrary, when participants were asked how they approached problem solving during homework students' indicated that they did not refer to school assigned textbooks. Much like the video game walkthrough guides compared to school assigned textbooks, students tend to rely on the teacher for instruction and the monitoring of their comprehension when they have not been provided multiple means of presentation. When students are not provided with free choice and multiple independent learning opportunities they rely on their teacher's guidance for feedback, and if video games were used as an everyday learning task may serve as a valuable educational tool (Barendregt & Bekker, 2011). Using video games regularly in the classroom to assess students' knowledge and providing those same supports outside of the classroom can unify the co-existence between the gaming and classroom environments (Shultz Colby & Colby, 2008).

Results of emerging studies have shown that playing video games can assist with students' problem solving skills and academic outcomes. An important finding by Adachi and Willoughby (2013) was that students who engaged in strategic role playing games for leisure also increased their self-reported problem solving skills. In another study on game based supports students were able to problem solve academic content at their own pace and were provided prompt feedback on their performances (Lin et al., 2013). Participating students increased their problem solving outcomes after using the game based interventions.

Video games are already being used in schools and the application for the purpose of learning and assessment has yet to be fully realized. McLean and Griffiths (2013) reported that the positive effects and features in gameplay must be considered alongside literature indicating video games to be counterproductive to students' learning outcomes. A number of studies have been conducted to measure or explore the negative attributes between users and video gameplay, however few studies have measured or explored the positive correlation of users and video gameplay (Adachi & Willoughby, 2012). Video games have characteristics and software capabilities that would allow game designers and educators to collaborate, building future GBL constructs. Students with disabilities can learn and represent their comprehension through the video gameplay. Traditional longstanding paper and pencil tasks used for assessing and grading students' comprehension does not have the video game accessibility features SWD can benefit from.

The use of video gaming in the classroom is often associated with already achieved student accomplishments. Often teachers and administrators perceive video games as a novelty that should only be used to reward students' achievements. In a personal account of a classroom observation video games were used in the classroom for two reasons

1. As a reward for academic achievement, and
2. As a reward for students reaching goals on individualized behavior plans.

Students were generally engaged in video games only on 'Fun Friday' or during the final minutes of a school day.

The video games played during observations were played on iPads and computer desktops. Students were playing educational video games individually or in an online multiplayer environment with peers from their school and players from outside of the school. The students were logging into the educational video games with their own personal profile based on the login features from the different video games they were playing. For every different video game accessed, profiles were not synched (i.e., one profile login access to play the different video games) across the numerous video games students were switching through. Students' game play data were available to each other within each video game. The students' video game play activities represented grade level content aligned with state standards they were learning at the time. Many of the missions, quests, and challenges they attempted through the video games served as supplemental classroom content support.

When video games were used as a content support the gameplay was supposed to translate to the traditional curriculum tasks or paper pencil assignments and assessments. In a study by Marino and colleagues (2014) on students with learning disabilities and the use of video games in a middle school science class, the researchers reported that students performed better after their teacher's test review than after engaging in a science video game. Marino and colleagues noted that the teacher review may have been more beneficial to the students' science test performance when compared to the video game-based support because the assessment was similar to the teacher's review and was conducted as a paper pencil task. The video gameplay providing the same content being tested was not taken as the students' final results to represent their knowledge of the science standard.

Annetta, Minogue, Holmes, and Cheng (2009) studied high school students using video games as a supplemental support to learn genetics and their engagement during gameplay. While learning outcome results were not significant, the researchers did report students' engagement during video gameplay (M=53.67) compared to the control group (M= 19.33) was statistically significant. Annetta and colleagues noted it important to consider that a disconnect may be present when assessing students with traditional paper pencil tests after they have used a technology software (e.g., video games) with accessibility features and multiple presentation modes. This disconnect is one of the issues related to limited research of video games in the K-12 education field. There is a noted lack of empirical studies investigating individuals' generalization of video gameplay to out-of-gameplay skills (Boot, Blakely, & Simons, 2011). Boot, Kramer, Simons, Fabiani, and Gratton (2008) recommended that there was a need for further research on video games used for enhancing individuals' skills as they were intended.

Students were more engaged and receptive to the innovative technologies and features that were in their classroom than to teachers' instruction (Muehrer, Jenson, Friedberg, & Husain, 2012). When creative and innovative lesson plans and activities such as video games are not used SWDs may display decreased effort and academic performance outcomes (Mazzotti, Test, & Wood, 2013). "As most parents and teachers have witnessed, many students with disabilities will work for hours to complete a video game to master a skill and level up, without complaint, parental nagging, or bribery" (Marino et al., 2014, pg. 28). The amount of time and level of mastery students are able to achieve in recreational video gaming should indicate this medium's applicability to increase content knowledge and assess student achievement. Student achievement in game-based assessment should be indicated on school progress monitoring reports. Canto, Proctor, and, Pervatt (2005) indicated that SWDs needed 'motivational' content materials to enhance learning persistence and successful learning accomplishments. With educational video games students can receive grades that accurately reflect what they have accomplished in game play and not on how the material generalized to traditional curriculum tasks or assessments.

Solutions and Recommendations

Sorensen (2014) reported that video games were a multi-billion dollar industry, with over 60% of the U.S. population engaging in video gameplay on a daily basis and schools building video game development programs. Today's youth will benefit from reformed education scoring and grading procedures. The goal of teaching content is students are able to generalize what they have learned when they enter higher education and the work force. It is important to consider video games as an advantageous component to the emerging field of modeling and simulation in education (Kincaid, Hamilton, Tarr, & Sangani, 2003).

Improving Perceptions of Video Gaming

Changing how video games are perceived and used in the inclusive classroom can be the platform for gaining acceptance to using video games as a measure for students' academic achievements.

In a study on teachers' perceptions of video game use in the classroom Kenny and McDaniel, (2011) found that teachers favored the use of a video game after using it though they were not as supportive of the idea before playing the video game. The researchers raised an important point on the approach taken to preparing future and current teachers during professional development and teacher education preparation program. They suggested that professional development needed to include video game learning and training to prepare to use video gaming in the classroom. Teachers are the key stakeholders for whether a technology tool or software introduced into their classroom is implemented to fidelity and accepted (Egenfeldt-Nielsen, 2004). Teachers' support and positive implementation of video games may influence parents' perceptions and attitudes towards their child's use of video games in the classroom (Bourgonjon, Valcke, Soetaert, de Wever, & Schellens, 2011).

Assessments, Grading, and Considerations

Similar to traditional assessments, games can be designed to capture either formative or summative data, or an integration of the two. Decisions regarding the nature of assessments and frequency should be made early on in the process along with the type of assessment, as there are also multiple approaches to assessing student-learning outcomes using GBL. Three types of assessments being used within GBL are:

1. Game scoring,
2. External assessments, and
3. Embedded assessments (Ifenthaler, Eseryel, & Ge, 2012).

Ifenthaler, Eseryel, and Ge (2012) define game scoring as a form of assessment that focuses on the player's time or number of accomplished tasks and obstacles the player overcomes. External assessments can be digital or paper-based, but the key is that they must not be part of the game environment. Finally, the type of assessment focused on in this chapter is an embedded assessment; which is comprised of rich data compiled from log files, clickstreams, and information trails that are in-game and do not interrupt play.

Theoretical models of GBL have been put forth as recommendations for successful implementation of educational games in classrooms (Kenny & Gunter, 2011; Ketelhut & Schifter, 2011). Some evidence supports the notion that there are four principles that can be followed to assist in successful implementation of an educational game (Ketelhut & Schifter, 2011). These principles have been identified as

1. Time,
2. Technical support,
3. Social support, and
4. Changes in the classroom structures including roles, behaviors, understanding, and perceived value of the tool being implemented (Schifter, 2008).

Within the literature of GBL and assessments two terms have often been used when describing video games that have monitoring and reporting capabilities; *serious games* and *stealth assessments*. Either can be used for formative or summative assessments, dependent on learning goals. Serious games differ from traditional games in that they are only intended for education or training (Shute, Ventura, Bauer & Zapata-Rivera, 2009). Stealth assessments emerged from research conjoining video games and embedded assessments (Shute et al., 2009). Stealth assessments have been characterized as being "seamlessly woven directly into the fabric of the instructional environment to support learning of important content and key competencies… and is intended to support learning and maintain flow" (Shute, 2011, p. 504). Another type of embedded assessments, *21st century dynamic assessments,* were identified by Quellmalz and colleagues (2012), who characterized the instruments as:

> *... assessments that capitalize on the affordances of technology to: (1) focus on complex, integrated knowledge structures and strategies; (2) provide rich, authentic task environments that represent significant, recurring problems; (3) offer interactive, immediate, customized, graduated scaffolding; and (4) analyze evidence of learning trajectories and proficiency. (p. 56)*

A factor that would influence implementation of different type of assessments for teachers would be knowledge of learning analytics (LA). A large difference between the types of assessments used in GBL is whether or not the game incorporates learning analytics. The use of learning analytics has emerged as a technique to measure student learning within alternative learning environments. A formalized definition is still emerging but the literature is defining it as the "measurement, collection, analysis, and reporting of data about learners and their contexts, for the purpose of understanding and optimizing learning and the environment in which it occurs" (Siemens, 2013, p. 1382). Essentially, LA is simply a series of algorithms that aggregate data. When LA are coupled with specific assessment points and parameters, the data points become valuable for learning. Algorithms aggregate data based on users responses, which include tracking in terms of time and cursor movement. Every click made ends up as a line in a log file on a server hard drive. Analysis and aggregation of these lines allow educators to derive meaning, based on the reports displayed in the dashboard (Verbert, Duval, Klerkx, Govaerts, & Santos, 2013). Learning analytics provide interpretation support through an algorithm which reviews data from many endpoints, aggregates them, and translates them into statistics to provide meaning to the data (Serrano-Laguna, Torrente, Moreno-Ger, & Fernandez-Manjon, 2012). The data are then reported as designed – either as feedback to the user or as reports to stakeholders. "Just as a good teacher continually uses formative assessment to adapt instruction to the needs of the students, a game-based assessment system should continually monitor the ability of the students and adapt itself accordingly" similar to successful commercial games that adapt to the player's ability level (Almond, Kim, Velasquez & Shute, 2014b, p. 123).

In an effort to keep the types of games and assessments tangible, three examples of games that adapt to each player's level during assessment will be discussed. The authors selected SimScientist (Quellmalz, Timms, Silberglitt, & Buckley, 2012), Betty's Brain (Segedy, Kinnebrew, & Biswas, 2013), and Newton's Playground (Shute, Ventura, & Kim, 2013) as landmark examples of games. Each game is comprised of different types of assessments and data collection. The main differences between the games are in the way that the learners interact with the content (structured or open) and how they are assessed (dynamic or static).

The first of the three, SimScientist is a serious game and a dynamic assessment (Quellmalz et al., 2012). In this game, the dynamic assessment collects multiple types of data for each learner through embedded assessments, reflections, and benchmark assessments (Herman, Dai, Htut, Martinez, & Rivera, 2011). The video game learning environment is supported with in-class curriculum, so students are able to take the more complex concepts from class and interact with the content individually in a learning environment that is tailored to their level. SimScientist specifically includes benchmark assessments in an effort to bridge alternative assessments with high stakes testing for SWD.

Differing from a serious game, Betty's Brain is an example of an *open-ended learning environment (OELE)*- an unstructured learning environment that is not bounded by the rules, goals, and objectives of more traditional games (Segedy et al., 2013). The OELE is a learning environment that has the tools needed to practice the skills being learned - which can change dependent on the complexity and nature of the task. Two examples of tailored features are discussed to show the adaptability of an OELE to specific content. Research on Betty's Brain, an OELE, investigated two types of metacognitive prompting through word phrasing, connecting declarative words, and conceptual phrases (Segedy et al., 2013). While the study showed no significance for metacognitive prompting, the results did "provide support for the effectiveness of meta-cognitive prompting" (p. 696) when participant outcomes were compared to those that did not receive any prompting, suggesting the method may be useful for instructional purposes (Fiorella, Vogel-Walcutt, & Fiore, 2012). Contrasting to previous findings, Hwang, Yang, and Wang (2013) indicated that when a concept-map embedded gaming approach is utilized, the concept-map can significantly improve the students' learning achievement and decrease their cognitive load, which is a helpful function for SWD. Furthermore, evidence supports the notion that students who learned with the proposed approach (concept mapping) revealed a significantly higher degree of perceived usefulness than those who learned with the conventional game-based learning approach (Hwang, Yang, & Wang, 2013).

The third example of an instructional game would be Newton's Playground, a serious game on qualitative physics (Shute et al., 2013). Research on Newton's Playground demonstrated how serious games could be incorporated without the use of embedded assessments or learning analytics. Within the primary research, findings supported transferability of knowledge from the game to a traditional assessment through pre-test and post-test scores (t (154) = 2.12, $p < .05$) for middle school science students. Furthermore, findings indicated "students playing the game improved in their qualitative, conceptual physics understanding over time" (Shute et al., 2013, p. 428).

When selecting a type of assessment, it should be noted that alignment of learning objectives and specific criteria for each objective should be clarified prior to implementation to determine what goals are being sought and how they are being measured because the key component for GBL assessments is the connections between the data points, which are interpreted into feedback. The feedback can be provided through multiple or single reports, but is only as valuable as the accuracy of the data point or collection of points to the learning objectives. If the feedback goes directly back to the player it can play "a particularly important role in highly self-regulated game-based learning environments because it facilitates the development of mental models and schemata" (p. 5), supporting long-term retention (Ifenthaler, Eseryel & Ge, 2012).

As more studies have been conducted on GBL, researchers have also reviewed evaluation models of SG and GBL tools (Hainey, 2010; Hainey, Connolly, Stansfield, & Boyle, 2011). Two such models have shown some success in capturing some of the multi-dimensional components of GBL but critics in the field have yet to identify a single evaluation framework for serious game evaluation research (Mayer et al., 2014). These evaluation models are: (1) the Four-Dimension Evaluation Framework (De Freitas & Oliver, 2006; De Freitas, Rebolledo-Mendez, Liarokapis, Magoulas, & Poulovassilis, 2010) and (2) the RETAIN model (Gunter, Kenny, & Vick, 2008; Kenny & Gunter, 2011). Mayer and colleagues (2014) have produced a list of 12 characteristics for an ideal evaluation framework, which include:

- A broad scope.
- Comparative.
- Standardized.
- Specific.
- Flexible.
- Triangulated.
- Multileveled.
- Validated.
- Expandable.
- Unobtrusive.
- Ease of use (fast and non-time consuming).
- Multi-purposed.

If and when a consistent level of GBL tools or add-ons adopt a standardized set of components and an evaluation framework, further examination of in game components (e.g., instructional strategies) can take place, continuing to support instructional guidance and best practices for all types of learners.

When evaluating games for learning, another important consideration is about the type of feedback incorporated into the learning environment. Depending on the instructional task, the feedback most helpful to the learners and the teacher should be considered when selecting or designing a game (Lockyer, Heathcote, & Dawson, 2013). The rapid progression of software and technologies has improved the interactive, individualized, and realistic video game experience (Goh, Ang, & Tan, 2008). Video games by nature were developed so that the player learned a skill or took on a self-initiated challenge to use problem solving skills to master a game (Charles, Charles, McNeill, Bustard, & Black, 2011). As the ongoing process of vetting educational video games takes place, the way students' academic performance outcomes are recorded should be considered. The academic grading system represents students' achievements in traditional curriculum and presentation. We recommend schools adopt an educational video game inventory for students to play. Teachers can then use the students' gameplay data to report out on performance outcomes from achievements in the video games. The students will still receive their traditional progress and report card grades along with the game-based grades. While SWDs may have lower grades from traditional curriculum assessments, their game-based grades may indicate that they are high achievers in the virtual learning environment. Game-based learning data can be collected and reported in various forms. One such method is the use of dashboards in learning management systems that can serve as a platform for the data aggregation and reporting of game based grades (Verbert, Duval, Klerkx, Govaerts, & Santos, 2013). Integration of learning management systems and games can be a practical method to get teachers exposed to game-based learning and assessment. While not all games or learning management systems are designed to connect, some may be able to be linked with existing data management systems or require only minor modifications. While this chapter is limited in breath and cannot cover all components of designing and implementing a learning analytics system, previous articles can be accessed on incorporating learning analytics into pre-existing educational software (e.g., Dyckhoff, Zielke, Bultmann, Chatti, & Schroeder, 2012).

Preparing Educators to Implement Video Gaming

In addition to creating a positive atmosphere in professional development and teacher preparation programs, the educational video game industry should build efforts to develop video game curricula exclusively for teacher preparation programs. One example of teacher and student dual participation of creating educational based video games indicated students were engaged and had high levels of understanding. In a pilot research project teachers created curriculum-based video games for their students learning and in return students were allowed to modify their teachers' video games (Annetta et al., 2013). Annetta and colleagues reported the students' involvement in the curriculum increased and resulted in higher comprehension of the content.

When new K-12 educational content and interventions are recognized and vetted through federal policies, teacher education programs must include those items into their teacher preparation curriculum (Smith, Robb, West, & Tyler, 2010). If teachers regularly engaged in training on the use of video games in the classroom they would both see and experience the benefits of an interactive, personalized learning environment. Teachers could then see the value in their video game assessment performance indicators and data. Teachers would be prepared to introduce video games as a learning tool instead of a novelty reward for their students, and in return the students would view the video games as a valuable tool for learning (Bourgonjon, Valcke, Soetaert, & Schellens, 2010). This could be a contributing piece within the field of education to take the adoption of video game technology in the classroom to the next level.

As video game research explores the different roles video games can have in diverse K-12 classrooms, it is important to consider the role they can play within higher education. Research into game based higher education curriculum models could initiate the use of game-based learning and assessment for future teachers, administrators, teacher preparation curriculum developers, and policy makers. One example of possible future research on video games for learning in the higher education realm can be on the investigation of doctoral level students and their initial introduction to new statistical, research terms and designs that can become the springboard to investigating the role of video games at the terminal degree level.

This is not a novel concept and has been used in fields outside of K-12 education, such as the training of medical professionals. The use of simulator based learning has been a valuable tool for teaching and learning (Billings, 2012). Video games possess many characteristics and abilities similar to simulator based virtual environments. The field of teacher education and preparation has, for the most part, taken to the possible qualities of video games in the classroom, but research on the generalizability of skills is in the classroom is still emerging (Blumberg, Altschuler, Almonte, & Mileaf, 2013). Assuming a great educational video game was designed with features that met requirements and standards for implementation, the general field of K-12 education would not know how to sustain its entertainment appeal within the curriculum (Squire, 2005). Young and colleagues (2012) suggested that criteria and definitions be developed within the research community for video game and simulation based learning environments, noting the importance of distinguishing different virtual learning environments used in studies addressing skills, learning, and interventions. The medical field has been using simulator based learning as a tool for learning, and according to Graafland, Schraagen, and Schijven (2012) there is potential within the field for game based learning environments (i.e., serious games) to serve as training tools. The researchers noted that it was crucial for video game designers and the stakeholders of their respective fields look to implement video game based learning initiatives to collaborate on the making of such learning tools (Graafland, Schraagen, & Schijven, 2012).

Some colleges and universities have already adopted virtual learning environments to build and measure university level students' course work. One example of a virtual learning environment used at the university level is TLE TeachLivE™ (TLE). Developed at the University of Central Florida this mixed-reality virtual classroom includes student and adult avatars in a school environment. Pre-service and practicing teachers enter the virtual classroom to interact with the avatars, practice evidence-based instructional strategies, and build classroom management skills. Results have indicated that practice in TLE can shape teacher behaviors generalizable to the regular classroom setting in as little as four 10-minute sessions (Dieker, Hughes, Hynes, & Straub, 2013). Feedback can be provided during, or immediately following a TLE session. Through partnerships with colleges and universities TLE has been used nationally and internationally to measure pre-service teachers' achievement and performance. Creating college level content delivery and learning objectives through vetted educational video game designs may contribute to the broader impacts of video game adoption and practices. The implications of the future research will contribute to educational video game research and development.

Including more educators from different classroom settings into the discussion of developing video games can begin to influence the field of education and bring to light the potential and benefits video games have in the classroom.

FUTURE RESEARCH DIRECTIONS

As video gaming assessment research continues it is important to explore a video game play grading system that includes cumulative gameplay grades with traditional grades or a separate gameplay assessment on students' progress reports and report cards. This will continue to add to the literature that explores how educational video gameplay interventions coincide with traditional assessments. Students with disabilities may be accomplishing amazing feats within the academic video game play while addressing specific content and then be given a worksheet with the same content and fail. This may result in a school grade that is below proficient, which may lead to additional tutoring time, after school interventions, Saturday school initiative tutoring, and identification as a poor performing student. The emerging delivery of content and assessment protocols within video games is continuing to take shape in the field of K-12 education. With video games serving as an alternative vehicle for delivering content and assessing understanding, there is a need for further research into the incorporation of accommodations through computer based assessments.

An issue for the emerging field of LA is a lack of conformity or standardization in the data being collected and reported. A trend in research supports the notion that data is tailored for the needs of clientele who may not incorporate rigorous methodologies to allow for a more global comparison and growth of the field. Individualized data may be very helpful for educators; however, researchers are not able to draw conclusions about the effectiveness of methods for learners when there is a high variance in what is being measured (DiCerbo, 2014). In the commentary surrounding Almond, Kim, Velasquez, and Shute's (2014a) publication on the impact of task features on evidence from assessments embedded in simulations and games, researchers indicated a strong need for linguistic bridge building between the professions involved in GBL and assessments; specifically identifying roles needed when utilizing task design, which include a game designer, a learning designer, assessment designer or *psychometrician,* and a computer programmer (Oliveri & Khan, 2014; Timms, 2014). Almond and colleagues also lead to a key issue that is commonly overlooked, indicating that many times "task features are determined by game or simulation logic rather than psychometric design" (2014a, p. 1), which can be an issue if the game is designed for assessment purposes.

Two organizations are attempting to research standardization of a common schema by which LA is stored, such as the Caliper or PAR Framework (Ice et al., 2012). The caliper framework standardizes the mechanisms to transmit, store, and aggregate LA data through the use of a common schema. The two frameworks are designed so they can be integrated to provide richer data. However, research in learning analytics is emerging and to date not enough empirical evidence has been reported to discuss directions or details on the developing frameworks for all learners, with inclusion of capabilities for special populations. To read more about frameworks of LA, see Dietz-Uhler & Hurn's (2013) report on LA tools and uses of data from several higher education institutions.

Issues in Complex Assessments

Lack of rigor in methodologies employed within the LA and gaming communities invalidates the research and data in the eyes of the scientific community, like educational researchers. However, within several advanced research communities like computer programming and medicine, we can draw from working models of effective technology use with the incorporation of 'constant edits' that are needed for the advancements of the field.

The technology and systematic methods can provide critical data to stakeholders just in time. Currently there is ongoing research about the information learning analytics can provide to teachers in real-time with meaningful data representation when they need it. Researchers are also looking to find new ways data can be presented in student reports to ensure clear interpretation by all stakeholders (e.g., teachers, principals, parents, etc.). Currently tools that aid in visualization of student data are receiving attention. Visualization of this data can look like graphs and charts and so far teachers' reports of usability and ease of interpretation are positive.

Learning analytics have the power to reinvent how we use data in education. Assessments are going digital and we now have the capability to capture and analyze descriptive statistics for each question, construct, and level of difficulty furthering the profile we can build on a learner to better support their needs and preferences. Researchers are also investigating the instructional power of a game-based learning and assessments that capture specific data to indicate a student's strengths and weaknesses. Learners are alerted to their performance and can make choices about their own learning and the games can inform the teacher about the progress about each student, groups, and general trends happening in their classroom.

Other future studies should also include SWD and their preference of video game materials. Mechling and Bishop (2011) studied the use of computer based assessments with students with severe and profound disabilities. Analysis of student preferences led them to the conclusion that computer screen size should be investigated further. Additional studies suggested are investigations that are conducted to identify SWDs' preferences of video game controllers, touch screen, motion capture, and voice activated control features in the video game environment.

The video game industry has created a niche for interactive educational video game genres. Further developments should include a video game curriculum for doctoral students pursuing terminal degrees in the field of education. The fundamental concepts of research designs and statistical procedures can be presented and assessed through video game format.

CONCLUSION

Using and assessing video gameplay for SWDs who are considered underperforming based on traditional grading and assessment systems, can represent their achievements in the more accessible video game environment. There are many features and content presentation modalities that support this innovative representation of learning. One of the benefits of video gameplay is students' opportunity to perform at or above proficient levels in academic tasks without the need of support from school personnel or additional tutoring. Video game software possibilities may include features where a virtual avatar character appears to the SWD on the screen of the device they are using during their academic video gameplay to assist with instructions and content support. Additional video game features may include an app feature where the student can click a button in the video game with the function of requesting the classroom teacher's assistance if the virtual avatar agent was not able to address the student's needs.

Many students, with and without disabilities, already engage in video gameplay; this is an opportunity to include all students in an environment where all diverse learners have an equal opportunity to participate, communicate, and problem solve with peers at a global level. Assessments through video games can serve as an individual assessment to measure one student's self-knowledge and introduce new constructs that address the issue of team building and teamwork assessments. Developing assessments through video games offers the field of education the opportunity to reconceptualize learning standards that address 21st century skills and tasks.

Kenny and McDaniel (2011) hypothesize that until there is a change in public policy on professional development and training, teachers will not put forth the effort to change their curriculum to integrate video games. Currently there is high potential for using GBL for assessments, but until research can provide support the hypothesis that effective learning outcomes are a derivative of GBL, the costs of such a tool as an assessment method will most likely be surpassed.

The significance of LA cannot be understated. As traditional brick and mortar schools become further and further stressed with new students many are turning to alternative models such as online and blended learning. It is quite common in the online K-20 setting to see 200 or more students enrolled to a single instructor. The reality is that most students are not going to need help from the instructor all of the time; that is where LA becomes critical. Educators can triage the struggling students and encourage those who are doing well. It is not inconceivable that in 20 years, we will look back on LA and wonder how we ever implemented online programs without it.

Virtual learning environments are now common in many day-to-day activities outside of the classroom. Students with disabilities have the opportunity to use video games as a 21st century advanced problem solving tool, and technology platform. Through video games students with disabilities can enter a realm where they are prompted to complete higher order thinking tasks and physical challenges. Video games are a generalizable tool that encompasses a global UDL approach of problem solving skills requiring collaboration, communication, missions, and objectives for mastery of levels. Students' abilities to rise to the challenge and master educational material through a video game should be reflected in reporting of students' academic outcomes.

REFERENCES

Acosta, A. M., Dewald, H. A., & Dewald, A. (2011). Pilot study to test effectiveness of video game on reaching performance in stroke. *Journal of Rehabilitation Research and Development*, *48*(4), 431–444. doi:10.1682/JRRD.2010.04.0052 PMID:21674392

Adachi, P. J. C., & Willoughby, T. (2012). Do video games promote positive youth development? *Journal of Adolescent Research*, *28*(2), 155–165. doi:10.1177/0743558412464522

Adachi, P. J. C., & Willoughby, T. (2013). More than just fun and games: The longitudinal relationships between strategic video games, self-reported problem solving skills, and academic grades. *Journal of Youth and Adolescence*, *42*(7), 1041–1052. doi:10.1007/s10964-013-9913-9 PMID:23344653

Almond, P., Winter, P., Cameto, R., Russell, M., Sato, E., & Clarke-Midura, J. … Lazarus, S. (2010). Technology-enabled and universally designed assessment: Considering access in measuring the achievement of students with disabilities—A foundation for research. *The Journal of Technology, Learning and Assessment, 10*(5). Retrieved from https://136.167.2.46/ojs/index.php/jtla/article/view/1605

Almond, R. G., Kim, Y. J., Velasquez, G., & Shute, V. J. (2014a). How task features impact evidence from assessments embedded in simulations and games. *Measurement: Interdisciplinary Research and Perspectives*, *12*(1-2), 1–33. doi:10.1080/15366367.2014.910060

Almond, R. G., Kim, Y. J., Velasquez, G., & Shute, V. J. (2014b). Rejoinder to comments on task features in simulations andg. *Measurement: Interdisciplinary Research and Perspectives*, *12*(3), 118–124. doi:10.1080/15366367.2014.939528

Annetta, L. A., Frazier, W. M., Folta, E., Holmes, S., Lamb, R., & Cheng, M.-T. (2012). Science teacher efficacy and extrinsic factors toward professional development using video games in a design-based research model: The next generation of STEM learning. *Journal of Science Education and Technology*, *22*(1), 47–61. doi:10.1007/s10956-012-9375-y

Annetta, L. A., Holmes, S. Y., Vallett, D., Fee, M., Cheng, R., & Lamb, R. (2013). Cognitive aspects of creativity: Science learning through serious educational games. In M. B. Gregerson, J. C. Kaufman, & H. T. Snyder (Eds.), Teaching creatively and teaching creativity (pp. 53–62). Springer New York; Retrieved from http://link.springer.com/chapter/10.1007/978-1-4614-5185-3_4 doi:10.1007/978-1-4614-5185-3_4

Annetta, L. A., Lamb, R., & Stone, M. (2011). Assessing serious educational games. In L. Annetta & S. C. Bronack (Eds.), Serious educational game assessment (pp. 75–93). SensePublishers. Retrieved from http://link.springer.com/chapter/10.1007/978-94-6091-329-7_5 doi:10.1007/978-94-6091-329-7_5

Annetta, L. A., Minogue, J., Holmes, S. Y., & Cheng, M. T. (2009). Investigating the impact of video games on high school students' engagement and learning about genetics. *Computers & Education*, *53*(1), 74–85. doi:10.1016/j.compedu.2008.12.020

Anstadt, S. P., Bradley, S., & Burnette, A. (2013). Virtual worlds: Relationship between real life and experience in Second Life. *International Review of Research in Open and Distance Learning*, *14*(4), 160–190.

Barendregt, W., & Bekker, T. M. (2011). The influence of the level of free-choice learning activities on the use of an educational computer game. *Computers & Education*, *56*(1), 80–90. doi:10.1016/j.compedu.2010.08.018

Bavelier, D., Green, C. S., Han, D. H., Renshaw, P. F., Merzenich, M. M., & Gentile, D. A. (2011). Brains on video games. *Nature Reviews. Neuroscience*, *12*(12), 763–768. doi:10.1038/nrn3135 PMID:22095065

Billings, D. R. (2012). Efficacy of adaptive feedback strategies in simulation-based training. *Military Psychology*, *24*(2), 114–133. doi:10.1080/08995605.2012.672905

Blumberg, F. C., Altschuler, E. A., Almonte, D. E., & Mileaf, M. I. (2013). The Impact of Recreational Video Game Play on Children's and Adolescents' Cognition. *New Directions for Child and Adolescent Development*, *2013*(139), 41–50. doi:10.1002/cad.20030 PMID:23483692

Boot, W. R., Blakely, D. P., & Simons, D. J. (2011). Do action video games improve perception and cognition? *Cognition*, *2*, 226. doi: 10.3389/fpsyg.2011.00226 PMID:21949513

Boot, W. R., Kramer, A. F., Simons, D. J., Fabiani, M., & Gratton, G. (2008). The effects of video game playing on attention, memory, and executive control. *Acta Psychologica*, *129*(3), 387–398. doi:10.1016/j.actpsy.2008.09.005 PMID:18929349

Bourgonjon, J., Valcke, M., Soetaert, R., de Wever, B., & Schellens, T. (2011). Parental acceptance of digital game-based learning. *Computers & Education*, *57*(1), 1434–1444. doi:10.1016/j.compedu.2010.12.012

Bourgonjon, J., Valcke, M., Soetaert, R., & Schellens, T. (2010). Students' perceptions about the use of video games in the classroom. *Computers & Education*, *54*(4), 1145–1156. doi:10.1016/j.compedu.2009.10.022

Brooks, B., Rose, F., Attree, E., & Elliot-Square, A. (2002). An evaluation of the efficacy of training people with learning disabilities in a virtual environment. *Disability and Rehabilitation*, *24*(11-12), 622–626. doi:10.1080/09638280110111397 PMID:12182802

Brown, R. T. (2014). A literature review of how videogames are assessed in library and information science and beyond. *Journal of Academic Librarianship*, *40*(5), 447–451. doi:10.1016/j.acalib.2014.06.009

Buzick, H. M., & Laitusis, C. C. (2010). Using growth for accountability measurement challenges for students with disabilities and recommendations for research. *Educational Researcher*, *39*(7), 537–544. doi:10.3102/0013189X10383560

Canto, A. I., Proctor, B. E., & Pervatt, F. (2005). Educational outcomes of students first diagnosed with learning disabilities in postsecondary school. *Journal of College Admission*, (187): 8–13.

Carnegie Mellon University. (n. d.). Whys & hows of assessment: Formative vs summative assessment. Retrieved from http://www.cmu.edu/teaching/assessment/howto/basics/formative-summative.html

CAST. (2013). Retrieved from http://www.cast.org/udl/index.html

Chan, J. C., Leung, H., Tang, J. K., & Komura, T. (2011). A virtual reality dance training system using motion capture technology. *Learning Technologies. IEEE Transactions on*, *4*(2), 187–195.

Charles, D., Charles, T., McNeill, M., Bustard, D., & Black, M. (2011). Game-based feedback for educational multi-user virtual environments. *British Journal of Educational Technology*, *42*(4), 638–654. doi:10.1111/j.1467-8535.2010.01068.x

Cortiella, C., & Horowitz, S. (2014). *The state of learning disabilities: Facts, trends, and emerging issues*. New York, NY: National Center for Learning Disabilities.

Courey, S. J., Tappe, P., Siker, J., & LePage, P. (2013). Improved lesson planning with Universal Design for Learning (UDL). *Teacher Education and Special Education: The Journal of the Teacher Education Division of the Council for Exceptional Children*, *36*(1), 7–27. doi:10.1177/0888406412446178

De Freitas, S., & Oliver, M. (2006). How can exploratory learning with games and simulations within the curriculum be most effectively evaluated? *Computers & Education*, *46*(3), 249–264. doi:10.1016/j.compedu.2005.11.007

De Freitas, S., Rebolledo-Mendez, G., Liarokapis, F., Magoulas, G., & Poulovassilis, A. (2010). Learning as immersive experiences: Using the four-dimensional framework for designing and evaluating immersive learning experiences in a virtual world. *British Journal of Educational Technology*, *41*(1), 69–85. doi:10.1111/j.1467-8535.2009.01024.x

de Mello Monteiro, C. B., Massetti, T., Dias da Silva, T., van der Kamp, J., de Abreu, L. C., Leone, C., & Savelsbergh, G. J. P. (2014). Transfer of motor learning from virtual to natural environments in individuals with cerebral palsy. *Research in Developmental Disabilities*, *35*(10), 2430–2437. doi:10.1016/j.ridd.2014.06.006 PMID:24981192

Delacruz, G. C., Chung, G. K. W. K., & Baker, E. L. (2010). Validity evidence for games as assessment environments (CRESST Report 773). Los Angeles, CA: University of California, National Center for Research on Evaluation, Standards, and Student Testing (CRESST).

DiCerbo, K. E. (2014). Game-based assessment of persistence. *Journal of Educational Technology & Society*, *17*(1), 17–28.

Dieker, L., Hughes, C., Hynes, M., & Straub, C. (2013). *TeachLivE™ national research project –year 1 results: Report to the Bill & Melinda Gates Foundation*. Orlando, FL: University of Central Florida.

Dietrichson, A. (2013). Beyond clickometry: Analysis for constructivist pedagogies. *International Journal on E-Learning*, *12*(4), 333–351.

Dietz-Uhler, B., & Hurn, J. E. (2013). Using learning analytics to predict (and improve) student success: A faculty perspective. *Journal of Interactive Online Learning*, *12*(1).

Durkin, K., Boyle, J., Hunter, S., & Conti-Ramsden, G. (2013). Video games for children and adolescents with special educational needs. *Zeitschrift fur Psychologie mit Zeitschrift fur Angewandte Psychologie*, *221*(2), 79–89. doi:10.1027/2151-2604/a000138

Dyckhoff, A., Zielke, D., Bultmann, M., Chatti, M., & Schroeder, U. (2012). Design and implementation of a learning analytics toolkit for teachers. *Journal of Educational Technology & Society*, *15*(3), 58–76.

Edyburn, D. L. (2013). Critical issues in advancing the special education technology evidence base. *Exceptional Children*, *80*(1), 7–24.

Egenfeldt-Nielsen, S. (2004). Practical barriers in using educational computer games. *On the Horizon*, *12*(1), 18–21. doi:10.1108/10748120410540454

Fiorella, L., Vogel-Walcutt, J. J., & Schatz, S. (2012). Applying the modality principle to real-time feedback and the acquisition of higher-order cognitive skills. *Educational Technology Research and Development*, *60*(2), 223–238. doi:10.1007/s11423-011-9218-1

Flanagan, S., Bouck, E. C., & Richardson, J. (2012). Middle school special education teachers' perceptions and use of assistive technology in literacy instruction. *Assistive Technology*, *25*(1), 24–30. doi:10.1080/10400435.2012.682697 PMID:23527428

Goh, D. H., Ang, R. P., & Tan, H. C. (2008). Strategies for designing effective psychotherapeutic gaming interventions for children and adolescents. *Computers in Human Behavior*, *24*(5), 2217–2235. doi:10.1016/j.chb.2007.10.007

Graafland, M., Schraagen, J. M., & Schijven, M. P. (2012). Systematic review of serious games for medical education and surgical skills training. *British Journal of Surgery*, *99*(10), 1322–1330. doi:10.1002/bjs.8819 PMID:22961509

Gunter, G. A., Kenny, R. F., & Vick, E. H. (2008). Taking educational games seriously: Using the RETAIN model to design endogenous fantasy into standalone educational games. *Educational Technology Research and Development*, *56*(5-6), 511–537. doi:10.1007/s11423-007-9073-2

Hainey, T. (2010). *Using games-based learning to teach requirements collection and analysis at tertiary education level* [Doctoral dissertation]. University of the West of Scotland.

Hainey, T., Connolly, T., Stansfield, M., & Boyle, E. (2011). The differences in motivations of online game players and offline game players: A combined analysis of three studies at higher education level. *Computers & Education*, *57*(4), 2197–2211. doi:10.1016/j.compedu.2011.06.001

Hall, L. O., Soderstrom, T., Ahlqvist, J., & Nilsson, T. (2011). Collaborative learning with screen-based simulation in health care education: An empirical study of collaborative patterns and proficiency development. *Journal of Computer Assisted Learning*, *27*(5), 448–461. doi:10.1111/j.1365-2729.2011.00407.x

Hamlen, K. R. (2012). Stochastic frontier estimation of efficient learning in video games. *Computers & Education, 58*(1), 534–541. doi:10.1016/j.compedu.2011.09.006

Hamlen, K. R. (2014). Video Game Strategies as Predictors of Academic Achievement. *Journal of Educational Computing Research, 50*(2), 271–284. doi:10.2190/EC.50.2.g

Herman, J., Dai, Y., Htut, A. M., Martinez, M., & Rivera, N. (2011). *Evaluation of the enhanced assessment grants (EAGs) SimScientists program: Site visit findings.* (CRESST Report No. 791). National Center for Research on Evaluation, Standards, and Student Testing (CRESST).

Honey, M., & Hilton, M. L. (Eds.) (2011). Learning science through computer games and simulations. Washington, D.C.: National Academies Press.

Hwang, G. J., Yang, L. H., & Wang, S. Y. (2013). A concept map-embedded educational computer game for improving students' learning performance in natural science courses. *Computers & Education, 69*, 121–130. doi:10.1016/j.compedu.2013.07.008

Ice, P., Díaz, S., Swan, K., Burgess, M., Sharkey, M., Sherrill, J., & Okimoto, H. et al. (2012). The PAR Framework Proof of Concept: Initial Findings from a Multi-Institutional Analysis of Federated Postsecondary Data. *Journal of Asynchronous Learning Networks, 16*(3), 63–86.

Ifenthaler, D., Eseryel, D., & Ge, X. (2012). Assessment for game-based learning. In *Assessment in game-based learning* (pp. 1–8). Springer New York. doi:10.1007/978-1-4614-3546-4_1

Izzo, M. V. (2012). Universal Design for Learning: Enhancing achievement of students with disabilities. *Procedia Computer Science, 14*, 343–350. doi:10.1016/j.procs.2012.10.039

Johnson-Harris, K. M., & Mundschenk, N. A. (2014). Working effectively with students with BD in a general education classroom: The case for Universal Design for Learning. *The Clearing House: A Journal of Educational Strategies, Issues and Ideas, 87*(4), 168–174. doi:10.1080/00098655.2014.897927

Jones, N. D., Buzick, H. M., & Turkan, S. (2013). Including students with disabilities and English learners in measures of educator effectiveness. *Educational Researcher, 42*(4), 234–241. doi:10.3102/0013189X12468211

Kagohara, D. M. (2011). Three students with developmental disabilities learn to operate an iPod to access age-appropriate entertainment videos. *Journal of Behavioral Education, 20*(1), 33–43. doi:10.1007/s10864-010-9115-4

Katz, J. (2013). The Three Block Model of Universal Design for Learning (UDL): Engaging students in inclusive education. *Canadian Journal of Education*, 1, 153.

Ke, F., & Abras, T. (2013). Games for engaged learning of middle school children with special learning needs. *British Journal of Educational Technology, 44*(2), 225–242. doi:10.1111/j.1467-8535.2012.01326.x

Kena, G., Aud, S., Johnson, F., Wang, X., Zhang, J., Rathbun, A., . . . Kristapovich, P. (2014). The condition of education 2014 (NCES 2014-083). Washington, DC. Retrieved from http://nces.ed.gov/pubsearch

Kenny, R., & Gunter, G. (2011). Factors affecting adoption of video games in the classroom. *Journal of Interactive Learning Research, 22*(2), 259–276.

Kenny, R. F., & McDaniel, R. (2011). The role teachers' expectations and value assessments of video games play in their adopting and integrating them into their classrooms. *British Journal of Educational Technology, 42*(2), 197–213. doi:10.1111/j.1467-8535.2009.01007.x

Ketelhut, D. J., & Schifter, C. C. (2011). Teachers and game-based learning: Improving understanding of how to increase efficacy of adoption. *Computers & Education*, *56*(2), 539–546. doi:10.1016/j.compedu.2010.10.002

Kincaid, J. P., Hamilton, R., Tarr, R. W., & Sangani, H. (2003). Simulation in education and training. In M. S. Obaidat & G. I. Papadimitriou (Eds.), Applied system simulation (pp. 437–456). Norwell, MA, USA: Kluwer Academic Publishers. Retrieved from http://dl.acm.org/citation.cfm?id=966015.966034 doi:10.1007/978-1-4419-9218-5_19

Lin, C.-H., Liu, E. Z.-F., Chen, Y.-L., Liou, P.-Y., Chang, M., Wu, C.-H., & Yuan, S.-M. (2013). Game-based remedial instruction in mastery learning for upper-primary school students. *Journal of Educational Technology & Society*, *16*(2), 271–281.

Lockyer, L., Heathcote, E., & Dawson, S. (2013). Informing pedagogical action: Aligning learning analytics with learning design. *The American Behavioral Scientist*, *57*(10), 1439–1459. doi:10.1177/0002764213479367

Lovett, B. J. (2010). Extended time testing accommodations for students with disabilities answers to five fundamental questions. *Review of Educational Research*, *80*(4), 611–638. doi:10.3102/0034654310364063

Manusos, D. O., Busby, J. R., & Clark, A. C. (2013). Authentic design in gaming: Changing the rules of play. *Technology and Engineering Teacher*, *72*(8), 8–13.

Marino, M. T., Basham, J. D., & Beecher, C. C. (2011). Using video games as an alternative science assessment for students with disabilities and at-risk learners. *Science Scope*, (5). Retrieved from https://login.ezproxy.net.ucf.edu/login?auth=shibb&url=http://search.ebscohost.com/login.aspx?direct=true&db=edsgao&AN=edsgcl.246179588&site=eds-live&scope=site

Marino, M. T., Becht, K., Vasquez, E., Gallup, J. L., Basham, J. D., & Gallegos, B. (2014). Enhancing secondary science content accessibility with video games. *Teaching Exceptional Children*, *47*(1), 27–34. doi:10.1177/0040059914542762

Marino, M. T., & Beecher, C. C. (2010). Conceptualizing RTI in 21st-century secondary science classrooms: Video games' potential to provide tiered support and progress monitoring for students with learning Disabilities. *Learning Disability Quarterly*, *33*(4), 299–311.

Marino, M. T., Black, A. C., Hayes, M. T., & Beecher, C. C. (2010). An analysis of factors that affect struggling readers' achievement during a technology-enhanced STEM astronomy curriculum. *Journal of Special Education Technology*, *25*(3), 35–47.

Marino, M. T., & Hayes, M. T. (2012). Promoting inclusive education, civic scientific literacy, and global citizenship with videogames. *Cultural Studies of Science Education*, *7*(4), 945–954. doi:10.1007/s11422-012-9429-8

Marino, M. T., Israel, M., Beecher, C. C., & Basham, J. D. (2013). Students' and teachers' perceptions of using video games to enhance science instruction. *Journal of Science Education and Technology*, *22*(5), 667–680. doi:10.1007/s10956-012-9421-9

Mayer, I., Bekebrede, G., Harteveld, C., Warmelink, H., Zhou, Q., van Ruijven, T., & Wenzler, I. et al. (2014). The research and evaluation of serious games: Toward a comprehensive methodology. *British Journal of Educational Technology*, *45*(3), 502–527. doi:10.1111/bjet.12067

Mazurek, M. O., Shattuck, P. T., Wagner, M., & Cooper, B. P. (2012). Prevalence and correlates of screen-based media use among youths with autism spectrum disorders. *Journal of Autism and Developmental Disorders*, *42*(8), 1757–1767. doi:10.1007/s10803-011-1413-8 PMID:22160370

Mazzotti, V. L., Test, D. W., & Wood, C. L. (2013). Effects of multimedia goal-setting instruction on students' knowledge of the self-determined learning model of instruction and disruptive behavior. *Journal of Positive Behavior Interventions, 15*(2), 90–102. doi:10.1177/1098300712440452

McLean, L., & Griffiths, M. D. (2013). The psychological effects of video games on young people. *Aloma: Revista de Psicologia, Ciències de l'Educació I de l'Esport, 31*(1). Retrieved from http://revistaaloma.net/index.php/aloma/article/view/184

Mechling, L. C., & Bishop, V. A. (2011). Assessment of computer-based preferences of students with profound multiple disabilities. *The Journal of Special Education, 45*(1), 15–27. doi:10.1177/0022466909348661

Messinger-Willman, J., & Marino, M. T. (2010). Universal Design for Learning and assistive technology: Leadership considerations for promoting inclusive education in today's secondary schools. *NASSP Bulletin, 94*(1), 5–16. doi:10.1177/0192636510371977

Morris, B., Croker, S., Zimmerman, C., Gill, D., & Romig, C. (2013). Gaming science: The "Gamification" of scientific thinking. *Frontiers in Psychology, 4*, 607. doi:10.3389/fpsyg.2013.00607 PMID:24058354

Muehrer, R., Jenson, J., Friedberg, J., & Husain, N. (2012). Challenges and opportunities: Using a science-based video game in secondary school settings. *Cultural Studies of Science Education, 7*(4), 783–805. doi:10.1007/s11422-012-9409-z

O'Rourke, J., Main, S., & Ellis, M. (2013). "It doesn't seem like work, it seems like good fun:" Perceptions of primary students on the use of handheld game consoles in mathematics classes. *Technology, Pedagogy and Education, 22*(1), 103–120. doi:10.1080/1475939X.2012.733537

Odum, M., McKyer, E. L. J., Tisone, C. A., & Outley, C. W. (2013). Elementary school personnel's perceptions on childhood obesity: Pervasiveness and facilitating factors. *The Journal of School Health, 83*(3), 206–212. doi:10.1111/josh.12016 PMID:23343321

Oliveri, M. E., & Khan, S. (2014). Further thoughts on "How task features impact evidence from assessments embedded in simulations and games.". *Measurement: Interdisciplinary Research and Perspectives, 12*(1-2), 51–53. doi:10.1080/15366367.2014.921034

Oswald, C. A., Prorock, C., & Murphy, S. M. (2014). The perceived meaning of the video game experience: An exploratory study. *Psychology of Popular Media Culture, 3*(2), 110–126. doi:10.1037/a0033828

Przybylski, A. K., Ryan, R. M., & Rigby, C. S. (2009). The motivating role of violence in video games. *Personality and Social Psychology Bulletin, 35*(2), 243–259. doi:10.1177/0146167208327216 PMID:19141627

Qi, S., & Mitchell, R. E. (2012). Large-scale academic achievement testing of deaf and hard-of-hearing students: Past, present, and future. *Journal of Deaf Studies and Deaf Education, 17*(1), 1–18. doi:10.1093/deafed/enr028 PMID:21712463

Quellmalz, E. S., Timms, M. J., Buckley, B. C., Davenport, J., Loveland, M., & Silberglitt, M. D. (2012). 21st century dynamic assessment. In M. C. Mayrath, J. Clarke-Midura, D. H. Robinson, & G. Schraw (Eds.), *Technology-Based assessments for 21st century skills: Theoretical and practical implications from modern research*, Charlotte, NC (pp. 55–89). Information Age Publishing.

Quellmalz, E. S., Timms, M. J., Silberglitt, M. D., & Buckley, B. C. (2012). Science assessments for all: Integrating science simulations into balanced state science assessment systems. *Journal of Research in Science Teaching*, *49*(3), 363–393. doi:10.1002/tea.21005

Rappolt-Schlichtmann, G., Daley, S. G., Lim, S., Lapinski, S., Robinson, K. H., & Johnson, M. (2013). Universal Design for Learning and elementary school science: Exploring the efficacy, use, and perceptions of a web-based science notebook. *Journal of Educational Psychology*, *105*(4), 1210–1225. doi:10.1037/a0033217

Retter, S., Anderson, C., & Kieran, L. (2013). iPad Use for accelerating gains in reading skills of secondary students with learning disabilities. *Journal of Educational Multimedia and Hypermedia*, *22*(4), 443–463.

Rose, D. H. (2000). Universal Design for Learning. *Journal of Special Education Technology*, *15*(1), 67–70.

Rowland, J. L., & Rimmer, J. H. (2012). Original research: Feasibility of using active video gaming as a means for increasing energy expenditure in three nonambulatory young adults with disabilities. *PM & R*, *4*(8), 569–573. doi:10.1016/j.pmrj.2012.03.011 PMID:22698849

Savoldelli, G. L., Naik, V. N., Park, J., Joo, H. S., Chow, R., & Hamstra, S. J. (2006). Value of debriefing during simulated crisis management: Oral versus video-assisted oral feedback. *Anesthesiology*, *105*(2), 279–285. doi:10.1097/00000542-200608000-00010 PMID:16871061

Schifter, C. C. (2008). *Infusing computers into classrooms: Continuous practice improvement*. Hershey, PA: IGI Global. doi:10.4018/978-1-59904-765-2

Segedy, J. R., Kinnebrew, J. S., & Biswas, G. (2012). The effect of contextualized conversational feedback in a complex open-ended learning environment. *Educational Technology Research and Development*, *61*(1), 71–89. doi:10.1007/s11423-012-9275-0

Serge, S. R., Priest, H. A., Durlach, P. J., & Johnson, C. I. (2013). The effects of static and adaptive performance feedback in game-based training. *Computers in Human Behavior*, *29*(3), 1150–1158. doi:10.1016/j.chb.2012.10.007

Serrano-Laguna, A., Torrente, J., Moreno-Ger, P., & Fernandez-Manjon, B. (2012). Tracing a little for big improvements: Application of learning analytics and videogames for student assessment. *Procedia Computer Science*, *15*, 203–209. doi:10.1016/j.procs.2012.10.072

Shaffer, D. W., & Gee, J. P. (2012). The right kind of GATE: Computer games and the future of assessment. In M. C. Mayrath, J. Clarke-Midura, D. H. Robinson, & G. Schraw (Eds.), *Technology-based assessments for 21st century skills: Theoretical and practical implications from modern research* (pp. 211–227). Charlotte, NC, US: Information Age Publishing.

Shultz Colby, R., & Colby, R. (2008). A pedagogy of play: Integrating computer games into the writing classroom. *Computers and Composition*, *25*(3), 300–312. doi:10.1016/j.compcom.2008.04.005

Shute, V. J. (2011). Stealth assessment in computer-based games to support learning. *Computer games and instruction, 55*(2), 503-524.

Shute, V. J., & Ventura, M. (2013). *Stealth assessment : measuring and supporting learning in video games*. Cambridge, Massachusetts: The MIT Press.

Shute, V. J., Ventura, M., Bauer, M., & Zapata-Rivera, D. (2009). Melding the power of serious games and embedded assessment to monitor and foster learning. In U. Ritterfeld, M. Cody, & P. Vorderer (Eds.), *Serious games: Mechanisms and effects* (pp. 295–321). New York, NY: Routledge.

Shute, V. J., Ventura, M., & Kim, Y. (2013). Assessment and learning of qualitative physics in Newton's playground. *The Journal of Educational Research, 106*(6), 423–430. doi:10.1080/00220671.2013.832970

Siemens, G. (2013). Learning analytics: The emergence of a discipline. *The American Behavioral Scientist, 57*(10), 1380–1400. doi:10.1177/0002764213498851

Simpson, E. S. (2009). Video games as learning environments for students with learning disabilities. *Children, Youth and Environments, 19*(1), 306–319.

Smith, D. D., Robb, S. M., West, J., & Tyler, N. C. (2010). The changing education landscape: How special education leadership preparation can make a difference for teachers and their students with disabilities. *Teacher Education and Special Education: The Journal of the Teacher Education Division of the Council for Exceptional Children, 33*(1), 25–43. doi:10.1177/0888406409358425

Sorensen, D. (2014). Utah's got game: Local schools are producing cutting-edge game developers. *Utah Business*, (8), 58.

Squire, K. (2005). Changing the game: What happens when video games enter the classroom. *Innovate: Journal of online education, 1*(6).

Steinberg, J., Cline, F., Ling, G., Cook, L., & Tognatta, N. (2014). Examining the validity and fairness of a state standards-based assessment of English-language arts for deaf or hard of hearing students. *Association of Test Publishers, 10*(2), 1–33.

Stone, E., & Davey, T. (2011). *Computer-adaptive testing for students with disabilities: A review of the literature. Research report. ETS RR-11-32*. Educational Testing Service; doi:10.1002/j.2333-8504.2011.tb02268.x

Thurlow, M. L., Lazarus, S. S., Thompson, S. J., & Morse, A. B. (2005). State policies on assessment participation and accommodations for students with disabilities. *The Journal of Special Education, 38*(4), 232–240. doi:10.1177/00224669050380040401

Timms, M. (2014). Commentary on "How task features impact evidence from assessments embedded in simulations and games" by Almond et al. *Measurement: Interdisciplinary Research and Perspectives, 12*(1-2), 54–56. doi:10.1080/15366367.2014.921035

Tindal, G., Heath, B., Hollenbeck, K., Almond, P., & Harniss, M. (1998). Accommodating students with disabilities on large-scale tests: An empirical study of student response and test administration demands. Retrieved from http://eric.ed.gov/?id=ED423632

Verbert, K., Duval, E., Klerkx, J., Govaerts, S., & Santos, J. (2013). Learning analytics dashboard applications. *The American Behavioral Scientist, 57*(10), 1500–1509. doi:10.1177/0002764213479363

Vlasak, E., & Ranaldo, M. (2012). Video games. *Exceptional Parent, 42*(6), 36–38.

Wilson, C. H., Brice, C., Carter, E. I., Fleming, J. C., Hay, D. D., & Hicks, J. D. … Weaver, J. (2011). Familiar technology promotes academic success for students with exceptional learning needs. Retrieved from http://eric.ed.gov/?id=ED530541

Ybarra, M. L., Huesmann, L. R., Korchmaros, J. D., & Reisner, S. L. (2014). Cross-sectional associations between violent video and computer game playing and weapon carrying in a national cohort of children. *Aggressive Behavior*, *40*(4), 345–358. doi:10.1002/ab.21526 PMID:24464267

Young, M. F., Slota, S., Cutter, A. B., Jalette, G., Mullin, G., Lai, B., & Yukhymenko, M. et al. (2012). Our Princess Is in Another Castle A Review of Trends in Serious Gaming for Education. *Review of Educational Research*, *82*(1), 61–89. doi:10.3102/0034654312436980

Zydney, J., & Hasselbring, T. (2014). Mini anchors: A Universal Design for Learning approach. *TechTrends: Linking Research & Practice to Improve Learning*, *58*(6), 21–28. doi:10.1007/s11528-014-0799-5

KEY TERMS AND DEFINITIONS

Accessibility: Access features embedded in materials for individuals with disabilities (e.g., text to speech, speech to text, read aloud feature, multiple font sizes, and closed captioning).

Dynamic Assessment: An assessment that captures multiple data point over time through the utilization of technology to analyze evidence of learning proficiency.

Feedback: Detailed description and information provided to an individual on their performances during or after a learning task.

Learning Analytics: An embedded or external program that collects, measures, analyzes, and reports of data about learners and their contexts, for the purpose of understanding and optimizing learning.

Mixed-Reality: A setting or simulation that is a combination of real world and virtual environments.

Psychometrics: The objective measurement of skills, knowledge, abilities, attitudes, personality traits, and achievement.

Serious Games: Digital games, simulations, virtual environments and mixed reality/media that provide opportunities to educate or train through responsive narrative/story, gameplay or encounters.

Static Assessment: An assessment taken at a singular point in time that does not provide additional feedback or evidence of learning to the learner or teacher outside of an individual or composite score.

Stealth Assessments: A type of embedded assessment that is integrated into the digital learning environment in a way that does not compromise the flow of the game while capturing multifaceted data on the learner.

Chapter 17
The Creation of a Rubric for the Evaluation of Language Teaching and Learning Videogames

Douglas A. Agar
Macquarie University, Australia

Philip J. Chappell
Macquarie University, Australia

ABSTRACT

This chapter reports on the creation and evaluation of the Language Education Videogame Evaluation Rubric (LEVER) which, it is hoped, will be of benefit to those involved in the teaching and learning of foreign languages. Based upon a sociocultural model of language development, this research is unique in the manner in which it draws on up-to-date best practice in the domains of both language pedagogy and videogame design. This chapter will then report on the application of the LEVER to two titles which have been created to teach a foreign language, in order to both to test the games for quality and the rubric itself for rigour and ease-of-use.

INTRODUCTION

Videogames, once seen as the preserve of adolescent boys, are now part of mainstream culture. The Digital Australia 2014 report by Australian Policy Online (apo.org.au), as conducted by Bond University, shows the development of this gaming culture since 2005, concluding that computer games have become a normal part of household activity across all age groups. Sixty-five per cent of Australians play videogames, 76 per cent of gamers are over the age of 18, and the average age of gamers is 32. Forty-seven per cent of gamers are female, 19 per cent of Australian gamers are aged over 51. Perhaps most relevant for educators is the finding that 98 per cent of homes with children have computer games, and that 81 per cent of mothers and 83 per cent of fathers play videogames. It must be noted, of course, there are now many more means to play videogames than

DOI: 10.4018/978-1-4666-9629-7.ch017

previously, with many older members of society only beginning to play in the last few years. Nonetheless, it is clear that videogames are virtually omnipresent in Australian homes, and are a valued medium of entertainment for those of school-going age. In this chapter, it is acknowledged that these significant trends are not taken advantage of in our educational settings. While schools are adopting technology in a number of ways, Anderson's (2012, p. 1) poignant description of the status of computer games in schools is our call to action.

Teachers are increasingly enthusiastic and confident about using ICT in teaching and schools are increasingly supportive; but there is this 'naughty child' sat in the corner and that's computer games.

We begin with an overview of the theoretical framework for the remainder of the chapter. This framework deals with views of language and language learning that are social and cultural in their origins, reflecting the fundamental belief that people's minds and their social lives reflect their culture and histories (Bruner, 1990). Indeed, we propose a powerful argument for adopting a view of language and learning that has at its heart acts of meaning, or semiosis. For foreign language classrooms, language is at the same time the content of lessons, the main mode of communicating that content, and the main mode of supporting the learning of that content. That is, language is both the object of learning and teaching activity as well as the medium through which it is enacted.

Introducing videogames into the range of foreign language curriculum materials adds another complexity to classroom learning and teaching, requiring the defining and delimiting of videogames in this context. This is a crucial issue for teachers, with the literature demonstrating they are not at all clear about what constitutes a worthy game and, if they can locate one, how it can be integrated into their curriculum activities. Thus, there is an early focus in this chapter not only on the application of videogames to language teaching, but also on their contribution to education in general. As far as this chapter is concerned, the term videogame will be used as a catch-all term to refer to games played on a number of different media. These include personal computers or laptops running Windows, Macintosh OS or Linux, tablet computers running iOS or Android and modern mobile phone technology, as well as dedicated gaming consoles such as SONY's PlayStation series, Microsoft's Xbox machines or Nintendo's Wii consoles, as well as their handheld iterations. At the time of writing, these three latter companies have recently released newer, more powerful versions of their popular home consoles. These machines, especially SONY and Microsoft's offerings, are extremely powerful machines which have the potential to offer unprecedented levels of immersion, depth and scale of gameplay. The term videogame will also be taken as being synonymous with the term computer game. As time has passed, the once clear distinction between these and other similar terms has blurred, and the perpetuation of such distinction is outdated and of little use within the parameters of this chapter.

A main part of this chapter is outlining a recent research project in which a rubric (*The Language Education Videogame Evaluation Rubric*, henceforth LEVER) for evaluating the worthiness of videogames was constructed and then used to evaluate a number of games. The rubric is based on the theoretical framework mentioned above and discussed in more detail below. It integrates best practices in education, language education and language pedagogy, and is notable for its approach, rather than past approaches that have focused more on practical considerations. The rubric is applied to two videogames in order to demonstrate the extremes of educational worthiness for the foreign language curriculum, and to provide a model for teachers and educators to follow when evaluating games for their own language learning and teaching contexts. It is only when our field has access to more of these evaluations, together with discussions of their findings and implications, that we can feel confident in knowing that viable videogames are able to find their place in the foreign language curriculum.

THEORETICAL CONSIDERATIONS

Socially-Based Perspectives on Language and Learning

When considering interactive gaming for foreign language learning, much can be gained from taking a view of language that foregrounds its social, goal-directed character. Such a perspective is found in Systemic Functional Linguistics (SFL) theory, whose starting point for language is its primary role as a meaning-making resource. Language is considered a social semiotic, a cultural tool whose very nature is determined by what it has evolved to do in the service of human activity (Halliday, 1978). Humans are inherently social beings, therefore it stands to reason that human social activity usually involves the use of language in communicative ways to build meanings that help coordinate the activity and achieve its goals. The artefacts of these forms of meaningful communication are texts. Texts are coherent passages of discourse that arise from, or constitute, human activity. They are imbued with meanings that are intimately linked to the social context of the activity. People's choices of language that make up these texts are influenced by the social and cultural settings in which the coordinated activity is taking place. Indeed, texts and their specific social contexts of use are in a co-constitutive relation. The context influences what language is used (the language choices of those involved) as much as the language choices influence the dynamics of the social setting. This allows for an understanding of the dynamics of the production of texts during an instance of human activity, such as an interactive digital game activity, which in turn presents the opportunity for teaching and learning language in authentic social settings. The forces that shape the particular social setting in which language plays a part and the forces that shape the language of that social setting are interrelated within a broader context of culture, whose role is discussed below. First, however, some comments on the relationship between a social view of language and a sociocultural perspective on language learning. The aim is to propose a unified view of a social theory of both language (as a social semiotic) and language learning (as semiotic mediation).

Language learning activity involving video games requires learners to use language to achieve communicative aims within virtual social contexts. This dual role for language – as the object of learning as well as the primary medium through which it is learned – reflects what Halliday (1993) has called a "language based theory of learning", in which language learning is viewed as the very foundation of learning itself. Language coordinates the joint activity of learners and teachers, enabling collective reflection on the activity together with its intended and actual results (Wells, 2007). These conscious reflections on pedagogic activity set the stage for subsequent teaching and learning decisions, which will be referred to as semiotic mediation.

Considerable efforts have been made to align Halliday's view of language as a social semiotic system with Vygotsky's developmental theory, based upon principles of semiotic mediation (Chappell, 2014; Hasan, 2004; Wells, 1994). Semiosis refers to learners interpreting the meaningful signs of others, which are mostly (but not exclusively) language-based signs. Mediation is the process whereby the interventions of one person are made in another's learning activity. Together, these represent pedagogic activity where people meaningfully interact with others during goal-directed activity with the educational intent of intervening in their learning. Language is the primary tool (sign system) to enable the intervention to be successful. The learner negotiates meaning out of the intervening act - the mediation - in order to make sense of the support that the other is offering. Language is what makes this understanding between minds possible (Vygotsky, 1997).

Semiotic mediation promotes learning in zones of proximal development (ZPD), where there is a relationship of learning leading development. Learning activity involving semiotic mediation is a precursor for individual development. This idea is apparent in the well-known definition of the ZPD:

What we call the Zone of Proximal Development ... is the distance between the actual developmental level as determined by independent problem solving, and the level of potential development as determined through problem solving [i.e. learning activity] under adult guidance or in collaboration with more capable peers. (Vygotsky, 1978, p. 86)

An important point to note here is that the ZPD is not an attribute of the individual learner but rather a potential for her or his development, awakened by the inter-mental interaction that occurs as the learner and other people cooperate in some activity when semiotic mediation occurs. Notably, this perspective privileges the primacy of the learner in language learning activity. Learning is driven by learners' needs and desires and is sensitive to the interactions with the more knowledgeable interactant. Rather than a situation where the pedagogue prescribes what should be learned, there is a dialectical relationship between teaching and learning that is captured in the Russian word "obuchenie". Teaching only exists when there also exists the ability of learners to learn. Teacher and learners are "intertwined within a mutually dependent relationship, and the process side of that relationship is what "obuchenie" means in Russian" (Valsiner, 1988, p. 163).

An important distinction between classroom-based, synchronous, face-to-face learning and teaching activity, and digital video game learning environments is the qualitative differences in the forms of semiotic mediation. There are opportunities for extensive and continual interconnection with other learners. Negotiation of roles and identities and extensive opportunities for communication and interaction present themselves. The role of the more capable peer reveals itself for multiple learner-players, setting up the potential for more equitable distribution of expertise (Beetham, 2013). This enriches the potential for ZPDs to emerge and semiotic mediation to take place to support language learning. Videogames can provide the learner with an environment which fulfils both the criteria of being socially-based and offering the player just enough support to reach beyond his or her current ability level so to grow and develop as a game player and as a language learner. They can also support language learning and teaching through activities that address learners' needs in a meaningful way, with tasks that are relevant for the learners and reflect their real-world interests (Wells, 1994; Vygotsky, 1978).

The anthropologist Malinowski (1923) had a profound influence on Halliday's theory of language as social semiotic, proposing that "language is essentially rooted in the reality of the culture" (p. 305). Socially and culturally appropriate use of language is not inherent to the individual, but rather to his or her cultural context. Without a cultural context, language does not have an environment in which to grow and develop. In schools, language use needs to be socially and culturally appropriate and meaningful (Ochs and Schieffelin, 1984). This raises two fundamental questions for language and literacy educators concerned with integrating videogames into the curriculum. Firstly, is the language taught in the school setting reflective of these two requirements? Secondly, is the use of video games likely to have a positive or negative impact on learners' abilities to understand and appropriately use a broad range of language types in a range of social contexts? From the viewpoint of the foreign language curriculum, this sociocultural aspect is crucial for videogames in the language classroom insofar as the language used therein must be appropriate to and reflective of the culture of the target language. That said, videogames are, as such, culturally relevant and meaningful to the contemporary learner, and if adopted appropriately have the power to link language, culture and the learner's developing mind in a clear and strong manner.

Just as video games are goal-directed, so too is language. Language is a cultural tool that enables people to get things done. For Malinowski:

> *[Each concrete use of language] has the aim and function of expressing some thought or feeling actual at that moment and in that situation, and necessary for some reason or other to be made known to another person or persons in order to serve purposes of common action, or to establish ties of purely social communion, or else to deliver the speaker of violent feelings or passions (Malinowski, 1923, p. 307).*

Thus, for Malinowski as well as for Halliday, language is a tool to coordinate human activity. Just as for Halliday text and social context are in a mutually constitutive relation, for Malinowski, so are language and human action. Martin (2007) refers to this as a principle of realisation - a dialectical process whereby language and social context co-evolve. This continues to hold true in the domain of video games, in which the mode of communication may take a number of forms, but the guiding principles remain the same. Many tasks in the traditional language curriculum are based around activities such as negotiating directions to the train station, buying clothes, or visiting the bank. As such, they are often delivered in isolation, in an artificial manner in which the main aim is simply to practise particular lexicogrammatical constructions performing limited and often contrived functions. How much more meaningful might it be for the learner to complete these tasks as part of a greater whole within the context of a living, breathing virtual environment? In this way, particular uses of language may be tied to a larger quest or adventure, or even a seemingly mundane visit to a foreign land, but these uses of language would be as instruments of action, logical, and working towards the completion of some meaningful goal. Rather than role-playing with nearby students in the classroom, the learner might find him or herself virtually (digitally) standing in a bank in Paris, or Berlin, or Madrid, and looking to complete a meaningful transaction, thus using language in a meaningful and relevant way.

OVERVIEW OF GAMES IN EDUCATION

Video games in education are a relatively new phenomenon, and despite recent research efforts, there remains a paucity of studies focused on the analysis of videogames as language-learning tools. Heift and Rimrott (2012) conducted a longitudinal study of beginner learners of German's (n=15) performance in CALL tasks, summarising (p. 540) that "we need to provide a wide variety of CALL tasks that allow learners to explore and practice the L2 given that their accuracy rates differ depending on which tasks they perform." Successful performance in limited tasks does not equate to overall mastery of the language. Chapelle (2009) presents a framework for the evaluation of CALL materials, focusing on six characteristics:

- Language learning potential,
- Meaning focus,
- Learner fit,
- Authenticity,
- Positive impact, and
- Practicality.

For Chapelle (p. 749) "[i]t is one thing to lay out important factors that go into good language learning materials and tasks, but evaluation requires that such perspectives be operationalized in a defensible evaluation of materials for a particular context." Thus Chapelle is advocating a step from the theoretical to the practical which appears to be lacking from the research up to this point. It must also be noted that much of the research to this point has been based around the use of CALL in general, and this research aims to build on the work of those such as Chapelle by establishing a precedent for analysing the language learning potential of videogames in particular within the broader area of CALL in general.

One of the main obstacles to implementing videogames in the classroom is a lack of knowledge of how this might be done. Lombardi (2012) argues that while many teachers view videogames positively, they are unaware of exactly how to incorporate them into the curriculum. This needs to be overcome, as videogames may prove themselves as powerful pedagogical tools for teaching and learning, provided they:

- Are clear in their teaching and learning outcomes,
- Exhibit a sound knowledge of the subject matter at hand, ('correctness')
- Offer the opportunity to demonstrate learning in a manner consistent with the game as a whole, and
- As language is learned socially, the opportunity to use learned language in an interactive manner and in realistic settings.

This also provides the opportunity for semiotic mediation by creating a more capable other, possibly through adding a mentor, a sidekick, any other NPC (Non-Player Character) or even through a narrator or commentator. The early parts of many videogames often use their early levels or scenes to assist the player in learning the rules and controls of the game. This is often achieved through modelling and demonstrating steps that are required to be completed to work towards the goal of the game. Modelling is an essential aspect of semiotic mediation and is usually a step that makes it easier for the learner to get started, and is prior to the "handover" step, where the learner is provided greater opportunities to work more independently (Bruner, 1983).

Videogames will not replace the teacher, nor will they take the place of the many tools and techniques which have been developed up to this point in the 21st century. To ignore them, though, is to miss out on an innovative and powerful language learning resource. Effective learning depends on sound pedagogy, and no amount of technology can make up for poor teaching strategies devoid of opportunities for semiotic mediation. Further, adopting digital technologies requires more than transforming an existing activity into a digital form. Simply adopting technology by itself is no guarantee that the resulting teaching and learning experiences will be any better than had the adoption not taken place at all (Blake, 2013). What is required is a unified push to inform educators of the possibilities and potentials of videogames in the classroom, as well as the creation of new generations of pedagogically sound videogames which take full advantage of the opportunities the technology provides to fundamentally change how subjects in general, and languages in particular, are taught and learned. This should not be an attempt to foist videogames on the curriculum purely for their own sake. Rather, videogames should be used to synthesise all the best parts of the various extant approaches to teaching and learning in an easily-accessible, enjoyable, but genuinely educational manner. As Thorne and Black (2007, p. 149) argue:

Education generally, and language education particularly, will need to accommodate emerging communication tools, their emergent and plastic cultures of use, as well as their attendant communicative genres that are, and have been for some years, everyday dimensions of competent social and professional activity.

It is imperative that education prepares students for the world of today and tomorrow, not the world of yesterday. The development of videogames as an integral component of the language curriculum will require sensitivity to learner needs and the teaching and learning context, as videogames offer a designed experience, privileging interactivity and the agency of the players (Squire, 2006). Videogames are "uniquely organized for a functional epistemology, where one learns through doing" (Squire, 2006, p. 22), and are thus a comfortable placeholder for the language curriculum whose point of departure is a socially derived perspective on language and language learning.

A number of titles are currently used in language classrooms which are uncharacteristic of a videogame in the true sense of the word. These are essentially on-screen versions of traditional pen-and-paper exercises with some added digital bells and whistles. These titles merely take exercises such as simple multiple-choice questions or cloze passages and make them digital. Many of the titles used in today's language classroom are exemplars of this style of title. Packages such as Language Perfect are claimed to be used by over one thousand schools worldwide (educationperfect.com), and Duolingo (duolingo.com) claims to be "the world's #1 language learning tool" with "over 80 million users". Such titles exhibit an extremely shallow form of gamification which, Blake (2013) cautions, offers little pedagogical innovation. To this end, a separate classification for such titles is presented here, termed 'digital wordgames', positioned in opposition to titles providing more complex and interrelated language learning opportunities. While this genre of games does offer instant feedback and positive reinforcement to the learner, the titles involved do not meet the criteria necessary for a videogame to be pedagogically effective. Such is the dearth of quality language-learning videogames, these low-quality programs are far and away the most common result of any Internet search for sites such as 'language learning games' or 'French language games'. They have become normalised as being representative of the potential of videogames in language learning and teaching, and have done very little to add to the reputation of technology in the language classroom. Arguably, the widespread adoption of these titles may have delayed the creation of deeper games built on a sociocultural model, and which offer content based on real-world interactions. Videogames have the potential to offer so much more than repetitive, shallow exercises that are simply coupled to tokenistic behaviourist rewards systems that do not really promote meaningful learning (Novak, 1998). These basic titles will not suffice for the learners of today, who are:

probably too smart to be cheated by the discount games that edutainment often are. [They lack] the coolness of the games industry, the state-of-the-art technology, the constant innovation in gameplay but perhaps, most importantly, the basic desire to produce entertaining products beyond anything else. (Egenfeldt-Nielsen, 2007, p. 41)

Lombardi (2012) calls for a ludic methodology privileging: the interpersonal aspects of learning contexts that promote cooperative learning and the co-construction of knowledge; the centrality of the learner as a complex, goal-directed, emotional being; meaningful learning activity linked to learners' prior experience; multi-sensuous engagement and motility redolent of total physical response methodology; and linguistic and cultural diversity. These principles are essential for effective language-learning using videogames. Exploration and culture (that is, experiencing another environment), present in some videogames, is also of considerable importance. The absence of these characteristics is liable to frustrate or alienate players. Teachers' lack of familiarity with videogame design can lead to poor pedagogical choices, resulting in the inclusion of digital wordgames at the expense of more effective alternatives. The educational videogame industry is often content to release poor-quality titles which are adopted in good faith by many educators. On the other hand, there are examples of educators successfully adopting off-the-shelf videogames in the classroom, for example, Pai (2011), who has achieved promising results in his own classroom by using a varied selection of well-chosen and appropriate videogames to improve student motivation and achievement.

Equally pertinent are those aspects of the game which focus on the material to be taught. Many commercial games, though not created for the express purpose of academic instruction, are by nature excellent at supporting the development of new abilities. They are structured in a manner which rewards risk-taking and exploration. Furthermore, the level structure of many videogames is surprisingly akin to how many school-based courses are designed. Firstly, a new ability is introduced, for example jumping, or, to offer a language-subject possibility, describing oneself. The player is presented with explicit instructions as to how this new ability works. S/he is then given opportunities to practise this ability in scenarios of increasing difficulty. Later, after successfully demonstrating this ability, s/he must again use it to defeat the 'end of level boss', much like students demonstrating their proficiency in an end-of-unit test. Having defeated this boss/passed this exam, a new ability is introduced and the cycle is repeated. These cycles continue until the player has learned all the abilities necessary to beat the game and defeat the 'big boss', just like learners sitting an end-of-course examination.

Learning to speak a new language involves learners developing a new identity, shaped by how they negotiate the social, historical, and cultural contexts in which their language learning takes place (Norton, 2000). As outlined earlier, the social view of language adopted for this chapter foregrounds the relationship between the language used by people in social activity and the social, cultural and historical contexts of that activity. It stands to reason that learners' newly developing identity can be enhanced by classroom materials, resources, communicative situations and interactions with others that are personally relevant and appealing for them. Indeed, Norton (2010, p. 358) suggests:

> *[t]here is growing recognition that when a learner engages in textual practices, both the comprehension and construction of the text is mediated by the learner's investment in the activity and the learner's identity.*

Videogames allow for a high level of investment in the learning process. The presence of a player's avatar creates a projective identity for the learner. The learner is seated remotely and safely in front of the screen, while the avatar takes the risks in presenting itself to the world using its developing second language system. The affective state of the learner is thus safeguarded from anxiety-producing errors and faux pas, helping the learner maintain a sense of dignity essential for collaborative learning in ZPDs (Mahn and John Steiner, 2002; Delwiche, 2006). That is, videogames offer engaging, safe, affective environments for the exploration of new linguistic, and therefore personal, identities. The virtual and safe conditions offer language learners the opportunity to socially interact in a manner that appears authentic (Rankin et al, 2006.) In many ways, this interaction not only appears but is authentic; it is simply digitally mediated rather than face to face. Crucially, videogames offer an environment in which it is even safe to fail. Jones (1997, cited in Delwiche, 2006, p. 165) reminds us that failure is not always a bad thing: "One can be told countless times, but making the mistake and the proper adjustment creates deeper connections with the content than simply trying to remember." Why would language teachers not take advantage of this phenomenon, which Kapur (e.g. 2008) labels "productive failure", and which is a cornerstone of semiotic mediation in ZPDs? Learners experiment with a number of approaches in an attempt to solve problems in their own way so to come to a better understanding of the issue at hand. It is by making errors that they will, under expert guidance, hopefully come to construct an accurate model of how these problems may be solved and how the phenomenon under study truly works. This is semiotic mediation in action, and the true spirit of obuchenie, where teaching and learning coexist and teachers and learners are intertwined in a mutually dependent relationship to achieve common goals (see below for a discussion of building into designs opportunities for semiotic mediation in ZPDs).

Language learning and teaching games work best when they are focussed on well-defined areas of the subject. There must be explicit pedagogical aims. It must be clear what is to be taught and learned in any given level or section. The game designer must have a clear idea of what he or she is trying to teach, as well as a sound subject knowledge related to that subject matter. This should be made clear to the player, either in general terms ("we're going to learn about clothes"), or more specific terms ("we're going to learn about items of clothing, colours, numbers, and the processes involved in buying an outfit in Paris.") The game must be structured so that appropriate topics are introduced at appropriate stages of the learning process, and at a point at which the student is ready to build on earlier learning. Crucially, the language used must be correct and accurate, as made clear by Shulman (1987), for whom (p. 8) "content knowledge" forms a crucial aspect of the knowledge base of the teacher. Ideally, they should offer alternative paths towards achieving the goals provided, as well as rewards for success. The player must want to continue playing, not only because of a desire to learn, but because s/he wants to progress through the game. This can be encouraged in a number of ways, perhaps – to use a phrase familiar to most gamers – by 'levelling up', by winning trophies or unlocking achievements, or even by being given items with which to personalise their avatar, their on-screen persona. This is particularly well handled in games which fall into the genre of Role Playing Games, in which player avatars are highly customisable. One of the most challenging aspects of marrying the two aspects, both ludic and pedagogic, is in attempting to balance both sides by ensuring that the game does not cloud the learning, but equally that the learning does not become detrimental to the enjoyment of the experience. There must be as little distinction as possible between the playing and the learning. The importance and difficulty of ensuring this balance is discussed in depth by, among others, Hyunh-Kim-Bang, Wisdom and Labat (2010, p. 7) who argue for two aspects of game design – learning and fun aspects.

Learning Aspects:

- How to make interaction instructive.
- How to initiate the reflective process.
- How to convey information without disturbing game immersion.

Fun Aspects:

- How to motivate users.
- How to help users advance in the game.

While both aspects need to be satisfied, they should be considered as complementing rather than opposing factors. This view is strongly emphasised by Purushotma, Thorne and Wheatley (2009), who decry designs that delineate fun from learning by encouraging a focus on one or the other rather than one and the other. There would be limited value, for example, in a title where a player is enjoying what he or she is doing, and suddenly encounters a tacked-on task which is anomalous to the game as a whole, which is an unenjoyable chore, and which is clearly there as a poorly-thought-out means of teaching a particular piece of lexis or construction, which, in short, prevents the learner from achieving a state of flow- an optimal state in which a participant is entirely engaged with the activity at hand, a state in which this participant may be at his or her most productive (Csikszentmihalyi, 2002).

Players must be allowed to get on with the game in order to enjoy it, and, in the case of an educational title, enter into this flow state in which effective learning is likely to take place. That said, adolescent learners are no fools, and they will know that games, when used in an educational setting, should have educational value. They will expect that they should be learning something from the activity. The key lies in making this educational aspect fit as neatly with the rest of the game as possible. You will never convince players that they are not playing an educational title, but they will appreciate being treated with respect and given a title that does not insult them either as gamers or learners.

EVALUATING GAMES

Having considered the principles for quality videogames that support foreign language learning, we now turn to a systematic method for evaluating such games. The method uses an evaluation rubric which practitioners and researchers can work with when considering the educational potential of such games. The aim has been to design a robust yet easy to use rubric that takes as a main starting-point the need to pay heed to both the ludic and pedagogical aspects of any title.

As has been emphasised thus far, it is imperative that attention be paid to two discrete but intertwined aspects of any videogame which is to be used in the classroom, namely the videogame as a game (ludic aspect), and the videogame as a teaching tool (pedagogical aspect). Neither of these criteria can be ignored. Failure to fulfil the former results in a game that is unenjoyable, a chore, and unlikely to attract repeat play by learners. If the latter aspect is weak, then the game becomes nothing more than a time-filling exercise, devoid of any true pedagogical value.

The importance of play within a Vygotskyean framework is discussed by Moran and John-Steiner (2002, p. 12):

Play is not just for fun; it is the work of childhood. Through play, children learn to give meaning to objects, to tease out relationships, to try on and practice different roles...as with other cultural behaviour, pretend play starts with social interaction with adults.

In this sense, play and learning are inextricably linked. Videogames offer the possibility of new, guided means of play, in which the child (or adolescent or even the adult) is presented with the means of developing new skills and abilities. Videogames are present in almost every social stratum. Indeed, in a very real sense, Huizinga's (1949) prophecy of Homo Ludens, Man The Player has been realised.

The LEVER (*The Language Education Videogame Evaluation Rubric* – see Appendix 1) consists of 37 statements which are designed to analyse the suitability of videogames for use in the language classroom. The LEVER was created by synthesising the literature which discusses best practice in both language education and game design. It was used with a number of titles in order to test its effectiveness, applicability, and accuracy, and to remove the instructor's own preferences and prejudices from the process of selecting titles for use. Appendix 1 sets out the individual aspects which we posit are integral to any high-quality language-videogames, as well as an example taken from the literature to justify the inclusion of each of these criteria. This justification adds to the robust nature of the LEVER as well as offering opportunities for the reader to undertake further research, if desired, on each of these points.

Twenty-three of the statements in the LEVER are related to Ludic Aspects, while 14 analyse the game from the point of view of Pedagogical Aspects. The game is given a rating of 0, 1, or 2 in relation to how closely it matches the descriptors in the rubric. Each title is thus given a score from a total of 46 for Ludic Aspects, and 28 for Pedagogical Aspects. This is not to imply that the former is in any way more important than the latter; a title should score highly in both areas in order to be considered for use. The final number of questions chosen, and the 0-1-2 scoring system, are the result of an in-depth review of the literature. An earlier iteration of the LEVER, involving fewer questions and a simple yes/no dichotomy was trialled and found to be unsatisfactory. In creating this rubric, an attempt has been made to balance rigour with ease of use. The final number of criteria included in the current iteration of the LEVER offers enough depth to provide a deep analysis of any title, while at the same time not being so complicated as to prove impractical. The twofold nature of analysis offered by the LEVER is useful for educators and game designers alike, and allows both groups to make up for a lack of expertise they may have in the creation of high-quality titles. In applying this rubric, educators may compensate for a lack of knowledge about videogames, while game designers may focus on the educational criteria which should be allowed for in the creation of such a videogame.

The first aspect to be treated here is the Ludic Aspect. Videogames are designed, in the main part, to be enjoyable. They offer an escape from reality, a break from boredom, and, in rare cases, an income due to success in gaming competitions. They are fun. If they were not, then why would anybody play them? Almost counter-intuitively, the sense of enjoyment which many people garner through playing videogames comes not from simplicity and success, but rather from the difficulties encountered in-game and the immense sense of achievement and satisfaction which comes from overcoming them. When the challenge is at just the right level, the player will rarely succeed at the first attempt, but through practice will learn how to overcome a particular problem. When this occurs while working with other learners, the possibilities for ZPDs to open up and allow semiotic mediation between peers present themselves in support of language learning.

In order to be a good, enjoyable game capable of attracting students and encouraging them to play, a title should display the following traits:

- A consistent, appropriate, and clear graphical, musical, and textual style,
- A well-laid-out, easy-to-use interface,
- Clear rules, gameplay and goals,
- A strong, story-driven plot,
- Characters and situations which provoke an emotional response in the player.
- Multiple paths which offer opportunities to explore and use different styles, tactics, and skills.
- Task-based, rather than taxonomic presentation of content.
- Feedback. The player must know whether or not they are "succeeding", however that may be defined in any particular situation.
- A sense of progress.
- Most of all, it must be fun. While this may be a difficult concept to pin down, a game without a strong element of fun will quite possibly not be played a second time.

These traits are broadly in line with those of Vandercruysse, Vandewaetere and Clarebout (2012), who stress the importance of fun or enjoyability, rules, goals and objectives, interaction, outcomes and feedback, problem solving, and story.

Opportunities for semiotic mediation can be explicitly built into an aspect or aspects of the design of the game. This is not only relevant to educational game design, but is also an accepted principle of videogame design in general. There are two means by which this may be achieved. The first is through the introduction of a character in the game who will act to support the player through certain parts of the game. Novak (2012, p. 128) offers two classic character archetypes which may be introduced as more capable others in a videogame: the mentor, "a character who often guides the hero toward some action [...] the mentor character provides the hero with the information needed to embark on the hero's journey" and the ally, "a character who helps the hero progress on the journey and may also assist the hero with tasks that might be difficult or impossible to accomplish alone." These character archetypes as described by Novak have the potential to offer roles conducive to semiotic mediation. Players will be familiar with these sorts of characters from commercial videogames; their presence in games as designed for educational purposes will not seem out of place or inappropriate. The second method which may be used to create the potential for learners working within ZPDs is by offering multiple approaches to task solving or adaptive difficulty levels based on prior achievements. This is perhaps the more difficult technique to implement, as it depends on the game having an analytical aspect that reacts to player actions, to "program the system to adjust to the difficulty level of the players as they play." (Fullerton, 2008, p. 296.) In a language game this may necessitate the player, through their avatar, or perhaps through the game interface or menu, actually asking for help. Alternatively, and this is the more difficult but perhaps more satisfactory scenario, the game may independently react to player failure by offering more or less support just as the more capable other would do in semiotic mediation. For example, a word may be translated for the player, or the criteria which need to be fulfilled for success may be subtly changed to allow for an alternative form of success. Players should have the option of accepting or declining assistance as they see fit. Sometimes these opportunities can be created in a language learning videogame by, for example, allowing players to click on or rollover a word in order to get a translation, synonym or further detail. This help is there if the player wants it; if he or she does not, then the option can remain unutilised. Thus the help offered is optional and contingent, allowing for learners at different levels of proficiency to play the game in a manner that suits their own needs.

Sorensen (2002, cited in Sorensen and Meyer, 2007, p. 563) offers a set of seven concepts integral to the development of any game for learning:

1. Challenges,
2. Reification,
3. Socialities,
4. Achievements,
5. Pleasure,
6. Exploration, and
7. Self interpretation.

It is interesting to reflect on these concepts for a moment; it is not coincidental that those same concepts could equally be applied to any educational or classroom activity. It is not unfair to say that this shows that videogames offer another stage in the evolution of pedagogy, and should fit comfortably within the spectrum of teaching and learning activities if used appropriately.

To sum up, a game which is to be used must be a good game in multiple respects, satisfying a range of criteria. The instructor must have a sound knowledge of the game if he or she is to successfully utilise it in the classroom. Novak's (2012) list, above, offers an excellent starting-point, and can be supplemented by that of Fullerton (2008), which also emphasises the importance of functionality, completeness and balance, and fun and accessibility. McGonigal (2011, p.21) argues for four key features: "[w]hen you strip away the genre differences and the technological complexities, all games share four defining traits: a goal, rules, a feedback system, and voluntary participation." While the notion of voluntary participation may be difficult to implement in the language classroom, it is not unfair to speculate that students should want to play the game. It should not be an imposition; it should be fun. Purushotma, Thorne and Wheatley (2009) refer to the importance of establishing a need for language use, providing learners with "support that allows them to navigate the game interface and learn whatever language concepts they need to complete the task at hand" and finally "creative feedback mechanisms that will allow them to improve their performance" (pp. 10-11).

Many gameplay and educational elements must be considered if a game is to be playable and enjoyable, and should be equally borne in mind by those who might wish to adopt or create a videogame for the foreign language classroom. Should a title be found lacking in any particular area, it may render it a much less enjoyable or immersive experience. Particularly with regards to a game for foreign language teaching, if the audio is poor, inaccurate, or even non-existent, then this clearly leaves the title open to criticism. Likewise if the interface is difficult to see or use, then any textual elements may frustrate and hinder player progress. It must be noted that in the last number of years there has been a sharp increase in the number of so-called casual games. These titles, in contrast to more traditional, hardcore games, often eschew fancy graphics and sounds in favour of low-resolution, low-budget alternatives, and place the emphasis squarely on gameplay and fun. Many people who now play videogames do not demand high-resolution, three-dimensional games – though they still inhabit a very large part of the market – but poor gameplay and frustrating interfaces will not be tolerated by this new generation of gamers. What is necessary is consistency of presentation and ease-of-use of the product. In a ruthless market which is saturated with many games of extremely varied quality, those which are not enjoyable will cease to exist, while a good game will thrive, regardless of style or budget. Videogames have become normalised as leisure activities, and are gaining widespread acceptance in society as a whole. This will eventually need to become the case in our schools.

EVALUATION OF TWO GAMES

Having finalised the criteria to be included in the LEVER, a number of titles were analysed. This chapter reports specifically on two of these titles: Duolingo and Language Trap, which are representative of the variety of titles available in his area. They were chosen to demonstrate the applicability of the rubric to a wide variety of titles, as well as to highlight the manner in which the popularity of a title does not necessarily correlate with its quality as a language-learning tool. Duolingo was chosen due to its large user-base and wide appeal, both as a classroom tool and individual study aid. The literature consistently shows that titles such as Duolingo do not offer the same depth of learning as other titles which are based upon a sociocultural model of language learning. This is backed up by analysis of this title by the LEVER.

Duolingo

Duolingo is a free, extremely popular program (at the time of writing it claims to have 38 million users) which is available both as a browser-based tool and as a mobile phone app. Duolingo allows the user to learn a number of foreign languages, including English for speakers of other languages. The Duolingo homepage claims that the system is scientifically proven to be an effective means of learning a foreign language. There is a strong emphasis on the gamified manner in which Duolingo approaches the teaching and learning of foreign languages.

Duolingo is exemplary of the digital wordgame. For many, titles like Duolingo are not generally considered to be true videogames, but, for a number of educators who are unfamiliar with videogames, they are perhaps their first venture into the use of interactive digital technology. The game revolves around the user translating phrases from English into the Target Language (TL), and occasionally completing short (one-sentence) dictations. There are also optional exercises in which the player speaks his or her translation into the computer's microphone rather than typing a response. The gamified aspect of the program is enacted through players losing hearts for offering incorrect answers, and receiving *lingots* (in-game jewels used as currency) for successfully completing challenges. The player can also link to other users, and see their achievements ranked against their scores, thus adding a competitive aspect to learning a language.

Ludic Aspects

Duolingo's score for Ludic Aspects, 20 out of 46, or just under 50%, reflects the manner in which the title lacks any true sense of being a videogame. Indeed, closer scrutiny of these scores shows that of these 20 points, 9 came from the criteria of *Consistent, appropriate, and clear graphical, musical, and textual style* and *Well-laid-out, easy-to-use interface*, indicating a significant lack of points in those areas such as *Strong, story-driven plot,* in which the title failed to score.

Upon signing up for Duolingo, the player completes a simple one-sentence translation, and is then invited to start the learning stage proper. The game offers a clear progression tree, allowing players to see what they have learned up to this point, and what they have yet to learn. This is not dissimilar to the type of interface often used by videogames, in particular Role Playing Games (RPGs), to visually represent character (player) progress and development. It is clear that this progress will be quite linear, although there are opportunities for stronger learners to be exempt from completing some of the easier tasks.

Due to the nature of the title, it is difficult to analyse Duolingo as a game. Gameplay consists of a number of variations on a theme of translation to and from the target language. These goals are made explicitly clear from the start, and the interface is free from visual clutter, and functions quite well within the overall aesthetic of the title. Duolingo is an example of the digitisation of older means of instruction without fully using the opportunities afforded by technology to improve the learning experience.

Pedagogical Aspects

The tasks in Duolingo are divided into units such as, for example, Animals, Food & Drink. After completing a number of these units, the player is then instructed to complete an entirely unrelated task: he or she is asked to translate a portion of an internet webpage. There may be no link between the vocabulary and structures encountered in this task and that which has just been learned, and this task is of a much higher difficulty level than any work completed up to that point. This exercise is how the player pays for using the game; real-world companies are charged for Duolingo's users translating their webpages into foreign languages.

While the grammar-translation method of instruction is outdated for language programs focusing on developing communicative competence – in particular when it is essentially the sole basis for a language learning videogame title – the form chosen by this particular title is arguably of limited use in the real world. The player, rather than progressing through conversations or dialogues, must complete a series of isolated sentence translations which are repetitive and contain situations which are unlikely to ever be encountered by the learner outside of the game. Some of the more unusual translations from a quick survey of game material are "The birds read the newspaper", "The shark is eating the dead elephant" and "I am dying alone". From a language-teaching point of view, not only does Duolingo depend on outdated skill-and-drill mechanics, but the language – or at least the syntactical choices made by the game's creators – bears little resemblance to the type of language encountered in everyday life. Furthermore, with the exception of the game's mascot, at no point does the player encounter any other characters, if only virtual. No effort is made to contextualise the learning. There is no sense of the use of language as an instrument of action, or of the player's use of language being linked to any real-world social and cultural contexts, nor of it having any real effect on the world. Regardless of the task being completed, or the lexical field in question, the player is presented with the same style of text on a broadly plain background. There is no sense of a realistic conversation or an appropriate setting such as a shop or hospital. This lack of real-world, sociopragmatic use of language, based on the grammar-translation method, combined with a behaviourist reward structure, results in Duolingo's score of 8 out of 28 for Pedagogical Aspects. While the user may learn individual words and short phrases in the target language by rote through using this title, it is debatable whether this will assist him or her to communicate in the TL. While it scores 2 for lexicogrammatical accuracy, it fails to score for sociopragmatic accuracy, as while the language used is correct at a basic level, it does not reflect real-life scenarios.

Duolingo is reflective of general trends in the domain of language education. A safe, traditional option has been taken, rather than attempting to change or revolutionise language teaching and learning. Indeed, this preference for titles which are easy and cheap to produce and distribute may arguably be a retrograde step when it comes to foreign languages in our classrooms. Those people who would produce titles with more complexity are in the minority, and may struggle to find a place among the many titles which already exist. In fact, the existence of many low-quality titles may cloud the vision of educators, and make them blind to the true potential of technology, and particularly videogames, in the classroom.

That is not to say that the digital wordgame as a genre is entirely without merit, as in spite of their limitations they may act as a stepping-stone towards a greater integration of digital technology in the language classroom. They offer tasks which are familiar to educators and students alike. While they may be based around teaching methods which have fallen out of favour in recent years, that is not to say that their pedagogical style should be entirely dismissed in certain circumstances. For the beginning language learner in particular, the repetitive nature of these titles may assist in the learning of isolated pieces of vocabulary, though not necessarily how to use this lexis in practical situations. In the early stages of learning a foreign language, it is difficult to make progress without simply learning certain words and phrases. Regardless of the pedagogical outlook of the instructor, novice learners cannot proceed to more social, realistic or practical utterances without first internalising the basic building blocks which make up these more complex phrases. If these digital wordgames act as a motivating factor in that endeavour, then they may well have a place in the foreign language classroom as long as educators are aware of their limits, and use them as only one of a number of appropriate tools and tasks in the classroom. Much like any learning task, they are best used in a targeted, well-thought-out manner. It is perhaps unrealistic to expect all educators to be willing to, or capable of, immediately adopting more complex videogames into their classroom activities. More simple titles, limited though they may be, may offer the opportunity to slowly become more adept in the use of technology as a part of language teaching and learning. This is perhaps best handled as part of a school, or at least faculty-wide policy of technology adoption which has clear goals in the longer term as to the overall progress which they aim to effect in this area. In short, these titles are of only limited worth if viewed in isolation. However, if taken as one facet of a larger set of policies and aims, they have the potential to act as a first step towards the integration of more complex titles into the curriculum.

Language Trap

Language Trap was created from the ground up by researchers in the University of Dublin, Trinity College, and is designed to help learners preparing for their Leaving Certificate (final high-school examinations) German examinations, and focusses particularly on the pragmatic choices one must make in conversations with others. There is also an unofficial version which was created to trial Irish language speech synthesis, access to which was kindly given for research purposes for this study. While not graphically rich, the visuals, in an isometric three-dimensional style are quite functional, and place the player in a hotel environment in order to solve a mystery. Neil Peirce, the creator, describes the thought processes behind the game (Peirce, 2014, personal correspondence):

The processes behind the design of the game were influenced by the nature of the learning content (language learning), the age, interests and ability of the learners, the environment in which the game would be trialled (secondary schools), best practices in educational game design, and the need for a game that could be personalised for each learner.

Ludic Aspects

Language Trap displays a high score for Ludic Aspects, scoring 35 out of 46. The title shows a number of strengths, particularly under the headings of *Consistent, appropriate, and clear graphical, musical, and textual style* (= 6/6), *Clear rules, gameplay, and goals* (= 6/6), and *Strong, story-driven plot* (= 6/6). Marks were mainly lost in the areas of *Multiple paths allowing for different styles and tactics* (= 1/4), *Immediate and appropriate feedback* (= 2/4), and *Sense of progress* (= 1/4). The title also scored well on *Learning tasks integrated within overall game* (= 4/4). As discussed below, the rubric has shown Language Trap to be reasonably effective as a language-learning game, in spite of a number of shortcomings.

Upon signing in to Language Trap, the player is presented with a back-story and scenario for the game. The title, based on a prescribed task for the German high-school-leaving examinations in Ireland, sends the player into the hotel as a secret agent who has been asked to liaise with another secret agent without blowing his or her cover. Although the back-story is short on detail, it is a viable attempt to draw the player in, and create rapport with the player's avatar. The game proceeds by the player guiding his or her avatar through the hotel in which the game is set, and interacting with various Non-Player Characters (NPCs) in order to gain information and make progress in solving the mystery that has been set. The user moves the on-screen pointer using the mouse, and the left mouse button controls all interactions, including moving the player's avatar (by clicking on a point on the background), interacting with NPCs (by clicking on them on-screen), and choosing responses to NPC prompts (by clicking on the chosen response from the list of potential responses provided). No other controls or interactions are available. This makes the game quite straightforward to play, and thus accessible to a large number of learners. (*Well-laid-out, easy-to-use interface* = 5/6.) Upon encountering a character, the player clicks on this character in order to greet them, and is given a set of three options in the Target Language. These three options vary in difficulty and complexity, but all are, to a greater or lesser extent, appropriate to the dialogue taking place. The player makes their choice as to what they will say, and the NPC responds appropriately, and thus the conversation continues until it reaches a conclusion. This will usually result in the player being given advice or information pertaining to what their next move should be.

Early in the game, the player meets a man in white who acts as a companion character for the duration of the game. Within the theoretical framework outlined earlier, this character takes the role of the expert other, offering forms of semiotic mediation to assist the player in adapting to the game world as well as synthesising the information he or she receives from other characters in the game. This approach towards semiotic mediation offers players assistance on demand to complete tasks which they find to be too difficult on their own. This reflects the role of the teacher in the language classroom, as well as older speakers of the language in society.

In Language Trap, there is an attempt to create an emotional bond between the player and his or her character. Thus the game gives the player a sense of agency (*In-game problems involve a sense of urgency and/or stress* = 2/2), although this affective aspect is not fully explored in the title due to the short, incomplete nature of the game. There is, however, a lack of customisability of the player's avatar, which may serve to disassociate the player somewhat from the game. The simple choice between a male or female character may seem lacking to the user who is used to playing role-playing games, for example, with highly customisable and upgradable avatars. The issue of ethnicity cannot be ignored, with both the male and female character options, as well as all NPCs in the game, being of Caucasian appearance.

Language Trap, while offering the player a sense of agency, does exhibit a rather linear storyline, which detracts somewhat from the immersive nature of the game. (*Sense of progress* = 1/4) To progress in the game as a story, every player will need to interact with the same NPCs in the same order. Indeed, some NPCs do not appear until this is triggered by a previous interaction with another NPC. This does not allow individual learners to approach the game in the manner which best suits them. There is no presence of true choice (*Multiple paths allowing for different styles and tactics* = 1/4). This may be a choice as to the order in which the player wishes to approach a number of tasks, or the manner in which these individual tasks are completed. This is not a possibility in Language Trap. This absence may frustrate those players who are more familiar with commercial videogames, while conversely making the game more readily accessible for newcomers to such media. The interactions with the NPCs are also tightly scripted. Given the nature of the game, it may have proven difficult to implement a more open style of interaction, and from a sociolinguistic point of view, what the game does it does it quite well. Although the interaction enacted is always between the player's avatar and computer-controlled characters (that is, the player never interacts with other real-life people), within the virtual world this is real interaction which is goal-based and socially mediated.

Pedagogical Aspects

Language Trap also scored very highly pedagogically, earning 24 marks out of 28. This is reflective of the manner in which the game is directly based on a curricular task, as well as providing an environment in which language is intrinsically linked to action and getting things done, and every choice made has consequences.

There is a strong socio-pragmatic aspect to the conversations encountered in Language Trap (*Language used is lexicogrammatically accurate* = 2/2 and *Language is sociopragmatically appropriate* = 2/2), (*Social, interactive use of language* = 4/4.) When interacting with an NPC, the player is given four choices of what they wish to say to this other character in order to start a conversation, make small-talk, or find out some information related to the goals of the game. The creator has made a rather interesting design choice which has both positive and negative aspects. Firstly, there are no incorrect answers offered as options, only those which are more or less appropriate and correct. When greeting an NPC, all four options offered are greetings, although it must be noted that choosing a less appropriate greeting may result in the NPC viewing the player's avatar in a less favourable light. This design choice emphasises the real-world pragmatic choices which may be encountered by the player, and exhibits a depth of thought which is lacking in less complex titles. However, when playing Language Trap, each of these options is accompanied by a star rating. The more appropriate the choice, the greater the number of stars received. There does not appear to be the opportunity to turn off this option. These earned stars can later be traded in for help or hints if the player cannot negotiate a particular aspect of the game. This ever-present star rating somewhat defeats the purpose of the game. It is possible to complete the game on auto-pilot without actually reading any of the options provided simply by picking the response with the highest star rating. While instant feedback is a highly valued characteristic of videogame technology, and this star rating may be of assistance as a learning tool, its implementation in Language Trap is flawed (*Immediate and appropriate feedback* = 2/4), and could be improved simply by offering the option to turn it off. The fact that each utterance offered is grammatically correct ensures that the user does not see and absorb any incorrect examples of the target language, rather, the focus is on choosing the most socially acceptable phrase on the list. This does, however, position the title at a level which is unsuitable for novice learners who may not yet be familiar with the many nuances of the language they are learning.

In Language Trap, conversation exists both as on-screen text and as spoken language, played through the computer's speakers. This use of both channels of transmission allows the player to make a link between the spoken and written word, as well as taking into consideration those users who may have hearing difficulties. Thus the player interacts on the level of auditory as well as visual channels; their reading and listening skills are both practised. Their writing and speaking skills are not explicitly developed within the boundaries of Language Trap, although listening to the authentic pronunciation as contained in the (unofficial) Irish-language version of the title may aid in improving the user's spoken language skills.

CONCLUSION

This chapter has drawn on best practice in both language pedagogy and videogame design to create a rubric which will assist in bringing the foreign-language classroom into the 21st Century, and has aimed to exemplify and showcase the manner in which videogames may be created and leveraged in order to best teach languages in light of a goal-driven, culturally-based model. Rather than adapting technology to the curriculum, educators must adapt the ways they teach to better reflect the realities of contemporary life, where technology is nothing less than an essential and integral part of how society functions, especially among those individuals designated as Gen Y or later. Indeed, the real and virtual are no longer two discrete domains, and the ability to leverage this blending of worlds creates a learning system which truly reflects the realities of life in the 21st Century.

Well-designed videogames may offer the opportunity to experience something of the foreign language and culture in a safe and easily accessible way, in which errors are not severely punished, and where learners can practise new constructions or vocabulary without fear of any tangible failure. They should be based upon models which allow for exploration and discovery, in which the learner finds out how to become a part of another society, to become an inhabitant of another culture, in which they learn to play a significant role, and all this perhaps without leaving the comfort, support, and safety of his or her own classroom.

As with any classroom task, the instructor must be aware that his or her own personal preferences may not be the same as a proportion of the target group. That said, our research would indicate that it appears that Role-Playing Games of various types offer most promise to the foreign language teacher, as their story- and narrative-based nature, coupled with the personalisation of avatars available to players, allow for deep immersion of players into the gameworld, and create the conditions to virtually explore the multiplicity of roles an individual may play in his or her life. Just as commercial videogames may allow the player to become a professional athlete, soldier, astronaut or assassin, albeit for a short time, well-designed language-learning videogames afford the ability to experience something of the souks of Marrakesh, the markets of Paris or the architecture of Buenos Aires. Even more, they provide the player with a true sense of agency and the ability to create his or her own narratives and experiences.

One shortcoming which appears repeatedly in educational videogames in general, and those designed to teach language in particular, is that many of them lack both an immersive aspect and an up-to-date pedagogical foundation. While behaviourist models may be of specific and limited use among beginning learners, particularly in relation to the learning of vocabulary, they are of less use when creating immersive environments for more advanced learners, and their success may be in part due to their accessibility and straightforward gameplay, as well as their undemanding nature technologically. It may equally be due to the lack of alternatives available to the end user, either the language learner or the educational institution. While these digital wordgames can be produced much more cheaply and quickly than more advanced titles, short-term economic considerations should not be the prime motivator in the sphere of education. If, however, there is a lack of interest on the larger scale in producing language-teaching videogames which attempt to reflect best practice, then it falls upon the shoulders of the classroom instructor, working either alone or with a team, to produce materials which attempt to allow the learner to experience a foreign language in new and interesting ways. This is clearly an ambitious aim, but one worthy of serious consideration if language education is to truly enter the twenty-first century.

At this point, it is appropriate once more to emphasise our findings that simply using videogames in the classroom will not necessarily improve learner outcomes. It is highly unlikely that an instructor would choose to use a coursebook, or a newspaper article, or a website with his or her class without first becoming familiar with the structure, content, and underlying meaning and ideology of that artefact. He or she would ensure that the material provided was linguistically rich and appropriate to the intended group. Thorne and Fischer (2012, section 48) carried out an in-depth review of language use within the online World of Warcraft, and found that "analysis [...] revealed a polarized distribution of sentences that clustered in two areas – those that are short and syntactically simple, and those that are long and highly complex." This is a pointed reminder that the instructor has an integral part to play in the design, implementation, and ongoing maintenance of any digitally-mediated tool which he or she chooses to use both in and out of the classroom. Any videogame or electronic resource must be appropriate to the level of the target learners. If the title has an online or chat-based aspect, then it must be borne in mind that this can be quite difficult for the instructor to monitor and control.

It is intended that the research findings reported above are useful in a number of ways. Firstly, the rubric as described in this chapter should prove useful for those instructors who wish to use existing videogames in their language classes, as each title's adherence or otherwise to the principles described in the LEVER is indicative of its suitability for use in the classroom. In addition, this rubric should also prove useful as a checklist for those who wish to create their own digital language-learning materials for use by their students. As technology becomes an ever greater aspect of our daily lives, it is incumbent upon educators to leverage these new tools to assist language students to learn in ever more efficient and immersive manners. The potential for learning offered by pedagogically sound, yet entertaining, videogames is huge. It is hoped and envisaged that over the next number of years education will by necessity fully embrace new technologies in a manner which will be truly transformative of the way in which we teach and learn. To fail to do so would be to do a great disservice to students and educators alike. While this will necessitate a willingness to change and upskill – and an admission that the role of the classroom teacher is in the process of changing dramatically and irreversibly – new technologies offer a multitude of new ways of engaging with other languages and cultures in a previously unimagined way. This will require a coming together of game design knowledge and foreign language pedagogy in order to create titles that both engage and educate the player in memorable, meaningful ways. At this point, we would like to echo the conclusions of Cornillie, Thorne and Desmet (2012, p. 245) who assert that "there clearly is strong pedagogical and research interest in gaming, but relatively few empirically supported studies have emerged that relate gaming experience to…gains on standard proficiency measures of L2 development." The next step along this path should be the creation and rigorous analysis of good-quality, pedagogically-sound language learning videogames, accompanied by qualitative, quantitative and longitudinal studies into their efficacy and insertion into the curriculum. It is hoped that the research outlined in this chapter may prove useful in that endeavour.

REFERENCES

Anderson, K. (2012). *Using computer games across the curriculum*. London: Bloomsbury.

Beetham, H. (2012). Designing for active learning in technology-rich contexts. In H. Beetham & R. Sharpe (Eds.), *Rethinking Pedagogy for a Digital Age: Designing for 21st Century Learning* (2nd ed., pp. 31–48). London: Routledge.

Blake, R. J. (2013). *Brave new digital classroom: Technology and foreign language learning* (2nd ed.). Washington, DC: Georgetown University Press.

Brand, J. E., Lorentz, P., & Mathew, T. (2014). Digital Australia 14. National research prepared by Bond University for the Interactive Games & Entertainment Association. Sydney. IGEA. Retrieved from http://igea.wpengine.com/wp-content/uploads/2013/11/Digital_Australia_2014_DA14.pdf

Bruner, J. S. (1983). *Child's talk: Learning to use language* (pp. 37–57). New York: W.W. Norton and Co.

Bruner, J. S. (1990). *Acts of meaning*. Cambridge, Mass.: Harvard University Press.

Chapelle, C. A., (2009). The Relationship Between Second Language Acquisition Theory and Computer-Assisted Language Learning. *The Modern Language Journal, 93* (Issue Supplement s1), 741-753.

Chappell, P. (2014). *Group work in the English language curriculum: Sociocultural and ecological perspectives on second language classroom learning*. London: Palgrave MacMillan. doi:10.1057/9781137008787

Cornillie, F., Thorne, S. L., & Desmet, P. (2012). Digital games for language learning: from hype to insight? Editorial for ReCALL special issue: Digital games for language learning: challenges and opportunities. *ReCALL, 24*(03), 243–256. doi:10.1017/S0958344012000134

Csikszentmihalyi, M. (2002). *Flow: The Classic Work on how to Achieve Happiness*. London: Rider.

Delwiche, A. (2006). Massively multiplayer inline games (MMOs) in the new media classroom. *Journal of Educational Technology & Society, 9*(3), 160–172.

Egenfeldt-Nielsen, S., (2006). Overview of research on the educational use of video games. *Digital Kompetanse* 3-2006, 184-213.

Fullerton, T. (2008). *Game Design Workshop: A Playcentric Approach to Creating Innovative Games*. (2nd ed.). Burlington, MA: Morgan Kaufmann.

Griffiths, M. D. (2002). The educational benefits of videogames. *Education for Health, 20*(3), 47–51.

Halliday, M. A. K. (1978). *Language as a social semiotic: The social interpretation of language and meaning*. Baltimore: University Park Press.

Halliday, M. A. K. (1993). Towards a language-based theory of learning. *Linguistics and Education*, *5*(2), 93–116. doi:10.1016/0898-5898(93)90026-7

Hasan, R. (2004). The concept of semiotic mediation. In J. Muller, B. Davies, & A. Morais (Eds.), *Reading Bernstein, Researching Bernstein* (pp. 30–43). London: Routledge Falmer.

Heift, T., & Rimrott, A. (2012). Task-Related Variation in Computer-Assisted Language Learning. *Modern Language Journal*, *96*(4), 525–543. doi:10.1111/j.1540-4781.2012.01392.x

Huizinga, J. (1949). *Homo Ludens: A Study of the Play-Element in Culture*. London: Routledge & Kegan Paul.

Huynh-Kim-Bang, B., Wisdom, J., & Labat, J. M. (2010). Design patterns in serious games: a blue print for combining fun and learning. *Project SE-SG*. Retrieved from http://seriousgames.lip6.fr/DesignPatterns

John-Steiner, V., & Moran, S. (2002). Creativity in the Making: Vygotsky's Contemporary Contribution to the Dialectic of Creativity & Development. Retrieved from www.unm.edu/~vygotsky/c_make.pdf

Kapur, M. (2008). Productive Failure. *Cognition and Instruction*, *26*(3), 3. doi:10.1080/07370000802212669

Kern, R. (2000). *Literacy and Language Teaching*. Oxford: Oxford University Press.

Lazzaro, N. (2008). Why We Play Games. In Fullerton, T., *Game Design Workshop: A Playcentric Approach to Creating Innovative Games*. (2nd ed.). Burlington, MA: Morgan Kaufmann.

Lombardi, I. (2012). Computer games as a tool for language education. *G|A|M|E. Games as Art, Media, Entertainment,* 1. Retrieved from http://www.gamejournal.it/computer-games- as-a-tool-for-language-education/

Mahn, H., & John-Steiner, V. (2002). The gift of confidence: A Vygotskian view of emotions. In G. Claxton & G. Wells (Eds.), *Learning for Life in the 21st Century: Socio-Cultural Perspectives of Future Education* (pp. 46–59). Oxford, UK: Blackwell. doi:10.1002/9780470753545.ch4

Malinowski, B. (1923). The problem of meaning in primitive languages. In C. K. Ogden, & I. A. Richards (Eds.), The Meaning of Meaning. London: Routledge.

Malinowski, B. (1966). Coral gardens and their magic: Vol. II. *The language of magic and gardening*. Bloomington: Indiana University Press.

Martin, J. R. (2007). Cohesion and Texture. In D. Tannen, H. E. Hamilton, & D. T. Schiffren (Eds.), *The Handbook of Discourse Analysis* (pp. 35–53). London: Blackwell Publishers.

McGonigal, J. (2011). *Reality Is Broken: Why Games Make Us Better and How They Can Change The World*. New York: Penguin Press.

Norton, B. (2000). *Identity and language learning: Gender, ethnicity and educational change*. Harlow, England: Longman/Pearson Education Limited.

Norton, B. (2010). Language and Identity. In N. Hornberger & S. McKay (Eds.), *Sociolinguistics and language education* (pp. 349–369). Bristol: Multilingual Matters.

Novak, J. (2012). *Game Development Essentials. An Introduction* (3rd ed.). New York: Cengage.

Ochs, E., & Schieffelin, B. B. (1984). Language acquisition and socialization: Three developmental stories and their implications. In R. A. Shweder & R. A. Levine (Eds.), *Culture theory: Essays on mind, self, and emotion*. Cambridge: Cambridge University Press.

Pai, A. (2011). Gamifying the Classroom. (Video.) Gamification Summit NYC 2011. Gamification Co. Retrieved from fora.tv/2011/09/16/Ananth_Pai_Gamifying_the_Classroom

Peirce, N., (2014). Personal correspondence.

Peterson, M. (2010). Massively multiplayer online role-playing games as arenas for second language learning. *Computer Assisted Language Learning*, *23*(5), 429–439. doi:10.1080/09588221.2010.520673

Purushotma, R., Thorne, S. L., & Wheatley, J. (2009). *10 key principles for designing video games for foreign language learning*. Retrieved from http://lingualgames.wordpress.com/article/10-key- principles-for-designing-video-27mkxqba7b13d-2/

Rankin, Y., Gold, R., & Gooch, B. (2006). 3D Role-Playing Games as Language Learning Tools. *Eurographics*, *25*(3), 211–225.

Shulman, L. S. (1987). Knowledge and Teaching: Foundations of the New Reform. *Harvard Educational Review*, *57*(1), 1–22. doi:10.17763/haer.57.1.j463w79r56455411

Sorensen, B. H., & Meyer, B. (2007). Serous Games in language learning and teaching – a theoretical perspective. *Situated Play, Proceedings of DiGRA 2007 Conference*.

Squire, K. (2006). From Content to Context: Videogames as Designed Experience. *Educational Researcher*, *35*(8), 19–29. doi:10.3102/0013189X035008019

Thorne, S. L., & Black, R. W. (2007). Language and Literacy Development in Computer-Mediated Contexts and Communities. *Annual Review of Applied Linguistics*, *27*, 133–160. doi:10.1017/S0267190508070074

Thorne, S. L., and Fischer, I., (2012). Online gaming as sociable media. *Alsic Apprentissage des Langues et Systèmes d'Information et de Communication*. (on-line), *15* (1) (last retrieved 22nd August 2014.)

Valsiner, J. (1988). *Developmental Psychology in the Soviet Union*. Indiana: Indiana University Press.

Vandercruysse, S., Vandewaetere, M., & Clarebout, G. (2012). Game-Based Learning: A Review on the Effectiveness of Educational Games. In M. M. Cruz-Cunha (Ed.), *Handbook of Research on Serious Games as Educational, Business, and Research Tools* (pp. 628–647). Hershey, PA: IGI Global. doi:10.4018/978-1-4666-0149-9.ch032

Vygotsky, L. S. (1997). Interaction between learning and development. In M. Gauvain, & M. Cole (Eds.), Readings on the development of children (2nd ed.). New York: W.H. Freeman and Company.

Vygotsky, L. S. (1997). Thinking and Speech. In R.W. Rieber and A.S. Carton (Eds.), The Collected Works of L. S. Vygotsky: Vol. 1. Problems of General Psychology (pp. 39–285). New York: Plenum Press.

Vygotsky, L. S. (1999). *The collected works of L.S. Vygotsky* (R.W. Rieber, Ed.) (Vol. 6). New York: Plenum Press.

Wells, G. (1994). The complementary contributions of Halliday and Vygotsky to a "language-based theory of learning". *Linguistics and Education*, *6*(1), 41–90. doi:10.1016/0898-5898(94)90021-3

Wells, G. (2007). The mediating role of discoursing in activity. *Mind, Culture, and Activity*, *14*(3), 160–177. doi:10.1080/10749030701316300

APPENDIX 1

Table 1. Lever element theoretical underpinnings

Ludic Aspects	
Criterion	**Justification/Reference**
Consistent, appropriate, and clear graphical, musical, and textual style	Novak (2012), principles of videogame design
Well-laid-out, easy-to-use interface	Purushotma, Thorne and Wheatley (2009), principles for designing video games for language learning; Novak (2012), principles of videogame design
Clear rules, gameplay, and goals	Vandercruysse, Vandewaetere and Clarebout (2012), Game-based Learning
Strong, story-driven plot	Novak (2012), principles of videogame design; Vandercruysse, Vandewaetere and Clarebout (2012), Game-based Learning
Creation of affective responses through characters and situations	Lazzaro (in Fullerton, 2008), 4 Fun Keys
Multiple paths allowing for different styles and tactics	Fullerton (2008), principles of videogame design
Immediate and appropriate feedback	McGonigal (2011); Purushotma, Thorne and Wheatley (2009), principles for designing video games for language learning
Sense of progress	Novak (2012), principles of videogame design;, Vandercruysse, Vandewaetere and Clarebout (2012), Game-based Learning
Learning tasks integrated within overall game (crossover with pedagogical aspects)	Lombardi (2012), Ludic Methodology
Pedagogical Aspects	
Criterion	**Justification/Reference**
Clear teaching and learning outcomes	Peterson (2010), previous work on MMORPGs and language learning; Blake (2013), titles must "support specific L2 learning tasks"; Griffiths (2002), "enlightenment not entertainment"
Sound knowledge of the subject matter ('correctness')	Shulman's, (1987) forms of teacher knowledge, especially "content knowledge".
Task-based presentation of content	Halliday (1993), Systemic Functional Grammar; Malinowski (1966), language is "primarily an instrument of action"
Provides mediation and support for learning	Vygotsky (1999), Zone of Proximal Development
Difficulty is appropriate to the learner	Vygotsky (1999), Zone of Proximal Development
Social, interactive use of language	Halliday (1978), Language as a Social Semiotic; Kern (2000), opposition to Structuralism; Egenfeldt-Nielsen (2006), opposition to Behaviourism
Cultural appropriacy	Malinowsi (1923), language is "rooted in the reality of the culture"; Ochs and Schieffelin (1984), language use must be "socially appropriate and culturally meaningful"; Lombardi (2012), Ludic Methodology

APPENDIX 2

Table 2. Duolingo analysis

Ludic Aspects	
Consistent, appropriate, and clear graphical, musical, and textual style	
Music and audio are appropriate, music can be turned off if desired	1
Visuals appropriate to setting	1
Textual style is appropriate to setting and curriculum	1
Well-laid-out, easy-to-use interface	
Buttons are clearly labelled	2
There is an option for "help" or "instructions"	2
In-game menus are clear, easily-accessible, and helpful	2
Clear rules, gameplay, and goals	
It is obvious to the player what he/she is to do	1
There are no unfair surprises or inconsistent rules	2
Gameplay achievements are allied to learning achievements	2
Strong, story-driven plot	
Themes relevant to target user group	0
Engaging complications in storyline	0
Theme relevant to curricular themes	0
Creation of affective responses through characters and situations	
Player character is "likeable" and can be customised	0
NPCs are fleshed out, and have personalities which are "likeable" or "dislikeable"	0
In-game problems involve a sense of urgency and/or stress	1
Multiple paths allowing for different styles and tactics	
More than one "correct" way to solve problems	0
Optional, more challenging situations are offered to more capable players	1
Immediate and appropriate feedback	
Feedback is in-game, and involves rewards as appropriate	2
Feedback is related to performance, and offers assistance as to possible improvements	2
Sense of progress	
Tasks become more difficult as the game progresses	0
On-screen avatar (if present) shows progress through new outfits, equipment etc.	0
Learning tasks integrated within overall game (crossover with pedagogical aspects)	
Tasks make sense within overall context of the game, not merely "tacked on"	0
Tasks reflect the curriculum and real-world scenarios	0

continued on following page

Table 2. Continued

Pedagogical Aspects	
Clear teaching and learning outcomes	
Tasks have clear learning objectives which reflect curricular demands	0
New learning is integrated with prior knowledge; information is recycled	0
Sound knowledge of the subject matter ('correctness')	
Language used is lexicogrammatically accurate	2
Language is sociopragmatically appropriate	0
Assessment of learning is integral to game progress	2
Task-based presentation of content	
New learning is used to 'do' things within the game	0
Provides mediation and support for learning	
In-game help is available on demand	1
'More capable other' is present (mentor, sidekick etc.)	1
Difficulty is appropriate to the learner	
Prior learning is taken into account	0
Tasks lie within the learner's ZPD (Goldilocks Zone: not too easy, not too hard)	0
Social, interactive use of language	
Players use language with other avatars/NPCs	0
A sense that the game takes place in a living, breathing setting	0
Cultural appropriacy	
Setting makes sense in the context of the target language	0
The game avoids sexism, racism etc.	2

APPENDIX 3

Table 3. Language Trap analysis

Ludic Aspects	
Consistent, appropriate, and clear graphical, musical, and textual style	
Music and audio are appropriate, music can be turned off if desired	2
Visuals appropriate to setting	2
Textual style is appropriate to setting and curriculum	2
Well-laid-out, easy-to-use interface	
Buttons are clearly labelled	2
There is an option for "help" or "instructions"	2
In-game menus are clear, easily-accessible, and helpful	1
Clear rules, gameplay, and goals	
It is obvious to the player what he/she is to do	2
There are no unfair surprises or inconsistent rules	2
Gameplay achievements are allied to learning achievements	2
Strong, story-driven plot	
Themes relevant to target user group	2
Engaging complications in storyline	2
Theme relevant to curricular themes	2
Creation of affective responses through characters and situations	
Player character is "likeable" and can be customised	1
NPCs are fleshed out, and have personalities which are "likeable" or "dislikeable"	1
In-game problems involve a sense of urgency and/or stress	2
Multiple paths allowing for different styles and tactics	
More than one "correct" way to solve problems	1
Optional, more challenging situations are offered to more capable players	0
Immediate and appropriate feedback	
Feedback is in-game, and involves rewards as appropriate	1
Feedback is related to performance, and offers assistance as to possible improvements	1
Sense of progress	
Tasks become more difficult as the game progresses	1
On-screen avatar (if present) shows progress through new outfits, equipment etc.	0
Learning tasks integrated within overall game (crossover with pedagogical aspects)	
Tasks make sense within overall context of the game, not merely "tacked on"	2
Tasks reflect the curriculum and real-world scenarios	2

continued on following page

Table 3. Continued

Pedagogical Aspects	
Clear teaching and learning outcomes	
Tasks have clear learning objectives which reflect curricular demands	2
New learning is integrated with prior knowledge; information is recycled	1
Sound knowledge of the subject matter ('correctness')	
Language used is lexicogrammatically accurate	2
Language is sociopragmatically appropriate	2
Assessment of learning is integral to game progress	2
Task-based presentation of content	
New learning is used to 'do' things within the game	2
Provides mediation and support for learning	
In-game help is available on demand	1
'More capable other' is present (mentor, sidekick etc.)	2
Difficulty is appropriate to the learner	
Prior learning is taken into account	1
Tasks lie within the learner's ZPD (Goldilocks Zone: not too easy, not too hard)	1
Social, interactive use of language	
Players use language with other avatars/NPCs	2
A sense that the game takes place in a living, breathing setting	2
Cultural appropriacy	
Setting makes sense in the context of the target language	2
The game avoids sexism, racism etc.	1

Chapter 18
Can Pre-Service Teachers Create Digital Game-Based Activities without Coding Knowledge?

Phu Vu
University of Nebraska at Kearney, USA

Martonia Gaskill
University of Nebraska at Kearney, USA

ABSTRACT

This chapter examined five cases of pre-service teachers' abilities and attitudes towards creating and using digital games in their future teaching. Participants included five pre-service teachers at a Midwest public university. The participants underwent the same research procedure including: pre-project open-ended interview, training session, and post-project open-ended interview. The researchers analyzed participants' responses to the interviews and the quality of the games they created, using the Educational Electronic Games Rubric. Results showed that students not only enjoyed learning about digital games, but also were able to create quality games without coding knowledge or advanced technology skills. Five participants indicated that they plan on creating and integrating digital games into their future teaching.

INTRODUCTION

I'm calling for investments in educational technology that will help create... educational software that's as compelling as the best video game. I want you guys to be stuck on a video game that's teaching you something other than just blowing something up. - President Obama, March 2011

Interest in game-based learning and integrating digital games or video games into education has risen in recent years (Garris, Ahlers, & Driskell, 2002; Moreno-Ger et al., 2008; Shaffer, Squire, Halverson, & Gee, 2005; Squire, 2003; Van Eck, 2006). In 2013, more than half of the Small Business Innovation Research (SBIR) Grant/Awards from the US Department of Education were given

DOI: 10.4018/978-1-4666-9629-7.ch018

to game-related projects (DeLoura & Metz, 2013). Recently the National Science Foundation (NSF) also offered many grant categories for game-related projects. Despite the priority and emphasis of integrating games into the classrooms, Epper et al. (2012) made the point that true adoption and institutional implementation of games into classrooms are still at the experimental stage. One of the biggest challenges for games to be integrated into classrooms is the fact that teachers lack the skills and knowledge to create games usable in their teaching. This suggests the need for extensive training and planning in pre-service education programs and in the schools. Most of game- creating platforms and/or programs require users a certain amount of coding skills and/or knowledge to be able to create a game applicable to classroom use. To that end, this research project seeks to solve the challenge by determining whether pre-service teachers without any code knowledge/expertise can create game-based activities usable for their student teaching after attending a short period of training, and what can be learned from that process. Specifically, the objective of the research project, which is a case study with five cases, is to answer the following research questions.

1. Can pre-service teachers without any coding skills be trained in a short period of time to create game-based activities usable for their student teaching?
2. What can be learned from that process?

REVIEW OF LITERATURE

Imagine if kids poured their time and passion into a video game that taught them math concepts while they barely noticed, because it was so enjoyable.
- Bill Gates, July 11, 2012

The use of games in education is not new. In fact, there are significant number of studies conducted in the 60's and 70's addressing the use of instructional game in the classroom. The first educational computer games made their way into the schools in the 80s when desktop computers were still considered a luxury. Computer games such as Oregon Trail and Carmen Sandiego enriched the classroom dynamics through gaming features such as characters, graphics and sound. It was the beginning of a journey that paved the way to sophisticated gaming technology such as simulation and augmented reality, namely Big Brain Academy and Bot Colony. Fields such as science and engineering have used gaming as learning tools for the longest time and continue to do so because of the authentic learning opportunities gaming has offer (Holand et al, 2003). Although gaming as an educational tool is finally starting to attract the education audience, it has not always been the case. Games have been long ignored by educators and researchers due to the lack of sound pedagogical standards and the infamous drill and practice approaches to game design widely used in the past (Gredler, 1996). It is worth to note that a common theme found in both earlier studies and recent research is that although gaming strategies have not necessarily improved learning outcomes, it has, however, significantly impacted student engagement and interest in participating in classroom activities.

Why Using Digital Games? Digital gaming, a term that includes digital video, computer, mobile and social media games is believed to have the potential to transform K-12 education and beyond (Prensky, 2001; Shaffer, Squire, Halverson & Gee, 2005). Jenkins (2002) states that games offer educators resources that are likely to bring life to their lessons and to motivate students to learn through rich and compelling problem solving. The authors further explain that gaming strategies can enhance gifted teachers instead of displacing them with impersonal technology. Vu et al (2014) argue that to enable students to learn how to learn and still perform well on standardized testing, the use of digital games must be implemented in the classroom. Another recent study by Takeuchi and

Vaala (2014) found that digital games have indeed entered K-8 classrooms with 74% of K-8 teacher participants using digital games for instruction. The study reports that gender did not predict digital game use in the classroom, however, younger teachers, teachers in low-income schools and teachers who play digital games themselves are more likely to use digital games with their students. Perhaps games are finally thriving in a time where video games and other innovative technologies have become, or are becoming, a standard tool in the hands of students and the population at large. It is also worthy to note that digital games are very different from what they used to be a decade ago. Current games are education- oriented, fun and for that reason alone they should be used for teaching and learning (Squire, 2008).

Pre-Service Teacher Preparation. Takeuchi and Vaala (2014) found that only 8% of K-8 teachers reported receiving pre-service training on digital game integration. This finding reveals the general lack of technology training in pre-service teacher programs. Many in-service teachers take advantage of online resources for just in time professional development and ideas. However, more adequate pre-service training and strategies to maximize professional development are needed (Takeuchi and Vaala, 2014).

Recent studies have also suggested that schools are failing generations of students due to the use of teaching approaches that are not aligned with students needs making the classroom environment a disconnected place for learners (Vu et al., 2014; Cross-Bystrom, 2010; Fudin, 2012; Gershenfeld, 2011; Squire, 2008). Such statement has serious implications to pre-service teacher preparation programs. Although little research has been conducted on the use of game base strategies with pre-service teachers, few recent studies offer some insights on the role of games in the educational process from pre-service teachers' perspective (Can & Cagiltay, 2006; Pastore & Falvo, 2010; Ruggiero, 2013; Sardone & Devlin-Scherer, 2010; Schrader, Zheng, & Young, 2006). These research studies have generally reported a positive attitude towards using games in both teaching and learning. Few studies revealed pre-service teachers' uncertainty towards successfully implementing games in the classroom (Hsu & Chiou, 2011; King, Schneider, Kozdras, Minick, Welsh, Brindley, Feger & Kirby, 2013). With President Obama's endorsement of video game implementation in K-12 classrooms, it is likely that teacher education programs will find ways to energize or revamp pre-service teachers' training to include current teaching and learning trends such as digital gaming and mobile learning initiatives. These are important trends that seem to address the perceived disconnect between schools and the digital learners.

METHODOLOGY

This is a case study with five cases. We used a case study approach for this project because it enables us to answer "how" and "why" type questions, while taking into consideration how a phenomenon is affected by the context within which it is situated (Baxter & Jack, 2008). In addition, the data collected in a case study is normally a lot richer and of greater depth than can be found through other experimental designs. Five pre-service teachers in a teacher education program at a Midwest public university were purposefully selected for this study. A stratified purposeful sample was based on the 2011 demographic profile of teachers in the U.S by Feistritzer (2011). Accordingly, 84% teachers in American public schools were female and 15% were male. In line with that demographic profile, four white female students and one male teacher candidates were included in this study. All five participants were between the ages of 19 and 24 and were earning their first college degree.

Data Collection

Several phases of data collection occurred over the course of the research project to make sure that the data sources are reliable and valid. We hoped that the five separate participants would affirm one another's stories for the purpose of triangulation.

The first phase involved structured open-ended interviews (Patton, 1990) with the five teacher candidates before they attended the game training sessions. The 45-minute interviews took place in one of the researchers' offices. After completing the interview, the participants scheduled 45-minute one-on-one training sessions with one of the researchers who was in charge of the training. During the training sessions, the research participants could either use their own iPads or the researchers' iPad to learn about the basic game-creating principles and how to create a digital game using a free app called TinyTap downloaded from the Apple's app store. After the training session, each participant had one week to create their own games and send the links to their games to the researchers for evaluation. The researcher used the Educational Electronic Games Rubric (please see the detailed rubric in the appendix section) by the California State University to evaluate whether the games could be utilized in the teaching situations. The rubric had three sets of criteria including organization and design, instructional design and delivery, and game-based learning. Each set of criteria had many sub-criteria. The levels of achievement were categorized into "Baseline" equivalent with zero point, "Effective" equivalent with three points, and "Exemplary" equivalent with five points. After the game was evaluated, the researcher did not reveal the evaluation result to the participants while they were in the second interview to avoid any possible bias. The third data collection phase include the structured open-ended interviews with the participants after they completed and sent the games they created to the researchers. The interviews were conducted in one of the researchers' offices and lasted 45 minutes. Five research participants' interview recordings before and after the one-one-one training and artifacts (digital game) were coded and put into five sub-folders named Participant 1, Participant 2, Participant 3, Participant 4, and Participant 5 for the ease of analysis, and confidentiality purposes.

Data Analysis

The constant comparative method (Glaser& Strauss, 1967) was used throughout this study to obtain a better understanding of the experiences of the teacher candidates in the process of learning and creating a digital game. As categories emerged from the coding of the interviews prior and post training sessions, they were compared to one another and among the five research participants. Analysis began with the transcriptions from the interviews. The transcripts were read and initial impressions noted in the margins. Interview transcripts of participants were read and sections were highlighted that seemed relevant to the research questions. Common themes were noted in the margins and became the codes. Below is an example of how our data were processed.

"I think video games are good for learning because when playing, the player can learn different skills such as quick decision making, and analysis.": Our code: useful

For the evaluation of the digital games created by the research participants, the researcher used the Educational Electronic Games Rubric to evaluate each of the digital game. Specific scores were given to each game. A game with a score range from 40-50 was considered "Exemplary"; a game with a score range from 30-39 was considered "Effective"; and a game with a score less than 30 was considered "Baseline".

Figure 1. Screenshot of the game by participant 1

FINDINGS

Case 1

Participant 1 was a white female teacher candidate. She did not have any experience or expertise in coding. In the interview prior to the training session, participant 1 stated that none of her teachers used games, so game-based learning or using games in classroom setting was a new concept to her. However, she noted that digital games should be integrated into classrooms to help students learn better. Recently she was in a classroom at a middle school to help a teacher. From her observation, she thought that games could have motivated students to perform better and to engage in the learning activities. She also indicated that she would definitely integrate digital games into her student teaching and future teaching practices when she had her own classroom. She acknowledged that one of the challenges of using games in the classroom was the fact that she did not know how to create digital games. There were many game-based learning resources available on the Internet; however, not all of the resources are usable in the classroom setting. Three days after the training, participant 1 sent the researchers a link to her game. The purpose of the game was to help students become familiar with the faces that helped the Patriots win the Revolutionary War. The game had four levels in which players had to listen to the oral description and select the correct images. Below is a screenshot of the game in the first level (see Figure 1).

Based on the Educational Electronic Games Rubric, this game received the score of 31, which was considered "effective" or acceptable to be used in the classroom setting. When asked if she noted any changes in her attitude toward using games in classrooms after going through the training session and being able to create her own digital game, she said that she was more confident in her ability to use games in her future classroom. She realized that creating digital games was not as difficult as it sounded because there were tools and technology available for teachers to create digital games without coding knowledge. She was excited to learn how to create new games and would continue exploring games to use in her future classroom. In her opinion, after her effort of creating her first game, the process of creating another game was a lot faster because she had the skills needed to develop a game. She noted that she was very excited to know that she was able to create her first game ever. She concluded that she could not wait to share her new skills with her friends and teachers.

Case 2

The participant 2 was also a white female teacher candidate. She did not have any experience or expertise in coding. In the interview prior to the training session, she indicated that sometimes her math teachers integrated games in the classroom, which she found to be very interesting. When asked if she wanted to use games in her future classroom, she said she was not sure about creating and using games in her future classroom because she did not know how to create games and it may take a lot of time to create game based materials to use with students. Shortly after the interview, participant 2 started her training session. The standard training procedures was used for consistency. Participant 2 seemed surprised when the researcher in charge of the training session indicated that she would be able to create her first digital games shortly. During the training, she talked about her ideas to incorporate in the game. The researcher helped participant 2 use mind map to create a storyboard for the game. The researcher and participant 2 agreed to create a draft game before she would create the final game. Participant 2 was thrilled to see how the draft version of her game worked and how easy it was to create a digital game. Five days after the training, she sent a link to her game, which was focused on recognizing famous art pieces of the Renaissance. Game players would view the famous paintings and listen to the description to recognize what art work was being described. Figure 2 shows a screenshot of the game.

Based on the Educational Electronic Games Rubric, this game received the score 40, which was considered "exemplary" or good to be used in the classroom setting. Participant 2 explained that her attitude toward games had changed considerably since creating her first game. "It's super easy to create games. I will definitely create more games for my teaching career", she stated. Before taking the training session, participant 2 thought that creating games was very difficult and time consuming. According to her, it took approximately 30 minutes to create her game. It

Figure 2. Screenshot of the game by participant 2

is interesting that she shared her game with her roommate, which in return asked her to show the process of creating a game. She concluded that she now realized that there were technologies out there for teachers to explore and use as long as they were willing to take the time to learn how to create and use games in the classroom.

Figure 3. Screenshot of the game by participant 3

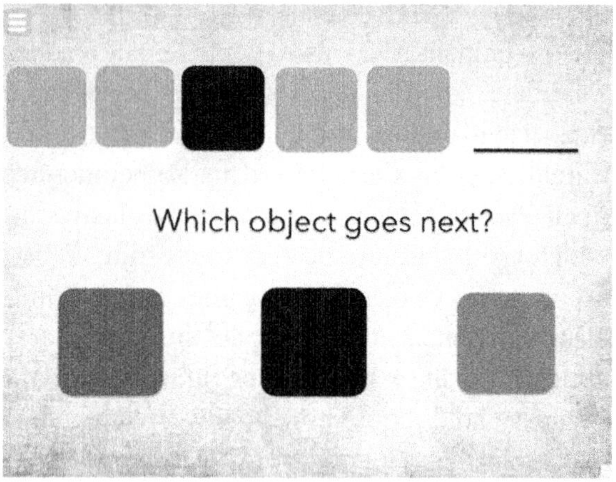

Case 3

The participant 3 was also a white female teacher candidate. She did not have any experience or expertise in coding. In the interview prior to the training session, she mentioned that none of her teachers in high school used games in her classes. She said since she did not have any background on using games in classrooms, she did not know whether games had any effect on students' performance. She also noted that she was not sure whether she would use games in her future teaching. She thought that it would be hard to create games for classroom use. Participant 3 noted that one of the most difficult tasks in integrating games into classroom was to make sure that the lesson was appropriately integrated into the games. Participant 3 also underwent the standard training procedure and sent the researchers a link to her game four days after attending the training session. Her game's title was "Complete the Pattern" and had four levels. To play the game, players had to look at the shapes available on the screen and decide what shape would come next. They would use their fingers to choose and drag the right shape into the right spot. Once the right shape was put in place, the next level page would appear automatically. Below is a screenshot of the game (see Figure 3).

Based on the Educational Electronic Games Rubric, the game received the score of 43, which was considered "exemplary" or good to be used in the classroom setting. Participant 3 stated that her attitude toward creating and using games in classroom changed after going through the training session and being able to create her very own game. According to her, it was much easier to create a game and integrate it into a lesson than she thought. She concluded that she would definitely create and incorporate games into her future teaching.

Case 4

Participant 4 was an Asian American male teacher candidate. He did not have any experience or expertise in coding. In the interview prior to the training session, participant 4 mentioned that none of his middle or high school teachers used games for learning purposes in the classroom. According to participant 4, games could get the kids engaged into the lessons. Although he did not have any background or experience in using games in classrooms, he wanted to incorporate games into his future teaching because he thought that it could be a fun way to learn since kids already enjoy playing games outside the classroom. He thought that some challenges of creating and integrating games into classrooms included time constraints, expertise needed to create games, and knowing ways to integrate games successfully for learning purposes. Among the five participants, participant 4 stood out as the most energetic and excited about integrating game-based materials into his future teaching. A week after attending the

Figure 4. Screenshot of the game by participant 4

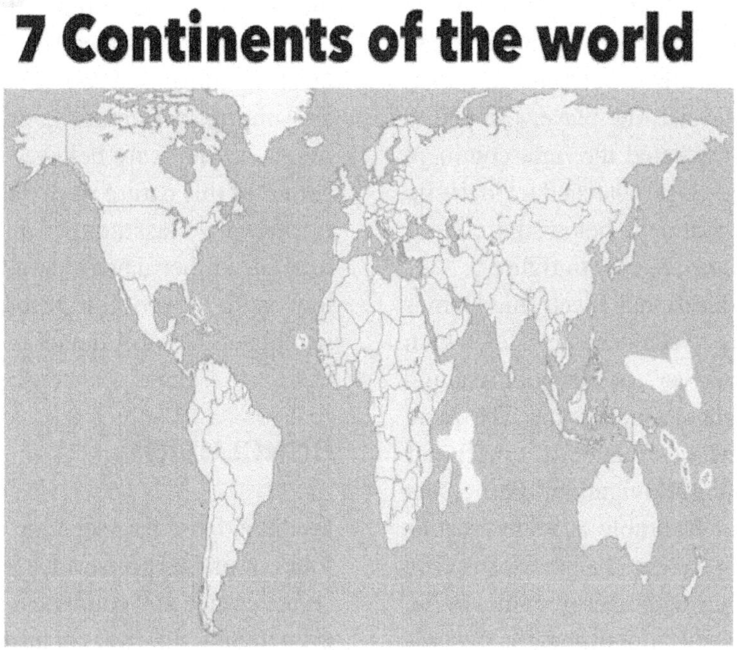

training session, participant 4 sent the link to his game, which was titled "The Seven Continents of the World". The game had six levels. Players had to pass level one to be able to move to level two. Each level had different sub-topics. For instance, level 1 topic was to identify the right continent by using a provided visual map. The second level was to identify the right flags of Asia countries. Below is a screenshot of the game at level 1 (see Figure 4).

Based on the Educational Electronic Games Rubric, this game received the score of 48, which was considered "exemplary" or good to be used in the classroom setting. Participant 4 stated that his attitude toward creating and using games in classroom changed considerably after taking the training session and being able to create his own game. According to him, "it is not hard to create games", and "students love to explore and play games". He also noted that he learned about a lot of cool stuff out there for teachers to create and use games in classrooms. He would create and use games in his future teaching. Participant 4 was also interested to know how his students liked and benefited from the games. Participant 4 assumption was that students in his classes would learn faster with game based materials and would enjoy learning while playing educational games.

Case 5

Participant 5 was a white female teacher candidate. She did not have any experience or expertise in coding, but in the interview prior to the training session, she indicated that while she was in high school, her teachers used games in the classroom and she enjoyed the experience of learning through games. According to her, she enjoyed the lessons better through playing the games than the traditional teaching method. Based on her experience in high school, she believed that she would definitely create and integrate games into her future teaching. However, like the other participants, she also acknowledged that one of the challenges of integrating games into teaching would be knowing how to create games that would motivate students. After undergoing the training session, participant 5 shared the game she had created. The game was a geographic in nature with two levels. In level 1, the player listened to the instructions and selected the right continent shape. In level 2, the player watched a video clip and identified the continent below the clip. A screenshot of the game appears in figure 5.

Based on the Educational Electronic Games Rubric, this game received the score of 28, which was considered "baseline" or not good enough to be used in the classroom setting. The main issue with this game was related to criterion 1 "Layout & Design" and "Navigation". Participant 5 explained that her favorable attitude towards game based learning did not change because she had always been a big supporter of games being incorporated into the educational process. According to her, creating that game on Tiny Tap only strengthened her initial position towards the use of games in education. Participant 5 believed that games can help keep students focused and keep their attention all while helping them learn vital information through fun and hands-on activities.

Participant 5 stated that creating a game for teaching purposes was challenging and time consuming, yet could be an extremely rewarding task. She truly believed that animation and games of this nature were the future of education in everyday classrooms, and she would take the time out of her day to learn how to utilize these tools at her disposal to insure that every student would get the most out of every lesson.

CONCLUSION

Findings from five separate cases indicated that four out of five pre-service teachers were able to create games that could be used in the classroom even though they did not have any coding knowledge or advanced technology skills. Three of them did not have any experience with using games as students prior to attending college. The common

Figure 5. Screenshot of the game by participant 5

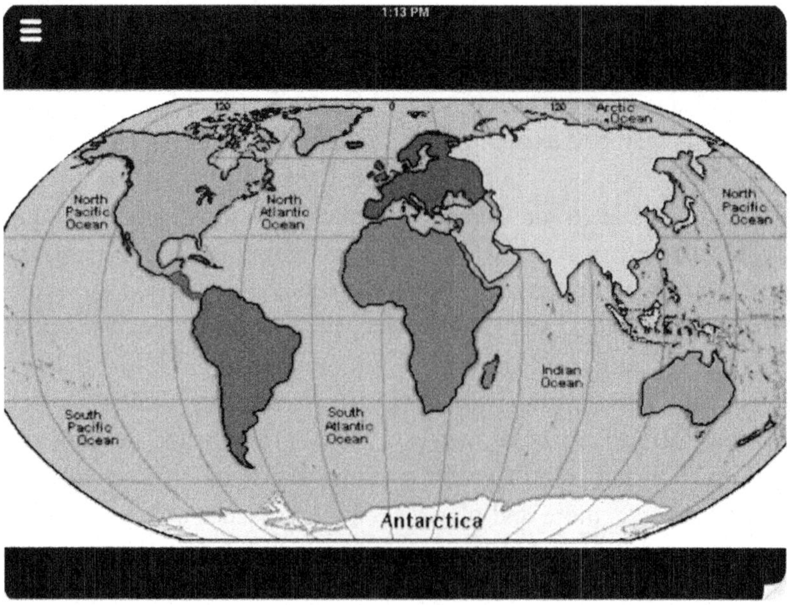

themes we found in the interviews prior to the training sessions were that participants all agreed that using games for learning purposes was a powerful strategy to get students engaged in the lessons and they would consider integrating games into their future teaching. Participants also agreed that the challenge of incorporating games into classrooms was the ability to create appropriate games suitable to their teaching context. After the training session and being able to create their first games, the pre-service teacher participants expressed their favorable attitude towards using games in classroom. They would consider creating more games and using them in their future teaching careers. Participants all seemed excited by the fact that they were able to create their own games using their own ideas. It is interesting to note that the game created by participant 5 was judged not to be usable in the classroom mainly due to issues with "Layout & Design" and "Navigation" features listed in the rubric. However, participant 5 provided deep insights on how she thought games could benefit learning and her determination to incorporate games into her future teaching.

From these five cases, many lessons could be learned.

1. Literally any pre-service teachers could be trained to create their own games usable for their teaching within a short period of time as long as we could find the right platform.
2. It is not necessary for pre-service teachers to have coding expertise or exposure to classrooms with games to be able to learn about the benefits of incorporating games into classrooms.
3. Pre-service teachers' attitudes toward using games in classrooms are important. Attitude can either encourage or discourage the candidates to learn, create and integrate games into their classrooms.

Educators have generally been known for being skeptical and even against the use of games as teaching and learning tools. However, this study revealed a new generation of teachers that have grown in the gaming era, and therefore are open to the possibilities that the medium can bring to the classroom environment. Gaming is an emerging and powerful trend that is gaining momentum in the education field due to criticism on the current state of the American educational system. Gaming is a strategy that can be integrated into a range of learning contexts and situations to enhance the failing traditional educational practices such as lectures, discussions, textbooks and testing. The 21st century learner expects to use gaming like tools in the schools because that is what they know and do at home and socially on a daily basis. There is already a strong relationship between young learners and technology and that seems to be a powerful and unique asset to take learning to the next level. However, challenges do exist. First, budget limitations to afford the implementation of educational gaming since quality commercial games are very expensive. Second, preparing teachers to be able to create and integrate gaming successfully in the classroom setting. Third, making a case for the importance of authentic learning in the face of the current emphasis on high stakes standardized testing. Utilizing game for learning under pressure to be standard focused could be seen more as a distraction than an educational tool.

In the end, we argue that it is in the best interest of students, teachers and the education process that we promote practical solutions to improve teaching and learning in the classroom. This study concluded that pre-service teachers with no coding or sophisticated technology skills are able to improve their teaching skills with their very own engaging digital games. The new generation of teachers can and are excited to create games for use in their future classrooms. Pre-service teachers are ready to play the game that matters and teacher education programs must focus on preparing them for the classrooms they will lead (Vu et al., 2014).

REFERENCES

Baxter, P., & Jack, S. (2008). Qualitative Case Study Methodology: Study Design and Implementation for Novice Researchers. *Qualitative Report*, *13*(4), 544–559. Retrieved from http://nsuworks.nova.edu/tqr/vol13/iss4/2

Can, G., & Cagiltay, K. (2006). Turkish prospective teachers' perceptions regarding the use of computer games with educational features. *Journal of Educational Technology & Society*, *9*(1), 308–321.

Cross–Bystrom, A. (2010, August 20). What you need to know about Generation Z. iMedia Connections: Connecting the Marketing Community. Retrieved from http://www.imediaconnection.com/content/27425.asp

Feistritzer, C. E. (2011). *Profile of teachers in the U.S. 2011*. Washington, DC: National Center for Education Information.

Fudin, S. (2012, March 29). Gen Z & What does it mean in your classroom? *Inside USC Rossier Online Blog*. Retrieved from http://rossieronline.usc.edu/gen-z-what-does-it-mean-in-your-classroom-2

Games-to-Teach Team. (2003). Design principles of next-generation digital gaming for education. *Educational Technology*, *43*(5), 17–33.

Gershenfeld, A. (2011, April 3) Game-based learning: Hype vs. versus reality. Retrieved from http://www.huffingtonpost.com/alan-gershenfeld/game-based-learning-education_b_843001.html

Gredler, M. E. (1996). Educational games and simulations: A technology in search of a research paradigm. In D.H. Jonassen (Ed.), *Handbook of research for educational communications and technology* (pp. 521–539). New York: MacMillan.

Holland, W., Jenkins, H., & Squire, K. (2003). Theory by design. In M.J.P. Wolf & B. Perron (Eds.), *The video game theory reader*. New York: Routledge.

Hsu, T. Y., & Chiou, G. F. (2011). Pre-service teachers' awareness of digital game-supported learning. In M. Koehler & P. Mishra (Eds.), *Proceedings of Society for Information Technology & Teacher Education International Conference 2011* (pp. 2135-2141). Chesapeake, VA: AACE.

Pastore, R., & Falvo, D. (2010). Video games in the classroom: Pre-service and in-service teachers' perceptions of games in K-12 classrooms. *International Journal of Instructional Technology and Distance Learning*, *7*(12), 49–57.

Prensky, M. (2001). *Digital game-based learning*. New York: McGraw-Hill.

Ruggiero, D. (2013). Video games in the classroom: The teacher point of view. Paper presented at the *Games for Learning workshop of the Foundations of Digital Games conference*, Chania, Greece.

Sardone, N., & Devlin-Scherer, R. (2010). Teacher candidate responses to Digital games: 21st Century skills development. *Journal of Research on Technology in Education*, *42*(4), 409–425. doi:10.1080/15391523.2010.10782558

Schrader, P. G., Zheng, D., & Young, M. (2006). Teachers' perceptions of video games: MMOGs and the future of Pre-service teacher education. *Innovate: Journal of Online Education, 2*(3), 1-10. Retrieved from http://www.slideshare.net/rredekopp/ijtie-the-use-of-games-in-preservice-teacher-education

Shaffer, D. W., Halverson, R., Squire, K. R., & Gee, J. P. (2005). Video games and the future of learning (WCER Working Paper No. 2005-4). Wisconsin Center for Education Research.

Squire, K. D. (2008). *Video Games and Education: Designing Learning Systems for an Interactive Age. Educational Technology Magazine: The Magazine for Managers of Change in Education, 48,* p. 17026. Mar-Apr.

Takeuchi, L. M., & Vaala, S. (2014). *Level up learning: A national survey on teaching with digital games*. New York: The Joan Ganz Cooney Center at Sesame Workshop.

Vu, P., Crow, S., & Fredrickson, S. (2014). Using games in online education: Is it a winning strategy? *Online Journal of Distance Learning Administration*, *17*(8).

KEY TERMS AND DEFINITIONS

Digital Game: An electronic game in which players control images on a television or computer screen.

Pre-Service Teachers: Students admitted to a teacher education program.

APPENDIX

Figure 6.

4/12/2015 Educational Electronic Games Rubric

Educational Electronic Games Rubric

Educational electronic games can be utilized in a variety of teaching situations. This rubric will help you evaluate your electronic game in an educational setting. If a criteria rating falls between two levels of achievement, you may score it with a point value between the two levels. To calculate your total score online: enter your score for each criteria, then click the *Calculate Totals* button below the Total Score box.

Evaluation of Total Score

CRITERIA	Levels of Achievement			Score
	Baseline	**Effective**	**Exemplary**	
Organization and Design				
Layout & Design	0 points There are few or no graphic elements, no variation in layout and/or the colors interfere with the readability.	3 points There are some graphic elements and limited variation in layout. Design elements sometimes assist students in understanding concepts and ideas.	5 points There are multiple graphic elements and variation in layout. Design elements assist students in understanding concepts and ideas.	0
Navigation	0 points Navigating the game is confusing and information cannot be found easily.	3 points Some navigation is unclear, resulting in a few places where students can become lost.	5 points The game is well-organized and easy to navigate. Students can clearly understand where they are and where to go next.	0
Instructional Design and Delivery				
Objectives	0 points Learning objectives are unclear or non-existent.	3 points Some learning objectives are identified.	5 points Learning objectives are clearly identified.	0
Different Learning Styles	0 points The game provides few auditory, kinesthetic, textual and/or visual activities to enhance student learning.	3 points The game provides some auditory, kinesthetic, textual and/or visual activities to enhance student learning.	5 points The game provides multiple auditory, kinesthetic, textual and/or visual activities to enhance student	0

http://www.csus.edu/indiv/k/kaym/rubric/edgamesrubric.html 1/3

Figure 7.

4/12/2015 Educational Electronic Games Rubric

			learning.	
Higher Level Learning Skills	0 points The game provides limited or no activities to help students increase their cognitive skills, such as analysis, synthesis and evaluation.	3 points The game provides some activities to help students increase their cognitive skills, such as analysis, synthesis and evaluation.	5 points The game provides multiple activities to help students increase their cognitive skills, such as analysis, synthesis and evaluation.	0
Game-Based Learning				
Rules	0 points Rules are not clearly stated.	3 points Some rules are given, but there is missing information. Students might be confused.	5 points Every rule is clearly stated.	0
Goals	0 points Goals are vague or incomplete.	3 points Goals are at least partially described.	5 points Goals are clearly stated and measure what students must know and be able to do to accomplish the game.	0
Feedback	0 points There are few or no opportunities for students to receive feedback on their performance.	3 points There are some opportunities for students to receive feedback on their performance.	5 points There are frequent opportunities for students to receive timely feedback on their performance.	0
Interaction	0 points Student-to-computer and student-to-student interactions are limited or non-existent.	3 points Student-to-computer and student-to-student interactions are at least partially identified.	5 points Student-to-computer and student-to-student interactions can be clearly identified. There is a definitive increase in social interaction.	0
	0 points	3 points	5 points	

http://www.csus.edu/indiv/k/kaym/rubric/edgamesrubric.html 2/3

Chapter 19
Exploring the Impact of Free-Form and Structured Digital Games on the Player Experience of Kindergarten and Primary School Students

Sotiris Kirginas
University of Athens, Greece

Dimitris Gouscos
University of Athens, Greece

ABSTRACT

The paper presents results of a study that was focused on testing the hypothesis that the levels of kindergarten and primary school students' positive emotions, engagement and positive experience will be significantly different while they play free-form and structured digital games. In the context of this study, students' emotion, engagement and experience were assessed through three corresponding questionnaires drawn from the literature. These questionnaires were completed for approx. 500 students of public kindergartens and primary schools located in Athens, Greece. From the analysis of the data collected, free-form digital games are found to lead students towards more positive emotions, higher engagement and more positive player experience. On top of that, a significant correlation is found between positive emotions, engagement and positive experience; the more positive the students' emotion while playing digital games, the higher appears to be their engagement and positive player experience.

DOI: 10.4018/978-1-4666-9629-7.ch019

INTRODUCTORY REMARKS

The work described in this paper forms part of a broader research effort which aims at:

1. Formalizing a concept of game structure, and be able to evaluate its presence/absence in different digital games; more specifically, the research aims at the formalization and, eventually, at the quantitative assessment of a concept of game structure in free-form and structured digital games, through representing the gameplay flow and states on diagrammatic formalisms such as State Transition Diagrams, and trying to arrive at typologies that will allow to place different digital games at various points on an axis between free creativity and rule-bound complexity
2. Formalizing a concept of player engagement in digital games and be able to evaluate the engagement produced by different digital games for kindergarten and primary school players; in this respect, and with a view to exploiting the knowledge already available in this area, the research aims at being able to assess player engagement using a variety of available tools such as observation and questionnaires and emerging approaches such as facial expression recognition or bio-feedback analysis
3. Exploring correlations between game structure and player engagement of preschool and primary school children, and find optimal relationships between these two variables; with a view to integrating digital games in educational settings, the research aims to identify if there are significant correlations between the quality of players' engagement and the kind of play that a digital game offers, depending on whether the latter focuses on the game dimension (structured games) or the play dimension (free-from games) of gameplay
4. Exploring the elements of game mechanics that digital games should have in order to exhibit a game structure that leads to optimal player engagement; the research intends, on the long term, to develop and validate a heuristic framework for designing optimally structured, and thus more engaging, digital games
5. Selecting and/or designing digital games for language learning for preschool and primary school children that exhibit this optimal game structure; the research aims at arriving, on the long run, to formulate and evaluate guidelines for selecting and/or designing digital games for learning which can exhibit an optimal structure and thus lead to an optimal engagement
6. Studying the learning outcomes of preschool and primary school children on language learning while playing these digital games, with a view to exploring and maximising the effectiveness of free-form and structured digital games for language learning.

BACKGROUND CONCEPTS AND RESEARCH

Player Emotion, Player Engagement, and Player Experience

Although the experience of playing digital games has been the focus of many theoretical and empirical studies, the concepts of engagement and player experience are still not well understood. Due to the lack of commonly accepted definitions of these concepts (Nacke et al. 2009; Bouvier et al. 2013), it is necessary to clearly define them.

The single most important factor that makes a digital game successful is the quality of players' experience. A digital game should be fun, challenging and exciting in order to provide the best gaming experience and produce positive emotions within the player. This player experience can be broadly defined as the experience of play, which includes elements such as how well the game supports and provides the type of fun players want to have, and what makes players having fun. The field of player experience research faces problems, such as indistinct concepts and lack of empirical research (Hassenzahl & Tractinsky 2006). These problems impede theoretical advancement and restrict our understanding of player experience as a theoretical notion and its further assessment and improvement in practice. Much of the empirical research is based on authors' and designers' personal experiences and often the players' point of view is ignored (Fabricatore et al. 2002). However, there are attempts towards a commonly accepted definition of player experience (e.g., Special Interest Group on User Experience - SIG-UX, http://www.cost294.org; Allaboutux, http://www.allaboutux.org/). Because many essential psychological components are included (e.g., feeling, satisfaction, need, mood, motivation, expectation, immersion) the evaluation of the subjective playing experience is a crucial part of the game development process (Kiili et al. 2014).

Experience, according to Dewey (1938) as presented in Almeida et al. (2013) and Calvillo-Gámez (2010), is both the process and outcome of the interaction of a user with the environment at a given time. It is an interactive experience (the process of playing the game) and an emotional experience (the outcome of playing) – an emotion (or a group of emotions) that results from playing. The interaction process is the way in which players play games. It is how they explore the game world; how they interact with other players, non-playable characters or objects; and how they make decisions. This process is limited by the game itself and influenced by the players' background, motivations, expectations and their current emotional experience which can possibly vary throughout the game, under the effects of the context within which the interaction occurs. The interaction process is also influenced by players' current emotional state: if players are anxious, they may be less capable of paying attention, which reflects on their ability to play and win; if they are relaxed and stress-free, they may find themselves in a state of flow where everything runs perfectly. This process will affect the gameplay result, which refers to the visible consequences of the game. These consequences can then influence the outcome of playing. When the emotional experience is positive, games can produce positive emotions within the player (e.g. satisfaction, enjoyment, excitement); if negative, they can produce negative emotions (anger, despair, indifference). It is also possible that positive or negative consequences can alter the interaction process by changing player motivations and actions (expectations). This bi-directional relationship can explain why occasionally players can feel at the same time enjoyment and frustration throughout the duration of the game (Almeida et al., 2013). Experience is personal and subjective, so evaluating experience is about evaluating a subjective appreciation of the user.

According to Roto (2007) there are 3 phases of player experience: (a) expected player experience (before a player starts to interact with a game), (b) player experience during interaction (experience that takes place while interacting with the game), and (c) overall player experience (experience after game ends). From the above three phases of player experience the most crucial one is player experience during interaction. Investigating the player experience during interaction is important in order to improve a game, as it is in this phase that features and components which create positive experience and others which do not can be observed. To understand player experience during the interaction phase, we need to see the effect of three aspects to player experience: the human aspect (predispositions, expectations, needs, motivation, mood, etc.), the system aspect (e.g. complexity, purpose, usability, functionality, etc.) and the contextual aspect (or the environment) within which the interaction occurs (e.g. organisational/social setting, meaningfulness of the activity, voluntariness of use, etc.) (Hassenzahl & Tractinsky 2006; Reiter et al. 2014). In this research we are leaving aside, on purpose, the social dimensions of playing video-games and we are focusing on the other two aspects, the system (game) and the human (user) aspect. The social dimensions of playing video-games have been documented (Lazzaro 2004), but they represent an additional aspect of playing, that follows once the connection between the player and the game has been established.

Engagement is one dimension of the player experience (Schoenau–Fog 2011) concerned with aspects related to the playing situation and focuses on what makes players want to continue playing and what it is that engages players so much that they want to keep playing. Engagement is understood as the level of continuation desire experienced in-game, during play or over a longer period of time, when players dedicate themselves to coming back and playing a game again and again (Schoenau–Fog 2011). It is a multidimensional concept which describe various qualities of an interactive experience and has been related to other concepts such as flow (Csikszentmihalyi 1990; Sweetser and Wyeth 2005; Wiebe et al. 2014), presence (Bracken et al. 2005; Takatalo et al. 2006), immersion (McMahan 2003; Brown and Cairns 2004; Ermi and Mäyrä 2005; Jennett et al. 2008), pleasure (e.g. Costello and Edmonds 2009), motivation (Przybylski et al. 2010; Malone and Lepper 1987; Rigby and Ryan 2011), enjoyment (Klimmt 2003; IJsselsteijn et al. 2008) and fun (Koster 2004; Poels, de Kort and IJsselsteijn 2007). Player engagement is furthermore related to a range of emotions (enjoyment, fun, satisfaction, etc.) and experiences (e.g. the feeling of being immersed, present or in flow) which may or may not be part of a player's experience of engagement, depending on both the player and the type of game played.

According to Brown & Cairns (2004) engagement is defined as the lowest level of involvement which must be experienced before the player can become engrossed or totally immersed. Ermi & Mäyrä (2005) present a gameplay experience model focused on immersion divided into three components: sensory, challenged-based and imaginative immersion. Imaginative immersion occurs when players become absorbed with the world and stories, or begin to empathise and/or identify with game characters. Sensory immersion is associated with the audiovisual elements of games and challenge-based immersion is concerned with the balance of challenges and abilities.

Brown and Vaughan (2009) propose that a central element of the concept of play is the desire to continue: "Play provides a continuation desire. We desire to keep doing it, and the pleasure of the experience drives that desire. We find ways to keep doing it. If something threatens to stop the fun, we improvise new rules or conditions so that the play doesn't have to end. And when it is over, we want to do it again".

Engagement has also been associated with enjoyment. Klimmt (2003) proposed that the enjoyment produced by a game depends on three experiential factors:

1. Experience of effectance or immediate feedback to the player,
2. Cyclic feelings of suspense and relief, and
3. The fascination of being drawn in to an alternative reality or a fiction world.

According to Klimmt, "enjoyment is the reason for players to begin, sustain, and repeat exposure to digital games".

Finally, other studies have often focused on the overall motivational aspects of games. Przybylski et al. (2010) and Rigby and Ryan (2011) explain that the underlying reasons why people play, and the ways in which digital games can motivate sustained engagement, stem from the ability of games to satisfy fundamental psychological needs for competence, autonomy (freedom of choice based on personal interests) and relatedness (interaction with others).

Although existing studies have contributed significantly in the research effort in the field of players' engagement and experience, they seem to overlook an important factor that affects the quality of players' engagement and experience, which is a player's emotion. Understanding players' emotions provides considerable advantages in various entertainment applications (Park et al. 2014). As games are self-motivating activities, emotion plays a big role in this. Appropriate emotions can help to focus on attention, make decisions, improve performance, create enjoyment and reward learning (Lazzaro 2007). In fact people cannot make choices without emotional systems (Damasio 1994). Because games are about making interesting choices, studying the emotional reactions of player serves a critical role in improving the quality of player engagement and experience. Due to this reason, we shall research the possible correlation between the variables of players' emotions, engagement and experience, with a view to investigating whether positive students' emotion while playing digital games actually leads to higher engagement and more positive experience.

Free-Form and Structured Digital Games

In game studies, play is defined as an activity that is fun, voluntary, intrinsically motivated, incorporates free choices/free will, offers escape, and is fundamentally exciting (Sutton – Smith, 1997).

Back in 1987, James Carse in his book Finite and Infinite Games introduced two new terms in order to express his thoughts about the two different kinds of games. One could be called finite, the other infinite. A finite game is played for the purpose of winning, an infinite game for the purpose of continuing the play. There is no game, finite or infinite, unless the players freely agree to play it. No one can play who is forced to play. This is an invariable principle of all play acts. If a finite game is to be won by someone, it must come to a definitive end. It will come to an end when someone has won. Winning is determined by agreement of the players. A finite game has a precise beginning and end, and exhibits clear spatial and numerical boundaries (the latter, as defined by Carse, having to do with the number of players that can simultaneously play together). There must be at least one opponent and, in most cases, there have to be teammates who are willing to play together. Only one person or team can win a finite game, but the other players may be ranked at the end of play. Infinite games, on the other hand, are the opposite of finite games in every way except for the principle of voluntarism. Infinite games have no spatial, temporal, or numerical boundaries, and no winners or rankings. Finite games are externally defined; infinite games are internally defined. The time of an infinite game is determined in the game itself.

Fundamental to the discussion of rules and freedom in play is the distinction Roger Caillois (2001) introduced by identifying two forms of play, *paidia* and *ludus*. According to Caillois, it is possible to approach each kind of game or play form with structures, rules, goals and limits (*ludus*), or with a more unstructured, spontaneous and free, not obligatory, act of play, separated from any sanctions, and circumscribed only by limits of space and time (*paidia*). The categories of *ludus* and *paidia* directly address a structural understanding of games, a continuum of relationships between structure and play. As play approaches closer to the *ludus* end of this continuum, for example, the rules become stricter and more influential. Located on the other end of the continuum, *paidia*-based play eschews strict formal structures in exchange for more free-form play.

Ludologist Gonzalo Frasca (2003) has developed Caillois' theory further and noted how certain games are more clearly designed for a formally defined *ludus* gameplay – they are typically focused on winning and losing, the counting of points, and they generally provide players with clearly defined goals during gameplay. In contrast, games designed with more open goals, exploration, experimentation and improvisation in mind are more likely to invite a *paidia* style of free, playful behaviors. As MacGregor (2008) notes, using Frasca's understanding of Caillois terms, the spectrum between *paidia* and *ludus* in relation to digital games operates between *ludus* as a structured goal-driven type of activity, with clearly defined or formalized rules, and *paidia* as a free-form type of activity, with undefined goals and undefined but implicit or informal cultural rules.

In their *book Rules of Play: Game design fundamentals* Kate Salen and Eric Zimmerman (2004), attempting to define what play is, divide the concept of play into three categories: "game play", "ludic activity" and "being playful". "Game play" is the narrowest category and requires both a structure and a formal set of rules, which make it easier to create replayability. To fall into this category, the activity must exhibit both structure and rules which limit the way in which a player plays. Without rules, the activity expands to a "ludic activity" the second category. "Ludic activities" do not have a formal set of rules, but do require structure. Such a basic structure allows the experience to be replicated, as the basis for replay. If players found the activity enjoyable, they can simply impose the same structure and reenter the Magic Circle associated with it. Finally, the third category of "being Playful" is the broadest and most inclusive category of all three and includes all other forms of play such as "ludic activities" and "game play". It refers not only to typical play activities, but also to the idea of being in a playful state of mind, where a spirit of play is injected into some other action. "Being playful", according to Salen and Zimmerman, is the only level of play that can exist without neither structure nor rules, and at the same time it can also lack the ability to be replayed.

At about the same time, in his book *Half-Real: Video Games between Real Rules and Fictional Worlds,* Jesper Juul (2005) argued that most digital games can be found on a scale between *emergence* and *progression*, and their game guides are consequently a combination of step-by-step descriptions and strategy guides. *Emergence* is the primordial game structure, where a game is specified as a small number of rules that combine and yield large numbers of game variations, which the players then design strategies for dealing with. This is found in card and board games and in most action and all strategy games. Emergence games tend to be replayable and tend to foster tournaments and strategy guides. *Progression* is the historically newer structure that entered the digital game through the adventure genre. A progression game can in many ways be less interesting than an emergence one. In a pure progression game, the player has to perform a predefined set of actions in order to complete the game. What is more, the player is simply presented with a series of challenges where all of the options and solutions have been explicitly described in the game rules. Progression games are also characterised by the fact that they can be completed, and that their replayability, as a consequence, can be low.

More recently, Konstantin Mitgutsch (2008) noted that while a number of digital games focus on the game-dimension of game play, such as rules, goals and structures (referred by Caillois as *ludus* there are other digital games that focus on the play-dimension of game play, such as unstructured, spontaneous and free act of play (referred by Caillois as *paidia*). He introduced the term "Digital Play-Based Learning" as "a phenomenon that refers not to a linear but to a circular process of learning and the unstructured act of play in games". According to Mitgusch, digital games that focus on the play dimension of gameplay are open virtual learning environments that can be characterised as frameworks for learning anew from negative instances experienced. The aim of these games is to teach the learners about their prior horizon of experience and to relativise their prejudgments and premature beliefs. Therefore, learning based on play does not only engage the learner by entertainment and challenge, but by confrontation and passion as well. This understanding of learning in games is not a substitution for Digital Game-Based Learning (Prensky, 2007), but it focuses on a different aspect of learning and playing.

On this basis it may be concluded that digital games categories can be considered to lie at various points on an axis of play between totally free-form activity and formally structured goal-driven activity:

The "formal" end of the axis focuses on the game-dimension of game play, such as rules, goals and structures. Games that would lie at this end comprise "structured" digital games which are more strictly defined since

1. They have an explicit set of winning and losing rules which force players to take specific paths to reach goals and ensure that all players take the same paths;
2. They have pre-determined and clear goals whether these are to beat players' high score, progress to the next level or complete the game in full, etc.;
3. They provide immediate feedback which lets players know immediately whether what they have done is positive or negative for them in the game, whether they are staying within or breaking the rules, moving closer to the goal or further away and how they are doing versus the competition;
4. They have structured designer-generated activities with linear gameplay which confront players with a fixed sequence of challenges; and
5. They have a defined space and time which include any narrative or story elements in the game.

The "free" end of the axis focuses on the play-dimension of game play, such as unstructured, spontaneous and free acts of play. Games that would lie at this end comprise "free-form" digital games that

1. Have no set of rules pre-determined by the game designers or if there are rules they are informal and flexible and the player has freedom to use them or not;
2. Exhibit no pre-defined goal but accommodate players' goals that are entirely intrinsic and personal;
3. Have no "winning plot", as they are more open-ended; and
4. Include nonlinear gameplay which allow greater player freedom than games with linear gameplay.

In free-form games the players have more freedom to decide what to do, to set their own individual goals and determine their rules, path, scenario and plot. As there is no system of rules that defines a victory or a defeat, a gain or a loss, the players' aim is not to win but rather to learn the game through exploration and discovery play. The players are the authors of the play and goals in digital games of this category, and this is the only decision made for the players by the game designers.

RESEARCH DESIGN

Research Focus and Hypotheses

The work reported in this paper aims to compare the levels of students' experience and engagement while they play with digital games that focus on different dimensions of gameplay.

More specifically, this study aims to (a) measure and compare the level of students' emotion, engagement and experience while they play free-form or structured digital games and (b) examine the possible correlations between the variables of students' emotion, engagement and experience. Based on the above objectives we formulate the following research hypotheses:

H1: The levels of kindergarten and primary school students' positive emotions, engagement and positive experience will be significantly different while they play free-form and structured digital games.

H2: There is a significant correlation between students' positive emotion, engagement and positive experience. The more positive the level of students' emotion, the higher is students' engagement and positive experience that can be expected.

Research Methodology and Organization

The study has been implemented in two urban public kindergarten and primary schools located in Athens, Greece. Four experimental groups were created for each kindergarten and primary school grade (1st, 2nd, 3rd, 4th and 5th grades). In the two primary schools all interventions were held in the computer lab. Due to the lack of computer lab in the two kindergarten schools, the interventions where held in a separate room with a laptop computer, where students played while their schoolmates were in the classroom with their teacher doing their daily activities.

The digital games' play activities were presented in a series of 30-minute classroom sessions twice for each kindergarten and primary school class. During the first intervention, students played for 30 minutes with the structured digital game that we selected as most appropriate for their age, while during the second intervention they played with a free-form digital game. In order to assess the effects of playing with these digital games on positive emotion, engagement and positive experience three questionnaires were completed by the students just after each play time.

It is worth noting that before the study a pilot evaluation was conducted in order to assess the time required to discover mistakes or failures (e.g. problems with questionnaires, processes, etc.) and issues which had not received enough attention. Completion of the interventions was followed by processing and analysis of the collected data in order to find answers to the initial research questions.

Criteria for Selecting the Digital Games Used in the Research

The digital games used in this research are distinguished in games with pre-designated goals and pre-designed gameplay paths, which are considered as "structured" games (Journey in the Land of Letters, Spark, Thunder and the suspect of the road of Winds and Natural Science); and games that, having no pre-designated goals, neither a single "winning plot", give room to many different player-generated gameplay paths and are considered as "free-form" games (Poisson Rouge, Magic Potion, Electro-room).

Since there are numerous free-form and structures digital games the following set of criteria were used to help select the most suitable games:

1. **Nonlinear Gameplay vs. Linear Gameplay:** Non linear gameplay means that games provide choices for players to make, different paths that the players can take to get from one point to another, from the game's beginning to its end. On the contrary, linear gameplay means that players have to follow a single path to one objective and there are no alternate paths or methods for accomplishing this objective. Players learn new things in the appropriate order and developers can make sure everything goes as pre-designed.
2. **Multiple Solutions to Challenges vs. Unique Solution to Challenges:** Free-form games allow multiple solutions to the game challenges and enable many different player-generated gameplay paths. Not every player will go about solving a situation in the same way and, given that these alternate solutions are reasonable, almost any challenge must have multiple ways for players to overcome

it. Structured games offer unique solutions to challenges (every player overcomes a challenge in the same way) and this does not allow players to come up with different ways to proceed in the game.

3. **Free Sequence of Challenges vs. Fixed Sequence of Challenges:** In free-form games players have the ability to choose the order in which they face challenges. Giving players choices of different challenges to overcome allows them to put aside a difficult challenge and occupy themselves with another one for a while. After completing the second challenge, players may return to the first gratified and less stressed/better concentrated, and thereby stand a better chance of overcoming it. On the contrary, structured games have structured designer-generated activities which confront players with a fixed sequence of challenges. Games with a fixed sequence of challenges allow players access to only one challenge at a time. In order to even attempt a second challenge, players must complete the first one. This is especially frustrating when players cannot overcome a particular challenge and can do nothing else until that challenge is successfully met.
4. **Selection of Challenges vs. Pre-Defined Set of Challenges:** Free-form games allow players to choose which challenges they want to overcome or not. From a games for learning perspective, in particular, such games can result in improving students' learning by increasing their interest due to the pleasant and attractive environment that they offer, often contrary to conventional learning environments. On the contrary, structured games have structured activities which confront players with a pre-defined set of challenges, that all need to be overcome.

Digital Games Used in the Research

Applying the above criteria, six digital games with different characteristics and gameplay types were selected and used in this research:

1. Poisson Rouge (www.poissonrouge.com),
2. Magic Potion (www.media.uoa.gr/epinoisi),
3. Electroroom (http://users.sch.gr/mtomara/ilektrodwmatio.swf),
4. Journey in the Land of Letters (http://www.siem.gr/en/product.html?id=0&shop=1),
5. Spark, Thunder and the Suspect of the Road of Winds (http://www.siem.gr/en/product.html?id=13), and
6. Natural Science (http://www.siem.gr/en/product.html?id=31).

A brief presentation of these games follows.

Poisson Rouge

Poisson Rouge is an interactive playground which contains fun and educational games and activities for children. The setting is a familiar one: a child's bedroom, full of toys. Each toy is clickable and can be played with. There are cubes with numbers and alphabets with animations, puzzles, games about coloring and color mixing, a variety of toys, a piano to learn music and much more. In this digital playground children can play music, be introduced to numbers and words in their own language or in others. No prior knowledge is necessary and in fact, it is a great tool for basic ICT skills. What makes the game promote creativity and exploration for children is that there are no instructions as to how to use anything on the game. Functionalities are either easy to find or non-essential. Through exploring the game's site, children find out the features offered and this discovery process is interesting in at least two ways: firstly, children are proud of their achievements and their findings and while this induces self-confidence, it also elicits language production as players want to share their discoveries with adults and other children; secondly, the very fact that there are things to discover teaches that one way to learn more is exploration in its own right.

Poisson Rouge can be considered as a free-form game given that it exhibits nonlinear gameplay, allows multiple solutions to the game challenges and enables many different player-generated gameplay paths, giving players the ability to choose the order in which they face challenges and allowing them to choose which challenges they want to overcome or not (see Figure 1).

Magic Potion

Magic Potion is an adventure game for learning which consists of four episodes (corresponding to the pursuit of the four colors of the rainbow) and comprises narrative scenes and some 20 micro-games in total (mathematics, language, everyday life skills). The game has a loosely-coupled structure, in the sense that episodes can be entered and exited at any time and in any turn, narrative scenes and micro-games can be played or skipped, and there is no memory (objects gained etc.) persistent beyond the boundaries of any single episode, which would impose some sort of in-game linear dependencies. The game involves several characters, all of which help each other to achieve the game objective of mixing a magic potion by collecting colors that are hidden into the game "world". The colors are earnt as a result of successfully completing specific activities that help learners build basic everyday life and communication skills as well as basic arithmetic and reading/writing skills. Development of The Magic Potion game has been led by a twofold objective: from a learning outcomes perspective, to provide modular game-based material for basic literacy, numeracy and social skills that contribute to everyday life autonomy; and from a learning process perspective, to provide an amusing gameplay experience that will mobilize students and enhance their self-confidence, hiding the educational agenda and taking away the feelings of stress and failure often inherent in educational processes.

Figure 1. Screenshot from "Poisson Rouge"

Magic Potion can be considered as a free-form game given that it exhibits nonlinear gameplay and enables players to choose the order in which they face challenges, making possible many different player-generated gameplay paths (see Figure 2).

Electroroom

Electroroom is an interactive educational game for natural science. The game is mainly intended for 11-12 years old students and intends to comply to the electricity subject matter of the official Greek curriculum for sciences in the 5th grade of primary school. The game results from an effort to implement a realistic interactive environment that simulates a real-world laboratory of electric circuits. It has been designed according to a discovery-based approach to knowledge, and incorporates features resulting from constructionist theories for learning. The prime objective of this game is to encourage learning through entertainment, and to this end it includes a large number of experiments, involving everyday life objects and appliances rather than laboratory-style experiments.

Electroroom can be considered as a free-form game, on the premise that it exhibits nonlinear gameplay, allows multiple solutions to the game challenges and enables many different player-generated gameplay paths, giving players the ability to choose the order in which they face challenges and allowing them to choose which challenges they want to overcome or not (see Figure 3).

Journey in the Land of Letters

Journey in the Land of Letters is an educational game for children aged between 4 and 7 that helps them to become familiar with reproduction, pronunciation and the method of writing the letters of the Greek alphabet. A book called Smarty is the hero of the game. This book is not like other books; instead of remaining motionless and silent on a dusty shelf on some bookcase, it can walk,

Figure 2. Screenshot from "Magic Potion"

Figure 3. Screenshot from "Electroroom"

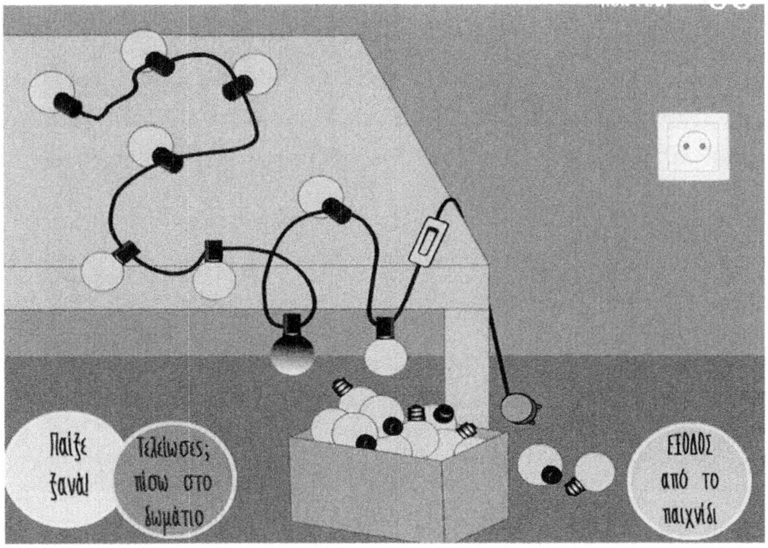

think and even talk. However, it is really unhappy, because there is not one single letter on any of its pages. So, one day, as it is sitting miserably in its room, it is suddenly struck by a wonderful idea: it will go on a journey around the Land of Letters to find letters and fill up its pages. In this quest Smarty visits 3 cities with 24 different houses inhabited by little human-like animals that talk, gesticulate, make faces and recite poems. The overall game consists of 10 educational and entertaining mini-games (shooting, crossword, pins, wheel, memory game, picture coloring, painting, fishing, slot-machine) in three rounds. Furthermore, there are activities that involve children with writing, painting and puzzle games for each letter of the Greek alphabet.

Journey in the Land of Letters can be considered as a structured game, since it exhibits linear gameplay, offers unique solutions to game challenges and at the same time confronts players with a pre-defined set of challenges, that all need to be overcome in a fixed sequence (see Figure 4).

Spark, Thunder and the Suspect of the Road of Winds

Spark, Thunder and the Suspect of the Road of Winds is an educational game that helps children become familiar with Greek as a native language at 3rd and 4th grades of primary school. Two children, Spark and Thunder are the heroes of the game. One summer afternoon the children decide to go for a walk in the city. But then, they are involved in an incredible adventure. A grouchy man falls over Thunder losing an electronic notebook. The children participate in strange experiments and they face strange and risky situations. The game offers a rich interactive environment.

Spark, Thunder and the Suspect of the Road of Winds can be considered as a structured game, as it exhibits semi-linear gameplay, offers unique solutions to challenges and confronts players with a a pre-defined set of challenges, that all need to be overcome in a fixed sequence (see Figure 5).

Figure 4. Screenshot from "Journey in Land of Letters"

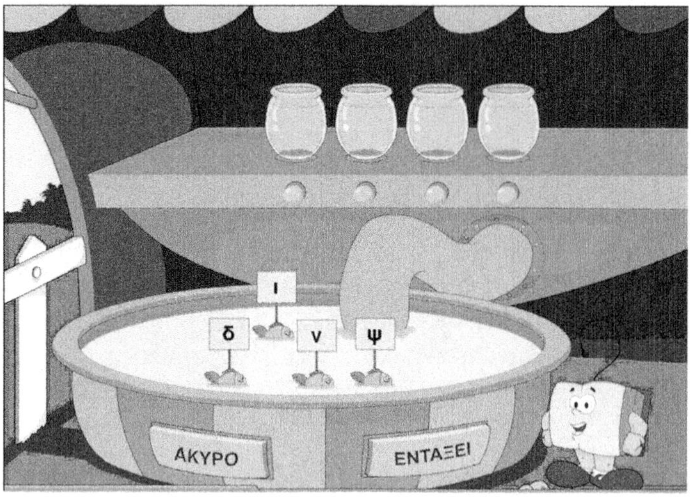

Natural Science

Natural Science is an educational game that helps children become familiar with issues of natural science for the 5th grade of primary school (Materials, Mixtures, Energy, Digestive system, Heat, Electricity, Light, Sound, Mechanics) through a variety of exercises, such as true-false, multiple choice, crossword, open-ended questions, classification, matching, gap filling, word search and word production. The game comes with a content management facility and an evaluation tool for both individual student progress and class progress during school time (with score, detailed results, level of difficulty for each exercise).

Natural Science can be considered as a structured game on the premise that it exhibits linear gameplay, offers unique solutions to game challenges and confronts players with a pre-defined set of such challenges that all need to be overcome in a fixed sequence (see Figure 6).

Figure 5. Screenshot from "Spark, Thunder and the Suspect of the Road of Winds"

Figure 6. Screenshot from "Natural Science"

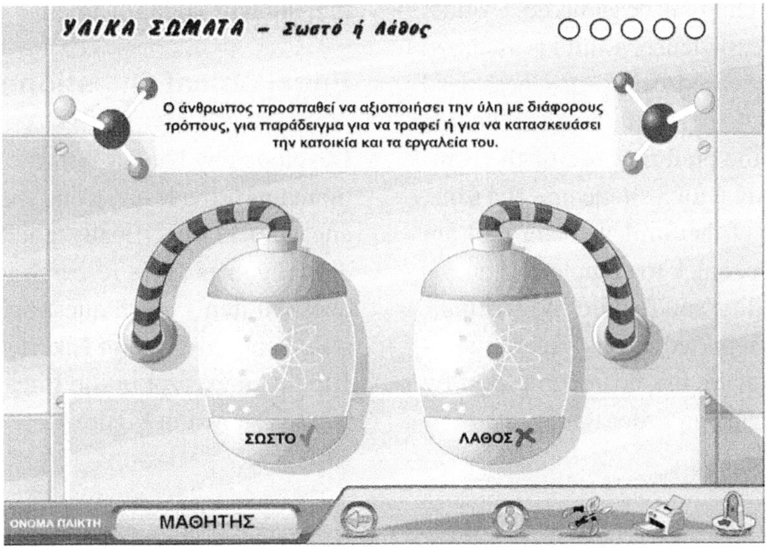

Research Participants

The participants in this research were 493 in total (238 boys and 255 girls) students from the kindergarten and primary schools, aged between 4 and 11 years old (mean=8.12, SD=1.74). From each participating school, teachers and students of two grades were involved in the study. In more detail, the participants comprise 74 in total (36 boys and 38 girls) students from kindergarten (4 to 5 years old) and 419 in total (206 boys and 213 girls) students from primary school grades (82 1st grade students (42 boys and 41 girls), 85 2nd grade students (41 boys and 43 girls), 84 3rd grade students (43 boys and 41 girls), 85 4th grade students (40 boys and 45 girls) and 83 5th grade students (40 boys and 43 girls).

Data Collection Methods

In order to collect the research data, three different questionnaires were used, aiming at measuring different dimensions of the plaeyrs' reactions and feedback. These questionnaires are described in detail below.

Smileyometer

This questionnaire is the first instrument of the Fun Toolkit which was developed by Read and MacFarlane (2000). It is a visual analogue scale with the coding based upon a 5-point Likert scale, with 1 relating to "Awful" and 5 to "Brilliant" as shown in Figure 7.The Smileyometer can be used before and after a child experiences a given

Figure 7. The Smileyometer

technology. By using it before, a measure of the expectations of the child can be gathered. Using it after a technology experience, a child is assumed to be reporting experienced feelings or experienced fun. If several technologies are being evaluated at the same time, the preferred use of the Smileyometer is to apply it for a single one at a time. The key attributes of the Smileyometer tool are that it is easy to use, quick to complete, requires limited reading ability, and requires no writing.

In the research reported in this paper, a Smileyometer questionnaire has been completed by all student participants in order to capture their feelings, moods and emotions while they were playing with digital games.

Engagement Questionnaire

Developed by Nicola Whitton (2010), this questionnaire provides a strong measure of levels of engagement specifically elicited while playing digital games. This research tool consists of 18 question items. Each question item consists of a statement on a 5-point Likert scale ranging from 1 to 5. An excerpt of the Engagement Questionnaire is shown in Figure 8.

Figure 8. The engagement questionnaire

Thinking about the activity you have just undertaken, please indicate the level to which you agree with the following statements:

	Strongly disagree	Disagree	Neither agree nor disagree	Agree	Strongly agree
I wanted to complete the activity	☐	☐	☐	☐	☐
I found the activity frustrating	☐	☐	☐	☐	☐
I felt that I could achieve the goal of the activity	☐	☐	☐	☐	☐
I knew what I had to do to complete the activity	☐	☐	☐	☐	☐
I found the activity boring	☐	☐	☐	☐	☐
It wasn't clear what I could and couldn't do	☐	☐	☐	☐	☐
It was clear what I could learn from the activity	☐	☐	☐	☐	☐
I felt absorbed in the activity	☐	☐	☐	☐	☐
The activity was pointless	☐	☐	☐	☐	☐
I was not interested in exploring the options available	☐	☐	☐	☐	☐
I did not care how the activity ended	☐	☐	☐	☐	☐
I felt that time passed quickly	☐	☐	☐	☐	☐
I found the activity satisfying	☐	☐	☐	☐	☐
The activity would not let me do what I wanted	☐	☐	☐	☐	☐
I could not tell what effect my actions had	☐	☐	☐	☐	☐
I did not enjoy the activity	☐	☐	☐	☐	☐
Feedback I was given was useful	☐	☐	☐	☐	☐
I found it easy to get started	☐	☐	☐	☐	☐

In the research reported in this paper, the Engagement Questionnaire has been completed by the student participants of the 2nd, 3rd, 4th and 5th grades of the two primary schools. Students of the kindergarten and 1st grade of primary school were not asked to complete this questionnaire, since in this age they are not yet experienced (or well-experienced) in reading and writing.

Kids Game Experience Questionnaire

The Kids Game Experience Questionnaire (KidsGEQ) is a self-reporting instrument to assess in-game experiences of young children aged 8-12 y.o. The structure of the KidsGEQ (Poels et al. 2008) is largely based on the Game Experience Questionnaire (GEQ) which has been developed for adults, but is adapted to a child-friendly format and wording. The core questionnaire consists of 21 items divided in 7 game experience dimensions: immersion (e.g. I could use my fantasy in the game); flow (e.g. While playing, I forgot everything around me); competence (e.g. I was good at it); tension (e.g. I was nervous during the game); challenge (e.g. I had to put a lot of effort in the game); positive affect (e.g. Playing the game was fun); and negative affect (e.g. I found it boring). Each question item consists of a statement on a 5-point Likert scale ranging from 1 to 5.

In the research reported in this paper the KidsGEQ questionnaire has been completed by student participants of 2nd, 3rd, 4th and 5th grades of the two primary schools, for the same reasons as above.

RESEARCH FINDINGS

The Smileyometer questionnaire was completed by all students (t=493). Students of kindergarten and 1st grade of primary school were not asked to complete the Engagement Questionnaire and KidsGEQ, since in this age they are not yet experienced (or well-experienced) in reading and writing. So the findings for kindergarten and 1st grade of primary school students listed in the following subsections should be considered as indicative, since they cannot be formally correlated with the variables of engagement and positive experience.

Impact of Free-Form and Structured Digital Games on Positive Emotion

The Smileyometer questionnaire has been completed by all students (t=493) after they played games from each of the two categories and the results are presented in Table 1.

A paired-samples t-test was used to compare the impact of free-form and structured digital games on students' positive emotion. This revealed a significant difference between the level of students' positive emotion while playing with free-form rather than structured digital games (t(492)=5.25 and p=0.034), whereby the level of students' positive emotion while playing free-form digital games had significantly higher mean strength scores than the level of students' positive emotion while playing structured digital games (for free-form digital games, M=3.93, SD=0.48; for structured digital games, M=2.42, SD=0.33).

Table 1. Level of students' positive emotion

	Kindergarten+1st	2nd+3rd	4th+5th	Mean	SD
Free-form games	4.10	3.95	3.75	3.93	0.48
Structured games	2.10	2.40	2.75	2.42	0.33
Paired-samples t-test: $t_{(492)} = 5.25$, p = 0.034					

Table 2. Level of students' positive emotion across gender

		Kindergarten	1st Grade	2nd Grade	3rd Grade	4th Grade	5th Grade
Boys	Free-form games	3.95	3.80	3.82	3.79	4.05	4.35
	Structured games	1.80	2.10	2.35	2.50	2.81	2.55
Girls	Free-form games	4.35	4.15	4.25	3.95	3.12	3.47
	Structured games	2.35	2.15	2.35	2.40	2.89	2.75

Furthermore, an analysis (Table 2) of the impact of free-form and structured digital games on students' positive emotion across gender showed that there are no significant differences which might have affected the subsequent analysis of the data. For both males and females, the most preferred (in the sense of generating positive emotion) kind of digital games are free-form games. Because different numbers of participants in different age groups could affect these results, we separated the game preferences by age group. The impact of free-form digital games on males' positive emotion is stronger than on females among 4th and 5th graders but not among kindergarten students, 1st, 2nd and 3rd graders. Among males, the impact of free-form digital games on students' positive emotion is stronger among 4th and 5th graders, and less so among kindergarten students, 1st, 2nd and 3rd graders. The impact of structured digital games on males' positive emotion is stronger among 2nd, 3rd, 4th and 5th graders and less by kindergarten students and 1st graders. Among females, the impact of free-form digital games on students' positive emotion is stronger by kindergarten students, 1st and 2nd graders and less so by 3rd, 4th and 5th graders. Structured games do not differ by age group among girls.

The results described above suggest that the level of students' positive emotion while playing free-form digital games is significantly higher than while playing structured digital games. More specifically, the analysis of research data showed that for both boys and girls, the most preferred kind of digital games are free-form games. Older boys (4th and 5th graders) and younger girls (kindergarten students, 1st and 2nd graders) preferred free-form digital games the most, while there are no significant differences on the level of students' positive emotion while playing structured digital games.

Impact of Free-Form and Structured Digital Games on Engagement

The engagement questionnaires data were analyzed with Cronbach's Alpha test in order for the internal consistency and reliability of the statements in the questionnaire to be assessed. The results showed an alpha of 0.70 ($\alpha=0.696$) which indicate that the questions in engagement questionnaires are internally consistent, so they can be summed up to an overall engagement score.

A paired-samples t-test was used to compare the impact of free-form and structured digital games on students' engagement (Table 3). This revealed a significant difference between the level of students' engagement while playing free-form versus structured digital games ($t(336)=20.75$ and $p = 0.031$), whereby the level of students' engagement while playing with free-form digital games had significantly higher mean strength scores than the level of students' engagement while playing with structured digital games (for free-form digital games, $M=3.26$, $SD=0.57$; for structured digital games, $M=2.43$, $SD=0.41$).

Furthermore, an analysis (Table 4) of the impact of free-form and structured digital games on students' engagement across gender showed that there are no significant differences which might have affected the subsequent analysis of the data.

Table 3. Level of students' engagement

	$2^{nd}+3^{rd}$	$4^{th}+5^{th}$	Mean	SD
Free-form games	3.21	3.31	3.26	0.57
Structured games	2.34	2.52	2.43	0.41
Paired-samples t-test: $t_{(336)} = 20.75$, $p = 0.031$				

Table 4. Level of students' engagement across gender

		2nd Grade	3rd Grade	4th Grade	5th Grade
Boys	Free-form games	2.98	3.10	3.25	3.45
	Structured games	2.24	2.42	2.34	2.78
Girls	Free-form games	3.30	3.45	3.07	3.47
	Structured games	2.30	2.40	2.32	2.62

For both males and females, the most preferred (in the sense of generating engagement) kind of digital games are free-form games. Because different numbers of participants in different age groups could affect these results, we separated the game preferences by age group. The impact of free-form digital games on males' engagement is stronger than on females among 4th and 5th graders but not among 2nd and 3rd graders. Among males, the impact of free-form digital games on students' engagement is stronger among 4th and 5th graders, and less so for 2nd and 3rd graders. The impact of structured digital games on males' engagement is stronger among 5th graders and less strong for 2nd, 3rd, 4th graders. Among females, the impact of free-form digital games on students' engagement is stronger for 2nd, 3rd and 5th graders and less so for 4th graders. Structured digital games generate stronger engagement for females among 5th graders and less so among 2nd, 3rd and 4th graders.

The results described above suggest that the level of students' engagement while playing free-form digital games is significantly higher than while playing structured digital games. More specifically, the analysis of research data showed that for both boys and girls, the most preferred kind of digital games are free-form games. Older boys (4th and 5th graders) preferred free-form digital games the most. Females' engagement was stronger for 2nd, 3rd and 5th graders and less so for 4th graders. Finally, there are no significant differences on the level of students' engagement while playing structured digital games.

Impact of Free-Form and Structured Digital Games on Positive Experience

The KidsGEQ data were analyzed through Cronbach's Alpha test in order for the internal consistency reliability of the statements in the game experience questionnaire to be assessed. The results showed an alpha of 0.83 (α=0.8296). These results indicate that the questions in KidsGEQ are internally consistent, so they can be summed up to an overall experience score.

A paired-samples t-test was used to compare the impact of free-form and structured digital games on students' positive experience (Table 5). This revealed a significant difference between the level of students' positive experience while playing free-form versus structured digital games ($t(336)=67.21$, $p=0.010$), whereby the level of

Table 5. Level of students' positive experience

Type of Game	$2^{nd}+3^{rd}$	$4^{th}+5^{th}$	Mean	SD
Free-form games	3.24	3.14	3.19	0.43
Structured games	2.12	2.22	2.17	0.65
Paired-samples t-test: $t_{(336)} = 67.21$, $p = 0.010$				

Table 6. Level of students' positive experience across gender

		2nd Grade	3rd Grade	4th Grade	5th Grade
Boys	Free-form games	2.90	3.15	3.05	3.26
	Structured games	2.05	2.16	2.05	2.55
Girls	Free-form games	3.35	3.55	2.97	3.15
	Structured games	2.10	2.15	1.98	2.30

students' positive experience while playing free-form digital games had significantly higher mean strength scores than the level of students' positive experience while playing structured digital games (for free-form digital games, M=3.19, SD=0.43; for structured digital games, M=2.17, SD=0.65).

Furthermore, an analysis (Table 6) of the impact of free-form and structured digital games on students' positive experience across gender showed that there are no significant differences which might have affected the subsequent analysis of the data. For both males and females, the most preferred (in the sense of generating positive experience) kind of digital games are free-form games. Because different numbers of participants in different age groups could affect these results, we separated the game preferences by age group. The impact of free-form digital games on males' positive experience is stronger than on females among 4th and 5th graders but not among 2nd and 3rd graders. Among males, the impact of free-form digital games on students' positive experience is stronger among 5th graders, and less so for 2nd, 3rd and 4th graders. The impact of structured digital games on males' positive experience is stronger among 5th graders and less by 2nd, 3rd, 4th graders. Among females, the impact of free-form digital games on students' positive experience is stronger for 2nd and 3rd graders and less so among 4th and 5th graders. Among females, the impact of structured digital games on positive experience is stronger among 5th graders and less strong among 2nd, 3rd and 4th graders.

The results described above suggest that the level of students' positive experience while playing free-form digital games is significantly higher than while playing structured digital games. More specifically, the analysis of research data showed that for both boys and girls, the most preferred kind of digital games are free-form games. Older boys (5th, 3rd and 5th graders) preferred free-form digital games the most. The positive experience of females was stronger for 2nd, 3rd and 5th graders and less so for 4th graders. Finally, there are no significant differences on the level of students' positive experience while playing structured digital games.

In addition, analysing the seven dimensions of KidsGEQ we found that the more positive dimensions of this questionnaire (immersion, flow, competence, challenge, positive affect) were experienced more positively for free-form digital games, while the more negative dimensions (tension, negative affect) were experienced less

Figure 9. Variation of the 7 dimensions of KidsGEQ by game type

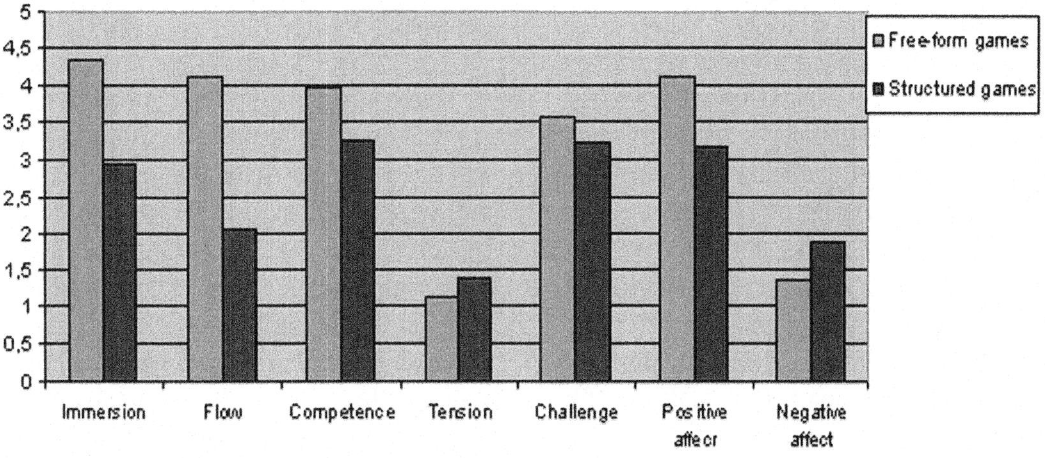

negatively (Figures 9, 10). The opposite was the case for structured digital games. A paired t-test revealed significant differences between free-form and structured games for immersion ($t(336)=7.37$, $p=0.002$) and flow ($t(336)=6.32$, $p=0.010$). This could indicate that free-form digital games would be better suited than structured games to create immersive and flow-generating gameplay.

Furthermore, we found a strong positive correlation between flow and immersion scores ($r=0.9310$, $SD=1.04$, $p<0.05$), potentially suggesting a mutual influence of these concepts for the games that were measured in this research.

More specifically, analyzing the seven dimensions of KidsGEQ across player gender we found that there were no significant gender differences

Figure 10. Variation of the 7 dimensions of KidsGEQ by player gender

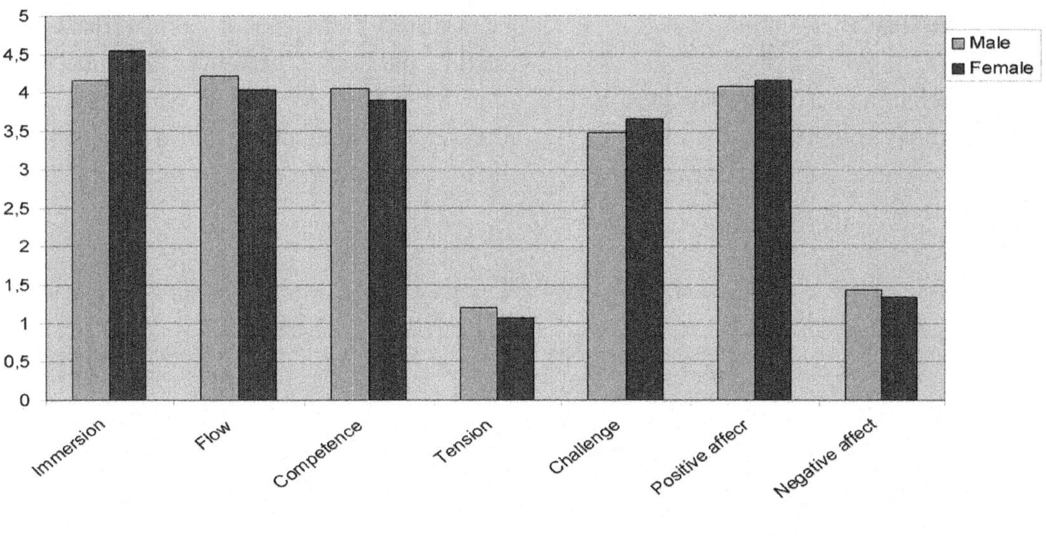

of students' positive experience while playing free-form digital games. Still, the results of multiple paired t-tests for individual dimensions of the KidsGEQ questionnaire revealed significant differences that merit particular attention. Firstly, there was a significant relationship between gender and reported levels of challenge (t(336)=7.37, p=0.002). The experience of competence was lower for female and higher for male players. Secondly, there was a marginally significant relationship between type of game and reported levels of flow (t(336)=-5.22, p<0.001). The experience of flow was lower for female than for male. Thirdly, there was a significant relationship between type of game and reported levels of immersion (t(336)=-4.07, p<0.005). The experience of immersion was lower for male than for female. These findings could indicate that free-form digital games would be better suited to male players in terms of flow experience and competence, while they are better suited to female players in terms of immersive experience.

Based on all these findings, we conclude that the kind of gameplay that a digital game offers, in terms of free-form vs. structured, seems to be crucial for a positively-rated game experience.

Correlation between Positive Emotion, Engagement, and Positive Experience

A Pearson's correlation coefficient was used to examine the relationship between the variables of player's positive emotion (coded as *Emotion*), engagement (coded as *Engagement*) and positive experience (coded as *Experience*). The results are presented in Table 7:

The Pearson's correlation coefficient shows that there is a strong positive correlation between the variables of positive emotion and engagement (r=0.9808, SD=0.88, p<0.05), between the variables of emotion and positive experience (r=0.9995, SD=0.85, p<0.05), as well as between the variables of engagement and positive experience (r=0.9848, SD=0.94, p<0.05). Therefore, the analysis of Pearson's correlation coefficient supports the view that there is a significant correlation between the variables of positive emotion, engagement and positive experience: increases in the level of students' emotion are correlated with increases in the level of students' engagement and positive experience.

In a much similar way, a line graph (Figure 11) shows a strong relationship between these three variables; the games which generated positive emotions to the players are also these which lead towards the players' higher engagement and more positive experience.

Finally, Figure 12 depicts these relationships in a more clear visual manner. As this figure shows, the variable of Game Type (formalizing the concept of free-form vs. structured digital games) affects the variables of players' Emotion, Engagement and Experience (as represented by the directed arrows between them); at the same time, the latter three variables are correlated (as represented by the undirected arrows connecting them). It should be noted, at this point, that Fig-

Table 7. Correlation between the variables of players' Emotion, Engagement and Experience

	Emotion	Engagement	Experience
Emotion	1		
Engagement	0,9808	1	
Experience	0,9995	0,9848	1

Figure 11. Correlation between the Emotion, Engagement and Experience variables

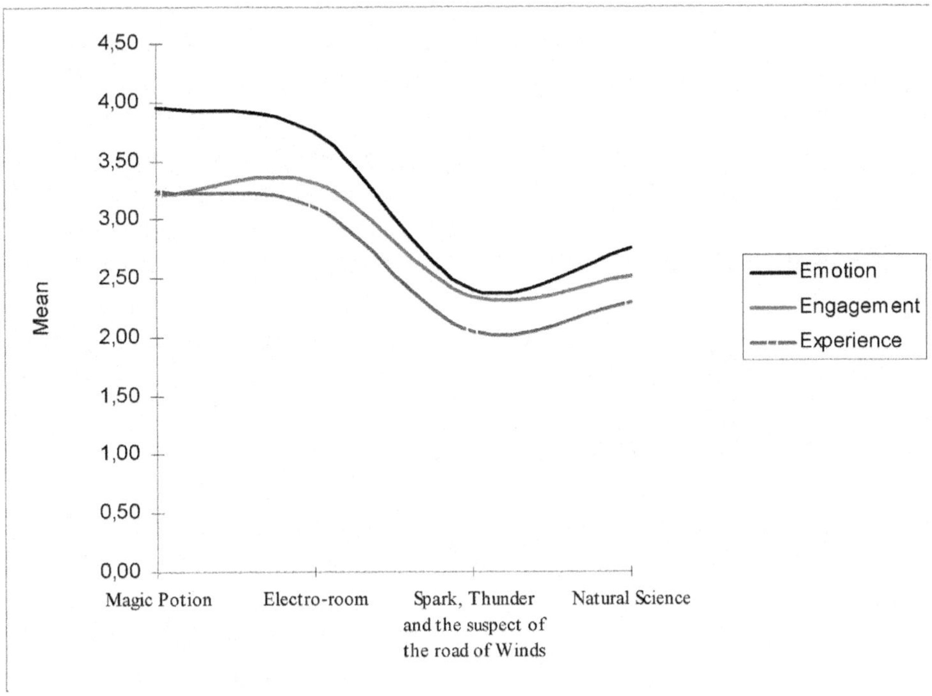

Figure 12. Relationships between the GameType, Emotion, Engagement and Experience variables

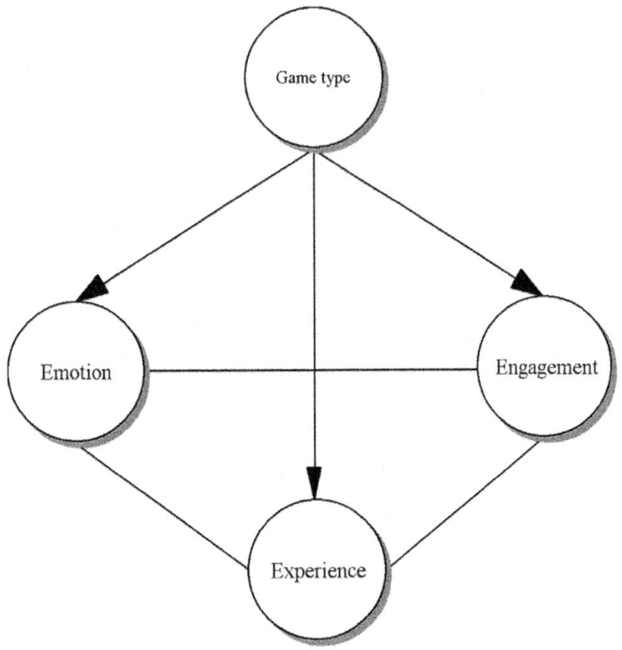

ure 11, although reminiscent of path diagrams or structural equation models, is not yet the result of such an analysis. Rather, based on the findings of the research reported in this paper, it represents a hypothesis of what the results of such an analysis could look like.

DIRECTIONS OF FURTHER RESEARCH

The findings of this research add to the body of research showing a direct correlation between the quality of players' experience and the kind of play that a digital game offers, depending on whether the latter focuses on the game dimension (structured games) or the play dimension (free-from games) of gameplay. Further research in this direction includes issues such as:

1. Exploring the relations between different kinds of gameplay, players' experience and players' age, in order to investigate whether specific digital games generate a player experience optimized for a particular age;
2. A survey of other factors that influence players' experience during gameplay such as immersion, flow, social context and the player's expectations from the game, as well as social interaction and competition between players; and
3. Ongoing work on measuring the quality of players' experience with more digital games in order to achieve more reliable results.

Alongside these research directions, however, further work is needed to explore all possible factors and features that make a digital game fun and enjoyable enough to lead to higher levels of positive emotion, engagement and positive experience.

CONCLUDING REMARKS

The findings of this study showed

1. That free-form digital games lead kindergarten and primary school children players to more positive emotions and, therefore, higher engagement and more positive experience, when compared to structured digital games;
2. That there are no significant differences on players' positive emotion, engagement and positive experience across gender which might have affected the subsequent analyses of the data; for both males and females, the most preferred kind of digital games are free-form games;
3. That free-form digital games may be better suited to male players in terms of flow experience and competence, whereas they may be better suited to female players in terms of immersive experience; and
4. That there is a significant correlation between the variables of positive emotion, engagement and positive experience: the more positive the level of players' emotion, the higher are their engagement and positive experience.

During this research, free-form digital games such as "Poisson Rouge", "Magic Potion", and "Electroroom" that generated higher levels of participating student players' positive emotions also generated higher levels of engagement and positive experience. On the contrary, structured digital games such as "Journey in the Land of Letters", "Spark, Thunder and the Suspect of the Road of Winds" and "Natural Science" that generated lower levels of positive emotion also generated lower levels of engagement and positive experience.

The above findings strongly suggest that there is a direct correlation between the quality of players' experience and the kind of play that a digital game offers, depending on whether the latter focuses on the game dimension (structured games) or the play dimension (free-from games) of gameplay.

Based on the findings of this research, combined with the findings of other studies (Mitgutsch 2008; Fabricatore 2000; Gee 2003), we would like to propose that free-form digital games, when compared to structured digital games, can lead to more engaging and more free-form learning processes, which can better support innovative approaches to learning and, more generally, to the acquisition of 21st century transferable skills. In the same line of thought, we would also like to propose and further investigate the view that that free-form digital games can be used across multiple learning subjects, put students at the centre and engage them actively in the learning process, promoting 21st century transferable skills such as discovery and experiential learning, collaboration, decision taking, active and critical thinking, creative thinking, problem solving skills. On these premises, school teachers and educators who want to encourage innovative learning processes could use free-form digital games in order to enrich their teaching methods and enhance students' learning.

On the other hand, one more implication of our findings is that a key factor for the design of effective digital games for learning seems to be the development of games that

1. Focus on the play dimension of gameplay, allowing for free, unstructured activities without pre-defined rules and pre-designed goals;
2. Create non-linear gameplay;
3. Allow multiple solutions to the game challenges and enable many different player-generated gameplay paths;
4. Give players the ability to choose the order in which they face game challenges; and
5. Allow players to choose which challenges they want to overcome or not.

Such games can result in improving students' learning by increasing their interest due to the pleasant and attractive environment that they offer, often contrary to conventional learning environments. When students play with free-form digital games they feel more motivated and engaged with free, non-obligatory and unstructured acts of play, without pre-defined rules and pre-designed goals. Students in such an environment have the freedom to determine their own learning paths via goals and rules. This, in our view, seems an important factor that makes free-form digital games more challenging than other learning environments. When students play with free-form digital games, the negative emotions caused by failure are weakened, exactly because success can be subjectively defined by the players themselves. Free, unstructured acts of play allow players to discover new skills, try and make mistakes or fail, and then try again without any negative real-world consequences. In such cases, a sense of continued engagement and intrinsic motivation can be sustained during gameplay especially when, according to Malone & Lepper (1987), games include representations of the real world and involve the players' fantasy. Fantasy can offer analogies or metaphors for real world processes that allow players to experience the same phenomenon from different perspectives. That means that skills may be learnt more easily when presented in an imaginative context rather than in a conventional learning environment.

Last but not least, it must be mentioned that the research conducted thus far has faced a number of limitations. Firstly, due to limits of time and practical constraints of the schools available to participate, a limited sample of six digital games had to be selected for this research from a large population of available free-form and structures games. Secondly, the period of the research has been relatively short and not allowed for long-term effects to be recorded. Thirdly, the fact that all participating kindergarten and primary schools are located in Athens, a major urban center of more than 5mn population, may introduce certain biases in the cultural and socio-economic profile of the student participants which could constrain the generalization potential of the research findings reported.

REFERENCES

Almeida, S., Veloso, A., Roque, L., Mealha, O., & Moura, A. (2013). The Video Game and Player in a Gameplay Experience Model Proposal. *Proceedings of Videojogos 2013 - 6th Annual Conference in the Science and Art of Video Games.* Coimbra, Portugal.

Bouvier, P., Lavoué, E., Sehaba, K., & Sébastien, G. (2013). Identifying Learner's Engagement in Learning Games - A Qualitative Approach based on Learner's Traces of Interaction. *Proceedings of the 5th International Conference on Computer Supported,* Aachen, Germany (pp. 339-350). SciTePress

Bracken, C. C., Lange, R. L., & Denny, J. (2005). Online video games and gamers' sensations of spatial, social, and co-presence. *Proceedings of the 2005 FuturePlay Conference*, East Lansing, MI.

Brown, E., & Cairns, P. (2004). A grounded investigation of immersion in games. In *ACM Conference on Human Factors in Computing Systems* (pp. 1297–1300). New York, NY: ACM Press.

Brown, S. L., & Vaughan, C. C. (2009). *Play: How it shapes the brain, opens the imagination, and invigorates the soul.* New York, NY: Avery Publishing Group.

Caillois, R. (2001). *Man, Play, Games.* Chicago, IL: University of Illinois Press.

Calvillo-Gámez, E. H., Cairns, P., & Cox, A. L. (2010). Assessing the Core Elements of the Gaming Experience. In R. Bernhaupt. (Ed.), Evaluating User Experience in Games London, UK (pp. 47 - 71). Springer Verlag. doi:10.1007/978-1-84882-963-3_4

Carse, J. P. (1987). *Finite and Infinite Games.* New York: Ballantine Books.

Costello, B., & Edmonds, E. (2009). A Tool for Characterizing the Experience of Play. *Proceedings of the Sixth Australasian Conference on Interactive Entertainment (pp.* 1-10*).* Sydney, Australia: ACM Press. doi:10.1145/1746050.1746052

Csíkszentmihályi, M. (1990). *Flow: The Psychology of Optimal Experience.* New York, NY: Harper & Row Publishers, Inc.

Damasio, A. R. (1994). *Descartes' Error: emotion, reason, and the human brain.* New York: Grosset/Putnam.

Dewey, J. (1938). *Experience & Education.* New York, NY: Kappa Delta Pi.

Ermi, L., & Mayra, F. (2005). Fundamental Components of the Gameplay Experience: Analysing Immersion. *Proceedings of Chancing Views – Worlds in Play* (Vol. 37, pp. 37–53). New York, NY: Peter Lang International Academic Publisher.

Fabricatore, C. (2000). *Learning and Videogames: an unexploited synergy.* Retrieved from www.learndev.org/dl/FabricatoreAECT2000.PDF

Fabricatore, C., Nussbaum, M., & Rosas, R. (2002). Playability in video games: A qualitative design model. *Human-Computer Interaction, 17*(4), 311–368. doi:10.1207/S15327051HCI1704_1

Frasca, G. (2003). *Simulation Versus Narrative: Introduction to Ludology*. Retrieved from http://www.ludology.org/articles/VGT_final.pdf

Gee, J. P. (2003). *What Video Games Have to Teach Us About Learning and Literacy*. New York: Palgrave Macmillan.

Hassenzahl, M., & Tractinsky, N. (2006). User Experience – a Research Agenda. *Behaviour & Information Technology, 25*(2), 91–97. doi:10.1080/01449290500330331

IJsselsteijn, W. A., Poels, K., & de Kort, Y.A.W. (2008). *The game experience questionnaire: Development of a self-report measure to assess player experiences of digital games* [Technical report]. Eindhoven, The Netherlands: TU Eindhoven.

Jennett, C., Cox, A. L., Cairns, P., Dhoparee, S., Epps, A., Tijs, T., & Walton, A. (2008). Measuring and defining the experience of immersion in games. *International Journal of Human-Computer Studies, 66*(9), 641–661. doi:10.1016/j.ijhcs.2008.04.004

Juul, J. (2005). *Half-Real: Video Games between Real Rules and Fictional Worlds*. Cambridge, MA: MIT Press.

Kiili, K., Ketamo, H., Koivisto, A., & Finn, E. (2014). Studying the user experience of a tablet based math game. *International Journal of Game-Based Learning, 4*(1), 60–77. doi:10.4018/IJGBL.2014010104

Klimmt, C. (2003). Dimensions and determinants of the enjoyment of playing digital games: A three-level model. In *Proceedings of the Digital Games Research Conference* (pp. 246-257). Utrecht, The Netherlands: Faculty of Arts, Utrecht University.

Koster, R. (2004). *A Theory of Fun for Game Design*. Scottsdale, AZ: Paraglyph Press.

Lazzaro, N. (2004). *Why we play games: Four keys to more emotion without story*. Retrieved from http://www.xeodesign.com/whyweplaygames/xeodesign_whyweplaygames.pdf

Lazzaro, N. (2007). Why We Play: Affect and the Fun of Games: Designing Emotions for Games, Entertainment Interfaces and Interactive Tools. In A. Sears & J. A. Sears (Eds.), *The Human-Computer Interaction Handbook: Fundamentals, Evolving Techniques, and Emerging Applications* (pp. 679–700). Mahwah, NJ: Lawrence Erlbaum Associates. doi:10.1201/9781410615862.ch34

Malone, T. W., & Lepper, M. R. (1987). Making Learning Fun: A Taxonomy of Intrinsic Motivations for Learning. In R. E. Snow & M. J. Farr (Eds.), *Aptitute, Learning and Instruction: III. Conative and affective process analyses* (pp. 223–253). Hilsdale, NJ: Erlbaum.

McGregor, G. (2008). Terra ludus, terra paidia, terra prefab: spatialization of play in videogames & virtual worlds. *Proceedings of the 5th Australasian Conference on Interactive Entertainment* (pp. 31-38), New York, NY: ACM Press. doi:10.1145/1514402.1514407

McMahan, A. (2003). Immersion, Engagement, and Presence: A Method for Analyzing 3-D Video Games. In M. J. P. Wolf & B. Perron (Eds.), *The video game theory reader* (pp. 67–86). New York: Routledge.

Mitgutsch, K. (2008). Digital Play-Based Learning. A philosophical-pedagogical perspective on learning and playing in computer games. *Journal for Information Technology Studies as Human Science, 9*(3), 18–36.

Nacke, L., Drachen, A., Kuikkaniemi, K., Niesenhaus, J., Korhonen, H. J., & van den Hoogen, W. M. (2009). Playability and Player Experience Research. *Proceedings of DiGRA 2009: Breaking New Ground: Innovation in Games, Play, Practice and Theory*. London, UK: DiGRA.

Park, K. S., Cho, Y., & Kim, D. K. (2014). A Framework for the creating, expressing and sharing of user's emotion. *International Journal of Multimedia and Ubiquitous Engineering*, *9*(1), 425–442. doi:10.14257/ijmue.2014.9.1.39

Poels, K., de Kort, Y. A. W., & IJsselsteijn, W. A. (2007). It is always a lot of fun! Exploring Dimensions of Digital Game Experience using Focus Group Methodology. *Proceedings of Futureplay 2007* (pp. 83–89). Toronto, Canada: ACM Press.

Poels, K., IJsselsteijn, W. A., & de Kort, Y. A. W. (2008). Development of the Kids Game Experience Questionnaire: a self report instrument to assess digital game experiences in children. Poster Presentation for Meaningful Play Conference, Michigan, USA.

Prensky, M. (2007). *Digital game-based learning*. St. Paul, MN: Paragon House.

Przybylski, A. K., Rigby, C. S., & Ryan, R. M. (2010). A Motivational Model of Video Game Engagement. *Review of General Psychology*, *14*(2), 154–166. doi:10.1037/a0019440

Read, J., & MacFarlane, S. (2000). Measuring Fun – Usability Testing for Children. Computers and Fun 3, York: England.

Reiter, U., Brunnström, K., De Moor, K., Mohamed-Chaker, L., Pereira, M., Pinheiro, A., You, J., & Zgank, A. (2014). Factors Influencing Quality of Experience. *T-Labs Series in Telecommunication Services*, 55-72.

Rigby, S., & Ryan, R. (2011). *Glued to games: How video games draw us in and hold us spellbound*. Santa Barbara, California: Praeger.

Roto, V. (2007). User Experience from Product Creation Perspective. In E. Law, A. Vermeeren, M. Hassenzahl, & M. Blythe (Eds.), Towards a UX Manifesto workshop, Lancaster, UK. COST.

Salen, K., & Zimmerman, E. (2004). *Rules of play: Game design fundamentals*. Cambridge, MA: MIT Press.

Schoenau-Fog, H. (2011). The player engagement process – an exploration of continuation desire in digital games. Proceedings of Think Design Play: Digital Games Research Conference. Utrecht School of the Arts & DiGRA, Utrecht, Netherlands: DiGRA.

Sutton-Smith, B. (1997). *The Ambiguity of Play*. Cambridge, Mass: Harvard University Press.

Sweetser, P., & Wyeth, P. (2005). GameFlow: A model for evaluating player enjoyment in games. *Computers in Entertainment*, *3*(3), 1–24. doi:10.1145/1077246.1077253

Takatalo, J., Hakkinen, J., Komulainen, J., Sarkela, H., & Nyman, G. (2006). Involvement and presence in digital gaming. Proceedings of the 4th Nordic conference on Human-computer interaction: changing roles, Oslo, Norway. ACM Press. doi:10.1145/1182475.1182520

Whitton, N. (2010). *Learning with digital games: a practical guide to engaging students in higher education*. New York: Routledge.

Wiebe, E., Lamb, A., Hardy, M., & Sharek, D. (2014). Measuring Engagement in Video Game-based Environments: Investigation of the User Engagement Scale. *Computers in Human Behavior*, *32*, 123–132. doi:10.1016/j.chb.2013.12.001

Chapter 20
Mission HydroSci:
Distance Learning through Game-Based 3D Virtual Learning Environments

James Laffey
University of Missouri, USA

Sean Goggins
University of Missouri, USA

Troy D. Sadler
University of Missouri, USA

Joseph Griffin
University of Missouri, USA

Ryan Nicholas Babiuch
University of Missouri, USA

ABSTRACT

Distance Learning through game-based 3D virtual learning environments has promise for helping rural and other communities that have become increasingly dependent upon online learning to meet the Next Generation Science Standards. The team developing Mission HydroSci (MHS) envisions a learning product that integrates a game-based 3D VLE with a learning progressions approach to curriculum and innovative methods for teacher support and learning analytics. MHS uses an eight level game which at each level immerses students in a simulation environment for learning about water systems and then requires the student to put that knowledge into practice in a context of developing their competencies for scientific argumentation. This chapter describes the vision for MHS at the beginning of the development process funded by a grant award from the Investing in Innovation (i3) Fund of the U.S. Department of Education.

INTRODUCTION

Serious concerns regarding science education for precollegiate learners have been voiced by educators, business leaders and policy makers in the United States. Put simply, most students do not become proficient enough in reasoning through scientific problems and using scientific practices to be well prepared for science-related careers or for dealing with scientific issues in their lives (NRC, 2011). Literature suggests that traditional methods of science instruction, heavily weighted to memorization and isolated laboratory experiences, need to be replaced (NRC, 2011). Scientists, Science

DOI: 10.4018/978-1-4666-9629-7.ch020

Educators and Policymakers are calling for a new orientation to science teaching and learning, an orientation that requires students to *engage with science* by applying core ideas from the disciplines through scientific practices. These ideas have been advanced through creation of new science standards, the *Next Generation Science Standards* (NGSS; NGSS Lead States, 2013). Knowing and learning science, as envisioned by the NGSS, require learners to develop understandings of and apply scientific ideas, principles and theories as they engage in meaningful scientific practices such as posing questions, carrying out investigations, developing models, and arguing from evidence. Implementation of NGSS is an ambitious challenge even in the most well-resourced classrooms, but as a nation we must also attend to students in diverse and constrained circumstances. Online learning, which includes students learning at a distance and in blended environments, is an approach to meet the needs of diverse students in diverse settings. However, substantial challenges must be overcome before online learning can readily deliver the deep engagement with scientific ideas and practices needed to achieve the vision of NGSS.

Finding teaching and learning practices that lead to *engaging with science* and that can be used in distance learning (DL) where the teaching and learning is fully mediated through computer experiences, is a substantial challenge. Recent surveys on the use of online education in K-12 report DL reached 1.5 million students in the 2009-10 school year alone and there are expectations for substantial growth in the future (Picciano & Seamen, 2009; Wicks, 2010). Small and rural schools, in particular, are turning increasingly to online DL as a way to overcome the challenges of attracting and keeping well qualified teachers and to offer a full range of courses for their students (Hannum et al., 2009). Therefore, in order to ensure equitable access to high quality science learning experiences for all students, including learners from small and rural communities who tend to be underrepresented in science related fields (Avery, 2013), new and innovative approaches for supporting online science education are necessary.

A recent review (NRC, 2011) of the role of games and simulation in science education suggests that games and simulation may be an important approach to meeting learning goals presented in the new standards. The report concludes that: "Simulation and games have potential to advance multiple science learning goals, including motivation to learn science, conceptual understanding, science process skills, understanding of the nature of science, scientific discourse and argumentation, and identification with science and science learning." (p. 54). In short, the potential of game-based learning aligns well with the NGSS. However, the same report also concludes that "Evidence for the effectiveness of games for supporting science learning is emerging, but is currently inconclusive. To date the research base is very limited" (p. 54). The report goes on to call for a research base that can accumulate across the variety of simulations and games and in the face of the constant innovation that characterizes them. While the research base is limited, some progress has been made on the design and development of games in science education. There are a few well-developed 3D game-based learning environments being successfully implemented in schools. However, these learning systems, such as Quest Atlantis (Barab et al., 2010), River City (Clarke et al., 2006), Mission Biotech (Sadler et al., 2013) and EcoMuve (Metcalfe et al., 2009) primarily are supplements to in-class teacher-led activity and do not attempt DL with both teachers and peers at a distance. Once the physical classroom is removed from the pedagogical process, the human-computer interaction and human-to-human via computer interaction of the learning system must meet the full requirements of delivering effective instruction and meet all the needs of the teacher and student as they take on teaching-learning practices. This chapter describes an approach to meeting those requirements so as to impact science education in schools and communities dependent upon DL.

BACKGROUND

The shift in focus to core ideas embedded within engagement in scientific practices, as articulated by the NGSS, is a relatively new development for the science education community. As such, extant research regarding the most effective ways of enacting NGSS-aligned teaching and learning is limited. Despite these limitations, we do know that in order to meet the goal of NGSS, students require rich learning contexts that make it possible to explore substantive science ideas through engagement in scientific practices (Quinn et al., 2012; Sadler, 2009). Virtual learning environments (VLE) can be leveraged to create these rich contexts and can be powerful tools for supporting science education in a range of contexts including formal face-to-face classrooms and informal science settings (Clark et al., 2013; Sadler et al., 2013). We see these forms of learning environments as needed and potentially powerful for addressing challenges associated with science education through online DL.

Video game play is becoming ubiquitous (58% of Americans play video games, ESA, 2013) and children are comparing the engaging, active experience of playing games with the rather placid and passive nature of being in a classroom (Project Tomorrow, 2008). Additionally many of these games place the player in an active, deeply engaging context where actions and decisions have consequences for progression in the game. Game play for entertainment also can encourage learning from failure, perseverance and sense of identity. Fortunately the technologies and techniques for virtualization and role playing experiences are also being applied, although with far less investment and more limited use, to 3D virtual learning and role playing games.

Laffey and colleagues (Laffey, Stichter & Galyen, 2013; Stichter, Laffey et al., 2013) have developed iSocial, a 3D VLE for youth with Autism Spectrum Disorders to develop social competency capabilities. The youth enter a 3D virtual world and participate with peers in guided activities to develop effective social practices. River City is a multi-user 3D VLE developed for middle-school students to learn inquiry skills and content related to biology and epidemiology (Clarke et al., 2006). Mission Biotech (Sadler et al., 2013; Sadler et al., 2015) supports student learning of basic biological principles through engagement in a series of virtual biotechnology investigations. Quest Atlantis (QA) is a set of multi-user 3D VLE for knowledge quests and interactive tasks and is designed to implement learning through transformational play (Barab, et al., 2007). As of 2009, 15 different QA worlds aligned with academic subject matter had been developed and used by thousands of students around the world (Barab et al., 2009). EcoMUVE (Metcalf et al. 2009) is a multi-user 3D VLE implemented as a two-week module focused on teaching students complex causality within ecosystems. Each of these systems demonstrates that 3D VLE can be engaging for students and impact significant learning outcomes. WolfQuest (Schaller et al. 2009) is a 3D wildlife simulation game designed to bring the immersive, emotionally compelling qualities of commercial videogames to informal science learning. SimCityEDU (Glasslab, 2013) is a game-based simulation for learning and assessment with middle school students. Students learn about human impacts on earth systems and systems thinking while taking on 6 pollution challenges in SimCityEdu. The SimCityEdu system has been designed to fit a classroom context and provide student reports to support the teacher.

One distinction that we note between our approach and the VLEs currently used in science education settings (e.g., SimCityEdu, Mission Biotech and Quest Atlantis) is that the current systems emphasize individuals performing certain tasks in a virtual world while interacting with peers and an instructor in a physical classroom. Typically, teachers monitor student work by walking around the class and observing physical behavior. In contrast, MHS will be designed so that all the learning activity and social interactions take place in the virtual world and the teacher observes students through analytics and uses the analytics to determine feedback. Fortunately, hardware, network and software technologies are advancing so that we can envision game-based, 3D immersive experiences augmented with learning analytics that engage and monitor students in scientific practices, even as complex as scientific argumentation. We are particularly interested in taking advantage of 3D environments with their potential to generate a sense of presence, fantasy and direct interaction (Squire 2011) as well as their ability to support learners' exploration of novel identities (Gee 2007). This configuration is part of our design because our delivery model envisions students learning at a distance where the student-teacher relationship is fully mediated through the VLE.

We believe that game-based, 3D VLEs can be an effective way to immerse students in the "stuff" of disciplinary core ideas and engage them in scientific practice. Further we believe that the game and technology-based environment we are building has potential to bring the goals of NGSS to students in diverse contexts with limited access to high quality teaching and learning. Our approach to using technology enables students to meet NGSS standards through distance and blended learning. While our focus is on students, particularly in small and rural communities, who may be dependent upon forms of online learning for science education, we also believe that the form of teaching and learning we are describing can benefit students in most educational settings because it prioritizes the engagement of students and motivates students through putting science understanding into practice. This can be difficult to achieve even in highly resourced educational environments. Additionally, even in highly resourced educational environments with highly qualified teachers, not all students respond well to traditional teaching and learning approaches. Games and game-based virtual learning environments like the project we are undertaking may be good approaches for students who need alternative approaches to traditional schooling.

We believe our vision of 3D game-based VLEs for distance learning is broadly applicable across disciplines and practices but we are developing a test-bed for our ideas and technologies in a learning system called Mission HydroSci (MHS). Our approach, for which MHS is an instantiation, includes a simulation environment for exploring and mastering disciplinary content and a practice environment for putting new knowledge and understandings into disciplinary practice, such as problem solving, reasoning and argumentation. Our approach also includes a learning analytics system which enables the VLE to be an adaptive system responsive to individual needs and also informs a performance support system to assist teachers as they monitor and guide learning.

MHS immerses students in learning about water systems and puts that knowledge into practice in a context of students developing their competencies for scientific argumentation. Since the fall of 2012 a small group of faculty, students and staff in the College of Education at the University of Missouri have undertaken an exploratory works project to advance a vision of virtual learning, test technological capabilities and build prototypes to see ideas come to life. In December of 2014, the Investing in Innovation (i3) Fund of the U.S. Department of Education awarded a development grant to this group and some additional partners to fully design, develop and test the potential of MHS to impact student achievement and engagement and teacher efficacy. This chapter provides an overview of our approach and a status for our vision by describing the design of MHS.

PROBLEM

While many middle school science classes and curricula address some aspects of water systems science, like various phases of the water cycle, most middle school science learners do not have opportunities to develop deep understandings of water systems while building competencies for scientific practices like argumentation. Therefore, students may learn terms and definitions for various aspects of the water cycle, but they tend not to engage in NGSS-aligned learning wherein the science of water is positioned as a dynamic system including drivers, constraints, physical and chemical processes, and multiple interactions through broader socio-ecological systems (Covitt et al., 2009; Gunckel et al., 2012). Furthermore, despite the significance of argumentation as a fundamental aspect of science (Duschl & Osborne, 2002), the practice of scientific argumentation tends not to be a prominently featured component of K-12 education (Berland & McNeill, 2010). The prevalence of argumentation in science classrooms is expanding with the advent of the new standards, but significant progress must be made in order to provide all students, particularly those learning science through online mechanisms, with opportunities to engage in and learn through scientific argumentation.

Predominant approaches used in online K-12 science courses often fail to provide the kinds of rich contexts necessary for meeting NGSS (Barko & Sadler, 2013). While all science educators are (or soon will be) negotiating the complexities of NGSS, supporting NGSS in online learning environments is especially challenging because of limited models for engaging learners in scientific practices through these venues. Prevalent forms of distance learning have attrition rates often exceeding 50%, and students report isolation, frustration and lack of support from information-centric teaching (Roblyer, 2006: LaPadula, 2003; de la Varre et al., 2011). To too large an extent these prevalent distance learning offerings are not consistent with what we know about how people learn (Bransford et al, 2000;) and what the science education community thinks students ought to learn (Donovan et al, 1999; NRC, 2011). However, online learning environments hold great promise because they present potential for reaching large audiences including a range of students from groups underrepresented in the sciences such as students from rural communities (Avery, 2013; Oliver, 2007; Versypt & Versypt, 2013).

INNOVATIVE APPROACH

MHS is an innovative learning technology based curriculum with objectives of deeply engaging students in scientific argumentation, scaffolding their learning to argue scientifically and integrating the practices of argumentation with disciplinary core ideas related to water systems. We argue that (1) the technology for creating immersive role playing 3D virtual environments with game engines, such as Unity, (2) the growing knowledge base for learning from and in virtual learning environments, and (3) the potential for using analytics to support interaction in the virtual learning environment and to include teachers in the process offer great potential for building new knowledge about and developing learning environments for addressing NGSS.

MHS is a virtual learning environment and curriculum to support middle school student learning of water systems science and scientific argumentation designed for implementation in online learning contexts. This will be a replacement unit for middle school science classes facilitated through blended or distance learning classes. We anticipate the full MHS unit to span approximately three weeks of playing/learning time (~ 12 to 15 hours). Learner experiences will be facilitated through interactions within the MHS virtual environment in which they will have opportunities to explore and experiment with water systems, collect evidence relative to challenging water-related problems, interact with non-player characters, and use the collected evidence as a basis for building and critiquing arguments. Students will progress through a series of eight units within the MHS system. Each unit will be

Figure 1. Illustrates a problem space (terrain land-mass) where the student must take on challenges (determining the amount of water that can be harvested) within a set of constraints (understanding of water flow, levels of terrain material for creating the land-mass, and levels of rain)

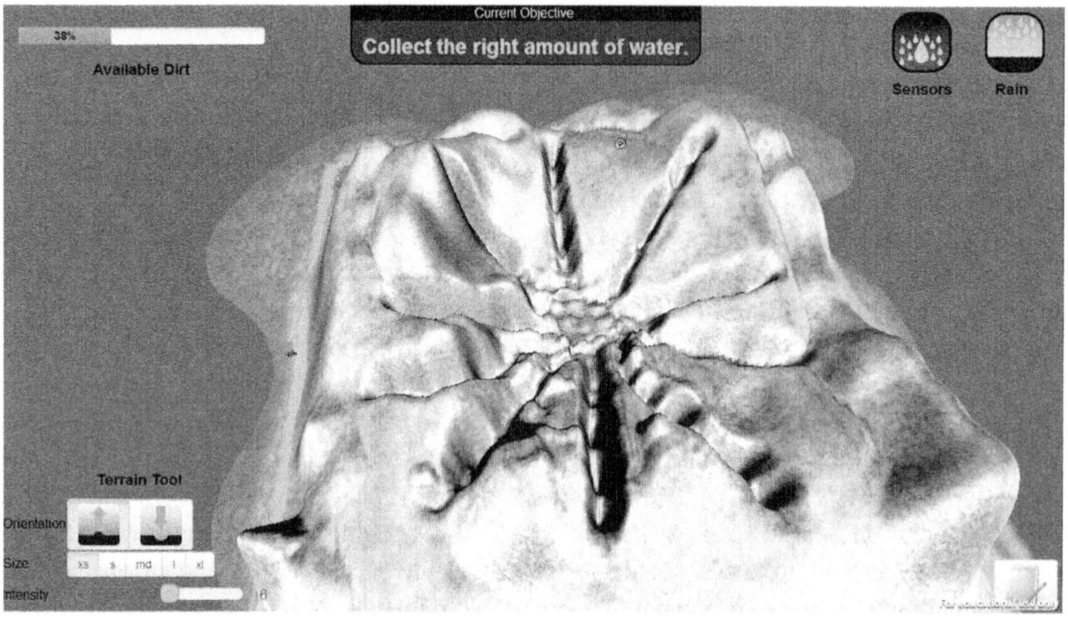

designed around a challenging problem or task and feature progressively more complex ideas about water systems as well as increasingly more challenging argumentation competencies. For example, the first unit challenges students to shape a continent (on a fantasy planet) such that they maximize flow of water though a particular location on the continent. This challenge has students negotiate ideas associated with watersheds and relationships among topography, the number of watersheds on a continent and the sizes of those watersheds. Figure 1 is a screenshot of a student manipulating a landmass to create a watershed as part of the first level. The student manages and places terrain material (bedrock, dirt, etc.) and has a meter in the upper left corner showing how much material is available for terrain building. In the lower left corner, the student has tools for manipulating the terrain structure and in the upper right corner the student has sensors that can be placed to assess water flow as well as a way to make it rain so as to test various scenarios. From the experience of testing scenarios the student will collect a set of data cards which represent evidence to be used in a successive level of the unit where the student must engage in argumentation to persuade decision makers about whether the mission should continue.

The MHS VLE incorporates several system elements: gaming, 3D virtualization, problem-solving context, social interactions, teaching and learning materials based on empirical learning progressions, opportunities for just-in-time instruction, scaffolding for argumentation, an empirically-grounded instructional model, and an analytics system. Our approach includes these elements within 4 key components as mechanisms for engaging students in challenging learning tasks, supporting teachers as they support students and achieving important learning outcomes at a distance. The four key components are: 1) a 3D virtual learning environment for learning through transformative play, 2) a science curriculum based on learning progressions, 3) a teacher support system, and 4) a learning analytics system. Figure 2 illustrates how these components contribute to the goal of meeting NGSS.

1. A 3D Virtual Learning System for Learning through Transformative Play

Barab and colleagues (Barab, Gresalfi & Arici, 2009; Barab, Gresalfi & Ingram-Goble, 2010; Barab, et al., 2007) have developed a theory of transformational play showing how specific design strategies can optimize the potential of games and play to lead to desired learning outcomes. Transformational play has been developed through decade-long research and the design of the game-like 3D VLE *Quest Atlantis (QA)*. The design strategies to enact transformational play include the student taking on the role of a protagonist who must use subject matter knowledge to make decisions and take action during play, and having these actions and decisions transform the problem-based situation (e.g., solving an environmental problem of a declining fish population and thus saving a community dependent on fishing). In turn the student's understanding of the subject matter is transformed and so is the student's identity (Gee, 2001). Techniques for virtualization and role playing experiences in virtual worlds are increasingly available to education, where realistic actions are possible and the consequences of actions can dynamically impact the world and the learner. These techniques along with advancing technology for virtualization and agent-based interactivity offer new promise for how transformational play can be enacted for virtual learning.

Figure 2. Illustrates how primary components of the MHS system are integrated to achieve student outcomes and teacher efficacy

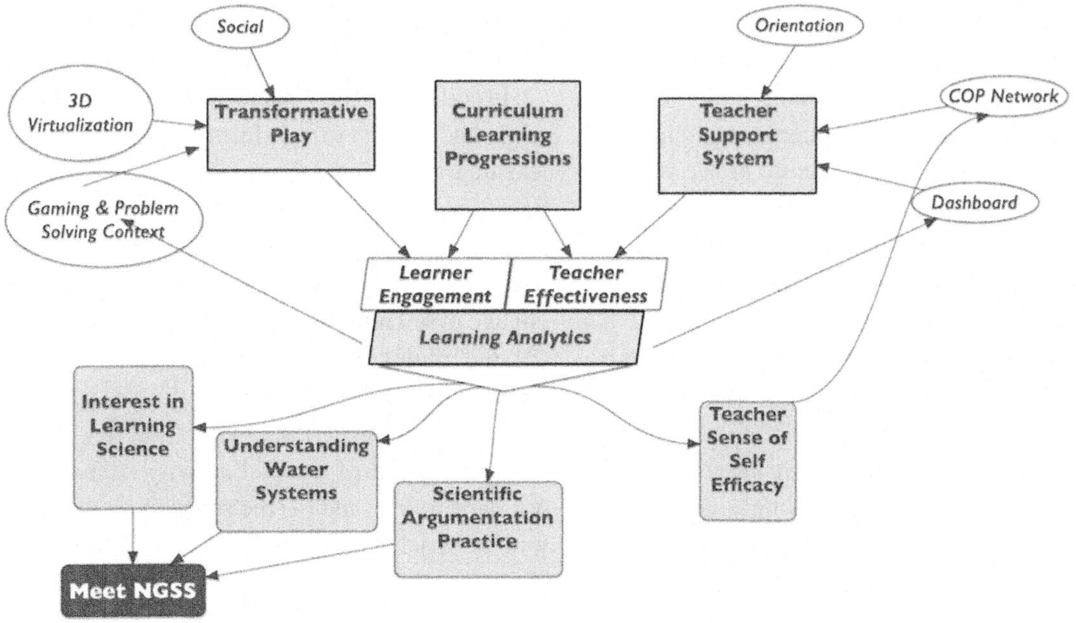

MHS includes two spaces for learner exploration and interaction: a water systems simulator (WSS) and a scientific argumentation environment (SAE). The interface between the WSS and the SA are data cards (drawn from simulations and experiments) and information cards (drawn from embedded learning materials). The MHS narrative brings players to a fantasy future where intergalactic travel is possible and earth's natural resources, like fresh water, have been overextended. After learning how to interact within the virtual environment, our student receives communication from world leaders back on Earth explaining that Earth is running out of potable water and outlining a mission to find a new source of water for a large population. Can the player manipulate the new planet's topography to create a watershed of sufficient size to achieve the mission directive? As the game progresses, the player will be able to shape topography of a continent, adjust the solar radiation received by the planet, explore and change the permeability of the continent's rocks, trace the flow of materials added to a watershed, and modify vegetative groundcover. Fortunately for our student, she will have access to a number of tools—some of which she may find in a present-day laboratory like water sensors and water quality testing materials—and other fantasy tools like excavation spaceships for shaping topography, a machine for looking into the future to see what the implications of choices will be and a host of other devices needed to support the narrative and undertake experiments related to the new planet's water system. The fantasy environment and tools are developed from models of how water systems on earth function, and provide the learner with a sense of agency that supports exploration. As the game unfolds, the player will receive missions that challenge her to explore increasingly complex dimensions of water systems such as relationships between atmospheric, surface and ground water as well as the links for these parts of the water cycle.

As the game progresses the learner is challenged to make the case for a solution to populating the landmass with a human community taking into account the requisite water needs. In the game, the learner is asked to be a scientist conducting experiments while testing and building the case for solutions. The learner is supported by non-player characters (NPCs) who can guide and assist the work; the learner also confronts NPC antagonists who challenge assertions made by the learner and her collaborators and in some instances introduce false claims to the discourse. At each level of the game, the learner receives missions to explore and test within the WSS, return to the SAE with data and information cards, and engage in discussion with NPCs to both explain the cards and use the cards in argumentation events. Figure 3 shows a student interacting with the General, an NPC, who must be convinced to keep the mission going. The figure illustrates the student using data cards from the WSS to support his argument. Following the argumentation events, the learner is either sent back to the WSS to collect and/or analyze additional evidence needed to strengthen her arguments, or the learner advances to the next unit. Advancement includes a process of reporting out to supervisors back on Earth what was accomplished so as to gain credits needed for the next unit.

In addition to the virtualization of the problem space and activity to transform that space through learning and using science constructs and practices, learners will experience MHS as a social learning space. By social we mean (1) the identities that learners create when given opportunities to engage in scientific practices and solve problems, (2) the dialog that collaboratively constructs knowledge (Stahl, 2006) through making sense in argumentation, (3) the motivation that comes from being part of a social activity (Baumeister & Leary, 1995), and (4) the sense of co-presence with a teacher that comes through designed activities and feedback. Anderson et al. (2001) provide a framework for understanding online teaching and learning through cognitive presence, social presence and teaching presence. Cognitive

Figure 3. When needing to make a claim or counter-claim students can place their data cards on the argumentation "white" board to construct their arguments. Here the student has placed 2 data cards on the white board and is continuing the conversation with one of the non-player characters.

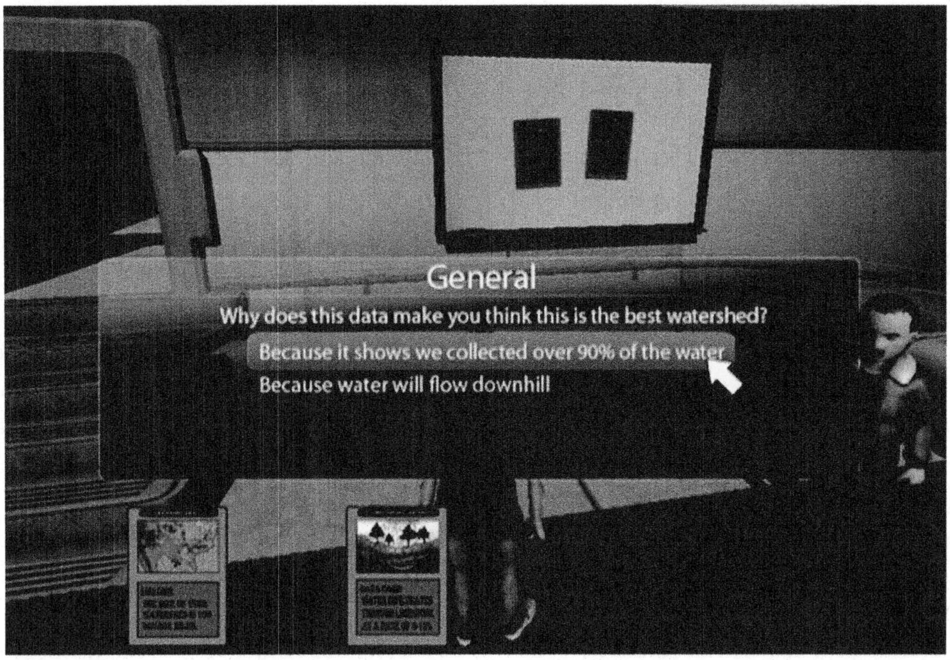

presence is created through instructional strategies that support meaning-making for students through active engagement and reflection. Social presence is achieved by creating an environment of trust and comfort through effective and open communication. Teaching presence refers to the facilitation of cognitive and social processes for the purpose of realizing personally meaningful and educationally worthwhile learning outcomes.

The social context of MHS includes learners assuming roles with responsibilities for saving Earth and interacting with NPCs (which have scripts designed to engage learners in argumentation and can also be shaped by teachers to meet individual needs). Learners also interact with peers as progress is made in developing argumentation competencies and with the teacher on an as needed basis. The primary set of interactions are with NPCs who play the roles of supporters and antagonists. Storyline, dialogue, avatar expression (movement, gesture, facial expressions) and role in problem solving will give these NPCs identities and, in turn, shape the identity of the learner. Additionally, the supporters represent the teacher and instructional designers in helping the learner succeed. In the culminating levels of MHS, the students will work in triads with peers to finally overcome their antagonists and evaluate competing arguments by providing reasons for why one argument is superior relative to several other evidence-supported claims.

2. The MHS Virtual Learning System Curriculum for Learning through Progressions

The sequencing of MHS missions are informed by empirical learning progressions of students understandings of water systems and scientific argumentation competencies. MHS represents one of the initial efforts to design a VLE that requires students to integrate core scientific knowledge with scientific practice. In the case of MHS, students first explore and gain understanding of water systems concepts and then employ their understandings of water systems through the practice of argumentation. Our project builds from extensive research related to students' ideas (and misconceptions) about water (e.g. Dickerson & Dawkins 2004; Endreny 2010; Shepardson et al. 2007) and empirically based learning progressions for water systems and associated assessments (Covitt et al., 2009; Gunckel et al., 2009). Levels of the learning progressions characterize learners' understandings and reasoning relative to various dimensions of water systems including movement of water through atmospheric, surface, and groundwater systems; representation of water at varying scales from molecules to watersheds; and processes that drive and constrain water flow and interactions.

Argumentation has long been recognized as a central epistemic practice within science (Kelly & Takao, 2002) and as an important goal for science education (Newton et al., 1999). We view scientific argumentation not as a simple skill, but rather as a competency that necessarily requires reasoning and the application of scientific content knowledge (Osborne et al., 2013). We also adopt the perspective that important differences exist between scientific explanation and argument (Osborne & Patterson 2011). Scientific explanation involves making sense of a phenomenon with scientific facts. Scientific argumentation, on the other hand, involves adjudication among multiple claims. It is entirely possible for an argument to focus on which of two or more explanations for a phenomenon is more plausible, but argumentation, as a scientific practice, involves the weighing of claims and evidence and not just providing an explanation of a phenomenon of interest. Toulmin's (1958) model for the structure of arguments has been widely used within science education to help define important elements of an argument (Erduran & Jimenez-Aleixandre, 2008). Based on this model, an argument begins with a claim, or the conclusion to be supported. Data are used to support the claim and warrants provide a link or justification between the data and claim. Warrants are often referred to as the reasoning that justifies how and why the data invoked support the claim (McNeill et al., 2006). Toulmin's model also identifies other argument components (e.g., qualifiers and backings), but several researchers have made the case that focusing on core argument structures (claims-warrants-data) is more productive for science education research and practice (e.g., Sadler & Donnelly, 2006). Over the last decade, the literature base on science learning and argumentation has expanded dramatically and researchers have consistently concluded that engaging in scientific argumentation is difficult for students and requires instructional supports (Cavagnetto, 2010). Students often struggle to support claims with appropriate and sufficient data and to provide warrants that link claims with data (McNeill & Krajcik 2007; Sandoval & Millwood 2005). Research also suggests that critiquing the scientific bases of others' claims can be particularly difficult for students (Erduran et al., 2004; Sadler, 2004). Despite the significance of argumentation for science learning and the difficulties that most students have with argumentation, most school science programs provide few opportunities for students to engage in argumentation (Hogan & Corey 2001; Berland & McNeill 2010).

Much of the current research on learning progressions has focused on students' scientific concepts (Alonzo & Gotwals, 2012); learning progressions for students' engagement in practices has been more limited (Schwarz et al., 2009). Berland and McNeill (2010) created an initial argumentation learning progression that focuses on coordination of instructional contexts, argumentative products and argumentative process based on a retrospective analysis of classroom argumentation studies. Osborne and colleagues (2013; 2014) have recently published a more empirically-based argumentation LP for middle school students. This work offers a progress map with twelve levels incorporating construction and critique of scientific arguments. The map builds on Toulmin's model and cognitive load theory (Pollock et al. 2002), and distinctions among the levels of the progress map are determined primarily by the complexity of connections among claims, data, and warrants. Figure 4 provides an illustration of the argumentation learning progression through a graphic depiction of three (of the twelve) proposed levels. In the lowest level of the progression, learners state or identify a claim. Intermediate levels require students to begin making links between claims and evidence with warrants. The highest level depicted in the figure represents learner evaluation of competing arguments. In this case, the learner makes and warrants a claim as to which of two arguments is superior and which is inferior. The most advanced level on the Osborne et al. (2013) progress map characterizes the construction or identification of a counter claim and justifying why it is superior to other competing arguments. We use this progression as a framework for design and assessment of argumentation within MHS.

As learners progress through MHS, they will be challenged (and scaffolded) to learn new concepts about water through carrying out tasks in a simulation environment and then put their understanding into practice with progressively more complex argumentation tasks. For example at unit 1 as part of their mission to find a new water supply for earth our students role playing scientists on a space mission will learn about surface water and water cycling by needing to build a water shed on a remote planet. They then engage with non-player characters on the mission representing mission commanders, politicians and other scientists to learn how to and practice supporting claims with evidence. Their ability to support claims with evidence determines if the mission continues or is aborted. In unit 2 they move onto a challenge of tracking a pollutant through their watershed. As they carry out this task they continue their learning about surface water and water cycling but add in a new feature of materials in water. After working through the tracking a pollutant task they move to interactions with the non-player characters where they must continue to support claims with evidence but now are also challenged to show the reasoning behind linking claims with evidence. The eight-unit game proceeds in this fashion to advancing challenges and learning progressions for water systems and argumentation.

Figure 4. Varying levels of argumentation competency predicted by the Osborne et al. (2013) argumentation learning progression

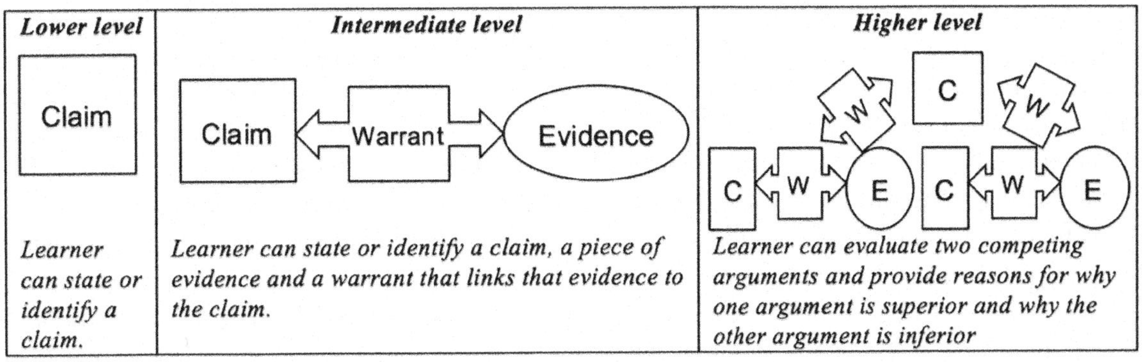

3. A Teacher Support System

MHS will be designed and developed specifically for implementation by a teacher in online middle school (including blended and distance) contexts. While we plan a version of MHS that will be tailored to a blended learning classroom, the target implementation is a class of students who interact online from their homes with their instructor for all of their teaching and learning activity. Typically teachers use a course management system with discussion boards, file sharing and online quizzes to engage students in learning activity. With MHS the student will download or access a web application (developing in Unity provides flexibility for one development and multiple formats of delivery) so that students could be working from a Windows machine, a Macintosh or a tablet. The students engage in a game-like experience of interaction, feedback and progress. The application uses built-in game and pedagogical mechanisms to shape its response to student actions based on context and the student's record of activity, but a log of their activity is also sent via the Internet to a central server where MHS analytics interprets the log, shapes the user profile for the next game session and sends reports to the teacher. The teacher views the class through a dashboard for seeing class progress and for managing individual student activity. We envision that at some point in the development of the analytics, the MHS server can also make recommendations for types of interventions for the teacher to try with the students, such as email messages, conferencing or adding support NPCs to MHS to help scaffold student learning and progress.

In both face-to-face and online environments, teachers shape how curriculum materials are enacted (Ball & Feiman-Nemser, 1988; Forbes & Davis, 2010). Remillard (2005) described the complex teacher-curriculum relationship as contextually based, dependent on both the teacher and the curriculum, and tightly interconnected with other teacher practices. In MHS, many curricular decisions (that might be made by teachers in other kinds of learning environments) are determined by designers of the VLE, but teachers will play a critical role in interpreting student progress, providing feedback, and ensuring learning. Therefore, MHS teachers will need to understand the MHS teaching and learning model, the analytics system, and ranges of responsive actions and feedback that can be offered to learners engaged in the environment.

To support coherent implementation and curriculum appropriate responses and actions by the teacher, we plan to implement 3 forms of teacher support. The first form is training materials and simulations that prepare the teacher to understand the hydrology and argumentation content of the game, the game play that students will experience and the processes and tools available to the teacher during student game play. The second form is a networked community of practice consisting of other teachers using MHS or artifacts from teachers who have used MHS. The third form of support for effective teaching is a dashboard representing data about the students during gameplay. This dashboard provides the teacher an up-to-date report from the learning analytics system as well as a recommender system for when and how to intervene for students. The dashboard will also provide "Just in Time" introductions to lesson activity and on-demand resources such as FAQs.

4. A Learning Analytics System

Hattie (2009) synthesized over 800 meta-analyses representing over 50,000 studies relating to educational achievement, and then provided rankings for the various interventions by their effect sizes. The mean effect size across all interventions was d=0.40. A key finding of his work was to identify "quality feedback" as the single most powerful influence enhancing student achievement. In discussing the finding on feedback Hattie says, "The mistake I was making was seeing feedback as something teachers provided to students—they typically did not, although they made claims that they did it all the time, and most of the feedback they did provide was social and behavioral. It was only when I discovered that feedback was most powerful when it is from the student to the teacher that I started to understand it better. When teachers seek, or at least are open to, feedback from students as to what students know, what they understand, where they make errors, when they have misconceptions, when they are not engaged—then teaching and learning can be synchronized and powerful. Feedback to teachers helps make learning visible." (2009, p. 173) The key for Hattie was to make teaching and learning visible so that the teacher and student could monitor how fluency is gained. He summarized implications of his findings in two principles: (1) having teachers see learning through the eyes of their students and (2) having students see themselves as their own teachers.

The principal goal of learning analytics systems is to make learning visible. Being visible helps students and teachers notice what impact behaviors or critical decisions in the VLE have on the path to problem solving and learning. Identifying behaviors that correspond with learning in a VLE is a complex endeavor that cannot be disembodied from the curriculum. Goggins' work developing a methodology and ontology for making sense of behavioral traces across a range of work and learning environments, called Group Informatics, provides a systematic foundation around which we build design iterations for MHS Analytics (Goggins, Mascaro & Valetto, 2013). The first step in developing any behavioral analytics system is abstracting the levels of organization within the system – the part of the trace data from which context can be reconstructed (Goggins & Petakovic, 2014). What traces do we have to work with by default? What other behavioral signals do we need to capture? And, most critically, how are a user's specific actions in the VLE connected to the curriculum being followed; what signals success, frustration or loss of interest? As the analytics lead researcher for Virtual Math Teams with Geogebra (VMTwG), Goggins developed a systematic approach for applying activity theory as a lens for processing raw traces, directly connected to curricular aims, showing statistically significant connections between group performance and participation on specific curriculum topics in VMTwG (Xing, Wadholm & Goggins, 2014). Further developing this approach, Xing, Petakovic & Goggins (2014) employed a genetic programming algorithm against activity theory in order to inform and reshape trace data to predict individual performance in a more user-understandable visualization in the VMTwG environment.

The MHS analytics follow a similar, systematic path as pioneered by Goggins. We are developing analytics that are focused on tracking individuals' specific choices and analyzing those discrete choices against a backdrop of learning outcomes and progression through the curriculum. Along with tracking choices, our approach tracks and systematically analyzes inscriptions (Borge & Goggins, 2014) created and used by students within the environment.

Capturing data of student behavior in the MHS learning space reveals patterns of behavior that provide information about student progress. This information about progress can be used to report to the teachers about student activity so that teachers are informed about each student's performance. Similarly the information about progress can be used to suggest interventions that the teacher may try with the student. The progress reports and suggestions provide feedback to the teacher and appear on the teacher dashboard for ease of use in understanding how the class is faring and for taking actions such as changing parameters in the game to help students succeed. In later iterations of MHS we may also utilize information about student behavior and progress to provide feedback directly to the student as messages about progress or recommendations or as direct impacts on the system, such as providing alternate paths through some learning sequences. MHS analytics also provide feedback to the designers in that seeing how students perform and how patterns of performance relate to success changes can be made to make MHS better fits for student characteristics or capabilities.

In summary, learning analytics is a powerful tool for providing feedback to teachers, students and designers. The feedback is not simply an a priori recognition that this behavior should be matched by this consequence, but rather is an understanding of a behavior in the context of how other students have behaved and subsequently performed so that the feedback is situated and made sense of through the collective experience of prior learners. This contextualization of learning activity connects the student and teacher and provides a basis for understanding progress and intervening as appropriate.

FUTURE DIRECTIONS

The Investing in Innovation (i3) Fund of the U.S. Department of Education awarded a 4-year development grant to our team at the University of Missouri and several partner organizations to develop and test MHS. The goal of i3 funding for development grants is to develop promising innovations that can serve as models and potentially be taken to scale based on demonstrated success. The i3 MHS project has 4 cycles to move from our early conceptualizations and prototypes to a product that can be tested for feasibility and efficacy in schools. The *first 3 cycles* are focused on advancing and informing the design and development process and learning about how components of the system should work. The *4th cycle* quantifies how able teachers are to implement MHS and the impact on student engagement and understanding of constructs and competencies in water systems and Scientific Argumentation.

In cycle 1 we design each level of MHS through a series of design activities including expert input, specification of learning outcomes and system requirements, writing scenarios and storyboarding each set of activities and scripting all interactions. From this design work we develop an implementation of Unit 1 and take it to *usability* testing in our lab. The usability testing uses protocols to engage students in game play and providing feedback to the tester. After the usability for Unit 1 is completed, we assess needs for change and produce Unit 2. This iterative process continues for each unit until units 1-4 have been developed. At this time a usability testing is repeated for students working through all 4 units. When units 1-4 have been developed and tested for usability we then proceed with a similar process to complete and test units 5-8.

Following Cycle 1 we will make whatever changes are needed to prepare all 8 units for a field site *usage* test. The field usage testing will take place in the Fall, 2016 at a local blended science classroom over a 3 to 4 week period and assess not only student engagement in MHS but also test the supports available for the classroom teacher. The teacher supports will include the first edition of orientation and training materials and a dashboard for monitoring and intervening with students. At the conclusion of cycle 2 we will have determined, or need to make changes to assure, MHS is sufficiently engaging for sustained effort by students, all functionality is usable by the students and teachers, and data are appropriately captured and used for the analytics.

Cycle 3 explores the *feasibility* of MHS in the online context of distance and blended courses. Two teachers, one with a distance class and one with a blended class, will implement MHS. The feasibility testing will require networked environments both for implementing MHS with the students and for supporting the teachers during the implementation. We will use both log data of the students experience in MHS and qualitative data from student questionnaires and teacher interviews to identify issues about the feasibility of implementing MHS in distance and blended classes.

Table 1. Unbalanced student distribution by treatment/comparison and distance/blended

	MHS Treatment	Comparison Intervention
Distance Learning Classes	140 students (14 classes)	60 students (6 classes)
Blended Learning Classes	700 students (28 classes)	300 students (12 classes)

Cycle 4 will use a cluster random assignment design to compare gains in water systems knowledge, scientific argumentation and interest in science with similar students who receive a comparable water systems curriculum but do not use MHS. Table 1 shows our goal for the number of students in each grouping.

At the conclusion of the 4 year project we plan to have a learning product that can be shared with schools, a framework that shows how to integrate a game-based 3D VLE with a learning progressions approach to curriculum and innovative methods for teacher support and learning analytics.

In planning for MHS there are a number of hurdles that can be anticipated. *First*, there are many pedagogical, artistic and technical choices that must be executed well to develop a powerful learning system. The primary approach to addressing this challenge is the iterative process and benefit of systematic feedback designed into our project. A *second* risk is that if the Learning Analytics are not effective, much of the pedagogical power of MHS and support for the teacher will be diminished. There are many challenges such as which data to mine, which processes to apply to the data and how to represent the results in meaningful ways to students and teachers. However, developing Learning Analytics is an iterative process where more trials can provide better results. Our plans are to continue data collection and analytics refinement after the i3 project is ended and MHS starts to be used in schools. A *third* risk is that teachers may feel overwhelmed by the new role and teaching tools/resources and fail to understand and carryout some aspects of the teaching. This is partially mitigated by designing the student experience to allow most students to succeed even if there is little teacher intervention. We will also use the analytics to examine teacher behavior in MHS so as to provide feedback to the teacher as well as notify the MHS network moderator if proactive support is needed in some cases. Of course there are also numerous hurdles which will emerge as the project progresses. While the specific hurdles cannot be clearly foreseen their potential impacts can be mitigated by our efforts to build a strong team and to be a part of a larger community of serious game design, science education and learning technologies.

CONCLUSION

In a way, what we consider to be an innovative conceptualization is an obvious and practical approach to improving online learning and bringing teaching and learning methods necessary for NGSS-aligned learning to small and rural communities.

- Games, especially video games, are readily adopted by youth.
- Prior efforts in designing commercial games for entertainment have tested and demonstrated that story, levels and virtualization of experience and feedback can be used to create problem solving contexts where the player must explore and learn the conditions of his-her world and then put knowledge into practice.
- Transformative play is a strong theory for mapping the engagement of game play to curriculum and projects like *Quest Atlantis* and the others previously described provide evidence for the promise of the theory and methods of game-based learning.

- Seeing curriculum as progressions through knowledge and competencies with end targets of putting knowledge into practice maps well to games.
- Integrating science practices, such as argumentation, into the classroom time used for science content, water systems, makes it more realistic that schools can adopt curriculum that addresses the NGSS.
- Analytics and the use of data that richly characterizes learners' activity and progression can be a powerful basis for how teachers can work in online learning.
- The economics of relatively high costs of producing learning systems but then easy and relatively cheap distribution of software means that if powerful and effective models can be created that a range of new solutions across the science education curriculum are possible.

For the reasons listed above we believe that MHS is a practical solution to meet the objectives of NGSS for learners in small and rural schools as well as having promise across most forms of education. If the MHS project can successfully enact our vision for 3D game-based learning related to water systems science and scientific argumentation and develop effective means to help teachers understand and adopt this new form of online learning, it will meet needs of small and rural schools and service providers to transform what should be expected from online learning.

REFERENCES

Alonzo, A. C., & Gotwals, A. W. (Eds.). (2012). *Learning progressions in science: Current challenges and future directions*. Springer. doi:10.1007/978-94-6091-824-7

Anderson, T., Liam, R., Garrison, D. R., & Archer, W. (2001). Assessing teacher presence in a computer conferencing context. *Journal of Asynchronous Learning Networks*, *5*(2), 1–17.

Avery, L. M. (2013). Rural science education: Valuing local knowledge. *Theory into Practice*, *52*(1), 28–35. doi:10.1080/07351690.2013.743769

Ball, D. L., & Feiman-Nemser, S. (1988). Using textbooks and teachers' guides: A dilemma for beginning teachers and teacher educators. *Curriculum Inquiry*, *18*(4), 401–423. doi:10.2307/1179386

Barab, S. A., Gresfali, M. S., & Arici, A. (2009). Why educators should care about games. *Educational Leadership*, *67*(1), 76–80.

Barab, S. A., Gresfali, M. S., & Ingram-Goble, A. (2010). Transformational play using games to position person, content and context. *Educational Researcher*, *39*(7), 525–536. doi:10.3102/0013189X10386593

Barab, S. A., Sadler, T. D., Heiselt, C., Hickey, D., & Zuiker, S. (2007). Relating narrative, inquiry, and inscriptions: Supporting consequential play. *Journal of Science Education and Technology*, *16*(1), 59–82. doi:10.1007/s10956-006-9033-3

Barko, T., & Sadler, T. D. (2013). Practicality in virtuality: Finding student meaning in video game education. *Journal of Science Education and Technology*, *22*(2), 124–132. doi:10.1007/s10956-012-9381-0

Baumeister, R. F., & Leary, M. R. (1995). The need to belong: Desire for interpersonal attachments as a fundamental human motivation. *Psychological Bulletin*, *117*(3), 497–529. doi:10.1037/0033-2909.117.3.497 PMID:7777651

Berland, L. K., & McNeill, K. L. (2010). A learning progression for scientific argumentation: Understanding student work and designing supportive instructional contexts. *Science Education*, *94*(5), 765–793. doi:10.1002/sce.20402

Borge, M., & Goggins, S. (2014). Towards the Facilitation of an Online Community of Learners: Assessing the Quality of Interactions in Yammer. *Proceedings from International Conference on the Learning Sciences*, Boulder, CO.

Bransford, J. D., Brown, A. L., & Cocking, R. R. (2000). *How people learn*. Washington, DC: National Academies Press.

Cavagnetto, A. R. (2010). Argument to foster scientific literacy. A review of argument interventions in K-12 science contexts. *Review of Educational Research*, *80*(3), 336–371. doi:10.3102/0034654310376953

Clark, D. B., Tanner-Smith, E. E., & Killingsworth, S. (2013). *Digital Games for Learning: A systematic review and meta-analysis*. Menlo Park, CA: SRI International.

Clarke, J., Dede, C., Ketelhut, D. J., Nelson, B., & Bowman, C. (2006). A Design-based research strategy to promote scalability for educational innovations. Educational Technology, 46(3), 27-36.

Covitt, B. (2013). Reasoning tools for understanding water systems. Retrieved from http://www.umt.edu/watertools/default.aspx

Covitt, B. A., Gunckel, K. L., & Anderson, C. W. (2009). Students' developing understanding of water in environmental systems. *The Journal of Environmental Education*, *40*(3), 37–51. doi:10.3200/JOEE.40.3.37-51

de la Varre, C., Keane, J., & Irvin, M. J. (2011). Dual perspectives on the contribution of on-site facilitators to teaching presence in a blended learning environment. *International Journal of E-Learning & Distance Education*, *25*(3).

Dickerson, D., & Dawkins, K. (2004). Eighth grade students' understandings of groundwater. *Journal of Geoscience Education*, *52*, 178–181.

Donovan, M. S., Bransford, J. D., & Pellegrino, J. W. (Eds.). (1999). *How people learn: Bridging research and practice*. Washington, DC: National Academies Press.

Duschl, R. A., & Osborne, J. (2002). Supporting and promoting argumentation discourse in science education. *Studies in Science Education*, *38*(1), 39–72. doi:10.1080/03057260208560187

Endreny, A. H. (2010). Urban 5th graders conceptions during a place-based inquiry unit on watersheds. *Journal of Research in Science Teaching*, *47*, 501–517.

Erduran, S., & Jiménex-Aleixandre, M. P. (2008). *Argumentation in science education: Perspectives from classroom-based research*. Dordrecht, The Netherlands: Springer.

Erduran, S., Simon, S., & Osborne, J. (2004). TAPing into argumentation: Developments in the application of Toulmin's argument pattern for studying science discourse. *Science Education*, *88*(6), 915–933. doi:10.1002/sce.20012

ESA. (2013). Essential Facts about the computer and video game industry. Retrieved from http://www.theesa.com/facts/pdfs/ESA_EF_2013.pdf

Forbes, C. T., & Davis, E. A. (2010). Curriculum design for inquiry: Preservice elementary teachers' mobilization and adaptation of science curriculum materials. *Journal of Research in Science Teaching*, *47*(7), 820–839. doi:10.1002/tea.20379

Gee, J. P. (2001). Identity as an analytic lens for research in education. *Review of Research in Education*, 99–125.

Gee, J. P. (2007). *What video games have to teach us about learning and literacy*. New York: Palgrave Macmillian.

GlassLab. About SimCityEDU. (2013). Retrieved from http://www.simcityedu.org/about/

Goggins, S., & Petacovic, E. (2014). Connecting theory to social technology platforms: A framework for measuring influence in context. *The American Behavioral Scientist*, 0002764214527093.

Goggins, S. P., Mascaro, C., & Valetto, G. (2013). Group informatics: A methodological approach and ontology for sociotechnical group research. *Journal of the American Society for Information Science and Technology*, *64*(3), 516–539. doi:10.1002/asi.22802

Gunckel, K. L., Covitt, B. A., & Anderson, C. W. (2009, June). Learning a secondary discourse: Shifts from force-dynamic to model-based reasoning in understanding water in socioecological systems. Proceedings of Learning Progressions in Science (LeaPS) Conference, Iowa City, IA.

Gunckel, K. L., Covitt, B. A., Salinas, I., & Anderson, C. W. (2012). A learning progression for water in socio-ecological systems. *Journal of Research in Science Teaching*, *49*(7), 843–868. doi:10.1002/tea.21024

Hannum, W. H., Irvin, M. J., Banks, J. B., & Farmer, T. W. (2009). Distance education use in rural schools. *Journal of Research in Rural Education*, *24*(3), 1–15.

Hattie, J. (2009). *Visible Learning; a synthesis of over 800 meta-analyses relating to achievement.* London: Routledge.

Hogan, K., & Corey, C. (2001). Viewing classrooms as cultural contexts for fostering scientific literacy. *Anthropology & Education Quarterly*, *32*(2), 214–243. doi:10.1525/aeq.2001.32.2.214

Kelly, G. J., & Takao, A. (2002). Epistemic levels in argument: An analysis of university oceanography students' use of evidence in writing. *Science Education*, *86*(3), 314–342. doi:10.1002/sce.10024

Laffey, J., Schmidt, M., & Galyen, K. (2013). Virtual gaming and learning environments as experience-tools for learning through problem solving. In M. Spector, B. Lockee, S. Smaldino, & M. Herring (Eds.), Learning, problem solving, and mindtools: Essays in honor of David H. Jonassen (pp. 105-125). New York, N.Y., Routledge.

LaPadula, M. (2003). A comprehensive look at online student support services for distance learners. *American Journal of Distance Education*, *17*(2), 119–128. doi:10.1207/S15389286AJDE1702_4

McNeill, K. L., & Krajcik, J. (2007). Middle school students' use of appropriate and inappropriate evidence in writing scientific explanations. *Thinking with data,* 233-265. In M. C. Lovett & P. Shah (Eds.), *Thinking with data*: The Proceedings of the 33rd Carnegie Symposium on Cognition. Mahwah, NJ. Erlbaum.

McNeill, K. L., Lizotte, D. J., Krajcik, J., & Marx, R. W. (2006). Supporting students' construction of scientific explanations by fading scaffolds in instructional materials. *Journal of the Learning Sciences*, *15*(2), 153–191. doi:10.1207/s15327809jls1502_1

Metcalf, S. J., Clarke, J., & Dede, C. (2009). Virtual worlds for education: River City and EcoMUVE. Proceedings of *MiT6 International Conference,* 1-6.

Newton, P., Driver, R., & Osborne, J. (1999). The place of argumentation in the pedagogy of school science. *International Journal of Science Education*, *21*(5), 553–576. doi:10.1080/095006999290570

NGSS Lead States. (2013). *Next Generation Science Standards: For States, By States*. Washington, DC: The National Academies Press.

NRC. (2011). *A framework for K-12 science education: Practices, crosscutting concepts, and core ideas*. Washington, DC: National Academies Press.

Oliver, J. S. (2007). Rural science education. In S. K. Abell & N. G. Lederman (Eds.), Handbook of Research on Science Education (pp. 345-369). Mahwah, NJ: Lawrence Erlbaum Associates.

Osborne, J., Henderson, B., MacPherson, A., & Szu, E. (2013). *Building a learning progression for argument in science.* Paper presented at the annual conference of the American Educational Research Association Conference, San Francisco, CA.

Osborne, J., Henderson, B., MacPherson, A., Wild, A., & Friend, M. (2014). *IRT analysis of items probing a unidimensional learning progression for argumentation of increasingly complex structure.* Paper presented at the annual conference of the National Association for Research in Science Teaching, Pittsburgh, PA.

Osborne, J. F., & Patterson, A. (2011). Scientific argument and explanation: A necessary distinction? *Science Education*, *95*(4), 627–638. doi:10.1002/sce.20438

Picciano, A. G., & Seaman, J. (2009). K-12 online learning: A 2008 follow-up of the Survey of U.S. School District Administrators. Retrieved from: http://sloanconsortium.org/publications/survey/k-12online2008.

Pollock, E., Chandler, P., & Sweller, J. (2002). Assimilating Complex Information. *Learning and Instruction*, *12*(1), 61–86. doi:10.1016/S0959-4752(01)00016-0

Project Tomorrow. (2008). 21st century students deserve a 21st century education. Retrieved from http://www.tomorrow.org/docs/National%20Findings%20Speak%20Up%202007.pdf

Quinn, H., Lee, O., & Valdes, G. (2012). *Language demands and opportunities in relation to Next Generation Science Standards for English Language Learners: What teachers need to know. Understanding Language Initiative*. Stanford, CA: Stanford University School of Education.

Remillard, J. T. (2005). Examining key concepts in research on teachers' use of mathematics curricula. *Review of Educational Research*, *75*(2), 211–246. doi:10.3102/00346543075002211

Roblyer, M. D. (2006). Virtually successful: Defeating the dropout problem through online school programs. *Phi Delta Kappan*, *88*(1), 31–36. doi:10.1177/003172170608800107

Sadler, T. D. (2004). Informal reasoning regarding socioscientific issues: A critical review of research. *Journal of Research in Science Teaching*, *41*(5), 513–536. doi:10.1002/tea.20009

Sadler, T. D. (2009). Situated learning in science education: Socio-scientific issues as contexts for practice. *Studies in Science Education*, *45*(1), 1–42. doi:10.1080/03057260802681839

Sadler, T. D., & Donnelly, L. A. (2006). Socioscientific argumentation: The effects of content knowledge and morality. *International Journal of Science Education*, *28*(12), 1463–1488. doi:10.1080/09500690600708717

Sadler, T. D., Romine, W. L., Menon, D., Ferdig, R. E., & Annetta, L. (2015). Learning biology through innovative curricula: A comparison of game- and nongame-based approaches. *Science Education*, *99*(4), 696–720. doi:10.1002/sce.21171

Sadler, T. D., Romine, W. L., Stuart, P. E., & Merle-Johnson, D. (2013). Game-Based curricula in biology classes. Differential effects among varying academic levels. *Journal of Research in Science Teaching*, *50*(4), 479–499. doi:10.1002/tea.21085

Sandoval, W. A., & Millwood, K. A. (2005). The quality of students' use of evidence in written scientific explanations. *Cognition and Instruction*, *23*(1), 23–55. doi:10.1207/s1532690xci2301_2

Schaller, D. T., Goldman, K. H., Spickelmier, G., Allison-Bunnell, S., & Koepfler, J. (2009). Learning in the wild: What Wolfquest taught developers and game players. Museums and the web 2009: Proceedings. Toronto: Archives & Museum Informatics. Retrieved from http://www. archimuse. com/mw2009/papers/schaller/schaller. html

Schwarz, C. V., Reiser, B. J., Davis, E. A., Kenyon, L., Achér, A., Fortus, D., & Krajcik, J. et al. (2009). Developing a learning progression for scientific modeling: Making scientific modeling accessible and meaningful for learners. *Journal of Research in Science Teaching*, *46*(6), 632–654. doi:10.1002/tea.20311

Shepardson, D. P., Wee, B., Priddy, M., Schellenberger, L., & Harbor, J. (2007). What is a watershed? Implications of student conceptions for environmental science education and the National Science Education Standards. *Science Education*, *91*(4), 554–578. doi:10.1002/sce.20206

Squire, K. (2011). *Video games and learning: Teaching and participatory culture in the digital age. Technology, Education-Connections (the TEC Series)*. New York, NY: Teacher College Press.

Stahl, G. (2006). *Group cognition: Computer support for building collaborative knowledge*. Cambridge, MA: MIT Press.

Stichter, J. P., Laffey, J., Galyen, K., & Herzog, M. (2013). iSocial: Delivering the social competence intervention for adolescents (SCI-A) in a 3D virtual learning environment for youth with high functioning autism. *Journal of Autism and Developmental Disorders*, *43*(7), 1–14. PMID:23104615

Toulmin, S. E. (1958). *The uses of argument*. Cambridge, UK: Cambridge University Press.

Versypt, J. J., & Versypt, A. N. F. (2013). *Mapping rural students' STEM involvement: Case studies of chemical engineering undergraduate enrollment in the states of Illinois and Kansas*. Paper presented at the American Society for Engineering Education, Atlanta, GA.

Wicks, M. (2010). A national primer on K-12 online learning. International Association for K-12 Online. Retrieved from http://www.inacol. org/research/bookstore/detail.php?id=22

Xing, W., & Petakovic, E., Goggins, S. (2014). Participation-based Student Performance Prediction Model through Interpretable Genetic Programming: Integrating Learning Analytics, Educational Data Mining and Theory. *Computers in Human Behavior*.

Xing, W., Wadholm, B., & Goggins, S. (2014). Learning analytics in CSCL with a focus on assessment: an exploratory study of activity theory-informed cluster analysis. *Proceedings of the Fourth International Conference on Learning Analytics And Knowledge* (pp. 59-67). ACM. doi:10.1145/2567574.2567587

KEY TERMS AND DEFINITIONS

3D Virtual Learning Environments: Computer generated, three-dimensional, graphical spaces developed as a pedagogical context which can be based on real or fantasy environments and in which users are typically represented as avatars.

Distance Learning: Delivering education to students who are not physically present in a traditional classroom.

Game-Based Learning: The act of playing a video game for the purpose of learning and the use of game thinking and mechanics to design a learning activity. AKA Serious Gaming.

Learning Analytics: Learning analytics is the measurement, collection, analysis and reporting of data about learners and their contexts, for purposes of understanding and optimising learning and the environments in which it occurs.

Learning Progressions: A sequence of teaching and learning expectations related to particular content and/or competency.

Scientific Argumentation: An epistemic practice critical to the generation and justification of new knowledge in science.

Social Learning: In a 3D virtual environment, learning that is promoted within a social context which leverages conversations, identity and co-presence as key elements.

Transformative Play: Playing transformationally involves (a) taking on the role of a protagonist (b) who must employ conceptual understandings (c) to make choices (d) that have the potential to transform (e) a problem-based fictional context and ultimately (f) the player's understanding of the content as well as of (g) herself as someone who has used academic content to address a socially significant problem. (Barab, Gresfali, & Ingram-Goble, 2010).

Chapter 21
Building Bridges:
Teachers Leveraging Game-Based Implicit Science Learning in Physics Classrooms

Elizabeth Rowe
Educational Gaming Environments group @ TERC, USA

Jodi Asbell-Clarke
Educational Gaming Environments group @ TERC, USA

Erin Bardar
Educational Gaming Environments group @ TERC, USA

Christina Shane-Simpson
New Knowledge Organization, USA

Su-Jen Roberts
New Knowledge Organization, USA

ABSTRACT

This chapter describes the analysis of 729 daily teacher logs from a 2013-14 national classroom implementation study with hundreds of high school physics students using the game, Impulse, finding classrooms using materials to bridge implicit and explicit science learning performed significantly better than control classrooms (Rowe et al., 2014). This effect was moderated by whether or not the class was a Honors/AP class. The authors examine the student and teacher demographics, science content, instructional materials and methods, and game-based pedagogies as potential explanations for those findings. The largest difference among Honors/AP vs. non-Honors/AP classrooms using any Bridge activities was their use of formal, teacher-led discussion.

INTRODUCTION

Game-based learning has been a growing field of research over the past decade or more (e.g. Gee, 2013; Squire, 2007), with many researchers using the data logs generated by digital games to study learning (Glasslab, 2014; Clarke, Nelson, Chang, D'Angelo, Slack, & Martinez-Gazza, 2011). Educational games are most often designed for use within classrooms and therefore include some formalizations such as content explanations and/or test questions that require explicit understanding of the material. These games typically differ from the games learners *choose* to play in their free time (Isbister, 2010), games that we call *free-choice* games.

DOI: 10.4018/978-1-4666-9629-7.ch021

Free-choice games are highly engaging, "sticky" environments that typically do not present any school-like interfaces. These games can still be designed with game mechanics that mirror authentic and idealized science. By aligning game mechanics (player actions in the game) with learning mechanics (learning goals designed into the game) and assessment mechanics (evidence for learning that can be seen through gameplay logs), researchers can support and examine *implicit* learning that takes place through well-designed gameplay (Plass et al., 2013), even gameplay that takes place outside class.

Implicit learning in games, however, does not ensure explicit (more formalized) learning that students are expected to demonstrate in class. The connection between implicit learning from experience and explicit classroom learning must be facilitated, typically through social interactions with a teacher and other learners (Hattie & Yates, 2013). This is true for game-based learning where the "big G Game" learning happens during interactions between peers, and between players and teachers, both of which can take place outside the game (Gee, 2013; Hayes & Gee, 2012).

In 2013-14 the authors conducted a national classroom implementation study with hundreds of high school physics students using the game, *Impulse* (Rowe, Asbell-Clarke, Bardar, Kasman, & MacEachern, 2014) where science learning was measured in classes that played the game and were provided with bridge activities--materials designed to help teachers bridge science content in the game with their formal instruction. For this chapter, we focus on the analysis of teachers logs from that implementation study to highlight the types of activities that occurred in implementation classes that can explain how these bridge activities were used in class. Our goal is to understand what resources teachers need, and what we can provide in terms of tools and professional development, to help STEM teachers leverage implicit learning in games to improve explicit learning in class.

Impulse is a free-choice game available for free from most app stores and can be played on the web or on a tablet. In *Impulse,* players are immersed in a physics simulator in which they must intuitively predict the Newtonian motion of a set of balls to successfully avoid collisions while navigating their ball to the goal. Players use an impulse (triggered by their click or touch) to apply a force to balls, all of which obey Newton's laws of motion and gravitation.

In the *Impulse* implementation study, teachers (and their students) were assigned to one of three conditions. Students in the Game group (209 students in 21 classes) were encouraged by their teachers to play *Impulse* outside of class. Students in the Bridge group (179 students in 18 classes) were encouraged to play the game outside of class and their teachers incorporated examples from the game into their classroom instruction on Newtonian mechanics. One hundred eight (108) students in 11 classes in the Control group neither played the game nor had game examples in class. Students in all groups completed assessments of their implicit understanding of the science concepts before and after the instruction on Newtonian mechanics.

Hierarchical Linear Modeling (HLM) analyses examined the relationship between study group—Bridge, Game Only, Control—and students' post-assessment scores. Results showed higher post-assessment scores for students in the Bridge classes, as compared to the Control classes after accounting for the students' pre-assessment scores, student characteristics, teacher characteristics, and school demographics. Relative to Control classrooms, significant improvements in science learning were seen for students in classes where they were encouraged to play the game and the teachers used class time for "bridging" between game-based learning and the related science classroom curriculum. While there was no significant overall difference between the Bridge and Game Only groups, the group effect was moderated by whether or not the class was Honors/AP. Honors/AP students in Game Only classrooms performed significantly worse than Honors/AP students in Bridge classrooms on post-assessments. Among students in non-Honors/AP classes, there was no difference between Bridge and Game Only classrooms, with both scoring significantly higher than Control classrooms. These results confirmed our conjecture that *Impulse* can help prepare some students for improved science learning in class. This chapter will explore two questions stemming from that work.

1. In what ways did Bridge classrooms differ from Control and Game classrooms? Did they differ in the use of game-centered pedagogy only or were there differences in student demographics, teacher background or science instruction methods or content that may have driven our results?
2. What types of strategies and classroom activities did Bridge teachers use to leverage implicit game-based science learning to improve classroom learning of Newtonian mechanics in Honors/AP and non-Honors-AP classrooms?

LEVERAGING IMPLICIT GAME-BASED LEARNING

Implicit learning can be considered foundational to explicit learning (Polanyi, 1966), yet presents a challenge for educational researchers because of the difficulty of direct measurement. As such, it is also difficult for teachers to leverage this foundational knowledge, because learners may struggle to express their implicit understandings. Researchers acknowledge, however, that implicit knowledge is key to cognitive development, a point emphasized most strongly by the misconception research community of STEM educators late in the last century (McCloskey, 1983; diSessa, 1993). We argue that digital games may provide a unique opportunity to promote and study implicit learning, providing an important new lens for learning science researchers (Asbell-Clarke et al., 2012; 2013; NRC, 2011).

Implicit knowledge (also called tacit knowledge) has a variety of forms or definitions, and has been a construct in psychological and sociological research for quite some time. Polanyi (1966), a philosopher and scientist, argued that tacit knowledge is foundational to all explicit knowledge. Within tacit knowledge, Collins (2010) distinguishes between somatic tacit knowledge of primal tasks such as walking and talking; collective tacit knowledge in a community such as language and humor; and tacit relational knowledge, the tacit knowledge that with effort can become related to explicit, or formalized, knowledge. As educational researchers, we focus on relational implicit knowledge because it has application to the explicit knowledge required in school settings. The importance of implicit knowledge was written about by Vygotsky (1978) as he described *preparedness for learning* — the abilities and understandings a learner brings to a learning situation that can be scaffolded by a teacher, environment, and tools. Late in the last century, much of the literature in US science education turned its attention to implicit learning in the form of misconceptions that may get in the way of a learner's conceptual development (e.g. McCloskey, 1983a, 1983b; Minstrell, 1982). diSessa (1993) notes the robustness of physics misconceptions, with over half of respondents agreeing with several common misconceptions about basic physics, such as Newton's Laws of Motion. diSessa also distinguishes between intuitive knowledge from expert understanding. A novice might have an intuitive feel that a book will not fall through a table or that a glowing filament is hot but still not be able to express an understanding of that phenomenon in formalisms or question it in a deeper sense. In contrast, experts not only think about a phenomenon in a more nuanced sense but also may seek consistency across phenomena to be able to abstract their experiences towards more general principles about the world (diSessa, 1993).

We suggest that while implicit learning is foundational and its measurement is an exciting new affordance for game-based learning researchers, we also see teachers as a key vehicle for bridging game-based implicit learning with the explicit learning required in classroom settings. Jim Gee (2007) and others argue that even a good educational game is only part of a complete learning experience. Post-game debriefing and discussions connecting gameplay with classroom learning are critical in helping students apply and transfer learning that takes place in games (Lederman & Fumitoshi, 1995; Ash, 2011; Ke, 2009). We extend that notion to include teachers' bridging of learning that takes place in free-choice games with classroom curricular content. Games can provide a venue for development of learners' implicit knowledge by giving them a place where they choose to dwell and persist so that they can grow their implicit knowledge over time. To exploit learning that happens in games, teachers need to build bridges between the students' "aha" moments while playing free-choice games and the STEM content being covered in the classroom.

The Game: Impulse

Impulse is a free-choice game for web or wireless devices that immerses players in an n-body simulation of gravitationally interacting balls. To succeed, players must get their ball to the goal without colliding with any ambient balls. To do this they must predict the Newtonian motion of the balls (see Figure 1). The motions of all balls in the game obey Newton's laws of motion and gravitation, including accurate gravitational interactions and elastic collisions among ambient balls with varying mass. Players use an impulse (triggered by their click or touch) to apply a force to balls. For a better understanding of this work, readers are encouraged to play Impulse at edge.terc.edu.

Impulse becomes more complex with each level as the number of balls increases and also vary in mass, requiring players to grapple with increasingly complex force interactions. Players only have 20 impulses (i.e., clicks) per level to navigate their ball to the goal and to negotiate the motion of the ambient balls. As players contend with the Newtonian motion of the balls, they de-

Figure 1. A screenshot from Impulse; the player is the green particle and is going towards the cyan goal in the bottom-left corner. Red, blue, and white particles have different masses.

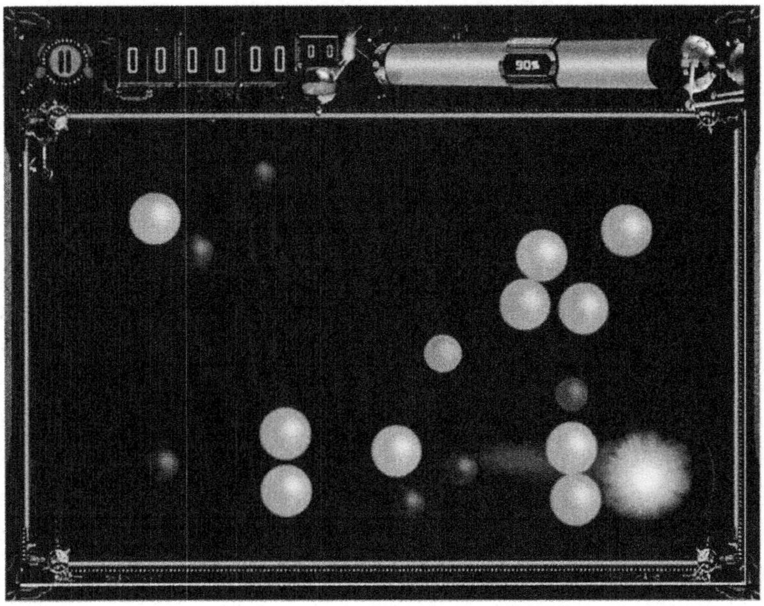

velop strategies to succeed that are recognizable as implicit understandings of Newton's first and second laws of motion.

Newton's first law of motion states that an object in constant motion will stay at constant motion unless acted upon by an external force. This law is actually a specific case of the more general Newton's second law of motion which states that the force acting on an object will result in its acceleration, the magnitude of which depends on its mass (or F=m*a). For example, predicting that the particle will keep floating at the same speed in the same direction when a player does not impact an impulse is consistent with an implicit understanding of Newton's first law. Even more directly, consistently imparting more force (more impulses) on a heavy particle than a light particle is consistent with an implicit understanding of Newton's second law.

OVERVIEW OF FINDINGS: IMPULSE CLASSROOM IMPLEMENTATION STUDY

The full results of the *Impulse* implementation study can be found in Rowe, Asbell-Clarke, Bardar, Kasman, and MacEachern (2014). In this study, 50 high school classes and 23 teachers were divided into three groups, Bridge, Game, and Control. Teachers in the Game and Bridge classes were asked to recruit students to play the game *Impulse* in their free time. In the 18 Bridge classes, teachers were provided video clips from the game along with talking points for leading a discussion on Newton's Laws of Motion using those video clips. In the Control class, students did not play the game and teachers did not use the game examples. All classes covered their typical content on Newton's Laws of Motion during the implementation period.

As part of the *Impulse* implementation study, researchers examined the conjecture that implicit learning in game play can help prepare students for classroom learning. Changes in assessment scores before and after classroom instruction were compared for the Game, Bridge, and Control groups using a series of hierarchical linear models using the SPSS MIXED linear models procedure, accounting for the clustering of students within classrooms and the clustering of classrooms by teachers. Results show higher post-assessment scores for students in the Bridge classes, as compared to the control classes after accounting for the students' pre-assessment scores, student characteristics, teacher characteristics, and school demographics.

Figure 2 shows the estimated marginal means, the result of the HLM models in terms of the predicted post-assessment score if the mean levels of all covariates were used (Rowe, et al., 2014). These results suggest the overall effect of Study Group is statistically significant ($F(2, 13.11)=3.9$, $p=0.047$), but pairwise comparisons show the Bridge group to be significantly higher than the Control group (Mean difference=0.527, $p=0.016$) but not significantly different from the Game group (Mean difference=0.275, $p=0.10$).

This group effect is moderated, however, by whether or not the class is a standard or Honor/AP science class. Figure 3 shows the predicted post-assessment scores (measured in effect sizes) for students scoring at the mean level of the pre-assessment. For students in Honors/AP classes, those in the Bridge study group earned mean level scores on the post-assessment 0.56 SD higher than students in Game classes and 0.31 SD higher than students in Control classes. Among students not in a Honors/AP class, those in Bridge and Game groups had similar mean post-assessments (a difference of 0.07 SD). Both were significantly higher than the mean post-assessment among students in the Control group (0.68 SD higher for Bridge classes, 0.61 SD higher for Game classes).

This moderating factor allows further exploration of the actual types of bridging activities that may explain the difference between Bridge and non-Bridge classes. By comparing the teacher

Figure 2. Estimated marginal mean post-assessment scores by study group

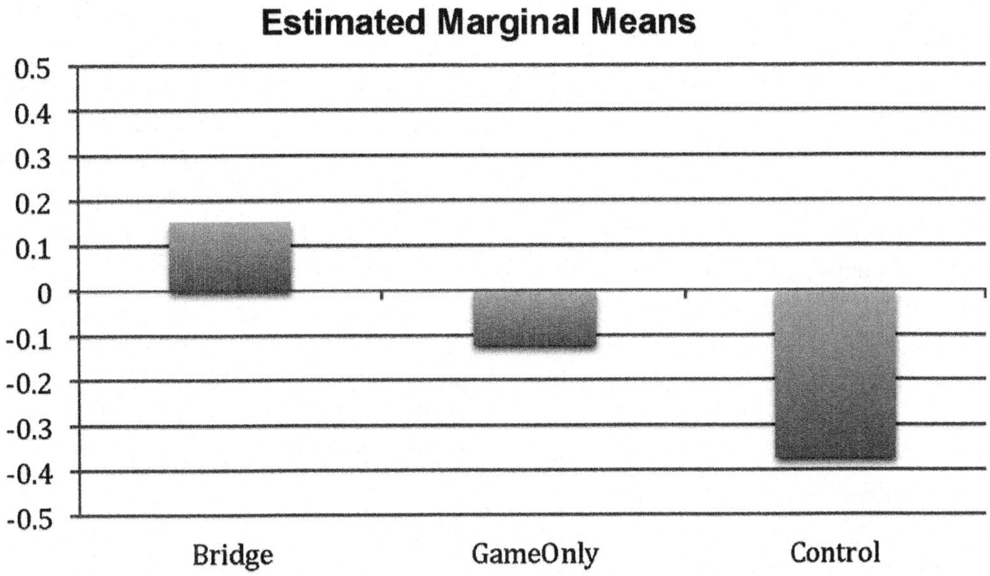

Figure 3. Predicted post-assessment scores across study conditions in Honors/AP classes versus non-Honors/AP classes

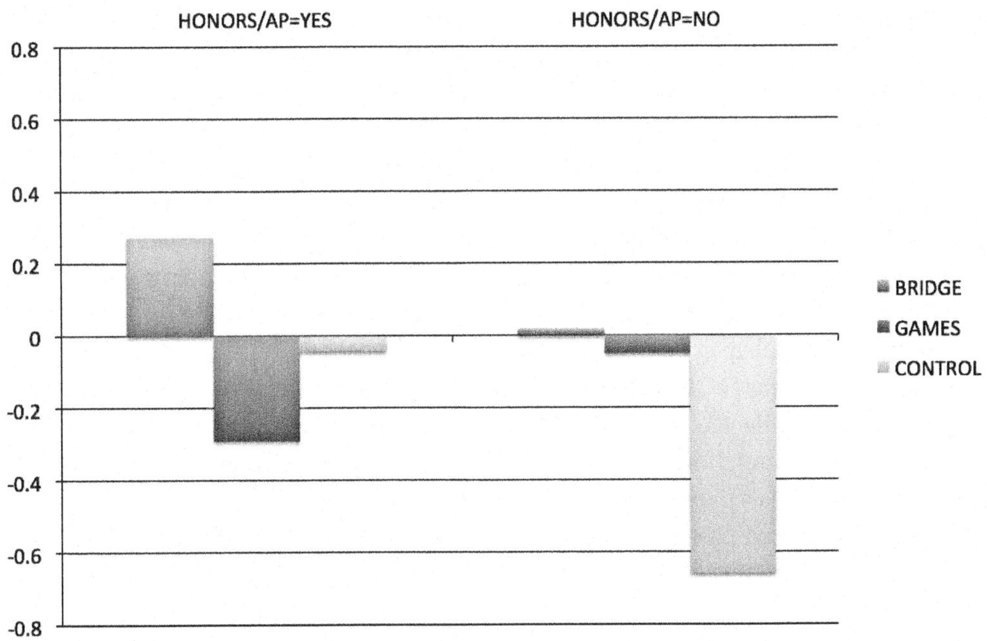

activities in non-honors/AP Bridge classes to honors/AP Bridge classes, we can examine if there are practices that teachers are doing in the honors/AP Bridge classes that is improving students' science learning.

One possible explanation for the difference between Honors/AP students and non-Honors/AP students is that students in Honors/AP classes might be more academic and served well by traditional curriculum, and that their counterparts may, on the whole, be more receptive to alternative curricula. This explanation is consistent with our findings in a previous survey of 1500 youth about gaming preferences, where it was found that youth who identified strongly with science preferred games that connected to science in the real world (Sylvan et al., 2013). The game, in this case, serves as an alternative form of scaffolding for the less academic students, but may be a disruption to academic students, causing them to falter when given the game without sufficient bridging to the class material.

While, overall, these findings confirm our conjecture that *Impulse* can help prepare some students for improved science learning in class, these findings highlight the need to examine whether there were important differences in game-based pedagogies in Honors/AP and non-Honors/AP classrooms. It is also possible that variations in science instruction, student demographics, and/or teacher background may explain these findings. It is important to explore these alternative explanations. The remainder of this chapter describes the teacher log data collected as part of the implementation study—how it was collected, from whom, how it was coded, and what relationship there is between teacher reports of classroom activity and student performance on the pre-post assessments. Specifically, this chapter explores two questions stemming from this work.

1. In what ways did Bridge classrooms differ from Control and Game classrooms? Was it primarily the use of game-centered pedagogy or were there other important differences in student demographics, teacher background or science instruction methods?
2. What types of strategies and classroom activities did Bridge teachers use to leverage implicit game-based science learning to improve classroom learning of Newtonian mechanics in Honors/AP and non-Honors-AP classrooms?

TEACHER LOG METHODS: INSTRUMENTS, CODING SYSTEM AND RELIABILITY

One hundred thirty-five (135) teachers applied to be part of the *Impulse* classroom implementation study. The primary selection criteria a teacher had to meet to be included in the study was teaching at least one class covering Newton's 1st and 2nd Laws during the 2013-14 academic year. Based on information in their applications and responses to emails, researchers assigned 42 teachers to the Bridge, Games, or Control group. Teachers were assigned to groups to ensure balance in terms of: the percentage of students at the school receiving free/reduced price lunch, the percentage of minority students, and student access to technology in and out of school. To a lesser degree, the authors also sought balance between private vs. public schools, years of science teaching experience, region of the country, and prior experience using educational games.

This chapter reports results from the 22 teachers (and 47 classes) participating in the study in the 2013-14 academic year who completed logs. Three teachers did not complete their logs and were excluded from these analyses. Teachers in all groups—9 Bridge, 8 Game Only, and 5 Control[1]—were asked to keep daily logs of activities for each study class and reflect on their practice before and after the study. Teachers were allowed to include up to three sections of the same class in the study (i.e., 3 sections of AP Physics) and up to three distinct classes (e.g., AP Physics, Honors Physics, and Conceptual Physics). Fourteen teachers had more than one section of the same class in the study. Four teachers had two distinct classes in the study--one Honors/AP, one non-Honors/AP. Teachers who completed the study—daily logs plus student completion of pre and post assessments—received stipends ranging from $300 for Control group teachers to $500 for Bridge group teachers.

Teacher Logs

The teacher logs utilized in the implementation study were modeled after the SCOOP Notebook developed by CRESST (Borko, Stecher & Kuffner, 2007). Teachers were asked to complete daily logs during the study as well as answer questions about their class before the study and reflect on their study experience afterwards. Each teacher in the study was given a personalized Google Drive folder containing all of the required "paperwork" for their participation in the research study, including blank log files. Google Drive allowed for instant sharing of classroom logs between teachers and EdGE researchers without requiring additional action from the teacher.

Pre-Study Questions

All teachers were asked to answer questions about their class before they began teaching Newton's Laws to their students. These questions included class title (e.g., AP Physics, Conceptual Physics, etc), the number of students enrolled in the class, the grade levels of those students, class population characteristics (e.g., AP, Honors, ELL), the textbook(s) and other primary support materials they used to teach forces and motion, and the dates they planned to start and stop teaching Newton's 1st Law, Newton's 2nd Law, and Forces and Motion (e.g., speed, inertia, acceleration). Table 1 provides a broad overview of the types of instructional materials teachers used to teach this science content. Textbooks were standard physics textbooks by major publishers. Six of the seven classes using only online materials were using ASU's Modeling Physics.

During the implementation period, teachers may have used additional support materials and resources (online and/or print) that were shared with researchers via their daily logs. Those details are not captured in Table 1.

Table 1. Percentage of classes using each combination of instructional materials, by study group and Honors/AP status

	Bridge		Game Only		Control	
	Honors-AP	Not Honors-AP	Honors-AP	Not Honors-AP	Honors-AP	Not Honors-AP
Textbook Only	100%	23%	50%	54%	67%	50%
Online Only	0%	46%	50%	8%	0%	50%
Textbook & Online	0%	23%	0%	0%	33%	0%
Textbook & Other Resources	0%	0%	0%	38%	0%	0%
None	0%	8%	0%	0%	0%	0%

Daily Log Questions

Teachers were instructed to complete separate daily log reports for each class or section participating in the study. In these logs, teachers were to provide detailed accounts of their classroom activities every day they taught content related to Newton's Laws/Forces and Motion.

Each teacher in the study was provided with 15 numbered daily log template files in his/her personalized Google Drive folder. Additional files were provided as necessary upon request for teachers whose units on Newton's Laws/Forces and Motion lasted more than 15 days. Teachers who taught the relevant content for fewer than 15 days were instructed to leave superfluous template files blank. In addition to blank log files, teachers were also provided with a sample completed daily log showing the length and level of detail we wanted them to include in their logs in order to paint as descriptive a picture as possible of everything that happened in their classrooms. Along with their completed log entries, teachers were also asked to share additional relevant materials from the day's lesson (worksheets, lesson plans, test questions, lab activities, media, etc.) via their Google Drive folder, email, or snail mail.

In their daily log entries, participating teachers were asked to respond to the following questions:

1. What were your objectives/expectations for student learning during this lesson?
2. Describe the lesson in enough detail so we understand how the materials were used or generated. Please make it clear what you would have done even if you were not participating in the study and what was changed because of the study.
3. Describe the conversations, if any, that took place in the classroom about the *Impulse* game. (Bridge & Game Only groups).
4. Thinking back to your original plans for the lesson, were there any changes in how the lesson actually unfolded?
5. Is there anything else you would like us to know about this lesson that you feel was not captured by this log?

Coding System

An emergent coding approach was used to perform the content analysis of the classroom logs. Two independent coders from EdGe reviewed two sets of class logs from each study condition (Control, Game, Bridge), chosen at random, and created a preliminary code list. These initial lists were compared against one another and refined to reflect the features of greatest relevance to the research. Daily logs were coded for: (1) Classroom activities; (2) Science content; and (3) Game-based pedagogies. Classroom activity codes characterize the nature of daily classroom practices and instruction (e.g., lecture, hands-on lab activities, gameplay, etc.). Content codes reflect science concepts related to Newton's Laws, forces, and motion that are typically covered in high school physics courses and are relevant to the game *Impulse*. Codes for game-based pedagogies (Game/Bridge conditions only) included Bridge activities (how teachers connected *Impulse* gameplay and classroom instruction), Gameplay (how teachers used the game *Impulse* in class), and Game discussion (how teachers and students talked about the game *Impulse* in class). Once the coding scheme was established, a comprehensive codebook of definitions, criteria, and examples was created to guide coders' analysis of the remaining log files.

To confirm the reliability of the coding system, an EdGE researcher and two external evaluators from New Knowledge Organization independently coded logs and supplemental classroom materials provided by teachers from 10 of the 47 classrooms. The EdGE researcher is an astrophysicist with a doctorate in science education. The NKO evaluators are social scientists with science education expertise. The EdGE team selected classes to ensure each was taught by a different teacher--4 Bridge, 4 Game Only, and 2 Control. Four classes were Honors/AP classes (2 Bridge, 1 Game Only, 1 Control). The remaining six classes were not Honors/AP classes. The EdGE researcher and one NKO evaluator double coded a total of 147 daily logs--58 from Bridge classrooms, 63 from Game Only classrooms, and 26 from Control classrooms. The team met to discuss code ambiguities and coding discrepancies. Once issues were resolved and consensus was reached on the coding scheme, the codebook was revised accordingly and select logs were re-coded. This coding was completed with an average Cohen's kappa of 0.71 across all codes (i.e., coders agree 71 percent more frequently than expected by chance). Only codes with reliability at or above 0.70 will be retained for subsequent analyses comparing Bridge, Game Only, and Control classrooms. While the selection of a cut-off value for kappas depends on the context, 0.70 is considered satisfactory for established systems and is an appropriately high bar for a new coding system when using the codes to make statistical comparisons. The EdGE researcher then coded all remaining logs and supplemental classroom materials (worksheets, tests, readings, etc.) provided by teachers.

Cohen's kappas for classroom activity codes are reported in Table 2. Teachers were not equally detailed in their logs, making it difficult to reliably code specific dimensions of classroom activity. Only codes for Bridge Activities, Lecture, Demo/Video/Provoking questions, Interactive/Exploratory activities, and Readings-based questions or guided note-taking were at or above 0.70. Abbreviated definitions for each of these classroom activities are reported in Table 2. For the complete list of codes, detailed definitions, and sample quotes, see the Appendix.

Table 3 reports the Cohen's kappas for science content codes. EdGE researchers divided the science content codes into four mutually exclusive categories: Newton's First Law, Newton's Second Law, Game-Related Science Content, and Other (non-game related) science content. Kappas for Newton's First Law, Newton's Second Law, and Other Science Content exceeded 0.70.

Table 4 reports the Cohen's kappas from the coding of 58 logs from the Bridge classrooms. The authors created four codes to capture these bridging activities—(1) discussion, (2) use of provided video clips, (3) in-class gameplay, and (4) other (teacher-created) materials. Coders reached the 0.70 kappa threshold only for the use of provided video clips. While the coders were able to reliably discern whether or

Table 2. Classroom activity code definitions and reliability

Classroom Activity Code and Definition	Cohen's Kappa
Lecture: Content delivered by teacher, with little or no student interaction/involvement; may include Powerpoint presentations.	0.83
Demo or Provoking Question/Scenario: Class included a teacher- or student-led demonstration, viewing video clip(s) not related to the game *Impulse*, or a thought-provoking question/scenario posed to students as a way to introduce a topic.	0.81
Interactive or Exploratory Activity/Hands On Lab: Students engaged in interactive or hands-on/laboratory work as whole class, in small groups, or as individuals (e.g., creating a class graph, doing a cart on a track lab, answering "clicker" questions).	0.72
Bridge Activity: Any activity that connects Impulse gameplay with content being covered in the classroom (e.g., using the EdGE-developed discussion guide or video clips in class as a way to talk about/illustrate how Impulse supports and/or demonstrates science concepts covered in class).	0.94
Reading or Reading-based questions, Guided Note Taking: Students were given a reading assignment to complete in class, responded to questions based on an assigned reading, or used a set of questions/prompts to guide reading or research on a given topic.	0.70
Review/Test Prep: Class time is devoted to reviewing or preparing for a non-EdGE quiz or test.	0.70

Table 3. Science content code definitions and reliability

Science Content Code Definition	Cohen's Kappa
Newton's First Law: This code includes explicit discussion of either Newton's First Law OR Inertia.	0.77
Newton's Second Law: This code includes explicit discussion of Newton's Second Law, Net Forces, OR Acceleration.	0.90
Game-related Science Content: This code includes explicit discussion of game-related science content such as Forces, Mass, Momentum, Impulse, Gravity, Velocity, Vectors, Collisions/Impact, OR Kinematics.	0.58
Other Science Content: This code includes explicit discussion of Newton's Third Law, Friction, Circular/Orbital Motion, Springs, OR History of Science.	0.71

not there was any Bridge activity, the level of details provided by teachers made it difficult to discern the exact nature of their bridging activity. Game-play and game-related discussion was coded in greater detail, with improved reliability in Tables 5 and 6.

There is some evidence teachers underreported their use of the game and discussion of the game in relation to content being covered in class. Three Game Only teachers (7 classes) indicated in their post-reflections that students played the game in class, yet did not report this in their daily logs. A

Table 4. Bridge Activity code definitions, sample quotes, and reliability

Bridge Activity Code Definitions	Sample Quotes	Cohen's Kappa
1. Discussion: Classroom activities for the day included a discussion related to the game *Impulse*. The nature of the discussion does not matter for this code. It could be about anything from whether or not students played the game to technical difficulties with the game or even an in-depth discussion of the physics represented in the game.	"I had planned to limit the discussion of the Impulse game to the questions assigned at the end of the period. However, the game examples came to be useful in discussing addition of forces and Newton's third law." (B138)	0.62
2. Use of EdGE-based video clips: Teacher logs mentioned use of EdGE-developed video clips of *Impulse* gameplay.	"While viewing the video clip, one of the students who played to an advanced level explained to the others that even though different colored particles appeared to be the same size, there were differences in mass - in fact, some particles were twice as massive as the others." (B132)	1.00
3. In Class Game Play: Class time was devoted to playing *Impulse* as a way to connect the game with explicit science content. This could include a teacher demonstration, group play, or individual students playing the game. However, gameplay without any intervention from the teacher that attempts to link the content of the game with science instruction (i.e., as part of the registration process or busy work), should not be coded as a bridge activity.	"I asked students how they would need to click on the screen in order to get the ball to move in a large circle. There were varying opinions, so I had them go to Level one on the game and try to do it. Once everyone was convinced that the force would need to be applied on the outside of the circle, directed inward, they very quickly made the link to the inward direction of acceleration when in uniform circular motion. This was an excellent application of the conceptual idea "the net force is ALWAYS pointed in the same direction as the acceleration." (B118)	0.35
4. Bridge Activity (other): Classroom activities developed by teacher to tie game into curriculum	"One of today's scenarios was a frictionless hover disc traveling at a constant velocity. Several students were tempted to draw a force in the direction of motion because "something has to be making it move." I used the green ball in the impulse game as a reference and asked them if they had to keep clicking it repeatedly to keep it moving once it was in motion. Most of them realized that it kept moving on its own and were able to use that idea to correct their force diagrams." (B120)	-0.02

Table 5. In-Class gameplay code definitions, sample quotes, and reliability

In-Class Gameplay Codes and Definitions	Sample Quotes	Cohen's Kappa
Teacher Demo: The game Impulse was played in class as a demonstration led by the teacher, projected for the entire class to watch.	"I used Impulse as a demonstration for initially presenting the concepts of inertia and net force…" (B134)	0
Group Activity: Students play the game Impulse in small groups or as a whole class with one student "driving" gameplay.	"This was our fourth session of gameplay in the computer lab. By today almost all the students had achieved Level 70, so this session was devoted to assisting those who had not achieved Level 70. Again, I was amazed at the level of collaboration and teamwork the student's displayed." (G172)	0
Individual Activity: Students play the game Impulse individually.	"I took the class to a computer lab so that every kids could be on a computer. I had written an assignment for them, Computer Activities for Unit 5, to guide their activities. We spent all period there. Almost every kid played Impulse up to level 20 or beyond." (B144)	0.27
Busy Work: Students were allowed/given the option to play the game Impulse during class as a "free-choice" activity or busy work after the primary lesson or activity for the day is completed.	"There were no conversations about Impulse today other than my mentioning that students were free to play as a reward for finishing their essays." (B136)	0.76
Primary/Major Part of Lesson: The teacher used Impulse gameplay as part of the primary lesson for the day (i.e., NOT as busy work).	"Today in class, I had students play Impulse for 15 minutes and then we talked about what they saw in the game."	0.58

different Game Only teacher reported allowing students to play Impulse in two class on "several occasions." Another Game Only teacher said "The logs are exactly what happened in class except for the few times I allowed the students to play the impulse game for short time increments when we had time." No in-class gameplay was mentioned in any of the daily logs for three classes, but the instructor's post-reflection log indicated that students played at least one time in conjunction with *BrainPlay* registration and perhaps on other occasions, though the frequency of additional in-class play (if it did occur) was unclear. One Game Only teacher and one Bridge teacher reported in-class gameplay just one time each in their daily logs (as busy work in the Game Only class and as part of *BrainPlay* registration in the Bridge class), but their post-reflections implied that there may have been more frequent use of the game during class time throughout the implementation period. Similarly, there were a couple known instances of under-representation of game discussion/bridging in the daily logs among 2 Bridge and 1 Game Only teachers. For example, the Game Only Instructor, who did not report any discussion of the game in his daily logs, said in his post-reflection, "I used teachable moments to make correlations to the Impulse game that the students were playing online. I view the online game as a tool in my teacher toolbox."

Table 5 reports the Cohen's kappas from the 121 logs in Game Only and Bridge classrooms related to in-class gameplay. The authors created 5 codes to describe in-class gameplay: teacher demo, individual gameplay, group gameplay, busywork, and whether the gameplay was a major part of the class (i.e., not busywork). Only the code for teachers using games as busy work was above 0.70. Similar to the generic science classroom activity codes, the level of detail reported by teachers varied greatly, making it difficult to discern exactly how the games were used in class.

Game discussion was coded for whether there was evidence of formal (teacher-led) integration, bridge materials being used, whether teachers provided incentives for the game, whether teachers

Table 6. Game Discussion code definitions, sample quotes, and reliability

Game Discussion Codes and Definitions	Sample Quotes	Cohen's Kappa
Formal Integration (teacher-led): The teacher initiated and led a discussion in class about the game Impulse and how it connects with science topics being covered in the curriculum.	"I emphasized that N2 is to be considered in terms of the sum of all forces, and that we name force vectors positive and negative to indicate right/left and up/down. I related this to the Impulse game by bringing up Newton's third law. The students mostly asserted that it is the moving object that exerts the force on the stationary object, even as they were able to recite N3 again. Upon questioning they came to agree that the moving object slowed down during the event and must therefore have experienced a force opposite to its direction of motion." (B138)	0.88
Formal Integration (EdGE docs): Same as the previous entry, but with specific mention of the EdGE Discussion Guide provided to teachers in their personalized Google Drive folders.	"At first I tried to run the video while asking the questions from the suggestion provided in the Video Clips suggestions and recording the question and answers" (B138)	0
Provided incentives for playing the game: Teacher discussed the game Impulse in class in the context of providing students with their own incentives to play the game (e.g., bonus points on a test, etc.), or telling students about incentives for student participation (e.g., a pizza party).	"In the remainder of the time of the class, I reviewed the expectations for the Impulse game and the prizes being offered, and I passed out instructions for students to register." (B118)	0.92
Encouraged/reminded students to play Impulse after school/in free time: Teacher discussed the game Impulse in the context of encouraging or reminding students to play Impulse outside of class/school time as part of their responsibilities as research study participants.	"I reminded this group about playing Impulse...." (B146)	0.73
Encouraged/reminded students to play Impulse in class/school: Teacher discussed the game Impulse in the context of encouraging or reminding students to play Impulse in class or school, perhaps as an option during "free-choice" time in class, after finishing an exam, as part of the day's lesson, etc.	"Since we were able to reserve a laptop cart ('Computer On Wheels' aka COW cart), students were able to obtain internet access within my classroom. I encouraged them to play Impulse after completing their rocket essay and reminded them that we have until December 1st to reach our goal." (B132)	0.12
Students talking about game in relation to physics content: Teacher log indicates that students were talking about the game Impulse in the context of peer-to-peer discussion in or out of class, or when the teacher did not specifically prompt a relationship between the game and what was being covered in class.	"...I heard them conversing with questions about the game and the physics involved. I heard some students describing the motion of the balls in the game as though surprised, while other students would respond that this is what is predicted by Newton's laws. They were very independent and had few questions for me." (B138)	0.32
Casual discussion: The game Impulse was discussed in class in more general, casual way (not related to class/physics content). For example, this type of discussion might be about what level they reached in the game, commentary on whether the game is hard/easy, etc.	"Before class began, students talked about the game as they entered the room. Comments that I received were that the game was difficult to use without a mouse, that after level 49 the game 'got hard' and that there were no directions on 'how to play'. One student asked where the game ended (i.e. what was the uppermost level)." (B132)	0.50

provided encouragement for students to play the games in their free time and/or in class, whether students explicitly discussed the science content in the game, and whether there was any casual discussion about the game among students. Table 6 reports the Cohen's kappas from the Game Only and Bridge classroom logs related to in-class game discussions. Only the codes for Formal Integration led by the teachers, Providing Incentives for playing the game, and Encouragement to Play in the Free Time reached a sufficient level of reliability to be included in subsequent analyses.

Post-Study Reflection Questions

Once teachers finished teaching the content related to the game *Impulse* and their students had taken the post-instruction assessment, they were instructed to provide their "Final Reflections" as the last piece of their required classroom logging activities. The purpose of the post-study reflections component of the classroom logs was to have teachers provide us with their honest impressions about participating in the research study and the impacts their participation had on their students and their classroom teaching practices. As with the other components of the classroom logs, a separate Final Reflections Log was to be completed for each class or section participating in the study, and EdGE provided a sample log as an exemplar. The post-study reflection questions for Bridge and Game Only teachers were:

1. How did your approach to teaching this class change as a result of using the games and/or bridge materials?
2. In what ways were these changes positive and/or negative?
3. Do you think your teaching will be impacted in any permanent way because of your experience in this study? If so, how?
4. What differences did you notice about students' learning of the related science during their experience in this study? Were they more or less engaged? Do you think they were able to learn less or more content? Skills?
5. What overall comments do you have about how students' classroom science learning may or may not be impacted by game-based learning?
6. How well does the set of descriptions and the materials you've included in your daily logs represent the spirit of what was going on in your class? What is not represented in what you've included and written here that you think is important for researchers to know about your teaching and your class during the implementation period?

Teachers' responses to these post-study reflection questions were coded to capture teachers' impressions of the overall impact that participating in the study had on their teaching and consequently, on their students' content knowledge and engagement. Specifically, we coded for the degree to which their teaching approach changed, the quality of the impact on their teaching, whether this change was permanent, and whether there were changes in students engagement and science learning. These class-level codes only had 10 data points (compared to over a hundred for most of the other codes) and any disagreement between coders had a much larger impact on the reliability. For this reason, we will include only codes that exceed 0.60 for this set of codes. Table 7 presents the Cohen's kappas for the class-level codes. Four codes exceeded 0.60: the type of impact on teachers perceived on their teaching; whether teachers thought the change in their teaching was permanent; the type of change teachers saw in their students' level of engagement; and the type of change teachers saw in their students' learning.

Teacher and School Demographics

In their applications to participate in the implementation study, teachers reported information about:

- The name of their school.
- Their school (private, public, public charter).
- The percentage of students their school receiving free-reduced price lunch (0-25%, 26-50%, 51-75%, 76-100%).
- The percentage of students in their school who are white (0-25%, 26-50%, 51-75%, 76-100%).
- The number of years they have taught science.
- The science courses they teach.
- Their prior experience using games in their teaching.
- The reason why they were interest in the study.

Table 7. Post study reflection code definitions, code values, sample quotes, and reliability

Class Level Code Definitions	Code Values	Sample Quotes	Cohen's Kappa
Degree of Change in Teaching Approach: Interpretation of teacher's self-evaluation of the degree to which using Impulse affected their teaching approach	Significant Minor No Change	"I used a few examples from the impulse game in class discussions, but for the most part, my approach was not drastically altered by either the game or the bridge materials." (B120)	0.41
Teaching Change Positive/Negative: Interpretation of teacher's self-evaluation of the type/quality of impact that using the game had on their teaching.	Positive Negative Mixed None Unsure	"Keeping in mind that few changes took place in my classroom teaching of this subject, I still have to report a positive influence on simply participating in the game study. The students were initially very excited about the process taking place in our poor school district and a few of them really enjoyed playing the game. I explained to them that they had the opportunity to make a difference in the development of a game and that made them feel like they made a difference." (G120)	0.65
Permanency of Change in Teaching: Teacher's reflections about whether their study experience will have long-term impacts on their pedagogy	Yes No Unsure	"I think that I will assign more simulations and game-like activities for students to do outside of class. It's given me the confidence that students will follow through with these activities." (B140)	1.00
Change in Student Engagement: Teacher's reflection about whether students were more or less engaged during the study.	More Less No Difference Unsure	"All of the students were initially engaged, but as time went on, some students dropped off the grid because they truly could not catch on to the ways in which they could have success in playing the game." (G152)	0.60
Change in Student Science Learning: Teacher's reflection about whether students learned more or less science content.	More Less No Difference Unsure	"...evidenced by the objective results of their chapter test, where the average picked up by approximately one letter grade. Obviously with a score increase there was more content being learned." (G120)	1.00

Note: All class-level codes allowed values of 'No Response' and 'Not Applicable'.

We verified the demographics of the students in public schools were verified with the 2011 Common Core of Data. While the CCD data is from two years year prior to this study, it is unlikely the characteristics of the entire high school student population change dramatically from year to year. Student demographic data is not available for private schools. Chi-square analyses of the distribution of classes across categories revealed uneven distributions among the percentage of minority students (Chi-square=32.1, 15 d.f., p<0.006) but not the percentage of students receiving free-reduced price lunch in each group (Chi-square=21.5, 15 d.f., p<0.122) (Table 8). While all of the Bridge classes were in schools with less than 50% minority students, Control and Game Only classes were spread across schools with low and high percentages of minority students.

All Bridge and Game Only Honors/AP teachers reported prior experience using games. Approximately half of the teachers in the remaining three groups reported prior experience using games. Two of the four Game Only, Honors/AP classes (the group with the lowest estimated mean) were taught by a teacher that never played Impulse despite both teachers reporting prior experience using games.

Table 8. School demographics, teacher science teaching experience, and teacher gameplay duration by study group and status

	Bridge		Game Only		Control	
	Honors-AP	Not Honors-AP	Honors-AP	Not Honors-AP	Honors-AP	Not Honors-AP
Number of Teachers	5	6	2	6	4	2
Number of Classes	6	12	4	14	8	3
Avg Number Classes/Teacher	1.2	2.0	2.0	2.3	2.0	1.0
Percentage of Classes Taught by:						
Male Teachers	33%	23%	50%	62%	22%	50%
Female Teachers	67%	77%	50%	38%	78%	50%
Percentage of Classes Taught by Teachers in:						
Public Schools	67%	77%	100%	62%	100%	100%
Private School	33%	23%	0%	38%	0%	0%
Percentage of Classes Taught by Teachers with:						
Less than 5 years science teaching experience	17%	8%	0%	62%	22%	0%
5+ years science teaching experience	83%	92%	100%	38%	78%	100%
Percentage of Classes in Schools with:						
0-25% Free-Reduced Lunch	17%	23%	50%	23%	56%	50%
26-50% Free-Reduced Lunch	50%	54%	0%	15%	22%	50%
51-75% Free-Reduced Lunch	0%	0%	50%	23%	22%	0%
Private School	33%	23%	0%	38%	0%	0%
Percentage of Classes in Schools with:						
0-25% Minority Students	33%	62%	50%	38%	44%	50%
26-50% Minority Students	67%	38%	0%	23%	33%	0%
51-75% Minority Students	0%	0%	0%	38%	0%	0%
76-100% Minority Students	0%	0%	50%	0%	22%	50%
Percentage of Classes taught by Teachers with Prior Experience using Games to Teach	100%	100%	100%	54%	44%	50%
Impulse Gameplay						
Mean Duration (minutes)	815	695	35	1460	--	--
Highest Level Reached	11	38	25	14	--	--
% Classes in which Teacher Never Played	17%	0%	50%	23%	--	--

Student Demographics

All student level characteristics were collected as part of the registration process into the game-based data collection system called *BrainPlay*. *BrainPlay* was developed by the EdGE team with our game development partners to organize and export pertinent data from each game along with player data from surveys. When registering in *BrainPlay*, students provided their gender, birth month, and birth year, which were used to calculate the student's age at the time of registration. *BrainPlay* also recorded all player interactions with the game, including the duration of gameplay and highest level of the game played. These measures of gameplay were included in this study as another alternative explanation of differences between Honors/AP and non-Honors/AP students in Bridge and Game Only classrooms in estimated post-assessment results. Table 9 shows the distribution of students across these groups.

In univariate analyses, there were significant differences between groups in the percentage who had 5+ years of science teaching experience (F=3.919, 5, 41 d.f., p=0.006), the percentage of teachers prior experience using educational games (F=3.269, 5, 41 df, p=0.014), and, among Bridge and Game Only classes, the highest level they reached in the game (F=3.946, 5, 41 d.f., p=0.019). The non-Honors/AP Game only classes were more likely than classes in the other groups to be taught be a teacher with less than 5 years of science teaching experience. If a lack of science teaching experience were related to poorer bridging, this group should have performed more poorly than the others. This was not the case.

Univariate analyses showed a significant difference in group membership by student age (F=70.6, 5, 467 d.f., p<0.001) but not gender (F=1.06, 5, 467 d.f., p=0.38). Pairwise contrasts show a moderating impact of study group and Honors/AP status (Figure 4).

Among Bridge classrooms, students in the non-Honors/AP classes were significantly older than those in the Honors/AP classes (mean difference=-0.4, p=0.002). The reverse pattern was true among Game Only classrooms (mean difference=1.2, p<0.001). There was no significant difference by Honors/AP status in Control classrooms (mean difference=0.13, p=0.56). Students in non-Honors/AP, Game-Only classrooms were significantly younger than students in all other groups.

RESULTS: COMPARISON OF BRIDGE CLASSROOMS TO CONTROL AND GAME CLASSROOMS

Bridge, Game Only, and Control classrooms were compared based on duration of participation (number of logs), how often each of five

Table 9. Student demographics by study group and Honors/AP status

Student Characteristic	Total	Bridge		Game Only		Control	
		Honors-AP	Not Honors-AP	Honors-AP	Not Honors-AP	Honors-AP	Not Honors-AP
Number of Students in Study	481	68	119	45	139	93	17
Student							
Female	270	46%	57%	62%	54%	58%	41%
Male	237	54%	43%	38%	46%	42%	59%
Student Age							
14	1%	0%	0%	45%	3%	0%	1%
15	16%	8%	0%	25%	3%	6%	16%
16	46%	29%	82%	16%	18%	12%	46%
17	37%	57%	18%	12%	48%	53%	37%
18	0%	5%	0%	1%	27%	29%	0%
Not Reported	0%	6%	0%	1%	0%	0%	0%

Figure 4. Mean student age by study group and Honors/AP status

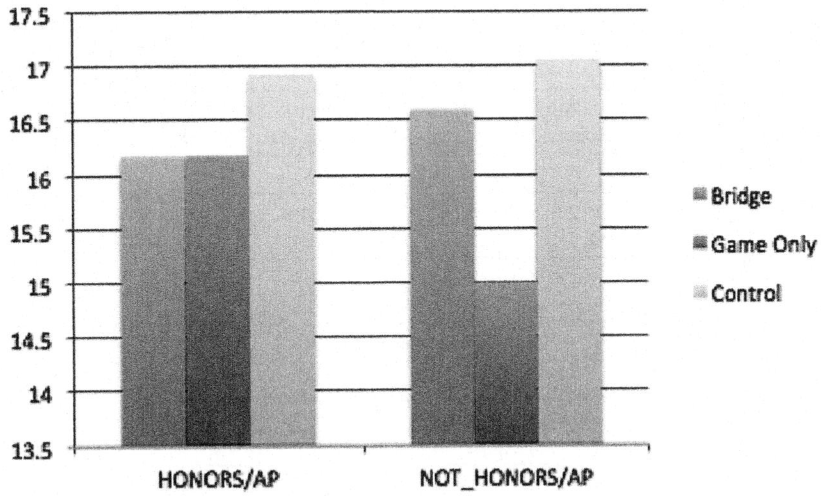

instructional practices were employed, and how often four science content areas were taught. To account for the varying durations of participation by each class within a study condition (Bridge, Game Only, Control), the mean percentage of class days, which is a very rough proxy for the amount of time a teacher spent engaging in that instructional activity or with that science content, was used for these comparisons. The actual amount of time spent covering material relevant to the game could vary widely, both across teachers and for a single teacher across days throughout the participation period, but the log data did not include the level of detail needed to determine that information. Without cost-prohibitive direct observations or more comprehensive (and therefore burdensome) questions in the daily teacher logs, it is difficult to make finer grain distinctions at the large scale needed to incorporate the log data in statistical models such as HLM. Univariate analyses are reported in Table 10.

The data indicated a significant relationship between Study Group (Bridge, Game Only, Control) and Honors/AP status with respect to the percentage of class time spent on interactive or exploratory/hands-on activities. Pairwise comparisons showed Honors/AP Game Only classes participated in interactive activities twice as often as non-Honors/AP Game Only classes (40% vs 21%, F=5.46, 5, 41 d.f., p<0.001).

There were few differences in the science content covered in these classes. However, one significant difference we found was in the prevalence of non-game-related science content (Newton's Third Law, Springs, etc.). Teachers in Bridge and Game Only classrooms, on average, covered these other science topics on more than half of their class days during the study, whereas teachers in Control classrooms only did so on one third of their class days (F=3.61, 5, 41 d.f., p=0.01). There were no significant differences in the mean number of topics covered per day, with all groups averaging between two and three topics (out of four categories) per day.

Overall, these results suggest classroom activities and science content are not a strong explanation for patterns found in pre-post assessment performance, where Honors/AP students in Game-only classrooms and non-Honors/AP students in Control classrooms underperformed

Table 10. Classroom activities and science content as a proportion of class time by study group and Honors/AP status

	Bridge		Game Only		Control		One-Way ANOVA	
	Honors-AP	Not Honors-AP	Honors-AP	Not Honors-AP	Honors-AP	Not Honors-AP	F-Value	p Value
Number of Classes	6	13	4	13	9	2		
Total Number of Logs Coded	60	276	72	204	102	15		
Mean Duration in Days (N Logs)	10	21	18	16	11	8	2.7	0.03
Mean Percentage of Class Days								
Lectures	6%	1%	5%	4%	5%	0%	0.60	0.70
Demo, Video, Provoking Questions or Scenarios	25%	32%	47%	22%	26%	59%	2.41	0.05
Interactive or Exploratory Activity/Hands-On Lab	36%	34%	40%	21%	54%	47%	5.46	0.00
Readings-based questions or guided note taking	24%	10%	10%	7%	12%	9%	1.34	0.27
Review/Test Prep	13%	17%	12%	10%	5%	0%	1.79	0.14
Mean Percentage of Class Days								
Newton's First Law	34%	34%	32%	45%	42%	32%	0.83	0.54
Newton's Second Law	85%	75%	74%	66%	68%	86%	1.34	0.27
Other, non-game related science content	68%	66%	59%	47%	32%	35%	3.61	0.01
Mean number of main topics per day	2.7	2.5	2.6	2.4	2.1	2.5	1.59	0.18

NOTE: The degrees of freedom for the one-way ANOVA tests are (5, 41) for all tests.

compared students in other classrooms (see Figure 3). Log data show that students in Control classrooms spent a greater proportion of their class days doing interactive, hands-on activities and were more focused on the content directly related to the game rather than other science content. Given the widespread belief in the efficacy of hands-on activities for enhancing science content learning, one might argue that students in Control classrooms should be outperforming students in the Bridge and Game Only classrooms. The fact that they are not suggests something related to the use of game-based pedagogies may be leading to the better performance of students in the Bridge classrooms relative to the Control classrooms.

RESULTS: GAME-BASED PEDAGOGIES

This section examines the game-based pedagogies used in Bridge & Game Only classrooms and whether they vary by Honors/AP status. Honors/AP status is a proxy both of students' prior science knowledge and teacher expectations for students' science learning in their current course. Three main bridging activities that were reliably coded are examined below—(1) gameplay; (2) teacher-led class discussions that explicitly connect gameplay with science content; and (3) the use of video examples of gameplay to illustrate specific science concepts.

Figure 5. Mean time (in minutes) spent playing Impulse by study group and Honors/AP status

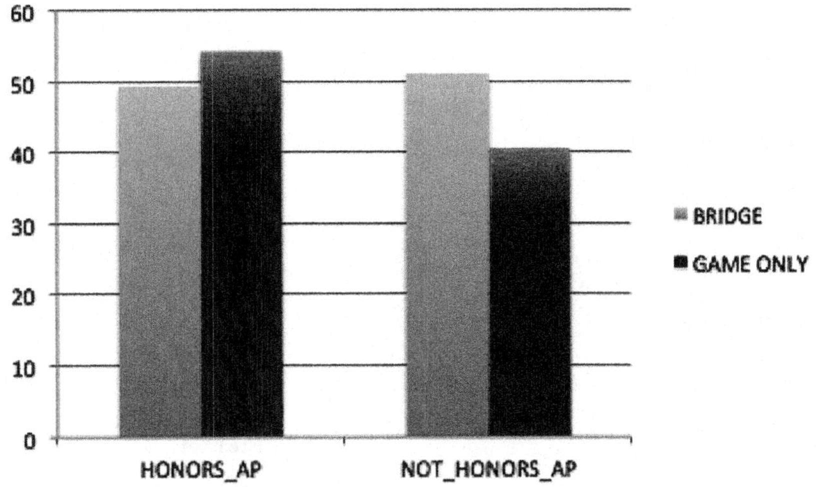

Figures 5 and 6 show the mean amount of time (in minutes) students in each of the four groups played *Impulse* and the mean highest level those students reached.[2] A univariate test comparing the mean number of minutes spent playing *Impulse* by students in these four groups was not significant (F=0.32, 3, 367 d.f., p=0.808) and neither were any of the group contrasts, which suggests all groups played Impulse for approximately the same amount of time. Univariate analyses also show no overall differences in the mean highest level reached in the game for each group (F=2.29, 3, 367 d.f., p=0.078).

Figures 7 and 8 report the percentage of all Bridge classes in which the teacher used each bridging strategy and the percentage of class

Figure 6. Average highest Impulse level reached by study group and Honors/AP status

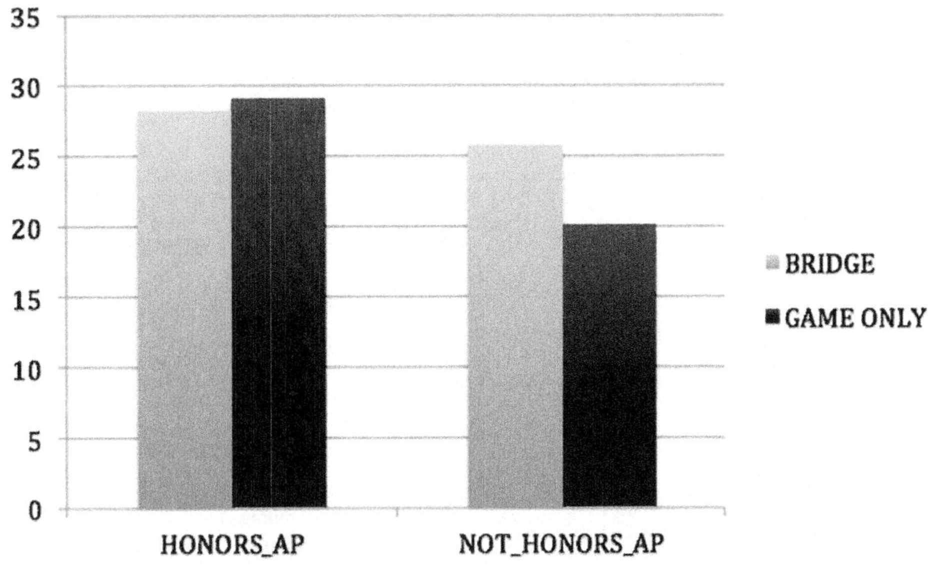

Figure 7. Percentage of Bridge teachers who engaged with specific bridging activities in at least one class period, by Honors/AP status

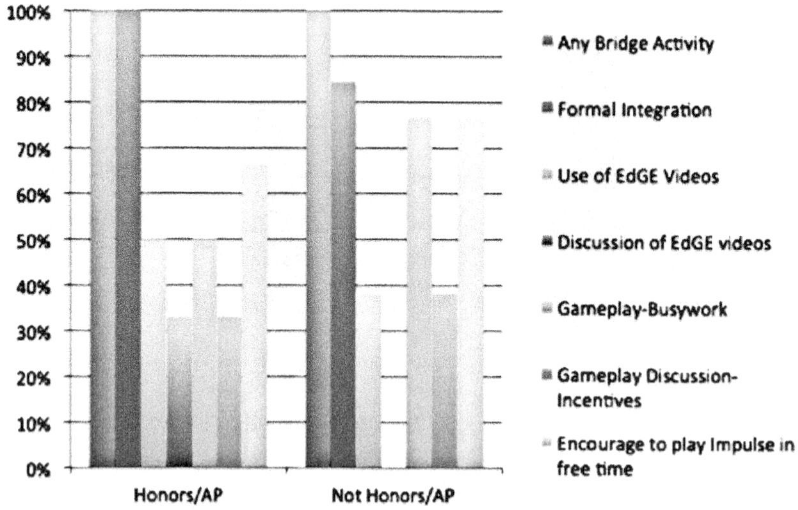

days the teacher used the strategy.[3] Teachers that did not use a strategy (0 percent) are included in these analyses to keep the number of classes constant. All Bridge Honors/AP classes had at least one class day with a teacher-led discussion connecting gameplay with science content. This was also true in all except one Bridge non-Honors/AP class. Teachers of Honors/AP classes, however, used this bridging strategy in an average of 40 percent of the class periods included in this study. Teachers of non-Honors/AP classes, led discussions of this type significantly less often, an average of 17 percent of their classes (F=10.4, 3, 32 d.f., p<0.001).

Figure 8. Mean percentage of Bridge class periods teachers spent on specific bridging activities, by Honors/AP status

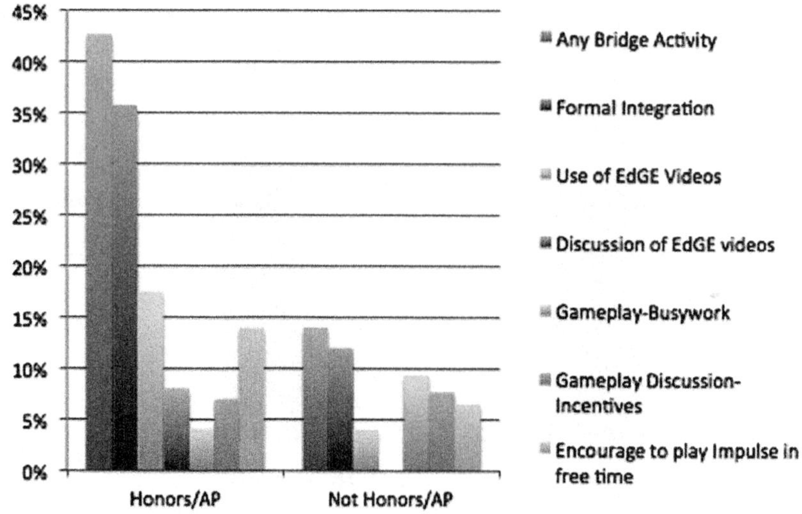

The use of videos of *Impulse* gameplay was reported less frequently than discussion. However, half of Honors/AP classes and 38 percent of non-Honors/AP classes reported using them at least once. Furthermore, 38 percent of Honors/AP classes reported also discussing those videos, while none of the non-Honors/AP classes did (F=5.13, 3, 32 d.f., p=0.005). Honors/AP Bridge teachers also reported using gameplay videos as a bridging activity in a larger proportion of their classes than did non-AP Bridge (average percentage was 18% for Honors/AP, 4% for non-Honors/AP, F=5.13, 3, 32 d.f., p=0.005).

IMPLICATIONS FOR GAME-BASED LEARNING IN SCIENCE CLASSROOMS

Prior analyses of a national classroom implementation study of *Impulse* suggest games can be effective tools for teaching science when accompanied by teacher bridging activities (Rowe et al., 2014). The direct effect of study group (Bridge, Game Only, Control) was moderated by whether the class was Honors/AP or not, so the Honors/AP status was incorporated into all analyses presented in this chapter. Before examining game-based pedagogies, the authors conducted analyses of student demographics, teacher demographics, teacher and student gameplay, science instruction, and science content to examine potential alternate explanations of the findings. Perhaps students in the Bridge group were more likely to have more experienced teachers or be in wealthier school districts? Perhaps their teachers provided more in-depth science instruction or that instruction was better aligned with the content of interest in the game (Newton's First and Second Laws)? Or, perhaps, Bridge teachers were more likely to have experience using games in their science instruction prior to this study? As it turns out, we did not find any of these to be true.

As seen in Figure 3, students in the Honors/AP Game Only classes fared worse on the post assessment than students in the Honors/AP Bridge classes after accounting for their pre-assessment performance and other student characteristics. Figure 5 shows that both groups of students spent an average of approximately 50-55 minutes playing the game, with both groups reaching the same average level in the game (Figure 6). When the game was played outside of class and without supporting peer and teacher discussion (as was the expectation in Game Only classes), the game may have only served as a distractor for more structured, traditional learners who may gravitate towards Honors/AP classes.

The greatest positive impact on learning was achieved by Honors/AP classes in the Bridge condition. When comparing classroom and teacher activities in these Honors/AP Bridge classes to non-Honors/AP classes, the authors found that the Honors/AP Bridge teachers were more likely to use video clips of gameplay during instruction than were non-Honors/AP teachers (Figures 7 and 8). It was also only the Honors/AP teachers who reported discussing those video clips with their students. While use of these EdGE-provided bridge materials may have been under-reported, there is no reason to believe under-reporting would vary by the type (Honors/AP vs. not) of class being taught.

The greatest difference between the Honors/AP and non-Honors/AP Bridge groups, and thus, the strongest candidate as the driver of the differences in science learning between the groups, was the use of game-related discussion. Honors/AP Bridge teachers used game-based discussion in a significantly higher proportion of their classes than non-Honors/AP Bridge teachers. The results of this study suggest that teachers should encourage their students play science-related games in and outside of class, and that the teachers should use bridge materials combined with formal game-related discussion to help connect implicit game-based learning to explicit classroom science learning.

The study also leaves many questions unanswered. *What types of discussions are making the most impact in scaffolding game-based learning? Are there critical points in lessons at which it is best to intervene to help bridge implicit game-based learning with explicit classroom learning? What kinds of teacher facilitation (if any) are needed to make peer-to-peer discussion fruitful for leveraging game-based learning?* Traditional methods, such as ethnography and discourse analysis, are hugely time-intensive and thus limit studies to small numbers of classes. To conduct statistical analyses with sufficient power, researchers need replicable and scalable methods to examine the social dynamics in game-based classrooms. These might include the use of a combination of sociometric badges (Pentland, 2014), natural language processing (McNamara, Graesser, McCarthy, & Cai, 2014), or other innovative technologies and data mining methods that can accurately depict more detailed interactions within large numbers of classrooms.

REFERENCES

Asbell-Clarke, J., Edwards, T., Larsen, J., Rowe, E., Sylvan, E., & Hewitt, J. (2012). Martian Boneyards: Scientific Inquiry in an MMO Game. *International Journal of Game-Based Learning, 2*(1), 52-76.

Asbell-Clarke, J., Rowe, E., & Sylvan, E. (2013, April). *Assessment Design for Emergent Game-Based Learning*. Paper presented at the ACM SIGCHI Conference on Human Factors in Computing Systems (CHI'13). Paris, France.

Ash, K. (2011). Gaming Goes Academic. *Education Week, 30*(25), 24–28.

Borko, H., Stecher, B., & Kuffner, K. (2007). *Using Artifacts to Characterize Reform-Oriented Instruction: The Scoop Notebook and Rating Guide.* CSE Technical Report 707. National Center for Research on Evaluation, Standards, and Student Testing (CRESST).

Clark, D. B., Nelson, B., Chang, H., D'Angelo, C. M., Slack, K., & Martinez-Garza, M. (2011). Exploring Newtonian mechanics in a conceptually-integrated digital game: Comparison of learning and affective outcomes for students in Taiwan and the United States. *Computers & Education, 57*(3), 2178–2195. doi:10.1016/j.compedu.2011.05.007

Collins, H. (2010). *Tacit & Explicit Knowledge*. Chicago: University of Chicago Press. doi:10.7208/chicago/9780226113821.001.0001

diSessa, A. A. (1993). Toward an Epistemology of Physics. *Cognition and Instruction, 10*(2/3), 105–225. doi:10.1080/07370008.1985.9649008

Gee, J. P. (2007). *What Video Games Have to Teach Us about Learning and Literacy* (2nd ed.). New York: Palgrave/Macmillan.

Gee, J. P. (2013). Discourses in and out of school. *Framing languages and literacies: Socially situated views and perspectives*, 51-82.

GlassLab. (2014). Psychometric Considerations In Game-Based Assessment. Institute of Play. Retrieved from http://www.instituteofplay.org/work/projects/glasslab-research/

Hayes, E., & Gee, J. P. (2012). Passionate affinity groups. Chapter. In C. Steinkuehler, K. Squire, & S. Barab (Eds.), *Games, learning, and society: Learning and meaning in the digital age*. London: Cambridge University Press.

Ke, F. (2009). A qualitative meta-analysis of computer games as learning tools. In R. E. Furdig (Ed.), *Handbook of Research on Effective Electronic Gaming in Education* (pp. 1–32). New York: IGI Global. doi:10.4018/978-1-59904-808-6.ch001

Lederman, L. C., & Fumitoshi, K. (1995). Debriefing the Debriefing Process: A new look. In D. C. K. Arai (Ed.), *Simulation and gaming across disciplines and cultures*. London: Sage Publications.

McCloskey, M. (1983). Intuitive Physics. *Scientific American, 248*(4), 122–130. doi:10.1038/scientificamerican0483-122 PMID:6227681

McNamara, D., Graesser, A., McCarthy, P., & Cai, Z. (Eds.). (2014). *Automated Evaluation of Text and Discourse with Coh-Metrix*. New York: Cambridge University Press. doi:10.1017/CBO9780511894664

National Research Council. (2011). M.A. Honey, & M.L. Hilton (Eds.), *Learning Science Through Computer Games and Simulations. Committee on Science Learning: Computer Games, Simulations, and Education*. Board on Science Education, Division of Behavioral and Social Sciences and Education. Washington, DC: National Academies Press. Retrieved from http://www.nap.edu/catalog/13078.html

Pentland, A. (2014). *Social Physics: How Good Ideas Spread-The Lessons from a New Science*. New York: Penguin Press.

Plass, J., Homer, B. D., Kinzer, C. K., Chang, Y. K., Frye, J., Kaczetow, W., & Perlin, K. et al. (2013). Metrics in Simulations and Games for Learning. In M. Seif El-Nasr, A. Drachen, & A. Canossa (Eds.), *Game Analytics: Maximizing the Value of Player Data* (pp. 694–730). London: Springer-Verlag. doi:10.1007/978-1-4471-4769-5_31

Polanyi, M. (2009). The Tacit Dimension (Original ed. 1966). London: Routledge (University of Chicago Press).

Reber, A. S. (1993). *Implicit learning and tacit knowledge: An essay on the cognitive unconscious*. Oxford, UK: Oxford University Press.

Rowe, E., Asbell-Clarke, J., Bardar, E., Kasman, E., & MacEachern, B. (2014, June). *Crossing the Bridge: Connecting Game-Based Implicit Science Learning to the Classroom.* Paper presented at the 10th Annual Meeting of Games+Learning+Society conference, Madison, WI.

Squire, K. D. (2007). Games, Learning, and Society: Building a Field. *Educational Technology, 4*(5), 51–54. Retrieved from http://website.education.wisc.edu/kdsquire/tenure-files/15-gls.pdf

Sylvan, E., Asbell-Clarke, J., Fraser, J., Plemons, K., & Rowe, E. (2013, August). *It's not who I am, its what I do: How Youth Gamer Identity and Beliefs about Social Perception Relates to Their Science Understanding*. Paper presented at the Digital Games Research Association (DiGRA) conference, Atlanta GA.

ENDNOTES

1 These numbers differ from our previous publications. When we examined the teacher logs we found one Game teacher who reported formally integrating the game into her instruction and should, therefore, be classified as a Bridge teacher. That change is incorporated into the analysis of the teacher logs, the focus of this chapter. Future HLM analyses will incorporate this change.

2 Five students had mean times exceeding 70K seconds (almost 20 hours) of gameplay. These values were outliers likely due to leaving the game running and dropped from the analyses of the duration of game play and mean duration per level.

3 To keep the number of bridge teachers constant in this figure, teachers who did not use a specific bridge activity have a value of '0'. Removing those teachers from the analysis would raise the means and increase the error. The overall pattern of results is the same in both, so the authors opted to retain all teachers for all analyses.

APPENDIX

Table 11. Detailed definitions of classroom activity codes with sample quotes

Classroom Activity Code and Definition	Sample Quote	Cohen's Kappa
Direct Instruction: Covers things like "I taught…," "I reviewed…," "Went over...," "Notes on the white board…," and other ambiguous statements about classroom activities.	"I started the class with a brief review of Newton's 2nd Law." (C118)	0.30
Lecture: Content delivered by teacher, with little or no student interaction/involvement; may include things like Powerpoint presentations. Teacher log should clearly indicate the activity is a lecture based on description provided by the teacher or include use of the term "lecture." If in doubt, choose "Direct Instruction."	"The lesson today was mostly lecture format outside of a demonstration of using Newton's first law to determine the frictional force of a book sliding on a table." (G108)	0.83
Impulse Gameplay: The game Impulse was used in class as a teacher-led demonstration, or students played the game as part of a group or individual activity.	"When this activity was done (and a homework sheet given out where the students draw the heads of the front and back car drivers as well as a ball in a wagon that gets pulled), the students were able to get an iPad so that they could play the game "Impulse"." (B126)	0.61
Demo or Provoking Question/Scenario: Class included a teacher- or student-led demonstration, viewing video clip(s) not related to the game Impulse, or a thought-provoking question/scenario was posed to students as a way to introduce a topic.	"I did show to 2nd period a video I found on the horse/cart problem. It shows again how action/reaction forces do NOT cancel and how other forces acting on the same object CAN combine and cause motion." (B126)	0.81
Interactive or Exploratory Activity/Hands On Lab: Students engaged in interactive or hands-on/laboratory work as whole class, in small groups, or as individuals. A lab is defined as an experience in the laboratory, classroom, or the field that provides students with opportunities to interact directly with natural phenomena or with data collected by others using tools, materials, data collection techniques, and models (NRC 2006, p. 3). During a lab, students should have opportunities to design investigations, engage in scientific reasoning, manipulate equipment, record data, analyze results, and discuss their findings. Examples might include things such as: creating a class graph, doing a cart on a track lab, answering "clicker" questions, etc.	"Students worked in groups using a spring scale to pull a person on roller blades. Students were asked to make and record observations as to how the roller blader moved when pulled with several constant forces. they were also asked to record the forces required to start the person moving and to keep them moving at a constant velocity. The lab titled balanced and unbalanced forces is in the forces folder." (C122)	0.72
Online-based simulation or activity (non-EdGE): The teacher or students (as a group or as individuals) conducted online research or used web-based materials or simulations. A simulation is defined as an imitation of a real-world process, phenomenon, or system over time (e.g., PhET simulations).	"Students immediately went down to the computer lab and logged onto the Forces in 1 Dimension PhET http://phet.colorado.edu/en/simulation/forces-1d. Students worked on visualizing both the force diagrams and the motion for objects on flat surfaces with varying applied and frictional forces. Students were asked to focus on the differences between balanced and unbalanced forces." (G128)	0.61
Small group work (not lab based): Students worked together in small groups to do things like discuss a reading, perform calculations, give presentations, etc. Use of the term 'jigsaw' may also refer to small group work. Small group work does NOT include lab work.	"Students worked in groups to solve Newtons 2nd law problems some one step some multiple step problems." (C124)	0.68
Class Discussion (non-game-related): Involves ongoing dialog between teacher and students, NOT including discussion of the game Impulse. Teacher's log entry may specifically include use of the word "discussion" or "conversation."	"The skydiver discussion seemed to be very revealing to most of the kids. The idea demystifies the explanation for what is actually observed when objects fall. In the end there was quite a bit of excited hands raised as the classes tried to process these ideas." (G110)	0.53

continued on following page

Table 11. Continued

Classroom Activity Code and Definition	Sample Quote	Cohen's Kappa
Bridge Activity: Any activity that connects Impulse gameplay with content being covered in the classroom (e.g., using the EdGE-developed discussion guide or video clips in class as a way to talk about/illustrate how Impulse supports and/or demonstrates science concepts covered in class).	"While viewing the video clip, one of the students who played to an advanced level explained to the others that even though different colored particles appeared to be the same size, there were differences in mass - in fact, some particles were twice as massive as the others." (B132)	0.94
Reading or Reading-based questions, Guided Note Taking: Students were given a reading assignment to complete in class, responded to questions based on an assigned reading, or used a set of questions/prompts to guide reading or research on a given topic.	"I used THE PHYSICS CLASSROOM http://www.physicsclassroom.com/Class/newtlaws/U2L2b.cfm for my students to read and take notes about the specifics of forces before I go into 1st and 2nd Laws. I'm slowly working my AP kids into gathering information on their own in order to get them into more of a college frame of reference instead of me giving direct instruction." (C112)	0.70
Worksheets/Problem-Solving: Students and/or teacher engaged in solving problems/performing calculations, etc. on the board as a class, individually, or in small groups.	"Newton's second law practice problems." (B112)	0.54
Independent Work: Students were given time to work independently on things like reading, homework, game play, etc.	"After the quest is completed, students could play the game "Impulse" or complete tonight's homework which is reading and answering questions based on the next chapter (Newton's Third Law)." (B126)	0.26
Consult an Expert: Students communicate with an expert from outside the school. This could include things like participation in an "adopt-a-physicist" program (or similar) or having a guest speaker/lecturer.	"Finally, students were given time to talk with their adopt-a-physicist and then read the Copernican Myths article from Physics Today (Dec. 2007)." (B108)	No cases in classes used for reliability analyses
Review/Test Prep: Class time is devoted to reviewing or preparing for a non-EdGE quiz or test.	"This class period was devoted to answering question covering the practice test and the questions in the textbook. When students would run out of questions I would ask my own covering what I thought was important for them to know." (G122)	0.70
Non-EdGE Assessment: Students took a quiz, test, or other assessment NOT developed by EdGE.	"We then took an assessment on 2nd Law math, which all but 1 student mastered at 100%." (C116)	0.88
Disruption: Any event or circumstance that interrupts or alters regularly planned classroom activities (e.g., school assembly, fire drill, sporting events, technical difficulties, etc.).	"Today's class period was a bit shorter as it was a 2-hr late start due to inclement weather." (G154)	0.41

Section 4
Gaming Innovations

Chapter 22
The Use of Smart Toys in Learning Games

Peter A. Smith
University of Central Florida, USA

Shelly Welch
University of Central Florida, USA

ABSTRACT

The use of toys and videogames in learning is becoming more and more established as mediums, however, the interaction between smart toys and videogames for learning is a wholly new endeavor. With the advent of new games like Activision's Skylanders, and Disney Infinity, kids are being introduced to a new level of interaction between the real and virtual. The ability to create stories in the virtual and relive them in the real, or vice versa, is changing the way kids are playing. Applying these technologies to learning games is the next logical step in the advancement of learning games for kids. This chapter will explore what smart toys are, how they are being used, and future applications of the technology.

INTRODUCTION

While there have been a few experiments with combining toys and videogames in learning, new technologies like NFC and RFID have supercharged the link between toys and games. These new Smart Toy powered Video Games have captured the attention of the youth with creative interactions that were not previously possible. In 2014, three out of every five accessory purchase was a Smart Toy from either *Disney Infinity* or *Skylanders* games, with *Skylanders* alone grossing over $2 Billion between 2011 and 2014 (CNET, 2014). These toys have captured the hearts and minds of players and are gaining more and more floor space in videogame stores. The magic behind these toys is simply the ability to play with the same characters inside and outside of the videogames. Kids are having experiences with characters in a videogame and then reliving them in the real world when they play with their toys. Research on toys in games and their potential benefit in P-12 education is paving the way for higher levels of interaction between learning games and learners. Reviewing the current use of games and toys for consumers and educators alike is laying the ground work for the ways in which Smart Toys are becoming pervasive games, blurring the lines

DOI: 10.4018/978-1-4666-9629-7.ch022

between virtual game worlds and physical play and already containing the potential for informal learning with toys in games.

Blast Theory and Mixed Reality Lab at the University of Nottingham, makers of a location-aware game called *Can You See Me Now* (CYSMN) posed an interesting question, "In what ways can we talk about intimacy in the electronic realm" (*Blast Theory*, 2014). . While this game primarily utilized mobile GPS and WiFi technology, they created an engaging experience that blended traditional and pervasive computer gaming. In their research, they explored the level of intimacy, or an emotional experience, between Smart Toys and the children using games like *Disney Infinity*. When playing in these worlds it does seem clear that this emotional experience, or intimacy, have an effect on their gameplay and interactions of players with the real world.

The key to understanding the users' experience may be heavily based on the users' state of mind when they play these games. In an article by McGonigal (2003), she spoke about players of pervasive games, describing concepts such as "willful suspension of disbelief" and the "Pinocchio Effect." She went on to state "pervasive games, at their heart, are the dream of the virtual to be real … [and] … the dream of the players for the real to be virtual" (McGonigal, 2003). So perhaps it is not merely the game that is invoking an emotional experience but a combination of immersive pervasive gameplay as well as the users' "conscious decision to prolong the pleasures of the play experience and to apply the skills acquired in gaming to real life." (McGonigal, 2003)

BACKGROUND: DEFINING TOYS IN GAMES

While toys can be used with games in many ways, the most interesting new developments are with Smart and Pervasive Toys. Toys are changing the gameplay experience for players both in the virtual world and the physical world. It is important to understand the types of toys and games that populate this portion of the market.

Pervasive Toys

So, to understand exactly how toys in games interact with their users in the real world, first look to pervasive games. Research by Magerkurth et al, defines pervasive games as ubiquitous in nature and "no longer confined to the virtual domain of the computer, but integrate the physical and social aspects of the real world" (2005). The authors go on to describe an extensive array of pervasive gaming genres, including Smart Toys, Augmented Table Top Games, Location-Aware Games, and Augmented Reality (AR). The key component in all of these types of games seems to be the increase in physical activity and social interaction combined with the real world to create a ubiquitous pervasive game. While *Disney Infinity* seems to land in the category of Smart Toys, it does use a unique combination of cross-platform gaming using Smart Toys that cross from the physical realm to the virtual world. This brings up ideas like seamless interaction, which seeks to integrate technology into the users' daily lives (Magerkurth et al., 2005). The ubiquitous nature of these Smart Toys tends towards seamless interaction for its users. Children mentally see their favorite Smart Toys as magical characters that both share a space on their bedroom shelves, but also play with them in the virtual spaces of their games.

Smart Toys

Smart Toys are toys that interact with videogames in interesting and often electronic ways. The most common example of these is *Skylanders*. This is a series of games developed by Activision and has sold billions of dollars in toys. The toys in *Skylanders* contain Near Field Communication (NFC) chips that allow them to communicate with the game. Players are able to put their toy on a "portal of power" the game's name for an NFC scanner, and play as the character they have selected in the game. Also, this communication is not one sided. Players can save their progress on the toy and level up their unique version of the character. They toy can then be taken to other systems and used, played with outside of the game, traded with friends, and collected as part of a series of toys.

In general, computer games add immersive illusion, interactivity, fantasy, challenge, and curiosity to its users (Magerkurth, Cheok, Mandryk, & Nilsen, 2005). However the gameplay involved with games like *Skylanders*, and its rival *Disney Infinity* makes them more than just a computer game. Coulton (2012), addressed the extensive array of intereaction options available in this type of game, especially *Skylanders*, these games provide "physicality within virtual worlds to objects that also have value to their owners within the real world" (Coulton, 2012). Furthermore, other researchers suggest that the tangible interaction of Smart Toys aid in learning by supporting collaboration, ability to help focus attention, promoting storytelling in physical play, as well as support of face-to-face social interaction (Bodén, Dekker, Viller, & Matthews, 2013).

Augmented Table Top Games

Another popular method of integrating toys into games in through Augmented Table Top Games. These games tend to use Augmented Reality Markers, like QR Codes, to integrate the real world into the game world. Both the Playstation Vita and the Nintendo 3DS come with augmented reality based card games. These games have the player place markers on a table and view the action through the camera on the device. The reliance on markers makes it easy to integrate but no information is stored outside of the game.

Some *Angry Birds* games have integrated a toy technology they call Tele-Pods. The Tele-Pods are toys that represent various characters in the game and unlock these characters for play. They contain small QR Codes on their base that are held over a mobile device camera to bring them into the game. The major difference between these toys and smart toys is that smart toys are able to have information written back to them. If this feature is not key to the games design, augmented reality markers are often a superior choice.

Location Aware Games

Toys and other artifacts tend to be a great way to bring games into the real world, and as such are brought into location aware games. These are games that leverage GPS or other physical real world markers to know where the player is. The most common example of a tangible artifact in a location based game is a map, but cards and other AR markers are often included.

Sorcerers of the Magic Kingdom invites the player to find locations on a map hidden around Disney's Magic Kingdom, and then use augmented reality based trading cards to cast spells, and rescue the park from Disney villains. In Universal Studios attendees are invited to buy wands to help cast spells around the Harry Potter section of the park. These toys increase interaction with the park, increase sales of collateral objects, and help alleviate congestion in the park by sending players to less busy sections for their next mission.

DISNEY INFINITY CASE STUDY

Disney Infinity is a unique combination of gameplay and human-computer interaction methods. There are multiple types of gameplay involved, including vast virtual worlds including action-adventure gameplay as well as a sandbox mode, called the "Toy Box" mode, where the user can create their own virtual worlds and gameplay. The game is available on virtually every major platform with few exceptions, including gaming consoles, mobile devices, and computers. Some versions differ from the core game, but most have the same core gameplay. With the vast array of platforms available, users can choose from multiple modes of interaction, from controllers, touchscreen, mouse and keyboard, and Smart Toys, that represent various Disney characters. Further, all of these platforms are networked to an account online, users' have the flexibility to play *Disney Infinity (2.0 Edition)* across multiple platforms. For example, a player could play on both a PS3 at home as well as an Apple iPad while waiting for the bus. Additionally, a player could bring their favorite Disney character over to a friend's house to play, all while continuing to track each character's level progress. This particular game combines all of these options with a unique set of toys as well as additional content that come in the form of Power Disks. Power Disks are additional NFC powered pieces of plastic that can be purchased in blind packages and traded with others, similar to trading cards, while also bringing additional content into the game. Some represent world elements, like a new skybox, while others give you character a boost in some way. These can actually be stacked under the character on the portal.

While our interactions within virtual worlds tend to be synchronous or asynchronous, as described in research by Hughes (2012), the virtual worlds found inside *Disney Infinity* allow for both. Asynchronous virtual worlds only allow for turn-based communication, where only one player communicates with the virtual world at a time. A few good example of this is *Sid Meier's Civilization*, a strategy game that allow for multiple players inside a virtual world, but where play is separated by turns – only one player allowed to interact with the world at a time. Synchronous play allows for multiple players in a single virtual world at one time. Some good examples of this include *Second Life* and *World of Warcraft*, where many players access the same virtual world and can play together simultaneously.

Disney Infinity lends itself to be played both asynchronously as well as synchronously, with play both locally (i.e. multiple players using controllers on a PS3) and online (i.e. multiple players logging in remotely into the same virtual world). The gameplay found in the "PlaySets", or adventure style virtual worlds, generally tends to lean toward asynchronous play – one player completing the missions outlined in the story. On the other hand, the gameplay found in the "Toy Box" mode, or sandbox style virtual worlds, allows for synchronous play – letting players create and share user-generated content with other players online to experience the worlds together. While there are many games very similar to *Disney Infinity* with methods of gameplay, some leaning more towards synchronous play, such as *Little Big Planet*, and others lean towards asynchronous play, *Disney Infinity* has a unique combination of both.

Disney Infinity "Toy Box" mode, the sandbox style portion of gameplay, as well as the *Disney Infinity* "PlaySets", the open world or adventure style portion of gameplay. Sandbox games give players the freedom to navigate within the virtual world as they choose as well as create their own content and game objectives, as opposed to the linear design of some other virtual worlds. Open worlds also allow players to freely navigate within the virtual world, however, as seen in the case of *Disney Infinity*'s "PlaySets", enforce specific game objectives and other limitations to the virtual world not present in "Toy Box" mode, such as creating and modifying elements within the virtual world and/or adding non-player characters (NPCs). Other more linear design virtual worlds have even greater limitations to player movement and interaction within the virtual world, such as single story paths.

ANALYZING THE POTENTIAL FOR INFORMAL LEARNING

Beyond the user experience, it is also important to look at the core functionality behind *Disney Infinity*, in this case augmented physical objects such as RFID and NFC based technologies, and how that technology may benefit informal learning. For example, research by Bodén et al. (2013) looked at augmenting physical play with their augmented reality (AR) based system *Save the Wild*. This system used simple storylines associated with a fiducial marker on an origami paper figure to teach sustainability and environmental consciousness in an informal learning setting. While the primary focus of this research was to find a more cost-effective and efficient way to integrate technology into the classroom, it also sought to enhance play-based learning through the use of AR in order to augment and guide the learners' own narrative (Bodén et al., 2013, p. 228). Specifically, this research emphasized the importance of AR, as well as physical objects, in play-based learning "where the activities are by nature more exploratory and self-directed" and that these Augmented Toys tie the physical object to the in-game experience allowing for a retelling of the narrative by children during physical play (Bodén et al., 2013, p. 230). This research goes on to discuss augmented learning and the importance of physical objects (i.e., physical artefacts) in supporting collaboration, engagement, conveying meaning, as well as their affordance towards semantic representations, spatial relationships, and supporting face-to-face social interaction (Bodén et al., 2013, p. 229-230).

Research conducted using the Augmented Knights Castle, by Lampe, Hinske, and Brockmann (2006), gave a great example of how similar technology can be utilized in gameplay. This research specifically looked at the touch-me paradigm, which used mobile devices to touch Smart Toys in order to access learning information and other media such as images, video, and sound. While the research stated the importance of children playing, including psychological, psychosocial, and social development, it also stressed that "the ideal entertainment experience then comes from the combination of physical experience, virtual content, storytelling and the imagination of the user" (Lampe et al., 2006).

Just as Smart Toy technologies have been studied for their benefit in informal learning and education, video games have as well. For example, research by Squire (2003) gave an excellent overview of videogames as educational media. Additionally, research by Garrido, Miraz, Ruiz, & Gómez-Nieto (2011) used NFC mobile technology to see if pervasive game technology encouraged learning and student motivation. They found students felt the technology was easy to use, which supported focusing on the game, and that it did indeed stimulate student motivation. Additionally, research by Riekki, Cortés, Hytönen, Sánchez, & Korkeamäki (2013) stated "this technology offers great potential, specifically for children, as it enables more natural learning by exploring and creating direct links between physical world and digital data, [and] therefore, NFC could be a key technology in edutainment, as it facilitates the implementation of game like learning applications" (2013).

ISSUES, CONTROVERSIES, PROBLEMS

The biggest issue with NFC based smart toys is that they increase the price of the game beyond the average sixty dollars consumers are used to spending. This means that a single game could cost upwards of three thousand dollars to experience all of the content available in the game. Many children will want to collect all the characters available and special variants only exasperate the problem. While this might seem normal when buying toys, baseball cards, and other things that people collect. It is expected that you can play an entire game when you make a large purchase. This is somewhat alleviated by platform holders requiring that enough toys to beat the game are included in the base package, but very little of the game will be experienced if players stick to that.

Many devices are including NFC in their base functionality, this includes Android Phones, the

Wii U, and the latest iPhone (though it is still reserved only for Apple Pay). Still many NFC powered toys are still released with their own scanners. This has to do with security and additional features (like scanning more than one tag at a time) but it causes users to maintain all of this extra hardware, and increases the base cost of the games.

The most controversial issue is, smart toys unlock content that is already on the disc when you buy the game, so you are actually paying to access something that you already own. This invariably upsets some players. The idea of paying for DownLoadable Content (DLC) upsets many players when it exists on the disk, but in this case they are paying even more, and can easily lose the toy and have to buy the content all over again.

Further, some are actually hard to find. This has led to them being stolen, and counterfeited. A popular Skylander variant is painted gold. This is hard to find in store, but surprisingly easy to find on eBay as many people are just painting the original versions and reselling them.

SOLUTIONS AND RECOMMENDATIONS

While the exact economics of a smart toy integrated game are not currently figured out, this is not a reason to avoid implementing smart toys if there is a good reason for them to be integrated into a game. Players will figure it out, if the game is fun.

Integrating smart toys into a learning game has great potential to increase the interaction with learning content. The idea that a player could experience learning in the game and then replay that experience later while playing with the toy outside of the game, could lead to opportunities for reflection on their learning experience. It could bring more of a connection to the learning and improve learning outcomes.

The toys could be used to store learning progress, and could even be turned in as a solution to a test. Their ability to maintain their history in internal storage opens new opportunities to engage learners in content across multiple platforms and even in various locations outside of the game world. For example, why not allow the user to scan a toy at a museum exhibit, and then return home and use the same toy on their playstation, carrying all the knowledge they gained outside back into the original game.

The important thing to think about with smart toys is to make sure that the player can still get the learning they need without having to buy a bunch of toys. Maybe combine them into content related play sets, or make sure each toy represents access to a competency. While collecting toys is fun, it is important that it doesn't block one's ability to learn.

FUTURE RESEARCH DIRECTIONS

While this much research already exists on Smart Toys in learning games, future research possibilities still exist. For example, as of May 2015, user testing began on research looking the user experience of the game Disney Infinity (2.0 Edition), also referred to as Disney Infinity or Disney Infinity: Marvel Super Heroes (2.0 Edition). This research specifically looked to determine what factors come into play when looking at the user experience involved with the video game Disney Infinity (2.0 Edition), more specifically, if the unique combination between sandbox and Smart Toy based gameplay present in Disney Infinity (2.0 Edition) offered an additional level of immersion (Welch, 2015). Much as the previous portions of this chapter spoke of the tangible interaction of Smart Toys between the physical world and the virtual world, this future research suggests that the gameplay present in games like Disney

Infinity (2.0 Edition) is more than just a virtual world playable on a video game console – it is a unique combination of vast virtual worlds, sandbox modes, and Smart Toys all playable across multiple platforms and linked through the Internet. Overall, this research also sought to determine if the unique combination between sandbox and Smart Toy based gameplay present in Disney Infinity (2.0 Edition) offers an additional level of immersion as well as what kinds of play to users prefer to engage in while using Disney Infinity (2.0 Edition).

The research begins by defining the gameplay existing in Disney Infinity (2.0 Edition), describing gameplay using previous research on Smart Toys, pervasive games, virtual worlds, and sandbox games, offering that the gameplay present in Disney Infinity (2.0 Edition) is a unique combination of all these types of gameplay and suggests there is a unique opportunity to study the effect of these types of gameplay on immersion using games similar to Disney Infinity (2.0 Edition). The study outlines a research design using a PS3 to study participants' immersion in gameplay using "Toy Box" mode, sandbox style version gameplay offered within Disney Infinity (2.0 Edition). The research study used a between-subject design with an independent variable being Smart Toys used. Participants were divided into two groups, and data was collected utilizing video capture and surveys. Care was taken in creating the research design in order to promote autonomy and volition, allowing for a carefully selected array of Smart Toys to choose from during testing, as well as freedom in gameplay choices within Disney Infinity (2.0 Edition) "Toy Box" mode in order to provide users the freedom to interact with the game as they preferred utilizing structured or unstructured game features.

As mentioned previously, this study analyzed the effect of Disney Infinity (2.0 Edition) on immersion while playing in "Toy Box" mode, as well as the users' preference and play tendencies outside of Disney Infinity (2.0 Edition) gameplay. Thus, this research sought to determine if the Smart Toys included with Disney Infinity (2.0 Edition) have any effect on immersion, determine how players play with Smart Toys both inside and outside of gameplay, and determine if players prefer playing with the Smart Toys. Data collected will then be analyzed in order to determine any effect on immersion and play preference in regards to Smart Toy use. Additionally data will be analyzed in order to determine if any small or larger (r=0.2 or greater) correlations exist between number of game elements used and immersion and/or average amount of gameplay experience and immersion for either group.

A High-Definition Personal Video Recorder (HD PVR) was used in order to measure game elements used. A game element was defined as any object the user placed into active gameplay by way of the "Toy Box", or any object that was customized by the user during active gameplay by way of the "Magic Wand". Examples include placing a piece of furniture from the "Toy Box" into a room or changing the wallpaper in a room by using the "Magic Wand". In order to measure immersion, a post survey was offered based off of similar research on serious educational games. The Game Immersion Questionnaire (GIQ), shown in research by Cheng, She, & Annetta (2014, p. 21-22), was modified for this research and was based off previous research on immersion by Brown & Cairns (2004) and Emri & Mäyrä (2005). The immersion section of the survey consisted of three dimensions of engagement, engrossment and total immersion using a 5-point Likert scale. Additional subcategories were created and included for play preference and video game experience. These sections include a similar 5-point Likert scale and open-ended questions.

While data has yet to be analyzed for this research, as of the date this chapter was published, this research hypothesizes that the unique combination of Smart Toys and pervasive gameplay utilized in Disney Infinity (2.0 Edition) will provide for a unique opportunity for increased immersion for players using Smart Toys.

Yet, the possibility for future work continues to grow and many research possibilities still go unexplored. For example, research could be conducted to study the effects of such gameplay on participants with learning or social disorders, such as children with autism and could expand on previous research looking at the benefit of creativity and/or play for children with similar learning or social disorders. Presently, research already exists looking at the value of virtual worlds for children in this population (Bai, Blackwell, & Coulouris, 2013; Bellani, Fornasari, Chittaro, & Brambilla, 2011; Rizzo, Schutt, & Linegar, 2012; Strickland, McAllister, Coles, & Osborne 2007), most frequently looking at different methods to aid social deficits typical present in children of this population. Thus, Disney Infinity's unique use of Smart Toys, aiding the idea of "functional play" versus "symbolic play", may aid generative ability and/or social skills in children with autism or similar learning and social disorders.

Additionally, gameplay could be controlled or modified to teach scientific concepts, as suggested by Short (2012) for the popular sandbox game Minecraft. Short (2012) describes various scenarios in which this sandbox game can and is beneficial to educators in the classroom, highlighting Minecraft's specific benefits towards subjects like biology, ecology, and physics. While Minecraft is predisposed to being used as teaching tool, seen through the addition of several educational "mods" and instructional lessons using the MinecraftEDU experience, other games have this same potential (Short, 2012, p.55). Perhaps, Smart Toy based games utilizing a sandbox gameplay such as Disney Infinity could be modified and expanded on as well in future work.

Similarly, these same Smart Toy and sandbox based games could be utilized to study creativity or creative perceptions. Over the years, researchers have tried to define creativity and understand whether it is a static trait or can be taught and learned, as seen through popular creativity tests such as the Torrance Tests of Creative Thinking, which continues to be widely used and adapted in creative research. Due to the wide array of possibilities present in sandbox games, as outlined previously the game Minecraft, they lend themselves to be ideal tools for expanding on creativity research. Previous creativity tests, such as the Torrance Tests of Creative Thinking, could be modified or expanded on to include Smart Toys and virtual sandbox environments, allowing for endless opportunities for learning about creativity and how these new Smart Toy based games could play a beneficial role.

However the research possibilities associated with Smart Toy based games are not limited to these areas. Given the vast array of platforms and gameplay options available in a single game such as *Skylanders* or *Disney Infinity*, there is a wide array of research possibilities comparing gameplay across platform types (i.e., mobile, PC/desktop, console, etc.), input styles (i.e., touch-screen, controller-based, gesture-based, mouse/keyboard input, etc.), and online social interactions (i.e., user-generated content, multiplayer online gaming, etc.) branching into the fields of user experience (UX) and Human-Computer-Interaction (HCI). For example, research could be developed to study the effect of different input styles on learning by using a single game but using different input styles such as a controller on a PS3 versus the touch-screen on an iPad. This would allow researchers to utilize the benefit of premade commercial games, like *Skylanders* or *Disney Infinity*, and aid in eliminating external factors which may cause unnecessary variations in study results as is sometimes the case when using different but similar games across different platforms or input styles. Additionally, much could also be discovered analyzing the effect of Smart Toys on user-generated content or even social interactions between players in multiplayer online environments.

CONCLUSION

As described earlier, researchers have spoken to the benefit of Smart Toys in informal learning ranging from aspects like psychological and social development benefits to engagement and spatial relationships. Furthermore, researchers have studied the effect of video game play on general user experiences, pointing out how pervasive games aid their users in continuing gameplay across both virtual and physical realms, allowing players to have an immersive and emotional experience. So while most popular games utilizing toys are generally designed for entertainment purposes, the unique combination of Smart Toys and pervasive gameplay utilized in these types of games could provide a unique opportunity for fostering informal learning.

Additionally, these Smart Toy and Pervasive Toy based videogames offer a vast array of research opportunities, not only for informal learning, but also exploring this new combination of gameplay styles, player social interactions, creativity, HCI and beyond. The popularity of games like *Disney Infinity* and *Skylanders*, are no doubt on a path towards continual profit and academic research, offering even more opportunities to utilize these commercial videogames in classrooms in the future

REFERENCES

Bai, Z., Blackwell, A. F., & Coulouris, G. (2013). *Through the looking glass: Pretend play for children with autism.* Paper presented at the Mixed and Augmented Reality 2013 IEEE International Symposium. doi:10.1109/ISMAR.2013.6671763

Bellani, M., Fornasari, L., Chittaro, L., & Brambilla, P. (2011). Virtual reality in autism: State of the art. *Epidemiology and Psychiatric Sciences*, *20*(03), 235–238. doi:10.1017/S2045796011000448 PMID:21922965

BlastTheory. (2014). Retrieved from http://www.blasttheory.co.uk/research/

Bodén, M., Dekker, A., Viller, S., & Matthews, B. (2013). *Augmenting play and learning in the primary classroom.* Paper presented at the Proceedings of the 12th International Conference on Interaction Design and Children. doi:10.1145/2485760.2485767

Brown, E., & Cairns, P. (2004). *A grounded investigation of game immersion.* Paper presented at the Computer-Human Interaction extended abstracts on human factors in computing systems. doi:10.1145/985921.986048

Byron, K., & Khazanchi, S. (2012). Rewards and creative performance: A meta-analytic test of theoretically derived hypotheses. *Psychological Bulletin*, *138*(4), 809–830. doi:10.1037/a0027652 PMID:22409506

Cheng, M., She, H., & Annetta, L. (2014). Game immersion experience: Its hierarchical structure and impact on game-based science learning. *Journal of Computer Assisted Learning*; Advance online publication. doi: 10.1111/jcal.12066

Corbit, M. (2002). Building virtual worlds for informal science learning (SciCentr and SciFair) in the Active Worlds Educational Universe. *Presence (Cambridge, Mass.)*, *11*(1), 55–67. doi:10.1162/105474602317343659

Coulton, P. (2012). Skylanders: Near Field in Your Living Room Now. *Ubiquity: The Journal of Pervasive Media*, 136-138.

Dickey, M. D. (2005). Three-dimensional virtual worlds and distance learning: Two case studies of Active Worlds as a medium for distance education. *British Journal of Educational Technology*, *36*(3), 439–451. doi:10.1111/j.1467-8535.2005.00477.x

Ermi, L., & Mäyrä, F. (2005). Fundamental components of the gameplay experience: Analysing immersion. Worlds in Play: International Perspectives on Digital Games Research, 37.

Garrido, P. C., Miraz, G. M., Ruiz, I. L., & Gómez-Nieto, M. Á. (2011). *Use of NFC-based pervasive games for encouraging learning and student motivation.* Paper presented at the 3rd International Workshop on Near Field Communication. doi:10.1109/NFC.2011.13

Jarmon, L., Traphagan, T., Mayrath, M., & Trivedi, A. (2009). Virtual world teaching, experiential learning, and assessment: An interdisciplinary communication course in Second Life. *Computers & Education*, *53*(1), 169–182. doi:10.1016/j.compedu.2009.01.010

Lampe, M., Hinske, S., & Brockmann, S. (2006). *Mobile Device based Interaction Patterns in Augmented Toy Environments.* Paper presented at the Third International Workshop on Pervasive Gaming Applications, PerGames 2006, Dublin, Ireland.

Magerkurth, C., Cheok, A. S., Mandryk, R. L., & Nilsen, T. (2005). Pervasive games: Bringing computer entertainment back to the real world. *Computers in Entertainment*, *3*(3), 4–4. doi:10.1145/1077246.1077257

McGonigal, J. (2003). A real little game: The performance of belief in pervasive play. *Proceedings of DiGRA 2003.*

Riekki, J., Cortés, M., Hytönen, M., Sánchez, I., & Korkeamäki, R. L. (2013). *Touching Nametags with NFC Phones: A Playful Approach to Learning to Read Transactions on Edutainment X* (pp. 228–242). Springer.

Riekki, J., Sanchez, I., & Pyykkonen, M. (2012). *NFC-based user interfaces.* Paper presented at the 4th International Workshop Near Field Communication 2012. doi:10.1109/NFC.2012.19

Rizzo, A., Schutt, S., & Linegar, D. (2012). Imagine that: creating a 'third space' for young people with high functioning autism through the use of technology in a social setting. Paper presented at the proceedings of the 24th Australian Computer-Human Interaction Conference. doi:10.1145/2414536.2414615

Short, D. (2012). Teaching scientific concepts using a virtual world-Minecraft. *Teaching Science. The Journal of the Australian Science Teachers Association*, *58*(3).

Shwe, H., & Francetic, A. (1999). Smarter play for smart toys: The benefits of technology-enhanced play. *Zowie Intertainment White Paper, 3208.*

Squire, K. (2003). Video games in education. *Int. J. Intell. Games & Simulation*, *2*(1), 49–62.

Squire, K. (2008). Open-ended video games: A model for developing learning for the interactive age. *Open-ended video games: A model for developing learning for the interactive age* (pp. 167-198).

Strickland, D., McAllister, D., Coles, C., & Osborne, S. (2007). An evolution of virtual reality training designs for children with autism and fetal alcohol spectrum disorders. *Topics in Language Disorders*, *27*(3), 226–241. doi:10.1097/01.TLD.0000285357.95426.72 PMID:20072702

Welch, S. (2015). The User Experience of Disney Infinity: Do Smart Toys Matter? [Unpublished M.F.A. thesis]. University of Central Florida, Orlando, Florida.

KEY TERMS AND DEFINITIONS

Informal Learning: A form of learning often defined as having no set objective in terms of learning outcomes and is often referred to as learning by experience or learning via participation and often includes socialization and play.

Near-Field Communication (NFC): Technology that uses radio communication between smartphones and other similar devices, like Smart Toys, by touching them together or bringing them into proximity.

Pervasive Games: Games that integrate both physical and social aspects of the real world, including Smart Toys, Affective Gaming, Augmented Table Top Games, Location-Aware Games, and Augmented Reality.

Pinocchio Effect: A term defined by McGonigal as the desire for a game to be transformed into real life, or conversely, for everyday life to be transformed into a game.

Radio-Frequency Identification (RFID): Technology that uses wireless signals and tags containing electronically stored information, which is attached to objects such as Smart Toys.

Smart Toys: Toys (also known as Augmented Toys) generally contain NFC or RFID technology, which enable them to exist both in the physical and digital realm.

Willing Suspension of Disbelief: A term coined by Samuel Taylor Coleridge and elaborated on by McGonigal, which describes the suspension of judgment concerning the implausibility of pervasive games.

Chapter 23
Minecraft Schooling:
Digital Learning for Junior Years

Leonard Busuttil
University of Malta, Malta

Christina Gruppetta
University of Malta, Malta

Vanessa Camilleri
University of Malta, Malta

ABSTRACT

Playing digital games is an important leisure activity for a large number of us. Research shows that a large number of children play digital games for leisure purposes. One of the games played is Minecraft. This chapter outlines how Minecraft is being used in junior year settings by referring to academic literature as well as communities of practice available on the internet. The authors outline a set of activities incorporating Minecraft aimed at seven year olds which were designed to introduce a series of curricular topics in a class in a Maltese school. Following qualitative data analysis the chapter outlines a series of outcomes that were extracted from this project

INTRODUCTION

Children of the present generation are being brought up in a digital environment ringed by the latest technology and extremely interactive games. It is common to observe children spending a vast amount of time playing either on tablets, mobile phones or hand-held consoles. Busuttil, Camilleri, Dingli and Montebello found that in Malta 97.6% of 3-6 year olds and 88.7% of 7-12 year olds play digital and video games. Other reports for Europe (GameVision Europe, 2010), Australia (Brand, 2012) and the US (Lenhart, Kahne, Middaugh, Evans, & Vitak, 2008) also provide similar figures. Children enjoy playing digital games since the majority of children in the primary age bracket play digital games in their free time for at least an hour every day. The study discussed in this chapter adopts a game-based learning approach by integrating the popular game Minecraft into teaching within an educational setting. This study was inspired by the amount of time Maltese children spend playing digital games.

DOI: 10.4018/978-1-4666-9629-7.ch023

BACKGROUND

New experiences are an essential prerequisite for mental growth. According to both Pringle (1986) and Isaacs (1968), it is the opportunity of new experiences that makes learning possible. A teacher can foster, limit or impair intellectual growth depending on the opportunity and encouragement given to the pupils in class. Schools should be child-centered and discovery orientated which regard pupils as active learners. Through play the child experiences a first-hand exploration of the world and learns to cope with it. Play is usually voluntary, engaging, intrinsically motivating and possesses a make-believe element. Salomon, Perkins and Globerson (1991) observe that children are able to achieve a state of 'mindfulness' if they are intrinsically motivated by something. This leads to the acquisition of meaningful and fruitful knowledge. Isaacs and Pringle both concluded that play is extremely important for the child's intellectual development since children learn best by doing. Play allows pupils to develop holistically and to acquire new knowledge about the world they live in. It is a form of self- expression which enables pupils to release their feelings in a safe way and deal with their emotions. Through play pupils are able to explore relationships, solve problems, take risks, and use trial and error to find things out about their world.

Educational, psychological and anthropological research point out that socialization and learning throughout a person's life can be encouraged and bolstered by play. Play and imitation are natural learning strategies for children, therefore asking children to play is like asking them to do what is natural. Piaget (1962) regarded play as an assimilation scheme and imitation as an accommodation strategy. Games provide essential opportunities for individuals to develop critical thinking and problem-solving skills.

Unfortunately play and games are easy targets for misconceptions and criticism hence reducing their likelihood of being used as learning tools. The word play can be misinterpreted since it is mistakenly believed that play is only directed towards young children (Rieber, 1996; Sutton-Smith, 1997). Provost (1990) points out that play is viewed as something which one has to cease to do as he grows up. Unlike work, play is also perceived as easy and is not respectable (Rieber, 1996). On the contrary, Rieber (1996) suggests that play is an activity which stimulates and engages individuals who in turn dedicate a great deal of effort and time to it. It also encourages them to persist in challenging and difficult quests (Rieber, 1996).

Postman (2011) believes that technological change is not just an addition to a toolbox but requires a cultural change. Drastic changes in the curriculum, ways of teaching and means of accessing knowledge should be the result of progress in technology. Technology is portrayed as a tool to enhance learning, communication and proficiency in specific content (West & Bleiberg, 2013). Simulations, games, amplified reality and the spectrum of new technologies used in education are promoting significant and powerful changes in today's education (West & Bleiberg, 2013).

The complexity of teaching encompasses a range of tedious tasks which require a substantial amount of time to be grasped by students. New technologies facilitate the recollection of necessary basic facts which in turn grants the teacher time to support those students who require individual aid (West & Bleiberg, 2013). Some educators are terrorized by the thought of technology taking over their teaching career. Even though technology can be pernicious it can serve as beneficial to the teaching profession if used properly (West & Bleiberg, 2013). Technology is not replacing the teacher but is in fact an extension of the teacher. As Bill Gates notes technology is just a tool, the teacher is vitally important to get the children motivated to work together (Walker & White, 2002). The teacher's role is now even more important than ever before because their role needs to change to facilitators of learning. Technology allows teachers to target higher-level thinking and more complex skills (West & Bleiberg, 2013). Hurley believes that a teacher who succeeds at using technology appropriately is able to reach remarkable goals with the students (Gregory & Burkman, 2011).

Rieber (1996) noted that a number of different environments which encourage exploration and discovery and kindle motivation through play can be created with computers. If education is based on the discoveries of the learner, gained from new experiences, it would lead to genuine learning and understanding (Gardner, 1969). Children benefit from technology as they grow older they tend to persist at difficult tasks later on in life (David, 2009).

GAME BASED LEARNING

The horizon report emphasizes that one of the six practices that are inclined to enter mainstream education is the adoption of a game-based learning approach. Game based- learning encourages the integration of games into teaching within an educational setting (Johnson, Adams, & Cummins, 2012). DeKanter (2004) believes that an authentic context in which constructivist learning can take place can be created through the incorporation of games in class. Kutner and Olson (2008) found that parents expressed some concerns about their children being exposed to video games. Certain issues such as on screen-violence, time-wastage and lack of physical exercise developed this worrisome behaviour in parents. This might have been the result of the parents' expectations of their children's behaviour compared to their experiences at that age. This preconception could be challenged by providing an insight into the benefits of vide o-gaming.

McGonigal (2012) notes that videogames are 'fullfilling genuine human needs'. Kebritchi (2008) believes that computer games can be pedagogically successful since they possess particular characteristics which render them ideal for educational use. These include the use of action instead of explanation, the accommodation of various learning styles, the provision of a decision-making context and the preparation of students for 21st century work.

Kickmeier-Rust et al. (2007) state that digital games generate a learning experience which is more engaging, effective and satisfying. They believe that the intrinsically motivating nature of digital games allows them to be successful educational tools. In addition the provision of immediate feedback, challenges, problem-solving contexts, interactivity and elements of surprise motivate students to proceed in the game and learn (Kickmeier-Rust et al., 2007).

Three research studies carried out at an East Coast University investigated game-based learning and its effects on students' academic achievement. Results show that students who incorporated video games in their learning process possessed higher means than students who did not. Differences between genders or ethnicities did not affect the scores (Blunt, 2007)

One of the best ways to learn a language is by immersion. Learning through play is built on the same concept. In fact microworlds are created so that individuals can learn a specific subject or area of interest by living it (Papert, 1980). Microworlds give the opportunity to individuals to 'live' in the world virtually. This encourages learning through doing and self-discovery. Microworlds are a simpler model of the domain and are adapted to the child's cognitive ability. Microworlds encourage children to learn by doing at their own pace. One example of an artificial microworld is the game 'Minecraft'. This videogame has the potential to develop children into self-regulated learners. These learners are self-evaluators, intrinsically motivated, able to plan, set goals and monitor their learning, and are able to adapt the environment to their personal learning style. Self-regulated learning is genuine and effective learning (Rieber, 1996).

A number of strategies are used by teachers to engage the students using face to face classroom sessions. These strategies include praise, rewards, fear of punishments, disapproval or failure. A few amount of choice, if any, is given to the pupil and the majority of tasks are directed or interrupted by the teacher. This should not be the case and other means to capture attention should be taken into consideration. Video games could be a means of capturing pupils' attention in school (De Castell & Jenson, 2004). De Castell and Jenson (2004) recognize the importance of video gaming as a means to capture and hold attention, motivate and immerse pupils. Video games possess contextual meaning whilst being pleasurable and give choice, power and freedom to the player. They help the individual develop new ways of thinking and new skills whilst enhancing previously acquired ones. These include; motor and perceptual skills, skills to complete complex tasks, intellectual skills, psychomotor skills and multi-tasking skills. The mentioned benefits resulted in the possibility of video games having an educative role; far more motivating than any other textual resource used in class. Video games have the potential to succeed at minimizing external control whilst maximizing self- regulation and voluntary attention. This implies that 'learning' tends to shift from the teacher to the virtual environment in which attention is voluntary instead of forced. The pupil's freedom to choose what and when to learn certain topics will be maximized whilst time waiting on teachers would be minimized. This will also result in engaging and motivating pupils to produce work at their own pace. Therefore video games should be considered as a gateway to capturing pupil's voluntary attention resulting in motivated and engaged pupils (De Castell & Jenson, 2004).

Game designers have discovered core aspects which kindle a sense of happiness in human beings. They argue that happiness cannot be achieved from a single event in life. Game designers believe that reality was not created to enhance a human being's emotional state or to magnify his potential. They conclude that the activity of persisting at certain tasks is what provides intrinsic rewards which in turn lead to the production of real happiness. These findings were used in order to create virtual worlds in games to create this peace of mind. Games can act as tools which enhance life experiences especially from an emotional point of view (McGonigal, 2012). Game designer Jane McGonigal (2012) thinks that we should go all the way.

The Horizon report examines the potential outcomes of applying a game-based learning approach within an educational environment. According to the Horizon Report games have shown effective results when used as educational tools. They encourage collaboration and enhance pupil engagement in the process of learning (Johnson et al., 2012). McGonigal (2012) argues that the human being's hunger for engagement can be satisfied through gaming. Games allow pupils to develop different viewpoints and attain worthwhile goals through effective engagement. Games succeed at immersing pupils into their own learning process as well as at developing an experiential learning approach in the children. They serve beneficial in boosting cognitive development and fostering soft skills among pupils. Such soft skills include problem-solving, communication and critical-thinking (Johnson et al., 2012). McGonigal (2012) also concludes that since games require cooperation with other players to conquer certain quests gamers are skilled problem solvers and collaborators. According to DeKanter (2005) games allow students to engage in inquiry by encouraging discovery leading to solving problems on their own. Videogames grant exciting rewards, thought-provoking challenges and outstanding victories which are scarcely incorporated in the real world (McGonigal, 2012). Motivation to advance and succeed in a game enhances active engagement in students (Johnson et al., 2012). DeKanter (2005) implies that game-based learning enhances collaboration between students since it encourages negotiation of knowledge.

DeKanter (2005) suggests that games encourage students to reflect on their personal learning process. The National Education Technology Plan declared that an optimal and effective way of carrying out student assessment is through the use of games since they grant instant feedback (as cited in Hattie & Anderman, 2012). Games are able to generate immediate and genuine assessment with no testing costs (West & Bleiberg, 2013). As concluded by the Horizon report it is apparent that gaming can produce effective outcomes if applied correctly. Game-based learning promotes the development of soft skills which schools attempt to foster in their pupils (Johnson et al., 2012).

Jackson et al. (2012) investigated the relationship between twelve year old children's use of technology and their creativity using Torrance's test of creativity. Various types of technology were acknowledged one of which was specifically video game playing. Others included computer use, internet use and cell phone use. From the four types of technology, videogame playing achieved an outstanding result in the amount of creativity since it covered all measures in the test. No relationship was found in the other types of information technology. The type of videogame, gender, or race did not influence the amount of creativity. The sole cause which determined this measure was the amount of time dedicated to videogame playing. Jackson et al. (2012) concluded that videogame playing can enhance the development of creativity and serve as a form of entertainment at the same time. Therefore if videogames are incorporated in the learning process of students the barriers between education and entertainment are likely to be diminished (Jackson et al., 2012).

Computer games make use of action instead of explanation, are intrinsic motivators, reinforce mastery skills, accommodate various learning styles and prepare students for 21st century work (Kebritchi & Hirumi, 2008). According to Kebritchi & Hirumi (2008) digital games provide a meaningful, rich and appealing learning environment, immediate feedback and a high level of interactivity. All this increases effectiveness, engagement, success and satisfaction in the pupils' learning (Kebritchi & Hirumi, 2008).

McGonigal (2012) points out that those who disregard games will suffer consequences in the future since gamers will be at an advantage. She believes that the future will belong to those who possess the ability to understand, create, and play games. The reason behind this is the fact that gamers will use the skills acquired from gaming in their own lives, communities and businesses (McGonigal, 2012). According to McGonigal (2012) gaming can improve lives, businesses and whole communities.

The Horizon report points out that educators have shown significant enthusiasm towards the idea of game-based learning. The ultimate cause of educators' Interest in game-based learning is because games present a safe setting for students to learn from their mistakes. This allows them to deal positively with failure with no perilous repercussions which in turn leads to motivation and persistence in achieving particular goals. Unfortunately the absence of necessary technology or supporting tools has acted as a barrier in applying a game-based approach. In fact educators who integrate games into their lesson plans and apply a game-based approach in their teaching are quite scarce (Johnson et al., 2012).

MINECRAFT

In the journal 'Well played, a journal on video games, value and meaning' rich literacy about specific games and their value has been developed and defined by a number of contributors (Duncan, 2011). According to Duncan (2011) through this contribution an expanded knowledge-base on video games and the variety of ways in which they can be played is established (Duncan, 2011). In the mentioned journal an in-depth analysis and detailed assessment of the video-game 'Minecraft' has been conducted by the development team. Minecraft is a compelling video game which has shown superiority in the world of video games due to its world-wide recognition and success. In fact, its developer, Markus Persson, attained a number of awards such as the 'Independent Game Festival Seumas McNally Grand Prize award' in 2011.

The most fundamentally distinct characteristic which generates such a fascinating atmosphere in Minecraft is its empowerment for creativity. This as well as its unique mechanics and aesthetic sensibility are to be held responsible for the game's success (Duncan, 2011). Minecraft is an unrestricted 'sandbox' computer game with no fixed game-play and undetermined goals. Playing Minecraft is similar to playing with blocks which is simple and targeted for different players (West & Bleiberg, 2013). Since it is an open sandbox Minecraft is targeted for different kinds of players ranging from the adventurous to the timid player (Duncan, 2011).

Minecraft Worlds

The presented worlds in Minecraft are constructed of a number of blocks and are all boundless and diverse. All material which can be found is constituted of blocks. The 'Education Technology success stories' report points out that the surface area of a Minecraft world is larger than that of Neptune's if each block has one-meter long sides. These worlds possess similar characteristics as Earth. In fact Minecraft generates different biomes such as forest, mountain, jungle and swamp which all incorporate a climate specific to them and an ordinary day night cycle (West & Bleiberg, 2013). Physics and chemistry principles as well as the laws of nature are maintained in Minecraft which enhance the accuracy of the simulation of Earth (Short, 2012). The stimulus to activity is the environment itself therefore organising it in a way which provokes the children to active and constructive learning is essential (Pringle, 1986). Minecraft's virtual worlds possess the potential to be developed into intellectual playgrounds which encourage exploration and discovery (West & Bleiberg, 2013).

MINECRAFT'S GAME-PLAY

Minecraft is a sandbox, construction-based game. Minecraft players collect resources which they use to construct items in-world. These items range from simple buildings to whole villages consisting of castles, electrical circuits and engines powered with coal (Duncan, 2011; West & Bleiberg, 2013). Minecraft features a range of different play modes. These include the 'Minecraft classic', the single-player mode, and a multi-player option. The virtual world of Minecraft grants the player two main objectives which include the creative and the survival elements. One can also choose to play in creative mode which eliminates the survival element so that the player can focus on the creative aspect of the game (Duncan, 2011).

The game itself encourages the players to quickly start creating something simple which will then lead to the creation of more elaborate structures within Minecraft. The initial step requires the creation of a world for the player to reside in. The whole game space is made up of a vast number of meter-square blocks similar to LEGO. These blocks range from material such as wool, coal and wood to trees, clouds and animals. A few empty slots for storing weapons are located at the bottom of the screen below the health of the player represented by a number of hearts. The constant presence of a block on the right hand side of the screen represents the hand of the player (Duncan, 2011).

The players have total freedom to construct and create anything from the provided material. No guidance or instruction is provided in the game's interface which affords more freedom to the player. After collected, building blocks and simple items from the world can be recombined to create more complex material using Minecraft's crafting interface. The player can then proceed into using the material to construct distinct buildings and create anything. Mastering crafting skills which lead to the creation of more efficient and stronger constructions develop whilst progressing in the game and making more effective use of the building blocks. In the survival mode of the game a number of monsters such as zombies and spiders roam at night therefore structures created have to provide a protective function (Duncan, 2011).

West & Bleiberg (2013) found that Minecraft succeeds as a game by allowing pupils of different skill levels to learn from it. They quote a number of teachers who incorporated Minecraft into their teaching and achieved outstanding results. These included enhancement of creativity skills and exploration skills, risk-taking and motivation. West & Bleiberg (2013) concluded that Minecraft, as a dynamic and flexible game, increases the opportunities for learning to occur. Motivational researchers attributed a number of characteristics to learning environments which are intrinsically motivating. These include; fantasy, control, curiosity and challenge (Lepper & Malone, 1987). Minecraft is able to meet these four important characteristics of intrinsic motivation.

The game's simplicity and flexibility allows players of different ages with varying skills to learn from it. It gives an opportunity to teachers to apply a constructivist approach and exploit the students' potential. Minecraft allows students of any background be active participators in their own learning process. Students playing the game are able to progress at a comfortable pace and be rewarded for their individual effort and talent (West & Bleiberg, 2013). It manages to assemble a number of players to move their way through the game and solve problems collaboratively. It is of a high educational value since its game-play requires leadership, team work and exploration (Johnson et al., 2012). Minecraft encourages constructivist learning since it allows students to gain accurate information through personal exploration in Minecraft's simulations. The players encounter a context which is familiar and relevant and which allows them to direct their own learning (West & Bleiberg, 2013). It succeeds at engaging the player within the game (Duncan, 2011) and manages to develop soft skills in children including problem solving, critical thinking, collaboration, communication and digital literacy (Johnson et al., 2012) This game also succeeds at satisfying the need for adventure which most children crave for since it encourages exploration (Duncan, 2011).

MINECRAFT IN EDUCATION

One of the five success stories featured in the 'Education Technology success stories' report is Minecraft (West & Bleiberg, 2013). Minecraft's user generated content lead to the game being adapted for different purposes in different contexts ranging from the development of other games to the generation of experiential experiments. The overall design of the game has cropped up an interest in various people to use it for other reasons rather than just for enjoyment purposes. In fact a number of educators recognised the educational value of incorporating Minecraft in their lesson plans. The game as an instructional space in which children can learn and explore as well as reach both educational and non-educational goals served as an awareness for the game's educational potential. Exploiting elements in Minecraft allows the individual to create unusual environments in which educational goals can be reached (Duncan, 2011).

According to Kebritchi & Hirumi (2008) a game has to possess the ability to adapt to the pupils' knowledge, skills, abilities and motivation .If these are not addressed the computer game fails to be an effective resource since a 'one size fits all' approach is not effective with every pupil. In fact according to Kickmeier-Rust et al. (2007) digital games which possess the ability to adapt to the students' knowledge, skills, motivation and abilities are the most effective. Fortunately, these characteristics are all incorporated into the game of Minecraft which allows it to move away from the 'one size fits all' approach of learning. This renders Minecraft's learning environment suitable for different individual needs and preferences resulting in more effective results. Minecraft is portrayed as a platform for adequate and effective improvement in Education (West & Bleiberg, 2013). In Minecraft, discovery and knowledge construction are key to solve problems and advance in the game. Managing to incorporate traditional educational topics so that they can be perceived as a natural part of the game-play is a recurring challenge in game-based learning (Johnson et al., 2012). Through the incorporation of Minecraft in the classroom this can be made possible. It is a powerful and extremely flexible game which is able to present educators with a new and effective way of instructing students. This educational game has the potential to help teachers give out high quality and valuable lessons (West & Bleiberg, 2013). In fact 'Minecraft' has been incorporated into lesson plans to teach the school curriculum by some educators (Johnson et al., 2012). It could also serve as freeing tool which decreases the teacher's demands and grants them with more time to teach (West & Bleiberg, 2013).

MINECRAFT IN SCHOOLS

A team of educators who individually possess a unique skill can work collaboratively to design interventions using Minecraft. Minecraft can be used as a self-directed learning tool across the whole curriculum in different subject areas. Using Minecraft as an assessment tool can help teachers assemble information and identify new talents, skills and masteries possessed by their students. During a literature lesson Minecraft can be used to recreate particular scenes from a book. Science principles can be experimented with and reinforced through the use of Minecraft. Minecraft provides an opportunity for teachers to teach digital citizenship since it introduces the concept of survival, problem-solving and cooperation. This digital-game also allows students to explore particular locations such as the Roman Coliseum, the Tower of Pisa and the Egyptian pyramids. The students' abilities and opportunities to visit such places are increased through Minecraft (West & Bleiberg, 2013).

Minecraft's flexibility has opened doors for different individuals to accommodate its setting for other essential experiences rather than just for enjoyment purposes. In fact exposure to Minecraft led various educators to use the game within other world-wide educational environments (Duncan, 2011). Kay, Groom, and Stuckey (2011) point out that teacher communities such as 'Massively Minecraft' which have emerged by time allow teachers to share experiences and explore different modes of using Minecraft across the curriculum (as cited in Duncan, 2011). Educators have developed a community to encourage the use of Minecraft in teaching. This community has created a Minecraft teaching wiki for lesson plans and research regarding the topic to be shared (West & Bleiberg, 2013).

In 2010, Joel Levin succeeded at creating a blog called 'The Minecraft Teacher' in which he recorded his experiences at using Minecraft in an educational setting with six and seven year olds (Duncan, 2011). Webster (2011) points out that Levin modified Minecraft to allow players to become resistant to any damage so that the focus remains on construction and the educational element (as cited in Duncan, 2011). According to Levin this encourages creativity in students (Duncan, 2011).

Other educators developed the ability to use Minecraft in order to teach specific topics and content areas which made way to new and exciting learning experiences (Schifter & Cipollone, 2013). At Yokohama International school in Japan 'Minecraft' is utilized in its humanities program. It is integrated into the following topics; early humans, earth and man, early civilizations, and Renaissance. It is primarily used as a way for helping eleven and twelve year old students to work together and explore different environments, models of buildings, architectural structures as well as the relationship between humans and the environment (Johnson et al., 2012).

In 2010, Michael Kolich, Alexi Chow, and Tim Mason, undergraduates at Miami University, succeeded at creating a game prototype called Circuit Madness. This game was designed within Minecraft and specifically targeted the teaching of logic. They built the needed environments and devices using common items found in Minecraft. The game required players to solve simple logical operators in order to advance to the next room (Duncan, 2011).

Jeffery Adams, a middle school science teacher in Toronto, incorporated Minecraft in his lessons which tackled sustainable planning. Building a sustainable city with minimum energy usage was the ultimate goal of this lesson. The majority of the students decided to use Minecraft in order to achieve this goal. They succeeded at creating these virtual city models and subsequently each was given a specific role including miner, builder and farmer. Two surveys conducted by Adams before and after the activity indicated that Minecraft served as a boost to the students' engagement and performance levels (West & Bleiberg, 2013). In fact eighty-six percent of the students expressed a desire to use Minecraft again and eighty percent considered gaming as a means to increase their creativity and freedom (Johnson et al., 2012).

An English teacher, Mr. Reeves, in a Northeastern U.S school used Minecraft to assess twenty students' understanding of point of view and characterization in narratives. Four of his female students hesitated to play the digital game and instead opted to use the school premises and a video camera. Mr Reeves observed that the students who used Minecraft took the task more seriously than the others who did not use Minecraft since their end result was extremely well developed. After evaluating the knowledge against an assessment rubric, Mr Reeves concluded that Minecraft helped students achieve higher levels of knowledge about characterization and plot (Schifter & Cipollone, 2013).

Yager and Weeding, teachers at an Australian school, integrated Minecraft into a science lesson conducted with 12-13 year old boys. The students were required to build a city model which is efficient in its energy use in five days. Ninety-six percent of them chose Minecraft as a form of presentation. The students encountered daily challenges in mathematics, science and languages in order to apply a multidisciplinary approach and maintain students' concentration. At the end of this project the teachers discovered that the students developed risk-taking skills and appreciated the freedom and flexibility granted by Minecraft (West & Bleiberg, 2013).

'It is games that give us something to do when there is nothing to do. We thus call games "pastimes" and regard them as trifling fillers of the interstices of our lives. But they are much more important than that. They are clues to the future. And their serious cultivation now is perhaps our own salvation' (Suits, 2005).

MINECRAFT IN A MALTESE SCHOOL: A PILOT STUDY

Following an overview of literature on Minecraft and game based learning this chapter now explores the study conducted in a Maltese school with a mixed ability year 4 (8 year old) group of students.

Planning the Minecraft Sessions

Six sessions that met the level of seven-year old children were planned over a six week period. Three topics were introduced to the students and each was integrated with the academic syllabus including the Maltese, English and Social Studies syllabus. Each topic was tackled in two one-hour sessions held every Friday for six consecutive weeks. Lesson plans as well as other resources related to the specific topics were prepared and presented to the children in the six sessions. The main resource used in these sessions was the digital game, Minecraft, which was installed on six tablets. Each student was given a tablet to work with in each session.

Children were given various tasks to carry out on Minecraft using the tablets provided. Pre/Post session questionnaires and ongoing observations provided the researchers with ample information to analyze the use of Minecraft as a main recourse to teach parts of the year four syllabus in a Maltese school. The researcher who carried out the sessions also kept a self-evaluation journal which was also used as a source of information during data analysis. The children's reactions and feedback were recorded both during the non-formal conversations between the researcher and the children and from the two questionnaires which were given prior and after the project.

The study aimed to anaylse whether Minecraft is a suitable educational tool to help students learn certain topics found in the local syllabus in a child-discovery oriented way. It also aimed to find out whether Minecraft is able to equip students with particular soft skills and allows students to progress at a comfortable pace. The study aimed to examine whether Minecraft increases the opportunities for learning to occur and to motivate students to develop knowledge through action and exploration.

Learning activities are 'the public face of instruction, a visible performance of learning and teaching'. In order for learning activities to be relevant, effective and appropriate they must be based on solid objectives. Sessions were planned out with clear objectives since as suggested by Reeves (2011), teachers should envision their teaching in terms of what the students' knowledge and abilities after the lesson rather than during the actual lesson.

According to Reeves (2011) human beings learn mostly through interacting with others and communicating ideas. If individuals understand the purpose for their learning they develop a better understanding. They enjoy moving about, solving problems, discovering new things, being creative, making things and learning how their world works. Students can experience these through cooperative learning, making presentations, peer feedback, brainstorming, discussions, discovery learning hands- on learning, playing games, field trips and problem solving activities. Unfortunately these activities are minimally encouraged through most teaching methods. Teachers can use Bloom's Taxonomy in order to help students move from the lowest levels of knowledge to the highest.

De Freitas and Oliver (2006) note that frameworks which help teachers evaluate the pupils' learning through games are crucial since they allow them to be reflective. A reflective practitioner becomes engaged in a reflective cycle that results in the development of new action theories and strategies as well as in change and increase in the effectiveness of both the learning environment and the educator's practice (Hallet, 2012). In order to assess the effectiveness of learning activities an assessment rubric tied with Bloom's Taxonomy was used in this study. This assessment rubric was used to assess the attainment of the students as well as a reflective instrument on the part of the teaching researcher. The teaching researcher used the assessment rubric to reflect on whether the higher levels of Bloom's taxonomy were reached during the class. Reeves (2011) suggests that by reflecting on their teaching methods teachers ted to improve their practice.

The study did not aim to find out the children's skill level at using Minecraft. It aimed at finding out the educational benefits of the exposure to Minecraft through the use of an assessment Rubric tied with Bloom's Taxonomy. This allowed the researchers to analyze and conclude whether Minecraft was a suitable teaching resource. Figure 1 shows the assessment rubric used by the researchers to assess the achievement of each child participant during the session, in this case the social studies session.

Figure 1. Assessment rubric for the social studies session

Name of Student:						
Sessions 5 & 6: Social Studies						
Levels of Bloom's Taxonomy	Criteria	Score				
		Excellent	Good	Fair	Needs Improvement	Not Assessed
Level 1: Knowledge	Answer questions about the video.					
	List the ways the team worked together.					
Level 2: Comprehension	Say what happened in the video in one's own words.					
	Discuss the message of the story.					
Level 3: Application	Discuss the importance of teamwork.					
	Distinguish elements between good and bad teamwork practices.					
Level 4: Analysis	List down places and things needed for survival in the village.					
	Discuss attitudes needed for good teamwork.					
Level 5: Synthesis	Create a plan of tasks assigned to each student.					
	Create part of a village on Minecraft.					
Level 6: Evaluation	Discuss the experience of working within a group.					
	Identify better ways for working in a group.					

Each rubric was accompanied with a marking sheet which helped the observer identify the level attained by the student observed. The following list is the marking sheet used for the assessment rubric in Figure 1.

1. Answer questions about the video.
   a. **Excellent:** Student is able to answer both higher order and lower order questions
   b. **Good:** Student is able to answer lower order questions
   c. **Needs improvement:** Student finds it hard to answer questions about the video
2. List the ways the team worked together.
   a. **Excellent:** Student is able to discuss the ways the team worked together and give the reasons behind the teamwork
   b. **Good:** Student is able to name some ways the team worked together
   c. **Needs improvement:** Student finds it hard to name the ways the team worked together
3. Say what happened in the video in one's own words.
   a. **Excellent:** Student is able to explain what happened in his own words whilst referring to the characters of the video and giving reasons behind their actions
   b. **Good:** Student is able to point out what happened in the video in his own words.
   c. **Needs improvement:** Student finds it hard to explain what happened in the video.
4. Discuss the message of the story.
   a. **Excellent:** Student is able to discuss the message of the story and supports it with logical reasons
   b. **Good:** Student is able to discuss the message of the story but does not support it with logical reasons

c. **Needs improvement:** Student finds it hard to discuss the message of the story

5. Discuss the importance of teamwork.
   a. **Excellent:** Student is able to discuss the importance of teamwork and supports his statements with logical reasons
   b. **Good:** Student is able to discuss the importance of teamwork of the but does not support his statements with logical reasons
   c. **Needs improvement:** Student finds it hard to discuss the importance of teamwork
6. Distinguish elements between good and bad teamwork practices.
   a. **Excellent:** Student is able to name the differences between good and bad teamwork practices and supports these with logical reasons
   b. **Good:** Student is able to name the differences between good and bad teamwork practices but does not support it with logical reasons
   c. **Needs improvement:** Student finds it hard to discuss differences between good and bad teamwork practices
7. List down places and things needed for survival in the village.
   a. **Excellent:** Student is able to suggest places and things needed for survival supported by logical reasons
   b. **Good:** Student is able to suggest places and things needed for survival supported but does not support his statement with logical reasons
   c. **Needs improvement:** Student is not able to suggest places and things needed for survival
8. Discuss attitudes needed for good teamwork.
   a. **Excellent:** Student is able to discuss attitudes needed for good teamwork supported with examples and logical reasons
   b. **Good:** Student is able to discuss attitudes needed for good teamwork but may not be supported with logical reasons
   c. **Needs improvement:** Student finds it hard to discuss attitudes needed for good teamwork
9. Create a plan of tasks assigned to each student.
   a. **Excellent:** Student is able to contribute in the discussion whilst giving reasons for his ideas
   b. **Good:** Student is able to contribute in the discussion but may not provide reasons for his ideas
   c. **Needs improvement:** Student finds it hard to contribute in the discussion or may suggest unsuitable ideas
10. Create part of a village on Minecraft.
   a. **Excellent:** Student is able to create the assigned part of the village on Minecraft according to the plan
   b. **Good:** Student is able to create the assigned part of the village on Minecraft but may deviate from the plan
   c. **Needs improvement:** Student finds it hard to create his part of the village on Minecraft and ignores the plan completely
11. Discuss the experience of working within a group.
   a. **Excellent:** Student is able to discuss the experience in great detail supporting the statements with logical reasons and examples from personal experience
   b. **Good:** Student is able to discuss the experience but may not support his statements with reasons and examples
   c. **Needs improvement:** Student finds it hard to discuss the experience or may point out irrelevant episodes of his experience

12. Identify better ways for working in a group.
    a. **Excellent:** Student is able to identify better ways and support with logical reasons
    b. **Good:** Student is able to identify better ways but may not support with logical reasons
    c. **Needs improvement:** Student finds it hard to identify better ways for working in a group and may deviate from the subject during his contribution in the discussion

Recruiting the Participants

The study was conducted as part of the one tablet per child pilot initiative which was researching the introduction of tablets in Maltese primary schools. A class from a volunteer school was chosen and six tablets were awarded to be used by students during this study. The number of tablets made available for this study resulted in limiting the number of participants to six too. Since the purpose of a qualitative study is to generate meaning and not to generalize or to be representative (Merriam, 2009) the limited sample size was not deemed to be a hindrance in this study. Notwithstanding, the authors feel the need to stress that had the study been carried out with another class/ group of students the same results might not have been achieved. The results obtained from this study are limited to this group of students.

Participants were recruited through a random sampling method from one year 4 classroom. All students were given two information sheets about the project one aimed at parents whilst the other aimed at the students. Children interested in participating in the study had to fill in both consent forms and hand them in to their class teacher. Since twelve participants were interested in participating in this project, six were selected through a random sampling technique. This allowed participants to be chosen in a fair manner. This group was taken out of their classroom for one hour on every Friday afternoon for six consecutive weeks. Each student was given a tablet for the first time and could participate in the previously-planned activities as outlined below

A Review of the Activities

The first and second sessions tackled the language of instruction. The Maltese syllabus for year 4 classes refers to the ability of children to be able to listen to instructions and directions in the native language whilst also giving directions and instructions to others.

In the first session a set of instructions were read out to the children. The students were then given a set of instructions in order to build a building on Minecraft. This allowed the students to familiarize themselves with Minecraft and provided the teaching researcher time to check whether the students were able to follow instructions. In the second session the students were asked to write a set of instructions for their peers. They were divided in pairs and asked to exchange their sets of instructions. To conclude students provided feedback to each other group on whether the building constructed tallied with the instructions.

The third and fourth session focused on creative writing linked with Julia Donaldson's book 'The Gruffalo'. These sessions were linked to the year 4 English syllabus sections which focus on participation in oral activities in the English language and to write a set of sentences based on their language ability. The third session the book entitled 'The Gruffalo' was read out to the students. They were then asked to sketch the house/territory where they think the Gruffalo lives. This sketch was later on transformed into a 3D model in Minecraft. During the fourth session students were asked to write a few sentences about their Gruffalo's house/territory by referring to particular details found in the 3D models created in Minecraft.

The fifth and sixth sessions focused on teamwork and communication skills which feature predominantly in the social studies syllabus. An animated teamwork video clip featuring the penguins of Madagascar was shown to the students. A discussion about the importance of teamwork for survival ensued. This discussion was followed by a collective brainstorming session. The list that resulted from the brainstorming sessions included different places, things and attitudes needed for survival in a Minecraft village. A task was assigned to each student by the teaching researcher. These tasks included building a food shop, building a hospital and building sheltered accommodation. Students were then left free to build their own village to live in whilst communicating with other students in class and respecting each other's work. To conclude a discussion about whether it was easy or difficult to work in a team and create a village together was carried out.

OUTCOMES OF THE PROJECT

In this section of the chapter we will focus on the outcomes of the Minecraft based activities held during this study. We will also look at how these outcomes relate to the literature outlined previously.

Participants' Views of Using Minecraft in the Classroom

Every participant found Minecraft easy to play. The study participants were motivated to play Minecraft on their own tablet and pointed out that they did not realize they were discussing topics from the year 4 syllabus whilst playing Minecraft. These sessions where experienced as 'play time' by the students who gained knowledge and persisted at difficult tasks. It is apparent that the researcher succeeded at creating play inspired activities since all participants agreed, in the post-questionnaire, that playing Minecraft in class was an enjoyable activity. Participants also acknowledged Minecraft's educational potential since all participants agreed that Minecraft can be used to help other students learn about a topic in the school syllabus.

Intrinsic Motivation and Persistence

From first hand observations of the researcher and feedback given by the participants it was evident that the students were intrinsically motivated with Minecraft. This corroborates Rieber (1996)'s view that play is usually voluntary, engaging and intrinsically motivating. This view was also apparent in the children's attitude during the sessions. Even though sessions were held on a Friday afternoon, which is usually the time in which children feel the most exhausted and lack motivation to work, the students still participated in lessons with great enthusiasm and effort. Participants showed their interest in Minecraft through their comments such as:

I bought a version of Minecraft to play at home

I searched YouTube on the procedure to use to build a fireplace in Minecraft

YouTube is full of videos on how to build in Minecraft and I found the videos extremely useful.

These comments indicate that participants were enjoying the sessions and were motivated to continue learning outside the classroom. This supports Jackson et al. (2012)'s belief that if videogames are incorporated in the learning process of students the barriers between education and entertainment are likely to be diminished.

Minecraft was able to satisfy the participant's hunger for engagement which resulted in the dedication of a great deal of effort and time to it. Rieber (1996) believes that play and imitation are natural learning strategies for children which in turn effectively engage individuals. It also backs up Kickmeier-Rust et al. (2007)'s statement that digital games generate a learning experience which is more engaging, effective and satisfying. This engagement allowed the participants to develop different viewpoints on certain topics since it targeted their different learning styles. This supports Johnson, Adams, & Cummins (2012)'s belief that games targeted at teaching specific content can assist students in developing different viewpoints and encourage them to tackle such content in diverse and more complex ways.

The researcher did not have to use an external motivation system such as a reward chart to control the students' behavior. Since students were engaged in-world in Minecraft they were intrinsically motivated by this digital game and there were no behavior problems whilst all the students participated wholeheartedly. The fact that every participant felt successful during the sessions decreased the feelings of anxiousness and frustration which resulted in more cooperation. This supports De Castell and Jenson (2004)'s assertion that video games provide a means of capturing pupils' attention in school and having the potential to succeed at minimizing external control whilst maximizing self- regulation and voluntary attention. This means that 'learning' shifts from the teacher to the virtual environment in which attention is voluntary instead of forced. The participants' intrinsic motivation led to the acquisition of meaningful and fruitful knowledge as Rieber (1996) suggested. Salomon, Perkins, & Globerson (1991) stress that children are able to achieve a state of 'mindfulness' if they are intrinsically motivated by something.

Persistence in certain tasks was also evident in the majority of the sessions. This can be seen in one instance when a child managed to construct a bunk bed even though this activity initially seemed like an impossible task to perform. Such episodes show that digital games encourage individuals to persist in challenging and difficult quests. It also supports Kebritchi & Hirumi (2008)'s stance that since digital games provide a meaningful, rich and appealing learning environment they increase effectiveness, engagement, success and satisfaction in the pupils' learning.

Self-Learning Skills

Results obtained from the assessment rubrics, observations and informal conversations indicated that the students acquired knowledge through their own discoveries and experiences on Minecraft. Some examples include their rational suggestions regarding improving their instruction writing after actually writing their own and following their peer's instructions. As suggested by Gardner (1969) these results support the idea that if education is based on the discoveries of the learner, gained from new experiences it would lead to genuine learning and understanding.

Students were able to advance in Minecraft by trying things out and making new discoveries. An important discovery which one of the students made affected the other participants during the social studies session. When a child, through trial and error, discovered how to make a bomb. In process most of the village being constructed was accidentally exploded. Students had to work together in order to put out the fire caused by the bombs and save their village from destruction. One of the students showed the rest of the group how to extinguish the fire by using buckets of water and everyone quickly followed suit. After managing to put out the fire, the students realized that their village was flooded. They had to collect all the water in empty buckets in order to save their village again. This incident created a situation where the children could engage in what Craft (2013) calls 'possibility thinking'. The children tried to identify different possibilities they could use to stop the floods from ruining their village .These included building a stone barrier around their village and digging out canals around their village through which water could drain. This episode allowed students to develop their critical thinking, communication and problem-solving skills as well as explore relationships, solve problems, take risks, and use trial and error strategies to find things out world.

During the sessions it was evident that Minecraft provided an ideal space for the students to learn through their own discoveries. The participants were allowed to explore the world, inventory, resources and different Minecraft terms on their own. The game also provided the players with immediate feedback and assessment. These results support DeKanter (2005)'s belief that games allow students to engage in inquiry by encouraging discovery, leading to solving problems on their own. The students were also given the responsibility to solve any disputes on their own during the social studies lessons. These instances allowed the students to learn through their own discoveries whilst the researcher provided some guidance in order to help them stay on task. This reinforces Wastiau et al. (2013)'s idea that when a game-based approach is incorporated, the teacher's main role is to guide while the students maintain control over their own learning.

From first hand observations of the researchers it is evident that the students were able to learn from their mistakes and develop an experiential learning approach. Minecraft allowed students to deal positively with failure in a safe environment. Students persisted in the tasks when they failed to succeed in on their first try and managed to attain good outcomes in more complex tasks such as building a bunk bed, a round cave, and a functioning barbeque. This supports Johnson et al. (2012)'s belief that games present a safe setting for students to learn from their mistakes with no perilous repercussions which in turn leads to motivation and persistence in achieving goals. This also supports West & Bleiberg (2013)'s conclusion that Minecraft, as a dynamic and flexible game, increases the opportunities for learning to occur.

Minecraft as an Assessment Tool

Minecraft allowed the researcher to immediately assess both the process and the product of the students' work. This provided the teaching researcher with opportunity to learn more about the students' needs, likes and learning styles. West & Bleiberg (2013) believe that Minecraft as an assessment tool can help teachers assemble information and identify new talents, skills and masteries possessed by their students. Since Minecraft awarded students with immediate feedback the students could easily assess their own work. This supports West & Bleiberg (2013)'s idea that games are able to generate immediate and genuine assessment with no testing costs.

Achieving Educational Goals

Through the use of Minecraft as a teaching resource the researcher was able to incorporate traditional educational topics so that they can be perceived as a natural part of the game-play. This allowed the researcher to reach some remarkable goals with her students. The Horizon report states that gaming can produce effective outcomes if applied correctly (Johnson et al., 2012). This supports Duncan (2011)'s belief that Minecraft allows the individual to create unusual environments in which educational goals can be reached. All of the pre-planned educational goals and lesson objectives were achieved through Minecraft, both in a direct and indirect manner. The first few levels of Bloom's taxonomy were achieved through the use of different resources such as the book 'The Gruffalo', the Gruffalo's toy model, video clips and games. However the challenge remains in the last few levels of Bloom's taxonomy. The students were able to reach these higher levels by using Minecraft as her main teaching tool.

Participants also believe that Minecraft can help other students learn more about certain topics through Minecraft. Reasons for their responses included the fact that Minecraft allowed them to use their imagination, to be more creative and to think and reflect about how they can create certain buildings. In addition students also agreed that Minecraft should be used at their school and incorporated into lessons.

High levels were scored on the assessment rubric based on Bloom's taxonomy because Minecraft allowed students to turn their abstract ideas into concrete concepts. One such example is the session in which students had to create the Gruffalo's territory. Minecraft was able to stimulate the students to write detailed sentences about the place where the Graffalo lives since they were able to visualise the imagined Graffalo adobe by creating it in Minecraft. This observation supports De Castell & Jenson (2004)'s statement that games provide the opportunity for pupils to choose what and when to learn certain topics resulting in the minimization of waiting time for the teacher's help. This resulted in the transformation of the students into self-regulated learners which was evident during the sessions. In fact students often evaluated their own work, set personal goals, created a plan, and adapted Minecraft's environment to their personal learning style. As a result the researcher was rewarded with more time to help the children who experienced difficulties. This ensures that all the students are on task at all times and therefore no learning time is wasted. When students experienced writer's block the researcher could easily ask them questions about their own creation on Minecraft in order to prompt them. This allowed the researcher to help students think more about their own work and their reasons behind it rather than about something abstract.

Another reason for these goal achievements is that even though all participants had different skills and abilities they were all able to learn from Minecraft and succeed in the game differently. This observation supports Kickmeier-Rust et al. (2007)'s idea that digital games which possess the ability to adapt to the students' knowledge, skills, motivation and abilities are the most effective. This resulted from the game's various characteristics which make it flexible resulting in children learning at their own pace. One of the participants had never even used a tablet before so she advanced in the game differently than two other students who had prior experience playing Minecraft. The students with prior Minecraft experience managed to create more complex and detailed buildings. This indicated that Minecraft was able to exploit the potential of each child even though they possessed different levels of expertise in the game. Minecraft was able to adapt to the participant's knowledge, skills, abilities and motivation which resulted in an effective learning tool. These observations support West & Bleiberg (2013)'s belief that Minecraft's simplicity and flexibility allows players of different ages with varying skills to learn from it. Students playing the game are able to progress at a comfortable pace and be rewarded for their individual effort and talent. This results in helping teachers move away from a 'one size fits all' approach to learning.

It was interesting to note that the teacher did not have to use a reward system to control the students' behavior. Students were engaged in Minecraft and were intrinsically motivated by this digital game. There were virtually no behavior problems and every student participated wholeheartedly. Through the use of Minecraft as a teaching resource the teacher was able to incorporate traditional educational topics as part of the game-play. This allowed the researcher to reach some remarkable goals with her students.

The perceptions of the children participants on the use of Minecraft during the classroom sessions is also important to take note of. In the post session questionnaire all of the students who participated in the sessions agreed that Minecraft should be used at their school and incorporated into lessons. The participants' reasons for these results included the fact that Minecraft allows students to use their imagination and to be more creative. Some of them also believe that Minecraft is fun to play and it is already a popular game amongst them.

One of the participants had a one-to-one learning support assistant (LSA) due to his inability to read and write on his own. During these Minecraft sessions the teacher allowed Liam[1] to participate on his own without the help of the assigned LSA. Minecraft provided a context in which the teacher could easily check that everyone was engaged and stayed on task. This allowed more time for the teacher to provide one to one help to Liam. The teacher built a stronger relationship with Liam. This supports West & Bleiberg (2013)'s idea that new technologies grant the teacher time to support those students who require individual aid. This finding merits further research since the study was conducted with a small group size and therefore a different result could have been obtained with a larger class.

Communication Skills

Communication skills between students were enhanced through Minecraft especially during the social studies sessions in which students had to build their own village in the same world. Participants had to communicate with one another in order to build the village according to the plan they created earlier with in class. Communication about in-world activities flowed into the class too. The class was filled with a buzz of activity during Minecraft time. Children communicated on the location of buildings, the colors used to and the location of primary materials in the Minecraft world. These observations supports West & Bleiberg (2013)'s point that technology is a tool which enhances learning and communication. In fact all of the participants in this Minecraft study believed that their communication skills have been developed through the Minecraft based activities.

The participants had to solve disputes which cropped up whilst creating their own village. Such conflicts resulted from their individualism and lack of group work skills. Students mostly quarreled when building space was limited due to others building in the same area. The participants realized that they had to reach compromises if they wanted to succeed and advance in the game. Their collaboration and problem solving skills were developed through solving their disputes and reaching compromises. In one such situation two students wanted to build structures in the same area. To solve the dispute one of the students offered to show his class mate how to build a fireplace as long as the class mate would in turn allowed him to build in the area. Children were using the game environment to engage in active mediation and conflict resolution. Johnson et al. (2012)'s are right when suggesting that Minecraft is of a high educational value since to succeed in the game-play leadership and team work skills are required. As McGonigal (2012) points out since games require cooperation with other players to conquer certain quests, gamers become skilled problem solvers and collaborators. Johnson et al. (2012) also state that games encourage collaboration and enhance pupil engagement in the process of learning.

Students were able to realize that communication was key in order to complete the assigned task. In fact the majority of the participants believe that the social studies sessions were the most enjoyable of the sessions were Minecraft was used in class. Reasons for their responses included the fact that these sessions included more action, teamwork and the sharing of ideas. This supports Duncan (2011)'s belief that Minecraft succeeds at satisfying the need for adventure which most children crave for.

Creative Skills

From first hand observations of the researcher and the participant's work it was evident that Minecraft enhanced the student's creative skills. This was most apparent during the English creative writing sessions in which students had to build a model of the Gruffalo's territory. The students used their imagination and creativity in order to create; caves, animals, barns, large doors, barbeque area, breakfast tables, a bunk bed and also large cakes labelled with the days of the week for the Gruffalo to eat. The participants managed to keep in mind that they were creating a house for the Gruffalo and reasoned every part of their creation. Results obtained from post-questionnaires indicate that Minecraft brought out the children's imagination and creativity.

These observations support the findings of Duncan (2011) when stating that the most fundamentally distinct characteristic which generates such a fascinating atmosphere in Minecraft is its empowerment for creativity (Duncan, 2011). Almost all of the participants in this study believe that their creative skills have been developed through Minecraft. Minecraft gave the children, even those who lack artistic ability, the opportunity to create a variety of complex buildings. This results in the enhancement of their self-esteem and sense of achievement. There were many reasons to this development. Some students believed that that Minecraft allowed them to create an unlimited variety of buildings and items. Other participants wrote that it helped them make more creative drawings since they could picture them in Minecraft. It was apparent in some of the children's reasons that Minecraft awarded them with free space in which they could develop their creative skills. The fact that no guidance or instruction is provided in the game's interface, affords more freedom to the player. This provided an ideal context in which students could express themselves and their creativity in a safe environment.

Digital Skills

Apart from the communication and creative skills mentioned above the students were able to develop their digital skills. All of the participants were able to master their tablet since they were responsible for switching it on, create new worlds on Minecraft, activate the Minecraft app and finally to switch the tablet off in a safe way. Results obtained from post-questionnaires indicated that most of the participants believed that their digital skills were developed through Minecraft. It was evident that in the last few sessions the student who never made use of a tablet before was able to master these crucial digital skills.

CONCLUSION

In this chapter the authors set out to identify different ways in which the popular game Minecraft is being used in schools by referring to communities of practice and studies outlined in journals. This chapter then set out to outline a study we conducted in a Maltese school aimed at assessing how Minecraft can serve as a suitable educational tool to help Maltese students engage more effectively with topics in the year 4 curriculum. Through the children's responses in the questionnaires, the authors' observations and the analysis of artefacts built in Minecraft the authors are confident in concluding that in this research project Minecraft did serve as a suitable educational tool. Minecraft is fun and easy to play while allowing students to engage effectively with a number of topics from the year 4 syllabus. Minecraft helped students develop a variety of soft skills including creative skills, problem-solving skills, digital skills, communication skills and teamwork skills. One can also conclude that Minecraft can serve as a suitable tool to gain and maintain the students' attention and intrinsically motivate them. The game also increased the opportunities for learning to occur. Whenever participants were faced with a challenge they were eager to figure out how to solve it. All of the students are able to progress at a comfortable pace in Minecraft and this was evident since even though the participants possessed different skills and knowledge regarding school subjects, Minecraft and technology use they still managed to achieve the similar goals. Knowledge and skill development was mostly done through trial and error, peer tutoring, and discovery-learning.

REFERENCES

Blunt, R. (2007, January). Does game-based learning work? Results from three recent studies. Proceedings of *the Interservice/Industry Training, Simulation & Education Conference (I/ITSEC)*, Orlando, Florida (Vol. 1).

Brand, J. E. (2012). *Digital Australia 2012 (DA12)*. Australia: School of Communication and Media Faculty of Humanities and Social Sciences Bond University.

Craft, A. (2013). Childhood, possibility thinking and wise, humanising educational futures. *International Journal of Educational Research, 61*, 126–134. doi:10.1016/j.ijer.2013.02.005

David, T. (2009). Young children's social and emotional development. *An Introduction to Early Childhood Studies,*, 78.

De Castell, S., & Jenson, J. (2004). Paying attention to attention: New economies for learning. *Educational Theory, 54*(4), 381–397. doi:10.1111/j.0013-2004.2004.00026.x

De Freitas, S., & Oliver, M. (2006). How can exploratory learning with games and simulations within the curriculum be most effectively evaluated? *Computers & Education, 46*(3), 249–264. doi:10.1016/j.compedu.2005.11.007

DeKanter, N. (2004). Gaming redefines interactivity for learning. *TechTrends, 49*(3), 26–31. doi:10.1007/BF02763644

Duncan, S. C. (2011). Minecraft, beyond construction and survival. *Well Played: A Journal on Video Games. Value and Meaning, 1*(1), 1–22.

GameVision Europe. (2010). *Video gamers in Europe 2010. Interactive Software Federation of Europe*. ISFE.

Gardner, D. E. M. (1969). *Susan Isaacs: The first biography*. London, UK: Cox & Wyman.

Gregory, G. H., & Burkman, A. (2011). Differentiated literacy strategies for english language learners, grades 7–12. London, UK: SAGE.

Hallet, E. (2013). *The reflective early years practitioner*. London, UK: Sage. doi:10.4135/9781473914919

Isaacs, S. (1968). The nursery years: The mind of the child from birth to six years.

Jackson, L. A., Witt, E. A., Games, A. I., Fitzgerald, H. E., von Eye, A., & Zhao, Y. (2012). Information technology use and creativity: Findings from the children and technology project. *Computers in Human Behavior, 28*(2), 370–376. doi:10.1016/j.chb.2011.10.006

Johnson, L., Adams, S., & Cummins, M. (2012). *NMC horizon report: 2012 K-12 edition*. Austin, TX: New Media Consortium.

Kebritchi, M., & Hirumi, A. (2008). Examining the pedagogical foundations of modern educational computer games. *Computers & Education, 51*(4), 1729–1743. doi:10.1016/j.compedu.2008.05.004

Kickmeier-Rust, M. D., Peirce, N., Conlan, O., Schwarz, D., Verpoorten, D., & Albert, D. (2007). *Immersive digital games: The interfaces for next-generation e-learning? Universal access in human-computer interaction applications and services* (pp. 647–656). Springer. doi:10.1007/978-3-540-73283-9_71

Kutner, L., & Olson, C. (2008). *Grand theft childhood: The surprising truth about violent video games and what parents can do*. New York: Simon and Schuster.

Lenhart, A., Kahne, J., Middaugh, E., Evans, C., & Vitak, J. (2008). Teens, video games, and civics.

McGonigal, J. (2012). *Reality is broken: Why games make us better and how they can change the world*. London: Vintage.

Merriam, S. B. (2009). *Qualitative research: A guide to design and implementation*. San Francisco: Jossey-Bass.

Papert, S. (1980). *Mindstorms: Children, computers, and powerful ideas*. New York: Basic Books.

Piaget, J. (1962). *Play, dreams and imitation in childhood*. New York: Norton.

Postman, N. (1992). *Technopoly: The surrender of culture to technology*. New York: Vintage Books.

Pringle, M. K. (1986). *The needs of children: A personal perspective*. London, UK: Hutchinson.

Provost, J. A. (1990). *Work, play, and type: Achieving balance in your life*. Davies-Black Publishing.

Reeves, A. R. (2011). *Where great teaching begins: Planning for student thinking and learning*. CA: ASCD.

Rieber, L. P. (1996). Seriously considering play: Designing interactive learning environments based on the blending of microworlds, simulations, and games. *Educational Technology Research and Development*, *44*(2), 43–58. doi:10.1007/BF02300540

Salomon, G., Perkins, D. N., & Globerson, T. (1991). Partners in cognition: Extending human intelligence with intelligent technologies. *Educational Researcher*, *20*(3), 2–9. doi:10.3102/0013189X020003002

Short, D. (2012). Teaching scientific concepts using a virtual world—Minecraft. *Teaching Science-the Journal of the Australian Science Teachers Association*, *58*(3), 55.

Sutton-Smith, B. (1997). *The ambiguity of play*. Cambridge: Harvard University Press.

Walker, T., & White, C. (2002). Technorealism: The rhetoric and reality of technology in teacher education. *Journal of Technology and Teacher Education*, *10*(1), 63–74.

Wastiau, P., Blamire, R., Kearney, C., Quittre, V., Van de Gaer, E., & Monseur, C. (2013). The use of ICT in education: A survey of schools in Europe. *European Journal of Education*, *48*(1), 11–27. doi:10.1111/ejed.12020

West, D. M., & Bleiberg, J. (2013). *Education technology success stories. Issues in Governance Studies, West, D. M. (2012). Digital schools: How technology can transform education*. WA: Brookings Institution Press.

ENDNOTE

1 Liam is not the real name of the participant but a name used to protect the identity of the student.

Chapter 24
Designing a Learning Analytic System for Assessing Immersive Virtual Learning Environments

Donna Russell
Walden University, USA

Steven E. Wallis
Capella University, USA

ABSTRACT

The purpose of this chapter is to develop a template for the evaluation of learning in an educational game. In this case, gaming is referred to as 3D immersive virtual learning environments. Problem-based learning is the design template for the IVLE as it engages learners in defined learning behaviors that have been shown to encourage advanced problem-based learning. As a result of this holistic design procedure the learning analytic system proposed in this chapter is an integrated system that can be linked to P-12 educational programs augmenting their traditional programs and providing alternative instructional procedures, alternative learning processes for students and a standards-based but a more individualistic and thus viable assessment of learning to replace an outdated learning assessment model.

INTRODUCTION

The purpose of this chapter is to develop a template for the evaluation of learning in educational games. In this case, gaming is referred to as 3D immersive virtual learning environments. Immersive virtual learning environments are defined for this chapter as learning environments designed to simulate a realistic scenario or environments that provide learners with the opportunity to practice skills, respond to content in context to solve problems and engage in interactions with others. An immersive virtual learning environment (IVLE) is a virtual world or scenario that engages learners in the simulation. Problem-based learning is the design template for the IVLE template described in this chapter as it engages learners in simulated problem spaces with defined learning behaviors that have been shown to encourage advanced problem-based learning (Jonassen, 2005; Russell & Schneiderheinze, 2005b). The learning analytic system proposed in this chapter is based on an

DOI: 10.4018/978-1-4666-9629-7.ch024

analytical research process cultural historical activity theory (CHAT) that defines and structures the learning responses from the Problem-based learning IVLE (Engestrom, 1987) for assessment . The types and quality of learning resulting from the IVLE will be assessed using rubrics based on Bereiter's Scheme of Knowledge (Bereiter, 2002), intersubjectivity (Hui & Russell, 2009), and Pfeiffer's task and role response (1979). As a result of this holistic design procedure the learning analytic system proposed in this chapter is an integrated system that can be linked to P-12 educational programs augmenting their traditional programs and providing non-traditonal instructional procedures, alternative learning processes for students and a standards-based but a differentiated, individualistic and thus viable assessment of learning to replace an out-dated learning assessment model.

BACKGROUND

The major issue in p-12 education today is the issue of how to assess learning. Currently high-stakes standardized testing is the norm for public schools in the U.S. Standardized testing mandated by the federal No Child Left Behind Act (NCLB) of 2001 and the attendent curriculum and instructional alignments has changed the nature of teaching and learning occurs in US schools. This bill was designed to hold schools accountable for learning but the current issue being debated is that the assessment of learning that the NCLB monitors is a low-level learning response for the testing process with the movement to develop a curriculum and instructional style that is not designed based on cognitive research and best-practice pedagogy but on standardized teaching model designed to disseminate information to all students in the same manner to prepare them for a test that removes information from context and meaning and instead focuses on memorization of facts.

Some of the problems with NCLB after 12 years include:

1. Test scores result in differing levels of funding with low performing districts tagged to the tests and unable to respond to their districts', schools' and students' needs as a result schools in low performing districts are counting down to the test as part of a continual cycle of teaching to the test.
2. The assessments are identifying the individual learner response to a low-level multiple choice test. This is not the type of learning needed to prepare learners to become knowledge workers of the future.
3. Teachers are held accountable for their students' scores and can lose their jobs if test scores go down. This means that teachers are adverse to any deviation from the standardized curriculum that is linked to the standardized tests even with the teacher's awareness of and training to respond to the individual needs of their learners.
4. Testings and preparing for testing takes up increasingly large amounts of instructional time. U.S. students spend approximately 900-1,000 hours of instructional time per year (Hull, J. & Newport, M., 2011).
5. Tests include cultural biases that push poorer districts and urban districts toward loss of accreditation,
6. Test results are not available to teachers to support students until the students are gone from their classroom, and
7. High stakes testing creates an antagonistic relationship between teacher, district, student and parents as teachers push students to do better on the tests without consideration of the emotional and cognitive needs of the students (Evans, J., 2013).

Standardized testing and the resulting standardization or nationalization of the curriculum and relevant instructional practice has resulted in the reduction of instructional practice based on learning theories and associated best practice in pedagogy. Additionally it has created inequalities that characterize segregated schooling in the United States (Kozol, 1992). No Child Left Behind (NCLB) was designed to support children who have, academically, been "left behind," a group in which poor Black and Hispanic children are over represented. The testing and accountability mandates of NCLB insure that even separate schooling is equal; however, the evidence indicates that the principal effect of NCLB on students "left behind" is a narrow, skills-based "pedagogy of poverty" (Haberman, 1991, p. 290) "alleged to be aligned with governmentally established goals and standards and . . . suited to what are regarded as 'the special needs and learning styles' of low-income children" (Kozol, 2005a, pp. 63-64). The danger is that a pedagogy of poverty by limiting low-income students' opportunities to experience rich, engaging curricula that characterizes the education of children in affluent schools, contributes to a process by which "intelligent, creative, cultured children [are] transformed . . . into seemingly 'slow,' deficited, acultured beings" (Gee, in Rogers, ix, 2003). "What is it about school that manages to transform children who are good at learning . . . regardless of their economic and cultural differences, into children who are not good at learning, if they are poor or members of certain minority groups?" (Gee, 2004, p. 10)

The standardization process has crept throughout education in response to the one size fits all assessment of learning. It is the premise of this chapter that this trend can be changed by focusing on constructivist learning theories, immersive learning processes, problem-based learning and an assessment model that is linked to these constructivist learning environments. Additionally it is the premise of this chapter that immersive virtual learning environments give educators the best prospect for implementation of constructivist learning environments when the IVLE is designed based on best-practice pedagogy and linked to a valid assessment model, in this case a learning analytic system based on cultural historical activity theory to define and gauge the learning.

MAIN FOCUS OF THE CHAPTER

In this chapter we propose an assessment model that will define the development of advanced learning in immersive virtual learning environments that are designed based on constructivist learning theories, with a curriculum model that is based on problem-based learning, defining the immersive learning occurs in immersive virtual learning environments, and a learning analysis system designed to be an interactive, reiterative process that is readily accessible by both the instructor and the learner. This integrated system provides a comprehensive assessment model for the development of advanced knowledge in virtual immersive learning environments. As learners interact and respond to simulations in virtual worlds their learning is not a result of isolated events. Rather it is a result of the immersion into the game resulting in potentially higher levels of learning but without the isolated, passivity of traditional education.

Immersive virtual learning environments is a term that refers to an online educational experience which is highly interactive in which the learning engages with the content to facilitate the learning. Immersive technology refers to an online educational experience which is highly interactive and engages the learner with the content to facilitate the learning. Immersive virtual learning includes educational games, online simulations and virtual learning worlds (Kapp & O'Driscoll). The principles that support the move to virtual immersive learning in the classroom are varied. It is a boost to learning itself as learning starts when information is processed in differing sensory modalities such as audio, visual and haptic (digital touch) interfaces available in virtual environments. In immersive virtual learning environments transitional objects are used to support translating personal experience into abstract symbols (Papert, 1988; Fosnot, 1992). Immersive virtual learning environments focus on how representations and applications can mediate interactions among learners and natural or social phenomena. Learers can immerse themselves in distributed, synthetic environments, becoming "avatars" who vicariously collaborate and engage in simulated real-world activities using virtual artifacts to construct knowledge (Walker, 1990). Matching these situated and distributed learning processes with the design of a problem-based virtual immersive learning environment further develops students' ability to apply abstract knowledge by situating education in immersive, authentic simulations similar to the environments in which learners' skills will be used (Dede, 1992) and providing the learners an opportunity to develop advanced knowledge and cognitive processes in a simulation with rules and consequences for iterative learning.

Research of the Open Habitat project, a collaborative learning and teaching platform in Second Life, identified eight benefits of 3D immersive simulations to develop advanced knowledge including:

1. Immersion in 3D provides an augmented sense of co-presence through embodiment as an avatar impacting affective, empathic and motivational aspects of the learning experiences,
2. Extended social interactions between individuals and communities, humans and objects and intelligent interaction between artifacts,
3. Community presence promoting a sense of belonging and purpose that coalesces groups, subcultures and geographies,
4. Exposure to authentic content and access to cultures that reflect diversity,
5. Opportunities for individual and collective identity and role play,
6. Content production tools that provide opportunities for creation and ownership of object,
7. Visualization and contextualization through the production and reproduction of normally inaccessible content including artifacts that may be historically lost, imaginary, futuristic, or impossible to see by the human eye, and
8. Simulations of existing real world contexts that may be too costly or dangerous in real-life (Warburton, S. & Garcia, M., 2009).

Another compelling reason to engage learners in immersive virtual learning environments is motivate students through the interactive experience. The immersive virtual learning environments (IVLE) provide multiple interactive, media-rich forums for the learner. This also means a higher level of engagement as the virtual worlds are designed to be visually rich and provide opportunities for the learner to interact with others in the environment through audio, text and visual media. Quest Atlantis (QA) is an international learning and teaching project that uses a 3D multi-user environment to immerse children, ages 9-16, in educational tasks. QA combines strategies used in the commercial gaming environment with lessons from educational research on learning and motivation. Participation in the game is designed to enhance the lives of children while helping them grow into knowledgeable, responsible, and empathetic adults. Quest Atlantis engages learners in an immersive process that involves them in collaborative learning, playing and helping. In Quest Atlantis, Questers can travel to virtual worlds where they learn about the theme of that world; complete various Quests; chat with other children and with mentors live, from around the world; and build their virtual persona shown to be a powerful motivator for engaging participation in online worlds (Turkle, 1995)

The potential for advanced learning resulting from immersive virtual learning environments designed based on problem-based learning authentic issues include

1. A real-world relevance (a meaningful application that drives student engagement),

2. Development of analytic skills (students can examine tasks from different perspectives using a variety of resources),
3. Collaboration,
4. Consequences of choice (reflection), and
5. Allowing a range of competing solutions with a diversity of outcomes (Jonassen, 1997).

These are critical skills as students prepare to enter a globally competitive job market with the ability to transform traditional learning into a system that permits the students' instant identification with real world application is invaluable. Virtual immersive learning environments have been shown to be productive learning environments if designed to focus on the development of clearly defined educational goals (Russell, D., Guenter, P. & Wood, L., 2013). Transitioning from technology-mediated interactions between students and phenomena to immersive virtual learning changes the focus of constructivist learning from superficially enhancing how a student interprets a typical interaction with the external world to shaping the fundamental nature of how learners experience their physical and social context by creating simulations of real-world environments and experiences. Through distributed simulations, a learner can be immersed in a synthetic, constructivist environment. The student acts and collaborates not as himself or herself, but through an "avatar": a surrogate persona in the virtual world thus providing a link to a distributed learning space (Lave & Wenger, 1999).

This higher, more immediate level of engagement in IVLE, telepresence, means that the learner can integrate more advanced knowledge and processes. Telepresence is the sense that a person using certain technologies has that he/she is present in a location other than their real world location. In the book Natural Born Cyborgs (2003) Andy Clark describes the ability of the human brain to develop new concepts using technological tools as opportunistic. He further states that " We should not underestimate the capacity of human brains in general—young human brains in particular—to simultaneously alter and grow so they can better exploit the problem-solving opportunities our technologies provide." (pp. 264). This concept was studied by Dr. Hayles who described telepresence as the extension of an embodied awareness in specific manners impossible without the electronic prosthesis (Hayles, 1999). Telepresence can allow the learner to feel high levels of engagement in the virtual environments and create the potential for high levels of learning responses. "The potential interactions among avatars and virtual cultures in this hypothetical synthetic environment illustrate how shared evolution of physical/social context, fluidity of identity, disinhibition, and mimesis can empower distributed, constructivist learning." (Dede, 1996 p.18).

Pedagogical Agents

The design of this problem-based learning IVLE incorporates the use of artificial intelligence in these virtual learning environments to develop student levels of telepresence and monitor student responses in the learning analytic system. When you correlate the natural language processing and reasoning control of artificial intelligence (AI) with a 3D character (avatar) it becomes a powerful personification of knowledge, called a pedagogical agent. The pedagogical agent is linked to the ontological knowledge base for the learning analytic system. This linkage results in modularity and dynamic abilities to change and update knowledge representation. With the pedagogical agent seeming to respond as a regular avatar does, social interaction and engagement among the learners are increased. The student level of telepresence is maintained by ongoing interactions with the pedagogical agents. These AI bots can be guides, mentors and even become points of assessment for the designer/facilitator. These pedagogical agents provide an ongoing formative and summative assessment system as their interactions with the learners and the context are tagged and coded for responses by the automated data management system.

The dialogs among the students and with the pedagogical agents creates the potential for evaluation of the level of student discourse using qualitative research methodologies, in this case cultural historical activity theory (Engestrom, 1983), and the assessment of student response using the principals of social cognitive science (Johnson, Rickel, & Lester, 2000). These ongoing interactions in the IVLE will be maintained by the pedagogical agents including access to information and web applications. In the learning analytic system there is an administrative dashboard that are triggered by flags or by choice, an educator can step in at any time to steer the conversation. Additionally web interfaces, widgets, are designed to guide conversation review. This means that administrators can review conversation logs and even enter desired responses to questions if the automatically generated replies are not desired. This allows the designer to develop surveys and measures of learning to assess the effectiveness of the interactions in the virtual environments when the teacher cannot be directly involved in these interactions. This means that the teacher can monitor and evaluate the learning of the students during and after their experiences in the virtual scenarios using the pedagogical agents.

It is a goal of the evaluative research of the development of an IVLE based on problem-based learning design principles (PBL) to study how the virtual interactions and the students' levels of telepresence are related to the development of both cognitive processes and content knowledge. This learner's sense of telepresence will be defined for research as an aspect of the collaborative virtual learning environment that is related to the development of cognitive apprenticeship as defined by Anderson (2001) who described this cognitive apprenticeship as a guided learning process where the guide mentors the learner by making the expert processes explicit. Additionally interactions with the virtual mentors will be correlated to the process of the development of learning in the Zone of Proximal Development as described by Vygtosky (1979) where a mentor scaffolds the learner through higher and higher levels of difficulty toward mastery. In the virtual worlds students will respond to surveys that define their relationship with the mentor guides and the teacher can then correlate this information to formative and summative assessments of their learning and knowledge responses. By relating the student's sense of telepresence to the quality of their learning experiences in these virtual worlds, researchers be able will assess the effectiveness of these interactions. The designers can modify these interactions based on the assessment feedback from the students about the avatar guides. For instance, one issue is the amount of avatar facial movement, gestures, characterization and personification develops the interaction with the students. Another issue is the emergent augmented reality devices that provide advanced visual, auditory and haptic senses engagement. Additionally there are full body sensory wear, such as the Tesla Suit (http://teslastudios.co.uk/), which links movement and haptic senses throughout the suit. This type of telepresence should be studied from the perspective of the cognitive sciences, best practice pedagogical design and technological affordances and constraints in an integrative and holistic research model.

As a result of the ongoing development of new technologies IVLE is becoming a more viable educational program. The purpose of this chapter is to define how to integrate these advanced technologies in a meaningful and valid way in P-12 education by linking the design of the IVLE with the potential for the new technologies, constructivist learning theories, a best-practice problem-based learning design template and a holistic learning analytic systems supported by a strong research base.

The purpose of this chapter is to discuss and justify the design of a learning analytic system based on constructivist learning theories using a template for curriculum design based problem-based learning principles and defining the immersive learning outcomes in the virtual worlds using a systemic analysis of learning to code and structure the evaluation of learning based on cultural historical activity theory (CHAT) (Illenov, 1978). The design of this CHAT- Learning Analytic System (CHAT-LAS) is based on constructivist learning theories. This CHAT-LAS is designed for assessment of learning outcomes in virtual learning environments designed based on constructivist learning theory, the pedagogy of problem-based learning model, the definition of learning activity using a specially design model of CHAT and the evaluation of learning responses using Bereiter's Scheme of Knowledge (2002), intersubjectivity, (Hui & Russell, 2009), and Roger's (1982) innovation theory.

Constructivist Learning Theory

The virtual learning analytic system is based on constructivist learning theories including situated theories of learning (Brown, Collins, & Druguid, 1989: Greeno, 1997; Lave & Wenger, 1991; Roschelle & Clancey, 1992; Roth & Bowen, 1995) and distributed cognition theory (Pea, 1993; Resnick, Levine, & Teasley, 1991; Salomon, 1993), which emphasize how the responses of the learner and the design of the learning environment influence the cognitive development of learners. Constructivism is a theory of how students acquire knowledge and skills. Unlike prior theories of learning that focused on the passive role of the learner and the student's ability to reproduce behaviors upon a stimulus provided by the teacher, constructivism focuses on how students are actively involved in the learning process. Students create meaning by comparing what they already know to new experiences. They either resolve the inconsistency by adapting or assimilating the new knowledge into their existing knowledge. Bruner (1990) called this process meaning making. In constructivist theory learning is an active and engaged process whereby "students are actively engaged in working at tasks and activities that are authentic to the environment in which they would be used" (Savery & Duffy, 1996, p. 37). The work of Dewey (1943), Piaget (1979), Bruner (1990), and Vygotsky (1979) provide a historical framework for understanding the theoretical assumptions of constructivism and placing this theory of learning within a framework of sociocultural learning theory. The four assumptions for learning based on a sociocultural learning theory. These include:

1. Knowledge and meaning are constructed, not dispensed, when students are engaged in meaningful activity;
2. Knowledge is anchored and categorized by the context in which the learning activity occurs and requires definition, expression, or representation;
3. Meaning making, which is prompted by a problem, is an attempt to resolve questions, confusion, disagreement, or dissonance, in the mind of the learner,
4. Meaning making and thinking are distributed throughout our tools, culture, and community and may also be socially constructed with others through activities (Vygotsky, 1978; Honebein, Duffy, & Fishman, 1993; Jonassen, Peck, & Wilson, 1999).

Instructional design grounded in constructivist principles engages learners in purposeful activity as they respond to a complex problem, overcome an obstacle, or negotiate a contradiction in their thinking (von Glasersfeld, 1998). The design of an immersive virtual learning environment based on constructivist learning principles allows students to apply their knowledge. (Brown, Collins, & Druguid, 1989). Through the process of responding to a virtual problem space or scenario, students acquire knowledge and skill that enable them to revise their theories, develop new theories, and compare their theories with other students through interactions in virtual spaces. In addition, an immersive virtual learning environment based on constructivist learning principles allows students to apply their knowledge more effectively under defined conditions in the virtual worlds (Collins, 1991). Jonassen (2000) refers to this as intentional learning since students are focusing their learning on satisfying their educational goals.

Sociocultural Learning Theory

Sociocultural theory defines human development as a fluid interaction between individual, group, and environmental artifacts. Proponents of sociocultural theory assert "mental action is situated in cultural, historical and institutional setting" (Wertsch, 1991, p.15). Cognition is described in sociocultural theory as "being shaped or even defined by the mediational means it employs to carry out a task" (Wertsch, 1995, p.14). An understanding of cognitive development based on a sociocultural perspective emphasizes "the transition from primitive remembering and involuntary attention to the higher mental processes of voluntary attention and logical memory" (Vygotsky, 1986, p.166). The holistic progressive aspects of sociocultural theory also give it functionality for designing virtual learning environments for students and the CHAT-LAS by providing a theoretical base for defining the learning processes and learning interactions in the virtual space.

The CHAT-LAS was designed to define learning outcomes by understanding human development based on the concepts of zone of proximal development. The zone of proximal development defines human development and learning through the interactions of the learner through his/her zone of proximal development. The zone of proximal development (ZPD) is the "actual developmental level as determined by independent problem solving under adult guidance or in collaboration with more capable peers" (Wertsch, 1991, p. 28). Using ZPD as a design metaphor the CHAT-LAS will isolate and code these learning interactions in the virtual immersive learning environments.

Problem-Based Learning

Problem-Based learning is the design model for the virtual immersive learning environment assessed using the CHAT-LAS. Problem-Based Learning (PBL) is an instructional method that addresses the complex knowledge and skill applications that students will face in the future by participating as problems solvers to tackle complex, ill-structured problems that resemble if not mirror real world problems. PBL proposes that learning experiences that build on the interdependent attributes of meaningful learning including authentic, intentional, active, constructive, and cooperative learning (Jonassen et al., 1999) and involve meaningful application of knowledge and skills. Problem-based learning design is a constructivist, distributed and situated learning environment.

Problem-Based Learning (PBL) is a design pedagogy that focuses on the complex knowledge and skill applications that students will face in the future by participating as problems solvers. Students tackle complex, ill-structured problems situated in real world problems. The IVLE PBL design template engages students in purposeful activity as the students attempt to tackle a complex problem, overcome an obstacle, or negotiate a contradiction in their thinking (Jonassen, 2000). In studies of collaborative virtual learning environments research have shown that learners can develop higher levels of awareness and knowledge as a result of their dialog and interactions in online problem-based learning environment (Russell, 2005). PBL immerses the students in a simulated problem space relevant to authentic problems. The students are active members of a community of learners within the context of the problem but respond with less risk and intensity than those in actual practice in a developmentally structured process designed to develop advanced knowledge (Barab, Kling, and Gray, 2006). As a result problem-based learning has an incredible potential to develop advanced learning and knowledge responses. Below is the PBL design template created to structure the design of PBL environments.

The Problem-Based Learning Design Template, Figure 1, incorporates the concepts of constructivist-based learning environments. Phase 1 of the PBL Design Template provides a means for engaging the learner in the relevance of the dilemma to begin challenging the students to recognize the legitimacy of the dilemma (Barab & Duffy, 2000) and develop a local context for the issues. This phase is an initial questioning phase to develop relevancy and encourage the student interactions. In Phase 2 the students work to develop an area of expertise within their inquiry process. This method of collaborative learning is supported by research on the nature of developing conceptual understanding of complex issues (Bruer, 1993; Brown & Campione, 1994; Brown, Ash, Rutherford, Nakagawa, Gordon, & Campione, 1993; Palinscar & Brown, 1984). In Phase 3 students present a strategy for solution of the problem. In this phase students create a model for a response to the issues and topics identified in the first two phases. This final phase is based on research on developing community of learners (Brown & Campione, 1990). The final phase groups are involved in an interactive process called a Jigsaw (Aronson, Blaney, Stephan, Sikes, & Snapp, 1978). This process is also supported by research on the nature of apprenticeship and expertise (Brown, Collins & Duguid, 1989). In this final phase learners are asked to bring together the areas of expertise and respond to the problem by identifying a course of action that resolves all the sub issues identified by the group. Learning to think critically, to analyze and synthesis information to solve problems in a variety of contexts and to work effectively in teams are crucial skills for knowledge workers of the future (Bransford, Goldman, & Vye, 1991).

Problem-Based Learning (PBL) in 3D IVLE

The 3D simulations of the learning environment of the 3D PBL design template shown below as Figure 2 were designed to develop advanced cognitive skills and knowledge through problem-based learning processes. It is based on the PBL design template identified as Figure 1. It defines the IVLE interactions based on the principles of the constructivist learning theories and research on virtual learning environments.

The CHAT-LAS will define the learning processes and interactions resulting from the problem-based learning design template using cultural historical activity theory and assess the level of learning response using relevant assessment models including Bereiter's Scheme of Knowledge (2002).

Assessment of Learning: Bereiter's Scheme of Knowledge

Carl Bereiter developed a Scheme of Knowledge in which he contends that knowledge implies the purposeful use, recombination, evaluation, and redistribution of information as the core abilities of a knowledge-based society (2002). The virtual PBL environment was designed to give learners the opportunity to develop expanded forms of communication, analysis, and expression (e.g., visualization tools, access to authentic issues and problems, ability for students to share work, access to primary and authentic resources, and opportunities to collaborate) that are needed to succeed in a knowledge-based society. Bereiter defines knowledge development as the development of the understandings of the relationship between culture, humans, objects, and tools.

In the CHAT-LAS learners' interactions and artifacts will be formatively and summatively evaluated using the Scheme of Knowledge's scale

Figure 1. PBL design template
(Russell, 2005b).

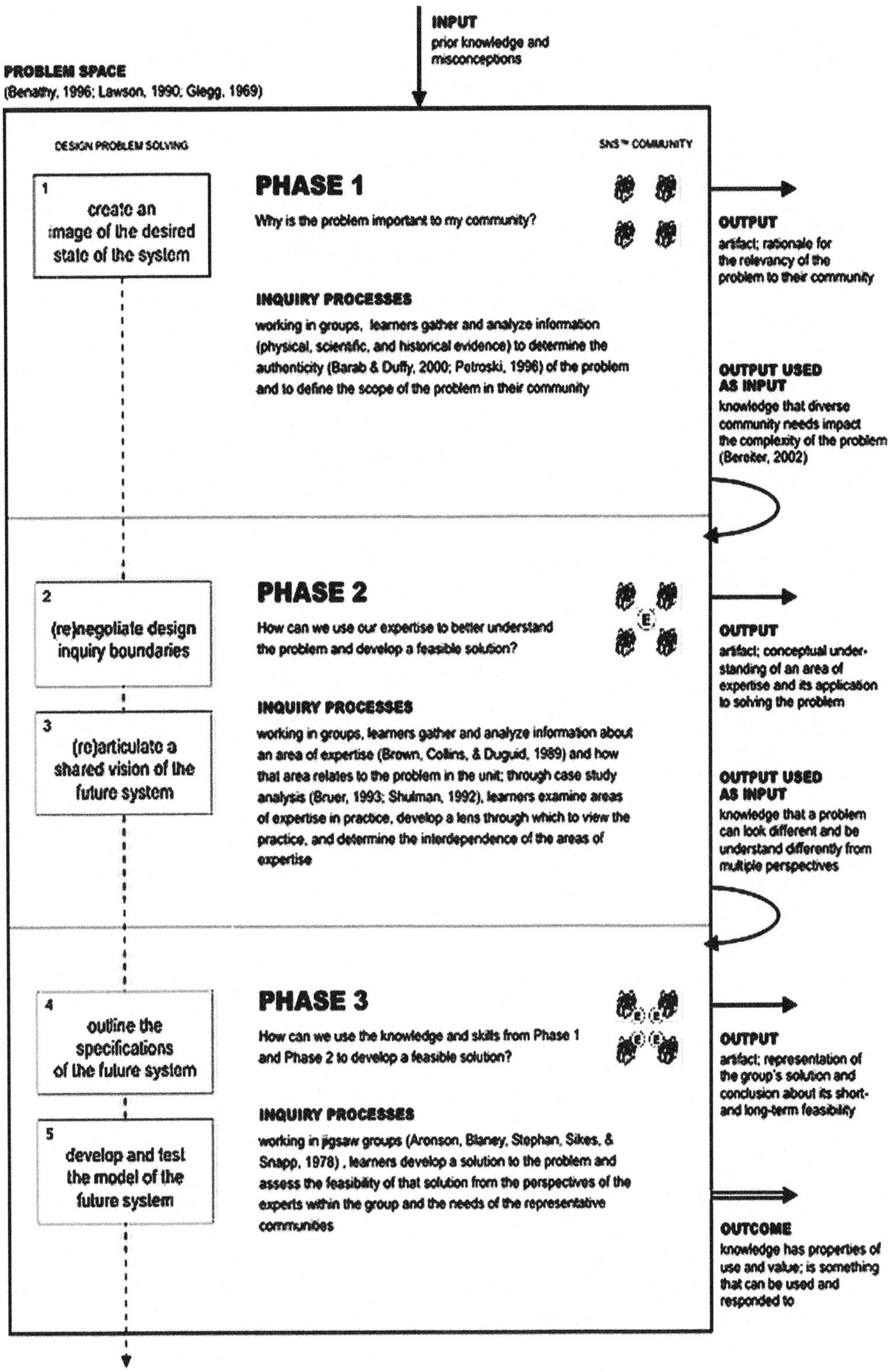

Figure 2. 3D PBL design

Virtual Design	Problem Space (Banathy, 1996; Lawson, 1990) Simulation designed as an interactive virtual environment that relates to a real world problem space.
Pedagogical Agent used as Guide to aid learners as they explore the problem space. **Output** Virtual artifact including a rationale for relevancy of the problem.	**PHASE 1** Why is the problem Important? **Inquiry Processes** Working in pairs, learners gather and analyze information in the virtual simulation to determine nature of the problem and to define the scope of the problem. (Barab & Duffy, 2000; Petroski, 1996). **Output used as input** Knowledge that a diverse community needs impact the complexity of the problem. (Bereiter, 2001).
Pedagogical Agent used as a Resource Mentor to answer questions and find resources. **Output** Virtual artifact including a conceptual understanding of an area of expertise and its application to solve the problem	**PHASE 2** How can we use our expertise to better understand the problem and develop a feasible solution? **Inquiry Processes** Working groups, learners gather and analyze information about an area of expertise (Brown, Collins & Duguid, 1989) and how that area relates to the problem, (Bruer, 1993, Shulman, 1992) learners examine areas of expertise in simulated environments, determine the interdependence of the areas of expertise. **Output used as input** Knowledge that a problem can look different and be understood differently from multiple perspectives.
Pedagogical Agent used as Survey Buddy to assess new knowledge and final projects. **Output** Virtual artifact including a representation of the group's solution and conclusion about its short-term and long-term feasibility.	**PHASE 3** How can we use the knowledge and skills from Phase 1 and Phase 2 to develop a feasible solution? **Inquiry Processes** Working in jigsaw groups (Aronson, Blaney, Stephan, Sikes & Snapp, 1978), learners develop a solution to the problem and assess the feasibility of that solution from the perspectives of the experts within the group and the needs of the community. **Outcome** Knowledge has properties of use and value; is something that can be used and responded to.

of 0-7 to evaluate the effectiveness of the virtual mentoring activities and the interactive aspects of the virtual environments in the development of knowledge as conceptual artifacts. These scaled responses are used to develop holistic rubrics, surveys, data coding structures and the analysis of interactions in the learning analytic system. Level 0 is knowledge as a truism, "the way things are" (p. 12). Thoughts are understood to be separate from the things themselves but they are not different than the reality of their existence. The learner does not modify the information to represent their understanding. In level 1, knowledge is understood as an individual response that is defined as something someone knows or does not know. The learner still responds to knowledge as a truism but defines their understanding as part of the learning process. In this case level 1 learning represents an brief essay or a project assessed by the occurance of facts or minimum criteria using a checklist. At level 2, knowledge becomes an object of manipulation. The learner can relate to others his or her understanding of the topic but without a concept of what the other students understands about the topic. Level 2 learning is represented by the creation of an object that is not dependent upon or gauged by the learner's awareness of others. This could be a project or a paper that is developed as the result of a checklist but not for presentation or to use in interactive projects. The assessment would be a checklist or a rubric but the rubric includes only minimum criteria for assessment.

In level 3, Bereiter describes the learner response to knowledge as "knowledge as representation" (p. 12). At this level the learner will understand that knowledge can be communicated to others. The learner will take into consideration that the others may have differing levels of understanding and interpretations. This is the first level where the understanding of others is taken into account in the structuring or response of the learner. In this level, the learner makes decisions about constructing a response based on how others will view or use the information. This is a project or paper that is part of a group activity and is assessed by a rubric that includes the level of the learner's awareness of how the object they created functions as a part of a whole. Level 4 represents a higher level of objectification. At this level the learner understands that knowing about something can look differently in different places, times, and when understood by other people. In this level the learner is assessed based on how well the object they created has potential to address differing levels of use and function based on context and purpose. This is assessed based on structuring of a rubric that can include self-evaluation surveys, and portfolios that includes functional use of the artifact such as a model.

Level 5 represents knowledge objectification as a learner who constructs understanding in a proactive response. This learner will see himself as the active creator of understandings. At this level there is switch to include not only learner creation but also learner as designer. This type of learning is possible on a project that is designed to give students choices initially and throughout. This is a project that is designed and sustained by the learners and graded in stages, formatively, and summatively, based on the ability to define, analyze and compare the characteristics of their object. At level 6, the learner becomes more holistically inclined. This learner response implies that the learner has defined knowledge as having properties of use, value and the lack of critical characteristic. This learner sees knowledge as a workable theory but also something that they use and respond to. In this level the learner has engaged in designing, building, and evaluating a learning object. The assessment will include formative and summative assessments that combine to provide a portfolio object assessed using a comprehensive rubric. At level 7, the learner has acquired a scientific perspective. This learner can understand that knowledge objects are independent of their understanding, use and value measurements: knowledge as "semi-autonomous artifacts" (Bereiter, 2001, p. 14). Thus knowledge can be a focus for describing how the world works. This stage means that the objectification is complete in that the learner understands that knowledge is something outside of themselves that can be used to create, and make sense of their reality. This highest level is the result of the design of a learning environment that provides the learners with opportunities to do design, research, build, and test their learning objects in as authentic manner as possible. This is advanced problem-based learning in a virtual simulation that is based on an authentic scenario such as global warming. Students would work over time to develop a strategy to address their local issue they defined such as drought that is an aspect of global warming. They then test their knowledge and revise and present their new project. Assessment is through a formative and summative process that includes both self-evaluation processes and a comprehensive rubric of their eportfolio.

Using Bereiter's Scheme of Knowledge the CHAT-LAS will be able to define and evaluate the level of response to the problem-based learning IVLE. Understanding knowledge development as learning, how the design of the learning environment provides opportunity for knowledge responses, and how to formatively and summatively assess this level of response is the integrated protocol for the CHAT-LAS.

SOLUTIONS AND RECOMMENDATIONS

The data structuring model for assessing the learning in the PBL IVLE utilizes cultural historical activity (CHAT) as a basis for understanding the types and qualities of interactions and subsequent learning developed in the immersive virtual learning environments based on sociocultural learning theory. CHAT provides a theoretical perspective for understanding how an educational game mediates players' understandings of new concepts while acknowledging the social and cultural contexts in which game is situated. CHAT defines learning as transformations that occur through the dynamic relations between subjects, artifacts, and mediating social structures. Using the CHAT model of systemic analysis of the development of learning, identified as the transforation of the object of the educational activity, the CHAT-LAS defines the learning activities and their effectiveness for meeting the learning goals of the individual learning and the educational outcomes of the program. It is the premise of the design of the CHAT-LAS that an immersive learning environment can be designed based on constructivist theories of sociocultural learning and problem-based learning to develop advanced knowledge (Vygotsky,1987; Jonassen, Peck, &Wilson, 1999; Bereiter, 2002). Cultural historical activity theory is based on the expansive learning process of transformation within activity theory (Engeström, 1987) and results in

Figure 3. CHAT model

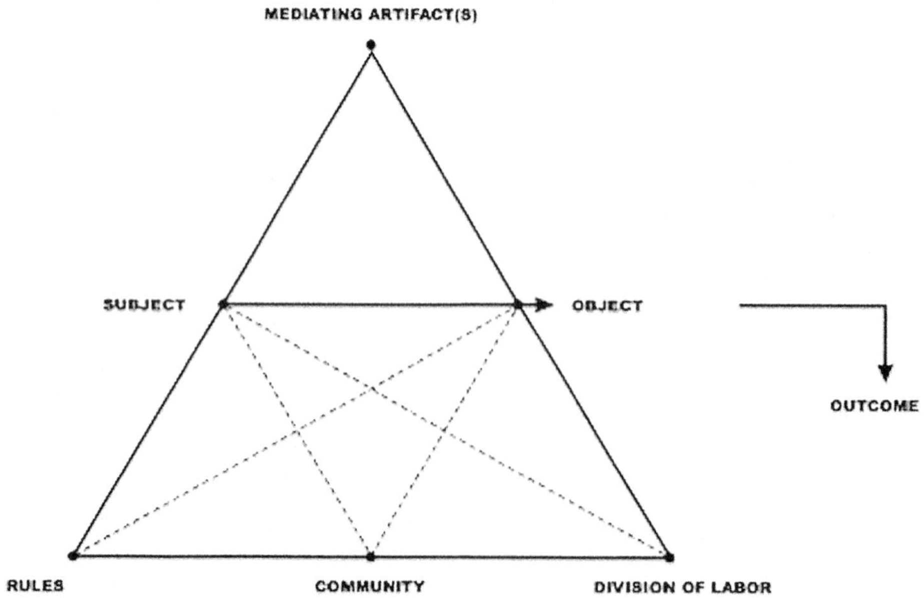

Table 1. Categories of CHAT-LAS

CHAT Category	Activities	Assessment
Mediation	Response to cultural artificats	LMS and game-based interactions including counts of time, location, learning objects and projects
Subject	Development of advanced cognitive processes	• Process oriented assessments incorporated into the learning analytics • Categories linked to rubrics completed by the instructor. • Rubrics assessments will be linked into the dashboard. • portfolio assessment
Context	Division of Labor: needed interactions to succeed	Assessment of grop interactions will use research on defining group roles and intersubjectivity to define interactions in context
	Community: Interactions with social rules and avatars in the game.	• Collected in the IVLE and LMS as time in game and count of response. • Interactions: evaluation of communication processes and skills
	Rules: Gaming Activities	• Context-based assessment of project • Assessment points designed into the game.

a complex, integrated description of how learners construct, validate, and reformulate the meaning of experience according to transformational learning theory (Mezirow, 1990). Below is the CHAT model as Figure 3. It defines the core model of CHAT including 1) mediational tools, 2) subject, and 3) context.

CHAT identifies system components that impact the development of the object, the new activity, that is the core of transformational learning. In this case the transformational activity is the development of the object, responding to the IVLE problem space. The subject are the students and teachers. The mediating artifacts are those new tools added to the system. In this case they are the immersive virtual learning environment, and interactive, immersive technologies. The object of the activity is the learning goals of the specific virtual immersive learning environment. The outcome of the activity is the development of advanced learning processes and content knowledge as a result of the activity. The bottom of the triangle defines the context including community, the interactions among other students, social groups and communication processes. The division of labor are those interactions among pedagogical agents, groups, instructors and mentors. The rules are the rules of the game-based learning environment and the structuring of all aspects of the evaluation of learning processes. A coding structure based on the CHAT model defines the learner response to these areas of influence for transformational activity. These defined, coded responses are then scaled for their effectiveness of response. The aspects of the CHAT model are listed below:

1. **Mediating Artifacts:** Aspects of immersive virtual learning environments.
2. **Subject:** Data on learning activities and responses.
3. **Object:** Successful completion of the gaming simulation.
    a. **Outcome:** Development of advanced knowledge, skills and concepts.
4. **Context:**
    a. **Rules:** Gaming rules.
    b. **Community:** Aspects of the social dynamic in the games.
    c. **Division of Labor:** Interaction with avatars, players that move the learner forward.

The IVLE categories and related assessment models are further defined in Table 1.

Utilizing this systemic model for identifying and evaluating learning in immersive virtual learning environments provides the structure for the development of online data management systems to structure assessment of learning, analyze the learning responses, provide a dashboard feedback for learners and educators and provide an evaluation model for the educational program for productivity and efficiency. There will be structuring categories for the data management system at the core of the CHAT-LAS based on the CHAT aspects listed above. These data structuring categories can be used to develop the holistic rubrics, the formative assessments such as game-based activites, and the project based checklists and self-evaluation surveys. Additionally these data structuring categories will be linked to all aspects of the IVLE to track student progress through the simulations and all learning responses. The tracking procedures will be an automated system that is based on semantic algorithms that collect and structure the data set based on the CHAT categories of transformative learning. The coding levels are described below.

Level 1 coding is the automated coding structures that collect defined data from the IVLE. Data is collected based on an ontological structuring of data. This is data is mapped into a graphical interface.

Level 2 coding is all interactive coding structures that are semantic and based on defining the types and qualities of interactions in the IVLE. These codings are semi-automatic and are a form of formative assessment that provide ongoing feedback to the educator for scaffolding if needed. This level 2 coding includes interactions with the pedagogical agents. This data is structured in a widget that identifies type and quality of responses based on the coding of task and role (Pfieffer & Jones, 1989) and intersubjectivisity (Hui & Russell, 2010) and is presented in the teacher and learner dashboards and at established intervals.

Level 3 coding are the summative assessment processes such as holistic rubrics, comprehensive rubrics and portfolio assessments that require educator assessment. These artifacts are collected within the IVLE and the Learning Management System and identified to the educator in the dashboard for evaluation. All rubrics, portfolios, surveys, and checklists are linked into a common data management system that oversees identification, coding, structuring and reporting of the data set in a data mashup.

In the following list are the specific coding structures for the three levels of coding structures.

Categories for Coding and Structuring Learning Responses Based on Cultural Historical Activity Theory: Cultural Historical Activity Theory-Learning Analytic System (CHAT-LAS)

Activity System:

1. **Individual Learning Processes (Bereiter, 2002):** Scaled rubrics of processes and product creation (Level 3 Coding Structure).
    a. **Level 1:** This is what I know.
    b. **Level 2:** Tell me what you know.
    c. **Level 3:** Tell us what you know.
    d. **Level 4:** Tell us how you came to know this.
    e. **Level 5:** Tell us why you think this is important.
    f. **Level 6:** Prove to us why this should be important.
    g. **Level 7:** Scientific research.
2. **Goal Directed Learning (Situated Learning; Distributed Learning):** Assessed through response to interactions and surveys. Behavioral coding and survey responses linked to database. (Level 2 Coding Structure).
    a. Scaled response to learning the goals for the game (Phiffer & Jones: 1989).
        i. Awareness,
        ii. Informational,

    iii. Personal,
    iv. Management,
    v. Consequence,
    vi. Collaboration,
    vii. Refocusing.

3. **Gaming Context:** Mediational responses to virtual learning environments (social cultural learning theory; mediational effects; distributed learning theory; innovation theory-Rogers) Quantitative user interactions are scaled based on factors below.
    a. **Tools:**
        i. **3D UI (Visual, Auditory, Haptic):** Accessibility, functionality, usability.
        ii. **Interactive Components (Pedagogical Agents, Avatars, Kiosks; Simulations):** Accessibility, functionality, usability.
        iii. **Learning Management System:** Accessibility, functionality, usability.
        iv. **Group Structures:** Accessibility, functionality, usability.
    b. **Interactive Tools:**
        i. Accessibility.
        ii. Functionality.
        iii. Usability.
4. **Interactions in Games (Sociocultural Learning Theory; Distributed Learning, CHAT):** Interactions of learners coded and scaled using Roger's theory of innovation and Phiffer's role behaviors.
    a. **Collaborative Activity (Level 2 Coding Structures) – Reformulation or Reinvention of Object:**
        i. **Disturbance Cluster:** Disturbance (anticipated, interactive, divergent), dilemma, innovation.
        ii. Questioning.
        iii. Interaction of difference voices.
    b. **Collaborative Activity (Level 2 Coding Structures) – Role Behaviors:**
        i. **Task Role:** Clarifying, following, information giving, information seeking, initiating, opinion seeking, orienting, reality testing, summarizing.
        ii. **Relationship Role:** Compromising, consensus taking, encouraging, gatekeeping, harmonizing, standard setting.
        iii. **Anti-Team Roles:** Avoiding, blocking, dominating, recognition seeking.
    c. **Individual Activity – Reformulation or Reinvention of Object:**
        i. **Phase 1:** Collaboration, goal-directed, inquiry, meaningful context, mediation, scaffolding.
        ii. **Phase 2:** Collaboration, goal-directed, inquiry, meaningful context, mediation, scaffolding.
        iii. **Phase 3:** Collaboration, goal-directed, inquiry, meaningful context, mediation, scaffolding.

LMS:

5. **Assessment of the Responses to the Learning Management System:** Standard user responses; LMS learning analytics system linked to Curriculum learning goals (Level 1 Coding Structures).
    a. Before the unit.
    b. During the unit.
        i. Phase 1.
        ii. Phase 2.
        iii. Phase 3.
    c. After the unit.
6. **Summative Learning Artifacts:** Assessment of learning artifacts using rubrics based on Bereiter Scheme of Knowledge; Rubrics linked to data base; (Level 3 Coding Structures).

a. Discussion board.
b. Project type:
    i. Excel chart/spreadsheet.
    ii. Sand box—virtual object design.
    iii. Inspiration concept map.
    iv. Poster.
    v. PowerPoint.
    vi. Review panel.
    vii. Media.
    viii. Word document.
c. Portfolio.

Strategic Knowledge Mapping

Strategic Knowledge Mapping will be the link between the CHAT LAS and the dynamic reporting of the learning in the IVLE. There is an alignment between the difficulty of strategic knowledge mapping and the difficulty of systems thinking. Strategic knowledge mapping is the process of designing a map of data collected by an organization to identify useful knowledge to support the goals of the organization. In this assessment model the CHAT systemic evaluation of learning defines the learning interactions based on the educational outcomes or goals. Strategic knowledge mapping is way to align the systemic analysis of learning resulting from CHAT in this educational program with the critical knowledge of strategic knowledge mapping. The game is based on notions of causality, measurability, complexity, and systems thinking. Educators' goal have been to simplify the process of understanding complexity, it is games are opportunities for creating an advanced game that will require a higher degree of experience and skill to play including problem-solving in simulations that recreate real-world scenarios (Wallis, 2014b).

Explorations in the literature suggest that more nuanced understandings await. These include abstraction (Wallis, 2014a), core/belt (Wallis, 2014c), orthogonal understandings of taxonomy, and others that await discovery on this new road to making better maps of learning in games. The SKM resulting from the learning analytics system provides educators and administrators with a mapping of the educational program and the ability to provide an integrated feedback record to the learners to support metacognitive processes. This systemic response to immersive virtual learning environments is a critical aspect of integrating an immersive learning process into a traditional educational setting. Providing teachers and learners with a holistic reporting of the learning replaces the need for standardized high-stakes testing with a learning assessment model matched to the immersive environment where it takes place.

The availability of metadata based on the Semantic Web technologies is recognized as a key asset that enables aggregation, provisioning, retrieval, reusability, adaptation, and personalization of (educational) multimedia content. In learning environments, Semantic Web technologies can integrate data about learning objects, learning activities and learners captured from various e-learning systems and tools. Other elements of the semantic web are expressed in formal specifications including Resource Description Framework (RDF), a variety of data interchange formats and notations such as RDF Schema (RDFS) and the Web Ontology Language (OWL), all of which provide a formal description of concepts, terms, and relationships within the categories and evaluative tools of the CHAT-LAS.

The use of the semantic web and data mining techniques provide the opportunity to link the CHAT model of categorization and analysis to identify 1) Context aspects in the immersive virtual learning environments including gaming rules, interactions in the game with avatars, and other learners' avatars, 2) Learning behaviors and level of learning responses which are the singular aspects of learning behaviors and initial structuring of the these defined responses based on the learning assessment structures including Scheme of Knowledge taxonomy for level of cognitive processes and learning response, intersubjectivity for dialogic analysis, and task and role response for collaborative activities and 3) mediational effects of the gaming environment. This first level of data structuring will collated in an online data management system with intial tags for context identification, learning, and mediational effects. At this point the data is structured through data management programs using the alogithms for search and restrieval based on CHAT principles to present the data set in meaningful ways for both the educator and the learner.

The CHAT-LAS will use dashboards to create user interfaces for review of learning responses, activities, and context. The CHAT-LAS dashboard will be a graphical presentation of the coded learning activities and responses and will be linked to the data mashups. A mashup is a lightweight web application that combines data from more than one source into an integrated and new, useful experience for the user. This data mashup, linked to the assessment model, incorporates a management information system, a dashboard, for user interface. The dashboard for this learning analytic system will provide clear representations of the learning in the immersive learning environments including the use of widgets. Widgets are users interfaces that connect information from other web pages. Linked with the data feeds from multiple data sets they are mashed together to provide learning assessment reports in the interface in the dashboard. These widgets are interactive components that feed responses to the educators and learners on their progress in the virtual learning environments. Built on a web-oriented architecture and leveraging lightweight, simple integration techniques this interaction between a learning assessment model based on cognitive theory and the development of a learning analytic system for a virtual immersive learning environment means that the learning resulting from games can become the most effective assessment model to understand the development of advanced functional knowledge.

The CHAT-LAS will use a MySQL database maintained on an Apache Web Server. Agents will communicate with each other through PHP. The user will add data through dynamic PHP web pages. For example a survey, project assessment, or project responses will be added by learners or instructors through these dynamic templates. This end-user annotation means that the designer of the IVLE will be able to provide templates that users will complete to add data to the LAS. The application converts these PHP pages to RDF statements through RAP API to add to the repository. The CHAT Learning Analytic System will structure the data using cultural historical activity theory and aligned metrics to create a metadata set that has been structured based on automatic structuring, semi-automatic structuring and instructor assessment structuring. The CHAT-LAS will then parse this metadata set to the user interfaces, the dashboard with the applicable widgets. An example would be a learner dashboard that includes an automated response widget that tells the learner what is current in the system such as last time in the IVLE, activities, contacts, projects. All those things that are counted automatically by the LAS. This can be a pedagogical agent that is linked the aligned database with a brief text hello and then a listing of activities, projects, etc. The learner will also see on his/her dashboard the semi-automated responses via a widget that identifies process, where they are in their group work, or a weekly response to assessments and interactions such as presentations, formative assessments. This widget could be a circular graph that shows progress reports. Finally the learner sees his/her assessments of summative projects and develop of cognitive processes in their projects and portfolio. Additionally the dashboard includes links to all aspects of the learning environment and resources such as calendars, courses' LMS, outside resources and interactive tools.

This comprehensive data management system using emergent online tools to develop an integrated learning analytic system that is based on research in the learning sciences and evaluative research models will be the first comprehensive assessment of learning from immersive virtual learning environments that are based on authentic pedagogical models designed to develop advanced learning and, as a result of this authentic design model, amendable to integration into current educational settings. In many ways, this level of learning response with this integration of online data management systems providing almost real-time feedback to educators and learners may only be possible in virtual learning environments. Additionally, immersive virtual learning environments, by providing the possibility to develop advanced learning and authentic learning may be the only viable potential for the productive integration of immersive learning environments that provide educators and learners with a viable alternative to traditional instruction and standardized testing to better serve their increasing diverse students and to empower them to become future knowledge workers.

CONCLUSION

The major issue in the assessment of learning in current educational settings that were established in the Industrial Age is that more human work in the current Knowledge Age deals with conceptual objects instead of the physical objects to which they are related (Bereiter, 2001). The Industrial Age of a standardized learning and instruction model is the source of the misalignment of standardized testing in education today. The rapid increase of information resulting from the internet can be defined using the Knowledge Doubling concept. In 1949 all human knowledge doubled every 100 years. It is now doubling every 13 months and is soon expected to double every 12 hours (IBM, 2013). The 19th century concept of learning and assessment as direct instruction and testing of recall of factoids does not match with the 21st century need for knowledge workers in a knowledge-based society.

The future of virtual immersive learning games and simulations to encourage advanced problem-based learning and the development of functional knowledge in P-12 education requires a learning analytic system that provides comprehensive learning assessment that creates a coherent report of the learning for both educators and learners. Virtual immersive learning environments can be a productive learning environment if designed to be incorporated in a comprehensive and integrated process with traditional curriculum and standards. Incorporated, not as singular gaming events, but as a comprehensive pedagogy with assessment the future of gaming to encourage authentic learning is immense.

Because an immersive virtual learning environment requires a great deal of communication and collaboration within the process of immersive learning activities in response to the rules of the virtual scenarios, the learner will build competency in communication, collaboration, decision making, systems thinking, meta analysis, and co-ordination. Educators' goal have been to simplify the process of understanding complexity, games are opportunities for creating an advanced IVLE that will require a higher degree of experience and skill to play including problem-solving in simulations that recreate real-world scenarios.

A few educational applications have sought to harness the power of these new virtual environments for teaching and learning purposes and more will surely follow. However, there are challenges to making an environment educational as well as immersive and engaging. A key challenge is to understand the nature of the social and cognitive experiences provided in the immersive virtual context and make sense of the growth and development potential that are part of those experiences.

There are four assumptions in the CHAT-LAS framework for assessment and making learning visible in IVLE. First, cultural historical activity theory (CHAT) as a conceptual orientation to the work of building a learning analytics framework. CHAT is based on established systems principles to provide a way to understand real world experiences and how individuals make sense of the world and develop their activity within it. Second, within a game all actions of the participants and conditions of the system can be monitored and captured for use in assessment. This full representation of action and conditions in the system provides a rich data set for mapping and making sense of the participants' actions. These semantic mappings will address both cognitive and social competence. Third, the streams of data and data sets of participant action and conditions can be related to expectations for learning and social behavior. Thus the system can monitor more than just what the participant explores but also the way they explore objects in the environment and if the ways of exploration are advancing along a schema of projected learning. These examples show a common form of assessment, that of comparing a behavior to an expected performance. We anticipate that assessment in the IVLE can apply a breadth and depth of behavioral data from activity with the system to inform these assessments against models or expected patterns of behavior. Fourth, the data over time and from multiple sources can be represented in a variety of forms from immediate feedback within the system to reports about learning and growth over time. A variety of visualization and notification techniques can be employed to fit the information about learning process and outcomes to appropriate decision making for the various stakeholders. Notifications can be used to keep parents and teachers informed about activity within the system as well as be used by the participants to make decisions about what to do next in the environment.

Immersive virtual learning environments are a black box for educators. What happens in the game that impacts and shapes the development of new knowledge and skills? The CHAT-LAS integrates multiple data sets to provide a comprehensive perspective on the learning responses of the student,provides the instructor and the students with an ongoing feedback model of the assessment of learning in immersive virtual learning environments. In comparison to the standardized model of testing that focuses on the isolation of content, traditional instructional methods and low level learning responses, this model of learning and assessment provides the opportunity for learners to build real-world authentic functional knowledge and an integrated assessment model. A method for understanding, assessing and representing learning within immersive virtual learning environments that parallels the richness of the immersive experience and takes advantage of a learning support system, that captures the actions of the user and always knows the state of the environment is a critical aspect of developing and integrating games in education. We need systems that relate the activity of participants to learning objectives and that make learning visible to students, teachers and educational decision makers. This prototype is an effort to articulate a vision and framework for making learning visible and a pathway to system requirements and methods for assessing learning. Additionally, this CHAT-based learning analytic system is also a systemic evaluation process that allows educators to revise educational programs to increase efficiency and effectiveness.

The long-term goal of the project is to develop a framework that can be broadly applied across fields to represent what is being learned in the gaming experience to key stakeholders (students, parents, teachers, educational leaders, and researchers/developers) and represent it in a way (timeliness, organization, visualization, etc) that will impact action and decision making. In the future researchers and designers can focus on integrative processes rather than disruptive processes based on outside pressures for supporting change in education. Reform in education should be based both on the emergent technologies and a solid theoretical and practical basis for change that focuses on the needs of the society to support the development of all students' knowledge, concepts and skills in order to become the future knowledge workers and global citizens.

REFERENCES

Anderson, J. R., Reder, L. M., & Simon, H. A. (1997). Situative versus cognitive perspectives: Form versus substance. *Educational Researcher*, *26*(1), 18–21.

Barab, S., Kling, R., & Gray, J. (2006). *Designing for Virtual Communities in the Service of Learning*. NY: Cambridge Publishing, Cambridge University Press.

Barab, S., Thomas, M., Dodge, T., Carteaux, R., & Tuzun, H. (2005). Making learning fun:Quest Atlantis, a game without guns. *Educational Technology Research and Development*, *53*(1), 86–107. doi:10.1007/BF02504859

Barab, S. A., & Duffy, T. (2000). From practice fields to communities of practice. In D. Jonassen & S. M. Land (Eds.), *Theoretical Foundations of Learning Environments* (pp. 25–56). Mahwah, NJ: Lawrence Erlbaum Associates.

Barab, S. A., Hay, K. E., & Yamagata-Lynch, L. C. (2001). Constructing networks of activity: An in-situ research methodology. *Journal of the Learning Sciences*, *10*(1&2), 63–112. doi:10.1207/S15327809JLS10-1-2_5

Bednar, A. K., Cunningham, D., Duffy, T. M., & Perry, D. J. (1992). Theory into practice: How do we link? In T. Duffy & D. Jonassen (Eds.), *Constructivism and the technology of instruction* (pp. 17–34). Hillsdale, NJ: Lawrence Erlbaum Associates.

Bereiter, C. (2002). *Education and mind in the knowledge age*. New York: Lawrence Erlbaum Assoc.

Bereiter, C., & Scardamalia, M. (1996). Rethinking learning. In D. Olson & N. Torrance (Eds.), *Handbook of education and human development: New models of learning, teaching, and schooling* (pp. 485–516). Cambridge, MA: Basil Blackwell.

Bereiter, C., & Scardamalia, M. (2001). *Beyond Bloom's taxonomy: Rethinking knowledge for the knowledge age: Developing higher-level approaches to knowledge*. Retrieved from http://unr.edu/homepage/luvisis/bereiter.html

Bransford, J. D., Brown, A. L., & Cocking, R. R. (Eds.). (1999). *How people learn: Brain, mind, experience, and school*. Washington, DC: National Academy Press.

Broussard, J. (2014). Why poor schools can't win at standardized testing. The Atlantic. Retrieved from http://www2.ed.gov/nclb/accountability/ayp/edpicks.jhtml?src=lnWhy

Brown, A. L., Ash, D., Rutherford, M., Nakagawa, K., Gordon, A., & Campione, J. C. (1993). Distributed expertise in the classroom. In G. Salomon (Ed.), *Distributed cognitions: Psychological and educational considerations*. NY: Cambridge University Press.

Brown, A. L., & Campione, J. C. (1990). Communities of learning and thinking or a context by any other name. *Contributions to Human Development*, *21*, 108–126. doi:10.1159/000418984

Brown, J. S., Collins, A., & Duguid, P. (1989). Situated cognition and the culture of learning. *Educational Researcher*, *18*(1), 32–42. doi:10.3102/0013189X018001032

Bruer, J. (1993). *Schools for thought*. Cambridge: The MIT Press.

Bruner, J. (1984). Vygotsky's zone of proximal development: The hidden agenda. In B. Rogoff, & J. Wertsch (Eds.), Children's learning in the zone of proximal development: New directions for child development. San Francisco: Jossey-Bass.

Bruner, J. (1990). *Acts of meaning*. Cambridge, MA: Harvard University Press.

Cole, M., & Engeström, Y. (1993). A cultural-historical approach to distributed cognition. In G. Salomon (Ed.), *Distributed cognition: Psychological and educational considerations*. Cambridge, MA: Cambridge University Press.

Collins, A. (1991). The role of computer technology in restructuring schools. *Phi Delta Kappan, 73*(1), 28–36.

Dede, C. (1996). Emerging Technologies and Distributed Learning. *American Journal of Distance Education, 10*(2), 2, 4–36. doi:10.1080/08923649609526919

Dede, C. (1997). The evolution of constructivist learning environments: Immersion in distributed, virtual worlds. In B. Wilson (Ed.), *Constructivist Learning Environments: Case Studies in Instructional Design*. Englewood Cliffs, NJ: Educational Technology Publications.

Dede, C. (2009). *Immersive Interfaces for Engagement and Learning Science*. 323, 66. DOI: Retrieved from http://www.sciencemag.org10.1126/science.1167311

Dewey, J. (1938). *Experience and Education*. New York, NY: Kappa Delta Pi.

Engeström, Y. (1987). *Learning by expanding: An activity-theoretical approach to developmental research*. Helsinki: Orienta-Konsultit.

Engeström, Y., Miettinen, R., & Punamaki, R. (Eds.). (1999). *Perspectives on activity theory*. Cambridge, U.K.: Cambridge University Press. doi:10.1017/CBO9780511812774

Evans, J. (2013). Problems with standardized testing. Retrieved from http://www.education.com/reference/article/Ref_Test_Problems_Seven/

Gee, J. (2003). What video games have to teach us about learning and literacy. *Computer Applications in Entertainment., 1*(1). doi: 10.1145/950566.950595

Gee, J. (2004). *Situated Language and Learning. A Critique of Traditional Schooling*. New York, NY: Routledge.

Greeno, J. G. (1997). On claims that answer the wrong question. *Educational Researcher, 26*(1), 5–17.

Haberman, M. (1991). The pedagogy of poverty versus good teaching. *Phi Delta Kappan, 73*(4), 290–294.

Hui, D., & Russell, D. L. (2009). Understanding the Effectiveness of Collaborative Activity in Online Professional Development with Innovative Educators through Intersubjectivity. In L. Tomei (Ed.), *Information Communication Technologies for Enhanced Education and Learning: Advanced Applications and Developments* (pp. 283–302). Hershey, PA: Information Science Reference; doi:10.4018/978-1-60566-150-6.ch020

Il'enkov, E. V. (1977). *Dialectical logic: Essays in its history and theory*. Moscow: Progress. http://nces.ed.gov/pubs2013/2013037.pdf

Jonassen, D. H. (2000). Toward a design theory of problem solving. *Educational Technology Research and Development, 48*(4), 63–85. doi:10.1007/BF02300500

Jonassen, D. H., Peck, K. L., & Wilson, B. G. (1999). *Learning with technology: A constructivist perspective*. Upper Saddle River, New Jersey: Merrill-Prentice Hall.

Kapp, K.M. & O'Driscoll, T. (2010) *Learning in 3D: Adding a New Dimension to Enterprise Learning and Collaboration*. San Francisco, CA: Wiley Publications

Kozol, J. (1991). *Savage Inequalities: Children in America's Schools*. New York, NY: Random House.

Kozol, J. (2005). *The Shame of the Nation: The Restoration of Apartheid Schooling in America* (pp. 63–64). New York, NY: Random House.

Laffey, J., Lin, G. Y., & Lin, Y. (2006). Assessing Social Ability in Online Learning Environments. *Journal of Interactive Learning Research*, *17*(2), 163–177.

Lave, J., & Wenger, E. (1991). *Situated learning: Legitimate peripheral participation*. Cambridge, UK: Cambridge University Press. doi:10.1017/CBO9780511815355

Moll, L. (1990). *Vygotsky and education: Instructional implications and applications of sociohistorical psychology*. Cambridge, UK: Cambridge University Press. doi:10.1017/CBO9781139173674

Moll, L. C., Tapia, J., & Whitmore, K. F. (1993). Living knowledge: The social distribution of cultural resources for thinking. In G. Salomon (Ed.), *Distributed cognitions: Psychological and educational considerations* (pp. 139–163). NY: Cambridge University Press.

National Center for Education Statistics. (2013). The Condition of Education 2013. U.S. Department of Education. Institute of Education Sciences. Retrieved from http://nces.ed.gov/pubs2013/2013037.pdf

Oshima, J., Bereiter, C., & Scardamalia, M. (1995). Information-Access Characteristics for High Conceptual Progress in a Computer-Networked Learning Environment. Proceedings of CSCL'95 conference.

Palinscar, A. S., & Brown, A. L. (1984). Reciprocal teaching of comprehension-fostering and comprehension-monitoring activities. *Cognition and Instruction*, *1*(2), 117–175. doi:10.1207/s1532690xci0102_1

Papamitsiou, Z., & Economides, A. (2014). Learning Analytics and Educational Data Mining in Practice: A Systematic Literature Review of Empirical Evidence. *Journal of Educational Technology & Society*, *17*(4), 49.

Pea, R. (1993). Practices of distributed intelligence and designs for education. In G. Salomon (Ed.), *Distributed cognitions: Psychological and educational considerations* (pp. 47–87). Cambridge, UK: Cambridge University Press.

Pea, R. D. (1985). Beyond amplification: Using the computer to reorganize mental functioning. *Educational Psychologist*, *20*(4), 167–182. doi:10.1207/s15326985ep2004_2

Pfeiffer, J. W., & Jones, J. E. (Eds.). (1974). *"Role nominations" A handbook of structured experiences for human relations training* (Vol. II). San Francisco, CA: Jossey Bass.

Piaget, J. (1952). *The Origins of Intelligence in Children*. New York, NY: International University Press. doi:10.1037/11494-000

Popham, J. (1999). Why standardized tests don't measure educational quality. Retrieved from http://www.ascd.org/publications/educational-leadership

Resnick, L., Levine, J., & Teasley, S. (Eds.), (1991). *Perspectives on socially shared cognition*. Washington, DC: American Psychological Association. doi:10.1037/10096-000

Rittel, H., & Webber, M. (1984). Planning problems are wicked problems. In N. Cross (Ed.), Developments in design methodology (pp. 135-144). New York, NY: Wiley Publications.

Rogers, E. M. (1995). *Diffusion of innovations* (4th ed.). NY: The Free Press.

Roschelle, J. M., Pea, R. D., Hoadley, C. M., Gordin, D. N., & Means, B. M. (2000). Changing how and what children learn in school with computer-based technologies. *Children and Computer Technology*, *10*(2), 76–101. PMID:11255710

Roth, W. M., & Bowne, G. M. (1995). Knowing and interacting: A study of culture, practices, and resources in a grade 8 open-inquiry science classroom guided by a cognitive apprenticeship metaphor. *Cognition and Instruction*, *13*(1), 73–128. doi:10.1207/s1532690xci1301_3

Russell, D. (2005b). Transformation in an Urban School: Using Systemic Analysis to Understand an Innovative Urban Teacher's Implementation of an Online Problem-Based Unit. *International Journal of Instructional Technology and Distance Learning*, *2*(2), 11–28.

Russell, D. (2006). Online professional development for educators: A Case student analysis using cultural historical activity theory. R. Sharma, & S. Mishra (Eds.), Cases on Global e-Learning Practices: Successes and Pitfalls (pp. 108-122). Hershey, PA: Information Science Publishing.

Russell, D. (2009). Group collaboration in an online problem-based university course. In O. Tan (Ed), Creativity and Problem-Based Learning (pp. 173-192). Australia: Cengage Learning.

Russell, D., Gentzler, P., & Wood, L. (2014). Mobile learning in nursing education: Lessons learned. In R. Huang, & C.N. Kinshuk (Eds.), *The New Development of Technology Enhanced Learning; Concept, Research and Best Practices*. Springer. DOI:http://link.springer.com/book/10.1007/978-3-642-38291-8

Russell, D., & Schneiderheinze, A. (2005a). Implementing an Innovation Cluster in Educational Settings In Order to Develop Constructivist-Based Learning Environments. *Journal of Educational Technology & Society*, *8*(2), 7–15.

Salomon, G. (1993). No distribution without individuals' cognition: A dynamic interactional view. In G. Salomon (Ed.), *Distributed cognitions: Psychological and educational considerations*. NY: Cambridge University Press.

Savery, J. R., & Duffy, T. M. (1996). Problem based learning: An instructional model and its constructivist framework. *Educational Technology*, *35*(5), 31–38.

Schank, R.C. (1994). Goal-based scenarios. In R.C.S.E. Langer (Ed.), *Beliefs, reasoning, and decision making: Psycho-logic in honor of Bob Abelson*. Hillsdale, NJ: Lawrence Erlbaum Associates.

Standardized Testing Costs Retrieved. (2015, January). *US Department of Education NCLB/Stronger Accountability*. Retrieved from http://www.huffingtonpost.com/2012/11/29/standardized-testing- costs_n_2213932.html

The Condition of Education. (2013). *US Department of Education. Institute of Education Sciences National Center for Education Statistics*. Retrieved from http://nces.ed.gov/pubs2013/2013037.pdf

von Glasersfeld, E. (1998). Cognition, construction of knowledge, and teaching. In M. R. Matthews (Ed.), *Constructivism in science education: A philosophical examination*. Norwell, MA: Kluwer Academic Publishers. doi:10.1007/978-94-011-5032-3_2

Vygotsky, L. (1986). *Thought and language*. Cambridge: The MIT Press.

Vygotsky, L. S. (1978). *Mind in society: The development of higher psychological processes*. Cambridge, MA: Harvard University Press.

Wallis, S., & Wright, B. (2014a, March 4-6) Strategic knowledge mapping: The co-creation of useful knowledge. Proceedings of the 42nd annual conference Association for Business Simulation and Experiential Learning (ABSEL). Las Vegas, NV.

Wallis, S. E. (2014b). Abstraction and insight: Building better conceptual systems to support more effective social change. *Foundations of Science*, *19*(4), 353–362. doi:10.1007/s10699-014-9344-4

Wallis, S. E. (2014c). A systems approach to understanding theory: Finding the core, identifying opportunities for improvement, and integrating fragmented fields. *Systems Research and Behavioral Science*, *31*(1), 23–31. doi:10.1002/sres.2159

Warburton, S., & Garcia, M. (2009). 3D design and collaboration in massively multi-user virtual environments (MUVEs). In D. Russell (Ed.), *Cases of Collaboration in Virtual Learning Environments: Processes and Interactions* (pp. 121–139). Hershey, PA: Information Science Reference.

Wertsch, J. (Ed.), (1995). *Studies of mind*. Cambridge, CT: Harvard University Press.

Wertsch, J., Resnick, L., Levine, J., & Teasley, S. (1991). *Perspectives on socially shared cognition*. American Psychological Association.

Wertsch, J. V. (1998). *Mind as action*. New York, NY: Oxford University Press.

Chapter 25
Navigating Through Virtual Worlds:
From Single Characters to Large Crowds

Norman Jaklin
Utrecht University, Netherlands

Roland Geraerts
Utrecht University, Netherlands

ABSTRACT

With the rise and success of digital games over the past few decades, path planning algorithms have become an important aspect in modern game development for all types of genres. Indirectly-controlled playable characters as well as non-player characters have to find their way through the game's environment to reach their goal destinations. Modern gaming hardware and new algorithms enable the simulation of large crowds with thousands of individual characters. Still, the task of generating feasible and believable paths in a time- and storage-efficient way is a big challenge in this emerging and exciting research field. In this chapter, the authors describe classical algorithms and data structures, as well as recent approaches that enable the simulation of new and immersive features related to path planning and crowd simulation in modern games. The authors discuss the pros and cons of such algorithms, give an overview of current research questions and show why graph-based methods will soon be replaced by novel approaches that work on a surface-based representation of the environment.

INTRODUCTION

Over the past decade, educational games have received increasing attention. By now, a large body of research has been carried out to determine how the principles behind engaging digital games can be utilized to improve learning. In general, this is an open research question with new methods still being developed, e.g. (Jeuring, van Rooij, & Pronost, 2014). It has been shown for particular cases that engaging virtual environments can yield a higher motivation and better learning results for students (Murray, Bogost, Mateas, & Nitsche, 2006; Ketelhut, Dede, Clarke, Nelson, & Bowman, 2007; Ketelhut, 2007; Gee, 2007; Schmitz, Specht, & Klemke, 2012).

DOI: 10.4018/978-1-4666-9629-7.ch025

A key requirement to achieve a high level of engagement and thus better learning results is the game being *immersive*. Immersion can be achieved in many ways, among which are the technological aspects of a game. Modern computer hardware and smarter algorithms have radically changed and shaped the overall appearance of digital games in general and educational games in particular. Technological aspects of games such as graphics, modeling or physics simulation have received much attention, and this led to a wide range of novel techniques to generate visually convincing and believable pictures, character models, and animations.

By contrast, the *paths* traversed by virtual characters[1] are often *not* visually convincing. Many educational games do not let their virtual characters move around autonomously. This is due to the fact that moving characters might not be necessary to achieve the learning goals. Furthermore, the computation of realistic and visually convincing paths is difficult and might even ruin a user's immersion when done in a cheap way. However, many educational games try to simulate a realistic virtual 3D environment to better match recent advances in entertainment games. An example of such a game is *The River City Project* (2002 - 2007). The game has been successfully used by teachers and students in the U.S., and results indicate that using virtual environments in education "might act as a catalyst for change in student's self-efficacy and learning processes" (Ketelhut, 2007). *The River City Project* simulates a virtual city from the late 19th century with buildings and different terrain, and the residents of the city are displayed as virtual 3D non-player characters. These, however, seem stationary and do not autonomously move around the city in a realistic way. We believe that state-of-the-art path planning and crowd simulation methods can improve such games with respect to the users' immersion and overall learning experiences.

Many games that *do* support moving characters rely on predetermined or scripted paths. In such games, a designer can manually create believable paths that are of high quality. While this does not ruin a user's immersion, it also limits the flexibility and design possibilities of a game. By contrast, games that are more flexible and allow unpredictable interactions among characters rely on *algorithms* to handle path planning.

In this chapter, we will discuss such algorithms. We focus on path planning for single virtual characters and large virtual crowds. The latter have become increasingly important in simulation software for mass events and evacuation training, e.g. (SportEvac, 2014), which could be used in school education to increase the students' awareness of potential dangers during such events.

The overall goal in this research field is to compute visually convincing and natural paths for a large number of characters in real-time to improve the user's immersion. We will discuss how this field and the methods used have changed over the past few decades, and give an overview of state-of-the-art techniques and open research problems.

We will start with discussing different ways to represent traversable space in a virtual environment. A classical approach is to use a grid or waypoint-graph representation. Path planning is then done using a graph-based search algorithm. We will explain why a graph representation is not adequate for many challenging path planning and crowd simulation problems.

A more recent approach to represent traversable space is to use a *navigation mesh*. We will discuss the advantages of navigation meshes over graph representations. In a believable and immersive game world, autonomous virtual characters need to react adequately to dynamic changes in the environment. Such dynamic changes might allow traversing paths that were previously blocked, or they might block paths that were previously traversable. Examples are parking cars on a sidewalk or an automatic door that opens and closes. Many games avoid solving these issues by using workaround techniques. Characters may be permitted to temporarily walk through obstacles, or the discs used for collision avoidance are very small. These workarounds may destroy a player's experience in an otherwise immersive world. A navigation mesh needs to be able to efficiently represent virtual environments that can dynamically change over time, and we will discuss cutting-edge research on this topic.

Some recent path planning methods that use a navigation mesh are based on a multi-level planning hierarchy. They compute a first rough path and then use advanced path following techniques that modify the input path to generate a smooth curve with certain desired properties. In this context, we will discuss the *Indicative Route Method*, which uses an augmented navigation mesh called *Explicit Corridor Map*. We also discuss its successor, the *Modified Indicative Routes and Navigation* method, which allows path planning in heterogeneous virtual environments that feature different region types. We will also give an overview of different collision-avoidance techniques and discuss their advantages and drawbacks.

Another topic we will discuss is social group behavior. While many of the aforementioned path planning methods solve issues related to single characters, they lack simulating social aspects for groups. In real life, people tend to form social groups and split up again after a while. Members of such groups try to stay in particular social formations whenever possible. Other people display different walking behavior when encountering a social group. For instance, social territories occupied by groups are usually avoided by other people. An immersive virtual world needs to reflect this.

Handling large virtual crowds requires different approaches. Virtual crowds that consist of hundreds of individual characters can be rendered with modern gaming hardware. In an educational game that features large crowds, however, only a small portion of the overall CPU power can be assigned to handle crowd simulation. Thus, coordinating and handling the navigation of crowds requires advanced strategies on a theoretical and practical level.

We now start by discussing different ways to represent traversable space in a virtual environment. Such representations form a basis on top of which path planning and crowd simulation can be performed.

REPRESENTING TRAVERSABLE SPACE

How should traversable space be represented in a game? The choice for a certain representation is strongly connected to the complexity and required efficiency of the application at hand. In this section, we discuss several representations of traversable space and their pros and cons.

Historically, digital games have been developed for entertainment purposes, while educational games are a comparably new phenomenon. Thus, we will consider examples from popular entertainment games when discussing traversable space. The same observations and conclusions can be applied to recent and future educational games.

Depending on the type of game, more or less effort needs to be spent on this matter. As an extreme example in which representing traversable space is a trivial task, consider the classic 2D arcade game *Space Invaders* (Taito Corporation, 1978). Here, the enemies move in a predetermined and scripted way, which does not involve any path planning. The player's traversable space is only a 1D straight-line segment at the bottom of the screen for which no complex representation is necessary. Note that there is no automated path planning for the directly-controlled player character either, but the player's traversable space is still important for collision avoidance with the left and right screen limits. A game that is more complex with respect to path planning is *Pac-Man*

(Namco, 1980). The enemies follow different strategies to catch the player. Here, the 2D game world consists of rectilinear tiles that are either traversable or blocked. Thus, a simple tile-based grid approach is a sufficient way to represent all traversable space. By contrast, many modern games tend to simulate an open world (e.g. *Grand Theft Auto V* (Rockstar Games, 2013)), or they provide a sandbox environment, which allows players to generate their own content (e.g. *Minecraft* (Mojang, 2009)). Both types of games feature highly dynamic multi-layered 3D environments with different terrain types. Characters in future variants of such game genres should not only plan collision-free paths, but also autonomously detect and use areas where climbing or jumping over gaps is possible to access difficult-to-reach areas in the game world. Such features require a representation of traversable space that is far from trivial and still open to future research.

The topology of the game world also influences the choice of how to represent traversable space. While the topology of the world in *Space Invaders* is a 2D plane, there are games with more complex topologies. In *Pac-Man*, characters are allowed to exit to the left and right screen edges to appear on the opposite side. This behavior follows the topology of a cylinder. An example of a game with the world topology of a torus is *Asteroids* (Atari Inc, 1979). The player's ship as well as asteroids and flying saucers can exit the screen to all four edges and appear on the opposite side. 3D Games that allow a character to fly, such as *Descent* (Parallax Software, 1994), feature a 3D space topology. In *Super Mario Galaxy*, the player can fully circumnavigate small planets and, hence, the world topology equals a sphere (Nintendo EAD Tokyo, 2007). In *Super Paper Mario* (Nintendo SPD, 2007), the player has to interactively switch between 2D and 3D perspectives to solve puzzles. In *Portal* (Valve Corporation, 2007), the player can create traversable connections between arbitrary points in particular areas of the game world. The game *Monument Valley* (Ustwo, 2014) features dynamic Escher-like worlds that are physically impossible. Other exotic topological spaces such as the *Möbius Strip* (Möbius & Listing (independently), 1858) or the *Klein Bottle* (Klein, 1882) require different path planning strategies, but may also enable novel gameplay elements.[2]

Note that we only discuss games that require two-dimensional traversable space representations. Even when the game world is technically a (multi-layered) 3D environment, a 2D representation is sufficient as long as characters need to traverse 2D surfaces only. For actual 3D path planning (e.g. for autonomous flying characters), the problems we discuss in this chapter are more complex and require even more advanced algorithms beyond the scope of this chapter.

For more information on world topologies and the concept of traversable space in digital games, we refer to the discussion *Theorizing Navigable Space in Video Games* (Wolf, 2009/2010). Its main focus is on space the *player* can traverse from an abstract level. For path planning purposes, however, we are interested in representing space for autonomous characters or player characters that are controlled in an indirect way (e.g. by assigning a goal position via a mouse click or a finger press on a touchpad). Therefore, we will now list several methods to represent traversable space that have been used in past and present digital games, and discuss their advantages and drawbacks.

Grids

Grids can be intuitively described as regular subdivisions of the plane into cells of a particular shape and with a particular grid resolution. From an abstract point of view, grids can be seen as a special case of *lattice structures*. This means that by adding so-called *generator* vectors to a given cell point in the grid, any neighboring cell point can be obtained. For a 2D grid, two generators representing the *up* and *right* directions are sufficient to obtain all grid cell points (LaValle, 2006).

Figure 1. Rectilinear, isometric and hexagonal grids

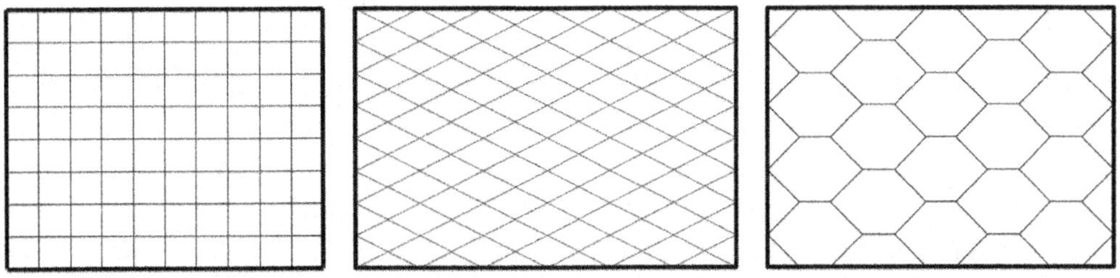

Grids are intuitive and easy to implement, which makes them a popular representation of traversable space. The most common types are rectilinear or square grids. However, other types have been widely used in games, too. Hexagonal grids are common, as well as grids with isometric diamond-shaped tiles; see Figure 1. From a topological point of view, isometric grids and rectilinear grids are equal. They are commonly used in 2D games to simulate an isometric view on pseudo-three-dimensional game worlds in which correct clipping is easily achieved by rendering objects on the grid from top to bottom along the screen. They are also used in many traditional and modern board games, and have also been widely used in *pen and paper role-playing games* to simulate combat scenarios.

When traversable space is represented using a grid, the actual path finding is usually performed on the *dual graph* of the grid cells. This is because a wide range of graph-search algorithm exists that can compute shortest paths efficiently (see Section "A* and its variants"). Furthermore, game objects are usually placed in the center of the grid cell. In the dual graph, each grid cell is represented as a vertex and adjacent cells are connected by an edge. While a rectilinear, square or isometric grid keeps its structure when considering its dual graph

Figure 2. Hexagonal grids and triangular grids are dual graphs of each other. Each point is a vertex in the triangular graph (red), and it corresponds to a hexagonal cell in its dual graph representation.

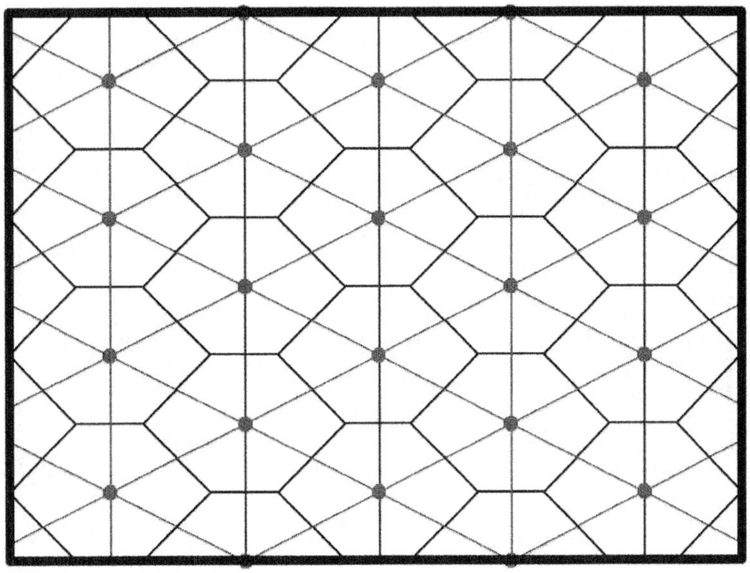

(except for an offset translation), hexagonal grids become triangular and vice versa, see Figure 2. Thus, using the center points of hexagonal cells as possible character positions is technically the same as performing path-finding on a triangular graph. In the case of square grids, typical variants are 4-neighbor and 8-neighbor square grids, depending on whether diagonal movement from one cell to another is allowed or not.

Path planning can also be done on the edges or vertices of the grid itself. *The Settlers II*, for instance, uses a hexagonal grid (Blue Byte Software (today: Ubisoft Blue Byte), 1996). The player can build roads along the edges and place flags along the vertices of the grid. Objects are then distributed and moved along the roads. The edges and vertices of the grid are also used in adaptations of abstract board games such as *Go* or in many puzzle games.

While grids are easy to implement, a major problem is that grids may not cover all of the traversable space visually shown to the player. Some corners of the game world and important passages between two obstacles might not be traversable due to a too coarse grid resolution; see Figure 3.

The question of how much a grid path deviates from a shortest path on the exact geometry has been mathematically answered via path-length analysis proofs. Nash (2012) presented a unified proof structure for upper bounds on the length of square, triangular, hexagonal and cubic 3D grid paths. The author showed that a grid path on a triangular, 4-neighbor square, 8-neighbor square, or hexagonal grid can be at most 2, 1.41, 1.08, or 1.15 times as long as an optimal (shortest) path, respectively. In addition, Jaklin, Tibboel, and Geraerts (2014) presented a path-cost analysis proof for 8-neighbor square grid paths in environments

Figure 3. Squared grid overlaid on a polygonal environment: Red (dark) squares count as obstacles because they are partially covered by polygons. Some passages are not traversable due to the too coarse grid resolution.

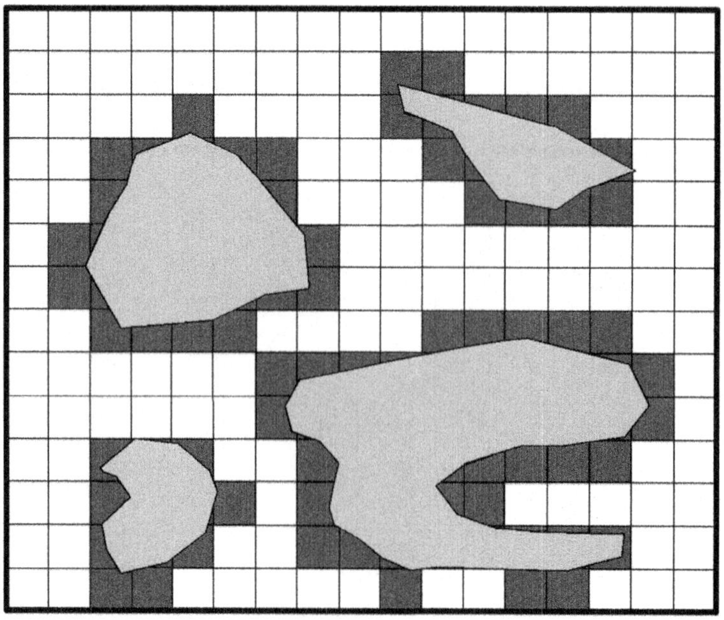

Figure 4. A waypoint graph for an environment with four obstacles

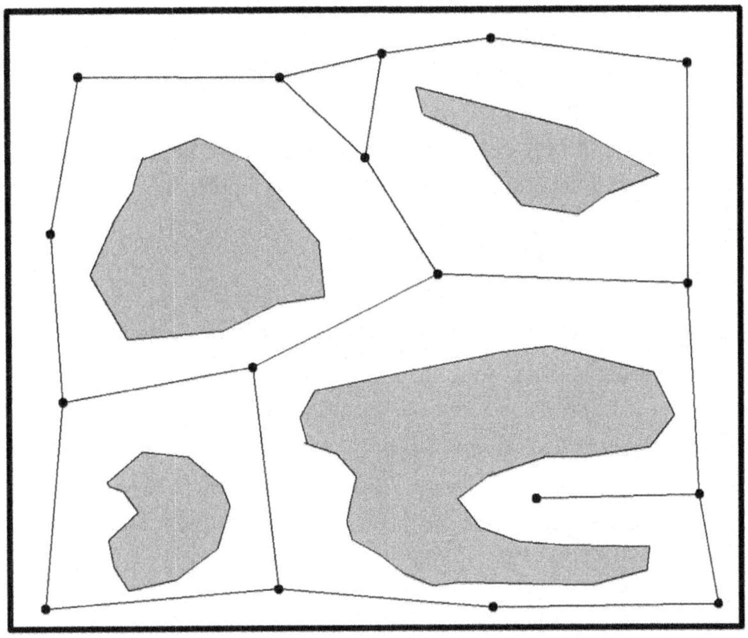

with multiple region types (e.g. different terrain types), where the cost for traversing a particular region is given as a weight .They showed that a grid path can be at most 5.08 times as long as an optimal path in this situation, when all regions are aligned with the grid.

Grids or their dual graphs are also inflexible because characters' motions are hard to coordinate when two or more characters follow the same edge bi-directionally. In addition, they impose only an infinitely small subset of all possible trajectories. Resulting motions may not be visually convincing because the underlying graph edges are not smooth and do not cover energy-optimal paths. Smoothing the paths can be expensive and often requires a global approach. This is undesired because digital games require real-time responses. Furthermore, the dual graph of a grid requires computationally expensive updates when the obstacles are inserted, deleted, or moved. Note that these issues also occur with other graph-based approaches such as waypoint graphs, which we discuss now.

Waypoint Graphs or Road Maps

Waypoint graphs and road maps are two interchangeable terms. The nodes (or waypoints) resemble locations in the game world in which a character can be located. An edge between two nodes in the graph resembles a straight-line path which characters can traverse without hitting obstacles; see Figure 4.

Waypoint graphs can be automatically generated based on the *visibility graph* of the environment or based on some other decomposition of the traversable space such as the *medial axis* of the environment (see Section "Navigation Meshes" and (de Berg, van Kreveld, Overmars, & Schwarzkopf, 2000). Other examples from the robotics community are *Probabilistic Road Maps* (Kavraki, Svestka, Latombe, & Overmars, 1996) and *Rapidly-Exploring Random Trees* (LaValle, 1998). The latter two are more general because they can be used to solve higher-dimensional problems, e.g. finding a path for a robot manipulator arm with six joints that has to grasp an object and move it through a cluttered 3D environment.

The nodes of a *visibility graph* are the vertices of the polygonal obstacles in the environment. An edge between two nodes is added in the visibility graph, if the straight-line segment between them does not intersect any obstacles, or, in other words, if the two nodes *see* each other; see Figure 5 (left). Note that the complexity of the visibility graph can be quadratic in the number n of polygon vertices. The graph can be computed in $O(n^2)$ worst-case optimal time (Welzl, 1985; Ghosh, 2007).

Laumond (1987) introduced the concept of the *generalized visibility graph*, which has been used for path planning by several authors (Yu, 2006; Masehian & Amin-Naseri, 2004; Wein, van den Berg, & Halperin, 2007). For a character that is represented as a disc with a maximum size $r \geq 0$, the obstacles in the generalized visibility graph are first inflated by r using Minkowski's operations. There are two types of nodes in the resulting graph. Vertices of the first type are concave corners of the inflated obstacles. Vertices of the second type are *fictitious vertices* that correspond to convex arcs of the inflated obstacles. In general, a shortest path in a polygonal scene consists of segments that are tangent to the borders of the obstacles. Therefore, it can be shown that all vertices of type one need not be connected by additional edges because they are never part of a shortest path. For the set of fictitious vertices, a generalized notion of visibility is used: Two fictitious vertices *see* each other, if and only if there is at least one pair of points on the corresponding two arc segments such that their straight-line connection is tangent to both arc segments. See Figure 5 (right) for an example. The generalized visibility graph is not only smaller in the number of edges, but it also makes a character automatically keep clearance from obstacles. Since the search for tangents can be performed in $O(n^2)$ time, the overall time complexity to compute the generalized visibility graph is the same as for the visibility graph.

Another common way to build a waypoint graph is to manually determine waypoints and edges for a given environment in the level design phase of game production. Some games such as real-time strategy games (e.g. *Starcraft II* (Bliz-

Figure 5. Left: A visibility graph for a scene with three obstacles. Dashed edges are pruned in the generalized visibility graph because their corresponding vertices in the generalized graph do not see each other. Right: A generalized visibility graph for the same scene with inflated obstacles and corresponding visibility edges.

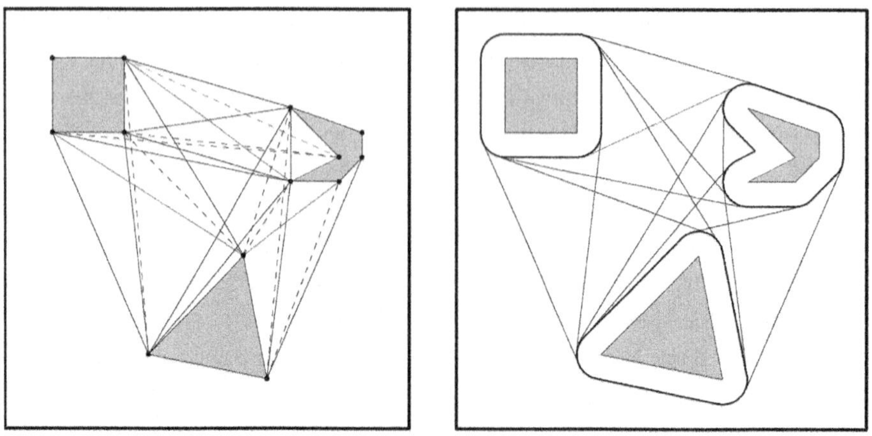

zard Entertainment, 2010)) even allow players to set waypoints themselves and use this as a tactical gameplay element.

As mentioned before, waypoint graphs are generally smaller in the number of nodes and edges compared to the dual graph of a grid. This decreases the time to perform a path-finding algorithm on that structure (see Section "A* and its Variants").

However, all graph-based techniques suffer from a range of problems that are inherent to these techniques. A graph does not provide information about the actual geometry of the scene, and it does not allow characters to deviate from their paths induced by the graph edges. This becomes an even bigger problem for a large crowd and collision-avoidance among the crowd members. The resulting paths may neither be natural nor visually convincing.

Given all these issues, we believe that the end of graph-based methods for advanced path planning has come. Recent techniques based on a surface-representation of the virtual environment - such as navigation meshes - are a promising next step into the future of digital games that feature large crowds or require other advanced navigational tasks.

Navigation Meshes

A *navigation mesh* is a set of two-dimensional simple polygons representing the traversable space in a game world. With this general definition, the aforementioned grids can also be seen as special types of navigation meshes. However, navigation meshes can be built with polygons representing the exact geometry of the environment, or with a sufficient approximation of it. Figure 6 shows an example of a navigation mesh.

Games that come with level editors and support path planning with navigation meshes either use an automatic navigation mesh generation algorithm or let the user define traversable space for the level geometry within the editor. For example, in *Counter-Strike: Source*, automatic navigation mesh generation for user-generated maps is done

Figure 6. A navigation mesh for the environment shown in Figure 3 and Figure 4

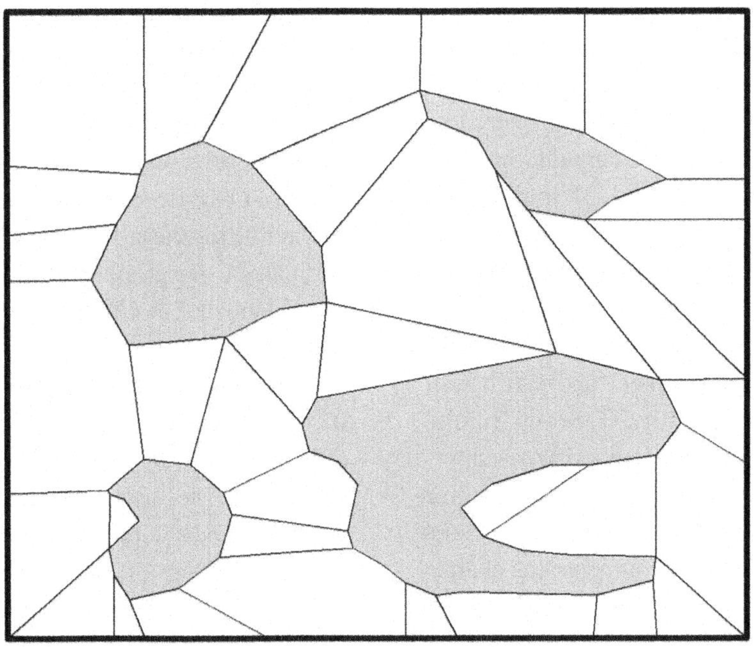

by a flood-filling algorithm (Valve Corporation, 2004). The user defines spawn-points for players on traversable parts of the game map. From those points, the algorithm computes all traversable space that can be reached from the initial positions. Additionally, the user can explicitly mark traversable areas in case the algorithm fails to detect some parts due to steep stairs or ramps.

An open source library to automatically construct navigation meshes out of 3D level geometry is the project *recastnavigation* (Mononen, 2009). *Recast* generates a voxel mold from the 3D level geometry and automatically detects and prunes non-traversable areas. The resulting walkable space is then divided into simple overlaid 2D regions with one single non-overlapping contour. By tracing the boundaries of the regions, the algorithm produces a set of traversable convex polygons as a final output. The resulting navigation mesh can be then used for path planning. For example, it can be fed into *Detour*, which is a path-finding toolkit accompanying *Recast*.

Kallmann (2010a) introduced a navigation mesh called a *Local Clearance Triangulation* (LCT). It can be used to answer path queries for characters of different size. Locally shortest paths can be computed in optimal time. If global optimality is required, an extended search is used to gradually improve the path. Furthermore, Kallmann discussed several algorithms and operations that are based on generic triangulation-based navigation meshes and on the LCT in particular (Kallmann, 2010b). Among these are methods for automatic agent placement, tracking moving obstacles, and ray-obstacle intersection queries. Kallmann's navigation mesh yields an exact representation of the environment and can handle dynamic updates efficiently. However, (multi-layered) 3D environments are not discussed.

Pettré et al. (2005) introduced a navigation mesh based on discs and cylindrical areas. It supports multi-layered 3D environments and characters of variable size. However, it does not support an exact representation of the navigable space and efficient dynamic updates of the environment.

A navigation mesh that combines the advantages of the aforementioned approaches is the *Explicit Corridor Map* (ECM) (Geraerts, 2010). It is based on the *medial axis* of the environment, which is the set of all points that are equidistant from at least two distinct closest obstacle points; see Figure 7.

The medial axis can be seen as a special type of waypoint graph in which all edges run through the center of the free space between pairs of obstacle polygons. For each vertex of the medial axis graph, there are either at least three obstacle polygons that have the same distance from that vertex, or the vertex is placed in a non-convex corner of an obstacle. An edge between two vertices of the medial axis consists of a sequences of straight-line segments and parabolic arcs, depending on the type of corresponding obstacles to its left and right, see Figure 7 (left). With each element in this sequence, its left and right closest obstacle points are stored. This partitions a 2D environment into a set of walkable areas in $O(n \log n)$ time and $O(n)$ space, where n is the total number of obstacle vertices. Each area corresponds to one particular obstacle polygon, as all points in that area are closer to that obstacle than to all other obstacles.

In the field of Computational Geometry, a similar structure is known as the *Generalized Voronoi Diagram* (GVD), and it has been widely studied during the last decades. It can be efficiently computed using graphics hardware (Hoff, Keyser, Lin, Manocha, & Culver, 1999): First, for each two-dimensional site (i.e. the obstacle polygons, lines or points) a three-dimensional *distance mesh* is computed and drawn by the graphics hardware, each mesh in a different color. By projecting the distance meshes back onto the 2D plane and tracing the boundary lines of the different regions in the color buffer, a feasible approximation of the GVD can be obtained. This approach requires

Figure 7. Left: Obstacles (shown in red; the center U-shape and the four bounding line segments), medial axis (solid blue), ECM vertices (large discs) and closest points, subdividing the free space into ECM cells (dotted gray lines). Right: a multi-layered 3D environment and its medial axis (van Toll, Cook IV, & Geraerts, 2012).

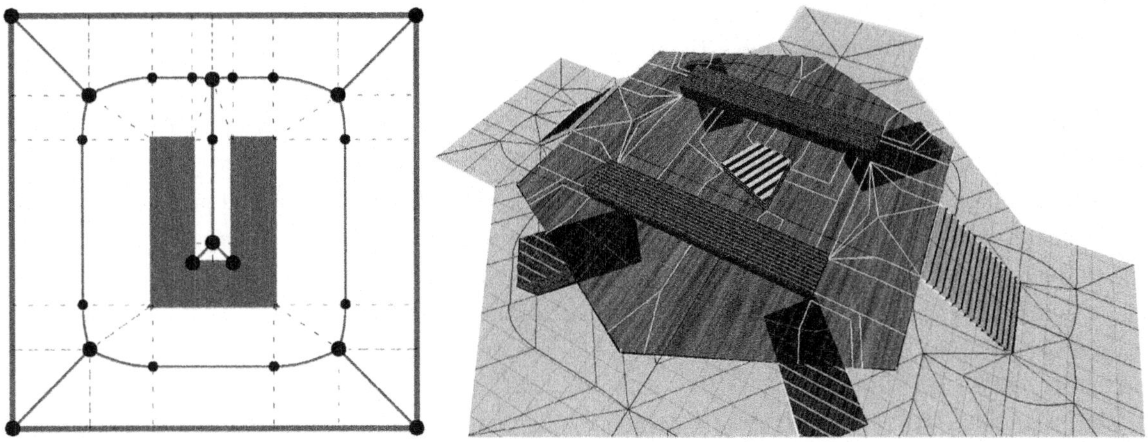

the obstacle polygons to be convex, so concave polygons are first subdivided into a convex ones. This yields edges and vertices that are not part of the GVD for the original scene. For path planning purposes, these additional edges are desired if they run into convex corners. Otherwise characters cannot access such corners. All other additional edges, however, are redundant. The medial axis is basically the same as the GVD, but with the redundant edges and vertices pruned.

The main drawback of the ECM is that it is difficult to implement in a robust way. There are software libraries available for computing GVDs (Held, 2011; The Boost C++ Library, 2015), but they often struggle with imprecision in the data due to numerical rounding errors, especially when a high level of detail is needed. Consequently, the input data (i.e. obstacles) need to be preprocessed.

Still, the ECM has many advantages. All traversable space is represented with respect to the correct topology of the environment. This resolves the issues that are inherent to all approximated representations that we discussed before. Furthermore, the ECM is space-efficient and supports time-efficient extraction of global paths with any desired amount of clearance from obstacles. The ECM works both for 2D and multi-layered 3D environments; see Figure 7. In addition, the ECM can be dynamically updated in real-time by only applying *local* changes to the mesh whenever an obstacle is inserted or deleted (van Toll, Cook IV, & Geraerts, 2012).

For more algorithms on automatic navigation mesh generation and related path planning topics, we refer the interested reader to the *AI Game Programming Wisdom* book series (Rabin, 2008). This concludes the first part on representing traversable space. We have discussed a wide range of representations, as well as their advantages and drawbacks. Now we will show how the corresponding structures can be queried to compute paths.

PATH PLANNING FOR SINGLE CHARACTERS

In this section, we will elaborate on both classic and recent path planning strategies. We start with the popular A* search algorithm on a graph. We then present the *Indicative Route Method* (IRM), and its successor, the *Modified Indicative Route and Navigation* (MIRAN) method. Afterwards, we give a general overview of local collision avoidance strategies.

A* and Its Variants

The A* algorithm (Hart, Nilsson, & Raphael, 1968) is one of the best known and probably the most used path-finding algorithm in the domain of digital games. This is because it can efficiently compute shortest paths in a graph and combines the advantages of *Dijkstra's algorithm* (1959) with a greedy *Best-First-Search* strategy. With only small and easy to implement variations, a wide range of variants (e.g. shorter computation time to find good paths rather than optimal ones) can be obtained.[3] This makes the A* algorithm a flexible and powerful tool for many path-finding applications (Trovato, 1996).

The main idea of A* is to combine actual traversal costs from a start node with heuristic values that estimate the distance to a target node. Given an edge-weighted graph with two designated nodes s and t, a function g assigns to each node n in the graph the costs of the currently known shortest path from s to n. Furthermore, a heuristic function h assigns to each node in the graph the estimated costs of a path from n to t. A* then starts to search for a path from s to t by computing $f = g + h$ for each node under consideration and expanding a node with minimum f-value in each step. The g-value of a node n is updated whenever a shorter path than the current one from s to n is detected. A* manages two lists of nodes, the *open list* and the *closed list*. While the open list stores all nodes that are currently under consideration, the closed list stores all nodes that have already been expanded and do not need to be visited again.

It can be proven, if the heuristic function h does not overestimate the actual costs for each node, that A* will always find an optimal (i.e. shortest) path. On the contrary, if h overestimates the costs for some or all nodes, the computation time of the search may be decreased, but the path may not be optimal.

If h is an exact estimation of the actual costs, then A* has the nice property to find a shortest path in optimal time. In this case only the nodes that are contained in a shortest path as well as their neighbors are expanded; see Figure 8 (bottom). Even if all paths in the graph are shortest, A* will expand only one of them depending on the sorting strategy of the open list. A theoretical approach to exploit this property could be to compute all costs of optimal paths for all pairs of nodes in the graph as a preprocessing step (without storing the paths themselves to save space). These costs could then be used as an exact heuristic to make A* compute optimal paths in optimal time. However, this is only practical for small graphs and is usually not a feasible solution in gaming applications.

If we do not consider the heuristic function h and let $f = g$, we get *Dijkstra's algorithm* (1959). If we only consider h and ignore all the g-values in each node (i.e. $f = h$), we get a greedy *Best-First-Search* strategy. Therefore, A* can be seen as generalization of both strategies. Figure 8 illustrates the three different strategies on a grid with uniform costs. It shows that Dijkstra's algorithm finds an optimal path, but expands a high number of nodes. The greedy strategy expands only a few nodes, but the resulting path is far from optimal. A* combines both strategies, finding an optimal path while expanding only a few nodes. Note that in the example, we assume to have an exact heuristic h, which reduces the number of expanded nodes to a minimum.

In general, finding a feasible heuristic can be difficult because the quality of the heuristic depends on the environment. The Euclidean distance is a popular choice. However, it is not well-suited for maze-like environments in which the length of a path between two points may differ a lot from the Euclidean distance between them.

There are many more variants and modifications of A*. As the size of the open list strongly influences the computation time for the final path,

Figure 8. Comparison of different search strategies on a grid with uniform costs. Obstacles are shown in grey, free space is shown in white. Expanded cells are shown in dark green. Cells that are part of the final path are shown in bright green (with arrows pointing towards the next node on the final path). Top Left: Dijkstra's algorithm expands many nodes, but finds an optimal path. Top Right: Best-First-Search expands only a few nodes, but finds a non-optimal path. Bottom: A combines both advantages (an exact heuristic is chosen to illustrate the strength of A*).*

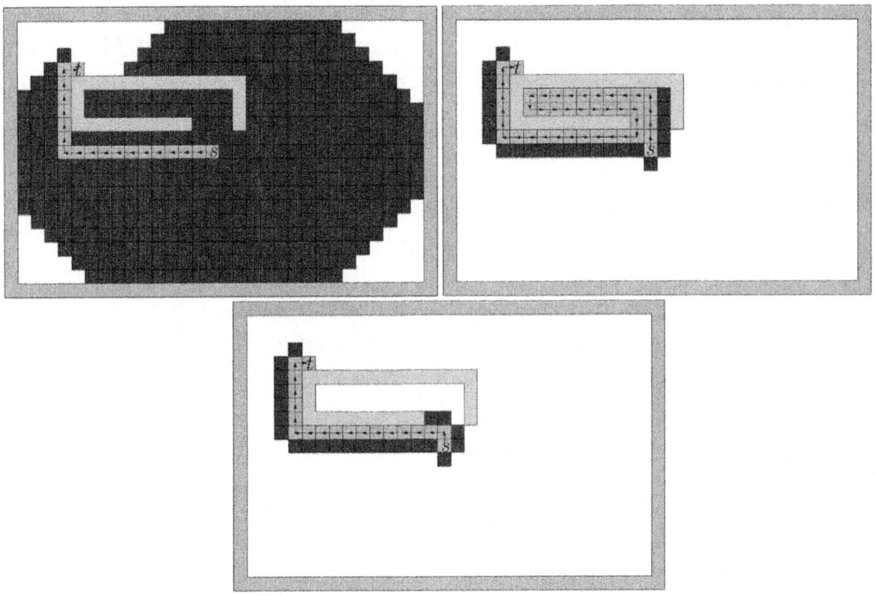

many variants aim at keeping the number of nodes in the open list small. For example, the size of the open list can be limited by a constant number of nodes, and nodes with the highest f -values can be dropped whenever the open list becomes bigger than that number (*beam search* (Lowerre & Reddy, 1980)).

Instead of generating one large set of opened and closed nodes, performance can also be improved by searching from s to t and from t to s simultaneously and stop when the two paths meet in the same node. However, the result is not guaranteed to be optimal.

Another concept is to inflate the h -values by some given weight $w \geq 1$ and to compute the f -values as $f = g + wh$. With this *weighted* A* variant (Pohl, 1970), additional emphasis is put on the heuristic. In this way, the expansion of nodes that appear to be closer to the goal are preferred, thus yielding a trade-off between computation time and quality of the path. This idea is further extended to *anytime variants* of A*, which start with a high weight for the heuristic values to compute a first rough solution quickly. This first solution is then improved over time by adjusting the weights. One of those anytime variants is ARA* (Likhachev, Gordon, & Thrun, 2004), in which the weight w is based on a linear trajectory and two additional user-controlled parameters. The user has to set the initial value of w together with a fixed step size Δw by which the weight is decreased between the computation of solutions. Another anytime variant of A* is called ANA* (*Anytime Non-parametric A**) (van den Berg, Shah, Huang, & Goldberg, 2011). It uses a novel criterion for deciding which node to expand next in each step. Instead of expanding the node with lowest weighted f -value, it expands the node that maximizes the term $e = (G - g) / h$, with G being the costs of the currently best solution (which is set to infinity in the first iteration). The term e can be intuitively understood as the ratio between the "budget" that is left to improve the current-best solution and the estimated costs between the node and the goal. Maximizing e corresponds to picking the largest weight w such that $f \leq G$, and to expanding the node that is most promising to improve the current-best solution. ANA* overcomes the user's problem in ARA* of finding appropriate parameters, and has comparable and in some cases better performance than ARA*.

Despite the fact that A* and its variants are widely used for path planning in digital games, it is not the final answer. Many open research questions cannot be answered by using A* on a graph. Recent approaches use the aforementioned navigation meshes and the possibility to store additional information. Solving advanced path planning and crowd simulation problems on 2D-surface representations of the environment rather than on 1D representations such as graphs require new strategies, which we will discuss in the following sections.

The Indicative Route Method

The *Indicative Route Method* (IRM) (Karamouzas, Geraerts, & Overmars, 2009) is a path planning strategy based on the *Explicit Corridor Map* (ECM); see Section "Navigation Meshes". The IRM combines the general concept of global planning using the ECM together with local force-based strategies. Given a character with a start position and a designated goal position, the method works as follows.

First, an indicative route is created. An indicative route is a route from the start to the goal position, and it functions as a guiding line and a rough estimation of the character's preferred route through the environment. This route can be either manually designed or automatically computed by a global path planning approach (e.g. by an A* search on a grid; see Sections "Grids" and "A* and its Variants"). We assume that the indicative route is given as a straight-line strip between a set of waypoints; see Figure 9 (left).

Second, the actual path is computed by letting the character move towards an attraction point in a number of discrete time steps. In each step, the character's current position x is *retracted* onto

Figure 9. Left: an indicative route with waypoints $w_0, \ldots, w_8$. Right: a character with center point x, its retraction point r on the medial axis, and attraction point α as the intersection of the indicative route and the maximum clearance disc (dashed) around r.

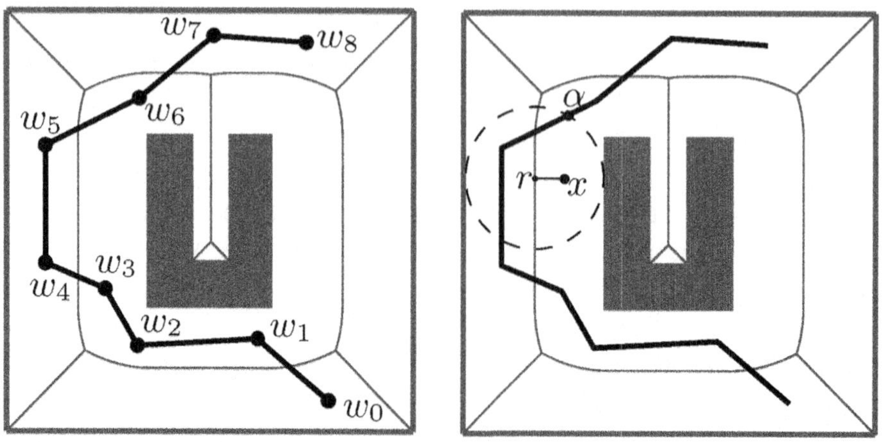

Figure 10. A smooth path computed by the Indicative Route Method using the Explicit Corridor Map (Geraerts, 2010)

the medial axis. This retraction works as follows: We trace the line between x and its closest obstacle point in opposite direction until it intersects the medial axis. This intersection point is the retraction point of x, and it is denoted by r; see Figure 9 (right). Now the radius of the maximum clearance disc around r is given as the distance between r and its closest obstacle point. In other words, the maximum clearance disc is the disc centered at r that is as large as possible before it intersects an obstacle. If the goal position is contained inside the disc, the character will be attracted to it. Otherwise, the attraction point $\boldsymbol{\alpha}$ is defined as the last point on the indicative route that intersects the boundary of the clearance disc; see Figure 9 (right). The attraction point $\boldsymbol{\alpha}$, the character's current position x and its preferred speed induce a preferred velocity for the character in each step of the simulation. This velocity is then integrated using Euler's integration (Butcher, 2008) or a similar integration scheme to produce smooth and natural paths; see Figure 10 for an example in a 3D city environment.

For a modest number of characters, the IRM runs at framerates suitable for real-time applications. However, the IRM has its drawbacks. For large crowds of tens of thousands of individual characters, the method is computationally inefficient. Furthermore, the retraction strategy requires indicative routes to have no self-intersections and backtracks, thus limiting the flexibility and power of the method for specific scenarios. Furthermore, as the definition of the attraction point depends on the available amount of free space around the character's current (retracted) position, the method causes undesired behavior in large areas of free space, but also in confined spaces. When there is a large area of free space around the character, the maximum clearance disc has a large radius. This results in attraction points being far ahead of the character's current position. The resulting path smoothes the indicative route to a great extent and skips parts that might be important. By contrast, in confined spaces such as a narrow but slightly winding and long passage, the maximum clearance is small. The IRM makes the character frequently change its orientation although a straight movement in the direction of the corridor is expected.

To address these limitations, the *Modified Indicative Routes and Navigation* method was developed. This method can be seen as a successor of the IRM, and we will describe it now in more detail.

The Modified Indicative Routes and Navigation Method

The *Modified Indicative Routes and Navigation* (MIRAN) method adopts from the IRM the concept of using an indicative route and computing an attraction point in each step of the simulation (Jaklin, Cook IV, & Geraerts, 2013). It computes several *candidate* attraction points in each step of the simulation. The best candidate is then picked according to a weight-function that takes region preferences into account.

MIRAN improves on the IRM in several aspects. Its main contribution is the simulation of heterogeneous environments for different character profiles. Each character profile has its own specific preferences for certain region types (roads, bike-lanes, sidewalks, lawns, etc.). MIRAN can be used for path following without requiring a copy of the navigable space for each character profile. Furthermore, the method allows the user to control how closely an indicative route should be followed and how much freedom a character has to deviate from or skip parts of it. Thus, the method is independent of local clearance information and overcomes the aforementioned problems of the IRM.

While MIRAN makes the above contribution, it has its limitations. MIRAN is defined for a character represented as a point in the environment, not a disc or similar 2D shape. Thus, different character sizes and arbitrary clearance from obstacles are not supported by this method. Furthermore, MIRAN does not handle collision avoidance with region-preferences. Characters do independently take regions into account while travelling, but they ignore this information as soon as collisions among them need to be avoided. Solving these issues is subject of current research.

Figure 11. The MIRAN method in a forest environment. An adult character (solid non-smooth indicative route and solid smooth path,) avoids puddles and dense wood, but is attracted to a region with a panoramic view (light grey). A child (dashed non-smooth indicative route and dashed smooth path) crosses puddles and climbs fallen tree logs (Jaklin, Cook IV, & Geraerts, 2013).

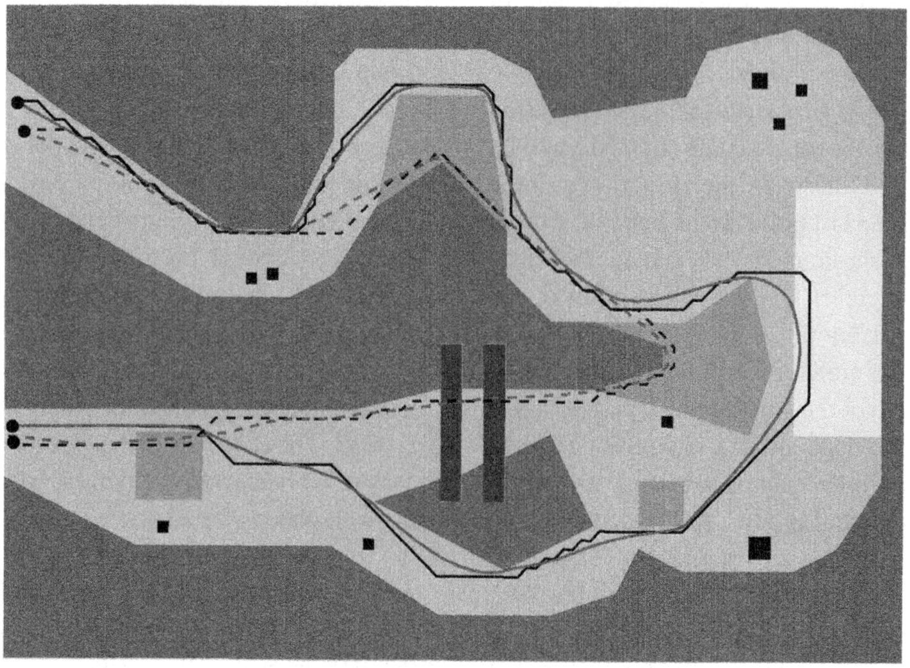

The quality of paths generated with the MIRAN method also depends on the quality of the indicative routes that are used. These can be computed by using A* on a grid (Jaklin, Cook IV, & Geraerts, 2013), but recent approaches rather consider the exact geometry of the environment (Jaklin, Tibboel, & Geraerts, 2014) (see Figure 11).

Local Collision Avoidance

In this section, we give an overview of different strategies to handle local collision avoidance between characters. The algorithms can generally be divided into three categories. First, *reactive steering* methods let the character adapt its path to dynamic and static obstacles. Second, *collision prediction* methods assume that a character moves with a constant velocity. Future motions are predicted by linearly extrapolating the character's current movement. In this way, collisions can be detected and avoided in advance. Third, *example-based* methods use a database of example behaviors from captured crowd data. A character selects an example behavior that closely matches its current state with respect to a given metric. We now discuss related work for each of the three collision avoidance categories.

Reactive steering methods originated from the robotics community. Force-based approaches are usually a variant of a potential field as described in Section "Potential Field and Flow-Based Methods". In the field of animation and crowd simulation, reactive steering was introduced by the seminal work of Reynolds on flocks, herds and schools (Reynolds C. W., 1987). In this model, three behavioral rules are applied to each flock member: avoiding collision with nearby flock members, matching velocity with the nearby flock members, and staying close to nearby flock members. Collision avoidance is achieved by repulsive forces that are exerted on nearby flock members. The shorter the distance between two flock members, the stronger the repulsive force. Velocity matching can be seen as predictive collision avoidance because flock members that successfully match their velocities are unlikely to collide. The three behavioral rules are ordered by priority and accumulated to produce the flock members motion. The order can be dynamically adapted during the simulation to temporarily split the flock for avoiding collisions.

Another reactive and force-based approach popular in the civil and traffic engineering community is the social force model introduced by Helbing and Molnár (1995). The behavior of pedestrian crowds is simulated by solving Newton's equations of motion, using both physical and socio-psychological forces. Repulsive and tangential forces are used to model interactions between individuals with respect to their relative distance, and to avoid collisions with obstacles. Heigas, Luciani, Thollot and Castagné (2003) propose an approach in which characters and obstacles are represented as particles. Interactions are represented by physically-based forces exerted between each pair of particles using a mass-spring-damper model. The distance between interacting particles influences the stiffness and viscosity of the model.

Reactive steering methods need not necessarily be force-based. Other reactive approaches comprise rule-based systems on a 2D grid (Loscos, Marchal, & Meyer, 2003) or by using cellular automata (Wolfram, 1994). Behavioral models such as the work of Terzopoulos, Tu, and Grzeszczuk (1994) to simulate artificial fish also belong to this category.

Reactive steering methods have the drawback that characters react to avoid collisions when other characters or obstacles get sufficiently close. This may result in unnatural trajectories because humans tend to resolve collisions in advance by the principle of least effort (Zipf, 1949). Furthermore, the resulting motions are often subject to oscillations.

Predictive methods address these issues. Reynolds (1999) presents a collection of steering behaviors, one of them being the *unaligned collision avoidance behavior*. Collisions are predicted by extrapolating current motions and resolving them by adjusting orientation and movement speed accordingly. Pettré, Ondřej, Olivier, Cretual, and Donikian (2009) describe a model based on experimental study. In this model, pedestrians take different roles during interactions (e.g. passing first or giving way). Adaptations of speed and orientation to avoid collisions depend on the specific roles of the characters. Among the predictive methods are also the more recent *vision-based* approaches. Those are based on the assumption that paths are most natural if decisions are based on the characters' visual stimuli. Ondřey, Pettré, Olivier, and Donikian (2010) combine visual stimuli with motor response laws. Fiorini and Shiller (1998) introduced the concept of a *Velocity Obstacle* (VO). For each character, the VO represents the set of all velocities that would lead to a collision with another character at some future time step. By taking the union of VOs for all characters under consideration, collisions can be avoided by selecting a velocity outside of the combined VO. Van den Berg et al. (2008) extended this concept to the *Reciprocal Velocity Obstacle* (RVO) that guarantees oscillation-free motions. A variety of models have improved on the VO and RVO concepts; see for example (Snape, Berg, Guy, & Manocha, 2009; Guy, et al., 2009; van den Berg, Guy, Lin, & Manocha, 2009). Vision-based approaches tend to be computationally expensive. This becomes particularly relevant when simulating crowds with high densities. In those scenarios, flow-based methods may be preferred (Treuille, Cooper, & Popovic, 2006). To further overcome the problems of short-range avoidance strategies, *long-range* collision avoidance has recently been taken into consideration (Golas, Narain, Curtis, & Lin, 2014; Anvari, Bell, Angeloudis, & Ochieng, 2014).

Among the example-based techniques are the works of Ju et al. (2010), Lee, Choi, Hong, and Lee (2007) and Lerner et al. (2007). Using a database of captured crowd behaviors, each character selects an example behavior that is close to its current state with respect to a given metric. Example-based models may simulate realistic motions and capture complex avoidance maneuvers based on actions taken by real members of a crowd. However, corresponding databases are limited to the number of different behaviors. Situations may occur in which all matching examples lead to collisions. In addition, the scenario must always be similar to the real-life scenario from which the examples were extracted. Lastly, example-based solutions are rather used for offline-simulations and are not applicable to real-time applications such as digital games due to a high computational complexity.

As we have described in this section, there is a great variety of strategies that all have its advantages and drawbacks. Factors that influence the choice for a specific method are: What number of characters does a game need to handle simultaneously? Does it have large crowds or few individual characters? What is the desired degree of realism? How many collisions are expected in each time frame, and how important are low computation times for resolving those collisions? How is traversable space represented, and what collision avoidance strategies are best suited for this representation? Answers to such questions need to be answered in the design phase of a game.

CROWD SIMULATION STRATEGIES

The strategies we discussed in the previous sections mainly focus on computing feasible path trajectories for individual characters. With modern hardware, they can be used to simulate a crowd by applying the corresponding techniques to all crowd members simultaneously and adding local collision-avoidance techniques. A different approach is to handle a crowd as one large entity by simulating the motion of each member as a per-particle energy minimization, thus handling a crowd similar to a fluid or gas. We now give an overview of such models.

Potential Fields and Flow-Based Methods

Using *Potential Fields* for path planning is an approach that has emerged from the field of robotics (Latombe, 1991). The general task in behavior-based robotics is to have a robot plan and execute its actions in three steps. First, it receives input through its sensors. Second, it evaluates the input to compute a desired behavior (i.e. *seek the goal point* or *avoid a wall*). Third, it maps this plan to a corresponding sequence of motor actions. For path planning in digital games, we are mainly interested in the second step of this approach. Potential Fields are widely used in this context because they are an intuitive and well-studied mathematical concept.

Moving characters in a potential field can be compared to a leaf floating on a stream of water, or a marble rolling through an environment of steep ramps or hills. The surrounding local topology or geometry of the environment directly influences the path of the moving object.

From an abstract point of view, a potential field can be described as a mapping from an input vector to an output vector. In robotics, the input vector usually describes the robot's current orientation and speed, and the same can be applied to moving characters in a digital game or simulation. The output vector describes a motion from the current position to the next. If the environment is represented by a finite and discrete approximation of all traversable space (e.g. by a grid, see Section "Grids"), the potential field can be visually shown as a *vector field.* It shows the union of all output vectors for every possible location of the character in the environment; see Figure 12. It might be necessary to compute the whole set of output vectors for large crowds that have a shared goal. However, when using potential fields for a small number of characters, the whole set of output vectors is hardly ever computed and only the ones are calculated that are actually necessary for the characters' motion.

For path planning purposes, a given goal point in the environment acts as an attractor for the character. The corresponding potential field applies forces on the character such that it is directed towards the goal; see Figure 12 (left). On the contrary, obstacles apply a repulsive force on the characters to avoid collisions; see Figure 12 (right).

Just like a rolling marble can get stuck in a hole or valley, characters can easily get stuck in local minima of the potential field. This is one of the main drawbacks when using potential fields

Figure 12. Left: an attractive potential field with a goal point. Right: a repulsive potential field with an obstacle.

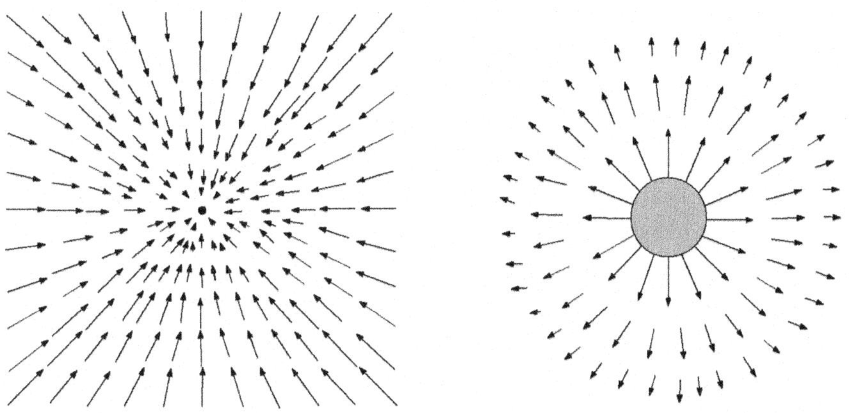

for path planning. Potential fields that are free of local minima do exist, but they are expensive to compute (Connolly & Grupen, 1992), (Rimon & Koditschek, 1992), (Sundar & Shiller, 1994). Workarounds are usually considered to handle this problem (e.g. predict the next few steps and change a character's motion if the current motion will lead to a local minimum).

Other flow-based methods have also been used for crowd simulation. Hughes (2003) modeled human pedestrians as a continuous density field, using partial differential functions to describe crowd dynamics. Treuille, Cooper, and Popovic (2006) presented a real-time crowd model based on continuum dynamics. Their model exhibits emergent phenomena observed in real crowds such as lane formation or vortex formation when several groups cross each other. Furthermore, it can be used in real-time applications. The authors showed that they can efficiently steer two opposing armies or let a crowd in a city react in panic to a user-controlled flying-saucer. Kerr and Spears (2006) presented a simulation model based on gas-kinetics for mobile robots. Pimenta, Michael, Mesquita, Pereira, and Kumar (2008) used a model based on Smoothed Particle Hydrodynamics to simulate swarms of mobile robots.

The main advantage of the abovementioned models is that they can efficiently simulate large numbers of characters, as long as there are only a few goal-states involved. In such cases, they usually outperform agent-based models in terms of computation times. However, the computational complexity of such models becomes too high for real-time applications when a large number of different crowds with different goal states needs to be simulated. Furthermore, flow-based models are not well-suited for low- to medium crowd densities, in which the individuality of each crowd member has a larger impact on the overall crowd behavior than in high-density scenarios. Lastly, none of the above models focuses on social interactions among crowd members. We now give an overview of models that simulate groups, formations and social interactions.

Groups and Formations

Simulating social interactions among the members of a crowd is a challenging step towards more immersive educational games. Pedestrians in a city environment such as *The River City Project* (2002 - 2007) should not walk individually, but form small social groups, walk together and automatically adapt to dynamic changes like spotting a friend in a crowd.

In this section, we give a brief overview of research on simulating small and large social groups of virtual characters. The basis for many of these approaches is the behavioral model by Reynolds to simulate flocks, herds, and schools (Reynolds C. W., 1987), which the author later extended by adding steering behaviors (Reynolds, 1999) and interactions within groups (Reynolds, 2000). Since this model mainly aims at simulating the behavior of groups of animals, other researchers have focused on autonomous *human* characters.

Musse and Thalmann (1997) presented a rule-based model for crowd behavior of multiple pedestrian groups. Characters in this model exhibit flocking behavior and are able to switch between groups based on sociological factors. The authors do not elaborate on how group coherence is being addressed, and the proposed collision-avoidance model yields undesired behavior compared to state-of-the-art methods described in Section "Local Collision Avoidance".

Kamphuis and Overmars (2004) proposed a path planning model that maintains group coherence and avoids spatial separation between members of the same group. The model focuses on large groups such as armies, and is thus well-suited for military games and applications rather than simulations of small groups in which social factors determine the overall behavior.

Kimmel, Dobson and Bekris (2012) also addressed the problem of maintaining group coherence. Their work is based on the *Velocity Obstacle* approach by Fiorini and Shiller (1998), and it extends this method by adding team behavior. The limitations of this model are that the characters all move at the same speed and that only one single formation is being kept.

Qiu and Hu (2010) presented a model to simulate dynamic groups based on utility theory and social comparison theory. Their model allows characters to dynamically leave and join groups based on spatial and social factors.

Park, Quek, and Cao (2012) presented a model that is based on *common ground theory*. This model aims at simulating the social interactions between group members. Each group has a leader, and group coherence is measured by the distance from a group member to its leader projected in the leader's direction of motion.

Karamouzas and Overmars (2012) presented a method of how to simulate local behavior of small pedestrian groups consisting of two or three individuals in city environments. Their approach is based on empirical studies regarding the spatial organization of such groups (Moussaïd, Perozo, Garnier, Helbing, & Theraulaz, 2010), (Peters & Ennis, 2009). From those empirical studies, they derived three formations that small groups tend to adapt to, namely *line-abreast, v-like* and *river-like* formations. The *line-abreast* formation functions as the default one when the group members communicate with each other while moving towards their goal. It is best suited for keeping the social interaction, provided there is enough space to do so. If the environment becomes more crowded or obstacles prevent the *line-abreast* formation, the *v-like* formation is taken. It still provides space for communication between the group members while adapting to the environmental situation. The *river-like* formation is taken when crowd density is too high to keep the *v-like* formation, or when the group has to move through a small hallway or an equivalent environmental setup. For groups of two pedestrians, the *v-like* formation is replaced by a more compact line-abreast formation that reduces the distance between the two members.

The model by Karamouzas and Overmars (2012) has been tested and visualized in different scenarios. Group interactions have been tested in a narrow corridor, a shopping mall and a busy crosswalk. The virtual shopping mall scenario was compared to original video footage of a real shopping mall. Different metrics have been defined to measure the quality of the results in a quantitative evaluation of the model.

Similar to collision-avoidance methods, it depends on the application at hand which crowd simulation model is best. A wide range of approaches and paradigms exist, and most of the recent models work well in specific scenarios. Some of them are beyond the scope of a typical gaming application, as they try to handle complex factors among social groups from fields such as sociology or psychology. With games becoming more and more realistic, though, these kind of factors might one day be a crucial and integral component of immersive gaming experiences, too.

FUTURE WORK

The advanced algorithms we have discussed in this chapter could be used in future educational games to enhance a player's immersion and thus the overall learning experience. Autonomous virtual characters could change their appearance from static, stiff and unnatural to lively, dynamic and more believable by using the methods we covered in this chapter.

For instance, in a game such as *The River City Project* (2002 - 2007), a navigation mesh such as the *Explicit Corridor Map* (Geraerts, 2010) could enable the residents to autonomously move around the city with respect to the exact geometry of the walkable space. Using a method such as MIRAN (Jaklin, Cook IV, & Geraerts, 2013) makes them stay on preferred terrain and avoid less attractive regions without treating such regions as hard obstacles, thus allowing more flexible behavior and creating smooth and visually convincing paths. Social-group methods such as (Karamouzas & Overmars, 2012) could be used to simulate the residents' social behavior. The characters could walk individually, but temporarily form small social groups to have conversations or walk together in socially-friendly formations. Novel crowd simulation models enable the simulation of large crowds at interactive rates for both low- and high-density situations (van Goethem, Jaklin, Cook IV, & Geraerts, 2015). These could be used to populate a virtual environment like *River City* with even more characters that coordinate their walking behavior and react to dynamic changes in the environment.

Furthermore, virtual crowds are essential in training software for evacuation scenarios and crowd management such as *SportEvac* (2014). Such games could not only be used by managers of mass events and safety personnel, but also in P-12 education to increase the students' awareness of potential dangers during such events.

The aforementioned methods could not only improve a player's immersion to a great extent, but they could also enable advanced gameplay and novel game-design elements in future educational games. For example, virtual characters that display social behavior could be used in a game that aims at training communication skills. A player's learning experience could be enhanced when the virtual characters not only react to the player's negative actions by simply stating that they are displeased, but actually start avoiding the player and tell their fellow characters about the incident, who in turn also display a negative attitude towards the player.

Future educational games could also simulate social-group behavior on a psychological level. The question of how individual characters meet, automatically form groups and depart has been addressed, but still leaves room for improvement. Studies from fields such as psychology and sociology should be used as a basis for more in-depth methods to simulate human behavior.

CONCLUSION

As discussed in the previous sections, educational games often lack realism when characters need to navigate through a virtual environment. Characters display stiff movements and lack flexibility in the paths they choose. For instance, paths are often scripted and manually created by a designer. The resulting repetitive behavior reveals the underlying technological aspects of a game, which in turn destroys a player's immersion and the overall learning experience.

Many different approaches have been taken to tackle path planning and crowd simulation issues in virtual environments. While the A* method on a grid is a flexible and general approach that has been widely and successfully used in the past, it is not the final answer to problems related to path planning and crowd simulation. We have discussed that surface-based representations of traversable space via navigation meshes gives developers the opportunity to create more advanced algorithms.

For all problems we have discussed in this chapter, a general and theoretically substantiated basis is missing. Therefore, novel approaches need to be taken, and new algorithms need to be developed to enhance future educational games with respect to their path planning and corresponding game design possibilities. We believe that the end of graph-based methods is near, and that the future lies in combining data structures and novel algorithms that work on a surface-based representation of the virtual environment.

In this chapter, we have mainly focused on the navigation aspects of path planning and crowd simulation for educational games. Other important aspects are behavioral patterns, visualization and animation. These are addressed in the book by Thalmann and Musse (2013).

Overall it can be said that the field of path planning and crowd simulation is continually growing and improving. Promising new ideas might soon evolve into algorithms providing many immersive features, thus enhancing a player's gaming experience and improving learning results in educational games for training and education purposes.

ACKNOWLEDGMENT

This work was funded by the COMMIT/ project, http://www.commit-nl.nl.

REFERENCES

Anvari, B., Bell, M. G. H., Angeloudis, P., & Ochieng, W. Y. (2014). Long-range Collision Avoidance for Shared Space Simulation based on Social Forces. *Transportation Research Procedia*, *2*, 318–326. doi:10.1016/j.trpro.2014.09.023

Atari Inc. (1979). USA: Asteroids.

Butcher, J. (2008). *Numerical Methods for Ordinary Differential Equations*. John Wiley & Sons. doi:10.1002/9780470753767

Connolly, C., & Grupen, R. (1992). Harmonic Control. *Proceedings of the 1992 International Symposium on Intelligent Control*, (pp. 503-506). doi:10.1109/ISIC.1992.225142

de Berg, M., van Kreveld, M., Overmars, M., & Schwarzkopf, O. (2000). *Computational Geometry: Algorithms and Applications* (2nd ed.). Springer-Verlag. doi:10.1007/978-3-662-04245-8

Dijkstra, E. (1959). A Note on two Problems in Connexion with Graphs. *Numerische Mathematik*, *1*(1), 269–271. doi:10.1007/BF01386390

Entertainment, B. (2010). *Starcraft II*. USA.

Fiorini, P., & Shillert, Z. (1998). Motion Planning in Dynamic Environments using Velocity Obstacles. *The International Journal of Robotics Research*, *17*(7), 760–772. doi:10.1177/027836499801700706

Gee, J. (2007). *What video games have to teach us about learning and literacy*. New York: Palgrave Macmillan.

Geraerts, R. (2010). Planning Short Paths with Clearance using Explicit Corridors. Proceedings of the *IEEE International Conference on Robotics and Automation* (pp. 1997-2004). doi:10.1109/ROBOT.2010.5509263

Geraerts, R., & Overmars, M. (2007). The Corridor Map Method: A general framework for real-time high-quality path planning. *Computer Animation and Virtual Worlds*, *18*(2), 107–119. doi:10.1002/cav.166

Ghosh, S. K. (2007). *Visibility Algorithms in the Plane*. Cambridge University Press. doi:10.1017/CBO9780511543340

Golas, A., Narain, R., Curtis, S., & Lin, M. C. (2014). Hybrid Long-Range Collision Avoidance for Crowd Simulation. *IEEE Transactions on Visualization and Computer Graphics*, *20*(7), 1022–1034. doi:10.1109/TVCG.2013.235 PMID:24080711

Grand Theft Auto V. (2013). Rockstar Games. USA.

Guy, S. J., Chhugani, J., Kim, C., Satish, N., Lin, M. C., Manocha, D., & Dubey, P. (2009). Clearpath: Highly parallel collision avoidance for mulit-agent simulation. Proceedings of the *ACM SIGGRAPH/EUROGRAPHICS Symposium on Computer Animation (SCA '09)* (pp. 177-187). doi:10.1145/1599470.1599494

Hart, P., Nilsson, N., & Raphael, B. (1968). A Formal Basis for the Heuristic Determination of Minimum Cost Paths. *IEEE Transactions on Systems Science and Cybernetics*, *4*(2), 100–107. doi:10.1109/TSSC.1968.300136

Heigeas, L., Luciani, A., Thollot, J., & Castagné, N. (2003). *A Physically-Based Particle Model of Emergent Crowd Behaviors*. Graphicon.

Helbing, D., & Molnár, P. (1995). Social force model for pedestrian dynamics. *Physical Review E: Statistical Physics, Plasmas, Fluids, and Related Interdisciplinary Topics*, *51*(5), 4282–4286. doi:10.1103/PhysRevE.51.4282 PMID:9963139

Held, M. (2011). VRONI and ArcVRONI: Software for and Applications of Voronoi Diagrams in Science and Engineering. *Proceedings of the 8th International Symposium on Voronoi Diagrams in Science and Engineering* (pp. 3-12). doi:10.1109/ISVD.2011.9

Hoff, K., Keyser, J., Lin, M., Manocha, D., & Culver, T. (1999). Fast computation of generalized voronoi diagrams using graphics hardware. *Proceedings of the 26th annual conference on Computer graphics and interactive techniques SIGGRAPH '99* (pp. 277-286). doi:10.1145/311535.311567

Hughes, R. (2003). The Flow of Human Crowds. *Annual Review of Fluid Mechanics*, *35*(1), 169–182. doi:10.1146/annurev.fluid.35.101101.161136

Jaklin, N., Cook, I.V.A. IV, & Geraerts, R. (2013). Real-time Path Planning in Heterogeneous Environments. [CAVW]. *Computer Animation and Virtual Worlds*, *24*(3), 285–295. doi:10.1002/cav.1511

Jaklin, N., Tibboel, M., & Geraerts, R. (2014). Computing High-Quality Paths in Weighted Regions. *Proceedings of the 7th International ACM SIGGRAPH Conference on Motion in Games (MIG 2014)* (pp. 77-86).

Jeuring, J., van Rooij, R., & Pronost, N. (2014). The 5/10 Method: A Method for Designing Educational Games. In Games and Learning Alliance (pp. 364-369). Springer International Publishing.

Ju, E., Choi, M. G., Park, M., Lee, J., Lee, K. H., & Takahashi, S. (2010). Morphable crowds. *ACM Transactions on Graphics*, *29*(6), 1. doi:10.1145/1882261.1866162

Kallmann, M. (2010a). Navigation queries from triangular meshes. *Proceedings of the Third international conference on Motion in Games* (pp. 230-241). Springer-Verlag.

Kallmann, M. (2010b). Shortest paths with arbitrary clearance from navigation meshes. *Proceedings of the Eurographics/SIGGRAPH Symposium on Computer Animation (SCA).*

Kamphuis, & Overmars. (2004). Finding paths for coherent groups using clearance. *Proceedings of the 2004 ACM SIGGRAPH/Eurographics Symposium on Computer Animation (SCA '04)* (pp. 19-28).

Karamouzas, I., Geraerts, R., & Overmars, M. (2009). Indicative routes for path planning and crowd simulation. *Proceedings of the 4th international conference on foundations of digital games FDG '09* (pp. 113-120). doi:10.1145/1536513.1536540

Karamouzas, I., & Overmars, M. (2012). Simulating and evaluating the local behavior of small pedestrian groups. *IEEE Transactions on Visualization and Computer Graphics*, *18*(3), 394–406. doi:10.1109/TVCG.2011.133 PMID:22241282

Kavraki, L. E., Svestka, P., Latombe, J.-C., & Overmars, M. (1996). Probabilistic Roadmaps for Path Planning in High-Dimensional Configuration Spaces. *IEEE Transactions on Robotics and Automation*, *12*(4), 566–580. doi:10.1109/70.508439

Kerr, W., & Spears, D. (2006). Robotic Simulation of Gases for a Surveillance Task. *Proceedings of the 2005 IEEE/RSJ International Conference on Intelligent Robots and Systems* (pp. 1160-1168).

Ketelhut, D. (2007). The Impact of Student Self-efficacy on Scientific Inquiry Skills: An Exploratory Investigation in River City, a Multi-user Virtual Environment. *Journal of Science Education and Technology*, *16*(1), 99–111. doi:10.1007/s10956-006-9038-y

Ketelhut, D., Dede, C., Clarke, J., Nelson, B., & Bowman, C. (2007). Studying situated learning in a multi-user virtual environment. In *Assessment of problem solving using simulations* (pp. 37–58). Lawrence Erlbaum Associates.

Kimmel, D., & Bekris (2012). Maintaining team coherence under the velocity obstacle framework. *Proceedings of the 11th International Conference on Autonomous Agents and Multiagent Systems (AAMAS '12)* (Vol. 1, pp. 247-256).

Klein, F. (1882). *Eric W. Weisstein - MathWorld–A Wolfram Web Resource.* Retrieved from http://mathworld.wolfram.com/KleinBottle.html

Latombe, J.-C. (1991). *Robot Motion Planning.* Kluwer Academic Publishers. doi:10.1007/978-1-4615-4022-9

Laumond, J. (1987). Obstacle growing in a non-polygonal world. *Information Processing Letters*, *25*(1), 41–50. doi:10.1016/0020-0190(87)90091-3

LaValle, S. M. (1998). Rapidly-exploring random trees: A new tool for path planning [Technical report].

LaValle, S. M. (2006). *Planning Algorithms.* Cambridge University Press. doi:10.1017/CBO9780511546877

Lee, K. H., Choi, M. G., Hong, Q., & Lee, J. (2007). Group behavior from video: a data-driven approach to crowd simulation. *Proceedings of the 2007 ACM SIGGRAPH/Eurographics Symposium on Computer Animation (SCA '07)* (pp. 109-118).

Lerner, A., Chrysanthou, Y., & Lischinski, D. (2007). Crowds by Example. *Computer Graphics Forum, 26*(3), 655-664.

Likhachev, M., Gordon, G., & Thrun, S. (2004). ARA*: Anytime A* with Provable Bounds on Sub-Optimality. Advances in Neural Information Processing Systems 16 *Proceedings of the 2003 Conference (NIPS-03).* MIT Press.

Loscos, C., Marchal, D., & Meyer, A. (2003). Intuitive crowd behaviour in dense urban environments using local laws. *Proceedings of the theory and practice of computer graphics.* IEEE Computer Society. doi:10.1109/TPCG.2003.1206939

Lowerre, B., & Reddy, D. (1980). The harpy speech understanding system. *Trends of Speech Recognition.*

Masehian, E., & Amin-Naseri, M. (2004, June). A voronoi diagram-visibility graph-potential field compound algorithm for robot path planning. *Journal of Field Robotics*, *21*(6), 275–300.

Minecraft. (2009). Mojang.

Möbius, F., & Listing (independently), J. B. (1858). *Eric W. Weisstein - MathWorld–A Wolfram Web Resource.* Retrieved from http://mathworld.wolfram.com/MoebiusStrip.html

Mononen, M. (2009). *recastnavigation.* Retrieved from https://github.com/memononen/recastnavigation

Monument Valley. (2014). Ustwo.

Moussaïd, M., Perozo, N., Garnier, S., Helbing, D., & Theraulaz, G. (2010). The walking behavior of pedestrian social groups and its impact on crowd dynamics. *PLoS ONE*, *5*(4), e10047. doi:10.1371/journal.pone.0010047 PMID:20383280

Murray, B., Bogost, I., Mateas, M., & Nitsche, M. (2006). Game design education: Integrating computation and culture. *Computer*, *39*(6), 43–51. doi:10.1109/MC.2006.195

Musse, & Thalmann. (1997, September 2–3). A model of human crowd behavior: Group inter-relationship and collision detection analysis. *Computer Animation and Simulation 97, Proceedings of the Eurographics Workshop in Budapest, Hungary* (pp. 36-51). Vienna: Springer.

Nash. (2012). *Any-Angle Path Planning* [PhD thesis]. University of Southern California.

Super Mario Galaxy. (2007 Nintendo, E.A.D. *Tokyo*, Japan.

Super Paper Mario. (2007). Nintendo SPD.

Ondřey, J., Pettré, J., Olivier, A.-H., & Donikian, S. (2010). A Synthetic-Vision Based Steering Approach for Crowd Simulation. *ACM Transactions on Graphics*, *29*(4).

Pac-Man. (1980). Namco. Japan.

Descent. (1994). Parallax Software.

Park, Q., & Cao. (2012). Modeling social groups in crowds using common ground theory. *Proceedings of the Winter Simulation Conference (WSC '12)* (pp. 1-12). doi:10.1109/WSC.2012.6465119

Pelechano, N., Allbeck, J. M., & Badler, N. I. (2007). Controlling individual agents in high-density crowd simulation. *Proceedings of the 2007 ACM SIGGRAPH / Eurographics Symposium on Computer Animation (SCA '07)* (pp. 99-108).

Peters, C., & Ennis, C. (2009). Modeling groups of plausivle virtual pedestrians. *IEEE Computer Graphics and Applications*, *29*(4), 54–63. doi:10.1109/MCG.2009.69 PMID:19798863

Pettré, J., Laumond, J.-P., & Thalmann, D. (2005). A navigation graph for real-time crowd animation and mulitlayered uneven terrain. *Proccedings of the first international workshop on crowd simulation (V-CROWDS'05).*

Pettré, J., Ondřej, J., Olivier, A.-H., Cretual, A., & Donikian, S. (2009). Experiment-based modeling, simulation and validation of interactions between virtual walkers. *Proceedings of the 2009 ACM SIGGRAPH/Eurographics Symposium on Computer Animation (SCA '09)* (pp. 189-198). doi:10.1145/1599470.1599495

Pimenta, L., Michael, N., Mesquita, R., Pereira, G., & Kumar, V. (2008). Control of Swarms Based on Hydrodynamic Models. *Proceedings of the 2009 IEEE International Conference on Robotics and Automation (ICRA 2009)* (pp. 1948-1953). doi:10.1109/ROBOT.2008.4543492

Pohl, I. (1970). Heuristic Search viewed as Path Finding in a Graph. *Artificial Intelligence*, *1*(3), 193–204. doi:10.1016/0004-3702(70)90007-X

Qiu, & Hu. (2010). Modeling group structures in pedestrian crowd simulation. *Simulation Modelling Practice and Theory, 18*(2), 190-205.

Rabin, S. (2008). *AI Game Programming Wisdom 4*. Charles River Media.

Reynolds, C. W. (1987). Flocks, herds, and schools: A distributed behavioral model. *Computer Graphics*, *21*(4), 25–34. doi:10.1145/37402.37406

Reynolds (1999). Steering Behaviors for Autonomous Characters. *Proceedings of the Game Developers Conference 1999* (pp. 763-782).

Reynolds. (2000). Interaction with groups of autonomous characters. *Game Developers Conference 2000* (pp. 449-460).

Rimon, E., & Koditschek, D. (1992). Exact robot navigation using artificial potential functions. *IEEE Transactions on Robotics and Automation*, *8*(5), 501–518. doi:10.1109/70.163777

Schmitz, B., Specht, M., & Klemke, R. (2012). An Analysis of the Educational Potential of Augmented Reality Games for Learning. *Proceedings of the 11th World Conference on Mobile and Contextual Learning 2012* (pp. 140-147).

INCONTROL Simulation Solutions. (2014). SportEvac.

Snape, J., Berg, J. v., Guy, S. J., & Manocha, D. (2009). Independent navigation of multiple mobile robots with hybrid reciprocal velocity obstacles. *IEEE/RSJ International Conference on Intelligent Robots and Systems*, (pp. 5917-5922).

Space Invaders. (1978Taito Corporation. Japan.

Sundar, S., & Shiller, Z. (1994). Optimal obstacle avoidance based on the hamilton-jacobi-bellmann equation. *ICRA*, *94*, 2424–2429.

Terzopoulos, D., Tu, X., & Grzeszczuk, R. (1994). Artificial fishes: Autonomous locomotion, perception, behavior, and learning in a simulated physical world. *Artificial Life*, *1*(4), 327–351. doi:10.1162/artl.1994.1.4.327

Thalmann, & Musse (2013). *Crowd Simulation*. Springer.

The Boost C++ Library. (2015). Retrieved from http://www.boost.org/

The River City Project. (2002 - 2007). Retrieved from http://muve.gse.harvard.edu/rivercityproject/index.html

The Settlers II (Original German title: Die Siedler II: Veni, Vidi, Vici). (1996). Blue Byte Software. Germany.

Treuille, A., Cooper, S., & Popovic, Z. (2006). Continuum Crowds. *ACM Transactions on Graphics*, *25*(3), 1160–1168. doi:10.1145/1141911.1142008

Trovato, K. (1996). *A* Planning in Discrete Configuration Spaces of Autonomous Systems* [PhD Thesis]. University of Amsterdam.

Counter Strike: Source. (2004). Valve Corporation. USA.

Portal. (2007). *Valve Corporation*. USA.

van den Berg, J., Guy, S. J., Lin, M. C., & Manocha, D. (2009). Reciprocal n-body collision avoidance. Proceedings of the *International Symposium on Robotics Research*.

van den Berg, J., Lin, M. C., & Machona, D. (2008). Reciprocal velocity obstacles for real-time multi-agent navigation. Proceedings of the *IEEE International Conference on Robotics and Automation* (pp. 1982-1935). doi:10.1109/ROBOT.2008.4543489

van den Berg, J., Shah, R., Huang, A., & Goldberg, K. (2011). ANA*: Anytime Non-Parametric A*. *Proceedings of the AAAI conference on artificial intelligence*.

van Goethem, A., Jaklin, N., Cook, I. V. A., & Geraerts, R. (2015). *On Streams and Incentives: A Synthesis of Individual and Collective Crowd Motion* [Technical Report UU-CS-2015-005]. Utrecht University.

van Toll, W., Cook, I. V. A. IV, & Geraerts, R. (2012). A navigation mesh for dynamic environments. *Computer Animation and Virtual Worlds*, *23*(6), 536–546. doi:10.1002/cav.1468

Wein, R., van den Berg, J., & Halperin, D. (2007). The visibility-voronoi complex and its applications. *Computational Geometry*, *36*(1), 66–87. doi:10.1016/j.comgeo.2005.11.007

Welzl, E. (1985). Constructing the Visibility Graph for n Line Segments in O(n^2) time. *Information Processing Letters*, *20*(4), 167–171. doi:10.1016/0020-0190(85)90044-4

Wolf, M. (2009/2010). *Theorizing Navigable Space in Video Games.* Retrieved from http://opus.kobv.de/ubp/volltexte/2011/4980/

Wolfram, S. (1994). *Cellular Automata and Complexity: Collected Papers*. Addison-Wesley.

Yu, K. (2006). Finding a natural-looking path by using generalized visibility graphs. *Proceedings of the 9th Pacific Rim international conference on Artificial Intelligence* (pp. 170-179). doi:10.1007/978-3-540-36668-3_20

Zipf, G. K. (1949). *Human Behavior and the Principle of Least Effort*. Addison-Wesley Press.

KEY TERMS AND DEFINITIONS

Character: Any moving entity in a digital game, either autonomous or controlled by the player.

Crowd: A large number of static or moving characters in a digital game, either with a shared goal or with individual goals.

Indicative Route: A rough path from a start to a goal position, indicating the approximate direction a character should follow. Used for guiding a character, but not used as a final path.

Local Collision Avoidance: The task to detect and avoid a collision among several moving characters on a local level, thus not taking global knowledge of the entire environment into account.

Navigation Mesh: A data structure to represent the traversable space in a digital game, consisting of 2D polygons.

Path Planning: The task to compute and follow a path from a given start to a given goal position in the game world.

Traversable Space: The space that can be traversed by characters in a digital game.

ENDNOTES

1 Throughout this chapter, we will refer to any moving entity as a *character*. Characters do not need to be humanoid, but can also be vehicles or any type of automated moving entities, depending on the specific gaming application.

2 Visit http://www.geometrygames.org/TorusGames/ for a collection of games such as *Chess* or *Tic Tac Toe* that run on a torus or a *Klein Bottle* topology (Klein, 1882). Accessed January 22, 2015.

3 Visit http://theory.stanford.edu/~amitp/GameProgramming/ for additional information on path planning with A*. Accessed January 22, 2015.

Chapter 26

Game-Based Learning with the Leap Motion Controller

Martin Ebner
Graz University of Technology, Austria

Norbert Spot
Graz University of Technology, Austria

ABSTRACT

Learning through games is a promising field for the future of education. In this research study the authors describe the development process of an educational application, a game targeting P-12 students. This application is meant to be used with the Leap Motion Controller, a small 3D infrared camera, which while in use, tracks the user's hands and finger movements in the 3D space. The chapter describes the application itself and presents the outcomes of a field study, which was carried out with a small group of students at an elementary school. It can be pointed out that there is a huge potential of using innovative input devices in school education.

INTRODUCTION

Computers have evolved rapidly and become part of people's everyday life. They spread into every field of industry and entertainment. People use computers almost everywhere, at work, at home, at schools and universities. Nowadays at least in middle Europe more than 90% of our youth (age 12-18) own a smartphone with mobile Internet access (Ebner et al, 2013). This affects of course also the field of education and therefore Prensky (2011) provokes by asking, whether today's students are the people our educational system was designed to teach or not? Since then several studies/publications has been carried out addressing a new generation of learners called digital natives (Prensky, 2011), netgeneration (Oblinger & Oblinger, 2005) or generation@ (Opaschowski, 1999). More a less all studies concluded that there is a change concerning the ownership of digital devices and also an increase of the digital literacy, but this did not affect the general learning behavior. (Conole et al, 2006) (Bullen et al, 2008) (Margaryan et al, 2011) (Nagler & Ebner, 2009). With other words students are equipped very well and can use all these devices professionally, but only rare for learning purposes.

DOI: 10.4018/978-1-4666-9629-7.ch026

Usually if people talk about using a computer, we imagine someone sitting at a table, typing on a keyboard, moving around with the mouse or tapping the touchpad and staring at the computer's screen. The way we interact with computers has not changed significantly since the 1960's when these peripherals were invented (Altman, 2013). This is slowly changing, though. Today, there are more and more innovative (input) devices on the market. On the one hand they differ from traditional ones and on the other hand they aim to change the way we interact with different kinds of computers. These peripheries however, do not intend to replace the traditional keyboard-mouse setup. They act as an addition, useful for diverse applications. Some of them represent also a more natural way of human-computer interaction. The computer can with the help of such peripheries sense motion in front of the screen or touch instead of getting input from the user by a keyboard and mouse. This more natural way of human-computer interaction enables a so-called Natural User Interface (Altman, 2013).

Prior to the works on this study, a literature study has been carried out about currently available innovative input devices aiming to find different ways for educational games. One of those found is the *MaKey MaKey*[1] seen on Figure 1. The device's name is a word play from the words "make" and "key". Essentially it is a printed circuit board with a micro controller running Arduino Leonardo firmware. It uses the Human Interface Device (HID) protocol to communicate with the computer, and it can send key presses, mouse clicks, and mouse movements. For sensing closed switches on the digital input pins, its engineers use high resistance switching to make it so that we can close a electric circuit even through materials like the human skin, leaves, and play-putty. That means we can create buttons from play-putty or just even draw a joystick with a pencil on a paper and use our "do it yourself" controllers to play a game. Or we can load up a piano software and instead of keyboard keys hook up the MaKey MaKey to bananas so that they become the piano keys. On the board itself there are six inputs on the front as shown in Figure 1, which can be attached to via alligator clips, soldering to the pads, or any other method. There are another 12 inputs on the back, 6 for keyboard keys, and 6 for mouse motion, which are accessible with jumpers via the female headers, paper clips, or by alligator clips

Figure 1. Makey Makey

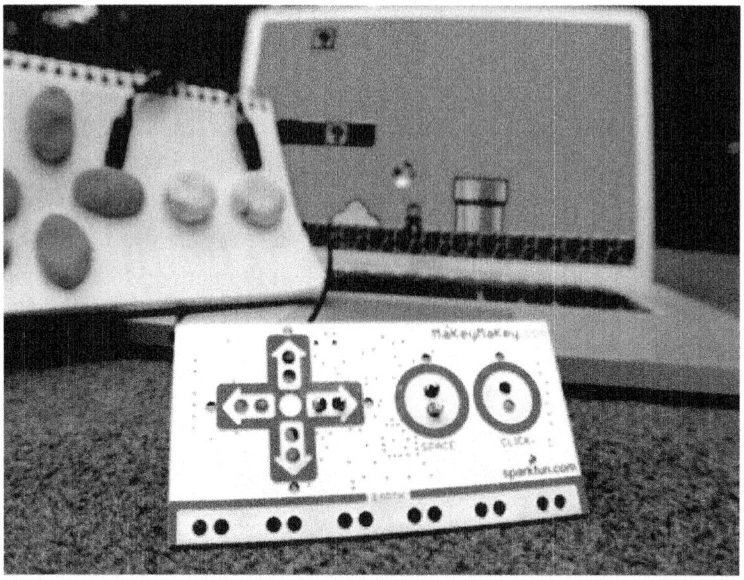

creatively around the headers. By reprogramming the Arduino environment different set of keys can be used or the behavior of the device can be changed. The biggest drawback of this device lies in its design requiring closed electrical circuits to make an action. This means the player has to be "connected" to the device with a wire so that he/she can act as a part of the electrical circuit. While the device has some potential and it is interesting, it did not meet our requirements in regards to collaboration and free real movements.

Another device on the list was the *Touch Board* from *Bare Conductive*.[2] It is a similar device to the *MaKey MaKey* capable of turning almost any material or surface into a sensor. It is designed as an easy-to-use platform for a huge range of projects, whether it is painting a light switch on the wall, making a paper piano or creating a custom interactive surface. It plays together with Bare Conductive's *Electric Paint*, which is essentially a non-toxic, air-drying, water-soluble conductive paint. It works smoothly on many materials including paper, plastic, textiles and conventional electronics. With the Electric Paint, we can draw our own circuit, our own light switch or keypads and use those as sensors. This device also utilizes the real world and it is a great tool for tinkering, but for our research purpose we are looking for a virtual environment. All these devices are well known in the Maker Movement, which is following the idea to "learn by making" (Schön et al, 2014). Papert described it stepwise as "learning by doing", "technology as building material", "big idea is hard fun", "learning to learn" (Papert, 1980).

The device, which has been chosen for the purpose of this research study, is the Leap Motion Controller. The Leap Motion is a consumer-grade sensor developed by a company with the same name. Along with the ability of creating a natural user interface, the requirements for the device needed for the research work included terms like *userfriendly*, *standalone*, *easy to use*. Considering these, the Leap Motion sensor is an optimal choice. This sensor is basically a small box in the size of a larger USB flash drive. The body of the sensor is made from aluminum with a black transparent plastic covering the insides. The device is similar to the Microsoft Kinect[3] sensor which is more widely known and popular, but as Weichert et al. (2013) point it out it is much more precise. It was designed to sense natural hand movements with high precision, instead of tracking the movements of the whole body. Therefore the device is able to let people using the computer in a new, unusual way, by pointing, waving, reaching, grabbing, or picking something up and moving it in the virtual world. However, it does not replace the keyboard, mouse, stylus, or trackpad. It is a new attractive addition to them. The Leap Motion is typically used as seen on Figure 2, as it lies on the table in front of the computer's monitor. But to make use of it, specifically for the device developed applications have to be used. Till September 2013 there have been 95 applications available through Airspace, the Leap Motion's application store, which has been renamed to App Store since then (Potter et al., 2013). These offered apps cover a broad field of games or educational and scientific apps, as well as apps for music and art.

"The Leap Motion Controller introduces a new gesture and position tracking system with sub-millimeter accuracy. In contrast to standard multi-touch solutions, this above-surface sensor is discussed for use in realistic stereo 3D interaction systems, especially concerning direct selection of stereoscopically displayed objects." (Weichert, 2013) The device is generally intended to be used with a minimal setup. It is designed for hand gesture and finger movement detection in interactive software applications. The sensor works by projecting infrared (IR) light upwards from the device and detecting reflections using monochromatic infrared cameras. Essentially it is an infrared stereoscopic 3D camera.

The Leap Motion Controller is capable of sensing movements done with our hands and fingers, or even with tools (pen etc.) in our hand. More precisely, it is 8 cubic feet (about 0,23m^3)

Figure 2. Leap Motion - interaction box (https://developer.leapmotion.com).

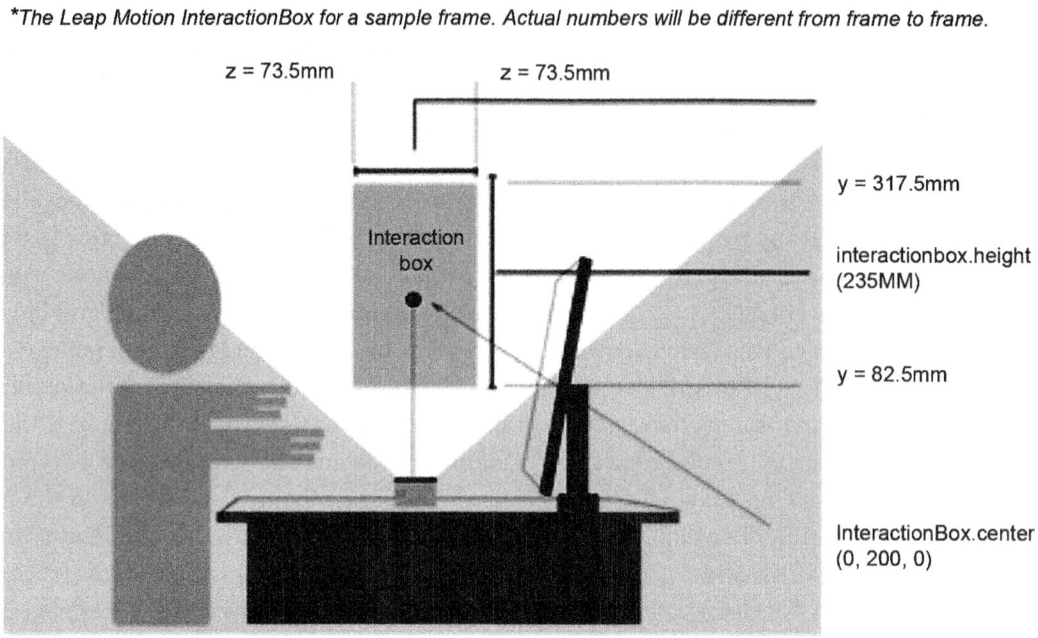

of interactive, three-dimensional space, which can be observed. This space is called the *interaction box* and it is shown in Figure 2. The device tracks all 10 fingers up to 1/100th of a millimeter and movements at a rate of over 200 frames per second. The company states that it is dramatically more sensitive than existing motion control technologies. It has a super-wide 150° field of view and a Z-axis for depth. The effective range of the Leap Motion Controller extends from approximately 25 to 600 millimeters above the device. This range is limited by how the IR light travels through space. Beyond a certain distance, it becomes much harder to detect the hand's position in 3D. The maximum current provided by the USB connection limits the intensity of the LEDs.[4]

In this research study a prototype is described, which has been developed for use with the Leap Motion with a special focus to the P-12 education. Finally the outcomes of a small-scale field study at an elementary school are presented.

RESEARCH DESIGN

The objective of this research study is to explore a way, how game-based learning (GBL) might, in cooperation with innovative controller devices, make the learning process more enjoyable (Shneiderman, 1998) and more motivating (Logan & Gording, 1981) (Holzinger, 1997) in P-12 education. GBL is close to problem-based learning, wherein specific problem scenarios are placed in a play framework (Barros & Tamblyn, 1980).

For our purpose, a prototype of an educational application has been developed following strictly the approach of prototyping (Alavi, 1984). Afterwards the application was evaluated at an elementary school within a small-scale field study with third grade students. Finally, the students' feedback has been recorded and evaluated.

PROTOTYPE

The prototype, which has been built for the purpose of this research study, is as mentioned before an educational game. The defined requirements were to develop a game, which should be easy to use, but the gameplay itself should be challenging and curious as well as it should also evoke players fantasy (Malone, 1980) to improve learning outcomes. With other words children should be able to learn by simply playing the game (Hannak et al, 2012). Furthermore, the game should offer a great and colorful user interface and it should be also fun to play so that learners will not get bored easily. Being a prototype, some features of a complete product have been left out. The application provides only basic graphics, it has no sounds and the gameplay is limited to 10 levels, which provide examples of basic multiplications only.

When designing for a motion controlled experience one of the first issues developers have to think about is in which environment is the application going to be used. People are quite adept at using their hands but the movements and gestures are sometimes subtle, sometimes not that precise. Furthermore we are not able to hold our hands perfectly steady. And if it comes to holding the arms for longer periods of time, it becomes quite exhausting. Furthermore depending on the application different ergonomic factors have to be considered. In our particular case the environment is a classroom and kids will use the application while standing or sitting at a desk. The interactions were designed with small rest periods so that the hands and arms don't get tired that fast.

We have decided to create a game which helps children to practice addition and subtraction between 1 and 100, and which makes them motivated to get to know the small multiplication chart and its practice. The current version of the prototype contains ten different levels with variable difficulty and with exercises for practicing the multiplication chart.

The game is placed into a 3D cartoon-like virtual world as shown in Figure 3. In this world there are colorful balloons floating in the air with different numbers on them. The player gets a mathematical exercise to solve, which is shown at the bottom of the screen. Afterwards he/she has to destroy the balloon, which carries the correct result of the exercise. When the player puts his or her hand above the sensor, a virtual robotic hand appears on the screen as seen on Figure 4, which replicates the movements of his/her hand. Punching the balloons to the ground with the virtual robotic hand pops/destroys them. So that the

Figure 3. The prototype

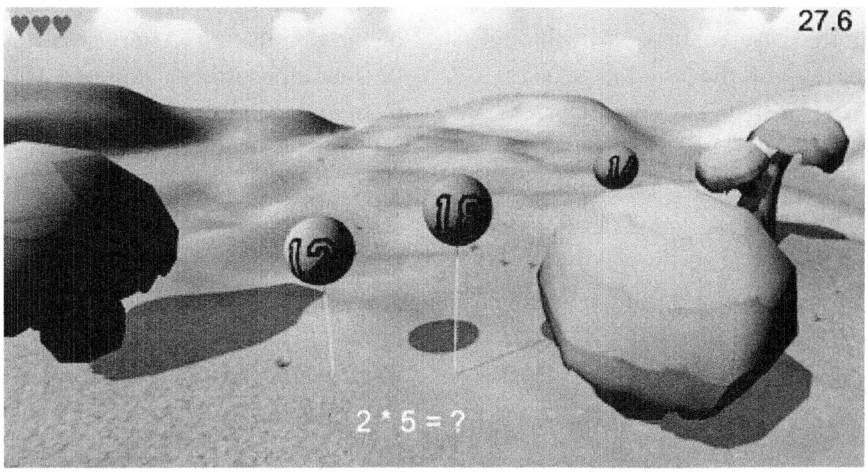

Figure 4. Robotic hand

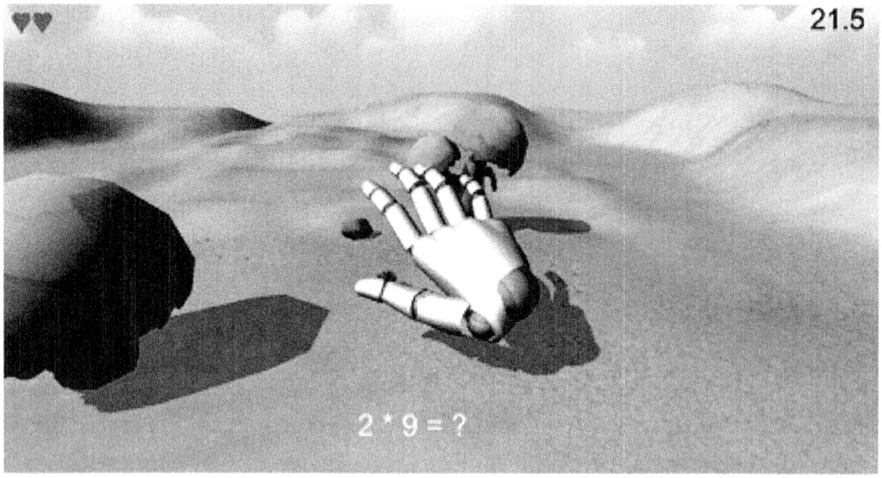

game is more challenging, the player is put under time pressure (in the right top corner). Sometimes the player even has to navigate through the world and search for the right balloon by forming a fist pointing in favorite direction. So a number of balloons are spread around and they might also be hidden behind trees or bushes. If the player pops the right balloon, he/she can continue to the next exercise, which is presented in the same way. After solving all the exercises of a given level there is a little pause for a tiny rest and then the next level is presented. If the player does not manage to solve the exercises within a given time or pops a balloon, which does not carry the correct result of the exercise, he/she loses one of the given lives. At the start the player owns three hearts, which are equal to lives. If the player manages to go through all the levels, or loses all the lives the game ends and the score is presented.

The power of Leap Motion is unleashed when used in a 3D environment. To create our 3D world Unity[5] has been used, a 3D game development ecosystem which holds a powerful rendering engine with a complete set of intuitive tools and rapid workflows to create interactive 3D and 2D content.

FIELD STUDY

To test out our prototype for game based learning with the Leap Motion in a real world scenario, it was given to 12 third grade children in an elementary school, which just learned the multiplication chart, so the game fits exactly to their learning process. The kids played with the application one-by-one. The research study concentrates on the one side how the Leap Motion and the application will perform in general with a special eye on school class environment and on the other side how the learners reacts and like the environment. The multi-level evaluation consists of an observation of the children as well as photo and audio documentation in parallel during their usage of the application. Afterwards oral feedback of the learners has been gathered using the cut-off-technique (Ebner et al, 2014).

First of all it has to be mentioned that there were some few performance issues during the test. The application sometimes behaved unstable, unplayable and the sensor did not work well. This might have been due to the strong lights in the classroom, or the fact that the application was each time run inside of Unity, and was not exported as a standalone app, or because the SDK was at the time of the trial still in beta, thus some performance issues might occur due to this fact. In the majority of cases however, it did work really well. The sensor had no problem also with the tracking of small hands of the kids.

Before the kids have started to play, they got basic instructions how to play. This is due to that the prototype does not include any graphics or other help files yet, which show how to play or work with such a device. All the kids reported, that they have never seen an application like this before. Therefore a short introduction is an absolute necessity. After they have seen the game in action for the first time they were eagerly waiting for their turn.

The kids really liked the interaction with the game menu. Some said they felt like magicians while starting the game. After the game has started it can be pointed out that the choice to simulate the robotic hand was good, as it did not scare the kids. The majority of children quickly learned how to move in the world with the "virtual joystick" and they were searching for the balloon with the right number on it. The most interesting part of the experiment however, was to observe how different kids played the game. Although the test group was small, it was possible to categorize the kids based on their performance in the game. There were basically four groups based on observation:

- The first group were kids who perform well at the class, they were also good in solving exercises in the game as well as having good hand-eye coordination skills and they had no problems with moving around in the virtual world, finding balloons and popping them. They really wanted to play the game again and again and this group enjoyed it.
- In another group, there were children, who were still good in solving exercises, but they had problems with coordination and finding the right balloons. Some of them had so much trouble playing the game that their experience was so frustrating they not really wanted to play the game again. For those kids from this group, who found the game a bit hard to play. It can be suggested to practicing similar games as can be found in the current store beforehand, which might have a positive influence on the hand-eye coordination skills. It is noticeable that they performed better as they played the game a second time.
- Those students, who were somewhat slower in solving exercises, made the third group. They had great coordination skills too and had no problems with game interaction. Playing the game for them was fun, and they wanted to play the game over and over again to be able to gain a better score. This game element was a big motivation. After each play, the kids were talking to each other and showing off their score. Those gaining higher were satisfied, while those who have earned a lower score wanted to try it again to make their score better. This form of virtual reward seems to work really well. It is motivational enough to make kids want to play a math game.
- In the last group there were the kids who performed not that well. They had problems with solving exercises in general. For them, solving math exercises and searching for balloons was not that fun. They quickly realized that the sensor can track two or more hands too, and that it is fun to play with the balloons with the virtual hands, or how cool it is when the virtual hands do the same as their own hands, when they clap and so on. They got bored really quickly.

The trial showed that the majority of kids loved the game. They were asked whether they want to play it again, and the response was positive. Almost all of them wanted to play the game again. They asked what is the name of the game, how and where can they play it. The sensor in general, especially how small it is and what it is capable of, impressed them. The kids enjoyed playing the game and they quickly forgot about math. It can be pointed out that the environment become immersive and they just wanted to find the right balloon, what obviously is possible only after solving the given examples, and finally they wanted to perform better and better to earn a higher score. This means they were practicing math while playing a game, and not thinking about school or exercises. The observation stated that incidental learning happens, where learners are learning while playing a game without thinking actively about the learning process anymore (Holzinger & Maurer, 1999).

The children were asked by the researchers how the game compares to the games they play daily on their iPads. The answer can be summarized as following: the iPad is nothing special anymore, and "this is much-much better" or "the best game I have ever played in my life". Of course children tend to overrate things and change their minds quickly over time. But they grew up in a world where there were smartphones and tablets everywhere, so they got used to it. They use iPads at the school where they have a couple of different apps for learning. They said that it is not a big deal to use a touch-screen "there you have to tap and touch it all the time, here you only swipe with your hands in the air and you play the game".

After the students played the game, they were interviewed with the help of the so-called cut-off technique (Ebner et al, 2014). A group of up to 4 children got 5 statements and different smiles (from sad to happy) and was asked to rank the statements as a group. Fischer (2007) mentioned that the ranking technique is highly interesting because it makes children to discuss about facts, bring them to reflect some circumstances and finally let them agree on one final decision. Of course due to the fact that a final decision must be done, minorities will be overruled, which can be seen as weakness of this methodology. On the other side this kind of evaluation will not deliver facts and figures rather than impressions, personal feelings and arguments. Figure 5 shows the five different cards for rating the statements.

These are the statements, which were given to the children:

1. I would like to play the game again.
2. It was easy to pop the balloons.
3. It was easy to find the balloons.
4. I think the exercises were easy.
5. I think the game was easy to play.

Figure 5. Rating of the statements

The group of children discussed the statement very detailed. Most of them had the idea to give the possible marks to each single point. Nevertheless those who had problems with the navigation and the gameplay voted against. This clearly points out, that for them it was quite hard to play the game due to the fact it was frustrating not to be able to find the right solution and pop the balloons. Table 1 describes in detail how the kids ranked the statements and what their decisions might mean.

The cut-off technique pointed out that in general children are very satisfied. Nevertheless in detail it can be stated might not be ideal for all types of students, particularly students with a need of special education or those, whose hand-eye coordination skill is not that well will have problems playing such games. The majority of children however tend to get used to things quickly. They can successfully use the widespread technology in their learning process, and our prototype has shown that bringing in fresh air, something different to them that can enhance their motivation.

Table 1. Statement rating

Statement	Rating of the Groups in Detail
I would like to play the game again	Got in general the best overall mark. The kids enjoyed playing the game, and they would love to play it again.
It was easy to pop the balloons	The majority of students voted to give the best mark, however some of them, which had problems popping the balloons, gave lower marks. They argue that popping the balloon is challenging. So it can be pointed out that the popping technique must be more appropriate.
It was easy to find the balloons	The majority of students vote for the highest mark. Few children mentioned some problems with the game play.
I think the exercises were easy	In general the groups seem to be satisfied and the difficulty level appropriate. Only some few argued that the time pressure is too hard.
I think the game was easy to play	Most of the students had no problems playing the game and therefore voted for the best mark.

DISCUSSION

The prototype development with Unity and the programming language C# runs smoothly. It provided all the tools and features, which were needed in the development process of the prototype. Nevertheless the prototype has not yet been done to a final stage and it has some reserves. As no sounds were added to the game, this would be an essential part of a possible future work to add sounds in the game menu as well as into the game. For example this could be environment sounds or music, or sound effects when popping the balloons. The addition of different physics forces like wind would also make the gameplay more interesting. The balloons might float in the wind and the player would need to catch and pop them. Otherwise the small research study pointed out, that the chosen development tools are satisfying for such a purpose.

As the Leap Motion is able to track two, or even more hands at the same time, a co-operation mode, where the players would help each other to get a higher score, might be also be a good addition, which would make the gameplay even more fun. Especially a team of two players with different skills can be helpful to overcome the problems of bad feelings of the gameplay.

Similar to other studies (Zechner & Ebner, 2011) it must be mentioned that games did not improve the learning behavior of those students who are performing not so well in the educational field the game was designed to. Nevertheless the majority of children tend to get used to things quickly. They can successfully use the widespread technology in their learning process, and our prototype has shown that bringing in fresh air, something new to them can boost their motivation.

CONCLUSION

The goal of this work was to make use of a new innovative controller device and to develop a prototype of a learning application for it, which would show a possible way to improve the game-based learning process at elementary schools.

After the field study at the elementary school we are able to point out that game-based learning might not be for everyone just like Whitton (2007) states. Especially students needing special education had trouble in succeeding the game. For other students however, such games utilizing innovative devices, which create a Natural User Interface, apart from the fact that students practice the school subject, might help to improve their hand-eye coordination skills. For well performing students with great coordination skills such games might mean a fun and novel way to practice the school subject.

It can be concluded, that game-based learning with innovative input devices such as the Leap Motion can significantly improve the learning process of some school subjects - if the applications are done right. Nevertheless it would need a longer and more rigorous scientific research study, which should be done in the next step. However, as we have seen in the classroom, such games can be motivational, engaging, challenging and fun to play to make students forget about the subject while still practicing it.

REFERENCES

Alavi, M. (1984, June). An assessment of the prototyping approach to information systems development. *Communications of the ACM*, *27*(6), 556–563. doi:10.1145/358080.358095

Altman, P. (2013). *Using MS Kinect Device for Natural User Interface*. Pilsen.

Barrows, H. S., & Tamblyn, R. M. (1980). *Problem-based learning: an approach to medical education (Springer series on medical education)*. New York: Springer.

Bullen, M., Morgan, T., Belfer, K., & Oayyum, A. (2008). *The digital learner at BCIT and implications for an e-strategy*. Paris, France: EDEN.

Conole, G., de Laat, M., Dillon, T., & Darby, J. (2006). *LXP: Student experiences of technologies. Final Report: JISC UK*. Retrieved from http://www.jisc.ac.uk/whatwedo/programmes/elearningpedagogy/learneroutcomes

Ebner, M., Nagler, W., & Schön, M. (2013). Architecture Students Hate Twitter and Love Dropbox" or Does the Field of Study Correlates with Web 2.0 Behavior? In *World Conference on Educational Multimedia, Hypermedia and Telecommunications 2013,* Chesapeake, VA (pp. 43-53). AACE.

Ebner, M., Schönhart, J., & Schön, S. (2014). Experiences with iPads in primary schools. In Profesorado, 18(3), 161-173.

Fischer, J. (2007). Detektivische Methode – Legetechnik. Retrieved from http://wissensreise.de/Intranet/Aufgabenkultur/forschen/Seiten/dMundLegetechnik.html

Hannak, C., Pilz, M., & Ebner, M. (2012). Fun - A Prerequisite for Learning Games. *Proceedings of World Conference on Educational Multimedia, Hypermedia and Telecommunications*, Chesapeake, VA (pp. 1292-1299). AACE

Holzinger, A. (1997). Computer-aided mathematics instruction with mathematica 3.0. *Mathematica in Education and Research*, *6*(4), 37–40.

Holzinger, A., & Maurer, H. (1999). Incidental learning, motivation and the Tamagotchi effect: VR-Friends, chances for new ways of learning with computers. Proceedings of Computer Assisted Learning CAL 99 (p. 70). London.

Logan, F. A., & Gordon, W. C. (1981). *Fundamentals of learning and motivation* (3rd ed.). Dubuque, IA: Brown.

Malone, T. W. (1980). What makes things fun to learn? Heuristics for designing instructional computer games. Proceedings of the *3rd ACM SIGSMALL symposium and the First SIGPC symposium on small systems* (pp. 162–169). doi:10.1145/800088.802839

Margaryan, A., Littlejohn, A., & Vojt, G. (2011). Are digital natives a myth or reality? University students' use of digital technologies. *Computers & Education*, *56*(2), 429–440. doi:10.1016/j.compedu.2010.09.004

Metz, R. (2013). *Leap Motion's Struggles Reveal Problems with 3-D Interfaces*. Retrieved from http://www.technologyreview.com/news/518721/leap-motions-struggles-reveal-problems-with-3-d-interfaces/

Nagler, W., & Ebner, M. (2009). Is Your University Ready For the Ne(x)t-Generation? Proceedings of the World Conference on Educational Multimedia, Hypermedia and Telecommunications 2009, Chesapeake, VA (pp. 4344 – 4351). AACE.

Oblinger, D. D., & Oblinger, J. L. (Eds.). (2005). *Educating the Net Generation*. Retrieved from http://www.educause.edu/educatingthenetgen

Opaschowski, H. W. (1999). *Generation @, Die Medienrevolution entlβt ihre Kinder: Leben im Informationszeitalter*. Hamburg, Ostfildern: Kurt Mair Verlag.

Papert, S. (1980). *Mindstorms: Children, Computers, And Powerful Ideas*. New York: Basic Books.

Potter, L. E., Araullo, J., & Carter, L. (2013). *The LeapMotioncontroller:Aviewonsignlanguage*. Adelaide, Australia. doi:10.1145/2541016.2541072

Prensky, M. (2001). Digital natives, Digital Immigrants. *On the Horizon*, *9*(5), 1–6. doi:10.1108/10748120110424816

Schön, S., Ebner, M., & Kurma, S. (2014, September). The Maker Movement. Implications of new digital gadgets, fabrication tools and spaces for creative learning and teaching. In eLearning Papers Special edition 2014 "Transforming Education through Innovation and Technology" (pp. 86-100).

Shneiderman, B. (1998). Relate-create-donate: A teaching/learning philosophy for the cyber-generation. *Computers & Education*, *31*(1), 25–39. doi:10.1016/S0360-1315(98)00014-1

Weichert, F., Bachmann, D., Rudak, B., & Fisseler, D. (2013). *Analysis of the Accuracy and Robustness of the Leap Motion Controller, Department of Computer Science VII*. Dortmund, Germany: Technical University Dortmund.

Whitton, N. (2007). *Motivation and computer game based learning*. In ICT: Providing choices for learners and learning. Proceedings of Ascilite Singapore 2007. Retrieved from http://www.ascilite.org.au/conferences/singapore07/procs/whitton.pdf

Zechner, J., & Ebner, M. (2011). Playing a Game in Civil Engineering. Proceedings of the 14th International Conference on Interactive Collaborative Learning (ICL2011) (pp. 417 – 422).

ENDNOTES

1 http://www.makeymakey.com
2 http://www.bareconductive.com/shop/touch-board/
3 http://www.microsoft.com/en-us/kinectfor-windows/
4 https://www.leapmotion.com/product
5 http://unity3d.com

Chapter 27

A Future Focus of Gaming: Soft Skills

DeAnna Proctor
Morehead State University, USA

Lenora Jean Justice
Morehead State University, USA

ABSTRACT

The authors discuss the instruction of soft skills by games and simulations as a future direction for the use of educational gaming in P-12 education. Technical or hard skills are taught in the educational curriculum; however, soft skills training, such as communication, collaboration, decision-making, problem-solving, negotiation, and leadership, are lacking. Soft skills training through games and simulations have been successful in areas such as the military, medicine, business, and disaster response, as well as those individuals with learning disabilities; therefore, the authors investigate the potential for soft skills training using games and simulations. In addition to instruction of soft skills, this article also addresses the inherent nature of games and simulations as teaching and assessment tools.

INTRODUCTION

Advancements in technology have increased opportunities for teaching through games and simulations. For instance, games and simulations have been successfully integrated as employee training of technical and soft skills in business, government training of military and service personnel, medical procedure simulations, and behavioral training for individuals with learning disabilities (Brown, Standen, Proctor, & Sterland, 2001; Carroll & Messenger, 2008; Chen & Levinson, 2006; Forssen & Haho, 2001; Gaba, 2004; Parsons & Mitchell, 2002). This successful integration of games and simulations has allowed people to learn potentially difficult and very technical information. Unfortunately, these hard skills are not the only types of training that are required throughout life. Despite the effort of students and personnel to study and acquire hard skills, they often do not possess the soft skills to effectively communicate their life skills and abilities and workforce potential. Furthermore, the influence of social media and mobile devices has exacerbated the loss of human interaction, which has particularly impacted the students of P-12 schools (Keller, 2013).

DOI: 10.4018/978-1-4666-9629-7.ch027

Unfortunately, even though the focus of many P-12 schools is often to provide some hard skills to help students reach their potential, many times the soft skills needed are either not practiced or addressed. Moreover, because basic soft skills are often more generic, the P-12 environment is a perfect place to begin these types of lessons. Consequently, with a demand for soft skills and an increase in the preference for independent learning, differentiated learning, and student-centered learning environments, educational institutions, particularly P-12 schools, can provide a solution through the development and implementation of a virtual soft skills training component adopted into the curriculum with games and simulations. Additionally, because today's student is networked in technology that can bridge the gap to a more engaging and immersive learning experience, why not promote the type of learning that students embrace? Although games are often blamed for a lack of soft skills in children, games, if designed appropriately, can facilitate learning, strengthen skills in collaboration, decision-making, and problem-solving, while also building confidence (Aldrich, 2005; Gee, 2003; Ke & Grabowski, 2007; Papastergiou, 2009; Robertson, 2012; Royle & Colfer, 2010; Shaffer, 2006; Shaffer, Squire, Halverson, & Gee, 2005; Squire, 2006; Vos & Brenan, 2010). For all of these reasons a future trend of the use of games and simulations in P-12 schools could easily involve the learning of soft skills.

Approximately 92% of American teens report going online daily to use social media, surf the Internet, play video games, and message others (Lenhart, 2015). Therefore, it is no wonder they prefer open learning environments where they have choices, driving their own education, through the use of technology. Games and simulations may be able to provide an effective and engaging method to teach soft skills to individuals who may belong to the most socially interactive generation so far, but who may also have the least amount of face-to-face interaction as well. Additionally, P-12 students of today may not understand the importance of soft skills as compared to technically specific hard skills, perhaps resulting in a lack of motivation to learn any soft skills. With this lack of understanding and motivation, the use of games and simulations, a teaching tool associated with high levels of motivation and engagement, may be the best way of reaching these independent learners that prefer using technology to more traditional methods of teaching.

This chapter discusses the instruction of soft skills by games and simulations as a future direction for the use of games and simulations in P-12 education. Additionally, current soft skills training strategies are reviewed to highlight the lack of compatibility with preferred learning strategies of (i.e., student-centered, differentiated, independent) current P-12 students.

This chapter will also address the use of games and simulations to teach soft skills. For example, the pedagogy and fail-safe nature of current games and simulations are used to describe some of the advantages of using this method of instruction. Additionally, incorporation strategies and specific games and simulations are referenced. Suggestions for future game and simulation designs, which incorporate the use of soft skills, are also included.

Overall, the authors predict that soft skills will be an educational gaming trend in the near future. The general application of soft skills needed throughout life makes it a perfect lesson for students at the P-12 level. Additionally, instruction with games and simulations is very compatible with P-12 student learning preferences (i.e., student-centered, differentiated, independent). All of the elements covered in this chapter support the authors' prediction.

BACKGROUND ON SOFT SKILLS

What Are Soft Skills?

Soft skills are people-related, personal skills in communication and collaboration in day-to-day situations via face-to-face, verbally and non-verbally, and written forms of correspondence that often reflect behavior and attitude exhibited toward others (Robles, 2012; Seetha, 2013). For example, soft skills can include teamwork and ability to take direction, work ethic, etiquette, decision-making, problem-solving, negotiation, and leadership. It is difficult to determine a specific list of soft skills since each situation in life has expected soft skills associated. For instance, in many of today's business careers, how one handles himself or herself, especially when the situation is critical, can make or break a negotiation effort. While technical skills can draw attention to one's resume, soft skills can complement the technical skills outlined as well as provide employers with a broader picture of the employee's potential contributions to the organization. Foundational soft skills can be applied throughout life in obtaining employment and succeeding in any career (Vijaya, 2013).

Therefore, soft skills are essential in providing a well-rounded individual that can communicate effectively and concisely in any surrounding. Those individuals who achieve higher levels of soft skills exhibit characteristics of a team member, good decision maker, problem-solver, and leadership for the organization.

The Disappearance and Increasing Demand of Soft Skills

Currently, technology has increased exponentially leading to large-scale training opportunities to build technical hard skills; however, soft skills, like effective communication, time management, critical and creative thinking, and problem-solving, seem to be diminishing. Although soft skills are the basis for individual success in both professional and personal lives, the ability to develop and build on soft skills is not an easy task, which suggests that they should be incorporated in an individual's educational curriculum as early as possible in order to build upon them throughout that individual's life.

Although there is a general consensus of the importance of soft skills, these skills seem to be in decline more recently (Keller, 2013). As students acquire hard skills for a position through education and training, it seems that increasingly they do not possess the soft skills to effectively communicate their skills and potential. One explanation for this deterioration seems to be today's technology driven environment which has overshadowed the need for soft skills in a face-to-face environment since email, text, and social media seems to be the preferred communication tools. Furthermore, the influence of social media and mobile devices seems to have exacerbated the loss of direct human interaction as society appears to have shifted from face-to-face communication to virtual communication such as email and text (Keller, 2013).

For example, over half of employers indicate challenges in hiring due to a lack of hard and soft skills training and/or education (The Indiana Youth Institute, 2012). Research conducted over the past two decades suggests soft skills, including customer service, communication, teamwork, critical thinking, positive attitude, integrity, ethics, time management, and professionalism, are as important to the success of an individual more so than traditional academic and technical skills (Fannon, 2003; Houghton & Proscio, 2001; International Youth Foundation, 2013; Office of Disability Employment Policy, 2010; Robles, 2012; Seetha, 2013). This makes sense in a globalized society where one must have the soft skills required to not only effectively communicate across cultures, but also to accurately communicate one's potential as a productive citizen within his community.

CURRENT TYPES OF SOFT SKILLS TRAINING AND STUDENT LEARNING

Although the focus of many P-12 schools is providing some hard or technical skills to help students reach their potential, many times the soft skills needed are either not practiced or not addressed (Pineteh, 2012; Pulko & Parikh, 2003; Zhang, 2012). While P-12 schools have yet to fully adopt games and simulations in the classroom in any form (Barjis, Gupta, Sharda, Bouzdine-Chameeva, Lee, & Verbraeck, 2012; Barron, 1998; Klopfer, Osterweil, Groff, & Hass, 2009), occupations in business and industry, technical fields, government, law enforcement, medicine, and social services for learning disabled have been successful in teaching essential soft skills through games and simulations (Brown et al., 2001; Carroll & Messenger, 2008; Chen & Levinson, 2006; Forssen & Haho, 2001; Gaba, 2004; Parsons & Mitchell, 2002).

Business Careers: Customer Service, Management, and Leadership

Business and industry are accustomed to providing face-to-face soft skills training as part of the hiring process and when company policies change. Games and simulations can reduce the costs of training financially as well as the amount of time employees are out of the office. Since success is tied to employee soft skills, many businesses traditionally hire expert training vendors or human resource personnel to provide training on the specific soft skills needed for the company; however, using resources to hire these outside trainers can be an issue. For example, business trainings tend to align more specifically toward soft skills such as leadership and management (Forssen & Haho, 2001; International Youth Foundation, 2013). A management classroom for business students could use a virtual office where communication and customer responsiveness are monitored to teach soft skills through active learning strategies rather than expending valuable resources on bringing in outside trainers (Houghton & Proscio, 2001; Nealy, 2005). Additionally, the use of role-play and simulations in management courses provides hands-on experience and practice in situations and behaviors encountered in business at reduced cost and less employee time out of the office. Role-playing techniques allow for complex situations to be developed in a realistic, yet risk-free environment, while providing immersion; whereas, simulations are learner-controlled since participants can interact at their own pace, spend time to think and reflect, and explore scenarios and decisions repeatedly (Chan, 2011).

In particular, businesses that operate globally often believe that individuals who possess soft skills improve customer and worker relations and increase productivity; therefore, they require soft skills in order to communicate and negotiate with such diverse clientele. Although this training is a high priority, many businesses use online training, including podcasts, blogs, wikis, and mobile devices, to reduce costs.

Technical Careers: Information Technology and Engineering

According to Chen and Levinson (2006) and Bancino and Zevalkink (2007), conventional approaches to technical areas, such as engineering and information technology, are dominated by analytical training which tends to deemphasize soft skills. They continue to point out that although experience is important to the learning process, often it is impossible to obtain experience when it might take unreasonable amounts of time or the risks and costs are too high to experiment in a real word situation; consequently, a simulation, which compresses time, cost, and risk, is ideal for learning while gaining some experience. Pineteh (2012) notes that the use of online teaching of communication skills training in first year information technology students promotes problem-solving and transference of knowledge in other educational subjects, as well as providing inclusion for those who are introverted or feel intimidated. Fundamental skills, including communication, presentation, collaboration, and conflict management tend to be lacking in technical fields and the Accreditation Board for Engineering and Technology (ABET) are imploring that soft skills be integrated into coursework (Zhang, 2012). More specifically, they suggest adding courses in business fundamentals, language, cultural differences and expectations, public speaking, diversity, and English skills in order to accurately convey messages in oral and written communications (Kesava Rao, 2012). This combination of soft and technical hard skills provides a combination that is exponentially increasing in a more global society.

Government, Service Personnel, and Medical Training Programs

Service personnel such as police, firefighters, various military positions, and employees of medical institutions already rely on soft skills training based on simulations (Chad Lane, Hays, Core, & Auerbach, 2013; Heinrichs, Youngblood, Harter, & Dev, 2008). Feedback and fidelity in virtual learning environments, like simulations, are essential design components when developing these types of environments. Therefore, this type of training provides a background to make decisions, act upon them, and witness the outcomes in a safe virtual environment where a wrong decision or miscommunication will not have an adverse effect in the real world.

Although interpersonal skills relevant to culture in a virtual environment currently cannot be compared to face-to-face effectiveness, virtual environments can be effective in improving basic communication skills (Chad Lane et al., 2013). Additionally, virtual environments, such as simulations, can be effective in areas requiring complex and difficult decision-making where the sense of presence is essential. Virtual environments utilize a learner's visual, auditory, and spatial abilities, which allow the learner to be immersed in the experience. Immersion has been identified as a key component of both gaming and the learning process (de Freitas & Oliver, 2006; de Freitas & Routledge, 2013). Also, virtual environments provide the opportunity for activities to be repeated as many times as necessary for mastery in a safe environment without consequences, and provide ownership and contextual learning, as well as the transference of newly learned skills from the virtual environment to the real world (Wahyudin, Hasegawa, & Dahlan, 2013).

Games have been used in the U.S. military since the 1970s and continue today in transforming decision-making, negotiation, problem-solving, and collaboration skills based on strategic missions through more advanced gaming options using the Sony™ Playstation 2® and Microsoft™ X-Box® (Macedonia, 2002). Tom Clancy's *Rainbow Six: Rogue Spear* has been used in military trainings since 2001 (Leonard, 2004), in addition to games such as *Delta Force 2,* Microsoft™ *Flight Simulator, C-Force,* and *Combat Systems XII* that focuses on communication, teamwork, decision-making and leadership (Macedonia, 2002).

As a result of September 11, 2001, and an increase in school shootings, the use of simulations in disaster preparedness and recovery is an area that has gained national attention (Gainey, 2009; Leonard, 2004; Simon & Teperman, 2001). In addition, natural disasters are a focus for the use of simulations. These game-based training simulations use mobile devices to practice hard and soft skills, like assessing critical areas of the situation, making decisions regarding equipment and personnel, team collaboration and time management, and communication with other responders and the public in a risk-free environment. These simulations provide assistance from non-playing virtual characters that can supply additional information and research similar incidents and responses.

Emergency responders and medical staff are trained in life-saving skills and interpersonal skills that are practiced and repeated in a risk-free environment through simulations that mimic real world ailments and procedures. These simulation scenarios introduce crisis incidents that users must analyze and assess to determine an appropriate and ethical solution in an immersive environment that is cost-efficient, risk-free, and allows participation from remote areas for individual and team training (Heinrichs et al., 2008). Simulation has made a huge impact in the medical field. For example, numerous simulators have been developed for medical purposes, the FDA has approved simulation training as part of new medical device approval, many major medical device companies use medical simulation as part of both initial and clinical trials and commercial rollout of new products, and board certification organizations are actively evaluating medical simulation as a tool to assess proficiency in procedure performance (Carroll & Messenger, 2008).

Development for Learning Disabilities

While recognizing difficulties in social behaviors at an early age is crucial to providing a path of learning and development for autistic individuals, studies indicate that communication, social skills, and behaviors can be enhanced through games, simulations, and other virtual environments (Beldarrain, 2006; Brown et al., 2001; Parsons & Mitchell, 2002; Simpson, 2009). Traditionally, operant conditioning principles that use a repetition of specific behaviors are utilized in developing new skills and behaviors; however, the ability to understand an action and resulting consequence is not always easily identified (Parsons & Mitchell, 2002). Individuals with autistic spectrum disorders can benefit from role-playing in a safe virtual environment. These safe situations provide the ability for unique learners to participate in role-playing activities that teach social skills in a safe and comfortable atmosphere, thus helping to reduce social anxiety (Parsons & Mitchell, 2002). Games, simulations, and other virtual environments provide learning spaces that support social development and alleviate anxiety as players learn to communicate and make decisions in a fail-safe environment.

Due to an increase in technology, virtual environments, including games and simulations, have been successful in cognitive rehabilitations in a variety of groups. These virtual environments can contribute to cognitive flexibility and transference, the ability to adapt to new conditions or knowledge, by manipulating the appropriate elements at the appropriate times, allowing for repetitive rote learning, and promoting prompt-fading or the need for a prompt is lessened, as new elements are introduced (Beldarrain, 2006). Communication and social skills can be taught, learned, and transferred from context to context if accomplished in an environment that is comfortable for the user and provides flexibility. The emerging technologies of today enable customization of content as well as level of interaction allowing a wide range of differentiation, where the learner chooses when and how to interact, which includes this distinct group of learners (Beldarrain, 2006).

JUSTIFICATION FOR TEACHING SOFT SKILLS TO P-12 STUDENTS

The educational arena has the opportunity to incorporate soft skills training including communication and teamwork, as well as activities to develop social skills and self-esteem skills, beginning as early as elementary school and continuing through graduation of secondary school. According to Harris and Rogers (2008), education generally provides the technical hard skills for a career, but, unfortunately, soft skills tend to be overlooked. There is no reason that these complementary hard and soft skills should not be developed throughout a student's educational career, enabling him or her to better compete in global society.

Current instructional methods in P-12 schools have yet to fully integrate technology in the delivery of soft skills training. Traditional face-to-face trainings include afterschool youth programs, facilitator instruction, on-the-job training, and classroom simulations through role-playing exercises (Junge, Manglallan, & Raskauskas, 2003; Office of Disability Employment Policy, 2010). Shute, Ventura, Bauer, and Zapata-Revira (2009) state that while P-12 education is substantially funded, students lack competencies as identified by scores based on traditional assessments to compete nationally and globally as learning remains primarily with texts and lectures. However, Kelly (2005) notes that using improved software and hardware, especially simulations, can repurpose the learning experience for soft skills and provide the ability to adapt to students learning styles and levels.

A few soft skills, such as sharing, working, and playing together, are already taught in elementary school; therefore, continuing these practices and building on them to include higher order skills such as communication, negotiation, decision-making, and problem-solving is a natural progression. Also, because learners build skills based on experiences and prior learning, the integration of soft skills instruction, using games and simulations, into the educational curriculum in P-12 should be a priority.

Learning Preferences of Current P-12 Students

Students of today are usually completely networked with their technology. They use the Internet as a research tool to help with school work; however, their primary use of their Internet connectivity is communication and socialization (Oblinger, 2004). They immerse themselves in activities, either for school or entertainment, and stay in touch with friends, family, and peers at every point. All of this communication may help learners since, as Kearns and Frey (2010) suggest, participation in a community of learners provides both academic and social benefits since participants provide social support as well as providing multiple learning strategies. Yardi (2006) corroborates this concept by indicating that there is an opportunity for active and collaborative learning through this back channel of communication and interaction. Other research suggests that students of today prefer to construct knowledge by actively engaging in the concepts they are learning through discussion, debate, questioning and explaining rather than passively receiving knowledge from a speaker (Boyle & Nicol, 2003; Pohl, Gehlen-Baum, & Bry, 2011).

Oblinger (2004) points out that students use technology to work, live, learn, and entertain. She continues to state that it has become so much a part of their culture that many students of today may have more experience playing video games than reading. Interestingly, this networking is often blamed for a lack of soft skills in children since they often use incomplete or fragmented sentences, Internet jargon, or emoji's to communicate or they immerse themselves for hours in a technology without using any soft skills (Bodomo, 2010). However, when it comes to technologies like games and simulations, if designed appropriately, learning can be facilitated, skills in collaboration, decision-making, and problem-solving can be strengthened, and confidence can be built (Balasubramanian & Wilson, 2005). For all of these reasons a future trend of using games and simulations as teaching tools in P-12 schools could easily involve the learning of soft skills.

Discussion of Compatibility of Training and Learning Preferences

The use of games and simulations in the training of soft skills are natural components of the socio-constructivist learning environment. For example, these methods of delivery provide reflection, scaffolding, facilitation, active learning, cooperative and collaborative modes, applied learning in real-life, risk-free environments, and assessment. Vygotsky (1978), known for the socio-constructivist theory, believed that learning constituted both social and cognitive development. He believed that children were born with innate discovery and learning skills and during growth these were developed through social interactions. Vygotsky's (1978) two main precepts are the More Knowledgeable Other and the Zone of Proximal Development, both of which can be demonstrated in games and simulations. The More Knowledgeable Other is a player within the virtual environment that has prior knowledge of skills, levels, and resources that other players can learn from and emulate, especially in multi-player conditions. In addition, the Zone of Proximal Development depends on the interaction of lower-skilled individuals practicing activities with higher-skilled individuals in a collaborative learning setting (Vygotsky, 1978).

Prior practices of instruction were linear and non-flexible; however, technology has enabled the curriculum to become more experiential for individuals to learn based on their styles and rates. Games and simulations provide flexibility, flow, and immersion in a non-linear, branching concept that gains and holds the attention of the learner (Chen & Levinson, 2006). Emmendorfer (2009) purports that soft skills can be taught through e-learning methods, such as games and simulations, by using a component-composite breakdown on learning tasks, by using real life examples and non-examples, and by requiring higher order thinking as learning progresses.

Chen and Levinson (2006) outline a simulation that models the effects of multiple variables in transportation networks. This allows engineers to create transportation patterns based on changes in population, land use, road speed, distance traveled, flow of traffic at various times of the day, and maintenance costs. This provides engineers an in-depth look at how each variable affects another and how to design a transportation network that is effective and efficient for travelers.

DESIGN OF SOFT SKILLS TRAINING WITH GAMES AND SIMULATIONS

The Office of Disability Employment Policy, U. S. Department of Labor (2010) recognizes that integrating technology into soft skills training can provide students with the hands-on experiences they need while effectively supporting, reinforcing, and augmenting classroom instruction. Advances in technology provide designers, instructors, and end-users with a variety of media formats lending various levels of engagement through auditory and visual elements; therefore, investigation and caution must be taken to choose an effective format for this type of lesson. For example, determining which training format to develop or pursue could be based on product competitiveness, end-user needs and/or available resources (e.g., technical, financial, personnel).

Games and game-based learning (GBL) have increased over the years as social networks and virtual reality have improved and provided a technical platform for providing skills training. According to a 2011 study by the National Research Council (as cited in McManus, Ebby-Rosin, & Kurshan, 2014, p. 1), "GBL has tremendous potential to impact teaching and learning because of its ability to 'individualize learning to match the pace, interests, and capabilities of each particular student and contextualize learning in engaging virtual environment.'" Since the Common Core State Standards (CCSS) do not include interpersonal or intrapersonal skills such as problem-solving, collaboration, and teamwork, the use of games as a resource in teaching provides an opportunity for students to learn these soft skills during classroom time (McManus et al., 2014).

Kriz (2003) outlines two types of learning simulations: closed (rigid rules) and open (free form), which use reflection, evaluation, and feedback to discuss cooperative actions between the simulation and real world. Alternative scenarios are presented, then tested and ranked in order to illustrate a variety of outcomes and interactions as players engage in different roles within the system. Consequently, these simulations and the feedback obtained can be effective in transferring learning to action through changes in dysfunctional and unacceptable work behaviors. Additionally, Klabbers (1999) noted that games and simulations represent networks of society with player interaction that are ideal environments for teaching soft skills.

The Potential of Game-Based Learning and the Fail-Safe Environment

Games and simulations have been widely acknowledged for the engaging, motivating, hands-on, learning by doing formats that can cause deep, meaningful learning (Aldrich, 2005; Becker, 2007; Chen & Levinson, 2006; Colby & Colby, 2008; Gee, 2003; Shaffer, 2006; van Staalduinen & de Freitas, 2011). Similarly acknowledged is that games and simulations offer an environment where it is not only safe to fail, but that a player is expected to fail and to learn from that failure. Becker (2008) goes a step further stating that gamers become persistent in playing since it is commonly known that there is a way to win. This knowledge encourages another try after every fail. This experimentation and fail-safe environment of games and simulations may account for part of the motivating factor of games. McGonical (2011) insinuates that there is no real comparison between games and reality. She suggests that games eliminate our fear of failure, improving our chances for success; whereas, reality is just hopeless. McGonical (2011) also points out that although no one likes to fail, gamers can spend 80% of their play failing (i.e., run out of time, lose the fight, do not solve the puzzle, die). She hypothesizes that positive failure feedback in a well-designed game is the reason. If a fail seems random or passive, the player could lose optimism and/or a sense of purpose. But, she argues that feedback that can be incorporated into a learning experience is valued and applied on the very next try.

Gee (2006, 2008) has a similar hypothesis in that good games use failure as a learning experience. But, he adds, the price of failure is also lowered in good games. For example, very often, good games will not make a player start completely over when he or she fails. Gee (2006, 2008) suggests that all of these features of failure in games allow players to take risks that might be too costly elsewhere, like classrooms, where failure is often seen as an end result.

For these reasons, games and simulations may be an optimal choice as a teaching tool in P-12 educational settings. Unfortunately, many schools use failure as an end result where students have high-stakes testing hanging over their heads. The low-stakes, reactive, rapid, unambiguous feedback that is characteristic of games and simulations may be well suited to soft skills that need to be practiced as well as learned.

Current Game and Simulation Designs and Their Pedagogy

Papert (1993) and Gee (2003) both affirm that learning can occur through games and simulations when designed through student-centered learning principles. The discussion of which learning principle or theory applies to games and simulations include the most notable: Gagne's (1985) Nine Events of Instruction, Reigeluth's (1979) Elaboration Theory, and Merrill's (2002) First Principles of Instruction. Although games and simulations have been heavily researched as overall instructional tools, less is known about what specific gaming elements influence learning outcomes (van Staalduinen & de Freitas, 2011). A few of the more recent frameworks and models that attempt to explain the relationship between educational outcomes and game design include Amory and Seagram's (2003) Game Object Model, Kiili's (2005) Experiential Gaming Model, and de Freitas and Oliver's (2006) Four-Dimensional Framework. Most designers can agree that the design of a game, simulation, or other similar virtual environment or web-technology should rely on the outcomes desired, participant base, and pedagogy (Morgan & Adams, 2009). They also have identified that the use of decision support systems involves problem recognition, alternative solutions, model formulation, what-if scenarios, decision-making, and implementation. Additionally, Causal Mapping ensures design efficiency and assessment of learning outcomes while providing for a participative and reflective teaching process in an environment that maintains a high degree of realism using pedagogy that is enhancing learning (Barjis et al., 2012).

As games and simulations grow in popularity as a training tool, more emphasis has been put on pedagogy (i.e., instructional techniques, training scenarios, communication/interaction with instructors). Those trainers who can afford it often create their own games and simulations. Their efforts are leading the way in researching game and simulation based learning. For example, Hill, Belanich, Chad Lane, Core, Dixon, Forbell, Kim, and Hart (2006) used five stages of development to design an immersive training system. They identified the objectives, developed storyboards, computer prototypes, and all the other major components to any game or simulation design. Interestingly though, one of the major differences is that at every level they not only consulted subject matter experts but also instructors who would implement the simulations. They discovered success in this strategy of training simulation design. Perhaps this is something to consider for future game and simulation designs.

Suggestions for Designers of Games and Simulations for Soft Skills Development

De Freitas and Routledge (2013) suggest a model for design of soft skills in simulation and gaming environments based on the e-Leadership and Soft Skills Educational Design Model (ELESS) that is centered on leadership development and soft skill development and implementation rather than game design or pedagogy. Leadership, social interactions, and immediate feedback engage and motivate learners while serving as a teaching tool, which provides reflection and practice, but can rather easily be incorporated into lessons (Matthews, 2011). Developing soft skills is more of a process of trial and error; hence, e-learning, games and simulations, and other fail-safe learning environments allow practice and can improve performance in these skills. Matthews (2011) suggests that a structured module on soft skills would include the following: describe the skill, provide relevant and insightful information, allow time for practice and reflection, and promote skill transfer to other situations while based on realistic scenarios and encounters that will legitimize the process. Also contributing their opinions on soft skills lessons, Petroski (2012) and Chan (2011) suggest that simulations are beneficial when decisions are based on large amounts of information, personalization of outcomes, real world situations, influence of information, branching progression, and varying scenarios. Additionally, simulations are based on cause-and-effect, providing an environment where soft skills, including communication, decision-making, and negotiation, can be exercised so that mistakes do not lead to irreparable damage; therefore, replaying the simulation and practicing skills reinforces good decisions (Doo, 2006). Balasubramanian and Wilson (2005) state that games and simulations encourage and stimulate student engagement and problem-solving skills while enhancing learning. They address five guidelines pertinent to the design of online simulations: design should challenge cognitive engagement, content should align with curriculum, acknowledgement of classroom and time constraints, feedback and assessment should relate to objectives, and resource guides should enhance classroom environment.

Chan (2011) purports that before integrating simulations into the curriculum a training needs analysis should be conducted describing the knowledge, skills, and attitudes of the participants.

Design and implementation should ensure learning objectives are stated, constraints are identified, and sufficient time is allotted with detailed and focused feedback (Chan, 2001; Morgan & Adams, 2009). This type of needs analysis would ensure that the lessons are relevant and taught at a level that would allow the player to successfully apply their knowledge in a real world scenario.

The design of soft skills training with games and simulations is in infancy even though research indicates the viability of delivery and learning (Linehan, Lawson, & Doughty, 2009). A lack of support could be a result of the lack of learning theories that specifically link game and simulation design to specific outcomes, as stated in the previous section. Additionally, a lack of common terminology and a division of instructional designers, subject matter experts, and game and simulation designers stalls the progress toward a uniformed structure for design, implementation, and assessment (van Staalduinen & de Freitas, 2011). However, in this particular case, the prominent barrier may be the inconsistencies to define and assess soft skills in order to transfer activities into a digital format that apply equally to varied learning domains. For example, most soft skill behaviors (i.e., communication, collaboration, listening) have a subtle and intrinsic nature, which means that the design of a game or simulation should not only consider the current level of soft skills for the individual, but also provide a myriad of scenarios that branch based on user response. Additionally, designers and developers of games and simulations for soft skills training in games and simulations should have standardized terminology. Also, standardizing categories, related to careers since different types of careers emphasize different types of soft skills, would help to identify levels and improvement in soft skills. For example, an employee of a customer service department would need a different type or level of soft skills than someone who is a computer programmer or pharmacist or military drill sergeant. Standardizing and/or categorizing soft skill users, abilities, and expectations may promote the design of this type of game or simulation much more than research into game or simulation pedagogy, design, or framework as games and simulations take elements from various pedagogical frameworks, yet must include the environment of the learner and social interaction as a blended design for academia and fun (deFreitas & Routledge, 2013).

INTEGRATING SOFT SKILLS TRAINING IN EDUCATIONAL CURRICULUM

Morgan and Adams (2009) suggest a pedagogy shift where learners are given more control over their own learning process through increased technologies. This shift toward the integration of technology leads to increased student engagement and motivation through multiple branching that supports student-centered, self-directed learning, including social software which soft skills training can be incorporated (McLoughlin & Lee, 2007). Games and simulations enable training with authentic and participatory learning, promoting a higher level of job performance and employability in an increasingly competitive global market demanding management, persuasion, and negotiation skills in order to discern an employee's ability to fit an organization.

Additionally, opportunities for teaching and learning soft skills through games and simulations provide students the opportunity to enhance communication skills, etiquette, interview techniques, collaboration, negotiation, motivation, problem-solving, and leadership for this wired generation (de Freitas & Routledge, 2013).

Suggested Games and Simulations and Potential Incorporation Strategies

As of the writing of this chapter, some of the virtual environments, including games, simulations, and computer applications (apps) used for helping students learn soft skills include:

Monster Interviews (Apple app), CUHK Soft Skills Mentor (Apple app), Good Communication Skills (Apple app), Interview Prep Training (Android app), Business Communication Skills (Android app), Communication Skills Book (Android app), My Interview Simulator (http://www.myinterviewsimulator.com), Everything Soft Skills (http://www.everythingsoftskills.com), Career4.me (http://www.career4.me/article/virtual-job-interview-simulator/), Game-Learn (http://www.game-learn.com), Quarantine (http://www.director-3d.com/quarantine), CyberNations (http://cybernations.net), Stop Disaster (http://www.stopdisastergame.org) and Connect-Ability (http://elearning.connect-ability.com). There are many good tools out there and more are created every day. Consequently, the authors suggest performing Internet searches and collaborating with peers to maintain one's own resource bank of soft skills lessons and practice.

Games and simulations lend to the use of a blended design incorporating online and face-to-face interaction that encourages learners to work together as a group in a collaborative social community (de Freitas & Routledge, 2013; Pineteh, 2012). Simulations may have no greater effect in teaching than traditional classroom training; however, when blended with a face-to-face course, students indicate that the simulation reinforces both factual and cognitive skills. A blended environment of traditional classroom-based methods with online components like simulations is preferred due to learning styles and discrepancies in experience and accessibility of technology (Pineteh, 2012).

Further research should be explored in the area of both instructor perception and learner perception related to the integration of technology such as games and simulations in the classroom. While students of today may be more comfortable with games and simulations, it is still unclear how effective games and simulations are related to learning. Research on this topic, relative to soft skills, should include learning styles, level of technological skills, established higher order thinking skills, and demographics (i.e., gender, social economic status, age).

Facilitator Preparation

While games and simulations have been shown as a successful tool for teaching, an essential component for the process is the preparation and acceptance of the facilitators (Fallon, 2010). Students are already on board for technology in their learning experiences; therefore, it is crucial that facilitators are trained in these delivery methods. The role of the facilitator is to guide students through the learning process using games and simulations in an engaging and motivating environment. In the case of learning soft skills, it can be stressful and frightening for many students; consequently, the facilitator must exhibit the ability to communicate, both listening and speaking, effectively to ensure that the learner feels comfortable. The facilitator must be able to evaluate and understand the student's current level of soft skills, as well as the student's learning style and align games and simulations as needed. While feedback is inherent in games and simulations, the facilitator must provide constructive feedback throughout the learning process based on the goals and objectives outlined by the game or simulation.

Fanning and Gaba (2007) note that adjudged levels of knowledge and skill of the facilitator is positively aligned to the experience and the level of participation from the student. Therefore, facilitators must provide a student-focused, engaging, and motivating learning environment that allows the student to actively learn through experience that produces greater understanding and transferability of soft skills to a variety of situations (Culpin & Scott, 2012).

GAMES AND SIMULATIONS AS ASSESSMENT TOOLS

The development of an assessment tool can be time consuming and must be designed to specifically address the measures that will be used to ascertain a student's level of achievement or competence. Traditional assessment tools include tests, surveys, interviews, and observations that provide evidence of learning and allow feedback for improvement. However, games and simulations have been used for decades in medicine, business, and military trainings as an assessment of user's knowledge, decision-making skills, and collaboration; however, education is hesitant to integrate games and simulations into the classroom (Gee & Levine, 2008; Kenny & Gunter, 2011; Koh et al., 2012). Interestingly, one of the identified barriers to using games and simulations in public schools is the accountability to high-stakes testing and the lack of patience for instructional strategies that have not been proven to raise scores on these assessments (Simpson & Stansberry, 2008). Traditionally, assessment has been limited by definition and antiquated methodology, yet games and simulations are valid assessment tools (Aldrich, 2001). Assessment is the process of gathering qualitative and quantitative data to validate that stated objectives are met, while providing feedback for areas of improvement (Chin, Dukes, & Gamson, 2009). Replacing the word assessment with game or simulation in the previous sentence is just as true, which suggests that games and simulations could be viewed as a type of assessment – for example, in many games, no matter the type, if you pass, you go on to the next level or if you fail, you lose a life or must start over. In general, games and simulations provide assessment elements through the data collected on character scores, acquisition of resources, and/or player development and progression (Chin et al., 2009).

Games and simulations are designed as an assessment since players develop skills and acquire knowledge of the game, players, and rules, while advancing to higher levels by overcoming obstacles and gaining resources for a higher score or enhanced character. Berlotti, Kapralos, Lee, Moreno-Ger, and Berta (2013) suggest that digital games have an advantage as a type of assessment since they keep track of every decision a player makes, provide differentiated learning that progresses to higher difficulties and different topics at the player's pace, and integrate pedagogy and gameplay to allow immersion, immediate feedback, and user adaptivity. However, potential issues with games and simulations as assessment tools include alignment with pedagogy, lack of instructor knowledge and enthusiasm for the new medium, open-ended nature of the design, and student use of cheat codes, which could compromise measuring what was actually learned from the session (Chin et al., 2009; van Staalduinen & de Freitas, 2010).

Forms of Assessment within Games and Simulations

Games provide a unique ability to incorporate automated scoring and assessments while providing an immersive environment that allows the player to perform without fear or stress of traditional testing. Therefore, both summative and formative assessment can be processed within games and simulations. Michael and Chen (2005) describe three primary types of assessment: (i) completion assessment, (ii) in-process assessment, and (iii) teacher assessment. In completion assessment, much like traditional classroom assessment, students are assessed after the game or simulation in order to determine understanding of the objective. However, in-process assessment analyzes the choices that a student makes within the virtual environment; whereas, teacher assessment uses these observations in order to evaluate student interaction and decision-making skills that are not generated by game scores and progress tracking. Michael and Chen (2005) refer to this repeating cycle as instruct and quiz.

Evidence-based assessment outlines the skills and knowledge that must be achieved as outlined by a pedagogical model or algorithm based on a predetermined measurable procedure such as pre-test versus post-test (Shute et al., 2009). Many researchers divide participants into a treatment group and a control group where each is given a pre-test, the treatment group interacts with a game or simulation while the control group receives a different form of instruction, followed by a post-test given to both groups in order to evaluate the effects of the game or simulation versus no interaction.

Simulations that provide face-to-face interaction with a trainer are a common form of performance-based assessment. The trainer works with participants in building soft skills aimed at the interview process using role-playing strategies; but unfortunately, many individuals find these face-to-face interactions intimidating. The incorporation of an online interview simulation with branching scenarios allows users to practice responses in a fail-safe environment, receive feedback throughout the interview, and repeat the process in order to gain confidence.

The future of games and simulations as assessment tools in education should be considered at all levels. Students of today expect and demand technology and the use of games and simulations provides an engaging process in developing both cognitive and non-cognitive skills in an environment that allows for assessment through tracking of student performance.

CONCLUSION

The ability to communicate, collaborate, make decisions, solve problems, think critically and creatively, negotiate, and provide leadership is essential in advancing both professionally and personally. Technology is changing education. Therefore, the use of technology, specifically games and simulations, for soft skills instruction in P-12 education should be examined and implemented.

Games and simulations provide users with well-defined goals, team play, tracking of level progression, change and challenges, consequences, personalization of environment and pace, and varying patterns for decision making (International Education Advisory Board, 2008). It is the opinion of the authors that games and simulations are proven and preferred instructional tools; therefore, education should integrate these forms of media into the P-12 curriculum. Games and simulations can provide the participant with expected outcomes such as completing a level, obtaining resources, achieving high scores, practicing skills, and, in multi-player games, communication and collaboration.

Since the youth of today are intrigued, engaged, and responsive to technology, the incorporation of games and simulations into the classroom as educational tools could be motivating, could be engaging, could provide differentiated instruction, could provide instant feedback, could be immersive, and could provide practice and application of lessons to validate student comprehension and learning. Because development of cognitive and non-cognitive skills is the outcome of these interactive learning activities, there is a demand for soft skills training, and there is an increase in online learning opportunities; therefore, the use of games and simulations in the learning environment to coach and promote or to assess soft skills should be further developed and implemented in the P-12 educational curriculum.

REFERENCES

Aldrich, C. (2001, September). The state of simulations: soft-skill simulations emerge as a powerful new form of e-learning. *OnLineLearning*.

Aldrich, C. (2005). *Learning By Doing: A Comprehensive Guide to Simulations, Computer Games, and Pedagogy in E-learning and Other Educational Experiences*. San Francisco: Pfeiffer.

Amory, A., & Seagram, R. (2003). Educational game models: Conceptualization and evaluation. *South African Journal of Higher Education*, *17*(2), 206–217.

Balasubramanian, N., & Wilson, B. G. (2005). Gaming and simulations. *ForeSITE, 1*.

Bancino, R. & Zevalkink, C. (2007, May). Soft skills: The new curriculum for hard-core technical professionals. *Association for Career and Technical Education* T*echniques*.

Barjis, J., Gupta, A., Sharda, R., Bouzdine-Chameeva, T., Lee, P. D., & Verbraeck, A. (2012). Innovative teaching using simulation and virtual environments. *Interdisciplinary Journal of Information, Knowledge, and Management*, *7*, 237–255.

Barron, T. (1998). The hard facts about soft-skills software. *Training & Development*, *52*(6), 48–51.

Becker, K. (2007). Pedagogy in commercial video games. In M. Prensky, D. Gibson, & C. Aldrich (Eds.), Games and Simulations in Online Learning: Research and Development Frameworks, 21-47. Hershey, PA, USA: IGI Global.

Becker, K. (2008). Video game pedagogy: Good games = good pedagogy. *Games: Purpose and Potential in Education* (pp. 73-125).

Beldarrain, Y. (2006). Distance education trends: Integrating new technologies to foster student interaction and collaboration. *Distance Education*, *27*(2), 139–153. doi:10.1080/01587910600789498

Berlotti, F., Kapralos, B., Lee, K., Moreno-Ger, P., & Berta, R. (2013). Assessment in and of serious games: An overview. *Advances in Human-Computer Interaction*, *2013*, 1–11. doi:10.1155/2013/136864

Bodomo, A. (2010). Is technology changing the way we communicate? In A. Bodomo (Ed.), *Computer-mediated communication for linguistics and literacy: Technology and natural language education* (pp. 9–16). Hershey, PA: Information Science Publishing. doi:10.4018/978-1-60566-868-0.ch002

Boyle, J., & Nicol, D. (2003). Using classroom communication systems to support interaction and discussion in large class settings. *Association for Learning Technology Journal*, *11*(3), 43–57. doi:10.1080/0968776030110305

Brown, D., Standen, P., Proctor, T., & Sterland, D. (2001). Advanced design methodologies for the production of virtual learning environments for use by people with learning disabilities. *Presence (Cambridge, Mass.)*, *10*(4), 401–415. doi:10.1162/1054746011470253

Carroll, J., & Messenger, J. (2008). Medical simulation: The new tool for training and skill assessment. *Perspectives in Biology and Medicine*, *51*(1), 47–60. doi:10.1353/pbm.2008.0003 PMID:18192765

Chad Lane, H., Hays, M. J., Core, M. G., & Auerbach, D. (2013). Learning intercultural communication skills with virtual humans: Feedback and fidelity. *Journal of Educational Psychology*, *105*(4), 1026–1035. doi:10.1037/a0031506

Chan, A. (2011). Learner receptivity toward role play simulation in teaching H.R.M. to university students in Hong Kong. *International Journal of Educational Research*, *2*(1), 1–16.

Chen, W., & Levinson, D. (2006). Effectiveness of learning transportation network growth through simulation. *Journal of Professional Issues in Engineering Education and Practice*, *132*(1), 29–41. doi:10.1061/(ASCE)1052-3928(2006)132:1(29)

Chin, J., Dukes, R., & Gamson, W. (2009). Assessment in simulation and gaming: A review of the last 40 years. *Simulation & Gaming*, *40*(4), 553–568. doi:10.1177/1046878109332955

Colby, R. S., & Colby, R. (2008). A pedagogy of play: Integrating computer games into the writing classroom. *Computers and Composition*, *25*(3), 300–312. doi:10.1016/j.compcom.2008.04.005

de Freitas, S., & Oliver, M. (2006). How can exploratory learning with games and simulations within the curriculum be most effectively evaluated? *Computers & Education*, *46*(3), 249–264. doi:10.1016/j.compedu.2005.11.007

de Freitas, S., & Routledge, H. (2013). Designing leadership and soft skills in educational games: The e-leadership and soft skills educational games design model (ELESS). *British Journal of Educational Technology*, *44*(6), 951–968. doi:10.1111/bjet.12034

Doo, M. Y. (2006). A problem in online interpersonal skills training: Do learners practice skills? *Open Learning*, *21*(3), 263–272. doi:10.1080/02680510600953252

Emmendorfer, J. (2009) *Yes you can! Teach soft skills with e-learning* [White Paper]. AME-Learning, Inc.

Fallon, G. (2010). Using avatars and virtual environments in learning: What do they have to offer? *British Journal of Educational Technology*, *41*(1), 108–122. doi:10.1111/j.1467-8535.2009.00991.x

Fanning, R., & Gaba, D. (2007). The role of debriefing in simulation-based learning. *Society for Simulation in Healthcare*, *2*(2), 115–125. doi:10.1097/SIH.0b013e3180315539 PMID:19088616

Fannon, K. (2003). 'Needle stick' – a role-play simulation: Transformative learning in complex dynamic social systems. *International Journal of Training Research*, *1*(2), 100–116.

Forssen, M., & Haho, P. (2001). Participative development and training for business processes in industry: Review of 88 simulation games. *International Journal of Technology Management*, *22*(1), 233–262. doi:10.1504/IJTM.2001.002963

Gaba, D. M. (2004). The future vision of simulation in health care. *Quality & Safety in Health Care*, *13*(Supplement 1), i2–i10. doi:10.1136/qshc.2004.009878 PMID:15465951

Gagne, R. M. (1985). *The Conditions of Learning* (4th ed.). New York: Holt, Rinehart & Winston.

Gainey, B. (2009). Crisis management's new role in educational settings. *The Clearing House: A Journal of Educational Strategies, Issues and Ideas*, *82*(6), 267–274. doi:10.3200/TCHS.82.6.267-274

Gee, J. P. (2003). *What Video Games Have to Teach Us About Learning and Literacy*. New York: Palgrave MacMillan.

Gee, J. P. (2006). Are videogames good for learning? *Curriculum & Leadership Journal, 5*(1).

Gee, J. P. (2008). Learning and games. In K. Salen (Ed.), The Ecology of Games: Connecting Youth, Games, and Learning, 3, 21-40. MIT Press.

Gee, J. P., & Levine, M. (2008). Let's get over the slump. *Education Week*, *8*(4).

Harris, K. S., & Rogers, G. E. (2008). Soft skills in the technology education classroom: What do students need? *Technology Teacher*, *68*(3), 19–24.

Heinrichs, W., Youngblood, P., Harter, P., & Dev, P. (2008). Simulation for team training and assessment: Case studies of online training with virtual worlds. *World Journal of Surgery*, *32*(2), 161–170. doi:10.1007/s00268-007-9354-2

Hill, R., Belanich, J., Chad Lane, H., Core, M., Dixon, M., & Forbell, E. et al. (2006). Pedagogically structured game-based training: Development of the ELECT BILAT simulation. *Proceedings of the 25th Army Science Conference* (pp. 1-8).

Houghton, T., & Proscio, T. (2001). *Hard work on soft skills: Creating a "culture of work" in workforce development*. Philadelphia, PA: Public/Private Ventures.

International Education Advisory Board. (2008) *Learning in the 21st century: Teaching today's students on their terms* [White Paper]. Certiport.

International Youth Foundation. (2013). *Getting youth in the door: defining soft skills requirements for entry-level service sector jobs*.

Junge, S. K., Manglallan, S., & Raskauskas, J. (2003). Building life skills through afterschool participation in experiential and cooperative learning. *Child Study Journal*, *33*(3), 165–174.

Ke, F., & Grabowski, B. (2007). Gameplaying for maths learning: Cooperative or not? *British Journal of Educational Technology*, *38*(2), 249–259. doi:10.1111/j.1467-8535.2006.00593.x

Kearns, L., & Frey, B. (2010). Web 2.0 technologies and back channel communication in an online learning community. *TechTrends*, *54*(4), 41–51. doi:10.1007/s11528-010-0419-y

Keller, M. (2013). Social media and interpersonal communication. *Social Work Today*, *13*(3), 10.

Kelly, H. (2005, Summer). Games, cookies, and the future of education. *Issues in Science and Technology*, 33–40.

Kenny, R., & Gunter, G. (2011). Factors affecting adoption of video games in the classroom. *Journal of Interactive Learning Research*, *22*(2), 259–276.

Kesava Rao, D. S. (2012). New strategies and materials for teaching soft skills to engineering students: The Indian context. *International Proceedings of Economics Development and Research*, *30*, 268–270.

Kiili, L. (2005). Digital game-based learning: Towards an experiential gaming model. *The Internet and Higher Education*, *8*(1), 13–24. doi:10.1016/j.iheduc.2004.12.001

Klabbers, J. (1999). Three easy pieces: A taxonomy on gaming. In D. Sounders & J. Severn (Eds.), *Simulation and Gaming Yearbook, Simulation and Games for Strategy and Policy Planning, (Vol. 7,* pp. 16–33). London: Kogan Page.

Klopfer, E., Osterweil, S., Groff, J., & Haas, J. (2009). Using the technology of today, in the classroom today [White Paper]. *The Education Arcade*, MIT.

Koh, E., Kin, Y., Wadhwa, B., & Lim, J. (2012). Teacher perceptions of games in Singapore schools. *Simulation & Gaming*, *43*(1), 51–66. doi:10.1177/1046878111401839

Kriz, W. C. (2003, December). Creating effective learning environments and learning organizations through gaming simulation design. *Simulation & Gaming*, *34*(4), 495–511. doi:10.1177/1046878103258201

Lenhart, A. (2015). Teens, social media & technology overview 2015. Pew Research Center, April.

Leonard, D. (2004). Unsettling the military entertainment complex: Video games and a pedagogy of peace. *Studies in Media and Information Literacy Education*, *4*(4), 1–8. doi:10.3138/sim.4.4.004

Linehan, C., Lawson, S., & Doughty, M. (2009). Tabletop prototyping of serious games for "soft skills" training. Paper presented at the *2009 Conference in Games and Virtual Worlds for Serious Applications*, Coventry, United Kingdom. doi:10.1109/VS-GAMES.2009.9

Macedonia, M. (2002). Games, simulation, and the military education dilemma. *Internet and the* University*: 2001 Forum*, 157-167.

Matthews, P. (2011, December). Can you learn soft skills from e-learning? *Training Journal,* 34-37.

McGonical, J. (2011). *Reality is Broken: Why Games Make Us Better and How They Can Change the World*. Penguin.

McLoughlin, C., & Lee, M. (2007). Social software and participatory learning: Pedagogical choices with technology affordances in the Web 2.0 era. Proceedings of ICT: Providing choices for learners and learning Ascilite Singapore 2007.

McManus, C., Ebby-Rosin, R., & Kurshan, B. (2014). Opportunities, obstacles and outcomes in educational gaming: Teaching to the common core, 21st century skills and beyond. *Philadelphia Social Innovation Journal, 17*, 1–11.

Merrill, M. D. (2002). First principles of instruction. *Educational Technology Research and Development, 50*(3), 43–59. doi:10.1007/BF02505024

Michael, D., & Chen, S. (2005, October). Proof of learning: assessment in serious games. Retrieved from http://www.gamasutra.com/view/feature/130843/proof_of_learning_assessment_in_.php

Morgan, G., & Adams, J. (2009). Pedagogy first: Making web-technologies work for soft skills development in leadership and management education. *Journal of Interactive Learning Research, 20*(2), 129–155.

Nealy, C. (2005). Integrating soft skills through active learning in the management classroom. *Journal of College Teaching and Learning, 2*(4), 1–6.

Oblinger, D. (2004). The next generation of educational engagement. *Journal of Interactive Media in Education*, (8): 1–18.

Office of Disability Employment Policy, U.S. Department of Labor. (2010, June). *Teaching soft skills through workplace simulations in classroom settings.*

Papastergiou, M. (2009). Digital game-based learning in high school computer science education: Impact on educational effectiveness and student motivation. *Computers & Education, 52*(1), 1–12. doi:10.1016/j.compedu.2008.06.004

Papert, S. (1993). *The Children's Machine*. New York: BasicBooks.

Parsons, S., & Mitchell, P. (2002). The potential of virtual reality in social skills training for people with autistic spectrum disorders. *Journal of Intellectual Disability Research, 46*(5), 430–443. doi:10.1046/j.1365-2788.2002.00425.x PMID:12031025

Petroski, A. (2012). Games vs. simulations: When simulations may be a better approach. *Training & Development, 66*(2), 27–29.

Pineteh, E. A. (2012). Using virtual interactions to enhance the teaching of communication skills to information technology students. *British Journal of Educational Technology, 43*(1), 85–96. doi:10.1111/j.1467-8535.2011.01193.x

Pohl, A., Gehlen-Baum, V., & Bry, F. (2011). Introducing Backstage – A digital backchannel for large class lectures. *Interactive Technology and Smart Education, 8*(3), 186–200. doi:10.1108/17415651111165410

Pulko, S. H., & Parikh, S. (2003). Teaching 'soft' skills to engineers. *International Journal of Electrical Engineering Education*, *40*(4), 243–254. doi:10.7227/IJEEE.40.4.2

Reigeluth, C. M. (1979). In search of a better way to organize instruction: The elaboration theory. *Journal of Instructional Development*, *2*(3), 8–15. doi:10.1007/BF02984374

Robertson, J. (2012). Making games in the classroom: Benefits and gender concerns. *Computers & Education*, *59*(2), 385–398. doi:10.1016/j.compedu.2011.12.020

Robles, M. (2012). Executive perceptions of the top 10 soft skills needed in today's workplace. *Business Communication Quarterly*, *75*(4), 453–465. doi:10.1177/1080569912460400

Royle, K., & Colfer, S. (2010). *Computer games and learning – Where next? The breadth and scope of the use of computer games in education. CeDARE.* Walsall, UK: University of Wolverhampton.

Seetha, S. (2013). Necessity of soft skills training for students and professionals. *International Journal of Engineering. Business and Enterprise Applications*, *4*(2), 171–174.

Shaffer, D. (2006). *How Computer Games Help Children Learn*. New York: Palgrave Macmillan. doi:10.1057/9780230601994

Shaffer, D., Squire, K., Halverson, R., & Gee, J. (2005). Video games and the future of learning. *Phi Delta Kappan*, *87*(2), 104–111. doi:10.1177/003172170508700205

Shute, V., Ventura, M., Bauer, M., & Zapata-Revira, D. (2009). Melding the power of serious games and embedded assessment to monitor and foster learning: Flow and grow. In U. Ritterfeld, M. Cody, & P. Vorderer (Eds.), *Serious Games: Mechanisms and Effects* (pp. 295–321). New York: Routledge.

Simon, R., & Teperman, S. (2001). The World Trade Center attack: Lessons for disaster management. *Critical Care (London, England)*, *5*(6), 318–320. doi:10.1186/cc1060 PMID:11737917

Simpson, E. (2009). Video games as learning environments for students with learning disabilities. *Children, Youth and Environments*, *19*(1), 306–319.

Simpson, E., & Stansberry, S. (2008). Video games and teacher development: Bridging the gap in the classroom. In K. McFerin, et al. (Eds.), *Proceedings of Society for Information Technology & Teacher Education International Conference 2008,* Chesapeake, VA (pp. 5326-5331). AACE.

Squire, K. (2006). From content to context: Videogames as designed experience. *Educational Researcher*, *35*(8), 19–29. doi:10.3102/0013189X035008019

The Indiana Youth Institute. (2012, March). *Soft skills: Beyond academic success* (Issue Brief March 2012). Indianapolis, IN.

van Staalduinen, J. P., & de Freitas, S. (2011). A game-based learning framework: Linking game design and learning. In M.S. Khine (Ed.), *Learning to Play: Exploring the Future of Education with Video Games* (Vol. 53, pp. 1–37). Peter Lang.

Vijaya, K. R. (2013). Teaching soft skills to technical professionals: Technology versus practical intelligence. *International Journal of Engineering Education*, *2*(3), 567–573.

Vos, L., & Brennan, R. (2010). Marketing simulation games: Student and lecturer perspectives. *Marketing Intelligence & Planning*, *28*(7), 882–897. doi:10.1108/02634501011086472

Vygotsky, L. (1978). *Mind in Society: The Development of Higher Psychological Processes.* Cambridge, MA: Harvard University Press.

Wahyudin, D., Hasegawa, S., & Dahlan, T. (2013). Mobile game based learning to develop ethical decision making skill of novice volunteer in disaster response. Paper presented at the *International Conference on Computers in Education*, Bali, Indonesia.

Yardi, S. (2006). The role of backchannel in collaborative learning environments. *Proceedings of the 7th International Conference on Learning Sciences* (pp. 852-858). International Society of the Learning Sciences.

Zhang, A. (2012). Cooperative learning and soft skills training in an IT course. *Journal of Information Technology Education: Research*, *11*, 65–79.

KEY TERMS AND DEFINITIONS

Assessment: The process of gathering qualitative and quantitative data to validate that stated objectives are met, while providing feedback for areas of improvement.

Communication: The ability to concisely state, either verbally or non-verbally, thoughts and ideas.

Employer Demand: The expectations of skills and knowledge from employees.

Fail-Safe: A situation that regardless of action, results in no harm.

Games: Activities considered competitive, rules based, and allow the player to master and advance through levels based on skills in the attempt to win.

Immersive: The feeling that one is physically, mentally, and emotionally a member of the environment.

P-12 Education: The system of academia that consists of pre-school through senior high year.

Simulations: Environments that facilitate immersive learning to represent real-world situations that allow for repeated experiences and branching opportunities.

Soft Skills: The characteristics used when interacting with another person.

Compilation of References

Grand Theft Auto V. (2013). Rockstar Games. USA.

The Settlers II (Original German title: Die Siedler II: Veni, Vidi, Vici). (1996). Blue Byte Software. Germany.

A.I. War: Fleet Command [Digital Game]. (2009). NC: Arcen Games, Arcen Games.

Aarseth, E. (2012). A narrative theory of games. *Proceedings of the International Conference on the Foundations of Digital Games* (pp. 129–133). DOI= doi:10.1145/2282338.2282365

Acosta, A. M., Dewald, H. A., & Dewald, A. (2011). Pilot study to test effectiveness of video game on reaching performance in stroke. *Journal of Rehabilitation Research and Development*, *48*(4), 431–444. doi:10.1682/JRRD.2010.04.0052 PMID:21674392

ACRL (Association for College and Research Libraries). (2015). ACRL information literacy framework for higher education. Retrieved from http://acrl.ala.org/ilstandards/wp-content/uploads/2015/01/Framework-MW15-Board-Docs.pdf

Adachi, P. J. C., & Willoughby, T. (2012). Do video games promote positive youth development? *Journal of Adolescent Research*, *28*(2), 155–165. doi:10.1177/0743558412464522

Adachi, P. J. C., & Willoughby, T. (2013). More than just fun and games: The longitudinal relationships between strategic video games, self-reported problem solving skills, and academic grades. *Journal of Youth and Adolescence*, *42*(7), 1041–1052. doi:10.1007/s10964-013-9913-9 PMID:23344653

Adams, E. (2014). *Fundamentals of Game Design* (3rd ed.). San Francisco, CA, USA: New Riders.

ALA (American Library Association). (2000). Information literacy standards. Retrieved from http://www.ala.org/acrl/standards/informationliteracycompetency#ildef

ALA AASL (American Association of School Librarians). (2007). Standards for the 21st century learner. Retrieved from http://www.ala.org/aasl/standards-guidelines/learning-standards

Alavi, M. (1984, June). An assessment of the prototyping approach to information systems development. *Communications of the ACM*, *27*(6), 556–563. doi:10.1145/358080.358095

Aldrich, C. (2001, September). The state of simulations: soft-skill simulations emerge as a powerful new form of e-learning. *OnLineLearning*.

Aldrich, C. (2005). *Learning By Doing: A Comprehensive Guide to Simulations, Computer Games, and Pedagogy in E-learning and Other Educational Experiences*. San Francisco: Pfeiffer.

Aldrich, C. (2009). *The complete guide to simulations and serious games: How the most valuable content will be created in the age beyond Gutenberg to Google*. San Francisco, CA: Pfeiffer.

All, A., Castellar, E.P.N., & Van Looy, J. (2014). Measuring Effectiveness in Digital Game-Based Learning: A Methodological Review. *International Journal of Serious Games*, *1*(2), 3–21. doi:10.17083/ijsg.v1i2.18

Allison, C., Campbell, A., Davies, C. J., Dow, L., Kennedy, S., McCafferty, J., & Perera, I. et al. (2012). Growing the use of virtual worlds in education: An OpenSim perspective. *Proceedings of the 2nd European Immersive Education Summit*.

Almeida, S., Veloso, A., Roque, L., Mealha, O., & Moura, A. (2013). The Video Game and Player in a Gameplay Experience Model Proposal. *Proceedings of Videojogos 2013 - 6th Annual Conference in the Science and Art of Video Games.* Coimbra, Portugal.

Almond, P., Winter, P., Cameto, R., Russell, M., Sato, E., & Clarke-Midura, J. … Lazarus, S. (2010). Technology-enabled and universally designed assessment: Considering access in measuring the achievement of students with disabilities—A foundation for research. *The Journal of Technology, Learning and Assessment, 10*(5). Retrieved from https://136.167.2.46/ojs/index.php/jtla/article/view/1605

Almond, R. G., Kim, Y. J., Velasquez, G., & Shute, V. J. (2014a). How task features impact evidence from assessments embedded in simulations and games. *Measurement: Interdisciplinary Research and Perspectives, 12*(1-2), 1–33. doi:10.1080/15366367.2014.910060

Almond, R. G., Kim, Y. J., Velasquez, G., & Shute, V. J. (2014b). Rejoinder to comments on task features in simulations andg. *Measurement: Interdisciplinary Research and Perspectives, 12*(3), 118–124. doi:10.1080/15366367.2014.939528

Alonzo, A. C., & Gotwals, A. W. (Eds.). (2012). *Learning progressions in science: Current challenges and future directions.* Springer. doi:10.1007/978-94-6091-824-7

Altman, P. (2013). *Using MS Kinect Device for Natural User Interface.* Pilsen.

Ambinder, M. (2009, March). Valve's Approach to Playtesting: The Application of Empiricism. Presentation and the Game Developers Conference. Retrieved from http://www.valvesoftware.com/publications/2009/GDC2009_ValvesApproachToPlaytesting.pdf

Ambinder, M. (2011, March). Biofeedback in Gameplay: How Valve Measures Physiology to Enhance Gaming Experience. Presentation at the Game Developers Conference. Retrieved from http://www.valvesoftware.com/publications/2011/ValveBiofeedback-Ambinder.pdf

American Association for the Advancement of Science. (1990). Science for All Americans. Retrieved from http://www.project2061.org/publications/sfaa/online/sfaatoc.htm

Ames, C., & Archer, J. (1988). Achievement goals in the classroom: Students' learning strategies and motivation processes. *Journal of Educational Psychology, 80*(3), 260–267. doi:10.1037/0022-0663.80.3.260

Amory, A., & Seagram, R. (2003). Educational game models: Conceptualization and evaluation. *South African Journal of Higher Education, 17*(2), 206–217.

Anderman, L. H. (2003). Academic and social perceptions as predictors of change in middle school students' sense of school belonging. *Journal of Experimental Education, 72*(1), 5–22. doi:10.1080/00220970309600877

Anderson, C. (2001). Situative versus cognitive perspectives: Form versus substance. *Educational Researcher, 26*(1), 18–21.

Anderson, K. (2012). *Using computer games across the curriculum.* London: Bloomsbury.

Anderson, M. L. (2003). Embodied cognition: A field guide. *Artificial Intelligence, 149*(1), 91–130. doi:10.1016/S0004-3702(03)00054-7

Anderson, T., Liam, R., Garrison, D. R., & Archer, W. (2001). Assessing teacher presence in a computer conferencing context. *Journal of Asynchronous Learning Networks, 5*(2), 1–17.

Anfara, V. A., & Mertens, S. B. (Eds.). (2007). *The young adolescent and the middle school.* IAP.

Annetta, L. A., Holmes, S. Y., Vallett, D., Fee, M., Cheng, R., & Lamb, R. (2013). Cognitive aspects of creativity: Science learning through serious educational games. In M. B. Gregerson, J. C. Kaufman, & H. T. Snyder (Eds.), Teaching creatively and teaching creativity (pp. 53–62). Springer New York; Retrieved from http://link.springer.com/chapter/10.1007/978-1-4614-5185-3_4 doi:10.1007/978-1-4614-5185-3_4

Annetta, L. A., Lamb, R., & Stone, M. (2011). Assessing serious educational games. In L. Annetta & S. C. Bronack (Eds.), Serious educational game assessment (pp. 75–93). SensePublishers. Retrieved from http://link.springer.com/chapter/10.1007/978-94-6091-329-7_5 doi:10.1007/978-94-6091-329-7_5

Annetta, L. A., Frazier, W. M., Folta, E., Holmes, S., Lamb, R., & Cheng, M.-T. (2012). Science teacher efficacy and extrinsic factors toward professional development using video games in a design-based research model: The next generation of STEM learning. *Journal of Science Education and Technology*, *22*(1), 47–61. doi:10.1007/s10956-012-9375-y

Annetta, L. A., Minogue, J., Holmes, S. Y., & Cheng, M. (2009). Investigating the impact of vid eo games on high school students' engagement and learning about genetics. *Computers & Education*, *53*(1), 74–85. doi:10.1016/j.compedu.2008.12.020

Anstadt, S. P., Bradley, S., & Burnette, A. (2013). Virtual worlds: Relationship between real life and experience in Second Life. *International Review of Research in Open and Distance Learning*, *14*(4), 160–190.

Anvari, B., Bell, M. G. H., Angeloudis, P., & Ochieng, W. Y. (2014). Long-range Collision Avoidance for Shared Space Simulation based on Social Forces. *Transportation Research Procedia*, *2*, 318–326. doi:10.1016/j.trpro.2014.09.023

ARISgames. (2014). ARIS. Retrieved from https://arisgames.org/

Arnold, N., & Ducate, L. (2011). Technology, CALL, and the Net generation: Where are we headed from here? In N. Arnold & L. Ducate (Eds.), Present and future promises of CALL: From theory and research to new directions in language teaching (pp. 1-22). CALICO Monograph Series, 5 (2).

Arnold, N. (2007). Technology-mediated learning ten years later: Emphasizing pedagogical or utilitarian applications? *Foreign Language Annals*, *40*(1), 161–181. doi:10.1111/j.1944-9720.2007.tb02859.x

Aronson, E., Blaney, N., Stephan, C., Sikes, J., & Snapp, M. (1978). *The jigsaw classroom*. Beverly Hills, CA: Sage Publications.

Asbell-Clarke, J., Edwards, T., Larsen, J., Rowe, E., Sylvan, E., & Hewitt, J. (2012). Martian Boneyards: Scientific Inquiry in an MMO Game. *International Journal of Game-Based Learning*, *2*(1), 52-76.

Asbell-Clarke, J., Rowe, E., & Sylvan, E. (2013, April). *Assessment Design for Emergent Game-Based Learning*. Paper presented at the ACM SIGCHI Conference on Human Factors in Computing Systems (CHI'13). Paris, France.

Ash, K. (2011). Gaming Goes Academic. *Education Week*, *30*(25), 24–28.

Atari Inc. (1979). USA: Asteroids.

Atkinson, J. W. (1957). Motivational determinants of risk-taking behavior. *Psychological Review; Psychological Review*, *64*(6p1), 359.

Aubusson, P., Fogwill, S., Barr, R., & Perkovic, L. (1997). What happens when students do simulation-role-play in science? *Research in Science Education*, *27*(4), 565–579. doi:10.1007/BF02461481

Aurasma (2014). Aurasma Augmented Reality Browser. Retrieved from http://www.aurasma.com/

Avery, L. M. (2013). Rural science education: Valuing local knowledge. *Theory into Practice*, *52*(1), 28–35. do i:10.1080/07351690.2013.743769

Aylett, R., & Louchart, S. (2003). Towards a narrative theory of virtual reality. *Virtual Reality (Waltham Cross)*, *7*(1), 2–9. doi:10.1007/s10055-003-0114-9

Bai, Z., Blackwell, A. F., & Coulouris, G. (2013). *Through the looking glass: Pretend play for children with autism.* Paper presented at the Mixed and Augmented Reality 2013 IEEE International Symposium. doi:10.1109/ISMAR.2013.6671763

Balasubramanian, N., & Wilson, B. G. (2005). Gaming and simulations. *ForeSITE, 1.*

Balfanz, R. (2009). *Putting middle grades students on the graduation path: A policy and practice brief.* Baltimore, MD: Johns Hopkins University, Everyone Graduates Center and Talent Development Middle Grades Program.

Ball, D. L., & Cohen, D. K. (1996). Reform by the book: What is: Or might be: The role of curriculum materials in teacher learning and instructional reform? *Educational Researcher*, *25*(9), 6–14.

Ball, D. L., & Feiman-Nemser, S. (1988). Using textbooks and teachers' guides: A dilemma for beginning teachers and teacher educators. *Curriculum Inquiry*, *18*(4), 401–423. doi:10.2307/1179386

Bancino, R. & Zevalkink, C. (2007, May). Soft skills: The new curriculum for hard-core technical professionals. *Association for Career and Technical Education Techniques.*

Bandura, A. (1986). *Social foundations of thought and action: A social cognitive theory*. Englewood Cliffs, NJ: Prentice Hall.

Bandura, A. (1997). *Self-efficacy: The exercise of control*. New York: Freeman.

Banks, J. A. (2008). Diversity, group identity, and citizenship education in a global age. *Educational Researcher*, *37*(3), 129–139. doi:10.3102/0013189X08317501

Barab, S. A., & Dodge, T. (2008). Strategies for designing embodied curriculum. In J. M. Spector, M. D. Merrill, J. van Merrienboër, & M. P. Driscoll (Eds.), *Handbook of research on educational communications and technology* (pp. 97–110). New York: Routledge.

Barab, S. A., Gresalfi, M., & Arici, A. (2009). Why educators should care about games. *Educational Leadership*, 76–80.

Barab, S. A., Gresfali, M. S., & Ingram-Goble, A. (2010). Transformational play using games to position person, content and context. *Educational Researcher*, *39*(7), 525–536. doi:10.3102/0013189X10386593

Barab, S. A., Hay, K. E., & Yamagata-Lynch, L. C. (2001). Constructing networks of activity: An in-situ research methodology. *Journal of the Learning Sciences*, *10*(1&2), 63–112. doi:10.1207/S15327809JLS10-1-2_5

Barab, S. A., Sadler, T., Heiselt, C., Hickey, D., & Zuiker, S. (2007). Relating narrative, inquiry, and inscriptions: A framework for socio- scientific inquiry. *Journal of Science Education and Technology*, *16*(1), 59–82. doi:10.1007/s10956-006-9033-3

Barab, S., & Dede, C. (2007). Games and immersive participatory simulations for science education: An emerging type of curricula. *Journal of Science Education and Technology*, *16*(1), 1–3. doi:10.1007/s10956-007-9043-9

Barab, S., & Duffy, T. (2000). From practice fields to communities of practice. In D. Jonassen (Ed.), *Theoretical Foundations of Learning Environments*. NJ: Lawerence Erlbaum Associates, Inc.

Barab, S., Kling, R., & Gray, J. (2006). *Designing for Virtual Communities in the Service of Learning*. Cambridge, UK: Cambridge University Press.

Barab, S., Thomas, M., Dodge, T., Carteaux, R., & Tuzun, H. (2005). Making learning fun:Quest Atlantis, a game without guns. *Educational Technology Research and Development*, *53*(1), 86–107. doi:10.1007/BF02504859

Barendregt, W., & Bekker, T. M. (2011). The influence of the level of free-choice learning activities on the use of an educational computer game. *Computers & Education*, *56*(1), 80–90. doi:10.1016/j.compedu.2010.08.018

Barjis, J., Gupta, A., Sharda, R., Bouzdine-Chameeva, T., Lee, P. D., & Verbraeck, A. (2012). Innovative teaching using simulation and virtual environments. *Interdisciplinary Journal of Information, Knowledge, and Management*, *7*, 237–255.

Barko, T., & Sadler, T. D. (2013). Practicality in virtuality: Finding student meaning in video game education. *Journal of Science Education and Technology*, *22*(2), 124–132. doi:10.1007/s10956-012-9381-0

Barlow, A., & Leston, R. (2012). *Beyond the blogosphere: information and its children*. Santa Barbara, CA: ABC-CLIO, LLC.

Barnea-Goraly, N., Menon, V., Eckert, M., Tamm, L., Bammer, R., Karchemskiy, A., & Reiss, A. L. et al. (2005). White matter development during childhood and adolescence: A cross-sectional diffusion tensor imaging study. *Cerebral Cortex*, *15*(12), 1848–1854. doi:10.1093/cercor/bhi062 PMID:15758200

Barron, T. (1998). The hard facts about soft-skills software. *Training & Development*, *52*(6), 48–51.

Barrows. H., (1983). Problem-based, self-directed learning, *Journal of the American Medical Association,* 250(30), 77-308.

Barrows, H. S., & Tamblyn, R. M. (1980). *Problem-based learning: an approach to medical education (Springer series on medical education)*. New York: Springer.

Barsalou, L. (1999). Perceptions of perceptual symbols. *Behavioral and Brain Sciences*, *22*(4), 637–660. doi:10.1017/S0140525X99532147 PMID:11301525

Bartle, R. A. (2005). Virtual worlds: Why people play. *Massively multiplayer game development, 2*, 3–18.

Bartle, R. A. (1996). Hearts, clubs, diamonds, spades: Players who suit MUDs. *Journal of MUD Research*, *1*(1). Retrieved from http://www.mud.co.uk/richard/hcds.htm

Basu, S., Sengupta, P., & Biswas, G. (2015). A scaffolding framework to support learning of emergent phenomena using multi-agent based simulation environments. *Research in Science Education*, *45*(2), 293–324. doi:10.1007/s11165-014-9424-z

Bateman, C., & Boon, R. (2005). *21st Century Game Design (Game Development Series). Newton Center*. MA: Charles River Media, Inc.

Bateman, C., Lowenhaupt, R., & Nacke, L. E. (2011, September). Player typology in theory and practice. *Proceedings of DiGRA*.

Baumeister, R. F., Bratslavsky, E., Muraven, M., & Tice, D. M. (1998). Ego depletion: Is the active self a limited resource? *Journal of Personality and Social Psychology*, *74*(5), 1252–1265. doi:10.1037/0022-3514.74.5.1252 PMID:9599441

Baumeister, R. F., & Leary, M. R. (1995). The need to belong: Desire for interpersonal attachments as a fundamental human motivation. *Psychological Bulletin*, *117*(3), 497–529. doi:10.1037/0033-2909.117.3.497 PMID:7777651

Bautista, A., Roth, W. M., & Thom, J. S. (2011). Knowing, insight learning, and the integrity of kinetic movement. *Interchange*, *42*(4), 363–388. doi:10.1007/s10780-012-9164-9

Bavelier, D., Green, C. S., Han, D. H., Renshaw, P. F., Merzenich, M. M., & Gentile, D. A. (2011). Brains on video games. *Nature Reviews. Neuroscience*, *12*(12), 763–768. doi:10.1038/nrn3135 PMID:22095065

Baxter, P., & Jack, S. (2008). Qualitative Case Study Methodology: Study Design and Implementation for Novice Researchers. *Qualitative Report*, *13*(4), 544–559. Retrieved from http://nsuworks.nova.edu/tqr/vol13/iss4/2

Beach, R., Campano, G., Edmiston, B., & Borgmann, M. (2010). Literacy tools in the classroom: Teaching through critical inquiry, grades 5-12. New York, NY: Teachers College Press.

Bear, D., Invernizzi, M., Templeton, S., & Johnston, F. (2012). *Words their way: Word study for phonics, vocabulary, and spelling instruction* (5th ed.). Upper Saddle River, NJ: Pearson Inc.

Beattie, J. (1809). *Remarks on the utility of classical learning*. Philadelphia: Hopkins and Earle.

Becker, D. A. (1997). The effects of choice on auditors' intrinsic motivation and performance. Retrieved from http://papers.ssrn.com/sol3/papers.cfm?abstract_id=2918

Becker, K. (2007). Pedagogy in commercial video games. In M. Prensky, D. Gibson, & C. Aldrich (Eds.), Games and Simulations in Online Learning: Research and Development Frameworks, 21-47. Hershey, PA, USA: IGI Global.

Becker, K. (2008). Video game pedagogy: Good games = good pedagogy. *Games: Purpose and Potential in Education* (pp. 73-125).

Becker, K. (2007). Digital game-based learning, once removed: Teaching teachers. *British Journal of Educational Technology*, *38*(3), 478–488. doi:10.1111/j.1467-8535.2007.00711.x

Becker, K. (2008). Video game pedagogy: Good games = good pedagogy. In C. T. Miller (Ed.), *Games: Purpose and potential in education* (pp. 73–125). New York, NY: Springer.

Bednar, A. K., Cunningham, D., Duffy, T. M., & Perry, D. J. (1992). Theory into practice: How do we link? In T. Duffy & D. Jonassen (Eds.), *Constructivism and the technology of instruction* (pp. 17–34). Hillsdale, NJ: Lawrence Erlbaum Associates.

Beetham, H. (2012). Designing for active learning in technology-rich contexts. In H. Beetham & R. Sharpe (Eds.), *Rethinking Pedagogy for a Digital Age: Designing for 21st Century Learning* (2nd ed., pp. 31–48). London: Routledge.

Beldarrain, Y. (2006). Distance education trends: Integrating new technologies to foster student interaction and collaboration. *Distance Education*, *27*(2), 139–153. doi:10.1080/01587910600789498

Bellani, M., Fornasari, L., Chittaro, L., & Brambilla, P. (2011). Virtual reality in autism: State of the art. *Epidemiology and Psychiatric Sciences*, *20*(03), 235–238. doi:10.1017/S2045796011000448 PMID:21922965

Benford, S., Greenhalgh, C., Reynard, G., Brown, C., & Koleva, B. (1998). Understanding and constructing shared spaces with mixed-reality boundaries. *ACM Transactions on Computer-Human Interaction*, *5*(3), 185–223. doi:10.1145/292834.292836

Bereiter, C., & Scardamalia, M. (2001). *Beyond Bloom's taxonomy: Rethinking knowledge for the knowledge age: Developing higher-level approaches to knowledge*. Retrieved from http://unr.edu/homepage/luvisis/bereiter.html

Bereiter, C. (2001). *Education and mind in the knowledge age*. New York, NY: Lawrence Erlbaum Assoc.

Bereiter, C. (2001). *Education and Mind in the Knowledge Age*. New York, NY: Lawrence Erlbaum Assoc.

Bereiter, C., & Scardamalia, M. (1996). Rethinking learning. In D. Olson & N. Torrance (Eds.), *Handbook of education and human development: New models of learning, teaching, and schooling* (pp. 485–516). Cambridge, MA: Basil Blackwell.

Bergen, D., & Fromberg, D. P. (2009). Play and social interaction in middle childhood. *Phi Delta Kappan*, *90*(6), 426–430. doi:10.1177/003172170909000610

Berk, L. J., Muret-Wagstaff, S. L., Goyal, R., Joyal, J. A., Gordon, J. A., Faux, R., & Oriol, N. E. (2014). Inspiring careers in STEM and healthcare fields through medical simulation embedded in high school science education. *Advances in Physiology Education*, *38*(3), 210–215. doi:10.1152/advan.00143.2013 PMID:25179609

Berland, L. K., & McNeill, K. L. (2010). A learning progression for scientific argumentation: Understanding student work and designing supportive instructional contexts. *Science Education*, *94*(5), 765–793. doi:10.1002/sce.20402

Berlotti, F., Kapralos, B., Lee, K., Moreno-Ger, P., & Berta, R. (2013). Assessment in and of serious games: An overview. *Advances in Human-Computer Interaction*, *2013*, 1–11. doi:10.1155/2013/136864

Berns, A., Gonzalez-Pardo, A., & Camacho, D. (2011). Implementing the use of virtual worlds in the teaching of foreign languages (level a1). *Proceedings of Learning a Language in Virtual Worlds: A Review of Innovation and ICT in Language Teaching Methodology* (pp. 33–40). Warsaw: Warsaw Academy of Computer Science.

Berns, A., Gonzalez-Pardo, A., & Camacho, D. (2013). Game-like language learning in 3-D virtual environments. *Computers & Education*, *60*(1), 210–220. doi:10.1016/j.compedu.2012.07.001

Best Selling Video Games. (2015). Retrieved from http://en.wikipedia.org/wiki/List_of_best-selling_video_games

Best, J. R. (2013). Exergaming in youth: Effects on physical and cognitive health. *Zeitschrift fur Psychologie mit Zeitschrift fur Angewandte Psychologie*, *221*(2), 72–78. doi:10.1027/2151-2604/a000137 PMID:25097828

Bianchi-Berthouze, N., Kim, W., & Patel, D. (2007). Does body movement engage you more in digital game play? And Why? In A. Paiva, R. Prada, R.W. Picard (Eds.), Lecture Notes in Computer Science: Affective Computing and Intelligent Interaction. (Vol. LNCS 4738, pp. 102-113). Berlin, Germany: Springer doi:10.1007/978-3-540-74889-2_10

Bianchi-Berthouze, N. (2013). Understanding the role of body movement in player engagement. *Human-Computer Interaction*, *28*(1), 40–75.

Big Brain Academy [Digital Game]. (2006). Kyoto, Japan: Nintendo.

Bigelow, B., & Diamond, N. (2007). The organic goodie simulation. In *Rethinking our classrooms: Teaching for equity and justice* (Vol. 1, pp. 100–102). Milwaukee, WI: Rethinking Schools.

Billings, D. R. (2012). Efficacy of adaptive feedback strategies in simulation-based training. *Military Psychology*, *24*(2), 114–133. doi:10.1080/08995605.2012.672905

Blake, R. J. (2013). *Brave new digital classroom: Technology and foreign language learning* (2nd ed.). Washington, DC: Georgetown University Press.

Blast Theory. (2014). Retrieved from http://www.blast-theory.co.uk/research/

Bloom, B. S., & Krathwohl, D. R. (1956). *Taxonomy of educational objectives: The classification of educational goals. Handbook I: Cognitive domain*. White Plains, NY: Longman.

Blumberg, F. C., Altschuler, E. A., Almonte, D. E., & Mileaf, M. I. (2013). The Impact of Recreational Video Game Play on Children's and Adolescents' Cognition. *New Directions for Child and Adolescent Development*, *2013*(139), 41–50. doi:10.1002/cad.20030 PMID:23483692

Blunt, R. (2007, January). Does game-based learning work? Results from three recent studies. Proceedings of *the Interservice/Industry Training, Simulation & Education Conference (I/ITSEC),* Orlando, Florida (Vol. 1).

Bodén, M., Dekker, A., Viller, S., & Matthews, B. (2013). *Augmenting play and learning in the primary classroom.* Paper presented at the Proceedings of the 12th International Conference on Interaction Design and Children. doi:10.1145/2485760.2485767

Bodomo, A. (2010). Is technology changing the way we communicate? In A. Bodomo (Ed.), *Computer-mediated communication for linguistics and literacy: Technology and natural language education* (pp. 9–16). Hershey, PA: Information Science Publishing. doi:10.4018/978-1-60566-868-0.ch002

Bogost, I. (2012). *Alien Phenomenology, Or What It's Like to Be a Thing*. University of Minnesota Press.

Boller, S. (2012, October 20). *Game-based learning – why does it work?* Bottom-line Performance. Retrieved from http://www.bottomlineperformance.com/

Boot, W. R., Blakely, D. P., & Simons, D. J. (2011). Do action video games improve perception and cognition? *Cognition*, *2*, 226. doi: 10.3389/fpsyg.2011.00226 PMID:21949513

Boot, W. R., Kramer, A. F., Simons, D. J., Fabiani, M., & Gratton, G. (2008). The effects of video game playing on attention, memory, and executive control. *Acta Psychologica*, *129*(3), 387–398. doi:10.1016/j.actpsy.2008.09.005 PMID:18929349

Borge, M., & Goggins, S. (2014). Towards the Facilitation of an Online Community of Learners: Assessing the Quality of Interactions in Yammer.*Proceedings from International Conference on the Learning Sciences*, Boulder, CO.

Borko, H., Stecher, B., & Kuffner, K. (2007). *Using Artifacts to Characterize Reform-Oriented Instruction: The Scoop Notebook and Rating Guide.* CSE Technical Report 707. National Center for Research on Evaluation, Standards, and Student Testing (CRESST).

Bourgonjon, J., De Grove, F., De Smet, C., Van Looy, J., Soetaert, R., & Valcke, M. (2013). Acceptance of game-based learning by secondary school teachers. *Computers & Education*, *67*, 21–35. doi:10.1016/j.compedu.2013.02.010

Bourgonjon, J., Valcke, M., Soetaert, R., De Wever, B., & Schellens, T. (2011). Parental acceptance of digital game-based learning. *Computers & Education*, *57*(1), 1434–1444. doi:10.1016/j.compedu.2010.12.012

Bourgonjon, J., Valcke, M., Soetaert, R., & Schellens, T. (2010). Students' perceptions about the use of video games in the classroom. *Computers & Education*, *54*(4), 1145–1156. doi:10.1016/j.compedu.2009.10.022

Bouvier, P., Lavoué, E., Sehaba, K., & Sébastien, G. (2013). Identifying Learner's Engagement in Learning Games - A Qualitative Approach based on Learner's Traces of Interaction. *Proceedings of the 5th International Conference on Computer Supported,* Aachen, Germany (pp. 339-350). SciTePress

Boyle, J., & Nicol, D. (2003). Using classroom communication systems to support interaction and discussion in large class settings. *Association for Learning Technology Journal*, *11*(3), 43–57. doi:10.1080/0968776030110305

Bracken, C. C., Lange, R. L., & Denny, J. (2005). Online video games and gamers' sensations of spatial, social, and co-presence.*Proceedings of the 2005 FuturePlay Conference*, East Lansing, MI.

Brain Age [Digital Game]. (2009). Kyoto, Japan: Nintendo.

Branch, R. M. (2008). *Instructional design: The ADDIE approach*. New York: Springer.

Brand, J. E., Lorentz, P., & Mathew, T. (2014). Digital Australia 14. National research prepared by Bond University for the Interactive Games & Entertainment Association. Sydney. IGEA. Retrieved from http://igea.wpengine.com/wp-content/uploads/2013/11/Digital_Australia_2014_DA14.pdf

Brand, J. E. (2012). *Digital Australia 2012 (DA12)*. Australia: School of Communication and Media Faculty of Humanities and Social Sciences Bond University.

Bransford, J. D., Brown, A. L., & Cocking, R. R. (2000). *How people learn*. Washington, DC: National Academies Press.

Bransford, J., Brown, A., & Cocking, R. (1999). *How people learn: Brain, mind, experience, and school*. Washington, DC: National Academy Press.

Brasell, H. (1987). The effect of real-time laboratory graphing on learning graphic representations of distance and velocity. *Journal of Research in Science Teaching*, *24*(4), 385–395. doi:10.1002/tea.3660240409

Britner, S. L., & Pajares, F. (2006). Sources of science self-efficacy beliefs of middle school students. *Journal of Research in Science Teaching*, *43*(5), 485–499. doi:10.1002/tea.20131

Brooks, B., Rose, F., Attree, E., & Elliot-Square, A. (2002). An evaluation of the efficacy of training people with learning disabilities in a virtual environment. *Disability and Rehabilitation*, *24*(11-12), 622–626. doi:10.1080/09638280110111397 PMID:12182802

Brophy, J. (1999). Toward a model of the value aspects of motivation in education: Developing appreciation for. *Educational Psychologist*, *34*(2), 75–85. doi:10.1207/s15326985ep3402_1

Broussard, J. (2014). Why poor schools can't win at standardized testing. The Atlantic. Retrieved from http://www2.ed.gov/nclb/accountability/ayp/edpicks.jhtml?src=lnWhy

Brown, A., & Campione, J. (1996). Communities of learning and thinking or a context by any other name. In Woods, P. (Ed), Contemporary Issues in Teaching and Learning. New York, NY: Routledge. 21,108-126.

Brown, E., & Cairns, P. (2004). A grounded investigation of immersion in games. In *ACM Conference on Human Factors in Computing Systems* (pp. 1297–1300). New York, NY: ACM Press.

Brown, A. L., & Campione, J. C. (1990). Communities of learning and thinking or a context by any other name. *Contributions to Human Development*, *21*, 108–126. doi:10.1159/000418984

Brown, A., Ash, D., Rutherford, M., Nakagawa, N., Gordon, A., & Campione, J. (1993). Distributed expertise in the classroom. In G. Salomon (Ed.), *Distributed cognitions: Psychological and educational considerations*. New York, NY: Cambridge University Press.

Brown, D., Standen, P., Proctor, T., & Sterland, D. (2001). Advanced design methodologies for the production of virtual learning environments for use by people with learning disabilities. *Presence (Cambridge, Mass.)*, *10*(4), 401–415. doi:10.1162/1054746011470253

Brown, E., & Cairns, P. (2004). A grounded investigation of game immersion. In E. Dykstra-Erickson & M. Tscheligi (Eds.), *CHI'04 Extended Abstracts on Human Factors in Computing Systems* (pp. 1297–1300). New York, NY: ACM; doi:10.1145/985921.986048

Brown, J. S., Collins, A., & Duguid, P. (1989). Situated cognition and the culture of learning. *Educational Researcher*, *18*(1), 32–42. doi:10.3102/0013189X018001032

Brown, R. T. (2014). A literature review of how videogames are assessed in library and information science and beyond. *Journal of Academic Librarianship*, *40*(5), 447–451. doi:10.1016/j.acalib.2014.06.009

Brown, R., & Kasper, T. (2013). The fusion of literacy and games: A case study in assessing the goals of a library video game program. *Library Trends*, *61*(4), 755–558. doi:10.1353/lib.2013.0012

Brown, S. L., & Vaughan, C. C. (2009). *Play: How it shapes the brain, opens the imagination, and invigorates the soul*. New York, NY: Avery Publishing Group.

Bruce, T. (2011). *Learning Through Play*. Hachette, UK: For Babies, Toddlers and Young Children.

Bruckman, A. (1999). Can educational be fun? Paper presented at the Game Developers Conference '99, San Jose, CA.

Bruer, J. (1993). *Schools for thought*. Cambridge: The MIT Press.

Bruner, J. (1984). Vygotsky's zone of proximal development: The hidden agenda. In B. Rogoff, & J. Wertsch (Eds.), Children's learning in the zone of proximal development: New directions for child development. San Francisco: Jossey-Bass.

Bruner, J. S. (1966). *Toward a theory of instruction*. Cambridge, MA: Belkapp Press.

Bruner, J. S. (1972). Nature and uses of immaturity. *The American Psychologist*, *27*(8), 28–60. doi:10.1037/h0033144

Bruner, J. S. (1983). *Child's talk: Learning to use language* (pp. 37–57). New York: W.W. Norton and Co.

Bruner, J. S. (1990). *Acts of meaning*. Cambridge, Mass.: Harvard University Press.

Bryant, L. (2011). *The Democracy of Objects*. http://quod.lib.umich.edu/o/ohp/9750134.0001.001

Bullen, M., Morgan, T., Belfer, K., & Oayyum, A. (2008). *The digital learner at BCIT and implications for an e-strategy*. Paris, France: EDEN.

Bulu, S. T. (2012). Place presence, social presence, co-presence, and satisfaction in virtual worlds. *Computers & Education*, *58*(1), 154–161. doi:10.1016/j.compedu.2011.08.024

Burchinal, M. R., Roberts, J. E., Zeisel, S. A., & Rowley, S. J. (2008). Social risk and protective factors for African American children's academic achievement and adjustment during the transition to middle school. *Developmental Psychology*, *44*(1), 286–292. doi:10.1037/0012-1649.44.1.286 PMID:18194027

Burgun, K. (2013). *Game Design Theory: A New Philosophy for Understanding Game*. Boca Raton, FL, USA: CRC Press.

Burns, H. L., & Capps, C. G. (1988). Foundations of intelligent tutoring systems: An introduction. In M. C. Polson & J. J. Richardson (Eds.), *Foundations of Intelligent Tutoring Systems* (pp. 1–19). Hillsdale, NJ: Lawrence Earlbaum Associates.

Butcher, J. (2008). *Numerical Methods for Ordinary Differential Equations*. John Wiley & Sons. doi:10.1002/9780470753767

Buzick, H. M., & Laitusis, C. C. (2010). Using growth for accountability measurement challenges for students with disabilities and recommendations for research. *Educational Researcher*, *39*(7), 537–544. doi:10.3102/0013189X10383560

Byford, J. M. (2012). *Behind the Iron Curtain: A teacher's guide to West Germany and Cold War activities*. Lanham, MD: University Press of America.

Byron, K., & Khazanchi, S. (2012). Rewards and creative performance: A meta-analytic test of theoretically derived hypotheses. *Psychological Bulletin*, *138*(4), 809–830. doi:10.1037/a0027652 PMID:22409506

Caillois, R. (2001). *Man, Play, Games*. Chicago, IL: University of Illinois Press.

Call of Duty: Modern Warfare 3 [Digital Game]. (2011). Santa Monica, CA: Activision, Infinity Ward Sledgehammer Games.

Calvillo-Gámez, E. H., Cairns, P., & Cox, A. L. (2010). Assessing the Core Elements of the Gaming Experience. In R. Bernhaupt. (Ed.), Evaluating User Experience in Games London, UK (pp. 47 - 71). Springer Verlag. doi:10.1007/978-1-84882-963-3_4

Cameron, B., & Dwyer, F. (2005). The effect of online gaming, cognition and feedback type in facilitating delayed achievement of different learning objectives. *Journal of Interactive Learning Research*, *16*(3), 243–258.

Can, G., & Cagiltay, K. (2006). Turkish prospective teachers' perceptions regarding the use of computer games with educational features. *Journal of Educational Technology & Society*, *9*(1), 308–321.

Cantin, S., & Boivin, M. (2004). Change and stability in children's social network and self-perceptions during transition from elementary to junior high school. *International Journal of Behavioral Development*, *28*(6), 561–570. doi:10.1080/01650250444000289

Canto, A. I., Proctor, B. E., & Pervatt, F. (2005). Educational outcomes of students first diagnosed with learning disabilities in postsecondary school. *Journal of College Admission*, (187): 8–13.

Carnegie Corporation of New York and The Center for Information and Research on Civic Learning and Engagement (CIRCLE). (2003). *The Civic Mission of Schools*. New York, NY: Author.

Carnegie Mellon University. (n. d.). Whys & hows of assessment: Formative vs summative assessment. Retrieved from http://www.cmu.edu/teaching/assessment/howto/basics/formative-summative.html

Carrington, V. (2006). *Rethinking middle years: early adolescents, schooling and digital culture*. Allen & Unwin.

Carroll, J., & Messenger, J. (2008). Medical simulation: The new tool for training and skill assessment. *Perspectives in Biology and Medicine*, *51*(1), 47–60. doi:10.1353/pbm.2008.0003 PMID:18192765

Carse, J. P. (1987). *Finite and Infinite Games*. New York: Ballantine Books.

Casby, M. W. (2003). The development of play in infants, toddlers, and young children. *Communication Disorders Quarterly*, *24*(4), 163–174. doi:10.1177/15257401030240040201

Casey, E. S. (1987). *Remembering: A Phenomenological Study*. Bloomington, IN: Indiana University Press.

Caskey, M.M., & Anfara Jr, V.A. (2007). Research summary: Young adolescents' developmental characteristics.

CAST. (2013). Retrieved from http://www.cast.org/udl/index.html

Castronova, E. (2005). *Synthetic Worlds: The Business and Culture of Online Games*. Chicago, IL, USA: University of Chicago Press.

Cavagnetto, A. R. (2010). Argument to foster scientific literacy. A review of argument interventions in K-12 science contexts. *Review of Educational Research*, *80*(3), 336–371. doi:10.3102/0034654310376953

Chad Lane, H., Hays, M. J., Core, M. G., & Auerbach, D. (2013). Learning intercultural communication skills with virtual humans: Feedback and fidelity. *Journal of Educational Psychology*, *105*(4), 1026–1035. doi:10.1037/a0031506

Chalmers, D. (2008). Foreword to Andy Clark's supersizing the mind. In A. Clark (Ed.), *Supersizing the mind: Embodiment, action, and cognitive extension* (pp. ix–xvi). New York, NY: Oxford University Press.

Chan, A. (2011). Learner receptivity toward role play simulation in teaching H.R.M. to university students in Hong Kong. *International Journal of Educational Research*, *2*(1), 1–16.

Chang, C. Y., Chien, Y. T., Chiang, C. Y., Lin, M. C., & Lai, H. C. (2013). Embodying gesture-based multimedia to improve learning. *British Journal of Educational Technology*, *44*(1), E5–E9. doi:10.1111/j.1467-8535.2012.01311.x

Chan, J. C., Leung, H., Tang, J. K., & Komura, T. (2011). A virtual reality dance training system using motion capture technology. *Learning Technologies. IEEE Transactions on*, *4*(2), 187–195.

Chao, K. J., Huang, H. W., Fang, W. C., & Chen, N. S. (2013). Embodied play to learn: Exploring Kinect-facilitated memory performance. *British Journal of Educational Technology*, *44*(5), 151–155. doi:10.1111/bjet.12018

Chapelle, C. A., (2009). The Relationship Between Second Language Acquisition Theory and Computer-Assisted Language Learning. *The Modern Language Journal, 93* (Issue Supplement s1), 741-753.

Chapelle, C. A. (2005). Interactionist SLA theory in CALL research. In J. Egbert & G. M. Petrie (Eds.), *CALL research perspectives* (pp. 53–64). Mahwah, NJ: Lawrence Erlbaum.

Chappell, P. (2014). *Group work in the English language curriculum: Sociocultural and ecological perspectives on second language classroom learning*. London: Palgrave MacMillan. doi:10.1057/9781137008787

Charles, D., Charles, T., McNeill, M., Bustard, D., & Black, M. (2011). Game-based feedback for educational multi-user virtual environments. *British Journal of Educational Technology*, *42*(4), 638–654. doi:10.1111/j.1467-8535.2010.01068.x

Checkland, P. (1999). Systems Thinking. In W. L. Currie & R. Galliers (Eds.), *Rethinking Management Information Systems* (pp. 45–56). Oxford: Oxford University Press.

Chee, Y. S. (2007). Embodiment, embeddedness, and experience: Game-based learning and the construction of identity. *Research and Practice in Technology Enhanced Learning*, *2*(1), 3–30. doi:10.1142/S1793206807000282

Chen, K. W., Hsu, F. C., Hsieh, Y. Z., & Chou, C. H. (2014). *To design an interactive learning system for child by integrating blocks with Kinect*. Paper presented at the Global Engineering Education Conference (EDUCON) (pp. 20-22). Istanbul, Turkey. IEEE

Cheng, M., She, H., & Annetta, L. (2014). Game immersion experience: Its hierarchical structure and impact on game-based science learning. *Journal of Computer Assisted Learning*; Advance online publication. doi: 10.1111/jcal.12066

Chen, W., & Levinson, D. (2006). Effectiveness of learning transportation network growth through simulation. *Journal of Professional Issues in Engineering Education and Practice*, *132*(1), 29–41. doi:10.1061/(ASCE)1052-3928(2006)132:1(29)

Cheok, A. D., Yang, X., Ying, Z. Z., Billinghurst, M., & Kato, H. (2002). Touch-space: Mixed reality game space based on ubiquitous, tangible, and social computing. *Personal and Ubiquitous Computing*, *6*(5), 430–442. doi:10.1007/s007790200047

Chi, M. T. H. (1978). Knowledge structure and memory development. In R. Siegler (Ed.), *Children's thinking: What develops?* (pp. 73–96). Hillsdale, NJ: Erlbaum.

Chi, M. T., Feltovich, P. J., & Glaser, R. (1981). Categorization and representation of physics problems by experts and novices. *Cognitive Science*, *5*(2), 121–152. doi:10.1207/s15516709cog0502_2

Chin, J., Dukes, R., & Gamson, W. (2009). Assessment in simulation and gaming: A review of the last 40 years. *Simulation & Gaming*, *40*(4), 553–568. doi:10.1177/1046878109332955

Chinn, C. A., & Malhotra, B. A. (2002). Epistemologically authentic inquiry in schools: A theoretical framework for evaluating inquiry tasks. *Science Education*, *86*(2), 175–218. doi:10.1002/sce.10001

Chinnici, J. P., Yue, J. W., & Torres, K. M. (2004). Students as "humans chromosomes" in role-playing mitosis and meiosis. *The American Biology Teacher*, *66*(1), 35–39. doi: 10.1662/0002-7685(2004)066[0035:SAHCIR]2.0.CO;2

Chou, Y.-K. (2013). Octalysis: Complete Gamification Framework. Yu-Kai Chou & Gamification. Retrieved from http://www.yukaichou.com/gamification-examples/octalysis-complete-gamification-framework/

Chuang, T. Y., & Chen, W. F. (2009). Effect of computer-based video games on children: An experimental study. *Journal of Educational Technology & Society*, *12*(2), 1–10.

Chung, H., Elias, M., & Schneider, K. (1998). Patterns of individual adjustment changes during middle school transition. *Journal of School Psychology*, *36*(1), 83–101. doi:10.1016/S0022-4405(97)00051-4

City of Heroes [Digital Game]. (2004). Seoul, Korea: NCsoft, Cryptic Studios.

Civilization V [Digital Game]. (2010). Novato, CA: 2K Games, Firaxis.

Clancey, W. J. (1997). *Situated cognition: On human knowledge and computer representations*. Cambridge, U.K.: Cambridge University Press.

Clapper, T. (2010). Role play and simulation. *Education Digest*, *75*(8), 39–43. doi: 10.1016/b978-0-7506-0617-2.50014-2

Clark, and M.L. Maher, The effects of a sense of place on the learning experience in a 3 virtual world, *Proc. 10th Association for Learning Technologies Conf. on Communities of Practice*, Sheffield, UK, 2003, 82-101.

Clark, D. B., Tanner-Smith, E., & Killingsworth, S. (revised and resubmitted). *Digital games, design, and learning: A systematic review and meta-analysis*. Review of Educational Research.

Clark, D., Nelson, B., Sengupta, P., & D'Angelo, C. (2009). Rethinking science learning through digital games and simulations: Genres, examples, and evidence. In Learning science: Computer games, simulations, and education workshop sponsored by the National Academy of Sciences, Washington, DC.

Clark, A. (1997). *Being there: Putting brain, body, and world together again*. Cambridge, MA: MIT Press.

Clark, A. (2003). *Natural Born Cyborgs; Minds, Technologies and the Future of Human Intelligence*. Oxford, UK: Oxford University Press.

Clark, A. (2008). *Supersizing the mind: Embodiment, action, and cognitive extension*. Oxford, U.K.: Oxford University Press. doi:10.1093/acprof:oso/9780195333213.001.0001

Clark, A., & Chalmers, D. (1998). The extended mind. *Analysis*, *58*(1), 7–19. doi:10.1093/analys/58.1.7

Clark, D. B., & Martinez-Garza, M. (2012). Prediction and explanation as design mechanics in conceptually integrated digital games to help players articulate the tacit understandings they build through game play. In C. Steinkuhler, K. Squire, & S. Barab (Eds.), *Games, learning, and society: Learning and meaning in the digital age*. Cambridge: Cambridge University Press. doi:10.1017/CBO9781139031127.023

Clark, D. B., Nelson, B., Chang, H., D'Angelo, C. M., Slack, K., & Martinez-Garza, M. (2011). Exploring Newtonian mechanics in a conceptually-integrated digital game: Comparison of learning and affective outcomes for students in Taiwan and the United States. *Computers & Education*, *57*(3), 2178–2195. doi:10.1016/j.compedu.2011.05.007

Clark, D. B., Sengupta, P., Brady, C., Martinez-Garza, M., & Killingsworth, S. (2015). Disciplinary Integration in Digital Games for Science Learning. *International STEM Education Journal*, *2*(2), 1–21. doi: 10.1186/s40594-014-0014-4

Clark, D. B., Tanner-Smith, E. E., & Killingsworth, S. (2013). *Digital Games for Learning: A systematic review and meta-analysis*. Menlo Park, CA: SRI International.

Clarke, J. (2013). Augmented reality, multimodal literacy and mobile technology: An experiment in teacher engagement. *QScience Proceedings*: Vol. 2013, 12th World Conference on Mobile and Contextual Learning (mLearn 2013), 28. Doi: 10.5339/qproc.2013.mlearn.28

Clarke, J., Dede, C., Ketelhut, D. J., Nelson, B., & Bowman, C. (2006). A Design-based research strategy to promote scalability for educational innovations. Educational Technology, 46(3), 27-36.

Classical Academic Press. (2014). Docendo Discimus. Classical Academic Press. Retrieved from http://classicalacademicpress.com/docendo-discimus/

Cohen, D. (Ed.). (2007). *The development of play*. Routledge.

Coiro, J., Knobel, M., Lankshear, C., & Leu, D.J. (Eds.), (2014). *Handbook of research on new literacies*. Routledge.

Cole, M., & Engeström, Y. (1993). A cultural-historical approach to distributed cognition. In G. Salomon (Ed.), *Distributed cognition: Psychological and educational considerations*. Cambridge, MA: Cambridge University Press.

Collins, A., White, B., & Fadel, C. (in preparation). What's worth learning: That school won't teach you.

Collins, A. (1991). The role of computer technology in restructuring schools. *Phi Delta Kappan*, *73*(1), 28–36.

Collins, A. (2011). A study of expert theory formation: The role of model types and domain frameworks. In M. S. Khine & I. Saleh (Eds.), *Models and Modeling: Cognitive Tools for Scientific Enquiry* (pp. 23–40). London: Springer. doi:10.1007/978-94-007-0449-7_2

Collins, A., & Ferguson, W. (1993). Epistemic forms and epistemic games. *Educational Psychologist*, *28*(1), 25–42. doi:10.1207/s15326985ep2801_3

Collins, H. (2010). *Tacit & Explicit Knowledge*. Chicago: University of Chicago Press. doi:10.7208/chicago/9780226113821.001.0001

Common Sense Media. (2015). Best reading games. Retrieved from https://www.commonsensemedia.org/lists/reading-games

Commonwealth of Australia. (2010). Literature review on the impact of playing violent video games on aggression. Retrieved from http://www.classification.govau/Pages/Public/Media-And-Student-Resources/Other%20Resources/Literature%20review%20on%20the%20impact%20of%20playing%20violent%20video%20games%20on%20aggression.pdf

Conati, C., & VanLehn, K. (2000). Toward computer-based support of meta-cognitive skills: A computational framework to coach self-explanation. *International Journal of Artificial Intelligence in Education*, *11*(1), 389–415.

Conklin, H. G. (2014). Toward more joyful learning: Integrating play into frameworks of middle grades teaching. *American Educational Research Journal*, *51*(6), 1227–1255. doi:10.3102/0002831214549451

Connolly, C., & Grupen, R. (1992). Harmonic Control. *Proceedings of the 1992 International Symposium on Intelligent Control*, (pp. 503-506). doi:10.1109/ISIC.1992.225142

Conole, G., de Laat, M., Dillon, T., & Darby, J. (2006). *LXP: Student experiences of technologies. Final Report: JISC UK*. Retrieved from http://www.jisc.ac.uk/whatwedo/programmes/elearningpedagogy/learneroutcomes

Contra [Digital Game]. (1988). Tokyo, Japan: Konami, Konami.

Cook, S. W., Mitchell, Z., & Goldin-Meadow, S. (2008). Gesturing makes learning last. *Cognition*, *106*(2), 1047–1058. doi:10.1016/j.cognition.2007.04.010 PMID:17560971

Cooper, S., Khatib, F., Treuille, A., Barbero, J., Lee, J., & Beenen, M. et al. (2010). Predicting protein structures with a multiplayer online game. *Nature*, *466*(7307), 756–760. doi:10.1038/nature09304 PMID:20686574

Corbett, A. T., Koedinger, K. R., & Anderson, J. R. (1997). Intelligent tutoring systems. In M. G. Helander, T. K. Landauer, & P. Prabhu (Eds.), *Handbook of human-computer interaction* (2nd ed., pp. 849–874). Amsterdam: Elsevier Science.

Corbit, M. (2002). Building virtual worlds for informal science learning (SciCentr and SciFair) in the Active Worlds Educational Universe. *Presence (Cambridge, Mass.)*, *11*(1), 55–67. doi:10.1162/105474602317343659

Cordova, D. I., & Lepper, M. R. (1996). Intrinsic motivation and the process of learning: Beneficial effects of contextualization, personalization, and choice. *Journal of Educational Psychology*, *88*(4), 715–730. doi:10.1037/0022-0663.88.4.715

Cornillie, F., Thorne, S. L., & Desmet, P. (2012). Digital games for language learning: from hype to insight? Editorial for ReCALL special issue: Digital games for language learning: challenges and opportunities. *ReCALL*, *24*(03), 243–256. doi:10.1017/S0958344012000134

Cortiella, C., & Horowitz, S. (2014). *The state of learning disabilities: Facts, trends, and emerging issues*. New York, NY: National Center for Learning Disabilities.

Costello, B., & Edmonds, E. (2009). A Tool for Characterizing the Experience of Play.*Proceedings of the Sixth Australasian Conference on Interactive Entertainment(pp.*1-10*)*.Sydney, Australia: ACM Press. doi:10.1145/1746050.1746052

Coulton, P. (2012). Skylanders: Near Field in Your Living Room Now. *Ubiquity: The Journal of Pervasive Media*, 136-138.

Counter Strike: Source. (2004). Valve Corporation. USA.

Counter-Strike [Digital Game]. (2000). Redwood City, CA: Electronic Arts, Valve.

Courey, S. J., Tappe, P., Siker, J., & LePage, P. (2013). Improved lesson planning with Universal Design for Learning (UDL). *Teacher Education and Special Education: The Journal of the Teacher Education Division of the Council for Exceptional Children*, *36*(1), 7–27. doi:10.1177/0888406412446178

Covitt, B. (2013). Reasoning tools for understanding water systems. Retrieved from http://www.umt.edu/watertools/default.aspx

Covitt, B. A., Gunckel, K. L., & Anderson, C. W. (2009). Students' developing understanding of water in environmental systems. *The Journal of Environmental Education*, *40*(3), 37–51. doi:10.3200/JOEE.40.3.37-51

Craft, A. (2013). Childhood, possibility thinking and wise, humanising educational futures. *International Journal of Educational Research*, *61*, 126–134. doi:10.1016/j.ijer.2013.02.005

Crawford, C. (1984). *The Art of Computer Game Design*. Berkeley, CA, USA: Osborne/McGraw-Hill.

Creech, S. (2001). *Walk Two Moons*. Pan Macmillan.

Creten, H., Lens, W., & Simons, J. (2001). The role of perceived instrumentality in student motivation. In A. Efklides, J. Kuhl, & R. M. Sorrentino (Eds.), *Trends and prospects in motivation research* (pp. 33–45). Dordrecht, The Netherlands: Kluwer Academic Publishers.

Cross–Bystrom, A. (2010, August 20). What you need to know about Generation Z. iMedia Connections. Retrieved from http://www.imediaconnection.com/content/27425.asp

Cross–Bystrom, A. (2010, August 20). What you need to know about Generation Z. iMedia Connections: Connecting the Marketing Community. Retrieved from http://www.imediaconnection.com/content/27425.asp

Csíkszentmihályi, M. (1990). *Flow: The Psychology of Optimal Experience*. New York, NY: Harper & Row Publishers, Inc.

Csikszentmihalyi, M. (1991). *Flow: The psychology of optimal experience*. New York, NY: Harper Perennial.

Csikszentmihalyi, M. (2002). *Flow: The Classic Work on how to Achieve Happiness*. London: Rider.

Cuendet, S., Bonnard, Q., Do-Lenh, S., & Dillenbourg, P. (2013). Designing augmented reality for the classroom. *Computers & Education*, *68*, 557–569. doi:10.1016/j.compedu.2013.02.015

Cushman, K., & Rogers, L. (2009). *Fires in the middle school bathroom: Advice for teachers from middle schoolers*. The New Press.

Damasio, A. R. (1994). *Descartes' Error: emotion, reason, and the human brain*. New York: Grosset/Putnam.

Dance Dance Revolution [Digital Game]. (2010). Tokyo, Japan: Konami.

David, T. (2009). Young children's social and emotional development. *An Introduction to Early Childhood Studies,*, 78.

Davis, J. P., Steury, K., & Pagulvan, R. (2005). A survey method for assessing perceptions of a game: The consumer playtest in game design. *The International Journal of Computer Game Research*, *5*(1).

de Berg, M., van Kreveld, M., Overmars, M., & Schwarzkopf, O. (2000). *Computational Geometry: Algorithms and Applications* (2nd ed.). Springer-Verlag. doi:10.1007/978-3-662-04245-8

De Castell, S., & Jenson, J. (2004). Paying attention to attention: New economies for learning. *Educational Theory*, *54*(4), 381–397. doi:10.1111/j.0013-2004.2004.00026.x

De Freitas, S., & Oliver, M. (2006). How can exploratory learning with games and simulations within the curriculum be most effectively evaluated? *Computers & Education*, *46*(3), 249–264. doi:10.1016/j.compedu.2005.11.007

De Freitas, S., Rebolledo-Mendez, G., Liarokapis, F., Magoulas, G., & Poulovassilis, A. (2010). Learning as immersive experiences: Using the four-dimensional framework for designing and evaluating immersive learning experiences in a virtual world. *British Journal of Educational Technology*, *41*(1), 69–85. doi:10.1111/j.1467-8535.2009.01024.x

de Freitas, S., & Routledge, H. (2013). Designing leadership and soft skills in educational games: The e-leadership and soft skills educational games design model (ELESS). *British Journal of Educational Technology*, *44*(6), 951–968. doi:10.1111/bjet.12034

De Groot, A. (1965). *Thought and choice in chess*. The Hague: Mouton.

de la Varre, C., Keane, J., & Irvin, M. J. (2011). Dual perspectives on the contribution of on-site facilitators to teaching presence in a blended learning environment. *International Journal of E-Learning & Distance Education*, *25*(3).

de Mello Monteiro, C. B., Massetti, T., Dias da Silva, T., van der Kamp, J., de Abreu, L. C., Leone, C., & Savelsbergh, G. J. P. (2014). Transfer of motor learning from virtual to natural environments in individuals with cerebral palsy. *Research in Developmental Disabilities*, *35*(10), 2430–2437. doi:10.1016/j.ridd.2014.06.006 PMID:24981192

Deci, E. L. (1975). *Intrinsic motivation*. New York: Plenum Press. doi:10.1007/978-1-4613-4446-9

Deci, E. L., Connell, J. P., & Ryan, R. M. (1989). Self-determination in a work organization. *The Journal of Applied Psychology*, *74*(4), 580–590. doi:10.1037/0021-9010.74.4.580

Deci, E. L., Koestner, R., & Ryan, R. M. (1999). A meta-analytic review of experiments examining the effects of extrinsic rewards on intrinsic motivation. *Psychological Bulletin*, *125*(6), 627–668. doi:10.1037/0033-2909.125.6.627 PMID:10589297

Deci, E. L., & Ryan, R. M. (1985). *Intrinsic motivation and self-determination in human behavior*. New York: Plenum. doi:10.1007/978-1-4899-2271-7

Dede, C. (2009). *Immersive Interfaces for Engagement and Learning Science*. 323, 66. DOI: Retrieved from http://www.sciencemag.org10.1126/science.1167311

Dede, C. (2014). Immersive interfaces for engagement and learning. Retrieved from http://isites.harvard.edu/fs/docs/icb.topic443490.files/Immersive%20Interfaces%20for%20Learning.pdf

Dede, C. (1996). Emerging Technologies and Distributed Learning. *American Journal of Distance Education*, *10*(2), 2, 4–36. doi:10.1080/08923649609526919

Dede, C. (1997). The evolution of constructivist learning environments: Immersion in distributed, virtual worlds. In B. Wilson (Ed.), *Constructivist Learning Environments: Case Studies in Instructional Design*. Englewood Cliffs, NJ: Educational Technology Publications.

DeKanter, N. (2004). Gaming redefines interactivity for learning. *TechTrends*, *49*(3), 26–31. doi:10.1007/BF02763644

Delacruz, G. C., Chung, G. K. W. K., & Baker, E. L. (2010). Validity evidence for games as assessment environments (CRESST Report 773). Los Angeles, CA: University of California, National Center for Research on Evaluation, Standards, and Student Testing (CRESST).

Delwiche, A. (2006). Massively multiplayer inline games (MMOs) in the new media classroom. *Journal of Educational Technology & Society*, *9*(3), 160–172.

Descent. (1994). Parallax Software.

Deterding, S., Dixon, D., Khaled, R., & Nacke, L. (2011, September). From game design elements to gamefulness: defining gamification.*Proceedings of the 15th International Academic MindTrek Conference: Envisioning Future Media Environments* (pp. 9-15). ACM. doi:10.1145/2181037.2181040

Deus Ex: Human Revolution [Digital Game]. (2011). Montreal: Square Enix, Eidos Studios.

Devlin-Scherer, R., & Sardone, N. (2010). Digital simulation games for social studies classrooms. *The Clearing House: A Journal of Educational Strategies, Issues and Ideas*, *83*(4), 138–144. doi:10.1080/00098651003774836

Dewey, J. (1938). *Experience & Education*. New York, NY: Kappa Delta Pi.

Dewey, J. (1938). *Experience and Education*. New York, NY: Kappa Delta Pi.

Di Blas, N., Paolini, P., & Poggi, C. (2004). Learning by playing. an eductainment 3D environment for schools. Presented at the World Conference on Educational Multimedia, Hypermedia and Telecommunications. Chesapeake, VA. ISBN 978-1-880094-53-2

Di Blas, N., Paolini, P., & Poggi, C. 3D worlds for edutainment: educational, relational and organizational principles. *Proc. 3rd IEEE PerCom2005 Workshops. On Pervasive eLearning*, Hawaii, (pp. 291-295). doi:10.1109/PERCOMW.2005.1

Diablo III [Digital Game]. (2012). Irvine, CA: Blizzard Entertainment, Blizzard Entertainment.

DiCerbo, K. E. (2014). Game-based assessment of persistence. *Journal of Educational Technology & Society*, *17*(1), 17–28.

Dickerson, D., & Dawkins, K. (2004). Eighth grade students' understandings of groundwater. *Journal of Geoscience Education*, *52*, 178–181.

Dickes, A., & Sengupta, P. (2013). Learning Natural Selection in 4th Grade with Agent-Based Models. *Research in Science Education*, *43*(3), 921–953. doi:10.1007/s11165-012-9293-2

Dickey, M. (2005). Three-dimensional virtual worlds and distance learning: Two case studies of Active Worlds as a medium for distance education. *British Journal of Educational Technology*, *36*(3), 439–451. doi:10.1111/j.1467-8535.2005.00477.x

Dickey, M. D. (2006). Girl gamers: The controversy of girl games and the relevance of female-oriented game design for instructional design. *British Journal of Educational Technology*, *37*(5), 785–793. doi:10.1111/j.1467-8535.2006.00561.x

Dickey, M. D. (2011). Murder on Grimm Isle: The impact of game narrative design in an educational game-based learning environment. *British Journal of Educational Technology*, *42*(3), 456–469. doi:10.1111/j.1467-8535.2009.01032.x

Dieker, L., Hughes, C., Hynes, M., & Straub, C. (2013). *TeachLivE™ national research project –year 1 results: Report to the Bill & Melinda Gates Foundation*. Orlando, FL: University of Central Florida.

Dietrichson, A. (2013). Beyond clickometry: Analysis for constructivist pedagogies. *International Journal on E-Learning*, *12*(4), 333–351.

Dietz-Uhler, B., & Hurn, J. E. (2013). Using learning analytics to predict (and improve) student success: A faculty perspective. *Journal of Interactive Online Learning*, *12*(1).

Dijkstra, E. (1959). A Note on two Problems in Connexion with Graphs. *Numerische Mathematik*, *1*(1), 269–271. doi:10.1007/BF01386390

diSessa, A. A. (1993). Toward an Epistemology of Physics. *Cognition and Instruction*, *10*(2/3), 105–225. doi:10.1080/07370008.1985.9649008

diSessa, A., Hammer, D., Sherin, B., & Kolpakowski, T. (1991). Inventing Graphing: MetaRepresentational Expertise in Children. *The Journal of Mathematical Behavior*, *10*, 117–160.

Donovan, M. S., Bransford, J. D., & Pellegrino, J. W. (Eds.). (1999). *How people learn: Bridging research and practice*. Washington, DC: National Academies Press.

Doody, O., & Condon, M. (2013). Using a simulated environment to support students learning clinical skills. *Nurse Education in Practice*, *13*(6), 561–566. doi:10.1016/j.nepr.2013.03.011 PMID:23602694

Doo, M. Y. (2006). A problem in online interpersonal skills training: Do learners practice skills? *Open Learning*, *21*(3), 263–272. doi:10.1080/02680510600953252

Dragon Age: Origins [Digital Game]. (2009). Redwood City, CA: Electronic Arts, BioWare.

Droll, J. A., & Hayhoe, M. M. (2007). Trade-offs Between Gaze and Working Memory Use. *Journal of Experimental Psychology. Human Perception and Performance*, *33*(6), 1352–1365. doi:10.1037/0096-1523.33.6.1352 PMID:18085948

Druckman, D., & Ebner, N. (2013). Games, claims, and new frames: Rethinking the use of simulation in negotiation education. *Negotiation Journal*, *29*(1), 61–92. doi:10.1111/nejo.12005

Duchesne, S., Ratelle, C. F., Poitras, S. C., & Drouin, E. (2009). Early adolescent attachment to parents, emotional problems, and teacher–academic worries about the middle school transition. *The Journal of Early Adolescence*, *29*(5), 743–766. doi:10.1177/0272431608325502

Duffy, T. M., & Cunningham, D. J. (2001). Constructivism: Implications for the design and delivery of instruction. In D. H. Jonassen (Ed.), *Handbook of Research for Educational Communications and Technology*. New York, NY: Simon and Schuster.

Duncan, S. C. (2011). Minecraft, beyond construction and survival. *Well Played: A Journal on Video Games. Value and Meaning*, *1*(1), 1–22.

Durkin, K., Boyle, J., Hunter, S., & Conti-Ramsden, G. (2013). Video games for children and adolescents with special educational needs. *Zeitschrift fur Psychologie mit Zeitschrift fur Angewandte Psychologie*, *221*(2), 79–89. doi:10.1027/2151-2604/a000138

Duschl, R. A., & Osborne, J. (2002). Supporting and promoting argumentation discourse in science education. *Studies in Science Education*, *38*(1), 39–72. doi:10.1080/03057260208560187

Duschl, R. A., Schweingruber, H. A., & Shouse, A. W. (Eds.). (2007). *Taking Science to School: Learning and Teaching Science in Grades K-8. National Research Council Board on Science Education, Center for Education, Division of Behavioral and Social Sciences and Education*. Washington, DC: The National Academies Press.

Duschl, R. A., Schweingruber, H. A., & Shouse, A. W. (Eds.). (2007). *Taking Science to School: Learning and Teaching Science in Grades K-8*. Washington, D.C.: The National Academies Press.

Dweck, C. S. (2006). *Mindset: The new psychology of success*. New York: Random House.

Dyckhoff, A., Zielke, D., Bultmann, M., Chatti, M., & Schroeder, U. (2012). Design and implementation of a learning analytics toolkit for teachers. *Journal of Educational Technology & Society*, *15*(3), 58–76.

Dzikovska, M., Steinhauser, N., Farrow, E., Moore, J., & Campbell, G. (2014). BEETLE II: Deep Natural Language Understanding and Automatic Feedback Generation for Intelligent Tutoring in Basic Electricity and Electronics. *International Journal of Artificial Intelligence in Education*, *24*(3), 284–332. doi:10.1007/s40593-014-0017-9

Ebner, M., Schönhart, J., & Schön, S. (2014). Experiences with iPads in primary schools. In Profesorado, 18(3), 161-173.

Ebner, M., Nagler, W., & Schön, M. (2013). Architecture Students Hate Twitter and Love Dropbox" or Does the Field of Study Correlates with Web 2.0 Behavior? In *World Conference on Educational Multimedia, Hypermedia and Telecommunications 2013,*Chesapeake, VA (pp. 43-53). AACE.

Eccles, J., Wigfield, A., & Schiefele, U. (1998). Motivation to succeed. In W. Damon (Series Ed.) & N. Eisenberg (Vol. Ed.), Handbook of child psychology: Vol. 3. Social, emotional, and personality development (5th ed., pp. 1017–1095). New York: Wiley.

Eccles, J., & Wigfield, A. (1995). In the mind of the actor: The structure of adolescents' achievement task values and expectancy-related beliefs. *Personality and Social Psychology Bulletin*, *21*(3), 215–225. doi:10.1177/0146167295213003

Edelson, D. C., Gordin, D. N., & Pea, R. D. (1999). Addressing the challenges of inquiry-based learning through technology and curriculum design. *Journal of the Learning Sciences*, *8*(3-4), 391–450. doi:10.1080/10508406.1999.9672075

Education Week. (2015). Oculus Rift fueling new vision for virtual reality in K-12. Retrieved from http://www.edweek.org/ew/articles/2014/08/27/02oculus.h34.html

Edyburn, D. L. (2013). Critical issues in advancing the special education technology evidence base. *Exceptional Children*, *80*(1), 7–24.

Egenfeldt-Nielsen, S., (2006). Overview of research on the educational use of video games. *Digital Kompetanse* 3-2006, 184-213.

Egenfeldt-Nielsen, S. (2004). Practical barriers in using educational computer games. *On the Horizon*, *12*(1), 18–21. doi:10.1108/10748120410540454

Egert, C. A., & Phelps, A. M. (2011). Motivating Science Education through Games. *Learning to Play: Exploring the Future of Education with Video Games*, *53*, 129.

Elder Scrolls: Skyrim [Digital Game]. (2011). Rockville, MD: Bethesda Softworks, Bethesda Game Studios.

Electronic Software Association. (2014, April) Essential facts about the computer and video game industry: 2014 sales, demographic, and usage data. Retrieved from http://www.theesa.com/wp-content/uploads/2014/10/ESA_EF_2014.pdf

Elliott, J. (2013) Analog Thinking: Digital Times. Invited workshop presentation at *American Education Research Association Annual Conference*, San Francisco, CA.

Elliott, E. S., & Dweck, C. S. (1988). Goals: An approach to motivation and achievement. *Journal of Personality and Social Psychology*, *54*(1), 5–12. doi:10.1037/0022-3514.54.1.5 PMID:3346808

Emmendorfer, J. (2009) *Yes you can! Teach soft skills with e-learning* [White Paper]. AME-Learning, Inc.

Endreny, A. H. (2010). Urban 5th graders conceptions during a place-based inquiry unit on watersheds. *Journal of Research in Science Teaching*, *47*, 501–517.

Engel, G., & Green, T. (2011). Cell Phones in the Classroom: Are We Dialing up Disaster? *TechTrends*, *55*(2), 39–45. doi:10.1007/s11528-011-0482-z

Engeström, Y. (1987). *Learning by expanding: An activity-theoretical approach to developmental research*. Helsinki: Orienta-Konsultit.

Engeström, Y., Miettinen, R., & Punamaki, R. (Eds.). (1999). *Perspectives on activity theory*. Cambridge, U.K.: Cambridge University Press. doi:10.1017/CBO9780511812774

Entertainment Software Association. (2014, September 25). *Millions of Americans embrace video games on mobile devices: New study reveals mobile games attract new players to video game community*. Retrieved from http://www.theesa.com/newsroom/release_detail.asp?releaseID=236

Entertainment, B. (2010). *Starcraft II*. USA.

Enyedy, N. (2005). Inventing mapping: Creating cultural forms to solve collective problems. *Cognition and Instruction*, *23*(4), 427–466. doi:10.1207/s1532690xci2304_1

Epper, R. M., Derryberry, A., & Jackson, S. (2012, August 9). Game-based learning: Developing and institutional strategy. Educause. Retrieved from http://www.educause.edu/

Erduran, S., & Jiménex-Aleixandre, M. P. (2008). *Argumentation in science education: Perspectives from classroom-based research*. Dordrecht, The Netherlands: Springer.

Erduran, S., Simon, S., & Osborne, J. (2004). TAPing into argumentation: Developments in the application of Toulmin's argument pattern for studying science discourse. *Science Education*, *88*(6), 915–933. doi:10.1002/sce.20012

Ermi, L., & Mäyrä, F. (2005). Fundamental components of the gameplay experience: Analysing immersion. In Worlds in Play: International Perspectives on Digital Games Research (37).

Ermi, L., & Mäyrä, F. (2005). *Fundamental Components of the Gameplay Experience: Analysing Immersion*. Paper presented at DiGRA 2005 Conference: Changing Views–Worlds in Play (pp. 88-115).Vancouver, Canada.

Ermi, L., & Mäyrä, F. (2005). Fundamental components of the gameplay experience: Analysing immersion. Worlds in Play: International Perspectives on Digital Games Research, 37.

Ermi, L., & Mayra, F. (2005). Fundamental Components of the Gameplay Experience: Analysing Immersion. *Proceedings of Chancing Views – Worlds in Play* (Vol. 37, pp. 37–53). New York, NY: Peter Lang International Academic Publisher.

Ertl, B. (Ed.). (2010). *E-Collaborative Knowledge Construction: Learning from Computer-Supported and Virtual Environments*. New York: IGI Global. doi:10.4018/978-1-61520-729-9

ESA. (2013). Essential Facts about the computer and video game industry. Retrieved from http://www.theesa.com/facts/pdfs/ESA_EF_2013.pdf

Eseryel, D., Law, V., Ifenthaler, D., Xun, G., & Miller, R. (2014). An Investigation of the Interrelationships between Motivation, Engagement, and Complex Problem Solving in Game-based Learning. *Journal of Educational Technology & Society*, *17*(1), 42–53.

EteRNA [Digital Game] (2011). Pittsburgh, PA: Carnegie Mellon University and Stanford University, Carnegie Mellon University. Retrieved from http://eterna.cmu.edu/

Evans, J. (2013). Problems with standardized testing. Retrieved from http://www.education.com/reference/article/Ref_Test_Problems_Seven/

EVE Online [Digital Game]. (2007). New York: Simon & Schuster Interactive, CCP TransGaming.

Fable II [Digital Game]. (2008). Redmond, WA: Microsoft, Lionhead Studios.

Fabricatore, C. (2000). *Learning and Videogames: an unexploited synergy*. Retrieved from www.learndev.org/dl/FabricatoreAECT2000.PDF

Fabricatore, C., Nussbaum, M., & Rosas, R. (2002). Playability in video games: A qualitative design model. *Human-Computer Interaction*, *17*(4), 311–368. doi:10.1207/S15327051HCI1704_1

FairTest. (2012, July). How Standardized Testing Damages Education. Retrieved from http://fairtest.org/how-standardized-testing-damages-education-pdf

Fallon, G. (2010). Using avatars and virtual environments in learning: What do they have to offer? *British Journal of Educational Technology*, *41*(1), 108–122. doi:10.1111/j.1467-8535.2009.00991.x

Fanning, R., & Gaba, D. (2007). The role of debriefing in simulation-based learning. *Society for Simulation in Healthcare, 2*(2), 115–125. doi:10.1097/SIH.0b013e3180315539 PMID:19088616

Fannon, K. (2003). 'Needle stick' – a role-play simulation: Transformative learning in complex dynamic social systems. *International Journal of Training Research, 1*(2), 100–116.

Farwell, N. (2014). *Minecraft: Redstone handbook.* New York, NY: Scholastic Inc.

Feiman-Nemser, S. (2001). From preparation to practice: Designing a continuum to strengthen and sustain teaching. *Teachers College Record, 103*(6), 1013–1055. doi:10.1111/0161-4681.00141

Feistritzer, C. E. (2011). *Profile of teachers in the U.S. 2011.* Washington, DC: National Center for Education Information.

Fenici, M. (2012). Embodied social cognition and embedded theory of mind. *Biolinguistics, 6*, 276–307.

Ferguson, R. C. (2006). *Teacher's guide: Research and benefits of chess.*

Ferrai, D. A. (2007). *An investigation on the relationships between immersion, body movements and extraversion in computer games play* [Unpublished master's thesis]. UCL. Retrieved from https://www.ucl.ac.uk/uclic/studying/taught-courses/distinction-projects/2006_theses/ferrai.pdf

Final Fantasy VII [Digital Game]. (1997). Foster City, CA: Sony Computer Entertainment, Square.

Final Fantasy XIII [Digital Game]. (2010). Tokyo, Japan: Square Enix.

Findley, M. J., & Cooper, H. M. (1983). Locus of control and academic achievement: A literature review. *Journal of Personality and Social Psychology. Journal of Personality and Social Psychology, 44*(2), 419–427. doi:10.1037/0022-3514.44.2.419

Fiorella, L., Vogel-Walcutt, J. J., & Schatz, S. (2012). Applying the modality principle to real-time feedback and the acquisition of higher-order cognitive skills. *Educational Technology Research and Development, 60*(2), 223–238. doi:10.1007/s11423-011-9218-1

Fiorini, P., & Shillert, Z. (1998). Motion Planning in Dynamic Environments using Velocity Obstacles. *The International Journal of Robotics Research, 17*(7), 760–772. doi:10.1177/027836499801700706

Fischer, J. (2007). Detektivische Methode – Legetechnik. Retrieved from http://wissensreise.de/Intranet/Aufgabenkultur/forschen/Seiten/dMundLegetechnik.html

Fishman, B., Riconscente, M., Snider, R., Tsai, T., & Plass, J. (2014). Empowering Educators: Supporting Student Progress in the Classroom with Digital Games. Ann Arbor: University of Michigan. Retrieved from gamesandlearning.umich.edu/agames

Fitó-Bertran, A., Beatriz Hernández-Lara, A., & Serradell-López, E. (2014). Comparing student competences in a face-to-face and online business. *Computers in Human Behavior, 30*, 452–459. doi:10.1016/j.chb.2013.06.023

Flanagan, S., Bouck, E. C., & Richardson, J. (2012). Middle school special education teachers' perceptions and use of assistive technology in literacy instruction. *Assistive Technology, 25*(1), 24–30. doi:10.1080/10400435.2012.682697 PMID:23527428

Flight Simulator X [Digital Game]. (2006). Redmond, WA: Microsoft, ACES Game Studio.

Flowerday, T., Schraw, G., & Stevens, J. (2004). The role of choice and interest in reader engagement. *Journal of Experimental Education, 72*(2), 93–114. doi:10.3200/JEXE.72.2.93-114

FoldIt [Digital Game]. (2008). Seattle, WA: University of Washington, University of Washington.

Fontichiaro, K. (2010). Research strategies grades 3-5. *School Library Monthly* [serial online]. 29 (3): 48-50. Retrieved from http://www.schoollibrarymonthly.com/articles/Fontichiaro2010-v27n3p12.html

Forbes, C. T., & Davis, E. A. (2010). Curriculum design for inquiry: Preservice elementary teachers' mobilization and adaptation of science curriculum materials. *Journal of Research in Science Teaching, 47*(7), 820–839. doi:10.1002/tea.20379

Forssen, M., & Haho, P. (2001). Participative development and training for business processes in industry: Review of 88 simulation games. *International Journal of Technology Management*, *22*(1), 233–262. doi:10.1504/IJTM.2001.002963

Fosnot, C. (Ed.). (2005). *Constructivism: Theory, perspectives, and practice*. New York, NY: Teachers College Press.

Fournier, S., & Avery, J. (2011). The uninvited brand. *Business Horizons, 54*(3), 193–207. DOI=10.1016/j.bushor.2011.01.001

Frasca, G. (2003). *Simulation Versus Narrative: Introduction to Ludology*. Retrieved from http://www.ludology.org/articles/VGT_final.pdf

Froese, T. (2009). *Sociality and the life-mind continuity thesis: A study in evolutionary robotics*. [Unpublished doctoral dissertation]. University of Sussex. U.K. Retrieved from https://www.academia.edu/584795/Sociality_and_the_Life-Mind_Continuity_Thesis_A_Study_in_Evolutionary_Robotics

Froese, T., & Di Paolo, E. A. (2009). Sociality and the life–mind continuity thesis. *Phenomenology and the Cognitive Sciences, 8(*4), 439-463.

Frost, J. L. (2009). *A history of children's play and play environments: Toward a contemporary child- saving movement*. Routledge.

Fudin, S. (2012, March 29). Gen Z & What does it mean in your classroom? Inside USC Rossier Online Blog. Retrieved from http://rossieronline.usc.edu/gen-z-what-does-it-mean-in-your-classroom-2

Fullerton, T. (2008). *Game Design Workshop: A Playcentric Approach to Creating Innovative Games*. (2nd ed.). Burlington, MA: Morgan Kaufmann.

Gaba, D. M. (2004). The future vision of simulation in health care. *Quality & Safety in Health Care, 13*(Supplement 1), i2–i10. doi:10.1136/qshc.2004.009878 PMID:15465951

Gagne, R. M. (1985). *The Conditions of Learning* (4th ed.). New York: Holt, Rinehart & Winston.

Gainey, B. (2009). Crisis management's new role in educational settings. *The Clearing House: A Journal of Educational Strategies, Issues and Ideas*, *82*(6), 267–274. doi:10.3200/TCHS.82.6.267-274

Galaga [Digital Game]. (1981). Chicago, IL: Namco, Midway.

Games-to-Teach Team. (2003). Design principles of next-generation digital gaming for education. *Educational Technology*, *43*(5), 17–33.

GameVision Europe. (2010). *Video gamers in Europe 2010. Interactive Software Federation of Europe*. ISFE.

Gardner, D. E. M. (1969). *Susan Isaacs: The first biography*. London, UK: Cox & Wyman.

Garrido, P. C., Miraz, G. M., Ruiz, I. L., & Gómez-Nieto, M. Á. (2011). *Use of NFC-based pervasive games for encouraging learning and student motivation.* Paper presented at the 3rd International Workshop on Near Field Communication. doi:10.1109/NFC.2011.13

Garris, R., Ahlers, R., & Driskell, J. E. (2002). Games, motivation, and learning: A research and practice model. *Simulation & Gaming*, *33*(4), 441–467. doi:10.1177/1046878102238607

Gates Foundation. (2011). Press release for innovative grants to develop new teaching and learning tools. Retrieved from http://www.gatesfoundation.org/Media-Center/Press-Releases/2011/04/Gates-Foundation-Announces-Portfolio-of-Innovative-Grants-to-Develop-New-Teaching-and-Learning-Tools-that-Support-Teachers-and-Help-Students

Gee, J. (2007). *What video games have to teach us about learning and literacy.* New York, NY: Palgrave Macmillan. ISBN-13: 9781-4039-8453-1

Gee, J. P. (2006). Are videogames good for learning? *Curriculum & Leadership Journal, 5*(1).

Gee, J. P. (2007). Good Video Games and Good Learning: Collected Essays on Video Games, Learning, and Literacy (New Literacies and Digital Epistemologies). New York: Peter Lang Pub Inc.

Gee, J. P. (2007b). What Video Games Have to Teach us About Learning and Literacy (2nd ed.). New York: Palgrave Macmillan.

Gee, J. P. (2008). Learning and games. In K. Salen (Ed.), The Ecology of Games: Connecting Youth, Games, and Learning, 3, 21-40. MIT Press.

Gee, J. P. (2013). Discourses in and out of school. *Framing languages and literacies: Socially situated views and perspectives*, 51-82.

Gee, J. P., & Levine, M. (2008). Let's get over the slump. *Education Week*, *8*(4).

Gee, J. (2004). *Situated Language and Learning. A Critique of Traditional Schooling*. New York, NY: Routledge.

Gee, J. P. (1990). *Social Linguistics and Literacies: Ideology in Discourses*. London: Falmer Press.

Gee, J. P. (2001). Identity as an analytic lens for research in education. *Review of Research in Education*, 99–125.

Gee, J. P. (2003). *What Video Games Have to Teach Us about Learning and Literacy*. New York, NY: Palgrave Macmillan.

Gee, J. P. (2003). *What Video Games Have to Teach Us About Learning and Literacy*. New York: Palgrave Macmillan.

Gee, J. P. (2003). What video games have to teach us about learning and literacy. *Computers in Entertainment*, *1*(1), 20–20. doi:10.1145/950566.950595

Gee, J. P. (2003/2007). *What video games have to teach us about learning and literacy*. New York: Palgrave Macmillan.

Gee, J. P. (2004). *Situated language and learning: A critique of traditional schooling*. Routledge.

Gee, J. P. (2005). *Why Video Games Are Good for Your Soul: Pleasure and Learning*. Common Ground.

Gee, J. P. (2007). *Good video games + good learning: Collected essays on video games, learning, and literacy*. New York, NY: Peter Lang.

Gee, J. P. (2007). *What video games have to teach us about learning and literacy: Revised and updated edition*. New York, NY: Palgrave MacMillan.

Gee, J. P. (2007a). *Good Video Games and Good Learning: Collected Essays on Video Games, Learning, and Literacy (New Literacies and Digital Epistemologies)*. New York: Peter Lang Pub Inc.

Gee, J. P. (2008). Video games and embodiment. *Games and Culture*, *3*(3-4), 253–263. doi:10.1177/1555412008317309

Geometry Wars [Digital Game]. (2003). Liverpool, U.K.: Bizarre Creations.

Geraerts, R. (2010). Planning Short Paths with Clearance using Explicit Corridors. Proceedings of the *IEEE International Conference on Robotics and Automation* (pp. 1997-2004). doi:10.1109/ROBOT.2010.5509263

Geraerts, R., & Overmars, M. (2007). The Corridor Map Method: A general framework for real-time high-quality path planning. *Computer Animation and Virtual Worlds*, *18*(2), 107–119. doi:10.1002/cav.166

Gershenfeld, A. (2011, April 3) Game-based learning: Hype vs. versus reality. Retrieved from http://www.huffingtonpost.com/alan-gershenfeld/game-based-learning-education_b_843001.html

Gershenfeld, A. (2011, April 3). Game-based learning: Hype vs. versus reality. Retrieved from http://www.huffingtonpost.com/education/

Ge, X., Natsuaki, M., Neiderhiser, J. M., & Reiss, D. (2007). Genetic and environmental influences on pubertal timing: Results from two national sibling studies. *Journal of Research on Adolescence*, *17*(4), 767–788. doi:10.1111/j.1532-7795.2007.00546.x

Ghosh, S. K. (2007). *Visibility Algorithms in the Plane*. Cambridge University Press. doi:10.1017/CBO9780511543340

Gibson, J. J. (1979). *The ecological approach to visual perception*. Boston, MA: Houghton Mifflin.

Giedd, J. N., Blumenthal, J., Jeffries, N. O., Castellanos, F. X., Liu, H., Zijdenbos, A., & Rapoport, J. L. et al. (1999). Brain development during childhood and adolescence: A longitudinal MRI study. *Nature Neuroscience*, *2*(10), 861–863. doi:10.1038/13158 PMID:10491603

Giere, R. N. (1988). *Explaining science: A cognitive approach*. Chicago: University of Chicago Press. doi:10.7208/chicago/9780226292038.001.0001

Ginsburg, K. R. (2007). The importance of play in promoting healthy child development and maintaining strong parent-child bonds. *Pediatrics*, *119*(1), 182–191. doi:10.1542/peds.2006-2697 PMID:17200287

GlassLab. (2014). Psychometric Considerations In Game-Based Assessment. Institute of Play. Retrieved from http://www.instituteofplay.org/work/projects/glasslab-research/

GlassLab. About SimCityEDU. (2013). Retrieved from http://www.simcityedu.org/about/

Glenberg, A. M., & Kaschak, M. P. (2002). Grounding language in action. *Psychonomic Bulletin & Review*, *9*(3), 558–565. doi:10.3758/BF03196313 PMID:12412897

Glenberg, A. M., & Robertson, D. A. (2000). Symbol grounding and meaning: A comparison of high-dimensional and embodied theories of meaning. *Journal of Memory and Language*, *43*(3), 379–401. doi:10.1006/jmla.2000.2714

Godwin-Jones, R. (2014). Emerging technologies. Games in language learning: Opportunities and challenges. *Language Learning & Technology*, *18*(2), 9–19.

Goggins, S. P., Mascaro, C., & Valetto, G. (2013). Group informatics: A methodological approach and ontology for sociotechnical group research. *Journal of the American Society for Information Science and Technology*, *64*(3), 516–539. doi:10.1002/asi.22802

Goggins, S., & Petacovic, E. (2014). Connecting theory to social technology platforms: A framework for measuring influence in context. *The American Behavioral Scientist*, 0002764214527093.

Goh, D. H., Ang, R. P., & Tan, H. C. (2008). Strategies for designing effective psychotherapeutic gaming interventions for children and adolescents. *Computers in Human Behavior*, *24*(5), 2217–2235. doi:10.1016/j.chb.2007.10.007

Golas, A., Narain, R., Curtis, S., & Lin, M. C. (2014). Hybrid Long-Range Collision Avoidance for Crowd Simulation. *IEEE Transactions on Visualization and Computer Graphics*, *20*(7), 1022–1034. doi:10.1109/TVCG.2013.235 PMID:24080711

Goldenberg, D., Andrusyszyn, M. A., & Iwasiw, C. (2005). The effect of classroom simulation on nursing students' self-efficacy related to health teaching. *The Journal of Nursing Education*, *44*, 310–314. Retrieved from http://europepmc.org/abstract/med/16094789 PMID:16094789

Gordon, P., Rogers, A., Comfort, M., Gavula, N., & McGee, B. (2001). A taste of problem-based learning increases achievement of urban minority middle school students. *Educational Horizons*, *79*(4), 171–175.

Gould, J., & Annenberg Public Policy Center. (2011). *Guardian of democracy: The civic mission of schools*. Retrieved from http://civicmission.s3.amazonaws.com/118/f0/5/171/1/Guardian-of-Democracy-report.pdf

Graafland, M., Schraagen, J. M., & Schijven, M. P. (2012). Systematic review of serious games for medical education and surgical skills training. *British Journal of Surgery*, *99*(10), 1322–1330. doi:10.1002/bjs.8819 PMID:22961509

Graham, S., & Weiner, B. (2012). Motivation: Past, present, and future. In K. Harris, S. Graham, T. Urdan, C. McCormick, G. Sinatra, J. Sweller (Eds.) APA Educational Psychology Handbook, Vol 1: Theories, Constructs, And Critical Issues (pp. 367-397). Washington, DC, US: American Psychological Association.

Gran Turismo 5 [Digital Game]. (2010). Foster City, CA: Sony Computer Entertainment, Polyphony Digital.

Grand Theft Auto IV [Digital Game]. (2008). New York: Rockstar Games, Rockstar North.

Grassian, E., & Kaplowitz, J. R. (2009). *Information literacy instruction: theory and practice* (2nd ed.). ALA Neal Schuman.

Grassian, E., & Trueman, R. (2013). What's in it for me?: Professional development in virtual worlds. In A. Sigal (Ed.), *Advancing Library Education: Technological Innovation and Instructional Design* (pp. 91–109). Hershey, PA: Information Science Reference. doi:10.4018/978-1-4666-3688-0.ch006

Gravemeijer, K., Cobb, P., Bowers, J., & Whitenack, J. (2000). Symbolizing, modeling, and instructional design. In P. Cobb, E. Yackel, & K. McClain (Eds.), *Symbolizing and communicating in mathematics classrooms: Perspectives on discourse, tools, and instructional design*. Mahwah, NJ: Lawrence Erlbaum Associates.

Gray, P. (2011). The decline of play and the rise of psychopathology in children and adolescents. *American Journal of Play*, *3*(4), 443–463.

Gredler, M. E. (1996). 17 educational games and simulations: A technology in search of a (research) paradigm. *Technology (Elmsford, N.Y.)*, *39*, 521–540.

Gredler, M. E. (1996). Educational games and simulations: A technology in search of a research paradigm. In D.H. Jonassen (Ed.), *Handbook of research for educational communications and technology* (pp. 521–539). New York: MacMillan.

Greenberg, B. S., Sherry, J., Lachlan, K., Lucas, K., & Holmstrom, A. (2010). Orientations to video games among gender and age groups. *Simulation & Gaming*, *41*(2), 238–259. doi:10.1177/1046878108319930

Greeno, (1997).

Greeno, J. G. (1997). On claims that answer the wrong question. *Educational Researcher*, *26*(1), 5–17.

Gregersen, A., & Grodal, T. (2009). Embodiment and interface. In Wolf (Ed.), The video game theory reader (pp. 65-85), New York, NY: Routlege

Gregory, G. H., & Burkman, A. (2011). Differentiated literacy strategies for english language learners, grades 7–12. London, UK: SAGE.

Gresalfi, M., Barab, S., Siyahhan, S., & Christensen, T. (2009). Virtual worlds, conceptual understanding, and me: Designing for consequential engagement. *On the Horizon*, *17*(1), 21–34. doi:10.1108/10748120910936126

Griffiths, M. D. (2002). The educational benefits of videogames. *Education for Health*, *20*(3), 47–51.

Griffiths, T., & Guile, D. (2003). A connective model of learning: Implications for work process knowledge. *European Educational Research Journal*, *2*(1), 56–73. doi:10.2304/eerj.2003.2.1.10

Gruber, M. J., Gelman, B. D., & Ranganath, C. (2014). States of Curiosity Modulate Hippocampus-Dependent Learning via the Dopaminergic Circuit. *Neuron*, *84*(2), 486–496. doi:10.1016/j.neuron.2014.08.060 PMID:25284006

Gruyer, N., & Toublanc, N. (n.d.). *Online classroom games for teaching economics*. Retrieved from http://economics-games.com/

Guild Wars 2 [Digital Game]. (2012). Seoul, Korea: NCsoft, ArenaNet.

Guitar Hero [Digital Game]. (2010). Santa Monica, CA: Activision, Vicarious Visions.

Gunckel, K. L., Covitt, B. A., & Anderson, C. W. (2009, June). Learning a secondary discourse: Shifts from force-dynamic to model-based reasoning in understanding water in socioecological systems. Proceedings ofLearning Progressions in Science (LeaPS) Conference, Iowa City, IA.

Gunckel, K. L., Covitt, B. A., Salinas, I., & Anderson, C. W. (2012). A learning progression for water in socio-ecological systems. *Journal of Research in Science Teaching*, *49*(7), 843–868. doi:10.1002/tea.21024

Gunter, G. A., Kenny, R. F., & Vick, E. H. (2008). Taking educational games seriously: Using the RETAIN model to design endogenous fantasy into standalone educational games. *Educational Technology Research and Development*, *56*(5-6), 511–537. doi:10.1007/s11423-007-9073-2

Guy, S. J., Chhugani, J., Kim, C., Satish, N., Lin, M. C., Manocha, D., & Dubey, P. (2009). Clearpath: Highly parallel collision avoidance for mulit-agent simulation. Proceedings of the *ACM SIGGRAPH/EUROGRAPHICS Symposium on Computer Animation (SCA '09)* (pp. 177-187). doi:10.1145/1599470.1599494

Haberman, M. (1991). The pedagogy of poverty versus good teaching. *Phi Delta Kappan*, *73*(4), 290–294.

Habgood, M. P. J., & Ainsworth, S. E. (2011). Motivating Children to Learn Effectively: Exploring the Value of Intrinsic Integration in Educational Games. *Journal of the Learning Sciences*, *20*(2), 169–206. doi:10.1080/10508406.2010.508029

Hadjistassou, S. (2012). An Activity Theory exegesis on conflict and contradictions in Networked discussions and feedback exchanges. *CALICO Journal*, *29*(2), 367–388. doi:10.11139/cj.29.2.367-388

Hainey, T. (2010). *Using games-based learning to teach requirements collection and analysis at tertiary education level* [Doctoral dissertation]. University of the West of Scotland.

Hainey, T., Connolly, T., Stansfield, M., & Boyle, E. (2011). The differences in motivations of online game players and offline game players: A combined analysis of three studies at higher education level. *Computers & Education*, *57*(4), 2197–2211. doi:10.1016/j.compedu.2011.06.001

Hallet, E. (2013). *The reflective early years practitioner*. London, UK: Sage. doi:10.4135/9781473914919

Halliday, M. A. K. (1978). *Language as a social semiotic: The social interpretation of language and meaning*. Baltimore: University Park Press.

Halliday, M. A. K. (1993). Towards a language-based theory of learning. *Linguistics and Education*, *5*(2), 93–116. doi:10.1016/0898-5898(93)90026-7

Hall, L. O., Soderstrom, T., Ahlqvist, J., & Nilsson, T. (2011). Collaborative learning with screen-based simulation in health care education: An empirical study of collaborative patterns and proficiency development. *Journal of Computer Assisted Learning*, *27*(5), 448–461. doi:10.1111/j.1365-2729.2011.00407.x

Hall, R., & Stevens, R. (1995). Making space: A comparison of mathematical work in school and professional design practices. In S. L. Star (Ed.), *The cultures of computing* (pp. 118–145). London, UK: Basil Blackwell.

Halo [Digital Game]. (2009). Redmond, WA: Microsoft, Bungie Software.

Hamlen, K. R. (2012). Stochastic frontier estimation of efficient learning in video games. *Computers & Education*, *58*(1), 534–541. doi:10.1016/j.compedu.2011.09.006

Hamlen, K. R. (2014). Video Game Strategies as Predictors of Academic Achievement. *Journal of Educational Computing Research*, *50*(2), 271–284. doi:10.2190/EC.50.2.g

Hannak, C., Pilz, M., & Ebner, M. (2012). Fun - A Prerequisite for Learning Games.*Proceedings of World Conference on Educational Multimedia, Hypermedia and Telecommunications*, Chesapeake, VA (pp. 1292-1299). AACE

Hannum, W. H., Irvin, M. J., Banks, J. B., & Farmer, T. W. (2009). Distance education use in rural schools. *Journal of Research in Rural Education*, *24*(3), 1–15.

Harackiewicz, B., & Pintrich, E. (2002). Revision of Achievement Goal Theory: Necessary and Illuminating. *Journal of Educational Psychology*, *94*(3), 638–645. doi:10.1037/0022-0663.94.3.638

Harman, G. (2001). Object-oriented philosophy. *Towards Speculative Realism: Essays and Lectures* (pp. 93-104). Ripley: Zero Books.

Harris, K. S., & Rogers, G. E. (2008). Soft skills in the technology education classroom: What do students need? *Technology Teacher*, *68*(3), 19–24.

Hart, P., Nilsson, N., & Raphael, B. (1968). A Formal Basis for the Heuristic Determination of Minimum Cost Paths. *IEEE Transactions on Systems Science and Cybernetics*, *4*(2), 100–107. doi:10.1109/TSSC.1968.300136

Hasan, R. (2004). The concept of semiotic mediation. In J. Muller, B. Davies, & A. Morais (Eds.), *Reading Bernstein, Researching Bernstein* (pp. 30–43). London: Routledge Falmer.

Hassenzahl, M., & Tractinsky, N. (2006). User Experience – a Research Agenda. *Behaviour & Information Technology*, *25*(2), 91–97. doi:10.1080/01449290500330331

Hattie, J. (2009). *Visible learning: A synthesis of over 800 meta-analyses relating to achievement*. New York, NY: Routledge.

Hattie, J. (2009). *Visible Learning; a synthesis of over 800 meta-analyses relating to achievement*. London: Routledge.

Hattie, J. (2012). *Visible learning for teachers: Maximizing impact on learning*. New York, NY: Routledge.

Hayenga, A. O., & Corpus, J. H. (2010). Profiles of intrinsic and extrinsic motivations: A person-centered approach to motivation and achievement in middle school. *Motivation and Emotion*, *34*(4), 371–383. doi:10.1007/s11031-010-9181-x

Hayes, E. R., & Gee, J. P. (2009). Public Pedagogy through Video Games. Handbook of public pedagogy: education and learning beyond schooling, 185.

Hayes, E., & Gee, J. P. (2012). Passionate affinity groups. Chapter. In C. Steinkuehler, K. Squire, & S. Barab (Eds.), *Games, learning, and society: Learning and meaning in the digital age*. London: Cambridge University Press.

Hayhoe, M. M., Shrivastava, A., Mruczek, R., & Pelz, J. B. (2003). Visual memory and motor planning in a natural task. *Journal of Vision (Charlottesville, Va.)*, *3*(1), 49–63. doi:10.1167/3.1.6 PMID:12678625

Hayles, N. K. (1999). How We Became Post-Human. Chicago, IL: University of Chicago Press. Retrieved from http://gamestudies.org/0102/squire/ doi:10.7208/chicago/9780226321394.001.0001

Heeter, C. (1992). Being there: The subjective experience of presence. *Presence (Cambridge, Mass.)*, *1*(2), 262–271.

Heift, T., & Rimrott, A. (2012). Task-Related Variation in Computer-Assisted Language Learning. *Modern Language Journal*, *96*(4), 525–543. doi:10.1111/j.1540-4781.2012.01392.x

Heigeas, L., Luciani, A., Thollot, J., & Castagné, N. (2003). *A Physically-Based Particle Model of Emergent Crowd Behaviors*. Graphicon.

Heinich, R., Molenda, M., Russell, J. D., & Smaldino, S. E. (1996). *Instructional media and technologies for learning* (5th ed.). Englewood Cliffs, NJ: Prentice Hall.

Heinrichs, W., Youngblood, P., Harter, P., & Dev, P. (2008). Simulation for team training and assessment: Case studies of online training with virtual worlds. *World Journal of Surgery*, *32*(2), 161–170. doi:10.1007/s00268-007-9354-2

Helbing, D., & Molnár, P. (1995). Social force model for pedestrian dynamics. *Physical Review E: Statistical Physics, Plasmas, Fluids, and Related Interdisciplinary Topics*, *51*(5), 4282–4286. doi:10.1103/PhysRevE.51.4282 PMID:9963139

Held, M. (2011). VRONI and ArcVRONI: Software for and Applications of Voronoi Diagrams in Science and Engineering.*Proceedings of the 8th International Symposium on Voronoi Diagrams in Science and Engineering* (pp. 3-12). doi:10.1109/ISVD.2011.9

Hennessy, S., Deaney, R., & Ruthven, K. (2006). Situated expertise in integrating use of multimedia simulation into secondary science teaching. *International Journal of Science Education*, *28*(7), 701–732. doi:10.1080/09500690500404656

Herman, J., Dai, Y., Htut, A. M., Martinez, M., & Rivera, N. (2011). *Evaluation of the enhanced assessment grants (EAGs) SimScientists program: Site visit findings*. (CRESST Report No. 791). National Center for Research on Evaluation, Standards, and Student Testing (CRESST).

Hestenes, D., Wells, M., & Swackhamer, G. (1992). Force concept inventory. *The Physics Teacher*, *30*(3), 141–158. doi:10.1119/1.2343497

Hew, K. F., & Cheung, W. S. (2010). Use of three-dimensional (3-D) immersive virtual worlds in K-12 and higher education settings: A review of the research. *British Journal of Educational Technology*, *41*(1), 33–55. doi:10.1111/j.1467-8535.2008.00900.x

Hidi, S. (1990). Interest and its contribution as a mental resource for learning. *Review of Educational Research*, *60*(4), 549–571. doi:10.3102/00346543060004549

Hill, V. (2012). Valibrarian's Anne Frank MOOC experience. Retrieved from http://www.livebinders.com/play/play?id=694451

Hill, V. (2014). Ethridge Minecraft digital citizens library. https://youtu.be/BQiBtD7fD1k

Hill, R., Belanich, J., Chad Lane, H., Core, M., Dixon, M., & Forbell, E. et al. (2006). Pedagogically structured game-based training: Development of the ELECT BILAT simulation.*Proceedings of the 25th Army Science Conference* (pp. 1-8).

Hill, V. (2015). Digital citizenship through game design in minecraft. *New Library World*, *116*(7/8), 369–382. doi:10.1108/NLW-09-2014-0112

Hill, V., & Lee, H. (2009). Libraries and immersive learning environments unite in second life. *Library Hi Tech*, *27*(3), 338–356. doi:10.1108/07378830910988487

Hinrichs, T. R. (1992). *Problem solving in open worlds: A case study in design*. Hillsdale, NJ: Lawrence Erlbaum Associates.

Hirsh-Pasek, K., Golinkoff, R. M., Berk, L. E., & Singer, D. (2008). *A mandate for playful learning in preschool: Applying the scientific evidence*. Oxford University Press. doi:10.1093/acprof:oso/9780195382716.001.0001

Hirumi, A., Appelman, R. L., Rieber, L. P., & Van Eck, R. (2010). Preparing Instructional Designers for Game-Based Learning: Part 2. *Techtrends. Linking Research & Practice to Improve Learning*, *54*(1), 19–27.

Hoff, K., Keyser, J., Lin, M., Manocha, D., & Culver, T. (1999). Fast computation of generalized voronoi diagrams using graphics hardware.*Proceedings of the 26th annual conference on Computer graphics and interactive techniques SIGGRAPH '99* (pp. 277-286). doi:10.1145/311535.311567

Hogan, K., & Corey, C. (2001). Viewing classrooms as cultural contexts for fostering scientific literacy. *Anthropology & Education Quarterly*, *32*(2), 214–243. doi:10.1525/aeq.2001.32.2.214

Holland, W., Jenkins, H., & Squire, K. (2003). Theory by design. In M.J.P. Wolf & B. Perron (Eds.), *The video game theory reader*. New York: Routledge.

Holmes, S. E. (2009) *Standardized testing and the No Child Left Behind Act: A failing attempt at reform*. Retrieved from http://www.ecu.edu/cs-lib/awards/upload/Sarah_Holmes_First_Place.pdf

Holzinger, A., & Maurer, H. (1999). Incidental learning, motivation and the Tamagotchi effect: VR-Friends, chances for new ways of learning with computers. Proceedings of Computer Assisted Learning CAL 99 (p. 70). London.

Holzinger, A. (1997). Computer-aided mathematics instruction with mathematica 3.0. *Mathematica in Education and Research*, *6*(4), 37–40.

Homer, B. D., Hayward, E. O., Frye, J., & Plass, J. L. (2012). Gender and player characteristics in video game play of preadolescents. *Computers in Human Behavior*, *28*(5), 1782–1789. doi:10.1016/j.chb.2012.04.018

Homer, B. D., Kinzer, C. K., Plass, J. L., Letourneau, S. M., Hoffman, D., Bromley, M., & Kornak, Y. et al. (2014). Moved to learn: The effects of interactivity in a Kinect-based literacy game for beginning readers. *Computers & Education*, *74*, 37–49. doi:10.1016/j.compedu.2014.01.007

Honey, M., & Hilton, M. L. (Eds.) (2011). Learning science through computer games and simulations. Washington, D.C.: National Academies Press.

Houghton, T., & Proscio, T. (2001). *Hard work on soft skills: Creating a "culture of work" in workforce development*. Philadelphia, PA: Public/Private Ventures.

Hou, H.-T. (2012). Analyzing the learning process of an online role-playing discussion activity. *Journal of Educational Technology & Society*, *15*(1), 211–222. Retrieved from http://www.ifets.info/journals/15_1/19.pdf

Hsu, T. Y., & Chiou, G. F. (2011). Pre-service teachers' awareness of digital game-supported learning. In M. Koehler & P. Mishra (Eds.), *Proceedings of Society for Information Technology & Teacher Education International Conference 2011* (pp. 2135-2141). Chesapeake, VA: AACE.

Huang, W. H., Huang, W. Y., & Tschopp, J. (2010). Sustaining iterative game playing processes in DGBL: The relationship between motivational processing and outcome processing. *Computers & Education*, *55*(2), 789–797. doi:10.1016/j.compedu.2010.03.011

Hubbard, P., & Levy, M. (2006). *Teacher education in CALL*. Amsterdam: John Benjamin Publishing Co. doi:10.1075/lllt.14

Hughes, F. P. (2009). Children, play, and development. *Sage (Atlanta, Ga.)*.

Hughes, R. (2003). The Flow of Human Crowds. *Annual Review of Fluid Mechanics*, *35*(1), 169–182. doi:10.1146/annurev.fluid.35.101101.161136

Hui, D., & Russell, D. L. (2009). Understanding the Effectiveness of Collaborative Activity in Online Professional Development with Innovative Educators through Intersubjectivity. In L. Tomei (Ed.), *Information Communication Technologies for Enhanced Education and Learning: Advanced Applications and Developments* (pp. 283–302). Hershey, PA: Information Science Reference; doi:10.4018/978-1-60566-150-6.ch020

Huitt, W., & Hummel, J. (2003). Piaget's theory of cognitive development. *Educational Psychology Interactive*, *3*(2), 1–24.

Huizinga, J. (1955). *Homo Ludens: A Study of the Play-Element in Culture*. Boston, MA: The Beacon Press.

Hurley, S. (2008). The shared circuits model (SCM): How control, mirroring, and simulation can enable imitation, deliberation, and mindreading. *Behavioral and Brain Sciences*, *31*(1), 1–22. doi:10.1017/S0140525X07003123 PMID:18394222

Hutchins, E. (1995). *Cognition in the Wild*. Cambridge, MA: MIT Press.

Hutchins, E. (2010). Enaction, imagination, and insight. In J. R. Stewart, O. Gapenne, & E. A. Di Paolo (Eds.), *Enaction: Towards a new paradigm for cognitive science* (pp. 425–450). Cambridge, MA: MIT Press. doi:10.7551/mitpress/9780262014601.003.0016

Huynh-Kim-Bang, B., Wisdom, J., & Labat, J. M. (2010). Design patterns in serious games: a blue print for combining fun and learning. *Project SE-SG*. Retrieved from http://seriousgames.lip6.fr/DesignPatterns

Hwang, G. J., Yang, L. H., & Wang, S. Y. (2013). A concept map-embedded educational computer game for improving students' learning performance in natural science courses. *Computers & Education*, *69*, 121–130. doi:10.1016/j.compedu.2013.07.008

Ice, P., Díaz, S., Swan, K., Burgess, M., Sharkey, M., Sherrill, J., & Okimoto, H. et al. (2012). The PAR Framework Proof of Concept: Initial Findings from a Multi-Institutional Analysis of Federated Postsecondary Data. *Journal of Asynchronous Learning Networks*, *16*(3), 63–86.

Ifenthaler, D., Eseryel, D., & Ge, X. (2012). Assessment for game-based learning. In *Assessment in game-based learning* (pp. 1–8). Springer New York. doi:10.1007/978-1-4614-3546-4_1

IJsselsteijn, W. A., Poels, K., & de Kort, Y.A.W. (2008). *The game experience questionnaire: Development of a self-report measure to assess player experiences of digital games* [Technical report]. Eindhoven, The Netherlands: TU Eindhoven.

Il'enkov, E. V. (1977). *Dialectical logic: Essays in its history and theory*. Moscow: Progress. http://nces.ed.gov/pubs2013/2013037.pdf

Im, M. H., Hughes, J. H., Kwok, O., Puckett, S., & Cerdia, C. A. (2014). Effect of retention in elementary grades on transition to middle school. *Journal of School Psychology*, *51*(3), 349–365. doi:10.1016/j.jsp.2013.01.004 PMID:23816229

INCONTROL Simulation Solutions. (2014). SportEvac.

InfoLit Ischool in Second Life. (2015). http://secondlife.com/destination/infolit-ischool

Ingold, T. (2011). *Being Alive: Essays on movement, knowledge and description*. London, New York: Taylor & Francis Group.

Institute of Play. (2014). Psychometric considerations in game-based learning assessment executive summary. Retrieved from http://www.instituteofplay.org/wp-content/uploads/2014/02/GlassLab_GBA1_Summary.pdf

International Education Advisory Board. (2008) *Learning in the 21st century: Teaching today's students on their terms* [White Paper]. Certiport.

International Youth Foundation. (2013). *Getting youth in the door: defining soft skills requirements for entry-level service sector jobs*.

iRacing [Digital Game]. (2008). Redmond, WA: iRacing.com Motorsport Simulations.

Isaacs, S. (1968). The nursery years: The mind of the child from birth to six years.

Isbister, K., Karlesky, M., Frye, J., & Rao, R. (2012). Scoop: A movement-based math game designed to reduce math anxiety. In J. A. Konstan, E. H. Chi, & K. Höök (Eds.), *CHI'12 Extended Abstracts on Human Factors in Computing Systems,* Austin, TX (pp. 1075–1078). ACM. doi:10.1145/2212776.2212389

Isenberg, J. P., & Quisenberry, N. (2002). A position paper of the Association for Childhood Education International PLAY: Essential for all Children. *Childhood Education, 79*(1), 33–39. doi:10.1080/00094056.2002.10522763

ISTE (International Society for Technology in Education). (2011). Understanding the holocaust project. Retrieved from http://sigve.iste.wikispaces.net/file/view/ISTE+2011+Newsletter+Final.pdf

Iyengar, S. S., & Lepper, M. R. (1999). Rethinking the value of choice: A cultural perspective on intrinsic motivation. *Journal of Personality and Social Psychology, 76*(3), 349–366. doi:10.1037/0022-3514.76.3.349 PMID:10101874

Izzo, M. V. (2012). Universal Design for Learning: Enhancing achievement of students with disabilities. *Procedia Computer Science, 14*, 343–350. doi:10.1016/j.procs.2012.10.039

Jackson, A., & Davis, G. A. (2000). *Turning points 2000: Educating adolescents in the 21st century*. New York, NY: Teachers College Press.

Jackson, L. A., Witt, E. A., Games, A. I., Fitzgerald, H. E., von Eye, A., & Zhao, Y. (2012). Information technology use and creativity: Findings from the children and technology project. *Computers in Human Behavior, 28*(2), 370–376. doi:10.1016/j.chb.2011.10.006

Jacob, B. A., & Rockoff, J. E. (2011). *Organizing schools to improve student achievement: start times, grade configurations, and teacher assignments*. Brookings Institution, Hamilton Project.

Jaimes, A., & Sebe, N. (2007). Multimodal human–computer interaction: A survey. *Computer Vision and Image Understanding, 108*(1-2), 116–134. doi:10.1016/j.cviu.2006.10.019

Jaklin, N., Cook, I.V.A. IV, & Geraerts, R. (2013). Real-time Path Planning in Heterogeneous Environments. [CAVW]. *Computer Animation and Virtual Worlds, 24*(3), 285–295. doi:10.1002/cav.1511

Jaklin, N., Tibboel, M., & Geraerts, R. (2014). Computing High-Quality Paths in Weighted Regions.*Proceedings of the 7th International ACM SIGGRAPH Conference on Motion in Games (MIG 2014)* (pp. 77-86).

Jalongo, M. R. (2003). A Position Paper of the Association for Childhood Education International: The Child's Right to Creative Thought and Expression. *Childhood Education, 79*(4), 218–228. doi:10.1080/00094056.2003.10521196

Jamestown: Legend of the Lost Colony [Digital Game]. (2011). Philadelphia: Final Form Games.

Jarmon, L., Traphagan, T., Mayrath, M., & Trivedi, A. (2009). Virtual world teaching, experiential learning, and assessment: An interdisciplinary communication course in Second Life. *Computers & Education, 53*(1), 169–182. doi:10.1016/j.compedu.2009.01.010

Järvinen, A. (2009). Game design for social networks: Interaction design for playful dispositions.*Proceedings of the 2009 ACM SIGGRAPH Symposium on Video Games* (pp. 95–102). doi:10.1145/1581073.1581088

Jauregi, K., Canto, S., de Graaff, R., Koenraad, T., & Moonen, M. (2011). Verbal interaction in Second Life: Towards a pedagogic framework for task design. *Computer Assisted Language Learning, 24*(1), 77–101. doi:10.1080/09588221.2010.538699

Jeffries, P. R. (2005). A framework for designing, implementing, and evaluating simulations used as teaching strategies in nursing. *Nursing Education Perspectives, 26*(2), 96–103. doi: 10.1043/1536-5026(2005)026%3C0096%3AAFWFDI%3E2.0.CO%3B2 PMID:15921126

Jennett, C., Cox, A. L., Cairns, P., Dhoparee, S., Epps, A., Tijs, T., & Walton, A. (2008). Measuring and defining the experience of immersion in games. *International Journal of Human-Computer Studies, 66*(9), 641–661. doi:10.1016/j.ijhcs.2008.04.004

Jensen, E. (2005). *Teaching with the brain in mind*. Alexandria, VA: Association for Supervision and Curriculum Development.

Jeuring, J., van Rooij, R., & Pronost, N. (2014). The 5/10 Method: A Method for Designing Educational Games. In Games and Learning Alliance (pp. 364-369). Springer International Publishing.

Johnson-Glenberg, M. C., Koziupa, T., Birchfield, D., & Li, K. (2011). Games for learning in embodied mixed-reality environments: Principles and results. In C. Steinkuehler, C. Martin, & A. Ochsner (Eds.), *Proceedings of the 7th International Conference on Games+ Learning+ Society Conference* (pp. 129-137). Madison, WI: ETC Press.

Johnson-Harris, K. M., & Mundschenk, N. A. (2014). Working effectively with students with BD in a general education classroom: The case for Universal Design for Learning. *The Clearing House: A Journal of Educational Strategies, Issues and Ideas*, *87*(4), 168–174. doi:10.1080/00098655.2014.897927

Johnson, J. H., Zerwic, J. J., & Theis, S. L. (1999). Clinical simulation laboratory: An adjunct to clinical teaching. *Nurse Educator*, *24*(5), 37–41. doi:10.1097/00006223-199909000-00016 PMID:10795255

Johnson, L., Adams, S., & Cummins, M. (2012). *NMC horizon report: 2012 K-12 edition*. Austin, TX: New Media Consortium.

Johnson, L., Laurence, F., Levine, A., & Smith, R. (2009). *The 2010 horizon report*. Austin, TX: The New Media Consortium.

Johnson, M. (1987). *The body in the mind: The bodily basis of imagination, reason, and meaning*. Chicago, IL: Chicago University Press.

Johnson, W., Rickel, J., & Lester, J. (2000). Animated pedagogical agents: Face-to-face interaction in interactive learning environments. *International Journal of Artificial Intelligence in Education*, *1*, 47–78.

John-Steiner, V., & Moran, S. (2002). Creativity in the Making: Vygotsky's Contemporary Contribution to the Dialectic of Creativity & Development. Retrieved from www.unm.edu/~vygotsky/c_make.pdf

Jonassen, D. (2000). Toward a design theory of problem solving. *Educational Technology Research and Development*, *48*(4), 63–85. doi:10.1007/BF02300500

Jonassen, D., Howland, J., Moore, J., & Marra, J. (2003). *Learning to Solve Problems with Technology: A Constructivist Perspective*. Upper Saddle River, NJ: Merrill-Prentice Hall.

Jonassen, D., Peck, K., & Wilson, B. G. (1999). *Learning with technology: A constructivist perspective*. Upper Saddle River, New Jersey: Merrill-Prentice Hall.

Jones, N. D., Buzick, H. M., & Turkan, S. (2013). Including students with disabilities and English learners in measures of educator effectiveness. *Educational Researcher*, *42*(4), 234–241. doi:10.3102/0013189X12468211

Ju, E., Choi, M. G., Park, M., Lee, J., Lee, K. H., & Takahashi, S. (2010). Morphable crowds. *ACM Transactions on Graphics*, *29*(6), 1. doi:10.1145/1882261.1866162

Junge, S. K., Manglallan, S., & Raskauskas, J. (2003). Building life skills through afterschool participation in experiential and cooperative learning. *Child Study Journal*, *33*(3), 165–174.

Juul, J. (2005). *Half-Real: Video Games between Real Rules and Fictional Worlds*. Cambridge, MA: MIT Press.

Kafai, Y. B., Heeter, C., Denner, J., & Sun, J. (2008). (Eds.), Beyond Barbie and Mortal Kombat: New Perspectives on Gender and Gaming. Cambridge, MA: MIT Press.

Kafai, Y. B., Fields, D. A., & Cook, M. S. (2010). Your Second Selves: Player Designed Avatar Designs. *Games and Culture*, *5*(1), 23–42. doi:10.1177/1555412009351260

Kafai, Y. B., Quintero, M., & Feldon, D. (2010). Investigating the ''why'' in whypox: Casual and systematic explorations of a virtual epidemic. *Games and Culture*, *5*(1), 116–135. doi:10.1177/1555412009351265

Kagohara, D. M. (2011). Three students with developmental disabilities learn to operate an iPod to access age-appropriate entertainment videos. *Journal of Behavioral Education*, *20*(1), 33–43. doi:10.1007/s10864-010-9115-4

Kail, R., & Cavanaugh, J. (2012). *Human development: A life-span view*. Cengage Learning.

Kalay, Y., Jeony, Y., & Kim, J. (2003). Virtual Learning Environments. *Journal of Information Technology in Mathematical Surfaces*. doi=10.1.1.120.8491

Kalay, Y., Jeong, S., Kim, W., & Lee, J. (n. d.). Virtual Learning Environments. *Proc. 9th CAADRIA2004 conf. on Culture, Technology and Architecture*, Seoul, Korea (pp. 871-890).

Kallmann, M. (2010b). Shortest paths with arbitrary clearance from navigation meshes. *Proceedings of the Eurographics / SIGGRAPH Symposium on Computer Animation (SCA).*

Kallmann, M. (2010a). Navigation queries from triangular meshes.*Proceedings of the Third international conference on Motion in Games* (pp. 230-241). Springer-Verlag.

Kalyuga, S. (2011). Cognitive Load Theory: How Many Types of Load Does It Really Need? *Educational Psychology Review, 23*(1), 1–19. doi:10.1007/s10648-010-9150-7

Kalyuga, S., Ayres, P., Chandler, P., & Sweller, J. (2003). The expertise reversal effect. *Educational Psychologist, 38*(1), 23–31. doi:10.1207/S15326985EP3801_4

Kamphuis, & Overmars. (2004). Finding paths for coherent groups using clearance. *Proceedings of the 2004 ACM SIGGRAPH/Eurographics Symposium on Computer Animation (SCA '04)* (pp. 19-28).

Kangas, M. (2010). Creative and playful learning: Learning through game co-creation and games in a playful learning environment. *Thinking Skills and Creativity, 5*(1), 1–15. doi:10.1016/j.tsc.2009.11.001

Kant, I. (1999). *Critique of pure reason.* Cambridge University Press.

Kapp, K. M. (2012, 2 Oct). The gamification of learning: What research says about simulations & serious games. Retrieved from http://www.slideshare.net/kkapp/spbt-kapp-keynote2012

Kapp, K. M. (2014, 11 Sep). Abstracts of Three Meta-Analysis Studies of Serious Games. Kapp Notes Blog. Retrieved from http://karlkapp.com/abstracts-of-three-meta-analysis-studies-of-serious-games

Kapp, K.M. & O'Driscoll, T. (2010) *Learning in 3D: Adding a New Dimension to Enterprise Learning and Collaboration.* San Francisco, CA: Wiley Publications

Kapur, M. (2008). Productive Failure. *Cognition and Instruction, 26*(3), 3. doi:10.1080/07370000802212669

Karamouzas, I., Geraerts, R., & Overmars, M. (2009). Indicative routes for path planning and crowd simulation.*Proceedings of the 4th international conference on foundations of digital gamesFDG '09* (pp. 113-120). doi:10.1145/1536513.1536540

Karamouzas, I., & Overmars, M. (2012). Simulating and evaluating the local behavior of small pedestrian groups. *IEEE Transactions on Visualization and Computer Graphics, 18*(3), 394–406. doi:10.1109/TVCG.2011.133 PMID:22241282

Karlova, N., & Fisher, K. (2013). A Social diffusion model of misinformation and disinformation for understanding human information behavior. *Information Research* [serial online], 18(1), 1-12. Retrieved from http://www.informationr.net/ir/18-1/paper573.html#VVEXW2RViko

Katz, J. (2013). The Three Block Model of Universal Design for Learning (UDL): Engaging students in inclusive education. *Canadian Journal of Education*, 1, 153.

Kavraki, L. E., Svestka, P., Latombe, J.-C., & Overmars, M. (1996). Probabilistic Roadmaps for Path Planning in High-Dimensional Configuration Spaces. *IEEE Transactions on Robotics and Automation, 12*(4), 566–580. doi:10.1109/70.508439

Kearns, L., & Frey, B. (2010). Web 2.0 technologies and back channel communication in an online learning community. *TechTrends, 54*(4), 41–51. doi:10.1007/s11528-010-0419-y

Keating, B., Gregor, S., Fitzgerald, R., Campbell, J., & Steele, J. (2014, December 8-10). *Information Systems Design Theory for Location-Based Educational Services in Informal Learning Environments.* Paper presented at the 25th Australasian Conference on Information Systems, Auckland, New Zealand.

Kebritchi, M., & Hirumi, A. (2008). Examining the pedagogical foundations of modern educational computer games. *Computers & Education, 51*(4), 1729–1743. doi:10.1016/j.compedu.2008.05.004

Kebritchi, M., Hirumi, A., Kappers, W., & Henry, R. (2009). Analysis of the supporting websites for the use of instructional games in K-12 settings. *British Journal of Educational Technology, 40*(4), 733–754. doi:10.1111/j.1467-8535.2008.00854.x

Ke, F. (2009). A qualitative meta-analysis of computer games as learning tools. In R. E. Furdig (Ed.), *Handbook of Research on Effective Electronic Gaming in Education* (pp. 1–32). New York: IGI Global. doi:10.4018/978-1-59904-808-6.ch001

Ke, F., & Abras, T. (2013). Games for engaged learning of middle school children with special learning needs. *British Journal of Educational Technology, 44*(2), 225–242. doi:10.1111/j.1467-8535.2012.01326.x

Ke, F., & Grabowski, B. (2007). Gameplaying for maths learning: Cooperative or not? *British Journal of Educational Technology, 38*(2), 249–259. doi:10.1111/j.1467-8535.2006.00593.x

Keirsey, D. (1998). *Please Understand Me II: Temperament, Character, Intelligence*. San Diego, CA: Prometheus Nemesis Book Company.

Keller, J. M. (2008). First principles of motivation to learn and e3-learning. *Distance Education, 29*(2), 175–185. doi:10.1080/01587910802154970

Keller, M. (2013). Social media and interpersonal communication. *Social Work Today, 13*(3), 10.

Kellough, R. D., & Kellough, N. G. (1999). Middle school teaching: A guide to methods and resources. Saddle River, NJ: Merrill.

Kelly, G. J., & Takao, A. (2002). Epistemic levels in argument: An analysis of university oceanography students' use of evidence in writing. *Science Education, 86*(3), 314–342. doi:10.1002/sce.10024

Kelly, H. (2005, Summer). Games, cookies, and the future of education. *Issues in Science and Technology*, 33–40.

Kena, G., Aud, S., Johnson, F., Wang, X., Zhang, J., Rathbun, A., . . . Kristapovich, P. (2014). The condition of education 2014 (NCES 2014-083). Washington, DC. Retrieved from http://nces.ed.gov/pubsearch

Kenny, R. F., & McDaniel, R. (2011). The role teachers' expectations and value assessments of video games play in their adopting and integrating them into their classrooms. *British Journal of Educational Technology, 42*(2), 197–213. doi:10.1111/j.1467-8535.2009.01007.x

Kenny, R., & Gunter, G. (2011). Factors affecting adoption of video games in the classroom. *Journal of Interactive Learning Research, 22*(2), 259–276.

Kern, R. (2000). *Literacy and Language Teaching*. Oxford: Oxford University Press.

Kerr, W., & Spears, D. (2006). Robotic Simulation of Gases for a Surveillance Task.*Proceedings of the 2005 IEEE/RSJ International Conference on Intelligent Robots and Systems* (pp. 1160-1168).

Kesava Rao, D. S. (2012). New strategies and materials for teaching soft skills to engineering students: The Indian context. *International Proceedings of Economics Development and Research, 30*, 268–270.

Ketelhut, D. J. (2007). The impact of student self-efficacy on scientific inquiry skills: An exploratory investigation in River City, a multi- user virtual environment. *Journal of Science Education and Technology, 16*(1), 99–111. doi:10.1007/s10956-006-9038-y

Ketelhut, D. J., Dede, C., Clarke, J., Nelson, B., & Bowman, C. (2007). Studying situated learning in a multi-user virtual environment. In E. Baker, J. Dickieson, W. Wulfeck, & H. O'Neil (Eds.), *Assessment of problem solving using simulations*. Mahwah, NJ: Lawrence Erlbaum Associates.

Ketelhut, D. J., & Schifter, C. C. (2011). Teachers and game-based learning: Improving understanding of how to increase efficacy of adoption. *Computers & Education, 56*(2), 539–546. doi:10.1016/j.compedu.2010.10.002

Khachatryan, G. A., Romashov, A. V., Khachatryan, A. R., Gaudino, S. J., Khachatryan, J. M., Guarian, K. R., & Yufa, N. V. (2014). Reasoning Mind Genie 2: An Intelligent Tutoring System as a Vehicle for International Transfer of Instructional Methods in Mathematics. *International Journal of Artificial Intelligence in Education, 24*(3), 333–382. doi:10.1007/s40593-014-0019-7

Khatib, F., Cooper, S., Tyka, M. D., Xu, K., Makedon, I., & Popovic, Z. et al. (2011). Algorithm discovery by protein folding game players. *Proceedings of the National Academy of Sciences of the United States of America, 108*(47), 18949–18953. doi:10.1073/pnas.1115898108 PMID:22065763

Kickmeier-Rust, M. D., Peirce, N., Conlan, O., Schwarz, D., Verpoorten, D., & Albert, D. (2007). *Immersive digital games: The interfaces for next-generation e-learning? Universal access in human-computer interaction applications and services* (pp. 647–656). Springer. doi:10.1007/978-3-540-73283-9_71

Kiili, K. (2007). *Foundation for problem-based gaming*. British Journal of Educational Technology. Doi: 10.111/j.1467-8535.2007.00704x

Kiili, K., Ketamo, H., Koivisto, A., & Finn, E. (2014). Studying the user experience of a tablet based math game. *International Journal of Game-Based Learning*, *4*(1), 60–77. doi:10.4018/IJGBL.2014010104

Kiili, L. (2005). Digital game-based learning: Towards an experiential gaming model. *The Internet and Higher Education*, *8*(1), 13–24. doi:10.1016/j.iheduc.2004.12.001

Kim, B., Park, H., & Baek, Y. (2009). Not just fun, but serious strategies: Using meta- cognitive strategies in game-based learning. *Computers & Education*, *52*(4), 800–810. doi:10.1016/j.compedu.2008.12.004

Kimmel, D., & Bekris (2012). Maintaining team coherence under the velocity obstacle framework. *Proceedings of the 11th International Conference on Autonomous Agents and Multiagent Systems(AAMAS '12)* (Vol. 1, pp. 247-256).

Kincaid, J. P., Hamilton, R., Tarr, R. W., & Sangani, H. (2003). Simulation in education and training. In M. S. Obaidat & G. I. Papadimitriou (Eds.), Applied system simulation (pp. 437–456). Norwell, MA, USA: Kluwer Academic Publishers. Retrieved from http://dl.acm.org/citation.cfm?id=966015.966034 doi:10.1007/978-1-4419-9218-5_19

King, J., Schneider, J., Kozdras, D., Minick, V., Welsh, J., Brindley, R., & Kirby, A. et al. (2013). The multiple ways technology supports pre-service teacher education: A foray into multimedia literacies. *Journal of Reading Education*, *38*(3), 14–20.

Kirriemuir, J., & Mcfarlane, A. (2004). Literature Review in Games and Learning. Retrieved from http://halshs.archives-ouvertes.fr/hal-00190453/

Kirsh, D. (1995). The intelligent use of space. *Artificial Intelligence*, *73*(1-2), 31–68. doi:10.1016/0004-3702(94)00017-U

Klabbers, J. (1999). Three easy pieces: A taxonomy on gaming. In D. Sounders & J. Severn (Eds.), *Simulation and Gaming Yearbook, Simulation and Games for Strategy and Policy Planning, (Vol. 7,* pp. 16–33). London: Kogan Page.

Klein, F. (1882). *Eric W. Weisstein - MathWorld–A Wolfram Web Resource*. Retrieved from http://mathworld.wolfram.com/KleinBottle.html

Klemmer, S. R., Hartmann, B., & Takayama, L. (2006). How bodies matter: Five themes for interaction design. In J. M. Carroll, S. Bødker, & J. Coughlin (Eds.), *Proceedings of the 6th Conference on Designing Interactive Systems* (pp. 140-149). University Park, PA. ACM. doi:10.1145/1142405.1142429

Klimmt, C. (2003). Dimensions and determinants of the enjoyment of playing digital games: A three-level model. In *Proceedings of the Digital Games Research Conference* (pp. 246-257). Utrecht, The Netherlands: Faculty of Arts, Utrecht University.

Klopfer, E., Osterweil, S., Groff, J., & Haas, J. (2009). Using the technology of today, in the classroom today [White Paper]. *The Education Arcade*, MIT.

Klopfer, E. (2008). *Augmented learning: Research and design of mobile educational games*. USA: MIT Press. doi:10.7551/mitpress/9780262113151.001.0001

Klopfer, E., Osterweil, S., & Salen, K. (2009). *Moving learning games forward*. Cambridge, MA: Education Arcade.

Klopfer, E., Yoon, S., & Perry, J. (2005). Using Palm technology in participatory simulations of complex systems: A new take on ubiquitous and accessible mobile computing. *Journal of Science Education and Technology*, *14*(3), 285–297. doi:10.1007/s10956-005-7194-0

Knuth, R. A., & Cunningham, D. J. (1993). Tools for constructivism. In T. M. Dufffy, J. Lowyck, & D. H. Jonassen (Eds.), *Designing environments for constructive learning* (pp. 163–188). Berlin, Heidelberg: Springer-Verlag. doi:10.1007/978-3-642-78069-1_9

Koerner, B. I. (2012). Popular science. *Wired Magazine*, July 2012, 138-145.

Koh, E., Kin, Y., Wadhwa, B., & Lim, J. (2012). Teacher perceptions of games in Singapore schools. *Simulation & Gaming*, *43*(1), 51–66. doi:10.1177/1046878111401839

Kolb, A. Y., & Kolb, D. A. (2009). The learning way meta-cognitive aspects of experiential learning. *Simulation & Gaming*, *40*(3), 297–327. doi:10.1177/1046878108325713

Kolb, D. A. (1984). *Experiential learning: Experience as the source of learning and development*. Englewood Cliffs, NJ: Prentice Hall.

Kolovou, A., & Heuvel-Panhuizen, M. V. D. (2010). Online game-generated feedback as a way to support early algebraic reasoning. *International Journal of Continuing Engineering Education and Lifelong Learning*, *20*(2), 224–238. doi:10.1504/IJCEELL.2010.036817

Koster, R. (2004). *A Theory of Fun for Game Design* (1st ed.). Phoenix, AZ: Paraglyph Press.

Kotler, P. (1986). The prosumer movement: a new challenge for marketers in NA - advances in consumer research eds. Richard J. Lutz, Provo, UT: *Association for Consumer Research,* (13): 510-513. Retrieved March 12, 2015, from http://acrwebsite.org/volumes/6542/volumes/v13/NA-13

Kozol, J. (1991). *Savage Inequalities: Children in America's Schools*. New York, NY: Random House.

Kozol, J. (2005). *The Shame of the Nation: The Restoration of Apartheid Schooling in America* (pp. 63–64). New York, NY: Random House.

Kriz, W. C. (2003, December). Creating effective learning environments and learning organizations through gaming simulation design. *Simulation & Gaming*, *34*(4), 495–511. doi:10.1177/1046878103258201

Kucklich, J. (2005). Precarious playbour: modders and the digital games industry. *Fibreculture,* 5. Retrieved from http://five.fibreculturejournal.org/fcj-025-precarious-playbour-modders-and-the-digital-games-industry/

Kuhlthau, C., & Maniotes, L. (2010). Building guided inquiry teams for 21st century learners. *School Library Monthly* [serial online], 26(5), 18-21. Retrieved from http://www.schoollibrarymonthly.com/articles/Kuhlthau&Maniotes2010-v26n5p18.html

Kuhn, D., Black, J., Keselman, A., & Kaplan, D. (2000). The development of cognitive skills to support inquiry learning. *Cognition and Instruction*, *18*(4), 495–523. doi:10.1207/S1532690XCI1804_3

Kukulska-Hulme, A., & Shield, L. (2008). An overview of mobile assisted language learning: From content delivery to supported collaboration and interaction. *ReCALL*, *20*(03), 271–289. doi:10.1017/S0958344008000335

Kutner, L., & Olson, C. (2008). *Grand theft childhood: The surprising truth about violent video games and what parents can do*. New York: Simon and Schuster.

Kzero Worldswide. (2014). Virtual world reports. Retrieved from http://www.kzero.co.uk/

Laffey, J., Schmidt, M., & Galyen, K. (2013). Virtual gaming and learning environments as experience-tools for learning through problem solving. In M. Spector, B. Lockee, S. Smaldino, & M. Herring (Eds.), Learning, problem solving, and mindtools: Essays in honor of David H. Jonassen (pp. 105-125). New York, N.Y., Routledge.

Laffey, J., Lin, G. Y., & Lin, Y. (2006). Assessing Social Ability in Online Learning Environments. *Journal of Interactive Learning Research*, *17*(2), 163–177.

Lainema, T. (2003). *Enhancing organizational business process perception: Experiences from constructing and applying a dynamic business simulation game*. [Unpublished doctoral dissertation]. Turku School of Economics and Business Administration, Turku, FIN

Lampe, M., Hinske, S., & Brockmann, S. (2006). *Mobile Device based Interaction Patterns in Augmented Toy Environments*. Paper presented at the Third International Workshop on Pervasive Gaming Applications, PerGames 2006, Dublin, Ireland.

Lanzilotti, R., & Roselli, T. (2007). An experimental evaluation of Logiocando, an intelligent tutoring hypermedia system. *International Journal of Artificial Intelligence in Education*, *17*(1), 41–56.

LaPadula, M. (2003). A comprehensive look at online student support services for distance learners. *American Journal of Distance Education*, *17*(2), 119–128. doi:10.1207/S15389286AJDE1702_4

Latombe, J.-C. (1991). *Robot Motion Planning*. Kluwer Academic Publishers. doi:10.1007/978-1-4615-4022-9

Latour, B. (1987). *Science in action: How to follow scientists and engineers through society*. Harvard University Press.

Laumond, J. (1987). Obstacle growing in a nonpolygonal world. *Information Processing Letters, 25*(1), 41–50. doi:10.1016/0020-0190(87)90091-3

LaValle, S. M. (1998). Rapidly-exploring random trees: A new tool for path planning [Technical report].

LaValle, S. M. (2006). *Planning Algorithms*. Cambridge University Press. doi:10.1017/CBO9780511546877

Lave, J., & Wenger, E. (1991). *Situated learning: Legitimate peripheral participation*. Cambridge, UK: Cambridge University Press. doi:10.1017/CBO9780511815355

Lazzaro, N. (2004). *Why we play games: Four keys to more emotion without story*. Retrieved from http://www.xeodesign.com/whyweplaygames/xeodesign_whyweplaygames.pdf

Lazzaro, N. (2008). Why We Play Games. In Fullerton, T., *Game Design Workshop: A Playcentric Approach to Creating Innovative Games*. (2nd ed.). Burlington, MA: Morgan Kaufmann.

Lazzaro, N. (2007). Why We Play: Affect and the Fun of Games: Designing Emotions for Games, Entertainment Interfaces and Interactive Tools. In A. Sears & J. A. Sears (Eds.), *The Human-Computer Interaction Handbook: Fundamentals, Evolving Techniques, and Emerging Applications* (pp. 679–700). Mahwah, NJ: Lawrence Erlbaum Associates. doi:10.1201/9781410615862.ch34

Lederman, L. C., & Fumitoshi, K. (1995). Debriefing the Debriefing Process: A new look. In D. C. K. Arai (Ed.), *Simulation and gaming across disciplines and cultures*. London: Sage Publications.

Lee, E. A.-L., & Wong, K. W. (2014). Learning with desktop virtual reality: Low spatial ability learners are more positively affected. *Computers & Education, 79*, 49–58. doi:10.1016/j.compedu.2014.07.010

Lee, J. J., & Hammer, J. (2011). Gamification in education: What, how, why bother? *Academic Exchange Quarterly, 15*(2), 146–151.

Lee, K. H., Choi, M. G., Hong, Q., & Lee, J. (2007). Group behavior from video: a data-driven approach to crowd simulation.*Proceedings of the 2007 ACM SIGGRAPH / Eurographics Symposium on Computer Animation (SCA '07)* (pp. 109-118).

Left 4 Dead [Digital Game]. (2008). Redwood City, CA, Kirkland, WA: Electronic Arts, Valve, Certain Affinity.

Lehrer, R., & Schauble, L. (2002). Symbolic communication in mathematics and science: Co-constituting inscription and thought. In E. Amsel & J. Byrnes (Eds.), *The development of symbolic communication*. Mahwah, NJ: Lawrence Erlbaum Associates.

Lehrer, R., & Schauble, L. (2006a). Cultivating model-based reasoning in science education. In R. K. Sawyer (Ed.), *The Cambridge Handbook of the Learning Sciences* (pp. 371–388). Cambridge, England: Cambridge University Press.

Lehrer, R., & Schauble, L. (2006b). In W. Damon, R. M. Lerner, K. A. Renninger, & I. E. Sigel (Eds.), Handbook of Child Psychology: Vol. 4. *Scientific thinking and science literacy: supporting development in learning in contexts* (6th ed.). Hoboken, NJ: John Wiley and Sons.

Lehrer, R., & Schauble, L. (2010). What kind of explanation is a model? In M. K. Stein (Ed.), *Instructional explanations in the disciplines* (pp. 9–22). New York: Springer. doi:10.1007/978-1-4419-0594-9_2

Lenhart, A. (2015). Teens, social media & technology overview 2015. Pew Research Center, April.

Lenhart, A., Kahne, J., Middaugh, E., Evans, C., & Vitak, J. (2008). Teens, video games, and civics.

Lenhart, A., Kahne, J., Middaugh, E., Macgill, A. R., Evans, C., & Vitak, J. (2008). *Teens, Video Games, and Civics: Teens' Gaming Experiences Are Diverse and Include Significant Social Interaction and Civic Engagement*. Pew Internet & American Life Project.

Lens, W. (2001). How to Combine Intrinsic Task-Motivation with the Motivational Effects of the Instrumentality of Present Tasks for Future Goals. In A. Efklides, J. Kuhl, & R. M. Sorrentino (Eds.), *Trends and Prospects in Motivation Research* (pp. 23–36). New York, NY: Kluwer Academic Publishers.

Leonard, D. (2004). Unsettling the military entertainment complex: Video games and a pedagogy of peace. *Studies in Media and Information Literacy Education, 4*(4), 1–8. doi:10.3138/sim.4.4.004

Lerner, A., Chrysanthou, Y., & Lischinski, D. (2007). Crowds by Example. *Computer Graphics Forum, 26*(3), 655-664.

Lesh, R. A., & Doer, H. (2003). Foundations of a models and modeling perspec-tive on mathematics teaching, learning, and problem solving. In H. Doer & R. A. Lesh (Eds.), *Beyond constructivism: Models and modeling perspectives on mathematics teaching, learning, and problem solving*. Mahwah, NJ: Erlbaum.

Leu, D. J., Kinzer, C. K., Coiro, J. L., & Cammack, D. W. (2004). Toward a theory of new literacies emerging from the Internet and other information and communication technologies. *Theoretical models and processes of reading, 5*(1), 1570-1613.

Likhachev, M., Gordon, G., & Thrun, S. (2004). ARA*: Anytime A* with Provable Bounds on Sub-Optimality.Advances in Neural Information Processing Systems16*Proceedings of the 2003 Conference (NIPS-03)*. MIT Press.

Limniou, M., Roberts, D., & Papadopoulos, N. (2008). Full immersive virtual environment CAVE^{TM} in chemistry education. *Computers & Education, 51*(2), 584–593. doi:10.1016/j.compedu.2007.06.014

Lin, C.-H., Liu, E. Z.-F., Chen, Y.-L., Liou, P.-Y., Chang, M., Wu, C.-H., & Yuan, S.-M. (2013). Game-based remedial instruction in mastery learning for upper-primary school students. *Journal of Educational Technology & Society, 16*(2), 271–281.

Linehan, C., Lawson, S., & Doughty, M. (2009). Tabletop prototyping of serious games for "soft skills" training. Paper presented at the *2009 Conference in Games and Virtual Worlds for Serious Applications*, Coventry, United Kingdom. doi:10.1109/VS-GAMES.2009.9

Li, Q., Lemieux, C., Vandermeiden, E., & Nathoo, S. (2013). Are you ready to teach secondary mathematics in the 21st Century? A study of Pre-service teachers' digital game design experience. *Journal of Research on Technology in Education, 45*(4), 309–337. doi:10.1080/15391523.2013.10782608

Liu, M., Toprac, P., & Yuen, T. (2009). What factors make a multimedia learning environment engaging: A case study. *Cognitive effects of multimedia learning*, 173-192.

Liu, M., Horton, L., Olmanson, J., & Toprac, P. (2011). A study of learning and motivation in a new media enriched environment for middle school science. *Educational Technology Research and Development, 59*(2), 249–265. doi:10.1007/s11423-011-9192-7

Locke, E. A., & Latham, G. P. (1990). *A theory of goal setting & task performance*. Englewood Cliffs, NJ: Prentice-Hall, Inc.

Lockyer, L., Heathcote, E., & Dawson, S. (2013). Informing pedagogical action: Aligning learning analytics with learning design. *The American Behavioral Scientist, 57*(10), 1439–1459. doi:10.1177/0002764213479367

Logan, F. A., & Gordon, W. C. (1981). *Fundamentals of learning and motivation* (3rd ed.). Dubuque, IA: Brown.

Lombardi, I. (2012). Computer games as a tool for language education. *G|A|M|E. Games as Art, Media, Entertainment,* 1. Retrieved from http://www.gamejournal.it/computer-games- as-a-tool-for-language-education/

Lord, G., & Lomicka, L. (2011). Calling on educators: Paving the way for the future of technology and CALL. In N. Arnold & L. Ducate (Eds.), Present and future promises of CALL: From theory and research to new directions in language teaching (pp. 441-470). CALICO Monograph Series, 5 (2).

Loscos, C., Marchal, D., & Meyer, A. (2003). Intuitive crowd behaviour in dense urban environments using local laws.*Proceedings of the theory and practice of computer graphics*. IEEE Computer Society. doi:10.1109/TPCG.2003.1206939

Lovett, B. J. (2010). Extended time testing accommodations for students with disabilities answers to five fundamental questions. *Review of Educational Research, 80*(4), 611–638. doi:10.3102/0034654310364063

Lowerre, B., & Reddy, D. (1980). The harpy speech understanding system. *Trends of Speech Recognition.*

Lwin, M. O., & Malik, S. (2012). The efficacy of exergames-incorporated physical education lessons in influencing drivers of physical activity: A comparison of children and pre-adolescents. *Psychology of Sport and Exercise*, *13*(6), 756–760. doi:10.1016/j.psychsport.2012.04.013

Lynch, M. (1990). The Externalized Retina: Selection and Mathematization in the Visual Documentation of Objects in the Life Sciences. In M. Lynch & S. Woolgar (Eds.), *Representation in Scientific Practice* (pp. 153–186). Cambridge, MA: MIT Press.

Macedonia, M. (2002). Games, simulation, and the military education dilemma. *Internet and the* University*: 2001 Forum*, 157-167.

Mackey, T. P., & Jacobson, T. E. (2011). Reframing information literacy as a metaliteracy. *College & Research Libraries*, *72*(1), 62–78. doi:10.5860/crl-76r1

Maddux, C., & Johnson, D. (n. d.). The need for a research Focus on the possible causal link between violent behavior and videogames. *Computers in the Schools*, *30*(1/2), 1–3.

Magerkurth, C., Cheok, A. S., Mandryk, R. L., & Nilsen, T. (2005). Pervasive games: Bringing computer entertainment back to the real world. *Computers in Entertainment*, *3*(3), 4–4. doi:10.1145/1077246.1077257

Mahn, H., & John-Steiner, V. (2002). The gift of confidence: A Vygotskian view of emotions. In G. Claxton & G. Wells (Eds.), *Learning for Life in the 21st Century: Socio-Cultural Perspectives of Future Education* (pp. 46–59). Oxford, UK: Blackwell. doi:10.1002/9780470753545.ch4

Makuch, E. (2014, February 26). *Minecraft passes 100 million registered users, 14.3 million sales on PC*. Retrieved from http://www.gamespot.com/articles/minecraft-passes-100-million-registered-users-14-3-million-sales-on-pc/1100-6417972/

Malinowski, B. (1923). The problem of meaning in primitive languages. In C. K. Ogden, & I. A. Richards (Eds.), The Meaning of Meaning. London: Routledge.

Malinowski, B. (1966). Coral gardens and their magic: Vol. II. *The language of magic and gardening*. Bloomington: Indiana University Press.

Malone, T. W. (1980). What makes things fun to learn? Heuristics for designing instructional computer games. Proceedings of the *3rd ACM SIGSMALL symposium and the First SIGPC symposium on small systems* (pp. 162–169). doi:10.1145/800088.802839

Malone, T. W. (1982). Toward a theory of intrinsically motivating instruction. *Cognitive Science*, *4*, 333–369.

Malone, T. W., & Lepper, M. R. (1987). Making Learning Fun: A Taxonomy of Intrinsic Motivations for Learning. In R. E. Snow & M. J. Farr (Eds.), *Aptitute, Learning and Instruction: III. Conative and affective process analyses* (pp. 223–253). Hilsdale, NJ: Erlbaum.

Maloy, R. W., & LaRoche, I. (2010). Student-centered teaching methods in the history classroom: Ideas, issues, and insights for new teachers. *Social Studies Research and Practice, 5*(2), 46-61. Retrieved from http://www.academia.edu/420967/Student-Centered_Teaching_Methods_In_the_History_Classroom_Ideas_Issues_and_Insights_for_New_Teachers

Maltese, A. V., & Tai, R. H. (2011, September01). Pipeline persistence: Examining the association of educational experiences with earned degrees in STEM among U.S. students. *Science Education*, *95*(5), 877–907. doi:10.1002/sce.20441

Malykhina, E. (2013, November 5). 8 apps that turn citizens into scientists. *Scientific American*, Retrieved from http://www.scientificamerican.com/article/8-apps-that-turn-citizens-into-scientists/

Mandler, J. M. (1984). *Stories, Scripts, and Scenes: Aspects of Schema Theory*. Hillsdale, NJ: Lawrence Erlbaum Associates.

Manning, M. L. (2002). Revisiting developmentally appropriate middle level schools. *Childhood Education*, *78*(4), 225–227. doi:10.1080/00094056.2002.10522187

Mäntylä, T. (2014). Nimenehdotuskilpailut netissä. Retrieved from http://tomibgt.wordpress.com/2014/02/04/nimenehdotuskilpailut-netissa/

Mäntylä, T., Lahti, I., Ketamo, H., Luimula, M., & Smed, J. (2014). Designing reality guides. Proceedings of the *Sixth International Conference on Virtual Worlds and Games for Serious Applications, VS-Games* (pp. 69–76).

Manusos, D. O., Busby, J. R., & Clark, A. C. (2013). Authentic design in gaming: Changing the rules of play. *Technology and Engineering Teacher*, *72*(8), 8–13.

Marczewski, A. (2013). *Gamification: A Simple Introduction*. Andrzej Marczewski.

Margaryan, A., Littlejohn, A., & Vojt, G. (2011). Are digital natives a myth or reality? University students' use of digital technologies. *Computers & Education*, *56*(2), 429–440. doi:10.1016/j.compedu.2010.09.004

Marino, M. T., Basham, J. D., & Beecher, C. C. (2011). Using video games as an alternative science assessment for students with disabilities and at-risk learners. *Science Scope*, (5). Retrieved from https://login.ezproxy.net.ucf.edu/login?auth=shibb&url=http://search.ebscohost.com/login.aspx?direct=true&db=edsgao&AN=edsgcl.246179588&site=eds-live&scope=site

Marino, M. T., Becht, K., Vasquez, E., Gallup, J. L., Basham, J. D., & Gallegos, B. (2014). Enhancing secondary science content accessibility with video games. *Teaching Exceptional Children*, *47*(1), 27–34. doi:10.1177/0040059914542762

Marino, M. T., & Beecher, C. C. (2010). Conceptualizing RTI in 21st-century secondary science classrooms: Video games' potential to provide tiered support and progress monitoring for students with learning Disabilities. *Learning Disability Quarterly*, *33*(4), 299–311.

Marino, M. T., Black, A. C., Hayes, M. T., & Beecher, C. C. (2010). An analysis of factors that affect struggling readers' achievement during a technology-enhanced STEM astronomy curriculum. *Journal of Special Education Technology*, *25*(3), 35–47.

Marino, M. T., & Hayes, M. T. (2012). Promoting inclusive education, civic scientific literacy, and global citizenship with videogames. *Cultural Studies of Science Education*, *7*(4), 945–954. doi:10.1007/s11422-012-9429-8

Marino, M. T., Israel, M., Beecher, C. C., & Basham, J. D. (2013). Students' and teachers' perceptions of using video games to enhance science instruction. *Journal of Science Education and Technology*, *22*(5), 667–680. doi:10.1007/s10956-012-9421-9

Martinez-Garza, M., & Clark, D. B. (2013). Teachers and Teaching in Game-Based Learning Theory and Practice. In M. Khine & I. Saleh (Eds.), *Approaches and Strategies in Next Generation Science Learning* (pp. 147–163). Hershey, PA: IGI Global; doi:10.4018/978-1-4666-2809-0.ch008

Martin, J. R. (2007). Cohesion and Texture. In D. Tannen, H. E. Hamilton, & D. T. Schiffren (Eds.), *The Handbook of Discourse Analysis* (pp. 35–53). London: Blackwell Publishers.

Marzano, R. J. (2010). The art and science of teaching/using games to enhance student achievement. *Educational Leadership*, *5*(67), 71–72.

Masehian, E., & Amin-Naseri, M. (2004, June). A voronoi diagram-visibility graph-potential field compound algorithm for robot path planning. *Journal of Field Robotics*, *21*(6), 275–300.

Mass Effect [Digital Game]. (2008). Redwood City, CA: Electronic Arts, BioWare.

Mass Effect 2 [Digital Game]. (2010). Redwood City, CA: Electronic Arts, BioWare.

Mastel, K., & Huston, D. (2009). Using video games to teach game design: A gaming collection for libraries. *Computers in Libraries*, *29*(3), 41–44.

Math Blaster! [Digital Game]. (1983). Torrance, CA: Davidson & Associates.

Matthews, P. (2011, December). Can you learn soft skills from e-learning? *Training Journal*, 34-37.

Maturana, H. R., & Varela, F. J. (1992). *The tree of knowledge: The biological roots of human understanding*. Boston, MA: Shambhala.

Mayer, I., Bekebrede, G., Harteveld, C., Warmelink, H., Zhou, Q., van Ruijven, T., & Wenzler, I. et al. (2014). The research and evaluation of serious games: Toward a comprehensive methodology. *British Journal of Educational Technology*, *45*(3), 502–527. doi:10.1111/bjet.12067

Mäyrä, F. (2007). The contextual game experience: On the socio-cultural contexts for meaning in digital play. In *Proceedings of DiGRA* (pp. 810–814).

Mazurek, M. O., Shattuck, P. T., Wagner, M., & Cooper, B. P. (2012). Prevalence and correlates of screen-based media use among youths with autism spectrum disorders. *Journal of Autism and Developmental Disorders*, *42*(8), 1757–1767. doi:10.1007/s10803-011-1413-8 PMID:22160370

Mazzotti, V. L., Test, D. W., & Wood, C. L. (2013). Effects of multimedia goal-setting instruction on students' knowledge of the self-determined learning model of instruction and disruptive behavior. *Journal of Positive Behavior Interventions*, *15*(2), 90–102. doi:10.1177/1098300712440452

McClarty, K., Orr, A., Frey, P., Dolan, R., Vassileva, V., & McVay, A. (2012). A literature review of gaming in education. Pearson Education. Retrieved from http://researchnetwork.pearson.com/wp-content/uploads/Lit_Review_of_Gaming_in_Education.pdf

McCloskey, M. (1983). Intuitive Physics. *Scientific American*, *248*(4), 122–130. doi:10.1038/scientificamerican0483-122 PMID:6227681

McCormick, M. J., Burton, T., & Werts, N. (2010). Case scenarios and simulations as techniques to facilitate asthma education and team building among health care students. *Journal of Asthma & Allergy Educators*, *1*(1), 18–22. doi:10.1177/2150129709355459

McCrae, R. R., & John, O. P. (1992). An introduction to the five-factor model and its applications. *Journal of Personality*, *60*(2), 175–215. doi:10.1111/j.1467-6494.1992.tb00970.x PMID:1635039

McGonigal, J. (2003). A real little game: The performance of belief in pervasive play.*Proceedings of DiGRA 2003.*

McGonigal, J. (2011). *Reality is broken: Why Games Make Us Better and How They Can Change the World.* London: The Penguin Press HC.

McGonigal, J. (2011). *Reality is broken: Why games make us better and how they can change the world.* New York, NY: Random House.

McGonigal, J. (2011). *Reality is Broken: Why Games Make Us Better and How They Can Change the World.* New York: Penguin Press.

McGonigal, J. (2011). *Reality Is Broken: Why Games Make Us Better and How They Can Change The World.* New York: Penguin Press.

McGregor, G. (2008). Terra ludus, terra paidia, terra prefab: spatialization of play in videogames & virtual worlds.*Proceedings of the 5th Australasian Conference on Interactive Entertainment* (pp. 31-38), New York, NY: ACM Press. doi:10.1145/1514402.1514407

Mclaughlan, R., & Kirkpatrick, D. (2005, April). *Online text-based roleplay-simulation: The challenges ahead.* Paper presented at the Simulation Industry Association of Australia (SIAA), Sydney, Australia. Retrieved from http://hdl.handle.net/10453/7195

McLean, L., & Griffiths, M. D. (2013). The psychological effects of video games on young people. *Aloma: Revista de Psicologia, Ciències de l'Educació I de l'Esport, 31*(1). Retrieved from http://revistaaloma.net/index.php/aloma/article/view/184

McLeod, S. A. (2010). Sensorimotor Stage. Retrieved from http://www.simplypsychology.org/sensorimotor.html

McLeod, S. A. (2012). Bruner. Retrieved from http://www.simplypsychology.org/bruner.html

McLoughlin, C., & Lee, M. (2007). Social software and participatory learning: Pedagogical choices with technology affordances in the Web 2.0 era. Proceedings of ICT: Providing choices for learners and learning Ascilite Singapore 2007.

McLuhan, M. (1964). *Understanding Media: The Extensions of Man.* New York, NY: McGraw Hill. 'Merriam Webster. Encyclopedia Britannica Company. Retrieved from http://www.merriam-webster.com/dictionary/augmented%20reality

McMahan, A. (2003). Immersion, engagement and presence. In M. J. P. Wolf & B. Perron (Eds.), *The video game theory reader* (pp. 67–86). New York, NY: Routledge.

McMahan, A. (2003). Immersion, Engagement, and Presence: A Method for Analyzing 3-D Video Games. In M. J. P. Wolf & B. Perron (Eds.), *The video game theory reader* (pp. 67–86). New York: Routledge.

McManus, C., Ebby-Rosin, R., & Kurshan, B. (2014). Opportunities, obstacles and outcomes in educational gaming: Teaching to the common core, 21st century skills and beyond. *Philadelphia Social Innovation Journal*, *17*, 1–11.

McNamara, D., Graesser, A., McCarthy, P., & Cai, Z. (Eds.). (2014). *Automated Evaluation of Text and Discourse with Coh-Metrix*. New York: Cambridge University Press. doi:10.1017/CBO9780511894664

McNeill, K. L., & Krajcik, J. (2007). Middle school students' use of appropriate and inappropriate evidence in writing scientific explanations. *Thinking with data,* 233-265. In M. C. Lovett & P. Shah (Eds.), *Thinking with data*: The Proceedings of the 33rd Carnegie Symposium on Cognition. Mahwah, NJ. Erlbaum.

McNeill, K. L., Lizotte, D. J., Krajcik, J., & Marx, R. W. (2006). Supporting students' construction of scientific explanations by fading scaffolds in instructional materials. *Journal of the Learning Sciences*, *15*(2), 153–191. doi:10.1207/s15327809jls1502_1

Mechling, L. C., & Bishop, V. A. (2011). Assessment of computer-based preferences of students with profound multiple disabilities. *The Journal of Special Education*, *45*(1), 15–27. doi:10.1177/0022466909348661

Mega Man [Digital Game]. (1990). Osaka, Japan: Hi Tech Expressions, Capcom.

Menary, R. (2010). *The extended mind*. Cambridge, MA: MIT Press. doi:10.7551/mitpress/9780262014038.001.0001

Merriam Webster. (2015). Online dictionary. Retrieved from http://www.merriam-webster.com/dictionary/gamification

Merriam, S. B. (2009). *Qualitative research: A guide to design and implementation*. San Francisco: Jossey-Bass.

Merriam-Webster, Inc. (2014a). Game. Merriam-Webster Online Dictionary. Retrieved from http://www.merriam-webster.com/dictionary/game

Merriam-Webster, Inc. (2014b). Augmented Reality. Merriam-Webster, Incorporated. Retrieved from http://www.merriam-webster.com/dictionary/augmented%20reality

Merriam-Webster. (n.d.). *Docendo discimus*. Retrieved from http://www.merriam-webster.com/dictionary/docendodiscimus

Merrill, M. D. (2002). First principles of instruction. *Educational Technology Research and Development*, *50*(3), 43–59. doi:10.1007/BF02505024

Messinger-Willman, J., & Marino, M. T. (2010). Universal Design for Learning and assistive technology: Leadership considerations for promoting inclusive education in today's secondary schools. *NASSP Bulletin*, *94*(1), 5–16. doi:10.1177/0192636510371977

Metcalf, S. J., Clarke, J., & Dede, C. (2009). Virtual worlds for education: River City and EcoMUVE. Proceedings of *MiT6 International Conference,* 1-6.

Metz, R. (2013). *Leap Motion's Struggles Reveal Problems with 3-D Interfaces*. Retrieved from http://www.technologyreview.com/news/518721/leap-motions-struggles-reveal-problems-with-3-d-interfaces/

Meyer, D. K., & Turner, J. C. (2006). Re-conceptualizing Emotion and Motivation to Learn in Classroom Contexts. *Educational Psychology Review*, *18*(4), 377–390. doi:10.1007/s10648-006-9032-1

Michael, D., & Chen, S. (2005, October). Proof of learning: assessment in serious games. Retrieved from http://www.gamasutra.com/view/feature/130843/proof_of_learning_assessment_in_.php

Millar, D., Patel, R., & Hornsby, A. J. (2011, November). Solving preadolescent anti socialism through play. *Proceedings of the 7th Australasian Conference on Interactive Entertainment* (p. 13). Interactive Entertainment.

Miller, L. (2015). Role-play games as a tool for STEM career inspiration and the development of scientific possible selves. In T. Bastiaens & G. Marks (Eds.), *Proceedings of Global Learn 2015* (pp. 385-389). Waynesville, NC: Association for the Advancement of Computing in Education (AACE). Retrieved From http://www.editlib.org/p/150883/proceeding_150883.pdf

Miller, L., Chaika, M., & Groppe, L. (1996). Girls' preferences in software design: Insights from a focus group. *Technology and Electronic Journal of the 21st Century,* *4*(2), 1-6.

Millstone, J., & Levy, A. (2012) *What do teachers really think about using video games in the classroom?* Paper presented at the 9th Annual Games for Change Summit, New York.

Minecraft. (2009). Mojang.

Mitgutsch, K. (2008). Digital Play-Based Learning. A philosophical-pedagogical perspective on learning and playing in computer games. *Journal for Information Technology Studies as Human Science*, *9*(3), 18–36.

Möbius, F., & Listing (independently), J. B. (1858). *Eric W. Weisstein - MathWorld–A Wolfram Web Resource.* Retrieved from http://mathworld.wolfram.com/MoebiusStrip.html

Mokros, J. R., & Tinker, R. F. (1987). The impact of microcomputer-based labs on children's ability to interpret graphs. *Journal of Research in Science Teaching*, *24*(4), 369–383. doi:10.1002/tea.3660240408

Molka-Danielsen, J., & Deutchmann, M. (2009). *Learning and teaching in the virtual world of Second Life.* Trondheim: Tapir Academy Press.

Moll, L. (1990). *Vygotsky and education: Instructional implications and applications of sociohistorical psychology*. Cambridge, UK: Cambridge University Press. doi:10.1017/CBO9781139173674

Moll, L. C., Tapia, J., & Whitmore, K. F. (1993). Living knowledge: The social distribution of cultural resources for thinking. In G. Salomon (Ed.), *Distributed cognitions: Psychological and educational considerations* (pp. 139–163). NY: Cambridge University Press.

Mononen, M. (2009). *recastnavigation.* Retrieved from https://github.com/memononen/recastnavigation

Monument Valley. (2014). Ustwo.

Moreno-Ger, P., Burgos, D., Martinez-Ortiz, I., Sierra, J., & Fernández-Manjón, B. (2008). Educational game design for online education. *Computers in Human Behavior*, *24*(6), 2530–2540. doi:10.1016/j.chb.2008.03.012

Morgan, G., & Adams, J. (2009). Pedagogy first: Making web-technologies work for soft skills development in leadership and management education. *Journal of Interactive Learning Research*, *20*(2), 129–155.

Morris, B., Croker, S., Zimmerman, C., Gill, D., & Romig, C. (2013). Gaming science: The "Gamification" of scientific thinking. *Frontiers in Psychology*, *4*, 607. doi:10.3389/fpsyg.2013.00607 PMID:24058354

Morrison, D., & Collins, A. (1995). Epistemic fluency and constructivist learning environments. *Educational Technology*, *35*(5), 39–45.

Moussaïd, M., Perozo, N., Garnier, S., Helbing, D., & Theraulaz, G. (2010). The walking behavior of pedestrian social groups and its impact on crowd dynamics. *PLoS ONE*, *5*(4), e10047. doi:10.1371/journal.pone.0010047 PMID:20383280

Muehrer, R., Jenson, J., Friedberg, J., & Husain, N. (2012). Challenges and opportunities: Using a science-based video game in secondary school settings. *Cultural Studies of Science Education*, *7*(4), 783–805. doi:10.1007/s11422-012-9409-z

Munz, U., Schumm, P., Wiesebrock, A., & Allgower, F. (2007). Motivation and learning progress through educational games. Industrial Electronics. *IEEE Transactions on*, *54*(6), 3141–3144. doi: 10.1109/TIE.2007.907030

Murphy, P. K., & Alexander, P. A. (2000). A motivated exploration of motivation terminology. *Contemporary Educational Psychology*, *25*(1), 3–53. doi:10.1006/ceps.1999.1019 PMID:10620380

Murray, B., Bogost, I., Mateas, M., & Nitsche, M. (2006). Game design education: Integrating computation and culture. *Computer*, *39*(6), 43–51. doi:10.1109/MC.2006.195

Murray, J. (1997). *Hamlet on the Holodeck: The Future of Narrative in Cyberspace*. Cambridge, MA: The MIT Press.

Murray, J. (2012). *Inventing the Medium: Principles of Interaction Design as a Cultural Practice.* Cambridge, MA: The MIT Press.

Musse, & Thalmann. (1997, September 2–3). A model of human crowd behavior: Group inter-relationship and collision detection analysis. *Computer Animation and Simulation 97, Proceedings of the Eurographics Workshop in Budapest, Hungary* (pp. 36-51). Vienna: Springer.

Myers, I. B., & Myers, P. B. (1980). *Gifts Differing: Understanding Personality Type.* Palo Alto, CA: Davies-Black Publishing.

Nacke, L. E., Bateman, C., & Mandryk, R. L. (2011). BrainHex: preliminary results from a neurobiological gamer typology survey. In Entertainment Computing–ICEC 2011 (pp. 288-293). Springer Berlin Heidelberg. doi:10.1007/978-3-642-24500-8_31

Nacke, L., Drachen, A., Kuikkaniemi, K., Niesenhaus, J., Korhonen, H. J., & van den Hoogen, W. M. (2009). Playability and Player Experience Research.*Proceedings of DiGRA 2009: Breaking New Ground: Innovation in Games, Play, Practice and Theory*. London, UK: DiGRA.

Nagler, W., & Ebner, M. (2009). Is Your University Ready For the Ne(x)t-Generation? Proceedings of the World Conference on Educational Multimedia, Hypermedia and Telecommunications 2009, Chesapeake, VA (pp. 4344 – 4351). AACE.

Nakamura, M., Kitajima, Y., Ota, J., Ogata, T., Huang, Z., Nagata, A., . . . Kanai-Pak, M. (2013). The relationship between nursing students' attitudes towards learning and effects of self-learning system using Kinect. In V.G. Duffy (Ed.), *4th international conference on digital human modeling and applications in health, safety, ergonomics, and risk management, part II: Human body modeling and ergonomics*. (Vol. LNCS 8026, pp. 111-116). Berlin, Germany: Springer.

Nash. (2012). *Any-Angle Path Planning* [PhD thesis]. University of Southern California.

Nash, P., & Shaffer, D. W. (2011). Mentor modeling: The internalization of modeled professional thinking in an epistemic game. *Journal of Computer Assisted Learning*, *27*(2), 173–189. doi:10.1111/j.1365-2729.2010.00385.x

National Center for Education Statistics. (2013). The Condition of Education 2013. U.S. Department of Education. Institute of Education Sciences. Retrieved from http://nces.ed.gov/pubs2013/2013037.pdf

National Research Council. (2003). *Engaging Schools: Fostering High School Students' Motivation to Learn*. Washington, DC: The National Academies Press.

National Research Council. (2011). M.A. Honey, & M.L. Hilton (Eds.), *Learning Science Through Computer Games and Simulations. Committee on Science Learning: Computer Games, Simulations, and Education*. Board on Science Education, Division of Behavioral and Social Sciences and Education. Washington, DC: National Academies Press. Retrieved from http://www.nap.edu/catalog/13078.html

Nealy, C. (2005). Integrating soft skills through active learning in the management classroom. *Journal of College Teaching and Learning*, *2*(4), 1–6.

Neely, J., Bowers, K. W., & Ragas, M. W. (2010). Virtual possibilities: A constructivist examination of the educational applications of Second Life. *Journal of Interactive Learning Research*, *21*(1), 93–110.

Nelson, B., Ketelhut, D. J., Clarke, J., Dieterle, E., Dede, C., & Erlandson, B. (in press). Robust design strategies for scaling educational innovations: The River City MUVE case study. In B. E. Shelton & D. A. Wiley (Eds.), *The educational design and use of computer simulation games*. Rotterdam, The Netherlands: Sense Press.

Nelson, D. L., & Blenkin, C. (2007). The power of online role-play simulations: Technology in nursing education. *International Journal of Nursing Education Scholarship*, *4*(1), 1–14. doi:10.2202/1548-923X.1263 PMID:17402925

Nersessian, N. J. (2002). The cognitive basis of model-based reasoning in science. In P. Carruthers, S. Stich, & M. Siegal (Eds.), *The cognitive basis of science* (pp. 133–155). Cambridge: Cambridge University Press. doi:10.1017/CBO9780511613517.008

New Media Consortium. (2010). 2010 Horizons Report: The K-12 Edition. *New Media Consortium*. Retrieved from http://wp.nmc.org/horizon-k12-2010/

Newland, L. A., Roggman, L. A., & Boyce, L. K. (2001). The development of social toy play and language in infancy. *Infant Behavior and Development*, *24*(1), 1–25. doi:10.1016/S0163-6383(01)00067-4

Newman, J. (2002b). The myth of the ergodic videogame. *Game studies*, *2*(1), 1-17.

Newman, J. A. (1998) *Gameworlds: Videogames, space and experience. Critically examining a player's perspective* [Unpublished doctoral dissertation]. Lancaster University (Edge Hill College), Lancashire, UK.

Newman, J. (2002a). In search of the videogame player: The lives of Mario. *New Media & Society*, *4*(3), 405–422. doi:10.1177/146144480200400305

Newton, P., Driver, R., & Osborne, J. (1999). The place of argumentation in the pedagogy of school science. *International Journal of Science Education*, *21*(5), 553–576. doi:10.1080/095006999290570

Ng, F., Zeng, H., & Plass, J. (2009) Research on Educational Impact of Games: A Literature Review. (Report No. 02/2009) New York, NY: Institute for Games for Learning, NYU/CUNY.

NGSS Lead States. (2013). *Next Generation Science Standards: For States, By States*. Washington, DC: The National Academies Press.

Nicholls, J. G. (1984). Achievement motivation: Conceptions of ability, subjective experience, task choice, and performance. *Psychological Review*, *91*(3), 328–346. doi:10.1037/0033-295X.91.3.328

Nijhar, J., Bianchi-Berthouze, N., & Boguslawski, G. (2012). Does movement recognition precision affect the player experience in exertion games? In A. Nijholt, H. Hondorp, & D. Reidsma (Eds.), *Intelligent technologies for interactive entertainment*(Vol. 9, pp. 73–82). Berlin, Germany: Springer. doi:10.1007/978-3-642-30214-5_9

Noë, A. (2004). *Action in Perception*. Cambridge, MA: The MIT Press.

Noormohammadi, S. (2012). Essential human qualities in strengthening place identity as expressed in Louis Kahn's architectural theory. In H. Casakin, & F. Bernardo (Eds), The Role of Place Identity in the Perception, Understanding and Design of Built Environments. Bentham eBooks. eISBN: 978-60805-413-8, 22-35.

Norbert-Schulz. (1971). *Existence, space and architecture*. New York, NY: Praeger Publishing.

Nørgård, R. T. (2011). The joy of doing: The corporeal connection in player-avatar identity. Paper presented at *Philosophy of Computer Games Conference*, Athens, Greece. Retrieved from https://gameconference2011.files.wordpress.com/2010/10/thejoy1.pdf

Norman, G., & Schidt, H. (1992). The psychological basis of problem-based learning: A review of the evidence. *National Institutes of Health*, 67(9), 557-65. Retrieved from http://www.ncbi.nlm.nih.gov/pubmed/1520409

Norman, D. A. (1993). *Things that make us smart: Defending human attributes in the age of the machine*. Reading, MA: Addison-Wesley Pub. Co.

Norton, B. (2000). *Identity and language learning: Gender, ethnicity and educational change*. Harlow, England: Longman/Pearson Education Limited.

Norton, B. (2010). Language and Identity. In N. Hornberger & S. McKay (Eds.), *Sociolinguistics and language education* (pp. 349–369). Bristol: Multilingual Matters.

Novak, J. (2012). *Game Development Essentials. An Introduction* (3rd ed.). New York: Cengage.

NRC. (2011). *A framework for K-12 science education: Practices, crosscutting concepts, and core ideas*. Washington, DC: National Academies Press.

O'Rourke, J., Main, S., & Ellis, M. (2013). "It doesn't seem like work, it seems like good fun:" Perceptions of primary students on the use of handheld game consoles in mathematics classes. *Technology, Pedagogy and Education*, *22*(1), 103–120. doi:10.1080/1475939X.2012.733537

O'Shea, P. & Elliott, J. (in press). Augmented reality in education: An exploration and analysis of currently available educational apps. *Research Highlights in Technology and Teacher Education* a publication of the Society for Information Technology and Teacher Education.

O'Shea, P., & Folkestad, J. (2010). *Evaluation of the augmented reality project at the School in the Park* [Unpublished Manuscript].

O'Shea, P., Mitchell, R., Johnston, C., & Dede, C. (2009). Lessons learned about designing augmented realities. *The International Journal of Games and Computer Mediated Simulations*, *1*(1).

Oblinger, D. D., & Oblinger, J. L. (Eds.). (2005). *Educating the Net Generation.* Retrieved from http://www.educause.edu/educatingthenetgen

Oblinger, D. (2004). The next generation of educational engagement. *Journal of Interactive Media in Education,* (8): 1–18.

Ochs, E., & Schieffelin, B. B. (1984). Language acquisition and socialization: Three developmental stories and their implications. In R. A. Shweder & R. A. Levine (Eds.), *Culture theory: Essays on mind, self, and emotion.* Cambridge: Cambridge University Press.

Odenwald, S. (n. d.) What is the speed of the Earth's rotation? Retrieved from http://image.gsfc.nasa.gov/poetry/ask/a10840.html

Odum, M., McKyer, E. L. J., Tisone, C. A., & Outley, C. W. (2013). Elementary school personnel's perceptions on childhood obesity: Pervasiveness and facilitating factors. *The Journal of School Health, 83*(3), 206–212. doi:10.1111/josh.12016 PMID:23343321

Office of Disability Employment Policy, U.S. Department of Labor. (2010, June). *Teaching soft skills through workplace simulations in classroom settings.*

Oliver, J. S. (2007). Rural science education. In S. K. Abell & N. G. Lederman (Eds.), Handbook of Research on Science Education (pp. 345-369). Mahwah, NJ: Lawrence Erlbaum Associates.

Oliveri, M. E., & Khan, S. (2014). Further thoughts on "How task features impact evidence from assessments embedded in simulations and games.". *Measurement: Interdisciplinary Research and Perspectives, 12*(1-2), 51–53. doi:10.1080/15366367.2014.921034

Olson, C. K. (2010). Children's motivations for video game play in the context of normal development. *Review of General Psychology, 14*(2), 180–187. doi:10.1037/a0018984

Ondřey, J., Pettré, J., Olivier, A.-H., & Donikian, S. (2010). A Synthetic-Vision Based Steering Approach for Crowd Simulation. *ACM Transactions on Graphics, 29*(4).

Opaschowski, H. W. (1999). *Generation @, Die Medienrevolution entlßt ihre Kinder: Leben im Informationszeitalter.* Hamburg, Ostfildern: Kurt Mair Verlag.

Operation: Resilient Planet [Digital Game]. (2008). Madison, WI: Filament Games.

Osborne, J., Henderson, B., MacPherson, A., & Szu, E. (2013). *Building a learning progression for argument in science.* Paper presented at the annual conference of the American Educational Research Association Conference, San Francisco, CA.

Osborne, J., Henderson, B., MacPherson, A., Wild, A., & Friend, M. (2014). *IRT analysis of items probing a unidimensional learning progression for argumentation of increasingly complex structure.* Paper presented at the annual conference of the National Association for Research in Science Teaching, Pittsburgh, PA.

Osborne, J. F., & Patterson, A. (2011). Scientific argument and explanation: A necessary distinction? *Science Education, 95*(4), 627–638. doi:10.1002/sce.20438

Oshima, J., Bereiter, C., & Scardamalia, M. (1995). Information-Access Characteristics for High Conceptual Progress in a Computer-Networked Learning Environment. Proceedings of CSCL'95 conference.

Oswald, C. A., Prorock, C., & Murphy, S. M. (2014). The perceived meaning of the video game experience: An exploratory study. *Psychology of Popular Media Culture, 3*(2), 110–126. doi:10.1037/a0033828

Owen, A. M., Hampshire, A., Grahn, J. A., Stenton, R., Dajani, S., & Burns, A. S. et al. (2010). Putting brain training to the test. *Nature, 465*(7299), 775–778. doi:10.1038/nature09042 PMID:20407435

Packman, J. (2002). *Group activity therapy with learning disabled preadolescents exhibiting behavior problems* [Doctoral dissertation]. University of North Texas.

Pac-Man. (1980). Namco. Japan.

Pai, A. (2011). Gamifying the Classroom. (Video.) Gamification Summit NYC 2011. Gamification Co. Retrieved from fora.tv/2011/09/16/Ananth_Pai_Gamifying_the_Classroom

Palinscar, A. S., & Brown, A. L. (1984). Reciprocal teaching of comprehension-fostering and comprehension-monitoring activities. *Cognition and Instruction, 1*(2), 117–175. doi:10.1207/s1532690xci0102_1

Papadimitriou, I., Komis, V., Tselios, N., & Avouris, N. (2006, December 8-10). Designing PDA mediated educational ctivities in the frame of a museum visit. IADIS Cognition and Exploratory Learning in Digital Age (CELDA) 2006 Conference, Barcelona, Spain.

Papamitsiou, Z., & Economides, A. (2014). Learning Analytics and Educational Data Mining in Practice: A Systematic Literature Review of Empirical Evidence. *Journal of Educational Technology & Society*, *17*(4), 49.

Papastergiou, M. (2009). Digital Game-Based Learning in high school Computer Science education: Impact on educational effectiveness and student motivation. *Computers & Education*, *52*(1), 1–12. doi:10.1016/j.compedu.2008.06.004

Papert, S. (1980). *Mindstorms: Children, computers, and powerful ideas*. Basic Books, Inc.

Papert, S. (1980). *Mindstorms: Children, Computers, And Powerful Ideas*. New York: Basic Books.

Papert, S. (1993). *The Children's Machine*. New York: BasicBooks.

Park, K. S., Cho, Y., & Kim, D. K. (2014). A Framework for the creating, expressing and sharing of user's emotion. *International Journal of Multimedia and Ubiquitous Engineering*, *9*(1), 425–442. doi:10.14257/ijmue.2014.9.1.39

Park, Q., & Cao. (2012). Modeling social groups in crowds using common ground theory.*Proceedings of the Winter Simulation Conference (WSC '12)* (pp. 1-12). doi:10.1109/WSC.2012.6465119

Parks, N. (2008). Video games as reconstructionist sites of learning in art education. *Studies in Art Education: A Journal of Issues and Research in Art Education*, 49(3), 235-250.

Parsons, S., & Mitchell, P. (2002). The potential of virtual reality in social skills training for people with autistic spectrum disorders. *Journal of Intellectual Disability Research*, *46*(5), 430–443. doi:10.1046/j.1365-2788.2002.00425.x PMID:12031025

Parten, M. B. (1932). Social participation among preschool children. *Journal of Abnormal and Social Psychology*, *27*(3), 243–269. doi:10.1037/h0074524

Pastore, R., & Falvo, D. (2010). Video games in the classroom: Pre-service and in-service teachers' perceptions of games in K-12 classrooms. *International Journal of Instructional Technology and Distance Learning*, *7*(12), 49–57.

Patall, E. A., Cooper, H., & Robinson, J. C. (2008). The effects of choice on intrinsic motivation and related outcomes: A meta-analysis of research findings. *Psychological Bulletin*, *134*(2), 270–300. doi:10.1037/0033-2909.134.2.270 PMID:18298272

Paulsen, G. (2006). *Hatchet*. Simon and Schuster.

Paus, T. (2005). Mapping brain maturation and cognitive development during adolescence. *Trends in Cognitive Sciences*, *9*(2), 60–68. doi:10.1016/j.tics.2004.12.008 PMID:15668098

Pavao, W. (2009). *Constitutional convention: A decision-making activity*. Retrieved from http://ssecamoreperfectunion.com/PDFs/Constitutional_Convention_Lesson_Plan_Web_Version_by_Pavao.pdf

Peake, J. (2010). If we teach today as we taught yesterday, we rob our children of tomorrow. *The Agricultural Education Magazine*, *83*(3), 4.

Pea, R. (1993). Practices of distributed intelligence and designs for education. In G. Salomon (Ed.), *Distributed cognitions: Psychological and educational considerations*. Cambridge, UK: Cambridge University Press.

Pea, R. D. (1985). Beyond amplification: Using the computer to reorganize mental functioning. *Educational Psychologist*, *20*(4), 167–182. doi:10.1207/s15326985ep2004_2

Peirce, N., (2014). Personal correspondence.

Pelechano, N., Allbeck, J. M., & Badler, N. I. (2007). Controlling individual agents in high-density crowd simulation.*Proceedings of the 2007 ACM SIGGRAPH / Eurographics Symposium on Computer Animation (SCA '07)* (pp. 99-108).

Pelletier, C. (2008). Gaming in context: How young people construct their gendered identities in playing and making games. In Y. B. Kafai, C. Heeter, J. Denner, & J. Y. Sun (Eds.), *Beyond Barbie and Mortal Kombat: New Perspectives on Gender and Gaming*. Cambridge, Mass: The MIT Press.

Pentland, A. (2014). *Social Physics: How Good Ideas Spread-The Lessons from a New Science*. New York: Penguin Press.

Perry, R., Hladkyj, S., Pekrun, R., & Pelletier, S. (2001). Academic control and action control in the achievement of college students: A longitudinal field study. *Journal of Educational Psychology*, *93*(4), 776–789. doi:10.1037/0022-0663.93.4.776

Peters, C., & Ennis, C. (2009). Modeling groups of plausivle virtual pedestrians. *IEEE Computer Graphics and Applications*, *29*(4), 54–63. doi:10.1109/MCG.2009.69 PMID:19798863

Peterson, M. (2010). Massively multiplayer online role-playing games as arenas for second language learning. *Computer Assisted Language Learning*, *23*(5), 429–439. doi:10.1080/09588221.2010.520673

Petroski, A. (2012). Games vs. simulations: When simulations may be a better approach. *Training & Development*, *66*(2), 27–29.

Pettré, J., Laumond, J.-P., & Thalmann, D. (2005). A navigation graph for real-time crowd animation and multilayered uneven terrain. *Proccedings of the first international workshop on crowd simulation (V-CROWDS'05).*

Pettré, J., Ondřej, J., Olivier, A.-H., Cretual, A., & Donikian, S. (2009). Experiment-based modeling, simulation and validation of interactions between virtual walkers. *Proceedings of the 2009 ACM SIGGRAPH/Eurographics Symposium on Computer Animation (SCA '09)* (pp. 189-198). doi:10.1145/1599470.1599495

Pew Research Center. (2015). Teens, social media, and technology overview 2015. Retrieved from http://www.pewinternet.org/topics/mobile/

Pfeiffer, J. W., & Jones, J. E. (Eds.). (1974). *"Role nominations" A handbook of structured experiences for human relations training* (Vol. II). San Francisco, CA: Jossey Bass.

Philip, S. (2010, September 23). Geek, Rebooted. *Top Gear*, (Front End), 53–58. Retrieved from http://www.iracing.com/wp-content/uploads/2010/10/Huttu-PDF.pdf

Piaget, J. (1952). *The origins of intelligence in children.* New York, NY: International Universities Press. doi:10.1037/11494-000

Piaget, J. (1954). *The construction of reality in the child.* New York, NY: Basic Books. doi:10.1037/11168-000

Piaget, J. (1962). *Play, dreams and imitation in childhood.* New York: Norton.

Picciano, A. G., & Seaman, J. (2009). K-12 online learning: A 2008 follow-up of the Survey of U.S. School District Administrators. Retrieved from: http://sloanconsortium.org/publications/survey/ k-12online2008.

Pickering, A. (1995). *The Mangle of Practice: Time, Agency, and Science*. Chicago: University of Chicago Press. doi:10.7208/chicago/9780226668253.001.0001

Piecka, D. C. B., Calinger, M., Wood, C., Shia, J., Kudlak, L., & Tabachnick, B. G. (2012, April). *Evaluation of a live high school clinical science education simulation.* Paper presented at the annual meeting of the American Educational Research Association, Vancouver, BC, Canada.

Pimenta, L., Michael, N., Mesquita, R., Pereira, G., & Kumar, V. (2008). Control of Swarms Based on Hydrodynamic Models.*Proceedings of the 2009 IEEE International Conference on Robotics and Automation (ICRA 2009)* (pp. 1948-1953). doi:10.1109/ROBOT.2008.4543492

Pineteh, E. A. (2012). Using virtual interactions to enhance the teaching of communication skills to information technology students. *British Journal of Educational Technology*, *43*(1), 85–96. doi:10.1111/j.1467-8535.2011.01193.x

Pintrich, P. R. (2003). A motivational science perspective on the role of student motivation in learning and teaching contexts. *Journal of Educational Psychology*, *95*(4), 667–686. doi:10.1037/0022-0663.95.4.667

Pintrich, P. R., & Schunk, D. H. (2002). *Motivation in education: Theory, research, and applications* (2nd ed.). Upper Saddle River, NJ: Prentice Hall.

Plass, J., Homer, B. D., Kinzer, C. K., Chang, Y. K., Frye, J., Kaczetow, W., & Perlin, K. et al. (2013). Metrics in Simulations and Games for Learning. In M. Seif El-Nasr, A. Drachen, & A. Canossa (Eds.), *Game Analytics: Maximizing the Value of Player Data* (pp. 694–730). London: Springer-Verlag. doi:10.1007/978-1-4471-4769-5_31

Poels, K., IJsselsteijn, W. A., & de Kort, Y. A. W. (2008). Development of the Kids Game Experience Questionnaire: a self report instrument to assess digital game experiences in children. Poster Presentation for Meaningful Play Conference, Michigan, USA.

Poels, K., de Kort, Y. A. W., & IJsselsteijn, W. A. (2007). It is always a lot of fun! Exploring Dimensions of Digital Game Experience using Focus Group Methodology. *Proceedings of Futureplay 2007* (pp. 83–89). Toronto, Canada: ACM Press.

Pohl, A., Gehlen-Baum, V., & Bry, F. (2011). Introducing Backstage – A digital backchannel for large class lectures. *Interactive Technology and Smart Education*, *8*(3), 186–200. doi:10.1108/17415651111165410

Pohl, I. (1970). Heuristic Search viewed as Path Finding in a Graph. *Artificial Intelligence*, *1*(3), 193–204. doi:10.1016/0004-3702(70)90007-X

Polanyi, M. (2009). The Tacit Dimension (Original ed. 1966). London: Routledge (University of Chicago Press).

Pollock, E., Chandler, P., & Sweller, J. (2002). Assimilating Complex Information. *Learning and Instruction*, *12*(1), 61–86. doi:10.1016/S0959-4752(01)00016-0

Popham, J. (1999). Why standardized tests don't measure educational quality. Retrieved from http://www.ascd.org/publications/educational-leadership

Portal [Digital Game]. (2007). Redwood City, CA: Electronic Arts - Valve, Valve Nuclear Monkey Software.

Portal. (2007). *Valve Corporation*. USA.

Postman, N. (1992). *Technopoly: The surrender of culture to technology*. New York: Vintage Books.

Potter, L. E., Araullo, J., & Carter, L. (2013). *The Leap Motion controller: A view on sign language*. Adelaide, Australia. doi:10.1145/2541016.2541072

Potvin, P., & Hasni, H. (2014). Interest, motivation and attitude towards science and technology at K-12 levels: A systematic review of 12 years of educational research. *Studies in Science Education*, *50*(1), 85–129. doi:10.1080/03057267.2014.881626

Prensky, M. (2001). *Digital game-based learning*. New York: McGraw-Hill.

Prensky, M. (2001). Digital natives, Digital Immigrants. *On the Horizon*, *9*(5), 1–6. doi:10.1108/10748120110424816

Prensky, M. (2005). Computer games and learning: Digital game-based learning. In J. Raessens & J. Goldstein (Eds.), *Handbook of Computer Game Studies* (pp. 97–122). Cambridge, MA: MIT Press.

Pringle, M. K. (1986). *The needs of children: A personal perspective*. London, UK: Hutchinson.

Project Tomorrow. (2008). 21st century students deserve a 21st century education. Retrieved from http://www.tomorrow.org/docs/National%20Findings%20Speak%20Up%202007.pdf

Provost, J. A. (1990). *Work, play, and type: Achieving balance in your life*. Davies-Black Publishing.

Przybylski, A. K., Rigby, C. S., & Ryan, R. M. (2010). A Motivational Model of Video Game Engagement. *Review of General Psychology*, *14*(2), 154–166. doi:10.1037/a0019440

Przybylski, A. K., Ryan, R. M., & Rigby, C. S. (2009). The motivating role of violence in video games. *Personality and Social Psychology Bulletin*, *35*(2), 243–259. doi:10.1177/0146167208327216 PMID:19141627

Pulko, S. H., & Parikh, S. (2003). Teaching 'soft' skills to engineers. *International Journal of Electrical Engineering Education*, *40*(4), 243–254. doi:10.7227/IJEEE.40.4.2

Purushotma, R., Thorne, S. L., & Wheatley, J. (2009). *10 key principles for designing video games for foreign language learning*. Retrieved from http://lingualgames.wordpress.com/article/10-key-principles-for-designing-video-27mkxqba7b13d-2/

Qi, S., & Mitchell, R. E. (2012). Large-scale academic achievement testing of deaf and hard-of-hearing students: Past, present, and future. *Journal of Deaf Studies and Deaf Education*, *17*(1), 1–18. doi:10.1093/deafed/enr028 PMID:21712463

Qiu, & Hu. (2010). Modeling group structures in pedestrian crowd simulation. *Simulation Modelling Practice and Theory*, *18*(2), 190-205.

Quellmalz, E. S., Timms, M. J., Buckley, B. C., Davenport, J., Loveland, M., & Silberglitt, M. D. (2012). 21st century dynamic assessment. In M. C. Mayrath, J. Clarke-Midura, D. H. Robinson, & G. Schraw (Eds.), *Technology-Based assessments for 21st century skills: Theoretical and practical implications from modern research*, Charlotte, NC (pp. 55–89). Information Age Publishing.

Quellmalz, E. S., Timms, M. J., Silberglitt, M. D., & Buckley, B. C. (2012). Science assessments for all: Integrating science simulations into balanced state science assessment systems. *Journal of Research in Science Teaching*, *49*(3), 363–393. doi:10.1002/tea.21005

Quinn, H., Lee, O., & Valdes, G. (2012). *Language demands and opportunities in relation to Next Generation Science Standards for English Language Learners: What teachers need to know. Understanding Language Initiative*. Stanford, CA: Stanford University School of Education.

Rabin, S. (2008). *AI Game Programming Wisdom 4*. Charles River Media.

Radoff, J. (2011). *Game On: Energize Your Business with Social Media Games*. Chichester, UK: John Wiley & Sons.

Radomski, N., & Russell, J. (2010). Integrated case learning: Teaching clinical reasoning. *Advances in Health Sciences Education: Theory and Practice*, *15*(2), 251–264. doi:10.1007/s10459-009-9195-x PMID:19760511

Railroad Tycoon [Digital Game]. (1990). Wilmington, DE: Micropose, Micropose.

Rambusch, J. (2006). The embodied and situated nature of computer game play. In proceedings of the workshop on the cognitive science of games and game play, Vancouver, Canada (pp. 1-8). Retrieved from http://jana-rambusch.net/publications/rambusch-vancouver.pdf

Rambusch, J., & Ziemke, T. (2005). The role of embodiment in situated learning. In B.G. Bara, L. Barsalou, & M. Bucciarelli (Eds.), *Proceedings of the 27th Annual Conference of the Cognitive Science Society* (pp. 1803-1808). Mahwah, NJ: Lawrence Erlbaum.

Rankin, Y., Gold, R., & Gooch, B. (2006). 3D Role-Playing Games as Language Learning Tools. *Eurographics*, *25*(3), 211–225.

Rapp, D. N., & Sengupta, P. (2012). *Models and modeling in science learning. Encyclopedia of the Sciences of Learning* (pp. 2320–2322). New York: Springer.

Rappolt-Schlichtmann, G., Daley, S. G., Lim, S., Lapinski, S., Robinson, K. H., & Johnson, M. (2013). Universal Design for Learning and elementary school science: Exploring the efficacy, use, and perceptions of a web-based science notebook. *Journal of Educational Psychology*, *105*(4), 1210–1225. doi:10.1037/a0033217

Raynor, J. O. (1969). Future orientation and motivation of immediate activity: An elaboration of the theory of achievement motivation. *Psychological Review*, *76*(6), 606–610. doi:10.1037/h0028291

Read, J., & MacFarlane, S. (2000). Measuring Fun – Usability Testing for Children. Computers and Fun 3, York: England.

Reber, A. S. (1993). *Implicit learning and tacit knowledge: An essay on the cognitive unconscious*. Oxford, UK: Oxford University Press.

Redekopp, R. (2013). Teaching digital games in preservice teacher education. *International Journal of Technology and Inclusive Education*, *2*(1), 124–129.

Reeves, A. R. (2011). *Where great teaching begins: Planning for student thinking and learning*. CA: ASCD.

Rehak, B. (2003). Playing at being. In M. Wolf & B. Perron (Eds.), *The Video Game Theory Reader* (pp. 103–127). New York, NY: Routledge.

Reigeluth, C. M. (1979). In search of a better way to organize instruction: The elaboration theory. *Journal of Instructional Development*, *2*(3), 8–15. doi:10.1007/BF02984374

Reigeluth, C., & Schwartz, E. (1989). An instructional theory for the design of computer-based simulations. *Journal of Computer-Based Instruction*, *16*(1), 1–10.

Reiss, S. (2002). Basic Desires that Motivate Our Actions Define Our Persona. *Who Am I*, 16.

Reiter, U., Brunnström, K., De Moor, K., Mohamed-Chaker, L., Pereira, M., Pinheiro, A., You, J., & Zgank, A. (2014). Factors Influencing Quality of Experience. *T-Labs Series in Telecommunication Services*, 55-72.

Relph, E. (2008). sense of place and emerging social and evnironmental challenges. In J. Eyeles, & A. Williams (Eds), Sense of place, health and quality of life (pp. 66-78). Burlington, VT: Ashgate.

Relph, E. (1976). *Place and placelessness*. London, UK: Pion Ltd.

Remillard, J. T. (2005). Examining key concepts in research on teachers' use of mathematics curricula. *Review of Educational Research*, *75*(2), 211–246. doi:10.3102/00346543075002211

Renninger, K. A., Hidi, S., & Krapp, A. (1992). *The role of interest in learning and development*. Hillsdale, NJ: Erlbaum.

Resnick, Levine, & Teasley (1991).

Resnick, L. (1987). Learning in school and out. *Educational Researcher*, *16*, 13–20.

Resnick, L., Levine, J., & Teasley, S. (Eds.), (1991). *Perspectives on socially shared cognition*. Washington, DC: American Psychological Association. doi:10.1037/10096-000

Retter, S., Anderson, C., & Kieran, L. (2013). iPad Use for accelerating gains in reading skills of secondary students with learning disabilities. *Journal of Educational Multimedia and Hypermedia*, *22*(4), 443–463.

Revenge of the Titans [Digital Game]. (2011). New York: Puppygames.

Rey, P.J. (2012). Gamification, playbor, and expoitation. *Cyborgology*. Retrieved from http://thesocietypages.org/cyborgology/2012/10/15/gamification-playbor-exploitation-2/

Reynolds (1999). Steering Behaviors for Autonomous Characters. *Proceedings of the Game Developers Conference 1999* (pp. 763-782).

Reynolds. (2000). Interaction with groups of autonomous characters. *Game Developers Conference 2000* (pp. 449-460).

Reynolds, C. W. (1987). Flocks, herds, and schools: A distributed behavioral model. *Computer Graphics*, *21*(4), 25–34. doi:10.1145/37402.37406

Rice, J. W. (2007). New media resistance: Barriers to implementation of computer video games in the classroom. *Journal of Educational Multimedia and Hypermedia*, *16*(3), 249–261.

Rideout, V. J., Foehr, U. G., & Roberts, D. F. (2011). *Generation M2: Media in the Lives of 8 to 18 year Olds: A Kaiser Family Foundation Study*.

Rieber, L. P. (1996). Seriously considering play: Designing interactive learning environments based on the blending of microworlds, simulations, and games. *Educational Technology Research and Development*, *44*(2), 43–58. doi:10.1007/BF02300540

Riekki, J., Sanchez, I., & Pyykkonen, M. (2012). *NFC-based user interfaces*. Paper presented at the 4th International Workshop Near Field Communication 2012. doi:10.1109/NFC.2012.19

Riekki, J., Cortés, M., Hytönen, M., Sánchez, I., & Korkeamäki, R. L. (2013). *Touching Nametags with NFC Phones: A Playful Approach to Learning to Read Transactions on Edutainment X* (pp. 228–242). Springer.

Rift [Digital Game]. (2011). Redwood Shores, CA: Trion Worlds.

Rigby, S., & Ryan, R. (2011). *Glued to games: How video games draw us in and hold us spellbound*. Santa Barbara, California: Praeger.

Rimon, E., & Koditschek, D. (1992). Exact robot navigation using artificial potential functions. *IEEE Transactions on Robotics and Automation*, *8*(5), 501–518. doi:10.1109/70.163777

Rittel, H., & Webber, M. (1984). Planning problems are wicked problems. In N. Cross (Ed.), Developments in design methodology (pp. 135-144). New York, NY: Wiley Publications.

Rizzo, A., Schutt, S., & Linegar, D. (2012). Imagine that: creating a 'third space' for young people with high functioning autism through the use of technology in a social setting. Paper presented at the proceedings of the 24th Australian Computer-Human Interaction Conference. doi:10.1145/2414536.2414615

Roaten, G. K., & Roaten, D. J. (2012). Adolescent Brain Development: Current Research and the Impact on Secondary School Counseling Programs. *Journal of School Counseling*, *10*(18), 18.

Robbins, P., & Aydede, M. (2009). *The Cambridge handbook of situated cognition*. Cambridge, U.K.: Cambridge University Press.

Robertson, J. (2012). Making games in the classroom: Benefits and gender concerns. *Computers & Education*, *59*(2), 385–398. doi:10.1016/j.compedu.2011.12.020

Robison, W. (2013, August). Stimulation, Not simulation: An alternate approach to history teaching games. *The History Teacher*, *46*(4), 577–588. Retrieved from http://www.societyforhistoryeducation.org/A13Preview.html

Robles, M. (2012). Executive perceptions of the top 10 soft skills needed in today's workplace. *Business Communication Quarterly*, *75*(4), 453–465. doi:10.1177/1080569912460400

Roblyer, M. D. (2006). Virtually successful: Defeating the dropout problem through online school programs. *Phi Delta Kappan*, *88*(1), 31–36. doi:10.1177/003172170608800107

Rocha, M. (2012). Cognitive, embodied or enacted? Contemporary perspectives for HCI and interaction. Retrieved from http://trans-techresearch.net/wp-content/uploads/2010/11/Rocha-01.pdf

Rocksmith [Digital Game]. (2011). Montreuil, France: Ubisoft San Francisco, Ubisoft.

Roeser, R. W., Eccles, J. S., & Sameroff, A. J. (2000). School as a context of early adolescents' academic and social-emotional development: A summary of research findings. *The Elementary School Journal*, *100*(5), 443–471. doi:10.1086/499650

Rogers, E. M. (1995). *Diffusion of innovations* (4th ed.). NY: The Free Press.

Rogers, S. (2014). *Level Up: The Guide to Great Video Game Design* (2nd ed.). Chichester, UK: John Wiley & Sons.

Roschelle, J. M., Pea, R. D., Hoadley, C. M., Gordin, D. N., & Means, B. M. (2000). Changing how and what children learn in school with computer-based technologies. *Children and Computer Technology*, *10*(2), 76–101. PMID:11255710

Roschelle, J., Knudsen, J., & Hegedus, S. (2010). From new technological infrastructures to curricular activity systems: Advanced designs for teaching and learning. In M. J. Jacobson & P. Reimann (Eds.), *Designs for Learning Environments of the Future: International Perspectives from the Learning Sciences* (pp. 233–262). New York: Springer. doi:10.1007/978-0-387-88279-6_9

Rose, D. H. (2000). Universal Design for Learning. *Journal of Special Education Technology*, *15*(1), 67–70.

Rosenman, M., Smith, G., Ding, L., Marchant D., & Maher, M.L. (2005). Multidisciplinary design in virtual worlds. *Proc. 11th CAAD Futures conf. on Learning from the Past – a Foundation for the Future*, Vienna, Austria (pp. 433-442).

Roth, W. M. (2010). Incarnation: Radicalizing the embodiment of mathematics. *For the Learning of Mathematics*, *30*(2), 8–17.

Roth, W. M. (2011). *Geometry as objective science in elementary classrooms. Mathematics in the flesh*. New York, NY: Routledge.

Roth, W. M., & Bowne, G. M. (1995). Knowing and interacting: A study of culture, practices, and resources in a grade 8 open-inquiry science classroom guided by a cognitive apprenticeship metaphor. *Cognition and Instruction*, *13*(1), 73–128. doi:10.1207/s1532690xci1301_3

Roto, V. (2007). User Experience from Product Creation Perspective. In E. Law, A. Vermeeren, M. Hassenzahl, & M. Blythe (Eds.), Towards a UX Manifesto workshop, Lancaster, UK. COST.

Rowe, E., Asbell-Clarke, J., Bardar, E., Kasman, E., & MacEachern, B. (2014, June). *Crossing the Bridge: Connecting Game-Based Implicit Science Learning to the Classroom.* Paper presented at the 10th Annual Meeting of Games+Learning+Society conference, Madison, WI.

Rowland, J. L., & Rimmer, J. H. (2012). Original research: Feasibility of using active video gaming as a means for increasing energy expenditure in three nonambulatory young adults with disabilities. *PM & R, 4*(8), 569–573. doi:10.1016/j.pmrj.2012.03.011 PMID:22698849

Rowlands, M. (2010). *The new science of the mind: From extended mind to embodied phenomenology.* Cambridge, MA: MIT Press. doi:10.7551/mitpress/9780262014557.001.0001

Rowling, J. K. (1999). *The Chamber of Secrets.* New York: Scholastic.

Royle, K., & Colfer, S. (2010). *Computer games and learning – Where next? The breadth and scope of the use of computer games in education. CeDARE.* Walsall, UK: University of Wolverhampton.

Rubin, K. H. (1982). Early play theories revisited: Contributions to contemporary research and theory. In D. J. Pepler & K. H. Rubin (Eds.), *The play of children: Current theory and research.* New York: Karger. doi:10.1159/000407155

Ruggiero, D. (2013). Video games in the classroom: The teacher point of view. Paper presented at the *Games for Learning workshop of the Foundations of Digital Games conference*, Chania, Greece.

Rushton, S., Juola-Rushton, A., & Larkin, E. (2010). Neuroscience, play and early childhood education: Connections, implications and assessment. *Early Childhood Education Journal, 37*(5), 351–361. doi:10.1007/s10643-009-0359-3

Russell, D. (2006). Online professional development for educators: A Case student analysis using cultural historical activity theory. R. Sharma, & S. Mishra (Eds.), Cases on Global e-Learning Practices: Successes and Pitfalls (pp. 108-122). Hershey, PA: Information Science Publishing.

Russell, D. (2009). Group collaboration in an online problem-based university course. In O. Tan (Ed), Creativity and Problem-Based Learning (pp. 173-192). Australia: Cengage Learning.

Russell, D., (2005b, February). Transformation in an Urban School: Using Systemic Analysis to Understand an Innovative Urban Teacher's Implementation of an Online Problem-Based Unit. *International Journal of Instructional Technology & Distance Learning*, 2(2).

Russell, D., Gentzler, P., & Wood, L. (2014). Mobile learning in nursing education: Lessons learned. In R. Huang, & C.N. Kinshuk (Eds.), *The New Development of Technology Enhanced Learning; Concept, Research and Best Practices.* Springer. DOI:http://link.springer.com/book/10.1007/978-3-642-38291-8

Russell, D. (2004a). *The Vashon Education Compact Youth Leadership and Technology Program: Community Renewal.* Presentation at the National Association of Multicultural Education, Kansas City, MO.

Russell, D. (2004b). Paradigm shift: A case study of innovation in an educational setting. *International Journal of Instructional Technology & Distance Learning, 1*(12).

Russell, D. (2005a). Implementing an Innovation cluster in educational settings in order develop constructivist-based learning environments. *Journal of Educational Technology & Society, 8*(2).

Russell, D. (2005b). Transformation in an Urban School: Using Systemic Analysis to Understand an Innovative Urban Teacher's Implementation of an Online Problem-Based Unit. *International Journal of Instructional Technology and Distance Learning, 2*(2), 11–28.

Russell, D. (2005b). Transformation in an urban school: Using systemic analysis to understand an innovative urban teacher's implementation of an online problem-based unit. *International Journal of Instructional Technology & Distance Learning, 2*(2).

Russell, D. (2007). The impact of group Collaboration on an online problem-based university course. In *O. Tan (Ed.), Problem-Based Learning and Creativity.* Singapore: Thomson Publications.

Russell, D., & Schneiderheinze, A. (2005a). Implementing an Innovation Cluster in Educational Settings In Order to Develop Constructivist-Based Learning Environments. *Journal of Educational Technology & Society, 8*(2), 7–15.

Ryan, R. M., & Deci, E. L. (2000). Intrinsic and Extrinsic Motivations: Classic Definitions and New Directions. *Contemporary Educational Psychology, 25*(1), 54–67. doi:10.1006/ceps.1999.1020 PMID:10620381

Sadler, T. D. (2004). Informal reasoning regarding socioscientific issues: A critical review of research. *Journal of Research in Science Teaching*, *41*(5), 513–536. doi:10.1002/tea.20009

Sadler, T. D. (2009). Situated learning in science education: Socio-scientific issues as contexts for practice. *Studies in Science Education*, *45*(1), 1–42. doi:10.1080/03057260802681839

Sadler, T. D., & Donnelly, L. A. (2006). Socioscientific argumentation: The effects of content knowledge and morality. *International Journal of Science Education*, *28*(12), 1463–1488. doi:10.1080/09500690600708717

Sadler, T. D., Romine, W. L., Menon, D., Ferdig, R. E., & Annetta, L. (2015). Learning biology through innovative curricula: A comparison of game- and nongame-based approaches. *Science Education*, *99*(4), 696–720. doi:10.1002/sce.21171

Sadler, T. D., Romine, W. L., Stuart, P. E., & Merle-Johnson, D. (2013). Game-Based curricula in biology classes. Differential effects among varying academic levels. *Journal of Research in Science Teaching*, *50*(4), 479–499. doi:10.1002/tea.21085

Salen, K., & Zimmerman, E. (2004). *Rules of play: Game design fundamentals*. Cambridge, MA: MIT Press.

Salen, K., & Zimmerman, E. (2004). *Rules of play: game design fundamentals*. Cambridge, MA: The MIT Press.

Salomon, G. (1993). No distribution without individuals' cognition: A dynamic interactional view. In G. Salomon (Ed.), *Distributed cognitions: Psychological and educational considerations*. NY: Cambridge University Press.

Salomon, G., Perkins, D. N., & Globerson, T. (1991). Partners in cognition: Extending human intelligence with intelligent technologies. *Educational Researcher*, *20*(3), 2–9. doi:10.3102/0013189X020003002

Salter, A. (2011, September 22). *Games in the classroom (part 2)* [Web log article]. Retrieved from http://chronicle.com/blogs/profhacker/games-in-the-classroom-part-2/36075

Salter, A. (2013, January 28). *Make games in the classroom with Inform 7.* [Web log article]. Retrieved from http://chronicle.com/section/Home/5

Salthouse, T. A. (2009). When does age-related cognitive decline begin? *Neurobiology of Aging*, *30*(4), 507–514. doi:10.1016/j.neurobiolaging.2008.09.023 PMID:19231028

Sandoval, W. A., & Millwood, K. A. (2005). The quality of students' use of evidence in written scientific explanations. *Cognition and Instruction*, *23*(1), 23–55. doi:10.1207/s1532690xci2301_2

Saracho, O. N., & Spodek, B. (1995). Children's play and early childhood education: Insights from history and theory. *Journal of Education*, *177*(3), 129–149.

Sardone, N., & Devlin-Scherer, R. (2010). Teacher candidate responses to Digital games: 21st Century skills development. *Journal of Research on Technology in Education*, *42*(4), 409–425. doi:10.1080/15391523.2010.10782558

Savery, J. R., & Duffy, T. M. (1995). Problem-based learning: An instructional model and its constructivist framework. *Educational Technology*, *35*(5), 31–38.

Savery, J. R., & Duffy, T. M. (1996). Problem based learning: An instructional model and its constructivist framework. *Educational Technology*, *35*(5), 31–38.

Savoldelli, G. L., Naik, V. N., Park, J., Joo, H. S., Chow, R., & Hamstra, S. J. (2006). Value of debriefing during simulated crisis management: Oral versus video-assisted oral feedback. *Anesthesiology*, *105*(2), 279–285. doi:10.1097/00000542-200608000-00010 PMID:16871061

Schaaf, R. (2012). Does digital game-based learning improve student time-on-task behavior and engagement in comparison to alternative instructional strategies? *The Canadian Journal of Action Research*, *13*(1), 50–64.

Schaller, D. T., Goldman, K. H., Spickelmier, G., Allison-Bunnell, S., & Koepfler, J. (2009). Learning in the wild: What Wolfquest taught developers and game players. Museums and the web 2009: Proceedings. Toronto: Archives & Museum Informatics. Retrieved from http://www.archimuse. com/mw2009/papers/schaller/schaller. html

Schank, R.C. (1994). Goal-based scenarios. In R.C.S.E. Langer (Ed.), *Beliefs, reasoning, and decision making: Psycho-logic in honor of Bob Abelson*. Hillsdale, NJ: Lawrence Erlbaum Associates.

Schell, J. (2008). *The Art of Game Design: A Book of Lenses*. Boca Raton, FL: CRC Press.

Schiefele, U., Krapp, A., & Winteler, A. (1992). Interest as a predictor of academic achievement: A meta-analysis of research. In K. A. Renninger, S. Hidi, & A. Krapp (Eds.), *The role of interest in learning and development* (pp. 183–212). Hillsdale, NJ: Erlbaum.

Schifter, C. C. (2008). *Infusing computers into classrooms: Continuous practice improvement*. Hershey, PA: IGI Global. doi:10.4018/978-1-59904-765-2

Schmitz, B., Specht, M., & Klemke, R. (2012). An Analysis of the Educational Potential of Augmented Reality Games for Learning.*Proceedings of the 11th World Conference on Mobile and Contextual Learning 2012* (pp. 140-147).

Schnotz, W., Fries, S., & Horz, H. (2009). Motivational aspects of cognitive load theory. (M. Wosnita, S. Karabenick, A. Efklides, & P. Nenniger, Eds.) Hogrefe & Huber, Contemporary motivation research: from multiple perspectives, 69–96.

Schoenau-Fog, H. (2011). The player engagement process – an exploration of continuation desire in digital games. Proceedings of Think Design Play: Digital Games Research Conference. Utrecht School of the Arts & DiGRA, Utrecht, Netherlands: DiGRA.

Schön, S., Ebner, M., & Kurma, S. (2014, September). The Maker Movement. Implications of new digital gadgets, fabrication tools and spaces for creative learning and teaching. In eLearning Papers Special edition 2014 "Transforming Education through Innovation and Technology" (pp. 86-100).

Schrader, P. G., Zheng, D., & Young, M. (2006). Teachers' perceptions of video games: MMOGs and the future of Pre-service teacher education. *Innovate: Journal of Online Education, 2*(3), 1-10. Retrieved from http://www.slideshare.net/rredekopp/ijtie-the-use-of-games-in-preservice-teacher-education

Schrader, P. G., Zheng, D., & Young, M. (2006). Teachers' perceptions of video games: MMOGs and the future of preservice teacher education. *Innovate: Journal of Online Education, 2*(3), 1–10.

Schuemie, M. J., Van Der Straaten, P., Krijn, M., & Van Der Mast, C. A. (2001). Research on presence in virtual reality: A survey. *Cyberpsychology & Behavior, 4*(2), 183–201. doi:10.1089/109493101300117884 PMID:11710246

Schumacher, D. (1998). *The transition to middle school. ERIC Clearinghouse on Elementary and Early Childhood Education*. University of Illinois.

Schunk, D. H. (1991). Self-efficacy and academic motivation. *Educational Psychologist, 26*(3-4), 207–231. doi:10.1080/00461520.1991.9653133

Schwarz, C. V., Reiser, B. J., Davis, E. A., Kenyon, L., Achér, A., Fortus, D., & Krajcik, J. et al. (2009). Developing a learning progression for scientific modeling: Making scientific modeling accessible and meaningful for learners. *Journal of Research in Science Teaching, 46*(6), 632–654. doi:10.1002/tea.20311

Seetha, S. (2013). Necessity of soft skills training for students and professionals. *International Journal of Engineering. Business and Enterprise Applications, 4*(2), 171–174.

Segedy, J. R., Kinnebrew, J. S., & Biswas, G. (2012). The effect of contextualized conversational feedback in a complex open-ended learning environment. *Educational Technology Research and Development, 61*(1), 71–89. doi:10.1007/s11423-012-9275-0

Seifert, T. L., & O'Keefe, B. A. (2001). The relationship of work avoidance and learning goals to perceived competence, externality and meaning. *The British Journal of Educational Psychology, 71*(Pt 1), 81–92. Retrieved from http://www.ncbi.nlm.nih.gov/pubmed/11307710 doi:10.1348/000709901158406 PMID:11307710

Sengupta, P. & Clark, D. B. (in preparation). Disciplinarily-integrated games: Shifting from perceptual and cognitive to developmental trajectories across the curriculum.

Sengupta, P. & Clark, D. B. (submitted). Playing Modeling Games in the Science Classroom: The Case for Disciplinary Integration. Educational Technology special issue on games and playful learning.

Sengupta, P., & Farris, A. V. (2012). Learning Kinematics in Elementary Grades Using Agent-based Computational Modeling: A Visual Programming Based Approach. *Proceedings of the 11th International Conference on Interaction Design & Children* (pp 78–87). ACM. doi:10.1145/2307096.2307106

Serge, S. R., Priest, H. A., Durlach, P. J., & Johnson, C. I. (2013). The effects of static and adaptive performance feedback in game-based training. *Computers in Human Behavior, 29*(3), 1150–1158. doi:10.1016/j.chb.2012.10.007

Serrano-Laguna, A., Torrente, J., Moreno-Ger, P., & Fernandez-Manjon, B. (2012). Tracing a little for big improvements: Application of learning analytics and videogames for student assessment. *Procedia Computer Science, 15*, 203–209. doi:10.1016/j.procs.2012.10.072

Shaffer, D. W. (2007). The educational value of computer games. Principle, March/April, 66-67.

Shaffer, D. W., Halverson, R., Squire, K. R., & Gee, J. P. (2005). Video Games and the Future of Learning (WCER Working Paper No. 2005-4). *Wisconsin Center for Education Research (NJ1).*

Shaffer, D. W., Halverson, R., Squire, K. R., & Gee, J. P. (2005). Video games and the future of learning (WCER Working Paper No. 2005-4). Wisconsin Center for Education Research.

Shaffer, D. W., Squire, K. R., & Halverson, R. (2005). Video Games and the Future of Learning. *Phi Delta Kappan, 87*(2), 104-111.\Siwek, S. (2014) Video games in the 21st century: The 2014 report. Retrieved from http://www.theesa.com/facts/pdfs/VideoGames21stCentury_2014.pdf

Shaffer, D., Hatfield, D., Svaronvsky, G., Nash, P., Nulty, A., Bagley, E., . . . Mislevey, R. (2009). Epistemic Network Analysis: A Prototype for 21st-Century Assessment of Learning. *International Journal of Learning and Media,* 1(2). MIT Press. Retrieved from http://www.mitpressjournals.org/doi/abs/10.1162/ijlm.2009.0013#VMb7qWTF8QU

Shaffer, D. W. (2008). *How Computer Games Help Children Learn*. New York, NY: Palgrave MacMillan.

Shaffer, D. W. (2009). Computers and the End of Progressive Education. In D. Gibson (Ed.), *Digital Simulations for Improving Education: Learning Through Artificial Teaching Environments* (pp. 68–85). Hershey, PA: IGI Global. doi:10.4018/978-1-60566-322-7.ch004

Shaffer, D. W., & Gee, J. P. (2007). Epistemic Games as Education for Innovation. In J. D. M. Underwood & J. Dockrell (Eds.), *Learning through digital technologies* (pp. 71–82). Leicester, UK: British Journal of Educational Psychology.

Shaffer, D. W., & Gee, J. P. (2012). The right kind of GATE: Computer games and the future of assessment. In M. C. Mayrath, J. Clarke-Midura, D. H. Robinson, & G. Schraw (Eds.), *Technology-based assessments for 21st century skills: Theoretical and practical implications from modern research* (pp. 211–227). Charlotte, NC, US: Information Age Publishing.

Shaffer, D., Squire, K., Halverson, R., & Gee, J. (2005). Video games and the future of learning. *Phi Delta Kappan, 87*(2), 104–111. doi:10.1177/003172170508700205

Shams, L., & Seitz, A. R. (2008). Benefits of multisensory learning. *Trends in Cognitive Sciences, 12*(11), 411–417. doi:10.1016/j.tics.2008.07.006 PMID:18805039

Shapiro, L. A. (2011). *Embodied cognition*. New York, NY: Routledge.

Sharp, L. A. (2012). Stealth learning: Unexpected learning opportunities through games. *Journal of Instructional Research, 1*(1), 42–48. doi:10.9743/JIR.2013.6

Shaw, C. M. (2012). Designing and using simulations and role-play exercises. In R. A. Denemark (Ed.), The International Studies Encyclopedia. New York, NY: Blackwell. Retrieved from http://webs.wichita.edu/depttools/depttoolsmemberfiles/carolynshaw/Shaw%20in%20Compendium.pdf

Shaw, D., Becker, H., Bransford, J., Davidson, J., Hawkins, J., Malcom, S., & Lehoczky, S. et al. (1998). Report to the president of the use of technology to strengthen k-12 education in the United States: Findings related to research and evaluation. *Journal of Science Education and Technology, 7*(2), 115–126. Retrieved from http://link.springer.com/article/10.1023/A:1022539822660#page-1 doi:10.1023/A:1022539822660

Sheets-Johnstone, M. (2009). *The corporeal turn: An interdisciplinary reader*. Exeter, UK: Imprint Academic.

Shepardson, D. P., Wee, B., Priddy, M., Schellenberger, L., & Harbor, J. (2007). What is a watershed? Implications of student conceptions for environmental science education and the National Science Education Standards. *Science Education*, *91*(4), 554–578. doi:10.1002/sce.20206

Shneiderman, B. (1998). Relate-create-donate: A teaching/learning philosophy for the cyber-generation. *Computers & Education*, *31*(1), 25–39. doi:10.1016/S0360-1315(98)00014-1

Short, D. (2012). Teaching scientific concepts using a virtual world-Minecraft. *Teaching Science. The Journal of the Australian Science Teachers Association*, *58*(3).

Short, D. (2012). Teaching scientific concepts using a virtual world—Minecraft. *Teaching Science-the Journal of the Australian Science Teachers Association*, *58*(3), 55.

Shulman, L. S. (1987). Knowledge and Teaching: Foundations of the New Reform. *Harvard Educational Review*, *57*(1), 1–22. doi:10.17763/haer.57.1.j463w79r56455411

Shultz Colby, R., & Colby, R. (2008). A pedagogy of play: Integrating computer games into the writing classroom. *Computers and Composition*, *25*(3), 300–312. doi:10.1016/j.compcom.2008.04.005

Shurchkov, O. (2012). Under pressure: Gender differences in output quality and quantity under competition and time constraints. *Journal of the European Economic Association*, *10*(5), 1189–1213. doi:10.1111/j.1542-4774.2012.01084.x

Shute, V. J. (2011). Stealth assessment in computer-based games to support learning. *Computer games and instruction, 55*(2), 503-524.

Shute, V. J., & Ventura, M. (2013). *Stealth assessment : measuring and supporting learning in video games*. Cambridge, Massachusetts: The MIT Press.

Shute, V. J., Ventura, M., Bauer, M., & Zapata-Rivera, D. (2009). Melding the power of serious games and embedded assessment to monitor and foster learning. In U. Ritterfeld, M. Cody, & P. Vorderer (Eds.), *Serious games: Mechanisms and effects* (pp. 295–321). New York, NY: Routledge.

Shute, V. J., Ventura, M., & Ke, F. (2015). The power of play: The effects of Portal 2 and Lumosity on cognitive and noncognitive skills. *Computers & Education*, *80*, 58–67. doi:10.1016/j.compedu.2014.08.013

Shute, V. J., Ventura, M., & Kim, Y. (2013). Assessment and learning of qualitative physics in Newton's playground. *The Journal of Educational Research*, *106*(6), 423–430. doi:10.1080/00220671.2013.832970

Shute, V., Ventura, M., Bauer, M., & Zapata-Revira, D. (2009). Melding the power of serious games and embedded assessment to monitor and foster learning: Flow and grow. In U. Ritterfeld, M. Cody, & P. Vorderer (Eds.), *Serious Games: Mechanisms and Effects* (pp. 295–321). New York: Routledge.

Shwe, H., & Francetic, A. (1999). Smarter play for smart toys: The benefits of technology-enhanced play. *Zowie Intertainment White Paper, 3208*.

Sicart, M. (2008). Defining game mechanics. *Game Studies*, *8*(2), 1–14.

Sicart, M. (2013). Moral dilemmas in computer games. *Design Issues*, *29*(3), 28–37. doi:10.1162/DESI_a_00219

Siegal, J. (2014, November 19). *Littlebigplanet 3 review: Small worlds after all*. Retrieved from http://bgr.com/2014/11/19/littlebigplanet-3-review/

Siemens, G. (2013). Learning analytics: The emergence of a discipline. *The American Behavioral Scientist*, *57*(10), 1380–1400. doi:10.1177/0002764213498851

Silvia, C. (2010). The impact of simulations on higher-level learning. *Journal of Public Affairs Education*, *18*, 397–422. Retrieved from http://www.naspaa.org/jpaemessenger/article/vol18-2/10_silva.pdf

SimCity [Digital Game]. (1989). Redwood City, CA: Electronic Arts, Maxis.

SimCity 4 [Digital Game]. (2003). Redwood City, CA: Electronic Arts, Maxis.

Simon, R., & Teperman, S. (2001). The World Trade Center attack: Lessons for disaster management. *Critical Care (London, England)*, *5*(6), 318–320. doi:10.1186/cc1060 PMID:11737917

Simpson, E., & Stansberry, S. (2008). Video games and teacher development: Bridging the gap in the classroom. In K. McFerin, et al. (Eds.), *Proceedings of Society for Information Technology & Teacher Education International Conference 2008,* Chesapeake, VA (pp. 5326-5331). AACE.

Simpson, E. S. (2009). Video games as learning environments for students with learning disabilities. *Children, Youth and Environments, 19*(1), 306–319.

Singer, D. G., Golinkoff, R. M., & Hirsh-Pasek, K. (Eds.). (2006). *Play= Learning: How play motivates and enhances children's cognitive and social-emotional growth.* Oxford University Press. doi:10.1093/acprof:oso/9780195304381.001.0001

Skinner, E., Zimmer-Gembeck, M., & Connell, J. (1998). Individual differences and the development of perceived control. *Monographs of the Society for Research in Child Development, 63(2–3,* Serial No. 254).

Slater, M., Linakis, V., Usoh, M., & Kooper, R. (1996). Immersion, presence, and performance in virtual environments: An experiment with tri-dimensional chess. Paper presented at ACM Virtual Reality Software and Technology Conference, Hong Kong (pp. 163–172). VRST. Retrieved from http://citeseerx.ist.psu.edu/viewdoc/download?doi=10.1.1.34.6594&rep=rep1&type=pdf

Slater, M., Steed, A., McCarthy, J., & Maringelli, F. (1998). The influence of body movement on subjective presence in virtual environments. *Human Factors: The Journal of the Human Factors and Ergonomics Society, 40*(3), 469–477. doi:10.1518/001872098779591368 PMID:9849105

Slater, M., Usoh, M., & Steed, A. (1995). Taking steps: The influence of a walking technique on presence in virtual reality. *ACM Transactions on Computer-Human Interaction, 2*(3), 201–219. doi:10.1145/210079.210084

Slator, B., Juell, P., McClean, P., & Saini-Eidukat, B., Schwert, D., White, D. A., & Hill. C., (1999). Virtual Environments in Education. paper presented at ED-MEDIA 99; AACE Conference.

Slavin, R. E., Madden, N. A., Chambers, B., & Haxby, B. (2009). *Two million children: Success for All.* CA: Corwin Thousand Oaks.

Smith, D. D., Robb, S. M., West, J., & Tyler, N. C. (2010). The changing education landscape: How special education leadership preparation can make a difference for teachers and their students with disabilities. *Teacher Education and Special Education: The Journal of the Teacher Education Division of the Council for Exceptional Children, 33*(1), 25–43. doi:10.1177/0888406409358425

Smith, E. T., & Boyer, M. A. (1996). Designing in-class simulations. *Political Science & Politics, 29*(4), 690–694. doi:10.1017/S1049096500045686

Snape, J., Berg, J. v., Guy, S. J., & Manocha, D. (2009). Independent navigation of multiple mobile robots with hybrid reciprocal velocity obstacles. *IEEE / RSJ International Conference on Intelligent Robots and Systems,* (pp. 5917-5922).

Sophocles. (n. d.). *Experiential learning.* Retrieved from http://www.psychology.pitt.edu/experiential-learning

Sorensen, D. (2014). Utah's got game: Local schools are producing cutting-edge game developers. *Utah Business,* (8), 58.

Sorensen, B. H., & Meyer, B. (2007). Serous Games in language learning and teaching – a theoretical perspective. *Situated Play, Proceedings of DiGRA 2007 Conference.*

Sowell, E. R., Thompson, P. M., Holmes, C. J., Jernigan, T. L., & Toga, A. W. (1999). In vivo evidence for post-adolescent brain maturation in frontal and striatal regions. *Nature Neuroscience, 2*(10), 859–861. doi:10.1038/13154 PMID:10491602

Space Invaders [Digital Game]. (1978). Tokyo, Japan: Taito, Midway.

SpaceChem [Digital Game]. (2011). Redwood City, CA: Zachtronics Industries.

Spires, H. A., Rowe, J. P., Mott, B. W., & Lester, J. C. (2011). Problem solving and game- based learning: Effects of middle grade students' hypothesis testing strategies on learning outcomes. *Journal of Educational Computing Research, 44*(4), 453–472. doi:10.2190/EC.44.4.e

Squire, K. (2002). Cultural framing of computer/video games. *The International Journal of Computer Game Research, 2*(1). Retrieved from http://www.gamestudies.org/0102/squire/

Squire, K. (2005). Changing the game: What happens when video games enter the classroom. *Innovate: Journal of online education, 1*(6).

Squire, K. (2008). Open-ended video games: A model for developing learning for the interactive age. *Open-ended video games: A model for developing learning for the interactive age* (pp. 167-198).

Squire, K. (2003). Video games in education. *Int. J. Intell. Games & Simulation, 2*(1), 49–62.

Squire, K. (2003). Video games in education. *International Journal of Intelligent Games & Simulation, 2*(1), 49–62.

Squire, K. (2003). Video games in education. *International Journal of Intelligent Simulations and Gaming, 2*(1), 49–62.

Squire, K. (2005). Changing the game: What happens when video games enter the classroom. *Innovate, 1*(6), 25–49.

Squire, K. (2006). From content to context: Videogames as designed experience. *Educational Researcher, 35*(8), 19–29. doi:10.3102/0013189X035008019

Squire, K. (2007). Cultural framing of computer/video games. *International Journal of Computer Games, 2*(1). Retrieved from http://www.gamestudies.org/0102/squire/

Squire, K. (2008). Video-game literacy: A literacy of expertise. In J. Coiro, M. Knobel, C. Lankshear, & D. Leu (Eds.), *Handbook of Research on New Literacies* (pp. 635–670). New York, NY: Rutledge - Taylor & Francis Group.

Squire, K. (2011). *Video Games and Learning: Teaching and Participatory Culture in the Digital Age*. New York, NY: Teachers College Press.

Squire, K. (2011). *Video games and learning: teaching and participatory culture in the digital age*. New York: Teachers College Press.

Squire, K. (2011). *Video games and learning: Teaching and participatory culture in the digital age*. New York: Teachers College Press.

Squire, K. (2011). *Video Games and Learning: Teaching and Participatory Culture in the Digital age*. New York: Teachers College Press.

Squire, K. (2011). *Video games and learning: Teaching and participatory culture in the digital age. Technology, Education-Connections (the TEC Series)*. New York, NY: Teacher College Press.

Squire, K. D. (2007). Games, Learning, and Society: Building a Field. *Educational Technology, 4*(5), 51–54. Retrieved from http://website.education.wisc.edu/kdsquire/tenure-files/15-gls.pdf

Squire, K. D. (2008). *Video Games and Education: Designing Learning Systems for an Interactive Age. Educational Technology Magazine: The Magazine for Managers of Change in Education, 48,* p. 17026. Mar-Apr.

Squire, K. D., & Jan, M. (2007). Mad city mystery: Developing scientific argumentation skills with a place-based augmented reality game on handheld computers. *Journal of Science Education and Technology, 16*(1), 1, 5–29. doi:10.1007/s10956-006-9037-z

Squire, K., Barnett, M., Grant, J. M., & Higginbotham, T. (2004). Electromagnetism supercharged!: Learning physics with digital simulation games.*Proceedings of the 6th International Conference of the Learning Sciences* (pp. 513–520).

Stahl, G. (2006). *Group cognition: Computer support for building collaborative knowledge*. Cambridge, MA: MIT Press.

Standardized Testing Costs Retrieved. (2015, January). *US Department of Education NCLB/Stronger Accountability*. Retrieved from http://www.huffingtonpost.com/2012/11/29/standardized-testing-costs_n_2213932.html

Stanford Center on Longevity. (2014, October 20). A consensus on the brain training industry from the scientific community. Retrieved from http://longevity3.stanford.edu/blog/2014/10/15/the-consensus-on-the-brain-training-industry-from-the-scientific-community/

Star Trek Online [Digital Game]. (2010). San Jose, CA: Atari, Cryptic Studios.

Star Wars: Knights of the Old Republic [Digital Game]. (2003). San Francisco: LucasArts, BioWare.

Starcraft [Digital Game]. (1998). Irvine, CA: Blizzard Entertainment.

Steinberg, J., Cline, F., Ling, G., Cook, L., & Tognatta, N. (2014). Examining the validity and fairness of a state standards-based assessment of English-language arts for deaf or hard of hearing students. *Association of Test Publishers*, *10*(2), 1–33.

Steinberg, L. (2011). Demystifying the adolescent brain. *Educational Leadership*, *68*(7), 42–46.

Steinkuehler, C. (2008). Massively multiplayer online games as an educational technology: An outline for research. *Educational Technology*, *48*(1), 10–21.

Steinkuehler, C., & Chmiel, M. (2006). *Fostering scientific habits of mind in the context of online play* (pp. 723–729). International Society of the Learning Sciences.

Steinkuehler, D., & Duncan, S. (2008). Scientific habits of mind in virtual worlds. *Journal of Science Education and Technology*, *17*(6), 530–543. doi:10.1007/s10956-008-9120-8

Steuer, J. (1992). Defining virtual reality: Dimensions determining telepresence. *Journal of Communication*, *42*(4), 73–93. doi:10.1111/j.1460-2466.1992.tb00812.x

Stichter, J. P., Laffey, J., Galyen, K., & Herzog, M. (2013). iSocial: Delivering the social competence intervention for adolescents (SCI-A) in a 3D virtual learning environment for youth with high functioning autism. *Journal of Autism and Developmental Disorders*, *43*(7), 1–14. PMID:23104615

Stipek, D. J., & Weisz, J. R. (1981). Perceived personal control and academic achievement. *Review of Educational Research*, *51*(1), 101–137. doi:10.3102/00346543051001101

StockTrack Global Portfolio Simulations. (2014). *National stock market simulation high school stock market game*. Retrieved from http://www.stocktrak.com/Public/products/National-SMS-High-School-Stock-Market-Game.aspx

Stone, E., & Davey, T. (2011). *Computer-adaptive testing for students with disabilities: A review of the literature. Research report. ETS RR-11-32*. Educational Testing Service; doi:10.1002/j.2333-8504.2011.tb02268.x

Strauch, B. (2003). *The primal teen: What the new discoveries about the teenage brain tell us about our kids*. New York: Doubleday.

Street Fighter [Digital Game]. (1988). Osaka, Japan: Capcom.

Strickland, D., McAllister, D., Coles, C., & Osborne, S. (2007). An evolution of virtual reality training designs for children with autism and fetal alcohol spectrum disorders. *Topics in Language Disorders*, *27*(3), 226–241. doi:10.1097/01.TLD.0000285357.95426.72 PMID:20072702

Suchman, L. A. (1987). *Plans and situated actions: The problem of human-machine communication*. Cambridge, U.K.: Cambridge University Press.

Sundar, S., & Shiller, Z. (1994). Optimal obstacle avoidance based on the hamilton-jacobi-bellmann equation. *ICRA*, *94*, 2424–2429.

Super Mario Bros. [Digital Game]. (1985). Kyoto, Japan: Nintendo R&D4.

Super Mario Galaxy. (2007 Nintendo, E.A.D. *Tokyo*, Japan.

Super Paper Mario. (2007). Nintendo SPD.

Sutton-Smith, B. (1997). *The Ambiguity of Play*. Cambridge, Mass: Harvard University Press.

Sutton-Smith, B. (2009). *The ambiguity of play*. Harvard University Press.

Sweetser, P., & Wyeth, P. (2005). GameFlow: A model for evaluating player enjoyment in games. *Computers in Entertainment*, *3*(3), 1–24. doi:10.1145/1077246.1077253

Sweller, J., Merrienboer, J. J. G. V., & Paas, F. G. W. C. (1998). Cognitive Architecture and Instructional Design. *Educational Psychology Review*, *10*(3), 251–296. doi:10.1023/A:1022193728205

Sylvan, E., Asbell-Clarke, J., Fraser, J., Plemons, K., & Rowe, E. (2013, August). *It's not who I am, its what I do: How Youth Gamer Identity and Beliefs about Social Perception Relates to Their Science Understanding*. Paper presented at the Digital Games Research Association (DiGRA) conference, Atlanta GA.

Tabak, I., & Reiser, B. J. (2008). Software-realized inquiry for cultivating a disciplinary stance. *Pragmatics & Cognition*, *16*(2), 307–355.

Takatalo, J., Hakkinen, J., Komulainen, J., Sarkela, H., & Nyman, G. (2006). Involvement and presence in digital gaming. Proceedings of the 4th Nordic conference on Human-computer interaction: changing roles, Oslo, Norway. ACM Press. doi:10.1145/1182475.1182520

Takeuchi, L. M., & Vaala, S. (2014). *Level up learning: A national survey on teaching with digital games*. New York: The Joan Ganz Cooney Center at Sesame Workshop.

Tan, O. (2003). *Problem-based learning innovation: Using problems to power learning in the 21st century*. Singapore: Thomson Learning.

Team Fortress 2 [Digital Game]. (2007). Redwood City, CA: Electronic Arts, Valve.

Terzopoulos, D., Tu, X., & Grzeszczuk, R. (1994). Artificial fishes: Autonomous locomotion, perception, behavior, and learning in a simulated physical world. *Artificial Life*, *1*(4), 327–351. doi:10.1162/artl.1994.1.4.327

Tetris [Digital Game]. (1989). Alameda, CA: Spectrum HoloByte.

Thalmann, & Musse (2013). *Crowd Simulation*. Springer.

The Boost C++ Library. (2015). Retrieved from http://www.boost.org/

The Condition of Education. (2013). *US Department of Education. Institute of Education Sciences National Center for Education Statistics*. Retrieved from http://nces.ed.gov/pubs2013/2013037.pdf

The Department of the Treasury. (2009). *President's advisory council on financial literacy: 2008 annual report to the President*. Retrieved from https://www.wdfi.org/_resources/indexed/ site/ymm/PACFL_ANNUAL_REPORT_1-16-09.pdf

The Escapist. (n. d.). *The adventurer's atlas*. Retrieved from http://www.theescapist.com/ypal/atlas.htm

The Independent. Photo of Anne Frank. Retrieved from http://www.independent.co.uk/incoming/article8673682.ece/alternates/w460/web-frank-rex.jpg

The Indiana Youth Institute. (2012, March). *Soft skills: Beyond academic success* (Issue Brief March 2012). Indianapolis, IN.

The Legend of Zelda: Ocarina of Time [Digital Game]. (1998). Kyoto, Japan: Nintendo EAD.

The New London Group. (2000). A pedagogy of multiliteracies: Designing social futures. In W. Cope & M. Kalantzis (Eds.), *Multiliteracies: Literacy learning and the design of social futures* (pp. 9–37). New York, NY: Rutledge.

The River City Project. (2002 - 2007). Retrieved from http://muve.gse.harvard.edu/rivercityproject/index.html

The SIFMA Foundation. (2013). The stock market game. Retrieved from http://www. stockmarketgame.org/impact.html

Thompson, E. (2007). *Mind in life: Biology, phenomenology, and the sciences of mind*. Cambridge, MA: The Belknap Press of Harvard University Press.

Thorne, S. L., and Fischer, I., (2012). Online gaming as sociable media. *Alsic Apprentissage des Langues et Systèmes d'Information et de Communication*. (on-line), *15* (1) (last retrieved 22nd August 2014.)

Thorne, S. L., & Black, R. W. (2007). Language and Literacy Development in Computer-Mediated Contexts and Communities. *Annual Review of Applied Linguistics*, *27*, 133–160. doi:10.1017/S0267190508070074

Thrash, T. M., & Elliot, A. J. (2001). Delimiting and integrating achieve-ment motive and goal constructs. In A. Efklides, J. Kuhl, & R. M. Sorrentino (Eds.), *Trends and prospects in motivation research* (pp. 3–21). Boston: Kluwer.

Thurlow, M. L., Lazarus, S. S., Thompson, S. J., & Morse, A. B. (2005). State policies on assessment participation and accommodations for students with disabilities. *The Journal of Special Education*, *38*(4), 232–240. doi:10.1177/00224669050380040401

Timms, M. (2014). Commentary on "How task features impact evidence from assessments embedded in simulations and games" by Almond et al. *Measurement: Interdisciplinary Research and Perspectives*, *12*(1-2), 54–56. doi:10.1080/15366367.2014.921035

Tindal, G., Heath, B., Hollenbeck, K., Almond, P., & Harniss, M. (1998). Accommodating students with disabilities on large-scale tests: An empirical study of student response and test administration demands. Retrieved from http://eric.ed.gov/?id=ED423632

Tiong, K., & Yong, S. (2008). Learning through computer game design: Possible success (or failure) factors. *Proceedings of the 16th International Conference on Computers in Education*, Taipei, Taiwan.

Torchlight [Digital Game]. (2009). Gardena, CA: Encore-Perfect World Entertainment, Runic Games.

Toulmin, S. E. (1958). *The uses of argument*. Cambridge, UK: Cambridge University Press.

Treuille, A., Cooper, S., & Popovic, Z. (2006). Continuum Crowds. *ACM Transactions on Graphics*, *25*(3), 1160–1168. doi:10.1145/1141911.1142008

Trilling, B., & Fadel, C. (2009). *21st century skills: Learning for life in our times*. John Wiley & Sons.

Trovato, K. (1996). *A* Planning in Discrete Configuration Spaces of Autonomous Systems* [PhD Thesis]. University of Amsterdam.

Trybus, J. (2014). *Game-based learning: What it is, why it works, and where it's going* (New Media Institute White Paper). Retrieved from http://www.newmedia.org/game-based-learning--what-it-is-why-it-works-and-where-its-going.html

Tüzün, H., Yılmaz-Soylu, M., Karakuş, T., İnal, Y., & Kızılkaya, G. (2009). The effects of computer games on primary school students' achievement and motivation in geography learning. *Computers & Education*, *52*(1), 68–77. doi:10.1016/j.compedu.2008.06.008

United States Chess Federation. (n. d.). Retrieved from http://www.quadcitychess.com/benefits_of_chess.html

Valsiner, J. (1988). *Developmental Psychology in the Soviet Union*. Indiana: Indiana University Press.

Van Calster, K., Lens, W., & Nuttin, J. R. (1987). Affective attitude toward the personal future: Impact on motivation in high school boys. *The American Journal of Psychology*, 1–13.

van den Berg, J., Guy, S. J., Lin, M. C., & Manocha, D. (2009). Reciprocal n-body collision avoidance. Proceedings of the *International Symposium on Robotics Research*.

van den Berg, J., Lin, M. C., & Machona, D. (2008). Reciprocal velocity obstacles for real-time multi-agent navigation. Proceedings of the *IEEE International Conference on Robotics and Automation* (pp. 1982-1935). doi:10.1109/ROBOT.2008.4543489

van den Berg, J., Shah, R., Huang, A., & Goldberg, K. (2011). ANA*: Anytime Non-Parametric A*. *Proceedings of the AAAI conference on artificial intelligence*.

Van Gelder, T. (1995). What might cognition be, if not computation? *The Journal of Philosophy*, *91*(7), 345–381. doi:10.2307/2941061

van Goethem, A., Jaklin, N., Cook, I. V. A., & Geraerts, R. (2015). *On Streams and Incentives: A Synthesis of Individual and Collective Crowd Motion* [Technical Report UU-CS-2015-005]. Utrecht University.

van Lier, L. (1996). *Interaction in the language curriculum: Awareness, autonomy, and authenticity*. New York: Longman.

van Lier, L. (2004). *The ecology and semiotics of language learning: A sociocultural perspective*. Boston: Kluwer. doi:10.1007/1-4020-7912-5

van Staalduinen, J. P., & de Freitas, S. (2011). A game-based learning framework: Linking game design and learning. In M.S. Khine (Ed.), *Learning to Play: Exploring the Future of Education with Video Games* (Vol. 53, pp. 1–37). Peter Lang.

van Toll, W., Cook, I. V. A. IV, & Geraerts, R. (2012). A navigation mesh for dynamic environments. *Computer Animation and Virtual Worlds*, *23*(6), 536–546. doi:10.1002/cav.1468

VandenBerghe, J. (2012). The 5 domains of play. Presentation at the Game Developers Conference 2012, San Francisco, CA, USA. Retrieved from http://www.darklorde.com/2012/03/the-5-domains-of-play-slides/

Vandercruysse, S., Vandewaetere, M., & Clarebout, G. (2012). Game-Based Learning: A Review on the Effectiveness of Educational Games. In M. M. Cruz-Cunha (Ed.), *Handbook of Research on Serious Games as Educational, Business, and Research Tools* (pp. 628–647). Hershey, PA: IGI Global. doi:10.4018/978-1-4666-0149-9.ch032

Vanquish, 2010 [Digital Game]. (2010). Tokyo, Japan: Sega, PlatinumGames.

Varela, A. H., Thompson, E., & Rosch, E. (1991). *The embodied mind.* Cambridge, MA: MIT Press.

Vawter, D. (2010). Mining the Middle School Mind. *Education Digest: Essential Readings Condensed for Quick Review, 75*(5), 47–49.

Verbert, K., Duval, E., Klerkx, J., Govaerts, S., & Santos, J. (2013). Learning analytics dashboard applications. *The American Behavioral Scientist, 57*(10), 1500–1509. doi:10.1177/0002764213479363

Versypt, J. J., & Versypt, A. N. F. (2013). *Mapping rural students' STEM involvement: Case studies of chemical engineering undergraduate enrollment in the states of Illinois and Kansas.* Paper presented at the American Society for Engineering Education, Atlanta, GA.

Vijaya, K. R. (2013). Teaching soft skills to technical professionals: Technology versus practical intelligence. *International Journal of Engineering Education, 2*(3), 567–573.

Vlasak, E., & Ranaldo, M. (2012). Video games. *Exceptional Parent, 42*(6), 36–38.

Vogel, J., Cannon-Bowers, J., Bowers, C., Muse, K., & Wright, M. (2006). Computer gaming and interactive simulations for learning: A meta-analysis. *Journal of Educational Computing Research, 6*(34), 229–243. doi:10.2190/FLHV-K4WA-WPVQ-H0YM

Vollmeyer, R., & Rheinberg, F. (2000). Does motivation affect performance via persistence? *Learning and Instruction, 10*(4), 293–309. doi:10.1016/S0959-4752(99)00031-6

von Glasersfeld, E. (1998). Cognition, construction of knowledge, and teaching. In M. R. Matthews (Ed.), *Constructivism in science education: A philosophical examination.* Norwell, MA: Kluwer Academic Publishers. doi:10.1007/978-94-011-5032-3_2

Vorderer, P., Hartmann, T., & Klimmt, C. (2006). Explaining the enjoyment of playing video games: The role of competition. In D. Marinelli (Ed.), *ICEC Conference Proceedings 2003: Essays on the Future of Interactive Entertainment* (pp. 107– 120). Pittsburgh, PA: Carnegie Mellon University Press.

Vos, L., & Brennan, R. (2010). Marketing simulation games: Student and lecturer perspectives. *Marketing Intelligence & Planning, 28*(7), 882–897. doi:10.1108/02634501011086472

Vroom, V. (1964). *Work and motivation.* Oxford, England: Wiley.

Vu, P., Crow, S., & Fredrickson, S. (2014). Using games in online education: Is it a winning strategy? *Online Journal of Distance Learning Administration, 17*(8).

Vygotsky, L. S. (1997). Interaction between learning and development. In M. Gauvain, & M. Cole (Eds.), Readings on the development of children (2nd ed.). New York: W.H. Freeman and Company.

Vygotsky, L. S. (1997). Thinking and Speech. In R.W. Rieber and A.S. Carton (Eds.), The Collected Works of L. S. Vygotsky: Vol. 1. Problems of General Psychology (pp. 39–285). New York: Plenum Press.

Vygotsky, L. (1978). *Mind in Society: The Development of Higher Psychological Processes.* Cambridge, MA: Harvard University Press.

Vygotsky, L. (1986). *Thought and Language* (Revised Edition). Cambridge, MA: The MIT Press.

Vygotsky, L. (1986). *Thought and language.* Cambridge: The MIT Press.

Vygotsky, L. S. (1967). Play and its role in the mental development of the child. *Journal of Russian & East European Psychology, 5*(3), 6–18. doi:10.2753/RPO1061-040505036

Vygotsky, L. S. (1978). *Mind in society. The development of higher psychological processes.* Cambridge: Harvard University Press.

Vygotsky, L. S. (1978). *Mind in society: The development of higher psychological processes.* Cambridge, MA: Harvard University Press.

Vygotsky, L. S. (1999). *The collected works of L.S. Vygotsky* (R.W. Rieber, Ed.) (Vol. 6). New York: Plenum Press.

Wahyudin, D., Hasegawa, S., & Dahlan, T. (2013). Mobile game based learning to develop ethical decision making skill of novice volunteer in disaster response. Paper presented at the *International Conference on Computers in Education*, Bali, Indonesia.

Walker, T., & White, C. (2002). Technorealism: The rhetoric and reality of technology in teacher education. *Journal of Technology and Teacher Education*, *10*(1), 63–74.

Wallis, S., & Wright, B. (2014a, March 4-6) Strategic knowledge mapping: The co-creation of useful knowledge. Proceedings of the 42nd annual conference Association for Business Simulation and Experiential Learning (ABSEL). Las Vegas, NV.

Wallis, S. E. (2014b). Abstraction and insight: Building better conceptual systems to support more effective social change. *Foundations of Science*, *19*(4), 353–362. doi:10.1007/s10699-014-9344-4

Wallis, S. E. (2014c). A systems approach to understanding theory: Finding the core, identifying opportunities for improvement, and integrating fragmented fields. *Systems Research and Behavioral Science*, *31*(1), 23–31. doi:10.1002/sres.2159

Warburton, S., & Garcia, M. (2009). 3D design and collaboration in massively multi-user virtual environments (MUVEs). In D. Russell (Ed.), *Cases of Collaboration in Virtual Learning Environments: Processes and Interactions* (pp. 121–139). Hershey, PA: Information Science Reference.

Ward, D., & Stapleton, M. (2012). Es are good: Cognition as enacted, embodied, embedded, affective and extended. *Advances in Consciousness Research*, *86*, 89–106. doi:10.1075/aicr.86.06war

Warhammer Online [Digital Game]. (2008). Redwood City, CA: Electronic Arts, Mythic Entertainment.

Wastiau, P., Blamire, R., Kearney, C., Quittre, V., Van de Gaer, E., & Monseur, C. (2013). The use of ICT in education: A survey of schools in Europe. *European Journal of Education*, *48*(1), 11–27. doi:10.1111/ejed.12020

Webber, S. (2013). Information literacy: A subject for the 21st century. *Pakistan Journal of Library and Information Science*. Retrieved from http://www.academia.edu/6956094/Information_Literacy_A_Subject_for_the_21st_Century

Weichert, F., Bachmann, D., Rudak, B., & Fisseler, D. (2013). *Analysis of the Accuracy and Robustness of the Leap Motion Controller, Department of Computer Science VII*. Dortmund, Germany: Technical University Dortmund.

Weinberger, A., Kollar, I., Dimitriadis, Y., Mäkitalo-Siegl, K., & Fischer, F. (2009). Computer-supported collaboration scripts. Perspectives from educational psychology and computer science. In N. Balacheff, S. R. Ludvigsen, T. de Jong, S. Barnes, & A. W. Lazonder (Eds.), *Technology-enhanced learning. Principles and products* (pp. 155–173). Berlin: Springer. doi:10.1007/978-1-4020-9827-7_10

Weiner, B. (2010). The development of an attribution-based theory of motivation: A history of ideas. *Educational Psychologist*, *45*(1), 28–36. doi:10.1080/00461520903433596

Wein, R., van den Berg, J., & Halperin, D. (2007). The visibility-voronoi complex and its applications. *Computational Geometry*, *36*(1), 66–87. doi:10.1016/j.comgeo.2005.11.007

Welch, S. (2015). The User Experience of Disney Infinity: Do Smart Toys Matter? [Unpublished M.F.A. thesis]. University of Central Florida, Orlando, Florida.

Wells, G. (1994). The complementary contributions of Halliday and Vygotsky to a "language-based theory of learning". *Linguistics and Education*, *6*(1), 41–90. doi:10.1016/0898-5898(94)90021-3

Wells, G. (2007). The mediating role of discoursing in activity. *Mind, Culture, and Activity*, *14*(3), 160–177. doi:10.1080/10749030701316300

Welzl, E. (1985). Constructing the Visibility Graph for n Line Segments in O(n^2) time. *Information Processing Letters*, *20*(4), 167–171. doi:10.1016/0020-0190(85)90044-4

Wenger, E. (1998). *Communities of practice: Learning, meaning, and identity*. Cambridge University Press. doi:10.1017/CBO9780511803932

Wentzel, K. (1991). Social competence at school: Relation between social responsibility and academic achievement. *Review of Educational Research, 61*(1), 1–24. doi:10.3102/00346543061001001

Wentzel, K. (1999). Social-motivational processes and interpersonal relationships: Implications for understanding students' academic success. *Journal of Educational Psychology, 91*, 76–97. doi:10.1037/0022-0663.91.1.76

Wentzel, K. (2000). What is it that I'm trying to achieve? Classroom goals from a content perspective. *Contemporary Educational Psychology, 25*(1), 105–115. doi:10.1006/ceps.1999.1021 PMID:10620385

Werbach, K., & Hunter, D. (2012). *For the win: How game thinking can revolutionize your business*. Philadelphia, PA: Wharton Digital Press.

Wertsch, J. (Ed.), (1995). *Studies of mind*. Cambridge, CT: Harvard University Press.

Wertsch, J. V. (1998). *Mind as action*. New York, NY: Oxford University Press.

West, D. M., & Bleiberg, J. (2013). *Education technology success stories. Issues in Governance Studies, West, D. M. (2012). Digital schools: How technology can transform education*. WA: Brookings Institution Press.

Wheeler, S. M. (2006). Role-playing games and simulations for international issues courses. *Journal of Political Science Education, 2*(3), 331–347. doi:10.1080/15512160600840814

Whitton, N. (2007). *Motivation and computer game based learning*. In ICT: Providing choices for learners and learning. Proceedings of Ascilite Singapore 2007. Retrieved from http://www.ascilite.org.au/conferences/singapore07/procs/whitton.pdf

Whitton, N. (2010). *Learning with digital games: a practical guide to engaging students in higher education*. New York: Routledge.

Wicks, M. (2010). A national primer on K-12 online learning. International Association for K-12 Online. Retrieved from http://www.inacol.org/research/bookstore/detail.php?id=22

Wiebe, E., Lamb, A., Hardy, M., & Sharek, D. (2014). Measuring Engagement in Video Game-based Environments: Investigation of the User Engagement Scale. *Computers in Human Behavior, 32*, 123–132. doi:10.1016/j.chb.2013.12.001

Wigfield, A. (1994). Expectancy-value theory of achievement motivation: A developmental perspective. *Educational Psychology Review, 6*(1), 49–78. doi:10.1007/BF02209024

Wigfield, A., & Eccles, J. S. (1989). Test anxiety in elementary and secondary school students. *Educational Psychologist, 24*(2), 159–183. doi:10.1207/s15326985ep2402_3

Wigfield, A., & Eccles, J. S. (1992). The development of achievement task values: A theoretical analysis. *Developmental Review, 12*(3), 265–310. doi:10.1016/0273-2297(92)90011-P

Wii Fit [Digital Game]. (2008). Kyoto, Japan: Nintendo, Nintendo.

Wilensky, U., & Reisman, K. (2006). Thinking like a wolf, a sheep or a firefly: Learning biology through constructing and testing computational theories – An embodied modeling approach. *Cognition and Instruction, 24*(2), 171–209. doi:10.1207/s1532690xci2402_1

Willis, J. (2007). Cooperative Learning Is a Brain Turn-On. *Middle School Journal (J1)*, 38(4), 4-13.

Wilson, C. H., Brice, C., Carter, E. I., Fleming, J. C., Hay, D. D., & Hicks, J. D. … Weaver, J. (2011). Familiar technology promotes academic success for students with exceptional learning needs. Retrieved from http://eric.ed.gov/?id=ED530541

Wilson, R. A., & Foglia, L. (2011). Embodied cognition. In E.N. Zalta (Ed.), *The Stanford Encyclopedia of Philosophy, Fall 2011 Edition*. Retrieved from http://plato.stanford.edu/archives/fall2011/entries/embodied-cognition

Wilson, M. (2002). Six views of embodied cognition. *Psychonomic Bulletin & Review, 9*(4), 625–636. doi:10.3758/BF03196322 PMID:12613670

Wilson, R. A. (2004). *Boundaries of the mind: The individual in the fragile sciences: Cognition*. Cambridge, U.K.: Cambridge University Press.

Witmer, B. G., & Singer, M. J. (1998). Measuring presence in virtual environments: A presence questionnaire. *Presence (Cambridge, Mass.)*, *7*(3), 225–240. doi:10.1162/105474698565686

Wolf, M. (2009/2010). *Theorizing Navigable Space in Video Games*. Retrieved from http://opus.kobv.de/ubp/volltexte/2011/4980/

Wolfram, S. (1994). *Cellular Automata and Complexity: Collected Papers*. Addison-Wesley.

World of Warcraft [Digital Game]. (2004). Irvine, CA: Blizzard Entertainment, Blizzard Entertainment.

Wouters, P., van der Spek, E. D., & Van Oostendorp, H. (2009). Current practices in serious game research: a review from a learning outcomes perspective. *Games-based learning advancements for multisensory human computer interfaces: techniques and effective practices* (pp. 232-255).

Wouters, P., van Nimwegen, C., van Oostendorp, H., & van der Spek, E. D. (2013). A meta- Analysis of the Cognitive and Motivational Effects of Serious Games. *Journal of Educational Psychology*, *105*(2), 249–265. doi:10.1037/a0031311

Xing, W., Wadholm, B., & Goggins, S. (2014). Learning analytics in CSCL with a focus on assessment: an exploratory study of activity theory-informed cluster analysis. *Proceedings of the Fourth International Conference on Learning Analytics And Knowledge* (pp. 59-67). ACM. doi:10.1145/2567574.2567587

Xing, W., & Petakovic, E., Goggins, S. (2014). Participation-based Student Performance Prediction Model through Interpretable Genetic Programming: Integrating Learning Analytics, Educational Data Mining and Theory. *Computers in Human Behavior*.

Xu, X., & Ke, F. (2014). From psychomotor to 'motor-psycho': Learning through gestures with body sensory technologies. *Educational Technology Research and Development*, *62*(6), 711–741. doi:10.1007/s11423-014-9351-8

Yan, B., & Slagle, M. (2006). School Start Time and Academic Achievement: A Literature Review. *Blue Valley School District Series*, 1-19.

Yang, Y.T.C. (2012). Building virtual cities, inspiring intelligent citizens: Digital games for developing students' problem solving and learning motivation. *Computers & Education*, *59*(2), 365–377. doi:10.1016/j.compedu.2012.01.012

Yardi, S. (2006). The role of backchannel in collaborative learning environments. *Proceedings of the 7th International Conference on Learning Sciences* (pp. 852-858). International Society of the Learning Sciences.

Ybarra, M. L., Huesmann, L. R., Korchmaros, J. D., & Reisner, S. L. (2014). Cross-sectional associations between violent video and computer game playing and weapon carrying in a national cohort of children. *Aggressive Behavior*, *40*(4), 345–358. doi:10.1002/ab.21526 PMID:24464267

Young, M. F., Schrader, P. G., & Zheng, D. (2006). MMOGs as learning environments: An ecological journey into Quest Atlantis and Sims Online. *Innovate: Journal of Online Education*, *2*(4), 1–7.

Young, M. F., Slota, S., Cutter, A. B., Jalette, G., Mullin, G., Lai, B., & Yukhymenko, M. et al. (2012). Our Princess Is in Another Castle A Review of Trends in Serious Gaming for Education. *Review of Educational Research*, *82*(1), 61–89. doi:10.3102/0034654312436980

Your Shape: Fitness Evolved [Digital Game]. (2010). Montreal, Canada: Ubisoft, Ubisoft Montreal.

Yu, K. (2006). Finding a natural-looking path by using generalized visibility graphs. *Proceedings of the 9th Pacific Rim international conference on Artificial Intelligence* (pp. 170-179). doi:10.1007/978-3-540-36668-3_20

Zahorik, P., & Jenison, R. (1998). Presence as being-in-the-world. *Presence (Cambridge, Mass.)*, *7*(1), 78–89. doi:10.1162/105474698565541

Zechner, J., & Ebner, M. (2011). Playing a Game in Civil Engineering. Proceedings of the 14th International Conference on Interactive Collaborative Learning (ICL2011) (pp. 417 – 422).

Zhang, A. (2012). Cooperative learning and soft skills training in an IT course. *Journal of Information Technology Education: Research*, *11*, 65–79.

Zheng, D. (2012). Caring in the dynamics of design and languaging: Exploring language learning in 3D virtual spaces. *Language Sciences*, *34*(5), 543–558. doi:10.1016/j.langsci.2012.03.010

Zheng, D., Newgarden, K., & Young, M. (2012). Multimodal analysis of language learning in World of Warcraft play: Languaging as values-realizing. *ReCALL*, *24*, 339–360.

Zipf, G. K. (1949). *Human Behavior and the Principle of Least Effort*. Addison-Wesley Press.

Zusak, M. (2007). *The Book Thief*. Knopf Books for Young Readers.

Zwaan, R. A., & Taylor, L. J. (2006). Seeing, acting, understanding: Motor resonance in language comprehension. *Journal of Experimental Psychology. General*, *135*(1), 1–11. doi:10.1037/0096-3445.135.1.1 PMID:16478313

Zydney, J., & Hasselbring, T. (2014). Mini anchors: A Universal Design for Learning approach. *TechTrends: Linking Research & Practice to Improve Learning*, *58*(6), 21–28. doi:10.1007/s11528-014-0799-5

About the Contributors

Donna Russell is adjunct faculty at Walden University's College of Education's Teaching, Learning and Innovation program. She is adjunct faculty at Capella University's School of Social and Behavioral Sciences' Educational Psychology program She has published extensively on the design and implementation of virtual learning environments. She has a bachelors and master's degree in Education specializing in Instructional Design. Her PhD is in Educational Psychology with an emphasis on cognition and technology. She has 15 years' experience teaching in P-12 educational settings.

James Laffey is a Professor in the School of Information Science and Learning Technologies and a former researcher and systems developer at Apple Computer, Inc. Dr. Laffey has a Ph.D. in Education from the University of Chicago and has won awards for the design of innovative, media-based computer systems. Through his design work and scholarship he is internationally recognized as an expert in the area of human-computer interaction. He currently teaches graduate level courses on development of systems to optimize HCI and learning, including approaches to game-based virtual learning. He has received over $8 million of funding during the past 15 years.

* * *

Deanne M. Adams currently works at Microsoft Studios as a User Researcher. Previously she held Postdoctoral Scholar positions at the University of Notre Dame and Vanderbilt University. Her research interests include the cognitive consequences of playing commercial video games, training spatial skills, navigation in virtual environments, multimedia learning, and cognitive tutors. Dr. Adams's more recent work has focused on value-added research with educational games such as incorporating worked examples. Dr. Adams received her Ph.D. from the University of California, Santa Barbara from the department of Psychological and Brain Sciences while working with Dr. Richard E. Mayer.

Douglas A. Agar is a research student in the Department of Linguistics at Macquarie University, Australia. His research interests are in the areas of appropriate and innovative uses of technology in language education, sociocultural models of language development, and multiple literacies. He has spent the last decade variously teaching Irish Gaelic and French in Irish and Australian high schools.

Jodi Asbell-Clarke is the director of the Educational Gaming Environments Group (EdGE) at TERC. TERC is a non-profit research and development organization focusing on innovative, technology-based math and science education. EdGE is a team of game designers, educators, and researchers who are studying implicit STEM learning in digital games. Jodi's background includes MA in Math, an MSc in Astrophysics and a PhD in Education. She was an onboard software verification analyst for IBM during the first 25 missions of the space shuttle and taught at the laboratory school at University of Illinois. In 2009, she co-founded EdGE at TERC.

Ryan Nicholas Babiuch is a game engineer at the University of Missouri within the School of Information Science and Learning Technologies leading and contributing to projects in research and development.

Erin Bardar is the Education Materials Director for the Educational Gaming Environments group (EdGE) at TERC. She works closely with game designers and teachers, focusing primarily on to how to bridge free-choice games and formal classroom science instruction. Erin has a background in physics and astronomy. She was a NASA Graduate Student Research Program (GSRP) fellow at Boston University where she earned a PhD in Astronomy for her research on introductory college students' understanding of light and spectroscopy. Erin is also the creator of the Light and Spectroscopy Concept Inventory, and has a U.S. patent for a binocular spectrometer.

Caitlyn A. Bukaty is a doctoral scholar and Presidential Fellow at the University of Central Florida. Prior to pursuing her PhD Caitlyn was a special educator in Western New York, teaching students of all ages and abilities. Caitlyn's research interests include creating innovative post-secondary opportunities for young adults with intellectual disabilities.

Leonard Busuttil is a resident academic at the Faculty of Education, University of Malta. His research interests are in game based learning and in introducing children to computational concepts. He has presented in conferences on digital game making by children and creativity.

Vanessa Camilleri is a resident academic at the Faculty of Education, University of Malta. Her research interests are mainly in technology-enhanced learning, more specifically involving Virtual Worlds technologies and their design for a more effective impact in the area of human-computer interaction. She has additionally delivered a series of talks and presentations at International Conferences relating to Mobile Learning applications and Serious Games, as well as Virtual Worlds and Digital Social Spaces.

Chris Campbell is a lecturer in ICT Education in the School of Education at The University of Queensland. Her teaching areas include teaching undergraduate students how to use technology in the classroom, including mobile learning tools. She has been involved in using the TPACK framework with Apps in mathematics education and her other research interests include integrating ICT as a learning tool into the classroom and other areas of research include topics such as learning design, virtual worlds research and augmented reality games research. Chris has also completed research on self-regulation and ICT in the classroom while her newer research includes learner response systems as well as self regulation when completing MOOCs and how teachers can use this to enhance their teaching.

Manetta Calinger has been a curriculum writer/designer for numerous educational curriculum packages and live role-playing simulations funded by diverse organizations including NASA, National Institutes of Health (NIH), National Institute of Occupational Safety and Health (NIOSH), National Oceanic and Atmospheric Administration (NOAA), the Mining and Safety and Health Administration (MSHA), the U. S. Army Corps of Engineers, and various foundations. She is a West Virginia certified general science and biology teacher with 25 years of classroom experience and administrative experience as a K-12 science department chair and curriculum committee member. She has developed and facilitated teacher professional development programs, delivering PD to educators teaching varying grade levels and subject matter specialties. During her tenure as a curriculum writer/instructional designer, Calinger has developed multiple live simulations, training modules, and functional exercises and has worked collaboratively with evaluators on the assessment/research components of these projects.

Philip J. Chappell is a Lecturer in the Linguistics Department at Macquarie University, Australia, where he convenes the Graduate Certificate of TESOL. His research interests are in classroom talk, sociocultural approaches to teacher cognition, dialogic pedagogy, and professional learning for English language teachers. Phil supervises higher degree research students at doctoral and masters level.

Douglas B. Clark, Professor of the Learning Sciences and Science Education at Vanderbilt, investigates the learning processes through which people come to understand core science concepts in the context of digital learning environments and games. This work focuses primarily on conceptual change, inquiry, modeling, explanation, collaboration, and argumentation. He is principal investigator on NSF and DOE grants on games.

Jody Clarke-Midura's research focuses on the design and evaluation of digital media for learning and assessment. She is interested in innovative approaches to assess and model learning. Prior to MIT, she was a researcher at the Harvard Graduate School of Education. She holds a master's degree and doctorate from the Harvard Graduate School of Education.

Erdem Demiroz is a PhD candidate at the University of Missouri-Kansas City (UMKC), in the School of Graduate Studies. His interdisciplinary PhD studies focus on Curriculum and Instructional Leadership and Mathematics and Statistics with emphasis on Information and Learning Technologies (ILTs) in Mathematics Education. He earned his MA in General Curriculum and Instruction and Learning Technologies at UMKC, and Bachelor of Arts in Computer Education and Instructional Technologies (CEIT) from Ege University in Turkey. His extensive background and experience in information and learning technologies underlie his teaching and research interests. He has taught graduate and undergraduate level courses which focus on teaching and learning with technology, educational assessment, and problem solving and creativity. His general research interests focus on the best practices of ILTs in K-12 education, the effects of technology on learning processes and on student learning outcomes with specific emphasis on course redesign & flipped learning with heavy use of ILTs, virtual learning environments, online teaching practices and design, learning theories in virtual learning, artificial intelligence, gaming and educational game design for P-12 education, human computer interaction, and kinesthetic learning in virtual settings.

Martin Ebner is currently head of the Department for Social Learning at Graz University of Technology and therefore responsible for all university wide e-learning activities. He holds the position of an Assoc. Prof. on media informatics and works also at the Institute for Information System Computer Media as a senior researcher. His research focuses strongly on e-learning, mobile learning, learning analytics, social media and Open Educational Resources. Martin gives a number of lectures in this area as well as workshops and keynotes at international conferences.

Scott Fredrickson is Professor and Graduate Program Chair of Instructional Technology at the University of Nebraska Kearney. He received his doctorate from Texas Tech University. He has been at the University of Nebraska Kearney for 23 years and prior to that he was at the University of Alaska Southeast in Sitka for four years. He was a computer science and government/social studies teacher at Lubbock (Texas) Independent School District for nine years. He has earned the Master Online Teacher certificate from the University of Illinois and the Certificated Online Administrator certification from the Online Learning Consortium. He has a Texas teaching endorsements in Computer Information Systems, Information Processing technology, Computer Literacy, Government, Political Science, and Broadfield Social Studies He has authored 38 peer-reviewed journal articles, six book chapters, 11 monographs, co-authored 17 peer-reviewed journal articles, and has presented at 42 national or international conferences.

Benjamin Gallegos is a doctoral student in the Exceptional Education Program at the University of Central Florida. He is a research associate on the Bill and Melinda Gates Foundation funded, UCF TeachLivE™ classroom. Ben began teaching in the southwest of the United States as a Preschool Programs for Children with Disabilities (PPCD) teacher and later in a fourth grade inclusive classroom. Ben's research interests are in using innovative, and promised based technologies for teacher practices and students learning achievements. Ben's research focus is on increasing STEM education outcomes, Universal Design for Learning Framework, and feedback features in the virtual learning environments for student with disabilities.

Martonia Gaskill is an Assistant Professor at the University of Nebraska at Kearney. She currently teaches graduate and undergraduate courses in the areas of instructional technology, research methods and general education. Her research interest includes online learning, technology integration, pre-service teacher education, digital cheating, MOOC learning environments and gaming in education.

Roland Geraerts is an assistant professor at the Games and Virtual Worlds group in the Department of Information and Computing Sciences at Utrecht University in the Netherlands. There, he obtained his PhD on sampling-based motion planning techniques. In addition, he studied quality aspects of paths and roadmaps. His current research focuses on path planning and crowd simulation in games and virtual environments. Furthermore, he teaches several courses related to games and crowd simulation. Roland has organized the Creative Game Challenge and is one of the co-founders of the annual Motion in Games conference.

Sean Goggins is an Associate Professor at Missouri's iSchool and the University of Missouri Informatics Institute. He teaches, publishes and conducts research on the uptake and use of information and communication technologies by small groups in medium to large scale sociotechnical systems; from Facebook, to online course systems and video games. Sean conceptualizes "group informatics" as a methodological approach and ontology (Goggins et al, 2013) for making sense of the interactions between people in medium to large scale social computing environments. His research examines the information behavior, knowledge construction, identity development, performance and structural evolution of small, online groups. The long tail of social computing bounds this work; large scale communities are approached from the bottom up in group informatics research. By understanding small groups of online learners, librarians or software engineers (to name just a few), and analyzing traces of their interactions, Group Informatics brings semantics to the clusters discovered in large scale social computing endeavors.

Susannah Gordon-Messer is a content manager for The Education Arcade. She is a content expert for high school math and science and works on developing game content as well as teacher materials that accompany games. She manages school and teacher partnerships, prototype testing with students, school implementations and leads professional development workshops. Prior to MIT, she was a postdoc with the Strategic Education Research Partnership (SERP) and developed curriculum for science literacy at the middle school level. Susannah worked for the Posse Foundation as the mentor for the inaugural group of Science Posse students and has volunteered designing programs at The Discover Museums in Acton, MA. She holds a PhD in Biophysics from Brandeis University and was a high school math teacher with Teach for America in Warrenton, NC.

Dimitris Gouscos is an Assistant Professor with the Faculty of Communication and Media Studies of the University of Athens, and a Research Fellow of the Laboratory of New Technologies in Communication, Education and the Mass Media. He is Editor-in-Chief of the Intl Journal of Electronic Governance and his research interests evolve around applications of social media, digital games and other interactive digital media to e-learning, e-participation and e-governance. More information available at http://www.media.uoa.gr/~gouscos.

Joseph Griffin is a doctoral student at Mizzou's School of Information Science and Learning Technology. He is interested in intelligent algorithms and serious games as methods of research into learning.

Christina Gruppetta is a 21- year old student at the University of Malta currently working on a B.Ed primary course. It is her last year at the University and she is expected to graduate in the upcoming December. She has a passion for teaching and trying out new teaching methods, leading to her interest in game-based learning. Her research study consisted of incorporating the use of the game Minecraft, in the classroom.

Stella K. Hadjistassou is a research fellow at the KIOS Research Center for Intelligent Systems and Networks. She has completed her Ph.D. in Rhetoric/Composition and Linguistics at Arizona State University, where she also taught multiple courses in ESL, sociolinguistics, English grammar, English composition, and technical and professional communication. Stella also participated in multiple research studies in the U.S. and Europe. She has also participated in multiple European funded projects and nationally funded projects in virtual worlds, second/foreign language teacher training, Web 2.0 technologies and gaming. She has also published extensively in this area.

Valerie J. Hill has served as a school librarian and instructor of library and information science for over twenty years. She earned her doctorate at Texas Woman's University in 2012 and her dissertation was "Factors Contributing to the Adoption of Virtual Worlds by Librarians". She is a National Writing Project trainer with interests that include children's and young adult literature, storytelling, multi-media, human-computer interaction, and emerging technology tools such as virtual and augmented reality for learning environments. Dr. Hill's research focus is centered on information literacy and the changing needs of learners in global participatory digital culture.

Patricia Hoehner is an Associate Professor in Educational Administration at the University of Nebraska, Kearney. Her research interests include online learning, leadership, and curriculum.

Norman Jaklin obtained a Diploma (BSc + MSc) in computer science in March 2011 from the Rheinische Friedrich-Wilhelms-Universität Bonn, Germany, with a strong focus on computational geometry. Since December 2011, he has been a PhD candidate in the Virtual Worlds division of the Department of Information and Computing Sciences, Utrecht University, the Netherlands. His research focuses on path planning and crowd simulation models for autonomous virtual agents. Such models are used in video games, CGI-enhanced movies, safety training simulations, and urban city planning.

Lenora Jean (Jeannie) Justice graduated with an Ed.D. in curriculum and instruction from the University of Florida. She has taught at the high school, GED/adult high school, undergraduate, and graduate levels for over 15 years. She currently teaches educational technology courses and advises both masters and doctoral students at Morehead State University in Morehead, Kentucky.

Michelle T. Kepple is a doctoral candidate at the University of Central Florida. Her research foci is in instructional strategies, game-based learning, and distance education. Prior to her doctoral studies, Ms. Kepple was a faculty instructor at Central Connecticut State University in the Educational Leadership department where she worked with preservice teachers on instructional technology and implementation.

Sotiris Kirginas is a primary school teacher and doctoral researcher at the Laboratory of New Technologies in Communication, Education and the Mass Media of the Faculty of Communication & Media Studies, National University of Athens. He holds a Bachelor Degree in primary education and a Master Degree in ICT in Education from the National University of Athens. His research focuses on exploring the significance of digital games-based learning in education and how does it relate to enhancing the learning process.

Eric Klopfer's research focuses on the development and use of computer games and simulations for building understanding of science, technology, engineering and mathematics. He works on mobile and online games designed to build understanding of scientific practices and concepts as well as critical knowledge. In the realm of simulations, Klopfer's work focuses on students understanding complex systems through, and connecting computer programming with, scientific practice, critical thinking, and real-world issues. He is the co-author of the books, "Adventures in Modeling", "The More We Know", as well as author of "Augmented Learning," Klopfer is also the co-founder, past President, and Board Member of the non-profit Learning Games Network.

Mario M. Martinez-Garza is a doctoral candidate of learning sciences and learning environment design at Vanderbilt University. His main areas of interest are investigating the potential of play as a vehicle for learning through cognitive perspectives, and applications of theory-based design principles to support learning through game environments of all kinds. He holds a Master's degree in Education and has served as a middle-school math and science teacher, and as a game designer for several commercial and educational games companies.

Judith Molka-Danielsen is a professor in Information Systems and Information Sciences at Molde University College where she is leader of the virtual learning and technology research group.

Patrick O'Shea is currently an assistant professor in instructional technology at Appalachian State University and an educational consultant working on Augmented Reality and Distributed Learning educational initiatives (e.g. student-authored textbooks written collaboratively with wiki technology). Before that he held a post-doctoral fellowship in learning technologies at Harvard's Graduate School of Education, where he directed the Handheld Augmented Reality Project. This project aimed to evaluate the educational applications of augmented reality technologies. O'Shea has professional experience working with educational technology, assessment, and program evaluation. He has taught online and in face-to-face settings and consulted nationally and internationally on educational projects, including working for the Bill & Melinda Gates Foundation in Africa and as a Fulbright Specialist in Sri Lanka.

Debra C. Burkey Piecka, Ed.D., is an evaluator and educational researcher with the Sponsored Research Programs department at Wheeling Jesuit University. She is the internal evaluator and educational researcher for the NIH grant, Pandem-Sim: Fighting Infectious Diseases Everywhere, where she performed a similar role for the NIH CyberSurgeons project. Piecka provided evaluation services for multiple projects including Micronauts (NASA Education), eLabs Virtual Science Labs (The Benedum Foundation), Mining and Industrial Safety Technology and Training (NIOSH), and the Bluestone Dam project (U.S. Army Corps of Engineers). She is also a contributing faculty member at Walden University's Educational Technology Ph.D. program. Piecka received her doctoral degree from Duquesne University in instructional technology along with graduate certificates in Interpretive and Qualitative Research Methods and Instructional Technology. She earned an M.B.A. from the University of Pittsburgh and a triple B.S.in Administration and Management Science, Economics, and Mathematics from Carnegie Mellon University.

DeAnna Proctor is currently a doctoral student in the Education Technology Leadership program at Morehead State University.

Su-Jen Roberts is a behavioral ecologist who joined NewKnowledge in 2014 as a researcher and analyst. She completed her PhD in the Ecology, Evolution, and Environmental Biology Department at Columbia University, where she studied primate behavior and reproduction. Additionally, Dr. Roberts has worked in museum research and evaluation at the Franklin Institute in Philadelphia and as a middle school teaching fellow in New York City. Her other research interests include wildlife, conservation biology, and STEM education.

Louisa Rosenheck manages the design, content, and development of educational games and simulations to be used with middle and high school students. She also oversees the research done on these projects exploring how games can be used most effectively in both formal and informal educational settings. Prior to becoming a researcher at MIT, Louisa worked in public media and Web site production, and also taught ESL to children and adults of all ages. She holds a B.A. in Computer Science from Brown University and an Ed.M. in Technology, Innovation, and Education from the Harvard Graduate School of Education.

Elizabeth Rowe, a senior researcher at TERC, studies and develops innovative uses of technology in and out of schools with a focus on game-based learning. Dr. Rowe is currently the Director of Research for the Educational Gaming Environments group at TERC where she oversees the research design, data collection, and data analysis for several NSF-funded EdGE projects including Leveling Up, Taking Games to School, SportsLab 2020, Revealing the Invisible, and the Finnish-US Network. Elizabeth's background includes a Bachelor's degree in Mathematics and a Ph.D. in Human Development and Family Studies.

Troy D. Sadler is a Professor of Science Education and serves as Director of the ReSTEM Institute: Reimagining & Researching STEM Education at the University of Missouri. He conducts research on the teaching and learning of science in the context of innovative learning environments and socio-scientific issues.

Pratim Sengupta, Assistant Professor of the Learning Sciences at the University of Calgary, designs and develops agent-based computational technologies for long-term, ecologically valid classroom integration, empirically grounded models of short-term conceptual change and long-term development of learners, and multi-agent models of complex social and natural phenomena. He is the recipient of an NSF CAREER award for his research on developing programming languages for K12 learners.

Christina Shane-Simpson is a researcher and analyst with New Knowledge, with a particular focus on dynamic interactions that occur among humans in digital environments. Mrs. Shane-Simpson studies college students' choices on social networking sites as they relate to self-esteem and general Internet use. She has also created technology-based interventions to assist students with autism and other disabilities to effectively navigate social networking sites. Mrs. Shane-Simpson has completed a Certificate in Interactive Technology and Pedagogy from The Graduate Center, while she currently teaches undergraduate psychology coursework at Hunter College.

Jouni Smed holds a PhD in Computer Science and acts as Senior Lecturer and Adjunct Professor in the University of Turku, Finland. He has organized and taught game development on diverse topics ranging from game algorithms and networking in multiplayer games to game software construction, game design and interactive storytelling. He is also the co-founder of Turku Game Lab, which aims at bringing together technologically- and artistically-oriented students to work on the same game projects and start their career in the game industry. His research interests range from code tweaking to software processes and from simple puzzles to multisite game development.

Peter A. Smith is currently an assistant Professor in the School of Visual Art and Design at the University of Central Florida, with over 10 years of experience working in the field of Serious Games and simulation. In this time he has worked on diverse catalog of gaming projects for the Navy, NSF, ADL, DAU, and many more. Peter received his Ph.D. in Modelling & Simulation from the University of Central Florida in 2012. He has presented internationally on the topic of Serious Games including the 2007 Serious Games Summit opening presentation on the Taxonomy of Serious Games. He is also a founder and previous chair of the Serious Games Showcase & Challenge a competition the highlights the best work in Serious Games held as an integral part of the I/ITSEC Conference for the last 9 years.

Anne Elizabeth Snyder is Director of Research and Learning Design at Second Avenue Learning. With a strong background in teaching and educational research, Anne is responsible for managing all instructional design and research efforts at Second Avenue Learning. Drawing from her experience in brick-and-mortar as well as online instruction, Anne applies best design and research practices to all proprietary and client products. Dr. Snyder holds a Ph.D. in Educational Psychology from Teachers College, Columbia University.

Norbert Spot is currently master student of computer science at Graz University of Technology. His master thesis is strongly focusing on Game Based Learning.

Tomi Suovuo is a graduate student at University of Turku Department of Information Technology, specialising in Games and Interaction.

Grant Van Eaton is a doctoral student in the learning sciences and science education at Vanderbilt University's Peabody College of Education. He previously taught high school biology in Washington, DC as a Teach For America corps member. Van Eaton remains active in new teacher training and development. His research explores teachers' and students' conceptual change as they interact with and incorporate technology in science classrooms.

Victoria Van Voorhis is founder and CEO of Second Avenue Learning.

Satyugjit Virk, postdoctoral scholar at Vanderbilt, completed his doctoral work with Dr. John Black at Teachers College, Columbia University. He was also previously director of product development and cognition at the autism gaming company Interactable, and has a diverse portfolio of industrial elearning and educational software experience. Sat focuses on cognitive science approaches to multi-representational systems with an emphasis on integrating causally related symbolic and semantic representations in STEM through interactive visualizations.

Sam von Gillern works at Iowa State University and is interested how educators can use games to promote learning outcomes in their classrooms. Additionally, he researches literacy and language development and cross-linguistic transfer. He teaches a variety of courses at Iowa State University and also works with young children promoting literacy development.

Phu Vu is an Assistant Professor in Instructional Technology at the University of Nebraska, Kearney. His research interests include online learning, educational technology, teacher education, and ESL online training.

Steven E. Wallis is a Fulbright Specialist focused on developing more effective strategy, policy, and theory for academic and research institutions. He is the director of meta-analysis at the ASK MATT division of Meaningful Evidence, LLC which uses a gamified approach to strategic planning and knowledge mapping. At Capella University, he mentors doctoral candidates in Industrial/Organizational Psychology.

Shelly Welch is a MFA student in Digital Media at the University of Central Florida. She is working with games, toys, and simulations in the areas of health, military, and education. She works at I.D.E.A.S. and will graduate in 2015.

Jane K. Ziebarth-Bovill is an associate professor in the department of teacher education at the University of Nebraska at Kearney (UNK). She received her B.A.E. degree in Social Science from Kearney State College, an M.A.E. degree in Comprehensive Social Science at Kearney State College, and a Ph.D. in Curriculum, Instruction, and Administration from the University of Nebraska at Lincoln. Dr. Ziebarth-Bovill teaches both undergraduate and graduate courses and supervises student teachers at UNK. Her research and teaching interests include field-based education, service-learning, classroom engagement strategies, academic advising, and Invitational Education.

Index

O

P

R

S

T

V

W

CPSIA information can be obtained at www.ICGtesting.com
Printed in the USA
BVOW09*0120271015

423562BV00008B/71/P